[

Classics in Psychoanalytic Technique

CLASSICAL PSYCHOANALYSIS AND ITS APPLICATIONS

A Series of Books edited by Robert Langs, M.D.

Classics in Psycho~ analytic Technique

Robert Langs, Editor

NEW YORK • JASON ARONSON • LONDON

CONTENTS

PART III
COUNTERTRANSFERENCE

PART IV
NONCOUNTERTRANSFERENCE

PREFACE

This book is a reader in psychoanalytic technique, broadly conceived. It collects under one cover what are in my opinion the most important and innovative investigations of the therapeutic relationship, interaction, setting, and experience ever to issue from the pens of psychoanalysts. In assembling them here, it is my wish to provide mental health practitioners of all persuasions the opportunity to read and study these now classic contributions. It is my belief that all true progress in the field must base itself on the questions and insights of these pioneers, even as many of their formulations are improved, elaborated, and finally surpassed.

In many ways, the present volume is an outgrowth of *The Therapeutic Interaction* (Langs 1976b), a work in which I abstracted over five hundred articles on this same subject, and then analyzed, criticized, and discussed the implications of that literature for both psychoanalytic theory and all types of therapeutic technique. All but a few of the papers included here were included in those volumes; as a result, the brief commentaries that I have prepared for each major section of this book, and for each individual paper, have been designed with conciseness and immediate perspective in mind. The interested reader will find far more extended critiques in the earlier book.

The papers are arranged by subject matter, though with much overlap, and chronologically within each of the parts. Such an arrangement allows the reader to sense the growth of psychoanalytic thinking in each of these critical areas. Starting, of course, with the basic writings of Freud, especially his revolutionary papers on psychoanalytic technique (1912a,b [chapters 1 and 38], 1913, 1914, 1915), one finds in the ensuing years many indications of evolution and growth. For example, in reading the papers on transference we see a steady expansion and revision of the concept. We begin with Freud's original presentation of its intrapsychic foundation and his oedipal emphasis, and proceed to a view which encompasses manifestations related to every stage of psychosexual development and which comprehends these expressions in terms of their interaction with reality—especially those within the therapeutic situation and relationship with the analyst. Developed too is the full interplay between transference expressions and actuality. There is a growing awareness of the nontransference aspect of the patient's relationship to the analyst, and eventually actual efforts by the patient to both harm and help the analyst are recognized. The almost exclusive initial stress on the patient's pathological functioning is ultimately counterbalanced with an extensive appreciation of his unconscious perceptiveness and constructive capacities. In addition, the early emphasis on displacements from the past and projections from the patient onto the analyst are ultimately placed into perspective through a growing appreciation of the introjective side of the analysand's experience.

In another area, the analyst's essentially sound and noncounter-transference-based functioning, outlined only briefly but with great perceptiveness in Freud's basic writings, has come under extensive scrutiny and clarification through the years. Countertransference, a subject Freud wrote little about, eventually became the focus of an extensive subliterature. Paula Heimann (1950; see chapter 11) provided a major impetus by writing not only of the detrimental aspects of countertransference but also of its constructive use, and thereby set the tone for a number of continuing debates. In the course of these struggles, our insights into the analyst's valid and disturbed functioning have been greatly expanded.

The interactional aspects of the analytic relationship, hardly touched upon by Freud, have also received growing attention and appreciation—largely due to the efforts of Kleinian writers. Strachey's remarkable paper (1934; see chapter 31) sets the tone here, though the subject has since been studied by both classicists and Kleinians, by the followers of Winnicott, and by a number of analysts with more independent leanings, such as Searles and myself. These writings, along with those related to the therapeutic alliance, and under the influence of considerations related to the ground rules and framework, have culminated for the moment in investigations of the bipersonal field (Baranger and Baranger 1966, Langs 1976a) and analytic space (Viderman 1974)—a broad meta-phoric view of the therapeutic experience and setting in which the intimate interplay between patient and analyst has come under extensive and productive scrutiny. Most recently, the role of the conscious and especially unconscious communicative interaction (Langs 1978a,b,d,e) has provided a basis for still further insight into the therapeutic experience.

Finally, beginning once again with Freud's first writings on technique (see especially 1912b, 1913) there is an expanding body of literature on the ground rules of analysis and the basic setting. While first viewed as a set of rules or tenets designed to provide secure conditions for the patient and to safeguard the analyzability of his transference expressions, this dimension of analysis has received an extended appreciation as a basic element of the patient-analyst relationship. Currently, it is seen as a means of providing both participants with a basic hold and container, necessary boundaries, and a viable communicative field within which sound analytic work can take place.

These papers, then, mark the struggles of individual analysts, and of analytic writers collectively, to identify and resolve uncertainties and errors, blind spots and unrecognized omissions, in the theory and practice of psychoanalytic technique. Written without benefit of a valid clinical methodology, these papers reveal themselves as the products of authors whose brilliance and perceptiveness nevertheless shine through. They represent the best in the history of a relatively young science, one in which psychoanalysts can even now take pride.

Still, the history of a science is by no means a matter of isolated facts and contributions, but is rather the subject of interpretation. Facts need a context. It is possible to consider these papers, and the history of psychoanalysis they are a part of, in a different perspective, and to emphasize, instead of development, an unfortunate sense of fixity and resistance to growth. One has only to consider that these forty-three papers have been culled from hundreds of others that reflect, in the main, an unimaginative rumination, a working over of the same ill-digested concepts to the point that one suspects the need for barriers to new ideas. These other writings indicate that for most psychoanalysts, a great many of Freud's early ideas on this subject persist as the central view of the therapeutic experience. No field can thrive under conditions of this kind, since growth and evolution is the most crucial sign of relevance, truth, and meaning in any endeavor. While certain core concepts are bound to prove relatively stable, the large bulk of the output from any era of writing and thinking should, over a reasonable period of time, be subjected to major revision. It is an important sign of vitality when each discovery is found to contain within itself the very seeds of its own revision and modification—sometimes, its total repudiation.

The signs of stultification, an especially serious matter for a field committed to search for the truth about both patient and analyst, their pathological and nonpathological functioning, can also be seen in the extent to which the writings of most major innovators in the field have failed to receive significant attention by those in the analytic mainstream. The Kleinians, and others with distinctly different ideas, have tended to be split off rather than integrated through an incorporative group process that would entail an eventual blending of the best of the classical and Kleinian viewpoints. This trend was decried by Greenson (1969), who just five years later (1974) was himself to write a scathing critique of their work. Similar fates have befallen most of the truly innovative and nonconforming analysts whose papers appear here. The envy, dread, and pervasive threat produced by new ideas prompt efforts in every psychoanalyst and psychotherapist to resist and destroy both the creative thinker and his innovation, despite avowed intentions to respond otherwise (see Langs 1978c).

For these reasons I have chosen to conclude this volume with a paper of my own. Having presented the papers which in my opinion best represent classical psychoanalytic thinking with respect to the analytic and therapeutic experiences, I offer as epilogue a reconsideration of the literature that puts on the agenda the question of whether these writings constitute a solid foundation or a facade. Although I fully acknowledge their lasting value, it is necessary, in any field in which growth and change are of the essence, to raise serious questions in the interest of greater understanding.

I wish to place this book at the center of the struggle, in which both analysts and therapists are presently engaged, to comprehend the therapeutic experience and its techniques. It is my hope that the reader, whatever his background or current opinions, will confront the diverse approaches reflected in these papers, and will integrate into his own thinking and clinical work what is sound in each of them. Because of limitations of space, it has been impossible to include a dozen or so additional papers which I believe fully deserve recognition as classics in psychoanalytic technique. Fortunately, the problem of selection proved difficult. In this regard, I am mindful of the decision to include a number of my own papers—a decision that required extensive thought and that remains filled with unresolved questions that only time and others will be able to set to rest.

Overall, then, this book is a tribute to those who struggled to advance the field of psychoanalysis, especially in the area of analytic and therapeutic technique, and who succeeded admirably where many had failed. I am grateful to them for what I have learned from their writings, and for the opportunity to present this volume as representative of the unique and superlative contributions of psychoanalysts to this most critical subject—the therapeutic interaction and experience.

Robert Langs, M.D.
New York, New York

PART I

TRANSFERENCE

This section contains a selection of papers that begins with Freud's fundamental delineation of transference in 1912 and concludes with Gill's 1979 effort to clarify the clinical manifestations of transference and the techniques they require. Much of the classical psychoanalytic literature on transference is essentially a restatement and elaboration of Freud's basic ideas. The papers selected for this section are included either because they very clearly epitomize the classical view of transference, or because they contribute relatively isolated but strikingly unique ideas.

With but a few exceptions, transference, as defined in these papers, refers to direct allusions to the analyst and readily identifiable displacements. It is almost unanimously viewed as an intrapsychic phenomenon with little or no interplay between this aspect of the patient's responses to the analyst and the analyst's own behaviors and communications to the patient. The term is often used to allude to the patient's entire relationship to the analyst, rather than being restricted to refer to the distorted and pathological elements; displacement from past important figures is seen as the central intrapsychic dynamism.

In the main, there are no empirical criteria with which one may confidently identify transference-based expressions, an issue that Szasz (1963; see chapter 4) alone considered in any major way. By contrast, Sandler et al. (1969; see chapter 5) asserted that analysts in general have a clear understanding of the clinical referents of transference.

Still it is fundamental, both theoretically and clinically, that the psychopathology of the patient finds expression in his relationship with the analyst, and that the interpretive-reconstructive understanding of the unconscious meanings and functions of transference expressions, in terms of their resistance and communicative properties, can serve as the essential vehicle of cure for the patient. Whatever the limitations of the classical concept of transference, it is this discovery that paved the way for an increasingly clear understanding of the nature of mental illness and the means by which it can be cured. A mastery of the concept, then, is in many ways fundamental to a basic grasp of the therapeutic experience, and can be extended by reading the closely related papers presented in Part V, The Therapeutic and Working Alliances, and Part VI, The Therapeutic Interaction—the latter presenting a conceptualization of transference more intimately embedded in the experiences between patient and analyst.

1

THE DYNAMICS OF TRANSFERENCE

Sigmund Freud

EDITOR'S NOTE
This paper is the first of five that Freud wrote on psychoanalytic technique (see also Freud 1912b [see chapter 38], 1913, 1914, 1915), in which he divided his attention between the manifestations of the patient's transference neurosis, as he termed it, and the means through which the analyst establishes and maintains the psychoanalytic setting. The paper was preceded by a number of earlier remarks regarding transference, especially those offered in his postscript to the case of Dora (1905), and is followed by a detailed investigation of the analyst's handling of transference-love (1915) and a number of shorter discussions of this subject in Freud's later writings.

The paper was selected for this volume because of its critical importance in identifying and clarifying the transference dimension of the patient's relationship to the analyst—perhaps the most fundamental of Freud's discoveries and a major stimulus for discussions of psychoanalytic technique. As the single most important embodiment of the unconscious basis for the patient's psychopathology, one that emerges directly in the relationship with the analyst, the recognition of transference proved to be the source of extensive insights into the nature of the analytic relationship and experience, and the key to the delineation of the analytic work necessary for the insightful, adaptive resolution of the patient's emotional disturbance—much of this based on the analysis of transference resistances. In many ways, then, the discovery of transference gave definitive meaning and function to psychoanalytic therapy, and, however modified in recent years, remains at the heart of analytic work.

As is characteristic of scientific discovery, Freud's innovative delineation of transference served as a selected fact (a realization that reorders and gives previously unrecognized meaning to disparate observations and data; see Bion 1963), while at the same time it has served—probably for Freud himself and certainly for his followers (see Szasz 1963 [see chapter 4], Chertok 1968)—as a barrier to other truths, many of them related to the analyst's counter-transferences. Thus, Freud's dictum—that the patient experiences his transferences as real and contemporaneous, while the analyst must search out their meanings in terms of the patient's past relationships—has all too often served as a means of denying the nondistorted aspects of many segments of the patient's responses and functioning within the analytic relationship, and has served also as a means of denying the analyst's disruptive inputs. This defensive function of the concept of transference has some bearing on Freud's relative neglect of the subject of countertransference, and on the tendency of psychoanalysts to maintain a view of transference as intrapsychic and as the overriding dimension of the patient's responses to the analyst.

The almost inexhaustible topic of transference has recently been dealt with by Wilhelm Stekel [1911b] in this journal[1] on descriptive lines. I should like in the following pages to add a few remarks to explain how it is that transference is necessarily brought about during a psycho-analytic treatment, and how it comes to play its familiar part in it.

It must be understood that each individual, through the combined operation of his innate disposition and the influences brought to bear on him during his early years, has acquired a specific method of his own in his conduct of his erotic life—that is, in the preconditions to falling in love which he lays down, in the instincts he satisfies and the aims he sets himself in the course of it.[2] This produces what might be described as a stereotype plate (or several such), which is constantly repeated—constantly reprinted afresh—in the course of the person's life, so far as external circumstances and the nature of the love-objects accessible to him permit, and which is certainly not entirely insusceptible to change in the face of recent experiences. Now, our observations have shown that only a portion of these impulses which determine the course of erotic life have passed through the full process of psychical development. That portion is directed towards reality, is at the disposal of the conscious personality, and forms a part of it. Another portion of the libidinal impulses has

been held up in the course of development; it has been kept away from the conscious personality and from reality, and has either been prevented from further expansion except in phantasy or has remained wholly in the unconscious so that it is unknown to the personality's consciousness. If someone's need for love is not entirely satisfied by reality, he is bound to approach every new person whom he meets with libidinal anticipatory ideas; and it is highly probable that both portions of his libido, the portion that is capable of becoming conscious as well as the unconscious one, have a share in forming that attitude.

Thus it is a perfectly normal and intelligible thing that the libidinal cathexis of someone who is partly unsatisfied, a cathexis which is held ready in anticipation, should be directed as well to the figure of the doctor. It follows from our earlier hypothesis that this cathexis will have recourse to prototypes, will attach itself to one of the stereotype plates which are present in the subject; or, to put the position in another way, the cathexis will introduce the doctor into one of the psychical 'series' which the patient has already formed. If the 'father-imago', to use the apt term introduced by Jung (1911, 164), is the decisive factor in bringing this about, the outcome will tally with the real relations of the subject to his doctor. But the transference is not tied to this particular

---

1. [The *Zentralblatt für Psychoanalyse,* in which the present paper first appeared.]

2. I take this opportunity of defending myself against the mistaken charge of having denied the importance of innate (constitutional) factors because I have stressed that of infantile impressions. A charge such as this arises from the restricted nature of what men look for in the field of causation: in contrast to what ordinarily holds good in the real world, people prefer to be satisfied with a single causative factor. Psychoanalysis has talked a lot about the accidental factors in aetiology and little about the constitutional ones; but that is only because it was able to

contribute something fresh to the former, while to begin with, it knew no more than was commonly known about the latter. We refuse to posit any contrast in principle between the two sets of aetiological factors; on the contrary, we assume that the two sets regularly act jointly in bringing about the observed result. Endowment and Chance determine a man's fate—rarely or never one of these powers alone. The amount of aetiological effectiveness to be attributed to each of them can only be arrived at in every individual case separately. These cases may be arranged in a series according to the varying proportion in which the two factors are present, and this series will no doubt have its extreme cases. We shall estimate the share taken by constitution or experience differently in individual cases according to the stage reached by our knowledge; and we shall retain the right to modify our judgement along with changes in our understanding. Incidentally, one might venture to regard constitution itself as a precipitate from the accidental effects produced on the endlessly long chain of our ancestors.

Reprinted from *The Standard Edition of the Complete Psychological Works of Sigmund Freud,* volume 12, pp. 97–108, trans. and ed. James Strachey, by permission of Sigmund Freud Copyrights Ltd., The Institute of Psycho-Analysis, The Hogarth Press Ltd., and (for U.S. rights) Basic Books Inc.

prototype: it may also come about on the lines of the mother-imago or brother-imago. The peculiarities of the transference to the doctor, thanks to which it exceeds, both in amount and nature, anything that could be justified on sensible or rational grounds, are made intelligible if we bear in mind that this transference has precisely been set up not only by the *conscious* anticipatory ideas but also by those that have been held back or are unconscious.

There would be nothing more to discuss or worry about in this behaviour of transference, if it were not that two points remain unexplained about it which are of particular interest to psycho-analysis. Firstly, we do not understand why transference is so much more intense with neurotic subjects in analysis than it is with other such people who are not being analysed; and secondly, it remains a puzzle why in analysis transference emerges as *the most powerful resistance* to the treatment, whereas outside analysis it must be regarded as the vehicle of cure and the condition of success. For our experience has shown us—and the fact can be confirmed as often as we please—that if a patient's free associations fail[3] the stoppage can invariably be removed by an assurance that he is being dominated at the moment by an association which is concerned with the doctor himself or with something connected with him. As soon as this explanation is given, the stoppage is removed, or the situation is changed from one in which the associations fail into one in which they are being kept back. At first sight it appears to be an immense disadvantage in psychoanalysis as a method that what is elsewhere the strongest factor towards success is changed in it into the most powerful medium of resistance. If, however, we examine the situation more closely, we can at least clear away the first of our two problems. It is not a fact that transference emerges with greater intensity and lack of restraint during psycho-analysis than outside it. In institutions in which nerve patients are treated

non-analytically, we can observe transference occurring with the greatest intensity and in the most unworthy forms, extending to nothing less than mental bondage, and moreover showing the plainest erotic colouring. Gabriele Reuter, with her sharp powers of observation, described this at a time when there was no such thing as psycho-analysis, in a remarkable book which betrays in every respect the clearest insight into the nature and genesis of neuroses.[4] These characteristics of transference are therefore to be attributed not to psycho-analysis but to neurosis itself.

Our second problem—the problem of why transference appears in psycho-analysis as resistance—has been left for the moment untouched; and we must now approach it more closely. Let us picture the psychological situation during the treatment. An invariable and indispensable precondition of *every* onset of a psychoneurosis is the process to which Jung has given the appropriate name of 'introversion'.[5] That is to say: the portion of libido which is capable of becoming conscious and is directed towards reality is diminished, and the portion which is directed *away* from reality and is unconscious, and which, though it may still feed the subject's phantasies, nevertheless belongs to the unconscious, is proportionately increased. The libido (whether wholly or in part) has entered on a regressive course and has revived the subject's infantile imagos.[6] The analytic treatment now proceeds to follow it; it seeks to track down the libido, to make it accessible to consciousness and, in the end, serviceable for reality. Where the investigations of analysis come upon the libido withdrawn into its hiding-place, a struggle is bound to break out; all the forces which have caused the libido to regress will rise up as 'resistances' against the work of analysis, in order to conserve the new state of things. For if the libido's introversion or regression had not been justified by a particular relation between the subject and the external world—stated in the most

---

3. I mean when they really cease, and not when, for instance, the patient keeps them back owing to ordinary feelings of unpleasure.

4. *Aus guter Familie*, Berlin, 1895.

5. Even though some of Jung's remarks give the impression that he regards this introversion as something which is characteristic of dementia praecox and does not come into account in the same way in other neuroses. — [This seems to be the first published occasion of Freud's use of 'introversion'. The term was first introduced in Jung, 1910b, 38; but Freud is probably criticizing Jung, 1911, 135–36*n.* (English translation, 1916, 487). Some further comment on Jung's use of the term will be found in a footnote to a later technical paper (1913c, p. 125 below) as well as in Freud's paper on narcissism (1914c, *Standard Ed.*, 14, 74) and in a passage towards the end of Lecture XXIII of the *Introductory Lectures* (1916–17). Freud used the term extremely seldom

in his later writings.]

6. It would be convenient if we could say 'it has recathected his infantile complexes'. But this would be incorrect: the only justifiable way of putting it would be 'the unconscious portions of those complexes'. — the topics dealt with in this paper are so extraordinarily involved that it is tempting to embark on a number of contiguous problems whose clarification would in point of fact be necessary before it would be possible to speak in unambiguous terms of the psychical processes that are to be described here. These problems include the drawing of a line of distinction between introversion and regression, the fitting of the theory of complexes into the libido theory, the relations of phantasying to the conscious and the unconscious as well as to reality—and others besides. I need not apologize for having resisted this temptation in the present paper.

general terms, by the frustration of satisfaction[7]— and if it had not for the moment even become expedient, it could never have taken place at all. But the resistances from this source are not the only ones or indeed the most powerful. The libido at the disposal of the subject's personality had always been under the influence of the attraction of his unconscious complexes (or, more correctly, of the portions of those complexes belonging to the unconscious),[8] and it entered on a regressive course because the attraction of reality had diminished. In order to liberate it, this attraction of the unconscious has to be overcome; that is, the repression of the unconscious instincts and of their productions, which has meanwhile been set up in the subject, must be removed. This is responsible for by far the largest part of the resistance, which so often causes the illness to persist even after the turning away from reality has lost its temporary justification. The analysis has to struggle against the resistances from both these sources. The resistance accompanies the treatment step by step. Every single association, every act of the person under treatment must reckon with the resistance and represents a compromise between the forces that are striving towards recovery and the opposing ones which I have described.

If now we follow a pathogenic complex from its representation in the conscious (whether this is an obvious one in the form of a symptom or something quite inconspicuous) to its root in the unconscious, we shall soon enter a region in which the resistance makes itself felt so clearly that the next association must take account of it and appear as a compromise between its demands and those of the work of investigation. It is at this point, on the evidence of our experience, that transference enters on the scene. When anything in the complexive material (in the subject-matter of the complex) is suitable for being transferred on to the figure of the doctor, that transference is carried out; it produces the next association, and announces itself by indications of a resistance—by a stoppage, for instance. We infer from this experience that the transference-idea has penetrated into consciousness in front of any other possible associations *because* it satisfies the resistance. An event of this sort is repeated on countless occasions in the course of an analysis. Over and over again, when we come near to a pathogenic complex,

the portion of that complex which is capable of transference is first pushed forward into consciousness and defended with the greatest obstinacy.[9]

After it has been overcome, the overcoming of the other portions of the complex raises few further difficulties. The longer an analytic treatment lasts and the more clearly the patient realizes that distortions of the pathogenic material cannot by themselves offer any protection against its being uncovered, the more consistently does he make use of the one sort of distortion which obviously affords him the greatest advantages—distortion through transference. These circumstances tend towards a situation in which finally every conflict has to be fought out in the sphere of transference.

Thus transference in the analytic treatment invariably appears to us in the first instance as the strongest weapon of the resistance, and we may conclude that the intensity and persistence of the transference are an effect and an expression of the resistance. The *mechanism* of transference is, it is true, dealt with when we have traced it back to the state of readiness of the libido, which has remained in possession of infantile imagos; but the part transference plays in the treatment can only be explained if we enter into its relations with resistance.

How does it come about that transference is so admirably suited to be a means of resistance? It might be thought that the answer can be given without difficulty. For it is evident that it becomes particularly hard to admit to any proscribed wishful impulse if it has to be revealed in front of the very person to whom the impulse relates. Such a necessity gives rise to situations which in the real world seem scarcely possible. But it is precisely this that the patient is aiming at when he makes the object of his emotional impulses coincide with the doctor. Further consideration, however, shows that this apparent gain cannot provide the solution of the problem. Indeed, a relation of affectionate and devoted dependence can, on the contrary, help a person over all the difficulties of making an admission. In analogous real situations people will usually say: 'I feel no shame in front of you: I can say anything to you.' Thus the transference to the doctor might just as easily serve to *facilitate* admissions, and it is not clear why it should make things more difficult.

---

7. [See the full discussion of this in the paper on "Types of Onset of Neurosis' (1912c), p. 231 ff. below.]

8. [Cf. the beginning of footnote 2, on the previous page.]

9. This, however, should not lead us to conclude in general that the element selected for transference-resistance is of peculiar pathogenic importance. If in the course of a battle there is a

particularly embittered struggle over the possession of some little church or some individual farm, there is no need to suppose that the church is a national shrine, perhaps, or that the house shelters the army's pay-chest. The value of the object may be a purely tactical one and may perhaps emerge only in this one battle.—[On transference-resistance see also p. 138.]

The answer to the question which has been repeated so often in these pages is not to be reached by further reflection but by what we discover when we examine individual transference-resistances occurring during treatment. We find in the end that we cannot understand the employment of transference as resistance so long as we think simply of 'transference'. We must make up our minds to distinguish a 'positive' transference from a 'negative' one, the transference of affectionate feelings from that of hostile ones, and to treat the two sorts of transference to the doctor separately. Positive transference is then further divisible into transference of friendly or affectionate feelings which are admissible to consciousness and transference of prolongations of those feelings into the unconscious. As regards the latter, analysis shows that they invariably go back to erotic sources. And we are thus led to the discovery that all the emotional relations of sympathy, friendship, trust, and the like, which can be turned to good account in our lives, are genetically linked with sexuality and have developed from purely sexual desires through a softening of their sexual aim, however pure and unsensual they may appear to our conscious self-perception. Originally we knew only sexual objects; and psychoanalysis shows us that people who in our real life are merely admired or respected may still be sexual objects for our unconscious.

Thus the solution of the puzzle is that transference to the doctor is suitable for resistance to the treatment only in so far as it is a negative transference or a positive transference of repressed erotic impulses. If we 'remove' the transference by making it conscious, we are detaching only these two components of the emotional act from the person of the doctor; the other component, which is admissible to consciousness and unobjectionable, persists and is the vehicle of success in psychoanalysis exactly as it is in other methods of treatment. To this extent we readily admit that the results of psycho-analysis rest upon suggestion; by suggestion, however, we must understand, as Ferenczi (1909) does, the influencing of a person by means of the transference phenomena which are possible in his case. We take care of the patient's final independence by employing suggestion in order to get him to accomplish a piece of

psychical work which has as its necessary result a permanent improvement in his psychical situation.

The further question may be raised of why it is that the resistance phenomena of transference only appear in psychoanalysis and not in indifferent forms of treatment (e.g. in institutions) as well. The reply is that they do show themselves in these other situations too, but they have to be recognized as such. The breaking out of a negative transference is actually quite a common event in institutions. As soon as a patient comes under the dominance of the negative transference he leaves the institution in an unchanged or relapsed condition. The erotic transference does not have such an inhibiting effect in institutions, since in them, just as in ordinary life, it is glossed over instead of being uncovered. But it is manifested quite clearly as a resistance to recovery, not, it is true, by driving the patient out of the institution—on the contrary, it holds him back in it—but by keeping him at a distance from life. For, from the point of view of recovery, it is a matter of complete indifference whether the patient overcomes this or that anxiety or inhibition in the institution; what matters is that he shall be free of it in his real life as well.

The negative transference deserves a detailed examination, which it cannot be given within the limits of the present paper. In the curable forms of psychoneurosis it is found side by side with the affectionate transference, often directed simultaneously towards the same person. Bleuler has coined the excellent term 'ambivalence' to describe this phenomenon.[10] Up to a point, ambivalence of feeling of this sort seems to be normal; but a high degree of it is certainly a special peculiarity of neurotic people. In obsessional neurotics an early separation of the 'pairs of opposites'[11] seems to be characteristic of their instinctual life and to be one of their constitutional preconditions. Ambivalence in the emotional trends of neurotics is the best explanation of their ability to enlist their transferences in the service of resistance. Where the capacity for transference has become essentially limited to a negative one, as is the case with paranoics, there ceases to be any possibility of influence or cure.

In all these reflections, however, we have hitherto

---

10. Bleuler, 1911, 43–4 and 305–6.—Cf. a lecture on ambivalence delivered by him in Berne in 1910, reported in the *Zentralblatt für Psychoanalyse*, 1, 266.—Stekel has proposed the term 'bipolarity' for the same phenomenon—[This appears to have been Freud's first mention of the word 'ambivalence'. He occasionally used it in a sense other than Bleuler's, to describe the simultaneous presence of active and passive impulses. See an

Editor's footnote, *Standard Ed., 14*, 131.]

11. [The pairs of opposite instincts were first described by Freud in his *Three Essays* (1905d), *Standard Ed.*, 7, 160 and 166–7, and later on in 'Instincts and their Vicissitudes' (1915c), *Standard Ed*, 14, 127 ff. Their importance in obsessional neurosis was discussed in the 'Rat Man' case history (1909d), *Standard Ed.*, 10, 237 ff.]

dealt only with one side of the phenomenon of transference; we must turn our attention to another aspect of the same subject. Anyone who forms a correct appreciation of the way in which a person in analysis, as soon as he comes under the dominance of any considerable transference-resistance, is flung out of his real relation to the doctor, how he feels at liberty then to disregard the fundamental rule of psycho-analysis[12] which lays it down that whatever comes into one's head must be reported without criticizing it, how he forgets the intentions with which he started the treatment, and how he regards with indifference logical arguments and conclusions which only a short time before had made a great impression on him—anyone who has observed all this will feel it necessary to look for an explanation of his impression in other factors besides those that have already been adduced. Nor are such factors far to seek: they arise once again from the psychological situation in which treatment places the patient.

In the process of seeking out the libido which has escaped from the patient's conscious, we have penetrated into the realm of the unconscious. The reactions which we bring about reveal at the same time some of the characteristics which we have come to know from the study of dreams. The unconscious impulses do not want to be remembered in the way the treatment desires them to be, but endeavour to reproduce themselves in accordance with the timelessness of the unconscious and its capacity for hallucination.[13] Just as happens in dreams, the patient regards the products of the awakening of his unconscious impulses as contemporaneous and real; he seeks to put his passions into action without taking any account of the real situation. The doctor tries to compel him to fit these emotional impulses into the nexus of the treatment and of his life-history, to submit them to intellectual consideration and to understand them in the light of their psychical value. This struggle between the doctor and the patient, between intellect and instinctual life, between understanding and seeking to act, is played out almost exclusively in the phenomena of transference. It is on that field that the victory must be won—the victory whose expression is the permanent cure of the neurosis. It cannot be disputed that controlling the phenomena of transference presents the psychoanalyst with the greatest difficulties. But it should not be forgotten that it is precisely they that do us the inestimable service of making the patient's hidden and forgotten erotic impulses immediate and manifest. For when all is said and done, it is impossible to destroy anyone *in absentia* or *in effigie*.[14]

---

12. [This seems to be the first use of what was henceforward to become the regular description of the essential technical rule. A very similar phrase ('the main rule of psycho-analysis') had, however, been used already in the third of Freud's Clark University Lectures (1910a), *Standard Ed.*, 11, 33. The idea itself, of course, goes back a long way; it is expressed, for instance, in Chapter II of *The Interpretation of Dreams* (1900a), *Standard Ed.*, 4, 101, in essentially the same terms as in the paper 'On Beginning the Treatment' (1913c) p. 134 below, where, incidentally, the subject will be found discussed in a long footnote.]

13. [This is elaborated in a later technical paper 'Recollecting, Repeating and Working-Through' (1914g), p. 150 ff. below.]

14. [Cf. the similar remark near the bottom of p. 152 below.]

2

THE ORIGINS OF TRANSFERENCE[1]

MELANIE KLEIN

EDITOR'S NOTE

Following Freud's delineation of transference, many papers appeared on the subject, most of them attempting to develop a more adaptive view and pointing in various ways to the influence of the current analytic situation and the analyst in generating transference manifestations. This paper by Melanie Klein deserves a special place in the history of the concept because of its stress on transference as a form of object relationship having preoedipal as well as oedipal roots, a relationship expressed in both libidinal and aggressive instinctual drive terms.

Extending a line of thought first expounded by Ferenczi (1909) and later elaborated by Strachey (1934), Klein developed the position that, in addition to the role of displacements from the past in transference expressions, projections onto the analyst of the patient's current inner mental world (self-representations and manifestations of id, ego, and superego) play an important role. She also extended the recognized range of transference expressions beyond direct references to the analyst and readily identifiable displacements, suggesting that every communication from the patient contains unconscious manifestations of the transference. Here Klein uses the term *transference* to refer to the patient's total relationship with the analyst, a common error quite in keeping with a tendency in Freud's own use of the term, despite his own definition of transference in terms of the distorting aspects of the patient's relation to the analyst. While few analysts have attempted an empirical study of the issues raised by Klein's discussion of the manifestations of transference, my own recent studies (1976a,b, 1978a,b) have validated her conception—so long as it is understood that she is actually referring to both transference and nontransference aspects (i.e., that every communication from the patient alludes on some level both to himself and to some aspect of his relationship with the analyst).

The present paper, then, significantly extended the criteria for what would count as transference expression and elaborated the underlying mechanisms and genetic factors. Projection and displacement are both seen as significant mechanisms, the former finding later elaboration in the writings of Klein's followers (see Part VI), who ascribed great importance to projective identification in the analytic interaction. This paper not only clarifies classical

1. Read at the 17th International Psycho-Analytical Congress, Amsterdam, August, 1951.

Freud thinking in regard to transference, but also endeavors to establish for this phenomenon the importance of Kleinian concepts of early childhood development. In many ways, then, the paper is a wellspring for both classical Freudian and Kleinian psychoanalysts in their attempts at further clarification of the concept.

In his *Fragment of an Analysis of a Case of Hysteria*[2] Freud defines the transference situation in the following way: —

What are transferences? They are new editions or fac-similes of the tendencies and phantasies which are aroused and made conscious during the progress of the analysis; but they have this peculiarity, which is characteristic for their species, that they replace some earlier person by the person of the physician. To put it another way: a whole series of psychological experiences are revived, not as belonging to the past, but as applying to the physician at the present moment.

In some form or other transference operates throughout life and influences all human relations, but here I am only concerned with the manifestations of transference in psycho-analysis. It is characteristic of psycho-analytic procedure that, as it begins to open up roads into the patient's unconscious, his past (in its conscious and unconscious aspects) is gradually being revived. Thereby his urge to transfer his early experiences, object-relations and emotions, is reinforced and they come to focus on the psycho-analyst; this implies that the patient deals with the conflicts and anxieties which have been reactivated, by making use of the same mechanisms and defences as in earlier situations.

It follows that the deeper we are able to penetrate into the unconscious and the further back we can take the analysis, the greater will be our understanding of the transference. Therefore a brief summary of my conclusions about the earlier stages of development is relevant to my topic.

The first form of anxiety is of a persecutory nature. The working of the death instinct within— which according to Freud is directed against the organism—gives rise to the fear of annihilation, and this is the primordial cause of persecutory anxiety.

Furthermore, from the beginning of post-natal life (I am not concerned here with pre-natal processes) destructive impulses against the object stir up fear of retaliation. These persecutory feelings from inner sources are intensified by painful external experiences, for, from the earliest days onwards, frustration and discomfort arouse in the infant the feeling that he is being attacked by hostile forces. Therefore the sensations experienced by the infant at birth and the difficulties of adapting himself to entirely new conditions give rise to persecutory anxiety. The comfort and care given after birth, particularly the first feeding experiences, are felt to come from good forces. In speaking of 'forces' I am using a rather adult word for what the young infant dimly conceives of as objects, either good or bad. The infant directs his feelings of gratification and love towards the 'good' breast, and his destructive impulses and feelings of persecution towards what he feels to be frustrating, i.e. the 'bad' breast. At this stage splitting processes are at their height, and love and hatred as well as the good and bad aspects of the breast are largely kept apart from one another. The infant's relative security is based on turning the good object into an ideal one as a protection against the dangerous and persecuting object. These processes—that is to say splitting, denial, omnipotence and idealization—are prevalent during the first three or four months of life (which I termed the 'paranoid-schizoid position' (1946)). In these ways at a very early stage persecutory anxiety and its corollary, idealization, fundamentally influence object relations.

The primal processes of projection and introjection, being inextricably linked with the infant's emotions and anxieties, initiate object-relations; by projecting, i.e. deflecting libido and aggression on to the mother's breast, the basis for object-relations is established; by introjecting the object, first of all the breast, relations to internal objects come into being. My use of the term 'object-relations' is based on my contention that the infant has from the beginning of post-natal life a relation to the mother (although focusing primarily on her breast) which is imbued with the fundamental elements of object-

---

2. 1905. Contained in *Collected Papers*, 3, p. 139.

relation, i.e. love, hatred, phantasies, anxieties, and defences.[3]

In my view—as I have explained in detail on other occasions—the introjection of the breast is the beginning of superego formation which extends over years. We have grounds for assuming that from the first feeding experience onwards the infant introjects the breast in its various aspects. The core of the superego is thus the mother's breast, both good and bad. Owing to the simultaneous operation of introjection and projection, relations to external and internal objects interact. The father too, who soon plays a role in the child's life, early on becomes part of the infant's internal world. It is characteristic of the infant's emotional life that there are rapid fluctuations between love and hate; between external and internal situations; between perception of reality and the fantasies relating to it; and, accordingly, an interplay between persecutory anxiety and idealization—both referring to internal and external objects; the idealized object being a corollary of the persecutory, extremely bad one.

The ego's growing capacity for integration and synthesis leads more and more, even during these first few months, to states in which love and hatred, and correspondingly the good and bad aspects of objects, are being synthesized; and this gives rise to the second form of anxiety—depressive anxiety—for the infant's aggressive impulses and desires towards the bad breast (mother) are now felt to be a danger to the good breast (mother) as well. In the second quarter of the first year these emotions are reinforced, because at this stage the infant increasingly perceives and introjects the mother as a person. Depressive anxiety is intensified, for the infant feels he has destroyed or is destroying a whole object by his greed and uncontrollable aggression. Moreover, owing to the growing synthesis of his emotions, he now feels that these destructive impulses are directed against a *loved person*. Similar processes operate in relation to the father and other members of the family. These anxieties and corresponding defences constitute the 'depressive position', which comes to a head about the middle of the first year and whose essence is the anxiety and guilt relating to the destruction and loss of the loved internal and external objects.

It is at this stage, and bound up with the depressive position, that the Oedipus complex sets in. Anxiety and guilt add a powerful impetus towards the beginning of the Oedipus complex. For anxiety and guilt increase the need to externalize (project) bad figures and to internalize (introject) good ones; to attach desires, love, feelings of guilt, and reparative tendencies to some objects, and hate and anxiety to others; to find representatives for internal figures in the external world. It is, however, not only the search for new objects which dominates the infants needs, but also the drive towards new aims: away from the breast towards the penis, i.e. from oral desires towards genital ones. Many factors contribute to these developments: the forward drive of the libido, the growing integration of the ego, physical and mental skills and progressive adaptation to the external world. These trends are bound up with the process of symbol formation, which enables the infant to transfer not only interest, but also emotions and phantasies, anxiety and guilt, from one object to another.

The processes I have described are linked with another fundamental phenomenon governing mental life. I believe that the pressure exerted by the earliest anxiety situations is one of the factors which bring about the repetition compulsion. I shall return to this hypothesis at a later point.

Some of my conclusions about the earliest stages of infancy are a continuation of Freud's discoveries; on certain points, however, divergencies have arisen, one of which is very relevant to my present topic. I am referring to my contention that object-relations are operative from the beginning of postnatal life.

For many years I have held the view that auto-erotism and narcissism are in the young infant contemporaneous with the first relation to objects—external and internalized. I shall briefly restate my hypothesis: auto-erotism and narcissism include the love for and relation with the internalized good object which in phantasy forms part of the loved body and self. It is to this internalized object that in auto-erotic gratification and narcissistic *states* a withdrawal takes place. Concurrently, from birth onwards, a relation to objects, primarily the mother (her breast) is present. This hypothesis contradicts

---

3. It is an essential feature of this earliest of all object-relations that it is the prototype of a relation between *two* people into which no other object enters. This is of vital importance for later object-relations, though in that exclusive form it possibly does not last longer than a very few months, for the phantasies relating to the father and his penis—phantasies which initiate the early stages of the Oedipus complex—introduce the relation to more than one object. In the analysis of adults and children the patient sometimes comes to experience feelings of blissful happiness through the revival of this early exclusive relation with the mother and her breast. Such experiences often follow the analysis of jealousy and rivalry situations in which a third object, ultimately the father, is involved.

Freud's concept of auto-erotic and narcissistic *stages* which preclude an object-relation. However, the difference between Freud's view and my own is less wide than appears at first sight, since Freud's statements on this issue are not unequivocal. In various contexts he explicitly and implicitly expressed opinions which suggested a relation to an object, the mother's breast, *preceding* auto-erotism and narcissism. One reference must suffice; in the first of two Encyclopaedia articles,[4] Freud said;

In the first instance the oral component instinct finds satisfaction by attaching itself to the sating of the desire for nourishment; and its object is the mother's breast. It then detaches itself, becomes independent and at the same time *auto-erotic,* that is, it finds an object in the child's own body.

Freud's use of the term object is here somewhat different from my use of this term, for he is referring to the object of an instinctual aim, while I mean, in addition to this, an object-relation involving the infant's emotions, phantasies, anxieties, and defences. Nevertheless, in the sentence referred to, Freud clearly speaks of a libidinal attachment to an object, the mother's breast, which precedes auto-eroticism and narcissism.

In this context I wish to remind you also of Freud's findings about early identifications. In *The Ego and the Id,*[5] speaking of abandoned object cathexes, he said; '. . . the effects of the first identification in earliest childhood will be profound and lasting. This leads us back to the origin of the ego-ideal; . . . .' Freud then defines the first and most important identifications which lie hidden behind the ego-ideal as the identification with the father, or with the parents, and places them, as he expresses it, in the 'prehistory of every person'. These formulations come close to what I describe as the first introjected objects, for by definition identifications are the result of introjection. From the statement I have just discussed and the passage quoted from the Encyclopaedia article it can be deduced that Freud, although he did not pursue this line of thought further, did assume that in earliest infancy both an object and introjective processes play a part.

That is to say, as regards auto-erotism and narcissism we meet with an inconsistency in Freud's views. Such inconsistencies which exist on a number of

points of theory clearly show, I think, that on these particular issues Freud had not yet arrived at a final decision. In respect of the theory of anxiety he stated this explicitly in *Inhibitions, Symptoms and Anxiety.*[6] His realization that much about the early stages of development was still unknown or obscure to him is also exemplified by his speaking of the first years of the girl's life as '. . . . lost in a past so dim and shadowy. . . .'[7]

I do not know Anna Freud's view about this aspect of Freud's work. But, as regards the question of auto-erotism and narcissism, she seems only to have taken into account Freud's conclusion that an auto-erotic and a narcissistic stage precede object-relations, and not to have allowed for the other possibilities implied in some of Freud's statements such as the ones I referred to above. This is one of the reasons why the divergence between Anna Freud's conception and my conception of early infancy is far greater than that between Freud's views, taken as a whole, and my views. I am stating this because I believe it is essential to clarify the extent and nature of the differences between the two schools of psycho-analytic thought represented by Anna Freud and myself. Such clarification is required in the interests of psycho-analytic training and also because it could help to open up fruitful discussions between psycho-analysts and thereby contribute to a greater general understanding of the fundamental problems of early infancy.

The hypothesis that a stage extending over several months precedes object-relations implies that— except for the libido attached to the infant's own body—impulses, phantasies, anxieties, and defences either are not present in him, or are not related to an object, that is to say they would operate *in vacuo.* The analysis of very young children has taught me that there is no instinctual urge, no anxiety situation, no mental process which does not involve objects, external or internal; in other words, object-relations are at the *centre* of emotional life. Furthermore, love and hatred, phantasies, anxieties, and defences are also operative from the beginning and are *ab initio* indivisibly linked with object-relations. This insight showed me many phenomena in a new light.

I shall now draw the conclusion on which the present paper rests: I hold that transference originates in the same processes which in the earliest stages determine object-relations. Therefore we have to

4. 'Psycho-Analysis', 1922. Contained in *Collected Papers,* 5, p. 119.

5. On the same page Freud suggests—still referring to these first identifications—that they are a direct and immediate identification which takes place earlier than any object cathexis.

This suggestion seems to imply that introjection even precedes object-relations.

6. 1926. Chapter 8, p. 96.

7. 1931. 'Female Sexuality'; contained in *Collected Papers,* 5, p. 254.

go back again and again in analysis to the fluctuations between objects, loved and hated, external and internal, which dominate early infancy. We can fully appreciate the interconnection between positive and negative transferences only if we explore the early interplay between love and hate, and the vicious circle of aggression, anxieties, feelings of guilt and increased aggression, as well as the various aspects of objects towards whom these conflicting emotions and anxieties are directed. On the other hand, through exploring these early processes I became convinced that the analysis of the negative transference, which had received relatively little attention[8] in psycho-analytic technique, is a precondition for analysing the deeper layers of the mind. The analysis of the negative as well as of the positive transference and of their interconnection is, as I have held for many years, an indispensable principle for the treatment of all types of patients, children and adults alike. I have substantiated this view in most of my writings from 1927 onwards.

This approach, which in the past made possible the psychoanalysis of very young children, has in recent years proved extremely fruitful for the analysis of schizophrenic patients. Until about 1920 it was assumed that schizophrenic patients were incapable of forming a transference and therefore could not be psycho-analysed. Since then the psycho-analysis of schizophrenics has been attempted by various techniques. The most radical change of view in this respect, however, has occurred more recently and is closely connected with the greater knowledge of the mechanisms, anxieties, and defences operative in earliest infancy. Since some of these defences, evolved in primal object-relations against both love and hatred, have been discovered, the fact that schizophrenic patients are capable of developing both a positive and a negative transference has been fully understood; this finding is confirmed if we consistently apply in the treatment of schizophrenic patients[9] the principle that it is as necessary to analyse the negative as the positive transference—that in fact the one cannot be analysed without the other.

Retrospectively it can be seen that these considerable advances in technique are supported in psychoanalytic theory by Freud's discovery of the Life and Death instincts, which has fundamentally added to the understanding of the origin of ambivalence.

Because the Life and Death instincts, and therefore love and hatred, are at bottom in the closest interaction, negative and positive transference are basically interlinked.

The understanding of earliest object-relations and the processes they imply has essentially influenced technique from various angles. It has long been known that the psycho-analyst in the transference situation may stand for mother, father, or other people, that he is also at times playing in the patient's mind the part of the superego, at other times that of the id or the ego. Our present knowledge enables us to penetrate to the specific details of the various roles allotted by the patient to the analyst. There are in fact very few people in the young infant's life, but he feels them to be a multitude of objects because they appear to him in different aspects. Accordingly, the analyst may at a given moment represent a part of the self, of the superego or any one of a wide range of internalized figures. Similarly it does not carry us far enough if we realize that the analyst stands for the actual father or mother, unless we understand which aspect of the parents has been revived. The picture of the parents in the patient's mind has in varying degrees undergone distortion through the infantile processes of projection and idealization, and has often retained much of its phantastic nature. Altogether, in the young infant's mind every external experience is interwoven with his phantasies and on the other hand every phantasy contains elements of actual experience, and it is only by analysing the transference situation to its depth that we are able to discover the past both in its realistic and phantastic aspects. It is also the origin of these fluctuations in earliest infancy which accounts for their strength in the transference, and for the swift changes—sometimes even within one session—between father and mother, between omnipotently kind objects and dangerous persecutors, between internal and external figures. Sometimes the analyst appears simultaneously to represent both parents—in that case often in a hostile alliance against the patient, whereby the negative transference acquires great intensity. What has then been revived or has become manifest in the transference is the mixture in the patient's phantasy of the parents as one figure, the 'combined parent figure' as I described it

---

8. This was largely due to the undervaluation of the importance of aggression.

9. This technique is illustrated by H. Segal's paper, *Some Aspects of the Analysis of a Schizophrenic* (*Int. J. Psycho-Anal.*, 31, 1950), and H. Rosenfeld's papers, 'Notes on the Psycho-

Analysis of the Super-ego Conflict of an Acute Schizophrenic Patient' (*Int. J. Psycho-Anal.*, 33, 1952) and 'Transference Phenomena and Transference Analysis in an Acute Catatonic Schizophrenic Patient' (see this volume, 457–464).

elsewhere.[10] This is one of the phantasy formations characteristic of the earliest stages of the Oedipus complex and which, if maintained in strength, is detrimental both to object-relations and sexual development. The phantasy of the combined parents draws its force from another element of early emotional life—i.e. from the powerful envy associated with frustrated oral desires. Through the analysis of such early situations we learn that in the baby's mind when he is frustrated (or dissatisfied from inner causes) his frustration is coupled with the feeling that another object (soon represented by the father) receives from the mother the coveted gratification and love denied to himself at that moment. Here is one root of the phantasy that the parents are combined in an everlasting mutual gratification of an oral, anal, and genital nature. And this is in my view the prototype of situations of both envy and jealousy.

There is another aspect of the analysis of transference which needs mentioning. We are accustomed to speak of the transference *situation*. But do we always keep in mind the fundamental importance of this concept? It is my experience that in unravelling the details of the transference it is essential to think in terms of *total situations* transferred from the past into the present, as well as of emotions, defences, and object-relations.

For many years—and this is up to a point still true today—transference was understood in terms of direct references to the analyst in the patient's material. My conception of transference as rooted in the earliest stages of development and in deep layers of the unconscious is much wider and entails a technique by which from the whole material presented the *unconscious elements* of the transference are deduced. For instance, reports of patients about their everyday life, relations, and activities not only give an insight into the functioning of the ego, but also reveal—if we explore their unconscious content—the defences against the anxieties stirred up in the transference situation. For the patient is bound to deal with conflicts and anxieties re-experienced towards the analyst by the same methods he used in the past. That is to say, he turns away from the analyst as he attempted to turn away from his primal objects; he tries to split the relation to

him, keeping him either as a good or as a bad figure; he deflects some of the feelings and attitudes experienced towards the analyst on to other people in his current life, and this is part of 'acting out'.[11]

In keeping with my subject matter, I have predominantly discussed here the earliest experiences, situations, and emotions from which transference springs. On these foundations, however, are built the later object-relations and the emotional and intellectual developments which necessitate the analyst's attention no less than the earliest ones; that is to say, our field of investigation covers *all* that lies between the current situation and the earliest experiences. In fact it is not possible to find access to earliest emotions and object-relations except by examining their vicissitudes in the light of later developments. It is only by linking again and again (and that means hard and patient work) later experiences with earlier ones and *vice versa,* it is only by consistently exploring their interplay, that present and past can come together in the patient's mind. This is one aspect of the process of integration which, as the analysis progresses, encompasses the whole of the patient's mental life. When anxiety and guilt diminish and love and hate can be better synthesized, splitting processes—a fundamental defence against anxiety—as well as repressions lessen while the ego gains in strength and coherence; the cleavage between idealized and persecutory objects diminishes; the phantastic aspects of objects lose in strength; all of which implies that unconscious phantasy life—less sharply divided off from the unconscious part of the mind—can be better utilized in ego activities, with a consequent general enrichment of the personality. I am touching here on the *differences*—as contrasted with the similarities—between transference and the first object-relations. These differences are a measure of the curative effect of the analytic procedure.

I suggested above that one of the factors which bring about the repetition compulsion is the pressure exerted by the earliest anxiety situations. When persecutory and depressive anxiety and guilt diminish, there is less urge to repeat fundamental experiences over and over again, and therefore early patterns and modes of feelings are maintained with less tenacity. These fundamental changes come

---

10. See *Psycho-Analysis of Children,* particularly Chapters 8 and 11.

11. The patient may at times try to escape from the present into the past rather than realize that his emotions, anxieties, and

phantasies are at the time operative in full strength and focused on the analyst. At other times, as we know, the defences are mainly directed against re-experiencing the past in relation to the original objects.

about through the consistent analysis of the transference; they are bound up with a deep-reaching revision of the earliest object-relations and are reflected in the patient's current life as well as in the altered attitudes towards the analyst.

Bibliography

Freud, Sigmund (1905). 'Fragment of an Analysis of a Case of Hysteria', *Collected Papers, 3*.

————(1922). 'Psycho-Analysis', *Collected Papers, 5*.

————(1923). *The Ego and the Id*.

————(1926). *Inhibitions, Symptoms and Anxiety*.

————(1931). 'Female Sexuality', *Collected Papers, 5*.

————Klein, Melanie (1932). *The Psycho-Analysis of Children*. Hogarth Press.

————(1946). 'Notes on Some Schizoid Mechanisms', *Int. J. Psycho-Anal.*, 27, also contained in *Developments in Psycho-Analysis*, by Melanie Klein, Paul Heimann, Susan Isaacs, and Joan Riviere. (London: Hogarth Press, 1952.)

————(1948). *Contributions to Psycho-Analysis, 1921–45*. Hogarth Press.

Rosenfeld, Herbert (1952). 'Notes on the Psycho-Analysis of the Super-ego Conflict of an Acute Schizophrenic Patient', *Int. J. Psycho-Anal.*, 33.

————(1952). 'Transference Phenomena and Transference Analysis of an Acute Catatonic Schizophrenic Patient' (this volume).

Segal, Hanna (1950). 'Some Aspects of the Analysis of a Schizophrenic', *Int. J. Psycho-Anal.*, 31.

3

THE ROLE OF TRANSFERENCE

PHYLLIS GREENACRE

EDITOR'S NOTE

This paper stands among the most lucid and sensitive delineations of the classical Freudian concept of transference. Greenacre's concept of basic and reactive transferences, which are related to Freud's earlier ideas (1905, 1912a [see chapter 1]) on deinstinctualized and instinctualized transferences, foreshadowed later discussions of the therapeutic alliance and transference—their distinctions and similarities (see Part V). The paper is also distinctive in regard to the author's discussion of the ground rules of analysis, in that the rationale for the maintenance of these tenets and the disruptive influence of their modification are spelled out in considerable detail—a position quite unique for a classical analyst (see Part VII). This study is the second in a series of contributions by Greenacre that served to clarify important dimensions of the analytic experience (see Greenacre 1971).

It is my intention to discuss some of the practical considerations in psychoanalytic treatment in their relationship to the role of the transference. I shall not enter into any extensive technical or historical survey but shall confine myself to a few problems expressed in nontechnical terms, and without benefit of quotation. I shall deal with these problems in the following order: (1) a discussion of the essentials of the transference relationship; (2) a brief outline of two different points of view regarding the utilization of the transference in therapy; and (3) a discussion of practical arrangements as they are determined by the transference.

I

First as to the nature of the transference relationship itself: If two people are repeatedly alone together some sort of emotional bond will develop between them. Even though they may be strangers engaged in relatively neutral occupations, not directed by one or the other for or against the "other one," it will probably not be long before a predominantly friendly or predominantly unfriendly tone will develop between them. The speed and the intensity of this development will be enhanced by the frequency of the periods in each other's company.

Human beings do not thrive well in isolation, being sustained then mostly by memories and hopes, even to the point of hallucination, or by reaching out to nonhuman living things (like Mendel and the beans). This need for sensory contact, basically the contact of warm touch of another body but secondarily experienced in the other senses as well (even the word "contact" is significant), probably comes from the long period of care which the human infant must have before he is able to sustain himself. Lonely infants fed and cared for regularly and with sterile impersonal efficiency do not live to childhood.

Even if the periods of repeated contact between two individuals do not comprise a major part of their time, still such an emotional bond develops and does so more quickly and more sensitively if the two persons are *alone* together; i.e., the more the spontaneous currents and emanations of feeling must be concentrated the one upon the other and not shared, divided, or reflected among members of a group. I have already indicated that I believe the matrix of this *is* a veritable matrix; i.e., comes largely from the original mother-infant quasi-union of the first months of life. This I consider the basic transference; or one might call it the primary transference, or some part of primitive social instinct.

Now if both people are adults but one is troubled and the other is versed in the ways of trouble and will endeavor to put the torchlight of his understanding at the disposal of the troubled one, to lend it to him that he may find his way more expeditiously, the situation more nearly approximates that of the analytic relationship. The analyst acts then like an extra function, or set of functions, which is lent to the analysand for the latter's temporary use and benefit.

Since this relationship may, in its most primitive aspects, be based on the mother-child relationship and since the patient is a troubled person seeking help, one can see at once that the relationship will not be one of equal mutual warming, but that there will be a tendency for the patient to develop an attitude of expectant dependent receptiveness toward the physician. It is the aim of treatment, however, to increase the patient's maturity, to realize his capacity for self-direction, his "self possession" (in the deeper sense of the word); and *not* to augment his state of helplessness and dependence, with which he in his neurotic suffering is already burdened.

How then is the patient's autonomy to be safeguarded and strengthened, in the very situation which might seem to favor its depletion? The chief safeguard is the analyst's sticking to the work of actually analyzing, and not serving as guide, model, or teacher, no matter how luring these roles may be. He must therefore genuinely leave matters of decision in the patient's own hands without guiding interference. We all know that the work of analysis consists very largely in helping the patient to rid himself of the tensions, patterned attitudes, and expectations which have arisen in the vicissitudes of the past and are impinging unhelpfully upon current situations, so much so that they actually distort his appreciation of and his reactive possibilities to the present problems of his life; and that this help of riddance is carried out through a mutual exploration of the forgotten past, using mainly the special techniques of free association and dream analysis.

The analytic relationship is used entirely for the benefit of the patient. Analysis is the profession of the therapist and he sets his fee and makes his time

arrangements with his patient in advance; and thereafter attempts to keep these constant except when extraordinary reality conditions intrude to force a dislocation of these elements of the reality framework. The analyst does not intrude his life, his point of view—moral, political or religious or any other—into his responses to his patient. His aim rather is to listen, to clarify and to communicate step by step an understanding of the patient's current dilemmas in relation to the intrusion into them of inappropriate emotional attitudes and action tendencies having their origin in the past. This sounds too mechanistic and too simple, but will be considered again in dealing further with the transference development. In the very neutrality and constancy of the physical arrangements of treatment, in their noncontamination by contributions from the analyst's own life, and in the essentially research and nondirective attitude of the analyst, many forces which might diminish the patient's autonomy are avoided.

It is quite apparent that in nonanalytic relationships, in just everyday give-and-take contacts, we react not merely on the basis of the realistic current elements of the situation but as these influence us additionally in accordance with their stirring memories of past experiences, whether or not these are available to direct recall. Indeed we seem to be more influenced when the memory is not available, and we mistake the feeling aroused by the past for one belonging intrinsically to the present. In each life situation, whole series of memory reactions of more or less related situations are re-evoked, and it is certainly not merely the present but a composite of past experiences which is influencing the attitudes and actions of the individual at any given time.

Now in the artificial situation of the analytic relationship, there develops early a firm basic transference, derived from the mother-child relationship but expressed in the confidence in the knowledge and integrity of the analyst and the helpfulness of the method; but in addition the nonparticipation of the analyst in a personal way in the relationship creates a "tilted" emotional relationship, a kind of psychic suction in which many of the past attitudes, specific experiences and fantasies of the patient are re-enacted in fragments or sometimes in surprisingly well-organized dramas with the analyst as the main figure of significance to the patient. This revival of past experiences with their full emotional accompaniment focused upon the analyst, is not only more possible but can be more easily seen, understood, and interpreted if the psychic field is not already cluttered with personal bits from the analyst's life.

This of course is the work with the neurotic symptoms and patterns as they occur in the transference; i.e., projected directly upon the analyst. Many times it is the most convincing medium of demonstration and interpretation to the patient and permits a greater degree of relief, probably because the memories are thus being actually experienced with their *full* emotional resonance, and not merely being reported and talked about with a *partial* reliving. One should recall that even in the matter of a confession, more relief is obtained if the events are specifically told, than if simply the recognition of wrongdoing is admitted in general terms.

So much time has been spent on these very elementary conditions for analysis because recently there has been a tendency to disregard them somewhat, and sometimes to ignore — on the basis that they are unnecessary, cumbersome or just so much rigid ritual anyway — the restrictions and to resent the deprivations which, admittedly artificial, are designed to promote the development of the full display of neurotic manifestations in the transference.

II

In regard to the role of the transference development, it seems that two fundamental and divergent points of view are represented more and more clearly among us. The one sees the transference relationship in its full development (permitting and even emphasizing the repetition in the transference of older, nuclear experiences) as the most delicate, subtle, and precious medium of work and considers that its development should be furthered, its existence safeguarded, and its content analyzed. The other (with which I am less familiar) regards the basic positive transference in the form of mutual respect and confidence as essential for the best progress of the work, very much as it is in any other therapeutic or co-operative working relationship, but considers intensity of transference relationship beyond this as largely a dependency reaction which should be diluted or dispersed as expeditiously as possible, by indicating to the patient that his reactions *are* those of different varieties of dependency, belonging to his childhood rather than to adulthood, and by encouraging him as quickly as possible to change his actions in the outer world, to undertake new experiences which will then, with the emotional support of the analyst, be of a different nature and configuration than those which he has experienced in the past. It is even said that the transference reactions needing specific interpretation should be avoided, and the relationship with the analyst is used for its emotional leverage in the enticement, direc-

tion or persuasion of the patient to his new undertakings. Thus hopefully, the patient will not remain dependent on the analyst because he will be throughout engaging himself in new and beneficial experiences in reality, although he is at the same time depending on the analyst's explanatory encouragement. Guided and suggested or at least supported by the analyst, he enters the "corrective experience," and is supposed to break the habitual neurotic constellation which has previously held him. This appears to be little more than the old-fashioned habit training with especially strong suggestive influencing. Or it might be compared to the re-conditioning experiences in which the approval of the analyst is the reward for running the new maze.

The contrast of these two points of view is summarized as, first, one which encourages, develops and utilizes the full transference reaction as a medium of re-experience and interpretation; and second, one which utilizes only the basic transference, avoids the intensity of the full transference development, directs by interpreting the dynamic lines and relationships rather than eliciting and interpreting specific past experiences, and encourages and promotes new experiences *per se* during the analytic work, often as quickly as possible. In the former there is a considerable reliance on the "working through" process, utilizing the analyst as an essential focus; in the latter a considerable reliance on the "working out" process, carrying into reality activity new behavior patterns under the suggestion and support of the analyst, and sometimes even with his stage management. The aim in the "working through" is a loosening of the neurotic tendencies at their source, since deepest emotional tensions are invested in the specific experiences; while in the "working out," counteracting, neutralizing or freshly coating experiences are relied upon to coerce the emotions into new patterns without paying too much specific attention to the old. One is a method of detailed analysis; the other of survey, and forward propulsion with the aid of the strong suggestion of personal attachment which will, however, presumably and paradoxically be without increased dependency. If we keep in mind these two divergent points of view, I think we may understand different emphases in technique and even in the maintenance of practical arrangements.

III

Much has been said in the recent past concerning the rules and rituals of analysis, the worshipful obedience which our organization is said to exact of its devotees. The magic numbers three, four and five seem to recur. But rules are the implementation of principles; i.e., the forms of their specific application, and no rule is very significant except as it represents the general practice of a desirable principle. In addition, there is no rule which may not have to be modified. It is from this angle of principles that practical procedures will be discussed here.

In the sort of psychoanalysis with which I am dealing, *the full transference relationship is accepted*, its establishment promoted and safeguarded, and its content examined and selectively interpreted. To the end of its speedy establishment, it is well to have analytic sessions spaced sufficiently close together that a sense of continuity of relationship (between analyst and analysand) and of content of material produced may be sustained. It would seem then that as nearly as possible a daily contact avoiding frequent or long gaps in treatment is desirable. In the setting of the organization of most lives, the analysis takes its place in the work of the week and accordingly five or six sessions are allocated to it. Later in many analyses it may be desirable to reduce the number of sessions, after the relationship between analyst and analysand has been consolidated, and the analyst has been able to determine the analysand's reactions to interruptions, first apparent in the reactions to week ends. If the analysand carries over a day's interruption well, without the relationship cooling off too much or the content being lost sight of, then it may be possible to carry the analysis on a three- or four-session-a-week basis, keeping a good rhythm of work with the patient. The desirability of this, however, can only be determined after the analyst has had a chance to gauge the patient's natural tempo and needs and the character of his important defenses; and this must vary from patient to patient. This initial period is generally at least a year, and more often longer.

There are three additional unfavorable factors here, however, which are seldom mentioned: (1) The actual prolongation of the treatment by spreading or infrequent spacing of sessions, in analytic work as well as in other psychotherapeutic approaches. If this prolongation is great, there is that much longer impact on other arrangements of the patient's life. "Brief psychotherapies" are sometimes paradoxically extended over very long times indeed, being repeatedly ended and reopened, because little was consolidated in the treatment and all sorts of extraneous and unnecessary interferences entered. (2) The larger the number of analytic patients possible at any given time when sessions per patient are less frequent, the greater the tax on the analyst in keeping at his mental fingertips the full range of facts and reactions belonging to each patient. The monetary recompense may, however, be greatly increased. Here again the feasibility of spacing must depend on some factors belonging to the analyst's special equipment and demands, combined with the patient's ability to "carry over," and there will inevitably be considerable variability in these. (3) The less frequent the therapeutic sessions the greater may be the risk of inadequate analysis of the negative transference. Especially with those patients where hours are made less frequent because the patient is thought by the analyst to be "wasting the hour" by what appears as unproductive talk or by silence, or where the analyst fears that the patient is feeling guilty over his silences, it has sometimes been recommended that the patient be given a vacation from treatment or that sessions be made less frequent. From my experience in the reanalysis of a number of patients, it has seemed to me rather that many of these periods are due to the patient's difficulty in expressing hostile or erotic feelings. It is about these feelings, rather than about his silence, that he feels guilty. Too often if he is given a rest or hours are made infrequent, these emotional attitudes are never brought out to be analyzed, and appear later on in disturbing forms. I am further impressed with the fact that those analysts who talk most about the dangers of dependence seem rarely to consider the reciprocal relationship between tenacious dependency and unanalyzed negative transference. In so far as negative attitudes toward the analyst are not analyzed or even expressed, the need of the patient to be reassured of the love and protection of the analyst becomes enormously increated and demanding. The analyst may see only this side of the picture and erroneously attempt to deal with it by greater spacing of contacts.

The length of the hour is, as a matter of practice, generally maintained at forty-five to sixty minutes. Certainly it is desirable that a sufficient span of time be permitted for a kind of natural organic pattern of productivity to occur during many of the sessions. The hour is our time unit in general use, perhaps because it does involve some kind of natural span of this kind, and is a feasible unit fitting into the working day. While there have been many experiments of speeding up analytic sessions to two a day or increasing the length to two hours at one session, no such practice has generally taken hold. It is my belief, however, that a regular allotment of time—the same duration and so far as possible on a prearranged and constant week-by-week schedule (in contrast to varying spans of time in sessions at irregular periods not expected in advance)—generally aids in the rhythm and continuity of the work and minimizes utilization of external situations as resistance by the patients.

The idea has been advanced by some that it would be wiser, when feasible, to have so flexible a schedule that it would be possible to see patients according to their sense of need, a kind of on-demand feeding programme; or such resiliency that hours could be lengthened or shortened according to the seeming current emotional state of the patient. While I have little doubt that this may be desirable in some open psychotic conditions, I do doubt its benefit in other conditions. I believe that in neurotic and even in many borderline states, patients gain a sense of strength in relation to reality and growing inner capacity in the ability to carry on regular work, tolerating some discomforts and anxieties, knowing that these will be worked with at a regular time, and have actually a lesser degree of (oral) dependency than where appointments are made on demand. This does not mean, however, that in situations of crisis from inner or outer reasons, extra appointments should necessarily be denied.

No discussion of practical arrangements for psychoanalytic therapy would be complete without paying one's respects to the question of whether the couch or the chair is to be used by the analysand during his treatment session. Indeed to many lay people and to some psychiatrists the use of the couch became sometimes the main or only index of whether the treatment was psychoanalytic or a discussion method. Couch meant psychoanalysis; chair meant no psychoanalysis. With the increased popularity of psychoanalysis, unfortunately some young psychiatrists became analysts through the purchase of a couch and the reading of the dream book; and with the increased interest in recent years in the hypnotic and drug and electroshock therapies, the couch is more or less routine equipment and no longer a mark of distinction. Although its use was originally probably derived from the hypnotic therapy with which analysis originated, it was retained—not as a residual organ—but because it was of service in inducing a state of mild relaxation and limiting gross movement in the analysand, a condition favorable for attention to the flow of associative thought so necessary for the exploration of unconscious connections. Furthermore with the analyst sitting at the head of the couch, the patient is not distracted by watching the analyst's facial expression and attempting to read it and accommodate to it, while the analyst can rest his face the more by not having to be looked at all day long and to inhibit or control the unconscious blend of reaction and reflection in his facial expression. As every analyst knows, there are some patients in marginal relationship with reality who find it very difficult to talk unless communication is maintained through visual as well as through spoken contact. Such patients naturally require to be treated vis-à-vis, but generally require other marked changes in analytic technique as well. Many analysts make a considerable distinction between what is said before the patient gets on the couch and immediately after he arises from it, from that which is couch born. Certainly there may be considerable significance in the difference in his postural relationship to the analyst and its connection with his utterances. One notices these things rather naturally with each patient and quite as naturally determines what importance to put upon them. Only a very compulsive analyst will want to determine an inexorable precision of rule of interpretation about these matters, or to prescribe every detail of the analyst's office. The general principle is to keep the physical arrangements of the office substantially the same throughout the treatment. Certainly this aids in limiting diverting influences and intrusions.

The safeguarding of the transference relationship is of prime importance. The relationship is an artificial one, arranged and maintained for the definite purpose of drawing the neurotic reactions into a sharp focus and reflecting them upon the analyst and the analytic situation. It is therefore just as necesary to keep the field pure for the clear reflection of the memories emerging from the past, as it is not to contaminate a field of surgical operation, or to avoid getting extraneous dirt onto a microscopic slide, which will blur or obscure the important findings, create artifacts and confuse interpretative understanding.

The two sets of considerations in safeguarding the transference field of work which seem most important to me are the strict maintenance of the confidences of the patient and, second, the elimination of other avenues of relationship with the patient than that of analysis. Both of these are difficult to maintain, but only by keeping the principles continually in mind, training oneself to respect safeguarding rules and closely examining any times in which violations occur, can an analyst really do justice to his work; and only if he is willing to maintain this degree of respect for his patient, himself, and his work, is he genuinely up to the job in hand. I cannot in the least agree with the remark of a quite eminent analyst, repeated to me several times, that so many analysts overstep the boundaries of the transference— even in grossly sexual ways—that therefore the best thing to do is to say nothing about these incidents.

It is only by discussing these possibilities (rather than by punishing the offenders) and by emphasizing their dangers to students and among ourselves that we can really develop our science to the research precision which must be aimed at in each clinical case.

In regard to maintaining the confidence of the patient, all would probably agree on the unwisdom of gossiping about patients, although even here, where should a person draw the line? It is not always easy to say where professional discussion ends and anecdotal interest starts. Further than this, seemingly less hazardous but in my opinion even more seriously endangering analytic work, is the giving and receiving of information directly about the patient to and from relatives, sincerely interested friends and even physicians. Here there is the danger not only of the breach of the patient's confidence, but the breakdown of the analyst's own integrity of work with the patient, his tendency to become prejudiced, seemingly paradoxically, by the supposed objective facts obtained from other sources. While it is undoubtedly true that an analyst's vision of the total situation may at certain points be seriously impaired by his need to stick to the microscopy of his work or by an overidentification with the patient, still it seems that this is in the long run less distorting—in that it leaves the autonomy of the patient intact and "objectivity" is obtained through the patient's changing activities and reality testing in the world—than if the analyst succumbs to the pressure of outside information, which is sometimes not in the least objective, and begins insidiously to exert "corrective" influential pressure in the analysis, sometimes without even being aware that he is doing so. Therefore it is a better principle to seek or to give specific information about a patient only with the patient's definite knowledge, understanding and wish.

It is almost self-evident that the same problems of breach of confidence, of insidious therapeutic pressure, and of the enormous complication of the changing transference identity of the analyst militate against sound analytic work in the simultaneous analysis of married couples or of those in close emotional relationships. While this may occasionally seem necessary under very extraordinary circumstances, it is at best a precarious proceeding. It has recently been sometimes justified on the basis of the wealth of factual background available to the analyst and the greater skill possible in handling the situation. That greater skill is demanded is evident; that that degree of skill is frequently possible seems dubious. In the reanalysis of analysts in my own practice,

I have sometimes found that such a strong wish on the part of the analyst represented rather an unusual degree of unresolved primal-scene scoptophilia in the analyst himself.

The need to avoid violation of the transference field by the establishment of other avenues of relationship with the patient demands a high degree of restraint and sacrifice on the part of the analyst. It demands, among other things the sacrifice on the part of the analyst of conspicuous public participation even in very worthy social and political "causes" to which he may lend his name or his activities. For in so far as the analyst is thrown into so active, even though general, a pressure role outside the analysis, his situation is the more complicated inside the analysis. It may be impossible for him to detect this if it means then that the patient just automatically does not dare to think of certain things which he unconsciously feels would cause him to be unacceptable to this particular analyst. Such deletions from the analysis only turn up on reanalysis or in the negative transference reactions which crop up after the termination of an analysis. The analyst must forego the privilege of eliciting the patient's admiration for his personal exploits.

Another form of contamination of the transference occurs when the analyst asks special favors, even seemingly minor ones, from his patient. This is frequently done and justified on the basis that the request is only a minor one; or, on the opposite basis, that the external situation is so important as to warrant breaking the rule; or that the analyst's skill is so great and his knowledge of his patient's inner situation so nearly perfect that he can afford to do so with impunity; or even that he is really doing it for the benefit of the patient; yet it may be followed by really severe disturbance. This rule about not entering into other relationships with the analysand is one which deserves always our most careful and respectful scrutiny.

This leads back again to consideration of that grosser overstepping of the transference limits in the establishment of a sexual relationship between analyst and analysand either during the analysis or relatively soon after it is officially terminated. That this is not so infrequent as one would wish to think becomes apparent to anyone who does many reanalyses. That its occurrence is often denied and the situation rather quickly explained by involved analysts as due to a hysterical fantasy on the part of the patient (indeed one knows how universal and necessary such fantasies are) is an indication of how great is the temptation. It would seem that there is a factor in this which is one of the not immediately observable implications of the setup of the analytic consulting room, with the patient in a passive-receptive position, and the whole situation one of intimacy and shutting out of the external world. Certainly such a situation is most provocative to a male analyst and a female patient.

It is my contention, however, that an equally distorting but not so obvious invasion of the transference relationship may occur with the female analyst, who may be drawn unconsciously into an overly protective, essentially maternal nursing attitude toward the suffering patient, whether man or woman. One must remember in considering the effects of such transgressions that the analytic situation *is* an artificial, tilted one; that there is none other in life that it really reproduces. In this very fact is its enormous force and capacity for utilization as a medium of establishing new integration. It is one which more nearly reproduces the demand of the child for a perfectly understanding parent, than any parent-child relationship can possibly approach, and it is the only one in life in which no emotional counterdemand is to be expected. It is produced for the purpose of drawing these infantile and childish reactions into a new life for the sake of their being understood and newly assimilated by the suffering adult whom the child has become. For this very reason, the carrying through into a relationship in life of the incestuous fantasy of the patient may be more grave in its subsequent distortion of the patient's life than any actual incestuous seduction in childhood has been.

Psychoanalysis is a hard taskmaster. Even in its practice it demands the accuracy, the fidelity, and the devotion of the true research worker. It is not something to be played with or even to be too lightly experimented with. The power of the unconscious is such that it "gets back" at those who work with it and treat it too lightly. There are some unfortunate sides to the markedly increased popularity of psychoanalysis since the last World War. Perhaps chief among these is the fact that because its importance, in its derived forms, was seen clearly under war conditions and attracted the attention of physicians and psychiatrists rather generally, the demand for training became so great that a growing temptation arose for the substitution of some of the therapies derived from psychoanalysis for psychoanalysis itself, at the risk of expediency being rationalized as tested theory.

4

THE CONCEPT OF TRANSFERENCE

Thomas Szasz

EDITOR'S NOTE

Szasz's comments on transference are truly unique, especially with respect to the classical psychoanalytic literature. Approaching the subject through the contrast between transference (distortion) and reality (nondistortion), Szasz points out that the designation by the analyst of a particular communication or behavior from the patient as transference-based entails considerable subjective evaluation. Though his paper falls short of offering definitive criteria for transference-based expressions, his detailed consideration of the implications of this realization remain valid and relatively untapped to this day. Not that the analyst's designation of a behavior as reality-based is necessarily an objective judgment; Szasz suggests that it often serves to defend the analyst against transference implications, just as the label of transference may defend against the recognition of reality. This point has wide-ranging implications, especially with respect to the use of the concept of transference and of so-called transference interpretations as a major means of denying the reality of the analyst's countertransferences (see Part III). The presence of insights of this kind might well explain the relative neglect of this unique contribution to our understanding of transference.

I. A Logical Analysis

Transference is one of the most significant concepts in psycho-analysis. It is therefore especially important that its meaning be clear, and its use precise. In this essay, my aim is to present a brief analysis of the principle meanings and uses of this concept. This contribution is part of a larger effort whose aim is to identify those activities that are specifically psycho-analytic, and thus distinguish psycho-analysis from other forms of psychotherapy (Szasz, 1957b, 1961).

Potentially, the subject of transference is as large as psycho-analysis itself. To make our task more manageable, I shall discuss transference under five separate headings as follows: (i) Transference and reality; (ii) transference in the analytic situation and outside it; (iii) transference and transference neurosis; (iv) transference as the analyst's judgement and as the patient's experience; (v) transference and learning.

Transference and reality

Logically, transference is similar to such concepts as delusion, illusion, and phantasy: each is defined by contrasting it with 'reality'. Freud's (1914) classic paradigm of transference, it will be recalled, was the phenomenon of transference love—that is, the female patient's falling in love with the male therapist. Just what is this phenomenon? According to

Reprinted from *International Journal of Psycho-Analysis* 44:432–443, 1963.

the patient, it is being in love with the analyst; according to Freud (1916–17), it is an illusion:

> The new fact which are thus unwillingly compelled to recognize we call *transference*. By this we mean a transference of feelings on to the person of the physician, because we do not believe that the situation in the treatment can account for the origin of such feelings (p. 384).

We have encountered this distinction elsewhere: between imaginary and real pain, and between psychogenic and physical pain (Szasz, 1957a). In these cases there is a conflict of opinion between patient and physician, which is not resolved by examination of the merits of the two views, but rather by the physician's autocratic judgement: his view is correct, and is considered 'reality'; the patient's view is incorrect, and is considered 'transference'.

This idea is expressed by Nunberg (1951), when, in reply to the question, 'What is transference?' he asserts:

> Transference is a projection. The term 'projection' means that the patient's inner and unconscious relations with his first libidinal objects are externalized. In the transference situation the analyst tries to unmask the projections or externalizations whenever they appear during the treatment (p. 1).

This view is uncritically repeated in every discussion of the subject. The most trivial examples of 'misidentification' are brought forward, again and again, as if they revealed something new. An excerpt from a recent paper by Spitz (1956) is illustrative:

> Take the case of that female patient of mine who, after nearly a year's analysis with me, in connection with a dream, expressed the opinion that I was the owner of a head of rich, somewhat curly brown hair. Confronting her with the sorry *reality* made it easy to lead her to the insight that the proprietor of that tonsorial adornment was her father, and thus to achieve one little step in the clarification of her insight both in regard to the emotions she felt towards me and to those which she had originally felt towards her father (italics added; p. 384).

On the face of it, there is nothing wrong with this account. But this is so only because the analyst's perception of the 'facts' is so obviously more accurate than the patient's. This obscures the complexities and pitfalls inherent in the tactic of classifying the analyst's view as reality, and the patient's as unreality (Fenichel, 1941). Here is a more challenging situation: the analyst believes that he is kindly and sympathetic, but the patient thinks that he is arrogant and self-seeking. Who shall say now which is 'reality' and which 'transference'? The point is that the analyst does not find the patient's reactions prelabelled, as it were; on the contrary, he must do the labelling himself. Hence, Nunberg's (1951) distinction between analytic and non-analytic work does not help much:

> The psycho-analyst and the non-psycho-analyst differ in their treatment and understanding of this phenomenon, in that the former treats the transference symptoms as *illusions* while the latter takes them at their face value, i.e., as *realities* (italics added; p. 4).

There is no denying, however, that the distinction between transference and reality is useful for psycho-analytic work. But so is the distinction between real pain and imaginary pain for the work of the internist or the surgeon. Practical utility and epistemological clarity are two different matters. Workmanlike use of the concept of transference should not blind us to the fact that the term is not a neutral description but rather the analyst's judgement of the patient's behaviour.

Transference in the analytical situation and outside it

There has been much discussion in the psychoanalytic literature about the precise relation between transference and the analytic situation. Freud emphasized from the outset that man's tendency to form transference is universal. Only the use we make of it is specific for analysis. Glover (1939) states this view succinctly:

> As the transference develops, feelings originally associated with parental figures are displaced to the analyst, and the analytic situation is reacted to as an infantile one. The process of transference is of course not limited to the psycho-analytic situation. It plays a part and a useful part in all human relations whether with concrete objects (both animate and inanimate) or abstract 'objects' (ideas). Hence, it is responsible for the most astonishing variations in the range of interests manifested by different individuals or by the same individual at different times (p. 75).

Despite the clarity and simplicity of this view, many analysts have tried to redefine transference as a uniquely analytic phenomenon. Two classes of transferences are thus created: one analytic, the other non-analytic.

Macalpine (1950) defines analytic transference as

'a person's gradual adaptation by regression to the infantile analytic setting'. Waelder (1956) also emphasizes the specificity of the analytic setting on the development of (analytic) transference:

> Transference may be said to be an attempt of the patient to revive and re-enact, *in the analytic situation* and *in relation to the analyst,* situations and phantasies of his childhood. Hence transference is a regressive process. Transference develops *in consequence* of the conditions of the analytic treatment, viz., of the analytic situation and the analytic technique (italics added; p. 367).

Menninger (1958) limits transference to the analytic situation:

> I define transference . . . as the unrealistic roles or identities unconsciously ascribed to a therapist by a patient in the regression of the psycho-analytic treatment and the patient's reactions to this representation derived from earlier experience (p. 81).

This interpretation, and others like it, are perhaps efforts at being 'operational'; but, if so, they overshoot the mark. To define transference in terms of the analytic situation is like defining microbes as little objects appearing under a microscope. The classic psycho-analytic position, exemplified by the writings of Freud, Fenichel, and Glover, though less pretentious, is more accurate. As the occurrence of bacteria is not limited to laboratories, so the occurrence of transference is not confined to the analytic situation; however, each is observed and studied best, not in its natural habitat, but under special circumstances.

This view does not imply that the analytic situation exerts no influence on the development of the transference. Of course it does. But so do all other situations in which transferences play a part, such as the doctor-patient relationship, marriage, the work situation, and so forth. The analytic relationship differs from all others in two ways: first, it facilitates the development of relatively intense transference reactions in the patient; second, it is a situation in which transferences are supposed to be studied and learned from, not acted upon.

Transference and transference neurosis

The difference between transference and transference neurosis is one of degree. Analysts generally speak of transferences when referring to isolated ideas, affects, or patterns of conduct which the patient manifests towards the analyst and which are repetitions of similar experiences from the patient's childhood; and they speak of transference neurosis when referring to a more extensive and coherent set of transferences (Hoffer, 1956; Zetzel, 1956).

The imprecision in this usage stems from a lack of standards as regards the quantity of transferences required before one can legitimately speak of a transference neurosis. In other words, we deal here with a quantitative distinction, but possess neither measuring instruments nor standards of measurement for making quantitative estimates. Thus, the distinction between transference and transference neurosis remains arbitrary and impressionistic.

Transference as the analyst's judgement and as the patient's experience

Traditionally, transference has been treated as a concept formed by the analyst about some aspect of the patient's conduct. For example, the female patient's declarations of love for the male analyst may be interpreted as unrealistic and due to transference. In this usage, the term 'transference' refers to the analyst's judgement.

In addition, the word 'transference' is often used, and indeed should be used, to describe a certain kind of experience which the analytic patient has, and which people in certain other situations may also have. The analytic patient may feel — with or without being told so by the analyst — that his love of the therapist is exaggerated; or that his hatred of him is too intense; or that his anxiety about the therapist's health is unwarranted. In brief, the patient may be aware that the therapist is 'too important' to him. This phenomenon is what I mean by transference as experience and as self-judgement.

Although the experience of transference can never be completely absent from analysis — if it were, how could it be analysed? — it has been curiously neglected in the theory of psycho-analytic treatment.

Fenichel (1941) mentions it, but fails to elaborate on it:

> Not everything is transference that is experienced by a patient in the form of affects and impulses during the course of an analytic treatment. If the analysis appears to make no progress, the patient has, *in my opinion,* the right to be angry, and his anger need not be a transference from childhood — or rather, we will not succeed *in demonstrating* the transference component in it (italics added; p. 95).

The fact is that the analyst's judgement of whether or not the patient's behaviour is transference may be validated by the patient; and conversely, the patient's experience and self-judgement may be validated by the analyst. Let us review briefly what such a process of cross-validation might entail.

To repeat, our premise is that the term 'transference' expresses a judgement—formed either by the therapist or by the patient—about some aspects of the patient's behaviour. Thus, a patient's action or feeling may be judged as: (1) transference—if it is considered an expression of interest 'basically' directed towards childhood objects, deflected to the analyst or to other figures in the patient's current life; (2) reality-adapted behaviour—if it is considered a valid feeling about, or reaction to, the person towards whom it is directed.

Since the analytic situation involves two persons, and since each has a choice of two judgements about any particular occurrence, there will be four possible outcomes:

(*a*) Analyst and patient agree that the behaviour in question is transference. This allows the analyst to interpret the transference, and the patient to experience it and learn from it.

(*b*) The analyst considers the patient's behaviour transference, but the patient does not. Instances of so-called 'transference love' or 'erotized transference' are illustrative. Regardless of who is correct, analyst or patient, such disagreement precludes analysis of the transference. The commonest reasons for this impasse are: (i) that the analyst is mistaken in his judgement; (ii) that the patient, though exhibiting transference manifestations, is unaware of doing so.

(*c*) Analyst and patient agree that the patient's behaviour is reality-oriented. This calls for no work that is specifically analytic. Needless to say, in this case as in all the others, both analyst and patient may be mistaken.

(*d*) The analyst may consider the patient's behaviour realistic, but the patient may know it is transference. This possibility, at least in this form, is rarely discussed in psycho-analysis. Consistent with its neglect, there are no formal examples—like 'transference love'—that could be cited to illustrate it. In general, the most common result is that the analyst 'acts out'. For example, he may engage in sexual acts with the patient, when in fact the patient was only testing him; or he may give up analysing—believing that the patient is too depressed, suicidal, or otherwise unanalysable—when, again, the patient was merely 'acting' difficult to test the analyst's perseverance in his efforts to analyse. This sort of occurrence cannot, of course, provide an opportunity for the analyst to make transference interpretations; it can, however, give the patient an opportunity to perform a piece of self-analysis, either during the analysis or, more often, afterwards.

The analysis outlined above helps to clarify the use of the word 'transference' in the treatment of so-called borderline or schizophrenic patients (Winnicott, 1956). In these cases, when analysts speak of transferences, they refer to constructions of their own which the patient does not share. On the contrary, to the patients, these experiences are invariably 'real'. The use of the term 'transference' in this context might be valid; but it is not valid to speak of 'analysing' such patients, because their so-called transferences can never be analysed (Szasz, 1957c).

Transference and learning

The patient's task in analysis is to discriminate between two aspects of his relationships: those based on transferences, and those based on reality. In other words, the patient must learn to distinguish his reactions to the analyst as a symbol and as a real person. The analytic relationship, if properly conducted, affords a particularly suitable—though not unique—situation for making this type of discrimination.

Phrased in terms of object relationships, we could say that the patient's task is to discriminate between the analyst as internal object and as external object. Internal objects can be dealt with only by intrapsychic defences; they can be tamed, but cannot be changed. To alter them, it is necessary to recognize the psychological existence of internal objects by their effects on actual, external objects. This can be accomplished only in the context of an actual human relationship. The analytic relationship—which allows the patient to invest the analyst with human qualities borrowed from others, but which the analyst neither accepts nor rejects, but only interprets—is thus designed to help the patient learn about his internal objects. This sort of psychotherapeutic learning must be distinguished from other learning experiences, such as suggestion or imitation. Only a theory based on the educational model can accommodate the role of transference in psychoanalytic treatment.

Summary of part I

1. The terms 'transference' and 'reality' are evaluative judgements, not simple descriptions of patient behaviour.

2. Transferences occur in all human relationships.

The analytic relationship differs from most others in (a) the ways in which it facilitates the development of transferences; and (b) the ways in which it deals with transferences.

3. The distinction between transference and transference neurosis is quantitative and arbitrary; there is no standard of the amount of transference required for a transference neurosis.

4. Human behaviour, especially in analysis, may be at once experienced and observed. Not only may the analyst consider the patient's behaviour either 'transference' or 'reality', but so may the patient himself. The analyst can interpret only what he recognizes as transference; the patient can learn only from what he experiences as and himself considers transference.

II. THE CONCEPT OF TRANSFERENCE AS A DEFENSE FOR THE ANALYST

In the first part of my paper I have reviewed the role of the concept of transference in the theory of psycho-analytic treatment. The aim of this second part is to demonstrate an unrecognized function of this concept: protecting the analyst from the impact of the patient's personality. In psycho-analytic *theory*, the concept of transference serves as an explanatory hypothesis; whereas in the psycho-analytic *situation*, it serves as a defence for the analyst. (Its function for the patient will not be considered in this essay.)

Types of data in the psycho-analytic situation

It is often assumed, and sometimes stated, that the analyst's data are composed of the patient's verbal utterances and non-verbal behaviour. Not only is this view seriously over-simplified, but completely false.

To begin with, we must distinguish between two different types of data available to the analyst—observation and experience. This is a familiar distinction; we are accustomed to speaking of the analysand's ego as being split into two parts, one experiencing, the other observing. This double ego-orientation, however, is not specific for analysis; most adults with adequately developed personalities, unless intensely absorbed in an experience, are capable of assuming both a concrete and an abstract attitude towards their actions and experiences (Goldstein, 1951).

Even a solitary person, if self-reflective, has two classes of data about himself. First, his self-experience; for example: 'I feel anxious'. Second, his judgement of the experience: 'It is silly, there is nothing to be afraid of.'

In the analytic situation, the data—that is, who experiences, observes, and communicates what and to whom—are far more complex. The information available to the participants in a two-person situation may be arranged in a hierarchical fashion, as follows:

(i) Each participant's own experience. (This is sometimes called 'subjective experience', but the adjective is superfluous and misleading.)

(ii) Each participant's judgement of his experience; the observing ego takes its own experience as its object of study. For example: transference as an experience of the patient's, countertransference as an experience of the analyst's.

(iii) Each participant's judgement of his partner's experience. For example: the analyst's judgement that the patient's bodily experiences are hypochondriacal; or, the patient's judgement that the analyst's friendliness is a façade.

(iv) Each participant's reaction to the partner's judgement of his experience. For example: the patient's reaction to the analyst's view that the patient is suffering from hypochondriasis: or, the analyst's reaction to the patient's view that the analyst is the most understanding person in the world.

(v–n) Logically, one reaction may be superimposed on another, *ad infinitum*; in actuality, we can experience and comprehend only a few back and forth movements in this sort of communicational situation.

Let us apply these considerations to the problem of transference in the practice of psycho-analysis. To start with the simplest example: the analyst decides that a certain behaviour by the patient is transference, and communicates this idea to him. The patient denies this, and claims that it is reality.

It is usually assumed that these two assertions contradict each other. Is this necessarily so? Only if each refers to the same object, occurrence, or relationship. This is the case when one person says, 'Boston is east of New York', and another says, 'No, Boston is west of New York'. In many other situations, however, where apparently contradictory statements are uttered, attention to detail reveals that the two speakers are not talking about the 'same thing'. For example, a hypochondriacal patient may say to his physician: 'I feel pains in my stomach'; the physician, having convinced himself that the patient is physically healthy, may counter with: 'No, you don't have any pains, you are just nervous'. These two people are talking about different things: the patient about his experiences, the physician about his medical judgement (Szasz, 1957a). Both statements may be true; both may also be false.

The point is that when the analyst communicates to the patient the idea that the latter has transferences, he is expressing a judgement; whereas when the patient denies this, he may be communicating one of two things: his experience, or his judgement of his experience. In the first instance, there is no contradiction between analyst and patient: they are not talking about the same thing. Only when the patient's denial refers to his own judgement of his allegedly transferential behaviour is there a contradiction between the assertions of the analyst and of the patient. But even then the two participants do not address themselves to and judge the 'same object': the analyst addresses himself to the patient's behaviour; whereas the patient addresses himself to (a) his own behaviour as experience, plus (b) his judgement of his own behaviour, plus (c) the analyst's interpretation of his behaviour as transference.

I think we are justified in concluding that the analytic situation is not a setting in which clearly formulated logical propositions are asserted, examined, and accepted as true or rejected as false. What may appear in the analytic situation as logical contradiction may be resolved, by psychological and semantic analysis, into two or more non-contradictory propositions.

Transference as logical construct and as psychological defence

We are now ready for the thesis of this essay—namely, that although in psycho-analytic theory the main function of the concept of transference is to serve as a logical construct, in the psycho-analytic situation it is to serve as a psychological defence for the analyst. In other words, in the context of psycho-analytical treatment, transference has a specific *situational significance,* which is lost in the setting of a psycho-analytic journal or book. What is this specific role which the concept of transference plays in the analytic situation?

To answer this question, we must try to recreate the psychological mood of the analytic situation. It is, of course, a very intimate situation: two people meet alone, frequently, and over a long period of time; the patient discloses his most closely guarded secrets; and the analyst pledges to keep his patient's confidences. All this tends to make the relationship a close one. In technical terms, we say that the analyst

becomes a libidinal object for the patient. But what is there to prevent the patient from becoming a libidinal object for the analyst? Not much. Patients do indeed become libidinal objects for analysts, up to a point. But if this were all that there was to analysis, the analytic relationship would not differ from that between trusted physician and patient, or legal adviser and client. What distinguishes the analytic relationship from all others is that patient as well as analyst are expected to make their relationship to each other an object of scientific scrutiny. How can they do this?

It is not as difficult as it is often made to seem. To begin with, the expectation of scrutiny of self and other is made explicit: the patient learns that it is not enough to immerse himself in the therapeutic relationship, and wait to be cured—as he might wait to have a tooth extracted. On the contrary, he is told (if he does not already know) that he must use to their utmost his powers of observation, analysis, and judgement. The analyst must do the same. We know, however, that human beings are not automatic thinking machines. Our powers of observation and analysis depend not only on our mental abilities, but also on our emotional state: powerful emotions are incentives to action, not to contemplation. When in severe pain, we want relief, not understanding of the causes of pain; when lonely, we want human warmth, not explanations of the causes of our loneliness; when sexually desirous, we want gratification, not rejection of our advances with the explanation that they are 'transferences'.

The analytic situation is thus a paradox: it stimulates, and at the same time frustrates, the development of an intense human relationship. In a sense, analyst and patient tease each other. The analytic situation requires that each participant have strong experiences, and yet not act on them. Perhaps this is one of the reasons that not only many patients, but also many therapists, cannot stand it: they prefer to seek encounters that are less taxing emotionally, or that offer better opportunities for discharging affective tensions in action.

Given this experientially intense character of the analytic encounter, the question is, how can the analyst deal with it? What enables him to withstand, without acting out, the impact of the patient's powerful feelings for and against him, as well as his own feelings for and against the patient? The answer lies in three sets of factors:

1. The personality of the therapist: he must be ascetic to an extent, for he must be able to bind powerful affects, and refrain from acting where others might not be able to do so.

2. The formal setting of analysis: regularly scheduled appointments in a professional office, payment of fees for services rendered, the use of the couch, and so forth.

3. The concept of transference: the patient's powerful affects are directed not towards the analyst, but towards internal objects.

In this essay, I shall discuss only the last element. The concept of transference serves two separate analytic purposes: it is a crucial part of the patient's therapeutic experience, and a successful defensive measure to protect the analyst from too intense affective and real-life involvement with the patient. For the idea of transference implies denial and repudiation of the patient's *experience qua experience*; in its place is substituted the more manageable construct of a *transference experience* (Freud, 1914).

Thus, if the patient loves or hates the analyst, and if the analyst can view these attitudes as transferences, then, in effect, the analyst has convinced himself that the patient does not have these feelings and dispositions towards *him*. The patient does not really love or hate the analyst, but some one else. What could be more reassuring? This is why so-called transference interpretations are so easily and so often misused; they provide a ready-made opportunity for putting the patient at arm's length.

Recognizing the phenomenon of transference, and creating the concept, was perhaps Freud's greatest single contribution. Without it, the psychotherapist could never have brought scientific detachment to a situation in which he participates as a person. There is historical evidence, which we shall review presently, to support the thesis that this could not be done before the recognition of transference; nor, apparently, can it be done today by those who make no use of this concept.

Not only may the analyst use the concept of transference as a defence against the impact of the patient's relationship with him (as person, not as symbol), but he may also use the concept of a reality relationship with the patient as a defence against the threat of the patient's transferences! We see this most often in analysts who treat borderline or schizophrenic patients. Indeed, the defensive use of the reality relationship has become one of the hallmarks of the Sullivanian modification of psycho-analysis. There are good reasons for this.

In the analysis of the normal-neurotic individual, one of the great dangers to the therapist is a *temptation*: the patient may appear too inviting as a person, as a sexual object, and so forth. To resist this, convincing himself that the patient is not interested in him as a real person is eminently useful. In the

therapy of the schizophrenic, however, one of the greatest dangers is *compassion*: the patient has suffered so horribly as a child that to recollect it might be too painful, not only for him but for the therapist as well. To counteract this danger, then, the therapist must convince himself that what the patient needs is not a review of his past misfortunes, but a good relationship with the therapist. This might be true in some instances; in others, it might be an example of the defensive use of the concept of a reality relationship (Szasz, 1957c).

To recapitulate: I have tried to show that in the analytic situation the concepts of 'transference' and 'reality'—as judgements of the patient's behaviour—may both be used defensively, one against the other. This phenomenon is similar to the defensive function of affects, for example of pain and anxiety: each may be used by the ego to protect itself from being overwhelmed by the other (Szasz, 1957a).

The reactions of Breuer and Freud to eroticism in the therapeutic situation

The cathartic method, which was the precursor of analytic technique, brought out into the open the hysterical patient's ideas and feelings about herself and her 'illness'. This, in turn, led to the recognition of the patient's sexual feelings and needs.

So long as hysterical symptoms were undisturbed—or were only chased after with hypnosis—patients were left free to express their personal problems through bodily signs and other indirect communications. Indeed, the medical, including psychiatric, attitudes toward such patients invited them to continue this type of communicative behaviour. Similarly, pre-Breuerian physicians were expected to respond to hysterical symptoms only in terms of their overt, common sense meanings: if a woman was neurasthenic, it was the physician's job to make her more energetic; if a man was impotent, he was to be made potent. Period. No other questions were to be asked. This state of affairs presented few problems to physicians (except that their therapeutic efficiency was low, but no lower than in organic diseases!), and led, of course, to no great changes in the patients. It was this *psychotherapeutically homeostatic situation between patients and doctors* which Breuer disturbed. He initiated the translation of the patient's hysterical body-language into ordinary speech (Szasz, 1961).

But Breuer soon discovered that this was not at all like deciphering Egyptian hieroglyphics. The marble tablet remained unaffected by the translator's efforts, but the hysterical patient did not. Thus, as Breuer proceeded in translating Anna O.'s symptoms into the language of personal problems, he found it necessary to carry on a relationship with her without the protection previously afforded by the hysterical symptoms. For we ought not forget that the defences inherent in the hysterical symptoms (and in others as well) served not only the needs of the patient, but also of the physician. So long as the patient was unaware of disturbing affects and needs—especially aggressive and erotic—she could not openly disturb her physician with them. But once these inhibitions were lifted—or, as we might say, once the translation was effected—it became necessary for the therapist to deal with the new situation: a sexually aroused attractive *woman,* rather than a pitifully disabled *patient.*

Breuer, as we know, could not cope with this new situation, and fled from it. Freud, however, could, and thereby established his just claim to scientific greatness.

My forgoing comments are based on the many historical sources of the origins of psychoanalysis made available to us, especially in the past decade. Instead of citing specific facts, most of which are familiar to analysts, I shall quote some passages from Jones's (1953) biography of Freud, which illustrate how the need for transference as a defence for the therapist arose, and the function it served for Breuer and Freud.

'Freud has related to me a fuller account than he described in his writing of the peculiar circumstances surrounding the end of this novel treatment. It would seem that Breuer had developed what we should nowadays call a strong counter-transference to his interesting patient. At all events he was so engrossed that his wife became bored at listening to no other topic, and before long jealous. She did not display this openly, but became unhappy and morose. It was a long time before Breuer, with his thoughts elsewhere, divined the meaning of her state of mind. It provoked a violent reaction in him, perhaps compounded of love and guilt, and he decided to bring the treatment to an end. He announced this to Anna O., who was by now much better, and bade her good-bye. But that evening he was fetched back to find her in a greatly excited state, apparently as ill as ever. The patient, who according to him had appeared to be an asexual being and had never made any allusion to such a forbidden topic throughout the treatment, was now in the throes of an hysterical childbirth (pseudocyesis), the logical termination of a phantom pregnancy that had been invisibly developing in response to Breuer's ministrations. Though profoundly shocked, he managed to calm her down by hypnotizing her, and then fled the house in a cold sweat. The next day he and his wife left for Venice to spend a second honeymoon, which resulted in the concep-

tion of a daughter; the girl born in these circumstances was nearly sixty years later to commit suicide in New York.

'Confirmation of this account may be found in a contemporary letter Freud wrote to Martha, which contains substantially the same story. She at once identified herself with Breuer's wife, and hoped the same thing would not ever happen to her, whereupon Freud reproved her vanity in supposing that other women would fall in love with *her* husband: "for that to happen one has to be a Breuer."

'The poor patient did not fare so well as one might gather from Breuer's published account. Relapses took place, and she was removed to an institution in Gross Enzerdorf. A year after discontinuing the treatment, Breuer confided to Freud that she was quite unhinged and that he wished she would die and so be released from her suffering. She improved, however, and gave up morphia. A few years later Martha relates how "Anna O.," who happened to be an old friend of hers and later a connection by marriage, visited her more than once. She was then pretty well in the daytime, but still suffered from her hallucinatory states as evening grew on.

'Frl. Bertha (Anna O.) was not only highly intelligent, but extremely attractive in physique and personality; when removed to the sanatorium she inflamed the heart of the psychiatrist in charge. Her mother, who was somewhat of a dragon, came from Frankfurt and took her daughter back there for good at the end of the eighties. Bertha, who was born and brought up in Vienna, retained her Viennese grace, charm and humour. Some years before she died she composed five witty obituary notices of herself for different periodicals. A very serious side, however, developed when she was thirty, and she became the first social worker in Germany, one of the first in the world. She founded a periodical and several institutes where she trained students. A major part of her life's work was given to women's causes and emancipation, but work for children also ranked high. Among her exploits were several expeditions to Russia, Poland, and Roumania to rescue children whose parents had perished in pogroms. She never married, and she remained very devoted to God.

'Some ten years later, at a time when Breuer and Freud were studying cases together, Breuer called him into consultation over an hysterical patient. Before seeing her he described her symptoms, whereupon Freud pointed out that they were typical products of a phantasy pregnancy. The recurrency of the old situation was too much for Breuer. Without saying a word he took up his hat and stick and hurriedly left the house' (pp. 224–226).

I should like to underscore the following items in this account:

1. Having effected the translation from hysterical symptom directed impersonally to anyone, to sexual interest directed to the person of Breuer himself,

Breuer panicked and fled. The relationship evidently became too intense for him.

2. Breuer protected himself from the danger of this relationship—that is, from his anxiety lest he succumb to Anna O.'s charms—first, by literally fleeing into the arms of his wife; and later, by convincing himself that his patient was 'very sick', and would be better off dead!

3. Freud, to whom Anna O.'s problem was essentially a theoretical one—he had no personal, therapeutic relationship with her—dealt with the threat of a too intense involvement with female patients by convincing himself that this could happen only to Breuer. I shall comment on this later.

Let us now take a look at the events preceding the publication of *Studies on Hysteria* (1893–95).

In the late eighties, and still more in the early nineties, Freud kept trying to revive Breuer's interest in the problem of hysteria or to induce him at least to give to the world the discovery his patient, Frl. Anna O., had made. In this endeavour he met with a strong resistance, the reason for which he could not at first understand. Although Breuer was much his senior in rank, and fourteen years older, it was the younger man who—for the first time—was entirely taking the leading part. It gradually dawned on Freud that Breuer's reluctance was connected with his disturbing experience with Frl. Anna O. related earlier in this chapter. So Freud told him of his own experience with a female patient suddenly flinging her arms around his neck in a transport of affection, and he explained to him his reasons for regarding such untoward occurrences as part of the transference phenomena characteristic of certain types of hysteria. This seems to have had a calming effect on Breuer, who evidently had taken his own experience of the kind more personally and perhaps even reproached himself for indiscretion in the handling of his patient. At all events Freud ultimately secured Breuer's cooperation, it being understood that the theme of sexuality was to be kept in the background. Freud's remark had evidently made a deep impression, since when they were preparing *Studies* together, Breuer said apropos of the transference phenomenon, "I believe that is the most important thing we both have to make known to the world" (Jones, 1953, p. 250).

In this account, the following facts deserve emphasis:

(i) The psychotherapeutic material on which Freud discovered transference concerned not his own patient, but someone else's: the *experiences* were Anna O.'s and Breuer's, the *observations* Freud's.

(ii) A heavy thread of denial runs through Freud's thinking in formulating the concept of transference; for example: for it to happen, '. . . one has to be a Breuer'; when he found that one does not, he concluded that the patient's love transference is due to the nature of the hysterical illness—under no circumstances must the patient's attraction to the therapist be considered 'genuine'.

(iii) Freud's concept of transference was vastly reassuring to Breuer.

We shall examine each of these topics in greater detail.

Transference as a defence for the analyst: Anna O., Breuer, and Freud

The fact that Anna O. was not Freud's patient has, I think, not received the attention it deserves. Possibly, this was no lucky accident, but a necessary condition for the discovery of the basic insights of psycho-analysis. In other words, the sort of triangular situation which existed between Anna O., Breuer, and Freud may have been indispensable for effecting the original break-through for dealing scientifically with certain kinds of highly charged emotional materials; once this obstacle was hurdled, the outside observer could be dispensed with.

It seems highly probable that Freud's position *vis-à-vis* both Breuer and Anna O. helped him assume a contemplative, scientific attitude towards their relationship. Breuer was an older, revered colleague and friend, and Freud identified with him. He was thus in an ideal position to empathize with Breuer's feelings and thoughts about the treatment of Anna O. On the other hand, Freud had no significant relationship with Anna O. He thus had access to the kind of affective material (from Breuer), which had been unavailable to scientific observers until then; at the same time, he was able to maintain a scientific attitude towards the data (which impinged upon him only by proxy).

It is sometimes said that the psycho-analytic method was discovered by Anna O. Actually, she discovered only the cathartic method and—as it turned out—its limited therapeutic usefulness. She was, however, a truly important collaborator in a more important discovery: the concept of transference. This concept is the cornerstone of psycho-analytic method as well as theory, and was created through the delicate collaboration of three people—Anna O., Breuer, and Freud. Anna O. possessed the relevant basic facts; Breuer transformed them into usable scientific *observations,* first by responding to them in a personal way, and second by reporting them to Freud; Freud was the *observer* and *theoretician.*

Subsequently, Freud succeeded in uniting the latter two functions in himself. In his self-analysis, he was even able to supply all three roles from within the riches of his own personality. It is unfortunate that Freud's self-analysis is sometimes regarded as a uniquely heroic achievement. To be sure, he might have been the first person ever to perform this sort of work (although one cannot be sure of this); he was certainly the first to describe and thus make public the methods he used. The discovery of Newton's laws and the principles of calculus were also heroic achievements; this does not prevent us from expecting high school students to master them and, indeed, to go beyond them. There is no reason to treat psycho-analysis differently.

To repeat: I have tried to show that because Anna O. was not Freud's patient it was easier for him to assume an observing role toward her sexual communications than if they had been directed towards himself.

Denial and transference

Let us now examine Freud's attempt to reassure his fiancée, by writing her that female patients could fall in love 'only with a Breuer', never with him.

Freud may have believed this to be true; or if not, he may have thought it would reassure Martha; or, he may have toyed with both possibilities, believing now one, now the other. The evidence for the probability of each of these hypotheses, though only suggestive, is worth pondering.

We must start with a contradiction: Freud asserted that female hysterical patients have a 'natural' tendency to form love transferences toward their male therapists; if so, one surely does not have to be a Breuer for this to happen. But then why did he write to Martha as he did?

We can only guess. Perhaps it was, as already mentioned, merely a device to reassure his fiancée. He might have done this, however, more effectively by explaining his concept of transference to her; it was, as we know, very reassuring to Breuer. There may have been two reasons why he did not do this. First, his concept of transference was perhaps not as clearly formulated when he wrote to Martha in 1883, as when he used it on Breuer nearly ten years later. Second, Freud was under the influence of a powerful, positive father transference to Breuer. From this point of view, Freud's assertion that women fall in love 'only with a Breuer' assumes new importance. It means that Breuer is the father, Freud the son. Thus, his statement to Martha would mean that women fall in love only with fathers (adult males), not with children (immature boys).

I mention these things, not to analyse Freud, but to cast light on the function of the concept of transference for the analyst. Freud's self-concept during the early days of psycho-analysis is relevant to our understanding of the work-task of the analyst. His self-depreciating remark is appropriate to the reconstruction offered above of the triangular relationship of Anna O., Breuer, and Freud. It seems that Freud had divided certain activities and roles between Breuer and himself: Breuer is the 'father', the active therapist, the heterosexually active male; Freud is the 'son', the onlooker or observer, the sexually inactive child. This, let us not forget, was the proper social-sexual role of the middle-class adolescent and young adult in the Vienna of the 1880s: aware of sexual desire, he was expected to master it by understanding, waiting, working, and so forth. The same type of mastery—not only of sexual tensions, but of all other kinds that may arise in the analytic situation—must be achieved by the analyst in his daily work.

When Freud was young—and presumably sexually most able and most frustrated—it may have been easier for him to believe that sexual activity with his female patients was impossible, than that it was possible but forbidden. After all, what is impossible does not have to be prohibited. A saving of defensive effort may thus be achieved by defining as impossible what is in fact possible.

Denial plays another role in the concept of transference. For, in developing this concept, Freud denied, and at the same time reaffirmed, the reality of the patient's experience. This paradox, which was discussed before, derives from the distinction between experience and judgement. To deny what the patient felt or said was not new in psychiatry; Freud carried on this tradition, but gave it a new twist.

According to traditional psychiatric opinion, when a patient asserts that he is Jesus Christ, the psychiatrist ought to consider this a delusion. In other words, what the patient says is treated as a logical proposition about the physical world; this proposition the psychiatrist brands as false. Psychiatrists and non-psychiatrists alike, however, have long been aware that the patient may, indeed, feel as though he were Jesus Christ, or be convinced that he is the Saviour; and they may agree with the fundamental distinction between affective experiences about the self, and logical propositions about the external world. The epistemological aspects of this problem, and their relevance to psychiatry, were discussed elsewhere (Szasz, 1961; and Part I of this paper). What is important to us now is to recognize that, in the concept of transference, Freud introduced this fundamental distinction into psychiatry, without, however, clarifying the epistemological foundation of the concept.

Thus, when Freud introduced the concept of transference into psychiatry, he did not deny the patient's self-experience: if the patient declares that she is in love with the analyst, so be it. He emphatically repudiated, however, the action-implication of the experience: the patient's 'love' must be neither gratified nor spurned. In the analytic situation, both of these common-sense actions are misplaced; in their stead Freud offered 'analysis' (Freud, 1914). He thus took what modern philosophers have come to describe as a *meta position* toward the subject before him (Reichenbach, 1947).

Transference and reassurance

The notion of transference is reassuring to therapists precisely because it implies a denial (or mitigation) of the 'personal' in the analytic situation. When Freud explained transference to Breuer, Breuer drew from it the idea that Anna O.'s sexual overtures were 'really' meant for others, not for him: he was merely a symbolic substitute for the patient's 'real' love objects. This interpretation reassured Breuer so much that he dropped his objections to publishing *Studies on Hysteria.*

The concept of transference was needed by Freud, no less than by Breuer, before either dared publish the sort of medico-psychological material never before presented by respectable scientists. The reaction of many medical groups confirmed Breuer's fears: this type of work was a matter for the police, not for doctors. More than just the prudery of German medical circles of the late nineteenth century is betrayed by this view; it suggested that, in psycho-analysis, what stands between obscenity and science is the concept of transference. This concept, and all it implies, renders the physician a non-participant with the patient in the latter's preoccupation with primary emotions (such as eroticism, aggression, etc.). Only by not responding to the patient on his own level of discourse and instead analysing his productions, does the analyst raise his relationship with the patient to a higher level of experience. Unable to comprehend the meaning of transference, Freud's early critics could not distinguish analytic work from indecent behaviour.

The concept of transference was reassuring for another reason as well. It introduced into medicine and psychology the notion of the *therapist as symbol*: this renders the *therapist as person* essentially invulnerable.

When an object becomes a symbol (of another object) people no longer react to it as an object; hence, its features *qua* object become inscrutable.

Consider the flag as the symbol of a nation. It may be defiled, captured by the enemy, even destroyed; national identity, which the flag symbolizes, lives on nevertheless.

The concept of transference performs a similar function: the analyst is only a symbol (therapist), for the object he represents (internal imago). If, however, the therapist is accepted as symbol—say, of the father—his specific individuality becomes inconsequential. As the flag, despite what happens to it, remains a symbol of the nation, so the analyst, regardless of what he does, remains a symbol of the father to the patient. Herein lies the danger. Just as the pre-Freudian physician was ineffective partly because he remained a fully 'real' person, so the psycho-analyst may be ineffective if he remains a fully 'symbolic' object. The analytic situation requires the therapist to function as both, and the patient to perceive him as both. Without these conditions, 'analysis' cannot take place.

The use of the concept of transference in psychotherapy thus led to two different results. On the one hand, it enabled the analyst to work where he could not otherwise have worked; on the other, it exposed him to the danger of being 'wrong' *vis-à-vis* his patient—and of abusing the analytic relationship—without anyone being able to demonstrate this to him.

If we agree that there is such an inherent error in psycho-analysis—and it is hard to see how anyone could dispute this today—it behooves us to try to correct it. Of course, there have been many suggestions, beginning with Freud's proposal that analysts should undergo a personal analysis, and ending with the current emphasis on so-called high standards in analytic institutes. All this is futile. No one, psycho-analysts included, has as yet discovered a method to make people behave with integrity when no one is watching. Yet this is the kind of integrity that analytic work requires of the analyst.

Summary of part II

My aim in this part of my essay has been to develop the thesis that the concept of transference fulfils a dual function: it is a logical construct for the psycho-analytic theoretician, and a psychological defence for the psycho-analytic therapist. To illustrate and support this thesis, the historical origins of the concept were re-examined. Breuer, it appears, was overcome by the 'reality' of his relationship with Anna O. The threat of the patient's eroticism was effectively tamed by Freud when he created the concept of transference: the analyst could henceforth tell himself that he was not the genuine object, but a mere symbol, of his patient's desire.

Transference is the pivot upon which the entire structure of psycho-analytic treatment rests. It is an inspired and indispensable concept; yet it also harbours the seeds, not only of its own destruction, but of the destruction of psycho-analysis itself. Why? Because it tends to place the person of the analyst beyond the reality testing of patients, colleagues, and self. This hazard must be frankly recognized. Neither professionalization, nor the 'raising of standards', nor coerced training analyses can protect us from this danger. Only the integrity of the analyst and of the analytic situation can safeguard from extinction the unique dialogue between analysand and analyst.

REFERENCES

Fenichel, O. (1941). *Problems of Psychoanalytic Technique.* (Albany, N.Y.: Psychoanal. Quart. Inc.)

Freud, S. (1914). 'Observations on Transference-Love (Further Recommendations on the Technique of Psycho-Analysis, III).' *S.E.* 12.

———(1916–17). *A General Introduction to Psycho-analysis.* (Garden City, N.Y.: Garden City Pub. Co., 1943.)

Glover, E. (1939). *Psycho-Analysis. A Handbook for Medical Practitioners and Students of Comparative Psychology.* (London: Staples, 1949.)

Goldstein, K. (1951). *Human Nature in the Light of Psychopathology.* (Cambridge, Mass.: Harvard Univ. Press.)

Hoffer, W. (1956). 'Transference and Transference Neurosis.' *Int. J. Psycho-Anal.,* 37.

Jones, E. (1953). *The Life and Work of Sigmund Freud,* Vol. I. (London: Hogarth.)

Macalpine, I. (1950). 'The Development of the Transference.' *Psychoanal. Quart.,* 19.

Menninger, K. (1958). *The Theory of Psycho-analytic Technique.* (New York: Basic Books.)

Nunberg, H. (1951). 'Transference and Reality.' *Int. J. Psycho-Anal.,* 32.

Reichenbach, H. (1947). *Elements of Symbolic Logic.* (New York: Macmillan.)

Spitz, R. A. (1956). 'Transference: The Analytic Setting and its Prototype.' *Int. J. Psycho-Anal.,* 37.

Szasz, T. S. (1957a). *Pain and Pleasure: A Study of Bodily Feelings.* (New York: Basic Books; London: Tavistock.)

———(1957b). 'On the Theory of Psycho-Analytic Treatment.' *Int. J. Psycho-Anal.,* 38.

———(1957c). 'A Contribution to the Psychology of Schizophrenia'. *A.M.A. Arch. Neurol. Psychiat.,* 77.

———(1961). *The Myth of Mental Illness. Foundations of a Theory of Personal Conduct.* (New York: Hoeber/Harper; London: Secker and Warburg, 1962.)

Waelder, R. (1956). 'Introduction to the Discussion on Problems of Transference.' *Int. J. Psycho-Anal.,* 37.

Winnicott, D. W. (1956). 'On Transference.' *Int. J. Psycho-Anal.,* 37.

Zetzel, E. (1956). 'Current Concepts of Transference.' *Int. J. Psycho-Anal.,* 37.

5

NOTES ON SOME THEORETICAL AND CLINICAL ASPECTS OF TRANSFERENCE

Joseph Sandler, Alex Holder, Maria Kawenoka,
Hanna Engl Kennedy and Lily Neurath

EDITOR'S NOTE

This paper is perhaps the most thoroughgoing historical survey of the classical psychoanalytic writings on the subject of transference, and the most careful effort in the literature to identify the various meanings of the term and concept. While the authors clearly distinguish their conception of transference from the one they impute to Melanie Klein, they share with her the position that the understanding of transference is founded on an in-depth consideration of the vicissitudes of object relationships.

The analytic situation is a variant of . . . human transference relationship.

—Willi Hoffer, 1956

I

Like many other psychoanalytic concepts, that of transference is one which has developed from the clinical situation of psychoanalytic practice. When we come to integrate it into our general psychoanalytic metapsychology we find—as with other concepts—that difficulties of conceptualization and definition may arise.

In this paper we should like to present some of the difficulties which arise in connection with the integration of a clinical concept into our general psychoanalytic psychology, to illustrate some of the problems with examples drawn mostly from analytic work with children, and to suggest a possible direction in which further research may proceed. No attempt will be made to present a systematic view of the literature, and this paper should be regarded as presenting a line of thought which has been stimulated by our work, and which will certainly require further elaboration and extension.

It is nearly three-quarters of a century since Freud first described the phenomenon which he called 'transference'. It appeared as a source of resistance to the analytic process, based on what he called 'a *false connexion*' between the person of the physician and 'the distressing ideas which arise from the content of the analysis' (1895). Ten years later Freud was referring to transferences as

new editions or facsimiles of the impulses and phantasies which are aroused and made conscious during the progress of the analysis; but they have this peculiarity, which is characteristic for their species, that they replace some earlier person by the person of the physician.

He pointed out that *past* experiences are revived as applying to the physician *in the present,* and remarked that

some of these transferences have a content which differs from that of their model in no respect whatever except for the substitution.

Using the analogy from publishing, he continues by saying that such transferences are merely *reprints* or *new impressions* of the old. But other transferences

are more ingeniously constructed . . . and they may even become conscious, by cleverly taking advantage of some real peculiarity in the physician's person or circumstances and attaching themselves to that. These . . . will no longer be new impressions, but revised editions (1905).

Freud later (1909) pointed out that

Transference arises spontaneously in all human relationships just as it does between the patient and the physician.

Reprinted from *International Journal of Psycho-Analysis* 50:633–645, 1969.

It is not *created* by psychoanalysis, but psychoanalysis merely *reveals* it and guides the psychical processes towards the desired goal. In 1912 Freud remarked that

unconscious impulses . . . endeavour to reproduce themselves in accordance with the timelessness of the unconscious and its capacity for hallucination.

The patient seeks 'to put his passions into action without taking any account of the real situation'. In the *Introductory Lectures* (1916–17) he comments that transference is present from the beginning of treatment, and is

for a while, the most important motive in its advance. We . . . need not bother about it so long as it operates in favour of the joint work of analysis. If it then changes into a resistance, we must turn our attention to it . . .

In his 'Autobiographical Study' (1925) Freud stressed again that transference

is a universal phenomenon of the human mind . . . and it in fact dominates the whole of each person's relations to his human environment.

Freud included under transference what we might perhaps call the transference of *authority* (Sandler, 1960). In his last work, *An Outline of Psychoanalysis* (1940), Freud speaks of the 'relation of transference' bringing with it two further advantages. One of these is that the patient reproduces part of his life story by 'acting it before us . . . instead of reporting it to us'.[1] The second advantage to the analysis of the relation of transference is described as follows:

If the patient puts the analyst in the place of his father (or mother), he is also giving him the power which his superego exercises over his ego, since his parents were, as we know, the origin of his superego. The new superego now has an opportunity for a sort of *after-education* of the neurotic.

It would appear that Freud saw transference as being predominantly a transfer of feelings about important objects from the past, to the person of the analyst in the present, and that they are experienced as real *in the present*. They may appear in their original form or they may be disguised and distorted.

They may include the transfer of *images* from the past as well as feelings, so that they influence the perception or apperception of the analyst by the patient, the altered perception integrating into it revived memory images. Transference of authority is seen as being within the framework of transference of feelings towards, and about, the parents. Moreover, transferences develop not only in the analytic situation, and towards the person of the analyst, but also in normal life.

The motive forces of transference are allocated, in all of this, primarily to the unconscious (we would nowadays say the *id*) in accordance with its blind thrust towards repetition, its domination by what Freud referred to as the 'repetition-compulsion'. It is a corollary of Freud's remarks about what has been referred to earlier as the 'transference of authority' that to the extent that superego functions as the internal representative of the parents, the superego introjects are invested with *feelings* of respect and authority, and the superego exercises its authority, in part at any rate, via such feelings (Sandler, 1960).

The advances in our understanding of the transference *since* Freud have, for the most part, been in the field of psychoanalytic technique. There has perhaps been an increase in our sensitivity to transference phenomena so that, for many analysts, transference appears to have replaced the dream as the 'royal road to the unconscious'.[2] We are more sensitive too to the ways in which the patient may attempt to manipulate or provoke the analyst to react in a particular way, attempting to *make him behave* in the present in the way in which the patient's infantile objects were seen (or fantasied) to behave in the past.

We are perhaps more aware of the ways in which patients defend against transference impulses, and more skilled in noticing transference manifestations *in statu nascendi*. Here the growing awareness of the role of the ego, particularly in regard to its defensive functions, has played a decisive part. But, in general, the contributions to the study of transference after Freud have not led to any fundamental advance on his views. This is particularly true in regard to what we can refer to as the metapsychology of transference, and this is perhaps surprising in view of the substantial developments which have taken place in ego psychology, and our increasing realization that object relationships belong as much to the ego as to

---

1. He refers here to the patient's transformation of present reality so that the past is re-experienced in the patient's perceptions and feelings in regard to the analyst in the present, as if they are emerging anew in the 'here-and-now'.

2. See Anna Freud (1965). We take the view, with Anna

Freud, that there are indeed many 'royal roads to the unconscious'; but there is no doubt that the analysis of transference phenomena has become an increasingly important part of psychoanalytic technique.

the id. True, there have been a number of major clarifying contributions, such as that of Nunberg (1951), Hoffer (1956) and, of course, Anna Freud's *The Ego and the Mechanisms of Defence* (1936).

When one reads the literature on transference and on transference neurosis, one cannot help but have the feeling that there is something which is being searched for, some elusive, slippery quality, inherent in the whole topic, and that this possibly provides one of the motive forces for our continuing preoccupation with the subject. Incidentally, with regard to transference neurosis (that intensification of the transference in which the patient's major conflicts become centred around the person of the analyst, so that his neurosis has become an analytic neurosis, so to speak, with a corresponding lessening of neurotic manifestations outside the analysis) Kepecs has recently shown (1966), in a review of the literature, that a great deal of confusion exists as to the precise distinction between transference and transference neurosis. The terms are often used interchangeably or in such a way that any differences in meaning may become obscured.

It is of interest to note at this point Hoffer's lucid account of the dynamics of the transference neurosis. He suggests that it

is not a reactive, but an active manifestation; it is not created by reality but by the spontaneous pressure of the Id. The infantile object relationships become intensified in the transference neurosis and remain there at first unrecognized. If the subsequent emergence of a transference neurosis is not interfered with by too brisk transference interpretations, symptomatic-neurotic suffering changes into feelings of inferiority and of mental pain due to frustrated infantile love (transference neurosis proper). Interpretations lead to the transformation of these transference feelings and actions into memories. Mental energy, invested in the repressed and disguised infantile object relations, is thus at first drained into the transference situation and then into memories of those relations . . . The painful actuality in the transference situation becomes transformed into memories of the past, and with it the patient's actual infantile relation towards his analyst will gradually become past as well and will relieve him from much actual suffering (1950).

Many of the difficulties in regard to the concept of transference arise from the fact that most workers have approached the subject from a frame of reference which is essentially related to clinical technique and that although they may *appear* to be considering aspects of the metapsychology of transference, their formulations are either implicitly or explicitly related to the analytical situation, and in particular to the

analytical situation when the patient is an adult, i.e. to so-called adult analysis.

This problem is not one specific to the area of transference. It is probably true that a great many analysts use a slightly different model (or at best a different frame of reference) when they are considering technical matters from that which they use when they consider theory. One has only to think of the extent to which the topographical model is used in connection with clinical work and technique, and to compare it with the use made of the structural model when theoretical issues are considered.

The importance of the frame of reference is evident when we come to examine the various definitions of transference. Consider, for example, the following definition given by Waelder (1956):

Transference may be said to be an attempt of the patient to revive and re-enact, in the analytic situation and in relation to the analyst, situations and phantasies of his childhood. Hence transference is a regressive process.

He goes on to say:

Transference develops in consequence of the conditions of the analytic experiment, viz. of the analytic situation and the analytic technique.

This is, of course, also a view expressed by many others, and although we are sure that Waelder would have agreed with Freud that extra-analytic transferences exist, the way in which he has related his definition to the analytic situation and to the analytic process makes it sound like a special analytic phenomenon, with the implication that it ultimately differs from relationships outside the analysis in aspects of quality as well as quantity. He (deliberately we believe) uses here a 'technical' frame of reference. One can have no quarrel with this, but such a technically oriented definition raises problems if we set our sights towards making psychoanalysis into a general psychology, an aim which Hartmann has so often stressed. Definitions of analytic concepts, from this point of view should ideally be applicable to extra-analytical phenomena as well as to those which arise in the clinical situation. Unless, of course, we specifically maintain, as some have done, that a concept such as transference is a clinical or technical one only. However, Freud himself extended his notion of transference outside the analytic situation, and our social experiences, as well as our clinical experience with non-analytic types of therapy, must surely tend to force us to do the same.

Consider a further definition, one recently given by Greenson (1965), which appears to be *more* general.

Transference is the experiencing of feelings, drives, attitudes, fantasies and defenses toward a person in the present which are inappropriate to that person and are a repetition, a displacement of reactions originating in regard to significant persons of early childhood. I emphasize that for a reaction to be considered transference it must have two characteristics: It must be a repetition of the past and it must be inappropriate to the present.

Although such a definition does not mention the analytic situation and can, on the face of it, be taken to apply to aspects of all relationships, analytic or otherwise, its use of the criterion 'appropriate-inappropriate' suggests that here again we have a frame of reference which is a technical one, for it is in the special analytic situation where appropriateness or inappropriateness can best emerge (although here again it is a question of judgement of the analyst, not always infallible). Moreover, the differentiation between what is appropriate and what is inappropriate in ordinary *non-analytic* relationships (in marriage, for example) must at best be an extremely arbitrary matter.

We may consider yet another example, this time from a British analyst. In a paper in 1930, Ella Freeman Sharpe commented on transference as follows:

Transference begins with the very first analytical session . . . just because everyone has thoughts about another human being when brought into close contact . . .

She goes on to describe the special conditions of the analytical situation:

In analysis, through the specially conditioned contact, we have potentially the freest field for phantasy concerning the analyst . . . From the first hour the patient will have thoughts and opinions about the analyst as in ordinary contacts, but the very fact of the phantasy-situation, the detachedness and isolation of the hour, the unknownness of the analyst, activates phantasy; and this, with the stimulus of dream-life and recollections of the past, brings about a very special relationship with the analyst. This relationship is the transference.

Anna Freud (1936) has given a definition of transference which is also in terms of the special analytic situation:

By transference we mean all those impulses experienced by the patient in his relation with the analyst which are not newly created by the objective analytic situation but have their source in early—indeed, the very earliest—object relations and are now merely revived under the influence of the repetition compulsion.

Interestingly, Anna Freud here contrasts transference with new relationships, as she puts it, 'created by the objective analytic situation'—showing here perhaps the influence of her experience with the analysis of children.

Instances of the sorts of definitions which we have quoted can be multiplied many times over (e.g. Hendrick, 1934; Glover, 1939, 1955; Silverberg, 1948; Klein, 1952; Menninger, 1958). However, a number of authors have emphasized strongly that transference should be regarded as a general phenomenon, and that its appearance and use in the psychoanalytic situation is a special, albeit highly intensified case of a more general process. Orr (1954), in a historical survey, echoes Freud in remarking that

Transference in its widest sense is regarded as a universal phenomenon in interpersonal relationships. In its most restricted sense, however, transference implies a specific relationship of patient to psychoanalyst.

Fenichel (1945), among others, spells out what distinguishes the more specific transference of the psychoanalytic situation from the more general and universal phenomenon. Speaking of the transference situations of everyday life, he says that

it is a general human trait to interpret one's experiences in the light of the past. The more that repressed impulses seek expression in derivatives, the more hampered is the correct evaluation of the differences between the present and the past, and the greater is the transference component of a person's behaviour.

In contrast to such transferences in everyday life, the psychoanalytic situation

promotes the production of transference in two ways: (1) The environment which is reacted to has a relatively uniform and constant character and therefore the transference component in the reactions becomes much more pronounced. (2) Whereas in other situations people react to a person's actions and words—thus provoking new reactions and creating new realities all of which obscures the transference character of the original action—the analyst, in contrast to this, provides no actual provocation to the patient and responds to his affective outbursts only by making the patient aware of his behaviour. Thus the transference character of the patient's feelings becomes clearer.

Similarly, Greenacre (1954) comments:

First as to the nature of the transference relationship itself: If two people are repeatedly alone together, some sort of emotional bond will develop between them.

She then describes the special developments in the artificial situation of the analytic relationship.

Now in the artificial situation of the analytic relationship, there develops early a firm basic transference, derived from the mother-child relationship but expressed in the confidence in the knowledge and integrity of the analyst and the helpfulness of the method; but in addition the non-participation of the analyst in a personal way in the relationship creates a 'tilted' emotional relationship, a kind of psychic suction in which many of the past attitudes, specific experiences and fantasies of the patient are re-enacted in fragments or sometimes in surprisingly well-organized dramas with the analyst as the main figure of significance for the patient. This revival of past experiences with the full emotional accompaniment focused upon the analyst, is not only more possible but can be more easily seen, understood, and interpreted if the psychic field is not already cluttered with personal bits from the analyst's life. This of course is the work with the neurotic symptoms and patterns as they occur in the transference; i.e. projected directly upon the analyst.

In a more recent paper, Greenacre (1966) comments that the phenomenon of transference is omnipresent in human relationships and is based on two essential psychological ingredients

first, the difficulty of the individual to exist long in emotional isolation; and second, the capacity to shift or transfer patterns of emotional relationship from one person to another, provided there is a connecting link between them.

She reiterates her view that the transference has its roots in the early and necessary relationship of infancy, and goes on to say:

However, in therapy, communication through bodily contact and direct gratification . . . is replaced as much as possible by verbal communication.

Similar points have been made by a number of other analysts, including Glover, Bornstein and Hoffer. Thus Hoffer (1956) sees the specific transference of the analytic relationship as a variant of human transference relationships in general and links it in particular to infantile experiences. He states:

The term 'transference' refers to the generally agreed fact that people when entering into any form of object-relationship and using objects around them for instinct gratification and for protection against anxieties (as a defence) *transfer* upon their objects those images which they encountered in the course of previous *infantile* experiences, and experienced with pleasure or learned to avoid (pleasure-pain principle). The term 'transference', stressing an aspect of the influence our childhood has on our life as a whole, thus refers to those observations in which people in their contact with objects, which may be real or imaginary, positive, negative or ambivalent, 'transfer' their *memories* of significant previous experiences and thus *'change the reality'* of their objects, invest them with qualities from the past, judge them and try to make use of them in accordance with their own past.

The analytic situation is a variant of such human transference relationship.

With the exception of a handful of authors, little work has been done on the psychological nature of the special bond that constitutes transference, other than to stress the fact that it involves a repetition of the past in the present, that it is in some way irrational, and that it can have an important social and adaptive function. Moreover, the assumption is often made that we are dealing with a *unidimensional* or unitary phenomenon, the differences between various types of transference phenomena, both within and without the analytic situation, being largely a matter of specific content, and of variations in the degree of complexity and intensity.

As with many other analytic concepts introduced by Freud, what appeared to be relatively simple in the beginning now turns out to be very complicated indeed.

We have suggested earlier that the problem of integrating the technical with the metapsychological frames of reference is an important one, and it arises in heightened form in relation to material derived from psychoanalytic work with children. Here the differences in the analytic setting, in the ways in which the patient communicates, in the therapeutic forces at work (for not all improvement during the course of child analysis can be attributed to the development of insight), together with the fact that the child's relationship to the analyst may at times be indistinguishable from extra-analytic relationships, and many other factors, all serve to make the differentiation between what is transference and what is not extremely difficult. Freud remarked in 1933 that, in the analysis of children as opposed to adults, 'Transference (since the real parents are still on the spot) plays a different part'.

But precisely *because* of the difficulties in distinguishing and defining transference in child analytic work (and a great deal has been written on the subject in recent years), the investigation of material from child analysis offers perhaps a most useful starting point for investigating both theoretical and technical aspects of transference in general—one can start by jumping in at the deep end, as it were. Accordingly we would like to present some of the results of the examination of relevant child analytic material from one of the studies conducted as part of the Hampstead Index Project.

II

We should like to preface this part of our paper with a few remarks about the role of transference in child analysis.

In Anna Freud's work on *The Psychoanalytic Treatment of Children* (1926), she expressed the view that although transference occurs in child analysis in the form of what she called transference reactions, a transference *neurosis* in the form in which it is seen in adults does not occur.[3] An exception to this might be the case where the child was living away from the real parents, for example in an institution. Anna Freud later altered her views on this, attributing the change to the developments which have occurred in the technique of child therapy, in particular the elimination of the introductory phase and the deliberate use of defence analysis. She now believes it possible for the child's transference reactions to develop into a transference neurosis.

In *Normality and Pathology in Childhood* (1965) she states:

I have modified my former opinion that transference in childhood is restricted to single 'transference reactions' and does not develop to the complete status of a 'transference neurosis'. Nevertheless, I am still unconvinced that what is called transference neurosis with children equals the adult variety in every respect.[4]

In *The Ego and the Mechanisms of Defense* (1936) Anna Freud had distinguished different types of transference phenomena according to the degree of their complexity. These are: (1) *transference of libidinal impulses,* in which instinctual wishes attached to infantile objects break through or attempt to break through towards the person of the analyst; (2) *transference of defence,* in which former defensive measures against the drives are repeated; and (3) *acting in the transference,* in which the transference intensifies and spills over into the patient's daily life.

Anna Freud has always maintained that in child analysis the analyst can be used by the child for multiple purposes—to play multiple roles—and only one of these is transference. Thus she has written of the analyst functioning as a 'new object' for the child, the healthy part of the child's personality displaying a 'hunger' (as she put it) for new objects, in contrast to the neurotic part of the child which uses the analyst for purposes of repetition. She also emphasizes the importance of the 'treatment alliance' (a concept which has come to replace that of the earlier 'introductory phase' in treatment). In addition, the analyst can also function as an object for externalization, externalization being a *subspecies* of transference but which should nevertheless be kept separate from transference proper. She put it in the following way:

Not all the relations established or transferred by a child in analysis are object relations in the sense that the analyst becomes cathected with libido or aggression. Many are due to externalizations, i.e. to processes in which the person of the analyst is used to represent one or other part of the patient's personality structure.

Thus the child restages in analysis his internal (intersystemic) conflicts as external battles with the analyst. Transference proper would be regarded as the repetition, by way of regression in the analysis, of the child's object relations from all levels of development.

All of this draws attention to the fact that distinctions can be made between various types of relationship to the analyst, some of which may be regarded as transference and others not. Here the definition of transference is one which is essentially related to the analytical situation and to the technique of analysis, and we are dealing with formulations which are basically within a technical frame of reference. This also applies to formulations regarding transference which have been put forward by other child analysts.

---

3. Bornstein (1945) expresses a very similar view. In child analysis 'the analyst may become the target of many of the child's sexual or aggressive impulses, and occasionally and within a limited scope he may play the part of one of the parents. And yet, as a rule, no transference neurosis in the proper sense of the term arises. The symptoms are not centered around the analyst's person nor around happenings during the analytic session.

There is a good reason why the child does not develop a transference neurosis, in the strict sense. There is no need for him to repeat his reaction vicariously since he still possesses his original love-objects, his parents, in reality'.

4. Similar views have been expressed, for instance, by Kut (1953), Brody (1961) and Fraiberg (1966).

The problem of integrating the clinical and theoretical frames of reference still remains.

In an attempt to investigate this problem further, a research group was set up within the framework of the Hampstead Index Project some years ago. Its specific task was to examine the accumulated child analytic material from the point of view of the clinical classification of those manifestations in analysis which could possibly be called transference, and then to consider these from a more theoretical, i.e. metapsychological, standpoint.

We had at our disposal in this project a mass of information collected in the Index under various headings which were relevant to the concept of transference. This material was examined in some detail, and in consequence a number of conclusions as to their classification were reached. We shall attempt to summarize some of these under a few broad headings, which are by no means mutually exclusive.

1. It very quickly became clear that the clinical and technical usage of the term 'transference' covered a very broad spectrum of phenomena. It became apparent, too, that this was not due to failure on the part of our therapists to apply what they had learned, but was connected with an intrinsic difficulty in regard to the definition of what was transference and what was not. However, we could group the material under a number of headings.

First we have all those manifestations which could be understood in terms of the way in which past experiences, impulses, fantasies and conflicts were *revived* in the course of the analysis, and which now relate to the person of the analyst in their manifest or latent content. We see here in particular how a repressed unconscious wish emerges as a new derivative of the unconscious, and which may combine with present reality (including the person of the analyst) in the expression of a revived wish, memory or fantasy. (For example, the wish for the exclusive possession of the therapist, representing a revival, in the analysis, of a boy's oedipal or pre-oedipal wish for the exclusive possession of the mother.) The particular content of such a transference from the past is influenced not only by present preconscious and conscious content but also by content derived from past memories and fantasies.

From a metapsychological point of view, transference of this sort could be considered as a derivative of the repressed Unconscious—or, from a structural point of view, as a derivative of the id. (Fenichel (1941) has elaborated the notion of

transference as a derivative—a point, of course, originally made by Freud.)

2. We had no doubt that a relationship which corresponds to the transference neurosis as it has been described in adult psychoanalytic work also occurs in a considerable number of child cases. The whole question of the occurrence of transference neurosis in the analysis of children is a controversial one, and, of course, much turns on the definition which one uses.

Our own definition of transference neurosis was arrived at after a considerable amount of thought and discussion, and we mean by it here the concentration of the child's conflicts, repressed wishes, fantasies, etc. on to the person of the analyst, *with the relative diminution of their manifestations elsewhere.* With this definition in mind, an examination of index instances of transference neurosis showed that, in some cases of what could appear to be a transference neurosis, the mechanism involved was not simply a concentration of the child's instinctual impulses on to the person of the analyst. Rather, the permissive attitude of the therapist allowed the child to express impulses which had to be restrained elsewhere, and this was accompanied by symptomatic improvement outside the analysis. The changes within the analytic situation were connected with changes in the direction of obtaining a more realistic ideal self-image.

3. We come now to the various forms of *externalization.* As mentioned earlier, Anna Freud has drawn our attention to the way in which the various major structures can be externalized during the course of the analysis, and although she suggests that this is a subspecies of transference which should be distinguished from transference proper, it worked out in practice to be impossible to avoid bringing externalization under the major heading of transference. Thus a patient may externalize his superego so that the analyst comes to bear for the patient the characteristics of the patient's own conscience, and is reacted to by the patient as if he were the patient's superego—an internal conflict has become an external one in the analysis. But it becomes extremely difficult to draw a dividing line between the externalization of the superego as a structure and the externalization of the introjects which form the basis of the superego, in which case we have the revival of a past object relationship (we mean here the psychic object relationship, not necessarily the real one which existed between patient and parents in the past); and we would very definitely have to call this a form of transference.

We have mentioned earlier Freud's remark that the analyst can take over the power of the patient's superego — here the *authority* of the introject is transferred rather than its content. The analyst does not reflect the superego introject — indeed one might say that the introject has not been externalized, but rather that the patient turns to an alternative authority — a transfer or displacement of authority (Sandler, 1960). This is, of course, of great importance as part of the mechanism of the therapeutic process.

Similarly, we might talk of externalization of the id — as, for example, when the patient sees the analyst as a seducer. But here again, how do we differentiate between externalization of the id and a projective defence against a revived instinctual impulse directed towards the person of the analyst in the present, as it was directed towards an object in the past?

Under the heading of *externalization* we can also include all those various forms which relate to the externalization of one or other aspect of the patient's own self-representation. This includes what we ordinarily understand by projection, in which an impulse of the patient towards the analyst is felt by the patient as being directed by the analyst towards him. But externalization of the self-representation includes far more; aspects of the patient's *ideal self* may be externalized, and this includes both positive and negative ideals. Or we may see the complicated but highly important mechanism in which the patient externalizes an aspect of his self-representation on to the analyst and at the same time identifies with a superego introject. This is sometimes loosely called projection, but it is in fact a rather more complicated mechanism — for example, when the patient feels *guilty* about an impulse of one sort or another, he may accuse the analyst of it, gaining at the same time a feeling of virtue through his own identification with his superego.

We can also get 'splitting' of the self-representation between analyst and patient in specific forms, as in the revival of the fantasy of having a twin, etc. The range of possible externalizations is infinite, and it is often extremely difficult to divorce externalization from the types of transference described earlier, for every libidinal or aggressive impulse carries with it some form of self-representation as well as some form of object-representation — and, of course, some form of relation between the two. Thus an unconscious exhibitionistic impulse carries with it an unconscious representation of the person exhibiting himself, some representation of the person exhibited to, and a representation of the act of the person exhibiting to the object.

Externalizations of aspects of the self-representations are, of course, paralleled by internalizations of various sorts, and the identifications and introjections that occur in the analytic situation belong in this category.

4. We come now to what we can call *displacements and extensions of other relationships*. Perhaps more noticeable in analytic work with children than with adults is the occurrence of displacements of *current* wishes, conflicts or reactions to persons outside the analysis into the analytic situation, or on to the person of the analyst. With children it is most frequently aspects of the relationship to the parents that are displaced or extended into the analysis in this manner. These current preoccupations may be largely reality-related (e.g. the child's reaction to a real rejection by the parent); or they may be a product or manifestation of the child's current level of functioning (e.g. the appearance of oedipal strivings as a consequence of the child's progressive development).

There can be little doubt that the interpretation and working through of these current preoccupations of the child extended into the analysis is one of the most important aspects of analytic work with children. It is perhaps of some interest that therapists vary in the degree to which they take up such material as relating specifically to the analytical situation. These displacements and extensions, which have been discussed in the literature (e.g. by Fraiberg), are what one could call 'transferences in breadth' as opposed to 'transferences in depth'.

5. The phenomena to which we have just referred bring us into the related field of what we might perhaps refer to as '*character transference*'. Here we see reactions, attitudes and relations manifested towards the therapist which can be considered to be habitual and characteristic for the patient concerned. Of importance in this connection is that these aspects of the patient's relationship to people (or to specific groups of people) are not in any way specific to the therapist, but are rather in the nature of character traits. Such reactions may be seen, and indeed very often are seen, in the *earliest* sessions of treatment, and may involve feelings of *the greatest intensity*. Typical of such manifestations is the occurrence in the analysis of a habitual tendency to placate or appease, or habitual demandingness, or a sado-masochistic tendency. From a purely technical point of view it may be correct and valuable to take these habitual or character transferences up in the analytic work as if they were specifically related to the analytical situation. However, there are occasions when the interpretation of such reactions of the patient (and we are thinking here of certain types of cases

with a so-called 'character disturbance') in terms of the intra-analytic situation is technically quite inappropriate.

6. We can comment briefly on certain other aspects of the analytic relationship. One of these is the so-called 'relationship to the analyst as a real person'—of particular importance in children who have suffered severe deprivations in their object relationships, but also seen, of course, in certain adult patients who may have had such early deprivations or who may be suffering from defects in the capacity to make full object relationships.

Another role of the analyst is his function, in certain cases, of being what has been referred to as an 'auxiliary ego'—something which we see particularly in borderline and psychotic cases, or in children with an organic defect, in blind children and so on.

To these we can add the function of the analyst in those instances where the patient relates to him simply on the basis of his being a person who can satisfy a need. What is significant here is that the analyst as a real and specific person plays no part—if the need arises then the demand is there for any person to satisfy it, and the analyst happens to be the person present. This is characteristic for certain patients who have not progressed far in their level of object-relations and in whom the need-satisfying components of their object-relationships predominate.

7. We come now to an aspect of the relationship to the analyst which has been much discussed in regard to both adult and child analysis. This is what has been called the 'therapeutic alliance' or the 'working alliance'. It is usually *contrasted* with transference—and refers to the treatment alliance between therapist and patient, based on the patient's conscious or unconscious wish to co-operate, and his readiness to accept the therapist's aid in overcoming internal difficulties. This is not the same as attending treatment simply on the basis of getting pleasure or some other form of gratification. In the treatment alliance there is an *acceptance* of the need to deal with internal problems, and to do analytic work in the face of internal or (particularly with children) external (e.g. family) resistance.

Although it is clear that we can distinguish between the treatment alliance and what we normally call transference, there can be little doubt that the success or failure of a treatment alliance depends, among other things, on the existence of what Greenacre (1954) has called a 'basic' or 'primary' transference. She considers that the basic transference originates from a primary need for sensory contact, for the warmth of contact with another body.

Greenacre stresses, incidentally, the need for a full adherence to the rules of analysis in order for the analytic process to develop within the matrix of the 'basic' or 'primary' transference.

The point we wish to emphasize here is that even though we may (and from a technical point of view *should*) contrast the treatment alliance with transference, a form of transference itself appears to be an essential ingredient of the treatment alliance. Indeed, the phrase 'positive transference' has often been used to denote the establishment of the basic transference to which Greenacre refers.

8. To conclude this section of the paper we would like to mention only briefly the whole host of fantasies and expectations which the patient may bring to treatment. These again have been referred to at times as transference manifestations, 'ready-made' transferences and the like; yet at the same time they are always contrasted with the forms of transference which develop as a consequence of regressive processes within the analytic situation.

It is perhaps of interest to hark back here to Greenson's two essential elements of (1) repetition of the past and (2) inappropriateness to the present—for these will on the whole apply also to the initial fantasies and expectations with which the patient comes to treatment. In contrast, a definition of the sort given by Waelder would not apply. Let us give an example recorded in the Index (this is a child who started analysis at the age of 3):

Sara played many games in which she showed that she saw the treatment situation as a repetition of her hospitalization, with the therapist as the doctor. When her fears about treatment were interpreted, she said to the therapist: 'You are a doctor'. She then took the role of the doctor and put plaster on the therapist's hand, saying it was bleeding.

We have spent some considerable time so far in describing some of the types of clinical phenomena which could conceivably be brought together under the general heading of transference, but we should like to emphasize at this point that we are not claiming that all these clinical manifestations *are* in fact transference. What we are saying is rather that it is extremely difficult to draw the line and to define transference in such a way that we can satisfactorily categorize our material into what is transference and what is not. If we start, as Freud did, from the view that transference represents the transferring of an impulse directed towards an infantile object, towards a new object—the analyst—in the present, we are limiting ourselves to a very narrow field, and excluding much of what is, in present-day usage, considered to be transference. The reader will recall that it was Anna Freud who, in 1936, spoke of *transference of defence* and who later referred to *externalization* as a *subspecies* of transference.

We should also like to emphasize that the problem in regard to transference is not necessarily a clinical one—we can assume that practising psychoanalysts know what they mean by transference—or the exact meaning of the term may not be important as long as one understands what the patient is doing, what mechanism is operating, and so on. The problem is basically a conceptual one, but as such it is also a problem in psychoanalytic communication, and consequently an important one in psychoanalytic teaching. When psychoanalysts speak to one another of transference, or teach their candidates about when to take up the transference or when to leave it alone, they may be in an area of pseudo-communication, unless they are sure that others understand the same thing by the term as they do. Indeed many avoidable technical errors are made by beginning analysts because they have been given 'rules of thumb' about when and when not to interpret material in the transference.

The objection may be raised at this point that the types of relationship which develop in analytic work with adults have a special quality and are more restricted in scope than those which can be discerned in analytic work with children, and that this is brought about because of the special structure of the adult psychoanalytic situation. We are accustomed to taking this special situation and the technique of adult analysis as our basic model, and to consider departures from the basic process as necessary variations in technique forced upon us by the needs of the patient. In this context Eissler (1953) has spoken of parameters of technique, referring here to necessary temporary deviations from the standard analytic procedure. From this point of view, the technique of child analysis is one which appears to involve parameters of the grossest sort, but although the differences between adult and child analysis have always been stressed, there are also marked similarities. In both, for example, we aim at creating a situation in which we allow the patient's material to develop and unfold, a situation in which internal and internalized conflicts can be externalized, interpreted and so on. Whereas in the adult analytic situation we have a set of rules which are appropriate to the fact that material can be brought in the form of free association, in child analysis we have a more flexible set of rules aimed in particular at providing suitable *modes of expression* to the child

so that he too can bring and develop his analytic material. We believe that child analysis has shown us that it is possible for the child analyst to step out of one role into another—for example, to initiate a game with a young child and at the same time to take sufficient distance in order to give an appropriate interpretation.

A great deal of adaptation to the limits, peculiarities and needs of the child goes on in child analysis, but even in the analysis of adults we often do something similar, except on a much more microscopic scale. Perhaps we should distinguish here between micro- and macroparameters of technique, the macroparameters being more characteristic of analytic work with children than with adults.

The point of saying all of this is to emphasize the conclusion, which is evident from the instances quoted earlier, that the types of relationship and the content of the material which emerge in child analysis do not essentially differ from that with which we are familiar from work with adults (although of course the technical procedures may be very different). All the instances we have referred to can be found in work with adults as well, but the child-analytic situation, operating as it does on a broader beam, with more flexible rules than adult analysis, enables us perhaps to see the range of relationships (which in the analytic situation could be called transference) in a more comprehensive way than we might otherwise do.

The concept of transference is one which has been developed from within psychoanalytic work—it derives historically from the understanding of particular types of resistance to the analytic process—and it has been extended outside the psychoanalytic situation into the general sphere of the psychology of interpersonal relationships. Freud himself did this when he referred to transference as a universal phenomenon. It is an inescapable conclusion that we have to view transference—the term is now used in a broad sense—as a *multidimensional* rather than as a unitary or unidimensional phenomenon. And if we want to conceptualize these dimensions from the point of view of psychoanalytic metapsychology, it is also evident that we need to consider the metapsychology of object relationships rather than that of transference as such. The term 'object-relationship' is used here with the qualification that it includes much more than the libidinal or aggressive cathexis of another person, but that it also refers to such things as the use of objects for externalizations and internalizations of all sorts, or as objects of displacement, or as objects to whom the relationship is entirely connected with reality matters. Thus there would appear to be as many dimensions to relationship as there are to transference in its broadest sense, and indeed the study of the one is, we believe, the study of the other. Freud, it will be remembered, spoke of 'the relation of transference'. Thus we are perhaps at a point at which we can proceed from psychoanalytic general psychology, from the more general field, to the study of the specific analytic phenomena—even though it may be that the analytic situation gives us the best insights into the general psychology of object relationships. But there is no doubt that there are other techniques—child observation, to quote but one example—which will also serve us well in this connection.

If we adopt this point of view we should then *not* ask ourselves: what is and what is not transference in the analytic situation, but rather *what dimensions of relationship enter into the specific and artificial analytic situation, and how are these involved in the process of treatment?*

We have used the term 'dimensions of relationship' in order to emphasize something which may become obscured when we view the development of object relationships in terms of the stages and phases which the child passes through in the course of his development. From a descriptive point of view we do see the replacement of an earlier type of relationship by different, more mature, forms. We see the replacement of the psychological reflection of the biological mother-infant relationship by anaclitic, so-called need-fulfilling, relationships, these in turn leading to further developments and so on. But in fact we probably do not ever get a real replacement of one type of relationship by another. What we see is rather the addition of various new types of object relationship developing collaterally, being integrated with and dominating the old, but not necessarily replacing them. Thus even in the person who has attained the most mature type of object love, the infantile aspects, for example the purely need-satisfying aspects, remain, although they may be subordinated to the higher-level developments. Sex is never entirely transformed into object love, but the same object may come to serve both aspects of the relationship. Included in the concept of relationship here are all those bonds which involve identification, externalization, and the like, and here too we have the development of parallel lines, so that even the most primitive state of primary identification, or primary confusion, as it is better called, persists alongside the more mature capacity to make secondary identifications once ego boundaries have been developed and are capable of being imposed. It has been suggested (Sandler & Joffe, 1967) that the first automatic response to the perception of another person is to be confused with them, but that normally this primary confusion or identification is dealt with by the rapid setting of self and object boundaries. Thus we have as part of normal development the attainment of the capacity to *disidentify,* a process which represents the inhibition of a genetically earlier state. Indeed, we would take the view that in normal ego functioning the ego has to expend a considerable amount of effort inhibiting earlier tendencies and solutions.[5] Thus so-called 'phase-dominance' is only descriptively a replacement of earlier forms of functioning by developmentally later ones. Dynamically, it involves a *subordination* of developmentally earlier trends which persist in the present in unconscious 'trial' form.

In normal life the elements of the past which enter into relationships may repeat themselves over and over again in the present. Or some degree of stability may be reached in an ongoing interpersonal relationship. The analytical situation, for both children and adults, owes its uniqueness and special properties to the fact that by means of a set of rules, conditions and procedures, the patient is enabled to recreate (among other things) the important aspects of his present and past internal and external object relationships in the analysis—all of which provides material for the ongoing analytic work. As a consequence of the analyst's interpretations, confrontations, reconstructions and other interventions, a process of further development within the analysis occurs, material shifts to a different level, and so on. We would like to stress the *process* aspect of analysis, for the analysis of resistances permits a development—including the relationships which we call transference—in a way and to a degree which would not be possible in normal life. Infantile impulses, fantasies, object relationships, conflicts and solutions become alive in the present, and with the cooperation of that part of the patient which is in alliance with the work of analysis, successful analytic work may ensue.

CONCLUSIONS

Transference is a clinical rather than a metapsychological concept. The concept as it has come to be used encompasses a whole variety of elements, all

---

5. The relaxation of this effort or constraint on the part of the ego in the analytic situation probably contributes in a substantial way to 'the return of the repressed' in the special (adult) psychoanalytic situation, in the forms which have been discussed in this paper.

of which enter into object relationships in general. The special psychoanalytic situation may facilitate the emergence of particular aspects of relationships, especially aspects of past relationships, but it is technically of the greatest importance to distinguish between these various elements ('dimensions' of transference) rather than to regard *all* aspects of the patient's relationship to the analyst as being a repetition of past relationships to objects.[6] In other words, transference, in the diluted sense in which it tends to be used today, should not be understood as only reflecting transference in the narrow sense in which it was originally conceived. The psychoanalyst must be ready to distinguish between the repetition of past relationships to objects, defences against this, the various forms of externalization, the displacements and extensions of other current relationships, so-called 'character' transferences and the like. Work with children shows the differences between these various elements most clearly, but they emerge as well, although in different proportions, in psychoanalytic work with adults.

ACKNOWLEDGEMENTS

The Hampstead Child-Therapy Clinic has been supported by the following foundations: the American Philanthropic Foundation; the Gustave M. Berne Foundation; the Field Foundation, Inc., New York; the Ford Foundation; the Foundations' Fund for Research in Psychiatry, New Haven, Conn., U.S.A.; the Anna Freud Foundation, New York; the Grant Foundation, Inc., New York; the Estate of Flora Haas, New York; the A. and M. Lasker Foundation; the Walter E. Meyer Research Institute of Law, New York; the National Institute of Mental Health, Bethesda, Md., U.S.A.; the New Land Foundation; the Old Dominion Foundation, U.S.A.; the Psychoanalytic Research and Development Fund, Inc., New York; the William Rosenwald Family Fund, New York; the Clement and Jessie V. Stone Foundation, Chicago; the Taconic Foundation, Inc., New York.

REFERENCES

Bornstein, B. (1945). Clinical notes on child analysis. *Psychoanal. Study Child* 1.

Brody, S. (1961). Some aspects of transference resistance in prepuberty. *Psychoanal. Study Child* 16.

Eissler, K. R. (1953). The effect of the structure of the ego on psychoanalytic technique. *J. Am. psychoanal. Ass.* 1, 104–143.

Fenichel, O. (1941). *Problems of Psychoanalytic Technique.* New York: Psychoanalytic Quarterly Inc.

Fenichel, O. (1945). *The Psychoanalytic Theory of Neurosis.* New York: Norton.

Fraiberg, S. (1966). Further considerations of the role of transference in latency. *Psychoanal. Study Child* 21.

Freud, A. (1926). *The Psychoanalytic Treatment of Children* London: Hogarth Press, 1950.

Freud, A. (1936). The Ego and the Mechanisms of Defence. London: Hogarth Press, 1954.

Freud, A. (1965). *Normality and Pathology in Childhood.* New York: Int. Univ. Press.

Freud, S. (1895). Studies on hysteria. *S.E.* 2.

Freud, S. (1905). Fragment of an analysis of a case of hysteria. *S.E.* 7.

Freud, S. (1909). Five lectures on psycho-analysis. *S.E.* 11.

Freud, S. (1912). The dynamics of transference. *S.E.* 12.

Freud, S. (1916–17). Introductory lectures on psychoanalysis. *S.E.* 15–16.

Freud, S. (1925). An autobiographical study. *S.E.* 20.

Freud, S. (1933). New introductory lectures on psychoanalysis. *S.E.* 22.

Freud, S. (1940). An outline of psycho-analysis. *S.E.* 23.

Glover, E. (1939). *Psycho-Analysis.* London: Staples Press, 1949.

Glover, E. (1955). *The Technique of Psycho-Analysis.* London: Ballière, Tindall & Cox.

Greenacre, P. (1954). The role of transference: practical considerations in relation to psychoanalytic therapy. *J. Am. psychoanal. Ass.* 2, 671–684.

Greenacre, P. (1966). Problems of over-idealization of the analyst and of analysis: their manifestations in the transference and countertransference relationship. *Psychoanal. Study Child* 21.

Greenson, R. R. (1965). The working alliance and the transference neurosis. *Psychoanal. Q.* 34, 155–181.

Hendrick, I. (1934). *Facts and Theories of Psycho-Analysis.* New York: Knopf, 1958.

Hoffer, W. (1950). Three psychological criteria for the termination of treatment. *Int. J. Psycho-Anal.* 31, 194–195.

Hoffer, W. (1956). Transference and transference neurosis. *Int. J. Psycho-Anal.* 37, 377–379.

Kepecs, J. G. (1966). Theories of transference neurosis. *Psychoanal. Q.* 35, 497–521.

Klein, M. (1952). The origins of transference. *Int. J. Psycho-Anal.* 33, 433–438.

Kut, S. (1953). The changing pattern of transference in

---

6. As does Melanie Klein (1952).

the analysis of an eleven-year-old girl. *Psycho-anal. Study Child* 8.

Menninger, K. (1958). *Theory of Psycho-Analytic Technique.* New York: Basic Books.

Nunberg, H. (1951). Transference and reality. *Int. J. Psycho-Anal.* 32, 1–9.

Orr, D. W. (1954). Transference and counter-transference: a historical survey. *J. Am. psycho-anal. Ass.* 2, 621–670.

Sandler, J. (1960). On the concept of superego. *Psychoanal. Study Child* 15.

Sandler, J. & Joffe, W. G. (1967). The tendency to persistence in psychological function and development, with special reference to fixation and regression. *Bull. Menninger Clin.* 31, 257–271.

Sharpe, E. F. (1930). *Collected Papers on Psycho-Analysis.* London: Hogarth Press, 1950.

Silverberg, W. V. (1948). The concept of transference. *Psychoanal. Q.* 17, 303–321.

Waelder, R. (1956). Introduction to the discussion on problems of transference. *Int. J. Psycho-Anal.* 37, 367–368.

6

NOTES ON TRANSFERENCE: UNIVERSAL PHENOMENON AND HARDEST PART OF ANALYSIS

BRIAN BIRD

EDITOR'S NOTE

For several reasons, this paper claims a special place in the classical psychoanalytic literature on transference. First, Bird offers a sensitive résumé and evaluation of the difficulties experienced by Freud in the development of this concept. Second, there is in the paper some recognition of the extent to which the analyst participates in the patient's transference neurosis, a recognition which suggests Bird's growing awareness of interactional considerations. This approach affords him a number of additional insights even though his paper stops short of a definitive exploration in this area. Third, the paper attempts to illuminate the transference neurosis, a concept first defined by Freud (1914) and discussed subsequently by a number of analysts.

Fourth, and perhaps most important, Bird quite seriously and carefully investigates the interaction between reality and transference. He is one of the first classical psychoanalysts to discuss in any detail the realistic consequences for the analyst of transference-based expressions from the analysand, including the patient's actual efforts to harm the therapist and the possibility that such destructive endeavors may be a response to countertransference-based, destructive interventions. This particular subject had earlier been studied rather extensively by Searles (1965), but his work has had little apparent influence on the writings of classical analysts; similarly, these important comments by Bird have not as yet gained the recognition they deserve.

As an introduction I would like to make a few general remarks about transference as I see it. Transference, in my view, is a very special mental quality that has never been satisfactorily explained. I am not satisfied, for instance, either with what has been written about it or with its use in analysis. To me, our knowledge seems slight, and our use limited. This view, admittedly extreme, is possible only because transference is such a very remarkable phenomenon, with a great and largely undeveloped potential. I am particularly taken with the as yet unexplored idea that transference is a universal mental function which may well be the basis of all human relationships. I even suspect it of being one of the mind's main agencies for giving birth to new ideas, and new life to old ones. In these several respects, transference would seem to me to assume characteristics of a major ego function.

I tend to go along with those who consider transference unique as it occurs in the analytic situation, and with those who hold that the analysis and

Reprinted from *Journal of the American Psychoanalytic Association* 20: 267–301, by permission of International Universities Press, Inc. Copyright © 1972 by American Psychoanalytic Association.

resolution of a transference neurosis is the only avenue to the farthest reaches of the mind. It is also my belief that transference, in one form or another, is always present, active, and significant in the analytic situation. From this it should follow that rarely is there a need to give up on the transference or to doubt that everything that goes on in analysis has a transference meaning. I would also be inclined to agree with those, perhaps few in number, who harbor the idea that analysts themselves regularly develop transference reactions to their patients, including periods of transference neurosis, and that these transference reactions play an essential role in the analytic process.

Finally, I want to point out that this paper is not a comprehensive study of transference. Nor is it a review paper, for, with the exception of a few references to some of Freud's writings, there is little or no mention of what has been written on the subject by others. As to how transference works, it seems likely there are more questions than answers. Therefore, I hope it will be understood that what I say is for question-raising, and anything sounding like an answer should be especially questioned.

SOME VIEWS ON FREUD AND TRANSFERENCE

As a prefatory remark about Freud and transference, the observation can be offered that Freud wrote only briefly about transference and did so, in the main, before 1917. Another observation which can rarely be made about Freud's works, and which everyone may not agree with, is that, with one or two exceptions, what he did write on transference did not reach the high level of analytical thought which has come to be regarded as standard for him. Some indication of what his contributions consist of is given by the editors of the Standard Edition, who list them in several places. One of the longer lists, in a footnote on page 431 of Volume 16, includes six references: "Studies on Hysteria" with Breuer (1895), the Dora paper (1905), "The Dynamics of Transference" (1912), "Observations on Transference-Love" (1915), the chapter on transference in the Introductory Lectures (1917), and "Analysis Terminable and Interminable" (1937). Although the editors in no sense suggest that these six papers include everything Freud wrote on the subject, it does seem evident that, considering the essential importance of transference to analysis, he wrote little. Moreover, the three papers in which transference is the specific theme, "The Dynamics of

Transference," "Transference-Love," and the transference chapter in the Introductory Lectures, come across as perhaps his least significant contributions.

Freud's first direct mention of transference occurs in "Studies on Hysteria" (1895). His first significant reference to it, however, did not appear until five years later when, in a letter to Fliess on April 16, 1900, he said (Freud, 1887–1902) he was "beginning to see that the apparent endlessness of the treatment is something of an inherent feature and is connected with the transference" (p. 317). In a footnote to this letter the editors state that, "This is the first insight into the role of transference in psycho-analytic therapy."

Despite these early references, it seems correct to say that yet another five years was to go by before the phenomenon of transference was actually introduced. Even then the introduction was far from prominent, for it was tacked on like an afterthought as a four-page portion of a postscript to what was perhaps Freud's most fascinating case history to date, the case of Dora (1905, pp. 116–120).

Using data from Dora's three-month-long, unexpectedly terminated analysis, and especially from her dramatic transference reactions which had taken him quite unawares, Freud now gave to transference its first distinct psychological entity and for the first time indicated its essential role in the analytic process. His account, although in general more than adequate—in fact elegant and remarkably "finished"—was brief, almost laconic, and perhaps not an entirely worthy introduction to such a truly great discovery. What was uniquely great was his recognizing the usefulness of transference. In his analysis of Dora he had noted not only that transference feelings existed and were powerful, but, much to his dismay, he had realized what a serious, perhaps even insurmountable, obstacle they could be. Then, in what seems like a creative leap, Freud made the almost unbelievable discovery that transference was in fact the key to analysis, that by properly taking the patient's transference into account, an entirely new, essential, and immensely effective heuristic and therapeutic force was added to the analytic method.

The impact on analysis of this startling discovery was actually much greater and much more significant than most people seem to appreciate. Although the role of transference as the *sine qua non* of analysis was and is widely accepted, and was so stated by Freud from the first, it has almost never been acclaimed for having brought about an entire change in the nature of analysis. The introduction of free association to analysis, a much lesser change, received and still receives much more recognition.

One of the reasons for the relatively unheralded entry of transference into analysis may have been the circumstances of its discovery. Although Freud's new ideas were recorded as if they arose as a sudden inspiration during the Dora analysis, they may in fact have developed somewhat later. In the paper's prefatory remarks, for instance, Freud (p. 13) said he had not discussed transference with Dora at all, and in the postscript (p. 119), he said he had been unaware of her transference feelings. Also pointing to a later discovery date is the extraordinary delay in the paper's publication. According to the editors' Note (p. 4), the paper had been completed and accepted for publication by late January 1901, but this date was then actually set back more than four and a half years until October 1905. The editors add: "We have no information as to how it happened that Freud . . . deferred publication." In my opinion, his reason may have been that only during those four and a half years, as a consequence of his own self-analysis, did he come to an understanding of the significance of the transference. Only then may it have been possible for him to turn again to the Dora case, to apply to it what he had learned in himself, to write his beautiful essay as part of the postscript, and at last to release the paper for publication.

Freud's self-analysis has been considered from many angles, but not significantly, as far as I know, from the standpoint of transference. Opponents of the idea that there is such a thing as definitive self-analysis, some of whom say it is impossible, generally object on the grounds that without an analyst there can be no transference neurosis. Freud clearly demonstrated, I think, the situation that may be necessary to fill this need: self-analysis may require at least a half-way satisfactory transference object. In Freud's case, the main transference object at this time seems to have been Fliess, who filled the role rather well. As with any analyst, his "real" impact on Freud was slight. He was essentially a neutral figure, relatively anonymous and physically separate. All of this, plus Fliess's own reciprocal transference reactions, made it possible for Freud to endow Fliess with whatever qualities and whatever feelings were essential to the development of Freud's transference, and it should be added, his transference neurosis. In the end, of course, the transference was in part resolved. Freud's eventual awakening to the realization of the presence within him of such strange and powerful psychological forces must have come as a stupendous disillusionment, directed not only toward Fliess but toward himself, and yet his subsequent working out of some of these transference attachments must have been both an intellectual triumph and an immensely healing and releasing process.

It was this event, the development, the discovery, and then the resolution within himself of the complexities of the transference neurosis, that constituted the actual center of his self-analysis, and it was this event that was the beginning of analysis as we know it.

In the years following this revolutionary discovery, the central role of transference in analysis gained remarkably wide acceptance, and it has easily held this central position ever since. What the substance of this central position consists of, however, is something of a mystery, for, in my opinion, nothing about analysis is less well known than how individual analysts actually use transference in their day-to-day work with patients. At a guess, because each analyst's concept of transference derives variably but significantly from his own inner experience, transference probably means many different things to different analysts.

In the same individually determined way, even Freud's own pupils must have differed on this issue, not only from him but from each other. Although some of their differences may have been slight, others may have contributed significantly to later analytic developments. A question could be raised, for instance, whether differences in handling the transference which at first were the property of one analyst gradually developed into formal clinical methods used by many, and whether these clinical methods, after having been conceptualized, served as the beginning of various divergent schools of analysis. Such an occurrence, consistent with my belief that analytic ideas do arise in this way, primarily out of transference experiences in the analytic situation, would lead to the question whether the history of the ideological differences among various schools might be found to be more consistently traceable to idiosyncratic differences in what was actually said and done in response to transference reactions than to any other factor. Whatever the case, many differences and divergencies did occur among the early analysts, and all of them, I suspect, had to do in some major way with differences in the handling of the transference.

Strangely, Freud himself seems to have taken little part in influencing this rapid and divergent period of growth. Usually accused of being too dominating in such matters, Freud seems to have done just the opposite during the development of this most critical aspect of analysis, the process itself, and, for reasons unknown, detached himself from it.

What was needed, one might be inclined to say,

was not leadership in the form of domination, but leadership in trying to provide what was lacking, and to me is still lacking, namely, an analytical rationale for transference phenomena. The question must be asked, of course, whether in fact this would have been a good thing at that particular time in psychoanalytic history. Perhaps not. The exercise of closure, which Freud's structuring might have amounted to, although adding to understanding and stability at a certain theoretical level, could at another level, as such closures have often done, have placed many obstacles in the way of further analytical developments. Thus, his leaving the matter of transference wide open, even though it led to confusion and uncertainty, may have been just as well.

In many ways the closest Freud ever came to establishing a formal analytical rationale for transference was his first attempt, in the postscript to the case of hysteria (1905). These few pages are, in my opinion, among the most important of all Freud's writings, outweighing by far the paper to which they are appended. Yet, I suspect, the case of Dora has always been taught as an entity rather than, as I would have it, ancillary to the essay on transference. In that essay Freud was clear: his ideas revealed tremendous insights and promised more to come. Imagine his being able to say at this early time that during analysis no new symptoms are formed, and that, instead, the powers of the neurosis are occupied in creating a new edition of the same disease. Just think of the analytical implications of his saying that this "new edition" consists of a special class of mental structures, for the most part unconscious, having the peculiar characteristic of being able to replace earlier persons with the person of the analyst, and in this fashion applying all components of the original neurosis to the person of the analyst at the present time. Surely as profound a statement as any he ever made.

Then he goes on to say that there is no way to avoid transference, that this "latest creation of the disease must be combated like all the earlier ones" (p. 116), and that, although this is by far the hardest part of analysis, only after the transference has been resolved can a patient arrive at a sense of conviction of the validity of the connections which have been structured during analysis.

He concludes by saying: "In psycho-analysis . . . all the patient's tendencies, including hostile ones, are aroused; they are then turned to account for the purposes of the analysis by being made conscious, and in this way the transference is constantly being destroyed. Transference, which seems ordained to be the greatest obstacle to psycho-analysis, becomes its most powerful ally . . ." (p. 117).

These remarkable observations, written in declarative style, with no hint of vacillation, vagueness, or ambivalence, convey a sense of deep conviction that could arise, one feels, only from Freud's own hard-won inner experience. Nowhere is there a suggestion that transference is a mere technical matter. Far from it. Here, in these few lines, Freud announces that he has come upon a new and exciting kind of mental function, or, as I believe, a new and exciting kind of ego function.

Very quickly, however, Freud's conviction seems to have failed him. Nothing he wrote afterward about transference was at this level, and most of his later references were a retreat from it. For instance, he never did develop the promising idea that the mind constantly creates new editions of the original neurosis and includes in them an ever-changing series of persons. Instead, he tended to become less specific, even referring to transference at times in broad terms as if it were no more than rapport between patient and analyst, or as if it were an interpersonal or psychosocial relationship, concepts which, of course, a great many analysts have since adopted, but which were not part of Freud's original ideas.

Perhaps his most persistent deviation was an on-and-off tendency to regard transference merely as a technical matter, often writing of it as an asset to analysis when positive and a liability when negative.

Significantly, because it indicated that an active struggle was still going on within him, Freud occasionally expressed once again, even though briefly, his earlier insights, particularly his idea that transference is an essential though unexplored part of mental life. An example of this appears in his otherwise quite indifferent account of transference in "An Autobiographical Study" (1925). Transference, he says, "is a universal phenomenon of the human mind . . . and in fact dominates the whole of each person's relations to his human environment" (p. 42). In these few words Freud again made the point, and in declarative fashion, that transference is a mental structure of the greatest magnitude. But he never really followed it up.

Rather extensive evidence of his departure from the original concept and of his continuing struggle with that concept is seen most clearly, I believe, in one of his last and one of his greatest works, "Analysis Terminable and Interminable" (1937). To my narrowly focused eyes, "Analysis Terminable and Interminable" is much more than a courageous, brilliant, and pessimistic appraisal of the difficulties and limitations of analysis. Although transference is little mentioned in the paper, a great deal about it comes through, some quite directly, some by easy inference. When looked at in this way, two themes stand out: Freud's personal frustrations with the enigmas of transference, and his tacit placing of transference in the very center of success and failure in analysis, both as a therapy and as a developing science. What also comes through, to me, is the perplexing realization of how far Freud had, by now, seemingly moved away from his original concepts. Or had he?

It is utterly perplexing, for instance, in reading his otherwise brilliant discussion of the ending of an analysis, to find that he makes no mention of what he had said so compellingly in this connection 30 years earlier: that for analysis to be effective, there must be a transference neurosis and that this neurosis must be resolved in the analytic situation.

His 1937 discussion of the negative side of transference is equally perplexing. Referring (pp. 221–222) to what is assumed to be Ferenczi's late-developing antagonism and to Ferenczi's rebuke that the negative transference should have been analyzed, Freud explains the situation rather lamely, it seems to me, by saying that even if such negative feelings had been detected in latent form, it was doubtful that the analyst had the power to activate them short of some unfriendly piece of behavior in reality on the analyst's part. Further on (p. 223), he also raises the question whether it is wise to stir up a pathogenic conflict which is not betraying itself. Contrast these views with his 1905 statement: "In psycho-analysis . . . all the patient's tendencies, including hostile ones, are aroused . . ." And in the next sentence, "Transference, which seems ordained to be the greatest obstacle to psycho-analysis, becomes its most powerful ally . . ." (p. 117). Here, it seems to me, Freud is saying that transference is precisely the power which is able to arouse "all the patient's tendencies," even latent ones, even ones which do not betray themselves, and that this arousal is not a matter of being wise or unwise but of being essential.

Other evidence of his strange and at least partial removal of transference from analysis appears where he says: ". . . we can only achieve our therapeutic purpose by increasing the power of analysis to come to the assistance of the ego. Hypnotic influence seemed to be an excellent instrument . . . but the reasons for our having to abandon it are well known. No substitute for hypnosis has yet been found" (1937, p. 230). As I read it, this statement seems to be a paradox. What about transference? Is not transference this very power, the power Freud now says we have not yet found? Indeed, what better definition of transference could there be than to say, using

Freud's words, that when properly taken into account, transference increases, in the most exquisite way, "the power of analysis to come to the assistance of the ego"? Is this not precisely what transference does? Is this not what Freud had earlier said its function was?

Again, toward the end of the paper (p. 247), in an otherwise masterful discussion of difficulties contributed by the individuality of the analyst, he fails almost completely to direct these difficulties to their most obvious source, the countertransference.

This fluid, inconstant, and ever-shifting state of Freud's views on transference may be explained, I believe, by the fact that for so much of his life he was himself deeply engaged in transference situations with many different persons. It should not be forgotten that Freud's discoveries were made primarily on himself. His primary sources were his own transference experiences. This, I suspect, was the principal executive agent of Freud's genius: his great capacity to become deeply involved in and to resolve myriad transference feelings, and then to derive from such experiences the basic principles governing them. One has to wonder, of course, whether this creative process was in any way unique with Freud. Perhaps not. Perhaps all great discoveries, or at least all "creative leaps," are made, via the transference, within the discoverer's own person. Perhaps all monumental breachings of the confines of the known depend not only upon the basic givens of genius but upon a capacity for greatly heightened cathexis of certain ego apparatuses, a development which, in turn, may require the kind of power generated by the ego only in a transference situation.

In this connection I would like to mention Isaac Newton, whose revolutionary discoveries were so far-reaching and so immense as to place him among the greatest geniuses of all time. My sketchy knowledge suggests that the circumstances of Newton's staggering creative breakthroughs might be profitably studied from the standpoint of transference and of transference's possible role in hypercathecting Newton's tremendously rich and expanded inner resources. The circumstances I refer to were unusual. In his third and fourth years at Cambridge as a bright but not remarkable student, he worked with and was encouraged by a gifted mathematician who was one of the few who recognized Newton as being something special. In 1665 the Great Plague forced the University to close for 18 months, and the students were dispersed. Newton went to his mother's house in the small village of his birth and he stayed there almost the entire time, completely cut off from all colleagues and practically isolated from the world. There, according to Andrade (1954), at the age of 23 and 24, alone with his mother and his thoughts, "the young Newton mastered the basic laws of mechanics; convinced himself that they applied to heavenly as well as to earthly bodies and discovered the fundamental law of gravitational attraction: invented the methods of the infinitesimal calculus: and was well on his way to his great optical discoveries" (p. 50). Other developments in Newton's long life might also be studied from the point of view of transference and creative productivity. Of particular interest are the intense and often stormy relations with his colleagues and the great impact these changing friendships and enmities may have had on his creativity.

In the case of Freud, the perplexing attitudes he took toward transference, his vacillations, contradictions, and omissions, his great insight and his apparent obtuseness, may all have reflected changes and phases of what was then going on in him with respect to the level and quality of his transference attachments to people, and his attempts to resolve and understand those attachments. In this respect, it might be scientifically rewarding to study Freud's personal data, particularly his letters, for evidence of transference reactions in his relations with various persons, and, taking the study a step further, for evidence of causal connections between the content or nature of these relationships and the particular analytic developments he was working on at the time.

Although the constant activity of Freud's great transference capacity was essential to his genius, it may also have been the very thing that prevented him from giving to transference itself the highly cathected and creative attention he gave, with such success, to many other subjects; and, because he did not, transference never attained a cohesive and stable analytic entity.

TRANSFERENCE: THE HARDEST PART OF ANALYSIS

Without being entirely aware of doing so, most of us have tended to follow and to extend Freud's somewhat meandering transference path. And, like Freud, we have moved steadily away from his original concepts.

How far we may have moved is uncertain, but a milestone of sorts, indicating how far we may have gone by 1952, is recorded in Orr's paper "Transference and Countertransference: A Historical Survey" (1954). Orr sums it up this way: "Most, if not all, recent psychoanalytic articles concerned with technique agree that handling of the transference continues to be the *sine qua non* of the treatment." But things were changing. "Increasingly," Orr says, ". . . 'handling' is taken to mean 'manipulation' in one form or another, and with the intensity of the transference or the depth of the therapeutic regression the points at issue." And although Orr could say that "The development, interpretation and resolution of the transference neurosis in the analytic relationship is still the hallmark of psychoanalysis for perhaps a majority of analysts today," he added the qualification that "for a considerable minority this is by no means the case, or at least not without considerable attenuation and modification" (p. 646).

By 1952, therefore, it seems possible that a great many analysts may have already given up on rigorous concepts of the transference neurosis and on a rigorous handling of it. The extent of this giving up, I think, is not surprising. Freud himself seems to have anticipated it even from the beginning, for in his 1905 paper, on page 116, he says: "This [the transference] happens . . . to be by far the hardest part of the whole task." Then he adds this most remarkable sentence: "It is easy to learn how to interpret dreams, to extract from the patient's associations his unconscious thoughts and memories and to practice similar explanatory arts . . ." This short statement, I believe, was intended to be a warning: the transference, Freud implies, is so hard to work with that we will be tempted to attenuate, modify, or even omit it. But if we do this, the warning goes on, analysis will be reduced to an explanatory art.[1]

The general sense of this warning seems clear, but Freud's stated reason why transference is so hard to work with scarcely matches the seriousness of the warning. "Transference," he says, ". . . has to be detected almost without assistance and with only the slightest clues . . ." Is this all there is to it? Or is Freud's warning in response to yet another reason? Is he saying, as I think likely, how very hard it is *on the analyst* to work effectively with the transference neurosis? We forget sometimes that a neurosis is based upon conflict and that what is specific about a transference neurosis is the active involvement of the analyst in the central crunch of this conflict. The wear and tear of this abrasive experience can be considerable and must surely be one of the major reasons some analysts pull away from the transference

---

1. Ten years later in "Transference-Love" (1915) Freud again makes the same point: ". . . the only really serious difficulties he [the analyst] has to meet lie in the management of the transference" (p. 159).

neurosis and away from analysis itself. Yet if analysis is to proceed successfully, if a transference neurosis is to develop and be analyzed, the analyst cannot pull away, cannot merely sit back, observe, interpret, and "practise similar explanatory arts." In addition, via the influence of the analytic situation, the patient must be enabled to include the analyst in his neurosis, or, as it were, to share his neurosis with the analyst. Only in this way, it seems, can the patient effectively reawaken the early stages of his neurosis, only in this way can its latent parts and forces be rendered sufficiently identifiable and functional to be available for analysis.

Accomplishing this is not easy. By the time a patient comes to analysis, his neurosis has moved a long way from where it began. Not only will it have gone through many changes and phases but, in all likelihood, it will have established itself as a rather fixed, walled-off, and independent institution. As a consequence, the drives and defenses originally involved in creating the neurosis may now act mainly within the confines of this neurotic institution and may no longer respond readily to extraneurotic influences. The only force powerful enough to bring the constituents of this encapsulated structure back into the main stream of the patient's mental functioning seems to be the transference neurosis. Bringing this about, calling as it does for the active inclusion of the analyst in the patient's neurosis, is probably, as perhaps Freud meant, the hardest part of analysis; but, as he also may have meant, it is what analysis is all about, it is what the analytic situation is set up to do, and it is why definitive analytic work leans so heavily upon the analyst's skilled fortitude.

Admittedly, many potential dangers attend the analyst's becoming involved in the patient's neurosis. The commonest would seem to be the analyst's unawareness of his own reciprocal transference reactions. A more subtle danger threatens when the analyst, although understanding his own transference, gains his insights so exclusively from this inner source that he pays little or no attention to the possible inapplicability of these insights to the patient's current transference developments. Although these and other problems with the analyst's transference involvement are obviously serious, the alternatives are not particularly inviting, for I have yet been unable to find evidence that a "safe" analysis, in which such dangers do not arise, has much chance of reaching the patient where he needs to be reached.

In view of how hard the whole thing is, can it be too speculative to believe that Freud's 1905 prediction may have come true, that, as an act of self-defense, handling of the transference has been steadily attenuated until analysis has finally become, in a great many hands at least, an explanatory art?

Transference and Transference Neurosis

Although things may not have gone quite this far, I do believe they have reached a point where most analysts nowadays work only with transference feelings. They either ignore the transference neurosis or believe, as anyone has a right to, that there are no significant differences between a transference neurosis and other transference reactions, that transference is simply transference. For myself, I believe just the opposite: there are differences, and they are significant. And I feel sure that if we could only learn more, a great deal more, about both transference and transference neurosis, life would be easier for the analyst and analysis would be better for the patient.

For me, the transference neurosis is essential to the analytic situation. Not the whole of it by any means, or even the most of it, but essential. Sharing a place with the transference neurosis are at least two other kinds of relationships: one based on ordinary transference feelings and the other on reality considerations—those of a patient to his doctor. These three share the time, as it were. All are important, all overlap, but each is specific. Each comes and goes, appearing and disappearing in response to a seemingly endless number of influences. The easiest relationship to maintain and to work with, and the one most generally used in analysis, is characterized by the patient's almost constant attribution of transference feelings to the person of the analyst. The most difficult relationship to establish and work with, the one most easily lost hold of, the one that is essential if definitive analytic work is to be done, is the transference neurosis. The one most likely to interfere with the others, and often the hardest to exclude, is the reality relationship.

In my view, as I have said, a transference neurosis differs fundamentally from those transference feelings which a patient experiences and expresses during much of the analytic time. When I think of transference, I think of feelings, of reactions, and of a repetition of past events; but when I think of transference neurosis, I think literally of a neurosis. A transference neurosis is merely a new edition of the patient's original neurosis, but with me in it. This new edition is created, for reasons I wish I knew more about and in ways that are quite perplexing, by the patient's shifting certain elements *of his neurosis* onto me. In this way he replaces *in his neurosis* mental representations of a past person, say his father, with mental representations of me. Although this maneuver would make it seem that the patient now regards me as his father, the actual situation is somewhat different. Because the maneuver is basically intrapsychic and deals with specific elements of his neurosis, I come to represent, not his father, but an aspect of his neurosis which, although contributed to by early, primarily oedipal experiences with his father, is now an intrapsychic structure of its own.

As I see it, this is quite different from what happens in a simple transference reaction. In a transference reaction, the patient displaces certain cathexes from early memories of his father to me, as if in the present. This is transference in its universal sense; it is the means of displacing feelings and attachments from one object to another, and of repeating the past in the present. In this process the two separate identities—the father and I—are merged, but the patient's own identity and my identity remain clear and separate. This is not the case with a transference neurosis. There the patient includes me somehow in the structure, or part structure, of his neurosis. As a result of this process, the identity difference between him and me is lost, and for the moment and for the particular area affected by the transference neurosis, I come to represent *the patient himself*. More specifically, I come to represent some complex of the patient's neurosis or some element of his ego, superego, drives, defenses, etc., which has become part of his neurosis. I do not, however, represent as such actual persons from the past, except in the form in which they have been incorporated into the patient's neurotic organization.

May I present an example of what I mean?

For the first two years of a young man's analysis, he became increasingly affected by one of his most crippling characteristics: an inability to get things done. Although generally stiff, rigid, and inhibited, there was more than this to his inability to act. Faced with a situation in which he should take specific action, he would balk and withhold such action in a procrastinating, stubborn, helpless, and often harmful way. Historically, throughout the patient's childhood, this characteristic led his mother into endless nagging at him to get things done, and when nagging did no good, in her frustration she wound up doing them for him. It was not surprising, I think, that in analysis I came to play the same role and that eventually my interpretations came to be regarded either as nagging or as my doing his work for him.

Although the patient easily recognized the similarity of this to what had gone on in childhood, disappointingly he gained nothing analytically useful from it.

One reason he did not, which took me quite a while to discover, was that the *act* of interpretation itself had become deeply involved in the transference. With this change, the *content* lost its importance, and instead he reacted to almost everything I said, interpretation or not, as if I were nagging him or doing something for him. But there was more to it than this. Upon realizing that such a shift had taken place, I became much less interpretive, in fact much more quiet all around. Surprisingly, the patient responded to my substantial quietness as if it did not exist. He went right on talking about one situation after the other in which he had failed to act, and went right on feeling that I was nagging and acting for him, although now I rarely even commented on what he reported.

This peculiar behavior, I suspected, indicated that still another shift had occurred. This was no longer a simple transference reaction, and I no longer represented a mother-object. This was a transference neurosis. In it his representation of me, now internalized, stood for certain elements of his neurosis, particularly, it seemed, elements of his ego and superego. In effect, the conflict was now remarkably self-contained; he was now nagging himself and doing things for himself. Upon noting this shift, I did my best to explain it to the patient and to speculate on what was revealed by it. What seemed most apparent was that in this way he was revealing a significant capacity to take over his own affairs and to be effective in getting things done, and that indeed the very strength of this drive might be a central factor causing his ego in his neurosis to react against it.

The patient responded to this formulation with a sense of its aptness. He began to appreciate the internal, personal, and conflicting nature of his neurosis and to accept some responsibility himself for his troublesome behavior. He also recalled periods of time when he had in fact been active and aggressive and had had no difficulty getting things done.

Following these inner discoveries, but only then, we were able to explore with meaning some of the origins of his problems as they concerned his relations with his mother.

In this particular instance, interpreting the transference neurosis in this specific way made a significant difference, a difference which effectively made this phase of the patient's analysis more than "an explanatory art." Very often, of course, this difference may not matter. The target, after all, is immense, and in whatever form an interpretation is made, if it is aimed generally in the right direction, it may have an impact. But when the difference does matter, as it commonly does, it may matter very much.

It is also true, of course, that the transference neurosis is not always available to work with. Being an on-and-off thing, as I believe it to be, there may be long periods when it is not in evidence. This means that the bulk of the bread-and-butter work of analysis is carried on largely in a transference relationship that is broader and less specific than a transference neurosis. Interpretations and constructions based on material evoked by these day-to-day transference reactions enable the patient's neurosis to unfold, and his character structure to come into clearer view. When the process goes further, as it may, the infantile neurosis may be retrieved from limbo and some of its vicissitudes may be traced. Doing this much is a great deal, but, much as it may seem, it will not reach all the way to the center of the patient.

This can happen, in my experience, only if the persistent and effective handling of the daily transference reactions, along with everything else it does, sets the stage for the appearance of episodes of transference neurosis. These may be short or long, clamorous or silent, but, in whatever way they appear, they will provide an opportunity to carry analysis the further step that does promise to reach the patient as nothing else can. It is this further step, however, which, because it is the hardest part of analysis, may never be taken.

Adding to whatever else makes this further step hard, are difficulties caused by transference itself: transference and transference neurosis are both subject to such serious limitations, interferences, and distortions that they may be very slow to develop, or they develop in such ways that long periods of analysis must go by before they reach a useful and workable state. Some of these interferences are iatrogenic, some seem to be a specific feature of the kind of disorder affecting the patient, and some may be inherent limitations in the phenomenon of transference itself. What I propose to do for the remainder of the paper is to comment on some of these interferences and limitations.

The Impact of Reality on Transference

"Reality" is a difficult word to use to everyone's satisfaction or even to one's own satisfaction. In this instance I use it rather arbitrarily to designate the direct, here-and-now impact of the analyst upon the patient. Reality, in this sense, contrasts with the impact the analyst has through his representation in the patient's fantasy life, neurosis, and transference. Since both kinds of impact seem always to coexist and since the former—the analyst's real impact—may be the worst enemy of the transference, the matter of their differentiation is possibly the most challenging aspect of analysis.

The analytic situation, which is set up to shut out ordinary reality intrusions, cannot and possibly should not exclude them all. In the beginning months, for instance, reality inevitably has the upper hand. The analyst, the office, the procedure, are all overwhelmingly real. Everything is strange, frightening and exciting, gratifying and frustrating. Until the patient can test it and orient himself to it, the impact of this reality is usually so great that even an ordinary useful transference relationship cannot be expected to develop.

Perhaps the most confusing aspect of this beginning period is the frequent appearance in it of what I regard as a false transference relationship. With great intensity and clarity, the patient may reveal, through transference-like references about the analyst, some of the deepest secrets not only of his neurosis but of its genesis. This pseudotransference, too good to be true, is almost sure to be nothing more than the patient's attempt to deal with the new situation: as completely as he can, he goes through, in respect to the person of the analyst, the entire spectrum of his various patterns of behavior. If, as it is easy to do, the analyst overlooks the likelihood that the patient's relationship with him at this time is real and that almost everything said about it is best related to this reality, analysis may get off to a very bad start. And if, as is even easier to do, the analyst interprets the genetic meanings of the openly exposed material, a good transference relationship may be seriously delayed and a workable transference neurosis may never appear. Even after initial reality has had time to fade, reality may continue to intrude in ways that are very hard to detect and that are very troublesome.

One of the most serious problems of analysis is the very substantial help which the patient receives directly from the analyst and the analytic situation. For many a patient, the analyst in the analytic situation is in fact the most stable, reasonable, wise, and understanding person he has ever met, and the setting in which they meet may actually be the most honest, open, direct, and regular relationship he has ever experienced. Added to this is the considerable helpfulness to him of being able to clarify his life story, confess his guilt, express his ambitions, and explore his confusions. Further real help comes from the learning-about-life accruing from the analyst's skilled questions, observations, and interpretations. Taken altogether, the total *real* value to the patient of the analytic situation can easily be immense. The trouble with this kind of help is that if it goes on and on, it may have such a real, direct, and continuing impact upon the patient that he can never get deeply enough involved in transference situations to allow him to resolve or even to become acquainted with his most crippling internal difficulties. The trouble in a sense is that the direct nonanalytical helpfulness of the analytic situation is far too good! The trouble also is that we as analysts apparently cannot resist the seductiveness of being directly helpful, and this, when combined with the compelling assumption that helpfulness is bound to be good, permits us to credit patient improvement to "analysis" when more properly it should often be recognized as being the result of the patient's using us, and the analytic situation, as model, preceptor, and supporter in dealing practically with his immediate problems.

Gross examples of this kind of reality-caused problem are common: a neurotically inept medical student who was able to stay in school for four years and graduate only because of the literal day-by-day support he took from visits to his analyst; a man with an unstable hold on his business whose analysis became little more than a source of real support needed to keep his business intact; and a woman whose analysis was almost completely absorbed in using it to keep a teetering marriage from collapsing. In none of these patients did any significant transference relationship develop. Instead, they clung to their actual dependence upon the analyst and the analytic situation. Because this problem so often goes unrecognized, and because even when recognized it is not sufficiently dealt with, this kind of usefulness may be one of the major reasons why analysis fails.

Perhaps I should mention one more difficult-to-handle intrusion of reality into the analysis. This is the definitive and final interruption of the transference neurosis caused by the reality of termination. Here, in a sense, the situation is reversed and the intrusion is analytically desirable, since ideally the impact of the reality of impending and certain termination is used to facilitate the resolution of the transference. As with the resolution of earlier episodes of transference neurosis, this final one is brought about principally by the analyst's interpretations and reconstructions. As these take effect, the

transference neurosis and, hopefully, along with it the original neurosis is resolved. This final resolution, however, which is much more comprehensive, is usually very difficult and may not come about at all without the help of the reality of termination. Accordingly, any attenuation of the ending, such as tapering off or casual or tentative stopping, should be expected to stand in the way of an effective resolution of the transference. Yet, it seems to me, this is what most commonly happens to an ending, and because of this a great many patients may lose the potentially great benefit of a thorough resolution and are forever after left suspended in the net of unresolved transference.

Yet, slurring over a rigorous termination seems understandable. As difficult as transference neurosis may be on the analyst at other times, this ending period, if rigorously carried out, simply has to be the period of his greatest emotional strain. There can surely be no more likely time for an analyst to surrender his analytic position and, responding to his own transference, become personally involved with his patient than during the process of separating from a long and self-restrained relationship. Accordingly, it may be better to slur over the ending lightly than to mishandle it in an attempt to be rigorous.

SOME SPECIAL TRANSFERENCE DIFFICULTIES IN THE CASE OF NEGATIVE, DESTRUCTIVE TENDENCIES

Various other difficulties with transference, both in its development and in its analysis, occur, as we all know, in respect to the nature of different forms of illness, e.g., acting out, psychosis, character disorders, etc.[2] But rather than discuss particular situations such as these, I would like to consider a different kind of difficulty, one which I think casts a very dark shadow on all transference manifestations and which may therefore be a severely limiting factor in analytic work generally.

This limiting factor, which may be universal, is the apparent inability of transference to reproduce with any verity the full range of man's negative, destructive tendencies. In contrast to libidinal drives, even the mildest and commonest negative ones seem to run into a good deal of trouble finding their way into the transference, ending up at best as

---

2. In two papers (Bird, 1954 and 1957) I have described some of the transference difficulties met with in a specific, narcissistic form of acting out.

wishes, feelings, and fantasies, while the more robust varieties, those involving literal destructive acts, seem to stand little chance of entering the transference at all.

The question why this limitation exists is not easy to answer. One suggestion, speculative to be sure, but nonetheless seeming to be worth serious consideration, is that negative, destructive tendencies are derivatives of a "death instinct" and as such are bound, not by ordinary principles of mental functioning, but by whatever principles do govern this elusive concept. Unfortunately, I believe, little study is being devoted to clarifying this important issue. Most analysts seem to have turned their back on the death instinct and on Freud's attempts to explore it. Many of us, with some logic, explain away our disinterest on grounds that the death instinct is a biological and not a psychological concept and therefore is not within our province.

Another somewhat less logical but perhaps more significant reason for our shying away from the death instinct is that analysts seem to shy away from everything touching on violence, destruction, and death. In our developmental theory, for instance, we prefer to regard the concepts of "killing of the parents" and "sexual union with the parents" as more or less antithetical equals, each suffering much the same fate at the instance of the ego's resolution of the Oedipus complex. In this way we are able to gloss over the differences between the two concepts and to avoid facing the apparent fact that, while the ego's oedipal impact does make it possible later on in life for sexual union to be normally carried out with a substitute for the parents, it does not make it possible for killing to be carried out normally at all. That there is no norm for whatever the killing drive consists of is not an insignificant matter. Most of us, of course, try to get around this difficulty by means of the somewhat fuzzy assumption that oedipal events do convert the killing drive into a much nicer one called aggression, which we regard as normal. Our accepting this rather broad assumption makes it easy to ignore the possibility that man's tendency to kill may not be basically changed by oedipal events, and to ignore the likelihood that whatever control the ego does have over violent tendencies is somewhat tenuous. Perhaps the most surprising thing we ignore is the overwhelming evidence of how uncertain the ego's control is, viz., the tremendous outbursts of violence that surround us in our daily life.

Even our analytic language, which leans heavily on euphemisms, seems designed to ignore the reality of destruction. We tend to use words like "negative," "aggressive," and "hostile" in describing patient behavior that may have caused actual damage. Or we speak of angry feelings, murder fantasies, castration wishes, and death wishes in respect to a patient's determined attempt to cause harm. To me, this language always seems at least once removed from what we are actually dealing with, or should be dealing with.

The inappropriateness of our language came home to me one day with a patient who, as we say so nicely, liked to "castrate" men. While listening to her describe some extreme behavior of this kind, I suddenly asked myself the question, What would I call this behavior outside of analysis? The answer was easy. I would call it vicious and destructive. So I told the patient what I had been thinking. She was shocked by these terms, but she admitted that the euphemisms we usually used had made it very easy for her to ignore the literal harm caused by her behavior.

In addition to failing to recognize a patient's violent intentions and actions for what they are, analysts sometimes further obscure the situation by regularly discouraging a patient from allowing his anger to deepen to the stage where its basic violent quality is unmistakable. Some of us sense a patient's "negative feelings" or "hostility" so accurately, and draw his attention to it so quickly, that nothing but superficial use can be made of it. Or when angry accusations do come from the patient, we nip them off too prematurely and may even couch our interpretations in just the right way to clear ourselves of the accusations.

Similarly, when a patient behaves violently in his daily life and reports this to us, we tend to get uneasy, and, although we may not tell him to stop, we may directly warn him of the consequences, or in our interpretations may feel compelled to add a subtle warning or in some way to introduce a suppressive note.

Why, one has to wonder, is this suppression needed? Is it because we all sense the limited extent to which actual destructive tendencies can enter into the transference neurosis, and thus the limited extent of their analyzability? Is this incapacity perhaps what we refer to when we say, as we commonly do, in the case of incompletely analyzed patients, that certain key aspects of their neurosis simply did not arise in the transference?

Was this, I wonder, the particular concept of transference which Freud had gradually come around to and which was responsible, especially in "Analysis Terminable and Interminable," for his becoming so cautious and pessimistic about the mobilization and analysis of negative elements?

Is this why he said of Ferenczi that even if latent negative feelings could have been aroused, it would probably not have been wise to do so? Should we, therefore, if we are to follow the line Freud seems to have taken, consider discarding altogether his 1905 statement, "In psychoanalysis . . . all the patient's tendencies, including hostile ones, are aroused; they are then turned to account for the purposes of the analysis by being made conscious, and in this way the transference is constantly being destroyed" (p. 117)? Or should we, while acknowledging the known and suspected limitations, nevertheless continue to search for evidence of significant negative representation in the transference? And, in doing this, should we perhaps concern ourselves not merely with watered-down versions of violence, such as aggressiveness, negative feelings, hostility, anger, etc., but with harmful actions, particularly actions directed against the analyst?

Tentatively, I would like to suggest what may be a rather common but generally unacknowledged way in which patients attempt to cause the analyst harm, and perhaps succeed at it more often than we think. This is to convert some element of the analytic situation into a weapon to use against the analyst. That a patient does use his analysis to attack and to injure others, especially his family, is well known. That he would try to injure the analyst by the same means should not be surprising. He has to use what is available to him, and the various elements of the analytic situation are about all he has.

Most suited to be used as weapons, I should think, are a patient's resistances. Almost any aspect of analysis can be used as a resistance, and almost any resistance carried a step further can be used as a more or less effective weapon. This further step is usually taken only after analysis is well along, and consists of the patient's clinging so determinedly to some form of behavior that it threatens to engulf and destroy the entire analysis. Although the resulting stalemate is terribly frustrating to the analyst, the patient himself is often unperturbed by it, even when it means that month after month, year after year, he shows no improvement. Typically, the resistance seems more directed against the fact of analysis than against any specific part of it and may strikingly lessen or disappear if the analyst, in despair, announces a termination date.

The best known and most talked-of resistance of this kind is the so-called negative therapeutic reaction. Such reactions, of course, have been written about by many authors, and there is probably little to add to what has been said about them. Except one thing! Rarely have these very serious, very difficult, and very puzzling reactions been regarded as an attack upon the analyst. Yet, in addition to whatever else they may mean, this is precisely what many, or even most, of them may be. Why they are not readily seen in this way is something of a mystery. Every analyst, I suspect, would be willing to regard these reactions as deadly serious and as imposing severe limitations on the outcome of even the best analyses. No one, it seems, is unaware that most analytic patients at some point in their analysis, in varying degrees and in various ways, take an unconscious but implacable stand against analytic advance; that some patients regularly and silently undo each step of progress, and that some even seem absolutely bent on destroying the analysis and with it their chance for various life successes. The self-destructive aims in such behavior are usually obvious, and it may even be obvious that along with this behavior the patient is trying, often unconsciously, to hurt the analyst.

This much seems clear. But it is probably rare for us as analysts to set our euphemisms aside and to suspect these stalemates, these therapeutically negative events, of being not merely hostile fantasies, wishes, or reactions, but very real destructive acts, actual attempts to injure us, the analyst. Is this not indeed probably the only way a patient can envision actually doing us serious harm? By and large, the analyst is immune to a patient's simple slings and arrows; they are chaff which the analyst blows away without being damaged. The patient's coming late, his delayed fee payments, his withholding of material, his carping criticisms, his open anger, his demands, his teasing, his acting out, even his outright quitting, are all, at most, irritating or unpleasant. But this other thing is different. The patient's largely unconscious determination to make the analysis go nowhere, his slow, often silent, and secret undermining of the analyst's every move, is not merely irritating, it hits the analyst in the very center of his functional life, and it may cause harm.

Peculiarly, although often sensing frustration, many of us do not suspect such resistances of being a personal attack. Perhaps, if we did, we would be in a better position to deal with them. That is to say, when, as I believe happens, resistances are used to attack the analyst, it would seem to follow that, in order to discover the neurotic meaning of these resistances, we must first discover and analyze their current "transference" use. Doing this would seem to begin by confronting the patient with what he is doing. I choose the word "confront" in place of "interpret" for the same reason that I prefer "destructive" and "harmful" to "hostile" and "negative," viz., to move from the concept of wish to the concept of deed, from hostile feelings to hostile acts. In my experience, resolving this destructive situation depends upon speaking of it directly, even assertively, in terms of action.

The patient's initial reaction to this confrontation depends upon many variables. A common reaction is a verbal attack in return, an attack which, perhaps for the first time, contains an injurious intent that is unmistakable to both patient and analyst. Sometimes the reaction is dramatic. One patient responded by telling me, with some wonderment in his voice, that for several weeks he had been carrying a gun in his car. Whatever the response, it will no doubt be a welcome relief, for the patient as well as for the analyst, from what has probably been a monotonous, many-months-long stalemate.

Significant success, however, can be counted only if the response leads to some rather detailed "chapter and verse" discoveries as to how and why the patient's malicious intent against the analyst was actually developed and carried out. This might include gaining some idea of how much the patient's attack was simply a matter of transference, how much it was caused by the analysis mobilizing his destructive impulses, and, finally, how much it was a retaliation for attacks made on him by the analyst.

Although it is tempting to attribute all occurrences of patient malice to transference, the opposite consideration is not without appeal. Is it possible that the ego's internalization of hostile-aggressive drive elements and their per se inclusion in intrapsychic structure is so limited that in the analytic situation they are represented more as a reality than as a transference fantasy?

With regard to the effect of the analytic process upon the patient's negative posture, it is again tempting to make an assumption, viz., the situation should improve as analysis goes along. It may, however, be just the reverse. The analysis of neurotic libidinal elements may gradually bring about, through a defusion-like process, a freeing of hostile-aggressive elements, which may then be increasingly applied to the analyst and to the analysis itself.

In regard to the third factor, how much the patient's destructive action is a retaliation, there surely must be many points of view. Ideally, it could be said, the analyst should do nothing hostile toward the patient. He should not make hostile remarks, should not phrase his interpretations as attacks, should not be silently hostile, and so on. Perhaps we can all agree on a policy of this sort, even while also agreeing that many of us do not always live up to it. Some of us, at least some of the time, do speak caustically, sarcastically, and accusingly, do put ridicule in our voice, and sullenness in our silence. Personally, I would be inclined to say that I am not too concerned about these overt, individually characteristic hostile acts. What concerns me more about the analyst is something different. To me, the analytic setting, in which the analyst remains constant as an objective, detached, uninvolved interpreter of the patient's productions, is almost sure to bring about a silent but significant built-up of the analyst's own unconscious negative-destructive impulses. As this goes on, the analyst can rarely avoid putting some of these impulses into action, and, like the patient, the analyst, being unable to represent these negative feelings fully in his own transference, will be forced to put them into action and will do so in about the only way available to him: by using elements of the analytic situation as a weapon. What I come to, then, is the proposition that a stalemate in the analysis, an implacable resistance, an unchanging negative therapeutic reaction—anything of this kind should be suspected of consisting of a silent, secret, but actual destructive act engaged in by *both* patient and analyst.

In this respect I would refer again to Freud's comments about Ferenczi in "Analysis Terminable and Interminable," where he implied that the patient's negative feelings for the analyst could have been mobilized only by an unfriendly act on the part of the analyst, the inference being, I believe, that the analyst should not say anything to the patient which might be regarded as unfriendly. My suspicion here is that we tend to lean too far backward on this issue, so far backward that our not confronting the patient becomes in itself not merely an unfriendly act but a destructive one. By not confronting the patient with the actuality of the patient's secret, silent obstruction of the analytic progress, the analyst himself silently introduces even greater obstructions.

I suppose what I am saying is that, to me, analysis, especially as it concerns negative destructive elements, is not merely an intellectual or an emotional experience; rather, it is as well a conflict, a conflict starting out within the patient's neurosis as an intrapsychic event and gradually becoming a conflict within the analytic situation. Only then, only when the analytic situation becomes, in a sense, an adversary situation, should we expect the kind of transference neurosis to develop that can admit to it a representation of destructive impulses strong enough and faithful enough to permit this aspect of the patient's neurosis to be effectively analyzed.

I do not mean by this that analysts should fight with their patients. Nor do I mean that an adversary situation per se is good. What I do mean is something rather different. I am referring specifically to the patient's intrapsychic neurotic life. In it, expectably, are many destructive elements. These elements, as I think many of us would assume, do not remain or perhaps do not even exist in isolation. They are engaged with other destructive elements, either as protagonist or antagonist or as both, to form an organized intrapsychic conflict. This organized conflict, which might be regarded more accurately as an adversary situation, seems to constitute a unitary neurotic structure and, as such, I believe, seems to stand a chance of finding representation in the transference neurosis. If it does, it should be expected to appear there as an adversary situation between patient and analyst. This is what I mean when I say that perhaps only when the analytic situation becomes an adversary situation should we suspect that a transference neurosis adequate enough to represent destructive impulses has developed.

In order for such a transference neurosis to come about, the analyst, through the analytic process, must somehow enable the patient to extend his intrapsychic conflicts to include the analyst. Whereupon the analyst becomes protagonist and the patient antagonist, or vice versa, in a real conflict within the analysis. In this way, through the patient's attributing one of the two or more adversary positions to the analyst, and through the patient's then being able to espouse more single-mindedly the opposing position, the patient's negative-hostile-destructive forces are likely to achieve a more personal, current, powerful, and real quality, a quality that hopefully makes them amenable to analysis.

In order for this to happen, I am tempted to believe, the analyst's own transference involvement is necessary. For one thing, his own transference may be the factor that enables him to accept an adversary role in the patient's neurosis. For another, it may be that only through the analyst's insight into his own "destructive" transference involvement can he understand and analyze the patient's destructive forces. The first thing he will be able to understand, I should think, is that the patient's literal attacks upon him, the patient's literal attempts to destroy the analyst, probably represent in the transference neurosis the patient's own intrapsychic destructive struggles, the patient's own attempts to destroy certain aspects of himself, and his own equally destructive attempts to preserve himself and instead to destroy others. The analyst, at this point of his understanding, will recognize most clearly that the patient's internal destructive forces are organized as an

intrapsychic adversary situation, an organization which, with some success and some failure, and perhaps at great expense, has prevented these destructive forces from completely annihilating either himself or others.

To say that the development and analysis of a transference neurosis of this kind is the hardest part of analysis, seems believable. For it to happen at all, I feel sure, requires major contributions from both analyst and patient. From the analyst it requires great perseverance, and, despite how tangled and acerbic and hopeless the analysis may seem to get, it requires rather strict adherence to the principles of the analytic method. There is nothing the analyst can do to deliberately create an adversary situation. He can only not stand in the patient's way. It is the patient's business to bring his adversary situation into the analysis. This is what is required of him — that he do what, hopefully, the analytic situation permits him naturally to do.

When the transference neurosis does develop, neither patient nor analyst may realize for awhile that it has. What they will realize, very likely, is only that the analysis has been caught up in a stalemate, a negative therapeutic reaction, a strong immovable resistance, or in some other seemingly impossible negative struggle between patient and analyst. Hopefully, this struggle will eventually be recognized as a transference neurosis, as a re-enactment in the transference of various destructive elements of the patient's neurosis, a re-enactment in which unconscious destructive acts of the analyst are likely to be involved.

This dark and ominous time, when both patient and analyst are about ready to call it quits, is, according to my thesis, perhaps the only kind of transference in which the patient's most deeply destructive impulses may be analyzable. If, as is sometimes possible, the analyst is able to work his way through this tremendously difficult, anger-laden impasse, the most effective, enduring analytical progress may be made.

CLOSING REMARKS:
NOTES ON TRANSFERENCE AS
AN EGO FUNCTION

The foregoing, on one score at least, brings me around to the paper's introduction and impels me to close the paper by commenting again on two ideas I opened with: the notion that an analyst's transference reactions are essential to the analyzing process, and the notion that transference is an ego function. Boiled down, these two ideas seem but one: if the analyst's transference is essential to the analyzing process, it could hardly be thought of as anything other than an ego function; and, conversely, if transference is an ego function, the analyst's transference would have to be seen as essential to his analyzing activity.

As to the nature of transference, there has never been much popular support for its designation as a regular function of the ego. This turn of affairs is somewhat surprising in view of Freud's early comments, especially in the Dora case (1905), where his description of transference was of a kind that could be reasonably attributed only to the ego. Perhaps failure to make this attribution is a consequence of our rather complete dependence upon transference in conducting clinical analysis. This dependence understandably may have established transference so securely as a technique that the analyst has seldom given himself the opportunity to wonder about its nature as a phenomenon, or about which agency of the mind it works with or belongs to. When these questions do come to mind, however, it is extremely difficult, for me at least, to escape the idea that transference must be regarded as one of the ego's principal structures, a very special, very powerful, and possibly even a very basic ego apparatus. Most remarkable is the closeness of its relationship to the drives. This closeness, amounting almost to an alliance with the drives, may make it possible, although seemingly paradoxical, to think of transference as being the ego's main antirepressive device. Such antirepressive action, so clearly exemplified by the usefulness of transference in analysis, may be seen as the power which in a general sense endows the ego with its crucial capacity to evoke, maintain, and put to use the past-in-the-present. It may also be this antirepressive force that enables transference to activate and expedite other parts of the ego, particularly, it would seem, the ego's conflict-free givens and its differentiating, synthesizing, and creative capacities.

If this is correct, if transference is indeed to be regarded as a significant ego function, a number of inferences are rather obvious. One is that analysis does not "cause" transference. Yet, although not caused by analysis, transference as it occurs in analysis does seem unique. What is unique, however, may not be transference itself but rather the effect upon transference of the unique conditions of the analytic situation. These conditions may affect most strongly such things as the choice of content of transference reactions, the intensity of these reactions, their exclusiveness, and their sharp focus on the person of the analyst. Although, as a result of these conditions, transference developments in analysis may differ from those occurring elsewhere, this does not mean that in analysis transference as a function is any different.

Another rather obvious inference, following from the first, is that transference can never be resolved. The content may be, but not the function. Through analysis, the symptomatic, neurotic, and historical complexes which have been brought into the transference may be resolved, but not the function itself. The function of transference, like other functions of the ego, may be affected by analysis in many ways, but it never goes away.

Still another inference is a general one concerning transference and the analyst. If transference is to be regarded as an ever active ego function, then the analyst's transference goes on all the time too, just like the patient's, and despite what he might wish to think, his transference has not been resolved in his own analysis. Admittedly the impact of the analytic situation upon the analyst is vastly different from what it is upon the patient, but many aspects of that situation do favor development in the analyst of transference reactions involving his patient. This does not mean, however, that it would be correct to believe the analyst should attempt to inhibit his transference function, much less disavow it. Yet what the analyst should do about his own transference is a question that has never been significantly pondered over. Aside from my belief that the analyst's transference is remarkably useful in the process of analyzing and may even be essential for certain aspects of analysis, what can be said?

Would it be wrong, I wonder, to propose that this ego function be dealt with in the same way the analyst deals with his other ego functions? Just as the analyst must consciously regulate his responses to other functions in order to create and sustain the analytic situation, should he not also regulate his responses to his transference activity? This does not mean, I should think, that the analyst must decide either whether or when a transference reaction to his patient exists. Such an attempt is beside the point on at least two counts. For one thing, significant transference reactions are usually not conscious; and, for another, transference activity in some form is always going on.

In view of these considerations, the simplest position for the analyst to take, and the one most likely to be helpful, may be to assume that *all* feelings and reactions of the analyst concerning the patient are *prima-facie* evidence of the analyst's transference.

Under this arrangement every feeling of warmth, pity, sadness, anger, hope, excitement, even interest; every feeling of coldness, indifference, disinterest, boredom, impatience, discouragement; and every absence of feeling, should be assumed to contain significant elements of the analyst's transference as focused on the patient. This would mean, essentially, that everything arising in the analyst about his patient is assumed to be part of the substance of analysis, that nothing represents merely the analyst's "real" reaction to his patient, and that especially when something seems most real it can be counted on to contain important aspects of the analyst's transference.

Were the analyst to take this rather imperative view of his own transference potential, he might be much more likely to remain abreast of the personal, neurotic meanings of the myriad but often subtle reactions and attitudes he develops toward his patient. This in turn might make it possible for him at least to keep his transference out of the patient's way and hopefully to use it to further the analysis.

The final inference I want to draw from all this is perhaps the most promising. This is that transference, if it indeed belongs to the family of ego functions, can be counted on to possess many of this family's characteristics. Thus, presently existing knowledge about the ego should provide many ready-made leads as to the nature of transference. The ego's ways of reality testing, for instance, its responses to internal and external stimuli, its uses of defense mechanisms, may all reveal much about the basic phenomenology of transference. Similarly, much may be surmised about transference's functional vicissitudes by assuming that transference suffers the same general developmental and neurotic deficiencies, distortions, limitations, and fixations to which various other functions of the ego are susceptible. A particularly important study would seem to be the special strengths of transference functioning, especially its way of joining with other agencies to serve and facilitate the individual's idiosyncratic interests and developments. Such a study, for instance, might center on the ego's object relations with reference to the question of whether transference is the ego function mainly responsible for their development.

Viewing transference in this way as an ego function means, of course, relinquishing certain elements of our existing viewpoints. One prominent feature of these existing viewpoints, no matter what form they take, is how hard they are to define or even to elicit. Another is how unquestioning we seem to be about the viewpoints we grew up with, how easily we assume transference to be but a therapeutically helpful given, an isolated psychological event having little to do with other psychological events, and, except in the analytic situation, to be lacking useful purpose. Assigned, without even wondering why, to neither ego nor id, it is usually dropped somewhere in between. Labeled but rarely described, it is most commonly called a projection or a repetition of the past, neither of them labels of great distinction.

Nevertheless, no matter how inadequate the form in which transference presently exists, it is a form that is deeply entrenched and that does not beg for change. Accordingly, wresting transference from its syntonic limbo is not likely to be easy and may be impossible; but doing so, bringing it out into open view where it can be contemplated as a major member of the ego family, is to me an utterly fascinating prospect, one that permits me to see transference not only as the best tool clinical analysis has, but possibly the best tool the ego has. It well may be, as Freud suggested, the basis of all human relationships and, as I have suggested, may be involved in all the ego's differentiating, integrative, and creative capacities. It is these aspects of transference that offer the most exciting questions, and it is with these questions that I wish to close my paper.

REFERENCES

Andrade, E., *Sir Isaac Newton*. New York: Doubleday, 1954.

Bird, B. (1954). Symposium on antisocial acting out. *Amer. J. Orthopsychiat.*, 24:685–689.

———(1957). A specific peculiarity of acting out. *This Journal*, 5:630–647.

Freud, S. [1887–1902]. *The Origins of Psycho-Analysis.* Letter 133. New York: Basic Books, 1954.

———(1905). Fragment of an analysis of a case of hysteria. *Standard Edition*, 7:3–122. London: Hogarth Press, 1953.

———(1912). The dynamics of transference. *Standard Edition*, 12:99–108. London: Hogarth Press, 1958.

———(1915). Observations on transference-love. *Standard Edition*, 12:158–171. London: Hogarth Press, 1958.

————(1917). Introductory lectures on psycho-analysis. *Standard Edition*, 16:431–447. London: Hogarth Press, 1963.

————(1925). An autobiographical study. *Standard Edition*, 20:3–74. London: Hogarth Press, 1959.

————(1937). Analysis terminable and interminable. *Standard Edition*, 23:211–253. London: Hogarth Press, 1964.

Freud, S. & Breuer, J. (1895). Studies on Hysteria. *Standard Edition*, 2. London: Hogarth Press, 1955.

Orr, D. (1954). Transference and countertransference: a historical survey. *This Journal*, 2:621–670.

7

THE ANALYSIS OF THE TRANSFERENCE

MERTON M. GILL

EDITOR'S NOTE

This paper offers a number of important insights into the nature of transference and the techniques it requires. Gill clarifies the distinction between resistances to the awareness of transference manifestations and those directed against interpretations designed to resolve the transference. Of particular importance is Gill's stress on the presence of early manifestations of transference which constitute important initial sources of resistance in analysis, and on the critical role played by precipitants within the analytic situation — implications of the analyst's attitudes and interventions — as stimuli for transference reactions. Gill offers a series of techniques through which transference expressions may be encouraged in the analytic interaction and indicates how a full realization of the stimuli for transference responses within the treatment situation facilitates both their interpretation and their being understood and worked through by the patient. Gill also argues persuasively that there is an element of transference in every communication from the patient.

While fully aware of the role of genetic transference interpretations, Gill stresses the analysis of transference in terms of the here-and-now of the current analytic interaction. This signals an important shift among classical psychoanalysts in the direction of an interactional conception of transference manifestations and their analytic understanding and resolution.

The analysis of the transference is generally acknowledged to be the central feature of analytic technique. Freud regarded transference and resistance as facts of observations, not as conceptual inventions. He wrote: ". . . the theory of psychoanalysis is an attempt to account for two striking and unexpected facts of observation which emerge whenever an attempt is made to trace the symptoms of a neurotic back to their sources in his past life: the facts of transference and of resistance . . . anyone who takes up other sides of the problem while avoiding these two hypotheses will hardly escape a charge of misappropriation of property by attempted impersonation, if he persists in calling himself a psychoanalyst" (1914a, p. 16). Rapaport (1967) argued, in his posthumously published paper on the methodology of psychoanalysis, that transference and resistance inevitably follow from the fact that the analytic situation is interpersonal.

Despite this general agreement on the centrality of transference and resistance technique, it is my impression, from my experience as a student and practitioner, from talking to students and colleagues, and from reading the literature, that the analysis of the transference is not pursued as

Reprinted from *Journal of the American Psychoanalytic Association* 27: 263–288 by permission of International Universities Press, Inc. Copyright © 1979 by American Psychoanalytic Association.

systematically and comprehensively as I think it could be and should be. The relative privacy in which psychoanalysts work makes it impossible for me to state this view as anything more than my impression. On the assumption that even if I am wrong it will be useful to review issues in the analysis of the transference and to state a number of reasons that an important aspect of the analysis of the transference, namely, resistance to the awareness of the transference, is especially often slighted in analytic practice, I am in this paper going to spell out these issues and reasons.

I must first distinguish clearly between two types of interpretation of the transference. The one is an interpretation of resistance to the awareness of transference. The other is an interpretation of resistance to the resolution of transference. The distinction has been best spelled out in our literature by Greenson (1967) and Stone (1967). The first kind of resistance may be called defense transference. Although that term is mainly employed to refer to a phase of analysis characterized by a general resistance to the transference of wishes, it can also be used for a more isolated instance of transference of defense. The second kind of resistance is usually called transference resistance. With some oversimplification, one might say that in resistance to the awareness of transference, the transference is what is resisted, whereas in resistance to the resolution of transference, the transference is what does the resisting.

Another more descriptive way of stating this distinction between resistance to the awareness of transference and resistance to the resolution of transference is between implicit or indirect references to the transference and explicit or direct references to the transference. The interpretation of resistance to awareness of the transference is intended to make the implicit transference explicit, while the interpretation of resistance to the resolution of transference is intended to make the patient realize that the already explicit transference does indeed include a determinant from the past.

It is also important to distinguish between the general concept of an interpretation of resistance to the resolution of transference and a particular variety of such an interpretation, namely, a genetic transference interpretation—that is, an interpretation of how an attitude in the present is inappropriate carry-over from the past. While there is a tendency among analysts to deal with explicit references to the transference primarily by a genetic transference interpretation, there are other ways of working toward a resolution of the transference. This paper will argue that not only is not enough

emphasis being given to interpretation of the transference in the here and now, that is, to the interpretation of implicit manifestations of the transference, but also that interpretations intended to resolve the transference as manifested in explicit references to the transference should be primarily in the here and now, rather than genetic transference interpretations.

A patient's statement that he feels the analyst is harsh, for example, is, at least to begin with, likely best dealt with not by interpreting that this is a displacement from the patient's feeling that his father was harsh but by an elucidation of some other aspect of this here-and-now attitude, such as what has gone on in the analytic situation that seems to the patient to justify his feeling or what was the anxiety that made it so difficult for him to express his feelings. How the patient experiences the actual situation is an example of the role of the actual situation in a manifestation of transference, which will be one of my major points.

Of course, both interpretations of the transference in the here and now and genetic transference interpretations are valid and constitute a sequence. We presume that a resistance to the transference ultimately rests on the displacement onto the analyst of attitudes from the past.

Transference interpretations in the here and now and genetic transference interpretations are of course exemplified in Freud's writings and are in the repertoire of every analyst, but they are not distinguished sharply enough.

Because Freud's case histories focus much more on the yield of analysis than on the details of the process, they are readily but perhaps incorrectly construed as emphasizing work outside the transference much more than work with the transference, and even within the transference, emphasizing genetic transference interpretations much more than work with the transference in the here and now (see Muslin and Gill, 1978). The example of Freud's case reports may have played a role in what I consider a common maldistribution of emphasis in these two respects—not enough on the transference and, within the transference, not enough on the here and now.

Before I turn to the issues in the analysis of the transference, I will only mention what is a primary reason for a failure to deal adequately with the transference. It is that work with the transference is that aspect of analysis which involves both analyst and patient in the most affect-laden and potentially disturbing interactions. Both participants in the analytic situation are motivated to avoid these interactions. Flight away from the transference and to the past can be a relief to both patient and analyst.

I divide my discussion into five parts: (1) the principle that the transference should be encouraged to expand as much as possible within the analytic situation because the analytic work is best done within the transference; (2) the interpretation of disguised allusions to the transference as a main technique for encouraging the expansion of the transference within the analytic situation; (3) the principle that all transference has a connection with something in the present actual analytic situation; (4) how the connection between transference and the actual analytic situation is used in interpreting resistance to the awareness of transference; and (5) the resolution of transference within the here and now and the role of genetic transference interpretation.

THE PRINCIPLE OF ENCOURAGING THE TRANSFERENCE TO EXPAND WITHIN THE ANALYTIC SITUATION

The importance of transference interpretations will surely be agreed to by all analysts, the greater effectiveness of transference interpretations than interpretations outside the transference will be agreed to by many, but what of the relative roles of interpretation of the transference and interpretation outside the transference?

Freud can be read either as saying that the analysis of the transference is auxiliary to the analysis of the neurosis or that the analysis of the transference is equivalent to the analysis of the neurosis. The first portion is stated in his saying (1913, p. 144) that the disturbance of the transference has to be overcome by the analysis of transference resistance in order to get on with the work of analyzing the neurosis. It is also implied in his reiteration that the ultimate task of analysis is to remember the past, to fill in the gaps in memory. The second position is stated in his saying that the victory must be won on the field of the transference (1912, p. 108) and that the mastery of the transference neurosis "coincides with getting rid of the illness which was originally brought to the treatment" (1917, p. 444). In this second view, he says that after the resistances are overcome, memories appear relatively without difficulty (1914b, p. 155).

These two different positions also find expression in the two very different ways in which Freud speaks of the transference. In "Dynamics of Transference," he refers to the transference, on the one hand, as "*the*

most powerful resistance to the treatment" (1912, p. 101) but, on the other hand, as doing us "the inestimable service of making the patient's . . . impulses immediate and manifest. For when all is said and done, it is impossible to destroy anyone *in absentia* or *in effigie*" (1912, p. 108).

I believe it can be demonstrated that his principal emphasis falls on the second position. He wrote once, in summary: "Thus our therapeutic work falls into two phases. In the first, all the libido is forced from the symptoms into the transference and concentrated there; in the second, the struggle is waged around this new object and the libido is liberated from it" (1917, p. 455).

The detailed demonstration that he advocated that the transference should be encouraged to expand as much as possible within the analytic situation lies in clarifying that resistance is primarily expressed by repetition, that repetition takes place both within and outside the analytic situation, but that the analyst seeks to deal with it primarily within the analytic situation, that repetition can be not only in the motor sphere (acting) but also in the psychical sphere, and that the psychical sphere is not confined to remembering but includes the present, too.

Freud's emphasis that the purpose of resistance is to prevent remembering can obscure his point that resistance shows itself primarily by repetition, whether inside or outside the analytic situation: "The greater the resistance, the more extensively will acting out (repetition) replace remembering" (1914b, p. 151). Similarly in "The Dynamics of Transference" Freud said that the main reason that the transference is so well suited to serve the resistance is that the unconscious impulses "do not want to be remembered . . . but endeavour to reproduce themselves . . ." (1912, p. 108). The transference is a resistance primarily insofar as it is a repetition.

The point can be restated in terms of the relation between transference and resistance. The resistance expresses itself in repetition, that is, in transference both inside and outside the analytic situation. To deal with the transference, therefore, is equivalent to dealing with the resistance. Freud emphasized transference within the analytic situation so strongly that it has come to mean only repetition within the analytic situation, even though, conceptually speaking, repetition outside the analytic situation is transference too, and Freud once used the term that way: "We soon perceive that the transference is itself only a piece of repetition, and that the repetition is a transference of the forgotten past not only on to the doctor but also on to all the other aspects of the current situation. We . . . find . . . the compulsion to repeat, which now replaces the impulsion to remember, not only in his personal attitude to his doctor but also in every other activity and relationship which may occupy his life at the time . . ." (1914b, p. 151).

It is important to realize that the expansion of the repetition inside the analytic situation, whether or not in a reciprocal relationship to repetition outside the analytic situation, is the avenue to control the repetition: "The main instrument . . . for curbing the patient's compulsion to repeat and for turning it into a motive for remembering lies in the handling of the transference. We render the compulsion harmless, and indeed useful, by giving it the right to assert itself in a definite field" (1914b, p. 154).

Kanzer has discussed this issue well in his paper on "The Motor Sphere of the Transference" (1966). He writes of a "double-pronged stick-and-carrot" technique by which the transference is fostered within the analytic situation and discouraged outside the analytic situation. The "stick" is the principle of abstinence as exemplified in the admonition against making important decisions during treatment, and the "carrot" is the opportunity afforded the transference to expand within the treatment "in almost complete freedom" as in a "playground" (Freud, 1914b, p. 154). As Freud put it: "Provided only that the patient shows compliance enough to respect the necessary conditions of the analysis, we regularly succeed in giving all the symptoms of the illness a new transference meaning and in replacing his ordinary neurosis by a 'transference neurosis' of which he can be cured by the therapeutic work" (1914b, p. 154).

The reason it is desirable for the transference to be expressed within the treatment is that there, it "is at every point accessible to our intervention" (1914b, p. 154). In a later statement he made the same point this way: "We have followed this new edition [the transference-neurosis] of the old disorder from its start, we have observed its origin and growth, and we are especially well able to find our way about in it since, as its object, we are situated at its very center" (1917, p. 444). It is not that the transference is forced into the treatment, but that it is spontaneously but implicitly present and is encouraged to expand there and become explicit.

Freud emphasized *acting* in the transference so strongly that one can overlook that repetition in the transference does not necessarily mean it is *enacted*. Repetition need not go as far as motor behavior. It can also be expressed in attitudes, feelings, and intentions, and, indeed, the repetition often does take such form rather than motor action. Such repetition is in the psychical rather than the motor sphere. The importance of making this clear is that Freud can be mistakenly read to mean that repetition in the psychical sphere can only mean remembering the past, as when he writes that the analyst "is prepared for a perpetual struggle with his patient to keep in the psychical sphere all the impulses which the patient would like to direct into the motor sphere; and he celebrates it as a triumph for the treatment if he can bring it about that something the patient wishes to discharge in action is disposed of through the work of remembering" (1914b, p. 153).

It is true that the analyst's effort is to convert acting in the motor sphere into awareness in the psychical sphere, but transference may be in the psychical sphere to begin with, albeit disguised. The psychical sphere includes awareness in the transference as well as remembering.

One of the objections one hears, from both analysts and patients, to a heavy emphasis on interpretation of associations about the patient's real life primarily in terms of the transference is that it means the analyst is disregarding the importance of what goes on in the patient's real life. The criticism is not justified. To emphasize the transference meaning is not to deny or belittle other meanings, but to focus on the one of several meanings of the content that is the most important for the analytic process, for the reasons I have just summarized.

Another way in which interpretations of resistance to the transference can be, or at least appear to the patient to be, a belittling of the importance of the patient's outside life is to make the interpretation as though the outside behavior is primarily an acting out of the transference. The patient may undertake *some* actions in the outside world as an expression of and resistance to the transference, that is, acting out. But the interpretation of associations about actions in the outside world as having implications for the transference need mean only that the choice of outside action to figure in the associations is codetermined by the need to express a transference indirectly. It is because of the resistance to awareness of the transference that the transference has to be disguised. When the disguise is unmasked by interpretation, it becomes clear that, despite the inevitable differences between the outside situations and the transference situation, the content is the same for the purpose of the analytic work. Therefore the analysis of the transference and the analysis of the neurosis coincide.

I stress this point particularly because some critics of earlier versions of this paper argued that I was advocating the analysis of the transference for its own sake rather than in the effort to overcome the neurosis. As I cited above, Freud wrote that the mastering of the transference neurosis "coincides with getting rid of the illness which was originally brought to the treatment" (1917, p. 444).

How the Transference Is Encouraged to Expand within the Analytic Situation

The analytic situation itself fosters the development of attitudes with primary determinants in the past, i.e., transferences. The analyst's reserve provides the patient with few and equivocal cues. The purpose of the analytic situation fosters the development of strong emotional responses, and the very fact that the patient has a neurosis means, as Freud said, that ". . . it is a perfectly normal and intelligible thing that the libidinal cathexis [we would now add negative feelings] of someone who is partly unsatisfied, a cathexis which is held ready in anticipation, should be directed as well to the figure of the doctor" (1912, p. 100).

While the analytic setup itself fosters the expansion of the transference within the analytic situation, the interpretation of resistance to the awareness of transference will further this expansion.

There are important resistances on the part of both patient and analyst to awareness of the transference. On the patient's part, this is because of the difficulty in recognizing erotic and hostile impulses toward the very person to whom they have to be disclosed. On the analyst's part, this is because the patient is likely to attribute the very attitudes to him which are most likely to cause him discomfort. The attitudes the patient believes the analyst has toward him are often the ones the patient is least likely to voice, in a general sense because of a feeling that it is impertinent for him to concern himself with the analyst's feelings, and in a more specific sense because the attitudes the patient ascribes to the analyst are often attitudes the patient feels the analyst will not like and be uncomfortable about having ascribed to him. It is for this reason that the analyst must be especially alert to the attitudes the patient believes he has, not only to the attitudes the patient does have toward him. If the analyst is able to see himself as a participant in an interaction, as I shall discuss below, he will become much more attuned to this important area of transference, which might otherwise escape him.

The investigation of the attitudes ascribed to the analyst makes easier the subsequent investigation of the intrinsic factors in the patient that played a role in such ascription. For example, the exposure of the fact that the patient ascribes sexual interest in him to the analyst, and genetically to the parent, makes easier the subsequent exploration of the patient's sexual wish toward the analyst, and genetically the parent.

The resistances to the awareness of these attitudes is responsible for their appearing in various disguises in the patient's manifest associations and for the analyst's reluctance to unmask the disguise. The most commonly recognized disguise is by displacement, but identification is an equally important one. In displacement, the patient's attitudes are narrated as being toward a third party. In identification, the patient attributes to himself attitudes he believes the analyst has toward him.

To encourage the expansion of the transference within the analytic situation, the disguises in which the transference appears have to be interpreted. In the case of displacement the interpretation will be of allusions to the transference in associations not manifestly about the transference. This is a kind of interpretation every analyst often makes. In the case of identification, the analyst interprets the attitude the patient ascribes to himself as an identification with an attitude he attributes to the analyst. Lipton (1977b) has recently described this form of disguised allusion to the transference with illuminating illustrations.

Many analysts believe that transference manifestations are infrequent and sporadic at the beginning of an analysis and that the patient's associations are not dominated by the transference unless a transference neurosis has developed. Other analysts believe that the patient's associations have transference meanings from the beginning and throughout. That is my opinion, and I think those who believe otherwise are failing to recognize the pervasiveness of indirect allusions to the transference — that is, what I am calling the resistance to the awareness of the transference.

In his autobiography, Freud wrote: "The patient remains under the influence of the analytic situation even though he is not directing his mental activities on to a particular subject. We shall be justified in assuming that nothing will occur to him that has not some reference to that situation" (1925, pp. 40–41). Since associations are obviously often not directly about the analytic situation, the interpretation of Freud's remark rests on what he meant by the "analytic situation."

I believe Freud's meaning can be clarified by reference to a statement he made in "The Interpretation of Dreams." He said that when the patient is told to say whatever comes into his mind, his associations become directed by the "purposive ideas inherent in the treatment" and that there are two such inherent purposive themes, one relating to the illness and the other—concerning which, Freud said, the patient has "no suspicion"—relating to the analyst (1900, pp. 531–532). If the patient has "no suspicion" of the theme relating to the analyst, the clear implication is that the theme appears only in disguise in the patient's associations. My interpretation is that Freud's remark not only specifies the themes inherent in the patient's associations, but also means that the associations are simultaneously directed by these two purposive ideas, not sometimes by one and sometimes by the other.

One important reason that the early and continuing presence of the transference is not always recognized is that it is considered to be absent in the patient who is talking freely and apparently without resistance. As Muslin and I pointed out in a paper on the early interpretation of transference (Gill and Muslin, 1976), resistance to the transference is probably present from the beginning, even if the patient is talking apparently freely. The patient may well be talking about issues not manifestly about the transference which are nevertheless also allusions to the transference. But the analyst has to be alert to the pervasiveness of such allusions to discern them.

The analyst should proceed on the working assumption, then, that the patient's associations have transference implications pervasively. This assumption is not to be confused with denial or neglect of the current aspects of the analytic situation. It is theoretically always possible to give precedence to a transference interpretation if one can only discern it through its disguise by resistance. This is not to dispute the desirability of learning as much as one can about the patient, if only to be in a position to make more correct interpretations of the transference. One therefore does not interfere with an apparently free flow of associations, especially early, unless the transference threatens the analytic situation to the point where its interpretation is mandatory rather than optional.

With the recognition that even the apparently freely associating patient may also be showing resistance to awareness of the transference, the formulation that one should not interfere as long as useful information is being gathered should replace Freud's dictum that the transference should not be interpreted until it becomes a resistance (1913, p. 139).

CONNECTION OF ALL TRANSFERENCE MANIFESTATIONS WITH SOMETHING IN THE ACTUAL ANALYTIC SITUATION

As a prelude to a further discussion of the interpretive technique for expansion of the transference within the analytic situation, I will argue that every transference has some connection to some aspect of the current analytic situation. Of course all the determinants of a transference are current in the sense that the past can exert an influence only insofar as it exists in the present. What I am distinguishing is the current reality of the analytic situation, that is, what actually goes on between patient and analyst in the present, from how the patient is currently constituted as a result of his past.

All analysts would doubtless agree that there are both current and transferential determinants of the analytic situation, and probably no analyst would argue that a transference idea can be expressed without contamination, as it were, that is, without any connection to anything current in the patient-analyst relationship. Nevertheless, I believe the implications of this fact for technique are often neglected in practice. I will deal with them as my next point. Here I want only to argue for the connection.

Several authors (e.g., Kohut, 1959, Loewald, 1960) have pointed out that Freud's early use of the term transference in "The Interpretation of Dreams," in a connection not immediately recognizable as related to the present-day use of the term, reveals the fallacy of considering that transference can be expressed free of any connection to the present. That early use was to refer to the fact that an unconscious idea cannot be expressed as such, but only as it becomes connected to a preconscious or conscious content. In the phenomenon with which Freud was then concerned, the dream, transference took place from an unconscious wish to a day residue. In "The Interpretation of Dreams" Freud used the term transference both for the general rule that an unconscious content is expressible only as it becomes transferred to a preconscious or conscious content and for the specific application of this rule to a transference to the analyst. Just as the day residue is the point of attachment of the dream wish, so must there be an analytic-situation residue, though Freud did not use that term, as the point of attachment of the transference

Analyst have always limited their behavior, both in variety and intensity, to increase the extent to which the patient's behavior is determined by his idiosyncratic interpretation of the analyst's behavior. In fact, analysts unfortunately sometimes limit their behavior so much, as compared with Freud's practice, that they even conceptualize the entire relationship with the patient a matter of technique, with no nontechnical personal relation, as Lipton (1977a) has pointed out.

But no matter how far the analyst attempts to carry this limitation of his behavior, the very existence of the analyst situation provides the patient with innumerable cues which inevitably become his rationale for his transference responses. In other words, the current situation cannot be made to disappear—that is, the analytic situation is real. It is easy to forget this truism in one's zeal to diminish the role of the current situation in determining the patient's responses. One can try to keep past and present determinants relatively perceptible from one another, but one cannot obtain either in "pure culture." As Freud wrote: "I insist on this procedure [the couch], however, for its purpose and result are to prevent the transference from mingling with the patient's associations imperceptibly, to isolate the transference and to allow it to come forward in due course sharply defined as a resistance" (1913, p. 134). Even "isolate" is too strong a word in the light of the inevitable intertwining of the transference with the current situation.

If the analyst remains under the illusion that the current cues he provides to the patient can be reduced to the vanishing point, he may be led into a silent withdrawal, which is not too distant from the caricature of an analyst as someone who does indeed refuse to have any personal relationship with the patient. What happens then is that silence has become a technique rather than merely an indication that the analyst is listening. The patient's responses under such conditions can be mistaken for uncontaminated transference when they are in fact transference adaptations to the actuality of the silence.

The recognition that all transference must have some relation to the actual analytic situation, from which it takes its point of departure, as it were, has a crucial implication for the technique of interpreting resistance to the awareness of transference, to which I turn now.

THE ROLE OF THE ACTUAL SITUATION IN INTERPRETING RESISTANCE TO THE AWARENESS OF TRANSFERENCE

If the analyst becomes persuaded of the centrality of transference and the importance of encouraging the transference to expand within the analytic situation, he has to find the presenting and plausible interpretations of resistance to the awareness of transference he should make. Here, his most reliable guide is the cues offered by what is actually going on in the analytic situation: on the one hand, the events of the situation, such as change in time of session, or an interpretation made by the analyst, and, on the other hand, how the patient is experiencing the situation as reflected in explicit remarks about it, however fleeting these may be. This is the primary yield for technique of the recognition that any transference must have a link to the actuality of the analytic situation, as I argued above. The cue points to the nature of the transference, just as the day residue for a dream may be a quick pointer to the latent dream thoughts. Attention to the current stimulus for a transference elaboration will keep the analyst from making mechanical transference interpretations, in which he interprets that there are allusions to the transference in associations not manifestly about the transference, but without offering any plausible basis for the interpretation. Attention to the current stimulus also offers some degree of protection against the analyst's inevitable tendency to project his own views onto the patient, either because of countertransference or because of a preconceived theoretical bias about the content and hierarchical relationships in psychodynamics.

The analyst may be very surprised at what in his behavior the patient finds important or unimportant, for the patient's responses will be idiosyncratically determined by the transference. The patient's response may seem to be something the patient as well as the analyst consider trivial, because, as in displacement to a trival aspect of the day residue of a dream, displacement can better serve resistance when it is to something trivial. Because it is connected to conflict-laden material, the stimulus to the transference may be difficult to find. It may be quickly disavowed, so that its presence in awareness is only transitory. With the discovery of the disavowal, the patient may also gain insight into how it repeats a disavowal earlier in his life. In his search for the present stimuli which the patient is responding to transferentially, the analyst must therefore remain alert to both fleeting and apparently trivial manifest references to himself as well as to the events of the analytic situation.

If the analyst interprets the patient's attitudes in a spirit of seeing their possible plausibility in the light of what information the patient does have, rather than in the spirit of either affirming or denying the patient's views, the way is open for their further expression and elucidation. The analyst will be respecting the patient's effort to be plausible and realistic, rather than seeing him as manufacturing his transference attitudes out of whole cloth.

I believe it is so important to make a transference interpretation plausible to the patient in terms of a current stimulus that, if the analyst is persuaded that the manifest content has an important implication for the transference but he is unable to see a current stimulus for the attitude, he should explicitly say so if he decides to make the transference interpretation anyway. The patient himself may then be able to say what the current stimulus is.

It is sometimes argued that the analyst's attention to his own behavior as a precipitant for the transference will increase the patient's resistance to recognizing the transference. I believe, on the contrary, that, because of the inevitable interrelationship of the current and transferential determinants, it is only through interpretation that they *can* be disentangled.

It is also argued that one must wait until the transference has reached optimal intensity before it can be advantageously interpreted. It is true that too hasty an interpretation of the transference can serve a defensive function for the analyst and deny him the information he needs to make a more appropriate transference interpretation. But it is also true that delay in interpreting runs the risks of allowing an unmanageable transference to develop. It is also true that deliberate delay can be a manipulation in the service of abreaction rather than analysis and, like silence, can lead to a response to the actual situation which is mistaken for uncontaminated transference. Obviously important issues of timing are involved. I believe an important clue to when a transference interpretation is apt and which one to make lies in whether the interpretation can be made plausibly in terms of the determinant I am stressing, namely, something in the current analytic situation.

A critic of an earlier version of this paper understood me to be saying that all the analyst need do is to interpret the allusion to the transference, but that I did not see that interpretation of why the transference had to be expressed by allusion rather than directly is also necessary. Of course I agree, and meant to imply this as well as other aspects of the transference attitude in saying that when the analyst approaches the transference in the spirit of seeing how it appears plausibly realistic to the patient, it paves the way toward its further elucidation and expression.

THE RELATIVE ROLES OF RESOLUTION OF THE TRANSFERENCE WITHIN THE ANALYTIC SITUATION AND BY GENETIC TRANSFERENCE INTERPRETATION

Freud's emphasis on remembering as the goal of the analytic work implies that remembering is the principal avenue to the resolution of the transference. But his delineation of the successive steps in the development of analytic technique (1920, p. 18) makes clear that he saw this development as a change from an effort to reach memories directly to the utilization of the transference as the necessary intermediary to reaching the memories.

In contrast to remembering as the way the transference is resolved, Freud also described resistance as being primarily overcome in the transference, with remembering following relatively easily thereafter: "From the repetitive reactions which are exhibited in the transference we are led along the familiar paths to the awakening of the memories, which appear without difficulty, as it were, after the resistance has been overcome" (1914b, pp. 154–155); and "This revision of the process of repression can be accomplished only in part in connection with the memory traces of the process which led to repression. The *decisive* part of the work is achieved by creating in the patient's relation to the doctor—in the 'transference'—new editions of the old conflicts. . . . Thus the transference becomes the battlefield on which all the mutually struggling forces should meet one another" (1917, p. 454; emphasis added). This is indeed the primary insight Strachey (1934) clarified in his seminal paper on the therapeutic action of psychoanalysis.

There are two main ways in which resolution of the transference can take place through work with the transference in the here and now. The first lies in the clarification of what are the cues in the current situation which are the patient's point of departure for a transference elaboration. The exposure of the current point of departure at once raises the question of whether it is adequate to the conclusion drawn from it. The relating of the transference to a current stimulus is, after all, part of the patient's effort to make the transference attitude plausibly determined by the present. The reserve and ambiguity of the analyst's behavior is what increases the ranges of apparently plausible conclusions the patient may draw. If an examination of the basis for the conclusion makes clear that the actual situation to which the patient responds is subject to other meanings than the one the patient has reached, he will more readily consider his pre-existing bias, that is, his transference.

Another critic of an earlier version of this paper suggested that, in speaking of the current relationship and the relation between the patient's conclusions and the information on which they seem plausibly based, I am implying some absolute conception of what is real in the analytic situation, of which the analyst is the final arbiter. This is not the case. My writing that what the patient must come to see is that the information he has is subject to other possible interpretations implies the very contrary to an absolute conception of reality. In fact, analyst and patient engage in a dialogue in a spirit of attempting to arrive at a consensus about reality, not about some fictitious absolute reality.

The second way in which resolution of the transference can take place within the work with the transference in the here and now is that in the very interpretation of the transference the patient has a new experience. He is being treated differently from how he expected to be. Analysts seem reluctant to emphasize this new experience, as though it endangers the role of insight and argues for interpersonal influence as the significant factor in change. Strachey's emphasis on the new experience in the mutative transference interpretation has unfortunately been overshadowed by his views on introjection, which have been mistaken to advocate manipulating the transference. Strachey meant introjection of the more benign superego of the analyst only as a temporary step on the road toward insight. Not only is the new experience not to be confused with the interpersonal influence of a transference gratification, but the new experience occurs together with insight into both the patient's biased expectation and the new experience. As Strachey points out, what is unique about the transference interpretation is that insight and the new experience take place in relation to the very person who was expected to behave differently, and it is this which gives the work in the transference its immediacy and effectiveness. While Freud did stress the affective immediacy of the transference, he did not make the new experience explicit.

It is important to recognize that transference interpretation is not a matter of experience, in contrast to insight, but a joining of the two together. Both are needed to bring about and maintain the desired changes in the patient. It is also important to recognize that no new techniques of intervention are required to provide the new experience. It is an inevitable accompaniment of interpretation of the transference in the here and now. It is often overlooked that, although Strachey said that only transference interpretations were mutative, he also said with approval that most interpretations are outside the transference.

In a further explication of Strachey's paper and entirely consistent with Strachey's position, Rosenfeld (1972) has pointed out that clarification of material outside the transference is often necessary to know what is the appropriate transference interpretation, and that both genetic transference interpretations and extratransference interpretations play an important role in working through. Strachey said relatively little about working through, but surely nothing against the need for it, and he explicitly recognized a role for recovery of the past in the resolution of the transference.

My own position is to emphasize the role of the analysis of the transference in the here and now, both in interpreting resistance to the awareness of transference and in working toward its resolution by relating it to the actuality of the situation. I agree that extratransference and genetic transference interpretations and, of course, working through are important too. The matter is one of emphasis. I believe interpretation of resistance to awareness of the transference should figure in the majority of sessions, and that if this is done by relating the transference to the actual analytic situation, the very same interpretation is a beginning of work to the resolution of the transference. To justify this view more persuasively would require detailed case material.

It may be considered that I am siding with the Kleinians who, many analysts feel, are in error in giving the analysis of the transference too great if not even an exclusive role in the analytic process. It is true that Kleinians emphasize the analysis of the transference more, in their writings at least, than do the general run of analysts. Indeed, Anna Freud's (1968) complaint that the concept of transference has become overexpanded seems to be directed against the Kleinians. One of the reasons the Kleinians consider themselves the true followers of Freud in technique is precisely because of the emphasis they put on the analysis of the transference. Hanna Segal (1967, pp. 173–174), for example, writes as follows: "To say that all communications are seen as communications about the patient's phantasy as well as current external life is equivalent to saying that all communications contain something relevant to the transference situation. In Kleinian technique, the interpretation of the transference is often more central than in the classical technique."

Despite their disclaimers to the contrary, my reading of Kleinian case material leads me to agree with what I believe is the general view that Kleinian transference interpretations often deal with so-called deep and genetic material without adequate connection to the current features of the present analytic situation and thus differ sharply from the kind of transference interpretation I am advocating.

The insistence on exclusive attention to any particular aspect of the analytic process, like the analysis of the transference in the here and now, can become a fetish. I do not say that other kinds of interpretation should not be made, but I feel the emphasis on transference interpretations within the analytic situation needs to be increased or at the very least reaffirmed, and that we need more clarification and specification of just when other kinds of interpretations are in order.

Of course it is sometimes tactless to make a transference interpretation. Surely two reasons which would be included in a specification of the reasons for not making a particular transference interpretation, even if one seems apparent to the analyst, would be preoccupation with an important extra-transference event and an inadequate degree of rapport, to use Freud's term, to sustain the sense of criticism, humiliation, or other painful feeling the particular interpretation might engender, even though the analyst had no intention of evoking such a response. The issue may well be, however, not of whether or not an interpretation of resistance to the transference should be made, but whether the therapist can find that transference interpretation which in the light of the total situation, both transferential and current, the patient is able to hear and benefit from primarily as the analyst intends it.

Transference interpretations, like extratransference interpretations, indeed like any behavior on the analyst's part, can have an effect on the transference, which in turn needs to be examined if the result of an analysis is to depend as little as possible on unanalyzed transference. The result of any analysis depends on the analysis of the transference, persisting effects of unanalyzed transference, and the new experience which I have emphasized as the unique merit of transference interpretation in the here and now. It is especially important to remember this lest one's zeal to ferret out the transference itself become an unrecognized and objectionable actual behavior on the analyst's part, with its own repercussions on the transference.

The emphasis I am placing on the analysis of resistance to the transference could easily be misunderstood as implying that it is always easy to recognize the transference as disguised by resistance or that analysis would proceed without a hitch if only such interpretations were made. I mean to imply neither, but rather that the analytic process will have the best chance of success if correct interpretation of resistance to the transference and work with the transference in the here and now are the core of the analytic work.

I close with a statement of a conviction designed to set this paper into a broader perspective of psychoanalytic theory and research. The points I have made are not new. They are present in varying degrees of clarity and emphasis throughout our literature. But like so many other aspects of psychoanalytic theory and practice, they fade in and out of prominence and are rediscovered again and again, possibly occasionally with some modest conceptual advance, but often with a newness attributable only to ignorance of past contributions. There are doubtless many reasons for this phenomenon. But not the least, in my opinion, is the almost total absence of systematic and controlled research in the psychoanalytic situation. I mean such research in contrast to the customary clinical research. I believe that only with such systematic and controlled research will analytic findings become solid and secure knowledge instead of being subject to erosion again and again by waves of fashion and what Ernst Lewy (1941) long ago called the "return of the repression" to designate the retreat by psychoanalysts from insights they had once reached.

CASE ILLUSTRATION

I believe the most faithful rendering of the therapeutic process is by a full session. No single session is likely to demonstrate all the points made in this paper. Nor can I find any session which is not open to one or another criticism.

I chose this session for the following reasons: Though the therapist may well be considered too intrusive, his very activity increases the number of illustrations of interpretation of the transference. Indeed, later in the session the therapist himself comments on the degree of his activity. (In a later session it becomes clear that the patient feels competitive in seeing connections and interprets the therapist's activity as besting him in this contest.) Since the patient is being seen only once a week most people would call this "psychotherapy." I am of the opinion that the range of settings (defined by frequency of sessions, couch or chair, type of patient, and experience of the therapist) in which the technique of analysis of the transference is appropriate is far broader than is usually thought; this illustration exemplifies this view. The session, only the second of the therapy, illustrates what I mean by employing this technique from the beginning. My comments will be largely restricted to how the analysis of the transference is being exemplified, though of course much else could be said.

This illustration of the analysis of transference is a summary of the second hour of a patient being seen once a week. The hours are also being audio-recorded and the patient understands that in return for being seen by an experienced therapist the recorded hours are being used for teaching purposes. The context of the hour is that after the first hour there was to have been a gap of three weeks because the therapist was to be away. His plans changed, however, and he phoned the patient to offer an earlier appointment. There was some difficulty in finding a mutually suitable time. The second hour took place ten days after the first. The account is given in summary rather than verbatim to save space, but it follows the transcript faithfully.

The patient began by saying he keeps a diary and had written something in it which he thought might be helpful. He asked if he should read it and the therapist said that was all right. It was an expression of great loneliness. The therapist asked if it had been written for him. The patient did not think so; rather, after having written it he thought it might be helpful to share it. In response to a question he said the central issue in the material he read is his loneliness. The therapist asked whether he had felt he could communicate this better by writing it down; he said he did. The therapist then asked when it was written and established that it was before he had phoned the patient. The therapist said that he nevertheless wondered if the loneliness was an implicit reference to the long time the patient had anticipated would elapse before his second appointment.

This interpretation suggests that material not manifestly about the relationship nonetheless alludes to it. It is made plausible by an event in the therapy—the anticipated long wait for the second appointment.

The patient said this might be true and that he was supposed to have had a last summing-up appointment with his previous therapist but he too has been away. This seems to be an indirect confirmation of the interpretation. The therapist suggested that this indicated there might be something

to what he had said; the patient replied, "What you're saying sounds valid and hits a nerve." He added that perhaps he is expecting a lot from the therapist. He referred to this as setting himself up, and the therapist suggested this meant he feared an awful letdown.

The patient agreed, but instead of following this up (as the therapist well might have) he asked what the patient's reaction had been to the phone call. He said he had been surprised and the therapist asked if that was all. When the patient said he had been angry because he had had to rearrange his schedule, the therapist asked why he hadn't refused the offer. The patient said it had seemed important to the therapist. When the therapist pointed out that the patient was accommodating him, the patient replied that he thought he was making himself look bad.

The therapist suggested that the patient apparently felt the therapist might react by feeling that it was inappropriate for the patient to talk as though he was doing the therapist a favor after the therapist had put himself out. The patient agreed.

The therapist asked whether the patient had speculated as to what had motivated the offer of an appointment. The patient said the therapist had wanted to maintain continuity. The therapist responded that apparently his concern was unnecessary since the patient had been prepared to wait. But after all, was it not true that the patient's loneliness did indicate that he was reacting to the long gap between appointments?

The therapist seems defensive here. He may indeed be reacting to the spurning of his concern. In fact his motivation may well have included a wish to have a session for the class he was teaching. It is not impossible that this was a speculation that had occurred to the patient (it has in other similar situations) and therapist and patient were colluding to keep this unspoken.

The therapist suggested that perhaps the patient's reaction was a denial of how strongly he felt about the long wait for the next appointment. The patient responded that this would sound dumb but that sometimes he feels he would like to abandon everything and just devote himself to working out his problems but after all he has a job and other responsibilities.

The therapist suggested that the patient had apparently interpreted the interpretation as a rebuke that he was not sufficiently interested in the therapy. This is an example of an interpretation of an allusion to the patient's experience of the relationship made plausible by what the therapist has said. It is an example of how the transference is an amalgam of past and present, or contributions from both therapist and patient.

The patient said the interpretation didn't "ring exactly true." The therapist tried to justify his interpretation by reminding the patient that he had introduced his response by saying it would sound dumb.

The patient still didn't accept the interpretation and said it was ironical that he had rushed away from a religious service to keep the appointment. But after all, he continued, this also was a cleansing of the soul.

The therapist inquired into a Hebrew expression the patient had used in his initial reading from his diary, and the patient explained that he had spent a year in Israel and was good at languages. The therapist had indicated he thought the patient's knowledge of Hebrew was extensive.

After a pause the patient said he was feeling intensely emotional and was surprised at this. The therapist asked for clarification of the feeling and the patient responded that he felt the therapist was "zeroing in" on sore spots the patient would prefer not to deal with. He was surprised at the therapist's ability to touch on important issues even though he doesn't know the patient very well.

The therapist asked for an illustration and the patient responded that it was the therapist's speaking of his loneliness; but then he recognized that he had introduced that topic himself. The therapist interpreted that the patient might be feeling two ways: on the one hand he wants to be understood, but on the other he would prefer that the therapist not deal with sore points so directly and rapidly.

The patient agreed and said he didn't feel ready to trust the therapist and was afraid of his own thoughts and feelings.

The therapist asked for a further clarification of what made the patient feel he was "zeroing in" so rapidly and the patient said he was not sure. The therapist asked if the patient was finding this therapy different from his previous one. The patient replied that he had built up a lot of trust in the previous therapist. He did not think the present therapist was acting differently from the people he was used to.

The therapist said he was concerned that he had been directing the conversation too much and he would wait for the patient to take the lead.

After a pause, the patient said he had a strange experience the week before. A girl had invited him to stay at her apartment because they came home very late from a date. He believes she expected him to make a sexual advance but he did not and he is concerned because he feels he should have.

The therapist might have interpreted here that this association—clearly spontaneous—was an illusion to the fact that the appointment had been initiated by the therapist's call, that is that the therapist had issued the invitation. The interpretation need not have included a sexual parallel.

The patient then spontaneously referred to his concern about homosexuality (possible evidence that the phone call was felt to be a homosexual seduction but probably premature to interpret). He said that a sexual experience relieved his loneliness a little, and that he felt like a "weirdo" because he had never had intercourse with a woman.

The patient had been pausing frequently and the therapist called attention to this, saying the patient apparently was not accustomed to speaking about himself in therapy without pausing for replies. He replied that his previous therapist said that he was afraid to get into the subject of his homosexuality and would start and stop in talking about it like a kind of bait. The therapist said he was not suggesting that the patient was using it as bait but was asking whether the patient was aware that he was not taking the initiative and whether he was concerned that he might be directing the conversation. The therapist explained they would more likely deal with the patient's concerns if he would take more initiative in the conversation. He disavowed that he necessarily wanted the patient to continue on the topic of homosexuality but raised the question of how the patient sees the relation between homosexuality and loneliness. He stopped himself, saying he was again directing, but asked whether the patient feared he would stress homosexuality and ignore the loneliness. The patient thought not, and that he was primarily wondering how the woman had interpreted his behavior.

After a pause the patient said he was concerned about his job because he had given notice some time before and it was finally being offered to someone else. The patient had introduced this by saying his language gave him away, and the therapist asked what he had been reluctant to reveal. The reply was that he feared to be told not to be so worried about his job. Then he said he feared he was second-guessing himself and that the therapist would think him a "total idiot."

The therapist suggested that this was perhaps why he was guarding his language. The patient said he wondered why he was guarding himself. The therapist suggested it was because he felt the therapist could see his sore spots too clearly, and he was reluctant to reveal them because he didn't know the therapist well enough to trust him. The patient responded that he wanted to give himself away and to hide himself at the same time.

The patient then said he could never please his father. The therapist asked whether the patient felt he was reacting in a way that he might with his father and whether the therapist had in some way indicated that the patient couldn't please him. This question by the therapist illustrates his dealing with the spontaneous comment about the past as a possible flight from the present. The patient thought not and that he himself was casting the therapist in that role, as he had his previous therapist.

He referred to his having thought in the previous session that the therapist had judged him, but the therapist had denied it. The therapist said it was understandable that the patient might not believe that since he knew so little about the therapist. This illustrates the therapist's emphasis on the plausibility of the patient's experience of the relationship.

The patient said his eyes keep tearing and the therapist said that was an example of his difficulty in admitting his feelings. He replied that he was ashamed, and the therapist said he apparently expected to be criticized and again it was understandable that he was in conflict about whether to trust the therapist so soon. He agreed.

When the hour was over he said he felt bad that his name was on the tape. The therapist at first said he would blank it out but then said that if the patient were to accept taping at all there was some degree of trust he would have to accept. He agreed and the therapist said he should nevertheless feel free to talk about the taping whenever he wished.

As he left he wished the therapist a good vacation, though the therapist had not given any reason as to why he would have been unable to see the patient for three weeks.

Summary

Let me summarize. I distinguish between two major different relationships between transference and resistance. One is resistance to awareness of the transference and the other is resistance to resolution of the transference.

I argue that the bulk of the analytic work should take place in the transference in the here and now. I detailed Freud's view that the transference should be encouraged to expand within the analytic situation. I suggested that the main technique for doing so, in addition to the analytic setup itself, is the interpretation of resistance to the awareness of transference by searching for the allusions to the transference in the associations not manifestly about the transference; that in making such interpretations one is guided by the connection to the actual analytic situation which every transference includes; the major work in resolving the transference takes place in the here and now, both by way of examining the relation between the transference and the actuality of the analytic situation from which it takes its point of departure and the new experience which the analysis of the transference inevitably includes; and that, while genetic transference interpretations play a role in resolving the transference, genetic material is likely to appear spontaneously and with relative ease after the resistances have been overcome in the transference in the here and now. Working through remains important, and it, too, takes place primarily in the transference in the here and now.

References

Freud, A. (1968), Acting out. *Writings*, 7:94–109. New York: International Universities Press, 1971.

Freud, S. (1900), The interpretation of dreams. *Standard Edition*, 5.

———(1912), The dynamics of transference. *Standard Edition*, 12: 99–108.

———(1913), On beginning the treatment (Further recommendations on the technique of psychoanalysis, I). *Standard Edition*, 12:123–144.

———(1914a), On the history of the psycho-analytic movement. *Standard Edition*, 14:7–66.

———(1914b), Remembering, repeating, and working through (Further recommendations on the technique of psycho-analysis, II). *Standard Edition*, 12:147–156.

———(1917), Introductory lectures on psycho-analysis. *Standard Edition*, 16.

———(1920), Beyond the pleasure principle. *Standard Edition*, 18:7–64.

———(1925), An autobiographical study. *Standard Edition*, 20:7–74. London: Hogarth Press, 1959.

Gill, M. & Muslin, H. (1976). Early interpretation of transference. *This Journal*, 24:779–794.

Greenson, R. (1967), *The Technique and Practice of Psychoanalysis*. New York: International Universities Press.

Kanzer, M. (1966), The motor sphere of the transference. *Psychoanal. Quart.*, 35:522–539.

Kohut, H. (1959), Introspection, empathy, and psychoanalysis. In: *The Search for the Self*. New York: International Universities Press, 1978, pp. 205–232.

Lewy, E. (1941), The return of the repression. *Bull. Menninger Clinic*, 5:47–55.

Lipton, S. (1977a), The advantages of Freud's technique

as shown by his analysis of the Rat Man. *Internat. J. Psycho-Anal.,* 58:255–274.

——(1977b), Clinical observations on resistance to the transference. *Internat. J. Psycho-Anal.,* 58:463–472.

Loewald, H. (1960), On the therapeutic action of psychoanalysis. *Internat. J. Psycho-Anal.,* 41:16–33.

Muslin, H. & Gill, M. (1978). Transference in the Dora case. *This Journal,* 26:311–328.

Rapaport, D. (1967), The scientific methodology of psychoanalysis. In: *Collected Papers,* ed. M. M. Gill. New York: Basic Books, 1967, pp. 165–220.

Rosenfeld, H. (1972), A critical appreciation of James Strachey's paper on the nature of the therapeutic action of psychoanalysis. *Internat. J. Psycho-Anal.,* 53:455–462.

Segal, H. (1967), Melanie Klein's technique. In: *Psychoanalytic Techniques,* ed. B. Wolman. New York: Basic Books, pp. 168–190.

Stone, L. (1967), The psychoanalytic situation and transference. *This Journal,* 15:3–57.

Strachey, J. (1934). The nature of the therapeutic action of psychoanalysis. Reprinted in: *Internat. J. Psycho-Anal.* (1969) 50:275–292.

PART II

NONTRANSFERENCE

It seems self-evident that transference (narrowly defined as the distorted, inappropriate, and pathological aspects of the patient's responses to the therapist or analyst) and nontransference (the valid, nondistorted component) are the poles of a continuum—one whose type is often encountered in considering dimensions of the therapeutic relationship and interaction. At one extreme (and probably never in pure form) are transference-based responses, perceptions, fantasies and the like, with the proportion of nontransference elements increasing as we move along the spectrum; at the other extreme are found (again, almost never in pure form) nontransference-based responses, with, as we approach the other pole, an increasing proportion of transference. In the middle range is an indefinite area of responses with relatively equal proportions of transference and nontransference components. It would appear, then, that the definition of the transference sector relies on an ability to appreciate the nontransference elements and to know and understand the nature of reality, especially its implicit and unconscious qualities—in large measure, those elements of the unconscious communicative interaction which can be consensually and psychoanalytically validated as realistic, appropriate, and nondistorted.

Viewing the matter in this way, we can recognize that Freud was indeed on solid ground in initiating the investigation of the patient's relationship with the analyst, and of the total analytic interaction, with an extended study of the transference component which, in the form of both resistances and more revealing manifestations, relates intimately to the unconscious fantasies, memories, and introjects on which the patient's psychopathology is based. It is this dimension that had defied clinical recognition and whose analytic comprehension proved essential for insightful, adaptive symptom resolution.

Nonetheless, the almost exclusive focus on transference carried with it a number of major dangers, to which Freud and most of his followers have succumbed. One of these dangers is the tendency to invoke the concept of transference as a defense against the actualities of the analyst's pathological contributions to the therapeutic interaction. Another is the failure to recognize that interactional realities, fraught with unconscious meanings and functions, contribute in major ways to the development—and resolution—of psychopathology. Thus, both transference and nontransference, reality and fantasy, must be appreciated and consistently investigated in the course of analytic work and in regard to the analytic interaction itself. Since it seems clear now that the greatest hindrance to the full and undistorted comprehension by any analyst of the truth of analytic material and experience lies in the realm of his countertransferences, an undue emphasis on the patient's transferences offers itself as a ready vehicle for countertransference expression.

Recent developments in ego psychology, the study of object relationships, and the investigation of the preoedipal years and their later influence have all brought to the fore the unconscious and pathogenic—as well as the conscious and constructive—aspects of reality, relatedness, and all interpersonal transactions. For these and other reasons, there is in recent years a growing number of attempts to more properly balance our picture of the patient in psychoanalysis and psychotherapy, and his relationship and interaction with the analyst or therapist.

As long as reality and nontransference are understood in depth, and as filled with unconscious implication, and not treated as the sole basis for the patient's responses to the analyst, a careful study of the nontransference dimension reaps many rewards. It enables us to define the patient's conscious and unconscious sectors of valid and nonpathological functioning within the analytic interaction, and to not only give them the appreciation they deserve, but also to draw upon them as an essential therapeutic resource. Such endeavors as the patient's unconscious corrective and curative efforts on behalf of the therapist, his unconscious communications through which he in fragmented form places the necessary rectifications and interventions into the therapist, and many other positive capacities can be both understood and utilized implicitly in therapeutic work. Similarly, the patient's actual destructive intentions toward therapy and the therapist can be understood more clearly both for its realities and for its unconscious basis.

Along different lines, the genetic dimension of the analytic experience is also clarified, in that links to the past are no longer viewed as definitive indicators of transference. Instead it is recognized that these may derive from either transference or nontransference-based experiences. Finally—and this by no means exhausts the implications of a full comprehension of the nontransference sphere—this type of more balanced approach provides full room for both the projective and the introjective aspects of the patient's experiences vis-à-vis the analyst, and paves the way for study of the conscious and unconscious dimensions of the analytic interaction itself (see Part VI).

There are some who prefer to think of the nontransference sphere of the patient's relationship to the analyst as the "real" relationship. Such a conception, however, proves most confusing in that the patient experiences his transference-based reactions to the analyst as quite real, and his valid functioning is consistently based on nondistorting unconscious elements intermingled with transference and distortion. In actual practice, this term has also promoted supposedly therapeutic work that is confined to surface realities and noninterpretive responses, rather than the investigation of unconscious implications and interpretations of admixtures of pathological and nonpathological components. In addition, the so-called real relationship alludes to but one aspect of the patient's nontransference responses and functioning, and would prove far too limiting for a full comprehension of the analytic relationship (for further discussion, see Langs 1976b).

As might be expected, then, the nontransference dimension has been relatively neglected by psychoanalysts. This neglect has by no means constituted a total avoidance, since from the outset Freud (1912a,b [see chapters 1 and 38], 1913, 1915, 1920) took into account the actual structure of the analytic relationship and setting, the relatively sublimated or essentially nontransference elements in the patient's relationship to the analyst, and efforts by the patient to create actual repetitions of past pathogenic experiences in his relationship with the analyst. Thereafter there appeared from time to time studies on such relevant topics as the impact of the analytic setting (e.g., Balint and Balint 1939), the influence of the actual analytic interaction (e.g., Strachey 1934), and the role of the personality of the analyst (e.g., E. Ticho 1972).

In addition, specific discussions of the patient's nontransference functioning and responses appeared, most of them by Greenson (1978), Searles (1965), and myself (1976a,b, 1978a,b). Concentrated primarily in the last ten years, these investigations have done much to establish a clinical and validatable basis for the distinction between transference and nontransference (and thus for their identification within intermixtures), and for a cataloging of the various ways in which patients function constructively and nonpathologically within the therapeutic interaction. The papers offered in this section are by those writers who have most carefully and extensively explored this dimension, and who have done so largely by isolating specific elements of nontransference. These papers may be supplemented in particular by Bird's paper (1972; see chapter 6) on transference, and by most of the papers in Parts V and VI, on the therapeutic alliance and the therapeutic interaction. I might also mention here my own "The Patient's Unconscious Perception of the Therapist's Errors" (1975).

There is little doubt that we have just begun to appreciate the ways in which, largely unconsciously, the patient functions adaptively and constructively within the therapeutic interaction. This balancing out of our image of the patient in therapy or analysis leads to an important revision of our concept of the nature of analytic work: these efforts entail not only the insightful cognitive and introjective adaptive modification of pathological unconscious fantasies, memories, and introjects, but also a freeing up and rendering available for conscious utilization the abundant unconscious resources of the patient already present when he enters analysis — resources severely curtailed by the pathological elements within himself, and the motivational and defensive barriers to his own inner fulfillment and realization.

8

THE "REAL" RELATIONSHIP BETWEEN
THE PATIENT AND THE PSYCHOANALYST

RALPH R. GREENSON

EDITOR'S NOTE

Ralph Greenson has established an exceptional place among psychoanalysts through his extensive and meticulous investigations of the analytic relationship. His paper on the genuine, nonfantasy aspects of the relationship between patient and analyst is one of a series of investigations of the nontransference aspects of the patient's relatedness in analysis, in which are included studies of the working alliance (1965; see Part V, chapter 28) and responses to the analysts errors in technique (1972).

Reacting strongly to a tendency among psychoanalysts to view the patient's relationship with them almost exclusively in terms of transference and distortion, Greenson here, as elsewhere, attempts to establish criteria for the patient's appropriate and inappropriate responses within the analytic situation, and to define the dimensions of the realistic aspect of that relatedness. While these efforts are somewhat limited by a restricted attention to manifest responses and content, this paper is part of Greenson's pioneering efforts to comprehend the true nature of the patient's experiences in the course of an analysis.

INTRODUCTION

This presentation is an attempt to explore further into the nature of the therapeutic processes which occur during psychoanalytic treatment. It has been the hallmark of psychoanalysis to emphasize the occurrence of transference and resistance during psychoanalytic therapy and to stress the decisive importance of interpreting these phenomena. This has led to a widely held view that all the patient's meaningful reactions to the person of the analyst are transference manifestations and the only important interventions are transference interpretations, a view common among Kleinian as well as the more

Reprinted from *The Unconscious Today*, ed. Mark Kanzer, pp. 213–232. New York: International Universities Press, 1971.

"conservative," classical analysts. These analysts may concede that other kinds of personal interactions take place in the analytic situation, but they are considered irrelevant and awkward impediments which are either to be circumvented or ignored. I base this last statement on the fact that I have never read a paper by an "Orthodox" or Kleinian analyst which indicated that any intervention besides interpretation was important in the patient-analyst relationship.

On the other hand, a survey of the recent psychoanalytic literature reveals that a significant number of psychoanalysts, a group too heterogeneous to be classified, do not deny the special value of transference phenomena and transference interpretations, but maintain that the total relationship between the patient and the analyst must be taken into account in order to fully understand and handle the vicissitudes of the psychoanalytic situation. They believe that a wide assortment of object relations, other than transference, takes place in the course of an analysis in both the patient and the therapist. It is their contention that the proper handling of these "nontransference," "extratransference," or "real" interactions are an indispensable ingredient for successful psychoanalytic treatment. I want to interpolate here that in this discussion I am emphasizing object relations including and beyond the scope of the concept of the therapeutic or working alliance as described by Zetzel (1956) and Greenson (1965). Stone (1961, 1967) and Fairbairn (1957, 1958) are the most outspoken on the subject of total object relations, but Anna Freud (1954, 1965), Gitelson (1952), Knight (1953), Winnicott (1955, 1965), Loewald (1960), and Erikson (1962), to mention only a few among many, have also pointed in this direction.

I want to quote from a few of the authors mentioned above in order to illustrate the areas of agreement despite the sharp differences in theoretical and technical points of view. Let me begin with the clearest statement of the problem, some remarks by Anna Freud published in 1954:

Just as "no two analysts would ever give precisely the same interpretations," we find on closer examination that no two of a given analyst's patients are handled by him ever in precisely the same manner. With some patients we remain deadly serious, with others humor, or even jokes, may play a part; with some the terms in which interpretations are couched have to be literal ones, others find it easier to accept the same content when given in the form of similes and analogies; there are differences in the ways we receive and send off patients, and in the degree to which we permit a real relationship to the patient to coexist with the transferred, fantasied one; there is, even with the strictness of the analytic setting, a varying amount of ease felt by analyst and patient. These wholly unintended and unplanned variations in our responses are imposed on us, I believe, not so much by the patient's neuroses but by the individual nuances of their personalities which may escape unobserved otherwise. If we become aware of these often minute variations in our own behavior and reactions, and cease to treat them as unimportant chance occurrences, their observation and scrutiny leads us directly to important findings. In the personal pressure which the patient exerts on us in this manner, he betrays the subtleties of his healthy personality, the degree of maturity reached by his ego, his capacity to sublimate, his intellectual gifts, and his ability to view his conflicts at least momentarily in an objective manner. In the variations of the analyst's "acting out" in technical behavior, we may, therefore, find new clues for the systematic study of character structures and personalities [pp. 609, 610].

Later on in the same paper Anna Freud goes on to say:

Further, I refer briefly to Dr. Stone's remarks concerning the "real personal relationship" between analyst and patient versus the "true transference reactions." To make such a distinction coincides with ideas which I have always held on this subject. . . . We see the patient enter into analysis with a reality attitude to the analyst; then the transference gains momentum until it reaches its peak in the full-blown transference neurosis which has to be worked off analytically until the figure of the analyst emerges again, reduced to its true status. But—and this seems important to me—so far as the patient has a healthy part of his personality, his real relationship to the analyst is never wholly submerged. With due respect for the necessary strictest handling and interpretation of the transference, I feel still that we should leave room somewhere for the realization that analyst and patient are also two real people, of equal adult status, in a real personal relationship to each other. I wonder whether our—at times complete—neglect of this side of the matter is not responsible for some of the hostile reactions which we get from our patients and which we are apt to ascribe to "true transference" only. But these are technically subversive thoughts and ought to be "handled with care" [pp. 618-619].

Fairbairn (1957), whose theoretical and technical orientation differs considerably from Freud's, wrote the following:

The relationship existing between patient and analyst is more important than details of technique; and it would seem to follow that the role of the analyst is not merely to fulfill the dual functions of (1) a screen upon which the patient projects his phantasies, and (2) a colourless instrument of interpretative technique, but that his personality and his motives make a significant contribution to the therapeutic process [p. 59].

It is interesting to observe how the different participants of a panel on "Variations in Classical Psycho-Analytic Technique" (Loewenstein, 1958) dealt with the problem of the nontransference relationship. Loewenstein (1958), Eissler (1958), and Rosenfeld (1958) look askance at any intervention other than interpretation and make no mention of any form of interpersonal relationship other than transference. Bouvet (1958) talks of the need to "manage" the relationship of patient and analyst. A. Reich (1958) describes helping her patient analyze her mother's behavior in order to free the patient from a crippling fixation. Nacht (1958) warns against taking the rule of neutrality and anonymity too rigidly and makes a plea for recognizing situations requiring the analyst's *"presence"* in the analytic situation.

Erikson (1962), pondering the issue of reality and actuality in the psychoanalytic situation, turned his attention to Freud's treatment of Dora in 1905. He raises the question which I would paraphrase as follows: What was it that Dora really needed from Freud that Freud would not or could not give her?

Stone (1967) writes the following:

The analyst is first perceived as a real object, who awakens hope of help, and who offers it, on the basis of his therapeutic competence. This operates in the patient's experience at all levels of integration, from that of actual and immediate perception, evaluation, and response, to the activation of original parental object representations and their cathexes.

This view does place somewhat heavier than usual emphasis on the horizontal coordinate of operations, the conscious and unconscious relation to the analyst as a living and actual object, who becomes invested with imagery, traits, and functions of critical objects of the past. The relationship is to be understood in its dynamic, economic, and adaptive meanings, in its current "structuralized" tenacity, the real and unreal carefully separated from one another [pp. 40, 41].

Roland (1967), emphasizing the need to activate a real reparative object relationship with the patient in order to overcome severe character resistances, quotes a hitherto overlooked contribution of Menaker in which she stated (1942):

It seems to us, however, important to distinguish between that part of the analytic experience which is relived *as* "real" (not to question the genuineness of this experience), and that part which *is* real, that is, which constitutes a direct human relationship between patient and analyst, which has an existence independent of the transference, and which is the medium in which the transference reactions take place [pp. 172, 173].

Finally, I want to quote one sentence from Freud himself which was brought to my attention by Anna Freud after I had already submitted the original draft of this paper. Freud is referring to his relationship to Ferenczi in "Analysis Terminable and Interminable" (1937, p. 222): "Furthermore, he added, not every good relation between an analyst and his subject during and after analysis was to be regarded as a transference; there were also friendly relations which were based on reality and which proved to be viable."

Different as their styles, their theoretical and technical orientations may be, all the authors cited above seem to be in accord with the idea that (1) personal interactions other than transference occur in the course of psychoanalysis, and (2) it is important to differentiate between the transference and the "real" relationship.

WORKING DEFINITIONS

At this point I want to attempt to briefly define the terms transference and the "real" relationship. Transference is the experiencing of feelings, drives, attitudes, fantasies, and defenses toward a person in the present which do not befit that person, but are a repetition of reactions originating in regard to significant persons of early childhood, unconsciously displaced onto figures in the present (Greenson, 1967). The two outstanding characteristics of a transference reaction are: (1) it is an undiscriminating, nonselective repetition of the past, and (2) it is inappropriate, it ignores or distorts reality.

The term "real" relationship is much harder to define. At best I can only describe what I mean by the concept. Like all object relations, it also consists of repetitions from the past; however, it differs from transference in being selective and discriminating in terms of what is repeated. Furthermore, a real relationship is modifiable by internal and external reality. In a real relationship between a husband and wife, for example, the wife may resemble the husband's mother in some bodily feature, but the resemblance does not bring with it all the instinctual and emotional components which were originally bound up with the mother. In addition, the wife will have traits that resemble other people in the past, both remote and recent. Consequently, such a wife becomes a unique entity, free from the fearful and guilt-laden infantile connections to the past. Finally, the real relationship to the wife will be influenceable and modifiable by changes occurring in each individual and the world they live in.

I must add that in all transference reactions there is some germ of reality, and in all relationships there is some element of transference. *All object relationships consist of different admixtures and blendings of real and transference components.* Although transference and real relationship are relative terms, they can and, as I hope to show, should be separated from one another. I also want to specify that the meaning of "real" in real relationship implies (1) the sense of being genuine and not synthetic or artificial, and (2) it also means realistic and not inappropriate or fantastic.

In ordinary usage, the term "real" has been employed for either genuine or realistic. I shall use the term "real relationship" only when I mean both.

Perhaps I can clarify these definitions if I point out that transference reactions are essentially unrealistic and fantastic, but they are felt as genuine, authentic, and sincere. Yet, here again this is only relatively true. Some transference reactions feel more genuine than others. When most of the ego is immersed in the experiencing of the feeling and only little of the rational ego is left untouched, the patient experiences the feeling as genuine. Other transference reactions may be experienced with "tongue in cheek," as though they are a "serious make-believe" (Stone 1967). In such instances, the experiencing ego and the observing ego are more or less of equal strength.

The working alliance, on the other hand, is essentially realistic, but more or less synthetic, artificial. In the analyst, the working alliance becomes part of his therapeutic character and personality, and in that sense it is genuine. But situations do arise when a strong countertransference will make it necessary for the analyst to call forth a therapeutic attitude by a conscious act of will. This state of affairs is even more likely to occur in a patient when he is in the throes of an intense transference reaction.

At this point I find it necessary to clarify the relationship between the working alliance and the real relationship. I described in an earlier paper how the patient and the analyst contribute to the working alliance (Greenson, 1965). The patient must have the capacity to form a relatively reasonable object relationship to the analyst and also fulfill the special requirements of the analytic situation. I also stated that certain transference hopes and longings contribute to the alliance.

As for the analyst, I wrote then that his consistent and unwavering pursuit of insight, as well as his concern and respect for his patient's predicament, contributed to the working alliance. His transference reactions, too, may support the alliance. I want to emphasize that the reliable, enduring core of the working alliance is the "real relationship" between the patient and the analyst, using the term as I defined it, the realistic and genuine relationship. The transference feelings, loving or hateful, from the most infantile to the most mature, may be helpful, but transference is an erratic and treacherous ally.

CLINICAL MATERIAL

It is an impressive clinical finding that in some patients the real relationship remains vaguely in the background and rarely becomes a noticeable issue in their psychoanalytic therapy. In other patients, the real relationship becomes a burning and crucial issue from the beginning to the end of treatment. In part, this may be due to the differences in the specific pathology and therapeutic needs of a given case. The situation is parallel to what one meets with in problems of identity. Patients in whom this issue is in the foreground are those who have had special difficulty in establishing an identity. The role of the real relationship in therapy may be determined by the patient, but also by the therapist's sensitivity or blindness to the issue of the real relationship. The personality or the theoretical orientation of the analyst may be the determining factor.

I shall first present clinical material demonstrating some of the difficulties patients have in dealing with their nontransference reactions to the analyst.

A young man, in his fifth year of analysis, hesitates after I have made an interpretation and then tells me he has something to say which is very difficult for him. He had been about to skip over it when he realized he had been doing just that for years. Taking a deep breath, he said: "You always talk a bit too much. You tend to exaggerate. It would be much easier for me to get mad at you and say you're cock-eyed or wrong or off the point or just not answer. It's terribly hard to say what I mean because I know it will hurt your feelings."

I believe the patient had correctly perceived some traits of mine and it was indeed somewhat painful for me to have them pointed out. I told him he was right on both counts, but I wanted to know why it was harder for him to tell it to me simply and directly as he had just done than to act in an angry fashion. He answered that he knew from experience I would not be upset by an exhibition of temper, since that was obviously his neurosis and I wouldn't be moved by it. Telling me so clearly about my talking too much and exaggerating was a personal criticism, and that would be hurtful. In the past he would have been worried that I might retaliate in some way, but now he knew it was not likely. Besides, he no longer felt my anger would kill him (Greenson, 1967, pp. 217, 218).

Here the difference between transference and nontransference reactions becomes clear. The patient had correctly perceived some characteristics of his analyst's way of working and had also quite realistically predicted that it would be painful for the analyst to have them pointed out. These are nontransference phenomena; they are contemporaneous, appropriate, and realistic. His earlier fantasies about a potentially retaliatory anger that might kill him were historically rooted carry-overs from his childhood anxieties: inappropriate exaggerations, and therefore transference distortions. The patient had developed a good working alliance in relation to his temper outbursts at the analyst, but this alliance could not maintain itself when it came to more realistic criticism. This development occurred only in his fifth year of analysis.

In the example cited the patient tried to hide his realistic perceptions and judgments by resorting to transference distortions. Other patients cling to some of the realistic traits they perceive in the analyst as a screen to ward off the awareness of other realistic traits or transference fantasies. One patient who felt I was annoyed in an hour insisted that it was a transference distortion. She "knew" I was a man of compassion and in good control of my emotions. I asked her what she would feel if I had really been annoyed with her. Only then did she realize how frightened she was of my being angry. She equated it with the rage of her brutal father. This patient tried again and again to keep me a "mirror-type" analyst whose every reaction was mild and benign. She either did not perceive reactions or traits in me which contradicted this or considered her perceptions to be inaccurate.

A male patient "knew" I was against sexual infidelity in marriage. He "knew" it because he felt a good analyst "must be" well analyzed, and if you are well analyzed you have a good sex life and a happy marriage and therefore don't need extramarital affairs. I responded to this somewhat stuffy portrayal of a psychoanalyst with a teasing question something like: "Why do you insist that I'm such a goody-goody?" This led to insight revealing the patient's need to use this image of me as a bulwark for his faltering superego because of his own promiscuous impulses. It also eventually uncovered another picture of me as Zorba the Greek, a man of great passions. In fact, it was the Zorba image he had perceived in a public lecture of mine which made him seek me out as an analyst in the first place. The Zorba image was subsequently camouflaged by other perceptions and transference distortions. Only later did the patient acknowledge that to him I was "really" more of a "Zorba" figure than a "goody-goody."

Lest you feel it is mainly the sexual and hostile reactions which are isolated or denied by the patient, let me cite the following illustration. A young man I sent into analysis with an analyst newly arrived from Europe told me how much he loved the "cute" mistakes in English and the bumbling physical clumsiness of this analyst. I knew the analyst personally and could verify that the young man had made accurate perceptions about him. I therefore asked him if he had brought this up in the analysis, to which he replied: "Hell, no. It's too embarrassing." I told him that it should be brought up, it belonged in the analysis. The young man said he would get around to it "sooner or later." Years later I asked if the cute errors and clumsiness had ever come up during treatment. He sadly said no. It became apparent to both of us at this point that these realistic perceptions and the loving and hostile transference derivatives had never entered his analysis.

I would now like to turn to the analyst's problems in dealing with the real relationship in our patients and ourselves. One source of error is the fact that a transference interpretation is not a neutral designation but our subjective judgment of the patient's behavior, a point Szasz (1963) has stressed. We have to know ourselves and our patient very well to be able to determine whether we are dealing with a transference or a realistic reaction. There is always the possibility that we are blind to some painful characteristic or behavior in ourselves. Furthermore, we may assign different values to certain traits than our patients do. For example, it may be that what I call straightforward speech may be perceived realistically by a patient of a different background as harsh and vulgar. It is not easy or always possible to determine which is correct.

It is important to keep in mind that our patients know us really far less than we know them. Their beliefs and judgments are based on much less evidence than is available to us. Yet, everything we do or say, or don't do or say, from the decor of our office, the magazines in the waiting room, the way we open the door, greet the patient, make interpretations, keep silent, and end the hour, reveals something about our real self, and not only our professional self.

Understandably, we analysts might be tempted to consider as transference manifestations all hurtful remarks made by the patient. In that way, we defend ourselves against recognizing our painful traits or behavior and our faulty interpretations.

I would now like to describe a flagrant example of the neglect of the nontransference relationship. Some years ago, I sent Mrs. E., a young woman I knew socially, into analysis with a psychoanalyst of another city whom I believed to be competently trained and a man of personal integrity. Although I continued my social relationship with Mrs. E., we did not discuss her analysis. About five years from the time I had recommended psychoanalysis to her, we had occasion to talk alone. She told me she had finished her analysis and that she had the greatest respect for psychoanalysis as a therapy and as a science despite the fact that her major symptoms had remained unchanged. I was puzzled and asked Mrs. E. why she had stopped treatment. She replied that, although her analyst was a brilliant man, an impeccable scientist of incorruptible character, she had found the analysis extremely painful from beginning to end. She had hated almost every minute of it. She believed her analyst had tried to help her, but something was wrong, something was missing. For example, she once asked if it were possible to stop the hour ten minutes early because she had an appointment with her child's school teacher. The analyst said nothing, and when she fell silent he repeatedly asked her just to say what came to her mind. He gave no indication that it was permissible for the patient to leave early, so she remained. He behaved in the same way when she occasionally asked for a change in the time for her appointment. He would either remain silent, ask her for associations, or inquire when had she done such things in the past. At the end of such an hour, he would usually interpret that it was her feelings of anger, hostility, or resistance, etc., transferred from some figure in her past, that were responsible for her request, and that would end the discussion. Mrs. E. felt that, although he was right, something was missing. I asked Mrs. E. if she had ever told her analyst of these feelings. She replied that she had, particularly in the beginning. "He only interpreted, he never conceded that my feelings or wishes had some merit. When I complained about it, he would interpret that, too, as transference. I finally gave up. I thought that is how psychoanalysis is supposed to be. I recently spoke to a friend who was analyzed and was struck by how different her experience had been. I know I need more analysis and I want it, but please send me to another kind of person."

No doubt Mrs. E. was an unusually submissive and masochistic patient. Nevertheless, I submit this material as an extreme example of the analyst's neglect of the real relationship between the patient and the therapist. I believe Mrs. E.'s analyst tried to interpret and dig out the original sources of the patient's transference resistances, but he neglected to recognize or acknowledge reality factors or his own contribution to some of the patient's resistances and hostile reactions. By "only interpreting" or "only analyzing," he interfered with the formation of a strong working alliance. His way of working signified to the patient that he was essentially detached and impersonal, there was little indication of concern or compassion (Stone, 1961). As a consequence, the real relationship remained thin and narrow, as did the working alliance and the transference neurosis. I believe that the whole school of analysts which believes that psychoanalytic treatment consists of "only interpreting" is guilty of using transference interpretations as a defense. Some of them seem to interpret the transference so frequently in the course of an hour because they are afraid of the painful affects that they or their patients might otherwise develop. Others of this group ignore the patient's correct and painful perceptions and judgments concerning the analyst and remain silent or pick up some interpretable material, no matter how trivial.

The harmful consequences of such a technique are many. At this point I want to stress three possibilities. By focusing constantly on the patient's transference distortions and ignoring the reality elements, we undermine his self-esteem and make him feel he is always wrong, sick, or crazy, beliefs which he has brought with him into the analysis. By acting as an ignorer of reality, we tempt the patient to live in the outside world as though all of life were lived on a gigantic psychoanalytic couch and people at large were either patients or psychoanalysts. By "only interpreting," we constrict the unfolding of the patient's transference neurosis and limit its development in accordance with our own theoretical biases.

If the patient has made a correct and accurate perception about the analyst, it should be acknowledged some time in that hour or in a subsequent hour. I am not claiming that this acknowledgment should precede or preclude interpretation of the patient's material: that will depend on many different factors. I do maintain that the analyst's confirmation of a patient's correct perception in regard to some trait, fault, or error in himself helps the patient learn to discriminate between reality and fantasy, something all our patients have difficulty with. It also helps break down the patient's infantile wish for us to be omnipotent and omniscient. Furthermore, it can keep the analyst from falling into the God-like conception of himself our work makes so easily possible. Acknowledging the correctness of a patient's perceptions or beliefs helps strengthen the patient's healthy capacity for object relations. Finally, an admission of fault or error indicates honesty, a basic and vital component of a "real relationship."

I have had many patients report to me that when I or their previous analyst responded to a complaint about our person by "only interpreting," we were saying to the patient, in effect, "Your perceptions or judgments are false, distorted, infantile, or unworthy of discussion." This was surely not the analyst's conscious intention, but the failure to acknowledge the correctness of the patient's perception in some way resulted in the patient's feeling humiliated and demeaned. There are analysts who behave as though the discovery of some interpretable unconscious material nullifies the possibility that the patient can also perceive and judge correctly.

Correct perceptions and beliefs can lead to transference reactions or to nontransference reactions or both. Let me illustrate how transference and realistic reactions may appear in an analytic hour. In the second year of his analysis, Mr. C., a 35-year-old sensitive and perceptive writer, begins the hour by attacking his wife verbally for her disorganization, forgetfulness, and irresponsibility, all of which lead him to jealousy fantasies concerning her sexual flirtatiousness with "some third-rate artist." My patient admits his fantasies have little basis in fact, but of late he cannot stop them. Mr. C. then goes on to talk about his wife's analyst, Dr. Z., whom he hates but admires and about whom he also has jealous fantasies. He feels that Dr. Z. considers him a bad husband for Mrs. C. and, further, that Dr. Z. would never tolerate his present behavior if he were in analysis with him. Mr. C. says that I put up with it because: "You are weak and full of shit. You like me, and you are wrong." I point out to the patient that he wants me to be tough like Dr. Z. so that I would control his bad behavior as his harsh father had done. When I am lenient, I become his mother, weak, full of shit, liking him, and wrong.

Mr. C. responds with an attack upon my "wishy-washy" attitudes, my repeatedly saying, "Let's try to understand this behavior," and my willingness to "wait and see." He shouts that he would rather have an answer about what to do, and no interpretations. He imagines Dr. Z. would give him a direct answer. I remain silent.

Mr. C. goes on. He does not trust psychoanalysis. There are no absolute standards for right and wrong. He pauses. Actually, he has been surprised about how well I understand him. He has the feeling, sometimes, that I must be a little bit like him to be so accurate about him. This embarrasses him, and it is probably wrong. Then Mr. C.'s tone changes: "Anyway, you can be fooled. You took me as a patient. You are supposed to be a big-shot analyst, it was so hard to get an appointment with you, and yet you accepted me as a patient. At first, I decided to fool you because I felt you would throw me out if I stopped throwing sand in your eyes. Why *did* you take me as a patient? You must be shit if you chose me. My God, I have felt this toward everybody who has ever liked me."

At this point, I say: "Yes. You felt this way toward your mother, your wife, and now toward me. A mixture of contempt, loving-closeness, and guilt." The patient then adds: "And I admire tough men who frighten me. I know you are not weak. There *is* a difference between warmth and weakness, only I forget sometimes. Now I recall something you have often told me: that I am afraid of warmth. It will make me like you too much, and I will become too dependent on you. I guess I am really more afraid of that than of the tough guys."

I intervene and tell the patient that I feel his last point is right. He was much more afraid of the warm me than he was of me as tough Dr. Z. He wishes I would be tough, and then he could fight me and keep me at a distance. Loving me made him vulnerable, dependent, and also full of jealousy. Mr. C. replies that he wished I would not use the word love, it made him feel squeamish: "But I know you. That is probably why you used it." He pauses, reflects and adds: "I suppose you are the third-rate artist I am jealous of."

I have chosen this clinical fragment to demonstrate how interwoven the transference relationship and the real relationship can be in a given hour. The main lines of the transference are quite obvious, and I shall condense my remarks. Mr. C. is jealous of me, a third-rate artist. He also fears and admires me as a tough, harsh analyst. He would like me to act the role of his severe father and control him. But he knows I will not, and then I become weak, full of shit, wrong, and "wishy-washy" like his mother and himself. From this point, Mr. C. goes on to speak of how I am a fool and a shit to have chosen him as a patient. He also recognizes how afraid he is to love and need me. It seems clear that all the above reactions are for the most part transference distortions.

In addition to these transference reactions, however, Mr. C. also indicates some realistic awareness of me as a person to whom he is relating. He knows that I like him, that I keep trying to understand him, and that I am persistent and patient. He is also aware that I can be fooled, I can be wrong, and at times harsh. Yet he senses I have a good grasp of his underlying feelings and impulses, I must resemble him in some way; I am warm, not weak, and also not afraid of upsetting him by choosing words which get to the heart of the matter. Furthermore, he also realizes that psychoanalysis has no absolute standards for right and wrong. I submit that these are not distortions, but accurate perceptions and judgments based on his observations of me and my work during the 18 months of treatment. They coexist with the transference reactions and do not negate them.

Correct perceptions may lead at first to realistic reactions and later to transference distortions. Let me turn now to another patient in whom the real relationship came into focus unusually early in the treatment. The main reason for this was that I had great doubts about the patient's motivation and suitability for psychoanalytic treatment which impelled me to confront him in one particular hour. Mr. D., a businessman in his mid-fifties, consulted me at the instigation of his young girl friend who told him he was sick because he was unable to commit himself to anybody or any activity he liked, for any length of time. His only loyalty was to business and to making money. The preliminary interviews confirmed the girl's main findings, and I was able to demonstrate to Mr. D. that this was a lifelong pattern which prevented him from enjoying a rich and full life. He seemed eager to embark upon treatment, and although I found him bright, psychologically minded, youthful in spirit, and interesting, I still wondered how much of his motivation was essentially a wish to please his lady friend and would evaporate when and if the love affair disintegrated or the hostile transference came into the foreground.

During one session in the third month of analysis, Mr. D. spent a good part of the hour talking about various people he knows and kept coming back to the theme that people give one impression upon first acquaintance and later turn out to be quite different. He included in this portrayal his recent girl friend, two unhappy marriage partners, several friendships, and a few hostile business partnerships. He ended this part of the session by stating: "You can't judge people by appearances, you never get to know anyone until you've lived with them." This prompted me to ask: "You have been living with me for three months now, what do you think of me?" Note that I did not ask him for free association, nor did I interpret that he was talking about me, the more traditional approaches. I wanted to highlight his nontransference reactions because of my concern for the working alliance. Although Mr. D. had brought into the analysis several fantasies and dreams about me as a transference figure he feared, resented, and idealized, he was taken aback by my question. He was silent a few moments, coughed uneasily, and then hesitantly replied: "When I first met you, you seemed very competent and sure of yourself, a little cocky perhaps, but straightforward. Now I would also describe you as essentially a kind person, but I still think you are too outspoken at times." The patient paused and then jokingly added: "Well, how did I do? Did I guess right? Or are you going to tell me this is also what you call transference?" I

replied that I would not answer him directly, that we would first have to explore the evidence on which he based his assumptions. Only then could we determine whether his reactions were realistic or transference.

Mr. D. was quite obsessional and very organized; thus, in the next several hours we uncovered material which explained how he had arrived at his opinions and attitudes. I am deleting other data in order to clarify my point. Mr. D. brought out that in the first sessions he found my approach to his complicated problems rather astute and my explanations very understandable. His previous sporadic exploratory experiences with psychiatrists had left him confused and unconvinced. Above all, he was surprised that I greeted him in my shirtsleeves and that I have no diplomas on my walls. This he interpreted to mean that I must be very sure of my professional status.

Mr. D. continued to pursue the question I had set before him. He felt I was generous because of my ample explanations and because I often permitted sessions to continue a few minutes beyond the 50-minute period. He considered this last trait poor business organization but good public relations. The patient did feel I was too outspoken and cocky because I talked of hate so readily, and besides I tended to use obscene words like "shit" and "fuck" more often than he considered to be in the best of taste. It was true he used such words upon occasion, but he believed it was not appropriate for a distinguished professional man.

In the course of the ensuing analysis, Mr. D. developed many different transference and nontransference feelings and attitudes toward me, some of which were triggered by the above-mentioned traits he had so early correctly detected.

Let me cite a few examples: What he once saw as competence and self-assurance, he later experienced as smugness and arrogance. My straightforwardness, outspokenness, and cockiness became the source of fantasies of me as vulgar and exhibitionistic, using interpretations as a brutal form of shock therapy and one-up-manship. The generosity he once admired turned into contempt and disgust for my homosexual seductiveness and my Jewish motherliness. What he once considered patience was only a façade for incompetence, slothfulness, senility, and timidity.

Mr. D., of course, experienced different varieties of love, dependency, and trust, as well as hostility, hate, and fear toward me. Sometimes the former took precedence, sometimes the latter; at other times both went on simultaneously. But Mr. D. did not remain in his analysis because his loving transference "neutralized" his hostile transference. I contend that in addition to his transference feelings, Mr. D. also had a real relationship with me which I think kept him in the analysis and which enabled us to work effectively.

The importance of the real relationship can be seen in the rigors of working through. A patient will break off an analysis of long standing when driven by a sudden eruption of an intense hostile transference. This may be understood as a failure to make the correct interpretations. Yet I have made many false interpretations which my patients knew or sensed, and they did not run away. The decisive factor was the relative strength of the real relationship existing between us, how much genuine and realistic liking and respect there was between us. Again I want to stress that the real relationship does not have to be verbalized or conspicuous, but it must be present to a sufficient degree for the analytic situation to endure the long and painful process of working through. A patient or an analyst will consider interrupting treatment if either realizes some basic aspect is not being properly understood. But this decision will be arrived at mutually. Unexpected crises or failures in psychoanalysis are the result of both incorrect interpretations and a failure in the real relationship. By and large, technical errors may cause pain, but they are usually repairable; human errors are much harder to remedy.

I would add that there are many indications which signal a change in the nontransference relationship. One typical clinical sign of a change in the patient's real relationship to the analyst is when a patient who has been coming to your office for months or years "sees" something for the first time. A patient in his fourth year of analysis will suddenly ask as he enters the treatment room, "Is that a new chair?" That chair was there, unchanged, from the first day he came to see me. What changed was something in his awareness of me and of himself as real persons.

Formulations, Hypotheses, and Conclusions

At this point, I would like to state some additional formulations and hypotheses which I have derived from my own clinical experience and the writings of others. In the course of a successful analysis, a patient will experience a wide range of *transference reactions* to his analyst from very primitive to quite mature, in terms of love, hate, sex, and aggression. In addition,

the patient will also experience realistic and genuine reactions toward the analyst and form a real relationship. I believe this must be present, to some extent from the beginning, in order for the patient to "get into" analytic treatment. All the qualities of the patient, realistic and unrealistic, genuine and synthetic, will play a role in determining the development and course of the transference and the real relationship. Intelligence, sensitivity, humor, empathy, education, temperament, and taste all play a part in shaping the transference and nontransference reactions. I believe all of this is true, albeit unequally, for both the patient and the psychoanalyst.

I furthermore believe that all patients have transference reactions, but only those who have the capacity for forming a real relationship to the analyst are analyzable. I contend that borderline and psychotic patients are analyzable only if and when they have the ability to form a real relationship to their analyst. (For a contradictory point of view see, above all, Rosenfeld, 1965.) In my opinion, most of them require preparatory therapy which consists essentially of *building* an object relationship. The reader is urged to refer to the writings on severely regressed adult patients by Federn (1952), Winnicott (1955, 1965), Fairbairn (1957, 1958), Wexler (1951, 1952, 1960), and Searles (1965). With regard to symbiotic or autistic children, see Mahler (1965) and Bettelheim (1963) and for borderline and neurotic children, Anna Freud (1965).

My clinical experience leads me to believe that the final resolution of the transference neurosis depends to a great extent on the transference neurosis being replaced by a real relationship. I do not share the traditional psychoanalytic point of view that interpretation alone can resolve the transference neurosis. Interpretation has to be supplemented by a realistic and genuine relationship to the person of the analyst, limited though it may be, for the transference neurosis to be replaced. This last subject deserves more elaboration but exceeds the boundaries of this presentation.

These deliberations concerning the importance and the role of the nontransference relationship between patient and analyst imply a significant reevaluation of some of the theory and technique of psychoanalytic therapy. I have only hinted at some of the possibilities in the clinical part of this paper. This will be pursued further and in greater detail when time and space permit.

I want to conclude this discussion by referring to the question of selecting certain therapeutic elements in accordance with the diagnostic category of a case (A. Freud, 1965). Most of our neurotic patients come to us with a mixed clinical picture. We ought to offer them the broadest range of therapeutic possibilities and not limit the changes of therapy to any single factor. I believe that "only interpreting" or "only analyzing" is insufficient for most of our patients.

REFERENCES

Bettelheim, B. (1963), *The Empty Fortress*. Glencoe, Illinois: Free *Press*.

Bouvet, M. (1958), Technical Variation and the Concept of Distance. *Internat. J. Psycho-Anal.*, 39:211–221.

Eissler, K. R. (1958), Remarks on Some Variations in Psycho-Analytical Technique. *Internat. J. Psycho-Anal.*, 39:222–229.

Erikson, E. H. (1962), Reality and Actuality. *J. Amer. Psychoanal. Assn.*, 3:451–474.

Fairbairn, W. R. D. (1957), Freud, the Psychoanalytic Method and Mental Health. *Brit. J. Med. Psychol.* 30:53–62.

———(1958), On the Nature and Aims of Psychoanalytic Treatment. *Internat. J. Psycho-Anal.*, 7:374–385.

Federn, P. (1952), *Ego Psychology and the Psychoses*. New York: Basic Books.

Freud, A. (1954), The Widening Scope of Indications for Psychoanalysis: Discussion. *J. Amer. Psychoanal. Assn.*, 2:607–620.

———(1965), *Normality and Pathology in Childhood*. New York: International Universities Press.

Freud, S. (1937), Analysis Terminable and Interminable. *Standard Edition*, 23:211–253. London: Hogarth Press, 1964.

Gitelson, M. (1952), The Emotional Position of the Analyst in the Psychoanalytic Situation. *Internat. J. Psycho-Anal.*, 33:1–10.

Greenson, R. (1965), The Working Alliance and the Transference Neurosis. *Psychoanal. Quart.*, 34:155–181.

———(1967), *The Technique and Practice of Psychoanalysis*, I. New York: International Universities Press.

Knight, R. P. (1953), Borderline States. In: *Psychoanalytic Psychiatry and Psychology*, ed. R. P. Knight & C. R. Friedman. New York: International Universities Press, pp. 97–109.

Loewald, H. (1960), On the Therapeutic Action of Psycho-Analysis. *Internat. J. Psycho-Anal.*, 41:16–33.

Loewenstein, R. M. (1958), Remarks on Some Variations in Psycho-Analytic Technique. *Internat. J. Psycho-Anal.*, 39:202–210.

Mahler, M. S. (1965), On the Significance of the Normal Separation-Individuation Phase. In: *Drives, Affects, Behavior*, ed. M. Schur. New York: International Universities Press, pp. 161–169.

Menaker, E. (1942), The Masochistic Factor in the Psychoanalytic Situation. *Psychoanal. Quart.*, 6:171–186.

Nacht, S. (1958), Variations in Technique. *Internat. J. Psycho-Anal.*, 39:235–237.

Reich, A. (1958), A Special Variation of Technique. *Internat. J. Psycho-Anal.*, 39:230–234.

Roland, A. (1967), The Reality of the Psycho-Analytic Relationship and Situation in Handling of Transference-Resistance, *Internat. J. Psycho-Anal.*, 48:504–510.

Rosenfeld, H. A. (1958), Contribution to the Discussion on the Variations in Classical Technique. *Internat. J. Psycho-Anal.*, 39:238–239.

———(1965), *Psychotic States: A Psychoanalytic Approach*. New York: International Universities Press.

Searles, H. F. (1965), Collected Papers on Schizophrenia and Related Subjects. New York: International Universities Press.

Stone, L. (1961), *The Psychoanalytic Situation*. New York: International Universities Press.

———(1967), The Psychoanalytic Situation and Transference: Postscript to an Earlier Communication. *J. Amer. Psychoanal. Assn.*, 15:3–58.

Szasz, T. S. (1963), The Concept of Transference. *Internat. J. Psycho-Anal.*, 44:432–443.

Wexler, M. (1951), The Structural Problem in Schizophrenia. *Internat. J. Psycho-Anal.*, 32:157–166.

———(1952), The Structural Problem in Schizophrenia: The Role of the Internal Object. In: *Psychotherapy with Schizophrenics*, ed. E. B. Brody & F. C. Redlich. New York: International Universities Press.

———(1960), Hypotheses Concerning Ego Deficiency in Schizophrenia. In: *The Out-Patient Treatment of Schizophrenia*, ed. S. S. Scher & H. R. Davis. New York: Grune and Stratton, pp. 33–45.

Winnicott, D. W. (1955), Metapsychological and Clinical Aspects of Regression within the Psychoanalytical Set-up. *Collected Papers*. New York: Basic Books, pp. 278–294.

———(1965), A Clinical Study of the Effect of a Failure of the Average Expectable Environment on a Child's Mental Functioning. *Internat. J. Psycho-Anal.*, 46:81–87.

Zetzel, E. R. (1956), Current Concepts of Transference. *Internat. J. Psycho-Anal.*, 37:369–376.

9

BEYOND TRANSFERENCE AND INTERPRETATION

RALPH R. GREENSON

EDITOR'S NOTE

Another in the series of investigations by Greenson of the patient's nontransference responses, this paper attempts to deal with aspects of the analytic interaction that lie beyond transference for the patient and interpretation for the analyst. Greenson sees considerable importance in the analyst's expression of his human qualities and advocates deviations in the basic interpretive stance under a variety of conditions. Prompted by his observations of insensitivities among analysts, Greenson's position in this respect is characteristic of most writings in this area by classical psychoanalysts (see Part VII).

This paper also includes a discussion of the analyst's errors and their technical management. Stress is placed on direct rather than implicit acknowledgment of such errors—a point with which I later took issue (Langs 1975b, 1976a,b, 1978b). Greenson concludes this paper with a consideration of the dangers of noninterpretive interventions, a discussion based mainly on an appreciation of the patient's realistic needs and responses.

In this paper I shall attempt to clarify some of the controversial issues raised in previous publications on the 'real' or 'non-transference' relationship between the patient and the psychoanalyst (see Greenson, 1967; Greenson & Wexler, 1969, 1970). I shall also try to demonstrate the importance of interventions other than interpretation as a necessary ingredient for the creation and maintenance of a productive analytic atmosphere. These statements are not meant to cast doubt upon the central role of the interpretation of transference and resistance for psychoanalytic therapy. However, I, along with a growing number of other psychoanalysts, contend that the technique of 'only interpreting', and the belief that all interactions between patient and analyst are transference phenomena, stifle or distort the development of the patient's transference neurosis and block his capacity to develop realistic object-relationships. 'Reality-relatedness proceeds always a bit ahead of, and makes possible, the progressive evolution and resolution of the transference . . .' (Searles, 1965). I shall use clinical examples to illustrate these points.

AN EXTRAORDINARY EVENT IN THE PATIENT'S LIFE

A 27-year-old woman, Mrs K., sought analysis because she felt out of things, numb, 'gone', like a zombie. She had been raised by a warm and promiscuous alcoholic mother, who married four times and never stayed married longer than three years. Mrs K. had recently married an older man, and it was the failure of her supposedly happy

Reprinted from *International Journal of Psycho-Analysis* 53:213–217, 1972.

marriage to resolve her inner numbness that motivated her to come for psychoanalytic treatment. In the third year of her analysis Mrs K. became pregnant and shortly thereafter her husband unexpectedly died. We analysed at great length the many anxieties stirred up by the thought of bringing a fatherless baby into the world. We also analysed how the foetus inside became good or bad, beautiful or deformed, destructive or destroyed. This depended on her internal body image, which in turn was determined by her transference *and* non-transference relationship to me.

When Mrs K. delivered a healthy baby girl she telephoned me from the hospital. I congratulated her, we chatted a few minutes about the delivery and I made an appointment to visit her in the hospital. I felt the unexpected loss of her husband and her past history made this a necessary and fitting act on my part. The patient's delight was visible when I arrived, but it was not long before she told me she also felt apprehensive and depressed. We then talked briefly but analytically about her anxieties and depression. I told Mrs K. I would visit her again the following week in her home, which I did, with approximately the same results, pleasure, anxiety and depression, emotions she could control and talk about. The baby was healthy, well formed and a good feeder, which reassured the patient.

When Mrs K. resumed analysis a month later, she often remarked how much my visits meant to her. She had always 'known' I was basically a kind person, but visiting her, giving up my lunch hour or work, added a sense of conviction about me as a humane person. From this point on, Mrs K. was able to re-experience the terror of being abandoned, the longing, rage and depression concerning her unreliable mother, with an intensity she had never dared let herself feel before. The usual starting point for these intense reactions were dreams and associations about me abandoning or rescuing her or her baby. Thus my non-interpretative actions in an extraordinary situation in a patient's life gave her a sense of security in her relationship to me which encouraged her to allow herself to have intense and regressive transference reactions that could be effectively analysed.

I want to contrast this with the case of a young analyst, Dr A., I supervised, who told me of an hour in which his patient unexpectedly appeared in the waiting room, swathed in bandages over his head and one arm. I asked the candidate: 'So, what did you do?' He smiled serenely, I thought. 'I just said hello as usual, then I sat behind the couch and waited. The patient was silent so I finally asked

him what was going on in his mind, but he remained very resistant and refused to talk.' At this point, I said, with difficulty, 'And what may have been going on in his mind?' He was sure, Dr A. replied, that the patient was thinking about the accident. It turned out that the evening before, while waiting for a light to change, he had been hit from the rear and thrown against the windscreen and steering wheel of his car. The patient was taken to an emergency hospital and given first aid for lacerations of the forehead and scalp and a dislocated elbow. He was furious with the man who had banged into him, and he hoped to collect a good deal of insurance. Dr A. was, he told me, puzzled that throughout the entire hour the patient seemed reluctant to express himself. At first he wondered if it were due to a mild brain concussion and then he thought the patient might be experiencing a transference reaction to him, because he sits behind the patient and perhaps the patient feels Dr A.'s interpretations also bang into him unexpectedly and cause pain. He suggested this to the patient, who remained uncommunicative.

I put it to the young analyst that though his interpretation may have been correct he may also have added to his patient's anger by his own unresponsiveness from the moment he first saw the bandaged man in the waiting room. Dr A. recalled he was startled at the sight of the patient, but did his best to suppress any sign of it. 'I did not want to show him I was upset, I did not want to upset him, and besides, I did not want to disturb the transference relationship.' I told the young analyst that I felt that the least he could have done was to permit himself to show that he was startled and also that he was concerned. It did not have to be done in words. His behaving as if nothing extraordinary had happened must have meant to the patient that the analyst either did not care or was terrified himself.

We spent a good deal of time discussing my belief that to preserve a patient's analysability, you must give indications of compassion for the patient when extraordinary or massive misfortunes befall him. We had plenty of time to discuss this hour because the patient had cancelled the remainder of the hours of that week. When he eventually did return, the analyst was able to confirm the fact that the patient had felt Dr A.'s reactions were inhuman, he had felt humiliated, hurt, and angry, but he did persuade himself to continue because, 'Maybe analysts *have* to behave that way . . . they are programmed that way.' This analysis never progressed to any great depth.

These two examples, I hope, illustrate the importance of the analyst's non-interpretative interventions and spontaneous human reactions to the patient undergoing extraordinary life situations. I would behave in similar ways if a patient were seriously ill, if there were a death of somebody close, if an important examination were passed or failed, etc. These reactions do not have to be put into words or actions, nor do they have to be intense. In comparison to the analyst's usual behaviour, ordinary responsiveness will stand out. For example, an analyst can express his sympathy when his patient reports flunking the bar examination, an accomplishment he had set his heart on, by merely allowing himself to sigh audibly. I would follow a similar policy with less dramatic events as well. I do not greet a patient after a six-week vacation as though I had seen him yesterday. Nor would I end the last hour before a lengthy separation as though I would see the patient tomorrow. The analyst's refusal to express any feelings may reveal him to be, or may make him seem, unfeeling or out of contact, which blocks the development of a trusting relationship and a productive analytic atmosphere.

Dealing with Errors in Technique and Lapses in Behaviour

Technical errors and behaviour lapses occur too frequently in every analysis to be completely omitted from this presentation. I shall limit myself, however, only to a few remarks and the briefest examples. Errors in technique may be caused by misunderstanding the goings on in a patient due to insufficient or faulty knowledge. This may be due to inexperience, ignorance or the clinging to a narrow set of theoretical beliefs and technical practices which are harmful to a given patient. Placing an acutely frightened paranoid or suicidal patient on a couch and sitting behind him silently would be an example of such an error. Unrecognized and uncontrolled countertransference reactions are another important source of errors. They may lead to technical mistakes or to behaving badly in human terms. Let me illustrate some of these points briefly.

I was analysing a young depressed divorced woman, Mrs L., for several years when I noticed to my surprise and dismay, that I always gave her some five to seven extra minutes. I do that occasionally with all patients because I do not like to interrupt either their or my flow of thought. In the case of Mrs L. it was a regular occurrence. Once I became aware of it I was determined to be more exact about the time, but without stopping the hour abruptly.

I also decided to do some self-analysis of my feelings for her. Mrs L. soon brought in material indicating her discontent with me and eventually said she felt I was giving her less time. I said she was right and told her I had recently become aware of giving her extra time and I considered that to be a mistake on my part. She was very curious about the reasons for this. I replied that giving her extra time had not been deliberate, but that I believed my personal unconscious reasons did not belong in her analysis. Then we analysed her many fantasies to my previous behaviour as well as to my asserting a right to privacy and to the inequality of the analytic situation.

In this case, I recognized and analysed a countertransference reaction and brought it under control. I did not bring it up in the analysis until the patient herself reacted to my change in behaviour. Then I admitted my error but did not burden or gratify her by revealing the unconscious determinants for my actions. The analysis proceeded more turbulently but more productively onwards. If I had changed my behaviour and only insisted on analysing her reactions without acknowledging my countertransference behaviour, I would be behaving like many parents do to a child. In effect, I would be saying, 'My behaviour is none of your business', or 'How dare you discuss me'.

One morning at 9 a.m. I came to my office door and found a note from my patient saying he had been there at 8, waited a half hour and left. I realized I had forgotten the appointment. I phoned the patient, apologized and told him I would see him the next day. The next day he attempted to deny his hurt feelings, anger and his jealousy fantasies, but in a short while he was able to express them with a good deal of intensity. When I asked him how he felt when I phoned to apologize, he said: 'That was very decent of you; in fact, I was ready to forget the whole thing, but you wouldn't let me.' Later on he added that he felt apologizing was beneath the dignity of a psychoanalyst. It took away the mystery and the magic. This was then analysed.

I believe it is right to apologize to a patient when your behaviour has been unnecessarily hurtful. Not to do so is to be disrespectful and impolite. Yet I have heard of psychoanalysts who have fallen asleep during a patient's hour and when awakened by the patient, remained silent or interpreted the event as a result of the patient's wish to put the analyst in a stupor. I believe the apology for behaving badly should be made before attempting any interpretations. Analysing before apologizing may be correctly perceived by the patient as an attempt to obscure or minimize the analyst's responsibility for his lapse in behaviour. I have found that apologizing does not interfere with the therapeutic process. On the contrary, failure to be forthright in such matters injects an element of hypocrisy and oppressiveness in the analytic situation.

IMPORTANT EVENTS IN THE COURSE OF THE ANALYSIS

I am referring here to the use of non-interpretative interventions when significant changes occur in the patient during the analysis. I believe that it is important to acknowledge or affirm that the patient has made an important step forward or backward in his struggle with his neurotic conflicts. I also acknowledge the patient's ability to perceive and judge correctly. This can be done in words or by tone, or woven into an interpretation, or by repeating the patient's discovery, etc. The following is a brief example.

For years, my patient, Mr Z., had expressed contempt and envy for his uncle Ben. He also despised his uncle's wife and was convinced theirs was a miserable marriage. I had tried for a long time to interpret from his material that perhaps underneath all these emotions, Mr Z. had had a wish to be loved by his uncle and that his contempt and envy had arisen only after he had felt rebuffed and rejected by his uncle. I also showed him how this was parallel to his reactions to me. His typical attitude for years had been: 'Who needs them', or, 'Who needs you', a denial of his infantile dependent yearning for love. The patient saw the parallel intellectually but could not feel it. Mr Z. began an hour some weeks after the last such interpretation by telling me that he had made a valuable discovery. At a family gathering, and after a few drinks, he felt a sudden surge of love and closeness towards his uncle Ben. He avoided close contact with him until he felt the effects of the alcohol had worn off. Then Mr Z. approached his uncle and engaged him in a conversation that lasted several hours. He was amazed to find how interesting and bright his uncle was and above all how warmly he felt towards him. The friendly conversation felt like being hugged and admired. Furthermore, when his uncle's wife entered their little group he realized how considerate and loving his uncle and aunt were to each other. It dawned on him then that he had distorted his evaluation of their marriage because he had felt like an outsider with them. Whenever he felt left out, people who were 'in'

became despicable, hypocritical and worthless. Mr Z. added, 'That is my usual angry defensive front, which I know chases people away from me and ends up creating the terrible loneliness I now hate.'

This was an important set of insights and I wanted Mr Z. to know that I realized it. I replied something as follows: 'Once you were able to recognize that underneath all the hateful feelings for your uncle, you really wanted to be loved by him, then you could allow yourself to make other important discoveries. Your uncle is a bright and interesting man and not a boor, and he does have a good relationship to his wife.' Mr Z. responded quickly: 'My aunt has her faults, but she is devoted to my uncle and she is quite attractive.' Then he drifted on to material of an oedipal nature which was new in this context.

I am using this example to illustrate the value of affirming the importance of a patient's insights. Too often we only speak when we can interpret some distortion in the patient's fantasies or behaviour. Acknowledgement of a good piece of insight on the patient's part encourages him to do more analytic work on his own, to work things through. It also fosters his independence and reminds him, *and us,* that he is not only made up of neurotic and infantile components. Such confirmations further his healthy identification with the analytic attitude of his analyst.

It is one of the vocational hazards of psychoanalysts to fall into the trap of habitually committing one-upmanship with one's patients. The overriding importance of interpretation tends to blur our awareness that by constantly confronting the patient with our discoveries of his unconscious distortions we may be repeating a damaging part of the patient's past relationship to his parents. As the patient's transference neurosis often makes him excessively submissive, he may yield to our interventions rather than cope with them. The analyst's constant pursuit of new derivatives of the neurotic conflicts may make him underestimate the importance of acknowledging the patient's budding capacities and accomplishments. Too often psychoanalysis assumes the nature of a contest between adversaries. We tend to forget the inequalities of the analytic situation. The patient is asked to reveal all of himself, the analyst is trained to expose as little of his personal self as he comfortably can. To be sure, we do not want our personality traits to intrude upon the patient's transference reactions; but we sometimes seem to use non-responsiveness and interpretations because they are safer and easier for us, rather than best for the patient.

I want to conclude this presentation with a few words about the dangers of permitting one's emotional responses, humanitarian concerns and reality considerations into the analytic situation. I have not stressed this aspect because traditional psychoanalytic training has always emphasized the hazards of not behaving as a relatively anonymous blank screen.

Visiting Mrs K. in the hospital led at first to her idealizing me as a saintly figure, self-sacrificing and extraordinarily compassionate. I had to repeatedly point out how exaggerated her reactions were, how they permitted her to indulge in pleasureful closeness fantasies and finally how she used them as a defence against her hostile feelings. My behaviour had made the demonstrability of the transference distortions *temporarily* more difficult, but her dreams and my repeated interpretations did lead to her being able to experience the childhood rage and terror I have described earlier.

Admitting technical errors or apologizing for lapses in behaviour can mislead a patient into believing the analytic situation is one between two equals. Some may construe this to mean that we are now friends in the conventional social sense. It then becomes necessary to point out that, however equal we may be in certain ways, in fact the patient may be my superior in some, nevertheless, in the psychoanalytic situation he is the patient and relatively unknowing and I am the expert, my errors notwithstanding.

Acknowledging that a patient has made a valuable insight often seduces the patient into attempting to make immediate interpretations of his own material. He becomes a 'junior psychoanalyst', a caricature of a working alliance. This has to be demonstrated and interpreted so that the analysis does not deteriorate into an educational seminar or a guessing game. Tact is required because we do not want to crush the patient's healthy wish to do some of the analytic work himself.

There is much more to be said about the dangers of non-interpretative interventions, but if the analyst is aware of the possible side effects of what he is doing, the patient's distortions are analysable and do not permanently interfere with the analytic process.

I hope the clinical examples in this paper have illustrated that civility towards the patient, compassion for his plight, respect for him as a human being, recognition of his achievements, and the acknowledgement of our own lapses when they become visible to the patient, are vital ingredients for a productive psychoanalytic atmosphere. These elements are beyond transference and interpretation, and are more difficult if not impossible to teach. They should not need to be taught. They should, however, be recognized as essential components of therapeutic psychoanalysis.

Acknowledgements

I am indebted to Milton Wexler, Nathan Leites and Alfred Goldberg for many helpful suggestions.

References

Greenson, R. R. (1967). *The Technique and Practice of Psychoanalysis*. New York: Int. Univ. Press.

Greenson, R. R. & Wexler, M. (1969). The non-transference relationship in the psychoanalytic situation. *Int. J. Psycho-Anal.* 50, 27–39.

Greenson, R. R. & Wexler, M. (1970). Discussion of 'The non-transference relationship in the psycho-analytic situation'. *Int. J. Psycho-Anal.* 51, 143–150.

Searles, H. F. (1965). *Collected Papers on Schizophrenia and Related Subjects*. New York: Int. Univ. Press.

The interested reader is advised to refer to the more comprehensive bibliography in the Greenson & Wexler paper of 1969.

10

THE PATIENT AS THERAPIST
TO HIS ANALYST

HAROLD F. SEARLES

EDITOR'S NOTE

Harold Searles stands prominent among the handful of analysts who have written innovatively over an extended period of time on the analytic relationship and interaction (see Searles 1965). The present paper is the culmination and crystallization of one important aspect of his extensive, careful, and quite unique explorations of the nontransference component of the patient's relationship with the analyst. Searles shows a remarkable sensitivity to the patient's unconscious perceptions and introjections of the analyst's valid and disturbed functioning, and of his sound and unsound unconscious communications. This serves Searles well in defining the dimensions of the nontransference sphere, and in discovering aspects almost totally neglected by other writers to this day.

In this paper, Searles convincingly and elaborately describes the patient's nonpathological unconscious strivings toward curing the analyst, an aspect of the therapeutic relationship first defined by Little (1951) and later studied by myself (Langs 1975a, 1976a,b, 1978a,b). While acknowledging the possibility of the admixture of transference-based elements, Searles focuses here on the mechanisms and genetics of the patient's valid attempts to cure the analyst; he shows a remarkable appreciation for the patient's nonpathological functioning.

This is a moving paper in many ways, and can serve as an important means of developing an appreciation for the scope of the patient's unconscious constructive functioning within the analytic relationship, most especially of his benevolence toward the analyst. While analysts were long delayed in acknowledging the patient's actual harmful intentions toward the analyst (see Part I, chapter 6), they were even more recalcitrant in identifying the patient's genuine curative efforts on behalf of both participants; to the present, these strivings have been acknowledged by only a handful of analytic writers. The present paper contributes, then, to a fuller appreciation of the actualities of the analytic experience for patient and analyst alike.

This paper is devoted to the hypothesis that innate among man's most powerful strivings toward his fellow men, beginning in the earliest years and even earliest months of life, is an essentially psychotherapeutic striving. The tiny percentage of human beings who devote their professional careers to the practice of psychoanalysis or psychotherapy are only giving explicit expression to a therapeutic devotion which all human beings share. As for the appreciably larger percentage of human beings who become patients in psychoanalysis or psychotherapy, I am suggesting here not merely that the patient wants to give therapy to, as well as receive therapy from, his doctor; my hypothesis has to do with something far more fundamental than that. I am hypothesizing that the patient *is ill because, and to the degree that,* his own psychotherapeutic strivings have been subjected to such vicissitudes that they have been rendered inordinately intense, frustrated of fulfillment or even acknowledgement, admixed therefore with unduly intense components of hate, envy, and competitiveness; and subjected, therefore, to repression. In transference terms, the patient's illness expresses his unconscious attempt to cure the doctor.

When I suggest that the patient is ill because of the developmental vicissitudes of this particular striving, from among the various emotional strivings which comprise the human affective equipment, I am putting the matter, of course, too simply. It is well-known that any neurotic or psychotic symptom is determined by a multiplicity of causes. I wish here to highlight a theme—a determinant of neurosis and psychosis—which would be erased by too many qualifications; therefore, I do, indeed, assert that *I know of no other determinant of psychological illness which compares, in etiologic importance, with this one.*

There is admittedly, at a glance, a jarring note of contrivance, of artificiality, about suggesting that a human infant can be viewed as an intended psychotherapist. It is more congenial to think in terms of human beings' love, or nascent capacities to develop love, for one another and of their desire to help the other to fulfill his or her human, psychological potentialities. I am endeavoring, of course, to be more specific and explicit than that, and above all I am focusing upon the situation of psychoanalytic therapy, wishing to highlight both the irony and the technical importance of the (to my mind) fact that the more ill a patient is, the more does his successful treatment require that he become, and be implicitly

Reprinted from *Tactics and Techniques in Psychoanalytic Therapy, Vol. II: Countertransference,* ed. Peter Giovacchini, pp. 95–151. New York: Jason Aronson, 1975.

acknowledged as having become, a therapist to his officially designated therapist, the analyst.

Parenthetically, throughout this paper henceforth I shall use the terms "therapist" and "analyst" interchangeably—a dubious procedure in a paper about this particular subject but necessary, in my opinion, to facilitate the exposition. I do not forget that the analyst, unlike the patient, has equipped himself with psychoanalytic training, and I shall touch later upon some of the difference this makes as regards their respective abilities to utilize effectively their mutually powerful, basically human, therapeutic strivings. At this juncture I wish to mention, as regards the special case of the patient who is himself a psychoanalyst or is acquiring psychoanalytic training, that I have done or am doing by now a considerable number of training analyses, and have found that, for the purposes of this paper, the therapeutic strivings at work in each of these patients, powerful as they are, are no more so than I have found in my nontraining analysands.

Later I shall briefly discuss the relatively scanty existing literature about this subject. At the moment, it is fair to say that psychoanalytic literature is written with the assumption that the analyst is healthy and therefore does not need psychological help from the patient, who is ill and is therefore in need of psychological help from, and unable to give such help to, the analyst. My own training analysis was a highly classical one and I emerged from it markedly less ill than I had been at the beginning; but it is a source of lasting pain to me that the analyst, like each of my parents long before, maintained a high degree of unacknowledgment of my genuine desire to be helpful to him.

In doing psychoanalytic therapy and in supervision of such work on the part of colleagues, I have found over and over that stalemates in treatment, when explored sufficiently, involve the analyst's receiving currently a kind of therapeutic support from the patient of which both patient and analyst have been unconscious. Thus ironically and, in the instances when this *status quo* does not become resolved, one can say indeed tragically, in those very instances wherein the analyst is endeavoring most anguishedly and unsuccessfully to help the patient to resolve the tenacious symptom, or the tenaciously neurotic or psychotic *modus vivendi,* at an unconscious level the analyst is most tenaciously clinging to this very mode of relatedness as being one in which he, the analyst, is receiving therapy from the patient, without the conscious knowledge of either of them.

This paper is allied with, and based upon, many of my previous writings (Searles, 1965, 1971, 1973).

In my first published paper (Searles, 1951) and in many subsequent ones, I have tried to highlight the analyst's unconscious gratifications in a treatment-resistant mode of patient-analyst relatedness which he is making every effort, consciously, to help the patient resolve. A still earlier, never published, paper (Searles, 1949) suggested that there is an element of reality in all the patient's distorted transference-perceptions of the analyst, in keeping with Freud's (1922) statement regarding projection that we do not project "into the sky, so to speak, where there is nothing of the sort already." One of my papers (Searles, 1972a), concerning my work over nearly twenty years with an awesomely psychotic woman, had as its main theme the highlighting of the reality-components (each of which had long remained unconscious to me) in her highly distorted, psychotic transference reactions.

One might think—erroneously, I believe—of the whole subject of this paper as being understandable in terms of the patient's fulfilling, in any one current situation under study, some neurotic or psychotic need on the part of the analyst. This view is erroneous for at least two reasons: (1) It does not credit the patient with potential therapeutic initiative, at a predominantly unconscious, if not conscious, level—the initiative being the active striving, to function or continue functioning as therapist to the analyst. (2) It does not take into account the dimensions of months and years of time. Patients manifest, over the course of months and years of treatment, an interest, a genuine caring, as to whether the analyst himself has been growing and thriving during and as a result of their therapeutic ministrations to him.

In 1961 I reported (Searles, 1961a) my experience in analytic work regarding the reality-relatedness between patient and analyst as differentiated from the transference-relatedness, "the evolving reality relatedness . . . pursues its own course, related to and paralleling, but not fully embraced by, the evolving transference relatedness over the years of the two persons' work together" (p. 378 in Searles, 1965). In another paper in 1961 I reported (Searles, 1961b) that "It has been my impression . . . that the evolution of the reality-relatedness proceeds always a bit ahead of, and makes possible, the progressive evolution and resolution of the transference, although to be sure the latter, in so far as it frees psychological energy and makes it available for reality-relatedness, helps greatly to consolidate the ground just taken over by the advancing reality-relatedness" (p. 557 in Searles, 1965). In the present paper I hypothesize a large step further: the evolution of the transference from, say, the patient's

transference-reaction to the analyst as being a harshly dominating father to perceiving the analyst as a much gentler but threateningly devouring mother-figure. Such involves a crucial element of the patient's success *in reality* as a therapist who has been attempting to help the analyst to modify the latter's *real* harsh-father identifications.

As in all my previous writings, I cannot hope to "prove" anything here; psychoanalytic work is too intuitive, too much dependent upon data which cannot be articulated in spoken, and even less in written words for that to be possible. But, as before, I hope that this paper, which emerges from my psychoanalytic experience, will prove sufficiently evocative, for colleagues, from their own psychoanalytic experiences, to acquire the subjectively convincing "proof" for them also. If my hypothesis is indeed valid as I obviously am convinced it is, then nothing less than a metamorphosis in our concepts of the nature of the curative process in psychoanalysis flows from it.

Space here allows me to include only a very few of the clinical experiences, from my work with neurotic and psychotic patients, typical of those which have caused me to formulate this hypothesis. The hypothesis is of particular significance for psychotic patients, for psychosis involves the patient's not having achieved, in infancy and childhood, the firm establishment of an individual human self, and in my view this tragedy is explicable primarily by the particularly severe vicissitudes with which his very early therapeutic strivings were met, beginning in late infancy and early childhood, prior to the time when he would normally have become able to achieve, and within his family setting would have been helped to achieve, individual selfhood. Instead, life consisted basically in his postponement, as it were, of his individuation, in the service of his functioning symbiotically as therapist to one or another of his family members, or to all collectively in a family symbiosis. For him now as a chronological adult in psychoanalytic treatment, the crucial issue is whether he and the analyst can function in such a manner that (1) a transference-symbiosis can develop, a symbiosis which will at first be highly distorted or pathological, as contrasted to that epitomized by the healthy-mother and healthy-infant symbiosis; (2) the nuclei of reality in this pathological symbiosis can become sufficiently evident to both patient and analyst that this symbiosis can gradually evolve into what I call a therapeutic symbiosis (Searles, 1959a, 1965, 1973), which is essentially a mutually growth-enhancing symbiosis like that of normal infancy; and (3) the mutual gratifications as well as further growth-frustrating aspects of this mode of relatedness can be dealt with, by both participants, such that a healthier individuation can occur, this time, for both of them.

In the course of phases (1) and (2) one encounters transference data, as I have come to see clearly only in recent years, which bring to light the patient's heretofore-unconscious, lifelong, guilt at having failed in his therapeutic effort, begun very early in life, to enable his ego-fragmented mother to become a whole and fulfilled mother to him. In my experience of recent years, it is only insofar as he can succeed in his comparable striving in the treatment, this time toward the therapist, that the patient can become sufficiently free from such guilt, and sufficiently sure of his symbiotic worth, so that he can now become more deeply a full human individual. Individuation has become free of its connotation of a murderous dismembering, or lethal abandonment of the mother for whom the patient has not only been made to feel responsible, but whom the patient has genuinely loved and wanted to somehow make whole and fulfilled.

Clinical examples: patient's therapeutic attempt to enable analyst to become free from some neurotic symptom or character trait in the latter

1. Mrs. A., a twenty-eight-year-old woman, clearly had had a strong parental relationship with the youngest of her three siblings, a brother five years younger than herself, and it was early evident to me that there was much repressed grief in her concerning the loss of this relationship which had become a most important area of her childhood and that of the brother. During the first three years of analysis she scarcely mentioned him from one year to the next, and then only most disparagingly and in passing, indicating that she thought of herself as having simply treated him in a disdainful, bullying manner.

But in the fourth year of the analysis, as her memories of their relationship began to emerge from repression, she recalled that the last several times she had fought with Eddie, when she was sixteen or seventeen years of age, he had won. "I guess that's why I stopped bringing them [i.e., their fist-fights] about. Actually, as I recall, I was quite pleased that he could beat me up. I guess that gave me some respect for him. I always thought he was a little drip; so after I found he could beat me up, I stopped . . ." She said all this in a tone that made clear that she had had a very loving motive toward him in all this— a motive of helping him to become a man. I conveyed

to her my impression of her tone, and suggested that she had been so motivated; but her dismissing response made clear that she was not yet able to accept anything like so loving an image of herself.

Later on in the session she said, in another context, "My [eldest] sister says I was horrible to Eddie; so I guess I was." It seemed clear to me, although not yet interpretable, that she was afraid, at an unconscious level, lest she kill her sister, were she—the patient— to come to see how cruel was the self-image which her sister had fostered in her in relation to their brother. She spoke in this session of how "cruel," in retrospect, had been her sister's pitying attitude toward Eddie as being a weakling, and her fostering in the patient a similar view of him. There were strong clues, partly accepted by her, that I was currently equivalent to Eddie in the transference relationship.

Later on in the session she said, again in reference to Eddie, that "After we stopped fighting, we stopped having anything to do with one another. We never acknowledge one another's existence. We never talk; we never phone; we never write." It was apparent, although not yet timely to interpret to her, that after having helped Eddie to become a masterful male toward her, she and he had to shun one another partly because of the sexual temptation with which their relationship was now imbued.

This brief example is typical of those in my experience, both in terms of indicating how deeply repressed have been the patient's therapeutic strivings toward the other family member(s), and in terms of the clarification of the transference relationship.

2. Miss B., a long-hospitalized woman forty years of age, devoted a considerable part of her time recurrently, over years of her treatment, reacting to me as being her ambivalence-ridden, indecisive and therefore unfirm father. It was clear that her own needs included a need for me to become a stronger, more firmly limit-setting father toward her; but it was equally clear that she was trying persistently to help me resolve the genuine flaw in myself which formed the nucleus of reality upon which her transference was based. Through outrageously and persistently obstreperous behavior, which involved both blatant sexual provocativeness as well as physical onslaughts of various kinds, she eventually succeeded in fostering in me a degree of decisiveness and firmness, expressed in masterful limit-setting, which I had not achieved before with anyone, either patients or other persons in my life. I worked for thirteen years with this woman, the most deeply ill patient I have ever treated, and over-all, I helped her much less than I wish it had been within my power to do. Still, I did help her considerably; I learned much from her; and

one of the most certain things I learned was that one of the important determinants of her illness had been a self-sacrificing effort to enable her father to become a man.

3. Mrs. C., a thirty-two-year-old attorney, had been beaten severely on occasion by her father when she was a child and he was a relatively young and physically vigorous man. In the later years of her upbringing, with the advent of adolescence and the father's aging and depression, his beatings had ceased. He was old and incapacitated with arthritis at the time she began analysis with me. As year after year went by in the analysis, years during which her loving and erotic, as well as murderously rageful feelings toward me as a father figure remained largely under repression, she became increasingly discouraged. At a conscious level, her discouragement had to do with the tenacity of the symptoms, for the relief of which she had sought analysis initially—namely, certain obsessive-compulsive rituals and a moderate but persistent alcoholism, both of which interfered appreciably with her professional work. Both these symptoms were expressions, in part, of her unconscious defiance toward me, as I represented her demanding, domineering father. At an unconscoius level, however, her discouragement was related also to her inability to galvanize me into being the vigorous and virile young father who had beaten her, despite year after year of contemptuously, defiant, acting-out behavior and various forms of verbal incitement. Her provocativeness clearly was not only expressive of an unconscious yearning for the erotic fulfillment which her father's beatings had provided her but it also was an effort to rejuvenate me, who was perceived as an aging, impotent, helpless father in the transference. Meanwhile, during that phase of analytic work, her grief about his aged and chronically ill condition was discernible directly only in brief glimpses.

4. After several years of analysis, Mr. D., a thirty-four-year-old man, said, in reference to his resistance to analysis, "I feel as though I won't participate—as though I sit down and refuse to take part . . ." I commented, "You say you feel as though you sit down and refuse to take part—*I'm* the one who's sitting down here." He agreed immediately, "Yeah—I've had the idea from time to time that you are depressed—and that I've got to do something to bring you out of yourself—to get you to blow up or—get you to lash out, or . . . [a few minutes later, without any further intervention from me]—When I think of my mother seated, she's always behind something—[clearly an allusion to my being seated behind the couch]—behind her sewing machine,

or behind her cookbooks, looking up recipes . . ."

In a later session, he confided that he had long desired to be able to experience, and convey to me, a fantasy so vivid "that you would be able to say, 'Boy, that's a marvelous fantasy!'" It was clear that he was giving expression to his long-familiar exasperation with himself for his relative inability to experience, and convey to me, anything but highly reality-bound associational material. But, at an apparently less conscious level, he was alluding also to my own characterologic inability to express undisguised, unambivalent enthusiasm for the contribution the other person has made, or is making. Thus, here again, was a glimpse of his therapeutic striving on behalf of his depressed mother, personified by me in the transference.

Upon hearing his statement, I was struck immediately by the fact of my adult life long inability to express such enthusiasm—an inability which I had never acknowledged openly in my work with him, and an inability which I manage, most of the time, to keep largely secret from myself. I well know that it was not entirely, nor not even primarily, due to any lack on his part of ability to experience and report fantasies, that I was unable to say, "Boy, that's a marvelous fantasy!", for no matter how abundantly suitable an occasion he might provide me for saying this, I am unable to say it. The inability emerged now, at this phase in the analysis after considerable growth in him (in this regard as well as in other ways). Although his therapeutic help had not proved sufficient to enable me appreciably to resolve my problem, he had helped me confront it much more clearly than I characteristically do—and that surely must be a help toward its eventual resolution.

I have dwelt at some length upon this brief clinical vignette because it comprises a typical example of how the analyst's psychopathology can remain masked—by introjective processes within the patient and projective processes within the analyst, and, by the same token, of how subtle is the patient's therapeutic striving—largely unconscious.

One might believe that this therapeutic striving of the patient is newly developed in the analysis; but my experience consistently has indicated quite otherwise—namely, that it has significant transference connections to his earlier life experience, and that it was indeed at work in him, though at an unconscious level, at the beginning of analytic work. When it emerges most clearly in the course of analysis, the transference connections between the analyst and earlier figures in the patient's life, toward whom this therapeutic striving has been devoted, are convincingly tangible.

5. Mrs. E., a forty-five-year-old woman, was sneezing, blowing her nose, and clearing her throat frequently in one of her analytic sessions. For years she had suffered from multiple allergies, and frequently had sinusitis with postnasal discharge, as she evidently did now. I felt, as I had felt during earlier years of her analysis regarding her allergic symptoms, that her physical discomfort was being used unconsciously by her in a neurotically hostile manner. In the course of this session she commented, while clearing her throat for the *n*th time, that she had many times to make an heroic effort to keep from vomiting here. I was familiar with such comments from her (as well as from occasional other patients) earlier in the analysis, and she seemed, as usual, quite unconscious of any sadistic gratification in making me feel recurrently threatened lest she suddenly vomit copiously all over my couch, carpet, and God knows what else in my office.

There emerged during this session data indirectly indicating that the theme of whether she was able to *feel* was unconsciously at work. Once, for example, she commented, in reference to pain in her sinuses exacerbated by her violent sneezes, that she evidently is able to feel, all right. Upon hearing that I felt like mentioning to her tartly that she was functioning, however, in a way which made *me* feel very *unfeeling* toward *her*; I felt convinced that she was projecting upon me her own subjective callousness and indifference to human suffering. I more than once felt like telling her that I found myself feeling that she could sneeze her goddam head off, for all I cared. I was reacting to her enormous, but still largely unconscious, demandingness—demands for sympathy, admiration, and so on; any list would be endless—and to her also largely unconscious hostility and threats. The implicit threat that she vomit was only one among a constellation of threats being conveyed to me. She gave me reason to feel intimidated. I feared her long-familiar capacity for character-assassinating me among her many social acquaintances, some of whom knew me personally. Thus, on more than one count I felt unfree to use, as shared investigative data, my "unfeeling" reaction that she could "sneeze her goddam head off," for all I cared.

Driving home at the end of the day I realized, with great relief, that my being "unfeeling" is *one* among the gamut of emotional responses available to me in my work with patients, and that this reaction can be as useful, for mutually exploratory analytic work, as any others among the many emotional reactions (jealousy, anger, tender feelings, sexual feelings, and so on) which I long ago had become accustomed

to using in my psychoanalytic work as data for the patient's analysis. The relief which accompanied this realization was tremendous, for until then I had found reason to fear, for several decades at crucial junctures in my personal and professional life, that I "really am" unable to feel, to care. That is, I had feared that this unfeeling one, subjectively not human, was the only real me—the only way, deep down in my core, that I really am.

In earlier years of this woman's analysis I had become aware of important ways in which work with her was proving of unusual therapeutic value to me (as well as of considerable such value, certainly, to her), and had found much evidence of powerful, and by no means entirely unconscious, therapeutic strivings on her part toward me. During the ensuing few days after this realization which I had experienced while driving home, I felt certain that it, like a number of analogous ones earlier in our work, had been predominantly a result of her therapeutic strivings—in this instance largely unconscious, so it appeared—on my behalf. My feeling in those few days was one of deep gratitude toward her. No one could possibly have helped me, so I felt, with anything more personally significant to me than this; this is where I had most been needing someone's help.

I am mindful of the transference aspects of the material of the session which I have mentioned though a discussion here is beyond the scope of this paper. I at no time lost sight of the fact that I was personifying for her a number of figures from her past, notably her mother, whom she tended to experience as being indifferent to her suffering. As I mentioned earlier, this paper is intended not to focus upon transference phenomena *per se*, but rather upon those real increments of the analyst's personality-functioning which serve, for the patient, as the nuclei of external reality and evoke his transference reactions.

Clinical examples of patient's therapeutic striving to enable the mother to become truly a mother

The healthy infant-mother symbiosis, which normally provides the foundation for later individuation, under tragic circumstances fosters the child's becoming not a truly human individual. He becomes what one might call a symbiotic therapist, whose own ego-wholeness is sacrificed throughout life in a truly selfless devotion, to complementing the ego-incompleteness of the mothering person, and of subsequent persons in his life who, in his unconscious, have the emotional meaning of similarly incomplete mothers. Their ego-functioning is dependent upon his being sustainingly a part of them. Such "negative" emotions as hatred and guilt, cited often in the literature concerning early ego development and the family dynamics of schizophrenia, are indeed a significant part of this etiological picture; but it is, I suggest, more than anything the patient's nascent capacity for love and for the development of mature human responsibility, which impels him to perpetuate this mode of relatedness.

Whereas the foregoing clinical examples, predominantly from neurotic patients, attempted to illustrate the patient's therapeutic effort to help the analyst resolve some neurotic symptom or character trait, in the following examples from patients who were suffering from some degree of schizoid or schizophrenic illness, the patient's therapeutic striving is referable more to a preindividuation, than postindividuation, developmental era. The patient's therapeutic striving is to function as mother to his biological mother (the latter's ego development in regard to her own mothering effort, being fixated at, or having regressed to, an infantile level) so as to enable her to become sufficiently integrated and mature that she will become able to function truly as a mother to the patient. This striving of the child is both "selfish" and "altuistic." The two aims are, at this level of primitive child-mother functioning, not as yet differentiated.

In a recent discussion of autism, I suggested (Searles, 1973) that for the analyst to help the autistic patient become able to participate in a therapeutic symbiosis (that is, a symbiosis similar in nature to a healthy infant-mother symbiosis), the analyst must first have become able to immerse himself in the patient's autistic world. This then fosters the patient's identifying with the analyst who can so immerse himself in the other's world: the patient, partly through such identification, becomes increasingly able to immerse himself in the analyst's more usual "own" world, and the rapid flux and interchangeability of a therapeutically symbiotic kind of relatedness flows from this. Khan (1963, 1964) has described the necessity for the analyst to come to function as the maternally protective shield (in my term, world) for such a patient, and I suggested that *the analyst must first accept the patient as comprising his (the analyst's) maternally protective shield* (functionally = "outer world," much as the womb is the outer world for the fetus).

Mrs. F., a thirty-year-old schizoid woman, early in the third year of her analysis mentioned that her parents were visiting her and her marital family at present. Mrs. F. had learned that her mother, in her distant home city, had been spending her time watching television or going to movie matinees. Mrs. F. said that her mother had been finding life boring and commented that her mother watched television and went to movies rather than getting a part-time job as a saleslady or secretary, or joining some women's social organizations.

"Somehow that seems to me such a waste; yet it's what she did so much of when I was a child," Mrs. F. reminisced, in a tone of regret and longing, ". . . movies and occasional romantic novels; I guess those were her only real interests . . ."

This was a glimpse, of which I came to see convincingly many—although, regrettably, I never found it feasible to interpret them to Mrs. F. as such—of her feeling of having failed to enable her mother to fulfill herself as a mother to her. The Oedipal-rivalry component in these data is also, of course, obvious.

In the preceding day's session she had mentioned having learned from her mother that the latter had given to the church library all the books which the daughter had acquired and treasured during childhood and adolescence, and thrown away all her daughter's stored clothing. "I had the feeling of being disposed of as deceased," she commented. The mother was showing her usual selfish-child concern with feeling inhospitably and inconsiderately treated by her husband and various of his relatives; and the patient added, in a tone more of genuine regret and sadness than blame, that on her own occasional trips with her husband and children to her parental home, "She (her mother) has *yet* to prepare a nice supper for us."

A few sessions earlier, there had occurred, as there had a great many times before, a predominantly silent session. But this one was different in quality. Before, the silences had been extremely tense ones which had often involved my having exasperated, frantic feelings of the sort which, I surmise, were largely at work in her emotionally rootless, discontented mother. During this particular session, she indicated that she was feeling unusually calm and relaxed, and asked whether I reacted differently when she is feeling so. Indeed I did, though I did not tell her so; I felt calm and relaxed, and experienced her as a source of nonverbal strength and solidity. In the course of this session she commented, "I can imagine my father holding me on his lap and cuddling me; but I can't imagine my mother." I had much misgiving, after that hour, about not having told her—confirmed for her—how I was feeling; I had never felt so with her before. Always before, her silences had been unpleasurable to me in one way or another.

In retrospect, I feel that I had withheld from her, unwisely and hatefully, a vitally needed confirmation of her at least partially successful mothering of me. Probably wisely, she discontinued our analytic work not many months thereafter.

Her having said, ". . . but I can't imagine my mother" is a testimony of the crucial significance, in one's therapeutic striving, of one's ability—or in this instance, inability—to achieve a fantasy of the other person's functioning in the striven-for manner, the manner fulfilling both for the other person and oneself. In my work with hospitalized schizophrenic patients, and in what I have heard from colleagues of their work with similar patients, the therapists' experiencing of nighttime dreams and daytime fantasies of the patient in which the latter—who in daily life is still very ill—is perceived as functioning as a healthy person, are crucial criteria of successful treatment.

With Mrs. G., a thirty-four-year-old woman whose psychodynamics are in some ways very similar to Mrs. F.'s, and whose analysis proceeds with strikingly little change year after year, I am becoming gradually much more receptive to her maternal effort to enable me to function as mother to her. Her effort is, as in all such instances, a highly ambivalent one, with strong rivalrous components (on negative-oedipal but also infantile-omnipotence grounds) to demonstrate that the mother is incapable of functioning as mother. However, the issue is proving to be more amenable to analysis than it was with Mrs. F. The resolution of particularly stalemated phases of the work involves my realizing, for example, how genuinely gratifying it is to me to go on being one of the fruits borne by the fruit tree which is one of her early-mothering images of herself. My often-exasperated efforts to encourage and insist upon her functioning more productively and spontaneously, as most neurotic analysands usually do, run aground upon the fact of my having (formerly unconscious) stakes in her continuing to maintain her usual early-mother orientation in the transference, as in her daily life.

Mr. H., 42 years of age, was suffering from ambulatory schizophrenia when he began analysis 15 months ago, but has improved to the point that his ego-dysfunctioning has been of no more than borderline-schizophrenic severity for some months now. Previously filled with hatred to a degree potentially dangerous to himself as well as to others, he has now become capable of relatively sustained, predominantly loving relations with his wife and children, as well as in the analytic setting; and he is manifesting a steadily strengthening kinship with his fellow human beings—although, in all these regards, such developments still encounter considerable disavowal on his part by persistent hostility and rejectingness.

His upbringing, like that of his older brother with whom there prevails a powerful and largely unconscious symbiosis, had been left largely to servants, and an abundance of evidence, from the beginning of the analytic work, indicating that their mother had been strikingly deficient in motherliness. Mr. H. was convinced that not only his nursemaids, but his mother as well, "despised" both himself and his brother; and he soon manifested, in our analytic work, a conviction that I, likewise, equivalent to such a mother or nursemaid, despised him.

The particular point I wish to make for this paper is that when, in a recent session, the patient said, "Mother didn't want anything to do with us," although this was said in an offhand attempt at glossing-over manner, there came through in it a feeling of deep, pervasive, and subjectively ineradicable shame. Moreover and most significantly, the shame had in it a perceptible quality that this was shame not so much that he and his brother had proved unworthy of the mother's caring for them but, much more meaningfully, that the two brothers had failed shamefully in their long-sustained effort to enable the mother to become, and to know the fulfillment of being, truly a mother. Space does not allow me to include the corollary data—abundant but significant mainly in its nuances of feeling which cannot be conveyed fully and convincingly in a written report such as this—which reassure me that his analogous effort in the transference situation is proving, this time, much more successful.

Miss J., a forty-two-year-old spinster who had become schizophrenic in the course of decades of living largely as a recluse in the service of her widowed and eccentric mother, became during the first year of her stay at Chestnut Lodge so emaciated, mute, and motionless that I, like the others concerned with her care, feared that she would die. The psychoanalytic contribution to the favorable change in this state of affairs consisted essentially, I believe, in my coming to function, over a period of some months, very much as a comfortably silent and unmoving inanimate object during our sessions. This seemed to provide her with a context in which she could become alive again. In retrospect, I now see that in order for me to have become able so to function, I had to become immersed, in a relatively unanxious, contented, self-gratifying way, in her seemingly inanimate world.

Over the ensuing months and, in fact, for many years, we had many stormy sessions, sessions in which she often reacted to me as being crazy, confused, and disorganized, meanwhile acting out, herself, a great deal of such psychopathology. During one phase of about two years in length, in about the fifth and sixth years of her treatment, the therapeutic sessions all took place in her room, and were therapeutically symbiotic in quality to the greatest degree that I have ever experienced with any of my patients; this, I feel sure, is related to the fact of her having had a better outcome than any others among my chronically schizophrenic patients thus far have achieved. During those two years I experienced her as winning a gentle victory over me: my earlier fury, contempt, and other "negative" feelings toward her for her inability (seemingly, her refusal) to come to my office for the sessions, gradually gave way to an atmosphere of the utmost shared contentment, in which I was receptive to and appreciative of her good mothering to me, and she, likewise, basked and throve in this symbiotic atmosphere. There were abundant indications of symbiotic processes at work during this time. Meanwhile her social worker told me one day in astonishment that she had had a dream the previous night of Miss J., in which Miss J. was a mother happily nursing her baby. Several others among the personnel members told me how amazed they were at the favorable changes they were seeing in Miss J.

One of the tenacious forms of resistance in Miss J.'s treatment has been her idealization of her upbringing. After many years of treatment, despite her having long ago become healthier than her family had ever known her to be, being relatively well-established in outpatient living, and functioning much of the time during the sessions more in a normal-neurotic fashion than a borderline schizophrenic fashion, she is still almost totally unable to remember and report any but conventionally "nice" memories and feelings about her parents and other family members. Meanwhile, there has been no lack of negative-transference phenomena, in which she has reacted to me as being essentially a crazy mother whose craziness is known only to Miss J. herself.

Her first reported memory of her mother which I heard as realistic, rather than her usual saccharine, idealized images, occurred after some three or four years of analysis. The content of the memory was mundane enough; but I thought it highly significant that it was reported during a session (in her room, as usual in that era) when the female patient who occupied the adjoining room, and who for weeks had frequently stormed in loud and overwhelming rage, was raging even more loudly than I had ever heard her. Whether Miss J. will ever be able to integrate her past experience of the mother's comparable behavior into a more realistic image of her mother, now long dead, I do not know. A "nervous breakdown," in the phrase of her siblings, which had incapacitated the mother for many months following the father's death, and had required the patient to leave high school and begin taking care of her, has never been remembered or acknowledged in any way by Miss J. as having occurred, despite many years of analysis.

Her move to outpatient living was very slow in coming about, and it gradually became clear that one of the many sources of her unconscious resistance to this move was her equating it, unconsciously, with a mother's abandoning of her little child. For example, my notes following a session early in the fifth year include this paragraph:

"She spoke with great disapproval of how mothers in effect abandon their children, as she sees in her trips into Rockville [the small city in which the sanitarium is located] where, she said, she sees mothers leave their children at loose ends, playing near the streets and so on, while they (the mothers) do their shopping. This I have heard a number of times before. But I was greatly interested when she said, this time, that she herself does not have a child, but that if she had one, she wouldn't want to 'keep running back' to the child. She would want it so well taken care of that she wouldn't 'have to keep running back.' This happens to be exactly the same terminology she has used [for years] in expressing her objection to moving out—namely, that such a move would be pointless because she 'would have to keep running back to the hospital.' I now realize that for her to move out of the hospital is unconsciously equivalent to a mother's abandoning her child (the child being me and, no doubt, various other persons in the hospital). [I would now add that the child was, much more largely, the sanitarium or 'hospital' as a whole]. I recall her saying recently that as a person gets older they become like a child, and agreeing with my comment, in response, that one may feel like a mother to one's own mother."

As her years in the sanitarium went on, she had a series of roommates in the various double rooms in which she lived. A number of these persons were highly psychotic and openly disturbed, and at least a few of them sufficiently homicidal that I was impressed with her ability to live with them in an increasingly firm, assertive, and forthright manner. Although I have not the slightest doubt that her poorly integrated, infuriating qualities stimulated many of the upsets of her various roommates, her conscious therapeutic concern for them seemed to me unmistakably genuine; and whereas a full four years elapsed, in one of the sanitarium cottages where she lived, before she ever set foot in the living room (lest, upon doing so, she immediately be held totally responsible for all that transpired there), she came to do so freely, and to participate in a generally much-appreciated and constructive way in the weekly or biweekly unit meetings of patients and staff.

The last roommate she had, for about a year before moving to an apartment of her own in Washington, was a highly psychotic woman whose verbal and physical behavior was often highly disorganized. Miss J. would state that Edna was, once again, "in a whirl." In one of her analytic sessions with me during that year, she asked me whether she could go to New York City on the following Sunday to visit her female cousin and miss her Monday hour. I said that it was all right with me; for reasons

I shall not detail here, I did not respond in an analytic-investigative manner as I would with a neurotic patient. She then said something about not being sure she could do it—i.e., make the trip to New York City alone. "I feel so little in New York. . . . I guess I always think of New York as a big city in a whirl. . . ."

The idea struck me that she projected onto New York City her own still largely repressed confusion, and tended to feel responsible—a responsibility overwhelmingly awesome to me as I sensed it—for what she perceived as the gigantic confusion of the big city. Her psychosis had first become overt, many years before, shortly following a visit to this cousin, and I felt that here I was being given a brief glimpse into the nature of her psychotic experience then. Later on, in looking over my notes, I realized that New York City was unconsciously equivalent to her overwhelmingly confused mother for whom the patient felt totally responsible.

About two years later, she was describing her weekly visit to her current social worker at Chestnut Lodge, a woman toward whom Miss J. has a mother-transference which involves, amidst clearly ambivalent feelings, a great deal of admiration, fondness of a sisterly sort, and maternal caring for the social worker. She said, "Recently she's been so busy, her office looks like a whirl!", making an illustrative whirling gesture with her arm as she said this.

Mrs. Joan Douglas (a pseudonym, of course), whose history and course thus far in psychotherapy I detailed in a recent paper (Searles, 1972a) and therefore shall touch upon only briefly here, was chronically and severely psychotic at the time when I began working with her, nearly twenty years ago. I have seen her four hours per week since then. For various reasons, carefully and recurrently considered, tranquilizing drugs have not been used in her treatment. For the past seven and one half years I have taped (with her knowledge) all the sessions, have earmarked and filed all these tapes, and have spent dozens of hours in careful playbacks of selected ones, in my attempt to better understand the processes, destructive as well as constructive, at work within and between us.

From the outset her ego-fragmentation was enormous and her delusions were innumerable and everchanging. She was long convinced, for example, that there were 48,000 Chestnut Lodges among which she was constantly being shifted; that there was literally a chain on her heart and machinery in her abdomen; that her head, as well as mine and other persons', was repeatedly being replaced by other heads. She often experienced both herself and me,

bodily and *in toto,* as being replaced by a succession of other persons during the psychotherapy hours. She was so vigorously and tenaciously opposed to psychiatry that for several years she refused steadfastly to come to my office at Chestnut Lodge, and had been there only some three or four times during the first 10½ years, after which she finally began coming with some regularity. During the past nine years, since I left Chestnut Lodge, she had been coming by taxicab to my office, some ten miles from the Lodge, and for the most recent several of those years, has been sufficiently reality-oriented and collaborative, despite continued severe psychosis, as to no longer need a nurse or aide to accompany her.

As regards her history, she apparently suffered from a significant degree of schizophrenia in childhood. Her mother, in the words of her eldest brother, had "loved to dominate" the girl, had beaten her brutally on occasion up into the teens, and generally had had an intensely ambivalent and therefore highly unpredictable relationship with her. As an example of the mother's unpredictable moods, which included both manic and depressive episodes, the brother described how she would return from Mass in a beatific mood, and within moments would be furiously throwing a kitchen pot at one or another of the children.

Although the patient had been able to complete high school with a brilliant academic record, to become accomplished in various athletics, and to marry and bear four children, she gradually had become overtly psychotic at the age of 33, within about a year following the death, from natural causes, of her mother. She had been overtly psychotic for about four years when I became her therapist. I was to learn that her relationship with her emotionally remote father had contributed importantly, also, to the foundation of her awesomely severe psychosis; but that relationship is less clearly relevant to the theme of this paper.

For many years her real identity was anathema to her to such a degree that, when one addressed her by her own name, one was met by a degree of unrelatedness from her which was often intolerable to me. She experienced a succession of personal identities, many of them nonhuman, and frequently changing *in toto* in the midst of a session, just as she usually perceived me as multiple at any one moment, as changing unpredictably, and frequently as being nonhuman. All these delusional experiences, while appreciably lessened in severity, are still present to a formidable degree.

In one session after some half dozen years of work, she explained to me, "You see, my mother was my mind," and this was said in such a tone as poignantly to convey the implication, "—and when I lost her, I lost my mind." It was painfully clear during the hour to what an awesome extent she indeed had lost her mind, as measured by the incredible depth of her confusion, quite unreproducible here. For years she had been performing various crazy actions, and had come to reveal more and more clearly that, in doing so, she was following obediently the directions which she heard coming from "that woman in my head," evidently an introject, no matter how greatly distorted by the patient's own anxiety and hostility, of the crazy mother of her childhood.

In one of the more amusing of our sessions in that era—sessions which much more often were far, indeed, from being amusing—she suddenly reported to me, "That woman in my head just said, 'Don't have anything to do with that frump out there'." She confirmed my amused assumption that "that frump" referred to me. At another point in the hour when I suggested, as had long been my custom, "Let's see what comes to your mind next," she protested vigorously, "You keep asking me what's in my *mind! She's* in my mind; but *she* has nothing to do with *me!*" She went on to make it evident that she felt that I utterly ignored her whenever I would endeavor to encourage her to express what she was experiencing. Usually we think of the person's mind as the locus and core of the self; but she emphasized that this was not true for her. It is now evident in retrospect that when I had been trying to help her explore and articulate what was in her mind, she had been reacting as though my effort had been to crush her emerging autonomy—to castrate her individuality (she had accused me on innumerable occasions of doing all sorts of physical violence to her), by making her introjected mother-image totally and permanently dominate her ego-functioning.

By the tenth year I had long since become impressed, in my work with all my schizophrenic patients, with the power and depth of the positive feelings between the to-become-schizophrenic child and his mother. My notes made following one of the sessions with her include the following:

"She was incredibly confused, as usual, throughout the hour. That is, she was no more confused than usual; but the degree of her confusion, present for several years now, I still find quite incredible. The bulk of it has to do with a tremendous confusion about identity.

"I bluntly mentioned to her, midway through the hour, that I found something like 90 % of what she told me to be gibberish, or words to that effect. My saying this was no doubt related to the significant things she said at the end of the hour, and I feel that my increasing bluntness is a useful part of the work. In this regard I recall that about six weeks ago I told her bluntly, 'You're a silly woman who is spending her life here in this looney bin, talking nonsense, while your life goes down the drain.'

"Despite her great confusion she managed to bring out, in a confused and indirect and displaced kind of way, the fact that her mother had run her life in an utterly single-handed and autocratic fashion up until Joan 'went into St. Thomas' Hospital', which I assume was at the age of eight when [as I had long known] she had had her mastoidectomy [the first of a series of surgical operations]. She went on to make clear that thereafter the doctors had taken over the management of her life, and that they had done a highly inefficient job. She had been speaking of her mother in the same admiring, loyal spirit as she has shown rather consistently in her references to her mother for several weeks now, while speaking in the same spirit of her older and only sister, Ellen. I then said, 'So perhaps, when you went into St. Thomas' Hospital and the doctors took over the management of your life, you couldn't help feeling guilty, couldn't help feeling that you were being disloyal to your mother, simply because these doctors were running your life now, instead of she.' Joan clearly and explicitly agreed.

"At the end of the hour as I went downstairs, she called after me loudly and defiantly, 'The doctors here haven't done a *goddam thing* for me; I'm *still* a blithering idiot!' I heard this as an expression of her loyalty to her mother, and of her determination not to let me and the others on the staff here be useful to her, because this would be tantamount to disloyalty to her mother.

"Also in the course of this hour, I was struck once again with how terribly confused a person the mother must have been; I felt that Joan's confusion is largely based upon introjection of this confused mother. When she was describing things that the mother used to say, I said, 'I suppose it would be hard for you to think that she may ever have been susceptible to being confused,' and Joan flatly disclaimed any such possibility. This is an indication of how Joan is struggling to maintain a picture of her mother as a very strong person [an effort to ward off unconscious disillusionment, guilt and grief in relation to the mother]."

Some three weeks later, I came to her session feeling fatigued and sick with hay fever and an external auditory canal infection. Therefore, I was relatively free from my compulsive, competitive, driving, coercing countertransference orientation, to which she is attuned and which she provokes. She, I am sure, partially in response to my changed feeling-state, was comfortably settled in her chair, and spoke unanxiously of feeling "set." She said, yawning comfortably, "I'm certainly a woman and I'm never going to be a men." For all the years, her confusion about her sexual identity, as well as mine, had been enormous; a man was, to her, still multiple, as I was usually a multiple transference figure to her—hence her saying "a men."

Later in the same hour she told me of a time when "my mother . . . was having a nervous breakdown . . ." This was, for me, a landmark dénouement. She described vividly her mother's having talked vehemently about "'When you were in Spain . . .,' where the girl had never been, and something about "'saving England'," and much other material on a par with the patient's own delusions. Joan went on, saying "I told her, 'You can't bear to have all those thoughts in your mind!'", in a tone of earnest and urgent solicitude. I suggested, "You wanted to relieve her of some of the burden of them." She promptly confirmed this, nodding and saying, "I was *trying* to." It was evident that she had been precisely as nonplussed, helpless and concerned as I had felt with her.

By this time, I had become aware of a number of instances in which her somatically experienced suffering was based on her perceiving various persons about her, for example, staff members and fellow patients in the cottage, or townspeople seen during her escorted trips into town, as suffering various forms of physical anguish, and her unconsciously taking those percepts into her own body image, in an attempt to heal them within herself. Despite the obvious defense which this represented against her largely unconscious sadism and murderous hostility toward these persons, it had become clear that her loving solicitude and therapeutic concern had an element of indubitable sincerity and genuineness.

Some three years later, during my supervision at another hospital of the psychotherapy of a borderline-schizophrenic young man, I was reminded of Joan when the patient said that he wanted to "sever the bonds of sickness to Mother. The way I'm bowing my head now is the way she does. It's like I have the struggles of a child still inside me." I regarded the image of the child, struggling within him, as being comprised not only of elements of his own childhood self, but also of elements of the child in mother, struggling against sickness, elements which he had taken, partly with a therapeutic motive, into his self-image. One of the striking aspects of this paper is the recurrent theme of how extremely immature are the areas of the parent's ego which are involved in these types of symbiotic fusion with the child, and how early in life the patient is called upon to try to function as a parent and therapist to the parent. Joan's inability to differentiate actual adults from actual children was extreme. One of her tenacious delusions was that

children are "arrested adults." For several years she recurrently called our sessions, derisively, her "babysitting" with me, and in more recent years she has made it clear that a major source of contention between herself and her mother, beginning in early childhood, was her insistence that *she* was the mother, and that her mother was the child or baby. Joan shows, to this day, a cynical-child quality that I have recognized as a defense against dependent needs in persons who had to function prematurely as parent to their parents, and who had very little childhood of their own. Joan once told me, "I grew up at the age of eight."

In the seventeenth year of our work, her consciously lovingly concerned and unconsciously murderously competitive efforts to bring surcease to various mother-figures was evident in a session, most of which is too delusionally distorted, too bewildering, to warrant reproducing here. It was beginning to dawn on me that she felt overwhelmed by my intended therapeutic devotion to her, devotion which presumably contained more murderous competitiveness than I could yet integrate (although I had long been familiar with sustained urges to murder her). Identifying with the aggressor, she spent most of the sessions in being preoccupied with how to rescue her delusionally distorted, gigantic but victimized mother. She incessantly felt unappreciated, unsuccessful and worst of all unacknowledged, in her endless striving to be of use, of help, to her mother.

She was looking tearful throughout most of this session. A very slowly developing capacity to grieve, bit by bit, was one of the major aspects of her therapeutic progress, and stood in marked contrast to the paranoid grandiosity which formerly had shielded her against feelings of loss; but the increments of healthy grief were accompanied by such intense affects of depression that I felt threatened by the possibility of her suicide. She looked earnest and very serious during this session.

At the beginning of the session she refused, as usual, to accept the name Joan, identifying herself as Barbara (one of innumerable names she applies to herself). Midway along the session, speaking of multiple, highly delusionally distorted, fragments of her image of her mother, she said, "I gave them to you [that is, literally put them into me, a familiar delusion], and you didn't help them. *I* couldn't; they hated *me*." She went on (and this clearly now had reference to her roommate, a highly psychotic young woman who was often placed into cold, wet-sheet packs), "I didn't want to make her *more* tense. . . . A couple of times I had to put them in straitjackets. . .

The way Mrs. Schultz [the name of her long-deceased mother; her mother transference to her roommate—her misidentification of her roommate as being literally her mother—had been evident before] talks about her life, it's always been terrible; she's always been the rubber outside the hemisphere, and rubber's always been hard to cure [a glimpse, here, of her irrepressible, usually caustic and mocking, wit] . . . . I spoke to Dr. Mitchell [the name of the former ward administrator many years before, whom she recurrently referred to as still being present] about them; *he* didn't make them any better."

I felt certain she was talking about her current young roommate when she said (in the excerpts below, my comments are in brackets):

". . . And that kid was in the room yesterday, and she wanted to behave well, I guess, and I started to talk to it [her hostility was often expressed in her experiencing others, including me in the sessions, as being nonhuman, and even inanimate], and somethin' grabbed it, 'cause it looked like *that* [she affected a shocked facial expression] at me—like a real baby. [Kid—'Kid'—ya mean the kid (realizing only now that she was speaking of her young roommate; one often had no way of knowing whether she were describing interactions with hallucinatory figures).] Yeah; the one who's knifed me to death. [Looked at ya very wide-eyed] I have *never*—uh—*felt as much antagonism,* and *hate,* and *loathing*—and I *grabbed it* by the shoulders, you know, and I said, 'Now your *mother* wants me to help her fix your head! And *she* doesn't have a license. *I* have a license.' I tried to reason with her, and at the end of that he [N.B.] *gave* me such a *sock*; he practically knocked my *head* off my *shoulders*! Now whaddya make of that?—and *no conversation, ever*. [From—the Kid?] Um (as a confirmation). A real baby . . . and [speaking now of some other delusionally distorted mother-figures] I gave them you as a doctor; but *you* didn't make them any better. You made them terrible—[Well, in a way that was a relief, wasn't it?] No. [You'd been trying *so* hard to help them. It would have been distressing if *I* had been *able* to, and *you* had *not*.] *Oh, no,* because I had to rely on *other* people to *help* them, they *really hate me*; they did *not like* me. [Spite of *all* your efforts, huh?] Yeah; I was just trying to make them feel more comfortable, less aggressive, and I couldn't understand why each person that went in there [That is, went, as a miniature, literally and bodily into the body of the person he or she was endeavoring to cure] had to make them *worse*. . . ." Later in the session she said, "The mother is at Chestnut Lodge, of course. . . . The mother doesn't want to be alone. . . . The women at the Lodge need a doctor. . . ." [This was one of the innumerable sessions during which I believed it was important to be careful about interpreting lest I say something that would lead to her suicide; her shockingly intense, murderous hostility tended to be directed, suicidally, against herself, now that her predominantly paranoid murderousness had shifted

gradually into depression. Previously my concern had been, not that she kill me but, during particularly stormy and enraging sessions, that I kill her.]

Seventeen months later (the nineteenth year of our work) during a particular session, she clearly expressed her therapeutic strivings.

When I motioned her into my office from the waiting room, as usual I did not address her by name. For the first ten minutes she was silent, as was not infrequent. She seldom looked at me. Her demeanor was one of helplessness, troubled feelings, bewilderment, vulnerability, and uncertainty as to whether she could trust me. She seemed to be listening to hallucinatory voices rather than thinking—many times before she had flatly stated that she had no mind, and was a radio through which people in the walls expressed themselves. A few times she nodded obediently, apparently in response to hallucinatory voices.

Then, she talked, and I felt she was giving me a tremendous working over by saying many caustically depreciatory things in a highly delusional way. I had long since realized that everything she said, no matter how delusional, consciously or unconsciously alluded to something in the immediate situation. She repeatedly implied, "If the shoe fits, wear it." I was often aware, through feelings of guilt, inadequacy and self-condemnation that the shoe fit all too well. Because her accusations were so indirect, I felt unable to retaliate with sufficient savagery to feel free.

Nonetheless this session proved to be more collaborative than many. She seemed largely unconscious of how much she was doing to make me feel discouraged and depressed; but she expressed the feeling that I did not need her in any way, even to feel entertained by her, an important revelation. Despite the accusing, reproachful, condemnatory, competitive, mocking, and beseeching working-over that she was giving me, she was still entertaining, by virtue of her caustic wit and the fabulously creative imagination which possessed her more than was possessed by her.

The collaborative yield of the session was evident in various ways. She made many realistic references to Chestnut Lodge—which, for her, was unusually good contact with reality. Parenthetically, during the past few years she has become aware that there is only one Chestnut Lodge where, she now realizes, she has lived for years. Forty-two minutes along in a two-hour session, she accusingly and reproachfully said: ". . . you hold onto me and push me away all at the same time . . .", a highly perceptive and succinct statement of reality, as I knew also from playbacks of tapes from earlier sessions. This was also a transfrence reaction; I represented her mother, who had simultaneously held her close while pushing her away. Some minutes later she protested: "You keep talking to me like my mother!"

Fifteen minutes later she despondently said, ". . . My mother . . . she doesn't seem to need me for nothin' . . .", and six minutes later, was saying of someone else she had invoked, "I amuse *her.*" She felt reproachful toward me, as a mother, since if she *is* able to amuse this other person, she fails in her therapeutic attempt to amuse *me* (that is, another mother).

She also made several realistic new comments about her ex-husband, of whom she had not spoken for many months. Later, she said, "I would *like* to engage a psychiatrist . . .", which was perhaps the greatest degree of verbal acceptance of psychiatry I had ever heard from her, apart from the marital connotation of the word *engage.*

I wish to highlight her efforts to entertain me (as the personification of her depressed mother).

Throughout nineteen years of treatment, confusion had been her predominant symptom, confusion defended against by innumerable and ever changing delusions. Only after some dozen years of my endeavoring primarily to rescue her from a life filled with manifold anguish, realistic as well as psychotic in nature, and permeated by this confusion, did I gradually come, bit by hard-won bit, to experience a kind of esthetic appreciation, at first highly guilt-laden and furtive, of her confusion. Her confusion had, from another viewpoint, a truly breathtaking creativity, far more fascinating, wondrous and, of course, alive than, for example, a beautiful and intricate Persian rug. With this gradual change in my orientation, which required some few years to become really well-established, I became also more receptive to, and appreciative of, her tremendous wit and her indomitable sense of humor. Of both her wit and her humor I had been well aware from the beginning.

Earlier, I had been so desperately concerned to help her that I had been largely unaware of how basically concerned she was in trying to be helpful and alleviating to me, if only by entertaining me with schizophrenic confusion which, for many years, was all she had to give me to relieve my depression. My depression was to a degree real but tremendously intensified, in her perceptions of me, by her depressed-mother-transference. Its reality was accentuated by much that she said and did, I believe largely unconsciously, which would be enough to greatly depress any psychotherapist.

In the next session, two days later, she said, "The human race is in a shambles," and she was able to recall realistic memories of her childhood, in which her mother had made repeated trips to Italy, evidently in line with her operatic ambitions, while leaving Joan and her siblings in the care of a succession of maids. She remembered not a succession but a chaotic myriad of vague parent-figures. The feeling tone of the session, significantly for this paper, was mutually enjoyable. I had learned that she throve in sessions in which, no matter how much reason for despair, we both were able genuinely to enjoy.

Two sessions and five days later, before inviting her in for the session, I confided briefly to my tape recorder my anxiety that she was invading my life so thoroughly that I would go crazy; the preceding session with her had been more disturbing to me than usual. But this session, a two-hour one as has been the case once each week for years, proved to be relatively collaborative and therapeutically fruitful. I was slowly becoming more appreciative of the healthy ingredients of her delusional thinking. For example, she expressed a delusion that she had been an architect in New York City and had designed many buildings there. Instead of my responding, as I usually had, to the arrogant grandiosity of her tone, I asked her what buildings she had designed, and I was impressed when she named a half dozen well-known buildings; this was, for her, a rare nugget of reality relatedness.

Later in the session I had occasion to suggest to her that maybe, while she was here in the office, she missed her current Chestnut Lodge roommate, to which she replied, seriously and thoughtfully, "Maybe so," a rare acknowledgement from her. For years I had noted that the form and content of the sessions were enormously influenced by her unconscious separation feelings toward the cab driver or the nurse or aide who had accompanied her to the session, or her unconscious feelings about having briefly left various sections of Chestnut Lodge.

Also in this session the role of her terror of her projected envy was becoming clearer in her saying, for example, ". . . this head [gesturing toward her head]—of course, it's not a head; it's just a piece of paper— . . ." In earlier years I had been sufficiently preoccupied with my own feelings of envy of her, for many well-founded reasons, and was so burdened with guilt about it, that I had failed to understand that her never experiencing her head as being her own head was because she feared her mother's envy. Her mother, in various ways, had lost her head in legendary outbursts of volcanic fury. Joan's therapeutic effort was aimed at protecting her mother from the realization of the mother's own state of deprivation.

Three weeks later, she was tearful, said, feeling burdened and intruded upon. There were indications that her identity was dominated by identification with memories of her mother, who was more disorganized than usual during a certain period of Joan's childhood. At that time the mother gave birth to twins, only one of whom, a male, had lived, whereas the other, a female, died shortly following delivery. During a session she made references to "the baby," a concept which encompassed both the dead baby girl and the live baby boy, and I had reason to know that she, as a child, had not only been invaded by the psychotic introject of the grief-crazed mother, but had striven thereby to rescue the mother by taking into herself the mother's burden of tragedy and psychotic reaction to tragedy.

Three weeks later she stated with conviction, as she frequently had before, that she is dead, this time explaining that she had died the night before in order that her mother not be killed. She stated that her Daddy had killed her over and over. Innumerable times in previous years she had accused me, when she perceived me as a remote and murderously omnipotent father in the transference, of murdering her. She was experiencing herself and her only living sister as being in effect, artificially conglomerated Siamese twins: she showed me one hand, saying, "That's me," and the other "is Mrs. Bradley" (her sister's married name). Never before had she conveyed so tangibly how important to her, how much a part of her, the sister is, the only one among all her numerous relatives who has found it endurable to keep on visiting Joan during the past ten years. She visits for a few days once or twice each year.

In the next session, two days later, I privately thought, as she walked into my office from the waiting room, that she looked like hell. She was wearing no lipstick; she was looking pale and old; her hair was unkempt; there was a button off the top of her familiar and unbecomingly tentlike Navy blue jumper; she was wearing sneakers rather than the reasonably attractive leather shoes she often wore, and no stockings. I thought, with a familiar dull hopelessness, of the setting in which she had lived her daily life for many years, amidst other chronically schizophrenic patients, and with a highly psychotic roommate—a setting where, despite the best efforts on the part of the administrative, nursing, and aide and other staff members, the alleviating of such chronic self-neglect seemed hopeless.

Throughout the whole hour her demeanor was one of tearfulness, vulnerability, and hurt; meanwhile, in her verbal communications, she was being her usual, extremely formidable self, giving me the usual tremendous working over throughout nearly the whole session.

Nonetheless, during the course of the session her communications provided realistic new glimpses of her parents' marriage, and valuable evidence that her tenacious self-neglect was part of an effort to evoke in me her mother who, as I knew, had striven incessantly and coercively to care for her clothing. It was apparent that she was trying to evoke this mother in me not only because she needed that mother, but as a way of resuscitating the mother who had been dead for 23 years.

She spoke, too, of "Ma" as being a "tempestuous woman," and indeed she had been. "He brawls," she went on; the mother indeed had had a strongly phallic quality, and had often run the home in a brawling manner. "I had a daughter," she later said, as indeed she has—a daughter as loathsome to her as is her own real identity, for between her and this daughter her conflicts with her own mother had raged, during Joan's daughter's childhood, to such a degree that years ago the two reached a point of denial of one another's existence. She later said, "I honestly don't know where my mother is"—a strikingly realistic statement, for her, and still later referred to ". . . that Mrs. Schultz [her mother] who was a good friend of mine [a memorable expression of positive feeling for her mother]," and went on to say that "I lived for centuries as an element" (in earlier years of our work she frequently had identified herself as being a boundless element—light, electricity, and so on—or as being filled with radioactive material), and stated, with a tone of partial accomplishment, that she has now become an animal, but is not yet a human being.

A prominent aspect of this session was my proving able not to be trapped into pursuing the bits of realistic reporting. I learned this was not only one of her ways of sadistically tantalizing me, but also one of her efforts to mobilize me as her mother, in a manner unconsciously intended to be therapeutic for this mother overwhelmed by depression and apathy. She was trying coercively to put her together—to put together the fragments of her healthy ego-functioning, out of the welter of psychotic material.

Five days later she was looking tearful and pensive. I felt that she was reacting primarily to the fact that Thanksgiving, with all its nostalgic connotations, was only two days off; only after the session did it occur to me that her sadness probably had more to do with the fact that Thanksgiving meant, also, the missing of our usual two-hour Thursday session. During this session it was evident that she was grieving particularly for the relationship with her daughter—new material, indeed—and she spoke repeatedly and realistically of her sister, also. Part of her delusional experience during this session was experiencing us as being in a gigantic statue. Someone was able to see out from the eyes of the statue and was reporting that no Coast Guard ship was approaching. She conveyed vividly the bleakness and remoteness of the scene, viewed from the eyes of the statue.

She asked of her mother, "Is she dead?" in full seriousness and as though this were the first time any such intimation had come to her, although many times and for many years I had told her, at times gently and at times with scornfully impatient harshness and bluntness, that her mother had died many years ago. "There's a lot of water behind the eyes of the statue," she said movingly.

She remarked later, "People who have murdered may pretend to be crazy," which clearly referred to us. Many times in past years she had accused me of having murdered her mother, and still feared, at an unconscious level, that if her mother were indeed dead, then she must have killed her—either in murderous rage or, more likely, through neglect.

Nine days later, as I was returning from the men's room in the middle of a two-hour session, I had thought that I had been having my psychosis vicariously in a controlled way through her over the years, with myself remaining safely apart from it, and that the hundreds of tapes of our sessions represented my psychosis. Half an hour later in the session she said, while wiping her face with her palms and pushing against her cheeks in a pathetic way, "I don't know how to run my expression . . . ." There was transitory, powerful, submerged anger detectible in her facial expression on occasion; but she was pathetically not in contact with it. A few minutes later she spoke of a "machine supposed to represent the mind of God." Since the early months of our work she had described, on occasion, either herself or me as being, quite concretely and literally, a machine.

Fourteen days later, I began feeling overwhelmed for a few seconds, with accompanying feelings of panic, when I realized that the things she was saying and feeling were based upon lampoons or satires, some conscious and many unconscious, of various real aspects of myself. Her outpourings felt like an avalanche. She still did not know the enormous impact her delusional thinking had upon me, as well as upon other persons in her daily life.

It was evident in this session that I was still emotionally unprepared to occupy the transference role she desperately needed me to occupy a gigantic but psychotically fragmented mother.

Five days later, in a session two days before Christmas, she looked very sad, unhappy, and tearful. She emphasized, as she had before, that people cannot have any emotional relatedness with one another unless they are members of the same parental family; her compulsive family loyalty had been one of the most powerful sources of her resistance. In this session, for the first time, she revealed that she had given her four children, with whom she had severed all ties many years before, to her mother. She wanted to provide her mother with fulfillment, at last, as a mother; it had long been evident that she had not found fulfillment in mothering Joan.

During this session her rapidly changing perceptions of myself and her were even more delusionally distorted than usual. For example she saw the eyes of many different persons fleetingly in my eyes. I experienced a submerged and disturbing agitation of an unusual degree. As far as I could discern, this was related to the intensity of this reality-unrelatedness between us. Only after the session did it occur to me that she had been more resistive, hostile, rejecting, and emotionally unrelated toward me than usual because of an increased need for closeness at the Christmas holiday. Such closeness was permissible, according to her superego standards, only with members of her family. Many years before I had seen her and her sister rush warmly into one another's arms during one of her sister's visits, in a manner which was expressive of genuine familial love, and in retrospect I could see that during this session, Joan had to vigorously defend herself against the expression of such feelings toward me at Christmas time.

A week later I found her to be more psychologically *here* in the session, more tangibly related to me, than she had been in a very long time—perhaps ever. Further, and significantly for the theme of this chapter, she emphasized that she had found that both her mother and father (each clearly related to me in the immediate transference situation) had regarded her as worthless and as contributing nothing worthwhile to either of them.

Three weeks later, I learned from the nurse in charge of her unit that Joan had been crying upon returning to Chestnut Lodge from her session with me on that day and had been talking, at the same time, of her mother's death—for the first time since this nurse had known Joan. Two sessions later, she spoke realistically of her mother's hatred of her:

"But I can't get over why she hates me so much . . . because my mother doesn't like me . . . ."

Five days later she said, gesturing toward her head, "I think I usta run in and out of myself," which I understood as meaning "in and out of fantasy." For many years I had been trying to help her differentiate between fantasy and reality, and this was a welcome indication of progress in that direction. She referred to herself at another point in the session as being an "earthquake"; I mention this as a sample of her persisting and incredible degree of identity distortion.

Regarding her going into and out of fantasy, I had much evidence, from both her psychotherapy as well as from the historical data provided by one of her siblings, that her mother also had gone into and out of fantasy a great deal. Four months later, the patient said, "My mother feels she can't survive unless she's playing a part." It was evident that Joan's childhood participation in her mother's fantasies, a result not only of the mother's domination of her but also of the patient's effort to help her mother survive, had been one of the main sources of Joan's chronically fantasy-ridden, schizophrenic mode of existence.

Four days later, I had just returned from a professional trip, a trip which I felt had been nothing less than triumphant for me in my part-career as an authority on the psychotherapy of schizophrenic patients. In my session with Joan on this day, I found myself feeling, as usual, completely inept and fully deserving of her delusionally expressed but demolishingly effective scorn toward me. It became increasingly clear that I had needed her to confirm, recurrently over the years, the lowest areas of my self-esteem—to reassure me that I am indeed worthless, as I privately feel oftentimes. To be sure, I could see transference connections between myself and her head-in-the-clouds mother who needed recurrently to be deflated down to earth, as well as between myself and her remote, intellectual father who had tenaciously ignored the interpersonal work at hand that desperately needed getting done; but there has been this significantly real core in her transference perceptions of me. In more recent times, as for various reasons my hunger for vilification has lessened somewhat, I gradually have become better able to weather her insults and hold her to our realistic collaborative task.

A week later, in the early part of the session, she suddenly, unexpectedly and very movingly became unusually tearful, protesting, "You keep looking at me so much, when there is someone in your right eye who needs your attention!" It seemed clear that she felt undeserving of my interest. A half hour later she spoke about an overzealous doctor, clearly a reference to me. As long as she felt therapeutically ineffective toward me as a transference figure, it only augmented her feelings of guilt and worthlessness whenever she did get a glimpse of me as genuinely wanting to be helpful to her.

Still later in the session she stated that her mother is not dead, and that she herself is dead, having been murdered. This I heard as typical of her unconscious guilt about her mother's death, but also of a genuinely loving devotion to her mother and a readiness, therefore, to sacrifice her own life in order that the mother might live. Repeatedly in the session she perceived "that man from Tunis" in my left eye—the origin of this perception, like that of most of her perceptions, I had no way of knowing ("Tunis" = twoness?)—and Al Capone in my right eye, and she repeatedly and forcefully accused me of multiple murders and other evil deeds, At one point I felt a rageful urge to beat the craziness out of her, and I sensed this urge as similar to those which had impelled her mother to repeatedly and brutally beat her daughter. One of the currents at work in this surely complex interaction was, I remain convinced on the basis of much corollary data, Joan's therapeutic struggle to resuscitate her dead (= depressed) mother, as personified by me.

Three weeks later she said to me, in the midst of the session, "You're the man from Pakistan." I had been confronted with such communications from her innumerable times before and this, like so many of the others, was said to me very decisively and directly. The new aspect of this instance is that I immediately asked, "Is this what the voices just told you?" and she agreed. I gained a deeper appreciation of the havoc wrought upon her sense of personal identity by her being assailed by such unexpected, forceful, and unequivocally emphatic hallucinatory voices, and realized, more clearly than before, that her incessant verbal barrage against my sense of personal identity was a reflection of what was happening to her during the session.

By contrast, material also emerged highlighting various gratifications which resulted from having no mind of her own—notably a freedom from feeling responsible for what would otherwise be her own thoughts. I had been familiar, from previous sessions, with her experiencing herself as a radio through which people in the walls, for example, were communicating. On some of the occasions when she has said such things—which of course tend totally to nullify my efforts with her—I have reminded her, ironically, that of course she realizes that I, too, am just a radio.

Eight days later, in an unusually collaborative and useful session she said, "You don't seem to realize you've interviewed nine hundred quaduary trillion people in this chair," gesturing toward her chair. This seemed only somewhat of an exaggeration of her stream of successive ego-identity fragments over the years. She was also able to say later ". . . but I got it all mixed up, I guess, in my mind . . ." which was a rare acknowledgement of her confusion.

Eleven days later, a major theme which ran through a session was her reproach toward me and others as being callous and brutal with extremely vulnerable, delicate structures. For example, she pointed out that the people at Chestnut Lodge are living inside a baby. As usual with her delusional thinking, she referred to this as though it were entirely obvious. She stays in her room most of the time, and remains very quiet so as not to damage the baby. Parenthetically, for years the ward staff have been concerned about her massive self-isolation. This building, too, she continued, is the inside of a baby. She was very harsh with me, as so often before, for being so unfeeling; there were innumerable allusions to my being callous and brutal as well as inept. A second and interrelated main theme emerged in the session with equal clarity: she was desperately in need of maternal assistance from me (as well as from others in her daily life), but manifested a fiercely destructive competitiveness with anyone's endeavor to provide such assistance. Early in the session there were unusually clear depictions of her childhood rivalry with her mother; they were involved in a chronic and unresolved power-struggle about who was the mother and who was the child. The prize was omnipotence, as well as the more conventional oedipal goals; and, for the patient, there was the motive of recurrently rescuing the mother from depression by provoking her with outrageously insolent and arrogant behavior.

A month later, during a session where as usual she seemed largely unaware of her castrative rivalry toward me and of the impact this was having upon me, she was able to say, "My mother has always been disgusted with me," a highly accurate statement of an important aspect of her childhood. She had told me that during childhood she suffered from vomiting, and that her mother's fury at her recurrent vomiting had often provoked the mother to beat her. The vomiting served, I believe, to bring the mother back to earth, so to speak, from her fantasyland.

Fifteen minutes later in this same session she concluded one of her usual bewilderingly delusional, dreamlike narratives with, ". . . — so that's where we are now." I realized that this meant that she is fixated at a particular point in an ongoing fantasy. Her intrapsychic life was now becoming sufficiently coherent that I could sense that currently her days were dominated by developing, continuing fantasies. Half an hour later in this two-hour session, she spoke of ". . . mother's . . . sublime . . . ethereal" qualities, so reminiscent of her brother's description of the mother returning from Mass in a beatific mood. Thus, I had a glimpse of how she identified with mother in her fantasy-dominated mode of living. Twenty minutes later, she said thoughtfully and simply, "Mrs. Schultz raised her children," a comment full of tremendous implications of grief and guilt, for she, by contrast, had abandoned her four young children to be raised by others. But here, too, emerged hints (similar to those I reported from an earlier session) that she had done so partly, if not primarily, to thus provide maternal fulfillment to other mother figures.

It occurred to me immediately following a session three weeks later that she cannot assume her real identity as long as I cannot be transformed into a gigantic mother. A month later I wrote the following note, after a session: "The main value of this session is that it is dawning upon me increasingly how *many*—I *now* surmise *all*—of her responses are founded predominantly upon identifications with me as she perceives me. It is dawning upon me how amazingly much she needs for me to *be* her *world,* in the transference relationship, for her to become well, and it seems to be exclusively interpretations of *this* that prove to be useful interpretations."

Perhaps the main reason why this has been so difficult for me to experience fully is that it has required my acknowledgment of her tremendous importance to me. Because of the particular symbiotic relationship she had with her mother, she became equivalent, in coutertransference terms, to my own early, symbiotic mother. I am convinced, not only from my work with Joan and other schizophrenic patients, but also from supervisory experiences with many therapists who were treating such patients, that *the more readily accessible to himself are the therapist's own symbiotic-dependent feelings, the better he is equipped to help the patient to become conscious of similar feelings, so that the patient need no longer act out symbiotic yearnings through the schizophrenic postponement of individuation.*

Within the first five minutes of a session one month later she stated her head was that of a fellow patient in her cottage whom I knew was chronically schizophrenic. She described in detail that the head contained a man in a bizarre position which was causing him much physical suffering. It was apparent that this distortion of her body image, typical of innumerable ones of which I had heard before but expressed more clearly than most, was based in part upon her primitive attempt to bring her fellow patient's suffering in for me, hopefully, to cure. As usual I felt mocked for my ineptitude as a therapist, but impressed once again with how thoroughly her existence depended upon her attempts to cure all her fellow patients as well as mankind in general, as an omnipotent therapist.

Her sister visited her a month later for two or three days, for the first time in some eight months. In her usual interview with me toward the end of her stay, she emphasized how impressive Joan's progress had been, although she did not disregard the persistent manifestations of her tenacious psychosis. In my interview with the patient a bit later during the sister's visit, I was both amused and impressed that Joan was equally oriented toward evaluating how much progress her patient, namely her sister, had made in the several months' interim since the previous visit. She detailed and caricatured, with consummate perception and mimicry, certain of the sister's lifelong compulsively driving characteristics, so much like some of mine, and expressed genuine distress that the sister was still incapable of sharing Joan's current orientation of taking life as it comes. Two days later it was apparent that her having taken "the Mrs. Bradleys" (her sister's married name; she perceived her sister, as usual, as being multiple figures rather than one person) into her own body image, protectively and restoratively, had been done not only out of loving feelings toward her sister, but also as a defense against projected murderousness and contempt toward her. Toward the end of this same month, she said of herself, "We're virtually the whole human race," in a tone both grandiose and burdened as well as simply human. I heard this as an expression of simple and profound truth on the part of one who had achieved, after a long and tragic struggle, kinship with fellow human beings, but had yet to come to terms with the psychotic conflict between her omnipotence-based murderousness toward her fellow human beings, and her at least equally intense loving and therapeutic concern for them.

DISCUSSION

1. *Goals and Techniques Involved in the Patient's Therapeutic Strivings:* One of the patient's strivings is to help the other person (in the treatment situation, the analyst) to fulfill his human potentialities. The patient strives to help the analyst to share those modes of interpersonal relatedness which are relatively anxiety-free for the patient, and anxiety-laden for the analyst; a simple example is the nonobsessive patient's teasing the analyst, in a way that is basically intended to be a helpful "come off it" about the latter's obsessive fussing with the ventilation, lighting, or what-not of the office. Another way of putting it is that the patient endeavors to help the analyst to share in the patient's relatively nonneurotic areas of ego functioning. He is endeavoring to contribute to the analyst's emotional growth, integration, and maturation.

Particularly in the instances of more severely ill — schizoid or schizophrenic — patients, such goals are relatively undifferentiated from the goal of the patient's endeavoring to provide himself with an increasingly constructive model for identification, in the person of the analyst, that can be used for the patient's further maturation.

The psychotherapeutic techniques which the patient utilizes frequently include one or another form of catharsis and various forms of verbal, and much more often nonverbal, reassurance. The most important mechanisms are the primitive unconscious processes of introjection of the analyst's more ill components, and projection upon the analyst of areas of relative strength of the patient's ego (Searles, 1972b). By the introjection the patient attempts to take the analyst's illness into himself and treat the "ill analyst" so that a healthier analyst can eventually be born out of the patient. This takes place during the course of and as a result of the symbiotic phase of treatment.

It is obvious that the patient is relatively unequipped, either consciously or unconsciously, to carry out the primary and paramount goal of the *psychoanalytic* psychotherapist, namely, the analysis of the transference. I shall touch on this matter again in Part 3 of this discussion.

2. *Technique of Interpreting, or Otherwise Acknowledging the Presence of the Patient's Therapeutic Strivings:* This is so complex a matter, so much a function of therapeutic intuition and timing, as to render unwise any attempt to generalize about the subject of when, and how, and to what extent the analyst interprets to the patient his striving to treat him. I rarely if ever acknowledge, in any explicit way, and surely not in any formal way, that I am receiving such help from the patient. The more I can comfortably accept these strivings as inherent to the treatment process, the more, I feel certain, does my whole demeanor convey an implicit acknowledgment that the therapeutic

process involves both of us. Certainly, I make transference interpretations which implicitly convey my acknowledgment that the patient's endeavor to be therapeutically helpful (and in my interpretations I use no such stilted a word as "therapeutic") to the mother is at the same time an endeavor to be similarly helpful toward me as the personification of the mother.

The analyst is technically on relatively solid ground when any indications which he gives that he is finding what is transpiring to be personally helpful to him, are given in a relatively nonanxious, nonguilty and therefore nonconfessional way, but rather as data which are being shared with a collaborator.

Beside the hazard of failing to recognize and interpret the patient's therapeutic strivings, is the hazard of prematurely interpreting them. Generally, as long as patient remains oppressed by feelings of guilty responsibility, he will react with intensified guilt to any intimation from the analyst that he is finding the sessions personally helpful. The patient, in addition to all his other burdens of guilty responsibility, has now also become responsible for the analyst's life, or for that particular aspect of it which the analyst has just revealed.

I cannot say simply that interpretations of the patient's therapeutic strivings should be reserved for relatively late in the analysis, for as a generalization I think that is untrue. But I can say that, in most instances, it is only after some years of analysis that one detects a shift in the feeling tone with which the patient speaks of his family's psychopathology. The feeling tone, which in the earlier years of the analysis had portrayed etiological family events or situations as burdens which were *imposed upon* him, gradually shifts in quality, as his more deeply repressed emotions of grief and loving devotion come to the fore, and conveys that he had also incorporated these burdens within himself in an active and lovingly devoted—what I am calling therapeutic—spirit. Transference interpretations of the patient's therapeutic strivings toward the analyst now are unlikely to intensify the patient's anxiety, confusion, or guilt. But I question whether this phase in the analysis can be reached, unless the analyst has engaged in interpretative activity at an earlier time, when it involves speaking with courage in the face of appreciable risk.

Relatively late in my preparation of this paper, a simple clinical vignette served to remind me how important is the timing of the analyst's interpretation of the patient's therapeutic strivings. A borderline schizophrenic woman from whom I have long been receiving therapeutic help of various kinds caused me to realize that it is not yet timely for me to begin interpreting this aspect of her ego functioning. She was reminiscing, as she often had before, of experiences with a previous therapist in which, seemingly at her initiative, he would soothingly hold her hand. This time she said, ". . . On other occasions he very much wanted to hold my hand, and I was very much aware that it wasn't what *I* needed; it got mixed up with what *he* needed . . .", and this was said with a tone of distinct regret.

She went on a moment later, "He seemed to believe in interaction; he wasn't like you at all. With you, nothing I do seems to matter; you're always the same way. I couldn't have *abided* someone like you [seizing her head in furious exasperation, as she had many times before in our sessions] you'd have driven me crazy! . . ." I felt convinced (particularly by her regretful reference to her previous therapist's need) that it was not yet timely for me to interpret her still largely unconscious therapeutic strivings toward me.

In general, to the degree that a patient is functioning in the treatment sessions in an autistic, infantile-omnipotent manner, he, like the woman just mentioned, is intolerant (despite all his complaints of the analyst's unresponsiveness) of the analyst's functioning in a tangibly alive and participative manner during the sessions—of the analyst's discernibly *contributing anything to* the analytic work, let alone *deriving anything from* it. The patient's infantile omnipotence would be greatly outraged. At a somewhat later phase of the patient's ego development, one finds instances in which the patient manifests a transference to the analytic *situation* as being a nursing mother, and to the analyst *himself* as being a rival sibling whom the patient is determined to keep barred out of this cherished situation of having mother all to oneself. But when this degree of object-relatedness has been achieved, the transference is more subject to interpretation. In any event I hope to have indicated here my cognizance of the fact that the patient's therapeutic strivings are not simply to be interpreted or otherwise acknowledged without considerable thought. The main theme of this chapter focuses upon the loss to both participants if the analyst, as the patient, remains unconscious of this dimension of the relationship and therefore fails to deal with it.

3. *Regression by the analyst, as it concerns his therapeutic strivings:* In a previous paper which included some discussion of patients' therapeutic strivings in the course of my developing another theme (Searles, 1967), I wrote of these patients that

"Their therapeutic techniques are outwardly so brutal that the therapeutic intent is seen only in the result. One apathetic, dilapidated hebephrenic patient of mine received considerable therapeutic benefit from a fellow patient, newly come to the ward, but, like him, a veteran of several years in mental hospitals, who repeatedly, throughout the day, gave my patient a vigorous and unexpected kick in the behind. From what I could see, this was the first time in years a fellow patient had shown any real interest in him, and my patient as a result emerged appreciably from his state of apathy and hopelessness."

During moments or even long phases of particularly intense anxiety in his work, the analyst undergoes regression such that his analytic orientation becomes primitivized (desublimated) to the level of relatively raw aggressive and sexual urges. This regression is a manifestation of the analyst's frustrated therapeutic strivings as well as those of the patient. In my work with the hebephrenic man just mentioned, it was only after some years of four hourly sessions per week, sessions filled with apathy and unrelatedness, punctuated only by moments of murderous rage, violent sexual urges, and acute fear, that I finally realized that it was possible for me to relate to him in some fashion other than the only two potential means heretofore available, those two means being, as I had thought of them, fucking him or killing him. To my enormous relief I realized that I could now be related to him without having either to kill him or fuck him.

It has long been my impression that a major reason for therapists' becoming actually sexually involved with patients is that the therapist's therapeutic striving has desublimated to the level at which it operated in childhood. He has succumbed to the illusion that a magically curative copulation will resolve the patient's illness which tenaciously had resisted all the more sophisticated psychotherapeutic techniques learned in his adult-life training and practice.

In my clinical experience, the temptation toward such activity is most intense in my work with patients whose childhood histories included the patient's having been involved in a relationship with a parent in which the child sensed the incestuous fulfillment would provide the parent with relief from neurotic or psychotic suffering. In such a childhood family situation, it is inordinately difficult for the child's therapeutic striving to become differentiated from, or sublimated beyond sexual strivings. All this becomes reexperienced in the transference relationship, with the analyst becoming the personification of the patient's child-self, feeling impelled to try to resolve the patient's neurotic or psychotic parental

identification (introject) through actual sexual activity.

Unacceptable incestuous urges become acceptable to the therapist's superego by clothing themselves in the guise of healing.

In many instances the primitive healing strivings are no less powerful than are the sexual strivings, and the therapeutic strivings can be the most powerful of all in bringing about a tragic deforming of the therapeutic endeavor, predatory sexual behavior by the therapist under the guise of the emancipated healer. A need for therapeutic omnipotence can lead the therapist to seize upon any available, intentionally therapeutic measures, including actual sexual involvement with the patient.

I touched upon this problem of regression in an earlier paper (Searles, 1959b) concerning integration and differentiation in schizophrenia. In discussing the group symbiosis which develops in the ward life of the hospitalized patient, I stated that:

"In the face of the increasingly intense conflictual feelings which permeate such a group symbiosis, regression deepens, not only in the patient's behavior but in that of the staff members as well. Not only do his demands become more infantile, but the personnel's mothering, good and bad, tends to assume more and more primitive forms. Just as he tends to become a suckling, demanding infant at the breast, they tend almost literally to offer him a breast, 'good' or 'bad' as the case may be, rather than provide more adult forms of mothering. . . ." (pp. 332–3 in Searles, 1965)

At that juncture I referred to one of Knight's (1953) articles on borderline psychosis, in which he described the treatment which a borderline-psychotic college girl had received from a woman dean and self-styled psychotherapist, prior to the girl's hospitalization. As the dean felt progressively cornered by the girl's demands, she allowed the sessions to go overtime, she allowed the girl to have sessions in the dean's home in the evenings and on weekends; she allowed the girl to use the dean's car; she allowed her to stay overnight in her home and, still later, to sleep in bed with her. Knight writes of the patient that

". . . At times she expressed irrational hatred of the dean and pounded her with her fists. At other times she wanted to be held on the dean's lap and fondled, and this wish was granted also. No real limits to her regressive behavior were set until she expressed a strong wish to suckle the dean's breasts. Here the dean drew the line. . . ."

Parenthetically, I now see in that material an

element I did not see when I wrote that paper and which Knight also had not mentioned: The patient's own therapeutic striving to enable the dean to become strong and decisive enough, when sufficiently cornered by the patient's demands (and, more importantly of course, by the dean's own unconscious ambivalence) to draw a line. But to provide another clinical example of the point I am presently making, namely, the regression which becomes manifest in the nature of the doctor's own therapeutic strivings, I mentioned (Searles, 1970) in a paper concerning autism and therapeutic symbiosis that

"I have been amused in retrospect—but only in retrospect—at something I would do from time to time when I would be feeling helpless in my work with one or another chronically paranoid patient who was sure I possessed the magic cure for his or her suffering, 'if you would only think nice thoughts about me,' or 'want me well.' I would have come, long since, to experience much fondness for the patient; but all my conventional analytic armamentarium had failed to help her resolve her psychotic symptoms. Now I would find myself smiling helplessly and pleadingly at the patient, with a feeling of wanting desperately to cure her, somehow, with my love. This, of course, like everything else I had found myself doing, did not work, and the intendedly magical love would be replaced by an equally omnipotence-based hatred, such that I would glare at the patient with, for example, a fantasy of burning out the inside of her skull."

To rephrase this point before going on to the next topic in this discussion, I am suggesting in essence that many instances of therapists' sexual acting-out with patients are motivated predominantly by the thwarting of the therapist's omnipotent healer strivings toward the patient. Surely this matter is related to a high percentage of negative therapeutic reactions: the resistive patient is holding out for the time when the therapist, out of his by now intolerable frustration and despair with the unceasingly futile results of his more conventional therapeutic efforts, will resort to throwing his sexuality onto the balance.

As it is with the therapist's sexual urges in his regressed omnipotent-healer state so, I suggest, it is with his aggressive urges also. At times my murderous urges toward a patient have taken the form of intended euthanasia—a rock-bottom urge to put him out of his misery. Since instances of therapists' barehanded murdering of patients are surely rare, indeed, by contrast to the apparently not-rare instances of sexual involvement between the two, one can surmise that the sexual involvement gives unconscious release, as well, to the two participants'

murderous urges toward one another. I have worked analytically with only one patient who had had an affair with a previous therapist, and I was not surprised to learn that powerful murderous urges evidently had been at work in both of them in the mutual omnipotent-healer strivings toward one another which had impelled them into that involvement with one another.

Turning to a less sensational area, in the course of our own work and in supervising the work of colleagues, we frequently see that a typical earmark of regression in the therapist, under the stress of his efforts to cope with his patient's intense ambivalence and his own responsive ambivalence, is that he, the therapist, has lost touch with the transference context of what is happening. His vision is narrowed by the anxiety and guilt aroused in him by his awareness that there are parts of himself which give immediate reality to the patient's transference to him. He cannot achieve sufficient emotional distance from the immediate interaction to view what is happening as a part of the patient's over-all life history. The realistic elements in the analyst may blind him to links between himself and earlier important figures in the patient's life, links between himself and the patient's childhood self, or evidence that the patient's present way of responding to him represents the activation of an important identification on the patient's part with some parent-image from the latter's childhood.

Here again, then, the therapist, in trying to carry through his therapeutic endeavor without, at this stressful time, the aid of his usual working knowledge and awareness of the dimension of transference, is himself very much like the typical patient in childhood who, in his or her efforts to bring therapeutic help to another family member has, of course, no awareness of the dimension of transference—a dimension which Freud, among his other fundamental contributions to mankind, discovered and enabled us, in turn, to recognize.

4. *Additional Etiological Aspects of Childhood and Family Relationships:* Any full description of the warping by the family of the child's therapeutic strivings would require a book in itself. I shall add here only a few comments to what I have said about this subject earlier in this paper.

Typically, the more ill the adult patient, the more powerful have been the parent(s) transferences (largely unconscious, of course) to him as being the latter's parent(s). Therefore, whenever the child showed any therapeutic concern for the parent, the latter reacted to the child as though the child were the parent's parent. This role reversal threatened to undermine the parent's status as parent and threatened fulfillment of incestuous aims. For these reasons the child's therapeutic striving (inevitably, in this context, impelling the child toward fulfilling a *parental* role in the family) had to be subjected to, or remain under, severe repression and be acted out, within the family, in a manner largely unconscious to all the family members including the child himself.

During the hundreds of teaching interviews in which I have participated, at various hospitals, with adolescent or young adult patients who have become psychotic in the course of attempted emancipation from their families, through going away to college or making analogous attempts to become established as separate individuals, I have found evidence in a high percentage of these interviews that the patient had become overwhelmed with psychotic defenses against unconscious rage, guilt, anxiety, and grief at having proved unable simultaneously to (a) be a successful young college student (or whatever), and (b) be a mother who in this same process of going away to college has abandoned children (namely, the parents and other family members) back home. The young person's individuation needs have come into unbearable conflict, that is, with his therapeutic strivings toward his family members.

It has further seemed to me—although this, now, is somewhat more conjectural—that the same course of events has involved the parents (and other family members) at home in their response to the youth off at college (let us say) as being an unconsciously hated (as well as loved) parent figure, and a feared and hated *parental* (i.e., father or mother) oedipal rival, to such an extent that the parents have seized this very time, when the offspring is making tenuous and of course ambivalent efforts to become established as an individual, defiantly to cast him off as being a hated authority figure to them. Thus, partly in their unconscious rage and hurt at this mother or father who has abandoned them, the actual parents have severed him from the genuinely parental support which he needs, and which most young people evidently receive in sufficient measure. The more one comes to appreciate the familywide, overwhelming tragedy in these situations, the less one feels a sense of blaming any of the family members.

5. *Concerning Gratitude:* More and more during the past several years, I have come at last to see something of how frequently the analyst has cause to feel gratitude toward the patient. Any discussion of gratitude, in the psychoanalytic literature, usually is conducted in the implicit assumption that gratitude is inherently, predominantly if not exclusively, unidirectional in nature: the *patient*, over the course of successful treatment, has increasing reason to experience gratitude toward the *analyst*, and if the former does not manifest this, he remains to that degree neurotic or psychotic. Hill (1955), for example, in the final chapter of his book concerning the psychoanalytic therapy of schizophrenic patients, notes that ". . . one hears very little about gratitude from these patients. . . ." (p. 206). Surely one hears little, likewise, of an analyst's gratitude toward his patient, and it has been only after decades of work in this field that I am becoming at all accustomed to such an emotion. I was still relatively rigorously defended, unconsciously, against experiencing gratitude toward patients when I discussed (Searles, 1966) the sense of identity as a perceptual organ:

"Following a single consultative interview (several years previously) with a schizophrenic man—one who had been making a thoroughgoing ass of himself with certain hebephrenic symptoms—I experienced myself, driving away from that hospital, as being an incredibly gifted and perceptive consultant. But then I caught myself and wondered what this was saying about the patient's dynamics. I was immediately struck with the likelihood that he tended to project onto other persons, including me, his own best ego capacities. This man, who had done such wonders, transitorily, for my self-esteem while abasing himself, committed suicide about two months later. We never know why about these things; but among the likely causes is the possibility that he came to find insupportable the burden which others placed upon him in their unconsciously exploiting him for the enhancement of their own subjective identities. . . ."

I am sure that I experienced, during that interview, no gratitude toward that man; one has no reason to feel gratitude toward someone who one perceives as being, whether consciously or unconsciously, victimized or exploited. It is only as I have come to sense and perceive the lovingly devoted, self-sacrificing, therapeutic-striving determinants of such behavior as he had manifested, that I have found reason to experience gratitude toward the patient. Nowadays, during and following sessions—whether with my own analytic patients or with patients seen in single consultative or teaching interviews such as that just mentioned—which have proved to be unusually fulfilling for me both personally and professionally, I find in myself feelings of heartfelt gratitude.

For example, during my teaching interview with a borderline schizophrenic young woman at a nearby hospital a year ago, I quickly began feeling that the interview was being not only of unusual therapeutic value for her, but was in the same vein, deeply fulfilling and confirming for me in my identity as someone wanting to be a useful psychoanalyst. I was sure that I was being of use to her and to the several psychiatric residents who were observing the interview. I felt that she and I both were being of rare growth value for one another. I have no doubt that my keen appreciating of her was evident in my demeanor. The group of staff members present fully shared, as was evident in the postinterview discussion, my appreciation of how much this patient had done for all of us. It struck me how illusory is any assumption that a therapist experiences such professional gratification as an expectable, everyday, mundane part of his work. I am trying here to suggest that the therapist has reason to feel as rare and memorable and intense a form of gratitude as has the patient whose therapist has effected, as we conventionally say, a remarkable cure.

On the very next day I had, at another nearby hospital, again in the presence of a group of staff members, an interview with a young man who was suffering from schizophrenia and drug addiction. This interview was in quality more like those to which I am accustomed, although this was one of the more extreme examples of this type. This interview gave me fantasies and feelings of giving up this profession entirely as a useless endeavor. The patient seemed to feel called upon chronically to justify his existence, and at the same time to feel unable to justify it. His impact upon me and upon the audience was as one not worth trying to save, and no one with the possible exception of myself—certainly not his therapist whose initial presentation of the case, prior to the patient's coming into the room, showed thoroughgoing disdain for the patient—seemed to feel at all interested in trying to save him. This interview served to enhance my gratitude toward the young woman I had interviewed on the previous day.

REVIEW OF RELEVANT LITERATURE

This review is not comprehensive. But the existing literature concerning the subject is scanty, indeed.

It is striking that this particular subject is so conspicuously absent from classical psychoanalytic papers concerning the analysis of nonpsychotic patients. For reasons of space I must resist quoting passages from such articles which would highlight their failure to acknowledge therapeutic strivings, conscious or unconscious, on the part of the patient.

Even in the literature concerning schizophrenia, in which illness the patient's therapeutic strivings are overwhelmingly significant and relatively easy to discern, most authors continue to view schizophrenic patients as basically parasitic. Typical of the abundant literature which views the patient as suffering from a crippling ego defect, as needful primarily of supplies from without, and as being oriented, therefore, toward receiving from, rather than giving to, his environment, is the volume by Burham, Gladstone and Gibson (1969), *Schizophrenia and the Need-Fear Dilemma:*

". . . a key element of our theoretical system . . . is the proposition that the schizophrenic person, because he lacks stable internal structure, is exceedingly dependent upon and vulnerable to the influence of external structure. . . ." (p. 13)

"We turn now to discuss the schizophrenic person's disordered object relations, particularly his intense need-fear dilemma. Because he is poorly differentiated and integrated, he lacks reliable internal structure and autonomous control systems. Accordingly he has an inordinate need for external structure and control. He requires others to provide the organization and regulation which he is unable to provide for himself. . . .

"The very excessiveness of his need for objects also makes them inordinately dangerous and fearsome since they can destroy him through abandonment. Hence he fears and distrusts them. He may attempt to alleviate the threat of abandonment by repeated pleas or demands for proof of the object's constancy. Such pleas are insatiable because much of the inconstancy of his percepts of objects stems from his inner instability. Another defensive tactic, also of limited value, is the attempt to deny his need and his fear of separation." (pp. 17–28)

The authors describe the patient as attempting to cope with his need-fear dilemma by object clinging, object avoidance, and object redefinition. Concerning object clinging, for example, they say that

"In this attempted solution . . . the patient, in effect, gives himself over to the need side of his conflict. He abandons efforts at differentiation and independence and attempts to fuse inseparably with others. A bewildering variety of terms has been employed to describe this type of relationship: symbiotic, narcissistic, orally fixated, object-addicted, anaclitic, self-centered, unilateral, possessive, overdependent, receptive, demanding, devouring, hunger-fulfilling, and others. These terms share common reference to the excessive need for supplies from the object, with little regard for the reciprocal needs of the object; in other words, a wish to receive but not give. . . . The schizophrenic person wishes the object to provide the inner balance and integration he has been unable to achieve for himself . . ." (p. 32).

Similarly Gibson (1966), in his paper, "The Ego Defect in Schizophrenia," while documenting a remarkably impressive degree of clinical improvement on the part of a chronically schizophrenic woman still in treatment with him, consistently portrays the patient as improving on the basis of strength borrowed from the therapist, portrayed as vastly more powerful than herself:

"This patient was struggling with a basic dilemma—the *need* for an object from which to borrow ego strength, and the *fear* of the same object because of its threat to ego organization. . . . The need-fear dilemma arises out of a deficit in ego functioning. I do not think of this defect as limited to a specific area of ego function; so perhaps it would be more accurate to speak of ego weakness rather than defect." (pp. 88–9)

Writing of the schizophrenic person in general, Gibson says that

". . . His vulnerability to disorganization of ego function makes him desperately need objects to provide the support and structure which he lacks. His lack of ego autonomy leaves him unable to resist the influence of objects and thus makes them frightening to him. The poor reality testing of the schizophrenic makes all object relations extremely tenuous." (p. 89)

Concerning the particular patient upon the treatment of whom his paper is mainly based, he says,

"I believe, to recapitulate, that this schizophrenic patient had an inordinate need for objects to compensate for an ego defect. . . ." (p. 92)

". . . At times, her prevailing feeling was one of extreme gratitude to me, and she took pleasure in our relationship. But, quite regularly, she felt threatened by the thought that she might lose it. At other times, she resented the enormous power over her that this gave me. She also feared that she would have to satisfy my dependency needs just as she had those of her parents. . . ."

"The inevitable vicissitudes of object clinging are illustrated by this sequence of events. Object clinging occurs as a response to the need-fear dilemma in the schizophrenic when the need is dominant. An effort is made to compensate for the ego defect through fusion with an object. The object becomes an auxiliary ego that shares the responsibility for organizing behavior, managing and controlling drives, and testing reality. This device may work remarkably well. Superficially at least, patients may seem fully intact so long as this kind of a relationship to an object is maintained."

". . . The patient will see in the therapist an object to which he can cling to strengthen his weakened ego, but this can rouse all of the fears I have just described. In addition the therapist may be seen as a controlling agent that will threaten the patient's autonomy." (p. 94)

Gibson describes the mother as having been extremely dependent upon the patient during the latter's childhood:

"The patient and sister (younger by three years) grew up with the mother, who was extremely dependent on both of her children, especially Eileen [the patient], and did everything she could to keep them from becoming independent. . . ." (p. 90)

But, although he writes that "She . . . feared that she would have to satisfy my dependency needs just as she had those of her parents" (p. 94), his account also includes no acknowledgment of any personal dependency feelings on his part toward her, of any anxiety lest he lose her, nor, by the same token, of any therapeutic strivings on her part toward him. It seems to me probable that such factors help to account for her maintenance of a predominantly positive transference toward him, of which he takes note in his account:

"Eileen required a fair degree of selective inattention to maintain the idealized view of me as an entirely benevolent helper. . . .By always displacing negative transference feelings onto someone other than the therapist, she was able to avoid any feelings of hostility toward the therapist that might have led to thoughts of terminating treatment. Such thoughts were intolerable to Eileen when she had to rely completely on me to serve as an auxiliary ego. . . ." (p. 96)

It is only in the most general terms that Gibson alludes to a conjectured dependency on the part of the therapist toward the patient when, early in his paper, he comments that

"To some extent, this need-fear dilemma is a part of the experience of all human beings capable of relating to an object." (p. 88)

and when, in his closing sentence, he conjectures, concerning what the therapist offers which proves therapeutic in this regard, that

". . . Perhaps most of all, the psychotherapist shares in the need-fear dilemma, and in so doing establishes a new kind of relationship for the patient—a relationship that nurtures ego growth." (p. 97)

As a portrayal of an important part of the state of affairs which one finds in the schizophrenic patient, the above-quoted descriptions by Burnham, Gladstone, and Gibson seem accurate enough. But the basic psychodynamics of such schizophrenic phenomena warrant, in my clinical experience, an utterly contrasting emphasis as being the truer one, and this emphasis is crucial for any successful psychotherapy of the schizophrenic person. His impairment in whole-ego functioning, his inability to function as a whole individual, is due most fundamentally to a genuinely selfless devotion to a mother, or other parent figure, the maintenance of whose ego functioning requires that the child not become individuated from her (or him). In the course of our work with him now as a chronological adult in psychotherapy, we entirely miss the main point, in my opinion, if we regard him as suffering most fundamentally from a crippling ego defect, a result of early deprivation or other trauma, and as needful of receiving supplies of various sorts from our own whole and intact ego. Ironically, the crucial issue is, rather, whether *we* can become and remain conscious of the symbiotic (pre-individuation) dependency which *we* inevitably develop toward *him,* and which is necessary for the success of the treatment.

In this regard we personify in transference terms the parent whose relationship with him over the preceding years has been fixated at a symbiotic level; but, as I have emphasized repeatedly, it is not "only transference." The therapist comes to feel that he *really* is, to a significant degree, at one with the patient, and to experience as a *real* question whether he, the therapist, can bear the loss to his own ego functioning of the individuation toward which the therapeutic endeavor is directed. Thus in retrospect the schizophrenic patient's "ego-defect" toward which it is so easy to feel a kind of pitying condescension, becomes translated as "a frightening degree of personal importance to the therapist's very self" (with the patient being emotionally equivalent, for example, to the therapist's heart or mind). The more *conscious* the therapist becomes, and remains, of these processes, the less likely is any acted-out *folie à deux.* If we never become conscious of them, we remain relatively comfortable in our condescending view of the schizophrenic patient, and he retains his usual status of someone we perceive as a pathetic and needful cripple. I can confidently say that the great bulk of our psychoanalytic and psychiatric literature is such as to make our recognition of the patient's symbiotic-therapist striving orientation toward us more, rather than less, anxiety-arousing, embarrassing, humiliating, and otherwise difficult for us.

Many authors in the field of psychotherapeutic work of all kinds acknowledge patients' contributions to our understanding of psychodynamics and of increasingly effective techniques of psychotherapy, but stop far short of perceiving the patient as needing to help the therapist. It is not uncommon for authors to dedicate books gratefully to their patients, though few acknowledge the patients' help so explicitly as does Milner (1969) in the dedication of her book:

"To all my teachers in psychoanalysis, especially my patients."

Jones (1953), in his biography of Freud, describes the following event as one of the landmarks of the Breuer period:

"Freud was still given to urging, pressing, and questioning, which he felt to be hard but necessary work. On one historic occasion, however, the patient, Frl. Elisabeth, reproved him for interrupting her flow of thought by his questions. He took the hint, and thus made another step towards free association." (pp. 243–4)

Although Freud and his patient together achieved this fundamental technical refinement as long ago as 1892 or shortly thereafter, it is still common to find technical psychoanalytic discussions that do not acknowledge patients' therapeutic strivings, which latter seem to me a necessary aspect of any adequate treatise on the subject of analytic technique in a truly interpersonal context. For example, Olinick et al. (1972), in their paper, "The Psychoanalytic Work Ego: Process and Interpretation," state that

". . . The timing of an interpretation is an acquired art that involved the synthesis of empathic and cognitive processes [and is in part, I suggest, the analyst's response to the patient's therapeutic strivings to enable the analyst to function, for example, as a successfully nursing mother or as a sexually potent father]. Partial and spontaneous interventions, of the kind described, are then further elaborated in the course of subsequent working through [which subsequent working through, I suggest, presumably consists in part in the consolidation of the analyst's therapeutic benefit at the hands of the patient]."

In the above-quoted passage, my rude intrusions of my own thoughts are attempts to depict how pervasively significant, to *any* of the much discussed psychoanalytic topics (such as interpretation and working through), is our cognizance of the patient's own therapeutic strivings toward the analyst. Similarly as regards the literature concerning the "therapeutic alliance" (for example, Zetzel 1956 and Greenson 1965 and 1967), where such writings imply that what is being discussed is alliance for therapy for the *patient,* I hold that what is actually at work is an alliance for therapy for *both* participants in the treatment situation.

The first writing, to my knowledge, which at all explicitly describes the patient's functioning as therapist to the doctor is Groddeck's (1923) *The Book of the It*. It is noteworthy that even this courageously pioneering statement portrays the therapeutic process at work as being, in essence, therapy *for the patient,* exclusively, in the long run; nonetheless, Groddeck is a pioneer of high courage in his reporting that

". . . His childlike attitude towards me—indeed, as I understood later, it was that of a child of three—compelled me to assume the mother's role. Certain slumbering mother-virtues were awakened in me by the patient, and these directed my procedure. . . . And now I was confronted by the strange fact that I was not treating the patient, but that the patient was treating me; or to translate it into my own language, the It of this fellow being tried so to transform my It, did in fact so transform it, that it came to be useful for its purpose. . . . Even to get this amount of insight was difficult, for you will understand that it absolutely reversed my position in regard to a patient. It was no longer important to give *him* instructions, to prescribe for *him* what I considered right, but to change in such a way that *he* could use *me*." (pp. 262–3)

Whitaker and Malone (1953), in discussing the motivations of the therapist, suggest that

"The enthusiasm and elation felt when contemplating the possibility that schizophrenic patients may be amenable to psychotherapy may reflect a perception that some residual needs can perhaps be answered only in therapeutic experiences with the schizophrenic." (p. 101)

This statement does not explicitly attribute a therapeutic motive to the patient, but implies that certain therapists, presumably more ill than most, may somehow find therapy for their own aberrant needs in their work with schizophrenic patients. Therefore the above statement is much more at odds with, than consonant with, the theme of this paper. Later on, the authors go far beyond the statement quoted above. In an extremely interesting chapter entitled, "Patient-Vectors ["vectors" meaning, so I gather, forces] in the Therapist," which they consider a more meaningful concept than that of countertransference (a view which I do not feel moved to embrace) they make the following statements, clearly in reference to patients generally (rather than exclusively schizophrenic patients) and to healthy therapists:

". . . the bilateral character of therapy constitutes its most effective dynamic basis. . . . In the best therapeutic relationship, the therapist recurrently brings his own patient-vectors to the patient. . . . Indeed, a therapeutic impasse can often be resolved only by the therapist's willingness to bring his patient-vectors to the patient quite overtly. This principle implies that were the therapist free of all patient-vectors, he would be no therapist at all." (p. 165)

They do not give any details as to how the therapist may usefully "bring his patient-vectors to the patient quite overtly." If by this they mean to recommend that the therapist on occasion share with the patient information about the therapist's own personal life, I must part company from them, for in my own work I probably do little more of this than does any classical psychoanalyst.

In 1968, Marie Coleman Nelson et al. published their volume, *Roles and Paradigms in Psychotherapy,* describing a method of psychoanalytic psychotherapy which they had developed during the previous ten years, and which they call *paradigmatic* psychotherapy. A paradigm is defined as demonstration by example, and paradigmatic psychotherapy is the systematic setting forth of examples by the analyst to enable the patient to understand the significant intrapsychic processes or interpersonal situations of his life, past and present. The authors see this technique as most appropriate for borderline patients who are unable to utilize the verbal interpretations basic to the usual psychoanalytic approach; but it is a technique which the authors convincingly demonstrate to have implications for the treatment of virtually every patient.

One of their standard techniques they term "siding with the resistance" (p. 75), which they further define as

". . . joining with the irrational aspects of a patient's responses and thus inducing him to oppose his own pathology, which the therapist has now taken over. When this technique is followed persistently, it soon appears that the patient is much more reasonable and healthy than the therapist, who then appears as a paradigm of the patient's own presenting pathology" (p. 75).

At the end of one of the clinical examples of the use of this technique, the author (Strean) formulates that

"Joining the patient's resistance in the above instance was narcissistically enriching [for the patient] instead of depleting. The patient and therapist were colleagues, with the former helping the latter. As the therapist enacted the role of the passve, naive, ignorant child, Mr. B. was in no way threatened by potential attack [whereas he had so reacted to more conventional psychoanalytic responses]. On the contrary, he could teach the therapist psychological facts. The therapist's role (the naive, ignorant part of Mr. B.) stimulated the patient to educate the therapist. For Mr. B., educating the therapist was, in effect, educating that part of himself which needed enlightenment but resisted it" (p. 183).

Despite a recurrent note of superficial game-playing, which in my opinion does far less than justice to the patient's genuine importance as therapist to the therapist, these authors' work is of much significance and value for anyone who wishes to pursue further the theme of this present paper. On occasion their accounts of their work convey a genuine and moving portrayal of their patients' functioning as therapists in the treatment situation, which go beyond what I can capture in these necessarily brief excerpts. For example, Strean (pp. 233–7), in his account of his work with a very withdrawn fourteen-year-old boy who could not read and who had been involved unsuccessfully with several previous therapists, describes his approaching the patient as being a consultant, with the patient's being in a position of "self-dosing," that is, providing his own prescription in the treatment situation. This came to involve the patient's functioning as teacher to the therapist:

". . . in the first interview . . . The patient was asked by the therapist, 'What should I do?' . . . Possibly he could teach the therapist techniques of passive resistance? . . . Joe stated that he might try for a little while to teach the therapist to be silent. . . . However, the patient insisted, 'You have to promise to say nothing. I'll be the boss around here.' . . .

"Several interviews passed uneventfully. Joe, instead of talking and teaching, remained silent. The therapist and patient merely looked at each other with no exchange except, 'Hello' and 'Good-bye.'

". . . When the therapist wondered if Joe could teach him something about electricity [in which he knew the boy was interested], Joe got up, walked out of the interview and stated dryly, 'You've got a lot to learn. I'll think about coming back and showing you.'

"Joe did return for two silent sessions, but without encouragement soon delighted in showing the therapist several electrical plans. Electricity became the sole mode of communication for several months, with Joe as teacher and the therapist as pupil. . . .

". . . Eventually, Joe entered a vocational school and specialized in electricity. . . .

"As he learned how to read and attained other academic and social successes, Joe suggested that 'the case be closed.' He wrote in his own handwriting, 'A Closing Summary on Mr. Strean' in which he both criticized and

praised the therapist, giving a colorful picture of the treatment process. . . .

"For the therapist, the relationship had enormous meaning. . . ." (pp. 235–6)

In 1969 Milner published her previously mentioned 412-page account of her psychoanalytic treatment, extending over nearly twenty years, of a schizophrenic woman. Milner's volume is richly creative, scholarly in its evaluation of the many psychoanalytic writings which she found relevant in the course of this long treatment endeavor, and inspiring in terms of the author's clinical devotion and the patient's clinical improvement. One of the many fascinating aspects of her book, to me, consists in Milner's very long-delayed, but eventually at least partial, recognition of the patient's therapeutic strivings toward her.

On page 107, for example, I noted that thus far one could find no evidence that Milner was yet aware of this patient's therapeutic strivings toward her, though such strivings were implicit in much data which she had been presenting from the patient. On page 120, although she surmises that the patient had endeavored, during the latter's upbringing, to cheer up her depressed mother, Milner shows no evidence that she finds this to be a factor in the transference relationship. On page 130, I noted that throughout the abundant data concerning mother-infant transference relatedness thus far, Milner assumes consistently that she is in the transference role of mother, and the patient in that of infant, whereas the reverse is often implied in the data from the sessions.

On page 177, referring to a time near the end of the seventh year of the treatment, Milner says that

"During the eight weeks of my summer break Susan wrote frequent letters to me from the hospital, sometimes four posted by different posts all in one day, calling me by my first name and ending 'with love'. . . . In the letters she said she was feeling quite terrible and was angry with the psychiatrist in charge, who, she said, had been tough with her and done nothing to help. . . ."

Milner seems to continue, here, to perceive the patient as being equivalent to a needful infant or child in relation to her as a mother, and not to perceive the patient's implicit maternal concern for the therapist as abandoned child—the patient's anxiety lest the therapist not be able to endure this separation, and her striving to assuage the therapist's loneliness and to reassure the latter of her, Milner's, indispensability.

On page 289, concerning a session in the fourteenth year, Milner makes a statement, for the first time in her account, which takes relatively full cognizance of the patient's therapist potentialities, and which is fully consonant with my own concepts about therapeutic symbiosis:

"What I seem to have said in the session was that she had difficulty in believing in a way of coming together with me that is psychical and not erotically physical, and which could lead to something new being created, her new self *and mine*. . . . [italics by HFS]"

On page 292 the author notes a theme, evident at that juncture (in the fourteenth year of the treatment), "of her attempt to avoid dependence on me by feeling she herself has all that she needs—and what I need as well." But the reader has no way of knowing, here, whether Milner conceptualizes "what I need as well" to be purely a distorted transference perception on the patient's part (if such were indeed possible), or whether there is a nucleus of reality in the patient's perception, here, of the analyst.

On pages 303 to 304, concerning a session a bit later in the fourteenth year, in which the patient did a drawing of a baby duck within a larger duck, Milner notes that

". . . there was not only the question of the part of herself, as the baby duck, being ready to come out from inside me, there was also the related task of her becoming able to let me out, let me be born out of her. . . ."

Still later in the fourteenth year, when the patient continued to be involved in a process lasting more than ten months of becoming ready to be born, Milner reports that

"On 27 July she says she remembers sitting on her mother's knee and feeling so depressed, and how her mother was always saying she [the mother] was going to die. Now she wonders if she was always trying to stop her from dying." (p. 322)

When, a few months later, the following material emerges, I would infer that the patient is concerned therapeutically to provide life to the analyst, a depressed mother not only in transference terms, but also, I would assume, to a degree *really* depressed. Mrs. Milner sees this *only* as a transference projection:

"On Thursday 25 November she brings a dream:
"She dreamed that I was telling her how my husband had left me his mummied heart in his will, and I was crying and so was she. But we were both quite separate from each other.

"Her own association to the dream . . . was that she could only give me a dead heart, which means that she will never get well. I said that in the dream she does seem to have a heart, because she is crying and feeling sorry. I said I thought the dream was more about artificially keeping a live heart dead than artificially preserving a dead one; that is, she has been trying to blot out the inner movement of feeling to do with love and sadness." (p. 347–8)

In my own similarly prolonged work with Mrs. Douglas, some aspects of which I have described at length earlier in this paper, I found, by contrast, that my real feelings of depression in addition to (or, in my terms, as a nucleus of) the patient's long-familiar transference perceptions of me as being the personification of her depressed mother, or of her depressed self, helped greatly to account for the tenacity of her "crazy talk" (as it has been referred to for many years in the sanitarium where she lives) during the sessions.

Specifically, innumerable times during recent years, as she has become more able to face her tremendous and long-repressed feelings of grief, this has involved our having to face a very considerable risk of her suicide; that is, her feelings of healthy grieving are not yet well-differentiated from those of a psychotically depressive nature. Partly as a function of this phase of my work with her (as well as from various other sources in my current life), I have found myself experiencing, concomitantly, feelings of depression of a formidable degree during our sessions. In fact, during at least one of our sessions some two years ago, I experienced considerable fear lest *one or the other* of us commit suicide immediately following the session.

Hence it is to a degree understandable to me that the following sequence occurred innumerable times in recent years, during a phase which now seems largely behind us, as she has become better able to grieve. She used to come into the session and instead of starting to pour forth her usual appallingly fragmented, yet irresistibly fascinating and in a sense entertaining "crazy talk," she would sit silently, appearing to be filled with mute grief and despair. Consciously I welcomed this development, in each such session. But each time when, after a few or many minutes of silence, she then started verbalizing her usual "crazy talk," and her demeanor came within a few minutes later still to show little if any of the feelings of grief and despair, *against my will* (so it felt) I would find myself feeling relieved at her being her long-familiar, chronically crazy self. There were abundant data, in such sessions, indicating that she tended to feel that she was thus keeping her mother (= HFS) alive, or bringing her mother back to life, by this craziness. If I had thought of such perceptions on her part, of me, as being "just transference," the remarkable tenacity of her craziness would have been much less understandable to me.

For a great many years following her admission to Chestnut Lodge, it was clear that her social role at the Lodge was of one whose craziness seemed designed to relieve depression in others. It was typical of her that when, a few days before a certain Christmas, while the patients were reacting with an intensively depressive pall to efforts on the staff's part to encourage them to join in carol singing, Joan's caustically scornful voice came loud and clear and masterfully sure over the group's tragically depressed and nostalgic efforts at singing, "What's the *matter* with you *idiots*, singing *Christmas carols?* Don't you realize it's *March the tenth?*" This broke up the crowd, staff members and patients alike, with relieved laughter at her craziness.

In the course of my careful reading of Milner's book, I recall no mention by the author of her feeling any such despair as has been so familiar to me in the work with Joan. On page 366 Milner describes her realization, in retrospect, of how caught up she had been in a compulsion to be helpful to her patient (much as I had described in a paper in 1955 [Searles, 1955]). In such a state one is in no position to discern the patient's therapeutic strivings toward oneself:

". . . my early tendency to do too much for her and to interpret too much in terms of the 'good object', not taking enough account of the 'good subject'. . . . my overanxiety to be a 'good' analyst in those early years of my practice, overanxiety leading to giving too many interpretations . . ." (p. 366).

The following passage, concerning a dream which the patient reported early in the 16th year of the analysis, shows how much more clearly the author has come to recognize the significance of the patient's own love — highly relevant, of course, to the theme of the present paper:

". . . So now I see the . . . dream as expressing this basic conflict she has been battling with all these years, the issue of whether she can accept any limitations on her loving, both in how she gives or how she takes; whether she can give up her belief that she can make herself one with what she loves by eating it, accept the fact that the food she eats is not actually the same as the breast that she loved, that she wished to become one with by eating; and also

whether she can accept limits in her giving, accept something less than an actual giving up her life; and find instead, by discrimination between inner and outer, a surrender that is not physical death." (p. 370)'

Somewhat later in the sixteenth year of the analysis, Milner describes that

"A few months after Susan's getting a room of her own her mother died; it was the ending of a long illness during which Susan had been very good to her, in spite of the fact that her mother could never recognize her devotion or give her any thanks; for instance, in the last year of her mother's life Susan would often visit her, taking her a box of chocolates, and her mother would eat them without ever offering Susan one. And when the nurse looking after her mother said, in front of them both, 'You have a very good daughter,' her mother had said nothing." (p. 388)

In a footnote to the above, Milner comments:

"This inability on the part of her mother to acknowledge her daughter's reparative activities highlighted important aspects of Susan's account of her childhood . . . [and] certainly tended to confirm the psychoanalytic view that the lack of opportunity for and recognition of reparative activities can greatly encourage psychotic states of mind." (p. 388)

It can be seen that what Milner (following her usual Kleinian conceptualization) terms reparative activities I would term therapeutic strivings, regarding these strivings as being more a part of the infant's primary potentialities for giving love than secondary to the individual's hostile strivings (and therefore expressive, in Kleinian terms, of an attempt at reparation for the fantasied damage wrought upon the mother, in past experiences with her, by one's own hostility).

It is my impression that an analyst's rigid adherence to a classically psychoanalytic orientation, his remaining oblivious of and unacknowledging of the nuclei of reality in the patient's transference responses to him, fosters his being precisely as unacknowledging of the patient's therapeutic strivings toward him as Susan's mother was toward Susan in the above-described situation. One is left with a nagging sense of doubt as to whether, or to what extent, Milner regards her patient's transference reactions to her as being based in a nucleus of reality when, in the following passage in her closing pages, she implies that in order to become free of psychosis a psychotic patient needs to create the analyst — *really* needs to, to a very significant and crucial degree:

". . . although I had myself been convinced through my own enquiries into painting [Milner, M., 1950] that the 'other' has to be created before it can be perceived, I had yet taken so long to realize the implications of this in clinical work, the full extent to which she had to be allowed to contribute from herself before she could feel that I was truly real for her. . . ." (p. 404)

The recent paper by Singer (1971), "The Patient Aids the Analyst: Some Clinical and Theoretical Observations," because of its high degree of consonance with the theme of this present paper, merits my quoting from it at length here. Singer begins,

"From their very beginnings most publications on psychoanalytic technique have stressed at least implicitly a dominant theme: that the analyst derives little personal satisfaction from his work other than the gratification the healer inevitably derives from the sense of a job well done and, of course, from the financial rewards attending his efforts. All other satisfactions arising in his working day have been suspect of countertransference tendencies rooted in the analyst's unresolved conflicts.

"Structuring the psychoanalytic relationship in these terms molded the process into a one-way street: the helping relationship was to be one in which the analyst aided the patient, in which he could not and should not expect any comparable aid from his client. . . .

"It is the purpose of this paper to explore . . . the potential power of the analyst's revealing his own life situation, thereby making it possible for the patient to be realistically helpful; and finally, as its main contribution, to support implications for a theory of personality development derived from these observations, implications at variance with those traditionally advanced in the psychoanalytic literature."

". . . unbending anonymity, while furthering the denouement of hidden destructive and other primitive tendencies, does not promote and activate reality-oriented and constructive qualities. . . ." (pp. 56-8)

Singer's paper resulted from the fact that his wife suddenly became seriously ill, which required him to cancel all his appointments until further notice, with a demeanor which he knew his patients had reason to detect as uncharacteristically anxious.

". . . My patients . . . sensed from my voice that this cancellation did not reflect a frivolous impulse and spontaneously inquired, 'What's up?' Too troubled to engage in lengthy conversations and hesitant about how much I wanted to say, I merely replied that I would explain when I saw them again. . . .

"With some trepidation I decided [in the interim] to tell them the truth. . . . I informed all patients about the reason for my absence.

"Their responses seemed to be astonishing, and that I was astonished reflected poorly on me. Concern, genuine sympathy, eagerness to be helpful with problems likely to arise, and, above all, efforts to be supportive and comforting—these reactions were eye-openers. As I listened, deeply moved and profoundly grateful, to the patients' efforts, it became apparent that each person expressed his desire to be helpful in his particular style, a manner which often, when occurring under different circumstances, had been identified as reflecting a pathological character orientation. I will give a few illustrations. . . . (pp. 58-9)

"I hope that these vignettes illustrate what I have learned: that the capacity to rise to the occasion when compassion and helpfulness are called for is part and parcel of the makeup of all human beings. Importantly, in no single instance did my disclosures have any ill effects; on the contrary, the insights, memories, and heightened awareness which followed my self-exposure proved remarkable, and I have the deep conviction that my frankness accelerated the therapeutic process in several instances.

". . . Strict psychoanalytic anonymity would have reduced my patients' opportunities to see their own strengths; and certainly it would have limited my knowledge of their caring and compassionate capacities. . . .

"My patients' efforts to search themselves much more seriously after my disclosures than ever before brought to light certain themes which up to now had never emerged or had at best been mentioned only fleetingly.

"Mrs. N., for instance, now genuinely attempted to grasp the truth of critical experiences and of the affect associated with certain of her present-day reactions to them. . . . With great pain Mrs. N. now began to reexperience instances of feeling totally unable to make any meaningful contributions to these all-knowing, all-successful, and seemingly 'need-less' people [i.e., her mother and her father] . . . . there is little doubt in my mind . . . that the admission of my pain made the vision of genuine usefulness a realistic possibility for her. . . . (pp. 62-3)

". . . much of the neurotic distress experienced by my patients seemed associated with their profound sense of personal uselessness and their sense of having failed as human beings because they knew that the only contributions they had made were embodied in nonconstructive reactions and behavior responding to equally nonconstructive demands. . . .

". . . those concerned with the origins of psychopathology and with efforts to rekindle emotional growth must give serious attention to the possibility that the most devastating of human experiences is the sense of uselessness. . . . (p. 65)

"This lack of authenticity in parent-child relations, the child's inadequate opportunities to express constructive relatedness, finds an analogue in the traditional analytic relationship. . . .

". . . For some patients the events described here accelerated a process of growth well underway. But others were reached emotionally for the first time in therapy by my disclosures and willingness to accept their help. . . ." (p. 67)

I have already indicated that I differ with one of Singer's main conclusions, namely that

". . . a marked reduction of the analyst's anonymity is essential to therapeutic progress. . . ." (p. 67)

In my own work, while I am relatively free about revealing feelings and fantasies which I experience during the analytic session itself, I tell patients very little of my life outside the office. But I feel sure that even the most critical reader of Singer's paper will find it difficult to write off his work as "wild analysis," for throughout the paper he manifests, recurrently, a commendably detailed, serious, and genuinely humble acknowledgment of the potential hazards of the departures from classical analysis which he is advocating. I myself regard the theme of this present paper as fraught with complexities; but it seems to me imperative that we enter this thicket and carve out of it some solid theoretical and technical area for our functioning as analysts, for in my opinion the classical analytic position contains an element of delusion to the effect that the analyst is not at all a real person to the patient, and therefore simply will not do. I find an analogy to this latter point in Lewin's (1958) charming little monograph, *Dreams and the Uses of Regression*. Lewin begins by saying that:

"Around the year 500 B.C., natural science began with a repudiation of the dream. . . ." (p. 11)

And then, toward the end of his essay, Lewin discloses the delightful irony that the view of the world as conceptualized by Descartes, the epitome of the natural scientists, is essentially dreamlike in nature:

"In short, I should like to hazard a hypothesis: when Descartes came to formulate his scientific picture of the world, he made it conform with the state of affairs in an ordinary successful dream. The picture of the dream world that succeeds best in preserving sleep . . . came to be the picture of the waking world that succeeded best in explaining it scientifically. . . ." (p. 50)

So, I feel, it is with classical psychoanalysis: to the degree that it is rigorously classical, it is essentially delusional.

Space does not allow for my trying to recapitulate all my own previous writings about the theme of this present paper; several of those have already been touched upon as I have gone along. The earliest published one is my paper (Searles, H., 1955) concerning dependency processes in the psychotherapy of schizophrenic patients, which includes a description of the role of the therapist's real dependency as it affects the patient.

SUMMARY

This paper advances the hypothesis that innate among the human being's emotional potentialities, present in the earliest months of postnatal life, is an essentially psychotherapeutic striving. The family-environmental warping of that striving is a major etiologic source of all psychopathology. The analyst's failure to recognize that long-repressed striving in the patient accounts, more than does any other interpersonal element in the treatment situation, for the patient's unconscious resistance to the analytic process. Despite the acknowledged complexities involved in our departing from classical psychoanalytic theory and technique in this regard, I believe that it is essential that we do so.

In this paper I place special emphasis upon the psychotic patient's therapeutic effort to enable the mother (and analogously in the analytic context, the analyst) to become a whole and effective mother (= analyst) to him.

A discussion of some of the relevant literature is included.

REFERENCES

Burnham, D. L., Gladstone, A. I., and Gibson, R. W. *Schizophrenia and the Need-Fear Dilemma*. New York: International Universities Press, 1969.

Freud, S. (1922). "Some Neurotic Mechanisms in Jealousy, Paranoia, and Homosexuality." *Standard Edition*, 18, London: Hogarth Press, 1922.

Gibson, R. W., "The Ego Defect in Schizophrenia." In *Psychoneurosis and Schizophrenia*, Usdin, G. L., ed., 88–97. Philadelphia and Montreal: J. B. Lippincott, 1966.

Greenson, R. R., "The Working Alliance and the Transference Neurosis." *Psychoanal. Quart.* 34:155–181 (1965).

———. *The Technique and Practice of Psychoanalysis*. Vol. I. New York: International Universities Press, 1967.

Groddeck, G. (1923). *The Book of the It.* (English translation pub. in 1950 by Vision Press, London; the original, *Das buch vom es,* pub. in 1923 by Psychoanalytischer Verlag, Vienna).

Hill, L. B., *Psychotherapeutic Intervention in Schizophrenia.* Chicago: University of Chicago Press, 1955.

Jones, E., *The Life and Work of Sigmund Freud, Vol. 1.* New York: Basic Books, 1953.

Khan, M. M. R., "The Concept of Cumulative Trauma." *Psychoanal. Study Child* 18:286–306 (1963).

———. "Ego Distortion, Cumulative Trauma, and the Role of Reconstruction in the Analytic Situation. *Int. J. Psychoanal.,* 45:272–78 (1964).

Knight, R. P. (1953). "Management and Psychotherapy of the Borderline Schizophrenic Patient." *Bull. Menninger Clinic* 17:139–50 (1953).

Lewin, B. D., *Dreams and the Uses of Regression.* New York: International Universities Press, 1958.

Milner, M. (1950). *On Not Being Able to Paint,* 2nd edition. New York: International Universities Press; also London: Heinemann, 1957.

———. *The Hands of the Living God—an Account of a Psychoanalytic Treatment.* New York: International Universities Press, 1969.

Nelson, M. C., Nelson, B., Sherman, M. H., and Strean, H. S. *Roles and Paradigms in Psychotherapy.* New York and London: Grune & Stratton, 1969.

Olinick, S. L., Poland, W. S., Grigg, K. A., and Granatir, W. L. (1972). "The Psychoanalytic Work Ego: Process and Interpretation." Presented at meeting of Washington Psychoanalytic Society, Washington, D.C., March 17, 1972.

Searles, H. F. (1949). (I) "Two Suggested Revisions of the Concept of Transference" and (II) "Comments Regarding the Usefulness of Emotions Arising in the Analyst During the Analytic Hour." Unpublished.

———. (1951). "Data Concerning Certain Manifestations of Incorporation." *Psychiatry* 14:397–413. Reprinted on pp. 39–69 of *Collected Papers* (see below).

———. (1955). "Dependency Processes in the Psychotherapy of Schizophrenia." *J. Amer. Psychoanal. Assoc.* 3:19–66 (1955). Also reprinted on pp. 114–156 of *Collected Papers* (see below).

———. (1959a). "Integration and differentiation in schizophrenia." *J. Nerv. and Ment. Dis.* 129:542–550. Also reprinted on pp. 304–316 of *Collected Papers* (see below).

———. (1959b). "Integration and Differentiation in Schizophrenia: An Over-all View." *Brit J. Med. Psychol.* 32:261–281. Also reprinted on pp. 317–

348 of *Collected Papers* (see below).

———. (1961a). "The Evolution of the Mother Transference in Psychotherapy with the Schizophrenic Patient," pp. 256–284 in *Psychotherapy of the Psychoses,* ed. by Burton, A; New York: Basic Books. Also reprinted on pp. 349–380 of *Collected Papers* (see below).

———. (1961b). "Phases of Patient-Therapist Interaction in the Psychotherapy of Chronic Schizophrenia." *Brit. J. Med. Psychol.* 34:169–193. Also reprinted on pp. 521–559 of *Collected Papers* (see below).

———. *Collected Papers on Schizophrenia and Related Subjects.* London: Hogarth Press, 1965; and New York: International Universities Press, 1965.

———. (1966). "Concerning the Development of an Identity." *Psychoanal. Rev.* 53:507–530, Winter 1966-67.

———. "The 'Dedicated Physician' in Psychotherapy and Psychoanalysis," pp. 128–143 in *Crosscurrents in Psychiatry and Psychoanalysis.* Gibson, R. W., ed., Philadelphia and Toronto: J. B. Lippincott, 1967.

———. "Autism and the Phase of Transition to Therapeutic Symbiosis." *Contemporary Psychoanalysis* 7:1–20, Fall, 1970.

———. (1971). "Pathologic Symbiosis and Autism," pp. 69–83 in *In the Name of Life-Essays in Honor of Erich Fromm,* ed. by Landis, B. and Tauber, E. S. New York, Chicago, and San Francisco: Holt, Rinehart and Winston.

———. "The Function of the Patient's Realistic Perceptions of the Analyst in Delusional Transference." *Brit. J. Med. Psychol.* 45:1–18 (1972a).

———. "Intensive Psychotherapy of Chronic Schizophrenia." *Int. J. Psychoanalytic Psychotherapy* 1:30–51 (1972b).

———. (1973). "Concerning Therapeutic Symbiosis: (a) the Patient as Symbiotic Therapist, (b) the Phase of Ambivalent Symbiosis, and (c) the Role of Jealousy in the Fragmented Ego." To be pub. in *The Annual of Psychoanalysis, Vol. 1,* ed. by Pollock, G. H. Chicago: Chicago Institute for Psychoanalysis, and New York: Quadrangle Books.

Singer, E. "The Patient Aids the Analyst: Some Clinical and Theoretical Observations," pp. 56–68 in *In the Name of Life-Essays in Honor of Erich Fromm,* ed. by Landis, B. and Tauber, E. S. New York, Chicago and San Francisco: Holt, Rinehart and Winston, 1971.

Whitaker, C. A., and Malone, T. P. (1953). *The Roots of Psychotherapy.* New York: Blakiston, 1953.

Zetzel, E. R., "Current Concepts of Transference. *Int. J. Psychoanal.* 37: 369–376 (1956).

PART III

COUNTERTRANSFERENCE

The papers in this section have appeared sporadically over the past thirty years or so. Selected for inclusion are papers whose main focus is on the effects of the psychopathology of the analyst or therapist—countertransference in its narrow sense. This usage may be contrasted with that of such analysts as Racker (1957), who have applied the term to the analyst's total experience with the patient, and then separated out pathological and nonpathological components.

Each of these studies involves some consideration of the analytic interaction, since considerations of countertransference, no matter how concentrated on the problems of the analyst, are virtually always developed with some attention to their relationship to the communications from the patient. In fact, one characteristic of the evolution of this concept of countertransference in these papers is a growing intensification of interactional considerations, to the point where there is an evident consensus that the countertransferences of the analyst cannot be understood without a full picture of what is happening with and within the patient.

The present papers can be supplemented by readings from Parts I and II, on transference and nontransference respectively, and especially from Parts IV and VI, on noncountertransference and the analytic interaction. As noted for the subject of countertransference itself, readings in these areas cannot be divorced from a careful consideration of every other dimension of the analytic experience.

Freud had little to say about countertransference. In the main, he identified its existence as a phenomenon within the analyst—in a paper written in 1910—and viewed it primarily as an obstacle and limiting factor to analytic work; in "Analysis Terminable and Interminable" (1937), he added a few remarks on the subject. This output stands in marked contrast to his extensive writings on transference and the analytic setting (see Parts I and VI), papers which are in the main focused on the patient and relatively divorced from considerations of his interaction with the analyst—though from time to time Freud did indeed offer brief comments in this regard. Still, his neglect of countertransference, and his relative exclusion of the analyst when trying to understand the analysand, set the tone for those who followed. There was therefore a rather long hiatus, during which little consideration was given to this subject in the psychoanalytic literature, until the early 1950s, when analysts became quite concerned about this topic. The papers reprinted here provide the reader an opportunity to experience and study a significant widening of the conceptualization by psychoanalysts of the manifestations of countertransference, their inevitability, their utility as well as their detrimental qualities, and their place both in the cure of the patient and as obstacles to that cure.

While many dimensions of countertransference have now been identified and traced out in terms both of the personal history of the psychoanalyst and of current dynamic realities within the unconscious therapeutic interaction, perhaps the single most neglected aspect remains the interplay between the analyst's countertransferences and the experiences of his own analysis. This is but one way of indicating that this entire subject is as yet by no means fully understood.

It is well to realize that there have been extremely few truly original contributions to the understanding of countertransference by analysts who have maintained a classical Freudian position. By contrast, the Kleinians, Winnicott and his followers, and a number of classical analysts who have extended the basic Freudian position into the interactional realm—e.g., Searles and myself, have rather courageously investigated what is for many analysts, as Little (1951) and others have noted, an anxiety-provoking subject that encroaches upon their own unresolved psychopathology and conflicts. These writers have provided us what is now a rather broad and balanced view of countertransference. Still, since it is here that analysts feel most vulnerable, it follows too that it is in this area that many of the most original discoveries related to the analytic interaction will be made.

11

ON COUNTER-TRANSFERENCE[1]

PAULA HEIMANN

EDITOR'S NOTE

This paper by Heimann is generally credited as the first definitive contribution to the literature in which the analyst's counter-transferences were viewed as constructive rather than entirely troublesome. It in no way diminishes Heimann's accomplishment to note that in 1933 Hann-Kende had enunciated this thesis, and that in 1948 Searles had written of this subject in considerable detail, though his paper did not appear until 1978. While Heimann here uses the term *countertransference* to cover all of the responses of the analyst to the patient, her presentation clearly implies that the analyst's pathological responses, while interfering and in need of self-analysis and rectification, can also be used as a means of understanding the patient.

This paper cleared the way for extensive investigations of the analyst's responses to his patient, whether noncountertransference (narrowly defined as the therapist's valid functioning and responses) or countertransference (narrowly defined as his disturbed and pathology-related functioning). As long as counter-transference was viewed entirely as a pathological manifestation of a disturbance within the analyst, and as an unfortunate and unwelcome disruptive influence on the analytic experience, investigations in this area were quite limited and could only stress the need for self-analysis and rectification.

The realization that despite their harmful effects there are constructive potentials to countertransference-based responses not only opened the path to more creative investigations of the analyst's experiences and functioning within the analytic interaction, but also served to lessen the morbid anxiety and tendency toward avoidance that was evident in analysts in regard to this aspect of their work—an attitude that has by no means been fully resolved. On the other hand, an understanding and acceptance of the positive nuclei within a disruptive countertransference-based response

---

1. Paper read at the 16th International Psycho-Analytical Congress, Zürich, 1949. After presenting this paper at the Congress my attention was drawn to a paper by Leo Berman: 'Countertransferences and Attitudes of the Analyst in the Therapeutic Process,' *Psychiatry*, Vol. XII, No. 2, May, 1949. The fact that the problem of the counter-transference has been put forward for discussion practically simultaneously by different workers indicates that the time is ripe for a more thorough research into the nature and function of the counter-transference. I agree with Berman's basic rejection of emotional coldness on the part of the analyst, but I differ in my conclusions concerning the use to be made of the analyst's feelings toward his patient.

carries with it the potential dangers of too ready an acceptance of the pathology of the analyst or therapist, and the lessening of efforts to continuously monitor and resolve these expressions and their underlying basis as they inevitably emerge. It is issues such as these that analysts have struggled with in the ensuing years.

This short note on counter-transference has been stimulated by certain observations I made in seminars and control analyses. I have been struck by the widespread belief amongst candidates that the counter-transference is nothing but a source of trouble. Many candidates are afraid and feel guilty when they become aware of feelings towards their patients and consequently aim at avoiding any emotional response and at becoming completely unfeeling and 'detached'.

When I tried to trace the origin of this ideal of the 'detached' analyst, I found that our literature does indeed contain descriptions of the analytic work which can give rise to the notion that a good analyst does not feel anything beyond a uniform and mild benevolence towards his patients, and that any ripple of emotional waves on this smooth surface represents a disturbance to be overcome. This may possibly derive from a misreading of some of Freud's statements, such as his comparison with the surgeon's state of mind during an operation, or his simile of the mirror. At least these have been quoted to me in this connection in discussions on the nature of the counter-transference.

On the other hand, there is an opposite school of thought, like that of Ferenczi, which not only acknowledges that the analyst has a wide variety of feelings towards his patient, but recommends that he should at times express them openly. In her warm-hearted paper 'Handhabung der Übertragung auf Grund der Ferenczischen Versuche' (*Int. Zeitschr. f. Psycho-anal.*, Bd., XXII, 1936) Alice Balint suggested that such honesty on the part of the analyst is helpful and in keeping with the respect for truth inherent in psycho-analysis. While I admire her attitude, I cannot agree with her conclusions. Other analysts again have claimed that it makes the analyst more 'human' when he expresses his feelings to his patient and that it helps him to build up a 'human' relationship with him.

For the purpose of this paper I am using the term 'counter-transference' to cover all the feelings which the analyst experiences towards his patient.

It may be argued that this use of the term is not

Reprinted from *International Journal of Psycho-Analysis* 31:81–84, 1950.

correct, and that counter-transference simply means transference on the part of the analyst. However, I would suggest that the prefix 'counter' implies additional factors.

In passing it is worth while remembering that transference feelings cannot be sharply divided from those which refer to another person in his own right and not as a parent substitute. It is often pointed out that not everything a patient feels about his analyst is due to transference, and that, as the analysis progresses, he becomes increasingly more capable of 'realistic' feelings. This warning itself shows that the differentiation between the two kinds of feelings is not always easy.

My thesis is that the analyst's emotional response to his patient within the analytic situation represents one of the most important tools for his work. The analyst's counter-transference is an instrument of research into the patient's unconscious.

The analytic situation has been investigated and described from many angles, and there is general agreement about its unique character. But my impression is that it has not been sufficiently stressed that it is a *relationship* between two persons. What distinguishes this relationship from others, is not the presence of feelings in one partner, the patient, and their absence in the other, the analyst, but above all the degree of the feelings experienced and the use made of them, these factors being interdependent. The aim of the analyst's own analysis, from this point of view, is not to turn him into a mechanical brain which can produce interpretations on the basis of a purely intellectual procedure, but to enable him, to *sustain* the feelings which are stirred in him, as opposed to discharging them (as does the patient), in order to *subordinate* them to the analytic task in which he functions as the patient's mirror reflection.

If an analyst tries to work without consulting his feelings, his interpretations are poor. I have often seen this in the work of beginners, who, out of fear, ignored or stifled their feelings.

We know that the analyst needs an evenly hovering attention in order to follow the patient's free associations, and that this enables him to listen simultaneously on many levels. He has to perceive the manifest and latent meaning of his patient's words, the allusions and implications, the hints to former sessions, the references to childhood situations behind the description of current relationships, etc. By listening in this manner the analyst avoids the danger of becoming preoccupied with any one theme and remains receptive for the significance of changes in themes and of the sequences and gaps in the patient's associations.

I would suggest that the analyst along with this freely working attention needs a freely roused emotional sensibility so as to follow the patient's emotional movements and unconscious phantasies. Our basic assumption is that the analyst's unconscious understands that of his patient. This rapport on the deep level comes to the surface in the form of feelings which the analyst notices in response to his patient, in his 'counter-transference'. This is the most dynamic way in which his patient's voice reaches him. In the comparison of feelings roused in himself with his patient's associations and behaviour, the analyst possesses a most valuable means of checking whether he has understood or failed to understand his patient.

Since, however, violent emotions of any kind, of love or hate, helpfulness or anger, impel towards action rather than towards contemplation and blur a person's capacity to observe and weigh the evidence correctly, it follows that, if the analyst's emotional response is intense, it will defeat its object.

Therefore the analyst's emotional sensitivity needs to be extensive rather than intensive, differentiating and mobile.

There will be stretches in the analytic work, when the analyst who combines free attention with free emotional responses does not register his feeings as a problem, because they are in accord with the meaning he understands. But often the emotions roused in him are much nearer to the heart of the matter than his reasoning, or, to put it in other words, his unconscious perception of the patient's unconscious is more acute and in advance of his conscious conception of the situation.

A recent experience comes to mind. It concerns a patient whom I had taken over from a colleague. The patient was a man in the forties who had originally sought treatment when his marriage broke down. Among his symptoms promiscuity figured prominently. In the third week of his analysis with me he told me, at the beginning of the session, that he was going to marry a woman whom he had met only a short time before.

It was obvious that his wish to get married at this juncture was determined by his resistance against the analysis and his need to act out his transference conflicts. Within a strongly ambivalent attitude the desire for an intimate relation with me had already

clearly appeared. I had thus many reasons for doubting the wisdom of his intention and for suspecting his choice. But such an attempt to short-circuit analysis is not infrequent at the beginning of, or at a critical point in, the treatment and usually does not represent too great an obstacle to the work, so that catastrophic conditions need not arise. I was therefore somewhat puzzled to find that I reacted with a sense of apprehension and worry to the patient's remark. I felt that something more was involved in his situation, something beyond the ordinary acting out, which, however, eluded me.

In his further associations which centred round his friend, the patient, describing her, said she had had a 'rough passage'. This phrase again registered particularly and increased my misgivings. It dawned on me that it was precisely because she had had a rough passage that he was drawn to her. But still I felt that I did not see things clearly enough. Presently he came to tell me his dream: he had acquired from abroad a very good second-hand car which was damaged. He wished to repair it, but another person in the dream objected for reasons of caution. The patient had, as he put it, 'to make him confused' in order that he might go ahead with the repair of the car.

With the help of this dream I came to understand what before I had merely felt as a sense of apprehension and worry. There was indeed more at stake than the mere acting-out of transference conflicts.

When he gave me the particulars of the car—very good, second-hand, from abroad—the patient spontaneously recognized that it represented myself. The other person in the dream who tried to stop him and whom he confused, stood for that part of the patient's ego which aimed at security and happiness and for the analysis as a protective object.

The dream showed that the patient wished me to be damaged (he insisted on my being the refugee to whom applies the expression 'rough passage' which he had used for his new friend). Out of guilt for his sadistic impulses he was compelled to make reparation, but this reparation was of a masochistic nature, since it necessitated blotting out the voice of reason and caution. This element of confusing the protective figure was in itself double-barrelled, expressing both his sadistic and his masochistic impulses: in so far as it aimed at annihilating the analysis, it represented the patient's sadistic tendencies in the pattern of his infantile anal attacks on his mother; in so far as it stood for his ruling out his desire for security and happiness, it expressed his self-destructive trends. Reparation turned into a masochistic act again engenders hatred, and, far from solving the conflict between destructiveness and guilt, leads to a vicious circle.

The patient's intention of marrying his new friend, the injured woman, was fed from both sources, and the acting-out of his transference conflicts proved to be determined by this specific and powerful sado-masochistic system.

Unconsciously I had grasped immediately the seriousness of the situation, hence the sense of worry which I experienced. But my conscious understanding lagged behind, so that I could decipher the patient's message and appeal for help only later in the hour, when more material came up.

In giving the gist of an analytic session I hope to illustrate my contention that the analyst's immediate emotional response to his patient is a significant pointer to the patient's unconscious processes and guides him towards fuller understanding. It helps the analyst to focus his attention on the most urgent elements in the patient's associations and serves as a useful criterion for the selection of interpretations from material which, as we know, is always over-determined.

From the point of view I am stressing, the analyst's counter-transference is not only part and parcel of the analytic relationship, but it is the patient's *creation*, it is part of the patient's personality. (I am possibly touching here on a point which Dr. Clifford Scott would express in terms of his concept of the body-scheme, but to pursue this line would lead me away from my theme.)

The approach to the counter-transference which I have presented is not without danger. It does not represent a screen for the analyst's shortcomings. When the analyst in his own analysis has worked through his infantile conflicts and anxieties (paranoid and depressive), so that he can easily establish contact with his own unconscious, he will not impute to his patient what belongs to himself. He will have achieved a dependable equilibrium which enables him to carry the rôles of the patient's id, ego, super-ego, and external objects which the patient allots to him or — in other words — projects on him, when he dramatizes his conflicts in the analytic relationship. In the instance I have given the analyst was predominantly in the rôles of the patient's good mother to be destroyed and rescued, and of the patient's reality-ego which tried to oppose his sado-masochistic impulses. In my view Freud's demand that the analyst must 'recognize and master' his counter-transference does not lead to the conclusion that the counter-transference is a disturbing factor and that

the analyst should become unfeeling and detached, but that he must use his emotional response as a key to the patient's unconscious. This will protect him from entering as a co-actor on the scene which the patient re-enacts in the analytic relationship and from exploiting it for his own needs. At the same time he will find ample stimulus for taking himself to task again and again and for continuing the analysis of his own problems. This, however, is his private affair, and I do not consider it right for the analyst to communicate his feelings to his patient. In my view such honesty is more in the nature of a confession and a burden to the patient. In any case it leads away from the analysis. The emotions roused in the analyst will be of value to his patient, if used as one more source of insight into the patient's unconscious conflicts and defences; and when these are interpreted and worked through, the ensuing changes in the patient's ego include the strengthening of his reality sense so that he sees his analyst as a human being, not a god or demon, and the 'human' relationship in the analytic situation follows without the analyst's having recourse to extra-analytical means.

Psycho-analytic technique came into being when Freud, abandoning hypnosis, discovered resistance and repression. In my view the use of counter-transference as an instrument of research can be recognized in his descriptions of the way by which he arrived at his fundamental discoveries. When he tried to elucidate the hysterical patient's forgotten memories, he felt that a force from the patient opposed his attempts and that he had to overcome this resistance by his own psychic work. He concluded that it was the same force which was responsible for the repression of the crucial memories and for the formation of the hysterical symptom.

The unconscious process in hysterical amnesia can thus be defined by its twin facets, of which one is turned outward and felt by the analyst as resistance, whilst the other works intrapsychically as repression.

Whereas in the case of repression counter-transference is characterized by the sensation of a quantity of energy, an opposing force, other defence mechanisms will rouse other qualities in the analyst's response.

I believe that with more thorough investigation of counter-transference from the angle I have attempted here, we may come to work out more fully the way in which the character of the counter-transference corresponds to the nature of the patient's unconscious impulses and defences operative at the actual time.

12

COUNTER-TRANSFERENCE AND THE PATIENT'S RESPONSE TO IT

Margaret Little

EDITOR'S NOTE

This paper is one of the most remarkable and sensitive in the psychoanalytic literature. Written at a time when counter-transference was given scant consideration, it is filled with insights into the analytic interaction, many of them largely unappreciated even to this day. In offering a study of the analyst's counter-transferences and the patient's responses to them, Little adopts an intensely interactional approach; the paper in fact might well have been placed in the interaction section of this volume. The result is a striking perspective on the role played by introjection and projection in the analytic experience, and a recognition and discussion of such issues as the analyst's reinforcement of the patient's resistances, the influence of his countertransference-based errors, and the patient's unconscious responses to these, including his curative efforts.

Little's perceptiveness in regard to the interdependence of patient and analyst enables her to explore many dimensions virtually ignored by those who approach either the patient or the analyst in relative isolation. She is therefore able to stress many of the patient's unconscious sensitivities and perceptions of the analyst, as well as a number of much neglected qualities of the analyst's constructive and destructive functioning.

This paper is one of several imaginative studies of the analytic experience and of the treatment of borderline patients by this author. While many have taken issue with Little's position that the analyst should, with discretion, communicate something of the nature of his errors (a position she herself later modified), this paper remains to this day one of the most original and valid considerations of the unconscious communicative interaction between patient and analyst.

I

I will begin with a story:

A patient whose mother had recently died was to give a wireless talk on a subject in which he knew his analyst was interested; he gave him the script to read beforehand, and the analyst had the opportunity of hearing the broadcast. The patient felt very unwilling to give it just then, in view of his mother's death, but could not alter the arrangement. The day after the broadcast he arrived for his analysis in a state of anxiety and confusion.

Reprinted from *International Journal of Psycho-Analysis* 32:32–40, 1951.

The analyst (who was a very experienced man) interpreted the patient's distress as being due to a fear lest he, the analyst, should be jealous of what had clearly been a success and be wanting to deprive him of it and of its results. The interpretation was accepted, the distress cleared up quite quickly, and the analysis went on.

Two years later (the analysis having ended in the meanwhile) the patient was at a party which he found he could not enjoy, and he realized that it was a week after the anniversary of his mother's death. Suddenly it came to him that what had troubled him at the time of his broadcast had been a very simple and obvious thing, sadness that his mother was not there to enjoy his success (or even to know about it), and guilt that he had enjoyed it while she was dead had spoilt it for him. Instead of being able to mourn for her (by cancelling the broadcast) he had had to behave as if he denied her death, almost in a manic way. He recognized that the interpretation given, which could be substantially correct, had in fact been the correct one at the time for the analyst, who had actually been jealous of him, and that it was the analyst's unconscious guilt that had led to the giving of an inappropriate interpretation. Its acceptance had come about through the patient's unconscious recognition of its correctness for his analyst and his identification with him. Now he could accept it as true for himself in a totally different way, on another level—i.e. that of his jealousy of his father's success with his mother, and guilt about himself having a success which represented success with his mother, of which his father would be jealous and want to deprive him. The analyst's behaviour in giving such an interpretation must be attributed to counter-transference.

II

Surprisingly little has been written on counter-transference apart from books and papers on technique chiefly meant for students in training. The writers of these all emphasize the same two points— the importance and potential danger of counter-transference and the need for thorough analysis of analysts. Much more has been written about transference, and a lot of that would apply equally well to counter-transference. I found myself wondering why, and also why different people use the term counter-transference to mean different things.

The term is used to mean any or all of the following:

(a) The analyst's unconscious attitude to the patient.

(b) Repressed elements, hitherto unanalysed, in the analyst himself which attach to the patient in the same way as the patient 'transfers' to the analyst affects, etc. belonging to his parents or to the objects of his childhood: i.e. the analyst regards the patient (temporarily and varyingly) as he regarded his own parents.

(c) Some specific attitude or mechanism with which the analyst meets the patient's transference.

(d) The whole of the analyst's attitudes and behaviour towards his patient. This includes all the others, and any conscious attitudes as well.

The question is why it is so undefined or undefinable. Is it that true isolation of counter-transference is impossible while the comprehensive idea of it is clumsy and unmanageable? I found four reasons.

(1) I would say that unconscious counter-transference is something which cannot be observed directly as such, but only in its effects; we might compare the difficulty with that of the physicists who try to define or observe a force which is manifested as light waves, gravity, etc. but cannot be detected or observed directly.

(2) I think part of the difficulty arises from the fact that (considering it metapsychologically) the analyst's total attitude involves his whole psyche, id and any super-ego remnants as well as ego (he is also concerned with all these in the patient), and there are no clear boundaries differentiating them.

(3) Any analysis (even self-analysis) postulates both an analysand and an analyst; in a sense they are inseparable. And similarly transference and counter-transference are inseparable; something which is suggested in the fact that what is written about the one can so largely be applied to the other.

(4) More important than any of these, I think there is an attitude towards counter-transference, i.e. towards one's own feelings and ideas, that is really paranoid or phobic, especially where the feelings are or may be subjective.

In one of his papers on technique Freud pointed out that the progress of psychoanalysis had been held up for more than ten years through fear of interpreting the transference, and the attitude of psychotherapists of other schools to this day is to regard it as highly dangerous and to avoid it. The attitude of most analysts towards counter-transference is precisely the same, that it is a known and recognized phenomenon but that it is unnecessary and even dangerous ever to interpret it. In any case, what is unconscious one cannot easily be aware of (if at all), and to try to observe and interpret something unconscious in oneself is rather like trying to see the back of one's own head—it is a lot easier to see the back of someone else's. The fact of the patient's transference lends itself readily to avoidance by projection and rationalization, both mechanisms being characteristic for paranoia, and the myth of the impersonal, almost inhuman analyst who shows no feelings is consistent with this attitude. I wonder whether failure to make use of counter-transference may not be having a precisely similar effect as far as the progress of psycho-analysis is concerned to that of ignoring or neglecting the transference; and if we can make the right use of counter-transference may we not find that we have yet another extremely valuable, if not indispensable, tool?

In writing this paper I found it very difficult to know which of the meanings of the term counter-transference I was using, and I found that I tended to slip from one to another, although at the start I meant to limit it to the repressed, infantile, subjective, irrational feelings, some pleasurable, some painful, which belong to the second of my attempted definitions. This is usually the counter-transference which is regarded as the source of difficulties and dangers.

But unconscious elements can be both normal and pathological, and not all repression is pathological any more than all conscious elements are 'normal'. The whole patient-analyst relationship includes both 'normal' and pathological, conscious and unconscious, transference and counter-transference, in varying proportions; it will always include something which is specific to both the individual patient and the individual analyst. That is, every counter-transference is different from every other, as every transference is different, and it varies within itself from day to day, according to variations in both patient and analyst and the outside world.

Repressed counter-transference is a product of the unconscious part of the analyst's ego, that part which is nearest and most closely belonging to the id and least in contact with reality. It follows from this that the repetition compulsion is readily brought to bear on it; but other ego activities besides repression play a part in its development, of which the synthetic or integrative activity is most important. As I see it, counter-transference is one of those compromise formations in the making of which the ego shows such surprising skill; it is in this respect essentially of the same order as a neurotic symptom, a perversion, or a sublimation. In it libidinal gratification is partly forbidden and partly accepted; an element of aggression is woven in with both the gratification and the prohibition, and the distribution of the aggression determines the relative proportions of each. Since counter-transference, like transference, is concerned with another person, the mechanisms of projection and introjection are of special importance.

By the time we have paranoia linked with counter-transference we have a mammoth subject to discuss, and to talk about the patient's response may be just nonsense unless we can find some simple way of approach. Many of our difficulties, unfortunately, seem to me to come from trying to over-simplify, and from an almost compulsive attempt to separate out conscious from unconscious, and repressed unconscious from what is unconscious but not repressed, often with an ignoring of the dynamic aspects of the thing. So once again I would like to say here that although I am talking mainly about the repressed elements in counter-transference I am not limiting myself strictly to this, but am letting it flow over into the other elements in the total relationship; and at the risk of being disjointed my 'simple approach' is chiefly a matter of talking about a few things and then trying to relate them to the main theme.

Speaking of the dynamic aspects brings us to the question: What is the driving force in any analysis? What is it that urges the patient on to get well? The answer surely is that it is the combined id urges of both patient and analyst, urges which in the case of the analyst have been modified and integrated as a result of his own analysis so that they have become more directed and effective. Successful combination of these urges seems to me to depend on a special kind of identification of the analyst with the patient.

III

Consciously, and surely to a great extent unconsciously too, we all want our patients to get well, and we can identify readily with them in their desire to get well, that is with their ego. But unconsciously we tend to identify also with the patient's super-ego and id, and thereby with him, in any prohibition on getting well, and in his wish to stay ill and dependent, and by so doing we may slow down his recovery. Unconsciously we may exploit a patient's illness for our own purposes, both libidinal and aggressive, and he will quickly respond to this.

A patient who has been in analysis for some considerable time has usually become his analyst's love object; he is the person to whom the analyst wishes to make reparation, and the reparative impulses, even when conscious, may through a partial repression come under the sway of the repetition compulsion, so that it becomes necessary to make that same patient well over and over again, which in effect means making him ill over and over again in order to have him to make well.

Rightly used, this repetitive process may be progressive, and the 'making ill' then takes the necessary and effective form of opening up anxieties which can be interpreted and worked through. But this implies a degree of unconscious willingness on the part of the analyst to allow his patient to get well, to become independent and to leave him. In general we can agree that these are all acceptable to any analyst, but failures of timing of interpretation such as that which I have described, failure in understanding, or any interference with working-through, will play into the patient's own fear of getting well, with all that it involves in the way of losing his analyst, and they cannot be put right until the patient himself is ready to let the opportunity occur. The repetition compulsion in the patient is here the ally of the analyst, if the analyst is ready not to repeat his former mistake and so once more strengthen the patient's resistances.

This unconscious unwillingness on the analyst's part to let his patient leave him can sometimes take very subtle forms, in which the analysis itself can be used as a rationalization. The demand that a patient should not 'act out' in situations outside the analysis may hinder the formation of those very extra-analytic relationships which belong with his recovery and are evidence of his growth and ego development. Transferences to people outside the analysis need not be an actual hindrance to the analytic work, if the analyst is willing to use them, but unconsciously he may behave exactly like the parents who, 'for the child's own good', interfere with his development by not allowing him to love someone else. The patient of course needs them just as a child needs to form identifications with people outside his home and parents.

These things are so insidious that our perception of them comes slowly, and in our resistance to them we are allying with the patient's super-ego, through our own super-ego. At the same time, we are showing our own inability to tolerate a splitting either of something in the patient, or of the therapeutic process itself; we are demanding to be the only cause of the patient's getting well.

A patient whose analysis is 'interminable' then may perhaps be the victim of his analyst's (primary) narcissism as much as of his own, and an apparent negative therapeutic reaction may be the outcome of a counter-resistance of the kind I have indicated in my story.

We all know that only a few of several possible interpretations are the important and dynamic ones at any given point in the analysis, but as in my story, the interpretation which is the appropriate one for the patient may be the very one which, for reasons of counter-transference and counter-resistance, is least available to the analyst at that moment, and if the interpretation given is the one that is appropriate for the analyst himself the patient may, through fear, submissiveness, etc., accept it in precisely the same way as he would accept the 'correct' one, with immediate good effect. Only later does it come out that the effect obtained was not the one required, and that the patient's resistance has been thereby strengthened and the analysis prolonged.

IV

It has been said that it is fatal for an analyst to become identified with his patient, and that empathy (as distinct from sympathy) and detachment are essential to success in analysis. But the basis of empathy, as of sympathy, is identification, and it is the detachment which makes the difference between them. This detachment comes about partly at least by the use of the ego function of reality testing with the introduction of the factors of time and distance. The analyst necessarily identifies with the patient, but there is for him an interval of time between himself and the experience which for the patient has the quality of immediacy—he knows it for past experience, while to the patient it is a present one. That makes it at that moment the patient's experience, not his, and if the analyst is experiencing it as a present thing he is interfering with the patient's growth and development. When an experience is the patient's own and not the analyst's an interval of distance is introduced automatically as well, and it is on the preservation of these intervals of time and distance that successful use of the counter-transference may depend. The analyst's identification with the patient needs of course to be an introjective, not a projective, one.

When such an interval of time is introduced the patient can feel his experience in its immediacy, free from interference, and let it become past for him too, so that a fresh identification can be made with his analyst. When the interval of distance is introduced the experience becomes the patient's alone, and he can separate himself off psychically from the analyst. Growth depends on an alternating rhythm of identification and separation brought about in this way by having experiences and knowing them for one's own, in a suitable setting.

To come back to the story with which I began, what happened was that the analyst felt the patient's

unconscious repressed jealousy as his own immediate experience, instead of as a past, remembered,
one. The patient was immediately concerned with
his mother's death, feeling the necessity to broadcast
just then as an interference with his process of
mourning, and the pleasure proper to it was transformed into a manic one, as if he denied his mother's
death. Only later, after the interpretation, when his
mourning had been transferred to the analyst and so
become past, could he experience the jealousy situation as an immediate one, and then recognize (as
something past and remembered) his analyst's
counter-transference reaction. His immediate reaction to the analyst's jealousy was a phobic one—
displacement by (introjective) identification, and
re-repression.

Failures in timing such as this, or failures to
recognize transference references, are failures of the
ego function of recognizing time and distance.
Unconscious mind is timeless and irrational, 'What's
yours is mine, what's mine's my own'; 'What's yours
is half mine, and half the other half's mine, so it's all
mine' are infantile ways of thinking which are used
in relation to feelings and experiences as much as to
things, and counter-transference becomes a hindrance to the patient's growth when the analyst uses
them. The analyst becomes the blind man leading
the blind, for neither has the use of the necessary two
dimensions to know where he is at any given
moment. But when the analyst can keep these intervals in his identification with his patient it becomes
possible for the patient to take the step forward of
eliminating them again and to go on to the next
experience, when the process of establishing the
interval has to be repeated.

This is one of the major difficulties of the student
in training or the analyst who is undergoing further
analysis—he is having to deal with things in his
patients' analysis which have still the quality of
present-ness, or immediacy, for him himself, instead
of that past-ness which is so important. In these
circumstances it may be impossible for him always
to keep this time interval, and he has then to defer as
full an analysis as the patient might otherwise
achieve until he has carried his own analysis further,
and wait until a repetition of the material comes.

V

The recent discussions here of Dr. Rosen's work
brought the subject of counter-transference to the
surface with a fresh challenge to us to know and
understand much more clearly what we are doing.
We heard how in the space of a few days or weeks
patients who for years had been completely inaccessible had shown remarkable changes which, from
some points of view at least, must be regarded as
improvement. But, what was not originally meant to
be in the bargain, they seem to have remained
permanently dependent on and attached to the therapist concerned. The description of the ways in
which the patients were treated, and of the results,
stirred and disturbed most of us profoundly, and
apparently aroused a good deal of guilt among us,
for several members in their contributions to the discussion beat their breasts and cried *mea culpa*.

I have tried to understand where so much guilt
came from, and it seemed to me that a possible
explanation of it might lie in the unconscious unwillingness to let patients go. Many seriously ill
patients, especially psychotic cases, are not able,
either for internal (psychological) reasons, or for
external (e.g. financial) ones, to go through with a
full analysis and bring it to what we regard as a satisfactory conclusion, that is with sufficient ego
development for them to be able to live successfully
in real independence of the analyst. In such cases a
superficial relationship of dependence is continued
(and rightly continued) indefinitely, by means of
occasional 'maintenance' sessions, the contact being
preserved deliberately by the analyst. Such patients
we can keep in this way without guilt, and the high
proportion of successes in the treatment of these
patients, it seems to me, may well depend on that
very freedom from guilt.

But over and above this there is perhaps a tendency to identify particularly with the patient's id in
psychotic cases generally; in fact it would sometimes
be difficult to find the ego to identify with! This will
be a narcissistic identification on the level of the
primary love-hate, which nevertheless lends itself
readily to a transformation into object-love. The
powerful stimulus of the extensively disintegrated
personality touches on the most deeply repressed
and carefully defended danger spots in the analyst
and, correspondingly, the most primitive (and incidentally least effective) of his defence mechanisms
are called into play. But at the same time a small
fragment of the patient's shattered ego may identify
with the ego of the therapist (where the therapist's
understanding of the patient's fears filters through to
him, and he can introject the therapist's ego as a
good object); he is then enabled to make a contact
with reality *via* the therapist's contact with it. Such
contact is tenuous and easily broken at first, but is
capable of being strengthened and extended by a
process of increasing introjection of the external
world and re-projection of it, with a gradually
increasing investment of it with libido derived
originally from the therapist.

This contact may never become sufficient for the patient to be able to maintain it entirely alone, and in such a case continued contact with the therapist is essential, and will need to vary in frequency according to the patient's changing condition and situation. I would compare the patient's position to that of a drowning man who has been brought to a boat, and while still in the water his hand is placed on the gunwale and held there by his rescuer until he can establish his own hold.

It follows from this perhaps, a truth already recognized, that the more disintegrated the patient the greater is the need for the analyst to be well integrated.

It may be that in those psychotic patients who do not respond to the usual analytic situation in the ordinary way, by developing a transference which can be interpreted and resolved, the countertransference has to do the whole of the work, and in order to find something in the patient with which to make contact the therapist has to allow his ideas and the libidinal gratifications derived from his work to regress to a quite extraordinary degree. (We may wonder, for instance, about the pleasure an analyst derives from his patients sleeping during their analytic sessions with him!) It has been said that greater therapeutic results are found when a patient is so disturbed that the therapist experiences intense feelings and profound disturbance, and the underlying mechanism for this may be identification with the patient's id.

But these outstanding results are found in the work of two classes of analysts. One consists of beginners who are not afraid to allow their unconscious impulses a considerable degree of freedom because, through lack of experience, like children, they do not know or understand the dangers, and do not recognize them. It works out well in quite a high proportion of cases, because the positive feelings preponderate. Where it does not the results are mostly not seen or not disclosed—they may even be repressed. We all have our private graveyards, and not every grave has a headstone.

The other class consists of those experienced analysts who have gone through a stage of overcautiousness, and have reached the point at which they can trust not only directly to their unconscious impulses as such (because of the modifications resulting from their own analyses) but also to being able at any given moment to bring the countertransference as it stands then into consciousness enough to see at least whether they are advancing or retarding the patient's recovery—in other words to overcome counter-transference resistance.

At times the patient himself will help this, for transference and counter-transference are not only syntheses by the patient and analyst acting separately, but, like the analytic work as a whole, are the result of a joint effort. We often hear of the mirror which the analyst holds up to the patient, but the patient holds one up to the analyst too, and there is a whole series of reflections in each, repetitive in kind, and subject to continual modification. The mirror in each case should become progressively clearer as the analysis goes on, for patient and analyst respond to each other in a reverberative kind of way, and increasing clearness in one mirror will bring the need for a corresponding clearing in the other.

The patient's ambivalence leads him both to try to break down the analyst's counter-resistances (which can be a frightening thing to do) and also to identify with him in them and so to use them as his own. The question of giving him a 'correct' interpretation is then of considerable importance from this point of view.

VI

When such a thing happens as I have quoted in this story, to neutralize the obstructive effect of a mistimed or wrongly emphasized interpretation giving the 'correct' interpretation when the occasion arises may not be enough. Not only should the mistake be admitted (and the patient is entitled not only to express his own anger but also to some expression of regret from the analyst for its occurrence, quite as much as for the occurrence of a mistake in the amount of his account or the time of his appointment), but its origin in unconscious countertransference may be explained, unless there is some definite contra-indication for so doing, in which case it should be postponed until a suitable time comes, as it surely will. Such explanation may be essential for the further progress of the analysis, and it will have only beneficial results, increasing the patient's confidence in the honesty and good-will of the analyst, showing him to be human enough to make mistakes, and making clear the universality of the phenomenon of transference and the way in which it can arise in any relationship. Only harm can come from the withholding of such an interpretation.

Let me make it clear that I do not mean that I think counter-transference interpretations should be unloaded injudiciously or without consideration on the heads of hapless patients, any more than transference interpretations are given without thought to-day. I mean that they should neither be positively avoided nor perhaps restricted to feelings which are justified or objective, such as those to which Dr. Winnicott refers in his paper on Hate in the Counter-Transference (*Int. J. Psycho-Anal.*, 30, 1949). (And of course they *cannot* be given unless something of the counter-transference has become conscious.) The subjectivity of the feelings needs to be shown to the patient, though their actual origin need not be gone into (there should not be 'confessions'); it should be enough to point out one's own need to analyse them; but above all the important thing is that they should be recognized by both analyst and patient.

In my view a time comes in the course of every analysis when it is essential for the patient to recognize the existence not only of the analyst's objective or justified feelings, but also of the analyst's subjective feelings; that is, the analyst must and does develop an unconscious counter-transference which he is nevertheless able to deal with in such a way that it does not interfere to any serious extent with the patient's interests, specially the progress of cure. The point at which such recognition comes will of course vary in individual analyses, but it belongs rather to the later stages of analysis than to the earlier ones. Occasionally, mistakes in technique or mistakes such as errors in accounts, etc., make it necessary to refer to unconscious mental processes in the analyst (i.e. to counter-transference) at an earlier time than one would choose, but the reference can be a slight one, sufficient only for the purpose of relieving the immediate anxiety. Too much stress on it at an early time would increase anxiety to what might be a really dangerous degree.

So much emphasis is laid on the unconscious phantasies of patients about their analysts that it is often ignored that they really come to know a great deal of truth about them—both actual and psychic. Such knowledge could not be prevented in any case, even if it were desirable, but patients do not know they have it, and part of the analyst's task is to bring it into consciousness, which may be the very thing to which he has himself the greatest resistance. Analysts often behave unconsciously exactly like the parents who put up a smoke-screen, and tantalize their children, tempting them to see the very things they forbid their seeing; and not to refer to counter-transference is tantamount to denying its existence, or forbidding the patient to know or speak about it.

The ever-quoted remedy for counter-transference difficulties—deeper and more thorough analysis of the analyst—can at best only be an incomplete one, for some tendency to develop unconscious infantile counter-transferences is bound to remain. Analysis cannot reach the whole of the unconscious id, and

we have only to remember that even the most thoroughly analysed person still dreams to be reminded of this. Freud's saying 'Where id was ego shall be' is an ideal, and like most other ideals is not fully realizable. All that we can really aim at is reaching the point at which the analyst's attitude to his own id impulses is no longer a paranoid one and so is safe from his patients' point of view, and to remember besides that this will still vary in him from day to day, according to the stresses and strains to which he is exposed.

To my mind it is this question of a paranoid or phobic attitude towards the analyst's own feelings which constitutes the greatest danger and difficulty in counter-transference. The very real fear of being flooded with feeling of any kind, rage, anxiety, love, etc., in relation to one's patient and of being passive to it and at its mercy, leads to an unconscious avoidance or denial. Honest recognition of such feeling is essential to the analytic process, and the analysand is naturally sensitive to any insincerity in his analyst, and will inevitably respond to it with hostility. He will identify with the analyst in it (by introjection) as a means of denying his own feelings, and will exploit it generally in every way possible, to the detriment of his analysis.

I have shown above that unconscious (and uninterpreted) counter-transference may be responsible for the prolonging of analysis. It can equally well be responsible for the premature ending, and I feel that it is again in the final stages that most care is needed to avoid these things. Analysts writing about the final stages of analysis and its termination speak over and over again of the way in which patients reach a certain point, and then either slip away and break off the analysis just at the moment when to continue is vital for its ultimate success, or else slip again into another of their interminable repetitions, instead of analysing the anxiety situations. Counter-transference may perhaps be the deciding factor at this point, and the analyst's willingness to deal with it may be the all-important thing.

I should perhaps add that I am sure that valuable unconscious counter-transferences may also very often be responsible for the carrying through to a successful conclusion of analyses which have appeared earlier to be moving towards inevitable failure, and also for quite a lot of the post-analytic work carried on by patients when analyses have been terminated prematurely.

In the later stages of analysis then, when the patient's capacity for objectivity is already increased, the analyst needs especially to be on the look-out for counter-transference manifestations, and for opportunities to interpret it, whether directly or indirectly, as and when the patient reveals it to him. Without it patients may fail to recognize objectively much of the irrational parental behaviour which has been so powerful a factor in the development of the neurosis, for wherever the analyst does behave like the parents, and conceals the fact, there is the point at which continued repression of what might otherwise be recognized is inevitable. It brings great relief to a patient to find that irrational behaviour on the part of his parents was not intended for him personally, but was already transferred to him from *their* parents, and to find his analyst doing the same kind of thing in minor ways can give conviction to his understanding and make the whole process more tolerable to him than anything else can do.

There will of course be phantasies in every analysis about the analyst's feelings towards his patient — we know that from the start — and they have to be interpreted like any other phantasies, but beyond these a patient may quite well become aware of real feelings in his analyst even before the analyst himself is fully aware of them. There may be a great struggle against accepting the idea that the analyst can have unconscious counter-transference feelings, but when once the patient's ego has accepted it certain ideas and memories which have been inaccessible till then may be brought into consciousness, things which would otherwise have stayed repressed.

I have spoken of the patient revealing the counter-transference to the analyst, and I mean this quite literally, though it may sound like the dangerous blood-sport of 'analysing the analyst'. The 'analytic rule' as it is usually worded nowadays is more helpful to us than in its original form. We no longer 'require' our patients to tell us everything that is in their minds. On the contrary, we give them permission to do so, and what comes may on occasion be a piece of real counter-transference interpretation for the analyst. Should he not be willing to accept it, re-repression with strengthened resistance follows, and consequently interruption or prolonging of the analysis. Together with the different formulation of the analytic rule goes a different way of giving interpretations or comments; in the old days analysts, like parents, said what they liked when they liked, as by right, and patients had to take it. Now, in return for the permission to speak or withhold freely, we ask our patients to allow us to say some things, and allow them too to refuse to accept them. This makes for a greater freedom all round to choose the time for giving interpretations and the form in which they are given, by a lessening of the didactic or authoritarian attitude.

Incidentally, a good many of the transference interpretations which are ordinarily given are capable of extension to demonstrate the possibility of counter-transference, for instance: 'You feel that I am angry, as your mother was when . . .' can include 'I'm not angry as far as I know, but I'll have to find out about it and, if I am, to know why, for there's no real reason for me to be.' Such things of course are often said, but they are not always thought of as counter-transference interpretations. In my view that is what they are, and their use might well be developed consciously as a means of freeing counter-transferences and making them more directly available for use.

In her paper read at the Zürich Congress (*Int. J. Psycho-Anal.*, 31, 1950) Dr. Heimann has referred to the appearance of some counter-transference feelings as a kind of signal comparable to the development of anxiety as a warning of the approach of a traumatic situation. If I have understood her correctly the disturbance which she describes is surely in fact anxiety, but a secondary anxiety which is justified and objective and brings a greater alertness and awareness of what is happening. She specifically states that in her opinion counter-transference interpretations are best avoided.

But anxiety serves first of all another purpose; it is primarily a method of dealing with an actual trauma, however ineffective it may be in this capacity. It can happen that this secondary anxiety with its awareness and watchfulness can mask very effectively anxiety of a more primitive kind. Below the level of consciousness analyst and patient can be sensitive to each other's paranoid fears and persecutory feelings, and become so to speak synchronized (or 'in phase') in them, so that the analysis itself can be used by both as defence and the analyst may swing over from an introjective identification with the patient to a projective one, with a loss of those intervals of time and distance of which I spoke earlier, while the patient may defend himself by an introjective identification with the analyst, instead of being able to project on to him the persecuting objects.

Resolution of this situation can come about through conscious recognition of the counter-transference either by the analyst or by the patient. Failure to recognize it may lead to either premature interruption of the analysis, or to prolonging it; in each case there will be re-repression of what might otherwise have become conscious, and strengthening of the resistances. Premature interruption is not necessarily fatal to the ultimate success of the analysis, any more than its prolongation is, for the presence of sufficient understanding, and some valuable counter-transference may make further progress possible even after termination, by virtue of other introjections already made.

The ideal analyst of course exists only in imagination (whether the patient's or the analyst's), and can only be made actual and living in rare moments. But if the analyst can trust to his own modified id impulses, his own repressions of a valuable kind, and to something positive in his patient as well (presumably something which helped to decide him to undertake analysis in the first place) then he can provide enough of that thing which was missing from the patient's early environment and so badly needed — a person who can allow the patient to grow without either interference or over-stimulation. Then a benign circle forms in the analytic situation which the patient can use to develop his own basic rhythmic patterns, and on those patterns to build up the more complex rhythms which are needed to deal with the world of external reality and his own continuously growing inner world.

VII

I have tried to show how patients respond to the unconscious counter-transferences of their analysts, and in particular the importance of any paranoid attitude in the analyst to the counter-transference itself. Counter-transference is a defence mechanism of a synthetic kind, brought about by the analyst's unconscious ego, and is easily brought under the control of the repetition compulsion; but transference and counter-transference are still further syntheses in that they are products of the combined unconscious work of patient and analyst. They depend on conditions which are partly internal and partly external to the analytic relationship, and vary from week to week, day to day, and even moment to moment with the rapid intra- and extra-psychic changes. Both are essential to psycho-analysis, and counter-transference is no more to be feared or avoided than is transference; in fact it *cannot* be avoided, it can only be looked out for, controlled to some extent, and perhaps used.

But only in so far as analysis is a true sublimation for the analyst and not a perversion or addiction (as I think it sometimes may be) can we avoid counter-transference neurosis. Patches of transitory counter-transference neurosis may appear from time to time even in the most skilled, experienced and well-analysed analysts, and they can be used positively to help patients towards recovery by means of their own transferences. According to the analyst's attitude to counter-transference (which is ultimately his attitude to his own id impulses and his own feelings) paranoid anxiety, denial, condemnation, or acceptance, and the degree of his willingness to allow it to become conscious to his patient as well as to himself, the patient will be encouraged to respond either by exploiting it repetitively, or to use it progressively to good purpose.

Interpretation of counter-transference along the lines which I have tried to indicate would make much heavier demands on analysts than before; but so did interpretation of transference at the time when it began to be used. Nowadays that is something which is taken for granted, and it has been found to have its compensations in that the analyst's libidinal impulses and creative and reparative wishes find effective gratification in the greater power and success of his work. I believe that similar results might follow a greater use of counter-transference if we can find ways of using it, though I must stress the tentativeness with which I am putting forward any of these ideas.

13

ON COUNTER-TRANSFERENCE

Annie Reich

EDITOR'S NOTE

Annie Reich has written several papers on countertransference and its various aspects. The present paper is included here for its sensitive presentation of the classical psychoanalytic position. Though treating countertransference rather implicitly as part of the analytic interaction, it focuses primarily on intrapsychic factors within the analyst. By virtue of this focus, the paper generates rewarding insights into the unconscious basis for countertransference expressions, as well as some understanding of the means through which they should be self-analytically resolved.

The stress here is almost entirely on the disruptive aspects of countertransference, although the hope is expressed that sublimation and desexualization can transform pathological attitudes so that they might serve the needs of the patient. The interested reader will find in Reich's second major paper on this subject (1960) a valuable critical discussion of several important works on this topic.

The act of understanding the patient's productions in analysis and the ability to respond to them skilfully is not based solely on logical conclusions. Frequently the analyst can observe that insight into the material comes suddenly as if from somewhere within his own mind. Suddenly the confusing incomprehensible presentations make sense; suddenly the disconnected elements become a *Gestalt*. Equally suddenly, the analyst gets inner evidence as to what his interpretation should be and how it should be given. This type of understanding impresses one as something which is experienced almost passively; 'it happens'. It is not the result of an active process of thinking, like the solution of a mathematical problem. It seems obvious that this kind of insight into the patient's problem is achieved *via* the analyst's own unconscious. It is as if a partial and short-lived identification with the patient had taken place. The evidence of what is going on in the patient's unconscious, then, is based on an awareness of what is now going on in the analyst's own mind. But this identification has to be a short-lived one. The analyst has to be able to swing back to his outside position in order to be capable of an objective evaluation of what he has just now felt from within.

Anyhow, the tool for understanding is the analyst's own unconscious. When Freud advises that the analyst should listen with free floating attention, he has exactly this in mind. The material should be absorbed by the analyst's unconscious; there should not be any aim-directed censoring or conscious elimination through the analyst's attempts at rational thinking. This method of listening will guarantee the analyst's ability to remember, in an effortless way, those parts of the patient's previous material which connect with or serve to explain the new elements which are presented.

It is obvious what hazards may arise. If the analyst has some reason of his own for being preoccupied, for being unable to associate freely, for

Reprinted from *International Journal of Psycho-Analysis* 32:25–31, 1951.

shrinking back from certain topics or if he is unable to identify with the patient, or has to identify to such a degree that he cannot put himself again outside the patient—to mention only a few of the possible difficulties—he will be unable to listen in this effortless way, to remember, to understand, to respond correctly.

Furthermore, there are more tasks for the analyst. He has to be the object of the patient's transference. He has to be the screen on to which the patient can project his infantile objects, to whom he can react with infantile emotions and impulses, or with defences against these. The analyst has to remain neutral in order to make this transference possible. He must not respond to the patient's emotion in kind. He must be able to tolerate love and aggression, adulation, temptation, seduction and so on, without being moved, without partiality, prejudice or disgust. It is, indeed, not an easy task to be able, on the one side, to feel oneself so deeply into another person as the analyst has to do in order to understand, and, at the same time, to remain uninvolved. Without having faced his own unconscious, his own ways and means of solving conflicts, that is, without being analysed himself, the analyst would not be able to live up to these difficult requirements.

To be neutral in relationship to the patient, to remain the screen, does not, of course, imply that the analyst has no relationship at all to the patient. We expect him to be interested in the patient, to have a friendly willingness to help him. He may like or dislike the patient. As far as these attitudes are conscious, they have not yet anything to do with counter-transference. If these feelings increase in intensity, we can be fairly certain that the unconscious feelings of the analyst, his own transferences on to the patient, i.e. counter-transferences, are mixed in. Intense dislike is frequently a reaction to not understanding the patient; or it may be based on deeper 'real counter-transference'. Too great, particularly sexualized, interest in the patient can most frequently be understood also as a counter-transference. We shall come back to this point.

A situation in which the analyst really falls in love with the patient is infrequent. In such a situation the analysis becomes impossible, and the patient should be sent to somebody else.

Counter-transference thus comprises the effects of the analyst's own unconscious needs and conflicts on his understanding or technique. In such cases the patient represents for the analyst an object of the past on to whom past feelings and wishes are projected, just as it happens in the patient's transference situation with the analyst. The provoking factor for such an occurrence may be something in the patient's personality or material or something in the analytic situation as such. This is counter-transference in the proper sense.

In a discussion before the psycho-analytic study group in Prague in 1938 between Dr. Otto Fenichel and myself on the topic of counter-transference, which Dr. Fenichel later on used as the basis of a paper entitled 'The Implication of the Didactic Analysis' (mimeographed by the Topeka Institute of Psychoanalysis), the conception of counter-transference was understood in a much wider sense. We included under this heading all expressions of the analyst's using the analysis for acting-out purposes. We speak of acting out whenever the activity of analysing has an unconscious meaning for the analyst. Then his response to the patient, frequently his whole handling of the analytic situation, will be motivated by hidden unconscious tendencies. Though the patients in these cases are frequently not real objects on to whom something is transferred but only the tools by means of which some needs of the analyst, such as to allay anxiety or to master guilt-feelings, are gratified, we have used the term counter-transference. This seemed to us advisable because this type of behaviour is so frequently mixed up and fused with effects of counter-transference proper that it becomes too schematic to keep the two groups apart. The simplest cases in the proper sense of counter-transference are those which occur suddenly, under specific circumstances and with specific patients. These are, so to speak, acute manifestations of counter-transference. I give you a simple example which was related to me recently:

An analyst was ill, suffering pain but being able to continue work with the help of rather large doses of analgesics. One of his patients chose this time to accuse the analyst of neglecting her, of not giving her enough time, and so on. The complaints were brought forth with the nagging persistence of a demanding oral aggressive individual. The analyst became violently annoyed with the patient and had great difficulty in restraining the expression of his anger. What had been going on is fairly obvious. The analyst resented the fact that the patient was able to make these aggressive demands for attention while he, the analyst, was in a situation which would have justified similar demands, but he had to control himself. The unexpressed demands then tie up with deeper material which is irrelevant in this connexion.

The analyst is here in a special situation in which

his mental balance is shaken by illness. In this condition, he cannot tolerate the patient who, as a mirror, reflects his own repressed impulses. The counter-transference reaction is based on an identification with the patient. Identifications of this kind belong to the most frequent forms of counter-transference.

Another example: A young analyst, not yet finished with his own training, feels irked by one of his patients and feels a desire to get rid of him. Why? The patient has expressed homosexual tendencies which the analyst is not inclined to face within himself. Here again the patient is the mirror that reflects something that is intolerable.

Counter-transference phenomena are by no means always manifestations of defence against the impulse, as in these last examples, but they may be simple impulse derivatives. I remember the case of a colleague who came for a second analysis because he had a tendency to fall in love with young attractive women patients. The analysis revealed that he was not really interested in these women but in identification with them, he wanted to be made love to by the analyst and in this way to gratify the homosexual transference fantasies which in his first analysis had remained unanalysed.

The sexual interest in the patient which could be called the most simple and direct manifestation of counter-transference is here the result of an identification with the patient. This is most typical. Most of the so-called 'simple' manifestations of that kind are built after that pattern. The patients are not really the objects of deeper drives but they reflect the impulses of the analyst as if they were fulfilled. But identification is certainly not the only possible danger. At other times, for instance, one is faced with counter-transference reactions which are provoked by the specific content of the patient's material. For instance: certain material of a patient was understood by an analyst as a representation of the primal scene. Whenever the material was touched upon by the patient the analyst reacted to it with the defence reaction he had developed in the critical situation in his childhood: he became sleepy and had difficulties in concentrating and remembering.

Sometimes the disturbances are of a more general nature, not dependent on any special situation of the analyst or special material. It is the analytic relationship as such and some special aspects of the relationship to patients which cause the analyst to be disturbed by manifestations of counter-transference. For instance, an inclination to accept resistances at face value, a feeling of inability to attack or analyse them, was based, in two cases which I could observe in analysis, on an unconscious identification with the patient, just because he was in the position of a patient. The analyst expressed in that identification a passive masochistic wish (in one case, a homosexual one; in the other case, of a woman analyst, a predominantly masochistic one) to change places with the patient and to be in the passive position. Both are tempted to let themselves be accused and mistreated by the patient. In both cases, to be a patient corresponded to an infantile fantasy.

Such manifestations of counter-transference, of course, do not represent isolated episodes but reflect permanent neurotic difficulties of the analyst. Sometimes the counter-transference difficulties are only one expression of a general character problem of the analyst. For instance, unconscious aggression may cause the analyst to be over-conciliatory, hesitant and unable to be firm when necessary. Unconscious guilt feelings may express themselves in boredom or therapeutic overeagerness. These attitudes naturally represent serious handicaps for the analyst.

Another example of this kind is a paranoid attitude which makes the analyst concentrate on 'motes' in other people's eyes in order not to see the 'beams' in his own. This can degenerate into complete projection of his own contents or may remain within the frame of usefulness and enable the analyst to develop an uncanny sense of smell, so to speak, for these particular contents. He does not invent them in his patients but is able to unearth them, even if they exist only in minimal quantities. Obviously the analytic situation is a fertile field for such behaviour. This mechanism may originally even have created the interest in analysis. Frequently, though, the analytic situation is not the only battleground for these forces, which extend also to other fields of life. This attitude cannot be considered as a pure counter-transference phenomenon in the proper sense any more. It belongs more to the 'acting-out' group, which I mentioned earlier, and of which I would like to bring just one example:

An analyst had the need to prove that he was not afraid of the unconscious, not afraid of his own unconscious drives. This led to a compulsion to 'understand' the unconscious intellectually, as if to say: 'Oh, I know and understand all that, I am not scared.' This caused a tendency to preserve a safe distance from the patient's unconscious by helping to keep up an intellectual isolation and induced the analyst to overlook the patient's defence mechanisms like isolations. The aim of this acting out was, of course, to master the analyst's anxiety. Such mechanisms are double-edged. They work only for a certain time and tend to break down when the intensity of anxiety becomes too great. The analyst, being afraid of his breakdown, was frightened by any emotional breakthrough or outburst of anxiety in his patient and avoided anything which could help the patient to reach greater emotional depth. Under such conditions it became important not to identify himself with the patient at all, or, at least, only with the resistances, which then were not recognized as such but were taken at their face value, this again seriously interfering with the analyst's tasks.

The bad relationship of the analyst with his own unconscious may lead to constant doubt of the veracity of the expressions of the unconscious. Such a doubt is sometimes overcompensated by the extraordinary stress which is placed on any bit of unconscious material that can be recognized. Deep interpretations are then given in a compensatory way to overcome the analyst's doubts before the patient is ready for them. In other cases I have seen a fear of interpretations.

I shall refrain from giving any other examples for 'acting out' in order not to overburden the reader with too many details. But there is one more group that should be mentioned. Here the analyst misuses the analysis to get narcissistic gratifications and assurances for himself.

A specific form of this kind might be called the 'Midas touch'. It is as if whatever the analyst touches was transformed into gold. He is a magic healer. He restores potency and undoes castration. His interpretations are magic gifts. His patients become geniuses just because they are *his* patients. It is obvious what enormous gratification the analyst can get from such an attitude and how dangerous it is. It easily can lead to unrealistic evaluations of the patients, to inability to observe soberly, to therapeutic over-ambition and hostility against the patient who fails to give his analyst the narcissistic gratification of becoming cured by him. In general, the slow cumbersome process of analysis makes high demands on the analyst's patience and narcissistic equilibrium. It is obvious how detrimental it may become if this equilibrium is shaky, that is, if the analyst depends on his patients for narcissistic supplies.

Related to this are attitudes which one might call pedagogic ones. The analyst feels tempted to fulfil thwarted infantile desires of patients and thus to teach them that the world is not as terrible as they in their childish ways of thinking assume. Thus anxiety is smoothed over, reassurance is given instead of real analysis of the anxiety. The psychotherapeutic past with which most of our students recently come to

analytic training presents us frequently with tendencies of this kind.

I remember the case of a colleague, for instance, who would constantly answer all the questions of a patient relating to the analyst's private affairs. The analyst was unable to let a frustration situation come to a peak, which would have led into the analysis of the childhood situation. Instead, he had to gratify and reassure the patient. It was as if he were saying to the patient: 'I am not treating you as you were treated, that is—mistreated—by your parents'. which means: 'I am not treating you as I was treated by my parents or by my former analyst. I am healing what they damaged.' Sometimes pedagogic attitudes like this may stand under the opposite sign: 'I shall treat you as I was treated. I will do to you what was done to me.' Here something that was originally passively experienced is transformed into something which is actively done to somebody else. This is one of the most effective forms of anxiety mastering.

I shall not continue to enumerate and describe here how the variety of possible disturbances in the activity of analysing is as manifold as the whole psychopathology of neuroses, character disturbances included. In all similar types of behaviour in which the activity of analysing is used in some way for extraneous unconscious purposes, mostly in order to keep up the analyst's inner equilibrium, the patient, as I mentioned before, is not a real object but is only used as a fortuitous tool to solve a conflict situation. Fenichel has coined a specific term to describe this situation: the patient is used as a witness to whom the analyst has to prove, for instance, that he can master the unconscious, or that he has no reason to feel guilty.

Let me stop here and look back. I have given many more examples of the permanent kind than of the acute one. This may be due to the material available to me, which after all was mostly contributed by analysts who came to analysis on account of some difficulty—but I am almost inclined to believe that indeed most counter-transference difficulties are of the permanent type. It is obvious that the acute ones are much easier to deal with than the others. Frequently a bit of self-analysis can reveal what is going on and bring about a complete solution of the conflict. The permanent and more generalized forms are consequences of deeply engrained personality difficulties of the analyst for which there is only one solution: thorough analysis. Freud, in his paper 'Analysis Terminable and Interminable', advises that the analyst after some years of practice should have some more analysis, even when the difficulties he has to struggle with are not as serious as those described. This is something we really should bear in mind.

The two forms of counter-transference manifestations could be compared with incidental hysterical symptoms in contrast to permanent character distortions. The attempt to keep these two types of counter-transference clearly separated is of course schematic. As mentioned before, there are transitions from one form to the other.

It would be impossible to attempt to give a complete description and classification of even the most frequent forms of counter-transference only. This would amount to a survey of the psychopathology of the analyst. We are most concerned with the effect these psychological mechanisms have on analytic technique. Nearly all the phenomena mentioned will interfere with the analyst's ability to understand, to respond, to handle the patient, to interpret in the right way. But on the other hand, the special talent and the pathologic are usually just two sides of the same; a slight shift in cathexis may transform an unconscious mechanism of the analyst from a living out of his own conflicts into a valuable sublimation. On the other hand, what is the preliminary condition for his psychological interest and skill may degenerate into acting out.

It appears to me highly desirable to reach a closer understanding about the conditions under which these unconscious elements do constitute a foundation for adequate or even outstanding functioning and when they serve to interfere with or at least to complicate the activity of analysing. We said before that the unconscious of the analyst is his tool. The readiness and faculty to use his own unconscious in that way obviously must have some deeper motivation in the analyst's psychological make-up.

The analysis of these deeper motives, which, as we said, are the necessary basis for the analyst's interest, leads us back to the unconscious drives which were sublimated into psychological talent. Sometimes this personal origin of the analyst's interest in his work is clearly discernible even without analysis. I know, for instance, a number of analysts who, after many years of work, are still fascinated by their being entitled to pry into other people's secrets; that is to say, they are voyeurs; they live out their infantile sexual curiosity. Curiosity is seriously considered by many analysts as an essential prerequisite for analysis, but this curiosity has to be of a special nature. It has to be desexualized. If it were still connected with sexual excitement, this would necessarily interfere with the analyst's functioning. It must be, furthermore, removed from the original

objects and has to be used for an interest in understanding their psychology and their structure. In this way the whole process is lifted above the original level of conflict.

I give here a piece of case material from the analysis of an analyst that throws some light on the psychologic background of such a sublimation; this may permit a somewhat deeper understanding of the structure of such a sublimation. The example I am choosing comes from a person who was capable and successful and had good therapeutic results. The counter-transference in his case, in spite of the rather pathological origin, was, one might say, tamed and harnessed for the benefit of the work. I shall limit myself to a few important elements.

One of the special gifts of this analyst was his keenness of observation, his ability to grasp little peculiarities of behaviour in his patients and to understand them—correctly—as expressions of an unconscious conflict. He was deeply interested in his work, to the exclusion of extraneous intellectual inclinations.

The genesis of his psychological interest could be reconstructed in analysis as follows: Dr. X. from early childhood was again and again an unwilling witness of violent fights between unhappily married parents, which frightened him and brought forth the wish to reconcile them and to undo whatever damage might have been done in their battles, which were misunderstood by the child as sadistic primal scenes. The father, strong and powerful, but intellectually the mother's inferior, was 'tearing pieces out of mother', as she complained whenever she wished to ward off his affectionate approaches. This left mother, the boy felt, castrated, sick, complaining and, at the same time, overambitious and demanding recompensation for her own deficiencies from her son, who had to become 'magnificent' to fill her narcissistic needs. Too frightened to identify with the father in his sadistic activities, the child rather early identified with the mother and felt passive and castrated like her. A mild attack of poliomyelitis during the height of the oedipal period served to engrave the mother identification more deeply. He now began to observe his own body as he had been observed anxiously by his mother who had been looking for signs of the illness. Overstress was now laid on any spark of masculinity, strength and perfection to contradict the inner awareness of his passivity and his fear of castration. In a partial regression he now became interested in his anal functions, following his mother here, too, who overanxiously watched his anal productions, willing to give him ample praise when she was satisfied. He now overevaluated himself just as his mother over-evaluated him. At that time a peculiar fantasy appeared: he is one with mother as if he and she were one body. He is her most precious part, that is, he is her penis. By being 'magnificent' as she wants him to be, his whole body becomes a big penis and in this way he undoes her castration. Both together they are complete.

This fantasy remained the basis for his tendency to self-observation, which thenceforward continued to exist. In this self-observation he plays two roles. He is identified with the anxious, castrated mother who watches him and at the same time he exhibits himself in order to gratify her. This narcissistic play now becomes a new source of gratification for himself. He is proud of his keenness of observation, his intelligence and knowledge. His thoughts are his mental products, of which he is as proud as of his anal achievements. In this way he is reconstructing what mother has lost. By self-observation he heals her castration in a magic way.

When he was nine, a little brother, the only other sibling, was born. This was a fulfilment of a desire for a child of his own which had already come to the fore in connection with his anal interests. Now he develops a motherly interest in the baby and succeeds in turning away his interest to a large degree from his own body to the baby and later to other outside objects. The self-observation turns into observation of other people, and thus the original play between him and mother is re-enacted by him in projection on to outside objects and thus becomes unselfish and objective. A necessary preliminary step in the direction of sublimation was made.

Furthermore, another important development can be now noticed. His interest in the little brother becomes a psychological one. He remembers a scene when the little one, not yet two years of age, had a temper tantrum, in his rage biting into the wood of the furniture. The older brother was very concerned about the intensity of emotion in the child and wondered what to do about it. Thus the interest which originally had to do with physical intactness had turned towards emotional experiences.

The psychological interest from now on played an important role in his life. The decision to study medicine and to choose psycho-analysis as his specialty impresses us as a natural development of these interests. Here he can build up a stable sublimation of his peculiar strivings. He can now continue to observe, not himself, but other people. He can unearth their hidden defects and signs of castration and can use the technique of analysis for healing them. He has a special talent for understanding other people's unconscious and their hidden resistance. In the relationship with the patient he relives his original interplay with mother. By curing the patient he himself becomes cured and his mother's castration is undone. The cured patient represents himself as a wonderful phallus that has returned to mother. It is obvious what tremendous narcissistic stress he laid on being a 'good analyst'. In this new position, as a 'magnificent' analyst, he represents his deepest ego-ideal as fulfilled, he is a phallic mother.

On a higher level, the patient also represents his child, his little brother, whom he wants to understand, in order to educate and help him.

The analytic faculties of this analyst are obviously based on an orginally rather pathologic and narcissistic self-interest. That he is interested in a patient is based on a projection of this self-interest; but what he observes remains objective and does not represent a projection of inner experiences and fantasies. This faculty for objective observation has to do with the fact that Dr. X., in spite of the at some time unstable boundaries between him and his mother, had had a warm and affectionate relationship with her and was capable of real object libidinal relationships. He sees what is there and not what is within himself, though his motive for seeing and his ability to understand are based primarily upon his preoccupation with the mother's and his own intactness or deficiency; though deep down he wants to be a magic healer he is able to content himself with the slow process of interpreting resistances, removing defences and unearthing the unconscious. Thus one can say that though his need to understand is the result of his highly pathological mother fixation he has succeeded in sublimating these infantile needs into true psychological interest. That he wishes to understand and to heal is motivated by the past. What he understands and how he tries to heal is based on objective reality. This is essential, as it represents the difference between acting out and a true sublimation.

I am aware that in representing this bit of case material I am not being fully successful in really shedding light on the finer prerequisites of this accomplishment. The problem why a sublimation is successful or not depends to a large degree on economic factors, and these are beyond the scope of this discussion. This is a problem, by the way, which is by no means specific for this type of sublimation.

The wish to heal and the psychological interest could be traced in this material to specific infantile set-ups. I do not feel entitled to assume that the wish to heal is typically based on a similar conflict situation. A further investigation of the origin of the interest in psychology and healing in a more general way would be a challenging problem.

What is of interest for us here is the similarity and the difference of the well-functioning sublimation and the aforementioned types of acting out. Here as well as there deep personal needs are fulfilled. But while in this sublimation the fulfilment is achieved *via* the route of desexualized psychological insight this transformation has not taken place in the pathological forms of counter-transference.

The double-edged character of such a sublimation is obvious. The intensity of interest, the special faculty of understanding lead to a high quality of work, but any disturbance of psychic equilibrium may bring about a breakdown of the sublimation and the satisfaction of personal needs may become over-important so that the objectivity in the relationship to the patient becomes disturbed.

What I should like to stress it that in this case of undisturbed functioning the psychological interest obviously is based on a very complicated 'counter-transference', which is desexualized and sublimated in character, while in the pathological examples the conflict persisted in its original form and the analytic situation was used either for living out the underlying impulses or defending against them or for proving that no damage has occurred in consequence of them.

Maybe we might come to the following conclusion: Counter-transference is a necessary prerequisite of analysis. If it does not exist, the necessary talent and interest is lacking. But it has to remain shadowy and in the background. This can be compared to the role that attachment to the mother plays in the normal object choice of the adult man. Loving was learned with the mother, certain traits in the adult object may lead back to her—but normally the object can be seen in its real character and responded to as such. A neurotic person takes the object absolutely for his mother or suffers because she is not his mother.

In the normally functioning analyst we find traces of the original unconscious meaning of analysing, while the neurotic one still misunderstands analysis under the influence of his unconscious fantasies and reacts accordingly.

14

COUNTERTRANSFERENCE[1]

Lucia E. Tower

EDITOR'S NOTE

This paper is the first extended description by an American classical analyst of the intensely interactional qualities of the analyst's countertransferences. It also offers the unique thesis that a countertransference disturbance develops in the course of every analysis and, further, that the resolution of the patient's transference constellation depends on and is parallel to the resolution of the countertransference-based syndrome.

Tower takes us a long way toward recognizing the inevitability of countertransference, its positive and negative effects, and the implications of its essential presence in respect to the actualities of the analytic experience and the process of cure. In part a reaction against the stress among classical analysts on interpretations as virtually the entire basis for adaptive symptom resolution, Tower's work provides a basis for recognizing that what has been broadly termed the transference-countertransference interaction, and its analytic resolution (for both parties) is a vital characteristic of sound analytic work—and, I would add, is fundamental to the salutary effects of interpretive endeavors.

There are many other valuable ideas and distinctions in this important paper. Of special note is Tower's tolerance of countertransference-based feelings and reactions, and her basic commitment to their gradual analysis and to the understanding of the patient's unconscious responses to their expression. She also suggests that the actual experiences of the analyst's errors offer the patient special opportunities for the modification of difficult transference resistances—a concept adumbrated by Winnicott (1956; see chapter 40), who viewed the patient's reactions to the analyst's actual failures as a new opportunity to rework the parents' past failures as they pertain to the illness of the analysand.

One can only wonder why it is that so little subsequent research and writing has been stimulated by this insightful paper. We can suspect again that an undue dread of the actualities of the unconscious communicative interaction, and of the analyst's pathological inputs, plays a significant role in this avoidance.

I. THEORETICAL CONSIDERATIONS

References to countertransference appeared very early in psychoanalytic literature. Originally, they paid mostly lip service to its existence, with unelaborated statements that, of course, analysts could have transference reactions to their patients. Little else was said, other than to imply that these were dubious reactions and should be controlled, and for analysts to discuss their countertransference reactions in public would be somewhat indecently self-revealing. about ten years ago, a moderate number of articles began to appear. The general overtone of these articles has been of a rather embarrassed sort, as though these were major imperfections in our therapeutic procedures, and of course certain countertransference phenomena are considered reprehensible in the extreme.

The literature on countertransference has recently been excellently reviewed by Douglass Orr (18). I shall make only cursory comments about this literature because my main purpose is to present some ideas of my own and some detailed case material. Despite wide agreement among analysts about transference, there has been wide disagreement about countertransference. Freud's first reference to it in 1910 was rather forbidding: "We have begun to consider the 'counter-transference' . . . arising as a result of the patient's influence on his [the physician's] unconscious feelings, and have nearly come to the point of requiring the physician to recognize and overcome this counter-transference in himself" (9, p. 289).

It is striking that a natural and inevitable phenomenon, so rich in potential for understanding, should have sustained so forbidding a tone toward its existence for forty-five years. I refer to the fact that no analyst has ever been presumed to have been so perfectly analyzed that he no longer has an unconscious, or is without susceptibility to the stirring up of instinctual impulses and defenses against them. The very phraseology of our training practices belies the mask of the "perfect analyst." We state that the student's personal analysis should "serve as a first-hand experience with the unconscious"; it should

gain him "working freedom from his own disturbing emotional patterns";[2] and it should enable him to continue his self-analysis on his own. At no time is it expected that he will have been perfectly analyzed. In addition, our recommendations for periodic reanalysis of analysts presuppose a large unconscious reservoir of sources for the development of new neurotic responses to emotional pressures from analytic patients upon the analyst's unconscious.

Conflicting conceptions of countertransference have covered a wide range. There were early ideas that it was the analyst's conscious emotional reaction to the patient's transference; attitudes that it covered every conscious or unconscious reaction about the patient, normal or neurotic; mechanistic constructions of the interpersonal relation between patient and analyst into some schematized oedipal picture (20); characterological disposition and personal eccentricities of the analyst were included; reactions to the patient as a whole have been considered transferences, and to partial aspects of the patient, countertransferences; anxiety in the analyst has been taken to be the common denominator to all countertransference reactions and every anxiety-producing response in the analyst considered countertransference (7); and finally, only sexual impulses toward patients have been regarded as countertransference. Major differences center around "seeing the analyst as a mirror — versus the analyst as a human being" (18). Countertransferences are considered as being simply transferences — and nothing else — versus their not being transferences and being almost anything else.

Other differences center around questions of whether or not to discuss countertransferences with patients;[3] whether countertransferences are always present and therefore reasonably normal; or whether they are always abnormal. "Carry over"[4] is mentioned several times as particularly ominous in its implications. Almost invariably there are explicit prohibitions against any erotic countertransference manifestations. Only once, I believe, is it suggested that unless there are periods or occasions of "carry over," the analysis will not be successful, and only once, I believe, is it suggested that there may be under normal, and perhaps even useful, circumstances

---

1. Read before the Chicago Psychoanalytic Society, May, 1955, and The American Psychoanalytic Association in New York, December, 1955.

2. Report of The Committee on Training Standards, Board on Professional Standards, American Psychoanalytic Association, November, 1953.

3. Some suggestions along this line seem to approach the "wild analysis" level.

4. "carry over": affects persisting in the analyst in response to and following an analytic interview.

something approaching a countertransference neurosis. Mostly the latter are strenuously criticized.

The forbidding nature of writings on the subject is indicated by the following typical quotes (slightly edited):

Our countertransference must be healthy [23].

It is assumed that the appropriate responses predominate [6].

At least some analytical toilet is part of the analyst's necessary routine [12].

Countertransference is the same as transference — it is then immediately obvious that countertransference is undesirable and a hindrance [8].

The [countertransference mistake] should be admitted, to allow the patient to express his anger, and he is entitled to some expression of regret from the analyst [16].

It is not safe to let even subtle manifestations of the countertransference creep inadvertently into the inter-personal climate. The analyst must recognize and control these reactions [1].

All of these — and similar attitudes — presuppose an ability in the analyst consciously to *control* his own unconscious. Such a supposition is in violation of the basic premise of our science — namely, that human beings are possessed of an unconscious which is *not* subject to conscious control, but which is (fortunately) subject to investigation through the medium of the transference (and presumably also the countertransference) neurosis.

Common evidences of countertransference are given as:

anxiety in the treatment situation;
disturbing feelings toward patients;
stereotypy in feelings or behavior toward patients;
love and hate responses toward patients;
erotic preoccupations, especially ideas of falling in love with a patient;
carry over of affects from the analytic hour;
dreams about patients and acting-out episodes.

The very recent literature on this subject includes a number of perceptive articles, rich with descriptive material and clinical examples, and with a much less forbidding tone.

I would employ the term countertransference *only* for those phenomena which are transferences of the analyst to his patient. It is my belief that there are inevitably, naturally, and often desirably, many countertransference developments in every analysis (some evanescent — some sustained), which are a counterpart of the transference phenomena. Interactions (or transactions) between the transferences of the patient and the countertransferences of the analyst, going on at unconscious levels, may be — or perhaps always are — of vital significance for the outcome of the treatment. The intellectual verbalizations, consisting of the communications of the patient, and the interpretive activity of the analyst are the media through which deep underground channels of communication develop between patient and doctor. Interpretations as such do not cure, nor will any analyst ever be remembered primarily for his interpretative brilliance by any patient with whom he has been successful. This is not, however, to depreciate the importance of interpretation in the analytic procedure. Obviously, only through the patient's verbal communications, and the painstaking, dispassionate, interpretative efforts of the analyst is it possible, little by little, so to peel away defenses that those deep insights and communications can be obtained that we know to be the essence of the curative effect of the analytic process.

Transferences and countertransferences are unconscious phenomena, based on the repetition compulsion, are derived from significant experiences, largely of one's own childhood, and are directed toward significant persons in the past emotional life of the individual. Habitual characterological attitudes should not be included as countertransference phenomena, since these will find expression in almost any situation, and nearly always in virtually the same form. They lack the specificity to a given situation of the countertransference phenomena. The fact that instinct derivatives have been permitted to become egosyntonic through being incorporated into the character structure makes such attitudes essentially conscious or preconscious in character, in contrast to the transference phenomena, which derive from deep unconscious conflicts, in a given situation at a given time, and in response to a given individual, in which are mobilized old, affectively significant experiences in relation to earlier important figures. Indoctrination of patients, for example, is probably not usually a countertransference phenomenon, but an impulse derivative. Many other things incorrectly discussed as "countertransferences" are simply defects in the analyst's perceptions or experience.

There are many difficulties in presenting counter-transference problems for discussion. There is a scarcity of good clinical material which derives substantially from the defensive systems of analysts toward the problem in general. The same resistances toward awareness of countertransference are seen among analysts in higher degree and in more insidious form than they are in patients in their resistances to transference insights. This is for good reason. The practicing analyst is under constant assault and has a precarious position to maintain. He has little motivation to change himself, and if he does develop such motivation, it is usually for personal reasons. The patient comes to the analyst for the purpose of being changed, and he values the procedure only if he feels changes are under way. The analyst, however, becomes anxious while he becomes aware of changes effected by emotional pressures from his patients, and there is no one except himself to push him into facing them.

Aside from the resistances of analysts to counter-transference explorations and the time not yet having been ripe, there are simple practical reasons for the scarcity of our information on the subject. During the treatment hour, an analyst habitually forces down fantasy about himself. It does take time to analyze anyone, including oneself, and a busy analyst, spending most of his day with patients, naturally pushes aside much potentially illuminating material about himself which comes into his own mind from time to time. Another factor is that many countertransference phenomena when catapulted into consciousness create a sort of emergency. Countertransference acting-out episodes, for example, confront the analyst with a situation of surprise necessitating rapid action and good judgment. He must concentrate on keeping the analytic situation in hand, and often the surprise and shock blot out memory of the processes leading up to the incident, probably due to repression out of the discomfort he experiences.

The decision long ago that analysts themselves should be analyzed before they practice analysis was a tremendous departure from any previous form of medical training. The idea of making a doctor into a patient before he can practice as a doctor is itself traumatic. After all one goes through to become an analyst, to have to become aware of the pervasiveness of countertransference phenomena is a threat and a letdown. The importance of analyzing the prospective analyst was recognized early. Carried into action, it was a major factor, probably, in the rapid advancement of our science. For many years, however, this was as far as it could go. In a sense,

the preparatory or personal analysis of the future analyst offered some of the protection which the dream offers our patients. They often regard the dream as a foreign body, over which they have no control, remote in time, and something for which they need not have any feeling of guilt. Similarly, the preliminary personal analysis is often regarded by the practicing analyst, remote in time, forced on him, and related to former problems, as having no connection with present operations, about which there may thus be a bolstering of defenses and rationalizations. The analysis (or observations) of the functioning analyst may be a most important future "royal road" toward understanding the treatment process. Analysts doing supervision are in a position to understand and to make such observations.

Group resistances to exploration of the unconscious of the analyst in the treatment situation follow well-known patterns. There is an unexpressed fear of studying the functioning analyst, as though to report any of his responses were to be permissive about reactions of dubious character. In almost every paper written on countertransference, some tribute has been paid to this group rigidity, in the form of moralizing and pious prohibition, despite intelligent and sympathetic discussion of countertransference problems. Virtually every writer on the subject of countertransference, for example, states unequivocally that no form of erotic reaction to a patient is to be tolerated. This would indicate that temptations in this area are great, and perhaps ubiquitous. This is the one subject about which almost every author is very certain to state his position. Other "countertransference"[5] manifestations are not routinely condemned. Therefore, I assume that erotic responses to some extent trouble nearly every analyst. This is an interesting phenomenon and one that calls for investigation. In my experience, virtually all physicians, when they gain enough confidence in their analysts, report erotic feelings and impulses toward their patients, but usually do so with a good deal of fear and conflict. The following story is typical:

A candidate who had had a partial therapeutic analysis prior to beginning his training, was talking about a very attractive woman patient whose treatment was winding up successfully. The patient had presented a prolonged and irritating resistance of silence. The candidate said: "This was the patient, perhaps, of all my patients, toward whom I have had

---

5. The quotation marks at this point are used because these responses are by no means all countertransference. Many should be quite simply regarded as psychophysiological.

the most sexual countertransference. I would sit and have sexual fantasies about her during those periods of silence. I used to think that if I ever went into a training analysis, I would never tell about this, because of what Dr. X [the previous analyst] said. When I had told him about it, he had seemed angry and had said [in effect], 'But how *can* you be interested in such a sick patient—and besides, you have no right to have any such fantasies toward any patient.' I am puzzled because I think I have gotten a lot of insight from my fantasies. I really never thought that I would be able to tell you about this, and I'm damned if I know how I was able to. I wish I knew what you had done to make me feel that it was alright to tell you. . . . Now I remember: once I had had been talking about being 'attracted' to a certain patient. I was being quite guarded and wasn't admitting that the attraction was sexual, only that I was attracted, and you said, 'But how do you know that your feelings toward her may not be really helpful to her?'[6] It was this that made it possible for me to talk about my sexual fantasies . . . *Now* I'm beginning to wonder: did your remark really include acceptance of sexual fantasies (i.e., feelings) or did it just refer to being attracted?"

This man was an excellent therapist and there was no acting-out behavior. Nevertheless, this man had an artificial fear of erotic and countertransference responses which was related to what he perceived to be the prohibitive attitude of the group to which he aspired to belong. Essentially he did not have within himself a feeling that there was anything wrong with his having these responses.

In our selection of candidates for training, we are disposed to pay close attention to the libidinal resources of the applicant, on the theory that large amounts of available libido are necessary to tolerate the heavy task of a number of intensive analyses. At the same time, we deride almost every detectable libidinal investment made by an analyst in a patient. There is much that is obscure about our understanding of the vicissitudes and functions of the analyst's libido in the treatment relationship. I believe this is a large and important topic in itself. It is not enough to talk just about dedication, empathy and rapport, important as these are. I have brought the analyst's libidinal responses into this discussion because they evoke so much countercathexis among analysts; I feel that this countercathexis belongs to the category of rigidity defenses of the analytic group. Suffice it to

---

6. This was said in the sense of: One could at least be open-minded to the idea that the patient's unconscious awareness of the positive nature of the therapist's countertransference was of specific value to this patient.

say that various forms of erotic fantasy and erotic countertransference phenomena of a fantasy and of an affective character are in my experience ubiquitous and presumably normal. Among the conspicuous characteristics of these phenomena are the facts that they are aim-inhibited in the sense of being virtually without impulse toward action, and are in most instances in high degree separated in point of time from erotic transferences of the patient.

Fantasies and feelings toward patients are profuse in all of us, and are now fairly generally accepted especially where they overlap reality based considerations. Almost all the rational and irrational feelings that we can have toward people in our daily lives, we may at times feel toward our patients. Feelings, however, which seem excessive or inappropriate to what the patient appears to be, or to what he is saying, and especially if they are associated with anxiety, undoubtedly have countertransference significance. Dreams about patients are, of course, usually significant and should always be explored for specific countertransference meaning.

I have for a very long time speculated that in many—perhaps every—intensive analytic treatment there develops something in the nature of countertransference structures (perhaps even a "neurosis") which are essential and inevitable counterparts of the transference neurosis. These countertransference structures may be large or small in their quantitative aspects, but in the total picture they may be of considerable significance for the outcome of the treatment. I believe they function somewhat in the manner of a catalytic agent in the treatment process. Their understanding by the analyst may be as important to the final working through of the transference neurosis as is the analyst's intellectual understanding of the transference neurosis itself, perhaps because they are, so to speak, *the vehicle for the analyst's emotional understanding of the transference neurosis.* Both transference neurosis and countertransference structure seem intimately bound together in a living process and both must be taken continually into account in the work which is psychoanalysis. In fact, I doubt that there is any interpersonal relationship between any two people, and for any purpose whatever, which does not involve, in greater or lesser degree, something in the nature of this living psychological process—interaction at an unconscious and transference level.

We cannot assume that we more than scratch the surface in the preparatory analyses of future analysts in regard to their understanding of themselves and their transference potentials in future analytic work. In addition I am inclined to believe that there are levels of transference which transcend any capacity we now have to gain access to them. There are perhaps even levels of transference to which we will never have access, at any rate by psychological means, because they lie at the borderline between that which is biological and that which is hereditary in us. The phenomenon of falling in love—so little comprehended dynamically—may lie at this borderline.

It is one thing, however, to be able, from experience and training, to formulate consciously the possible occurrence of given countertransference problems. It is another thing to be able to fulfill the cautions with which one charges oneself with 100 per cent efficiency as one goes deeper and deeper into an analytic treatment, week after week, month after month, and year after year, becoming more and more identified with, interested in, and deeply aware of a patient and his problems. If nothing else, too much attention to possible unfavorable countertransference reactions could lead an analyst to some kind of a fixed defense by virtue of which very significant material could be overlooked. Every analyst of experience knows that as he gets deeper and deeper into an analysis, he somehow or other loses a certain perspective on the total situation.

I would conjecture that the development of countertransference neurotic structures in an analyst over a long period of time might be something like Einstein's theory of relativity. This theory has to do with the fact that light is supposed to travel in a straight line from one point to another, and actually does so in our own little world and with our own short distances of measurement. However, when light travels the gigantic distances known to us in terms of millions of light years, other factors previously never understood or even conceived of enter into the picture; and Einstein proved that over these vast reaches of time and space, there is a drift from the straight line in the beam of light. So, too, the hypothetically perfectly trained and perfectly analyzed analyst should be able to pursue an utterly straight course of avoiding all those countertransference pitfalls which his personal analysis should have taught him to anticipate and to avoid. And, undoubtedly, by and large, he is increasingly able to do so and over considerable periods of time. Ultimately, however, it would appear that even under the most ideal circumstances there are bound to be certain drifts, so to speak, from the utterly straight direction of the analyst's performance and understanding of a case, and it is these very slow almost imperceptible drifts which develop in him in unconscious response to hidden pressures and moti-

vations from his patient, which I think constitute the essence of the development of a countertransference structure in and of itself. It is irrelevant to this thesis that these may be most minor excrescences on a very large total structure—the treatment situation. I simply do not believe that any two people, regardless of circumstance, may closet themselves in a room, day after day, month after month, and year after year, without something happening to each of them in respect to the other. Perhaps the development of a major change in the one, which is, after all, the purpose of the therapy, would be impossible without at least some minor change in the other, and it is probably relatively unimportant whether that minor change in the other is a rational one. It is probably far more important that the minor change in the other, namely the therapist, be that which is specifically important and necessary to the one for whom we hope to achieve the major change. These changes in the therapist would be compounded in my view from the ego adaptive responses and the unconscious countertransferences of the analyst, interacting upon each other in such a way as to expand his ego integrative powers specifically to cope with the particular patient's transference resistances. It is in the nature of the transference resistances as they are built up by the patient that they should ferret out and hurl themselves against the weakest spots in the therapist's armamentarium.

Focusing in this manner on one small aspect of a long and involved treatment procedure may inadvertently create an impression that I do not at all wish to create—namely, an illusion that the matter under study is felt to be quantitatively of major importance or qualitatively very different from the bulk of our experience. It is the defensiveness of the analytic group about countertransference phenomena which makes it necessary to caution against such misinterpretation.

I do not like the term "countertransference neurosis" and would not employ it. It has, however, crept into our literature, and it has some reason for existence through analogy with the term "transference neurosis." However, this latter is perhaps also a misnomer, in view of what actually occurs in an analysis. In general, the transference phenomena are experienced in multiple and varying forms throughout any analytic experience, and by both patient and therapist. A discrete, well-structured, easily describable transference neurosis as such probably seldom occurs, and by the same token even less frequently does a discrete countertransference neurosis develop. The term neurosis is very loosely used in our literature. It is employed as an epithet (with the specificity of the word rheumatism) or a well-defined psychiatric diagnosis, or as a catch-all for any and all of the immaturities, eccentricities, and emotional conflicts of those people who come to us for assistance. It is easy for us to say that their transferences to us comprise another neurosis to be given the test tube treatment, but it is another matter entirely to concede that our own transferences to them are similar in kind, though—hopefully—microscopic in quantity by comparison.

I reserve for further and future thought understanding of the nature and meaning of countertransference affect, or lack of it, in psychoanalysis. Increasing personal and group maturity should make its contemplation scientifically a little more tolerable. To some extent this has already begun to occur, but it is still most gingerly approached. A paper presented to The Chicago Psychoanalytic Society four years ago by Adelaide Johnson touched tangentially on this problem and evoked the most massive anxiety and countercathexis in the audience I have observed in many years of psychoanalytic meetings. This reaction seemed all out of proportion to the valid objections which could be raised against the argument of the paper.

If one accepts the premise that countertransferences should be understood as transferences of the analyst, and that they are normal and ubiquitous, countertransference affects have a theoretical *raison d'être* in the universally accepted dictum that true insight is achieved in analysis of transferences only with accompanying and appropriate releases of affect. The fact that the analytic group, despite its vaunted preliminary personal analyses as a means of removing "blind spots," should still defend itself strenuously against applying to its own operations the same dynamic interpretations that it systematically applies to its patients' operations is further testimony to the interminability of the analytic process and the strengths of the repressive forces of the ego.

II. Clinical Material

I have selected for discussion countertransference elements from the analyses of four of my own patients, as I have been able to perceive these. In three cases, countertransference affects of fair intensity played a role at times. Two cases were reasonably successful analyses, one perhaps should have been more successful. I believe my fear of countertransference involvements in this case limited the results. One relatively unsuccessful case was marked by little countertransference affect; an inability to clarify in my own mind my countertransference involvement, if any, and little deep emotional communication between myself and the patient. I wish to emphasize that I believe in general an external observer could not have detected anything out of the ordinary in any one of these analyses.

I have chosen material which I felt demonstrated rather simply some of the points under discussion in Part I. In addition, I chose material which I could be reasonably comfortable about presenting. None of these cases were really painful failures. Also, I selected material from long, fairly "classically" conducted analyses, for reasons which should be obvious. All of the patients seemed to be both analyzable and to require thorough analysis. I do not believe the experiences I had with these patients are particularly unusual in comparison with many other cases of my own and cases I have supervised with other analysts, except for somewhat striking and above or below average countertransference.

I will begin with an example of a specific countertransference reaction with acting out. Many years ago a patient, referred after a near-psychotic reaction, to an "analysis" with an untrained person was utterly enraged at the referral, because of the frustration of her claims upon the previous therapist. Week after week, and month after month, she raged at me in a vituperative manner, despite my having the greatest of patience with her. I endured a quantity of abuse from her, such as I have never taken from any other patient. At times, I would get irritated with the abuse, but mostly I rather liked the patient, was genuinely interested in helping her and was somewhat surprised at my ability to control my irritation with her. I eventually came to understand that what was for the most part a desirable therapeutic attitude, offered a certain countertransference complication. The following episode brought this problem to my attention.

One beautiful spring day I walked out of my office, twenty minutes before this patient's hour, with my appointment book lying open on my desk. I had a delicious luncheon, alone, which I enjoyed more than usual, and strolled back to the office, in time for my next appointment, only to be informed that my patient had been there and had left extremely angry. It was obvious that I had forgotten her appointment, unconsciously and purposely, and it suddenly came over me that I was absolutely fed up with her abuse to the point of nonendurance. At this point, I began to be angry at my patient, and between this time and the next time she came in, I was in a substantial rage against her. Part of this rage I related to guilt, and part to some anxiety about how I would handle the next treatment interview, which I expected would surpass all previous abuse, and I was now aware of the fact that I was no longer going to be able to tolerate this abuse. I fantasied (which of course was a hope) that my patient would terminate her treatment with me. At her next appointment, she glared at me and said, in an accusatory manner, "Where were *you* yesterday?" I said only, "I'm sorry, I forgot." She started to attack me, saying she knew I had been there shortly before, and went on with her customary vituperation. I made no comment, for the most part feeling it was better that I say nothing. This went on for five or ten minutes and abruptly she stopped. There was a dead silence and all of a sudden she started to laugh, saying, "Well, you know, Dr. Tower, really I can't say that I blame you." This was absolutely the first break in this obstinate resistance. Following this episode, the patient was much more cooperative and after one or two short recurrences of the abusiveness, probably to test me, the defense disappeared entirely, and she shortly went into analysis at deep transference levels. At first glance, this seems so unimportant an episode that it hardly warrants description. One would say I was irritated with the patient and missed her hour because of aggression, which of course was true. But the real countertransference problem was not that. Actually, my acting-out behavior was reality-based and brought a resolution to the countertransference problem which was that I had been patient with her too long. This tendency in myself I could trace in detail from certain influences upon me in my earliest childhood. I had gotten into difficulties from this tendency from time to time during my development. I understood this in part, and yet it was not sufficiently resolved in my personality. This prolonged abusive resistance need not have lasted so long, had I been freer to be more aggressive in the face of it. The manner in which I repressed my aggression and allowed it to accumulate to a point where I was forced to act it out, was not an entirely desirable therapeutic procedure. Thus, a theoretically good therapeutic attitude, namely, that of infinite patience and effort to understand a very troubled patient, was actually in this situation a negative countertransference structure, virtually a short-lived countertransference neurosis, which undoubtedly wasted quite a bit of the patient's time, and but for my sudden resolution of it through acting out might well have gone on for a considerably longer time. I gave this little episode a good deal of thought in subsequent years, and eventually came to understand more of its true significance.

However, it is only recently that I might have questioned whether this countertransference reaction which had such clear negative implications at certain levels in this treatment, might perhaps at other levels have had equally positive implications. This particular disposition of mine might well have facilitated this patient's eventual ability to deal fully and affectively with her most highly defended problem—the passive homoerotic aspect of the transference—for it had been an acute paranoid type reaction that brought her into treatment with me.

In the following material I attempt to trace countertransference developments in two analyses which lend themselves to many comparisons.

This is material from the cases of two men, both successful business men of fairly similar backgrounds, near my own age, both liked me as a person, and I liked both of them as people. Both were intelligent, married and had children; both had long analyses. One analysis was successful in a working through at the very deepest transference levels, of an intense transference neurosis, resulting in great symptomatic improvement, much maturation and increased success. In the second, there was no real working through of a transference neurosis, the analysis was unsatisfactory to me, and I felt insecure about the patient's future. There was symptomatic improvement, and the patient was not too dissatisfied, but I eventually counseled him to seek analysis with someone else, which he did after a considerable resistance.

I was initially more favorably inclined toward the second patient, who seemed highly motivated for treatment, more adequate, and whose psychosexual development seemed more normal. The first and more successful patient, on the other hand, was initially ambivalent, derisively hostile, and created early doubts in me about taking him for treatment.

Both parental marriages had been stable, the fathers being somewhat passive but reasonably successful. Both mothers seemed compulsive, and both patients seemed to have suffered deep developmental defects in relation to the mother, the first, and successful patient, perhaps less so. The course and content of his analysis suggested mainly regression from oedipal conflict, while this as a dominant feature was by no means as demonstrable in the second case.

Both patients presented severe problems of inhibition of masculine assertiveness with passive homosexual reaction formations. Both had deep, unconscious problems of an oral sadistic, murderous disposition toward a female sibling; both had developed fairly serious neurotic symptomatology in late adolescence, and in both there were schizoid features. Both reacted against homosexual problems by early flight into marriages with aggressive, controlling, narcissistic women. Both wives were attractive, compulsive, disturbed, and so highly defended that neither would consent to treatment, despite the fact that both marriages were stormy. The husbands were devoted, and struggled to keep the marriages going. The wives resented their husbands' treatment and attempted to sabotage it. I had occasion to become acquainted with both wives, although this was not sought by me. I did not experience troublesome negative feelings about either of them, despite their anxiety-ridden efforts to undercut the husbands' treatment.

With both men, I was quite aware of the contributions which they themselves made to the difficulties with their wives, namely, that both were too submissive, too hostile, in a sense too devoted, and both wives were frustrated for lack of sufficient uninhibited masculine assertiveness from their husbands. In both instances, this was extensively interpreted and worked over, but without much change in the picture.

Obviously, this was a problem that could not be satisfactorily worked through without thorough analysis of its deep sources in conflict which each had toward the female sibling, and behind that, the murderous rage toward the mother, as an oral sadistic regression from oedipal conflict. I went through phases of (countertransference?) protectiveness, in both cases; that with the first man was toward the marriage and the wife; with the second it was toward the man himself. Both patients confronted me, in transference material, with suggestions that I was being too protective and as I became conscious of this, I believe I was reasonably able to correct this.

In the first case, the protectiveness was directed toward avoiding secondary disturbance in the wife. She had at one time been thought by a psychiatrist to be psychotic, and I wished, realistically, not to provoke a blowup in her with all of the disruptive effects upon a family that such an episode can have. The protectiveness in the second case was directed toward the patient himself, and on a similar basis. This patient himself had once been thought to be psychotic. There was a Rorshach examination of this patient which, in brief, showed the case to be a deeply set neurosis; analytic treatment was indicated though it could be expected to be very difficult. It was a very productive record, with no schizophrenic material. While energy and drive appeared extremely high, the personality organization was such as to lead to expectation of a boiling over of affects into the world at large. Imagination was limited and there were reduced avenues of escape into an inner life.

The symptomatology which brought these patients to treatment was similar: diffuse anxiety with some depression, a strong awareness of massive inhibition, and a certain amount of confusion, particularly regarding sexual roles. Both, thus, would be classed as anxiety neurosis. The more normal psychosexual development of the second case, and my initial more favorable feeling toward him, would suggest theoretically that if my own libidinal organization approached the so-called "normal" and if I were to develop countertransference deviations, these would be more likely to be manifested toward the second patient, rather than the first, who when he came into treatment presented some not too attractive psychosexual problems. In fact, exactly the reverse proved to be the case.

Both patients presented irritating difficulties in communication: mumbling, halting speech, circumstantiality, repetitiveness, minutiae. There were times in both analyses when I became quite irritated with the communication problem. Only late in the treatment of both, as the infantile neuroses unfolded, did I begin to perceive some of the differences between what appeared to be fairly similar speech difficulties. The communication problem in the first case was a highly structured resistance, with the concealed purpose of destroying my power as an analyst and getting revenge upon me for my attentions to any and all other siblings and all males. The speech blocks in this case concealed biting, sardonic, destructive, object-oriented impulses, and disappeared with the working through in the transference of the deep oral sadistic problem. The communication problems of the second patient appeared to be an extension of the hidden anaclitic character of his ego, were essentially clinging in character and designed to acquire an object rather than to destroy a frustrating one, and were never in any substantial way relieved. Despite my long and conscientious effort to help this man, I do not think that I succeeded in any way commensurate with the amount of time and energy expended by both of us upon the attempt.

At this point, one might say that it has long been known that cases which we classify as transference neuroses, as our first patient would seem to be, are far more accessible to analytic procedures than the narcissistic neuroses, as was apparently the diagnosis of our second patient. Why should one have to bring in considerations of countertransference as a factor in the ultimate success of these treatments? This is all very true and, at the same time, too simple. It was, indeed, a very long time before I could differentiate sharply between these two cases, as I have just done, and it is also after the fact, so to speak. For a long time the first patient appeared to be most narcissistic. Certain delinquencies in this man and his much more severe psychosexual problems pointed this up. Additionally, I am not trying to prove that countertransference neurotic phenomena are the sole, or even major, factors involved in therapeutic progress. My purpose is to attempt to demonstrate their existence in a far more pervasive and perhaps significant manner than is generally conceded; to offer some evidence that they may be of crucial importance under certain circumstances, and to make some small contribution toward tracing their origins, development and resolution in the course of an analytic treatment.

This brings me to crucial turning points in the analyses of these two men. So far, I have discussed the emotional and practical situations with which I was confronted, and the background material which seems pertinent to a framework in which I might or might not develop some relatively organized countertransference response. Both men presented me with a specific problem, calculated potentially to stir up some countertransference responses of a reasonably normal character, in any female analyst who might be somewhat off guard. I refer to the fact that both these rather nice men were dependently attached to wives who defensively resented and made efforts to undermine the analyses, who were possessive of their husbands, and depreciating of them in a refined kind of way. Both men had much aggression against their wives, of which both were afraid, and had varying forms of overcompensatory behavior in regard to this. Both were therefore bound, sooner or later, to make efforts to play the analyst off against their wives, and both were bound, eventually, to attempt to exploit the analyses in the heterosexual transference for whatever gratification they might be able to seduce from the analyst. Both were, of course, inevitably bound to succeed or fail, to some extent in terms of the deeper aspects of the resolution of the oedipus conflict in the analyst's own personality. Of all of this I was, of course, theoretically aware from very early in the treatment of both men, and was consistently and reasonably well on guard to watch my own reactions, especially toward the large amount of complaining material brought against the wives. I was equally on guard against letting myself become irritated with the respective wives for their subversive behavior in regard to their husbands' treatment.

The turning point in the first case developed as follows: Toward the end of the second year of this analysis, despite much intellectual knowledge of his difficulties, when there seemed virtually no improvement in the marital situation, the communication

block or in his dependency defense, the patient's wife developed a severe psychosomatic illness. I took careful note of this fact at the time, speculating to myself that this illness might bind her anxiety which seemed so prepsychotic. I wondered if this might not be an out for her, in that she could now abandon her controlling, attacking behavior and lean on her husband more, without too much ego anxiety. I thought this might benefit the marital relation. What I took note of consciously, however, must have remained detached from what already was developing unconsciously in me as the nucleus of a small countertransference reaction toward the total situation. I believe this man's developing transference neurosis was slowly and inexorably pushing me in the direction of actually being to him, in some small measure, the overconcerned and overidentified mother figure (which he felt his wife was not) who, regardless of the merits of the situation, would see things much more in terms of his evaluation of them, and would identify with his hostilities, rather than being the completely dispassionate observer. I believe that, despite my cautions, I had been imperceptibly pushed by his transference pressures into regarding his wife as more of a problem than she had initially appeared to be. At any rate, I failed to observe that she had actually slowly become somewhat less of a problem, for, despite the patient's chronic, exasperating resistance, he *was* dealing with his domestic situation with more firmness and gentleness. Whether this was concealed from me by the patient, or I, for my own unconscious reasons, was blind to it, is beside the point. Very probably both were true. By this time the ego satisfactions of an improved functioning outside of the treatment was disrupted by strong, unconscious, frustrated libidinal drives in the transference neurosis. These were to make the most of the possession of a truly interested, maternally perceived person out of those transference needs as well as out of whatever unconscious potential I had to offer in the direction of fulfilling them.

This man's mother had, in reality, twice in his life deserted him emotionally at very crucial periods. There was a remoteness between mother and son which I never did fathom, but which inclined me to consider whether this was not a quite detached mother. Some of the later phases of the analysis of his transference neurosis bore this out, and revealed why it was perhaps of crucial importance for this particular patient that he literally be able to seduce me, to some small extent, into a countertransference deviation toward the side of his hostile dependent defenses against his wife, before he would be able to trust me with his deepest transference neurotic needs of me. These, I believe, are some of the factors which led to my intellectual speculations about the meaning of the wife's psychosomatic illness, remaining detached from the slowly developing countertransference blindness about the wife.

This all came to a head about a year later. I had been getting both uneasy and frustrated with the monotonous masochistic and depressive character of this patient's resistance. I suddenly had a dream which so startled me that it blotted out all recollection of what led up to it. The dream was very simply that I was visiting in this patient's home. Only his wife was there, she seemed glad to have me, and was being most hospitable and gracious. The general tone of the visit was much like that of an afternoon chat of friendly wives, whose husbands were, perhaps, friends or colleagues. The dream vaguely disturbed me.

As I started to think about it, I realized that I had known for some time, but had not taken note of the fact, that the wife was no longer interfering in her husband's treatment. This was due to his better adjustment, to a developing confidence that I was no true threat to her, and a decreasing direct envy of her husband's relationship to me. I also remembered, at this point, that almost a year previously I had speculated about the meaning of the wife's psychosomatic illness and had then largely forgotten it. In other words, I realized that I had unconsciously developed a somewhat fixed attitude of being too afraid of her psychotic potential, and had ignored her improvement. The dream pointed up to me that I had been derelict in identifying with her in the marital situation; that in effect she really did want me to come into her home and would welcome my having a better prospective upon her. The dream said that the wife was much more positively oriented toward me than I had given her credit for during the past year, and that it was time that I look in on the domestic scene from her point of view.

After I had given all of this very careful thought and felt fairly sure of my ground, I went into action. First, I picked up the analysis of the subtle acting out on his part against his wife within the domestic situation, a point which had been neglected for some time. I became very direct in discussing the aggression against his wife through the mechanism of his masochism and his dependent hostility, which we both now understood much better than in the earlier analysis of these problems. Following this, I discussed again and more actively his attempts to play off his wife and myself against each other, and how he had exaggerated and prolonged the bad marital situation for purposes of transference gratification.

All of this had been previously extensively worked over, but with insufficient effect. It is, of course, obvious that in my own unconscious some resurgent oedipal conflict in the form of an overdetermined competition with and fear of another woman in a triangular situation lay behind my countertransference response.

Following this active repairing of the holes in the analysis, so to speak the patient shortly took over the analysis very assertively. From a complaining, lowvoltage approach for nearly the three years, he began moving with the greatest directness. He began subjecting me to intense emotional pressures; he himself carried the analysis back into a comprehensive review of his entire development, with new insights into crucial life experiences, and with minute attention to reconstructing the infantile situation. There were new recoveries of early memories, especially of primal scene material and of a peculiarly unexpressed remoteness between the parents.

Following extensive reworking over of the oedipal material—without, however, enough reliving of castration anxiety to make me feel secure about a working through—the patient switched to the deepest oral material. This had been displaced from the sister born when he was about two, to the sister born during the height of the oedipal period. With the opening up of this material the first intense, undefended affect of the entire analysis made its appearance. There was a long period characterized by profound depressive feelings and naked rage, feelings largely confined to the analytic hours. With this outpouring of affect, the patient's block in communication disappeared permanently. Dream and fantasy material in this phase included almost every form of sadistic attack or indignity conceivable. This was, of course, phallic sadism couched in oral language. During this period the relationship between us was very tense. The quantity of the patient's affect alone would have constituted a severe burden upon any one attempting to deal with it. In addition, he subjected me to the most persistent, minute and discomforting scrutiny, as though tearing me apart—cell by cell. My every move, my every word, was watched so closely that it literally felt to me that if I made even one slightest false move, all would be lost. The threat, however, was not to myself. The affect created in me was more of the following order: if I were to fail to meet this test, he would fall apart, and would never again trust another human being. On several occasions I experienced dreams which directly anticipated oncoming material, as though from my own unconscious came forewarning of what was to come,[7] and fortified me to deal with the massive quantity of his affect when it hit.

During this period, every hour was exhausting and often the feelings engendered in me during the hour would carry over. On several occasions, I began to be worried about the extent of this carry-over. All my disposition to become morbid about this was dispelled rather suddenly and amusingly. I was to go off one afternoon for a vacation, having seen the patient that morning. This had, in itself, stepped up both the sadistic and depressive feelings with which he burdened me. I went off feeling at a very low ebb and on the verge of anger with the whole business. The depression and irritation in me lasted for several hours and then suddenly disappeared completely. Nothing extraneous happened to dispel it, nor did I make any conscious effort to do so. I doubt that I even thought of this patient, except in the most casual way throughout the entire vacation. The fact that this could happen so spontaneously led me to the reassuring conclusion that my disturbing feelings did not of themselves mean that I was getting involved in any quantitatively excessive countertransference problem which might prove to have unfavorable implications, either for him or for myself. It seemed to me only that what had been going on was that my unconscious had somehow finally become sufficiently attuned to his unconscious; that I was able to tolerate the affect connected with his feelings of utter despair, because of affects and attitudes in myself over which I had no conscious control, but which *were* appropriate to his needs, in order to work this problem through. As I have thought it over since, to understand what had been going on in myself in response to this patient, it seems compounded of two factors. On the one hand there developed in me, on a transient basis, an amount of masochism sufficient to absorb the sadism which he was now unloading, and which had terrified him throughout his entire life. The other ingredient of my affective response was, I believe, a joining with him and a supporting of him, through identification, in a true unconscious grief reaction. This, I believe, was similar to the "sadness" of affect in the therapist, of which Adelaide Johnson (15) and Michael Balint (3) have written. As he unloaded his sadism, free from fear of loss of control, and of any fear of retaliation, I believe that this man's ego was finally and permanently freed of the binding of this sadism into his superego. The depressive affect had become wholly free of self-depreciation and guilt and

had taken on the quality of a true mourning for a lost love object.

Following this, the patient returned to the oedipal situation, and with intense affect. The repressed competition with the father was brought out in the transference in a quite usual way, with fantasies about men in the analyst's life, competition with father surrogates, and real fear derived from competitive impulses toward these men as erotic transference impulses arose toward the analyst. With this final working through of the oedipal material, the patient went on to termination. The improvement and personality change in this patient have now been sustained for some time, and I have the impression that the wife's difficulties are largely intrinsic only, and are not being contributed to by her husband.

Interestingly, it was only with the development and resolution of my countertransference response to the marital situation, and the breaking through of the patient's resistance against communication, with the outpouring of long stored-up affect, that I began to have feelings of very much liking this man as a person. I do not mean that I had previously disliked him. Precisely here, I believe, lies evidence that in this case the countertransference response had a beneficial effect. I am inclined to think that it was only after this man's unconscious perceived that he had *actually* forced me into a countertransference response that he became sufficiently confident of his powers to influence me, and of my willingness, at least in small part, to be influenced or subjugated by him. It was only then that he could finally allow me to penetrate his masochistic defense, and give me access to the deep unconscious sadism so long bound into his superego, for it now became both possible and necessary to turn that sadism upon me. This massive sadism, deriving presumably from an infantile depression, had been re-experienced in the oedipal situation, causing strong regressive admixtures of oral sadism into the phallic sadism of the oedipal conflict. I do not believe that without the experience, perceived by his unconscious, of actually having been able in some small way to bend me affectively to his needs, this man would have succeeded in going into these deepest sources of his neurosis. That he was able so to bend me to his will, simultaneously repaired the wound in his masculine ego, and eliminated his *infantile* fear of *my* sadism in the mother transference. It would seem that he had finally achieved an inner confidence that his controls were *in fact* adequate, and that I *in fact* trusted them.[8]

---

7. Mostly disguised masochistic response to sadism.

8. I hope that it is entirely clear that nothing of my affective response was *ever* made a manifest element in the treatment.

Interestingly, his unconscious also perceived that I had changed in my feeling about him. During this period, he made a number of comments about my affection for him, which bore no references to sexual love. They were simple statements of fact. I do not think he ever gave conscious thought to whether I had changed. He never asked for any confirmation, never indicated that he felt not liked previously; these were simple and causal statements of a perception of something, which from his point of view was timeless, incontrovertible and unambivalent. His unconscious *had* correctly perceived something which had actually developed in me. In fact, I think it is possible that any final successful working through of a deep and thorough analysis involves some development of this sort. That there are many more or less successful analyses, which are nevertheless partial analyses in fact, is well known to all of us. Many, clearly, never should be other than partial. I doubt that there is any thorough working through of a deep transference neurosis, in the strictest sense, which does not involve some form of emotional upheaval in which *both* patient and analyst are involved. In other words, there is both a transference neurosis and a corresponding countertransference "neurosis" (no matter how small and temporary) which are both analyzed in the treatment situation, with eventual feelings of a substantially new orientation on the part of both persons toward each other.

I do not know whether the crucial episode which seemed to me to be a turning point in the second case was a sudden perception on my part of the reality that this man was unanalyzable by me, and the real countertransference difficulty was my illusion that I could treat this man. The resistance described earlier had become chronic. Slowly, there *were* gains which in all honesty I would have to look upon as psychotherapeutic largely. Slowly, I became aware of a subtle smeary overtone in his attitudes toward his wife, and also toward me in the analysis. It lay, however, so nebulously concealed behind the manifest oral sadistic and oral dependent material that somehow I was never able to bring it out into the open where it could be dealt with. Even now I wonder if it were not really some derivative of the fuzziness in this man's ego boundaries. I found myself slowly and increasingly identified with and sympathetic for his wife, related primarily to my perception of this vaguely smeary attitude toward her. I was aware also, step by step, of changes in her attitudes, how her interference gradually slowed down, how she began to cooperate with him about his analysis, and finally turned to me with despair because there

were no significant changes for the good in his attitude toward her. This patient made intense protestations of dependent and erotic need for me in a manner in which such material usually appears. From hindsight, I would say the reason I was not moved by this was that it was not structured and was thus interpretively intangible, and that deep down this man did *not* have a mobilizable strength capable of bending me to *his* will, as did the first patient. I believe that with his deep anaclitic ego organization, his maximum potential would have been to seduce me into bending him toward *my* will. Consequently, I must have always felt that these protestations were overcompensatory, not contained, and not truly transference.

The turning point in this case came when he suddenly and unpredictably developed a schizoid depressed state. I had no warning that this was coming, had little material with which to understand it, and before I could evaluate what was happening, he came for a five o'clock appointment one day, following several days of intense anxiety and obsessive suicidal fantasies. He became severely agitated, the suicidal fantasies suddenly gave way to a violent outburst of murderous feelings, such that I became truly alarmed. I felt he was very close to an ego break and might very well go out the window, or off the fire escape, out of fear of the murderous ideas. The office was deserted, the secretaries having gone home. I announced quickly and calmly that I thought he was far too upset to discuss his problems that evening, would he please go home, take a sedative, try to find distraction and return first thing in the morning when he might feel more calm. The patient followed my request, in a trance-like state, and left. Slowly I was able to pull him out of this acute apparently near-psychotic state. After this episode I never again had confidence in my ability to do anything with this man psychoanalytically, nor did I ever see him again outside of office hours. Eventually I terminated his relationship with me and arranged his treatment with someone else. I felt that perhaps this might be worked through with a male analyst whom he would perceive as a person able to control him. We eventually parted company with mutual good feeling, rather of a surface character. However, out of all this long effort at therapy, I think little in the way of really deep mutual (i.e., nonverbal) communication of feeling ever occurred between us.

If this man was unanalyzable by me—or by a woman—I would conjecture that the reason lay in that the defect in his masculine ego was reparable only by identification and actual incorporation of a masculine ego in a treatment situation with a man, and perhaps only after experiencing an intense passive homoerotic transference. Apparently I could not offer him this, and neither was I able to mobilize any affect in the homoerotic material he did bring. In contrast, the defect in the masculine ego of the first man was apparently actually repaired by a small victory over me in the transference. In other words, there were built-in controls in his ego, which I unconsciously perceived, and this permitted me without undue anxiety to respond in very small but perhaps crucial measure to this man as woman to man, at the same time that my dominant relation to him was that of physician to patient. Built-in controls appeared absent in the second case, and would have to be acquired by identification and incorporation before he could live out affectively his underlying sadism, or move me to trust him as woman.[9]

A number of years ago I analyzed a young man who had essentially the same problems and personality structure as the first of the two cases just discussed, and whose analysis reached virtually the same depth with similar mutual affective intensity. This case was not carried through to a fully successful result, and I believe that it should have been. There were further countertransference complications in this case, in that I could never decide whether this was one of those rare cases in which the analyst should actively foster a divorce. In retrospect, I believe two important factors were operative in me. First, my discomfort with the transference-countertransference affect blocked me in a full working through of this problem. Secondly, I was probably intimidated by the pressures of an older and very aggressive analyst, who was treating the wife and who was openly determined that this marriage be successful. I terminated the case prematurely, with all the usual supposedly mutual understandings and rationalizations between us about indications for terminating. The fact that the patient's unconscious correctly perceived what I had unconsciously done to him, and why, was proved by some rage-motivated, fairly serious acting out he did against me afterward, which I understood immediately but which unfortunately did not come to my attention until far too late for me to do anything about it. Fortunately, the young man later obtained further analysis with someone else.

9. At a conscious level I had for a long time a reverse impression of the element of control in these two patients.

III. SUMMARY AND CONCLUSIONS

An attempt has been made to clarify present conceptions of psychoanalysts about countertransference and to bring some clinical material to bear upon a thesis that these conceptions need simplification and modification, and that countertransference phenomena are inherently dynamically operative in all treatment procedures.

It is emphasized that countertransference is only one of a number of responses of the analyst of equal or greater importance to the treatment situation. (Empathy, rapport, intuition, intellectual comprehension and ego-adaptive responses are, of course, other very significant elements.)

The treatment situation between patient and analyst at its deepest and nonverbal levels probably follows the prototype of the mother-child symbiosis so sensitively described by Benedek and involves active libidinal exchanges between the two through unconscious nonverbal channels of communication. Thus, broadly speaking, patients do affect their analysts. At these deep levels of interchange the dominant trends of constructive or of destructive use of the treatment situation by the patient are probably derivatives of the earliest relationships to the mother.

In the successful analysis the patient not only brings out in full form his *own* worst impulses, but perhaps, in addition, accomplishes a similar purpose, in minor form, with reference to the analyst, in part as a testing, in part as a becoming deeply aware of the analyst as a human being with limitations. At the same time, he accomplishes, for the purposes of his own ego strengthening, a capacity to handle the analyst's defects constructively, to forgive him for his aggression, his countertransference acting out, and to establish a mature adequately positive libidinal relationship with him, despite these imperfections.

The term countertransference should be reserved for transferences of the analyst—in the treatment situation—and nothing else. As such, they are syntheses of the analyst's unconscious ego, and together with the patient's transferences, both are products of the combined unconscious work of patient and analyst. They are multiple and varied in their origins and manifestations, and change from day to day and from patient to patient. They are normal phenomena, taking root in the repetition compulsion. They become "abnormal," or perhaps better described as interfering, excessive, fixed, or unworkable, on the basis of both qualitative and quantitative factors in their synthesis, as well as the manner in which they impinge on the analytic situation.

An effort has been made to explore the concept and the possible functions of a countertransference "neurosis" as such. There is evidence that structured formations may occur more consistently than generally supposed and that they may under certain circumstances perform useful functions. This usefulness may be a more or less temporary phenomenon and derive from the source and the character of the structure itself. On the other hand its uncovering, analysis, and resolution by the analyst may be useful to a deeper emotional understanding by the analyst of the transference neurosis.

I believe that in all instances where anything more than the most superficial relationship develops between patient and therapist, and inevitably, in truly deep analytic procedures, there are many countertransference reactions and that something in the nature of a countertransference neurosis develops, which, no matter how small, may be of great significance for the course of the treatment, in the sense of a catalytic agent. By definition, a catalyst is an ordinarily inert substance which in a given milieu is capable of accelerating, or of decelerating, a chemical process. It does not seem too unrealistic to think that there may be similar phenomena at those deep levels of interpersonal relationship which one finds in the psychoanalytic treatment process.

Scientific study of the psychoanalyst's unconscious in the treatment situation should improve our therapeutic efficiency and do much to provide a solid scientific basis upon which to evaluate treatment techniques. Such study would likewise illuminate that which is defensive and acting out upon the therapist's part, and that which is scientifically and demonstrably constructive.

BIBLIOGRAPHY

1. Alexander, F. Some quantitative aspects of psychoanalytic technique. *This Journal*, *2*:692–701, 1954.
2. Balint, A. and Balint, M. On transference and countertransference. *Internat. J. Psychoanal.*, *20*:223–230, 1939.
3. Balint, M. Changing therapeutical aims and techniques in psycho-analysis. *Internat. J. Psychoanal.*, *31*:117–124, 1950.
4. Benedek, T. Adaptation to reality in early infancy. *Psychoanal. Quart. 7*:200–215, 1938.
5. Benedek, T. Countertransference in the training analyst. *Bull. Menninger Clin.*, *18*:12–16, 1954.
6. Berman, L. Countertransference and attitudes of the analyst in the therapeutic process. *Psychiatry*, *12*:159–166, 1949.
7. Cohen, M. B. Countertransference and anxiety. *Psychiatry*, *15*:231–243, 1952.
8. Fliess, R. Countertransference and counteridentification. *This Journal*, *1*:268–284, 1953.
9. Freud, S. (1910) The future prospects of psychoanalytic therapy. *Collected Papers*, *2*:285–296. London: Hogarth Press, 1946.
10. Frosch, J. et al. (Eds.) *Annual Survey of Psychoanalysis*, *1*:237–248. New York: International Universities Press, 1950.
11. Gitelson, M. The emotional position of the analyst in the psycho-analytic situation. *Internat. J. Psychoanal.*, *33*:1–10, 1952.
12. Glover, E. *Technique of Psycho-Analysis*. New York: International Universities Press, 1955.
13. Greenson, R. Panel discussion on "Sublimation." *This Journal*, *3*:525–527, 1954.
14. Heimann, P. On counter-transference. *Internat. J. Psychoanal.*, *31*:81–84, 1950.
15. Johnson, A. Transference and countertransference in late analysis of the oedipus. (To be published.)
16. Little, M. Counter-transference and the patient's response to it. *Internat. J. Psychoanal.*, *32*:32–40, 1951.
17. Lorand, S. *Technique of Psychoanalytic Therapy*. New York: International Universities Press, 1946, pp. 209–222.
18. Orr, D. W. Transference and countertransference: a historical survey. *This Journal*, *2*:621–670, 1954.
19. Payne, S. M. Notes on developments in the theory and practice of psycho-analytic technique. *Internat. J. Psychoanal.*, *27*:12–18, 1946.
20. Racker, H. A contribution to the problem of countertransference. *Internat. J. Psychoanal.*, *34*:313–324, 1953.
21. Reich, A. On counter-transference. *Internat. J. Psychoanal.*, *32*:25–31, 1951.
22. Rioch, J. The transference phenomenon in psychoanalytic therapy. *Psychiatry*, *6*:147–156, 1943.
23. Sharpe, E. F. The psycho-analyst. *Internat. J. Psychoanal.*, *28*:1–6, 1947.
24. Tauber, E. S. Exploring the therapeutic use of countertransference data. *Psychiatry*, *17*:331–336, 1954.
25. Winnicott, D. W. Hate in the counter-transference. *Internat J. Psychoanal.*, *30*:69–74, 1949.
26. Round-table Discussion: Doctor-patient relationship in therapy. *Am J. Psychoanal.*, *15*:3–21, 1955

15

THE MEANINGS AND USES OF COUNTERTRANSFERENCE

Heinrich Racker

EDITOR'S NOTE

Heinrich Racker, a gifted South American psychoanalyst, has produced an extensive series of investigations into transference, countertransference, and the interplay between the two (for further references and discussion, see Racker, 1968, Langs 1976b). The present paper is a remarkably wide-ranging study of issues related to countertransference, there being almost no aspect of the subject that Racker does not consider and brilliantly illuminate. Notable are his discussion of a subject seldom broached—countertransference difficulties stemming from the analyst's own so-called didactic or training analysis—and his attempts to identify specific transference-countertransference constellations.

The paper is grounded in a deep appreciation for the interactional aspects of countertransference and investigates important countertransference and noncountertransference functions in the analyst (terms used here in the narrow sense—Racker himself uses *countertransference* in its broadest meaning). There is a detailed consideration of the two major forms of identificatory processes within the analyst, a most important contribution to the study of his valid functioning (see Part IV). Racker writes from a Kleinian vantage point, and countertransference is discussed largely in terms of internal object relations as influenced by events within the analysis. His thinking turns as well to interactional pathology—vicious circles of pathological transference and countertransference which serve to repeat rather than modify the pathogenic past and reinforces the present psychopathology (see also Strachey 1934 [chapter 31]).

Racker is deeply concerned about the defenses within psychoanalysts that lead them to avoid writing on countertransference and recognizing its manifestations in their work with patients. This surely is one factor that led him to study the subject in such detail, and to document his clinical findings with so many telling vignettes. The paper is quite lucid and readable regardless of one's orientation, and possesses a perceptiveness and originality from which every reader can benefit.

I

Freud describes transference as both the greatest danger and the best tool for analytic work. He refers to the work of making the repressed past conscious. Besides these two implied meanings of transference, Freud gives it a third meaning: it is in the transference that the analysand may relive the past under better conditions and in this way rectify pathological decisions and destinies. Likewise three meanings of countertransference may be differentiated. It too may be the greatest danger and at the same time an important tool for understanding, an assistance to the analyst in his functioning as interpreter. Moreover, it affects the analyst's behavior; it interferes with his action as object of the patient's re-experience in that new fragment of life that is the analytic situation, in which the patient should meet with greater understanding and objectivity than he found in the reality or fantasy of his childhood.

What have present-day writers to say about the problem of countertransference?[1]

Lorand (16) writes mainly about the dangers of countertransference for analytic work. He also points out the importance of taking countertransference reactions into account, for they may indicate some important subject to be worked through with the patient. He emphasizes the necessity of the analyst being always aware of his countertransference, and discusses specific problems such as the conscious desire to heal, the relief analysis may afford the analyst from his own problems, and narcissism and the interference of personal motives in clinical purposes. He also emphasizes the fact that these problems of countertransference concern not only the candidate but also the experienced analyst.

Winnicott (24) is specifically concerned with 'objective and justified hatred' in countertransference, particularly in the treatment of psychotics. He considers how the analyst should manage this emotion: should he, for example, bear his hatred in silence or communicate it to the analysand? Thus Winnicott is concerned with a particular countertransference reaction insofar as it affects the behavior of the analyst, who is the analysand's object in his re-experience of childhood.

Heimann (11) deals with countertransference as a tool for understanding the analysand. The 'basic

assumption is that the analyst's unconscious understands that of his patient. This rapport on the deep level comes to the surface in the form of feelings which the analyst notices in response to his patient, in his countertransference.' This emotional response of the analyst is frequently closer to the psychological state of the patient than is the analyst's conscious judgment thereof.

Little (15) discusses countertransference as a disturbance to understanding and interpretation and as it influences the analyst's behavior with decisive effect upon the patient's re-experience of his childhood. She stresses the analyst's tendency to repeat the behavior of the patient's parents and to satisfy certain needs of his own, not those of the analysand. Little emphasizes that one must admit one's countertransference to the analysand and interpret it, and must do so not only in regard to 'objective' countertransference reactions (Winnicott) but also to 'subjective' ones.

Annie Reich (21) is chiefly interested in countertransference as a source of disturbances in analysis. She clarifies the concept of countertransference and differentiates two types: 'countertransference in the proper sense' and 'the analyst's using the analysis for acting out purposes'. She investigates the causes of these phenomena, and seeks to understand the conditions that lead to good, excellent, or poor results in analytic activity.

Gitelson (10) distinguishes between the analyst's 'reactions to the patient as a whole' (the analyst's 'transferences') and the analyst's 'reactions to partial aspects of the patient' (the analyst's 'countertransferences'). He is concerned also with the problems of intrusion of countertransference into the analytic situation, and states that, in general, when such intrusion occurs the countertransference should be dealt with by analyst and patient working together, thus agreeing with Little.

Weigert (23) favors analysis of countertransference insofar as it intrudes into the analytic situation, and she advises, in advanced stages of treatment, less reserve in the analyst's behavior and more spontaneous display of countertransference.

In the first of my own two papers on countertransference (17), I discussed countertransference as a danger to analytic work. After analyzing the resistances that still seem to impede investigation of countertransference, I attempted to show without reserve how oedipal and preoedipal conflicts as well as paranoid, depressive, manic, and other processes persist in the 'countertransference neurosis' and how they interfere with the analyst's understanding,

---

1. I confine myself in what follows to papers published since 1946. I have referred to a previous bibliography in another paper (17).

Reprinted from *Psychoanalytic Quarterly* 41:487–506, 1972.

interpretation, and behavior. My remarks applied to 'direct' and 'indirect' countertransference.[2]

In my second paper (*18*), I described the use of countertransference experiences for understanding psychological problems, especially transference problems, of the analysand. In my principal points I agreed with Heimann (*11*), and emphasized the following suggestions. 1. Countertransference reactions of great intensity, even pathological ones, should also serve as tools. 2. Countertransference is the expression of the analyst's identification with the internal objects of the analysand, as well as with his id and ego, and may be used as such. 3. Countertransference reactions have specific characteristics (specific contents, anxieties, and mechanisms) from which we may draw conclusions about the specific character of the psychological happenings in the patient.

The present paper is intended to amplify my remarks on countertransference as a tool for understanding the mental processes of the patient (including especially his transference reactions), — their content, their mechanisms, and their intensities. Awareness of countertransference helps one to understand what should be interpreted and when. This paper will also consider the influence of countertransference upon the analyst's behavior toward the analysand, — behavior that affects decisively the position of the analyst as object of the re-experience of childhood, thus affecting the process of cure.

Let us first consider briefly countertransference in the history of psychoanalysis. We meet with a strange fact and a striking contrast. The discovery by Freud (*7*) of countertransference and its great importance in the therapeutic work gave rise to the institution of didactic analysis which became the basis and center of psychoanalytic training. Yet countertransference received little scientific consideration over the next forty years. Only during the last few years has the situation changed, rather suddenly, and countertransference become a subject examined frequently and with thoroughness. How is one to explain this initial recognition, this neglect, and this recent change? Is there not reason to question the success of didactic analysis in fulfilling its function if this very problem, the discovery of

which led to the creation of didactic analysis, has had so little scientific elaboration?

These questions are clearly important, and those who have personally witnessed a great part of the development of psychoanalysis in the last forty years have the best right to answer them.[3] I will suggest but one explanation.

The lack of scientific investigation of countertransference must be due to rejection by analysts of their own countertransferences, — a rejection that represents unresolved struggles with their own primitive anxiety and guilt. These struggles are closely connected with those infantile ideals that survive because of deficiencies in the didactic analysis of just those transference problems that later affect the analyst's countertransference. These deficiencies in the didactic analysis are in turn partly due to countertransference problems insufficiently solved in the didactic analyst, as I shall show later. Thus we are in a vicious circle; but we can see where a breach must be made. We must begin by revision of our feelings about our own countertransference and try to overcome our own infantile ideals more thoroughly, accepting more fully the fact that we are still children and neurotics even when we are adults and analysts. Only in this way — by better overcoming our rejection of countertransference — can we achieve the same result in candidates.

The insufficient dissolution of these idealizations and underlying anxieties and guilt feelings leads to special difficulties when the child becomes an adult and the analysand an analyst, for the analyst unconsciously requires of himself that he be fully identified with these ideals. I think that it is at least partly for this reason that the oedipus complex of the child toward its parents, and of the patient toward his analyst, has been so much more fully considered than that of the parents toward their children and of the analyst toward the analysand. For the same basic reason transference has been dealt with much more than countertransference.

The fact that countertransference conflicts determine the deficiencies in the analysis of transference becomes clear if we recall that transference is the expression of the internal object relations; for understanding of transference will depend on the analyst's capacity to identify himself both with the analysand's

---

2. This differentiation accords in essentials with Annie Reich's two types of countertransference. I would add, however, that also when the analyst uses the analysis for his own acting out (what I have termed 'indirect' countertransference), the analysand represents an object to the analyst (a 'subtransferred' object), not merely a 'tool'.

3. Michael Balint (*2*) considers a similar problem, the scarcity of papers on the system of psychoanalytic training. Investigation of this problem leads him to several interesting remarks on the relationship between didactic analysts and candidates. (See footnote 5.)

impulses and defenses, and with his internal objects, and to be conscious of these identifications. This ability in the analyst will in turn depend upon the degree to which he accepts his countertransference, for his countertransference is likewise based on identification with the patient's id and ego and his internal objects. One might also say that transference is the expression of the patient's relations with the fantasied and real countertransference of the analyst. For just as countertransference is the psychological response to the analysand's real and imaginary transferences, so also is transference the response to the analyst's imaginary and real countertransferences. Analysis of the patient's fantasies about countertransference, which in the widest sense constitute the causes and consequences of the transferences, is an essential part of the analysis of the transferences. Perception of the patient's fantasies regarding the countertransference will depend in turn upon the degree to which the analyst himself perceives his countertransference processes, — on the continuity and depth of his conscious contact with himself.

To summarize, the repression of countertransference (and other pathological fates that it may meet) necessarily leads to deficiencies in the analysis of transference, which in turn lead to the repression and other mishandling of countertransference as soon as the candidate becomes an analyst. It is a heritage from generation to generation, similar to the heritage of idealizations and denials concerning the imagoes of the parents, which continue working even when the child becomes a father or mother. The child's mythology is prolonged in the mythology of the analytic situation,[4] the analyst himself being partially subject to it and collaborating unconsciously in its maintenance in the candidate.

Before illustrating these statements, let us briefly consider one of those ideals in its specifically psychoanalytic expression: the ideal of the analyst's objectivity. No one, of course, denies the existence of subjective factors in the analyst and of countertransference in itself; but there seems to exist an important difference between what is generally acknowledged in practice and the real state of affairs. The first distortion of truth in 'the myth of the analytic situation' is that analysis is an interaction between a sick person and a healthy one. The truth is that it is an interaction between two personalities, in both of which the ego is under pressure from the id, the superego, and the external world; each personality has its internal and external dependences, anxieties, and pathological defenses; each is also a child with its internal parents; and each of these whole personalities — that of the analysand and that of the analyst — responds to every event of the analytic situation.[5] Besides these similarities between the personalities of analyst and analysand, there also exist differences, and one of these is in 'objectivity'. The analyst's objectivity consists mainly in a certain attitude toward his own subjectivity and countertransference. The neurotic (obsessive) ideal of objectivity leads to repression and blocking of subjectivity and so to the apparent fulfilment of the myth of the 'analyst without anxiety or anger'. The other neurotic extreme is that of 'drowning' in the countertransference. True objectivity is based upon a form of internal division that enables the analyst to make himself (his own countertransference and subjectivity) the object of his continuous observation and analysis. This position also enables him to be relatively 'objective' toward the analysand.

II

The term countertransference has been given various meanings. They may be summarized by the statement that for some authors countertransference includes everything that arises in the analyst as psychological response to the analysand, whereas for others not all this should be called countertransference. Some, for example, prefer to reserve the term for what is infantile in the relationship of the analyst with his analysand, while others make different limitations (Annie Reich [21] and Gitelson [10]). Hence efforts to differentiate from each other certain

---

4. Little (15) speaks, for instance, of the 'myth of the impersonal analyst'.

5. It is important to be aware of this 'equality' because there is otherwise great danger that certain remnants of the 'patriarchal order' will contaminate the analytic situation. The dearth of scientific study of countertransference is an expression of a 'social inequality' in the analyst-analysand society and points to the need for 'social reform'; this can come about only through a greater awareness of countertransference. For as long as we repress, for instance, our wish to dominate the analysand

neurotically (and we do wish this in one part of our personality), we cannot free him from his neurotic dependence, and as long as we repress our neurotic dependence upon him (and we do in part depend on him), we cannot free him from the need of dominating us neurotically.

Michael Balint (2) compares the atmosphere of psychoanalytic training with the initiation ceremonies of primitives and emphasizes the existence of superego 'intropressure' (Ferenczi) which no candidate can easily withstand.

of the complex phenomena of countertransference lead to confusion or to unproductive discussions of terminology. Freud invented the term countertransference in evident analogy to transference, which he defined as reimpressions or re-editions of childhood experiences, including greater or lesser modifications of the original experience. Hence one frequently uses the term transference for the totality of the psychological attitude of the analysand toward the analyst. We know, to be sure, that real external qualities of the analytic situation in general and of the analyst in particular have important influence on the relationship of the analysand with the analyst, but we also know that all these present factors are experienced according to the past and the fantasy, — according, that is to say, to a transference predisposition. As determinants of the transference neurosis and, in general, of the psychological situation of the analysand toward the analyst, we have both the transference predisposition and the present real and especially analytic experiences, the transference in its diverse expressions being the resultant of these two factors.

Analogously, in the analyst there are the countertransference predisposition and the present real, and especially analytic, experiences; and the countertransference is the resultant. It is precisely this fusion of present and past, the continuous and intimate connection of reality and fantasy, of external and internal, conscious and unconscious, that demands a concept embracing the totality of the analyst's psychological response, and renders it advisable, at the same time, to keep for this totality of response the accustomed term 'countertransference'. Where it is necessary for greater clarity one might speak of 'total countertransference' and then differentiate and separate within it one aspect or another. One of its aspects consists precisely in *what is transferred* in countertransference; this is the part that originates in an earlier time and that is especially the infantile and primitive part within total countertransference. Another of these aspects — closely connected with the previous one — is *what is neurotic* in countertransference; its main characteristics are the unreal anxiety and the pathological defenses. Under certain circumstances one may also speak of a countertransference neurosis (*15, 17*).

To clarify better the concept of countertransference, one might start from the question of what happens, in general terms, in the analyst in his relationship with the patient. The first answer might be: everything happens that *can* happen in one personality faced with another. But this says so much that it says hardly anything. We take a step forward by bearing in mind that in the analyst there is a tendency that normally predominates in his relationship with the patient: it is the tendency pertaining to his function of being an analyst, that of understanding what is happening in the patient. Together with this tendency there exist toward the patient virtually all the other possible tendencies, fears, and other feelings that one person may have toward another. The intention to understand creates a certain predisposition, a predisposition to identify oneself with the analysand, which is the basis of comprehension. The analyst may achieve this aim by identifying his ego with the patient's ego or, to put it more clearly although with a certain terminological inexactitude, by identifying each part of his personality with the corresponding psychological part in the patient — his id with the patient's id, his ego with the ego, his superego with the superego, accepting these identifications in his consciousness. But this does not always happen, nor is it all that happens. Apart from these identifications, which might be called *concordant* (or *homologous*) *identifications,* there exist also highly important identifications of the analyst's ego with the patient's internal objects, for example, with the superego. Adapting an expression from Helene Deutsch, they might be called *complementary identifications.* [6] We will consider these two kinds of identification and their destinies later. Here we may add the following notes.

1. The concordant identification is based on introjection and projection, or, in other terms, on the resonance of the exterior in the interior, on recognition of what belongs to another as one's own ('this part of you is I') and on the equation of what is one's own with what belongs to another ('this part of me is you'). The processes inherent in the complementary identifications are the same, but they refer to the patient's objects. The greater the conflicts between the parts of the analyst's personality, the greater are his difficulties in carrying out the concordant identifications in their entirety.

2. The complementary identifications are produced by the fact that the patient treats the analyst as an internal (projected) object, and in consequence the analyst feels treated as such; that is, he identifies himself with this object. The complementary identifications are closely connected with the destiny of the concordant identifications: it seems that to the degree to which the analyst fails in the concordant identifications and rejects them, certain complementary

---

6. Helene Deutsch (*4*) speaks of the 'complementary position' when she refers to the analyst's identifications with the object imagoes.

identifications become intensified. It is clear that rejection of a part or tendency in the analyst himself, — his aggressiveness, for instance, — may lead to a rejection of the patient's aggressiveness (whereby this concordant identification fails) and that such a situation leads to a greater complementary identification with the patient's rejecting object, toward which this aggressive impulse is directed.

3. Current usage applies the term 'countertransference' to the complementary identifications only; that is to say, to those psychological processes in the analyst by which, because he feels treated as and partially identifies himself with an internal object of the patient, the patient becomes an internal (projected) object of the analyst. Usually excluded from the concept countertransference are the concordant identifications, — those psychological contents that arise in the analyst by reason of the empathy achieved with the patient and that really reflect and reproduce the latter's psychological contents. Perhaps it would be best to follow this usage, but there are some circumstances that make it unwise to do so. In the first place, some authors include the concordant identifications in the concept of countertransference. One is thus faced with the choice of entering upon a terminological discussion or of accepting the term in this wider sense. I think that for various reasons the wider sense is to be preferred. If one considers that the analyst's concordant identifications (his 'understandings') are a sort of reproduction of his own past processes, especially of his own infancy, and that this reproduction or re-experience is carried out as response to stimuli from the patient, one will be more ready to include the concordant identifications in the concept of countertransference. Moreover, the concordant identifications are closely connected with the complementary ones (and thus with 'countertransference' in the popular sense), and this fact renders advisable a differentiation but not a total separation of the terms. Finally, it should be borne in mine that the disposition to empathy, — that is, to concordant identification, — springs largely from the sublimated positive countertransference, which likewise relates empathy with countertransference in the wider sense. All this suggests, then, the acceptance of countertransference as the totality of the analyst's psychological response to the patient. If we accept this broad definition of countertransference, the difference between its two aspects mentioned above must still be defined. On the one hand we have the analyst as subject and the patient as object of knowledge, which in a certain sense annuls the 'object relationship', properly speaking; and there arises in its stead the approximate

union or identity between the subject's and the object's parts (experiences, impulses, defenses). The aggregate of the processes pertaining to that union might be designated, where necessary, 'concordant countertransference'. On the other hand we have an object relationship very like many others, a real 'transference' in which the analyst 'repeats' previous experiences, the patient representing internal objects of the analyst. The aggregate of these experiences, which also exist always and continually, might be termed 'complementary countertransference'.[7]

A brief example may be opportune here. Consider a patient who threatens the analyst with suicide. In such situations there sometimes occurs rejection of the concordant identifications by the analyst and an intensification of his identification with the threatened object. The anxiety that such a threat can cause the analyst may lead to various reactions or defense mechanisms within him, — for instance, annoyance with the patient. This — his anxiety and annoyance — would be contents of the 'complementary countertransference'. The perception of his annoyance may, in turn, originate guilt feelings in the analyst and these lead to desires for reparation and to intensification of the 'concordant' identification and 'concordant' countertransference.

Moreover, these two aspects of 'total countertransference' have their analogy in transference. Sublimated positive transference is the main and indispensable motive force for the patient's work; it does not in itself constitute a technical problem. Transference becomes a 'subject', according to Freud's words, mainly when 'it becomes resistance', when, because of resistance, it has become sexual or negative (8, 9). Analogously, sublimated positive countertransference is the main and indispensable motive force in the analyst's work (disposing him to the continued concordant identification), and also countertransference becomes a technical problem or 'subject' mainly when it becomes sexual or negative. And this occurs (to an intense degree) principally as a resistance, — in this case, the analyst's, — that is to say, as counterresistance.

This leads to the problem of the dynamics of countertransference. We may already discern that the three factors designated by Freud as determinant in the dynamics of transference (the impulse to repeat infantile clichés of experience, the libidinal need, and resistance) are also decisive for the

---

7. In view of the close connection between these two aspects of countertransference, this differentiation is somewhat artificial. Its introduction is justifiable only considering the abovementioned circumstances.

dynamics of countertransference. I shall return to this later.

III

Every transference situation provokes a counter-transference situation, which arises out of the analyst's identification of himself with the analysand's (internal) objects (this is the 'complementary countertransference'). These countertransference situations may be repressed or emotionally blocked but probably they cannot be avoided; certainly they should not be avoided if full understanding is to be achieved. These countertransference reactions are governed by the laws of the general and individual unconscious. Among these the law of talion is especially important. Thus, for example, every positive transference situation is answered by a positive countertransference; to every negative transference there responds, in one part of the analyst, a negative countertransference. It is of great importance that the analyst be conscious of this law, for awareness of it is fundamental to avoid 'drowning' in the counter-transference. If he is not aware of it he will not be able to avoid entering into the vicious circle of the analysand's neurosis, which will hinder or even prevent the work of therapy.

A simplified example: if the patient's neurosis centers round a conflict with his introjected father, he will project the latter upon the analyst and treat him as his father; the analyst will feel treated as such, — he will feel treated badly, — and he will react internally, in a part of his personality, in accordance with the treatment he receives. If he fails to be aware of this reaction, his behavior will inevitably be affected by it, and he will renew the situations that, to a greater or lesser degree, helped to establish the analysand's neurosis. Hence it is of the greatest importance that the analyst develop within himself an ego observer of his countertransference reactions, which are, naturally, continuous. Perception of these countertransference reactions will help him to become conscious of the continuous transference situations of the patient and interpret them rather than be unconsciously ruled by these reactions, as not seldom happens. A well-known example is the 'revengeful silence' of the analyst. If the analyst is unaware of these reactions there is danger that the patient will have to repeat, in his transference experience, the vicious circle brought about by the projection and introjection of 'bad objects' (in reality neurotic ones) and the consequent pathological anxieties and defenses; but transference interpretations made possible by the analyst's awareness of his countertransference experience make it possible to open important breaches in this vicious circle.

To return to the previous example: if the analyst is conscious of what the projection of the father-imago upon him provokes in his own countertransference, he can more easily make the patient conscious of this projection and the consequent mechanisms. Interpretation of these mechanisms will show the patient that the present reality is not identical with his inner perceptions (for, if it were, the analyst would not interpret and otherwise act as an analyst); the patient then introjects a reality better than his inner world. This sort of rectification does not take place when the analyst is under the sway of his unconscious countertransference.

Let us consider some applications of these principles. To return to the question of what the analyst does during the session and what happens within him, one might reply, at first thought, that the analyst listens. But this is not completely true: he listens most of the time, or wishes to listen, but is not invariably doing so. Ferenczi (6) refers to this fact and expresses the opinion that the analyst's distractability is of little importance, for the patient at such moments must certainly be in resistance. Ferenczi's remark (which dates from the year 1918) sounds like an echo from the era when the analyst was mainly interested in the repressed *impulses,* because now that we attempt to analyze resistance, the patient's manifestations of resistance are as significant as any other of his productions. At any rate, Ferenczi here refers to a countertransference response and deduces from it the analysand's psychological situation. He says '. . . we have unconsciously reacted to the emptiness and futility of the associations given at this moment with the withdrawal of the conscious charge'. The situation might be described as one of mutual withdrawal. The analyst's withdrawal is a response to the analysand's withdrawal, — which, however, is a response to an imagined or real psychological position of the analyst. If we have withdrawn, — if we are not listening but are thinking of something else, — we may utilize this event in the service of the analysis like any other information we acquire. And the guilt we may feel over such a withdrawal is just as utilizable analytically as any other countertransference reaction. Ferenczi's next words, 'the danger of the doctor's falling asleep . . . need not be regarded as grave because we awake at the first occurrence of any importance for the treatment', are clearly intended to placate this guilt. But better than to allay the analyst's guilt would be to use it to promote the analysis, — and indeed so to use the guilt would be the best way of alleviating it. In fact, we encounter here a cardinal problem of the relation between transference and countertransference, and of the therapeutic process in general. For the analyst's withdrawal is only an example of how the unconscious of one person responds to the unconscious of another. This response seems in part to be governed, insofar as we identify ourselves with the unconscious objects of the analysand, by the law of talion; and, insofar as this law unconsciously influences the analyst, there is danger of a vicious circle of reactions between them, for the analysand also responds 'talionically' in his turn, and so on without end.

Looking more closely, we see that the 'talionic response' or 'identification with the aggressor' (the frustrating patient) is a complex process. Such a psychological process in the analyst usually starts with a feeling of displeasure or some anxiety as a response to this aggression (frustration) and, because of this feeling, the analyst identifies himself with the 'aggressor'. By the term 'aggressor' we must designate not only the patient but also some internal object of the analyst (especially his own superego or an internal persecutor) now projected upon the patient. This identification with the aggressor, or persecutor, causes a feeling of guilt; probably it always does so, although awareness of the guilt may be repressed. For what happens is, on a small scale, a process of melancholia, just as Freud described it: the object has to some degree abandoned us; we identify ourselves with the lost object;[8] and then we accuse the introjected 'bad' object,—in other words, we have guilt feelings. This may be sensed in Ferenczi's remark quoted above, in which mechanisms are at work designed to protect the analyst against these guilt feelings: denial of guilt ('the danger is not grave') and a certain accusation against the analysand for the 'emptiness' and 'futility' of his associations. In this way a vicious circle—a kind of paranoid ping-pong—has entered into the analytic situation.[9]

Two situations of frequent occurrence illustrate both the complementary and the concordant identifications and the vicious circle these situations may cause.

1. One transference situation of regular occurrence consists in the patient's seeing in the analyst his own superego. The analyst identifies himself with the id and ego of the patient and with the patient's dependence upon his superego; and he also identifies himself with the same superego,—a situation in which the patient places him,—and experiences in this way the domination of the superego over the patient's ego. The relation of the ego to the superego is, at bottom, a depressive and paranoid situation; the relation of the superego to the ego is, on the same plane, a manic one insofar as this term may be used to designate the dominating, controlling, and accusing attitude of the superego toward the ego. In this sense we may say, broadly speaking, that to a 'depressive-paranoid' transference in the analysand there corresponds—as regards the complementary identification—a 'manic' countertransference in the analyst. This, in turn, may entail various fears and guilt feelings, to which I shall refer later.[10]

2. When the patient, in defense against this situation, identifies himself with the superego, he may place the analyst in the situation of the dependent and incriminated ego. The analyst will not only identify himself with this position of the patient; he will also experience the situation with the content the patient gives it: he will feel subjugated and accused, and may react to some degree with anxiety and guilt. To a 'manic' transference situation (of the type called 'mania for reproaching') there corresponds, then,— as regards the complementary identification,—a 'depressive-paranoid' countertransference situation.

The analyst will normally experience these situations with only a part of his being, leaving another part free to take note of them in a way suitable for the treatment. Perception of such a countertransference situation by the analyst and his understanding of it as a psychological response to a certain transference situation will enable him the better to grasp the transference at the precise moment when it is active. It is precisely these situations and the analyst's behavior regarding them, and in particular his interpretations of them, that are of decisive importance for the process of therapy, for they are the moments when the vicious circle within which the neurotic habitually moves,—by projecting his inner world outside and reintrojecting this same world,—is or is not interrupted. Moreover, at these decisive points the vicious circle may be

---

8. It is a partial abandonment and it is a threat of abandonment. The object that threatens to abandon us and the persecutor are basically the same.

9. The process described by Ferenczi has an even deeper meaning. The 'emptiness' and 'futility' of the associations express the empty, futile, dead part of the analysand; they characterize a depressive situation in which the analysand is alone and

abandoned by his objects, just as has happened in the analytic situation.

10. Cesio (3) demonstrates in a case report the principal countertransference reactions that arose in the course of the psychoanalytic treatment, pointing out especially the analyst's partial identifications with objects of the patient's superego.

re-enforced by the analyst, if he is unaware of having entered it.

A brief example: an analysand repeats with the analyst his 'neurosis of failure', closing himself up to every interpretation or repressing it at once, reproaching the analyst for the uselessness of the analysis, foreseeing nothing better in the future, continually declaring his complete indifference to everything. The analyst interprets the patient's position toward him, and its origins, in its various aspects. He shows the patient his defense against the danger of becoming too dependent, of being abandoned, or being tricked, or of suffering counter-aggression by the analyst, if he abandons his armor and indifference toward the analyst. He interprets to the patient his projection of bad internal objects and his subsequent sado-masochistic behavior in the transference; his need of punishment; his triumph and 'masochistic revenge' against the transferred parents; his defense against the 'depressive position' by means of schizoid, paranoid, and manic defenses (Melanie Klein); and he interprets the patient's rejection of a bond which in the unconscious has a homosexual significance. But it may happen that all these interpretations, in spite of being directed to the central resistance and connected with the transference situation, suffer the same fate for the same reasons: they fall into the 'whirl in a void' (*Leerlauf*) of the 'neurosis of failure'. Now the decisive moments arrive. The analyst, subdued by the patient's resistance, may begin to feel anxious over the possibility of failure and feel angry with the patient. When this occurs in the analyst, the patient feels it coming, for his own 'aggressiveness' and other reactions have provoked it; consequently he fears the analyst's anger. If the analyst, threatened by failure, or to put it more precisely threatened by his own superego or by his own archaic objects which have found an *agent provocateur*' in the patient, acts under the influence of these internal objects and of his paranoid and depressive anxieties, the patient again finds himself confronting a reality like that of his real or fantasied childhood experiences and like that of his inner world; and so the vicious circle continues and may even be re-enforced. But if the analyst grasps the importance of this situation, if, through his own anxiety or anger, he comprehends what is happening in the analysand, and if he overcomes, thanks to the new insight, his negative feelings and interprets what has happened in the analysand, being now in this new positive countertransference situation, then he may have made a breach—be it large or small—in the vicious circle.[11]

---

11. See Chap. V, example 8.

IV

We have considered thus far the relation of transference and countertransference in the analytic process. Now let us look more closely into the phenomena of countertransference. Countertransference experiences may be divided into two classes. One might be designated 'countertransference thoughts'; the other 'countertransference positions'. The example just cited may serve as illustration of this latter class; the essence of this example lies in the fact that the analyst feels anxiety and is angry with the analysand, —that is to say, he is in a certain countertransference 'position'. As an example of the other class we may take the following.

At the start of a session an analysand wishes to pay his fees. He gives the analyst a thousand peso note and asks for change. The analyst happens to have his money in another room and goes out to fetch it, leaving the thousand pesos upon his desk. During the time between leaving and returning, the fantasy occurs to him that the analysand will take back the money and say that the analyst took it away with him. On his return he finds the thousand pesos where he had left it. When the account has been settled, the analysand lies down and tells the analyst that when he was left alone he had fantasies of keeping the money, of kissing the note goodbye, and so on. The analyst's fantasy was based upon what he already knew of the patient, who in previous sessions had expressed a strong disinclination to pay his fees. The identity of the analyst's fantasy and the patient's fantasy of keeping the money may be explained as springing from a connection between the two unconsciouses, a connection that might be regarded as a 'psychological symbiosis' between the two personalities. To the analysand's wish to take money from him (already expressed on previous occasions), the analyst reacts by identifying himself both with this desire and with the object toward which the desire is directed; hence arises his fantasy of being robbed. For these identifications to come about there must evidently exist a potential identity. One may presume that every possible psychological constellation in the patient also exists in the analyst, and the constellation that corresponds to the patient's is brought into play in the analyst. A symbiosis results, and now in the analyst spontaneously occur thoughts corresponding to the psychological constellation in the patient.

In fantasies of the type just described and in the example of the analyst angry with his patient, we are dealing with identifications with the id, with the ego, and with the objects of the analysand; in both cases, then, it is a matter of countertransference reactions.

However, there is an important difference between one situation and the other, and this difference does not seem to lie only in the emotional intensity. Before elucidating this difference, I should like to emphasize that the countertransference reaction that appears in the last example (the fantasy about the thousand pesos) should also be used as a means to further the analysis. It is, moreover, a typical example of those 'spontaneous thoughts' to which Freud and others refer in advising the analyst to keep his attention 'floating' and in stressing the importance of these thoughts for understanding the patient. The countertransference reactions exemplified by the story of the thousand pesos are characterized by the fact that they threaten no danger to the analyst's objective attitude of observer. Here the danger is rather that the analyst will not pay sufficient attention to these thoughts or will fail to use them for understanding and interpretation. The patient's corresponding ideas are not always conscious, nor are they always communicated as they were in the example cited. But from his own countertransference 'thoughts' and feelings the analyst may guess what is repressed or rejected. It is important to recall once more our usage of the term 'countertransference', for many writers, perhaps the majority, mean by it not these thoughts of the analyst but rather that other class of reactions, the 'countertransference positions'. This is one reason why it is useful to differentiate these two kinds of reaction.

The outstanding difference between the two lies in the degree to which the ego is involved in the experience. In one case the reactions are experienced as thoughts, free associations, or fantasies, with no great emotional intensity and frequently as if they were somewhat foreign to the ego. In the other case, the analyst's ego is involved in the countertransference experience, and the experience is felt by him with greater intensity and as true reality, and there is danger of his 'drowning' in this experience. In the former example of the analyst who gets angry because of the analysand's resistances, the analysand is felt as really bad by one part of the analyst ('countertransference position'), although the latter does not express his anger. Now these two kinds of countertransference reaction differ, I believe, because they have different origins. The reaction experienced by the analyst as thought or fantasy arises from the existence of an *analogous situation* in the analysand, — that is, from his readiness in perceiving and communicating his inner situation (as happens in the case of the thousand pesos), — whereas the reaction experienced with great intensity, even as

reality, by the analyst arises from *acting out* by the analysand (as in the case of the 'neurosis of failure'). Undoubtedly there is also in the analyst himself a factor that helps to determine this difference. The analyst has, it seems, two ways of responding. He may respond to some situations by *perceiving* his reactions, while to others he responds by *acting out* (alloplastically or autoplastically). Which type of response occurs in the analyst depends partly on his own neurosis, on his inclination to anxiety, on his defense mechanisms, and especially on his tendencies to repeat (act out) instead of making conscious. Here we encounter a factor that determines the dynamics of countertransference. It is the one Freud emphasized as determining the special intensity of transference in analysis, and it is also responsible for the special intensity of countertransference.

Let us consider for a moment the dynamics of countertransference. The great intensity of certain countertransference reactions is to be explained by the existence in the analyst of pathological defenses against the increase of archaic anxieties and unresolved inner conflicts. Transference, I believe, becomes intense not only because it serves as a resistance to remembering, as Freud says, but also because it serves as a defense against a danger within the transference experience itself. In other words, the 'transference resistance' is frequently a repetition of defenses that must be intensified lest a catastrophe be repeated in transference (20). The same is true of countertransference. It is clear that these catastrophes are related to becoming aware of certain aspects of one's own instincts. Take, for instance, the analyst who becomes anxious and inwardly angry over the intense masochism of the analysand within the analytic situation. Such masochism frequently rouses old paranoid and depressive anxieties and guilt feelings in the analyst, who, faced with the aggression directed by the patient against his own ego, and faced with the effects of this aggression, finds himself in his unconscious confronted anew with his early crimes. It is often just these childhood conflicts of the analyst, with their aggression, that led him into this profession in which he tries to repair the objects of the aggression and to overcome or deny his guilt. Because of the patient's strong masochism, this defense, which consists of the analyst's therapeutic action, fails and the analyst is threatened with the return of the catastrophe, the encounter with the destroyed object. In this way the intensity of the 'negative countertransference' (the anger with the patient) usually increases because of the failure of the countertransference defense (the therapeutic action) and the analyst's subsequent increase of anxiety over a catastrophe in the countertransference experience (the destruction of the object).

This example also illustrates another aspect of the dynamics of countertransference. In a previous paper (*20*), I showed that the abolition of rejection[12] in analysis determines the dynamics of transference and, in particular, the intensity of the transference of the 'rejecting' internal objects (in the first place, of the superego). The 'abolition of rejection' begins with the communication of 'spontaneous' thoughts. The analyst, however, makes no such communication to the analysand, and here we have an important difference between his situation and that of the analysand and between the dynamics of transference and those of countertransference. However, this difference is not so great as might be at first supposed, for two reasons: first, because it is not necessary that the free associations be *expressed* for projections and transferences to take place, and second, because the analyst communicates certain associations of a personal nature even when he does not seem to do so. These communications begin, one might say, with the plate on the front door that says *Psychoanalyst* or *Doctor*. What motive (in terms of the unconscious) would the analyst have for wanting to cure if it were not he that made the patient ill? In this way the patient is already, simply by being a patient, the creditor, the accuser, the 'superego' of the analyst; and the analyst is his debtor.

V

The examples that follow illustrate the various kinds, meanings, and uses of countertransference reaction. First are described situations in which the countertransference is of too little intensity to drag the analyst's ego along with it; next, some situations in which the intense countertransference reaction intensely involves the ego; and finally, some examples in which the repression of countertransference prevents comprehension of the analysand's situation at the critical moment.

1. A woman patient asks the analyst whether it is true that another analyst named N has become separated from his wife and married again. In the associations that follow she refers repeatedly to N's first wife. The idea occurs to the analyst that the patient would also like to know who N's second wife is and that she probably wonders whether the second wife was a patient of N. The analyst further supposes that his patient (considering her present transference situation) is wondering whether her own analyst might not also separate from his wife and marry her. In accordance with this suspicion but taking care not to suggest anything, the analyst asks whether she is thinking anything about N's second wife. The analysand answers, laughing, 'Yes, I was wondering whether she was not one of his patients'. Analysis of the analyst's psychological situation showed that his 'spontaneous thought' was possible because his identification with the patient in his oedipal desires was not blocked by repression, and also because he himself countertransferred his own positive oedipal impulses, accepted by his conscious, upon the patient.

This example shows how, in the analyst's 'spontaneous thoughts',—which enable him to attain a deeper understanding,—there intervenes not only the sublimated positive countertransference that permits his identification with the id and the ego of the patient but also the (apparently absent) 'complementary countertransference',—that is, his identification with the internal objects that the patient transfers and the acceptance in his conscious of his own infantile object relations with the patient.

2. In the following example the 'spontaneous thoughts', which are manifestly dependent upon the countertransference situation, constitute the guide to understanding.

A woman candidate associates about a scientific meeting at the Psychoanalytic Institute, the first she had attended. While she is associating, it occurs to the analyst that he, unlike most of the other didactic analysts, did not participate in the discussion. He feels somewhat vexed, he thinks that the analysand must have noticed this, and he perceives in himself some fear that she consequently regards him as inferior. He realizes that he would prefer that she not think this and not mention the occurrence; for this very reason, he points out to the analysand that she is rejecting thoughts concerning him in relation to the meeting. The analysand's reaction shows the importance of this interpretation. She exclaims in surprise: 'Of course, I almost forgot to tell you'. She then produces many associations related to transference which she had previously rejected for reasons corresponding to the countertransference rejection of these same ideas by the analyst. The example shows the importance of observation of countertransference as a technical tool; it also shows a relation between a transference resistance and a countertransference resistance.

3. On shaking hands at the beginning of the session the analyst, noticing that the patient is

---

12. By 'abolition of rejection' I mean adherence by the analysand to the fundamental rule that all his thoughts are to be expressed without selection or rejection.

depressed, experiences a slight sense of guilt. The analyst at once thinks of the last session, in which he frustrated the patient. He knows where the depression comes from, even before the patient's associations lead him to the same conclusion. Observation of the countertransference ideas, *before* and *after* the sessions, may also be an important guide for the analyst in understanding the patient's analytic situation. For instance, if a feeling of annoyance before entering the consulting room is a countertransference response to the patient's aggressive or domineering behavior, the annoyance may enable the analyst to understand beforehand the patient's anxiety which, at the most superficial layer, is fear of the analyst's anger provoked by the patient's behavior. Another instance occurs in the analyst who, before entering his consulting room, perceives a feeling of guilt over being late; he realizes that he often keeps this analysand waiting and that it is the analysand's pronounced masochistic submission that especially prompts him to this frustrating behavior. In other words, the analyst responds to the strong repression of aggression in the patient by doing what he pleases and abusing the patient's neurosis. But this very temptation that the analyst feels and yields to in his behavior, and the fleeting guilt feelings he experiences for this reason, can serve as a guide for him to comprehend the analysand's transference situation.

4. The following example from analytic literature likewise shows how the countertransference situation makes it possible to understand the patient's analytic situation in a way decisive for the whole subsequent course of the treatment. It is interesting to remark that the author seems unaware that the fortunate understanding is due to an unconscious grasp of the countertransference situation. I refer to the 'case with manifest inferiority feelings' published by Wilhelm Reich (*22*). After showing how, for a long period, no interpretation achieved any success or any modification of the patient's analytic situation, Reich writes: 'I then interpreted to him his inferiority feelings toward me; at first this was unsuccessful but after I had persistently shown him his conduct for several days, he presented some communications referring to his tremendous envy not of me but of other men, to whom he also felt inferior. And then there emerged in me, like a lightning flash, the idea that his repeated complaints could mean only this: "The analysis has no effect upon me, — it is no good, the analyst is inferior and impotent and can achieve nothing with me". The complaints were to be understood partly as triumph and partly as reproaches to the analyst.' If we inquire into the origin of this 'lightning idea' of Reich, the reply must be, theoretically,

that it arose from identification with one of his internal objects. The description of the event, however, leaves little room for doubt that the latter, the 'complementary countertransference', was the source of Reich's intuition, — that this lightning understanding arose from his own feeling of impotence, defeat, and guilt over the failure of treatment.

5. Now a case in which repression of the countertransference prevented the analyst from understanding the transference situation, while his later becoming conscious of the countertransference was precisely what brought this understanding.

For several days a patient had suffered from intense anxiety and stomach-ache. The analyst does not understand the situation until she asks the patient when it first began. He answers that it goes back to a moment when he bitterly criticized her for certain behavior, and adds that he has noticed she has been rather depressed of late. What the patient says hits the nail on the head. The analyst has in truth felt somewhat depressed because of this aggression in the patient. But she has repressed her aggression against the patient that underlay her depression and has repressed awareness that the patient would also think, consciously or unconsciously, of the effect of his criticism. The patient was conscious of this and therefore connected his own anxieties and symptoms with the analyst's depression. In other words, the analyst scotomatized the connection between the patient's anxiety and pain and the aggression (criticism) perpetrated against her. This scotomatization of the transference situation was due to repression of the countertransference, for the aggression that the patient suspected in the analyst, and to which he responded with anxiety and gastric pains (self-aggression in anticipation) existed not only in his fantasy but also in the analyst's actual countertransference feelings.

The danger of the countertransference being repressed is naturally the greater the more these countertransference reactions are rejected by the ego ideal or the superego. To take, for instance, the case of a patient with an almost complete lack of 'respect' for the analyst, it may happen that the analyst's narcissism is wounded and he reacts inwardly with some degree of annoyance. If he represses this annoyance because it ill accords with the demands of his ego ideal, he deprives himself of an important guide in understanding the patient's transference; for the patient seeks to deny the distance between his internal (idealized) objects and his ego by means of his manic mechanisms, trying to compensate his inferiority feelings by behavior 'as between equals' (in reality inverting this situation with the idealized objects by identification with them) and defending himself in this way against conflict situations of the greatest importance. In like manner, sexual excitement in the analyst may point to a hidden seductive behavior and erotomanic fantasies in the analysand as well as to the situations underlying these. Repression of such countertransference reactions may prevent access to the appropriate technique. What is advisable, for instance, when the patient exhibits this sort of hypomanic behavior is not merely analytic 'tolerance' (which may be intensified by guilt feeling over the countertransference reactions), but, as the first step, making the patient conscious of the countertransference reactions of his *own* internal objects, such as the superego. For just as the analyst reacted with annoyance to the almost total 'lack of respect' in the patient, so also do the patient's internal objects; for in the patient's behavior there is aggressiveness against these internal objects which the patient once experienced as superior and as rejecting. In more general terms, I should say that patients with certain hypomanic defenses tend to regard their conduct as 'natural' and 'spontaneous' and the analyst as 'tolerant' and 'understanding', repressing at the same time the rejecting and intolerant objects latently projected upon the analyst. If the analyst does not repress his deeper reactions to the analysand's associations and behavior, they will afford him an excellent guide for showing the patient these same repressed objects of his and the relationship in which he stands toward them.

6. In analysis we must take into account the *total* countertransference as well as the total transference. I refer, in particular, to the importance of paying attention not only to what has existed and is repeated but also to what has never existed (or has existed only as a hope),—that is to say, to the new and specifically analytic factors in the situations of analysand and analyst. Outstanding among these are the real new characteristics of this object (of analyst or of analysand), the patient-doctor situation (the intention to be cured or to cure, to be restored or to restore), and the situation created by psychoanalytic thought and feeling (as, for instance, the situation created by the fundamental rule, that original permission and invitation, the basic expression of a specific atmosphere of tolerance and freedom).

Let us illustrate briefly what is meant by 'total transference'. During a psychoanalytic session, the associations of a man, under treatment by a woman analyst, concern his relations with women. He tells of the frustrations and rejection he has endured, and his inability to form relationships with women of culture. There appear sadistic and debasing tendencies toward women. It is clear that the patient is transferring his frustrating and rejecting imagoes upon the analyst, and from these has arisen his mistrust of her. The patient is actually expressing both his fear of being rejected by the analyst on account of his sadism (deeper: his fear of destroying her and of her retaliation) and, at bottom, his fear of being frustrated by her,—a situation that in the distant past gave rise to this sadism. Such an interpretation would be a faithful reflection of the transference situation properly speaking. But in the total analytic situation there is something more. Evidently the patient needs and is seeking something through the session as such. What is it? What is this specific present factor, what is this prospective aspect, so to speak, of the transference situation? The answer is virtually contained in the interpretation given above: the analysand seeks to connect himself with an object emotionally and libidinally, the previous sessions having awakened his feelings and somewhat disrupted his armor; indirectly he is asking the analyst whether he may indeed place his trust in her, whether he may surrender himself without running the risk of suffering what he has suffered before. The first interpretation refers to the transference only as a repetition of what has once existed; the latter, more complete interpretation refers to what has existed and also to what has never existed and is hoped for anew from the analytic experience.

Now let us study an example that refers to both the total transference and total countertransference situations. The illustration is once again drawn from Wilhelm Reich (*22*). The analysis has long centered around the analysand's smile, the sole analyzable expression, according to Reich, that remained after cessation of all the communications and actions with which the analysand had begun treatment. Among these actions at the start had been some that Reich interpreted as provocations (for instance, a gesture aimed at the analyst's head). It is plain that Reich was guided in this interpretation by what he had felt in countertransference. But what Reich perceived in this way was only a part of what had happened within him; for apart from the fright and annoyance (which, even if only to a slight degree, he must have felt), there was a reaction of his ego to these feelings, a wish to control and dominate them, imposed by his 'analytic conscience'. For Reich had given the analysand to understand that there is a great deal of freedom and tolerance in the analytic situation and it was this spirit of tolerance that made Reich respond to these 'provocations' with nothing but an interpretation. What the analysand aimed at doing was to test whether such tolerance really existed in the analyst. Reich himself later gave him this interpretation, and this interpretation had a far more positive effect than the first. Consideration of the total countertransference situation (the feeling of being provoked, *and* the 'analytic conscience' which determined the fate of this feeling) might have been from the first a guide in apprehending the total transference situation, which consisted in aggressiveness, in the original mistrust, *and* in the ray of confidence, the new hope which the liberality of the fundamental rule had awakened in him.

7. I have referred above to the fact that the transference, insofar as it is determined by the infantile situations and archaic objects of the patient, provokes in the unconscious of the analyst infantile situations and an intensified vibration of archaic objects of his own. I wish now to present another example that shows how the analyst, not being conscious of such countertransference responses, may make the patient feel exposed once again to an archaic object (the vicious circle) and how, in spite of his having some understanding of what is happening in the patient, the analyst is prevented from giving an adequate interpretation.

During her first analytic session, a woman patient talks about how hot it is and other matters which to the analyst (a woman candidate) seem insignificant. She says to the patient that very likely the patient dares not talk about herself. Although the analysand was indeed talking about herself (even when saying how hot it was), the interpretation was, in essence, correct, for it was directed to the central conflict of the moment. But it was badly formulated, and this was so partly because of the countertransference situation. For the analyst's 'you dare not' was a criticism, and it sprang from the analyst's feeling of being frustrated in a desire; this desire must have been that the patient overcome her resistance. If the analyst had not felt this irritation or if she had been conscious of the neurotic nature of her internal reaction of anxiety and annoyance, she would have sought to understand why the patient 'dared not' and would have told her. In that case the lack of courage that the analyst pointed out to the patient would have proved to be a natural response within a dangerous object relationship.

Pursuing the analyst's line of thought and leaving aside other possible interpretations, we may suppose that she would then have said to the analysand that something in the analytic situation (in the relationship between patient and analyst) had caused her fear and made her thoughts turn aside from what meant much to her to what meant little. This interpretation would have differed from the one she gave the patient in two points: first, the interpretation given did not express the object relationship that led to the 'not daring' and, second, it coincided in its formulation with superego judgments, which should be avoided as far as possible.[13] Superego judgment was not avoided in this case because the analyst was identified in countertransference with the analysand's superego without being conscious of the identification; had she been conscious of it, she would have interpreted, for example, the feared aggression from the superego (projected upon the analyst) and would not have carried it out by means of the interpretation. It appears that the 'interpretation of tendencies' without considering the total object relationship is to be traced, among other causes, to repression by the analyst of one aspect of his countertransference, his identification with the analysand's internal objects.

Later in the same session, the patient, feeling that she is being criticized, censures herself for her habit of speaking rather incoherently. She says her mother often remarks upon it, and then she criticizes her mother for not listening, as a rule, to what she says. The analyst understands that these statements relate to the analytic situation and asks her: 'Why do you think I'm not listening to you?' The patient replies that she is sure the analyst is listening to her.

What has happened? The patient's mistrust clashes with the analyst's desire for the patient's confidence; therefore the analyst does not analyze the situation. She cannot say to the patient, 'No, I will listen to you, trust me', but she suggests it with her question. Once again interference by the uncontrolled countertransference (the desire that the patient should have no resistance) converts good understanding into a deficient interpretation. Such happenings are important, especially if they occur often. And they are likely to do so, for such interpretations spring from a certain state of the analyst and this state is partly unconscious. What makes these happenings so important is the fact that the analysand's unconscious is fully aware of the analyst's unconscious desires. Therefore the patient once again faces an object that, as in this case, wishes to force or lure the patient into rejecting his mistrust and that unconsciously seeks to satisfy its own

---

13. If the interpretations coincide with the analysand's judgments, the analyst is confused with the superego, sometimes with good reason. Superego judgments must be shown to the analysand but, as far as possible, one should refrain from uttering them.

desires or allay its own anxieties rather than to understand and satisfy the therapeutic need of the patient.

All this we infer from the reactions of the patient, who submits to the analyst's suggestion, telling the analyst that she trust her and so denying an aspect of her internal reality. She submits to the previous criticism of her cowardice and then, apparently, 'overcomes' the resistance, while in reality everything is going on unchanged. It cannot be otherwise, for the analysand is aware of the analyst's neurotic wish and her transference is determined by that awareness. To a certain degree, the analysand finds herself once again, in the actual analytic situation, confronting her internal or external infantile reality and to this same degree will repeat her old defenses and will have no valid reason for really overcoming her resistances, however much the analyst may try to convince her of her tolerance and understanding. This she will achieve only by offering better interpretations in which her neurosis does not so greatly interfere.

8. The following more detailed example demonstrates: (a) the talion law in the relationship of analyst and analysand; (b) how awareness of the countertransference reaction indicates what is happening in the transference and what at the moment is of the greatest significance; (c) what interpretation is most suitable to make a breach in the vicious circle; and (d) how the later associations show that this end has been achieved, even if only in part—for the same defenses return and once again the countertransference points out the interpretation the analysand needs.

We will consider the most important occurrences in one session. An analysand who suffers chiefly from an intense emotional inhibition and from a 'disconnection' in all his object relationships begins the session by saying that he feels completely disconnected from the analyst. He speaks with difficulty as if he were overcoming a great resistance, and always in an unchanging tone of voice which seems in no way to reflect his instincts and feelings. Yet the countertransference response to the content of his associations (or, rather, of his narrative, for he exercises a rigid control over his ideas) does change from time to time. At a certain point the analyst feels a slight irritation. This is when the patient, a physician, tells him how, in conversation with another physician, he sharply criticized analysts for their passivity (they give little and cure little), for their high fees, and for their tendency to dominate their patients. The patient's statements and his behavior meant several things. It was clear, in the first place,

that these accusations, though couched in general terms and with reference to other analysts, were directed against his own analyst; the patient had become the analyst's superego. This situation in the patient represents a defense against his own accusing superego, projected upon the analyst. It is a form of identification with the internal persecutors that leads to inversion of the feared situation. It is, in other words, a transitory 'mania for reproaching' as defense against a paranoid-depressive situation in which the superego persecutes the patient with reproaches and threatens him with abandonment. Together with this identification with the superego, there occurs projection of a part of the 'bad ego', and of the id, upon the analyst. The passivity (the mere receptiveness, the inability to make reparation), the selfish exploitation, and the domination he ascribes to the analyst are 'bad tendencies' of his own for which he fears reproach and abandonment by the analyst. At a lower stratum, this 'bad ego' consists of 'bad objects' with which the patient had identified himself as a defense against their persecution.

We already see that it would be premature to interpret this deeper situation; the patient will first have to face his 'bad ego': he will have to pass in transference through the paranoid-depressive situation in which he feels threatened by the superego-analyst. But even so we are still unsure of the interpretation to be given, for what the patient said and did has even at the surface still further meanings. The criticism he made to the other physician about analysts has the significance of rebellion, vengeance, and provocation; and, perhaps, of seeking for punishment as well as of finding out how much freedom the analyst allows, and simultaneously of subjugating and controlling this dangerous object, the analyst.

The analyst's countertransference reaction made clear to the analyst which of all these interpretations was most strongly indicated, for the countertransference reaction was the living response to the transference situation at that moment. The analyst felt (in accordance with the law of talion) a little anxious and angry at the aggression he suffered from the patient, and we may suppose that the patient in his unconscious or conscious fantasy sensed this annoyance in the internal object toward which his protesting behavior was directed, and that he reacted to this annoyance with anxiety. The 'disconnection' he spoke of in his first utterance must have been in relation to this anxiety, since it was because of this 'disconnection' that the analysand perceived no danger and felt no anxiety. By the patient's projection of that internal object the analyst is to the patient a tyrant who demands complete submission and forbids any protest. The transgression of this prohibition (the patient's protest expressed to his friend, the physician) must seem to the analyst—in the patient's fantasy—to be unfaithfulness, and must be responded to by the analyst with anger and emotional abandonment; we deduce this from the countertransference experience. In order to reconcile the analyst and to win him back, the patient accepts his anger or punishment and suffers from stomach-ache;—this he tells in his associations but without connecting the two experiences. His depression today is to be explained by this guilt feeling and, secondarily, by the object loss resulting from his increased 'disconnection'.

The analyst explains, in his interpretation, the meaning of the 'disconnection'. In reply the patient says that the previous day he recalled his conversation with that physician and that it did indeed cause him anxiety. After a brief pause he adds: 'and just now the thought came to me, well . . . and what am I to do with that?' The analyst perceived that these words once again slightly annoyed him. We can understand why. The patient's first reaction to the interpretation (he reacted by recalling his anxiety over his protest) had brought the analyst nearer to satisfying his desire to remove the patient's detachment. The patient's recollection of his anxiety had been at least one forward step, for he thus admitted a connection that he usually denied or repressed. But his next words frustrated the analyst once again, for they signified: 'that is of no use to me, nothing has changed'. Once again the countertransference reaction pointed out to the analyst the occurrence of a critical moment in the transference, and that here was the opportunity to interpret. At this moment also, in the patient's unconscious fantasy, must have occurred a reaction of anger from the internal object,—just as actually happened in the analyst,—to which the interpretation must be aimed. The patient's anxiety must have arisen from just this fantasy. His anxiety,—and with it his detachment,—could be diminished only by replacing that fantasied anger by an understanding of the patient's need to defend himself through that denial ("well . . . what am I to do with that?"). In reality the analyst, besides feeling annoyed, had understood that the patient had to protest and rebel, close himself up and 'disconnect' himself once again, deny and prevent any influence, because if the analyst should prove to be useful the patient would fall into intense dependence, just because of this usefulness and because the patient would be indebted to him. The interpretation increased this danger, for the patient felt it to

be true. Because of the analyst's tyranny,—his dominating, exploiting, sadistic character,—this dependence had to be prevented.

The analyst by awareness of his countertransference understood the patient's anxiety and interpreted it to him. The following associations showed that this interpretation had also been accurate.

The patient said shortly afterward that his depression had passed off, and this admission was a sign of progress because the patient was admitting that there was something good about the analyst. The next associations, moreover, permitted a more profound analysis of his transference neurosis, for the patient now revealed a deeper stratum. His underlying dependence became clear. Hitherto the interpretation had been confined to the guilt feelings and anxiety that accompanied his defenses (rebellion, denial, and others) against this very dependence. The associations referred to the fact that a mutual friend of the patient and of the analyst had a few days before told him that the analyst was going away on holiday that night and that this session would therefore be his last. In this way the patient admits the emotional importance the analyst possesses for him, a thing he always used to deny. We understand now also that his protest against analysts had been determined beforehand by the imminent danger of being forsaken by his analyst. When, just before the end of the session, the analyst explains that the information the friend gave him is false, the patient expresses anger with his friend and recalls how the friend has been trying lately to make him jealous of the analyst. Thus does the patient admit his jealousy of the analyst, although he displaces his anger onto the friend who roused his anxiety.

What has happened? And how is it to be explained?

The analyst's expected journey represented, in the unconscious of the patient, abandonment by internal objects necessary to him. This danger was countered by an identification with the aggressor; the threat of aggression (abandonment by the analyst) was countered by aggression (the patient's protest against analysts). His own aggression caused the patient to fear counteraggression or abandonment by the analyst. This anxiety remained unconscious but the analyst was able to deduce it from the counteraggression he perceived in his countertransference. If he had not interpreted the patient's transference situation, or if in his interpretation he had included any criticism of the patient's insistent and continuous rejection of the analyst or of his obstinate denial of any bond with the analyst, the patient would have remained in the vicious circle between his basic fear of abandonment and his defensive identification with the persecutor (with the object that abandons); he would have continued in the vicious circle of his neurosis. But the interpretation, which showed him the analyst's understanding of his conduct and of the underlying anxiety, changed (at least for that moment) the image of the analyst as persecutor. Hence the patient could give up his defensive identification with this image and could admit his dependence (the underlying stratum), his need for the analyst, and his jealousy.

And now once again in this new situation countertransference will show the content and origin of the anxiety that swiftly drives the analysand back to repetition of the defense mechanism he had just abandoned (which may be identification with the persecutor, emotional blocking, or something else). And once again interpretation of this new danger is the only means of breaking the vicious circle. If we consider the nature of the relationship that existed for months before the emotional surrender that occurred in this session, if we consider the paranoid situation that existed in the transference and countertransference (expressed in the patient by his intense characterological resistances and in the analyst by his annoyance), — if we consider all this background to the session just described, we understand that the analyst enjoys, in the patient's surrender, a manic triumph, to be followed of course by depressive and paranoid anxieties, compassion toward the patient, desires for reparation, and other sequelae. It is just these guilt feelings caused in the analyst by his manic feelings that may lead to his failure adequately to interpret the situation. The danger the patient fears is that he will become a helpless victim of the object's (the analyst's) sadism, — of that same sadism the analyst senses in his 'manic' satisfaction over dominating and defeating the bad object with which the patient was defensively identified. The perception of this 'manic' countertransference reaction indicates what the present transference situation is and what should be interpreted.

If there were nothing else in the analyst's psychological situation but this manic reaction, the patient would have no alternative but must make use of the same old defense mechanisms that essential constitute his neurosis. In more general terms, we should have to admit that the negative therapeutic reaction is an adequate transference reaction in the patient to an imagined or real negative countertransference in the analyst.[14] But even where such a negative

countertransference really exists, it is a part only of the analyst's psychological response. For the law of talion is not the sole determinant of the responses of the unconscious; and, moreover, the conscious also plays a part in the analyst's psychological responses. As to the unconscious, there is of course a tendency to repair, which may even create a disposition to 'return good for evil'. This tendency to repair is in reality a wish to remedy, albeit upon a displaced object, whatever evil one may have thought or done. And as to the conscious, there is, first, the fact that the analyst's own analysis has made his ego stronger than it was before so that the intensities of his anxieties and his further countertransference reactions are usually diminished; second, the analyst has some capacity to observe this countertransference, to 'get out of it', to stand outside and regard it objectively; and third, the analyst's knowledge of psychology also acts within and upon his psychological response. The knowledge, for instance, that behind the negative transference and the resistances lies simply thwarted love, helps the analyst to respond with love to this possibility of loving, to this nucleus in the patient however deeply it be buried beneath hate and fear.

9. The analyst should avoid, as far as possible, making interpretations in terms that coincide with those of the moral superego.[15] This danger is increased by the unconscious identification of the analyst with the patient's internal objects and, in particular, with his superego. In the example just cited, the patient, in conversation with his friend, criticized the conduct of analysts. In so doing he assumed the role of superego toward an internal object which he projected upon the analyst. The analyst identified himself with this projected object and reacted with unconscious anxiety and with annoyance to the accusation. He inwardly reproached the patient for his conduct and there was danger that something of this reproach (in which the analyst in his turn identified himself with the conduct of the patient as superego) might filter into his interpretation, which would then perpetuate the patient's neurotic vicious circle. But the problem is wider than this. Certain psychoanalytic terminology is likely to re-enforce the patient's confusion of the analyst with the superego. For instance 'narcissism,' 'passivity', and 'bribery of the superego' are terms we should not use literally or in paraphrase in treatment without careful reflection, just because they increase the danger that the patient will confuse the imago of

---

14. *Cf.* Little (*15*, p. 34).

15. Something similar, although not connected with counter-

transference, is emphasized by Fairbairn (*5*).

the analyst with that of his superego. For greater clarity two situations may be differentiated theoretically. In one, only the patient experiences these or like terms as criticism, because of his conflict between ego and superego, and the analyst is free of this critical feeling. In the other, the analyst also regards certain character traits with moral intolerance; he feels censorious, as if he were indeed a superego. Something of this attitude probably always exists, for the analyst identifies himself with the objects that the patient 'mistreats' (by his 'narcissism', or 'passivity', or 'bribery of the superego'). But even if the analyst had totally solved his own struggles against these same tendencies and hence remained free from countertransference conflict with the corresponding tendencies in the patient, it would be preferable to point out to the patient the several conflicts between his tendencies and his superego, and not run the risk of making it more difficult for the patient to differentiate between the judgment of his own superego and the analyst's comprehension of these same tendencies through the use of a terminology that precisely lends itself to confusing these two positions.

One might object that this confusion between the analyst and the superego neither can nor should be avoided, since it represents an essential part of the analysis of transference (of the externalization of internal situations) and since one cannot attain clarity except through confusion. That is true; this confusion cannot and should not be avoided, but we must remember that the confusion will also have to be resolved and that this will be all the more difficult the more the analyst is really identified in his experience with the analysand's superego and the more these identifications have influenced negatively his interpretations and conduct.

VI

In the examples presented we saw how to certain transference situations there correspond certain countertransference situations, and vice versa. To what transference situation does the analyst usually react with a particular countertransference? Study of this question would enable one, in practice, to deduce the transference situations from the countertransference reactions. Next we might ask, to what imago or conduct of the object, — to what imagined or real countertransference situation, — does the patient respond with a particular transference? Many aspects of these problems have been amply studied by psychoanalysis, but the specific problem of the

relation of transference and countertransference in analysis has received little attention.

The subject is so broad that we can discuss only a few situations and those incompletely, restricting ourselves to certain aspects. We must choose for discussion only the most important countertransference situations, those that most disturb the analyst's task and that clarify important points in the double neurosis, *la névrose à deux*, that arises in the analytic situation, — a neurosis usually of very different intensity in the two participants.

1. What is the significance of countertransference anxiety?

Countertransference anxiety may be described in general and simplified terms as being of depressive or paranoid character.[16] In depressive anxiety the inherent danger consists in having destroyed the analysand or made him ill. This anxiety may arise to a greater degree when the analyst faces the danger that the patient may commit suicide, and to a lesser degree when there is deterioration or danger of deterioration in the patient's state of health. But the patient's simple failure to improve and his suffering and depression may also provoke depressive anxieties in the analyst. These anxieties usually increase the desire to heal the patient.

In referring to paranoid anxieties it is important to differentiate between 'direct' and 'indirect' countertransference (*17*). In direct countertransference the anxieties are caused by danger of an intensification of aggression from the patient himself. In indirect countertransference the anxieties are caused by danger of aggression from third parties onto whom the analyst has made his own chief transferences, — for instance, the members of the analytic society, for the future of the analyst's object relationships with the society is in part determined by his professional performance. The feared aggression may take several forms, such as criticism, reproach, hatred, mockery, contempt, or bodily assault. In the unconscious it may be the danger of being killed or castrated or otherwise menaced in an archaic way.

The transference situations of the patient to which the depressive anxieties of the analyst are a response are, above all, those in which the patient, through an

---

16. See Klein (*12, 13*). The terms 'depressive', 'paranoid', and 'manic' are here used simply as descriptive terms. Thus, for example, 'paranoid anxieties' involve all the fantasies of being persecuted, independently of the libidinal phase or of the 'position' described by Klein. The following considerations are closely connected with my observations upon psychopathological stratification (*19*).

increase in frustration[17] (or danger of frustration) and in the aggression that it evokes, turns the aggression against himself. We are dealing, on one plane, with situations in which the patient defends himself against a paranoid fear of retaliation by anticipating this danger, by carrying out himself and against himself part of the aggression feared from the object transferred onto the analyst, and threatening to carry it out still further. In this psychological sense it is really the analyst who attacks and destroys the patient; and the analyst's depressive anxiety corresponds to this psychological reality. In other words, the countertransference depressive anxiety arises, above all, as a response to the patient's 'masochistic defense', — which at the same time represents a revenge ('masochistic revenge'), — and as a response to the danger of its continuing. On another plane this turning of the aggression against himself is carried out by the patient because of his own depressive anxieties; he turns it against himself in order to protect himself against re-experiencing the destruction of the objects and to protect these from his own aggression.

The paranoid anxiety in 'direct' countertransference is a reaction to the danger arising from various aggressive attitudes of the patient himself. The analysis of these attitudes shows that they are themselves defenses against, or reactions to, certain aggressive imagoes; and these reactions and defenses are governed by the law of talion or else, analogously to this, by identification with the persecutor. The reproach, contempt, abandonment, bodily assault, — all these atittudes of menace or aggression in the patient that give rise to countertransference paranoid anxieties, — are responses to (or anticipations of) equivalent attitudes of the transferred object.

The paranoid anxieties in 'indirect' countertransference are of a more complex nature since the danger for the analyst originates in a third party. The patient's transference situations that provoke the aggression of this 'third party' against the analyst may be of various sorts. In most cases, we are dealing with transference situations (masochistic or aggressive) similar to those that provoke the 'direct' countertransference anxieties previously described.

The common denominator of all the various attitudes of patients that provoke anxiety in the analyst is to be found, I believe, in the mechanism of 'identification with the persecutor'; the experience of being liberated from the persecutor and of triumphing over him, implied in this identification, suggests our designating this mechanism as a manic one. This mechanism may also exist where the manifest picture in the patient is quite the opposite, namely in certain depressive states; for the manic conduct may be directed either toward a projected object or toward an introjected object, it may be carried out alloplastically or autoplastically. The 'identification with the persecutor' may even exist in suicide, inasmuch as this is a 'mockery' of the fantasied or real persecutors, by anticipating the intentions of the persecutors and by one doing to oneself what they wanted to do; this 'mockery' is the manic aspect of suicide. The 'identification with the persecutor' in the patient is, then, a defense against an object felt as sadistic that tends to make the patient the victim of a manic feast; and this defense is carried out either through the introjection of the persecutor in the ego, turning the analyst into the object of the 'manic tendencies', or through the introjection of the persecutor in the superego, taking the ego as the object of its manic trend. Let us illustrate.

An analysand decides to take a pleasure trip to Europe. He experiences this as a victory over the analyst both because he will free himself from the analyst for two months and because he can afford this trip whereas the analyst cannot. He then begins to be anxious lest the analyst seek revenge for the patient's triumph. The patient anticipates this aggression by becoming unwell, developing fever and the first symptoms of influenza. The analyst feels slight anxiety because of this illness and fears, recalling certain previous experiences, a deterioration in the state of health of the patient, who still however continues to come to the sessions. Up to this point, the situation in the transference and countertransference is as follows. The patient is in a manic relation to the analyst, and he has anxieties of preponderantly paranoid type. The analyst senses some irritation over the abandonment and some envy of the patient's great wealth (feelings ascribed by the patient in his paranoid anxieties to the analyst); but at the same time the analyst feels satisfaction at the analysand's real progress which finds expression in the very fact that the trip is possible and that the patient has decided to make it. The analyst perceives a wish in part of his personality to bind the patient to himself and use the patient for his own needs. In having this wish he resembles the patient's mother, and he is aware that he is in reality identified with the domineering and vindictive object with which the patient identifies him. Hence the patient's illness seems, to the analyst's unconscious, a result of the

---

17. By the term 'frustration' I always refer to the subjective experience and not to the objective facts. This inner experience is determined by a complementary series at one end of which is primary and secondary masochism and at the other end the actual frustrating happenings.

analyst's own wish, and the analyst therefore experiences depressive (and paranoid) anxieties.

What object imago leads the patient to this manic situation? It is precisely this same imago of a tyrannical and sadistic mother, to whom the patient's frustrations constitute a manic feast. It is against these 'manic tendencies' in the object that the patient defends himself, first by identification (introjection of the persecutor in the ego, which manifests itself in the manic experience in his decision to take a trip) and then by using a masochistic defense to escape vengeance.

In brief, the analyst's depressive (and paranoid) anxiety is his emotional response to the patient's illness; and the patient's illness is itself a masochistic defense against the object's vindictive persecution. This masochistic defense also contains a manic mechanism in that it derides, controls, and dominates the analyst's aggression. In the stratum underlying this we find the patient in a paranoid situation in face of the vindictive persecution by the analyst, — a fantasy which coincides with the analyst's secret irritation. Beneath this paranoid situation, and causing it, is an inverse situation: the patient is enjoying a manic triumph (his liberation from the analyst by going on a trip), but the analyst is in a paranoid situation (he is in danger of being defeated and abandoned). And, finally, beneath this we find a situation in which the patient is subjected to an object imago that wants to make of him the victim of its aggressive tendencies, but this time not in order to take revenge for intentions or attitudes in the patient, but merely to satisfy his own sadism, — an imago that originates directly from the original sufferings of the subject.

In this way, the analyst was able to deduce from each of his countertransference sensations a certain transference situation; the analyst's fear of deterioration in the patient's health enabled him to perceive the patient's need to satisfy the avenger and to control and restrain him, partially inverting (through the illness) the roles of victimizer and victim, thus alleviating his guilt feeling and causing the analyst to feel some of the guilt. The analyst's irritation over the patient's trip enabled him to see the patient's need to free himself from a dominating and sadistic object, to see the patient's guilt feelings caused by these tendencies, and also to see his fear of the analyst's revenge. By his feeling of triumph the analyst was able to detect the anxiety and depression caused in the patient by his dependence upon this frustrating, yet indispensable, object. And each of these transference situations indicated to the analyst the patient's object imagoes, — the fantasied or real countertransference situations that determined the transference situations.

2. What is the meaning of countertransference aggression?

In the preceding pages, we have seen that the analyst may experience, besides countertransference anxiety, annoyance, rejection, desire for vengeance, hatred, and other emotions. What are the origin and meaning of these emotions?

Countertransference aggression usually arises in the face of frustration (or danger of frustration) of desires which may superficially be differentiated into 'direct' and 'indirect'. Both direct and indirect desires are principally wishes to get libido or affection. The patient is the chief object of direct desires in the analyst, who wishes to be accepted and loved by him. The object of the indirect desires of the analyst may be, for example, other analysts from whom he wishes to get recognition or admiration through his successful work with his patients, using the latter as means to this end (17). This aim to get love has, in general terms, two origins: an instinctual origin (the primitive need of union with the object) and an origin of a defensive nature (the need of neutralizing, overcoming, or denying the rejections and other dangers originating from the internal objects, in particular from the superego). The frustrations may be differentiated, descriptively, into those of active type and those of passive type. Among the active frustrations is direct aggression by the patient, his mockery, deceit, and active rejection. To the analyst, active frustration means exposure to a predominantly 'bad' object; the patient may become, for example, the analyst's superego which says to him 'you are bad'. Examples of frustration of passive type are passive rejection, withdrawal, partial abandonment, and other defenses against the bond with and dependence on the analyst. These signify frustrations of the analyst's need of union with the object.

In summary, we may say that countertransference aggression usually arises when there is frustration of the analyst's desires that spring from Eros, both those arising from his 'original' instinctive and affective drives and those arising from his need of neutralizing or annulling his own Thanatos (or the action of his internal 'bad objects') directed against the ego or against the external world. Owing partly to the analyst's own neurosis (and also to certain characteristics of analysis itself) these desires of Eros sometimes acquire the unconscious aim of bringing the patient to a state of dependence. Hence countertransference aggression may be provoked by the rejection of this dependence by the patient who rejects any bond with the analyst and refuses to surrender to him, showing this refusal by silence, denial, secretiveness, repression, blocking, or mockery.

Next we must establish what it is that induces the patient to behave in this way, to frustrate the analyst, to withdraw from him, to attack him. If we know this we shall know what we have to interpret when countertransference aggression arises in us, being able to deduce from the countertransference the transference situation and its cause. This cause is a fantasied countertransference situation or, more precisely, some actual or feared bad conduct from the projected object. Experience shows that, in somewhat general terms, this bad or threatening conduct of the object is usually an equivalent of the conduct of the patient (to which the analyst has reacted internally with aggression). We also understand why this is so: the patient's conduct springs from that most primitive of reactions, the talion reaction, or from the defense by means of identification with the persecutor or aggressor. In some cases it is quite simple: the analysand withdraws from us, rejects us, abandons us, or derides us when he fears or suffers the same or an equivalent treatment from us. In other cases it is more complex, the immediate identification with the aggressor being replaced by another identification that is less direct. To exemplify: a woman patient, upon learning that the analyst is going on holiday, remains silent a long while; she withdraws, through her silence, as a talion response to the analyst's withdrawal. Deeper analysis shows that the analyst's holiday is, to the patient, equivalent to the primal scene; and this is equivalent to destruction of her as a woman, and her immediate response must be a similar attack against the analyst. This aggressive (castrating) impulse is rejected and the result, her silence, is a compromise between her hostility and its rejection; it is a transformed identification with the persecutor.

To sum up: (a) The countertransference reactions of aggression (or of its equivalent) occur in response to transference situations in which the patient frustrates certain desires of the analyst. These frustrations are equivalent to abandonment or aggression which the patient carries out or with which he threatens the analyst, and they place the analyst, at first, in a depressive or paranoid situation. The patient's defense is in one aspect equivalent to a manic situation, for he is freeing himself from a persecutor.[18]

(b) This transference situation is the defense against certain object imagoes. There may be an object that persecutes the subject sadistically, vindictively, or morally, or an object that the patient defends from his own destructiveness by an attack against his own ego (*19*); in these, the patient attacks, — as Freud and Abraham have shown in the analysis of melancholia and suicide, — at the same time the internal object and the external object (the analyst). (c) The analyst who is placed by the alloplastic or autoplastic attacks of the patient in a paranoid or depressive situation sometimes defends himself against these attacks by using the same identification with the aggressor or persecutor as the patient used. Then the analyst virtually becomes the persecutor, and to this the patient (insofar as he presupposes such a reaction from his internal and projected object) responds with anxiety. This anxiety and its origin is nearest to consciousness, and is therefore the first thing to interpret.

3. Countertransference guilt feelings are an important source of countertransference anxiety; the analyst fears his 'moral conscience'. Thus, for instance, a serious deterioration in the condition of the patient may cause the analyst to suffer reproach by his own superego, and also cause him to fear punishment. When such guilt feelings occur, the superego of the analyst is usually projected upon the patient or upon a third person, the analyst being the guilty ego. The accuser is the one who is attacked, the victim of the analyst. The analyst is the accused; he is charged with being the victimizer. It is therefore the analyst who must suffer anxiety over his object, and dependence upon it.

As in other countertransference situations, the analyst's guilt feeling may have either real causes or fantasied causes, or a mixture of the two. A real cause exists in the analyst who has neurotic negative feelings that exercise some influence over his behavior, leading him, for example, to interpret with aggressiveness or to behave in a submissive, seductive, or unnecessarily frustrating way. But guilt feelings may also arise in the analyst over, for instance, intense submissiveness in the patient even though the analyst had not driven the patient into such conduct by his procedure. Or he may feel guilty when the analysand becomes depressed or ill, although his therapeutic procedure was right and proper according to his own conscience. In such cases, the countertransference guilt feelings are evoked not by what procedure he has actually used but by his awareness of what he might have done in view of his latent disposition. In other words, the analyst identifies himself in fantasy with a bad internal object of the patient and he feels guilty for what he has provoked in this role, — illness, depression,

---

18. This 'mania' may be of 'superego type', as for instance 'mania for reproaching' (identification with the persecuting moral superego) which also occurs in many depressive and masochistic states. It may also be of a 'pre-superego type' (belonging to planes underlying that of moral guilt) as occurs for instance in certain erotomanias, for erotic mockery is identification with the object that castrates by frustrating genitally (*19*).

masochism, suffering, failure. The imago of the patient then becomes fused with the analyst's internal objects which the analyst had, in the past, wanted (and perhaps managed) to frustrate, make suffer, dominate, or destroy. Now he wishes to repair them. When this reparation fails, he reacts as if he had hurt them. The true cause of the guilt feelings is the neurotic, predominantly sadomasochistic tendencies that may reappear in countertransference; the analyst therefore quite rightly entertains certain doubts and uncertainties about his ability to control them completely and to keep them entirely removed from his procedure.

The transference situation to which the analyst is likely to react with guilt feelings is then, in the first place, a masochistic trend in the patient, which may be either of a 'defensive' (secondary) or of a 'basic' (primary) nature. If it is defensive we know it to be a rejection of sadism by means of its 'turning against the ego'; the principal object imago that imposes this masochistic defense is a retaliatory imago. If it is basic ('primary masochism') the object imago is 'simply' sadistic, a reflex of the pains ('frustrations') originally suffered by the patient. The analyst's guilt feelings refer to his own sadistic tendencies. He may feel as if he himself had provoked the patient's masochism. The patient is subjugated by a 'bad' object so that it seems as if the analyst had satisfied his aggressiveness; now the analyst is exposed in his turn to the accusations of his superego. In short, the superficial situation is that the patient is now the superego, and the analyst the ego who must suffer the accusation; the analyst is in a depressive-paranoid situation, whereas the patient is, from one point of view, in a 'manic' situation (showing, for example, 'mania for reproaching'). But on a deeper plane the situation is the reverse: the analyst is in a 'manic' situation (acting as a vindictive, dominating, or 'simply' sadistic imago), and the patient is in a depressive-paranoid situation (*19*).

4. Besides the anxiety, hatred, and guilt feelings in countertransference, there are a number of other countertransference situations that may also be decisive points in the course of analytic treatment, both because they may influence the analyst's work and because the analysis of the transference situations that provoke such countertransference situations may represent the central problem of treatment, clarification of which may be indispensable if the analyst is to exert any therapeutic influence upon the patient.

Let us consider briefly only two of these situations. One is the countertransference boredom or somnolence already mentioned which of course assumes great importance only when it occurs often.

Boredom and somnolence are usually unconscious talion responses in the analyst to a withdrawal or affective abandonment by the patient. This withdrawal has diverse origins and natures; but it has specific characteristics, for not every kind of withdrawal by the patient produces boredom in the analyst. One of these characteristics seems to be that the patient withdraws without going away, he takes his emotional departure from the analyst while yet remaining with him; there is as a rule no danger of the patient's taking flight. This *partial* withdrawal or abandonment expresses itself superficially in intellectualization (emotional blocking), in increased control, sometimes in monotony in the way of speaking, or in similar devices. The analyst has at these times the sensation of being excluded and of being impotent to guide the course of the sessions. It seems that the analysand tries in this way to avoid a latent and dreaded dependence upon the analyst. This dependence is, at the surface, his dependence upon his moral superego, and at a deeper level it is dependence upon other internal objects which are in part persecutors and in part persecuted. These objects must *not* be projected upon the analyst; the latent and internal relations with them must not be made present and externalized. This danger is avoided through various mechanisms, ranging from 'conscious control and selection of the patient's communications to depersonalization, and from emotional blocking[19] to total repression of any transference relation; it is this rejection of such dangers and the avoidance and mastery of anxiety by means of these mechanisms that lead to the withdrawal to which the analyst may react with boredom or somnolence.

Countertransference anxiety and guilt feelings also frequently cause a tendency to countertransference submissiveness, which is important from two points of view: both for its possible influence upon the analyst's understanding, behavior, and technique, and for what it may teach us about the patient's transference situation. This tendency to submissiveness will lead the analyst to avoid frustrating the patient and will even cause the analyst to pamper him. The analyst's tendency to avoid frustration and tension will express itself in a search for rapid pacification of the transference situations, by prompt 'reduction' of the transference to infantile situations, for example, or by rapid reconstruction of

---

19. This emotional blocking and, in particular, the blocking of aggression seems to be the cause of the 'absence of danger' for the analyst (the fact that the analysand does not run away or otherwise jeopardize the analysis), which seems to be one of the conditions for occurrence of countertransference boredom.

the 'good', 'real' imago of the analyst.[20] The analyst who feels subjugated by the patient feels angry, and the patient, intuitively perceiving this anger, is afraid of his revenge. The transference situation that leads the patient to dominate and subjugate the analyst by a hidden or manifest threat seems analogous to the transference situation that leads the analyst to feel anxious and guilty. The various ways in which the analyst reacts to his anxieties, — in one case with an attitude of submission, in another case with inner recrimination, — is also related to the transference attitude of the patient. My observation seems to indicate that the greater the disposition to real aggressive *action* in the analysand, the more the analyst tends to submission.

VII

Before closing, let us consider briefly two doubtful points. How much confidence should we place in countertransference as a guide to understanding the patient? And how useful or how harmful is it to communicate to the patient a countertransference reaction? As to the first question, I think it certainly a mistake to find in countertransference reactions an oracle, with blind faith to expect of them the pure truth about the psychological situations of the analysand. It is plain that our unconscious is a very personal 'receiver' and 'transmitter' and we must reckon with frequent distortions of objective reality. But it is also true that our unconscious is nevertheless 'the best we have of its kind'. His own analysis and some analytic experience enables the analyst, as a rule, to be conscious of this personal factor and know his 'personal equation'. According to my experience, the danger of exaggerated faith in the messages of one's own unconscious is, even when they refer to very 'personal' reactions, less than the danger of repressing them and denying them any objective value.

I have sometimes begun a supervisory hour by asking the candidate how he has felt toward the patient that week or what he has experienced during the sessions, and the candidate has answered, for instance, that he was bored, or that he felt anxious because he had the impression that the patient wanted to abandon the analysis. On other occasions I have myself noticed annoyance or anxiety in the candidate relative to the patient. These countertransference responses have at times indicated to me

in advance the central problem of the treatment at whatever stage it had reached; and this supposition has usually been verified by detailed analysis of the material presented in the supervisory hour. When these countertransference reactions were very intense they of course referred to unsolved problems in the candidate, and his reactions were distorted echoes of the objective situation. But even without such 'intensity' we must always reckon with certain distortions. One candidate, for instance, reacted for a time with slight annoyance whenever his analysands were much occupied with their childhood. The candidate had the idea that only analysis of transference could further the treatment. In reality he also had a wish that the analysands concern themselves with him. But the candidate was able by analyzing this situation quickly to revive his interest in the childhood situations of the analysands, and he could also see that his annoyance, in spite of its neurotic character, had pointed out to him the rejection of certain transference situations in some analysands.

Whatever the analyst experiences emotionally, his reactions always bear some relation to processes in the patient. Even the most neurotic countertransference ideas arise only in response to certain patients and to certain situations of these patients, and they can, in consequence, indicate something about the patients and their situations. To cite one last example: a candidate, at the beginning of a session (and before the analysand, a woman, had spoken), had the idea that she was about to draw a revolver and shoot at him; he felt an impulse to sit in his chair in a defensive position. He readily recognized the paranoid character of this idea, for the patient was far from likely to behave in such a way. Yet it was soon clear that his reaction was in a certain sense appropriate; the analysand spontaneously remarked that she intended to give him 'a kick in the penis'. On other occasions when the candidate had the same idea, this patient was fantasying that she was the victim of persecution; in this case also the analyst's reaction was, in a way, appropriate, for the patient's fantasy of being persecuted was the consequence and the cause of the patient's sadistic impulses toward the transferred object.

On the other hand, one must critically examine the *deductions* one makes from perception of one's own countertransference. For example, the fact that the analyst feels angry does not simply mean (as is sometimes said) that the patient wishes to make him angry. It may mean rather that the patient has a transference feeling of guilt. What has been said above concerning countertransference aggression is relevant here.

---

20. Wilhelm Reich (*22*) stressed the frequent tendency in analysts to avoid negative transference. The countertransference situation just described is one of the situations underlying that tendency.

The second question,—whether the analyst should or should not 'communicate' or 'interpret' aspects of his countertransference to the analysand,—cannot be considered fully here.[21] Much depends, of course, upon what, when, how, to whom, for what purpose, and in what conditions the analyst speaks about his countertransference. It is probable that the purposes sought by communicating the countertransference might often (but not always) be better attained by other means. The principal other means is analysis of the patient's fantasies about the analyst's countertransference (and of the related transferences) sufficient to show the patient the truth

(the reality of the countertransferences of his inner and outer objects); and with this must also be analyzed the doubts, negations, and other defenses against the truth, intuitively perceived, until they have been overcome. But there are also situations in which communication of the countertransference is of value for the subsequent course of the treatment. Without doubt, this aspect of the use of countertransference is of great interest; we need an extensive and detailed study of the inherent problems of communication of countertransference. Much more experience and study of countertransference needs to be recorded.

REFERENCES

1. Balint, Alice: *Handhabung der Übertragung auf Grund der Ferenczischen Versuche.* Int. Ztschr. f. Psa., XXII, 1936, pp. 47–58.
2. Balint, Michael: *On the Psychoanalytic Training System.* Int. J. Psa., XXIX, 1948.
3. Cesio, F.: *Psicoanálisis de una melancholía con ataques histero epilépticos.* Rev. de Psicoanálisis, IX, 1952.
4. Deutsch, Helene: *Okkulte Vorgänge während der Psychoanalyse.* Imago, XII, 1926, pp. 418–433.
5. Fairbairn, W. R. D.: *The Repression and the Return of Bad Objects.* Brit. J. Med. Psychology, XIX, 1943.
6. Ferenczi, Sandor: *Missbrauch der Assoziationsfreiheit.* In: *Bausteine zur Psychoanalyse, II.* Vienna: Int. Psa. Verlag, 1927, p. 41.
7. Freud: *The Future Prospects of Psychoanalytic Therapy* (1910). Coll. Papers, II.
8. ———: *Further Recommendations in the Technique of Psychoanalysis. On Beginning the Treatment* (1913). Coll. Papers, II.
9. ———: *The Dynamics of the Transference* (1912). Coll. Papers, II.
10. Gitelson, Maxwell: *The Emotional Position of the Analyst in the Psychoanalytic Situation.* Int. J. Psa., XXXIII, 1952.
11. Heimann, Paula: *On Countertransference.* Int. J. Psa., XXXI, 1950.
12. Klein, Melanie: *A Contribution to the Psychoanalysis of Manic-Depressive States.* Int. J. Psa., XVI, 1935.
13. ———: *On the Criteria for the Termination of a Psychoanalysis.* Int. J. Psa., XXXI, 1950.
14. Libermann, D.: *Fragmento del análisis de una psicosìs paranoide.* Rev. de Psicoanálisis, IX, 1952.
15. Little, Margaret: *Countertransference and the Patient's Response to It.* Int. J. Psa., XXXII, 1951.
16. Lorand, Sandor: *Technique of Psychoanalytic Therapy.* New York: International Universities Press, Inc., 1946.
17. Racker, Heinrich: *Contribution to the Problem of Countertransference* (1948). Int. J. Psa., XXXIV, 1953, pp. 313–324.
18. ———: *Observaciones sobre la contratransferencìa como instrumento ténico* (1951). Rev. de Psicoanálisis, IX, 1952, pp. 342–354.
19. ———: *Contribution to the Problem of Psychopathological Stratification.* Int. J. Psa., XXXVIII, 1957, pp. 223–239.
20. ———: *Notes on the Theory of Transference,* This Quarterly, XXIII, 1954.
21. Reich, Annie: *On Countertransference.* Int. J. Psa., XXXII, 1951.
22. Reich, Wilhelm: *Character Analysis* (1933). New York: Orgone Institute Press, 1945.
23. Weigert, Edith: *Contribution to the Problem of Terminating Psychoanalyses.* This Quarterly, XXI, 1952.
24. Winnicott, D. W.: *Hate in the Countertransference.* Int. J. Psa., XXX, 1949.

21. Alice Balint (*1*), Winnicott (*24*), and others favor communicating to the patient (and further analyzing) certain countertransference situations. Heimann (*11*) is among those that oppose doing so. Libermann (*14*) describes how, in the treatment of a psychotic woman, communication of the countertransference played a very important part. The analyst freely associated upon unconscious manifestations of countertransference which the patient pointed out to him.

16

ON A SPECIFIC ASPECT OF COUNTERTRANSFERENCE DUE TO THE PATIENT'S PROJECTIVE IDENTIFICATION

Leon Grinberg

EDITOR'S NOTE

In this paper Leon Grinberg identifies a specific type of counter-transference expression—projective counteridentification—which occurs in the presence of intense projective identifications by the patient (see Part VI, and Langs 1976a,b, 1978a,b, for more extended considerations of the role of projective identifications in analysis and therapy). Most investigations of countertransference have implicitly or explicitly, whether interactionally founded or not, been restricted to the cognitive sphere. In addition, most studies of pathological projective identification have concentrated on instances where it stems from the patient; collaterally, they assume an adaptively responding psychoanalyst, capable of *reverie* (Bion 1963)—the adaptive containing and metabolizing of patho-logical projective identifications toward interpretive insight. The analyst's own pathological projective identifications and his diffi-culties with those deriving from the patient have both been relatively neglected.

It falls, then, to this paper to bring to our attention the difficulties that an analyst may have in containing and metabolizing the patient's pathological interactional projections, and the dangers of countertransference-based responses, including pathological repro-jection of nonmetabolized or nondetoxified contents. Grinberg stresses the detrimental aspects of this type of response, while leav-ing room for constructive possibilities as well.

In previous papers (3, 4) I have dealt with some changes in the analytic technique resulting from the analysands' massive use of projective identification. The excessive use of this mechanism, in certain situations, gives rise to a specific reaction in the ana-lyst, who is unconsciously and passively 'led' to play the sort of role the patient hands over to him. For this particular reaction, I suggest the term 'projective counter-identification'.

I then pointed out that it had to do with a very

specific and partial aspect of the countertransference. But I consider it especially important to stress this aspect in order to show the difference existing be-tween the response I have in mind and the counter-transference reactions resulting from the analyst's own emotional attitudes, or on his neurotic rem-nants, reactivated by the patient's conflicts. With a view to making this difference clearer, I should like to describe in a schematic form the two processes which co-exist in the analyst's mind.

In process A the analyst is the active subject of the patient's introjective and projective mechanisms. In this process, and based on Fliess's remarks (2), three important phases can be described: (i) when the

Reprinted from *International Journal of Psycho-Analysis* 43:436–440, 1962.

analyst selectively introjects the different aspects of the patient's verbal and nonverbal material, together with their corresponding emotional charges; (ii) when the analyst works through and assimilates the identifications resulting from the said identification of the patient's inner world; and (iii) when the analyst (re)projects the results of this assimilation by means of interpretations.

On the other hand, in process B, the analyst is the *passive object* of the analysand's projections and introjections. In this case, however, two further situations may still develop: (i) that the analyst's emotional response may be due to his own conflicts or anxieties, intensified or reactivated by the patient's conflicting material. (ii) That the emotional response may be quite independent from the analyst's own emotions and appear mainly as a reaction to the analysand's projections upon him.

The second process presents for us considerable interest, especially in connexion with the problem raised in this paper. In one phase, it is the analysand who, in an active though unconscious way, projects his inner conflicts upon the analyst, who acts in this case as a passive recipient of such projections.

This projective-identification process being constant, the analyst's reactions to it will be similar to his reactions toward the material he has already introjected by an active process of selection. On some occasions, however, the analysand's projective identification mechanism may become too active — owing either to an exaggerated intensity of its emotional charges or to the violence with which this same mechanism was imposed on him during childhood.

Melanie Klein's papers (5, 6), especially those dealing with her concept of projective identification, are sufficiently known to require further comments. I consider that her paper 'On Identification' constitutes, at present, the most complete study of the contents and functioning of the projective identification mechanism; according to her description, it implies a combination of the splitting mechanism, the subsequent projection of the split parts onto another person, with the ensuing loss of those parts, and an alteration of the object-perception mechanism. This process is bound up with the processes that take place during the first three or four months of life (paranoid-schizoid position), when splitting is at its maximum height, with a predominance of persecutory anxieties.

It follows, then, that the essential aspect in the functioning of that mechanism is that the subject projects his own conflicts, emotions, or parts into the object. But should we assume that the analyst does not play a part in this process, that he does not react to his patient's active projective identification? In my opinion, there is quite often a specific response more or less intense on the part of the analyst; this fact has been confirmed by experience.

Let me first point out that although there is a dual participation in the process I am describing — as always happens in the analytic situation — the main emphasis should be attributed to the extreme violence of the projective identification mechanism of the analysand. I shall show, later on, in some clinical examples, how the particular intensity of this mechanism is usually related to traumatic infantile experiences, during which the patient suffered the effect of violent projective identifications.

Whenever the analyst has to meet such violent projective identifications, he may react in a normal way, i.e. by properly interpreting the material brought by the patient and by showing him that the violence of the mechanism has in no way shocked him. Sometimes, however, the analyst may be unable to tolerate it, and he may then react in several different ways:

(a) By an immediate and equally violent rejection of the material which the patient tries to project into him.

(b) By ignoring or denying this rejection through a severe control or some other defensive mechanism; sooner or later, however, the reaction will become manifest in some way or other.

(c) By postponing and displacing his reaction, which will then become manifest with another patient.

(d) By suffering the effects of such an intensive projective identification, and 'counter-identifying' himself, in turn.

In fact, the response of the analyst will depend on his degree of tolerance.

When this counter-identification takes place, the normal communication between the analysand's and the analyst's unconscious will obviously be interrupted. In this case, the unconscious content rejected by the analysand will be violently projected onto the analyst, who, as the recipient object of such projective identifications, will have to suffer its effects. And he will react as if he had acquired and assimilated the parts projected on to him in a *real and concrete way*.

In certain cases, the analyst may have the feeling of being no longer his own self and of unavoidably becoming transformed into the object which the patient, unconsciously, wanted him to be (id, ego, or some internal object). For this particular situation, I propose the term 'projective counter-identification', i.e. the analyst's specific response to the violent projective identification from the patient, which is not consciously perceived by the former. In such a case, even if this situation prevails only for a short time (although occasionally it may persist, with the ensuing danger) the analyst will resort to all kinds of rationalizations in order to justify his attitude or his bewilderment.

Some clinical examples will serve as a basis for the above considerations.

(i) A woman patient came to her first session fifteen minutes late; she lay down on the couch and then remained still and silent during a few minutes. After that, she said she felt the same as she used to feel when passing an oral examination (which usually caused her great anxiety). Then she associated the analytic session with her wedding night, when, even though she was feeling extremely frightened, she was told that she looked like a statue.

I told her then that what she felt was that she was having with me the same experience that she had had at her oral examinations and during her wedding night, because she feared I might deflower her, introduce myself into her to look at things and examine them. Here, too, she was behaving like a statue; the rigidity and stillness she showed at the beginning of her session were intended to disguise her anxiety, but also to prevent the actual possibility of being penetrated.

Although I realized that this interpretation of her paranoid anxiety was correct, I had the feeling that there was something wrong in it; still, I could not understand the reason for such a feeling. I guessed that my interpretation had been rather superficial and that the facts I had pointed out to her were too near her consciousness. I had to find out the deeper motives of her exaggerated fear of my going into her.

On the other hand, her initial attitude of stiffness had particularly attracted my attention, and I found myself, not without considerable amazement, having the phantasy of analysing a corpse. A thought came at once into my mind, which took the form of a popular Spanish saying: 'She is trying to force the dead into me' (which meant that she wanted to burden me with the whole responsibility and guilt). This thought showed me my own paranoid reaction, aroused by the feeling that she was trying to project her fears into me, through projective identification.

Based on this countertransferential feeling, I told her that with her rigidity and silence she wanted perhaps to mean something else, besides the representation of a statue; she wanted to express in this way some feeling of her own, related to death.

This interpretation was a real shock to her; she began to cry and told me that when she was 6 years old her mother, who suffered from cancer, had committed suicide. The patient felt responsible for her mother's death, because she had hanged herself in her presence, and it had been actually on account of her delay in warning the rest of the family that the death could not be prevented, as had been done in former attempts. She remembered having watched all the arrangements her mother made and being greatly impressed by them; then she went out and waited for a long while (perhaps fifteen minutes, she said); only then did she run for help, but when her father came it was too late.

I had the feeling that with her corpse-like rigidity the patient was not only trying to show that she carried inside a dead object, but also, at the same time, to get rid of it by projective identification. From that moment on, she wanted me unconsciously to take over the responsibility, to bear 'the dead'. As a defence against her violent projective identification, with which she tried to introduce into me a dead object, I reacted with my first interpretation, which in fact inverted the situation: she was the one who was afraid of my piercing her. Later on, I managed to grasp the actual meaning of the whole situation, I had a much clearer understanding of the deepest sources of her paranoid anxieties and gave her a correct and more complete interpretation.

I am in agreement with Hanna Segal's suggestion[1] that the particular violence of the projective identification process is generally related to infantile experiences, during which the child has been subject to violent projective identifications on the part of his or her parents. In the case I am referring to, it is very likely that the utter violence of the patient's projective identification was the result of her mother's intense projective identification, not only during the traumatic episode of her suicide, but also on other occasions.

(ii) A student under psycho-analytic training came to his session after having analysed a 'difficult' patient. During the session with his own patient, he had had the feeling of 'killing himself', owing to his very active interpretations, without, however, obtaining any satisfactory result. He was depressed by the feeling of failure, and after communicating his experience and mood to his training analyst, he remained silent. While listening to his analyst's interpretations, which momentarily did not modify his state of mind, the student had the impression that the same situation he had been complaining about was being repeated, although with inverted

---

1. Personal communication.

roles: he realized that now it was his analyst who was killing himself to obtain some reaction from him, while he was acting in the same way as his patient had done. When, with some surprise, he communicated his impression to the analyst, the latter showed him that his behaviour during the session had 'compelled' (his own word) him to identify himself with the patient. The interpretation was then completed in the sense that the student envied his analyst for having better and 'easier' patients (the student himself). A very intense projective identification had thus taken place, by means of which the student unconsciously wanted his analyst to experience his own difficulties. The student recurred to splitting and projected his hampered and dissatisfied professional part on to the analyst, remaining himself with the part of himself identified with his own patient, 'who makes one work and does not gratify'. The training analyst had in turn 'succumbed', so to speak, to the analysand's projection, and felt unconsciously compelled to counter-identify himself with the introjected part.

When this occurs—and this process is much more frequent than is usually believed—the analysand may have the magical unconscious feeling of having accomplished his own phantasies, by 'placing' his parts on the object, which also may arouse in him, in certain cases, a maniacal feeling of triumph over his analyst.

(iii) During a certain period of a patient's analysis, with a positive outcome, I observed a strange and uncommon reaction in myself. Throughout a number of sessions, every time he spoke about the possibility of getting married, I felt invaded by an intense drowsiness, which interfered with my relationship to him and his subject. It was not due to boredom, since this was a new and very important aspect in his life; on the contrary, the patient himself spoke cheerfully and with great enthusiasm of his projects. Neither could it be attributed to a general weariness on my part, since the drowsiness appeared only in connexion with this particular patient. What surprised me most was my own reaction, which was indeed so strange to my nature. I remembered, though, that at the beginning of his analysis, drowsiness had been a frequent characteristic of this patient, and I was able then, by reinterpreting previous material, to realize that marriage unconsciously meant for him transforming his wife into a servant and a prostitute, as he felt his father had done with his mother.

His intense guilt, not yet definitely overcome, prevented him from accepting a situation that had for him the profound significance of damaging his mother's image. In this case, however, his resistance was placed on me through the projective identification process and, owing to my counter-identification reaction, I actually experienced his drowsiness, which in turn inhibited my interpretations and the progress of his analysis.

This reaction of mine—which resulted from very personal characteristics of the patient—is, in fact, a solid argument to show that my attitude was, in this particular case, a direct and specific consequence of his projective identification.

I then interpreted the whole situation and made him conscious of his resistance, which I had been able to perceive through my own sensations.

The patient then confessed that at times, during the sessions, he had had the phantasy that I had fallen asleep; instead, however, of considering this as a disturbing fact, he felt that he should respect my sleep, because I had already done too much for him. This showed that he had set up a limit, beyond which he neither wanted nor dared to progress, owing to his unconscious guilt. His reparative attitude of letting me rest and deliver myself from the servitude to which he felt he was submitting me, just as he wished to do with his mother, was also evident. On another level, it also meant that he had pushed into me his own drowsiness to avoid seeing the primal scene, because of his envy and his unconscious phantasies.

(iv) The following episode with a patient who during a certain period of her analysis presented hypochondriacal material referred to certain bodily sensations, was reported to me by Marie Langer. During a session, after a prolonged silence, the analyst felt, at a given moment, a sudden need to move. On the basis of this sensation, she pointed out that the patient was becoming rigid. The latter, however, answered that on the contrary she felt very relaxed, and then asked the analyst why she had said this. The analyst explained to the patient her countertransferential sensation; then the patient did confess that her right leg had actually become rigid, but that she had not said so before because she considered it as something independent of herself. It was evident that the patient had unconsciously perceived her projective identification, owing to the strange and foreign character attributed to the symptom: it no longer belonged to her; it was outside her, because she had placed it in the analyst who had incorporated it through counter-identification.

I should like to add now some further considerations regarding several facts presented by Hanna Segal in her paper 'Depression in the Schizophrenic' (7), which, in my opinion, are closely related with the process I have called 'projective counter-identification'. These facts refer, especially, to the projection of the patient's depressive anxieties into the object (analyst) by means of projective identification, and to the specific response aroused in the analyst as a result of such identification, as it should appear from some expressions used by Segal. Let us examine some phrases extracted from her paper: '. . . Then one day as she was dancing round the room, picking some imaginary things from the carpet and making movements as though she was scattering something round the room, *it struck me* that she must have been imagining that she was dancing in a meadow, picking flowers and scattering them, and it occurred to me that she was behaving exactly like an actress playing the part of Shakespeare's Ophelia. The likeness to Ophelia was all the more remarkable in that, in some peculiar way, the more gaily and irresponsibly she was behaving, *the sadder was the effect, as though her gaiety itself was designed to produce sadness in her audience,* just as Ophelia's pseudo-gay dancing and singing is designed to make the audience in the theatre sad.' [My italics.]

'Projective counter-identification' was successfully dealt with by Segal by integrating it in an adequate interpretation of her patient's attitude. She pointed out to her that she (the patient) had put into her (the analyst) all her depression and guilt, thereby transforming her into the sad part of herself and, at the same time, into a persecutor, since she felt that the analyst was trying to push her unwanted sadness back into her.

In some cases, projective counter-identification may become a positive element in the analysis, since it clarifies to the analyst some of the patient's contents and attitudes determined by projective identification, and makes possible certain interpretations, whose emergence could not be otherwise explained.

When I read lately Bion's paper on 'Language and the Schizophrenic' (1) I found my own ideas confirmed in certain interpretations given to a patient; in view of this, I think it may be interesting to transcribe here a paragraph of Bion's paper. 'The patient had been lying on the couch, silent, for some twenty minutes. During this time I had become aware of a growing sense of anxiety and tension which I associated with facts about the patient which were already known to me from work done with him in the six months he had already been with me. As the silence continued *I became aware* of a fear that the

patient was meditating a physical attack upon me, though I could see no outward change in his posture. As the tension grew I felt increasingly sure that this was so. Then, and only then, I said to him, "You have been pushing into my inside your fear that you will murder me." There was no change in the patient's position, but I noticed that he clenched his fists till the skin over the knuckles became white. The silence was unbroken. At the same time I felt that the tension in the room, presumably in the relationship between him and me, had decreased, I said to him, "When I spoke to you, you took your fear that you would murder me back into yourself; you are now feeling afraid you will make a murderous attack upon me." I followed the same method throughout the session, waiting for impressions to pile up until I felt I was in a position to make my interpretation. *It will be noted that my interpretation depends on the use of Melanie Klein's theory of projective identification, first to illuminate my countertransference, and then to frame the interpretation which I give the patient.*' [My italics.]

I am not quite sure whether, in this last assertion, Bion considers the process in the same way as I have approached it in these pages, and as shown in the examples I have given.

I do not know, on the other hand, to what extent Bion would agree in denominating 'projective counter-identification' his countertransference illuminated by the patient's projective identification which gave place to his interpretations. In any case, I feel sure that we coincide a great deal in our appreciation of this type of phenomenon.

SUMMARY

This paper deals with the disturbance in technique arising from the excessive interplay of projective identification and what is termed 'projective counteridentifications'. The latter came about specifically, on some occasions, as the result of an excessive projective identification, which is not consciously perceived by the analyst, who, in consequence, finds himself 'led' into it. The analyst then behaves as if he had *really and correctly* acquired, by assimilating them, the aspects that were projected on to him. The various considerations are supported by relevant clinical examples.

REFERENCES

(1) Bion, W. R. 'Language and the Schizophrenic.' In: *New Directions in Psycho-Analysis,* ed. Klein *et al.* (London: Tavistock, 1955.)

(2) Fliess, R. (1942). 'Metapsychology of the Analyst.' *Psychoanal. Quart.,* 11.

(3) Grinberg, L. (1958). 'Aspectos mágicos en la transferencia y en la contratransferencia: Identificación y contraidentificación proyectivas.' *Rev. de Psicoanál.,* 15.

(4) ———— (1957). 'Perturbaciones en la interpretación por la contraidentificación proyectivas. *Rev. de Psicoanál.,* 14.

(5) Klein, M. (1946). 'Notes on Some Schizoid Mechanisms.' *Int. J. Psycho-Anal.,* 27.

(6) ————'On Identification'. In: *New Directions in Psycho-Analysis* (see (1)).

(7) Segal, H. (1956). 'Depression in the Schizophrenic.' *Int. J. Psycho-Anal.,* 37.

17

COUNTERTRANSFERENCE

Otto F. Kernberg

EDITOR'S NOTE

This paper offers a valuable résumé and discussion of the distinction between the classical conception of countertransference and the totalistic one. Where the former emphasizes the pathological dimension, the latter is all-embracing. Kernberg himself adopts the totalistic conception, though he incorporates into his theory the valuable aspects of both positions.

The heart of this paper, however, is its consideration of countertransferences evoked by patients who severely regress in the course of analysis. Kernberg defines the potential sources of danger that derive from this regression, the nature of the safeguards available to the analyst in preventing an uncontrolled countertransference-based response and parallel regression in himself, and the detrimental consequences to the patient of the vicious circles so created. The paper is also notable for Kernberg's attempts at exploring specific genetic factors in the analyst's countertransferences. He offers too a discussion of concern as a noncountertransference-based trait that serves the analyst in the mastery of his countertransferences and thus in his work with the patient. This paper is one of the earliest in a series of extensive investigations by this writer of the analytic relationship and interaction in the treatment of patients with borderline and narcissistic syndromes (see Kernberg 1975).

The Concept of Countertransference

Two contrasting approaches in regard to the concept of countertransference could be described. Let us call the first approach the "classical" one, and define its concept of countertransference as the unconscious reaction of the psychoanalyst to the patient's transference. This approach stays close to the use of the term as first proposed by Freud (8) and

Reprinted from *Journal of the American Psychoanalytic Association* 13: 38–56 by permission of International Universities Press, Inc. Copyright © 1965 by American Psychoanalytic Association.

to his recommendation that the analyst overcome his countertransference (9). This approach also tends to view neurotic conflicts of the analyst as the main origin of the countertransference.

Let us call the second approach the "totalistic" one; here countertransference is viewed as the total emotional reaction of the psychoanalyst to the patient in the treatment situation. This school of thought believes that the analyst's conscious and unconscious reactions to the patient in the treatment situation are reactions to the patient's reality as well as to his transference, and also to the analyst's own reality needs as well as to his neurotic needs. This second approach also implies that these emotional reactions of the analyst are intimately fused, and that although countertransference should certainly be resolved, it is useful in gaining more understanding of the patient. In short, this approach uses a broader definition of countertransference and advocates a more active technical use of it. Some radical proponents of this approach disciuss, under certain circumstances, the effect of the countertransference with the patients as part of the analytic work.

Reich (32, 33), Glover (15), Fliess (6), and to some extent Gitelson (14), are the main exponents of the "classical" approach. Among the main exponents of the "totalistic" approach are Cohen (2), Fromm-Reichmann (11), Heimann (16), Racker (31), Weigert (43), Winnicott (45, 46) and to some extent Thompson (41). Little's (23, 24) definition of countertransference is closer to the "classical" approach, but her use of it is closer to the "radical" wing of the "totalistic" approach. She has been the most important proponent of the use of countertransference as material to be communicated to the patient. Menninger (26) and Orr (29) occupy an intermediate position.

The classical approach's main criticism of the totalistic approach is that the broadening of the term countertransference to include all emotional phenomena in the therapist is confusing and makes the term countertransference lose all specific meaning. The classical approach implies that the broadening of the concept of countertransference tends to exaggerate the importance of the analyst's emotional reaction, with a detrimental shift away from the position of neutrality in which the analyst should ideally remain. Adherents of the classical approach also point out the danger of an excessive intervention of the analyst's personality when his emotional reaction is put so much in the foreground. On the other hand, Reich (33) points out that adherents of the totalistic approach tend to do the classical position injustice when stating that the analyst's neutrality implies detached coolness and lack of humanity on the part of the analyst. Freud (10) states quite clearly that neutrality does not mean loss of spontaneity and of the natural warmth of the analyst, and that "listless indifference" on the analyst's part may in itself bring about resistances in the patient.

The totalistic orientations' main criticisms of the classical approach are the following: (i) The restricted definition of countertransference tends to obscure its importance by the implication that countertransference is something basically "wrong." Thus, this criticism continues, a phobic attitude of the analyst toward his emotional reaction is fostered, limiting his understanding of the analytic situation. (ii) The fusion of influences of the patient's transference and his reality on the one hand and of the therapist's past and present reality on the other gives much important information about the nonverbal communication between patient and analyst, which tends to get lost when the efforts center on eliminating the analyst's emotional reaction rather than focusing on it and on its sources. When the analyst feels that his emotional reaction is an important technical instrument for understanding and helping the patient, the analyst feels freer to face his positive and negative emotions evoked in the transference situation, has less need to block these reactions, and can utilize them for his analytic work. (iii) An important group of patients—those presenting severe character disorders and those with borderline and psychotic levels of organization who nonetheless seem able to benefit from analytically oriented psychotherapy—tend, by their intense, premature, and rapidly fluctuating transference, to evoke intensive countertransference reactions in the therapist which may at times give the most meaningful understanding of what is central in the patient's chaotic expression (19).

I want to develop further some of the positions of the totalistic approach. Not only in the patient's transference but also his reality (both in the analytic situation and in his extra-analytic life) may elicit strong emotional reactions in the analyst which are actually quite justified. Winnicott (45) points out that there exists an "objective countertransference," that is, natural reactions of the analyst to rather extreme manifestations of the patient's behavior toward him. Also, as Fromm-Reichmann (11) mentions, there are aspects of the therapist's reaction to the patient which are determined by the therapist's special professional nature since he does not work in a vacuum but represents a professional standard, status, and group. These are reality aspects of the therapist in his work with any patient.

Racker (30) refers to what he calls "indirect countertransference," that is, the therapist's emotional reaction to third persons somehow involved in the treatment program. Tower (42) analyzes the influences of the analyst's own training analyst in his therapeutic dealings.

Gitelson (14) also considers all these reality aspects as part of countertransference reactions, but different in type from what he calls the "transference reactions" of the analyst. He states that transference reactions of the analyst are his "total" reactions to the patient's personality which tend to appear especially at the beginning of treatment and may even disqualify the analyst from continuing his work with that patient. Countertransference reactions, in contrast, Gitelson continues, are of a partial type, fluctuating, changing according to the nature of the material that the patient presents. Yet, as Cohen (2) points out, these "total" reactions to the patient's personality are present during the whole course of the analysis and not at all limited to the initial period, and implicitly cannot be differentiated from countertransference reactions in Gitelson's terms. Heimann (18) formulates a critique similar to Cohen's. Thompson (41) states that the boundary between the analyst's normal reaction to the patient and his reaction based on his own problems is difficult to evaluate.

A totalistic concept of countertransference does justice to the conception of the analytic situation as an interaction process in which past and present of both participants, as well as their mutual reactions to their past and present, fuse into a unique emotional position involving both of them. Sullivan (39, 40) makes this concept of interpersonal interaction process a cornerstone of his theories; Menninger (26) specifically underlines it in its connection with countertransference.

Most examples of countertransference in the literature refer to emotional reactions of the analyst which usually are conscious, with the unconscious aspects appearing as transitory "blind spots" in the therapist which he later overcomes by bringing his emotional reaction out into the open. One might say, of course, that only the initial, unconscious "blind spot" is countertransference, but this would not do justice to the fact that very often the problem for the therapist is not so much to find out one aspect of his feeling of which he might not have been aware but rather how to deal with the very strong emotions which he experiences and which influence the treatment. Menninger (26) states that "the manifestations of the countertransference may be conscious although the intrapsychic conditions resulting in its appearance may be unconscious." This has relevance for the management of countertransference, in that it implies the possibility of the analyst's understanding of the function of his countertransference reaction in the concrete analytic interaction, although the part of its origin stemming from his own past may remain concealed from him. Although the analyst may not be able to discover the past roots of a certain countertransference position, he may still become aware not only of the intensity and meaning of his emotional reaction but also to what extent this reaction is determined by the reality of both patient and analyst, and thus delimit the participation of the analyst's own past.

Reich (32, 33) separates "permanent countertransference" reactions from "acute countertransference" reactions, referring to the former as due to character disorder of the analyst, and the latter as determined by the different transference manifestations of the patient. She feels that permanent countertransference reactions are more difficult to deal with and ideally would require more analysis of the analyst. Yet, even countertransference reactions which reflect predominantly unresolved character problems of the therapist are intimately connected with the analytic interaction with the patient. Through the mechanism of emphatic regression in the analyst, certain conflicts of the patient may reactivate similar conflicts of the analyst's past; this regression may also reactivate previously abandoned, old character defenses of the analyst. Also, when strong negative countertransference reactions extend over a long period of time, whatever their origin, the analyst may revert to former neurotic patterns in his interaction with a particular patient which had been given up in his contact with other patients and in his life outside the analytic hours. The analyst, so to speak, becomes his worst in his relationship with a certain patient. Operating with a restricted concept of countertransference, it is tempting to write the whole reaction off as a character problem of the analyst and not consider sufficiently the specific way in which the patient provokes this reaction in the analyst.

One can describe a continuum of countertransference reactions ranging from that related to the symptomatic neuroses on one extreme to psychotic reactions at the other, a continuum in which the different reality and transference components of both patient and therapist vary in a significant way. As we proceed from the "neurotic pole" of the continuum toward the "psychotic pole," transference manifestations become increasingly predominant in the patient's contribution to the countertransference reaction of the therapist, displacing the importance of those countertransference aspects which arise from the therapist's past. When dealing with borderline or severely regressed patients, as contrasted to those presenting symptomatic neuroses and many character disorders, the therapist tends to experience rather soon in the treatment intensive emotional reactions having more to do with the patient's premature, intense and chaotic transference, and with the therapist's capacity to withstand psychological stress and anxiety, than with any particular, specific problem of the therapist's past. In other words, given reasonably well-adjusted therapists, all hypothetically dealing with the same severely regressed and disorganized patient, their countertransference reactions will be somewhat similar, reflecting the patient's problems much more than any specific problem of the analyst's past. Little (23) states that the more disintegrated the patient the greater is the need for the analyst to be well integrated, and that with psychotic patients, countertransference may have to do the whole of the work, with the underlying mechanism probably being identification with the patient's id. Will's (44) observations point in the same direction.

Thus, countertransference becomes an important diagnostic tool, giving information on the degree of regression in the patient and the predominant emotional attitude of the patient toward the therapist and the changes occurring in this attitude. The more intense and premature the therapist's emotional reaction to the patient, the more threatening it becomes to the therapist's neutrality, and the more it has a quickly changing, fluctuating, and chaotic nature—the more we can think the therapist is in the presence of severe regression in the patient. At the other extreme of the continuum, working with patients suffering from symptomatic neuroses and not too severe character disorders, such intensive emotional reactions of the therapist occur only temporarily, after a "build-up" over a period of time (generally past the initial period of treatment), and are of a much less threatening nature in so far as the stability and neutrality of the analyst are concerned.

REGRESSION AND IDENTIFICATION
IN THE COUNTERTRANSFERENCE

Fliess (5) states that the analyst's attitude is based on empathy, which in turn depends on a "transient trial identification" with the patient. Spitz (38) states that this process of trial identification may be considered a form of regression in the service of the ego. In a later article, Fliess (6) describes the transient trial identification when a major degree of regression in the countertransference occurs. Such regression motivates what Fliess calls "counteridentification" in the analyst, that is, an excessive and more permanent identification with the patient, involving a duplication in the analyst of some constituent identification of the patient. Counteridentification, he says, interferes permanently and severely with the analyst's work. Reich (33) elaborates on Fliess's concept, and states that countertransference is exactly what is implied in the failure of the transient trial identification and in the appearance of "counteridentification." She says that one consequence of this failure is the return of impulses following the Talion

principle, the analyst now tending to return love for love and hate for hate, or to "get stuck" in an identification which gives him narcissistic gratification.

What Fliess considers a constituent identification in the therapist and a duplication of the equivalent constituent identification of the patient is related to what Erikson (3, 4) might call an early identity of the ego, that is, a precipitate of identifications involving very early object relationships. The danger of "getting stuck" in such a "constituent identification" has to do with the fact that it involves a repressed or dissociated early identity containing painful or traumatic interpersonal experiences that the ego could not integrate at the time when these early identifications occurred. This dissociated early ego identity also contains the derivatives of pregenital aggressive impulses, the identifications involved being of a very hostile nature because of the activation, projection, and reintrojection of these aggressive impulses in early interactions. Finally, this ego identity also involves archaic defensive operations of the ego, among which the mechanism of projective identification as described by Klein (20, 21), Heimann (17), and Rosenfeld (34, 35) seems to me to be of special interest.

I suggest in Chapter 1 projective identification may be considered an early form of the mechanism of projection. In terms of structural aspects of the ego, projective identification differs from projection in that the impulse projected onto an external object does not appear as something alien and distant from the ego because the connection of the self with that projected impulse still continues, and thus the self "empathizes" with the object. The anxiety which provoked the projection of the impulse onto an object in the first place now becomes fear of that object, accompanied by the need to control the object in order to prevent it from attacking the self when under the influence of that impulse. A consequence or parallel development of the operation of the mechanism of projective identification is the blurring of the limits between the self and the object (a loss of ego boundaries), since part of the projected impulse is still recognized within the ego, and thus self and object fuse in a rather chaotic way.

When very early conflictual object relationships become manifest in the transference, as frequently is the case in severe character disorders and more disorganized patients, the therapist is involved in a process of empathic regression in order to continue his emotional contact with the patient. At some point of regression, the therapist's own early identifications may become reactivated, together with the mechanism of projective identification. The therapist is now faced by several dangers from within: (1) the reappearance of anxiety connected with early impulses, especially those of an aggressive nature which now are directed toward the patient; (ii) a certain loss of his ego boundaries in the interaction with that particular patient; and (iii) the strong temptation to control his patient in consonance with an identification of him with an object of the analyst's own past.

Fliess and Reich point out the dangers of such developments in the countertransference. Yet, the emotional experience of the analyst at that point can also be useful. It may provide information of the kind of fear the patient is undergoing at that time and of the fantasies connected with it, because this process in the analyst has come about by "duplicating" a process in the patient. Also, when the therapist is able to face the awareness of his own aggressive impulses without feeling too threatened by them, this may provide the basis for a most helpful transmission of emotional security to the patient.

Fortunately, there are important compensatory mechanisms operating in the analyst. Some aspects of his ego remain intact, while others are involved in the empathic regression to the patient where projective identifications occur as part of the activation of a "constituent identification" in him. What remains functioning at a mature level in the analyst is the main part of his ego, including his advanced ego identity and the adaptive and cognitive structures connected with it. Projective identification involves loss of ego boundaries in the analyst only in the sector of his interaction with the patient, and in compensation special stress is exerted on his more advanced ego functions which normally keep the ego boundaries well delimited.

Even with severely regressed patients, the therapist may have lost his "analytic objectivity" during the hour, but after leaving the sessions or a few hours later slowly regains his equilibrium. A process of working through occurs in the therapist by which the stable, adaptive and cognitive structures formed around his later and more mature ego identity act, one might say, in a supportive way toward the part of his ego in which primitive identifications, defense mechanisms, and impulses have been activated and where ego boundaries have become fluid. When this process fails, the analyst gradually loses his capacity to "snap out" of the countertransference position created by a certain patient. Over a period of days or weeks or months, the analyst finds himself more and more involved in a permanent emotional distortion in regard to that patient. Some symptoms of this "fixed" countertransference position are, other than those general symptoms of countertransference reaction as mentioned in the literature (2, 15, 24, 26, 46), the development of suspiciousness in connection with that particular patient, even paranoid fantasies about unexpected attacks from him and the form that these might take; a broadening of the inner reaction to that particular patient so that other people are involved in emotional reactions of the therapist which have to do with the relationship with that particular patient; and finally, the development of a kind of "microparanoid" reaction in the analyst. What has happened is that the working through within the analyst's ego has failed, mainly because the patient has successfully managed to destroy the more stable and mature ego identity of the analyst in their relationship, and the analyst is duplicating the patient's emotional position, without ego control.

We have to keep in mind that the analyst experiences a regression in the service of the ego, in order to keep in touch with the patient, and not as a reaction to the onslaught of the patient's behavior. The very tolerance and neutrality toward the patient, which is part of the analyst's efforts to keep in emotional touch with him, may reinforce the danger of the analyst's being unprotected in facing the inappropriate, especially aggressive behavior of borderline patients. In fact, some analysts especially interested in working with severely regressed patients unwillingly become the passive victims of the patient's behavior because so much of the analyst's efforts are absorbed by the struggle with his inner emotional reactions triggered off by that patient.

Ego identity depends on the continuity and confirmation of the self concept, and this holds true also for the analyst in his relationship with any patient. In the particular interaction with a patient who threatens the analyst both by inducing an important countertransference regression and by his behavior, this confirmation does not take place. The analyst's identity is continuously undermined and finally the very forces—the structures of his mature ego identity—which otherwise would compensate for his regression in the service of the ego are no longer available. From a practical point of view, this consideration underlines the importance of some external structure as part of the analytic work with severely regressed patients, a certain limit to what the patients can do and will be permitted to do, a limit to which the analyst must then firmly and unwaiveringly adhere, direct indications to the patient that certain behavior is not permitted in the hour, increased structure through hospitalization, or other adjunctive treatment devices.

Racker (31) further develops the utilization of countertransference reactions of the analyst to obtain information about the inner emotional constellation of the patient, classifying the identifications that take place in the countertransference reaction in two types: "concordant identification" and "complementary identification." "Concordant identification," according to Racker, is an identification of the analyst with the corresponding part of the patient's psychic apparatus: ego with ego, superego with superego. Under the influence of concordant identification, the analyst experiences in himself the central emotion that the patient is experiencing at the same time, and, Racker states, one might consider empathy as a direct expression of concordant identification.

"Complementary identification" (a concept first expressed by Helene Deutsch) refers to the identification of the analyst with the transference objects of the patient. In that position, the analyst experiences the emotion that the patient is putting into his transference object, while the patient himself is experiencing the emotion which he had experienced in the past in his interaction with that particular parental image. For instance, the analyst may identify with a superego function connected with a stern, prohibitive father image, feeling critical and tempted to control the patient in some particular way, while the patient may be experiencing fear, submission, or rebelliousness connected with his relationship to his father. Racker states that the analyst fluctuates between these two kinds of countertransference identifications.

It is precisely at the level of regression in which projective identification in the analyst occurs where the maximal development of complementary identification takes place. And, as stated, while the analyst is struggling with the upsurge of primitive impulses in himself and the tendency to control the patient as part of his efforts to control these impulses, he also thus reproduces the early relationship with a significant parental image of the patient. Thus a highly meaningful and specific situation is brought about which, when understood and worked through, may provide a cornerstone of the analytic work with that particular patient. Under these circumstances, the analyst may bring about fundamental changes in the ego structure of the patient through the corrective experience implied in the analytic situation. In contrast, the greatest danger confronting the analytic situation at this point is the threat of a traumatic repetition of the early frustrating childhood experience of the patient in the analytic situation. What the analyst does when he becomes unable to "snap out" of his countertransference bind is to re-establish the vicious circle of the patient's interaction with the parental image.

SOME CHRONIC COUNTERTRANSFERENCE FIXATIONS

The reappearance of the previous neurotic character structure of the analyst, which had been generally abandoned but which becomes reactivated strongly in his dealings with a particular patient, has already been mentioned. Its reappearance frequently acquires a peculiar form, so that the analyst's particular pathology becomes molded in the therapeutic interaction and resembles the patient's own personality structure or complements it in such a way that the patient and therapist seem "prematched" to each other. This kind of chronic countertransference bind is, of course, very harmful to both participants. What happens in these circumstances is that the neurotic character defenses of the analyst are his safest defense against rather primitive anxieties that tend to emerge in his countertransference, and the peculiar complementary character formation that he establishes with the patient is the product of the mutual influence of projective identification in both of them.

With borderline and psychotic reactions, or at times of very deep regression in all kinds of patients in analytic treatment, conflicts around pregenital aggression have been found to occupy a central position (12, 13, 20, 22, 24, 36, 46). Throughout the literature, the examples of the most serious countertransference disturbances and difficulties in handling it are those involving this kind of severe, archaic aggression in the patient, expressed typically by the therapist's emotional reaction to the patients who always seem to have to bite the hand that feeds them. Wherever one stands in regard to the controversy about whether there exists a death instinct or whether aggression is secondary to frustration, there is sufficient evidence that there is a strong predisposition in the psychic apparatus to turn aggression against the self. Aggression and aggression against the self are fused in the patient's efforts to destroy the analyst's capacity to help him, and both elements are also present in the analyst's emotional response to this situation.

In very simple terms, the experience of giving something good and receiving something bad in return, and the impossibility of correcting such experience through the usual means of dealing with reality, is a dramatic part of the analyst's work. It resembles that other basic experience in which building up of what Erikson calls "basic trust" fails, or what Melanie Klein calls the "securing of the good inner object" fails. It is as if in his relationship with that particular patient, the analyst would have to lose confidence in the forces that could neutralize aggression; this in turn reactivates the analyst's masochism. Money-Kyrle (28) points out how the patient's aggression feeds into the superego functions of the analyst, provoking in him paranoid fears or depressive guilt.

In dealing with borderline personality organization, dedicated therapists of all levels of experience may live through phases of almost masochistic submission to some of the patient's aggression, disproportionate doubts in their own capacity, and exaggerated fears of criticisms by third parties. During these phases, the analyst comes to identify himself with the patient's aggression, paranoid projection, and guilt. Secondary defenses against this emotional position of the analyst, especially his characterological defenses, may obscure this basic situation.

The reappearance of the old neurotic character structure of the analyst in a peculiar complementary integration with the patient's characterological pathology is one form this chronic countertransference bind may take. One other frequent secondary defense is narcissistic withdrawal or detachment of the therapist from the patient, so that empathy is also lost and the possibility of continuing an analytic approach with that patient is threatened. There are cases which are discontinued, emotionally speaking, quite some time before an unsuccessful termination actually occurs. One other defensive solution, perhaps more pathological than the one mentioned, is the narcissistic withdrawal of the analyst from reality, with the appearance of unrealistic certainty of being able to help this patient (one might say, the reappearance of archaic omnipotence). The therapist now tends to establish himself in a kind of island with such a particular patient, helps the patient to deflect his aggression from the analyst to external objects, and absorbs some of this aggression in masochistic submission to the patient, rationalized as "total dedication," which also provides some narcissistic gratification. After a period of time this latter defensive operation tends to break down, frequently in a rather abrupt way, after which the symptomatology of the patient reappears and simultaneously treatment often comes to an end. Such a "Messianic spirit" is quite different from authentic

concern for the patient, because mature concern has to include reality.

Narcissistic withdrawal from the patient in the form of passive indifference or inner abandonment by the therapist, and narcissistic withdrawal from external reality in a complementary relationship with that patient, are potential dangers particularly in analysts whose narcissism has not been sufficiently worked through in their own analysis. Such analysts fall back more easily on their narcissistic character defenses; this happens not only because of the defensive return to old character patterns, but also because these character defenses themselves are so often directed against pregenital conflicts involving early aggression. Countertransference regression is especially threatening in these cases.

THE IMPORTANCE OF CONCERN AS A GENERAL TRAIT OF THE ANALYST

One important force active in neutralizing and overcoming the effect of aggression and self-aggression in the countertransference is the capacity of the analyst to experience concern. Concern in this context involves awareness of the serious nature of destructive and self-destructive impulses in the patient, the potential development of such impulses in the analyst, and the awareness by the analyst of the limitation necessarily inherent in his therapeutic efforts with his patient. Concern also involves the authentic wish and a need to help the patient in spite of his transitory "badness." On a more abstract level, one might say that concern involves the recognition of the seriousness of destructiveness and self-destructiveness of human beings in general and the hope, but not the certainty, that the fight against these tendencies may be successful in individual cases. In an analysis of the importance of hope as a basic human tendency, Menninger (27) describes hope as the manifestation of the life instinct against the forces of destructiveness and self-destructiveness. Money-Kyrle (28) says that concern for the patient's welfare stems from the combination of reparative drives in the analyst counteracting his early destructive tendencies, and from his parental identifications. Frank (7), in a different context, stresses the importance of the therapist's faith in himself and his technique as a prerequisite for therapeutic success. One might, in addition, describe concern also negatively, saying that it does not mean an abandonment of the analytic position, of the analyst's neutrality;

concern for the patient cannot mean abandonment of reality either.

Psychoanalysts of different orientations would describe different genetic and dynamic conditions underlying the capacity for concern. Winnicott (47) suggests that concern stems from modulated and restricted guilt feelings. He suggests that the child's successful working through of repeated cycles of aggression, guilt, and reparation makes this development possible. Whatever its origin, the manifestations of the analyst's capacity for concern may be described in connection with the immediate reality of the treatment situation of any particular patient. In concrete terms, concern implies ongoing self-criticism by the analyst, unwillingness to accept impossible situations in a passive way, and a continuous search for new ways of handling a prolonged crisis. It implies active involvement of the therapist as opposed to narcissistic withdrawal, and realization of the ongoing need of consultation with and help from one's colleagues. The last point is important: willingness to review a certain case with a consultant or colleague, as contrasted with secrecy about one's work, is a good indication of concern.

There are professional pressures on the analyst tending to restrict his capacity to accept his limitations and his efforts to overcome them. During his analytic training, the candidate has to struggle with the temptation to use his patients narcissistically because their treatment may be a requisite for his graduation: the wish to keep a "good" patient and to get rid of a "bad" patient may represent a countertransference reaction strongly influenced by the candidate's wishes or fear in connection with the fulfillment of his requirements. Benedek (1) further describes some of the countertransference complications arising in the analyst within the setting of a psychoanalytic society. Pressures which act on the analyst when he is part of a complex treatment setting also influence his countertransference and may limit, realistically or in his fantasy, his inner freedom to deal with difficult treatment situations. Savage (37) mentions this point in connection with psychoanalytically oriented therapy of schizophrenic patients in a hospital setting. Main (25) conducted an illustrative research involving the study of countertransference reactions occurring in a hospital setting.

Not all difficulties or crises in treatment, however, involve countertransference binds. The therapist's lack of experience or of technical or theoretical knowledge has to be differentiated from his counter-transference reaction. This is not easy because these two factors influence each other.

The analyst's insight into the meaning of his countertransference reaction does not itself help the patient. What helps the patient is the analyst's using this information in his transference interpretations; the analyst's taking the necessary steps to protect himself and his patient from treatment situations which might realistically be impossible to handle; and the analyst's providing the patient, through their relationship, evidence of the analyst's willingness and capability to accompany the patient into his past without losing the sight of the present.

SUMMARY

Contrasting views of countertransference and its clinical use are outlined. It is suggested that countertransference may be helpful in evaluating the degree of regression in the patient and in clarifying the transference paradigms in borderline personality organization.

Patients with the potential for severe regression in analysis or expressive psychotherapy tend to foster serious countertransference complications, especially "counteridentification."

It is suggested that countertransference complications in the form of "counteridentification" are related to the partial reactivation of early ego identifications and early defensive mechanisms in the analyst. While these counteridentifications may be the source of important information about the analytic situation, they are also a serious threat to the analysis, and predispose the analyst to the development of "chronic countertransference fixation."

The following signs of chronic countertransference fixation are described: reappearance of abandoned neurotic character traits of the analyst in his interactions with a particular patient; "emotional discontinuation" of the analysis; unrealistic "total dedication"; "micro-paranoid" attitudes toward the patient. These countertransference complications present themselves especially in the treatment of patients with a potential for severe regression, particularly in borderline personality organization.

The importance of "concern" as a general trait of the analyst, helpful in protecting him from the countertransference complications mentioned, is described. Some of the characteristics, preconditions, and realistic limitations of the development of concern are mentioned.

BIBLIOGRAPHY

1. Benedek, T. Countertransference in the training analyst. *Bull. Menninger Clin.*, 18:12–16, 1954.
2. Cohen, M. B. Countertransference and anxiety. *Psychiatry*, 15:231–243, 1952.
3. Erikson, E. H. Growth and crises of the healthy personality (1950). In: *Identity and the Life Cycle* [*Psychological Issues*, 1:50–100]. New York: International Universities Press, 1959.
4. Erikson, E. H. The problem of ego identity. *J. Am. Psychoanal. Assoc.*, 4:56–121, 1956.
5. Fliess, R. The metapsychology of the analyst. *Psychoanal. Quart.*, 11:211–227, 1942.
6. Fliess, R. Countertransferences and counteridentification. *J. Am. Psychoanal. Assoc.*, 1:268–284, 1953.
7. Frank, J. D. The dynamics of the psychotherapeutic relationship. *Psychiatry*, 22:17–39, 1959.
8. Freud, S. The future prospects of psycho-analytic therapy (1910). *Standard Edition*, 11:139–151. London Hogarth Press, 1957.
9. Freud, S. Recommendations for physicians on the psycho-analytic method of treatment (1912). *Standard Edition*, 12:109–120. London: Hogarth Press, 1958.
10. Freud, S. *Psychoanalysis and Faith: The Letters of Sigmund Freud and Oskar Pfister*, ed. H. Meng & E. L. Freud. New York: Basic Books, 1963, p. 113.
11. Fromm-Reichmann, F. *Principles of Intensive Psychotherapy*. Chicago: University of Chicago Press, 1950.
12. Fromm-Reichmann, F. Some aspects of psychoanalytic psychotherapy with schizophrenics. In: *Psychotherapy with Schizophrenics*, ed. E. B. Brody & F. C. Redlich. New York: International Universities Press, 1952.
13. Fromm-Reichmann, F. Basic problems in the psychotherapy of schizophrenia. *Psychiatry*, 21:1–6, 1958.
14. Gitelson, M. The emotional position of the analyst in the psycho-analytic situation. *Int. J. Psychoanal.*, 33:1–10, 1952.
15. Glover, E. *The Technique of Psycho-Analysis*. New York: International Universities Press, 1955.
16. Heimann, P. On counter-transference. *Int. J. Psychoanal.*, 31:81–84, 1950.
17. Heimann, P. A combination of defence mechanisms in paranoid states. In: *New Directions in Psycho-Analysis*, ed. M. Klein, P. Heimann, & R. E. Money-Kyrle. London: Tavistock Publications, 1955, pp. 240–265.
18. Heimann, P. Countertransference. *Brit. J. Med. Psychol.*, 33:9–15, 1960.
19. Kernberg, O. Manejo de la contratransferencia en la escuela analitica de Washington. Presented to the Chilean Society of Psychoanalysis, December, 1960.
20. Klein, M. Notes on some schizoid mechanisms. *Int. J. Psychoanal.*, 27:99–110, 1946.
21. Klein, M. On identification. In: *New Directions in Psycho-Analysis*, ed, M. Klein, P. Heimann, & R. E. Money-Kyrle. London: Tavistock Publications, 1955, pp. 309–345.
22. Lidz, R. W. & Lidz, T. Therapeutic considerations arising from the intense symbiotic needs of schizophrenic patients. In: *Psychotherapy with Schizophrenics*, ed. E. B. Brody & F. C. Redlich. New York: International Universities Press, 1952.
23. Little, M. Countertransference and the patient's response to it. *Int. J. Psychoanal.*, 32:32–40, 1951.
24. Little, M. Countertransference. *Brit. J. Med. Psychol.*, 33:29–31, 1960.
25. Main, T. F. The ailment. *Brit. J. Med. Psychol.*, 30:129–145, 1957.
26. Menninger, K. A. *Theory of Psychoanalytic Technique*. New York: Basic Books, 1958.
27. Menninger, K. A. Hope. *Amer. J. Psychiat.*, 116:481–491, 1959.
28. Money-Kyrle, R. E. Normal countertransference and some of its deviations. *Int. J. Psychoanal.*, 37:360–366, 1956.
29. Orr, D. W. Transference and countertransference: a historical survey. *J. Am. Psychoanal. Assoc.*, 2:621–670, 1954.
30. Racker, H. A contribution to the problem of countertransference. *Int. J. Psychoanal.*, 34:313–324, 1953.
31. Racker, H. The meaning and uses of countertransference. *Psychoanal. Quart.*, 26:303–357, 1957.
32. Reich, A. On countertransference. *Int. J. Psychoanal.*, 32:25–31, 1951.
33. Reich, A. Further remarks on countertransference. *Int. J. Psychoanal.*, 41:389–395, 1960.
34. Rosenfeld, H. Remarks on the relation of male homosexuality to paranoia, paranoid anxiety and narcissism. *Int. J. Psychoanal.*, 30:36–47, 1949.
35. Rosenfeld, H. Transference-phenomena and transference-analysis in an acute catatonic schizophrenic patient. *Int. J. Psychoanal.*, 33:457–464, 1952.
36. Rosenfeld, H. Notes on the psychoanalysis of the super-ego conflict in an acute schizophrenic patient. In: *New Directions in Psycho-Analysis*, ed. M. Klein, P. Heimann, & R. E. Money-Kyrle. London: Tavistock Publications, 1955, pp. 180–219.
37. Savage, C. Countertransference in the therapy of schizophrenics. *Psychiatry*, 24:53–60, 1961.
38. Spitz, R. A. Countertransference: comments on its varying role in the analytic situation. *J. Am. Psychoanal. Assoc.*, 4:256–265, 1956.
39. Sullivan, H. S. *Conceptions of Modern Psychiatry*. New York: Norton, 1953.
40. Sullivan, H. S. *The Interpersonal Theory of Psychiatry*. New York: Norton, 1953.
41. Thompson, C. M. Countertransference. *Samiksa*, 6:205–211, 1952.

42. Tower, L. E. Countertransference. *J. Am. Psychoanal. Assoc.,* 4:224-255, 1956.

43. Weigert, E. Contribution to the problem of terminating psychoanalyses. *Psychoanal. Quart.,* 21:465-480, 1952.

44. Will, O. A. Human relatedness and the schizophrenic reaction. *Psychiatry,* 22:205-223, 1959.

45. Winnicott, D. W. Hate in the countertransference. *Int. J. Psychoanal.,* 30:69-75, 1949.

46. Winnicott, D. W. Countertransference. *Brit. J. Med. Psychol.,* 33:17-21, 1960.

47. Winnicott, D. W. The development of the capacity for concern. *Bull. Menninger Clin.,* 27:167-176, 1963.

18

THE ADAPTATIONAL-INTERACTIONAL DIMENSION OF COUNTERTRANSFERENCE

ROBERT LANGS

EDITOR'S NOTE

In this paper I investigate countertransference in the light of specific adaptive sequences occurring within the therapeutic or analytic bipersonal field. By shifting from the more usual broad consideration of countertransference to a minute investigation of its interactional manifestations and functions, this contribution is able to document the interrelatedness of the experiences of both participants: it unmistakably indicates that no aspect of these happenings can be considered meaningfully in isolation, thereby rendering interactional considerations of countertransference a necessity. To that end are presented investigations of countertransference-based expressions not only in regard to the analyst's interpretations on the cognitive level, but in respect as well to the areas of (1) containing, metabolizing, and interpreting the patient's projective identifications and (2) management of the ground rules or framework. The latter proves to be an extremely common area for countertransference-based expression. The influence of countertransference on the analyst's holding and containing capacities is detailed here for the first time. There is also an investigation of the effects of the patient, the ground rules, and the setting—their qualities of stability and holding—on the analyst and his countertransferences. This contribution succeeds, I think, in embedding the concept of countertransference in the totality of the therapeutic interaction.

It is the basic purpose of this paper to outline, discuss, and synthesize a series of clinical postulates regarding countertransference, developed through an adaptational approach to this dimension of therapeutic and analytic relationships. These postulates are based on clinical observations and an extensive review of the psychoanalytic literature (Langs 1976a,c), and were shaped with a view toward enhancing our understanding of the treatment interaction and with some stress on their pertinence to

analytic and therapeutic technique.[1] The present investigation of countertransference is somewhat different than the prior explorations I have undertaken (1974, 1976a,c), in that I shall focus here almost exclusively on the interactional aspects of countertransference and shall concentrate on recent conceptions developed largely since those earlier publications—some of which have not previously been considered at all, either by myself or by others. I shall adopt an approach that concentrates on the delineation, elaboration, and clinical illustration of these postulates and, while the ideas presented here have been contributed to significantly by earlier writers, I will not provide an historical survey since I

* Reprinted from *Technique in Transition*, by Robert Langs, pp. 501–536. New York: Jason Aronson, 1978. This paper has appeared also in *Contemporary Psychoanalysis* 14:502–533 (1978).

have done so in an earlier work (1976c). Without further introduction, then, I shall turn now to the basic definitions that we will need in order to define and comprehend the interactional dimension of countertransference.

BASIC DEFINITIONS

I shall proceed in outline form, offering only the essentials (the interested reader may find the elaborating literature in Langs 1973a,b, 1974, 1975a,b,c, 1976a,c, 1978a,b).

1. *The bipersonal field* (Baranger and Baranger 1966, Langs 1976a,c) refers to the temporal-physical space within which the analytic interaction takes place. The patient is one term of the polarity; the analyst is the other. The field embodies both interactional and intrapsychic mechanisms, and every event within the field receives vectors from both participants. The field itself is defined by a framework—the ground rules of psychoanalysis—which not only delimits the field, but also, in a major way, contributes to the communicative properties of the field and to the analyst's hold of the patient and containment of his projective identifications.

Communications within the field take place along an interface determined by inputs from both patient and analyst, and possessing a variety of characteristics, including, among others, psychopathology, depth, and stability. The major interactional mechanisms in the field are those of projective and introjective identification, although other interactional defenses, such as denial, splitting, the creation of bastions (split-off sectors of the field; see Baranger and Baranger 1966), and additional unconsciously shared forms of gratification and defense are also characteristic. The major intrapsychic defenses are those of repression, displacement, and the other well-known classically described mechanisms.

2. The investigation of the communicative medium provided by the frame of the field and the communicative mode of each participant is essential for an understanding of the analytic interaction and therapeutic work. The basic communications from each participant occur verbally and nonverbally, through words and actions serving a variety of meanings and functions. As a fundamental means of categorizing these communications, they can be classified as manifest content and as Type One and Type Two derivatives (Langs 1978a,b). The first term refers to the surface nature and meaning of a communication, while a Type One derivative constitutes a relatively available inference or latent theme extracted from the manifest content. In contrast, a Type Two derivative is organized around a specific *adaptive context*—the precipitant or instigator of the interactional and intrapsychic response—and entails definitive dynamic meanings and functions relevant to that context. Further, within a given bipersonal field, every communication is viewed as an interactional product, with inputs from both participants.

3. On this basis, we may identify three basic styles of communicating and three related forms of interactional field (Langs 1978a). The Type A style or field is characterized by the use of symbolic communications, and the bipersonal field itself becomes the realm of illusion and a transitional or play space. In general, the patient's associations can be organized around a seris of specific adaptive contexts, yielding a series of indirect communications that constitute Type Two derivatives. These latent contents and themes fall into the realm of unconscious fantasy, memory, and introject on the one hand, and unconscious perception on the other. For the development of a Type A field, both patient and analyst must be capable of tolerating and maintaining a secure framework; in addition, the analyst must have the ability to offer symbolic interpretations of the patient's communications.

The Type B field or style is one in which action, discharge, and the riddance of accretions of psychic disturbance is central. The primary mechanism in this field is that of projective identification and living (acting) out, and both language and behavior are utilized as means of discharge rather than as vehicles for symbolic understanding.

While the Type A and Type B fields are positively communicative, each in its own way, the essential characteristic of the Type C field is the destruction of communication and meaning, and the use of falsifications and impervious barriers as the main interactional mode. Here, language is used as a defense against disturbed inner mental contents. The Type C field is static and empty, and is further characterized by the projective identification of both emptiness and nonmeaning, finding its only sense of meaning in these efforts to destroy communication, links, and meaning itself. While resistances in the Type A field are characterized by the availability of analyzable derivatives, and those in the Type B field are amenable to interpretation based on the defensive use of projective identification, defenses and resistances in the Type C field have no sense of depth and possess a persistent, amorphous, and empty quality.

4. Within the bipersonal field the patient's

relationship with the analyst has both transference and nontransference components. The former are essentially distorted and based on pathological, intrapsychic unconscious fantasies, memories, and introjects, while the latter are essentially nondistorted and based on valid unconscious perceptions and introjections of the analyst, his conscious and unconscious psychic state and communications, and his mode of interacting. Within the transference sphere, in addition to distortions based on displacements from past figures (genetic transferences), there are additional distortions based on the patient's current intrapsychic state and use of interactional mechanisms (projective distortions). Further, nontransference, while valid in terms of the prevailing actualities of the therapeutic interaction, always includes important genetic components—though essentially in the form of the actual repetition of past pathogenic interactions (for details, see Langs 1976c).

The analyst's relationship with the patient is similarly constituted in terms of countertransference and noncountertransference. The former entails all inappropriate and distorted reactions to the patient, whatever their source, and may be based on displacements from the past as well as on pathological projective and introjective mechanisms. Factors in countertransference-based responses range from the nature of a particular patient, the quality and contents of his communications, the meaning of analytic work for the analyst, and interactions with outside parties—other patients and others in the analyst's nonprofessional and professional life.

The noncountertransference sphere of the analyst's functioning entails his valid capacity to manage the framework, to understand the patient's symbolic communications and offer meaningful interpretations, and a basic ability to contain, metabolize, and interpret symbolically the patient's projective identifications. There are a wide range of additional aspects of the analyst's valid and noncountertransference-based functioning which will not be detailed here (see Langs 1976c).

INTERACTIONAL POSTULATES REGARDING COUNTERTRANSFERENCE

Postulate 1: As a dimension of the bipersonal field, countertransference (as well as noncountertransference) is an interactional product with vectors from both patient and analyst.

Among the many implications of this generally accepted postulate, some of which have not been specifically identified and discussed in the literature, I will consider those most pertinent to psychoanalytic technique and to the identification and resolution of specific countertransference difficulties. In this context, it is well to be reminded that countertransference-based interventions and behaviors are often not recognized as such by the analyst, due largely to the fact that countertransference is itself rooted in unconscious fantasies, memories, introjects, and interactional mechanisms. The adaptive-interactional approach to countertransference greatly facilitates their recognition and resolution.

This initial postulate implies that each countertransference-based response from the analyst has a specific and potentially identifiable adaptive context. While this stimulus may reside in the personal life of the analyst or in his work with another patient, it most often entails stimuli from the relationship with the patient at hand and is, as a rule, evoked by the communications from that patient. Any unusual feeling or fantasy within the analyst, any failure by the patient to confirm his interventions (whether interpretations or management of the framework), any unusual or persistent symptom or resistance in the patient, or any regressive episode in the course of an analysis should alert the analyst to the possible presence of countertransference factors.

The interactional approach proves to be of special value in these pursuits in three important ways: (1) by establishing the finding that the patient's communications and symptoms may be significantly derived from the countertransferences of the analyst; (2) by indicating that through the process of introjective identification the patient becomes a mirror and container for the analyst, in the sense that the patient's communications will play back to the analyst the metabolized introjects derived from his countertransference-based interventions (and his valid, noncountertransference-based interventions as well); and (3) by directing the search for the form and meaning of countertransferences to the sequential interaction of each session.

If we consider these sequential clues first, we may recognize that the immediate precipitant for a countertransference-based reaction can be found in the material from the patient that precedes the erroneous intervention (inappropriate silences, incorrect verbalizations such as erroneous interpretations, and mismanagements of the framework). While there is often a broader context to the countertransference-based intervention in the ongoing relationship between the analyst and his patient, and while there may be, as I have noted, additional inputs derived from relationships outside of the immediate bipersonal field, clinical experience indicates that these immediate adaptive contexts provide extremely important organizing threads for the detection and comprehension of the underlying countertransference fantasies. When dealing with a countertransference-based positive intervention (as compared to silence, which I would consider a negative intervention), it is, of course, the last of the patient's associations that prompts the analyst's response. If this communication is viewed within the overall context of the patient's material, and understood in terms of manifest and latent content, and if all of this is addressed in interaction with the manifest and latent content of the analyst's erroneous intervention, the amalgam provides important and immediate clues as to the nature of the analyst's underlying difficulty.

Thus, the interactional sequence for a countertransference-based response is (1) adaptive context (especially the stimulus from the patient at hand), (2) the analyst's erroneous reaction (positive or negative intervention, whether interpretation or management of the frame), and (3) response by the patient and continued reaction by the analyst. If countertransferences are to be understood in depth, they must be organized around their specific adaptive contexts, so the analyst may understand himself in terms of Type Two derivatives, including both unconscious fantasies and perceptions. Without such an effort, he would be restricted to an awareness of the manifest content of his erroneous intervention or to readily available inferences—both fraught with possible further countertransference-based effects.

This sequence also implies that the analyst may recognize the presence of a countertransference difficulty at one of several junctures—as the patient is communicating disturbing material, while he is intervening, or after he has intervened—and that this recognition may be based either on his own subjective reactions or on subsequent communications from the patient. Much has already been written regarding subjective clues within the analyst who has a countertransference problem, while less consideration has been given to those leads available from the patient; let us now examine these latter more carefully.

The bipersonal field concept directs the analyst to the investigation of his countertransferences when any resistance, defense, symptom, or regression occurs within the patient or himself. Since the adaptational-interactional view considers all such occurrences as interactional products, it generates as a technical requisite the investigation of unconscious factors in both participants at such moments in therapy. As a rule, these disturbances, when they occur within the patient (to take that as our focus), will have unconscious communicative meaning. In the presence of a prevailing countertransference-based communication from the analyst, they will reflect the patient's introjective identification of this disturbance, his unconscious perceptions of its underlying basis, and his own realistic and fantasied metabolism of the introject. The patient's reactions to the disturbed intervention from the analyst may include exploitation, the creation of misalliances and bastions, and use of the intervention for the maintenance of his own neurosis (a term used here in its broadest sense), as well as unconscious efforts to detoxify the introject and cure the analyst.

In terms of the patient's associations and behaviors following an incorrect intervention, the interactional model directs us to the intervention itself as the adaptive context for the patient's subsequent association. In this way, the patient's material can, as a rule, be treated as Type Two derivatives in response to the particular adaptive context. I term these associations *commentaries* on the analyst's intervention, in that they contain both unconscious perceptions and unconscious fantasies.

It is here that we may identify a particular hierarchy of tasks for the analyst, based in part on the recognition that this discussion implies that the patient's associations always take place along a *me/not-me interface* (Langs 1976c, 1978a) with continuous references to self and analyst. Thus, valid technique calls for the monitoring of the material from the patient for conscious and unconscious communications related to the analyst before establishing those related to the patient; actually, the one cannot be identified without an understanding of the other. In addition, in both spheres—self and analyst—the analyst must determine the patient's valid perceptions, thoughts, and fantasies before identifying those that are distorted and inappropriate; here too, the identification of one relies on a comprehension of the other. Ultimately, of course, these determinations have as their most essential basis the analyst's self-knowledge, and especially his in-depth understanding of the conscious and unconscious meanings of his communications to the patient.

In the adaptive context, then, of the analyst's interventions, the patient's responsive associations are an amalgam of unconscious perceptions of the manifest and latent qualities of the intervention, on the one hand, and, on the other, their subsequent elaboration in terms of the patient's valid and distorted functioning. Thus, in addition to determining whether such associations truly validate the analyst's intervention by providing genuinely new material that reorganizes previously known clinical data (i.e., constitutes a *selected fact*, as Bion, 1962, has termed it) and evidence for positive introjective identification, the analyst must also consider this material in terms of the patient's experience and introjection of his communication—valid and invalid. This introjective process takes place on the cognitive level as well as in terms of interactional mechanisms. The analyst must therefore be prepared to recognize that both cognitive-symbolic communications and projective identifications are contained in his interventions; in fact, he must be prepared to recognize his use of interventions as facades, clichés, falsifications, and barriers as well (see below).

This interactional approach enables the analyst to make full use of his patient's conscious and unconscious resources, and of the analysand as an unconscious teacher and therapist. The analytic bipersonal field is not, of course, designed primarily for such a use of the patient, but these occurrences are inevitable in every analysis, since countertransferences can never be totally eliminated. In addition, in actuality, these experiences often have enormously therapeutic benefit for the patient (see Searles 1975), so long as the analyst has not deliberately misused the analysand in this regard, and is in addition capable of understanding and responding appropriately to the patient's curative efforts. In this respect, it is essential that the analyst make silent and unobtrusive use of his patient's introjection of his countertransferences and of his additional therapeutic efforts on his behalf, responding without explicit acknowledgment and with implicit benefit. This latter implies the analyst's ability to follow the patient's leads and benefits through efforts at self-analysis based on the patient's unconscious perceptions and therapeutic endeavors; it also requires a capacity to actually rectify—correct or modify—any continued expression of the countertransference difficulty and to control all, if not most, subsequent possible expressions. In addition, it may entail the analyst's *implicit* acknowledgment of an error in technique and a full analysis of the patient's unconscious perceptions and other responses in terms that accept their validity—work that must in addition address itself eventually to the patient's subsequent distortions, and to the pathological misappropriations and responses to these countertransference-based difficulties within the analyst.

Postulate 2: The analyst's unconscious countertransference fantasies and interactional mechanisms will influence his three major functions vis-à-vis the patient: his management of the framework and capacity to hold the patient; his ability to contain and metabolize projective identifications; and his functioning as the interpreter of the patient's symbolic associations, projective identifications, and efforts to destroy meaning. A complementary postulate would state that the analyst's countertransferences can be aroused by, and understood in terms of, not only the patient's associations and behaviors, but also in terms of the analyst's responses to the framework of the bipersonal field, and to the holding and containing capacities of the patient.

While some analysts, such as Reich (1960) and Greenson (1972), have questioned the invariable relationship between technical errors and countertransference, my own clinical observations clearly support such a thesis. However, virtually the entire classical psychoanalytic literature prior to my own writings (see especially 1975b,c, 1976a,c, 1978a) considered as the sole vehicle of countertransference expression the analyst's erroneous verbal interventions, especially his errors in interpreting. A number of Kleinian writers, especially Grinberg (1962) and Bion (1962, 1963, 1965, 1970) have also investigated countertransference influences on the analyst's management of projective identifications and on his containing functions. A full conceptualization of possible avenues of countertransference expression would include all these areas, as well as the analyst's management of the ground rules and his capacity to hold the patient.

As we have already seen in the discussion of the first postulate, the adaptational-interactional view helps to deepen and render more specific our understanding of the interplay between countertransference and the analyst's interpretive interventions. Not unexpectedly, it leads us to include missed interventions and inappropriate silences among the expressions of countertransference, and provides us extensive means for identifying, rectifying, and interpreting the patient's responses to these errors. Much of this has been discussed above, tends to be familiar territory for most analysts, and has been considered rather extensively in prior publications (see especially Langs 1976a,c); I will therefore restrict myself here to a consideration of those aspects of this postulate that have been relatively disregarded.

Perhaps the single most neglected arena for the expression of the analyst's countertransferences is that of his management of the ground rules—the framework of the bipersonal field. In part, because virtually every analyst has to this day been analyzed within a bipersonal field whose framework has been modified, the influence of countertransferences on the analyst's management functions has been virtually ignored by all. Nonetheless, I have garnered extensive evidence for the basic and necessary functions of a secure framework (Langs, 1975c, 1976a, 1978a), demonstrating its importance in creating a therapeutic hold for the patient, in establishing the necessary boundaries between patient and analyst, and in affording the bipersonal field its essential open and symbolic communicative qualities.

However, the maintenance of a secure framework requires of the analyst a tolerance for his patient's therapeutic regression and related primitive communications, a renunciation of his pathological and countertransference-based needs for inappropriate gratification and defenses, and a capacity to tolerate his own limited regression and experiences of anxiety, which are inevitable under these conditions. Thus, because the management of the frame is so sensitively a function of the analyst's capacity to manage his own inner state, and to maintain his psychic balance, his handling of the framework is in part a direct reflection of the extent to which he has mastered his countertransferences. Further, because of the collective blind spots in this area and the sanction so implied, analysts will tend to monitor their verbal interventions for countertransference-based influences, while neglecting to do so in regard to their management of the frame. Clearly, any alteration in the framework can provide the analyst countertransference-based and inappropriate gratifications, as well as defenses and nonadaptive relief from anxiety and other symptoms; all possible deviations in the frame should therefore be explored for such factors (see Langs, 1975c).

Interactionally, one of the analyst's basic functions is to receive, contain, metabolize, and interpret the patient's projective identifications (interactional projections) and other interactional inputs. Due to underlying countertransferences, an analyst may be refractory to such containment and impervious to both the patient's communications and his interactional efforts. Much of this is based on what Bion (1962, 1970) has described as the container's dread of the contained, and which he has characterized as fears of denudation and destruction. An analyst may indeed dread the effects on himself of the patient's communications and projective identifications, and may respond on a countertransference basis with nonlistening, with distancing or breaking the link with the patient (Bion 1959), or by undertaking active efforts to modify the patient's disturbing communications and projections—often through the use of irrelevant questions, distinctly erroneous interpretations, and sudden alterations in the framework.

A second form of countertransference-based disturbance in the analyst's containing function may occur in regard to the processing or metabolizing of the patient's projective identifications (see Langs 1976b). Grinberg (1962) has termed this *projective counteridentification*: a situation in which the analyst receives a projective identification, remains unconscious of its contents, meanings and effects, and inappropriately and unconsciously reprojects the pathological contents back into the patient—either directly or in some modified but not detoxified form. Bion (1962) has termed this containing function the capacity for *reverie,* and has stressed the importance of the detoxification of dreaded and pathological projective identifications, leading to reprojections back into the patient that are far more benign than the original projective identifications. In my terms, this detoxification process entails the appropriate *metabolism* of a projective identification, the awareness in the analyst of its conscious and unconscious implications, and the symbolic interpretation of these contents in terms of defense-resistance functions and the revelation of pathological introjects. In this regard, countertransference-related anxieties, introjects, and disruptive fantasies may disturb the metabolizing and detoxifying process within the analyst, and may render him incapable of becoming aware of the nature of the patient's projective identifications and unable to interpret them. Under these conditions, he will, as a rule, pathologically metabolize the introject in terms of his own inner disturbance, and reproject into the patient—through verbal interventions and mismanagement of the framework—a more terrifying and pathological projective identification than that which originated from the analysand.

A third type of containing pathology entails what I have described as a pathological need for introjective identifications—a countertransference-based need to inappropriately and excessively contain pathological introjects (Langs 1976a,b). This tends to be expressed through provocative interventions—whether interpretive or in respect to the frame—that are unconsciously designed as intrusive projective identifications into the patient, intended to evoke responsive pathological projective identifications from the analysand. These analysts have a hunger for pathological expressions from their patients, and find many means of inappropriately disturbing their patients and generating ill-timed pathological projective identifications.

The analytic bipersonal field is designed for the cure of the patient, and for the analytic resolution, through cognitive insight and implicit positive introjective identifications, of his psychopathology. It has proved difficult for analysts to accept that a valid and secondary function of the same bipersonal field—valid only so long as it is, indeed, secondary—is that of the analytic resolution of more restricted aspects of the analyst's psychopathology. This idea is often misunderstood to imply a belief in the use of the patient and the analytic situation as a primary vehicle for the cure of the analyst. Despite explicit disavowal of such intentions, the recognition that this will inevitably be a second-order phenomenon is viewed as exploitation of the patient, rather than as a relatively silent and actually indispensable benefit that will accrue to the well-functioning analyst. In the course of overcoming the many resistances against accepting this postulate—more precisely, a clinical observation—it has become evident that this attribute is an essential component of the bipersonal field, and that it is unlikely that the analyst could function adequately in its absence. Without it, it would be virtually impossible for him to master the inevitable anxieties and disturbances that will occur within him, as interactional products, in the course of his analytic work with each patient. Their inevitable presence has not only a potential therapeutic effect on his behalf, but also renders him a far more effective analyst for his patients.

The basic framework—the ground rules—of the psychoanalytic situation provides a hold, appropriate barriers, and the necessary communicative medium for analyst as well as patient. This hold affords him a valuable and appropriate sense of safety, a means of defining his role vis-à-vis the patient, assistance in managing his inappropriate impulses and fantasies toward the patient (his countertransferences), and insures the possibility of his use of language for symbolic interpretations (it is therefore essential to his interpretive capacities).

Just as certain aspects of the analyst's behavior and stance are essential dimensions of the framework, the patient too offers a hold to the analyst. Such factors as the regularity of his attendance at sessions, his being on time, his payment of the fee, his complying with the fundamental rule of free association, his listening to and working over the analyst's interpretations, and his own adherence to the ground rules and boundaries of the analytic relationship contribute to a holding effect experienced by the analyst. Further, the patient will inevitably serve as a container for the analyst's projective identifications—both pathological and nonpathological—a function through which, once again, the analyst may implicitly benefit.

As for the influence of countertransference in these areas, these may derive from undue or pathological (instinctualized: aggressivized or sexualized) holding needs, and an unconscious fear of, or need to repudiate, the patient's hold, a dread of the patient as container, and an excessive need to utilize the patient's containing capacities. These countertransference influences are manifested through the analyst's mismanagement of the frame, his erroneous interventions, his failures to intervene, and, overall, through conscious and unconscious deviations in the analyst's central commitment to the therapeutic needs of the patient. The analyst who inordinately requires a rigid and unmodified frame will be intolerant of his patient's alterations of that frame; these may take the form of latenesses, missed sessions, necessary requests to change the time of an hour because of changed life circumstances, unnecessary requests for such changes in schedule, and a variety of gross and subtle efforts to alter the basic ground rules of analysis—such as efforts to engage the analyst in conversation after an hour.

It is my empirically derived conclusion (Langs 1975c, 1976a,c) that it is the analyst's main responsibility to maintain, to the extent feasible, the framework intact in the face of all inappropriate efforts at deviation. I am therefore in no way advocating conscious—or unconscious—participation in inappropriate modifications of the frame. I wish to stress, however, that analysts with pathological needs for a rigid frame—in contrast to the necessary rigorous frame (Sandler, in Langs et al., in press)—will have difficulty in recognizing those rare valid indications for an alteration in the framework (e.g., a suicidal emergency), a change that is in essence a revised version of the basic framework without its destruction or defective reconstitution. In addition, such an analyst will have a great deal of difficulty in dealing with his patient's efforts to modify the framework and in recognizing such endeavors as a crucial adaptive context for the organization of the analysand's subsequent material. He also will have major problems in understanding the unconscious implications of these intended or actual alterations in the frame, and in carrying out effective, relevant analytic work. Further, he will dread those interpretations to his patient that might generate moments of hostility and rejection, and which might unconsciously prompt the patient to modify in some way his usual, implicit hold of the analyst.

Those analysts for whom the patient's inevitable hold generates a threat, whether related to fears of intimacy, instinctualization of the patient's holding capacities in terms of seductive and aggressive threats, or the dread of the necessary and therapeutic regression evoked by such a hold, unconsciously will make efforts to disturb the patient's holding capacities. It seems evident that the patient derives a degree of implicit and necessary gratification in regard to his capacity to safely hold the analyst, a satisfaction that is not unlike those derived from his unconscious curative efforts on the analyst's behalf (Searles 1965, 1975, Langs 1975b, 1976a,c). Thus, the repudiation on any level of the patient's appropriate holding capacities not only generates active countertransference-based inputs into the bipersonal field, but also denies the patient a form of growth-promoting gratification that forms an important complementary means of achieving adaptive structural change, in addition to the more generally recognized means derived from affect-laden insights and inherent positive introjective identifications. It is evident too that the analyst's need to repudiate the patient's appropriate hold will prompt him to generate interventions and mismanagements of the framework designed unconsciously to disturb that holding function, create artificial and undue distance, and erect pathological and inappropriate barriers between himself and the patient.

Every analyst at some time in the course of an analytic experience, and a number of analysts in the course of much of their work with all of their patients, will be burdened by countertransference pressures that prompt the inappropriate use of the patient as what I have termed a *pathological container* for his own disturbed inner contents (Langs 1976a). At such junctures, the analyst's interventions are not primarily designed for the meaningful insight of the patient and for the appropriate maintenance of the framework, but instead unconsciously function as efforts at projective identification as a means of placing into the patient the analyst's burdensome psychopathology and inappropriate defensive needs. And while, as I have mentioned above, the patient can indeed accrue adaptive benefit from his own unconscious capacities to function as a pathological container for the analyst's projective identification and from his curative efforts on the analyst's behalf, such gains are dangerously intermixed with the destructive aspects of such interactions. These include the overburdening of the patient with the analyst's pathology to a degree that evokes a pathological regression that not only will be difficult to manage and interpret, but also may be essentially misunderstood by the analyst who has unconsciously evoked the regressive process and who maintains his

unconscious disturbed needs for the patient's containing ability. Failures by the patient to contain the analyst's pathological projective identifications, and to metabolize them, however unconsciously, toward insights for the analyst, will be unconsciously resented by the analyst, and will considerably complicate the analytic interaction. The influence on the patient of the pathological introjects generated by the analyst also may be quite destructive, and may in a major way reinforce the patient's own pathological introjects and defenses. In large measure, such an interaction may constitute the repetition of an important past pathogenic interaction which helped to generate the patient's emotional problems in his formative years.

On the other hand, the analyst may dread any even momentary and limited use of the patient as a container—not only for his pathological projective identifications, but for his valid interventions as well. Under these conditions he will experience an extreme constriction in his capacity to interpret to the patient and excessive anxiety in communicating freely to him, however consciously these interventions are founded on a wish to be appropriately helpful. Often, the dread of containing the patient's projective identifications is based on conscious and unconscious fears of being driven crazy by the patient, and related fears of psychic disintegration or loss of control; fears of similar effects on the patient may inhibit the analyst's necessary projective communications to the analysand.

Postulate 3: Countertransferences have a significant influence on the communicative properties of the bipersonal field, and on both the analyst's and the patient's style of communicating.

It is evident that the communicative style of the analyst (and of the bipersonal field of which he is a part) is a function of a wide range of factors, the most immediately obvious being inborn tendencies; acute and cumulative genetic experiences; personality and character structure; ego resources; ego dysfunctions; intrapsychic conflicts; unconscious fantasies, memories, and introjects; and the overall extent of emotional health or psychopathology. The focus here on the influence of countertransference is, then, an attempt to delineate simply one vector among many that coalesce to effect a particular communicative style and field.

Initial clinical evidence suggests that the ideal analyst basically employs the Type A mode of communication, with its essential symbolic qualities, and that he has a capacity to manage the framework of the analytic situation in order to create with the patient a potential field for a Type A communicative interaction. Such an analyst would undoubtedly, from time to time, and based on many factors, momentarily shift to the Type B, action-discharge mode of communication and to the Type C, barrier-negation mode. He would, however, through his own awareness and through communications from his patient, be capable of recognizing these shifts in communicative style, of self-analyzing their underlying basis, of rectifying their influence on the patient and the therapeutic bipersonal field, and of interpreting to the patient his conscious and unconscious perceptions of this communicative shift and its unconscious meanings and functions.

In contrast to the Type A therapist, the Type B therapist experiences repeated difficulty in deriving symbolic formulations of his patient's associations and in generating symbolic interpretations. While his conscious intentions may well be to offer such interventions—there is considerable lack of insight within analysts in regard to their communicative mode—his use of language will be unconsciously aimed at projective identification into the patient and internal relief-producing discharge. While at times patients may undoubtedly derive some type of symptom relief from such therapeutic interactions—based primarily on relatively benign projective identifications from the analyst and on positive self-feelings derived from unconscious curative efforts and containing responses to his pathology—such gains are not embedded in valid cognitive insights and modulating, positive introjective identifications. As a result, they are quite vulnerable to regression and are without the necessary substantial foundation characteristic of lasting adaptive structural change. In addition to their use of verbal interventions that function interactionally as pathological projective identifications, these analysts are quite prone to unneeded modifications of the framework which similarly serve their needs for pathological projective identification, action, and discharge. Elsewhere (Langs 1976a,c) I have designated as *misalliance and framework cures* the noninsightful, unstable symptom relief, in either patient or analyst, that may be derived in a Type B communicative field.

The analyst who is prone to a Type C communicative style will seldom be capable of a truly symbolic interpretation. His verbal interventions make use of language not primarily as communication, but as a form of noncommunication and as an effort to destroy meaning. These analysts make extensive use of the psychoanalytic cliché and, unconsciously, their interventions and mismanagements of the framework are designed to destroy the communicative qualities of the bipersonal field and to render it frozen and static. Based on the massive defensive barriers and falsifications offered by these analysts, patients will from time to time experience symptom relief through reinforcement of their own Type C communicative style or through the development of impermeable defensive barriers that momentarily serve as a protection against disruptive underlying contents—fantasies, memories, and introjects. This type of *misalliance cure* (Langs 1975b, 1976a,c) may well account for a large percentage of symptom relief among present-day psychotherapeutic and psychoanalytic patients, and within their therapists and analysts as well.

The Type A therapist will, of course, tend to be rather comfortable with a Type A patient, and will be capable of interpreting his communications. Countertransference-based anxieties may occur because of the regressive pressures that he experiences in a Type A field and, in addition, will arise when the communications from the Type A patient touch upon areas of continued vulnerability. With a Type B patient, he will be capable of containing, metabolizing, and interpreting his patient's projective identifications, though countertransference difficulties may intrude when these projective identifications are massive or touch upon areas of excessive sensitivity. Some Type A analysts experience discomfort with the action-prone, projectively identifying Type B patient, and will experience difficulties in containing, metabolizing, and interpreting their interactional projections.

A Type C patient may be quite boring to the Type A analyst, who will consciously and unconsciously experience the envy, destruction of meaning, and attack on the analyst's ability to think and formulate that is characteristic of these patients. The Type A analyst may be vulnerable to these qualities of the negative projective identifications of these patients, and he may also have difficulty in tolerating their use of massive, impenetrable, and uninterpretable defensive barriers. Still, he is in the best position to identify the qualities of a Type C communicative style and to patiently interpret the primary defensive aspects. In addition, he is best prepared to tolerate, contain, and interpret the underlying psychotic core of these patients.

While clinical evidence indicates that it is possible to conduct a successful analysis with a Type B or Type C patient (Langs 1978a), it appears likely that the reverse is not true: Type B and Type C analysts cannot be expected to generate bipersonal fields characterized by an openness of communication, the use of symbolic language, the rendering of symbolic interpretations that lead to cognitive insight and mastery, and the interactional experience of positive projective and introjective identifications—all culminating in adaptive structural change and growth for the patient. While, as I have noted above, Type B and Type C analysts may indeed afford their patients periods of symptom relief, and while these may on occasion structuralize and lead to the disappearance of symptoms, the underlying basis for these symptomatic changes are infused with pathological mechanisms and are quite vulnerable to regressive pressures. There can be no substitute for a personal analysis and for the self-analytic efforts designed to master a given analyst's propensities for the Type B and Type C communicative modes.

In concluding this delineation of interactional postulates related to countertransference, two points implicit to this discussion deserve to be specified. First, in virtually every countertransference-based intervention there is a nucleus of constructive intention and effect. While in general, this kernel of valid effort is by no means sufficient to compensate for the hurt and damage done by a countertransference-based intervention—effects that may range from the relatively modifiable to the quite permanent—this positive nucleus often can be used as the center of constructive therapeutic work during the therapeutic interludes evoked by the consequences of an unconscious countertransference fantasy or introject. Second, it follows from this observation, and from more general clinical impressions, that considerable insightful analytic work can prevail throughout the rectification-analysis phase of such countertransference-dominated interludes. Thus, we must maintain a balanced view of the effects of the analyst's countertransferences: to some degree, they damage the patient and reinforce his neurosis (a term I again use here in its broadest sense), and thereby perpetuate or even intensify his psychopathology; in addition, however, so long as the countertransference-based effects are recognized, rectified, and fully analyzed with the patient—and of course, subjected to self-analysis by the analyst— these experiences also can provide extremely moving, insightful, positive introjective moments for both patient and analyst.

CLINICAL VIGNETTE

I will now present a single condensed clinical vignette as a means of illustrating these postulates. Because of my commitment to total confidentiality regarding my direct work with patients, this material will be drawn from a supervisory seminar. While this approach is somewhat limiting in the area of countertransference, the interested reader will find additional data in several recent and pending publications (Langs 1976a,b, 1978a); most important, he should have ample opportunity to clinically document these postulates in his own therapeutic endeavors.

Mr. A. was married, in his mid-thirties, depressed, and afraid of growing old and dying. Early in his analysis, during sessions in which his analyst took notes and intervened largely in terms of questions and reflections of the patient's anxiety about initiating treatment, the patient seemed concerned with a certain deadness in the analytic situation: it was, he said, like talking into a tape recorder. He spoke a great deal of tennis, of the homosexual discussions of his closest male friend, and of his fears of divorce, despite feelings that his marriage was killing him. His wife, he said, often loses control and acts crazy; she is overdependent on him. He also expressed wishes that he could invent a machine that could do psychoanalysis. He spoke of friends who fared poorly in analysis, and the analyst suggested that the patient had doubts about his own treatment. The patient disagreed, but said, however, that he wanted it to be quiet and peaceful, like smoking pot. He was not afraid of talking about homosexuals, though he felt that a physician who worked for him had many such fears.

In the next session, he reported a dream in which he found himself in bed with two women. Earlier that day, he had lingered at his tennis club after one of the members had died of a heart attack or sudden stroke. Mr. A. had fantasies of dropping dead on the tennis court, but spoke instead of feeling quite alive and interested in some medically related research in which he and a male friend were engaged.

The analyst asked the patient how he felt in the dream and inquired about other details. The twosome reminded the patient of a harem and of how he often thinks of other women during intercourse with his wife. He thought of a madam in a movie who had been destructive toward the girls who worked for her, and added that he never understood women and feared them. Further questions along these lines by the analyst led to additional allusions to discussions with friends about homosexuality and to curiosity about what was going on in the analyst's mind. When he plays tennis, the patient said, he thinks of nothing—his mind is blank. The analyst pointed out that the patient seemed frightened of his thoughts concerning homosexuality, but that having two women at one time could hardly be called "homosexual."

In response, Mr. A. wondered why he comes to analysis at all. When his friends told him that homosexuals hate women, he panicked; these women were his slaves. He spoke of his hatred for his mother and of his close relationship with a research physician, and wondered what he saw in him; he was always involved with other men; it would be awful to be homosexual.

In the next hour, Mr. A. reported a dream of being late for his session. He was standing outside his analyst's office. The analyst came out to move his car and everybody started to laugh. His tire hit a rock, which then hit a taxicab and disabled it. A black woman got out of the cab and called the analyst crazy; he then pushed the cab around because it couldn't go. In associating, the patient alluded to the previous session and how analysis was a dangerous field because the wrong people can influence you. He feels constricted in what he says while on the couch. The dream followed tennis. He can't be close with anyone; he fights with his wife; everything he does brings him unhappiness.

The analyst asked a series of questions related to the manifest dream, and the patient spoke of how his friends and father think that he is crazy for coming to analysis, though in the dream people are calling the analyst crazy. His father accuses him of trying new things and dropping them. After some rumination, the patient spoke of feeling constricted in the sessions and of possible envy of the analyst; he had to arrange his life in keeping with the analyst's schedule. The analyst responded that the patient skips out in the dream, but the patient rejoined that it was the analyst who had been late—not he. He said he recognized that he is not the analyst's only patient and that the analyst's life doesn't center around him, as is true for himself in relation to the analyst. If he missed an appointment, he mused, would the analyst lie down? That would be reversing their roles and would make the analyst the crazy one. The analyst responded that the patient seemed afraid of being laughed at, and the patient agreed, suggesting again that the whole thing was a big reversal. The analyst emphasized again that the dream reflected the patient's fears of being laughed at, criticized, and going crazy.

The patient was late for the next session and spoke of a friend who had become a college professor; the patient felt guilty that he had not taken the right path for his own life. There were further references to being crazy, to being in analysis, and to the static qualities of his marriage. The research center at which the patient had done his postgraduate work was probably going to close because it could not get enough funds or students. Many of the staff had died, and the patient spoke of a fear of cancer that he had felt since beginning his analysis. He had had gastrointestinal symptoms; his mother was always preoccupied with gynecological problems; and at his engagement party he had suffered food poisoning. When the father had had his recent surgery, the patient had experienced an intense fear of dying. His father was seldom available when Mr. A. was a child and would never play tennis with him. Mr. A. recalled several accidents in his childhood, and spoke considerably of his father's disinterest, coldness, and lack of care; if he had been different, the patient would have realized his potential far more than he had. His mother, on the other hand, would get hysterical to the point that no one could talk to her; she was only concerned when he was hurt.

At this point, the analyst suggested that the patient write a short biography of himself for the analyst. Without responding directly, the patient continued to associate: he could always make his mother cry and yet she never hated him as did his father, who held grudges.

In the next hour the patient reported that he had not written the biography; he hadn't had time. He spoke of his research physician friend who had come to Mr. A.'s office to get some downers (sleeping pills) that the patient kept on hand. This doctor was a man worried about aging, and yet Mr. A. still idealized him. He was, however, beginning to see new things and maybe this doctor friend was becoming more human. He felt at any rate that he was more honest with himself than this other man was, and Mr. A. was thinking of leaving the area. He wondered if he should get a nursemaid for his infant daughter and spoke again of his tennis club. He wished his wife would be more aggressive and wondered how women ever develop into good mothers. If he left her, he said, she'd fall apart, and all the time he spends with his men friends interferes with his love for her. So much of this had happened since he started analysis, and it came up too because he'd been talking to his physician friend about that analytic jargon about homosexuality and castration anxiety. His friend felt that analysis is actually insignificant and that one day Mr. A. would have a gnawing pain somewhere, and they'd open him up and find something that would mean that everything would soon be over. Mr. A. would sometimes think about childhood and sex, but not about his parents in that respect. He said he felt he should have read more before he came into analysis, and here the analyst noted that the patient seemed to be looking for some kind of guidelines. The patient said that analysis is like an examination, and he spoke of his secret purchase of nudist magazines. His parents never talked about sex. He had his first sexual relations quite late in life; it was a difficult experience and he had trouble getting an erection and had considered turning on with some kind of drug.

I will focus here solely on those aspects of this material that are pertinent to this discussion. The early fragments of this material are in part an unconscious response to the analyst's note-taking and questions—nonanalytic work with manifest contents. At the time this material was presented, the supervisee indicated some sense of confusion with this patient and stated that the note-taking was an effort to get a better idea about what was going on in this analysis; it was also based on a wish to discuss this case with colleagues. The patient's unconscious perceptions and experiences of the note-taking serve us well in attempting to define its unconscious implications, especially those related to the analyst's countertransferences: the analyst is not alive, but a tape recorder and analytic machine; his wife loses control and acts crazy; craziness is connected with homosexuality; his wife is excessively dependent; and there is worry about a physician who worked for the patient.

I will take this as sufficient commentary on the note-taking, and will not attempt to trace out its implications in the additional clinical material. We can therefore pause here and suggest that the note-taking did indeed serve as a significant adaptive context for the patient's associations. It is a meaningful organizer of these communications from the patient, which may be viewed as symbolic in nature and largely in terms of Type Two derivatives: disguised unconscious perceptions of, and fantasies about, the analyst. Much of this falls into the realm of unconscious perceptiveness, and conveys possibly valid unconscious fears, motives, and needs within the analyst that have prompted him to take notes— motives of which the analyst was largely unaware, if we are to take his justifications as reflecting the extent of his insight into himself. It would be difficult here to identify and establish the patient's own unconscious homosexual anxieties and fantasies, fears of losing control and going crazy, and needs for mechanical protective devices, since he can justifiably project and conceal them within the analyst's own evident similar anxieties, efforts at inappropriate gratification, and pathological defenses, expressed, however unconsciously, through the note-taking.

In terms of the postulates developed here, I also would suggest that this patient is making extensive efforts at Type A communication and toward the development of a Type A bipersonal field. The analyst, for his part, both through the alteration in the framework reflected in his note-taking and through his use of noninterpretive interventions—questions directed at the surface of the patient's associations— is utilizing a Type C mode of communication and is endeavoring to create a static, surface-oriented, falsifying communicative field. While there are, in this material, occasional efforts by the analyst at projective identification which I will soon consider, many of his interactional projections are attempts to place a sense of emptiness and void into the patient, and to develop impenetrable, clichéd defenses—the negative type of projective identification characteristic of the Type C field. The main hypothesis, then, is to the effect that the note-taking and the surface-oriented interventions are unconsciously designed by this analyst to satisfy his own needs for a Type C barrier and, actually, to destroy the patient's openness to symbolic communication—to the expression of anxiety-provoking contents that are too disturbing for this analyst.

This hypothesis is supported by the patient's material, and while under other conditions these associations might well reflect the patient's own need for a Type C field, here the data suggest that this is not at all the case: the patient seems to be making repeated efforts at Type A communication, and his allusions to Type C mechanisms appear to be based on introjective identifications with the analyst.

The patient's associations, then, support the formulation that the note-taking and questioning unconsciously reflect impairments in the analyst's capacity to safely hold the patient and to contain the patient's projective identifications. The analyst's behaviors also convey his inappropriate needs to be held by the patient and for the patient to contain his anxieties—implications to which the patient is quite sensitive. On a communicative level, these interventions reflect an unconscious effort by the analyst to modify this potential Type A field into a Type C field in which he would feel better held and safer, especially in regard to disturbing communications and projective identifications from the patient.

The very act of writing down every word from the patient, with its striking containing and incorporative qualities, reflects a dread of actually containing in an affective way the patient's projected contents and a distinct incapacity to metabolize them toward interpretation. Instead, much as the patient unconsciously perceives the therapist's interventions—in respect to the frame and verbally—the note-taking is an effort to deaden the analytic situation, to make it mechanical, and to render it static. The mention of the tape recorder, and the later reference to a psychoanalytic machine, are metaphors of the analyst's containing functions rendered inanimate, probably because of inordinate fears of the patient's projective identifications—the container's fear of the contained (Bion 1962). To state this another way, in terms of the patient's unconscious perceptions and Type Two derivative communications, the therapist fears being driven crazy by his patient and his material, and attempts a Type C mode of expression and set of defenses in a massive effort to seal off this potential craziness and to prevent the contained contents from destroying him—a formulation quite in keeping with an earlier delineation of the Type C field and its function (Langs 1978a).

Among these terrifying contents and projective identifications, those related to latent homosexual themes, uncontrolled destructiveness, and annihilation seem most prominent. While, as I pointed out earlier, the patient may well have intense anxieties in each of these areas, for the moment these formulations apply very directly to the analyst. These countertransferences and their manifestations must be rectified in actuality, and the patient's responses to them analyzed, before the latter's own disturbances could surface in derivative and analyzable form in this bipersonal field. The patient himself refers to the conditions of this field, in which the communicative interface, and the elements of psychopathology it contains, has shifted toward the analyst by referring to efforts to put himself in the analyst's shoes and the reference to role reversal. The analyst's unneeded deviations in the frame and inappropriate interventions unconsciously express his countertransferences and his wish to have the relevant contents contained by the patient and in a sense, therapeutically modified.

In this context, the analyst's intervention that the patient seemed to have many doubts about treatment may be seen as what I have termed a *psychoanalytic cliché*—a psychoanalytically derived generalization based on manifest content or Type One derivatives that primarily serves to destroy the true underlying meaning of the patient's communications, and to substitute a defensive falsification (Bion 1965, 1970, Langs 1978a). The patient's response to this intervention, in which he referred to feeling peaceful when he smoked pot, reflects again the unconscious obliterating qualities of the analyst's interventions—a characteristic of almost all the interventions described in this vignette—and suggest in addition that the patient's own propensities toward the Type C mode are being intensified in this therapeutic interaction. The patient rather wisely concludes this hour with a further allusion to the underlying homosexual anxieties unconsciously shared by both himself and the analyst.

In a general way, the analyst confirmed aspects of this formulation in indicating that he was having a difficult time understanding this patient's material and that he was feeling somewhat anxious about the patient's pathology and the initial course of this analysis. These conscious feelings and thoughts are related to the analyst's difficulty in holding this patient and in containing his projective identifications; they also suggest a countertransference difficulty related to the patient's hold of the analyst. In some way, this patient's material and reactions were not providing the analyst a sense of safety. But rather than tracing out the sources of the analyst's discomfort, he turned to note-taking as a means of artificially and mechanically (how well the patient senses this!) providing himself with a holding device and a containing substitute that will protect him from the postulated dreaded inner destruction—denudation and annihilation, as Bion (1962, 1970) terms it.

In addition, it may well be that the analyst's sense of dissatisfaction regarding the hold that he is experiencing in this analytic interaction has been intensified, rather than reduced, by his own alteration in the framework: his note-taking. Unconsciously, analysts tend to have anxieties in regard to their need to take notes, their anticipation of presenting such material to colleagues and exposing their vulnerabilities, and their use of what I have termed *framework cures* (Langs 1975c, 1976a,c) to resolve underlying countertransference problems. The note-taking itself is often distracting. The entire constellation, conscious and unconscious, actually disrupts the analyst's sense of security rather than enhancing it.

In evaluating the next hour, it would appear that in addition to continuous specific precipitants (the analyst's note-taking and erroneous interventions—questions and generalizations) there was a specific and related adaptive context in the patient's outside life: the death of a member of his tennis club. This day residue can be readily related not only to the patient's fears of death, but also to his unconscious perception of similar anxieties in the analyst—based on earlier material not presented here. However, in the actual session, these day residues were not integrated with the dream, which appears to have been a response to these precipitants; instead the analyst chose to focus on the manifest content of the dream and to its postulated role as a defense against homosexual fantasies and anxieties.

Keeping to ideas relevant to this presentation, it would appear that interventions of this kind, offered without a specific adaptive context and in terms of manifest content and Type One derivatives—the direct reading of a manifest dream and limited associations for latent content, rather than the use of an adaptive context to generate dynamically meaningful Type Two derivatives—characteristically serve to reinforce the Type C, falsified and static qualities of the bipersonal field. As this session illustrates, such interventions almost always are designed to avoid a specific adaptive context which connects on some level to the patient's relationship with the analyst, and usually they are designed to cover over the patient's unconscious perceptions of the analyst's countertransference-based interventions. This approach facilitates an emphasis on the patient's pathology, and on his unconscious fantasies rather than his unconscious perceptions, and often deals with anxieties extraneous to the analytic relationship; they are a major form of defensiveness in respect to the influence of the analyst's countertransferences on the analytic interaction, the bipersonal field in which it occurs, and the analysand.

Interventions of this type are experienced by patients in terms of an impaired sense of holding, and especially as a reflection of the analyst's refractoriness in regard to his containing functions. Here, the unconscious communication from the analyst is to the effect that death, and especially sudden death, is to be denied, rendered nonexistent, and split off into a bastion of the bipersonal field (Baranger and Baranger, 1966). A more general and widespread effort at obliteration may follow, creating a Type C field.

To some extent, these hypotheses are supported by the patient's response to the analyst's general interpretation of the patient's concerns about homosexuality and the dream of the two women as defensive in this regard. The patient rightly wonders why he comes to analysis at all, implying that if important meanings are to be destroyed in the analytic bipersonal field, effective analytic work will be impossible. There are also further indications of his doubts regarding the analyst's capacity to contain, manage the frame, and interpret, and, in respect to his stress on underlying homosexual anxieties, it might be asked whether these are primarily the analyst's concerns, and whether as such they serve as a deflection from more disturbing worries.

In the following hour, the patient had a dream that he immediately linked to the previous session. In terms of the patient's associations, it alludes to the analyst's craziness and his fear of doing damage—and by implication, of being damaged. The patient comments on the dangers of being an analyst, a point quite pertinent to the present discussion. He also describes his sense of constriction in the sessions, conveying both the extent to which the Type C mode is being imposed upon him and his unconscious perceptions of the analyst's own needs to constrict. It is then that the patient refers to his envy of the analyst and his security. On one level, this alludes to the analyst's massive defensiveness and the protection it affords him; while on another level, it is an introjective identification of the analyst's envy of the patient, who feels secure enough to communicate his unconscious fantasies, introjects, memories, and anxieties—a communicative mode that is quite difficult or perhaps even impossible for this analyst.

It is also noteworthy that when the analyst attempts to suggest that the dream reflects the patient's wish to leave analysis, the patient points out that it is the analyst who had the problem in the dream—a formulation in keeping with the assessment of this material being offered here. It is in this context that the patient implies the projection into himself by the analyst of the wish that patient become therapist in this bipersonal field—the reversal of roles. The analyst's rejoinder is to emphasize the patient's paranoid feelings and anxieties, partially, it seems, to deny his own concerns and partially to projectively identify them into the patient as well.

In the next hour, the patient was late and the analyst felt concerned about the course of the analysis. Patients frequently respond to failures in the analyst's holding, containing, and interpretive capacities with disruptions in the framework that impart to the analyst a sense of being held poorly and a related sense of disturbance.

The hour itself begins with direct and indirect allusions to having made a mistake in entering analysis. The patient then returns to the theme of death and his own fear of cancer—an image that would suggest, in the context of this discussion, both the patient's dread of containing the analyst's pathological projective identifications and the analyst's comparable fear. It is a metaphor of the container's fear of the contained, and is the reprojection of the analyst's pathological projective identification in a form that is further imbued with toxicity and destructiveness. The patient's reference to food poisoning conveys similar implications.

The interactional qualities of this material is supported by the patient's reference to his own fears, as well as those of his mother, and his allusion to his father's surgery. Unconsciously, he then reprimands the therapist for his insensitivity and distance, but sees it as an alternative to utter loss of control—hysteria.

It was at this point in the session that the analyst experienced an intense sense of disquietude and concern about the patient's pathology and asked him to write a biography. Consciously, he had been concerned about the dream of the previous hour, in which he had appeared undisguised, and while he wondered whether this was an indication of some type of countertransference difficulty, most of his thoughts related to anxieties about serious underlying pathology in the patient. The request for the biography was made by the analyst as another effort to learn more about the patient in order to understand his pathology more clearly.

Once again, we will allow the patient's response to guide us in evaluating this intervention—another alteration in the frame. First, he did not write the biography, and he soon spoke of a physician friend who asked him for some sedatives. This consciously idealized physician was now being seen as human and vulnerable, and in some sense, as dishonest with himself. Here we have a metaphor for the analyst's projective identification into the patient of his own anxieties and need for noninsightful, artificial, drug-based relief. It is the patient who is to offer a healing reprojection—the pill or the biography—to relieve the analyst of his inappropriate anxieties. The danger, as the patient put it in Type Two derivative form, is that the analyst might fall apart; the dread is of something deadly inside. Exhibitionism, voyeurism, sexual impotence, and homosexuality are all implied as related anxieties and themes.

At this point in his presentation, the analyst was able to describe some unresolved anxieties regarding death. He soon realized that the request of the patient that he write a biography was an effort to undo these anxieties by creating a permanent, indestructible record of the patient with which he—the analyst—could reassure himself. It is interesting that this patient refused to serve as a pathological container for the analyst's anxieties, at least on this level, and that he also refused to join in the sector of misalliance and in the framework cure offered by the analyst. Apparently recognizing unconsciously that the biography was an effort at artificial communication and an effort to erect a barrier to the disturbing contents that were emerging in this analysis, the patient unconsciously communicated these perceptions to the analyst and became engaged in additional unconscious efforts at cure—largely through a series of insightful unconscious interpretations related to the analyst's need to obliterate, his wish for

the patient to serve him as a nursemaid and good mother, his homosexual and bodily anxieties, and his fears of death, containing, and sexuality.

While considerably more could be said in regard to this vignette, I will conclude this discussion by suggesting that only a series of self-insightful efforts directed toward resolution of the analyst's underlying countertransference difficulties, and the actual rectification of his difficulties in holding, containing, interpreting, and creating a Type A rather than a Type C communicative field—and the full interpretation of the patient's unconscious perceptions, introjections, and reactions to these inputs by the analyst—could redirect the interface of this bipersonal field to the pathology of the patient, and provide him a Type A communicative medium and an opportunity for insightful therapeutic work.

CONCLUDING COMMENTS

I will not attempt a comprehensive discussion of these postulates regarding countertransference, nor will I endeavor to delineate further the special advantages of viewing countertransference as an interactional product of the bipersonal field. I shall conclude by simply emphasizing the importance of an adequate and full listening process, of a validating clinical methodology, and of self-knowledge in applying these concepts regarding countertransference in the clinical situation, and more broadly in the expansion of psychoanalytic knowledge.

As many other analysts have noted (Langs 1976a), transference was first seen by Freud as the major enemy and obstacle to psychoanalysis, and only later recognized as its greatest ally—a quality that is by no means full appreciated even to this day, so that the patient as the enemy and as resisting dominates the analyst's unconscious images, while the patient as ally and as curative is still far less appreciated. Similarly, with an even greater sense of dread, countertransference was first viewed as an enemy to analytic work; and while Freud never specifically acknowledged its constructive aspects, later analysts have indeed attempted to do just that. There has been a recent trend toward identifying the constructive dimensions of countertransference, and these very much deserve to be put into perspective.

However, it is well to conclude this discussion with a recognition that despite the many parallels between transference and countertransference (in their narrowest sense), there are important differences. While both are inevitable in the course of an analysis, transference manifestations are absolutely vital to the analytic work and are bound to be a major component of the patient's constructive experiences with the analyst and of his unconscious communications to him. By contrast, it is essential that countertransference expressions be kept to a reasonable minimum, that they not dominate the experiences and communications of the analyst, and that they not overfill the bipersonal field. However human such expressions are, and however meaningful their rectification and analysis with the patient may be, countertransference-based communications do traumatize the patient to some degree and these effects must be fully appreciated. It can be seen, then, that a properly balanced view of countertransference is extremely difficult to maintain. It is my hope that the present paper has enabled the reader to develop a more sensitive conception of this most difficult subject.

NOTE

1. The clinical observations and formulations to be developed in this paper are equally pertinent to psychotherapy and psychoanalysis. Since almost all the prior literature on this subject is derived from the psychoanalytic situation, I will adopt that as my model for this presentation.

REFERENCES

Baranger, M., and Baranger, W. (1966). Insight and the analytic situation. In *Psychoanalysis in the Americas*, ed. R. Litman, pp. 56–72. New York: International Universities Press.

Bion, W. (1959). Attacks on linking. *International Journal of Psycho-Analysis* 40:308–315.

———(1962). *Learning from Experience*. New York: Basic Books. Reprinted in W. Bion, *Seven Servants*. New York: Jason Aronson, 1977.

———(1963). *Elements of Psycho-Analysis*. New York: Basic Books. Reprinted in W. Bion, *Seven Servants*. New York: Jason Aronson, 1977.

———(1965). *Transformations*. New York: Basic Books. Reprinted in W. Bion, *Seven Servants*. New York: Jason Aronson, 1977.

Greenson, R. (1972). Beyond transference and interpretation. *International Journal of Psycho-Analysis* 53:213–217.

Grinberg, L. (1962). On a specific aspect of countertransference due to the patient's projective identification. *International Journal of Psycho-Analysis* 43:436–440.

Langs, R. (1973a). The patient's view of the therapist: reality or fantasy? *International Journal of Psychoanalytic Psychotherapy* 2:441–451.

———(1973b). *The Technique of Psychoanalytic Psychotherapy* Vol. 1. New York: Jason Aronson.

———(1974). *The Technique of Psychoanalytic Psychotherapy* Vol. II. New York: Jason Aronson.

———(1975b). Therapeutic misalliances. *International Journal of Psychoanalytic Psychotherapy* 4:77–105.

———(1975c). The therapeutic relationship and deviations in technique. *International Journal of Psychoanalytic Psychotherapy* 4:106–141.

———(1975a). The patient's unconscious perception of the therapist's errors. In *Tactics and Techniques in Psychoanalytic Therapy, Vol. II: Countertransference*, ed. P. Giovacchini. New York: Jason Aronson.

———(1976a). *The Bipersonal Field*. New York: Jason Aronson.

———(1976b). On becoming a psychiatrist: discussion of "Empathy and intuition in becoming a psychiatrist" by Ronald J. Blank. *International Journal of Psychoanalytic Psychotherapy* 5:255–279.

———(1976c). *The Therapeutic Interaction*. 2 vols. New York: Jason Aronson.

———(1978a). Some communicative properties of the bipersonal field. *International Journal of Psychoanalytic Psychotherapy* 7:89–161.

———(1978b). Validation and the framework of the therapeutic situation. *Contemporary Psychoanalysis* 14: 98–124.

Langs, R. et al. (in press). *Psychoanalytic Dialogues III: Some British Views on Clinical Issues*. New York: Jason Aronson.

Reich, A. (1960). Further remarks on countertransference. *International Journal of Psycho-Analysis* 41: 389–395.

Searles, H. (1965). *Collected Papers on Schizophrenia and Related Subjects*. New York: International Universities Press.

———(1975). The patient as therapist to his analyst. In *Tactics and Techniques in Psychoanalytic Therapy, Vol. II: Countertransference*, ed. P. Giovacchini. New York: Jason Aronson.

PART IV

NONCOUNTERTRANSFERENCE

The literature on the analyst's appropriate or valid functioning vis-à-vis the patient—what I call noncountertransference—is founded on two fundamental papers by Freud (1912b [see chapter 38], 1913) in which he made a series of recommendations to the practitioners of psychoanalysis. A wide variety of investigations have followed, including studies of the analyst's basic attitude and stance, his mode of listening, his management of the basic setting, and his formulation and offer of interventions. In particular, the processes of empathy and identification have received extensive scrutiny, as have the specific forms of intervention.

While the papers in this section tend to focus on the non-conflicted aspects of the analyst's functioning and are designed to heighten these capacities, they also consider to some extent the nature and basis for disturbances in this regard. Consequently, the papers in Parts III and IV, countertransference and noncountertransference, overlap significantly.

There is little sense of historical development here but instead a quality of examination and reexamination. For example, Ferenczi (1919), one of the first analysts after Freud to consider this aspect of the analyst's functioning, delineated the analyst's contradictory tasks: permitting a freedom of associations in fantasy and open responsiveness to the patient's material, and yet subjecting this material and his reactions to it to logical scrutiny and understanding. Some years later, Fliess (1942; see chapter 19) carefully examined aspects of the analyst's empathy and identification with the analysand, and as recently as 1974 (see chapter 23) Beres and Arlow returned productively to the same topic.

The reworking and clarification of noncountertransference is typified by Bion's extension of Freud's concept of the analyst's use of evenly suspended attention into the suggestion that he should enter each session without desire, memory, or understanding (Bion 1967, 1970), thereby modifying his own defensive need to rediscover what he already knows. Instead, Bion insists, he should open himself to the unknown and the nonsensual. In another vein, Sandler (1976; see chapter 24) specifically defined the therapist's need to maintain an openness to the role (and image) responses that the patient attempts to evoke in the analyst, doing so as a means of understanding object-relational efforts to re-create the pathogenic past in the actual relationship with the analyst.

These extensions of Freud's basic concepts, the latter based on Freud's own clinical writings (1914, 1920), represent some of the most insightful work in this area in recent years. My own study of the analyst's interventions resulted in a series of proposals for basic revisions in our understanding of their nature and the form they should take, and indicates the considerable potential for innovative studies of this dimension of the analytic interaction.

19

THE METAPSYCHOLOGY
OF THE ANALYST

ROBERT FLIESS

EDITOR'S NOTE

Relying heavily on Freud's and Ferenczi's (1919) pioneering studies of the analyst's nonconflicted, noncountertransference-based functioning in the analytic situation, this study of the metapsychology of the analyst offers a careful and detailed consideration of his empathic functioning and the process of trial identification. Fliess introduces the term *working metabolism* for the internal processing of the introjects so derived, and he also coins the term *work ego* for the analyst's total functioning vis-à-vis the patient. Fliess briefly considers disturbances within the analyst that influence these processes, a subject that he investigated in greater detail in a second contribution (Fliess 1953).

Of the two persons involved in the analytic situation, one, customarily not considered a problem, is the object of this brief metapsychologic study. While in the course of the analytic procedure the patient, gradually sloughing off the personality epitomized in his diagnosis, moves towards becoming truly an individual, the analyst remains from beginning to end what he always is while at work: essentially a 'categorical person'. It is this person that we shall attempt to describe by subjecting him to as close a scrutiny as the present state of our theory warrants.

The psychoanalyst is molded out of the raw material presented by the individual who intends to devote himself to the calling. Our educational recipe directs us to select a physician with mental health, psychiatric training, and psychological aptitude. After completing a training analysis, lectures and seminars, he will be able to analyze patients, although he will for a while need our periodic advice. Everything in the curriculum of this student consists, as in any other curriculums of professional training, in imparting rational knowledge and experience. Even the training analysis can here hardly be considered as an exception, for the purpose of this procedure—which, as Freud in one of his latest papers has said, as an analysis 'can only be short and incomplete'—is accomplished 'if it imparts to the novice a sincere conviction of the existence of the unconscious, enables him through the emergence of repressed material in his own mind to perceive in himself processes which otherwise he would have regarded as incredible, and gives him a first sample of the technique which has proved to be the only correct method in conducting analyses. . . .'[1]

This curriculum is quite in accord with a good deal of the analyst's therapeutic activity which actually consists in the application of very specialized knowledge to the understanding and correcting of pathological mental conditions in his patients. No one could, however, conduct an analysis with results if he limited himself to such an application. He would be bound to become hopelessly caught in the ambiguities of interpretation and would never convince anyone because he would never have convinced himself of the true nature of what he sees. He would come to feel that he must have overrated his

Reprinted from *Psychoanalytic Quarterly* 11:211-227, 1942.

---

1. Freud: *Analysis Terminable and Interminable*. Int. J. Psa. XVIII, 1937, p. 401.

instruction which had not taught him how to grasp the real character of his patient's utterances before it had him render them subject to an at least potentially correct interpretation.

This is precisely the point where the analytic technique appears as but a very particular kind of practical psychology, and where it draws on what the training requirements rightly call 'psychological aptitude', which they are equally right in requiring the future analyst to possess as a prerequisite for his training instead of expecting it to appear as a result of it. We may hence turn from his curriculum to the history of our man and acknowledge that we expect nature and possibly infancy to do the better part of the work in creating the infrequent combination of 'born psychologist' and passionate theoretician that is indispensable for the mastery of our profession.[2]

This acknowledgment leaves us, however, still curious as to the character of that quality, 'psychological aptitude'. We are therefore compelled to begin all over again with the candid question: on what does the so called born psychologist's keenness in sizing up his object's utterances depend? Essentially on his ability to put himself in the latter's place, to step into his shoes, and to obtain in this way an inside knowledge that is almost first-hand. The common name for such a procedure is 'empathy'; and we, as a suitable term for it in our own nomenclature, should like to suggest calling it *trial identification*.[3]

A correct metapsychological description of this process would be as follows. We know that the nuclear process in identification is introjection (6). The analyst's identifying with the patient, however, cannot possibly mean—as the idiom 'stepping into somebody's shoes' would suggest—that he introjects himself into the patient's mind, for it is in the analyst's mind that everything has to occur. It can only mean that he introjects the patient's mind.[4] But would this be desirable? Would it not convert the analyst partially into the patient, and thereby of necessity restrict affectively the free use of his perception and of his faculty of elaboration? The answer is given by the complete (although merely dynamic) formulation of the process: a person who uses empathy on an object *introjects this object transiently, and projects the introject again onto the object*. This alone enables him in the end to square a perception from without and one from within; it is a trick that one can see operated by anyone who attempts anywhere a psychological evaluation. Any practical psychologist, analytic or nonanalytic, has to be able to perform this particular test just as quickly and reliably and as undisturbedly as, for example, the tea taster, who introjects materially a small sample only long enough to be able to taste it. The psychoanalyst, however, in contradistinction to any other psychologist, will have to apply empathy in a very special situation. It is this unique application, specific for

---

2. The occurrence of such a combination is naturally much rarer than that of its elements; hence the ever repeated attempts made by so many to dispense with the intricacies of Freud's theoretical contributions, and the lifelong endeavor of others to substitute the application of theory for a full-fledged experience of their own.

3. Reik (7) questions that the mechanism is really an identification. 'it is said', he explains, 'that in order to comprehend another person we must be able to imitate in our own experience what is going on in the other's mind. To me that assumption seems misleading, not because it suggests a difference in the intensity of the experience, but also because at the same time it denotes essential difference in the quality' (p. 194, ff.). It is these doubts which we have to call unjustified, or in other words, the evaluation by Reik of his own description, not the description as such, which is well deserving of quotation, at least of its high lights.

The actor (whom the author uses for exemplification) 'has developed in his art what we have all possessed in embryo since our childhood: the capacity to share in the experience of others, not *like* our own, but *as* our own' (p. 196; italics Reik's). . . . 'The psychological condition of analytic conjecture of repressed impulses is a like unconscious change in the ego for the fraction of a minute together with subsequent reversion to the former state, and the power to discern our own former transformed ego objectively in the other person' (p. 196). . . . 'Thus comprehension is preceded by a reproduction of what goes on in the other person's mind: it is an unconscious sharing of emotion seized upon by endopsychic perception. The observation of another is

here diverted into observation of the ego, or rather to the observation of a part of the ego, transformed by taking some object into itself' (p. 198).

Why is this not a transient identification? Because it uses one's *own* latent possibilities? That is characteristic of *any* identification: the material out of which I erect the other person in me cannot but be my own. It is ultimately for this very reason that the popular description is able to reverse the process by calling it 'stepping into somebody else's shoes (*'sich in jemanden hineinversetzen', 'se mettre dans la peau de quelqu'un'*). These locutions seem to follow the subjective accompanying experience, which apparently is an object-libidinal one, and as such is nearer to consciousness than the narcissistic concomitant that it entails. This concomitant we saw correctly designated by Reik as the 'observation of a part of the ego transformed by taking some object into itself'. Could the fact, finally, that only *a part of the ego* participates in the identification be a reason for his withholding the term? This fact, a topographical state of affairs (for which we will account hereafter) makes indeed for what Reik calls a 'difference in the quality of the experience' and designates as 'essential'. The use of this adjective in a matter purely experiential is of course indisputable. What we wish to dispute, however, is its use in the corresponding conceptual evaluation. There it obscures the truly essential fact that this 'difference in the quality of the experience' is the result of a topographical peculiarity only, not of one concerning the *mechanisms* involved. These mechanisms are illustrated in Reik's own description, and wherever they operate the result can only be called an identification.

our particular work, which demands here the closest possible study.

The least accessible and the most important phase of the curative process in therapeutic analysis (comparable almost to the commercial factory secret in an industrial manufacturing process) is the transformation of practically each and every[5] neurotic conflict into a transference conflict. For only in the transference can any conflict effectively be resolved. The analyst must therefore manage to lend himself to becoming an ideal transference object—not a personal but a merely categorical one. Technique requires him to serve as what might be called a 'transference dummy', to be dressed up by the patient, i.e., to be invested with the various traits of his infantile objects. This means no less than that with whomever the patient has had any conflicts, he will temporarily have these conflicts with the analyst.

If we now apply our concept of empathy to the transference, we shall be laying the first theoretical hold on a sequence of intrapsychic events in the analyst during the analytic session. For the formula which we obtain by such application informs us that the patient's transference conflicts, while passing through what might be called the psychic 'working metabolism' of the analyst, have temporarily to become intrapsychic conflicts in the latter.

Could we artificially isolate a particular striving of the patient in a transference conflict and view what happens to it when subjected to the analyst's empathy in detail, we should discover the following four phases in this 'metabolic' process. (1) The analyst is the object of the striving; (2) he identifies with the subject, the patient; (3) he becomes this subject himself; (4) he projects the striving, after he has 'tasted' it, back onto the patient and so finds himself in the possession of the inside knowledge of its nature, having thereby acquired the emotional basis for his interpretation.

Such abstraction has the advantage of making comment possible on each of these phases separately, and of thus acquainting the analyst with the dangers specific to each. He will be able to learn when and how he is threated with failure in each particular part of his performance.

In the first phase, in which he is the object of the striving of his patient, an instinctual response will be stimulated in the analyst. This is called the 'countertransference', but it deserves this name only in the case of the further complication that such response repeats an infantile one and uses the patient as a substitute for its infantile object. The problem of what to do with this induced striving becomes therefore identical with the problem of 'handling the countertransference', only with the same qualification. If we say that if handled properly the instinctual forces aroused in the analyst will be transformed so as to reinforce his sole and only purpose of intellectual penetration, we pronounce a truism, but afford at the same time a deduction as to the economics of the procedure. For performance will here depend on the completeness of such a transformation, i.e., on all the energy of the striving having been used up in the process of its sublimation.[6] If it has been, it will so to speak furnish the momentum for the analyst's entry into the next phase in order to lay hold of the emotional correlate of the object of his curiosity by means of a transient identification.

It is expedient to review this second phase, the identification with the subject of a striving directed at the analyst, in conjunction with the next. For with this third phase the identification has been accomplished: the patient's striving has been transformed into a narcissistic one in the analyst, who by now has become its subject as well as its object.

This formulation enables any one familiar with metapsychological terminology to recognize the situation (of which it so far describes the dynamics only) as a 'danger situation' (Freud),[7] and therefore prone to stimulate any of the appropriate reactions. It is the analyst's narcissistic equilibrium that is in danger at this point; in other words, his activity potentially threatens his mental health. The more conscientious the worker, the less will he be able to evade this situation or retreat from it. He may consequently find himself in the grip of the unfortunate alternative of either having the situation revert into an object relation utterly inconsistent with his work, or of suffering any of the ill consequences of a damming up of narcissistic libido. If the patient's striving in question is a libidinous one, this damming

---

4. More correctly, the patient's ego as the hypothetical subject of the utterances to which empathy is to be directed.

5. I am conscious here of differing from Freud, who in *Analysis Terminable and Interminable* declares this impossible. (*Loc. cit.,* p. 388). My own experience compels me to call it a test of the proper conduct of an analysis that no pathogenic conflict is allowed to escape from temporarily entering the transference.

6. We feel entitled to use this concept here for what it is worth.

Its discussion requires a different context and does not yield anything that is specific for our subject.

7. It will be recalled that Freud understood this term—danger situation—as implying the threat of an impending situation which he called the traumatic situation, and that he defined the trauma, the anticipation of which constitutes the danger situation, as a breaking through of the defense against an excessive stimulus (*Reizschutzdurchbruch*).

of libido will be particularly likely to seek a way out by transforming itself into object libido. The resulting libidinal relation to the patient is bound to interfere with the analyst's rôle as a transference object in the sense that we found requisite here. But it will equally hamper him in the rest of his functions; for elation will dull the keenness of his watchful psychological penetration and lure him into overstepping his rôle of observer. If the patient's striving is aggressive, the analyst's corresponding reaction on the object-libidinal level could only be masochistic. But the attitude resulting from such a reaction—an attitude comparable to that of the martyr—is not propitious in analytic therapy. It is no more propitious here than it is, for example, in 'progressive' education where it constitutes one of the typical and most frequent misapplications of Freud's findings, and results from an apparently identical constellation: identification with the aggressor, in this instance the child. On the level of narcissism the corresponding response is bound to be a tendency towards depression[8] or the disposition to physical illness.

The fourth phase, that of reprojecting the striving in question after it had been the analyst's for the brief moment of trial identification, presupposes its having been kept free from admixtures.[9] It is here as

---

8. It is not an atypical experience to find this masochistic attitude in an analyst who asks for technical advice, and to be consulted later by the same individual about disturbances of a depressive nature.

But while the 'masochistic technique' has no counterpart in the experienced, the depressive disequilibration has one in the normal. For even the steadiest and most proficient workers will have noticed at times at least mild oscillations in their *Selbstgefühl*, their narcissistic equilibrium; and I feel that this part of analytic activity, the intrapsychic elaboration of the patient's transference impulses, particularly his aggressive ones, accounts for a symptom which all analysts are likely to develop occasionally: a fatigue, physical as well as mental, that is not quite in proportion to an hour spent in a comfortable chair at a work which while he was doing it did not even impress the analyst as imposing any particular strain.

Here, by the way, is the place to credit Ferenczi with having been the first to ask of the future a special 'hygiene' for the analyst in his paper on *The Elasticity of the Psychoanalytic Technique* (4). The passage, which could almost serve as a motto for our study, is well worth quoting: 'As a problem thus far untouched I wish to point out a possible metapsychology of the psychic processes of the analyst during analysis. His cathexes oscillate between identification (analytic object love) and self-control, and/or intellectual activity. He can afford the enjoyment of a free living-out of his narcissism and egoism only for brief moments in fantasy, not at all in reality. I do not doubt that such an onus, hardly occurring elsewhere in life, will necessitate sooner or later the creation of a special hygiene for the analyst.'

Freud (1) himself became well aware of the 'dangers of analysis threatening not the passive but the active partner in the analytic situation', and the suggestion, which he finally made, that the analyst turn analysand every five years, may well be taken as his contribution towards such a hygiene.

In between the times of Ferenczi's and Freud's publications Simmel dealt analytically with the psychology of the medical therapist and discussed the well-known phenomenon that the specialist is so frequently a patient in the very field in which he is a physician. Simmel (5) writes: 'I am calling such "specialists" "partialists" (*"Partialärzte"*)'; and explains that he does so because 'their professional activities are, viewed psychoanalytically, the equivalent of a perversion. . . . What occurs is a kind of organ fetishism which as a countercathexis serves as the energy-source for the repression. For instead of "transferring" onto the patient, the specialist identifies with him. Instead of reviving the organ of the patient he tries to lay hold of it by introjection, to "repress" it; by doing so he is bound to become ill himself from the libido-congestion of his ego (or the organ). He reintroverts the relation to his patients, and thus regresses from understanding to introjection, from the communicative "utterance" to action, from "Mit-Leid" (sympathy) to "Mit-Leiden" (sym-pathos, suffering-with, suffering-in-common). I have seen stomach specialists fall ill of gastric diseases, psychiatrists of psychoses, psychoanalysts (from counteridentification instead of countertransference) of neuroses and depressions.'

We see the author end his description, which is excellent but for its terminological insufficiencies (They reflect a period in our science when formulating separately the fate of narcissistic and object libido was as yet hardly possible; the reader may be left to correct them for himself.), by directly applying it to our theme, for he states tersely that the analyst's field—and hence danger spot—is the psyche.

9. Barbara Low (6) in dealing with *The Psychological Compensations of the Analyst* gives a description in contravention (at least of its consequences) to ours, of what in this paper has been called the trial identification, and has been applied especially to the transference. 'The essential process', Miss Low writes, 'appears to be a form of introjection and projection directed towards the material presented by the patient, a situation which parallels the relationship between the artist and the external world upon which he works'. 'The artist', she later explains, quoting Freud, '(for artist here we may substitute analyst) in contact with the external world (for which we may substitute patient) obtains his material, molds and illuminates it by fusion with his own unconscious, and presents it again, thus reshaped, in forms acceptable to reality demands and to the unconscious of the world (the patient)'.

This description is quite consistent with the one the author gives of the analyst as '"eating his own meal" side by side with the patient's and so 'reliving his own inner sequence'. ('The production and assimilation of this material,' she explains, actually 'has the closest parallel to the taking in and recombining of actual food material, and the pleasure-activity accompanying the processes.') It is inconsistent, however, with our request that the patient's striving, passing through what we called the analyst's 'working metabolism', be kept free from admixtures. The term 'working metabolism' we arrived at by modifying Abraham's 'psychic metabolism'. This modification was predicated upon full awareness of the difference between the narcissistic constellations in analyzing and in other activities such as mourning for instance, or for that matter, artistic creation. The sober metaphor of the tea taster was chosen not because we deny the existence at certain points of an analogy between artistic and therapeutic 'creation', but because the point in question seems to us precisely one wherein they differ.

it is in bacteriology, where we may transfer a bacterium from an animal onto a medium and back again, and where we have to be sure that it has remained uncontaminated by anything that the medium might carry. In other words, we have been able to guarantee that no instinctual additions of our own distort the picture after the reprojection of the striving onto the patient.

The foregoing description has the typical disadvantages of its kind. It is forced to dissociate elements that are in actuality inseparable, and must fail in its attempt to adapt the rigidity of its conceptual abstractions to the flow of events. It could therefore no more cover the fact that the trial identification depicted at such length is but one of the several activities amongst which the analyst steadily oscillates, than it could include an account of the topical qualities of the personality venturing on this trial identification. Such account will have to be given separately and may start with drawing upon another characteristic of the analyst's therapeutic activity.

The psychoanalyst has to proffer towards the patient's utterances what Freud calls 'free-floating attention'. His activity when he complies with this technical requirement seems to be correctly covered by the term: 'conditioned daydreaming'. The word 'conditioned' is used here as it is in 'conditioned associations', in contradistinction to free ones. The analyst certainly does not indulge in ordinary 'free' daydreaming, where the stimuli comes largely from within, for his daydreaming is almost entirely stimulated from without, and by one particular source: the patient's reactions. He keeps close watch on these reactions but restricts this vigilance almost exclusively to one sensory sphere, that of hearing. The eye serves as but an accessory to the ear; smell is almost, the sense of touch completely, excluded, for he reciprocates his patient's motor restrictions. Thereby is obtained one of the prerequisites for daydreaming, which requires a relative restriction of mobility in the same way as night dreaming requires a complete one.

The foremost metapsychological characteristic of the dreamer's personality is its topographical redifferentiation: the dreamer's ego is reduced to a sort of perceptory surface of the id, whose unconscious contents appear as hallucinations restricted only by the superego whose activity is reduced to that of the dream censor. In dayreaming, reality testing is not lost but is temporarily renounced, and the ego obtains, at the price of this renunciation, free access at least to the whole range of the preconscious psychic content. This state of affairs is commonly reflected in the relative coherence of a daydream as compared to a dream; for the primary process has only a limited influence on its formation. By availing ourselves of our preconscious psychic content and of the help of primary processes in elaborating, by means of conditioned daydreaming, upon our analytic perceptions, i.e., the patient's material, we supplement most efficiently our rational elaboration upon this material, both in the transference and elsewhere.

The problem is only how to exploit the advantages of the situation just outlined without incurring its disadvantages. For obviously we can neither at any time renounce the use, without the slightest restriction, of our faculty of reality testing, nor can we ever allow any impairment of the keen operation of any of our intellectual functions (the critical penetration of the material offered, the determining of the course of the treatment as we intend to conduct it after due consideration of a variety of aspects of the case, such of our activities as might be called educational, etc.).

This problem[10] appears at first sight insoluble, because advantages and disadvantages are brought about by the same topographical change; it seems therefore impossible to abolish the latter without losing the former. It is true that we constantly oscillate between the two topographical states, that of full and that of partial differentiation; but this obviously cannot make available to us the uninterrupted use of faculties which seem to depend on one of the two conditions between which the oscillation occurs.[11]

The answer is that the analyst must make possible what rightly seems impossible, because it is actually impossible for the average person, and must do so by becoming a very exceptional person during his work

---

10. Ferenczi (*4*) saw this problem as early as 1918 and formulated it as concisely as could be done without the use of metapsychological terms not available at that time. In *The Control of the Countertransference* (p. 189) he writes: 'Analytic therapy . . . makes claims on the doctor that seem directly self-contradictory. On the one hand it requires of him the free play of association and fantasy, the full indulgence of his own unconscious . . . on the other hand the doctor must subject the material submitted by himself and the patient to a logical scrutiny, and in his dealings and communications may only let himself be guided exclusively by the result of this mental effort. . . . This constant oscillation between the free play of fantasy and critical scrutiny presupposes a freedom and uninhibited motility of psychic excitation on the doctor's part, however, that can hardly be demanded in any other sphere.'

11. We may assume that it was the lack of metapsychological orientation that caused Ferenczi in the paper just quoted to go no further than to require of the analyst the mere ability to perform such oscillation.

with the patient. To this end he will have to acquire a 'work-ego' with the special structure which we are attempting to analyze by means of our metapsychological description. While we have above indicated the peculiarities of this ego in several of its basic functions (perceptions, motor function, sublimation,) and thereby touched upon two of its three fundamental relationships, those to id and environment, we have so far neglected its relation to the superego.

This relation is of a particular kind, tends to elude formulation, and yet constitutes the foremost characteristic of the analyst's work-ego. We have seen this ego subjected to the severest restrictions: its environment is narrowed down to one object: this object, the patient, becoming a categorical one (i.e., an individual as a member of his particular category alone); intercourse with this object is restricted practically to one sphere of perception and one of motor activity, and operating under the obligation to utilize any instinctual stimuli for the sublimated purposes of its work.[12] But we have disregarded the economic aspect in our description.

Economically such an ego transformation is feasible for the limited working period of the analytic hour largely because the voluntary submission to these severe deprivations constitutes a proportionately intense superego gratification. This results in an ego-superego relation in which the ego, by means of its renunciations, under the conditions and for the duration of the analytic situation, induces the superego to lend its specific powers to the ego's free use. The superego's judicial function becomes thereby what might be called the analyst's 'therapeutic conscience'[13] and its function of critical self-observation enables the analyst's ego to achieve that singular detachment towards its own psychic content, conscious as well as preconscious, which we found so indispensable for his work.

While we are able to formulate this result, we cannot yet state what brings it about, for a precise description of the ego-superego relation referred to is not afforded by our existing metapsychological symbols.[14] We can at present do no more than, following Freud, indicate the mechanism that seems responsible for the change in relationship.

This mechanism falls under the libido theory; the term for it is displacement of cathexis (*Besetzungsverschiebung*), and Freud, although frequently using this term, only once made a truly topographical application of it. This application occurs in his paper on Humor (2) and is the more suited to serve as a model for our own in that it concerns itself with the identical topic, the ego-superego relation. Freud explains that the humorist's attitude is brought about by a shifting of the psychic accent (*Verlegung des psychischen Akzents*) effected by displacing substantial quantities of cathexis (*Verschiebung grosser Besetzungsmengen*) between superego and ego. With this application the concept of displacement of cathexis graduates, as it were, is admitted by Freud to full membership in terminology, and is even prophesied an important future. When once our reluctance to analyze normal psychic phenomena is overcome, he says, we shall apply the concept of a shift in cathexis to the 'explanation of a good many phenomena of normal psychic life' and thus recognize how great a rôle 'their understanding requires us to ascribe to the static conditions as well as to the dynamic changes in the quantities of energy cathected'.

The analysis of the analyst analyzing has undoubtedly to be called such an instance. It reveals a divagation (*Ausnahmezustand*) in the normal, that is characterized by the very topographical alteration which displacement of cathexis is supposed to afford. Without entering into the discussion of the concept of displacement of cathexis as such, which would lead us too far into that of narcissism in general, we

---

12. These restrictions are apt to produce in the analyst an instinctual blocking (*Triebstauung*). If the urge towards discharge finds a path in professional elaboration, it results in technical innovations, especially when supported by other motives for rebellion. Collectively considered, most of these improvements actually consist (as in view of their origin one would expect them to do) in reintroducing all the activities into the situation of which Freud gradually divested it in his period of trial and error in technique.

13. An analogous transformation of the superego, and on analogous terms, may be obtained by individuals while engaging in other work, e.g., scientific research. Would we hesitate to call the result of such transformation the scholar's 'scientific conscience'?

Nietzsche, in a penetrating remark on the genesis of what he calls the 'scientific character' seems to indicate the very same

metasychological conception when he writes: '*Die Gewissenhaftigkeit im kleinen, die Selbstkontrolle des religiosen Menschen war eine Vorschule zum wissenschaftlichen Charakter: vor allem die Gessinnung welche Probleme ernst nimmt, noch abgesehen davon, was persönlich dabei für einen herauskommt . . .*' (*Der Wille zur Macht, Drittes Buch.* p. 469).

'Conscientiousness in small things, the self-control of the religious man was a preparatory school for the scientific character, as was also, in a very preeminent sense, the attitude of mind which makes a man take problems seriously, irrespective of what personal advantage he may derive from them . . .' (*The Will to Power*, Third Book, p. 469. Trans. by A. M. Ludovici.)

14. I shall at some other time suggest an addition to these symbols which will increase their formulative powers sufficiently to cope with problems such as this description.

might, nevertheless, profit by a comparison between humorist and psychoanalyst in reference to the character of their respective ego-superego relations. Both are *Zustände* (Freud), states of mind in so far as they concern us here; both are normal, both transient. But while humor, as Freud explains, 'rejects reality, serves an illusion', analysis operates in a (laboratory) situation from which so much of the characteristics of ordinary reality are eliminated that the superego can afford to adopt the same formal character in its attitude towards the ego as in humor, but without the subject's meeting with the disturbing factors that could only be disposed of by indulgence in an illusion. As to their content the two attitudes are of course antithetic; for in humor the attitude is one of disposing of a reality by means of a joke implying its illusory evaluation; in analysis it is one of acknowledging and evaluating properly a reality which became 'psychic reality' by reduction through laboratory conditions. If, however, we disregard this difference in content (which by the way does not fail to reflect itself in the antithesis 'reconstruction'— 'delusion', as discussed by Freud in his last technical paper [3]), the formal analogy becomes evident. To make it clearly discernible we can even use Freud's own oratoric illustration. He has Humor say: 'Look here, this is the world which looks so dangerous. Child's play—just the thing to be joked about.'[15] We could have the analyst say: 'Look here, this is the (inner) world that seems so dangerous. A child's world—just the thing to be analyzed, i.e., to be reexperienced, and to be understood.' Both speeches are soliloquies since it is in both cases a narcissistic constellation which they are meant to depict.

As a countercheck for the correctness of our analogy we shall find that we may apply verbally Freud's description of the experience of the humorist's hearer to the daily experience—conscious or unconscious—of the analysand; for he too expects that the analyst 'will show signs of some affect; will get angry, will complain, express grief, fright, horror, perhaps even

despair and the onlooker-listener is ready to follow him by allowing himself to be stirred by the same emotions. But he becomes frustrated in his readiness for emotion, for the other fails to show affect, and instead makes a joke; the emotional outlay thus saved finds its employment in the enjoyment of humor.' An analogous frustration of the patient's readiness for emotions helps to constitute the 'abstinence-situation' in which analyzing is done; and the emotional outlay thus saved the analysand finds its indispensable use in the dynamics of the therapeutic process to which he is subjected. The object's experience, however, as described here, but reflects in ours as in the humorist's case the subject's inner experience in analysis as in humor.

The fact, finally, that the narcissistic constellation which makes for this experience is a transient one, truly answers the pseudovocational problem discussed by Freud, who assures the analyst of his 'sincere sympathy in the very exacting requirements of his practice. It almost looks', he says, 'as if analysis were the third of these "impossible" professions in which one can be sure of only unsatisfactory results. . . .' And yet, he goes on to explain, 'we cannot demand that the prospective analyst should be a perfect human being so that only persons of this rare and exalted perfection should enter the profession'. The solution lies precisely in the transient character of the work-ego. It is not the analyst as an individual who approaches that 'rare and exalted perfection', but the temporarily built-up person who does so under the circumstances and for the period of his work. The ability in the analyst to achieve (not to feign) this particular transformation is an indispensable although perhaps an 'exacting requirement of his practice' . . .[16]

We may summarize our findings in the following inclusive formulation:

The predominant characteristics of the analyst's work-ego (Arbeitsich) *consists of a special temporary displacement of*

---

15. The quotations from this paper are retranslations of the originals, in which, e.g. Humor's fictitious little speech reads *'Sieh' her, das ist nun die Welt, die so gefährlich aussieht. Ein Kinderspiel, gerade gut, einen Scherz darüber zu machen!'* (Freud: Ges. Schr., XI, p. 409). This in its colloquial simplicity, its measured brevity, its musical overtones, as it were, imperceptibly suggests all the qualities of a friendly 'talking-down'. It could almost be termed a glorified nursery speech given by the parent derivative in us to the child in us, as envisaged by a literary writer. A translation that lacks this peculiar terseness of the original can appeal only to the rational in the reader.

16. Freud's *Analysis Terminable and Interminable* which incorporates implicitly all his previous technical writing, supplied the chief stimulus for our study. Freud does not in this paper extract

the *concept* of the analyst-at-work, which we did, and yet deals with the problem of how to obtain this person *in practice*, which we have neglected. In answer to this latter problem Freud writes: '. . . we hope and believe that the stimuli received in the candidate's own analysis will not cease to act upon him when the analysis ends, that the processes of ego transformation will go on of their own accord and that he will bring his new insight to bear upon all his subsequent experience. This does indeed happen, and just in so far as it happens it qualifies the candidate who has been analyzed to become an analyst'. The cautiousness of this unimpeachable formulation suggests at first sight that it is incomplete, but any supplementing of it lies outside the scope of this paper.

cathexis (Besetzungswandel), *at present not fully describable, between ego and superego, whereby the latter's function of critical self-observation is utilized for the recognition of instinctual material which has transiently been acquired by identification with the patient. Thus, by virtue of its habitual faculty of practicing self-observation independent of the degree of consciousness of the material observed, the superego enlarges the ego's faculty of perception. By limiting its critical function to that of a 'working conscience', it abstains at the same time from acting as daydream censor and from restricting any of the ego's abilities necessary for the work.*

This formula confines itself, as does the present paper, to what is specific for the psychoanalyst in his therapeutic activity. It deliberately neglects the fact that being a therapist — someone who, for a remuneration (in principle) endeavors to cure — implies a very definite personality in itself; one that in our instance will furnish the frame as it were for the analyst's personality as delineated above.

Since this study was undertaken to lay a systematic foundation for dealing with certain clinical problems, it has had to restrict itself to their theoretical aspects. Thus conciseness of scientific abstraction became mandatory for an author who as a clinician would advocate almost anything rather than a rigidity in behavior.

REFERENCES

1. Freud: *Analysis Terminable and Interminable.* Int. J. Psa., XVIII, 1937, pp. 373–405.
2. ———: *Der Humor.* Ges. Schr. XI. (Trans. in Int. J. Psa., IX, 1928.)
3. ———: *Constructions in Analysis.* Int. J. Psa., XIX, 1938, pp. 377–387.
4. Ferenczi, Sandor: The Control of the Countertransference. Fourth Chapter of a paper called On the Technique of Psychoanalysis in *Further Contributions to the Theory and Technique of Psychoanalysis.* London: Institute of Psychoanalysis and Hogarth Press, 1926. Also *Die Elastizität der psychoanalytischen Technik* in *Bausteine zur Psychoanalyse,* Vol. III. Berne: Hans Huber Verlag, 1939.
5. Simmel, Ernst: *The 'Doctor-Game', Illness and the Profession of Medicine.* Int. J. Psa., VII, 1926, pp. 470–483.
6. Low, Barbara: *The Psychological Compensations of the Analyst.* Int. J. Psa., XVI, 1935, pp. 1–8.
7. Reik, Theodor: *Surprise and the Psychoanalyst.* New York: E. P. Dutton & Co., 1937.
8. Graber, Gustav Hans: *Die zweierlei Mechanismen der Identifizierung.* Imago, XXIII, 1937, pp. 24–48.
9. Christoffel, Hans: *Bemerkungen über zweierlei Mechanismen der Identifizierung (im Anschluss an G. H. Graber).* Imago, XXIII, 1937, pp. 49–62.

20

EMPATHY AND ITS VICISSITUDES[1]

RALPH R. GREENSON

EDITOR'S NOTE

Another in a series of careful and sensitive investigations of the analytic relationship by this author, this paper is also one of several important studies of empathy to have appeared during this period, Roy Schafer's "Generative Empathy in the Treatment Situation" (1959) being of particular note. The present chapter is included in this volume for its scope, clinical applicability, extended consideration of disruptive influences, and definitive interactional tone—the recognition that empathy within the analyst is influenced considerably by the patient. In some ways, this paper anticipates the notable contribution of Beres and Arlow (1974; see chapter 23).

Most experienced psycho-analysts will agree that in order to carry out effective psychotherapy a knowledge of psycho-analytic theory and the intellectual understanding of a patient is not sufficient. In order to help, one has to know a patient differently—emotionally. One cannot truly grasp subtle and complicated feelings of people except by this 'emotional knowing'. It is 'emotional knowing', the experiencing of another's feelings, that is meant by the term empathy. It is a very special mode of perceiving. Particularly for therapy, the capacity for empathy is an essential prerequisite. Although I believe these points are well known it is striking how little psycho-analytic literature exists on the subject of empathy. In their technical papers, Freud (11, 12), Ferenczi (8), Glover (13), Sharpe (23), and Fenichel (6) comment only briefly on this important topic. There seems to be a tendency among analysts either to take empathy for granted or to underestimate it. There also seems to be some antagonism between theory and empathy.[2] The systematic theoreticians have neglected this field and the empathic clinicians write little theory and then unsystematically (Reik (21, 22)). Finally, one frequently hears the phrase that empathy cannot be taught or learned; one either, has it or one hasn't. Perhaps all these elements play some role in the relative obscurity of this important chapter.

Before proceeding further, I would like to attempt a preliminary definition of empathy as we use the term in psycho-analysis. To empathize means to share, to experience the feelings of another person. This sharing of feeling is temporary. One partakes of the quality and not the degree of the feelings, the kind and not the quantity. It is primarily a preconscious phenomenon. The main motive of empathy is to achieve an understanding of the patient.

Empathy is to be differentiated from sympathy since it does not contain the element of condolence, agreement, or pity essential for sympathy. There are other vicarious experiences besides empathy, where one participates in the joys and sorrows of another person, for example, as in the theatre; but the aim is quite different. Imitation and mimicry also bear

---

1. Enlarged version of paper read at the 21st Congress of the International Psycho-Analytical Association, Copenhagen, July 1959.

Reprinted from *International Journal of Psycho-Analysis* 41:418–424, 1960.

2. An exception to this statement is the recent paper: Schafer, Roy, 'Generative Empathy in the Treatment Situation', *Psychoanal. Quart.*, 1959, 28, pp. 342–373, which was published after this paper had been presented.

some resemblance to empathy, but they are conscious phenomena and limited to the external behavioural characteristics of a person. Finally, empathy needs to be differentiated from identification, although there seems to be a close relationship between them. Identification is essentially an unconscious and permanent phenomenon, whereas empathy is preconscious and temporary. The aim of identification is to overcome anxiety, guilt, or object loss, while empathy is used for understanding (Olden (19)). Perhaps the relationship between empathy and identification will become clearer later on.

PATHOLOGY OF EMPATHY

My attention was drawn to problems of empathy by studying the errors in dosage, timing, and tact of interpretation which I had opportunity to observe in my own work and during supervisory work with psycho-analytic students. The crucial questions in estimating dosage and timing can be formulated as follows: How can I present this insight so as to be sufficiently meaningful and yet not traumatic to the patient? Essentially one has to be able to assess the patient's ego capacities at the given moment and then one has to imagine the effect of the particular interpretation upon the patient's ego structure. It is true that lack of clinical experience may be occasionally responsible for errors in dosage, timing, and tact. However, in my opinion, disturbances of empathy are usually the decisive factor. I have seen beginners who already had considerable skill in this regard; and I have seen analysts of long clinical experience who made repeated errors. I believe one can differentiate between two different types of disturbance in the capacity for empathy.

(i) Inhibition of empathy

There are some students who have repeated difficulty in recognizing the affects and motives, particularly the subtle affects and unconscious motives, of their patients. (This is not only true of students, but in this presentation I shall use the term student to refer to those with difficulties, since most of my *quotable* clinical observations have come from students.) I have found this difficulty to exist in intelligent, astute, and otherwise perceptive people. It is quite typical for such students to be extremely silent and passive in their work with their patients. They seem bent upon collecting more and more data, waiting

for additional evidence, before confronting the patient. They remain oblivious despite the clarity of the patient's material. For example, a student related to me how a young woman patient recounted, for the first time in her analysis, how she succumbed to the temptation to masturbate. Then the patient fell silent. The student went on to describe her behaviour on the couch in such a way that I could visualize the patient's feeling of embarrassment and shame; yet the student had no idea about what was going on. He waited silently, looking for more verbal material and further clues, trying to remember her previous dreams, etc. The patient talked trivia the rest of that hour and for several hours thereafter, yet the student who was bright and conversant with psycho-analytic theory was completely in the dark. He had failed to recognize that the patient had *confessed* something to him in the previous hour and therefore overlooked the obvious connexion between the masturbation and the ensuing silence. He missed her shame reaction because at that particular time and on that subject he was unable to feel along with the patient, to empathize with her.

I have observed students give very painful interpretations to patients early in the analysis and then be surprised when the patient seemed traumatized. They could answer correctly in a seminar if asked 'How will the patient react if one gives an excessively painful interpretation?' Clinically, however, they fell into this error because they were unable to feel along with the patient. They did not anticipate via empathy what repercussions the painful insight would have.

Such inhibitions in the capacity to empathize with the patient may be transient or chronic, generalized or localized. They may occur in students during a particular phase of their own analysis and be a result of some temporary neurotic disturbance within them. The transient and localized inhibitions of empathy have a good prognosis, whereas the chronic and generalized inhibitions have a poor prognosis. The latter type is frequently found in those who have a chronically precarious mental equilibrium, or with a deep mistrust of their feelings, impulses, and their unconscious. These people often prove to be rigid, severe compulsive-obsessives, or else schizoid personalities struggling to maintain their hold on reality.

(ii) Loss of control of empathy

In doing supervisory work and also in a retrospective examination of my own work I have often come upon another type of disorder in the capacity to empathize. In such situations the therapist begins by being able to empathize with his patient, but this empathy does *not* lead to understanding and then to the proper confrontation of the patient. Some other reaction intervenes, and the understanding is either blocked or is misused, or only takes place after a detour. Let me give an example.

A student was analysing a difficult patient and in the course of an analytic session detected that the patient was hinting to him about some sexually provocative behaviour she had indulged in, in regard to her child. The patient did not overtly relate this, nor did she completely evade it; she hinted about it, testing the student's reaction. The student readily picked up this rather subtle behaviour because he was in good empathic contact with the patient. The patient suddenly changed her mode of talking and directly asked the student whether it was harmful to a child when a mother expressed sexual feelings towards her son. The student, instead of dealing with the meaning of this question, impulsively answered the patient. He assured her that a parent's sexual feelings towards a child were natural and even good for a child. When the student reported this clinical experience to me, I noticed that he was ill at ease and upset. When I questioned the correctness of his procedure he readily admitted that he was puzzled by his own behaviour and could not understand why he did this. I did not attempt to explain his error, but only indicated that this might be brought up in his own analysis. A week later he voluntarily told me that he now understood his actions. Apparently he had acted out with his patient the role he wished his own analyst would take with him, namely to absolve him of his guilt for sexual impulses and feelings he had towards his own child. In this instance, empathy led not to understanding but to a counter-transference reaction.

There are many other examples which come to mind as illustrations of the loss of control of empathy. Perhaps the most typical situations are those in which the young analyst picks up the sexual or hostile undercurrent of feelings in his patient via empathy and then permits himself to prolong his reaction to the patient, which then interferes with his capacity for objectivity and understanding. Or the student detects some subtle resistance in the patient but sympathetically identifies with the resistance instead of demonstrating it to the patient.

It should be mentioned that one often sees combinations of both types of disturbances in the capacity to empathize.

PRELIMINARY FOUNDATIONS

On the basis of the clinical material sketched and indicated above, I believe we can now attempt some preliminary formulations about the function of the capacity to empathize.

(i) Since to empathize means to share, to participate partially and temporarily, it means that the therapist must become involved in the emotional experiences of the patient. This implies a split and a shift in the ego functioning of the analyst. In this process, it is necessary for the analyst to oscillate from observer to participant and back to observer (Sterba (23)). Actually, the role of observer is shorthand for designating the different functions of analysing, i.e. observing, remembering, judging, thinking, etc.

(ii) The inhibited empathizer is afraid to get involved with the patient. He is unconsciously unwilling to leave the isolation of the position of the uninvolved observer. He is able to think, remember, observe, but he is afraid to feel the affects, impulses, or sensations of the patient and he therefore misses all the subtle, non-verbal communications and their meanings.

(iii) The uncontrolled empathizers do participate in the emotional experiences of their patients, but tend to become too intensely involved and therefore cannot readily become uninvolved. They make the transition from observer to participant but run into difficulties regaining the position of observer or analyser. They tend to identify or act out or have strong instinctual reactions, all of which interfere with their ability to observe and to analyse.

(iv) The aim of empathy in psycho-analysis is to understand the patient. When the patient becomes an object mobilizing strong sexual feelings or aggression or guilt or anxiety, the patient has probably become a transference figure for the therapist. The therapists in group (i) are afraid of their counter-transference and inhibit their reactions. The 'uncontrolled' therapists give in to and act upon their counter-transference reactions instead of using them for the analytical work (3).

(v) The wish to understand is a derivative of oral introjective aims, skin eroticism, anal mastery, sexual curiosity, and scoptophilic impulses and drives (Fenichel (7)). Under ideal conditions the ability to understand is a neutralized, autonomous ego function (Hartmann (15)). In the examples given above, the wish to understand has been reinvaded by its genetic predecessors. The inhibited behaviour in the one group and the uncontrolled behaviour in the other would indicate that a reinstinctualization has occurred. Understanding by empathy has become an instinctual temptation which is either a danger to be avoided or a pleasure to be enjoyed. In either case the capacity for empathy will be disturbed.

(vi) It seems that it is essential for the development of the optimum capacity for empathy that the therapist be able to become both detached and involved—the observer and the participant—objective and subjective—in regard to his patient. Above all, the therapist must be able to permit transitions and oscillations between these two sets of positions. Freud (12) described the suspended, even-hovering attention and listening which is preferable and necessary for the analyst. This implies the partaking of both detached and involved positions and oscillations between them. Only from the evenly suspended position can one readily shift from observer to participant and back. Ordinarily, this occurs automatically and preconsciously, but these shifts can be consciously initiated and interrupted. Ferenczi (8), Sharpe (22), Reik (21), and Fliess (9) also have described the need to oscillate between observation and introspection.

PSYCHOLOGY OF EMPATHY

All the foregoing is mainly a description of some of the more obvious findings in disorders of empathy, and I would now like to attempt to probe a little deeper into the phenomenon of empathy—in the therapist. I should like to use a clinical example to illustrate some of the points I want to make, but it is not easy to find an appropriate one. I shall have to use myself as the example, because in my experience I have only been able to study empathy in a very fragmentary way in others since the pursuit of this subject led in a direction contrary to my therapeutic task with my patients. No matter what example I may choose, there is some amount of distortion, because essentially the process of empathy is an automatic process and one observes it only in retrospect. Furthermore, in order to clarify the various events one has to magnify the intervals and separate steps in an occurrence in which much seems to happen very rapidly and perhaps simultaneously. Finally, the best examples of empathy and the clearest occur where there is some difficulty in the empathy. In using the approach I have chosen, two

questions immediately come to the fore: Is this state of affairs true for all analysts? Is this state of affairs valid for empathy in general or only for empathy in psycho-analytic work?

The clinical example I have chosen is a relatively simple and innocuous situation:

I had been treating a woman for several years and usually with good empathic understanding. In one hour she recounted the events of a weekend and focused in particular on a Saturday night party. Suddenly she began to cry. I was puzzled. I was not 'with it'—the crying left me cold—I couldn't understand it. I realized that I had been partially distracted by something she had said. At the party she mentioned a certain analyst and I had become side-tracked, wondering why he was present. Quickly reviewing the events she had recounted, I found no clues. I then shifted from listening from the 'outside' to participant listening. I went to the party as if I were the patient. Now something clicked—an 'aha' experience. A fleeting event told to me as the outsider had eluded me; now in my empathy this event illuminated the crying. At the party a woman had graciously served the patient with a copious portion of food. To me as the observer, this event was meaningless. But to me as the experiencer, this woman instantly stirred up the picture of the patient's good-hearted and big-breasted nursemaid. The 'aha' I experienced was my sudden recognition of this previously anonymous figure. Now I shifted back to the position of observer and analyser. Yes, the longing for the old nursemaid had come up in the last hour. In the meantime the patient herself had begun to talk of the nursemaid. My empathic discovery seemed to be valid. When the analyst's association precedes and coincides with the patient's, it confirms that the analyst is on the right track.

The sequence of events

(i) Listening, observing, thinking about the patient's material was insufficient. There was the recognition of not being in good emotional, non-verbal contact—feeling 'out of it'. She cried and I was puzzled.

(ii) I shifted—from listening and observing from the outside to listening and feeling from the inside. I permitted part of myself to become the patient.

(iii) As I had worked with this patient day by day, I had slowly built up within me a working model of the patient. This consisted of her physical appearance, her affects, her life experiences, her modes of behaviour, her attitudes, defences, values, fantasies, etc. This working model was a counterpart or replica of the patient that I had built up and added to from my new observations and insights. It is this working model which I now shifted into the foreground of my listening. I listened through this model.

More precisely: I listened to the patient's words and transformed her words into pictures and feelings from *her* memories and *her* experiences and in accordance with her ways. To put it another way: The events, words, and actions the patient described were now permitted to permeate the working model. The model reacted with feelings, ideas, memories, associations, etc. In the above example, the working model of the patient produced the significant association to the nursemaid.

(iv) By shifting the working model of the patient into the foreground, the rest of me was relatively de-emphasized and isolated. Only those personal experiences and reactions of mine similar to the patient's remained near the model or might be used to fill out the working model. All that is peculiarly or uniquely me was shifted into the background.

(v) If the empathy is successful I shall feel in emotional contact with the patient and the patient's communications will be likely to stir up some kind of an 'aha' experience. I use the term 'aha' experience to epitomize that involuntary and pleasant sensation of suddenly grasping and understanding something hitherto obscure. (Sometimes in listening to patients one also has 'oi weh' or 'ach' experiences.)

(vi) The 'aha' experience indicates that an association in the working model has alerted my analysing ego, which had been relatively distant from the proceedings. This analysing ego may now come to the fore and attempt to formulate the meaning of the goings-on in the model.

(vii) The analysing ego may now be used to determine the desirability of making some communication to the patient by testing out the proposed intervention on the working model. Again there is the shift and oscillation between observer and participant. The reaction within the working model will determine the dosage, timing, and tact of interpretation.

Usually all this happens automatically, preconsciously, and quickly. The steps do not go in a straight sequence, but there are oscillations and variations and simultaneous occurrences.

Some qualifying additions

(i) The working model of the patient within me is not merely a replica of the patient. If that were so, the model would have the same resistances as the patient and would not supply me with clues. The model has resistances and defences similar in quality but less in degree. It is close enough not to distort, but different enough to be of help.

Clinical Note: For proper empathy it is necessary to forget and re-repress *almost* as the patient does. Reading and memorizing notes about the patient interferes with empathy. Data gathered from external sources also create the same kind of obstacle.

(ii) The working model is not identical with the patient in that the model also contains our expectations and anticipations of the patient's potentials (4). We listen to the way the patient reacts with the inner awareness of alternative reactions the patient might have had—often an 'Oi' experience. These potentials of the patient influence the interpretations and change during the course of psycho-analysis.

(iii) The working model also contains insights and interpretations which have not yet been given but are close to the patient's consciousness. Our theoretical knowledge and past clinical experiences are also lightly sketched into the model.

(iv) Thus the working model consists of:

(*a*) All I know of the patient: experiences, modes of behaviour, memories, fantasies, resistances, defences, dreams, associations, etc. All this is the skeleton and basic structure.
(*b*) I diminish the quantity of resistance.
(*c*) I add my conception of his potentials.
(*d*) I add my theoretical knowledge and clinical experience.
(*e*) In addition all my experiences with similar kinds of people and situations—real or fantasied.

All these additions fill out the model and give it a three-dimensional form. My unique experiences are isolated—for emergency use only. It is important to differentiate what is the patient, what is the model, what is me.

(v) Empathy is to some extent a two-way relationship (Bond (1)). One's capacity for empathy can be influenced by the other person's resistance or readiness for empathic understanding. There are patients who consciously and unconsciously want to remain ununderstood; they dread being understood. For them to be understood may mean to be destroyed, devoured, unmasked, etc. The analyst's attempts at empathy leave the analyst frustrated and the patient untouched. In one such case I was surprised to find myself refusing to try to empathize; I was annoyed. When I recognized this it occurred to me that perhaps the patient preconsciously wanted this. She wanted to remain ununderstood—mainly to hide a secret so terrible, she thought its revelation would cause me to throw her out. My interpretation led to confirmatory material.

Patients eager for empathic understanding increase the empathy in the therapist. Also, patients pick up the analyst's lack of empathy. I have seen this kind of reaction between speakers and listeners, actor and audience, artists and audience (Tidd (24)). This is also to be seen in candidates being supervised or in presenting cases: The fear to be understood, i.e. revealed, in the candidate may cause the supervisor difficulty in empathizing.

(vi) There are special problems of empathy in supervisory work, since it is necessary to empathize with the candidate as well as his patient. Actually, in doing psycho-analytic therapy one not only empathizes with the patient, but one needs to do so with the other significant persons in the patient's life; only in this way can one form some perspective and be able to evaluate the patient's behaviour.

(vii) One begins to empathize with the patient as soon as one goes to open the door, even before seeing him. This might explain the special preoccupied look of the analyst which many patients notice. The patient may believe the analyst is preoccupied with other patients, whereas actually he is partly preoccupied with the working model of the present patient. The analyst is looking then at both the patient and the working model. This might also explain the special startle reaction which happens to analysts when they find the wrong patient in the waiting room. It is more than the astonishment at the unexpected; there is something disorienting about it, due I believe to the cathexis of the internal working model.

Some Metapsychological Considerations

(i) Empathy, as we use it in analytic work, requires the capacity for controlled and reversible regressions in ego functions. The primitivization and progression of the ego in the building of the working model bears a marked resemblance to the creative experience of the artist as formulated by Kris (17).

(ii) The conception of a working model of the patient implies a special kind of internal object representative. It is an internal representation which is not merged with the self and yet is not alien to the self (14). By cathecting the working model as a supplement to the external patient one approaches the identificatory processes. Empathy may be a forerunner, an early, tentative form of identification (Fenichel (5), Goldberg (14), Ekstein (2)).

The capacity to empathize seems dependent on one's ability to modulate the cathexis of one's self-image. The temporary de-cathexis of one's self-image which is necessary for empathy will be readily undertaken only by those who are secure in their sense of identity. Analysts with too restricted an identity or with amorphous or multiple identities will probably be inhibited or unreliable empathizers (cf. Erikson (4)).

(iii) Empathy begins in non-verbal, skin, touching, intonational relationship of mother and child (Katan (16), Olden (18)). The mother shares the child's experiences by feel or touch, and at a distance by visual and auditory signs. The child learns to recognize and share the mother's feelings by primitive perceptions where perception and mimicry are very close to each other (Fenichel (7)). Less verbal mothers are more prone to empathize; loving mothers too.

(iv) One might express these clinical ideas in terms of ego psychology, i.e. neutralization and conflict-free, autonomous ego functions (Hartmann (15)).

Some Remaining Questions

(i) Is the hypothesis on the formation of the internal working model the only means of explaining empathy? Fliess' (9) ideas about transient identifications pursue another line of thought.

(ii) Empathy and intuition are related. Both are special methods of gaining quick and deep understanding. One empathizes to reach feelings; one uses intuition to get ideas. Empathy is to affects and impulses what intuition is to thinking. Empathy often leads to intuition. The 'aha' reaction is intuited. You arrive at the feelings and pictures via empathy, but intuition sets off the signal in the analytic ego that you have hit it. Intuition picks up the clues that empathy gathers. Empathy is essentially a function of the experiencing ego, whereas intuition comes from the analysing ego. Yet there are antitheses between the two. Empathic people are not always intuitive and intuitive people are often unreliable empathizers. Intuitive people may use intuition to avoid empathy, i.e. involvement. It is less emotionally demanding. Intuition may warn you *not* to empathize.

Both intuition and empathy give one a talent for psychotherapy; the best therapists seem to have both. Empathy is the more basic requirement; intuition is an extra bonus.

(iii) Is empathy teachable? One can remove inhibition and misuse of empathy—the disorder may be cured—but the *capacity* for empathy cannot be taught. If it is available one can be taught how to use it properly.

(iv) Since empathy originates in the early mother-child non-verbal communications, it has a definite feminine cast (A. Katan (16)). For men to be empathic they must have come to peace with their motherly component.

(v) Empathy and depression. One empathizes to re-establish contact—with an elusive object. One resorts to empathy when more sophisticated means of contact have failed and when one *wants* to regain contact with a lost object. To not understand is a form of losing or rejecting an object. One makes a model—an internal object—an introject of sorts. This is in accordance with Freud's view on the process of grief and mourning in regard to the lost love object (10). This formulation is also similar to Rapaport's ideas on hallucinatory wish-fulfilment by cathecting memory traces of lost need-satisfying objects (20).

For the empathizer, the ununderstood patient is a kind of a lost, need-fulfilling love object. Empathy, then, may be an attempt at restitution for the loss of contact and communication. In line with this formulation, I have the impression that people with a tendency to depression make the best empathizers.

BIBLIOGRAPHY

(1) Bond, Douglas. Personal communication.

(2) Ekstein, Rudolf. Personal communication.

(3) Ekstein, Rudolf, and Wallerstein, Robert S. *The Teaching and Learning of Psychotherapy*, p. 177. (New York: Basic Books, 1956.)

(4) Erikson, Erik H. (1956). 'The Problem of Ego Identity.' *J. Amer. Psychoanal. Assoc.*, 4, 56-121.

(5) Fenichel, Hanna. Personal communication.

(6) Fenichel, Otto. *Problems of Psychoanalytic Technique*, pp. 5-8. (Albany, New York: Psychoanal. Quart., 1941.)

(7) ———*Psychoanalytic Theory of Neurosis*. (New York: Norton, 1945.)

(8) Ferenczi, Sandor (1928). 'The Elasticity of Psychoanalytic Technique.' In: *Problems and Methods of Psychoanalysis*, pp. 7-102. (New York: Basic Books, 1955.)

(9) Fliess, Robert (1953). 'Countertransference and Counteridentification.' *J. Amer. Psychoanal. Assoc.*, 1, 1268-1284.

(10) Freud, Sigmund (1917). 'Mourning and Melancholia.' *S.E.*, 14.

(11) ———(1921). 'Group Psychology and Analysis of the Ego.' *S.E.*, 28, 110.

(12) ———(1924). 'Recommendations to Physicians Practising Psycho-Analysis.' *S.E.*, 12, 111-120.

(13) Glover, Edward. 'Defence Resistance.' In: *The Technique of Psychoanalysis*, p. 52. (New York: Int. Univ. Press, 1955.)

(14) Goldberg, Alfred. Personal communication.

(15) Hartmann, Heinz. *Ego Psychology and the Problem of Adaptation*. (New York: Int. Univ. Press, 1958.)

(16) Katan, Anny. Personal communication.

(17) Kris, Ernst (1950). 'On Preconscious Mental Processes.' *Psychoanal. Quart.*, 19.

(18) Olden, Christine (1956). 'On Adult Empathy with Children.' In: *Psychoanal. Study Child*, 8, 111-126.

(19) ———(1958). 'Notes on the Development of Empathy.' In: *Psychoanal. Study Child*, 13, 505-518.

(20) Rapaport, David. *Organization and Pathology of Thought*. (Columbia Univ. Press., 1951.)

(21) Reik, Theodor. *Surprise and the Psychoanalyst*. (London: Kegan Paul, 1936.)

(22) ———*Listening with the Third Ear*. (New York: Farrar, Straus, 1948.)

(23) Sharpe, Ella Freeman. 'The Analysand. Papers on Technique.' In: *Collected Papers on Psychoanalysis*. (London: Hogarth, 1950.)

(24) Sterba, Richard (1960). 'Dynamics of the Dissolution of the Transference Resistance.' *Psychoanal. Quart.*, 9, 363.

(25) Tidd, Charles. Personal communication.

21

ON THE FORMULATION OF THE INTERPRETATION[1]

Geneviève T. de Racker

EDITOR'S NOTE

In the extensive literature on the analyst's interventions, especially his interpretations and reconstructions, two approaches have prevailed: first, classification according to manifest form and properties (e.g., Bibring 1954, Langs 1974) and, second, investigations from the vantage point of language and linguistics (e.g., Edelson 1975, Rosen 1974, Shapiro 1970).

Apart from this, a number of studies have periodically appeared that derive primarily from clinical observation. De Racker's investigation of the formulation of interpretations stands high among them (see also Zac 1972, Langs 1978d). It has been included in this volume because of its sensitive understanding of the interactional dimension of the analyst's interpretations—the extent to which they are and should be a product of the patient's communications. While this tenet is widely recognized, de Racker's thesis, that unconsciously the patient places into the analyst the qualities and fragments of meaning that he needs to have interpreted back, has important implications for an understanding of the therapeutic process. The patient will place into the analyst, in a scattered and disguised form requiring only conscious integration, everything the analyst needs to formulate his intervention. And this idea leads naturally into another, namely, that every session should be its own creation.

Beyond these important insights into technique, there is an imaginative and rather beautiful quality to de Racker's writings which affords the reader a special feeling regarding the analytic interaction and the ways in which we may understand and write about this very human and perplexing experience.

Studies of the infant's emotional life, both through clinical observation (6, 7, 8) and deep analyses have shown that the mother's contact with her child is of the greatest importance. This resides not only in the *fact* of contact as such, but also—and sometimes even more—in the *manner* of this contact, since it is the expression of the unconscious relation towards the baby (the *real* contact, transmitted through the *manner* of the external contact). It is not the fact—fundamental of course—of feeding the infant or of changing his diapers, but the subtleties of the way in which this is done, which conditions his experience

1. Paper presented at the Argentine Association, 2 October, 1956.

Reprinted from *International Journal of Psycho-Analysis* 42:49–54, 1961.

and therefore his response, his beginning relation to the object.

According to the conclusions drawn by Klein and her collaborators (5), the fundamental aspect of this first object-relation — given the interdependence between internal and external world through the process of projection and introjection — resides in the fact that the characteristics of the external world (those of the object) represent a decisive factor for the modification or reassertion of internal anxieties. Basically these spring from the death instinct, and seem to be more acute in the measure in which they are not sufficiently counteracted and mitigated by the life instinct, that is, the more deficient the degree of fusion between both instincts. The outward projection of 'the bad' (on to the object) is then all the more intense. If owing to its characteristics the object is actually 'bad' for the infant, he simply reintrojects the projected 'badness' without modification, or even in a reinforced manner. On the other hand, if the way in which the breast is given to him (without forcing him, for instance) imprints this breast with a 'good' character, a modification of the projected 'badness' is brought about (by his encounter with 'the good' received), and the introjection that follows already initiates an internal transformation in favour of integration. In the last instance it could then be said that the mother's adequate 'manner' comes to be — in the moment in which it is brought about — the active 'merger' of her child.

If I here emphasize the well-known importance of the mother's 'manner' of contact with her baby, it is because I would like to establish a parallel with what takes place in the psycho-analytic process, since its aim is precisely the rebuilding of the patient's internal world. If, in order to be able to modify internal anxieties, what is fundamental in the child — beyond the basic fact of receiving food and care — is the way in which this is accomplished, if this is fundamental for the transformation processes of the internal world, it is evident that this *way* must also play a very important part within the psycho-analytic process.

Thus, the manner in which the food-interpretation is given, that is to say, its formulation, is just as important for the patient, and conditions his response just as the child's response is conditioned, and therefore brings about, or not, a modification within the patient. And here we find another similarity between the situation of infant and patient. The healthier the infant is at birth the more he is disposed to receive, the more openly he seeks the relation to the mother, and for her he is likely to be a 'lovable child' as a natural response, and she will know how to be a 'loving mother' towards him. Thus, also, the less severe the patient's splitting, the more disposed he is to receive the interpretations, and to place his own 'good' in the analyst together with aggression, so that he offers no major difficulty for the analyst's natural response, i.e. the adequate formulation of the interpretations.

The problem becomes severe when strong or even absolute rejection exists in the child towards any and all contacts with the mother. But it is precisely in these cases that contact with the object becomes essential as the only means of modifying overwhelming anxiety, which would lead the child to die by the rejection even of food. And this is where the mother's 'manner' may be decisive, since upon it depends that the child who needs to receive will accept receiving. Only it is precisely in these cases that it becomes more difficult for the mother to find the adequate 'manner', since she receives nothing 'lovable' (nothing 'good') from the child which might bring forth her own 'loving' ('good') response; she only receives rejection (Thanatos, what is 'bad').

Nevertheless, it is undeniable that any baby, even the most rejecting one, also seeks to live, and that this same rejection — even though it may seem paradoxical — is an expression of his desire for life, inasmuch as (in one aspect) it is a protection from the destruction he expects from the world, owing to his paranoid anxieties. And it is probably this perception (the 'reception' within herself) of her baby's concealed desire for life (of 'the good') which — permitting her 'good' response — enables the mother to know intuitively what would be 'good' for him, that is to say, the decisive 'manner' in which to transform paranoid rejection into acceptance.

In analysis the same serious problem arises in face of the absolute rejection of interpretations by markedly paranoid patients, rejection which implies the total impossibility of modifying the situation.[2] It came to my notice that precisely in this type of patient certain formulations of interpretations were able to transform their rejection into acceptance, and I then attempted to understand — in a previous paper[3] — the characteristics of such formulations, which were

---

2. I would like to recall the papers on countertransference and related subjects by H. Racker, Cesio, Liberman, Grinberg, González, and others, who have extensively described the psychological effects produced in the analyst by the patient's paranoid states and the danger to the analysis which arises from these effects (the danger of the transference-countertransference 'vicious circle', etc.).

3. 'Considerations on the Formulations of the Interpretations' read to the Argentine Psychoanalytic Association, Annual Symposium, 1956.

experienced as being 'good', as well as the mechanisms from which they arose (2, 3).

Firstly, I shall refer to the two examples presented in that paper and to the conclusions drawn from them, because they imply certain facts which I consider important for the development of the present study. On the other hand, these facts are intimately related to the decisiveness of the 'manner' of the mother's contact with her child, as I shall try to show later.

Before presenting these cases, I would like to point out that under the appearance of exclusively placing the 'bad' in the analyst—a typically paranoid mechanism—with the resulting necessity for keeping it isolated, a permanent placing of good parts existed, although totally split off from the associative material at hand; nevertheless, the material contained these good parts, though they were 'hidden' in it, in a manner similar to that in which the autistic person hides the 'good' within himself in order to preserve it.

The fact that the patient is inevitably giving good parts of himself can already be understood in that the analyst, who was consciously sought in the hope of obtaining 'something good', represents an idealized object for the unconscious; the patient is deeply dependent on that object because from the beginning the 'something good' expected is, in the unconscious phantasy, 'all the good'. In this first phantasy the patient has already placed 'all his own good' (that which is gratifying) on to the object, and with this—idealized—image he will keep projecting, depositing, his good parts, even though 'hiding' them from the other image—the 'bad' one.

A pre-psychotic woman, 32 years of age, experienced a frankly paranoid transference. Her attitude was exceedingly aggressive and her associations revealed the most varied criminal phantasies towards me; furthermore, she exercised her sadism by any possible means: mockery, recrimination, 'dirtying' and 'destroying' me (my reputation) as analyst by speaking very badly of me outside of the analysis, etc. But a remarkable feature existed in all her associations: they were aesthetic: her 'way' of saying things was really beautiful.

I noticed that, after the first impact of her intense aggression had passed, I also found myself formulating my interpretations in a 'beautiful' way, a thing which did not occur in other cases. Furthermore, I noticed that she experienced my interpretations very differently when they were given in a 'beautiful' way than when they were not so given: the 'not beautiful' interpretations were victims of her paranoid sadism or were simply ignored. The 'beautiful' ones were taken in and clearly operated a change in her state of mind; the defensive, paranoid attitude diminished for the moment and the depressive, so much rejected, phantasies appeared. As was to be expected, for a long time this brought on the immediate return of paranoid anxieties, but here again a 'beautiful' interpretation re-established contact, while the 'not beautiful' one simply fell into the vicious circle.

Later on I was able to understand the opposite meaning which the two types of interpretation had for her even though they were identical in content. The 'beautiful' aspect of her associations was her own 'good' part which she deposited in me as an idealized and omnipotent object, in so far as she supposed that I could make her 'beautiful'. If my interpretations did not contain the 'beautiful' it meant the danger of re-introjecting the 'bad' part which she had projected on to me; then it was I as a bad object who answered her; the 'good' one had remained split off, 'outside' my interpretation. Another of her experiences was for instance that her own 'good' part (beautiful part) had been destroyed inside me, or that I had robbed her of it, or directly, that she was full only of ugly and destroyed things, etc.

The importance which the reception (apprehension) and inclusion of her good parts ('beautiful' parts) in the interpretation had for her can then be understood, since the interpretation was transformed, as she experienced it, from a dangerous element towards which she 'closed' herself into a 'good' element she could incorporate. This transformation was largely due to the fact that this type of interpretation each time represented an active and concrete integration (*de facto*, one could say) of the split-off object within her, at the same time representing a re-integration, a return of her good parts.

Another, predominantly hysterical, patient, 23 years old, comes to her session after the holidays in a state of frank hostility. She begins to ridicule the fact of being in my house again, or being with me. After a somewhat prolonged silence she reproaches me violently for not having been able to communicate with me by telephone. Again she remains silent, always with an angry expression on her face. I interpret her wish to recover me, to be united with me once more (communicate by telephone), but at the same time her need to hinder, to destroy our union (by her ridicule, by not talking to me) inasmuch as I have become bad and dangerous because she supposes that now I have inside me all the aggression she had ejected into me when I left her to take my holiday.

The interpretation remains without effect: she persists in her silence. I wait and then tell her that first she was doing to me what she felt I had done to her by forsaking her: I had laughed at her and at our union, and destroyed it. But then I am just as angry with her as she was with me, and to protect herself from my aggression she must not let my words enter and puts silence as a barrier between us. This interpretation does not modify the situation either, and her following associations show the paranoid phantasy even more clearly. I continue interpreting and relating the present situation with past experiences, with the mother, but it is in vain. Until one interpretation, which was formulated in a very different, and to me unaccustomed, manner, provoked a surprising change. Her last association had been: 'Besides, you cause me a lot of trouble . . . for example, I will have to tell Mama that I come here and she is going to come down on me.' I then pointed out that at this moment she felt the need to tell me: 'Mama! I come here, you see that I want to be with you, united, but . . .' and here I had to interrupt myself, though I intended to complete the interpretation by saying that this exposed her to the danger that I as the bad mother 'would come down on her'—a similar interpretation to the one I had first given her. But I had to interrupt myself because in that same instant she began to cry desperately.

Somewhat calmer, she then told me: 'I am not crying because of what you said, I couldn't hear everything . . . I cry because you said "Mama!" like that. I felt something inside . . . that transformed me . . . this crying hurts, but it is so good too . . . that it fills me again. Besides, it's strange, the pains I felt in my whole body have gone.' Then, and as a response to an interpretation I gave her and which she could already take in, the repressed depressive phantasy emerged which had led her to those persecutory fears. Her crying and her words show that the word 'Mama' had achieved her reunion with me, at the same time re-uniting (integrating) her inwardly. Pain and happiness, good and bad were together and she was 'full' again.

I must emphasize that in the association to which I responded with the efficient formulation she had not said 'my mother', as she usually did, but 'Mama', which roused my attention but did not consciously motivate me to formulate the interpretation in that way. Nevertheless, considering it afterwards, it is clear that this affectionate word she had chosen enclosed—and I would say 'hid'—the mother's 'good' image, the one who does not forsake, who stays united, i.e. the image which in that moment remained split off from her, but which in this manner she placed upon me, 'hidden away' from my 'bad' image.

As in the former case, here the interpretation which could be experienced as being 'good' and therefore taken in, in fact represented an active and concrete integration of 'the good' which had been split off. In this patient and in that moment, what had been isolated was the desire to unite with me. And that word 'Mama' re-united her with me. At the margin of all the magic-infantile value of the mother's recovery which this word still contains in the unconscious, I believe that the decisive fact resided in that I said in this way 'Mama' and not 'your Mama', for example. She herself expresses it: 'Because you said thus: "Mama".' The specific aspect is that I had spoken *for* her, and it had been effective then, that at that moment, in that word, I was she saying 'Mama'; that is to say, I was she and myself at the same time: we were, in fact, a unity.

The conclusion drawn in the above-mentioned paper was the following: 'The two examples described—and the observation of others—show that what permitted and even more *shaped* the effective interpretation was:

(i) the apprehension of the good parts which the patient was placing in the "good" analyst, "hidden away" from the "bad" one, and "capsulated" in some way in her formulation of the associations; and

(ii) the inclusion (here intuitive) of the "good parts" of the patient in the interpretation given, inclusion which shaped its formulation ("the beautiful" in the first case, "Mama" in the second).'

I would like to return to an aspect which, although pointed out in that paper, has not been sufficiently taken into account in the conclusions, although it follows from them. It is the fact that the inclusion of the patient's 'good parts' in the formulation of the interpretation achieves, in its moment, such positive effects in the measure in which this formulation is a *de facto* integration (already effected) of the split-off parts of the patient. Within himself the analyst has fulfilled the function which the patient was incapable of realizing for himself. The resulting formulation is the concrete expression of the integration operated, and—as a consequence—operative: it can be seen, for instance, in the fact that if the patient can take in this interpretation, it is because the object (what it gives) has stopped being 'totally bad'; simultaneously this implies that the patient himself is more integrated, since otherwise his paranoid projection would persist, and with it his rejection of the object. On the other hand, in the cases presented, the integrative effect of those formulations, observable in the patient's emotional response, cannot be doubted. Thus the essential value of these 'good' formulations was that of working as an actively integrative instrument when, given the severeness of splitting, all contact was rejected.

Here again a clear similarity with the mother's adequate 'manner' is put in evidence, which in the last instance operates—as was pointed out—as an active 'merger' of her child.

The other two points (closely interrelated) to which I shall refer concern certain features present in the two examples given and later observed in other cases which will be presented further on.

The first one refers to the fact that the 'good parts' of these patients were enclosed in the 'bad parts'; as a matter of fact, the 'totally bad' aggressive current they ejected upon me, carried their 'good parts', hidden and clearly isolated, within itself. That is to say, their rejection 'enclosed' their search for union with me—just as the baby's ejection 'encloses' his search for life.

As will be remembered, what 'shaped' the integrative interpretation was not the perception of this desire to unite, but—and this seems to me the most important point—those patients had subtly transmitted to me their 'form' of receptiveness through their 'way' of expressing the 'bad aspects'. Here I say 'expression' of 'the bad' and not 'ejection' because their manner of expressing themselves, within the whole paranoid rejection towards me, was precisely the only 'island' of 'not rejection', since it meant communicating with me (uniting with me). Specifically that is where 'the good' was placed, and their 'form' of expression indicated then the form of what was 'good' for them.

The first patient expressed her rejection and aggression by means of aesthetic phrases, and by means of aesthetic formulations she was able to receive. In the second patient, it was also a peculiar form of expression which caused the 'form' of the interpretation which—in that moment—corresponded to her receptiveness. Something similar probably happens in the mother/child relationship which permits the mother to know intuitively which 'form' of contact is 'good' for her baby (*how* to hold, wrap, breast-feed, calm him, etc.).

For instance, the baby who rejects passively (who ignores the nipple or falls asleep), suggests with this to his mother that 'the good' is to stimulate him, to 'wake' his desire, etc. On the contrary, the baby who rejects actively (screaming and struggling) indicates that 'the good' is evidently not to force him. But this is only the most rudimentary aspect, because, since at the same time it is necessary to give to him, the mother must subtly perceive *how* he needs to be given in order not to 'feel forced'. And there is 'something' in her child which 'tells' her how to do it.

The session I shall now transcribe refers precisely to an attitude of 'active rejection' where the form of expression indicated this 'how' to give.

N, a young schizoid girl, comes to her session with an angry face. She lies down and remains silent. After a while I try to interpret something in relation to her silence, but she interrupts me at once, exclaiming vehemently: 'I don't want to listen to anything! Do you know that? Leave me alone!' I want to interpret that she does not want to listen because she fears that I will force something very bad into her (through her ears). But again she interrupts, saying: 'That's enough! All right? . . .' I then attempt to show her (relating this to her angry expression on coming into my room) her phantasy of having herself forced her own 'bad' part ('anger') into me, as the basis of her fear and rejection. But it was useless, she could not listen this time either. As soon as I began to speak she interrupted me once more with 'Didn't I tell you to leave me in peace?'

It is evident—her paranoid rejection being so absolute—that here it was not a matter of the correctness of those interpretations, since she did not even hear them.

On the other hand, to 'leave her in peace' (as she demanded) would have been mistaken, even though it is true that such an attitude might have been experienced, apparently, as the attitude of a 'good' object (an understanding one). But, as it was the result of her 'control', it would actually only have been a 'tamed' (paralysed) bad object which she managed to keep outside herself. Thus the introjection of the 'good' integrative element would have been lacking, the only means of modifying anxiety within her.

Not knowing what to do, I remained silent, mentally reviewing her attitude and her words, and trying to understand the situation. My attention was then roused by the fact that every time she rejected me she had used the interrogative form: 'Do you know that?' 'All right?' 'Didn't I tell you?' It seemed useful to point this out to her, which I did in the form of a question, although without having a determined purpose.

This time she listened until the end, and then, with a completely different tone of voice, already without aggression, she told me: 'I was like this, nervous, because I had a stomach-ache. . . . I felt ill since this morning . . . maybe it was because of that awful discussion with my stepmother. We said every kind of thing to each other . . . and in what a way! Upon interpreting[4] this material (which confirmed my first attempts at interpretation) and relating it to her attitude at the beginning of the session, she could again 'receive' what I gave to her, and in her turn give to me 'giving' associations in return. The union (integration) had been achieved.

In principle, this change in her attitude could be ascribed to the fact that my intervention consisted only in pointing something out to her, and not in interpreting, i.e. to the fact that I was not 'forcing' myself into her intimacy, into her inside, but that in some way I remained 'outside', in as much as I limited myself to pointing at an 'external' detail (her form of expression). But if it is taken into account that with my former attempts she interrupted me the moment I began to speak (that is to say, without yet knowing what I was going to say to her) and that this time she let me proceed (risking with this that I might 'force' an interpretation into her) it is evident that the element which from the start transformed her experience of my speaking, did not reside in its content—since she could not know it yet—but in its *formulation*. In fact, what was characteristic of my formulation—interrogatory—could be perceived by her from the start in its peculiar intonation. Thus she herself, by means of her form of expression (although it was the expression of 'the bad') had transmitted to me her form of being able to receive. She could receive inasmuch as my formulation was shaped

4. She and her stepmother had been mutually and violently forcing 'every kind of thing' into each other. Then I—stepmother—am full of 'all' the bad she forced into me, and I want to force it back into her (through her ears), just as she, upon entering, felt that she 'put into me' (into my room) the bad she had inside herself (her anger, illness).

by her own 'good' part. At that moment, therefore, asking represented her own 'good' part which she had been placing on to me, thus indicating—exactly like the baby who expresses his rejection actively—'how' she needed to be given in order not to 'feel forced'. At that moment her specific paranoid anxiety was in fact that I would force something into her, and by *asking* me she was 'entering into me' (investigating, exploring me) but without forcing me, inasmuch as to ask implies a proposal, as opposed to an imposition. Thus she herself was 'bad' (rejecting) towards me when *imposing* silence, and in a completely separated and concealed way, she was 'good' in *proposing* to me a union with herself. And I was 'bad' inasmuch as I *imposed* (forced something into her) and I had been 'good' in *proposing* that she receive me (listen to me).

This example presents the three aspects I wished to point out in relation to the formulation. But I must admit that I find it difficult to present others just as clearly, because one very seldom finds a case which does not offer any doubts whatsoever in regard to the formulation of the interpretation being the decisive factor for the modification of certain paranoid situations. The fact that at a given moment the analyst feels that the formulation has been the most important factor in breaking the absolute rejection does not eliminate the possibility that the interpretation's content may have had at least the same importance. This is what really happens in the great majority of cases. Nevertheless, sometimes it is the patient himself who through his experience of the interpretation expresses the importance of a given formulation, as the following example will show.

At the beginning of his analysis, a young schizoid man, 22 years old, used to remain silent and quiet during most of the session. I spoke to him, and apparently he did not react (like the baby who passively rejects the breast). Little by little this initial lapse into silence became progressively shorter, and in the same measure his contact with me increased; he began to react to my interpretations and later on to tell me his experiences in relation to me. Thus one day, when telling me how he had experienced the beginning of his analysis, he said 'It's that you told me so many things and so softly. You talked and talked to me in such a special way. . . . How well you knew how to fill my silence!' Here it can be seen that what he then experienced was that fact that I talked to him (1) (independently of its content) and that I did so in the 'abundant

and soft way', that I 'especially knew *how* to fill his silence' (4). In this respect I remember that in fact I talked 'abundantly', and that it seemed important to do so, but the 'special way' which he felt was evidently indicated to me in some 'way' by himself.

It can also be seen that his silence—his way of expressing rejection—was at the same time the manifestation of his 'emptiness' (hunger) in order that I should be able to 'fill' him; that is to say, the manifestation of his 'desire to live' (his 'good' part manifested within the form of expressing the 'bad' one, i.e. the rejection).

CONCLUSION

The child connects with the world through that first piece of external world which is the mother. The greater his anxiety or his rejection, the greater the importance of the mother's manner in making this contact possible.

The analyst also has the function of being a bridge towards a new and unknown world, the internal one, which is feared and rejected. In moments of intense paranoid rejection, the manner of the analyst's interpretation—that first piece of internal world—may also be decisive in order to produce real insight.

The cases here presented permit the following conclusions:

(i) Given the concrete inclusion of the patient's 'good' part the formulation is (for certain states of splitting) the (momentary) active integrator which simultaneously accomplishes the union within the patient and with the object; thus the paranoid rejection of the interpretation as such disappears.

(ii) The isolated 'good' part which is hidden with the 'bad' one (the rejection) expressed by the patient, is located within the way in which this rejection of the analyst is expressed, inasmuch as the form (the way) of expressing oneself is the form of communicating, that is to say, of uniting with the object, and as a consequence is also the form in which the object can unite with oneself.

(iii) The patient's modality of expression would therefore indicate his modality of receptiveness (the 'recipe', the 'good ingredient' which food must have in order that he may 'eat' it).

REFERENCES

(1) de Alvarez de Toledo, Luisa G. (1954). 'El análisis del asociar, del interpretar y de las palabras.' *Rev. de Psicoanálisis*, 11, 3.

(2) Freud, S. (1912). 'Recommendations for Physicians on the Psycho-Analytic Method of Treatment.' *S.E.*, 12.

(3) ———(1937). 'Constructions in Analysis.' *C.P.*, 5.

(4) González, A. (1956). 'Observaciones sobre el significado de los aspectos inespecíficos de la interpretación.' (Unpublished paper presented at the First Latin-American Psycho-Analytic Congress, Buenos Aires, 1956.)

(5) Klein, M. *Developments in Psycho-Analysis.* (London: Hogarth, 1952.)

(6) Middlemore, M. *The Nursing Couple.* (London: Hamish Hamilton, 1941.)

(7) Ribble, M. A. 'Infantile Experience in Relation to Personality Development.' In: *Personality and the Behavior Disorders,* ed. Hunt. (New York: Ronald Press, 1944.)

(8) Spitz, R. A. (1945). 'Hospitalism.' *Psychoanal. Study Child,* 1-2.

22

NOTES ON MEMORY AND DESIRE

W. R. Bion

EDITOR'S NOTE

This highly aphoristic paper is one of two significant addenda to Freud's remarkable delineation (1912b; see chapter 38) of the analyst's basic attitude toward the patient in terms of the use of evenly suspended, free-floating attention (see also chapter 24). In advocating the suspension of memory and desire, Bion is trying to help the analyst approach each session in a state that facilitates immediate experiencing, the detection of unconscious implications, and the search for the nonsensuous and the unknown. What is already known should be set aside because of its tendency to serve as a defense or barrier to what is not known. In a later work Bion (1970) added understanding to the list of things the analyst should dare to leave behind as he enters the session. No desire, no memory, no understanding. The resultant state of mind he termed "faith."

Many analysts have resisted this reconceptualization, and have failed to understand the importance Bion places on the search for the unknown, the intensity of the analyst's resistances in this regard, and the critical role played by the interactional and passive form of recall and understanding that is generated as each unique session is allowed to unfold on its own terms. The present paper is but one of the many contributions, both direct and indirect, made by this writer to the understanding of the analytic interaction and experience. It only hints at the remarkable originality of this writer, whose works fully deserve to be read in their entirety.

Memory is always misleading as a record of fact since it is distorted by the influence of unconscious forces. Desires interfere, by absence of mind when observation is essential, with the operation of judgment. Desires distort judgment by selection and suppression of material to be judged.

Memory and Desire exercise and intensify those aspects of the mind that derive from sensuous experience. They thus promote capacity derived from sense impressions and designed to serve impressions of sense. They deal respectively with impressions of sense. They deal respectively with sense impressions of what is supposed to have happened and sense impressions of what has not yet happened.

Psychoanalytic "observation" is concerned neither with what has happened nor with what is going to happen but with what *is* happening. Furthermore it is not concerned with sense impressions or objects of sense. Any psychoanalyst knows depression, anxiety, fear and other aspects of psychic reality whether those aspects have been or can be successfully named or not. These are the psychoanalyst's real world. Of its reality he has no doubt. Yet anxiety, to take one example, has no shape, no smell, no taste; awareness

Reprinted from *Psychoanalytic Forum* 2:271–280, 1967, ed. J. Lindon. Permission granted by the Psychiatric Research Foundation.

of the sensuous accompaniments of emotional experience are a hindrance to the psychoanalyst's intuition of the reality with which he must be at one.

Every session attended by the psychoanalyst must
have no history and no future.

What is "known" about the patient is of no further
consequence: it is either false or irrelevant. If it is
"known" by patient and analyst, it is obsolete. If it is
"known" by the one but not the other, a defense or
grid category 2 element (1, 2) is operating. The only
point of importance in any session is the unknown.
Nothing must be allowed to distract from intuiting
that.

In any session, evolution takes place. Out of the
darkness and formlessness something evolves. That
evolution can bear a superficial resemblance to
memory, but once it has been experienced it can
never be confounded with memory. It shares with
dreams the quality of being wholly present or un-
accountably and suddenly absent. This evolution is
what the psychoanalyst must be ready to interpret.

To do this he needs to discipline his thoughts.
First and foremost, as every psychoanalyst knows,
he must have had as thorough an analysis as possible; nothing said here must be taken as casting
doubt on that. Second, he must cultivate a watchful
avoidance of memory. Notes should be confined to
matters which *can* be recorded — the programme of
appointments is an obvious example.

Obey the following rules:

1. *Memory*: Do not remember past sessions. The
greater the impulse to "remember" what has been
said or done, the more the need to resist it. This
impulse can present itself as a wish to remember
something that has happened because it appears to
have precipitated an emotional crisis: *no* crisis should
be allowed to breach this rule. The supposed events
must not be allowed to occupy the mind. Otherwise
the evolution of the session will not be observed at
the only time when it can be observed — while it is
taking place.

2. *Desires*: The psychoanalyst can start by avoiding
any desires for the approaching end of the session (or
week, or term). Desires for results, "cure" or even
understanding must not be allowed to proliferate.

These rules must be obeyed *all* the time and not
simply during the sessions. In time the psychoanalyst will become more aware of the pressure of
memories and desires and more skilled at eschewing
them.

If this discipline is followed there will be an
increase of anxiety in the psychoanalyst at first, but
it must not interfere with preservation of the rules.
The procedure should be started at once and not
abandoned on any pretext whatever.

The pattern of analysis will change. Roughly
speaking, the patient will not appear to develop over
a period of time but each session will be complete in
itself. "Progress" will be measured by the increased
number and variety of moods, ideas and attitudes
seen in any given session. There will be less clogging
of the sessions by the repetition of material which
should have disappeared and, consequently, a
quickened tempo within each session every session.

The psychoanalyst should aim at achieving a state
of mind so that at every session he feels he has not
seen the patient before. If he feels he has, he is treating the wrong patient.

This procedure is extremely penetrating. Therefore the psychoanalyst must aim at a steady exclusion of memory and desire and not be too disturbed
if the results appear alarming at first. He will
become used to it and he will have the consolation of
building his psychoanalytic technique on a firm basis
of intuiting evolution and NOT on the shifting sand
of slight experience imperfectly remembered which
rapidly gives way to experience but neurologically
certain decay of mental faculty. The evolving session
is unmistakable and the intuiting of it does not deteriorate. If given a chance it starts early and decays
late.

The foregoing is a brief account distilled from putting the precepts advocated into practice. The theoretical implications can be worked out by each
psychoanalyst for himself. His interpretations should
gain in force and conviction — both for himself and
his patient — because they derive from the emotional
experience with a unique individual and not from
generalized theories imperfectly "remembered."

BIBLIOGRAPHY

1. Bion, W. R. (1963). *Elements of Psycho-Analysis.* New
York: Basic Books.

2. ———. (1965). *Transformations.* New York: Basic Books.

23

FANTASY AND IDENTIFICATION IN EMPATHY

David Beres and Jacob A. Arlow

EDITOR'S NOTE

This paper is important for several reasons. First, it attempts to integrate empathic and intuitive experiences within the analyst with an understanding of his fantasy activity, both conscious and unconscious. Second, it carefully scrutinizes a variety of empathic experiences and attempts to understand their conscious meanings and functions. Third, as an interactionally tinged investigation by two well-known classical psychoanalysts, it demonstrates that both patient and analyst are increasingly being considered within such a framework. And finally, in addition to the authors' general perceptiveness and careful use of clinical vignettes, the paper offers their unique comments on the need to validate so-called empathic and intuitive experiences—a critical consideration much neglected in this body of literature.

It is easy to cloathe Imaginary Beings with our own Thoughts & Feelings; but to send ourselves out of ourselves, to *think* ourselves in to the Thoughts & Feelings of Beings in circumstances wholly & strangely different from our own . . . and who has achieved it? Perhaps only Shakespere . . . a great Poet must be implicitè if not explicitè, a profound Metaphysician. He may not have it in logical coherence, in his Brain & Tongue; but he must have it by *Tact*/for all sounds, & forms of human nature he must have the *ear* of a wild Arab listening to the silent Desart, the eye of a North American Indian tracing the footsteps of an Enemy upon the Leaves that strew the Forest; the *Touch* of a Blind Man feeling the face of a darling child.

—Samuel T. Coleridge, 1802

Empathy, which we consider of focal significance in our work as psychotherapists, is something that is too easily taken for granted. We expect a good therapist to be empathic and we search for this quality in the candidates whom we select for training in psychoanalysis. Criteria indicating the presence of empathic tendencies, however, are hard to define, and the literature does not make clear whether this quality is a given or whether it represents something which can be developed through training and personal analysis. Disturbances of empathy, on the other hand, are easier to detect, and consequently more has been written and discussed about them; they are frequently introduced in connection with countertransference difficulties during supervised work with candidates. This communication will limit itself to discussion of the nature of empathy and its mode of operation.

With the exception of material dealing with problems candidates demonstrate during training, precise and documented data concerning empathic phenomena are difficult to find in the literature. There are many reasons for this. Because empathic communication is so fundamental to our work and constitutes a welcome, if unconscious, adjunct to our technical procedures, we do not tend to wonder as much as we should how such an interaction comes about. Furthermore, the phenomenon is an old and familiar one, known to us from our daily experience outside the therapeutic situation. It is only within

Reprinted from *Psychoanalytic Quarterly* 43:155–181, 1974.

the therapeutic situation, however, that we exercise with disciplined attention the necessary consistent self-observation which illuminates the vicissitudes of empathy. This part of our experience has an aesthetic quality and is one we tend to regard and mistakenly believe to be beyond the realm of scientific analysis. Hence, it is easy for us to think of empathy as part of the art of therapy, imbricated into a mystique which has come to envelop probing into the unconscious mind of man.

There is another, even more important factor that accounts for the scarcity of documented reports on empathy. Such documentation has to be self-revealing, especially about the personal response of the therapist to his patient's productions. Very few of us have the courage to expose for public scrutiny the record of our inner processes, as Freud did in The Interpretation of Dreams.[1] It should be noted, also, that today the audience for such exposure is much larger, more sophisticated and highly skilled in the technique of psychoanalytic interpretation. Recording a few surface phenomena can be more revealing than they were in Freud's time.

The problem of how to enter into the mind of another person is an old and fundamental one. Freud (1915) spoke of the difficulty of apprehending the conscious workings of another's mind. He well knew that consciousness made us aware only of ourselves but that by identification could be extended by the ego to others. 'But', he wrote, 'even where the original inclination to identification has withstood criticism—that is, when the "others" are our fellowmen—the assumption of a consciousness in them rests upon an inference and cannot share the immediate certainty which we have of our own consciousness' (p. 169). If this, indeed, is the difficulty encountered in understanding the conscious functioning of other minds, how much more difficult then is the task of grasping *unconscious* processes in the minds of others. In this task empathy and intuition play a basic role. And, in turn, they are buttressed by the analyst's conscious knowledge of psychic functioning and psychopathology.

In his advice on therapeutic technique, Freud (1915 [1914]) recommends that the beginning analyst should not be too concerned with trying to master the patient's data in a cognitive fashion. The correct interpretation, he suggests, comes into the analyst's mind in the form of a free association.

What Freud was actually describing is the fact that we rely heavily on the process of intuition, that is, on the immediate knowing or learning something without the conscious use of reasoning. As in any form of creative scientific work, the vast stores of information available to the investigator are organized into meaningful configurations outside of the scope of consciousness, and the results of this process are later brought into relationship in a rational, disciplined, and cognitive fashion with the data of observation. This does not mean that every association which comes to the mind of the therapist during his work constitutes an accurate interpretation of the data presented to him (*cf.*, A. Reich, 1961). Somewhere in the course of the introspective activity which the analyst exercises, he becomes aware of the end product of a highly complicated process which has been going on outside of the scope of consciousness. The awareness and the perception of this end product is the result of intuition; the validation of the interpretation thus presented to the consciousness of the therapist is a further process upon which the analyst must then embark.

In order to illustrate the problems surrounding the utilization of empathy in clinical interpretation, the following data from a therapeutic session are introduced. From this data, it was possible to reconstruct the nature of the underlying, unconscious fantasy, and to examine to some extent the process by which this reconstruction became possible.

CLINICAL EXAMPLE

On his return from the long Thanksgiving holiday a patient reported:

I am not so sure that I am glad to be back in treatment even though I did not enjoy my visit with my mother and father in the Midwest. I feel I just have to be free. My visit home was depressing. My mother hasn't changed a bit. She is as bossy, manipulative, and aggressive as always. My poor father. He says nothing. At least in the summertime he could retreat to the garden and work with flowers. But my mother watches over him like a hawk—a vulture—she has such a sharp tongue and a cruel mouth. You know, each time I see my father now, he seems to be getting smaller and smaller. Pretty soon, he will disappear and there will be nothing left of him. She does that to

---

1. A notable exception is a recent communication by Miller (1972) in which with rigorous honesty he reports his reactions to falling asleep while listening to a patient. He ascribes this to a manifestation of his countertransference, the result of the simultaneous appearance in the therapist and the patient of an analogous unconscious fantasy.

people. I always felt that she was hovering over me, ready to swoop down on me. She has me intimidated, just like my wife. I don't feel like getting involved, but when you are married, there isn't much you can do about it.

I was furious this morning. When I came to get my car, I found that someone had parked in such a way that I was hemmed in. It took a long time and lots of work to get my car out. During the time I realized how anxious I was. The perspiration was pouring down the back of my neck.

I feel restrained by the city. I need the open, fresh air. I have to breathe. I have to stretch my legs, I'm sorry I gave up that house in the country. Next week, I am going up to Massachusetts to look around for property. I have to get away from this city. I really can't afford to buy another house now, but at least I'll feel better if I can look.

If only business were better, I can maneuver more easily. I hate this feeling of being stuck in an office from nine until five. My friend Bob has the right idea. He arranged for retirement and now he's free to come and go as he pleases. He travels; no officers, no board of directors to answer to. I love my work, but I can't stand the restrictions it imposes on me. But I am ambitious, so what can you do?

At this point, the therapist called attention to the recurrence in the material of the theme of being trapped and confined. The patient continued:

I do get symptoms of claustrophobia from time to time. They are mild, just a slight anxiety. I begin to feel that perspiring feeling at the back of my neck, and begin to have a sense of restlessness. It happens when the elevator stops between floors or when a train gets stuck between stations. I begin to worry how I'll get out. You know, I have the same feeling about starting an affair with Mrs. X. She wants the affair, and I guess I want it too. Getting involved is easy. It's getting uninvolved that concerns me. How do you get out of an affair once you are in it?

I am really chicken. It's a wonder I ever was able to have relations at all and to get married. No wonder I didn't have any intercourse until I was in my twenties. My mother was always after me. 'Be careful about getting involved with girls—they will get you into trouble. They will be after you for your money. If you have sexual relations you can pick up a disease. Be careful when you go into public toilets. You can get an infection, etc., etc.' She made it all sound dangerous. You could get hurt from this, you could get hurt from that. It reminds me of the time I saw two dogs having intercourse. They were stuck together and couldn't separate. The male dog was yelping and screaming in pain. I don't know how old I was then, maybe five or six, perhaps seven, but I was definitely a child, and I was frightened.

By the time the therapist communicated to the patient the simple observation that he seemed to be concerned about being hemmed in or confined, he had already concluded that the patient was suffering to some degree from claustrophobia. At this point, the existence of claustrophobia could be deduced in a rational way from clues presented in the material of the session. Although the idea of being confined had appeared in a few similar or parallel expressions and the theme repeated several times, claustrophobia was a new element in the treatment. The experience of anxiety was a factor common in all the elements mentioned.

While the data in this case corresponded to a pattern recognizable from clinical experience and reported in the literature, it is hard to say to what extent the therapist was aware of the configurations and interrelationships of the data at the times he was perceiving them. More often than not, in such instances, most therapists appreciate only in retrospect the rich and subtle interconnection of the inner logic of the material. For the most part, but by no means exclusively, the data is conceptualized outside of awareness. First, it is intuited, and then, it is rationalized. (The term 'rationalized' is used here in its strict sense, not as a form of defense.)

But there was another idea that presented itself to the therapist's inner perception. This was the idea that the patient was under the influence of an unconscious fantasy in which his penis would be trapped or injured if it entered a vagina, originally his mother's. A corollary of this notion was that the patient fantasied his whole body as his penis, and it, too, would be subject to the same danger that threatened his penis in the preceding fantasy. Concerning this insight, there was much less evidence than for the conclusion regarding claustrophobia. Yet certain clues, more subtle ones it is true, could be identified. The factor of contiguity was important. The material conveying the sense of anxiety about being confined followed immediately upon a train of thoughts dealing with his fearsome mother and her destructive, hawklike beak.

While the factor of contiguity is suggestive, it is not definitive. It is true, however, that in claustrophobia fantasies which unconsciously equate the fear of enclosure with the vagina are common. In addition, there was the earlier knowledge of this patient's sexual inhibitions which accurately fit into the configuration of the data suggested by the second fantasy.

In this clinical vignette, it should be noted that beyond the cognitive organization of the data there was an immediate, noncognitive sharing with the patient of a fantasy of which he was still unaware—

namely, the fantasy of a *vagina dentata*. There can be no doubt that at this point technical knowledge and training were very important in organizing the data in the analyst's mind and helped to facilitate in concrete terms the formulation of the underlying unconscious fantasy.

How is it possible for the therapist to select and collate out of the myriad of observations available to him those necessary elements that he organizes as his insight into the patient's unconscious mental processes? Beyond the rational activities that may operate either within or outside of the scope of consciousness, a further element must enter. This element we call empathy.

IDENTIFICATION AND EMPATHY

The dictionary defines empathy as the projection of one's own personality into the personality of another in order to understand him better. This is essentially the usage of the term to which Kohut (1959) subscribes when he considers empathy 'vicarious introspection'. Greenson (1960) speaks of empathy as a form of 'emotional knowing', the experiencing of another's feelings, a special mode of perceiving. He considers empathy primarily a preconscious phenomenon to be distinguished from sympathy because it does not contain the elements of condolence, agreement, or pity. Definitions of empathy often include concepts concerning the genetic origin of the phenomenon. Loewald (1970) assumes that emphatic communication tends to approximate the kind of deep, mutual empathy which we see in the mother-child relationship. Similarly, Burlingham (1967), H. Deutsch (1926) and others consider the infant's sensitive response to the mother's affective state as a manifestation of empathy. Perhaps the most extreme statement of this position is by Ferreira (1961) who sees empathy as rooted in the primary umbilical unity of the infant and the mother. A corollary of his view is the idea that empathy is primitive and archaic and gradually tapers off and decreases through the years. Such concepts which view empathy as recapitulating the early mother-child unity emphasize a merging of analyst and patient, of subject and object in the therapeutic interaction. Schafer (1968, p. 153) also speaks of infantile forms of empathy as being based on merging.

The literature contains many references to the importance of 'being with the patient' as a desirable technical approach. The fact is, for all its implication of human warmth, this may be detrimental to the

therapeutic process. Brierley (1943) has made a useful distinction between thinking *with* the patient and thinking *about* the patient. Thinking with the patient is not necessarily empathy. Sometimes it may indicate countertransference, projection, or a degree of identification with the patient that implies merging and can be detrimental to therapeutic work. This point has been emphasized particularly by A. Reich (1960).

There is general agreement that identification is indeed involved in empathy, but this form of identification must be separated from other forms. Empathy may play a role in feelings of sympathy or pity, but it is not identical to these feelings. There are two distinguishing features to empathy: one, it is a transient identification; second, the empathizer preserves his separateness from the object. It is hard to say just when the individual develops the capacity for empathy, but evidence indicates that it is not present in infancy: the essential component of empathy, which is lacking in the infant, is the capacity to separate self from nonself. Stable self- and object representations or the state of object constancy are not established until later. In Mahler's (1968) terms, the infant has not completed the necessary process of separation-individuation. In addition, the capacity for empathy requires such functions as memory, thought, comprehension, and conceptualization. Only then can the cues that perception affords lead to empathy. Empathy consists of more than an immediate affective response; it requires considerable ego development. Accordingly, the capacity for empathy increases with age and experience, especially experiences of suffering.

While there is no question that the good mother empathizes with her infant, there is also a potential danger. Olden (1953) has described a pathological mother-child relationship which is essentially symbiotic and merging in nature and not empathic. When a child is hurt, for example, the empathic mother will react to his pain and anxiety but will maintain her separate existence as a mother; her identification with the child's pain and anxiety is evoked, but it is transient and serves to mobilize behavior appropriate to the emergency. The nonempathic mother, on the other hand, may narcissistically withdraw from the situation or so completely identify with the child that she suffers along with him to the point where she shares the child's helplessness. She merges with her child in identification; she suffers with the child and not about the child.

This is what Beres (1968a) emphasizes concerning the transient identification in empathy. Such identification implies only a temporary sense of one-ness with the object, followed by a sense of separate-ness in order to appreciate that one has felt not only *with* the patient but *about* him. This point is impor-tant in evaluating the genetic precursors of the pro-cess of empathy mentioned above.

In general, narcissistic individuals have difficulty in empathizing because of their tendency to merge with the object for the purpose of narcissistic gratifi-cation and because of their inability to maintain a sense of separateness from the object. This is most apparent in the repetitive love relationships of cer-tain narcissistic patients. They plunge into every relationship with great emotional intensity. To be separated from the lover gives rise to intense anx-iety. They are totally submissive and will accept humiliation and even physical abuse. At the same time, they make demands on the lover for attention and are intolerably possessive. As self and object are one in their fantasy, the love object has no real exis-tence and serves only as a prop. Such individuals merge with a lover in identification; there is no sepa-rateness of self from the other.

SIGNAL AFFECT AND EMPATHY

So far we have emphasized two ideas concerning empathy: first, the sense of transient identification and second, the complementary sense of separate-ness. Several authors (e.g., Greenson, 1960; Racker, 1958; Little, 1951) have emphasized the sharing of the patient's affect in the process of empathy. The reaction of the empathizing therapist is a complex one, a mixture of affect and cognition. The affect experienced by the therapist we suggest is in the nature of a signal affect, a momentary identifi-cation with the patient which leads to the awareness, 'This is what my patient may be feeling'. It does not necessarily follow that the mood of the therapist duplicates what the patient is experiencing (*cf.,* A. Reich, 1960). The therapist need not be depressed when his patient is depressed, nor anxious when his patient is anxious. He knows what it feels like to be depressed or anxious, but after his momentary iden-tification with the patient he avoids further partici-pation in his affective state.

The affect which the therapist experiences may correspond precisely to the mood which the patient has sought to stimulate in him as, for example, the masochist who tries to evoke criticism and attack. Empathy in such instances consists of recognizing that this is precisely what the patient wishes to

provoke in the analyst. The affect experienced is a signal affect alerting the therapist to the patient's motivation and fantasy. If the therapist does not recognize this, then empathy has failed and counter-transference takes over.

The technical implications of these observations were succinctly stated by Little (1951) when she said: 'The analyst necessarily identifies with the patient, but there is for him an interval of time be-tween himself and the experience which for the patient has the quality of immediacy—he knows it for past experience, while to the patient it is a pres-ent one. That makes it at that moment the patient's experience, not his, and if the analyst is experiencing it as a present thing he is interfering with the patient's growth and development' (p. 35).

FANTASY AND EMPATHY

The therapist empathically sharing the patient's affective state, an affect which we regard as a signal affect, leads to the question of the significance of the signal. Clinical observations suggest that the signal portends the emergence of an unconscious fantasy, and that the quality of the affect is appropriate to the nature of that fantasy. This was suggested in the pre-ceding clinical vignette and the material which fol-lows makes the same point. In addition, however, it demonstrates the instant communication of an unconscious fantasy shared in common between therapist and patient.

A middle-aged professional man tormented by feelings of guilt and depression, demonstrated a rather typical masochistic character formation. Much of his problem centered around an unresolved feminine attitude and erotic longing for an uncle who had served as a father surrogate during his early years.

The patient was the youngest of three children and the only boy. When he was two years old his father left the family in Europe and came to the United States. The family was not reunited until the patient was ten years old. During the absence of his father the patient's uncle, his mother's younger brother, played the role of father surrogate. Illusions of grandeur concerning the missing father were soon displaced onto the young uncle: to the little boy, he became an idol—he was strong, self-reliant, gay, and always helpful. When the time came for the family to join the father in the United States, the patient became depressed; he did not want to leave his uncle, with whom he had played and whose bed he had shared.

The patient found it difficult to reconcile himself to his father in the new country. He yearned for the uncle and tried to get his sisters to join him in saving money to bring the uncle to the United States, but the uncle had no intention of leaving Europe. The aggrandized image of his uncle from his childhood fell far short of reality. The uncle was a ne'er-do-well and lived primarily by his wits. However, this information, to which the patient was privy in his later years, had no effect upon the image of the uncle he retained. For example, when war broke out and the Nazis seized his home town, the patient was certain that his uncle would survive; his bravery and resourcefulness would see him through. In spite of the fact that no word had been heard from him for years, the patient was certain that his uncle must have outwitted the Nazis and found his way to Israel. Later, during his analysis, the patient went to Israel and learned his uncle's fate: he had been shot the first day the Germans occupied the village because of some foolhardy and defiant gesture.

One day, the patient began the analytic session by saying:

Last night I had the following dream. I saw myself in a house with some cousin of mine in the country. It was not yet dark, but it was no longer light, and I seemed to be all alone in the house. My cousin was elsewhere; I could not see him. I called out 'Peter' and somebody, in a joking way, called back 'Joey'.

The therapist heard no more than this of the patient's material when suddenly he found himself having a vivid visual fantasy. He saw himself at a European airport, standing in the terminal. It was the kind of airport typical of many European cities: the passengers debark from the plane at some distance from the terminal and are brought in by bus. As the therapist was standing and waiting a bus approached the terminal. Among the passengers, he recognized his father who had been dead for a number of years. Many thoughts came into his mind about this fantasy. As a matter of fact, the last time he had seen his father alive had indeed been at an airport except that the circumstances had been reversed; his father was waiting for him at the airport in New York upon his return from a visit to Europe. The visit had included a sentimental journey. The therapist had made a trip to his father's native land, and had, in fact, gone out of his way to visit the city where his father had spent his youth. It

suddenly came to him that he was in a twilight zone between life and death, in that in-between land where it is possible for the living and the dead to be reunited.

The therapist's next thought was the patient's dream. The patient had been in a house in the country; it was not yet dark, but it was no longer light. The patient, too, was in the twilight zone, and the therapist realized immediately that the names Peter and Joey, which occurred in the dream, were actually anglicized forms of the names the patient and his uncle used to call each other. At this point, the therapist began to emerge from his intrusive visual fantasy and heard his patient speaking: 'Last night I was watching television. The show was "Twilight Zone" . . .'.

It was not hard to interpret the patient's dream. It expressed the wish to be reunited with his uncle. The dream was based upon the unconscious fantasy of reunion in a twilight area where the living and dead find each other once again. The patient and the therapist both had the same 'dream' and, with no immediate associations to the manifest content, an unconscious fantasy of the therapist's congruent with that of the patient's appeared in his mind. Without the benefit of associations to the dream, and before the process of intuition could become operative, the therapist had grasped the meaning of the patient's dream and responded with his own version of the identical unconscious fantasy. In truth, the therapist had created his own unconscious fantasy before he had any conscious awareness of the meaning of the patient's dream.

Clearly, this empathic process by which the patient's fantasy stimulated the therapist's own had taken place entirely at an unconscious level. An identification between the two of them had been effected through this shared unconscious wish that led in turn to an almost identical fantasy in both their minds. What happened next, however, was a rupture of the sense of the momentary identification and the sudden awareness on the therapist's part that his inner experience, which seemed so personal and idiosyncratic, was in effect a commentary on the patient's material. The correct interpretation had come into the therapist's mind in the form of a fantasy. It then required a set of cognitive operations for him to be able to translate this fantasy into an interpretation. At this point, the identification was broken off and was replaced by an object relationship. Thinking and feeling *with* the patient was replaced, as Brierley (1943) and Beres (1968a) put it, by thinking *about* the patient.

SHIFTING IDENTIFICATION IN EMPATHY

Empathic understanding of the patient is much more complicated than simply the sharing of affects, presumably experienced by the patient at the time. Sometimes the process of identification in empathy goes through several phases and undergoes vicissitudes and transformations. This is illustrated in the following excerpt.

The main complaint of a patient in his middle thirties was pathological jealousy of one of his girlfriends. Although he had many transient love affairs, they did not seem to bother him. As the analysis proceeded, a pattern of hostile aggressiveness against women, expressed in these multiple affairs, became clear but the motive for this aggression was not clear. At least two possibilities had been suggested by the material but up until this time neither had seemed predominant. The first possibility was that the pattern of hostility toward women represented a displacement of his anger against his adulterous mother; the second was that this sadism was used as a defense against his masochistic, passive, feminine identification.

During one session the patient described a date with one of his girlfriends. It was a long and somewhat startling record of one provocative statement after another. He took advantage of every feeling of inferiority or sense of insecurity that the girl exhibited in order to put her on the defensive. As this was only their second date, the girl tried her best to make a favorable impression; with each fresh assault by the patient, she tried a new tack which she hoped would make her seem agreeable and friendly, all to no avail. At one point in the conversation the young lady mentioned the fact that as a result of strenuous efforts she had recently lost quite a bit of weight. 'You're still too plump', the patient said. The woman responded, 'Oh I have pictures of myself some months ago. I was much plumper then.' 'I don't believe it', the patient said, to which the woman responded, 'Would you like me to show you the pictures?', and she rose to fetch them.

At this point in the session, the therapist had a quasi-visual image of this hapless young woman. He felt terribly sorry for her, and could practically see her with a small, wistful, desperate smile on her lips, trying to do everything to please this man and yet feeling that nothing would be of any help. He indeed felt very sorry for her. If empathic feelings had been aroused, the therapist's identification was completely with her and not with his patient.

The patient continued. He said, 'I was amazed to think that she would really get up and fetch those pictures for me. How foolish can anyone get? Why would she take my cruelty the way she did?' Beyond the triumph in the patient's voice, the therapist detected a note of remorse, a feeling of how terrible it must be to be in this young woman's position. At this point, the therapist had another empathic reaction, but with his patient. He recalled how, during his adolescence and on a few other occasions later in life, he had himself behaved in a similar way.

The therapist was struck by this two-phase experience of empathy; first, with the patient's feminine victim, and then, with the patient himself, especially with that aspect of the patient's productions which suggested an identification with his own victim. It made the therapist think immediately that the second possibility mentioned above—namely, that the patient's behavior constituted an aggressive defense against his own feminine masochistic wishes—was probably the more important element in his unconscious fantasy life at this time. But this was as far as he could go in trying to reconstruct the unconscious wish at that time.

Material elucidating the nature of the unconscious wish was not long in coming. In the next session, the patient recollected some feelings of sensitivity about having called the therapist's attention to the patient's dress. He then reported that he had had a restless night. Before falling asleep he had a fantasy of being on the couch in the office, getting very angry and feeling that he did not want to listen to the therapist any more. In his fantasy he got up, pointed a finger at the therapist, and began to shout: 'Now you listen here. There are some things that I want to tell you.' After reporting this fantasy, the patient laughed and said, 'I realize I had nothing to say. I don't understand what I was so angry about.'

He then reported a dream of being both a pursuing and a pursued person. The dream culminated in a struggle with a man at the edge of a brown, muddy pit. He was being very aggressive toward his adversary and tried to hit him, but could not quite do it. He woke from the dream in great fright, so much so that in regressive fashion he had to turn on the lights and go to the front door to make sure that it had been properly bolted to protect him against the possibility of intruders. His associations had to do with his fear that he might discover that he had homosexual trends, and with a number of recollections from his boyhood when he had placed himself in a sexually awkward and dangerous position with men; one of the men had fondled his buttocks.

This material confirmed the interpretation suggested by the therapist's double empathic response to the woman victim and to the patient, and, in effect, this double identification repeated the elaboration of the patient's conflict—first, the awareness of his defensive need to assault the woman, and second, the emergence of his own masochistic feminine wish. This would seem to be a clinical validation of the point made by H. Deutsch (1926) that in empathy the analyst may identify not only with the patient but with his objects as well.

NONVERBAL COMMUNICATION AND EMPATHY

There are other derivatives of unconscious fantasy activity, some of which find expression in the form of nonverbal communication, especially motor activity. From our knowledge of gesticulation, mimicry, and the dance, we know how emotion can be transmitted through an identification by way of the emotion we see in action (cf., Fenichel, 1926). Jacobs (1973) has recently called attention to motor activity which analysts often engage in unconsciously during sessions. On investigation, he was able to determine that these constituted empathic responses to the patient's unconscious mental activity. These are colleagues who seek to penetrate the meaning of the patient's associations by repeating certain gestures or hand movements which they have observed in the patient. In this way, they feel that they can enter into his mood more easily and better understand the nature of his conflicts.

In a paper on nonverbal communication in psychoanalysis, Arlow (1969c) observed that certain specific configurations of the fingers as they appear in photographs or in works of art are, in effect, motor metaphors through which the musculature in action captures and conveys important affective states. Gombrich (1972) discussed this point in connection with artistic representation of symbolic images. F. Deutsch (1947, 1952) reported similar observations in his studies of the posture patients assume on the analytic couch.

An example of empathy in nonverbal communication was reported by a patient. While in the kitchen his wife asked him to prepare the tuna fish for their son's sandwich, pointing out that the boy whom they both dearly loved liked to have the tuna fish chopped in a certain way. As he was preparing the food according to his wife's instructions, the patient was suddenly overwhelmed by a powerful feeling of the kind of affection that he felt his wife must have for their son. This emerged by way of his identification with her in the act of preparing the food. Through this identification he could understand not only her feeling but could be brought into closer awareness with his own very intense affectionate feelings of a maternal nature which he ordinarily warded off.

Also pertinent to this discussion is the analyst's empathic responses to the patient's silence, which may be an important clue to the mental content being suppressed or repressed during the periods of silence (Arlow, 1961). Blos, Jr. (1972) has also emphasized the communicative significance of the patient's silence and the importance of the analyst's feelings and reactions to the silent patient.

RESISTANCE AND EMPATHY

In addition to empathizing with the affective ideational and motor components of the patient's fantasies and conflicts, the therapist must be able to empathize with the patient's state of resistance. This has an important bearing on the timing and the wording of interpretation. Ferenczi (1928) emphasized this point when he stated that empathy is the precondition for tact. Ferenczi makes the further point that a proper empathic understanding and tact would dictate 'when one should keep silent and await further associations and at what point the further maintenance of silence would result only in causing the patient useless suffering'.

Shapiro (1974) draws attention to variations in the capacity of a patient to empathize with others in his environment. There is, further, one aspect of empathy that is frequently overlooked in the therapeutic setting: the lack of empathy of the patient as his present self with his past self—a kind of discontinuity of identity which is occasioned by conflict and narcissistic influences. By resolving unconscious conflicts, psychoanalysis enables a patient to see himself in a continuum from his early life and to accept and tolerate hitherto repudiated aspects of himself. One result of treatment is the enriched capacity of the patient to empathize with himself.

Another aspect of the problem of empathy is the capacity of the individual to empathize with others whose experiences and background differ markedly from his own. This point has been raised in connection with the analyst's treatment of patients with different sex, race, social, and economic background. Except for the most extreme circumstances, the therapist, even as the artist, must have the capacity to empathize with the feelings and thoughts of others different from himself.

PERCEPTION AND FANTASY IN EMPATHY

In the clinical material cited above, we emphasized how the process of empathy reflects the awareness of the affective tone enveloping an emerging unconscious wish or fantasy. In previous communications Arlow (1969a, 1969b) attempted to define the relationships between persistent unconscious fantasy and perception and reality testing. He emphasized the reciprocal effects that unconscious fantasy and the data of sensory registration have upon each other. Unconscious fantasy activity establishes the mental set against which the data of sensory registration are selectively perceived, inhibited, disregarded, or transformed. Conversely, the data of perception have the power to reactivate or facilitate the emergence of unconscious fantasy activity. Sensory registrations outside the realm of consciousness can also affect the emergence of unconscious fantasy, and conscious fantasy activity may facilitate, alter, transform, or repress the registered sensory impressions even before they achieve mental representation in consciousness.

Clinical material obtained in the treatment situation may be examined from the vantage point of these principles. The sensory input, the analyst's perceptions, consists of the patient's productions. A measure of the analyst's empathic capacity lies in his ability to be stimulated by the patient's unconscious fantasy when the analyst himself is not yet aware of the existence or the nature of the patient's unconscious fantasy.

The process described above is basic in psychoanalytic experience. It furnishes, as we know from Freud (1908[1907]), Sachs (1942), Abraham (1935), Rank (1932), Kris (1952), Beres (1962), Arlow (1961b), and others, the fundamentals for the understanding of mythology, religion, group formation, and artistic experience from a psychoanalytic point of view. All of these shared experiences which hinge on the transmission of emotion have as one of their essential components the emergence of an unconscious fantasy that is shared in common (Sachs, 1942). In religious groups and in aesthetic experience, it is the leader or the poet who creates the frame of reference that evokes in his listeners, readers, or members of his audience unconscious fantasies which correspond to his own.

In previous studies on the analogy between aesthetic experience and the psychoanalytic experience, Beres (1957, 1968b) has demonstrated the parallel between the therapist and the patient on the one hand and the poet and the audience on the other. The devices which make poetry and enable the poet to transmit to others the emotion he experiences are the same ones which make the patient's material assume configurations that transmit meaning and emotion to the therapist, making empathy possible. Contiguity, repetition, symbolism, allusion, contrast, and, above all, metaphor (*cf.*, Sharpe, 1935, 1940; Arlow, 1969b) are the most important of these devices. In addition to the consciously experienced fantasies, what the poet presents to the audience are derivative expressions of fantasies of which he is completely unaware. These derivative expressions are congruent with the unconscious fantasies that members of the audience share in common with him. The universally shared early biological experiences of mankind form the basis of universal fantasies, facilitating empathic communication between person and person, and person and groups. Thus poet and audience respond to similar but not necessarily identical unconscious fantasies, though neither of them is aware of the infantile, instinctual roots of his emotions. Only the process of analysis can bring these fantasies into consciousness. The interaction between audience and poet, like the interaction between patient and therapist, is an empathic one based upon the communicability of unconscious fantasy. Psychotherapy and art both serve to place a distance between the individual and his unconscious conflicts, a distance from which he can contemplate with comfort derivatives of his unconscious fantasies. In art, for reasons of defense, the experience remains at the level of derivative expressions of unconscious fantasy. In analysis, on the other hand, one seeks to overcome the defenses and reconstruct the unconscious fantasies in order to alter their persistent intrusiveness and destructive effect on the individual's functioning.

INTUITION AND EMPATHY

There is an important relationship between intuition and empathy. Neither intuition nor empathy are mystical phenomena based on some kind of innate capacity to comprehend or experience. When the therapist appears to arrive intuitively at an understanding of his patient he is actually becoming aware of the end product of a series of mental operations carried on outside the scope of consciousness.

Intuition, however, differs from empathy. Empathy involves identification, although transient, with a mental activity of another person. Intuition does not involve identification; it is an immediate apprehension of an idea, a thought, or a fantasy. Empathy furnishes the clue which alerts the therapist to the emergence of the correct interpretation. The intuitive understanding of the therapist follows his empathic response.

The therapeutic situation requires that empathy and intuition go on to interpretation and insight; otherwise, we would have no more than a mutuality of experience—for the patient a transference experience and for the therapist a countertransference experience.

The final step in our discussion of empathy is the issue of validation. Greenson (1960) says that when the therapist's associations precede or coincide with a patient's, this confirms that the therapist is on the right track. While we agree with the statement, we would add that this phenomenon is suggestive but not necessarily confirmatory. Both the empathic and the intuitive responses which arise in the mind of the therapist have to be subjected to disciplined validation. The technical implications of these observations have been considered in detail by A. Reich (1960). Empathy is an essential tool in psychoanalytic work. It facilitates the emergence of intuition and leads by way of interpretation to insight.

SUMMARY

This communication considers the clinical and theoretical aspects of empathy, emphasizing the role of identification and the distinction between the self and the nonself. We have stressed how empathy is mediated by the communication of unconscious fantasy shared by the patient and the analyst. The cues for this communication are both verbal and nonverbal: they emanate from words, gestures, and behavior.

The empathic process which is central to the psychotherapeutic relationship between patient and therapist is also a basic element in all human interaction and finds its highest social expression in the shared aesthetic experience of the artist and his audience, as well as in religion and other group phenomena.

From the theoretical point of view it is necessary to consider the relation of empathy to identification, projection, and countertransference, as well as the distinction between self and objects.

Empathy serves as a signal affect and leads to intuition. These are not mystical, innate phenomena and demand disciplined clinical validation.

REFERENCES

Abraham, Karl (1935): *The History of an Impostor in the Light of Psychoanalytic Knowledge.* This Quarterly, IV, pp. 570-587.

Arlow, Jacob A. (1961a): *Silence and the Theory of Technique.* J. Amer. Psa. Assn., IX, pp. 44-55.

——(1961b): *Ego Psychology and the Study of Mythology.* J. Amer. Psa. Assn., IX, pp. 371-393.

——(1969a): *Unconscious Fantasy and Disturbances of Conscious Experience.* This Quarterly, XXXVIII, pp. 1-27.

——(1969b): *Fantasy, Memory, and Reality Testing.* This Quarterly, XXXVIII, pp. 28-51.

——(1969c): Motor Behavior as Nonverbal Communication. Read before *Panel on Nonverbal Communication in the Analysis of Adults.* J. Amer. Psa. Ass., XVII, pp. 955-967.

Beres, David (1957): *Communication in Psychoanalysis and in the Creative Process: A Parallel.* J. Amer. Psa. Assn., V, pp. 408-423.

——(1962): *The Unconscious Fantasy.* This Quarterly, XXXI, pp. 309-328.

——(1968a): *The Role of Empathy in Psychotherapy and Psychoanalysis.* J. Hillside Hospital, XVII, pp. 362-369.

——(1968b): *The Humanness of Human Beings: Psychoanalytic Considerations.* This Quarterly, XXXVII, pp. 487-522.

Blos, Peter, Jr. (1972): *Silence: A Clinical Exploration.* This Quarterly, LXI, pp. 348-363.

Brierley, Marjorie (1943): *Theory, Practice, and Public Relations.* Int. J. Psa., XXIV, pp. 119-125.

Burlingham, Dorothy (1967): *Empathy between Infant and Mother.* J. Amer. Psa. Assn., XV, pp. 764-780.

Coleridge, Samuel T. (1802): Letter to William Sotheby, July 13th. In: *Collected Letters of Samuel Taylor Coleridge, Vol. II.* Edited by Earl Leslie Griggs. Oxford: Oxford University Press, 1956.

Deutsch, Felix (1947): *Analysis of Postural Behavior.* This Quarterly, XVI, pp. 195-213.

——(1952): *Analytic Posturology.* This Quarterly, XXI, pp. 196-214.

Deutsch, Helene (1926): Occult Processes Occurring during Psychoanalysis. In: *Psychoanalysis and the Occult.*

Edited by George Devereux. New York: International Universities Press, Inc., 1953, pp. 133–146.

Fenichel, Otto (1926): Identification. In: *Collected Papers of Otto Fenichel, Vol. I*. New York: W. W. Norton & Co., Inc., pp. 97–112.

Ferenczi, Sandor (1928): The Elasticity of Psychoanalytic Technique. In: *Final Contributions to the Theory and Technique of Psycho-Analysis. The Collected Papers of Sandor Ferenczi, Vol. III*. New York: Basic Books, Inc., 1955, pp. 87–101.

Ferreira, Antonio J. (1961): *Empathy and the Bridge Function of the Ego*. J. Amer. Psa. Assn., IX, pp. 91–105.

Freud, (1908[1907]): *Creative Writers and Day-Dreaming*. Standard Edition, IX, pp. 141–153.

——(1915[1914]): *Observations on Transference-Love. (Further Recommendations on the Technique of Psycho-Analysis III)*. Standard Edition, XII, pp. 157–171.

——(1915): *The Unconscious*. Standard Edition, XIV, pp. 159–215.

——(1921): *Group Psychology and the Analysis of the Ego*. Standard Edition, XVIII, pp. 65–143.

Gombrich, Ernst H. (1972): *Symbolic Images*. London: Phaidon Press Ltd.

Greenson, Ralph R. (1960): *Empathy and Its Vicissitudes*. Int. J. Psa., XLI, pp. 418–424.

Jacobs, Theodore J. (1973): *Posture, Gesture, and Movement in the Analyst: Cues to Interpretation and Countertransference*. J. Amer. Psa. Assn., XXI, pp. 77–92.

Kohut, Heinz (1959): *Introspection, Empathy, and Psychoanalysis. An Examination of the Relationship between Mode of Observation and Theory*. J. Amer. Psa. Assn., VII, pp. 459–483.

Kris, Ernst (1952): *Psychoanalytic Explorations in Art*. New York: International Universities Press, Inc.

Little, Margaret (1951): *Counter-Transference and the Patient's Response to It*. Int. J. Psa., XXXII, pp. 32–40.

Loewald, Hans (1970): Psychoanalytic Theory and the Psychoanalytic Process. In: *The Psychoanalytic Study of the Child, Vol. XXV*. New York: International Universities Press, Inc., pp. 45–68.

Mahler, Margaret S. (1968): *On Human Symbiosis and the Vicissitudes of Individuation, Vol. I, Infantile Psychosis*. New York: International Universities Press, Inc.

Miller, Ira (1972): *Inhibition of Empathy Caused by Unconscious Fantasy*. Int. J. Psa. Psychotherapy, I, pp. 107–116.

Olden, Christine (1953): On Adult Empathy with Children. In: *The Psychoanalytic Study of the Child, Vol. VIII*. New York: International Universities Press, Inc., pp. 111–126.

——(1958): Notes on the Development of Empathy. In: *The Psychoanalytic Study of the Child, Vol. XIII*. New York: International Universities Press, Inc., pp. 505–518.

Racker, Heinrich (1958): *Psychoanalytic Technique and the Analyst's Unconscious Masochism*. This Quarterly, XXVII, pp. 555–562.

Rank, Otto (1932): *Art and Artist: Creative Urge and Personality Development*. New York: Tudor Publishing Co.; Alfred A. Knopf.

Reich, Annie (1960): *Further Comments on Counter-Transference*. Int. J. Psa., XLI, pp. 389–395.

Sachs, Hanns (1942): *The Creative Unconscious. Studies in the Psychoanalysis of Art*. Cambridge, Mass.: Sci-Art Publishers.

Schafer, Roy (1968): *Aspects of Internalization*. New York: International Universities Press, Inc.

Shapiro, Theodore (1974): *The Development and Distortions of Empathy*. This Quarterly, XLIII, pp. 4–25.

Sharpe, Ella Freeman (1935): *Similar and Divergent Unconscious Determinants Underlying the Sublimations of Pure Art and Pure Science*. Int. J. Psa., XVI, pp. 186–202.

——(1940): *Psycho-Physical Problems Revealed in Language: An Examination of Metaphor*. Int. J. Psa., XXI, pp. 201–213.

24

COUNTERTRANSFERENCE AND ROLE-RESPONSIVENESS

Joseph Sandler

EDITOR'S NOTE

Earlier I mentioned Bion's paper on memory and desire (chapter 22) as one of two major addenda to Freud's concept of the analyst's use of evenly suspended attention. The other is this paper by Joseph Sandler. It has as its basis Freud's ideas (1914, 1920) concerning the patient's efforts to repeat rather than remember past pathogenic experiences in the relationship with the analyst, and thereby to engage the analyst in a reenactment, on some level, of that past. What is new and significant here is Sandler's specific identification of the need for free-floating interactional responsiveness to the roles and images that the patient tries to have the analyst experience. Sandler's distinction between the object relationship point of view, which his paper reflects, and the position of the Kleinians, who emphasize projective identification as basic to the therapeutic interaction, provided a basis for my investigations of the listening process, which I defined in terms of three fundamental spheres: the cognitive, the object relational, and the projective-introjective (see Langs 1978a).

As we know, the term 'countertransference' has a great many meanings, just as the term 'transference' has. Freud first saw countertransference as referring to the analyst's blind spots which presented an obstacle to the analysis. From the beginning, countertransference was consistently seen by Freud 'as an obstruction to the freedom of the analyst's understanding of the patient.' In this context Freud regarded the analyst's mind as an 'instrument . . ., its effective functioning in the analytic situation being impeded by counter-transference'. Countertransference in the analyst was equated with the resistance in the patient (Sandler, Dare & Holder, 1973).

As far as *transference* is concerned, it will be remembered that Freud saw it first as a hindrance, but later regarded it as an indispensable vehicle for the analytic work. However, he did not take a similar step in regard to countertransference, but this inevitable step was taken after Freud. It was a crucial development in the psychoanalytic literature when the countertransference 'began to be seen as a phenomenon of importance in helping the analyst to understand the hidden meaning of material brought by the patient. The essential idea . . . is that the analyst has elements of understanding and appreciation of the processes occurring in his patient, that these elements are not immediately conscious and that they can be discovered by the analyst if he monitors his own mental associations while listening to the patient' (Sandler, Dare & Holder, 1973). The first explicit statement of the *positive* value of countertransference was made by Paula Heimann (1950). Others have written on and developed the topic. However, the two papers by Paula Heimann

Reprinted from *International Review of Psycho-Analysis* 3:43–47, 1976.

(1950, 1960) have to be singled out as landmarks in the change of view of countertransference. She started by considering countertransference as referring to all the feelings which the analyst may experience towards his patient. Heimann remarks that the analyst has to be able to '*sustain* the feelings which are stirred up in him, as opposed to discharging them (as does the patient), in order to *subordinate* them to the analytic task in which he functions as the patient's mirror reflection'. She assumes 'that the analyst's unconscious understands that of his patient. This rapport on the deep level comes to the surface in the form of feelings which the analyst notices in response to his patient, in his "countertransference"' (Heimann, 1950).

I shall not mention the other important writings in this field, except to say that, of course, countertransference had been written about before Heimann's work and it had been pointed out that countertransference is a normal phenomenon. But what seems to have been stressed has been the differences between what one might call the 'appropriate' and 'useful' countertransference on the one hand and the 'dangerous' or 'undesirable' countertransference response on the other. Heimann's contribution was to show clearly that the reaction of the analyst may usefully be the first clue to what is going on in the patient.

In *The Patient and the Analyst* the literature on transference was discussed in some detail (Sandler, Dare & Holder, 1973) and we concluded by commenting that, in our view,

. . . transference need not be restricted to the illusory apperception of another person . . ., but can be taken to include the unconscious (and often subtle) attempts to manipulate or to provoke situations with others which are a concealed repetition of earlier experiences and relationships. It has been pointed out previously that when such transference manipulations or provocations occur in ordinary life, the person towards whom they are directed may either show that he does not accept the role, or may, if he is unconsciously disposed in that direction, in fact accept it, and act accordingly. It is likely that such acceptance or rejection of a transference role is not based on a conscious awareness of what is happening, but rather on unconscious cues. Transference elements enter to a varying degree into all relationships, and these (e.g. choice of spouse or employer) are often determined by some characteristic of the other person who (consciously or unconsciously) represents some attribute of an important figure of the past.

In our conclusions about transference we took the step of extending the notion of the patient's *projection* or *externalization* of some aspect of the past or of a figure of the past, on to the person of the analyst, to *all* his attempts to manipulate or to provoke situations with the analyst. I believe such 'manipulations' to be an important part of object relationships in general, and to enter in 'trial' form into the 'scanning' of objects in the process of object choice. In the transference, in many subtle ways, the patient attempts to prod the analyst into behaving in a particular way and unconsciously scans and adapts to his perception of the analyst's reaction. The analyst may be able to 'hold' his response to this 'prodding' in his consciousness as a reaction *of his own* which he perceives, and I would make the link between certain countertransference responses and transference via the behavioural (verbal and non-verbal) *interaction* between the patient and the analyst. Paula Heimann went as far as to point out that the analyst's response to the patient can be used as a basis for understanding the patient's material, often by something which he catches and holds in himself. I should like to try to take this a little further.

No one can doubt the value of the analyst's continuing analysis of his countertransference. We can, I believe, start by assuming that the understanding of countertransference *is* important. My own interest in the subject has, in recent years, run parallel with an interest in the psychoanalytic psychology of object relationships, and what I present in the following is based on the assumption that a relationship or, to say the least, an interaction, develops between the two parties to the analytic process. We are all aware of the special features of the analytic situation, with its capacity to induce the regressive revival of the past in the present, in a way which is usually entirely unconscious in or rationalized by the patient. On the other hand, we have the use made by the analyst of his special skills, including the employment by him of such capacities as that for free-floating attention, for self-analysis and for the maintenance of what Winnicott (1960) has called the 'professional attitude'. By free-floating attention I do not mean the 'clearing of the mind' of thoughts or memories, but the capacity to allow all sorts of thoughts, day-dreams and associations to enter the analyst's consciousness while he is at the same time listening to and observing the patient.

I have mentioned the interaction between the patient and the analyst, and this is in large part (though, of course, not wholly) determined by what I shall refer to as the intrapsychic role-relationship which each party tries to impose on the other. One aspect of such a role-relationship can be appropriate to the task in hand, i.e. to the work of analysis.

Certainly from the side of the *patient* we may see a whole variety of very specific role-relationships emerge. What I want to emphasize is that the role-relationship of the patient in analysis at any particular time consists of a role in which he casts himself, and a *complementary* role in which he casts the analyst at that particular time. The patient's transference would thus represent an attempt by him to impose an interaction, an interrelationship (in the broadest sense of the word) between himself and the analyst. Nowadays many analysts must have the conviction (or at least the uneasy feeling) that the conceptualization of transference as the patient's libidinal or aggressive energic cathexis of a past object being transferred to the image of the analyst in the present is woefully inadequate. The patient's unconscious wishes and mechanisms with which we are concerned in our work are expressed intrapsychically in (descriptively) unconscious images or fantasies, in which both self and object in interaction have come to be represented in particular roles. In a sense the patient, in the transference, attempts to *actualize*[1] *these in a disguised way*, within the framework and limits of the analytic situation. In doing so, he resists becoming aware of any infantile relationship which he might be attempting to impose. I want to underline, at this point, the difference between the manifest content of what the patient brings and the latent unconscious content (in particular the infantile role-relationships which he seeks to express or enact, as well as the defensive role-relationships which he may have constructed). If the patient keeps to the rules he will report rather than enact, and our clues, as analysts, to the unconscious inner role-relationship which the patient is trying to impose, come to us via our perceptions and the application of our analytic tools.

One could regard even the simplest instinctual wish as, from early in life, a wish to impose and to experience a *role-relationship* as a vehicle of instinctual gratification. However, what I have to say here applies not only to unconscious instinctual wishes, but *to the whole gamut of unconscious (including preconscious) wishes related to all sorts of needs, gratifications and defences.*

Parallel to the 'free-floating attention' of the analyst is what I should like to call his *free-floating responsiveness*. The analyst is, of course, not a machine in absolute self-control, only experiencing on the one

hand, and delivering interpretations on the other, although much of the literature might seem to paint such a picture. Among many other things he talks, he greets the patient, he makes arrangements about practical matters, he may joke and, to some degree, allow his responses to depart from the classical psychoanalytic norm. My contention is that in the analyst's overt reactions to the patient as well as in his thoughts and feelings what can be called his 'role-responsiveness' shows itself, not only in his feelings but also in his attitudes and behaviour, as a crucial element in his 'useful' countertransference.

Let me give one or two examples to illustrate what I mean.

1. This patient, aged 35, had not had any previous analysis and had very little knowledge of the analytic process. He was referred to me because of extreme anxiety about making public presentations of his work, although he felt absolutely competent and at ease in private and informal discussions. He had had a very narrow education, was the son of Eastern European immigrants, but because of his great financial and organizational skills had risen to a very high position in an extremely large financial organization. In the initial interview I found that he responded extremely well to trial interpretations, and I felt that work with him was going to be rewarding and a pleasure. During the first week or two of his analysis I found that I was talking very much more than I usually do. I should say that I am not an unduly silent analyst. After a little while I felt that something was making me anxious in regard to this patient, and some self-analytic reflexion on my part showed me that I was afraid that he would leave, that I was anxious to keep him, to lower his anxiety level so that he would stay in analysis and that I was talking more than usual in order to avoid the aggressive side of his ambivalent feelings. When I saw this, I felt relieved and reverted to my more usual analytic behaviour. However, I noticed at once the urge to talk during the session and became aware that the patient, by a slight inflexion of his voice, succeeded in ending every sentence with an interrogation, although he did not usually formulate a direct question. This gave me the opportunity to point out to him what he was doing (he was quite unaware of it, just as I had been unaware of it in him) and to show him how much he needed to have me reassure him by talking. He then recalled how he

---

1. I want to use the term *actualization* in the dictionary sense of the word, not in the specific technical senses in which it has been used by certain writers. The *Oxford English Dictionary* defines *actualization* as 'a making actual; a realization in action or fact', and *actualize* as 'to make actual, to convert into an actual fact, to realize in action'.

would feel extremely anxious as a child when his father returned home from work, and would compulsively engage his father in conversation, asking him many questions in order to be reassured that his father was not angry with him. His father had been a professional fighter, was very violent, and the patient was terrified of him but needed his father's admiration and love, to be the preferred child. (Later in the analysis we were, as one might expect, to see his fear of his own hostility to his father.) He told me that his father had the habit of not listening and not responding, and how frightening this was. The patient then realized that from early childhood onwards he had developed the trick of asking questions without directly asking them, and this had become part of his character, being intensified in situations where he feared disapproval and needed supplies of reassurance from authority figures.

The point I want to make here is that, apart from the 'ordinary' elements in his analytic work, the analyst will often respond overtly to the patient in a way which he feels indicates *only* his own (the analyst's) problems, his own blind spots, and he may successfully resort to self-analysis in order to discover the pathology behind his particular response or attitude to the patient. However, I want to suggest that very often the irrational response of the analyst, which his professional conscience leads him to see entirely as a blind spot of his own, may sometimes be usefully regarded as a compromise-formation between his own tendencies and *his reflexive acceptance of the role which the patient is forcing on him.*

Naturally, some analysts will be more susceptible to certain roles than others, and also the proportion of the contribution from the side of the patient and from the side of the analyst will vary greatly from one instance to another. And, of course, not all the irrational actions and reactions of the analyst are reflexions of the role into which he is manoeuvred by the patient. What I wanted to show in this example was simply how the patient, by a rather subtle element in his behaviour, evoked an overt response from the analyst which, at first sight, seemed to be *only* irrational countertransference. Let me say emphatically that I am absolutely opposed to the idea that all countertransference responses of the analyst are due to what the patient has imposed on him.

Let me give a further example.

2. This refers to a patient in her late twenties and a schoolteacher. She came to treatment because of social and sexual difficulties, and after some time it became clear that she was terrified of her penis-envy and of her hostility towards her mother, had multiple phobic anxieties and needed, mainly through intellectualization and organizational control of others, including her teaching, to 'structure' her world so that she always knew exactly 'where she was'. Her need to do this emerged in the transference, and after some three years of analytic work her psychopathology had become very much clearer and she was much improved and happier. However, there was one strand of material which had remained rather obscure. From the beginning she had cried during each session, and I had routinely passed her the box of tissues whenever she began to cry. Now I did not know why I did this but, having begun the practice, I did not feel inclined to change it without some good reason. Without knowing why, I had not felt it appropriate to take up her failure to bring her own tissues or a handkerchief, although with other patients I would have done this. There were many determinants of her crying, including her mourning for the mother she wanted to kill off, for the father she felt she had to give up, and so on. It transpired that when she was about two years old and a second child, a brother, had been born, she felt that she had lost her mother's attention, and remembered that at about two and a half years of age she was relegated to playing on her own in the back-yard while her brother was being washed and changed. At this time she had also been sent to a kindergarten, and she had the memory of being very withdrawn and climbing into the rabbit hutch at the nursery school and cuddling a white rabbit. She then told me that she had later learned that after a short while at this school she was diagnosed as 'autistic' by the school psychologist, and was apparently very regressed and had uncontrollable rages and tantrums. By this point in her analysis we were able to get at the repetition in the present of her fear of soiling and disgracing herself, and her need to control her objects as she had to control her sphincters. However, there was clearly something which was an important unconscious fantasy for her and which had not been elicited. I had the feeling that we were somewhat 'stuck' in the analytic work. One day something rather unusual happened in the analysis. She had begun to cry silently but this time I failed to respond, and she suddenly began to upbraid me and criticize me for not passing her the tissues. She became quite panicky and began to accuse me of being callous and uncaring. I responded by saying that I did not know why I had not passed her the tissues at that particular point, but if she could go on talking perhaps we could both understand more about it. What emerged then was material which lent a great deal of specificity to something which we had not been able to

crystallize previously. It became clear that her great need for control and for 'structures' in her life was based not on a fear of soiling herself, but rather on a fear that she would soil or wet herself *and that there would not be an adult around to clean her up*. This turned out to be the fear which dominated her life. It was a specific fantasy which seemed to have been elaborated during the late anal phase, under the impact of the mother's withdrawal from her because of the birth of the second child. The discovery and working through of this specific fantasy marked a crucial point in her analysis. I do not want to go into any more detail about her material, except to say that I think that I must have picked up unconscious cues from the patient which prompted me to behave in a certain way in her analysis, both to keep passing her the tissues and then to omit doing so. (It would be pure speculation to link the two and a half years of analysis with the age when her anxiety started.) I believe that this patient had forced me into a role, quite unconsciously on her part and on mine, a role corresponding to that of a parental introject, in which I enacted the part, first of the attentive mother and then suddenly that of the parent who did not clean her up. In the session I was not around to make sure that she was clean, just as she felt that, with the birth of her brother, her mother had not been around to clean her, being busy paying attention to the new baby.

Because of the length of this presentation is limited I cannot go into this rich topic any further, and in conclusion I shall restrict myself to one or two points. I have suggested that the analyst has, within certain limits, a free-floating behavioural responsiveness in addition to his free-floating conscious attention.

Within the limits set by the analytical situation he will, unless he becomes aware of it, tend to comply with the role demanded of him, to integrate it into his mode of responding and relating to the patient. Normally, of course, he can catch this counter-response in himself, particularly if it appears to be in the direction of being inappropriate. However, he may only become aware of it through observing his own behaviour, responses and attitudes, *after these have been carried over into action*. What I have been concerned with in this paper is the special case of the analyst regarding some aspect of his own behaviour as deriving entirely from within himself when it could more usefully be seen as a *compromise* between his own tendencies or propensities and the role-relationship which the patient is unconsciously seeking to establish. I should add that I do not find the terms 'projection', 'externalization', 'projective identification' and 'putting parts of oneself into the analyst' sufficient to explain and to understand the processes of dynamic interaction which occur in the transference and countertransference. It seems that a complicated system of unconscious cues, both given and received, is involved. This is the same sort of process that occurs not only in the aspects of transference and countertransference discussed here but in normal object relationships and in the process of temporary or permanent object choice as well.

REFERENCES

Heimann, P. (1950). On counter-transference. *Int. J. Psycho-Anal.* 31, 81–84.

Heimann, P. (1960). Counter-transference. *Br J. med. Psychol.* 33, 9–15.

Sandler, J., Dare, C. & Holder, A. (1973). *The Patient and the Analyst: The Basis of the Psychoanalytic Process*. London: Allen & Unwin.

Winnicott, D. W. (1960). Countertransference, *Br. J. med. Psychol.* 33, 17–21.

25

INTERVENTIONS IN THE BIPERSONAL FIELD

ROBERT LANGS

EDITOR'S NOTE

Here interventions are examined using the listening and validating processes (Langs 1978a). The result of this detailed study of unconscious communications in the therapeutic interaction is the delineation of six basic interventions, some of them new to the literature. Fundamentally interactional in its approach, this paper considers the patient's unconscious interventions, the role of countertransference, and a methodology for the derivation and confirmation of the analyst's efforts. Particularly notable is the division of the analyst's interventions into those related to the ground rules—setting, hold, containing, and framework factors, all elements of the background of therapy—and those related to the foreground—the ongoing analytic interaction and the dynamic contents of the patient's associations. The study of interventions in terms of distinctive communicative fields and styles, and in respect to cognitive, interactional, and object relational aspects, are additional innovative features of this contribution. Finally, there is a brief consideration of the countertransference element in every intervention, and a preliminary discussion of the far-reaching implications of this insight.

It is my purpose in this paper to reconceptualize the nature and function of interventions, consequent to a study of their effects within the bipersonal field. I will take an adaptational-interactional approach to the unconscious communicative interaction between patient and therapist or analyst,[1] in contrast to existing studies of interventions, which appear based upon a classification founded on their manifest properties, rather than on their implications within the therapeutic interaction.

THE PREVIOUS LITERATURE

The literature related to the analyst's intervention has confined itself almost entirely to the sphere of verbal efforts designed to generate cognitive insight within the patient. This tone was set by Freud, who, with the exception of his paper on reconstructions (1937), did not offer a systematic study of the analyst's interventions. There are virtually no references to interpretations in the Standard Edition; these are confined to a few brief remarks on the importance of the interpretation of transference resistances (see especially Freud 1913), and scattered efforts at dream interpretation (perhaps best illustrated in his analysis of the two dreams reported by his patient, Dora; Freud 1905). Implicit in Freud's endeavors is the important role of unconscious fantasies, especially

Reprinted from *Technique in Transition* by Robert Langs, pp. 627–678. New York: Jason Aronson, 1978. This paper has appeared also in *Contemporary Psychoanalysis* 15:1–54.

transference fantasies, in the patient's symptoms and neurosis, and the use of interpretations of their derivative expression, especially at times of resistance, as a means of making unconscious contents and the related defensive mechanisms conscious to the patient. Throughout these writings, however, there is consistent evidence for Freud's grasp of the need for validation from the patient of both interpretations and reconstructions, essentially through what he termed *indirect material* (Freud 1937).

Perhaps the single paper most often referred to in discussions of intervening is that of Bibring (1954), who synthesized the scattered writings on the subject by distinguishing five techniques, verbal and nonverbal, expressed in the behaviors of the therapist and intended to affect the patient in the direction of the goals of analysis. These techniques he designated suggestive, abreactive, manipulative, clarifying, and interpretive.

In brief, suggestion refers to the therapist's induction of ideas, impulses, emotions, and actions in the patient, to the relative exclusion of the latter's rational or critical thinking. Abreaction alludes to the emotional discharge and reliving, through which intense feelings and responses to traumas are ventilated. Manipulation includes advice, guidance, directives, efforts to neutralize certain emotional forces, the mobilization of certain conflicts, and a wide range of comparable measures. Clarification is any effort by the therapist to enable the patient to see more clearly the nature of his feelings, thoughts, and other communications; it is generally developed on a conscious level and alludes to contents or implications of which the patient is not sufficiently aware. Finally, interpretations are an attempt to identify unconscious material, defenses, and warded-off instinctual drive tendencies, related to the hidden meanings of the patient's behaviors and their unconscious interconnections. Interpretations include constructions and reconstructions of unconscious processes assumed to determine manifest behavior. They are the essential vehicle through which the patient is afforded insight, and become effective through the process of assimilation, which is related to working through, and which leads to reorientation and readjustment.

Virtually every work on psychoanalytic technique has regarded interpretation and working through as the ultimate expression of the analyst's interventions, the means through which the patient gains insight and adaptive structural change. Greenson (1967) is representative in this regard, and he leaned heavily on the contribution of Bibring (1954). He suggested that the analysis of transference or the transference neurosis is the central therapeutic effort in psychoanalytic treatment. It involves demonstrating the transference through confrontations and the use of evidence; clarification of the transference, which includes at times, a pursuit of the transference trigger; interpretation of the transference in terms of the relevant affects, impulses, and attitudes, which entails tracing the antecedents of the transference figure and a full exploration of the transference fantasy; and the working through of transference interpretations. For Greenson, to interpret means to make an unconscious phenomenon conscious. In addition, he commented on the necessity for validation, and while not exploring this aspect in any detail, he did note that verification is essential in determining the correctness of an interpretation and that it often takes the form of the patient's adding some new embellishing material.

My own clinical delineation of the therapist's interventions (1973) used and expanded the basic contributions of Bibring and Greenson. However, certain additional trends are evident. First, I included silence among the therapist's basic interventions, to which I added questions, clarifications, confrontations, interpretations, and reconstructions. Second, while maintaining the usual psychoanalytic focus on the formal characteristics and conscious intentions of these interventions, I also alluded to a variety of unconscious meanings and communications inherent in both valid and essentially erroneous interventions. For perhaps the first time in the literature, there was specific consideration of the misuses of the various interventions and of the influence of the therapist's countertransferences in this regard. Third, I offered an extended discussion of confirmation and nonconfirmation of interventions, and attempted to develop specific clinical criteria for the validity of an intervention.

Finally, in a chapter that in many ways is the forerunner of the findings and hypotheses to be described here, I reexamined the therapist's so-called supportive (supposedly positive, through noninterpretive) interventions (Langs 1973: Chapter 16). Through an investigation of the patient's unconscious (indirect and derivative) responses to such measures, it became evident that they were experienced as destructive manipulations, invasions of privacy, infringements upon the patient's autonomy, and the like, and that despite conscious acceptance on the part of the patient, the unconscious repercussions were uniformly negative.

In the five years since publication of the technique books, my studies of the analytic and therapeutic situations have evolved more and more in terms of adaptive and interactional considerations. With the use of the metaphor of the bipersonal field, the unconscious interaction between patient and analyst, and their unconscious communicative exchange, began to take on increasingly greater importance. As this perspective widened, the formal attributes and goals of an intervention, while still critical, were viewed as but one dimension of the therapist's communications to the patient, and their unconscious communicative qualities and functions became the subject of extensive investigation.

The bipersonal field concept also led to an elaborate study of the nature and functions of the ground rules or framework of the therapeutic and analytic situations. This led to the specific delineation of a major sphere of interventions that previously had not been separated from the therapist's interpretive endeavors: the establishment, management, and rectification of the frame. Many new hypotheses were generated and validated, leading to fresh perspectives on the therapeutic interaction (Langs 1976a,b, 1978a,b,c,d). In the course of this work, new insights were developed in regard to many aspects of the therapist's interventions, and these form the substance of this paper.

BASIC METHODOLOGY: THE LISTENING AND VALIDATING PROCESS

The listening process itself entails the first application of the validating process. In the course of listening and formulating, the analyst generates *silent hypotheses* which must be silently validated from the patient's continued associations—e.g., through a coalescence of unconscious meaning—before the analyst intervenes. The second application of the validating process occurs after the intervention, and entails a search for confirmation in both the cognitive and the interactional spheres (see Langs 1976b, 1978b,d for details).

Two basic propositions must be stated: first, that the full application of the listening process consistently reveals that the most significant unconscious communications and adaptive reactions within the patient derive from his relationship with the analyst. This implies that this relationship and interaction must be the essential realm of the analyst's interventions, and that interventions based on outside adaptive contexts and unconscious reactions must in some way be related to the therapeutic relationship (Langs 1978b).

The second proposition involves the essential methodology for the present study of the analyst's interventions. This may be stated in general as the complete application of the full range of the listening and validating processes. Beyond that, however, a particular aspect of these processes plays a major role: the role of every intervention by the analyst, whatever its nature, as the essential adaptive context for the patient's subsequent communications. These responses are considered as validating or nonvalidating on one level but, on another, are viewed as a rich *commentary* (Langs 1978b) on the unconscious implications of the intervention at hand.

In distinction from the usual view of the patient's material as essentially transference-based and distorted, and as falling largely in the realm of fantasy, attending to such material as a commentary implies that the patient's associations and behaviors will be organized as Type Two derivatives in the adaptive context of the analyst's intervention, taking fully into account its unconscious implications. Here, the me/not-me interface is fully applied, revealing the manner in which the patient has unconscious experienced and introjected these unconscious qualities of the analyst's intervention (Langs 1978b,c,d).

In keeping with principles already stated, the patient's manifest and latent response is seen as a mixture of reality and distorted fantasy, of veridical perception and pathological misperception. This material therefore contains both truths and falsifications regarding analyst and patient alike; it is essential to sort out the different components of this mixture. As is true with every aspect of the listening process, which is greatly influenced by the whole gamut of factors within the analyst, this crucial step in the listening process—the distinction of the veridical from the distorted—relics on the self-awareness of the analyst, his capacity to maintain perspective, and his understanding of internal and external reality as it applies to both himself and the patient. By maintaining an openness for valid unconscious perceptions and introjects based on the patient's internal processing of the therapist's interventions (in addition to investigating these reactions for their pathological components), the analyst has a rich opportunity to ascertain the unconscious qualities of his therapeutic endeavors. This basic resource is supplemented by the analyst's own subjective responses to his interventions, his reconsideration of what he has said or done, his thoughts and feelings about it, and the like—his own conscious commentary and efforts at validation, which can themselves be processed for unconscious meaning.

The evaluation of an intervention, then, is based on the totality of these applications of the listening and validating processes. Validating sequences tend to confirm the analyst's conscious intentions, and to reflect minimal disturbing inputs on the unconscious communicative level — an aspect that is, of course, always present, though it need not be essentially pathological. Nonvalidating responses contain derivatives related both to the correct intervention required for the moment and to the unconscious, countertransference-based inputs reflected in the erroneous intervention. A revised formulation — silent hypothesis — that is subsequently subjected to silent validation can then be interpreted to the patient, and the entire sequence subjected to a second effort at interactional validation.

It is evident that this methodology has little use for an assessment as to whether a given intervention is designed as an interpretation, a question, or whatever. It treats all interventions as conscious and unconscious communications, identifies their conscious form and purpose, and then extensively explores the unconscious intentions, functions, and communicative roles. It does so in a manner that is repeatedly subjected to validation, and it is efforts of this kind that have yielded the findings and hypotheses to which I will now turn.

Six Basic Interventions

On the basis of this clinical research, I will propose an armamentarium for the analyst (or therapist) of six basic interventions (I will discuss below those interventions excluded from this classification): silence; the establishment, management, and rectification of the framework; interpretations-reconstructions; the playing back of derivatives in the absence of a clear-cut adaptive context (one usually related to the therapeutic relationship); the metabolization of a projective identification; and the identification of metaphors for the Type C field and their function. The latter four interventions reflect what I would broadly term the *interpretive efforts* of the analyst, and occur in two basic forms: *definitive interventions* and *transversal interventions*.

I will comment briefly on these fundamental tools.

1. *Silence* is, of course, absolutely basic to the analyst's repertory of interventions. It is filled with non-verbal and unconscious implications, which may vary from moment to moment and from session to session, within the context of the dynamic interaction between patient and analyst. It implies holding the patient, containing his communications and projective identifications, and permitting him to build the analyst's interventions out of fragments

that need only be synthesized and organized. It implies entering each session without desire, memory, or understanding (Bion 1970, Langs 1978b), and permitting the patient to create unconsciously the analyst's understanding and intervention. It implies too a capacity for the adequate management of internal conflicts, tensions, and the like within the analyst, and it certainly conveys a wish to understand and help the patient. It represents the analyst's free-floating attention (Freud 1912), free-floating role-responsiveness (Sandler 1976), and openness to the metabolism of projective identifications (Langs 1976a, 1978b). It embodies the analyst's wish to listen, contain, understand, and offer constructive help in keeping with the patient's appropriate needs.

It is also self-evident that silence can be misused and inappropriately extended in the service of countertransference-based needs within the analyst. This occurs in all situations that call for a positive intervention from the analyst, at which point his silence no longer serves the therapeutic needs of the analysand. However, with the exception of preliminary efforts in the technique book (Langs 1973; see also Langs 1976a, for additional references), there has been little effort to empirically delineate the characteristics of appropriate silence and the definitive properties of moments at which its maintenance is no longer tenable. The matter is extremely complex, though it can be definitively stated that the evaluation of the functions of the analyst's silences calls for full use of the validating process. Silence is by far the best way of facilitating the patient's free association, communication of indirect, derivative contents and mechanisms, and unconscious interactional thrusts; it is the optimal means through which expressions of the patient's neurosis become available for interpretation.

There are, then, two major indications for the use of silence: first, the need to wait and allow the patient to build up a neurotic communicative network, to communicate the role evocations, cognitive derivatives, and interactional pressures that provide the substance through which a positive intervention can be made; and second, the absence of truly analyzable material, of interpretable derivatives, role pressures, and interactional processes. There is a tendency among analysts to intervene more actively under the latter conditions, with the expectation that such interventions ultimately will promote derivative expression by the patient; my own observations indicate that this is a deceptive rationalization and that active interventions under the conditions just described have no such effect. Silence, then, is the preferred intervention in the absence of interpretable material. Inappropriate silences lead to the problem of failures to intervene, a subject that will be discussed in the section on countertransference-based influences.

2. *Establishing, managing, and rectifying the framework, and analyzing infringements* constitute a major group of relatively unrecognized and consistently crucial interventions. Included here is the series of interventions through which the analyst establishes the analytic contract and the conditions of treatment (Langs 1973, 1976b). Interventions in this area also involve responses to efforts by the patient to modify the framework, and in addition, any necessary steps involved in rectifying an alteration in the ground rules. Included here, too, is the announcement of any change in the usual course of the sessions (e.g., a vacation by the analyst), and any other major or minor modification in the basic agreement and tenets of the psychoanalytic situation.

Elsewhere (Langs 1975a,b, 1976a,b, 1978a,b,c), I have rather extensively defined the basic framework of psychoanalysis and psychoanalytic psychotherapy, and have clinically demonstrated and discussed its multiple meanings and functions for both patient and analyst. In essence, the framework contributes to the basic ego-enhancing therapeutic hold offered by the analyst to the patient, a security that permits therapeutic regression and the unfolding of analyzable expressions of the patient's intrapsychic pathology—primarily within the analytic interaction. Similar support is inherently afforded the analyst by these conditions, and both patient and analyst have available a secured container for pathological projective identifications and other pathological communications. In addition, the framework is the single most essential factor in determining the nature of the communicative medium and whether language will be used for insight and understanding, or instead for pathological projective identifications, for inappropriate and pathological forms of defense and gratification, and as massive defensive barriers.

Since the conditions of the analytic situation as constituted by the framework are one of the most basic actualities of treatment, the patient is extremely sensitive to the most minor alteration in the frame; deviations will consistently function as traumatic adaptive contexts engendering intense unconscious reactions. Deviations in the frame, no matter what the reason (even in emergencies), are experienced unconsciously as in part disruptive and threatening, and as filled with danger and countertransference (when the analyst has participated). They consistently disturb the communicative properties of the biper-

sonal field and tend to shift the field from a Type A mode, if present, to a Type B or Type C modality.

As an essential determinant of the communicative medium of psychoanalysis, responses to alterations in the framework are among the most crucial indications for intervention. Interventions in such situations should be designed to restore a secure frame in actuality—rectification—and should include the interpretation of the extensive implications that both the alteration and the rectification have had for the patient. These efforts are productive of extensive insight and positive introjective identifications, and are a major vehicle of adaptive structural change and cure.

It is the analyst's responsibility in the first hour to establish the analytic contract with clear and firm definition. Such an approach cannot be characterized as rigid, though it is rigorous, since it is designed for the patient's therapeutic needs (and has been extensively validated in the clinical situation as offering the best medium for the patient's analysis).

As a matter of principle, then, the analyst endeavors to maintain the framework as defined in the initial hour, without exception. For example, the unexpected need on his part to be absent for a session will entail its cancellation without the offer of a make-up appointment; similarly, vacations are taken as anticipated and hours are not made up. In all other ways, the analyst strives to maintain the frame—a point also made by Viderman (1974).

Any effort on the part of the patient to modify the basic framework (e.g., the wish to change an hour, to have an insurance form filled out, to take a unilateral vacation, etc.) is met with the basic response of silence (the absence of any direct reaction), permitting the patient to continue to free associate. When under pressure, the analyst must avoid both participation and direct refusal to participate, and must maintain his basic analytic attitude: it is essential that the patient continue to free associate. On that basis, the patient's subsequent material serves as a commentary on his proposal, and will reveal in derivative form both its unconscious meanings and the appropriate response for the analyst, which, remarkably enough, always turns out to be—adherence to the established frame. The analyst is then in a position to use the material from the patient as a means of deriving his management response—adhering to the principle of permitting the patient to shape every intervention—and to interpret the unconscious meanings for the patient. The latter interventions take the form of the interpretation of Type Two derivatives around the adaptive context of the proposed alteration in the frame, and are almost always expressed in the

Type A mode. Such work clearly entails additional communications beyond the analyst's interpretive efforts; he has no choice but to establish his position regarding the frame in reality, although I must stress again that this can always be done at the prompting of the patient's unconscious communications.

In situations in which there has been a deliberate or inadvertent alteration of the frame, it is essential to both rectify the frame and interpret the entire experience. Rectification is the essential first step, since it is vital to the restoration of the therapeutic alliance and the positive communicative properties of the bipersonal field, as well as to the necessary interpretive work. When the frame has been altered, unconsciously the analyst is seen as dangerous, the boundaries are unclear, the implications of his verbal and behavioral communications are uncertain, and the patient feels endangered. Rectifying measures—e.g., no longer signing insurance forms, shifting hours, or extending sessions, and desisting in nonneutral interventions—should always be accompanied by interpretive efforts. Examples will be provided and discussed in the clinical section of this paper.

3. *Interpretations-reconstructions* allude to the analyst's basic efforts to make unconscious contents, processes, defenses, interactional mechanisms—fantasies, memories, introjects, self- and object-representations, and the like—conscious for the patient within a dynamic and affective framework. It is well beyond the scope of this presentation to discuss the mechanics of interpretation and reconstruction, or to explore many issues involved in the development and offer of an interpretive and reconstructive intervention (see Kris 1947, Loewenstein 1951, 1957, Ekstein 1959, Greenson 1960, Shapiro 1970, Fine, Joseph, and Waldhorn 1971, Zac 1972, Levy 1973, Langs 1973, Rosen 1974, Viderman 1974, Edelson 1975, Davis and O'Farrell 1976). Here my focus will be on certain properties of interpretations and reconstructions (I will offer my discussion mainly in terms of the former) which are brought to the fore by the adaptational-interactional approach. While these two interrelated interventions play a central role in generating cognitive insight and adaptive structural change as the basis for symptom alleviation, interpretations can serve their intended function only if the bipersonal field has a secure frame. In its absence, intended interpretations consistently serve as vehicles for the analyst's pathological projective identifications or as a means of creating Type C barriers.

Within the bipersonal field, then, every interpre-

tation should be developed around an adaptive context and in terms of Type Two derivatives. These interventions must in addition be appended to the therapeutic interaction, even in the presence of a central outside adaptive context (even here, the outside adaptive context will allude on some level to an aspect of the patient's therapeutic experience). Further, the analyst must be prepared to interpret both unconscious fantasies and unconscious perceptions, since the neglect of either or the confusion of one with the other is disruptive of the analytic process. Much so-called analytic work is carried out in disregard of these essential principles, and is maintained through a suspension of the validating process and a denial of the patient's unconscious perceptions and their elaboration.

Clearly, then, the formal classification of a particular intervention says relatively little about its communicative properties. Every interpretation contains inputs both from the analyst's countertransferences and from his noncountertransference functioning. A valid interpretation minimizes the former, while an erroneous intervention is relatively saturated with the latter.

In preparing an interpretation and in listening to it as it is spoken, the analyst can initiate a process through which he endeavors to become aware (of necessity, partly in retrospect) of the essential unconscious communications it contains. He should begin by identifying the manifest content of his effort; next he should attempt to identify the particular adaptive context, and to monitor the patient's responses for unconscious fantasies, introjects, defenses, and interactional efforts. At times he will be able to relate this delineation to a particular therapeutic context—symptoms, resistances, etc.—and, in addition, to introduce from the patient's material specific genetic links.

However, beyond the analyst's conscious intentions, the range of unconscious communication is infinite. As is well known, much is conveyed in the tone, style, wording, affective investment, timing, tact, and other verbal and nonverbal qualities of an intervention. In undertaking to restructure the relatively dispersed or fragmented communications from the patient into a meaningful whole organized around a particular adaptive context, the analyst will inevitably be selective. There is a need for him to be definitive and to be understood without becoming overrepetitive or confusing; if he is to succeed in this, he must deal not with too many facets of the complex communicative networks he faces. This danger of being overinclusive is of course countered by that of being too restrictive. The proper balance falls within a rather ill-defined range, and errors in either direction may be viewed as communicative blind spots.

The possibilities for error here are endless. The analyst may identify a wrong adaptive context or attempt to intervene without having identified the primary adaptive task. There may be interventions based largely on the analyst's associations rather than on the patient's: fragments of the analyst's own fantasies may be introduced, or, more subtly, material from other sessions which for the moment is quite dormant within the patient (every session should, in its entirety, be its own creation). Other instances of error are the need to exclude particular types of derivatives, and the failure to be sufficiently selective, giving the impression of disorganization and uncertainty.

Any fragment or thread that extends beyond the patient's own unconscious communications tends to be derived from the analyst's countertransferences. In subjectively reviewing an intervention, the analyst must be able to identify relatively quickly his own idiosyncratic contributions. He will be guided in this task by the associations from the patient, which will often address the countertransference-based aspects of the analyst's communication before those elements that are essentially valid and helpful. While this is an aspect of the listening process that is beyond the scope of this paper (see Langs 1978b), it is to be stressed that these commentaries from the patient occur almost always in derivative form. Subsequent interventions from the analyst must therefore address the patient's introjection and processing of any pathological communication from the analyst, though not to the exclusion of other aspects of the patient's material. A fully balanced, perceptive interpretive approach is difficult to achieve, but an important ideal to strive for.

As for reconstructions my concern lies, first, in the possibility of the analyst's introducing countertransference-based elements because of the climate of uncertainty in these interventions and the consequent need to postulate; second, in the tendency to invoke a genetic reconstruction primarily in the service of countertransference-based defenses and needs within the analyst. Clinically, it is not uncommon to discover that an analyst has introduced a genetic reconstruction entirely divorced from the present analytic interaction, or one that treats current experience almost entirely in terms of the patient's distortions and fantasies. Such reconstructions serve defensive needs in the analyst and are often invoked when he has placed disturbing, countertransference-based interventions into the analytic bipersonal field, and the patient has introjected and perceived them unconsciously, and is working them over in a rather disturbed climate. The shift to genetics and the past becomes a major invitation to the patient to desist in his conscious and unconscious responses to the analyst's countertransference-based interventions. In this context, when a reconstruction evokes new memories and genetic material, these communications must be understood as having *functional meaning* (Langs 1978b) that pertain not only to the past, but to the current analytic experience. In principle, then, reconstructions should be offered in terms of prevailing adaptive contexts within the therapeutic interaction, and in a manner that accords meaning to both past and present.

4. *The playing back of selected derivatives* is an important technical measure that is often used in the absence of an adaptive context acknowledged by the patient, a context almost always related to the therapeutic interaction. The analyst is aware of the adaptive context (e.g., the patient has been absent in the prior hour, the analyst has announced his vacation, there has been some extraanalytic contact, etc.), but the patient has not alluded to it or provided any clear-cut bridge to it in his associations in the hour. Such an omission reflects significant intrapsychic, and sometimes interactional, defenses, and efforts at pathological instinctual drive gratification; these should not be bypassed or gratified by the introduction of the missing element by the analyst. The analysis of such defenses is fostered by the analyst's silences until the relevant material has surfaced. At times, however, the missing adaptive context is also a crucial therapeutic context; here there are important reasons to intervene.

In a session of this kind, while maintaining an openness for additional adaptive contexts, the analyst organizes the patient's material around the unmentioned primary adaptive task. Virtually always, the patient's indirect communications will convey a commentary on that context, in terms of both unconscious fantasies and unconscious perceptions. They will be filled with unconscious implications and Type Two derivatives related to the context, and in the later part of the session, sound technique calls for the playback of these selected derivatives in a form that leaves open the possibility of fantasy and perception, as well as allusions to both patient and therapist. This is a quality that is essential to what I term a *transversal intervention*, which alludes equally to seemingly contradictory possibilities.

This type of playback is designed to create a tension state or preconception (Bion 1962) in the patient, which can be alleviated or saturated into a conception only through an identification of the organizing adaptive context. Quite often, the patient responds in a way that fulfills this expectation, permitting subsequent interpretive work around the now identified adaptive context.

It is evident that the technique of playing back selected derivatives can be seen as a form of confrontation, but I prefer to discard the latter term largely because of its many destructive implications and misapplications. In general, confrontations address the surface of the patient's communications, while the playing back of derivatives is a transversal communication that embodies both manifest and latent contents. It is designed as a bridge to the patient's unconscious communications and is not fixated at the surface. It fosters expression of the necessary missing communicative elements, including the unconscious basis for the patient's resistances. Further, it minimizes the possibility of countertransference-based inputs from the analyst at a time when he is frustrated in not having sufficient material from the patient for interpretation. It is an extremely useful technique, and I will illustrate its use in the section on clinical material.

5. *The interventional processing—or metabolization—of a projective identification* is related to each of the four interventions I have so far identified, and is based on listening and experiencing the communications from the patient in terms of interactional pressures and projections (Langs 1978b). All formulations built on subjective experiences of this kind must be considered *silent hypotheses* to be validated largely through the cognitive material from the patient. The insightful metabolism of a projective identification from the patient will yield cognitive understanding that ultimately can be conveyed to the patient through an interpretation.

These considerations are equally applicable to interventions in the object relational sphere, as they pertain to unconscious efforts on the part of the patient to evoke role responses, self-images, and other reactions in the analyst in keeping with the patient's unconscious transference fantasies and the real or imagined behaviors of earlier objects—as well as of the analyst in the present (the countertransference aspect; see Langs 1978b). Because of the major element of subjectivity, the need for silent validation is again essential.

In intervening in regard to a projective identification or role evocation, the analyst should maintain the principle of initiating his comments with an adaptive context whenever possible. In the absence of such a context, his remarks should be modeled on the playing back of derivatives, though these must be expressed largely in the interactional sphere. In general, though he should be aware of the adaptive context, however disguised, in the face of massive efforts at interactional projection he may find it necessary to intervene without a clear-cut precipitant. In so doing, he must either state or hint that the adaptive organizer is lacking, and he must make every effort to use Type One derivatives and unconscious inferences; there is a major danger of adhering to the surface of a projective identification rather than delving into its unconscious contents and functions.

When an adaptive context is available, the interactional projection elements are organized as Type Two derivatives and interpreted in terms of the analytic interaction. In the absence of an adaptive context, it is necessary to minimize the introduction of idiosyncratic elements that are open to significant countertransference-based inputs. The patient's projective identifications often impinge upon the framework of the analytic situation, and maintenance of the frame is essential for their effective processing.

6. *Identifying metaphors related to the Type C field and their function* is a special intervention designed to cope with patients who make use of the Type C communicative style. The material from these patients is flat and lacking in derivatives, and as a rule lends itself neither to interpretations nor to the playing back of selected derivatives. It is only after interventions related to the patient's unconscious metaphorical representation of his communicative style and defenses that derivative material, usually quite chaotic and regressive, becomes momentarily available for interpretive work. With such patients, long periods are spent in silent listening and in the occasional presentation of these metaphors (see also Langs 1978b,c).

Wherever possible, the metaphorical representation should be linked to an adaptive context and its defensive-barrier function hinted at or directly stated. Such barriers often serve as massive defenses against an active psychotic disturbance. Unconsciously, the patient is aware of his defensiveness and will from time to time permit a metaphor to communicate this awareness. Typical metaphors of this sort include allusions to safes, tanks, walls, dead ends, voids, unrelatedness, lies and deceptions.

TRANSVERSAL INTERVENTIONS

Finally, I wish to discuss an aspect of intervening that may apply to interpretations-reconstructions, the playing back of selected derivatives, and the interpretive processing of projective identifications. I refer to the *transversal* quality or form of an intervention, a necessary aspect of technique with which the analyst responds to the patient's *transversal communications* (Langs 1978b). Such communications are characterized by the manner in which they traverse two realms: reality and fantasy, patient and analyst, transference and nontransference, or perception and distortion. Every communication, whether from patient or analyst, has dormant transversal qualities in that it condenses opposite elements of one kind or another (a possible exception occurs in the Type C field, where apparent communications are actually attempts to destroy meaning; but even this is only a tendency, as the attempt is often betrayed by the appearance of Type C metaphors). We will reserve the term *transversal communication,* however, for those associations and behaviors whose heavy investment with ambiguity makes itself felt; when a communication is so experienced, is is almost always found to arise from and to express a specific adaptive context; where this is not found, the experience must itself be examined, in the case of the analyst, for countertransference inputs.

Often, when the patient has unconsciously perceived and introjected the countertransference-based aspect of an intervention from the analyst, the working over and commentary by the analysand will be heavily invested in both veridical perceptions and pathological distortions. In intervening, it is essential that the analyst acknowledge the validity of the patient's perceptions, while not neglecting the distorted aspects that derive from the patient's own pathological unconscious fantasies and the like. Similar considerations apply to associations that meaningfully though unconsciously allude to both the patient himself and the analyst—both must be acknowledged through a transversal interpretation.

This position is in contrast to the usual approach to interpretations, especially those related to transference and resistances, which are based on the premise that the patient's communications are essentially distorted and based on pathological fantasies. Such an approach, while it might acknowledge an occasional reality element or adaptive context, views the patient's communications as usually related to himself alone, and to the realm of fantasy. In contrast, other analysts will adhere to the manifest content of the patient's associations, and will deal only with realistic and nondistorted elements. Occasionally, when there is an acute countertransference-based input, the focus will be on the analyst's inappropriate communications, often with the neglect of the patient's distorting addenda.

In contrast, to all of these attitudes, the *transversal intervention* consistently acknowledges all aspects condensed in the patient's communications—both reality and fantasy. This concept will become clearer, I trust, when illustrated in the final section of this paper.

THE VALIDATION OF INTERVENTIONS

Elsewhere (Langs 1976b, 1978b,d), I have offered rather extended comments on the validating process in psychoanalytic psychotherapy and psychoanalysis. It has become increasingly evident that many analysts and therapists make little or no effort to validate either their silent formulations or their actual interventions to the patient. I will stress here only the importance of taking each intervention as the adaptive context for the patient's subsequent associations, and the need to listen to this material, first, as a *commentary* on the intervention—an amalgam of unconscious fantasy and perception, valid and invalid responses offered in derivative form (a variety of *transversal communication*)—and, second, as the means through which the correctness of an intervention is assessed.

In this latter regard, true validation is seen in the cognitive sphere by the report of new, previously repressed associations that lend genuinely new meaning to the prior material. This constitutes the appearance of a *selected fact* (Bion 1962), a realization that reorganizes the previous material so that it yields up a meaning not previously evident. Lesser validation is seen in associations which, in some genuinely new manner, add to the richness of the material under analysis. Direct confirmation of an intervention, its genuine surface acceptance, comments that extend it in ways already known, and the repetition of earlier material—all are linear and nonvalidating. They call for reformulation and a renewed period of silence on the part of the analyst, so that the patient may assist him in the search for the prevailing adaptive context, the crucial unconscious meanings and functions of his communications, and the working over of the countertransference elements and bias in the analyst's error.

In the interactional sphere, validation is expressed

through the report of positive introjects, usually in terms of some outside figure who has functioned constructively or of some reference to a positive attribute of the patient himself. Both cognitive and interactional validation can be achieved only by organizing the subsequent material around the analyst's intervention, thereby throwing into relief the critical Type Two derivatives. Every meaningful and curative intervention from the analyst, whether interpretations or managements of the ground rules and frame, should find validation through Type Two derivatives from the patient, and any intervention not so confirmed must be considered in error and explored for countertransference-based inputs.

DISCARDED INTERVENTIONS

The six interventions I have described should serve all the therapeutic needs of the patient. They are to be maintained even in situations of emergency, although it is more than evident that in some crises, in part because of the usual presence of countertransference-based inputs, the analyst will be at a loss for a valid interpretive intervention and may have to resort to emergency directives. Nonetheless, even though used as a lifesaving measure (and the emergency should be of such proportions), there are uniformly negative repercussions within the patient, many of them expressed in derivative form under the guise of conscious gratitude. Since I have elsewhere established my position on the detrimental consequences of most of the interventions I have discarded (Langs 1973, 1975b, 1976a, 1978b), my discussion here will be brief.

As for methodology, my position is based on repeated empirical tests of the unconscious functions, communications, and meanings conveyed in the actual interaction between patient and therapist or analyst by each of the interventions to be described. Each application was taken as an adaptive context, and the patient's responses studied in terms of Type Two derivatives as commentaries in terms of both meaning and validity. I shall now briefly indicate my findings.

Questions and clarifications are used largely because of confusion as to the nature of neurotic communications and the best means of obtaining derivatives from patients. Rather than recognizing that silence and a secure frame offer the conditions that best facilitate the patient's expressing himself in derivative and analyzable form, some analysts mistakenly believe that pertinent questions and clarifi-

cations foster these expressions. This attitude also reflects basic confusions regarding the listening process and particular difficulties in identifying adaptive contexts and Type Two derivatives (see Langs 1978b).

Both questions and clarifications direct the patient toward manifest content and the surface of his communications. A remarkable number of these interventions occur at a point in a session in which the patient is unconsciously working over, through displaced and disguised derivatives, an aspect of his relationship with the analyst—usually a countertransference-based input. Typically, the analyst intervenes with a question or clarification directed toward an outside relationship or an aspect of the manifest content. These interventions constitute the offer of Type C barriers to the patient (Langs 1978b), and serve to defend both patient and analyst against more meaningful derivatives related to a more catastrophic aspect of the analytic interaction. Empirically, these interventions almost never foster the expression of analyzable derivatives (see Langs 1978b); they tend instead to detract from that level of communication (for earlier discussions, see Olinick 1954, 1957, Langs 1973).

Confrontations have been placed in the present delineation by the technique of playing back selected derivatives organized around an unspoken adaptive context and by the identification of metaphors of Type C barriers and falsifications. The very term *confrontation* conveys a sense of forcefulness and attack that, unfortunately, characterizes all too well a major unconscious function that this intervention serves for many analysts (see Adler and Myerson 1973, Langs 1973). In addition, despite the conscious intention to use this intervention as a means of developing derivative communication, observations of actual clinical interactions indicate that this seldom proves the case.

Confrontations tend to address the surface of the patient's material, to elicit direct and manifest responses, and to fix the patient on a relatively superficial level of communication. In addition, their use, all too common, without an adaptive context entails the risk of major countertransference-based inputs, largely designed to gratify the analyst's unconscious pathological fantasies and defensive needs; often harshly seductive, punitive, and attacking qualities prevail. As a result, the patient's material will unconsciously center around the introjection and working over of the analyst's countertransferences and the disruptive elements of his confrontation, rather than constructively and unconsciously elaborating in a new and meaningful manner those themes, contents, and defenses relevant to the analyst's manifest intervention.

There are a wide range of noninterpretive and nonneutral interventions that may be classified under such rubrics as supportive, directly responsive, self-revealing, gratuitious, and extraneous. In my previous writings (1973, 1975a,b, 1978b,d), I have, based on repeated empirical documentation, demonstrated that such seemingly well-meaning interventions evoke responses in the patient that are, as a rule, split: manifestly and consciously, the patient is grateful, while unconsciously — in his derivative communications — he uniformly experiences the unconscious communications contained in these interventions as seductive, destructive, and nonsupportive, and as a violation of his autonomy, an assault on his ego- and self-boundaries, and a reflection of the analyst's lack of faith in the patient's ego capacities. These interventions are essentially in the service of the analyst's unresolved countertransferences. Sometimes, though quite rarely, a direct response to the patient is needed (for example, when a patient forgets the date of the analyst's vacation); even then, clarification must be delayed until a full analysis and working through of the unconscious implications of the analysand's failure to remember has been completed.

Finally, there are a wide range of inappropriate alterations in the ground rules and framework of the analytic interaction, implicit and explicit, that entail interventions that consistently reflect the analyst's countertransferences and which find nonvalidating responses from the patient. Similarly, repetitions or elaborations by the analyst of an intervention without clear-cut validation are in the service of pathological needs within the analyst, and will evoke further nonvalidating reactions in the patient.

These comments should serve as a reminder that seemingly innocuous interventions are filled with significant unconscious implications and are not to be treated lightly.

INTERVENTIONS: INDICATIONS AND TIMING

At present, analysts have an extremely loose conception of when they should intervene. In general, the principle has been to maintain an interpretive focus on transference resistances, expecting to clear the way for the revelation of core unconscious transference fantasies, memories, and introjects — so-called contents — which are then subjected to both interpretation and reconstruction. This led to the maxim that one interprets defenses and resistances before contents, a tenet usually supplemented by some vague recognition that interventions are indicated also by ruptures in the therapeutic alliance, acting out, and unexpected symptomatic and regressive episodes.

In an early paper (Langs 1972), I labeled all such indications for intervening *indicators*. Later I termed these indicators the *therapeutic context* (Langs 1973). This term implies that there are specific communications and behaviors on the part of the analysand that create conditions under which the analyst should be inclined to intervene — in keeping with the needs of the patient. In addition, the term suggests that once the material in the session has been organized around a specific adaptive context and identified for Type Two derivatives, the entire constellation should be reorganized around the therapeutic context as a means of revealing the unconscious meanings and functions of the particular indicator.

The major therapeutic contexts, as generally accepted, are resistances; ruptures in the therapeutic alliance; living out; acute regressions, symptoms, or crises within the patient; and any other disturbance within the analysand or the analytic situation. A second, seldom identified group of therapeutic contexts derive from the behaviors of the analyst, and pertain to his erroneous interventions — whether mismanagements of the frame or verbal misinterventions. In keeping with the principles described below, there is a hierarchy of therapeutic contexts: the analyst must interpret the patient's responses to his own errors before responses to essentially internally derived psychopathological reactions. Still, it is important to remember that every disturbance within the bipersonal field, whether within the patient or the analyst, receives vectors from both participants. Sound interpretive work takes into account the contributions of each, and often entails the use of transversal interpretations.

The presence of a therapeutic context, however, does not place the analyst under a total obligation to intervene. It expresses a need within the patient for an intervention, to which the analyst responds if the material permits. The analyst must maintain a sense of balance and proportion, and must evaluate the acuteness of the therapeutic context. He is likely to intervene even in the face of material that is not clearly formulated if the situation is one of emergency proportions or has been evoked by an error in technique; he is less likely to do so in the absence of an acute therapeutic context, since he then has time to allow the material to unfold to the point of permitting a clear-cut interpretive intervention.

It is well to stress that initially, even in a crisis, it is best to maintain the basic listening process, in order to identify the crucial adaptive context and to be able to intervene in terms of Type Two derivatives. The analyst should also safeguard his interpretive efforts by consistently developing silent formulations and searching for silent validation before intervening to the patient.

This said, we may state as a principle that every intervention should be placed into the analyst by the patient. The latter conveys derivatives or scattered fragments that require organization by the analyst around a particular adaptive context. Interventions should be confined to the material from the session at hand, since each session should be allowed to be its own creation (see also de Racker 1961, Bion 1970, and Langs 1978b).

In keeping with the observation that, almost always, the major unconscious and neurotic communications from the patient are organized around the analytic interaction, another important principle of intervening may be stated as follows: the analyst should not intervene unless he has identified the prevailing adaptive context, organized the material in terms of Type Two derivatives along the me/not-me interface as it pertains to the analytic relationship, and has obtained a definitive manifest bridge from the patient's indirect, derivative communications to the therapeutic relationship itself. While there are occasions in which the analyst will, because of an acute therapeutic context, have no choice but to intervene in terms of Type One derivatives or without a direct bridge to the analytic relationship, these situations should be extremely rare. They occur at times of crisis or when the patient is in acute distress, when he communicates relatively intense, often primitive projective identifications, or when he is involved in disruptive behaviors in the analytic situation itself—the so-called acting in (Zeligs 1957, Langs 1976b).

The presence of massive projective identifications may require a processing intervention not included in my list of six. The analyst's first goal here should be to validate his subjective experiences and to deal with the material in terms of derivative communication to the greatest extent feasible. It is a common technical error under these conditions, largely because of the patient's disruptive interactional projections and the analyst's countertransference responses, to respond either with inappropriate silence or with premature interventions, many of them in terms of manifest content. The patient will find such comments the reflection of a failure to

properly metabolize his projective identifications, and often he will use them as intellectualized material with which to form interactional obsessive defenses. The patient then continues to communicate on a manifest level in a manner consistent with the intervention, and true validation through Type Two derivatives is lacking.

Another indication for intervening occurs when the analyst has identified an adaptive context, related it to the analytic interaction, and formulated a series of relevant unconscious memories and fantasies in terms of Type Two derivatives. He then silently validates his formulation by finding additional coalescing derivatives. There is in such a process a point of saturation, a shift from preconception to conception (Bion 1962), and the fullness of the communicative network and the presence of silent confirmation serve as an indication to intervene. This is best done, again, when there is a bridge to the analytic relationship.

Finally, there are a number of priorities for interventions, which I would state as follows: resistance before content, interactional resistance before intrapsychic resistance, defense before content, framework before all other material (content or defense), medium before content, communicative style before content, reality before fantasy, analyst before patient.

INTERVENTIONS WITHIN THE THREE BASIC COMMUNICATIVE FIELDS

In the Type A field, both patient and analyst use language and behavior for symbolic communication, illusion, and transition (Langs 1978c). The patient communicates essentially through Type Two derivatives organized around sequential adaptive contexts. Whether the prevailing attitude is resistance or revelation, in very little time the derivatives necessary to interpret the unconscious fantasies, memories, introjects, and perceptions on which the defensiveness or core fantasy is based become available. In this field, the analyst offers the patient a secure hold and container by defining and maintaining the framework. He then interprets the patient's behaviors and verbal associations, whether they impinge upon the ground rules or serve as a communicative medium. The analytic work takes place mainly in the cognitive sphere, though there may be occasional episodes of interactional projection and efforts at role evocation. There is a general sequential alteration between periods of resistance and revelation, with interpretive resolution of the inevitable obstacles and insight into their unconscious sources and meanings, supplemented by similar insight into core fantasies and memories and the like.

The Type A field, then, is one in which silence, interpretations-reconstructions, and occasional management responses to infringements by the patient on the framework prevail. At times of acute anxiety or conflict, these patients may repress allusions to important adaptive contexts within the analytic relationship, and the playing back of selected derivatives pertinent to that adaptive context proves a valuable intervention.

In the Type B field, established largely through the patient's use of projective identification and action-discharge, the analyst's main function is to receive, contain, and metabolize toward cognitive understanding the patient's interactional pressures. The silent hypotheses developed in this way should consistently be subjected to validation both through the reception of further interactional pressures from the patient, and through the latter's cognitive material. The major intervention in this field is that of processing a projective identification, and of interpreting the implications of role and image evocations. At times the playing back of selected derivatives can be important and quite often management and interpretation of impingements on the framework will also require responses from the analyst.

It is well to remember that projective identifications may serve both defensive and revealing functions, and often expresses efforts at resistance. Still, this is a valid mode of communication for the patient, and should be accepted as such so that the analyst can intervene in an interpretive manner. Often the analyst is under considerable pressure to intervene with these patients, and, while he must develop the capacity to silently tolerate interactional pressures until they can be cognitively understood, there will be a need to intervene more frequently with these patients at times of crisis.

In the Type C field, silence is an essential tool for the analyst. While there may be efforts to modify the frame from time to time, characteristically these patients accept the frame as established and make few impingements in any direction. There is little or no use in playing back apparent derivatives to these patients in the hope of identifying a hidden adaptive context, since they maintain their opaque defenses and interpersonal distance quite intensely and will

seldom provide missing links—in part, because such a revelation would reestablish the link between patient and analyst.

A limited form of interpretation proves the primary verbal tool for the analyst in this type of field, and can be characterized as identification of the patient's metaphors for the barriers, void, destruction of meaning, falsifications, and destruction of relatedness that prevails in the Type C field. Using sometimes minor bridges to the therapeutic interaction, these metaphors must be interpreted in terms of the nature of the patient's communicative style. Validation is generally found in momentary expression of the tumultuous inner mental world that these defenses serve to seal off.

Work with Type C analysands requires much patience of the analyst. There are long periods of uninterpretable resistance and noncommunication, and the communicative mode itself functions to conceal the underlying basis for these resistances rather than to reveal them in the form of Type Two derivatives. The analyst must tolerate the Type C narrator (Langs 1978b,c) and must recognize that his elaborate communications serve essentially to destroy meaning. He must refrain from attempting to interpret the contents of the material; his doing so would be met with nonvalidation and, sometimes, a sense of triumph over the analyst, who has permitted himself to be fooled by these nonmeaningful series of verbiage. It is in this sphere that the analyst's tolerance and capacity to contain a void—what I term *negative projective identifications* (Langs 1978b)—proves crucial.

As mentioned, the occasional modifications of a Type C barrier will lead to an interlude during which the inner chaos—the psychotic core within patient, analyst, or bipersonal field—that has been sealed off by the Type C barrier will emerge in the material from the analysand. At such moments, interpretations-reconstructions, playing back selected derivatives around an unmentioned adaptive context, and even the metabolizing and processing of projective identifications will be required. The patient will, however, soon restore the Type C barriers and the analyst must shift back to the use of interpretations of the patient's metaphorical representations of the Type C communicative mode.

In all, the analyst's interventions are distinctive for each communicative bipersonal field or particular style of communication by the patient. The timing, pace, and nature of these interventions will vary considerably for each field, and it is essential to identify the patient's communicative mode and work accordingly (see Langs 1978c for details).

THE ROLE OF NONCOUNTERTRANSFERENCE AND COUNTERTRANSFERENCE

It is beyond the scope of this paper to identify and fully discuss the multitude of factors within the analyst that influence his style of intervening (see Langs 1976a,b, 1978a,b,c). Here, to be brief, it is well to note that every analyst has his own style of listening and intervening. Some analysts prefer the cognitive mode and tolerate poorly the Type B and Type C communicative styles in their patients. Others prefer to process interactional projections and are less responsive to symbolic communication. Clearly, the variations are considerable (see Langs 1978c), and it is essential for the analyst to be aware of his preferences in this regard. He must be aware of his capacity or incapacity to tolerate ambiguity or closeness, as well as for synchronized and discordant communication, holding, and containing—to name but a few of the important aspects that deserve fuller discussion.

The analyst must carefully examine through self-analysis, and through his understanding of the patient's commentary responses to his interventions, the true unconscious nature and function of his verbal interventions and efforts to manage the framework. He must be prepared to discover in himself the presence of unconscious projective identifications and Type C barriers—psychoanalytic clichés (Langs 1978b,c). These aspects are mentioned specifically because they extend beyond the usual discussions of the influence of the analyst's unconscious countertransference fantasies on his interventions, in which stress is placed on unresolved conflicts, special areas of vulnerability, the misuse of interventions for seductive and hostile purposes, the presence of defensive blind spots, and unconscious wishes for inappropriate gratification (see, for example, Langs 1974).

I wish to emphasize in this discussion a single tenet which, once stated, will seem self-evident. It is a principle, however, that has taken several years to develop, and that required a departure from the usual view of interventions as essentially correct or incorrect. It is as follows: every intervention made by the therapist—interpretively or in terms of the management of the framework—contains some element of countertransference-based expression.

To my knowledge, this principle and its many implications, most of which cannot be traced out here, has not been explicitly stated in the literature. It implies a continuum of interventions, ranging from those with only a modicum of countertransference to those in which its influence is overridingly significant. It suggests too that the timing of an intervention, the material selected for comment, the associations that are not picked up on, the therapist's linguistic style and tone, his use of innuendo or of concrete thinking, and many other dimensions of intervening leave extensive room for the expression of countertransference no matter how essentially valid a particular intervention may be. This implies too that both countertransference and noncountertransference are ever-present in the therapeutic interaction, as are, of course, both transference and nontransference on the patient's part.

There is therefore an element of countertransference in every moment of the communicative interaction, and the patient will respond continuously to this aspect along with his reactions to the noncountertransference elements in the therapist's interventions, including his silences. It becomes essential now to recognize that when we have spoken of a valid intervention we have been characterizing its predominant qualities, just as when we have considered erroneous interventions we have been stressing major countertransference-based influences—to which, quite often, there has been an added acknowledgement of what I have called a valid core or noncountertransference element (Langs 1976a).

In evaluating a therapist's intervention, then, it becomes essential to identify both its valid and invalid aspects, and to at least be aware of any measure of error in an essentially correct intervention. It seems likely that it is this continuous stream of countertransference-based inputs that provides the patient a greater or lesser degree of external and interactional pathology to which he responds in terms of his own both distorted and valid repertory of reactions. This tenet becomes another means through which the crucial importance of therapeutic work within the framework of the therapeutic interaction is established. On the one hand, the countertransference-based inputs serve on some level as a repetition of past pathogenic experiences and in the actual therapeutic interaction constitute a means, however modified, through which the patient's neurosis is actually restimulated in the present—in a form that is open to analysis only so long as (1) the therapist ultimately becomes aware of the true nature of the unconscious communicative interaction, and (2) these inputs are, by and large, relatively small. On the other hand, the valid, constructive, and essentially noncountertransference-based components of the therapist's interventions provide the patient previously unavailable adaptive resources, cognitive insights, and inevitable adaptive introjective identifications crucial to analytic cure.

Under those conditions in which countertransference factors take on major proportions, a traumatic repetition of the pathological past will prevail, as will an offer of interactional defenses and resistances, of inappropriate and pathological gratification and sanction, and of misalliance and bastion formations (Langs 1975a, 1976a). It is the use of validating process and of self-knowledge that provides safeguards in this respect, and offers a means through which the therapist may detect these elements in his intervening—making use both of the patient's unconscious communications and of self-analysis.

In this context, it can be stated again that every erroneous intervention contains its constructive nucleus, and that the rectification and analysis of therapeutic interludes related to essentially erroneous interventions may provide both the patient and the therapist significant opportunity for insight, adaptive inner change, and growth—so long as the situation is identified and corrected, and is not part of a repetitive, countertransference-dominated interaction. Clearly, the optimal therapeutic work takes place in a situation in which the countertransference-based elements are, most of the time, a relatively minor component of the therapist's interventions. This provides a setting within which the analyst's constructive interpretations and management of the framework provide a predominantly positive tone to the therapeutic interaction and to the vital work that centers around the patient's introjections of the therapist's pathology and his projection of his own inner disturbances.

THE PATIENT'S INTERVENTIONS

The usual study of the analytic situation has considered only the analyst's interventions, while neglecting those of the patient. It is supposed that the patient simply free associates, and that these communications are designed to reveal his inner conflicts, unconscious fantasies, defenses, projections onto the therapist, and the like. A careful investigation of the analytic interaction reveals, however, that this characterization is limited, and that the patient will from time to time, depending on

the underlying nature of the analytic interaction, offer major conscious and unconscious interventions to the analyst. Since we now realize that countertransference is ever present, activities of this kind undoubtedly occur at a low level of intensity throughout the therapeutic experience. Major inputs of this type occur when the analyst has placed significant aspects of his own countertransferences into the bipersonal field and patient; they may also occur when the patient wishes unconsciously to offer a model intervention to the analyst, one that neither participant has been able to generate consciously.

As a rule, the patient's valid interventions—i.e., those that the analyst is able ultimately to confirm through Type Two derivatives organized around the adaptive context of the patient's intervention—are offered in derivative form, unconsciously (Little 1951, Searles 1975, Langs 1975a, 1976a). On occasion, the patient will consciously and directly rectify the frame or confront the analyst with an aspect of the latter's implicit psychopathology or explicit errors. A conscious, valid interpretation is extremely rare. However, unconsciously the patient will consistently offer interpretations in derivative form in response to the analyst's pathological inputs; he will also convey models of valid functioning to the analyst, directives toward the rectification of the frame, and the like. The unconscious resourcefulness of the patient has been insufficiently appreciated. These efforts should be silently accepted by the analyst as offering ameliorating insights and directives. This is feasible, however, only if he tries to be aware of the unconscious communications contained in his own interventions, and if he is prepared to treat his patient's responses to his therapeutic endeavors as commentaries filled, as a rule, with rich and valid understanding—this in addition to their pathological qualities.

CLINICAL MATERIAL

I shall present several condensed clinical vignettes to illustrate the basic techniques of intervening. My formulation will center around these issues, and little effort will be made to discuss other aspects of the material.

Mr. A was in once-weekly psychotherapy with a therapist who had offered family therapy to his brother, sister, and parents. He was now the only member of his family seeing the therapist, and these excerpts took place after a year and a half of treatment for periods of depression, problems in dating, and fears of becoming a homosexual. The patient was twenty-seven and single.

In the first session of this sequence, the patient spoke in great detail of feeling criticized at work, especially by a woman supervisor who had called him irresponsible for allowing a grade-school class that he taught a free period in the schoolyard. This assistant principal had quarreled with another assistant principal, who had attempted to protect the patient, and of whom the patient had had some homosexual thoughts.

After hearing many details, the therapist suggested that the patient was talking about women and men, feelings of irresponsibility, and two people who are fighting over him. The patient felt accused of being irresponsible by the therapist, and stated that he had not behaved in any such manner. The therapist responded by apologizing, saying that he had not meant to imply that he believed the patient irresponsible; he then attempted to clarify that he had meant to imply that the patient himself was concerned about taking responsibility. The patient agreed that this was a possibility, and he ruminated about his responsibilities at work.

To comment briefly on these interventions: this is a session in which the therapist was unable to identify a specific adaptive context related to the therapeutic interaction, and with some lack of certainty he took as the context the accusation made against the patient at work. In our supervisory discussion, the therapist felt in retrospect that he had probably intervened in the previous hour in a manner that was critical of the patient and irresponsible; this may well have been the primary adaptive task that had evoked this material, which could then be seen as Type Two derivatives related to the patient's unconscious fantasies and perceptions in response to the intervention.

This therapist quite consistently alternated between rather effective and helpful interventions, and sudden lapses during which he became noninterpretive, critical, and confused in his responses. The material suggests the possibility that the two assistant principals represent the patient's unconscious split image of the therapist. Considered along the me/not-me interface, the allusions to homosexuality may be a form of unconscious perception and interpretation to the therapist regarding the underlying basis for his problems in intervening—his unconscious homosexual anxieties and countertransferences. These difficulties serve to mask the patient's own homosexual conflicts and divided self, and would have to be rectified before the patient's pathology could clearly emerge within this bipersonal field.

The unconscious perception of the therapist as having homosexual conflicts which are expressed in the therapeutic interaction appears, based on my knowledge of his work, to be a transversal communication that contains valid perceptiveness and some minor degree of internal distortion—a mixture of reality and perception, nontransference and transference. These comments are of course quite tentative in light of the brief extract offered here, and are offered primarily as models for the type of clinical referents that pertain to the formulations offered in the theoretical and discussion sections of this paper.

If we turn now to the therapist's first intervention, which lacked a definitive adaptive context (Langs 1978b), we can identify it as a type of confrontation with the manifest content of the patient's outside relationships. It was not organized as a playback of selected derivatives around a known unmentioned adaptive context that exists within the therapeutic interaction. The confrontation is designed unconsciously to steer the patient away from that interaction, and to place the burden of prevailing difficulties within the patient—the therapist's contributions are totally set aside. The patient's nonvalidating response seems to allude to the therapist's efforts to blame the patient for the sense of difficulty, and to the irresponsible qualities of this intervention, which failed to take into account derivatives and unconscious communication.

In the face of direct negation, it is well for the therapist to sit back, become silent, listen, and reformulate. The therapist's efforts at apology and clarification are noninterpretive interventions which treat the patient's disclaimer in terms of its manifest content, rather than as a derivative communication which serves as a commentary on the therapist's intervention, and which contains both unconscious fantasies and perceptions—especially the latter. It shifts the patient and the therapist to the surface of their respective communications, offers the patient an interactional obsessional defense and misalliance, and creates a bastion which seals off derivatives and more direct communications related to the therapeutic interaction. Rumination follows within the patient, as a representation of these interactional defenses.

In the next session, the patient began by saying that he hated to talk about his sister (the one whom the therapist had treated); he thought it a waste of time. However, she had threatened suicide because her fiancé had been critical of her and she felt that no one could help her. His mother had said that his sister was fine and the patient had seen her. She told him a dream in which her leg is injured and bleeding; she turns to her mother, who walks away. The dream was depressing, and later his parents fought and the patient felt quite helpless. He remembered times when his father would not allow him to help at work.

The therapist intervened and suggested that the patient had been counseling his sister. He noted that in the dream someone was not being helped, and he pointed out that this sister had been in treatment with him and that the dream must have implications regarding therapy. In fact, he suggested, the image of someone not getting help could tie into treatment, and he pointed out that after the patient had talked to his sister he had become depressed. He also had been unable to help his mother and father, and had recalled his father not allowing the patient to help him. With his sister, he had also been in a helping situation and ended up feeling inadequate and helpless.

The patient agreed that he had been counseling his sister, and thought he deserved a handsome fee. He now felt like crying and remembered a time at supper when he started to wheeze at the dinner table and left for a moment. When he returned, his sister had been given the steak that he wanted and his protests were to no avail—his parents thought he had finished dinner.

In evaluating this session, we must take the prior hour, and in particular the therapist's interventions, as the initial adaptive context for this material. It is striking that the patient began the hour by talking about how he had been wasting his time in therapy—a relatively valid commentary on the prior session and the therapist's interventions. His sister's suicide threat and dream represents, on one level, something of the patient's own depression and bodily anxieties, to which he rather directly adds his own sense of helplessness and the failure of his father to call on him for assistance at work.

However, if we monitor this material along the me/not-me interface in the context of the ineffective interventions made by the therapist in the previous hour, and if we keep in mind the possibility of a latent adaptive context related to the modification in the framework of this therapy that compromised the one-to-one relationship between patient and therapist, it is possible to suggest tentatively that the patient experienced the therapist's need to treat multiple family members as a defense against depressive and suicidal feelings, and as a reflection of his own helplessness. The images certainly convey a

disturbance in the working relationship between patient and therapist, and as commentary on the altered frame the patient seems to be suggesting that under these conditions there is no sense of therapeutic hold and no protection against suicidal fantasies.

As for the therapist's interventions, there was a failure to wait for a bridge to the therapeutic relationship and to identify a specific adaptive context in that area. Had the therapist played back a series of seemingly pertinent Type One derivatives related to the general context of therapy not being helpful, the patient might well have revealed a more specific adaptive context and clearer, Type Two derivatives. In general, however, I would recommend continued silence, offering a secure hold, and allowing the patient an opportunity for meaningful derivative communication.

Rather than adhering to the principle of permitting the patient to build the therapist's intervention in its entirety, the therapist rather dramatically introduced the fact that the patient's sister had been in treatment with him; it was also he who suggested the bridge between the allusions to failures to be helpful and the treatment situation. The intervention also has a transversal quality, in that the therapist alludes both to certain realities regarding conditions of treatment, and to the patient's experience of not being helped—without suggesting that the latter is either well founded or distorted.

Still, the focus is almost entirely on the patient's experience, without any indication of specific contributions from the therapist—a point that I make in assessing the intervention, and not as a suggestion for a proposed intervention. (For the moment, technically, I would have allowed the derivatives to build further in the hope of obtaining a bridge to the treatment situation; failing that, I would have played back selected derivatives taken from the material from the patient with the expectation that he would then communicate with less disguised derivatives, in terms of both unconscious fantasies and perceptions.) Finally, we should note that the therapist intervened in a rather confused manner, scattering his comments and shifting back and forth from one theme to another. This type of disjointed intervention is not uncommon in the absence of a reference to an organizing adaptive context, and in itself suggests an underlying sense of helplessness, rather than mastery.

The patient's response to this intervention (which was partially correct, though premature) has another type of transversal quality: it seems both confirmatory and nonconfirmatory. In the main, however, it lacks definitive validation. On the positive side, it may be seen as containing Type Two derivatives related to the prevailing problems in the therapeutic situation; these imply that under conditions in which the one-to-one relationship is altered, the patient is open to illness, and further, that the particular deviation is experienced as favoritism toward the sister and deprivation. As a model, an intervention made on the basis of such a formulation would constitute an effort at interpretation—the identification of a specific adaptive context and the patient's derivative unconscious perceptions and fantasies. In this respect there is a transversal quality in that there is truth to the patient's appreciation of his actual vulnerability under these conditions, and to his sense of favoritism and deprivation, although the oral qualities of his fantasies seem to derive at least in part from within himself. It is an open question as to whether it would be possible for the therapist to be analytically helpful to the patient after having seen the siblings and parents previously.

It is, as I have indicated, a fundamental principle that each intervention should be treated as the adaptive context for the associations that follow, and that the latter be treated as a commentary on the intervention—an unconscious appraisal with mixtures of perceptiveness and distortion. In this context, the patient's acknowledgment of his counseling efforts, and his comment that he deserved a high fee, seem to be a response to the positive elements in the therapist's comment. In supervision, I had previously suggested that the intervention had a valid core; that is, it was an effort to approach the truth of what was really disturbing the patient, though it was undertaken rather prematurely and with some sense of confusion. The patient's response appears to appreciate that mixture: there are the positive elements just noted, an appreciation of the positive endeavors of the therapist which hint at a new understanding of the consequences of the altered frame. On the other hand, the memory of deprivation implies that there is something lacking in the intervention and that the patient had not been adequately fed—a transversal, oral model of the analytic interaction that contains both unconscious truth and unconscious fantasy.

In the next hour, the patient began by saying that he had little on his mind, but was glad to be at the session. He had begun to think about women sexually (a new development), and was masturbating less. He felt he might be responding to the pressures of his mother, who kept insisting that he was doing much better of late—and it was true.

The patient had talked with a young man who was serving as his assistant teacher. He had had homosexual fantasies about being in bed with this man and embracing him, though without having an orgasm. He imagined this student needing help, and helping him sexually. He stopped the fantasy, lest he imagine actual sexual contact.

The patient had been with a friend who had also been a patient of the therapist. For the first time since early in therapy, he described the overt homosexual relationship between the two of them, and how it had developed when they had been classmates and their parents had become friends. Initially, the friend had been the aggressor and the patient had eventually stopped him, only to reinitiate the sexual contact later on. The friend had resisted stimulation to orgasm, but the patient had insisted to the point where they performed mutual fellatio.

The patient was pleased to have told all of this to the therapist, and stated that he now had the wish to go out with a woman. The therapist responded by pointing out that the patient had had a daydream about the assistant teacher which did not reach closure and that he had prevented himself from imagining orgasm. He noted that the patient had gone on to talk about women, fears of exposure, fears of being found inadequate, and a need to cover up. He also pointed out that the patient had stressed how his friend would not look at his penis and denied having had an orgasm, stressing once again the qualities of hiding and secretiveness.

The patient responded by saying that the image of secrets stirred him up, and he then recalled a series of childhood secrets: finding his father's pictures of nude women and having an erection; not being able to undress in the locker room in high school in front of the guys; having nocturnal emissions that his mother commented on in a humiliating way; being bathed by his mother; and first masturbating with great fears of damaging himself.

We may note that in the adaptive context of the therapist's intervention in the previous session— which entailed an attempt to rectify the frame (in actuality, the therapist had stopped all contact with other family members and had also desisted from such practices as note-taking and answering the telephone during sessions) and to interpret the implications of the previously impaired frame to the patient—the patient indicated that he was doing well and described both homosexual fantasies and a previous homosexual relationship with a former patient of the therapist. This material too has a transversal quality, in that it suggests that the patient now feels safe enough to reveal and explore his homosexual relationships and fantasies, largely in the form of an effort to resolve the underlying pathology and to move toward heterosexuality. At the same time, these communications serve as Type Two derivatives in the adaptive context related to the framework, and suggest that the patient had experienced the alterations in the frame as a seduction and as an expression of unresolved homosexual fantasies and needs within the therapist.

The therapist attempted to play back derivatives around the unmentioned adaptive context of the alterations in framework, though once again he did so in a confusing manner which impaired his efforts to stress the patient's concern about secret sexual contact and needs to cover up. The intervention was stated in a manner that left no room for the patient's unconscious perceptions of the therapist, and did not constitute a definitive interpretation. It is therefore especially interesting to review the many new memories that emerged subsequently. While they undoubtedly reveal aspects of the patient's psychopathology—his overstimulation as a child, the seductiveness of his mother, his intense castration anxiety—it must be recognized also that they function as unconscious communications related to the qualities of the therapeutic situation as experienced under the conditions of this therapy.

Any isolated intervention related to this material, one directing itself entirely toward the patient's earlier experiences in an effort to help him understand the unconscious basis for his homosexuality and fears of women, would include a major defensive element: it would deny the patient's unconscious perceptions of the therapist and the therapeutic interaction, perceptions which have served as the immediate adaptive context for this material, and to which it is also attached. A more appropriate interpretation would have a transversal quality: it would take the conditions of treatment, both past and present, as the adaptive context, would attempt to show the patient that he is currently experiencing the earlier deviant conditions as a repetition of the pathogenic past, and would detail the relevant unconscious perceptions and their extension into fantasy. The material might then permit an interpretation of the patient's awareness of the differences that have been developing with the restructuring of the framework. The therapist could then delineate some of the patient's anxieties within the more clearly defined therapeutic situation—his fears of a therapeutic regression (Langs 1976a). Technically, however, such an intervention could not be made

until the patient provided a clear-cut bridge to the therapeutic interaction. To develop such a communication, the selected playing back of derivatives would serve well, including some allusion to the friend in a way that might hint at the fact that he too had been in treatment with the therapist.

It is, of course, the revelations regarding the homosexual relationship with the friend that are the closest derivatives of the patient's unconscious perceptions and fantasies of his relationship with the therapist. As a major transversal communication, these derivatives contain elements of truth and distortion, of transference and nontransference: there is indeed a seductive aspect to family treatment, and the hypothesis that it satisfies and protects against the therapist's unconscious homosexual fantasies would probably be validated if it could be tested out. On the other hand, the therapist had never been directly seductive, was not overtly homosexual, and had made every effort to manage and master expressions of his unresolved homosexual countertransferences. We would therefore have to see this material as containing both kernels of truth and extensive distortions based on the patient's own unconscious homosexual fantasies and conflicts, and their genetic sources. An intervention designed to interpret the implications of this material would have to take into account the diametrically opposed qualities of these associations from the patient—it would have to be stated in transversal form.

In the following hour, the patient described his discomfort in the waiting room (which was in the hospital at which the therapist was associate director), stating that there were too many sick people around. He felt better for what he had discussed in the previous session, and described how well he was doing at work, where he was receiving admiration and was now ready for either a promotion or for a new job at a higher level. His main concern was leaving his job and having a farewell party, during which he might break down emotionally. He had been praised by the principal of the school and had had homosexual thoughts about him. He wondered if he should leave or not.

The therapist pointed out that the patient had said that he felt strange and uptight in the waiting room, and that this was connected to some ambivalence regarding change and his concern about public exposure. He suggested that there were various meanings to the themes the patient was talking about. The patient responded that he had no thought of leaving treatment, if that's what the therapist had in mind, and he reviewed again his concern about leaving his job and becoming too upset and crying at a farewell party. His mother had once attended the funeral of a near stranger and had made a fool of herself by carrying on. He thought of his sister's depression and how he still gets somewhat upset when he has to speak in front of his class. There's no place where he can cry—not at home, not with friends, and not in treatment.

The therapist said that the patient had now brought up his mother and sister, and that they were somehow related to facing a problem in changing jobs, speaking in public, and speaking freely. He added that the patient seemed to feel a similar problem here in therapy, where he is unable to cry. The patient responded that actually therapy had changed considerably since the therapist had stopped being a friend. At first the patient hated it and felt betrayed, but now it was working out well. Before, the therapist was a member of the family, but now there seemed to be a change and the patient felt safer. He could talk and he felt more secure when, as just a moment ago, the therapist no longer answered the telephone. Still, there was his fear of revealing himself, and he wondered now if it had been induced by the therapist and if he then took it outside. The therapist said that there might well be a kernel of truth in that, and the patient went on to talk about the recent differences in the therapist, and his own improvement of late. He thought then of his anxieties and of his hand-shaking, and how he controlled it with strangers. He felt like he keeps up a facade. He is two people living in a shell: one part is a stranger, but confident and liked, and now top dog and interested in women, and doing well; while the other part is the little boy under the covers, masturbating and afraid of exposure.

The therapist said that the patient had mentioned his—the therapist's—involvement with his family and had gone on to talk of exposure, adding that there were two parts to himself: one strong and the other immature. The therapist added that he thought that the patient was referring to therapy, and that he was feeling better about it and safer, and was now revealing more. This was related in part, the therapist said, to his involvement with the patient's sister and mother, which had been inappropriate and not right.

The patient said that he had been flooded by a number of additional thoughts, but there was time to share only one: he had stopped going to pornographic movies and to the backrooms of pornographic shops where he used to masturbate. He felt he no longer needed them because he now had privacy in treatment.

In brief, the patient appears to be working over his reactions to both the previously modified frame and the currently secured one. The therapist, in his first intervention, played back a series of themes expecting to hear from the patient that he was, indeed, having some thoughts about terminating. It should be noted that the therapist's use of the word *ambivalence* runs the risk of intellectualization and carries with it a certain clichéd quality. It is best to intervene using the patient's language, and to do so without technical terms.

The playback of derivatives was clearly organized around the therapeutic situation and made use of the material from the patient. It may have been a bit premature, since the adaptive context was not as yet clear, and there was still a good deal of time available to allow the patient the freedom of direct and indirect expression.

The patient responded by denying thoughts of leaving treatment, although the therapist felt that there had been improvement to the point where such an issue might soon appropriately arise. The expressed fears of humiliation and exposure now appear to relate to the patient's dread of his own inner mental world, which would emerge within the therapeutic situation as secured by the frame. The therapist again played back derivatives, attempting to develop further the patient's insight into his feelings about the previous family therapy and the current therapeutic situation. This led to entirely new material about the patient's experience of the rectification of the frame, associations that reveal considerable conscious appreciation of the differences between the two treatment situations.

The therapist's acknowledgment that he may have contributed to the patient's symptoms, while clearly a constructive and honest effort, nonetheless addresses itself to the manifest content and serves as a kind of confession. This could more adequately have been done within the context of a more definitive interpretation. If we now take this intervention as the adaptive context for the associations that follow, it appears that the patient is unconsciously perceiving striking variations in the therapist's capacity to intervene: one moment rather effectively, the next moment based on anxieties. According to the patient's unconscious interpretation, the latter is based on continued unresolved sexual countertransferences.

The intervention—the therapist's acknowledgment of error—is an attempt to address the adaptive context of the alterations in the framework; it alludes to both the patient's unconscious perceptions and his unconscious fantasies. It is somewhat confused once again, and while addressing the contributions of the therapist, it stresses the split within the patient without clearly relating it to the distinct alterations—the split—in the therapist's interpretations and managements of the framework. Still, it seems clear that the patient appreciated the valid efforts contained in this intervention (and they certainly stand in contrast to earlier interventions that failed to appreciate the implications for the patient of the family therapy). The patient's response appears validating in that it reflects an unconscious positive introject of the therapist, who had secured the frame and brought under control a major segment of his unconscious sexual countertransferences. This introject helps modify an earlier pathological introject that had, as the associations reveal, actually contributed to the patient's homosexuality and other perversions. The material suggests that the patient's voyeurism and masturbation had been an interactional symptom based in part on the therapist's countertransferences as expressed in the family therapy situation, and in part derived from the family interaction and the patient's intrapsychic conflicts and pathology.

The therapist's final intervention, then, implies the rectification of the framework, and a transversal interpretation of the unconscious fantasies and perceptions involved in the patient's experience of the altered frame. The patient's allusion to his renunciation of pornography validates the intervention through Type Two derivatives that derive special transversal meaning in the adaptive context of the intervention. It serves too, as a selected fact (Bion 1962) that provides new meaning to the previous material; it reveals the unconscious sexual implications, both reality and fantasy, for both patient and therapist, of the altered framework.

Let us turn now to another brief vignette:

Mr. B. was a young man in psychotherapy for about a year on a once-weekly basis. He was afraid that he might be crazy and had intense homosexual fantasies and anxieties; he had been impotent with women. The therapist was aware that he was having considerable difficulties in treating this patient and found that his interventions consistently seemed to miss the mark and to evoke responses within the patient that reflected a view of the therapist as monstrous and destructive.

The patient began one hour by saying that he felt he was not getting anywhere in therapy. He was ruminating about the daily events of his life without getting into things, as the therapist had pointed out in the previous hour. He bullshits, as the therapist had said, and the therapist was also right when he told the patient that he accuses everyone else of being crazy, when he is really the one who is struggling with these feelings (a gross distortion of the therapist's intervention).

The patient was bothered because he can't really get into what bothers him. He had had a bad scene with his sister and brother-in-law. He had been critical of how his sister had dressed, and she had then told her husband, who became angry with the patient. The patient tried to apologize, but it wasn't accepted. He had been less depressed in the past week, and felt that his sister and brother-in-law had overreacted and had been too attacking in their comments.

The therapist intervened and said that the patient was relating things to the session in the previous week, that he was indicating that the therapist had made him apprehensive and upset, just as his brother-in-law was trying to do.

The patient responded by becoming ruminative again, talking about how immature and selfish he is, how bad he is, and how he did bad things as a child and got his mother angry again and again. When he came to therapy he thought he'd be able to get rid of all the bad things inside himself and become clean and pure, walking the streets free of the bad things inside of him. He thought the therapist would sweep out all of that bad stuff. The therapist responded by saying that he now felt a sense of disorganization as the patient spoke. He suggested that it must relate to the patient's comment about bad things in himself; the bad stuff had somehow gotten out of him, into the room and into the therapist. The therapist went on: he was now coping with a sense of fear, helplessness, and disorganization, which he felt existed in the patient and was now within himself—in the room. The patient responded that he had always been frightened of being crazy and sick, and had always thought of others as nuts. He constantly thinks the other person is crazy so that he himself won't feel crazy.

Briefly, this is a Type B communicative field, which reflects a therapeutic situation in which the patient is engaged in efforts at pathological projective identification, to which the therapist is responding with efforts at metabolism and cognitive interpretation, though it seems evident that he is unable to maintain this level of functioning and ultimately responds with unconscious pathological projective identifications of his own. As a result, the therapeutic situation appears stalemated and disturbed.

The patient's initial associations allude not only to his own difficulties in communicating meaningfully, but to the nature of the therapist's interventions as well (a point confirmed, in part, by the therapist's own subjective awareness). The patient's recollection of the previous hour was filled with distortions to the point where the therapist felt attacked, angry, crazy, and under pressure to see himself as bad. The shift in the patient's associations to the sister and brother-in-law provided a moment of relief for the therapist, but he nonetheless intervened in an effort to process the material in terms of the interactional pressures that seemed to prevail. Much of the intervention, however, is stated in terms of manifest content, and to some extent is an effort to blame the patient for distorting everything the therapist says and for feeling attacked when the therapist has no such intention.

A more adequate intervention might well have been derived if the therapist had continued to process the patient's projective identifications in terms of efforts to destroy his grasp on reality, attack him, and drive him crazy—a transversal communication that unconsciously alludes to both patient and therapist, and that has some representation in the cognitive material. This intervention could have been related to the adaptive context of the therapist's specific interventions in the previous session, which although unreported here, did indeed have qualities of attacking the patient, disturbing his grasp of reality, and driving him crazy.

We can see then that this material is part of a spiraling exchange of pathological projective identifications between patient and therapist. Any intervention that would adequately process this material would have to allude to this spiraling interaction, to the patient's experiences of the therapist's interventions, and to the patient's attempts to place these disturbances back into the therapist. It would have to be stated in transversal form, alluding to patient and therapist, reality and fantasy, nontransference and transference, and noncountertransference and countertransference.

Such an intervention should not be offered to the patient until silently validated in the cognitive material. The associations to the sister and brother-in-law provide validation to some degree, but it is wise to wait for the patient's associations to form a new bridge back to the therapeutic interaction. There is a danger here of intervening prematurely in a way that would constitute a further unconscious attack on the patient and a further projective identification of disruptive defenses and contents into him. Granted this bridge, however, the therapist could have pointed out that the patient seems to be experiencing the therapeutic interaction in a manner not unlike what had happened with his sister and brother-in-law:

there is a sort of spiraling interaction without relief in which both himself and the therapist are being seen as attacking, blaming, and accusatory. The patient is experiencing the therapist as provocative and destructive, and as placing crazy and destructive contents into him, and he responds in kind by overreacting, distorting as had the brother-in-law, and by attempting to disturb the therapist in turn.

Such a transversal intervention, initiated in terms of a specific adaptive context, draws upon both Type One and Type Two derivatives. It is an attempt to understand the nature of the unconscious interactional mechanisms as they exist in this bipersonal field, and in both patient and therapist. The therapist might add, if the material permitted, that the patient seems to feel he is being cast in the role of someone who is sick and crazy, someone to be demeaned, and that in turn he attempts to have the therapist feel and behave similarly. To the extent that this interpretive processing is valid, the patient would then respond cognitively with new material and, quite likely, with important genetic links; interactionally, there would be a positive introjective identification based on the therapist's valid containing and metabolizing functions, and his ability to interpret this unconscious exchange of pathological interactional projections.

In response to the rather mixed intervention that actually was offered, the patient describes an accusatory relationship between himself and his mother, one that it seems is unconsciously being repeated in the therapeutic interaction, rather than interpreted. The patient then alludes to fantasies of projectively identifying and discharging his bad inner stuff into the therapist. In the adaptive context of the antecedent intervention, this is an acknowledgment of some of the inappropriate qualities of the therapy, as it is being misused by both participants, though this is conveyed largely on a manifest level. It also contains, as Type Two derivatives along the me/not-me interface, an unconscious perception of the therapist who is using his own interventions as a means of attempting to get rid of the bad stuff within himself. In a sense, too, the patient's comments appear to convey a refusal to contain the therapist's badness and an effort unconsciously to interpret the therapist's unconscious projective identifications.

The therapist's final intervention is a direct self-revelation which has no place in the techniques being described here. The therapist's attempt to use his subjective experiences and to hold the patient responsible for them reveals no effort to understand the basis for his own subjective responses. As is true of all such noninterpretive interventions, his comments serve as a confession of his own disorganization and as an effort to further attack the patient to engender guilt, and to blame him for the therapist's pathology. The therapist presents himself as a victim of the persecutions of the patient, in a form that now makes the patient a victim of the therapist's persecutions. The patient's responsive expression of his own fears of being crazy and his need to think of others as nuts, organized as Type Two derivatives in the adaptive context of this intervention, presents a compelling introject of this therapist's unconscious communications.

We turn now to a final vignette:

Mr. C. was in once-weekly psychotherapy at a point when the therapist had brought up the possibility of termination. He had apparently decompensated during an earlier period in his life, and now had secured powerful barriers against this psychotic part of his personality. In the session to be described, he reported a dream of a man who seemed to be chasing him out of his own apartment. There was the danger of rape, but the patient then found himself in an empty vault with the door closed, safe and protected.

In associating, Mr. C. spoke of mistrusting his banker, and conveyed thoughts of changing his bank because he no longer felt appreciated as a customer; still, he put the matter out of his mind. When conflicted, he makes his mind a blank and feels relief. The therapist pointed out that the patient has a tendency to seal himself off from the dangers and to seek safety in voids, and suggested that this is reflected not only in his dream, but in the way in which he was communicating in the session. In response, the patient recalled childhood fears of bombs and explosions, and recent fantasies of attacking his boss for firing a friend whom the patient very much liked. He then wondered if this had anything to do with the recent discussion of the termination of his therapy, and recognized that he felt much better and that perhaps it was time to think about it after all.

In this brief excerpt, the therapist attempts to interpret several metaphors of the patient's use of Type C barriers, doing so, of course, without identifying a specific adaptive context since one was not available in the material. The intervention is confirmed through Type Two derivatives, through which the patient expresses his need for vaults and blankness as a protection against inner disintegration; on another level, validation is reflected in the recollection of the fantasies of attacking the boss who had fired a friend. This latter derivative led the patient directly to termination, and to a continued working through of his anxieties and reactions to the therapist's proposal in this regard.

CONCLUDING COMMENTS

Despite the lengthy clinical material, it has been possible to discuss within that context only a limited number of aspects of the intervening process. The main thrust of this paper has been to offer a series of basic postulates, to selectively illustrate them, and to point toward future studies.

In concluding, it seems appropriate to reflect upon the need for some rather major alterations in the prevailing conception of the analyst's interventions. The current approach stresses the formal nature of interventions and addresses only the rather gross contradictory unconscious communications contained in them. It neglects the continuous unconscious inputs from the analyst. If one shifts instead to a study of the unconscious communicative interaction, a new and more sensitive appreciation of the analyst's work emerges. It confronts us as therapists with our continual countertransference-based inputs, however major or minor, but fosters their mastery and a more effective approach to the therapy of the patient.

NOTE

1. The observations, tenets, and principles to be developed in this paper are equally applicable to both psychotherapy and psychoanalysis. Because most of the relevant literature has addressed itself to the psychoanalytic situation, I will use that as my basic model.

REFERENCES

Adler, G., and Myerson, P. (1973). *Confrontations in Psychotherapy*. New York: Jason Aronson.
Bibring, E. (1954). Psychoanalysis and the dynamic therapy. *Journal of the American Psychoanalytic Association* 2: 745-770.

Bion, W. (1962). *Learning from Experience.* In W. Bion, *Seven Servants.* New York: Jason Aronson, 1977.

———(1970). *Attention and Interpretation.* In W. Bion, *Seven Servants.* New York: Jason Aronson, 1977.

Davies, G., and O'Farrell, V. (1976). The logic of transference interpretation. *International Review of Psycho-Analysis* 3:55–64.

Edelson, M. (1975). *Language and Interpretation in Psychoanalysis.* New Haven: Yale University Press.

Ekstein, R. (1959). Thoughts concerning the nature of the interpretive process. In *Readings in Psychoanalytic Psychology,* ed. M. Levitt, pp. 221–247. New York: Appleton-Century-Crofts.

Fine, B., Joseph, E., and Waldhorn, H. (1971). *Recollection and Reconstruction: Reconstruction in Psychoanalysis.* New York: International Universities Press.

Freud, S. (1905). Fragment of an analysis of a case of hysteria. *Standard Edition* 7:3–122.

———(1912). Recommendations to physicians practicing psychoanalysis. *Standard Edition* 12:111–120.

———(1913). On beginning the treatment (further recommendations on the technique of psycho-analysis III). *Standard Edition* 12:121–144.

———(1937). Constructions in analysis. *Standard Edition* 23:255–270.

Greenson, R. (1960). Problems of dosage, timing, and tact in interpretation. *Bulletin of the Philadelphia Association of Psychoanalysis* 10:23–24.

———(1967). *The Technique and Practice of Psychoanalysis,* Vol. I. New York: International Universities Press.

Kris, E. (1947). The nature of psychoanalytic propositions and their validation. In *Freedom and Experience,* ed. S. Hook and M. Konwitz. Ithaca, N.Y.: Cornell University Press.

Langs, R. (1972). A psychoanalytic study of material from patients in psychotherapy. *International Journal of Psychoanalytic Psychotherapy* 1(1):4–45.

———(1973). *The Technique of Psychoanalytic Psychotherapy,* Vol. I. New York: Jason Aronson.

———(1974). *The Technique of Psychoanalytic Psychotherapy,* Vol. II. New York: Jason Aronson.

———(1975a). Therapeutic misalliances. *International Journal of Psychoanalytic Psychotherapy* 4:77–105.

———(1975b). The therapeutic relationship and deviations in technique. *International Journal of Psychoanalytic Psychotherapy* 4:106–141.

———(1976a). *The Bipersonal Field.* New York: Jason Aronson.

———(1976b). *The Therapeutic Interaction.* 2 vols. New York: Jason Aronson.

———(1978d). Validation and the framework of the therapeutic situation. *Contemporary Psychoanalysis* 14:98–124.

———(1978c). Some communicative properties of the bipersonal field. *International Journal of Psychoanalytic Psychotherapy* 7:89–161.

———(1978a). The adaptational-interactional dimension of countertransference. In R. Langs, *Technique in Transition,* New York: Jason Aronson, 1978.

———(1978b). *The Listening Process.* New York: Jason Aronson.

Leavy, S. (1973). Psychoanalytic interpretation. *Psychoanalytic Study of the Child* 28:305–330.

Loewenstein, R. (1951). The problem of interpretation. *Psychoanalytic Quarterly* 20:1–14.

———(1957). Some thoughts on interpretation. *Psychoanalytic Study of the Child* 12:127–150.

Olinick, S. (1954). Some considerations of the use of questioning as a psychoanalytic technique. *Journal of the American Psychoanalytic Association* 2:57–66.

———(1957). Question and pain, truth and negation. *Journal of the American Psychoanalytic Association* 5:302–324.

de Racker, G. (1961). On the formulation of the interpretation. *International Journal of Psycho-Analysis* 42:49–54.

Rosen, V. (1974). The nature of verbal interventions in psychoanalysis. *Psychoanalysis and Contemporary Science* 3: 189–209.

Sandler, J. (1976). Countertransference and role-responsiveness. *International Review of Psycho-Analysis* 3:43–47.

Shapiro, T. (1970). Interpretation and naming. *Journal of the American Psychoanalytic Association* 18:399–421.

Viderman, S. (1974). Interpretation in the analytic space. *International Review of Psycho-Analysis* 1:467–480.

Zac, J. (1972). An investigation of how interpretations arise in the analyst. *International Journal of Psycho-Analysis* 53:315–320.

Zeligs, M. (1957). Acting in. *Journal of the American Psychoanalytic Association* 5:685–786.

PART V

THE THERAPEUTIC AND WORKING ALLIANCES

In his basic papers on technique, Freud (1912a) distinguished between relatively sublimated positive transferences, and those which remained instinctualized and derive from unconscious erotic fantasies. The former were seen as the basis for the patient's cooperation with the analyst, while the latter were at the heart of the analytic work with the patient's so-called transference neurosis. In 1934 (chapter 26) Sterba, and in a less definitive manner Bibring (1937), identified the alliance sector and, while acknowledging elements of transference, stressed its distinction from that sphere. Then, in 1956, Zetzel (chapter 27) firmed up the concept *therapeutic alliance* and attempted to map its dimensions—a pursuit she then clarified in a variety of ways in the years that followed (see Zetzel 1970).

While from time to time papers appeared which addressed this aspect of the therapeutic relationship, it was Greenson's study of the working alliance (1965; see chapter 28) that provided a major impetus for a consideration of this dimension of the analytic experience. Recent investigations have included an effort by Dickes (1975) to distinguish the working and therapeutic alliances and careful critiques by Kanzer (1975; see chapter 30) and Brenner (1979). My own investigation of therapeutic misalliances (1975a) has offered an extensive interactional study of major aspects of disturbance in this area.

These papers on the therapeutic alliance are of interest for two reasons. First, it is mainly through a consideration of the alliance sector that classical analysts have taken a closer look at the interactional aspects of the analytic experience. This trend is of considerable importance in that it allows this group of analysts to modify their tendency to isolate intrapsychic happenings within the patient from other dimensions of the therapeutic experience. Since the concept of alliance of its very nature calls for an investigation of the interplay between patient and analyst, studies in this area, especially as they broaden in scope, should lead to a growing appreciation in all quarters for the interactional dimension.

The second reason for interest in these papers is that they allow us to pinpoint the dangers, both theoretical and technical, that arise when analysts consider the alliance sector in relative isolation. There is a tendency to emphasize the autonomous ego functions deemed necessary for a secure alliance, and to couple this with a disregard of the transference aspect on the one hand, and of the continuous influence of the analyst or therapist on the other. Often such an approach leads to surface-oriented thinking, noninter-pretive interventions, and what are often defended as efforts to establish and maintain the therapeutic alliance. These measures, characteristically somewhat manipulative, tend to be accepted consciously by the patient, while proving indirectly and unconsciously disruptive on all levels, including that of the alliance itself.

There is considerable evidence that the alliance sector is best established and maintained through the creation of a stable analytic setting, adherence to the ground rules, and an essentially interpretive approach. The literature on the therapeutic and working alliances can be viewed in this perspective as a record of how classical analysts have explored dimensions of the therapeutic relationship beyond the transference component, thereby bringing to the fore important interactional considerations. This then promotes analytic work with the pathology of both patient and analyst — the latter on his own of course — as it interferes with their basic working relationship and the ultimate cure of the patient.

26

THE FATE OF THE EGO
IN ANALYTIC THERAPY

Richard Sterba

EDITOR'S NOTE

With its roots in Freud's original division (1912a; see chapter 1) of positive transference into friendly or affectionate feelings, and those derived from erotic sources that extend into the unconscious, Sterba's contribution specifically delineates a division within the patient's ego, one part focused on reality and the other functioning at the behest of instinctual and defensive energies. Through his recognition of this type of dissociation in the ego, Sterba was able to suggest that the analyst, through his interpretations, effects an alliance with one part of the ego against the forces of instinct and repression. He thereby provides one of the first references in the literature to what later was termed the working or therapeutic alliance.

This development, stemming from increasing understanding of the ego's defenses, the healthy portions of the ego, and the nature of object relationships, proved a wellspring for later investigations of the different aspects of the patient's functioning within the therapeutic relationship, as well as of the cooperative qualities of the patient-analyst relationship. Sterba's suggestion that the alliance sector is reinforced on the side of the patient through certain aspects of positive transference and through an identification with the analyst is a reminder that this dimension of the analytic relationship relies not only upon relatively autonomous ego functions, but also on a variety of unconscious, transference-based factors that include notable contributions from the analyst himself.

That part of the psychic apparatus which is turned towards the outside world and whose business it is to receive stimuli and effect discharge-reactions we call the ego. Since analysis belongs to the external world, it is again the ego which is turned towards it. Such knowledge as we possess of the deeper strata of the psychic apparatus reaches us by way of the ego and depends upon the extent to which the ego admits it, in virtue of such derivatives of the Ucs as it still tolerates. If we wish to learn something of these deeper strata or to bring about a change in a neurotic constellation of instincts, it is to the ego and the ego alone that we can turn. Our analysis of resistances, the explanations and interpretations that we give to our patients, our attempts to alter their mental attitudes through our personal action upon them — all these must necessarily start with the ego. Now amongst all the experiences undergone by the ego during an analysis there is one which seems to me so specific and so characteristic of the analytic situation that I feel justified in isolating it and presenting it to you as the 'fate' of the ego in analytic therapy.

The contents of this paper will surprise you by

Reprinted from *International Journal of Psycho-Analysis* 15:117–126, 1934.

their familiarity. How could it be otherwise, seeing that it is simply an account of what you do and observe every day in your analyses? If, nevertheless, I plead justification, it is because I believe that, in what follows, adequate recognition is given for the first time to a factor in our therapeutic work which has so far received too little attention in our literature. The nearest approach to my theme is to be found in a paper on character-analysis by Reich,[1] in which he talks of 'isolating' a given character-trait, 'objectifying' it and 'imparting psychic distance' to it, referring thereby no doubt to that therapeutic process which I shall now prsent in a much more general form.

For the purposes of our incomplete description it will suffice if we regard the ego in analysis as having three functions. First, it is the executive organ of the id, which is the source of the object-cathexis of the analyst in the transference; secondly, it is the organization which aims at fulfilling the demands of the super-ego and, thirdly, it is the site of experience, i.e. the institution which either allows or prevents the discharge of the energy poured forth by the id in accordance with the subject's previous experiences.

In analysis the personality of the analysand passes first of all under the domination of the *transference*. The function of the transference is twofold. On the one hand, it serves to satisfy the object-hunger of the id. But, on the other, it meets with opposition from the repressive psychic institutions — the super-ego, which rejects it on moral grounds, and the ego, which, because of unhappy experiences, utters a warning against it. Thus, in the transference-resistance the very fact of the transference is utilized as a weapon against the whole analysis.

We see, then, that in the transference a dualistic principle comes into play in the ego: instinct and repression alike make themselves felt. We learn from the study of the transference-resistance that the forces of repression enter into the transference no less than the instinctual forces. Anti-cathexes are mobilized as a defence against the libidinal impulses which proceed from the Ucs and are revived in the transference. For example, anxiety is activated as a danger-signal against the repetition of some unhappy experience that once ensued from an instinctual impulse, and is used as a defence against analysis. Here the repressive forces throw their weight on the side of the transference because the revival of the repressed tendency makes it the more imperative for the subject to defend himself against it and so put an end to the dreaded laying bare of the Ucs.

In order to bring out the twofold function of the transference let me sketch a fairly typical transference-situation such as arose at the beginning of one of my analyses.

A woman patient transferred to the analyst an important object-cathexis from the period of early childhood. It represented her love for a physician to whom she was frequently taken during her fifth year on account of enlarged tonsils. On each occasion he looked into her mouth, without touching the tonsils, afterwards giving her some sweets and always being kind and friendly. Her parents had instituted these visits in order to lull her into security for the operation to come. One day, when she trustfully let the doctor look into her mouth again, he inserted a gag and, without giving any narcotic or local anesthetic, removed the unsuspecting child's tonsils. For her this was a bitter disillusionment and never again could she be persuaded to go to see him.

The twofold function of the transference from this physician to the analyst is obvious: in the first place it revived the object-relation to the former (a father-substitute), but, in the second place, her unhappy experience with him gave the repressive forces their opportunity to reject the analyst and, with him, the analysis. 'You had much better stay away, in case he hurts you', they warned her, 'and keep your mouth shut!' The result was that the patient was obstinately silent in the analysis and manifested a constant tendency to break it off.

This typical example shews how the ego manages in the transference to rid itself of two different influences, though in the shape of a conflict. For the establishment of the transference is based on a conflict between instinct and repression. Where the transference-situation is intense, there is always the danger that one or other of the conflicting forces may prevail: either the analytic enterprise may be broken up by the blunt transference demands of the patient, or else the repressive institutions in the mind of the latter may totally repudiate both analyst and analysis. Thus we may describe the transference and the resistance which goes with it as the conflict-laden result of the struggle between two groups of forces, each of which aims at dominating the workings of the ego, while both alike obstruct the purposes of the analysis.

In opposition to this dual influence, the object of which is to inhibit the analysis, we have the corrective influence of the analyst, who in his turn, however, must address himself to the *ego*. He approaches it in its capacity of the organ of perception and of the testing by reality. By *interpreting* the transference-situation he endeavours to oppose those elements in

---

1. *Internationale Zeitschrift für Psychoanalyse,* Bd. XIV, 1928.

the ego which are focussed on reality to those which have a cathexis of instinctual or defensive energy. What he thus accomplishes may be described as a *dissociation* within the ego.[2]

We know that dissociations within the ego are by no means uncommon. They are a means of avoiding the clash of intolerable contradictions in its organization. 'Double consciousness' may be regarded as a large-scale example of such dissociation: here the left hand is successfully prevented from knowing what is done by the right. Many parapraxes are of the nature of 'double consciousness', and abortive forms of this phenomenon are to be found in other departments of life as well.

This capacity of the ego for dissociation gives the analyst the chance, by means of his interpretations, to effect an alliance with the ego against the powerful forces of instinct and repression and, with the help of one part of it, to try to vanquish the opposing forces. Hence, when we begin an analysis which can be carried to completion, the fate that inevitably awaits the ego is that of *dissociation*. A permanently unified ego, such as we meet with in cases of excessive narcissisms or in certain psychotic states where ego and id have become fused, is not susceptible of analysis. The therapeutic dissociation of the ego is a necessity if the analyst is to have the chance of winning over part of it to his side, conquering it, strengthening it by means of identification with himself and opposing it in the transference to those parts which have a cathexis of instinctual and defensive energy.

The technique by which the analyst effects this therapeutic dissociation of the ego consists of the explanations which he gives to the patient of the first signs of transference and transference-resistance that can be interpreted. You will remember that in his recommendations on the subject of technique Freud says that, when the analyst can detect the effects of a transference-resistance it is a sign that the time is ripe for interpretation. Through the explanations of the transference-situation that he receives the patient realizes for the first time the peculiar character of the therapeutic method used in analysis. Its distinctive characteristic is this: that the subject's consciousness shifts from the centre of affective experience to that of intellectual contemplation. The transference-situation is *interpreted,* i.e. an explanation

is given which is uncoloured by affect and which shews that the situation has its roots in the subject's childhood. Through this interpretation there emerges in the mind of the patient, out of the chaos of behaviour impelled by instinct and behaviour designed to inhibit instinct, a *new point of view of intellectual contemplation.* In order that this new standpoint may be effectually reached there must be a certain amount of positive transference, on the basis of which a transitory strengthening of the ego takes place through identification with the analyst. This identification is induced by the analyst. From the outset the patient is called upon to 'co-operate' with the analyst against something in himself. Each separate session gives the analyst various opportunities of employing the term 'we', in referring to himself and to the part of the patient's ego which is consonant with reality. The use of the word 'we' always means that the analyst is trying to draw that part of the ego over to his side and to place it in opposition to the other part which in the transference is cathected or influenced from the side of the unconscious. We might say that this 'we' is the instrument by means of which the therapeutic dissociation of the ego is effected.

The function of interpretation, then, is this: Over against the patient's instinct-conditioned, or defensive behaviour, emotions and thoughts it sets up in him a principle of intellectual cognition, a principle which is steadily supported by the analyst and fortified by the additional insight gained as the analysis proceeds. In subjecting the patient's ego to the fate of therapeutic dissociation we are doing what Freud recommends in a passage in *Beyond the Pleasure Principle* (p. 18): 'The physician . . . has to see to it that some measure of ascendancy remains [in the patient], in the light of which the apparent reality [of what is repeated in the transference] is always recognized as a reflection of a forgotten past.'

The question now suggests itself: What is the prototype of this therapeutic ego-dissociation in the patient? The answer is that it is the process of *super-ego-formation.* By means of an identification—of analysand with analyst—judgements and valuations from the outside world are admitted into the ego and become operative within it. The difference between this process and that of super-ego-formation is that,

---

2. It may be doubted whether 'dissociation' is an appropriate term for non-pathological processes in the ego. This point is answered by the following passage in Freud's *New Introductory Lectures on Psycho-Analysis,* a work which has appeared since this paper was read: 'We wish to make the ego the object of our study, our own ego. But how can that be done? The ego is the subject *par excellence*: how can it become the object?

There is no doubt, however, that it can. The ego can take itself as object; it can treat itself like any other object, observe itself, criticize itself, do Heaven knows what besides with itself. In such a case, one part of the ego stands over against the other. The ego can, then, be split; it becomes dissociated during many of its functions, at any rate in passing. The parts can later on join up again' (p. 80).

since the therapeutic dissociation takes place in an ego which is already mature, it cannot well be described as a 'stage' in ego-development: rather it represents more or less the opposition of one element to others on the same level. The result of super-ego-formation is the powerful establishment of moral demands; in therapeutic ego-dissociation the demand which has been accepted is a demand for a revised attitude appropriate to the situation of an adult personality. Thus, whilst the super-ego demands that the subject shall adopt a particular attitude towards a particular tendency in the id, the demand made upon him when therapeutic dissociation takes place is a demand for a balancing contemplation, kept steadily free of affect, whatever changes may take place in the contents of the instinct-cathexes and the defensive reactions.

We have seen, then, that in analysis the ego undergoes a specific fate which we have described as therapeutic dissociation. When analysis begins, the ego is subject to a process of 'dissimilation' or dissociation, which must be induced by the analyst by means of his interpretation of the transference-situation and of the resistance to which this gives rise.

As the analyst proceeds, the state of 'dissimilation' in the ego is set up again whenever the unconscious material, whether in the shape of instinctual gratification or of defensive impulses, fastens on the analyst in the transference. All the instinctual and defensive reactions aroused in the ego in the transference impel the analyst to induce the therapeutic process of ego-dissociation by means of the interpretations he gives. There is constituted, as it were, a standing relation between that part of the ego which is cathected with instinctual or defensive energy and that part which is focussed on reality and identified with the analyst, and this relation is the filter through which all the transference-material in the analysis must pass. Each separate interpretation reduces the instinctual and defensive cathexis of the ego in favour of intellectual contemplation, reflection and correction by the standard of reality.

However, once the analyst's interpretations have set up this opposition of forces — the ego which is in harmony with reality versus the ego which acts out its unconscious impulses — the state of 'dissimilation' does not last and a process of *'assimilation'* automatically begins. We owe to Hermann Nunberg our closer knowledge of this process, which he calls 'the synthetic function of the ego'. As we know, this function consists in the striving of the ego, prompted by Eros, to bind, to unify, to assimilate and to blend — in short, to leave no conflicting elements within its domain. It is this synthetic function which, next to therapeutic dissociation of the ego, makes analytic therapy possible. The former process enables the subject to recognize intellectually and to render conscious the claims and the content of his unconsciousness and the affects associated with these, whilst when that has been achieved, the synthetic function of the ego enables him to incorporate them and to secure their discharge.

Since there are in the transference and the transference-resistance two groups of forces within the ego, it follows that the ego-dissociation induced by the analyst must take place in relation to each group, the ego being placed in opposition to both. At the same time the interpretations of defensive reactions and instinctual trends become interwoven with one another, for analysis cannot overcome the defence unless the patient comes to recognize his instinctual impulses, nor put him in control of the latter unless the defence has been overthrown. The typical process is as follows: First of all, the analyst gives an interpretation of the defence, making allusion to the instinctual tendencies which he has already divined and against which the defence has been set up. With the patient's recognition that his attitude in the transference is of the nature of a defence, there comes a weakening in that defence. The result is a more powerful onslaught of the instinctual strivings upon the ego. The analyst then has to interpret the infantile meaning and aim of these impulses. Ego-dissociation and synthesis ensue, with the outcome that the impulses are corrected by reference to reality and subsequently find discharge by means of such modifications as are possible. In order that all these interpretations may have a more profound effect, it is necessary constantly to repeat them; the reason for this I have explained elsewhere ('Zur Dynamik der Bewältigung des Übertragungswiderstandes,' *Internationale Zeitschrift für Psychoanalyse.* Bd. XV, 1929).

Now let us return to the case I cited before and see how it illustrates what I have just said. The patient's resistance, which began after a few analytic sessions, took the form of obstinate silence and a completely negative attitude towards the analyst. Such meagre associations as she vouchsafed to give she jerked out with averted head and in obvious ill-humour. At the close of the second session an incident occurred which shewed that this silence and repellent attitude were a mode of defence against a positive transference. At the end of the hour she asked me if I had not a cloakroom where she could change her clothes as they were all crumpled after she had lain on the sofa for an hour. The next day she said to me in this connection that, after her analysis, she was going to meet a woman friend, who would certainly wonder where the patient had got her dress so crushed and whether she had been having sexual intercourse. It was clear that, as early as the second session, her ego had come under the influence of the transference and of the defence against it. Of course, she herself was completely unconscious of the connection between her fear of being found out by her friend and the attitude of repudiation which she assumed in analysis.

The next thing to do was to explain to the patient the *meaning* of her defence. As a first step, the defensive nature of her attitude was made plain to her, for of this, too, she was unconscious. With this interpretation we had begun the process which I have called therapeutic ego-dissociation. When the interpretation had been several times repeated the patient gained a first measure of 'psychic distance' in relation to her own behaviour. At the start her gain was only intermittent and she was compelled almost at once to go on acting her instinctual impulses out. As, however, the positive transference was sufficiently strong, it gradually became possible to enlarge these islands of intellectual contemplation or observation at the expense of the process of acting the unconscious impulses out. The result of this dissociation in the ego was that the patient gained an insight into the defensive nature of her attitude in analysis, that is to say, she now began to work over preconsciously the material which had hitherto been enacted unconsciously in her behaviour. This insight denoted a decrease in the cathexis of those parts of the ego which were carrying on the defence.

Some time afterwards there emerged the memory of her visits to the kind throat-specialist and of the bitter disillusionment in which they had ended. This recollection was in itself a result of the synthetic function of the ego, for the ego will not tolerate within itself a discrepancy between defence and insight. The effect of the infantile experience had, it is true, been felt by the ego, but this effect had been determined from the unconscious; it now became incorporated in the preconscious in respect of its causal origin also. It is hardly necessary for me to point out that the discovery of this infantile experience of the patient with the physician was merely a preliminary to the real task of the analyst, which was to bring into consciousness her experiences with her father and especially her masochistic phantasies relating to him.

In overcoming the transference-defence by the method of therapeutic ego-dissociation we were not merely attacking that part of the ego which was using

the patient's unhappy experience with the physician in her childhood to obstruct the analysis; we were, besides, counteracting part of the super-ego's opposition. For the defensive attitude was in part also a reaction to the fear that her friend might find out the patient had been having sexual intercourse. Now she had developed an obvious mother-transference to this particular friend, and the mother was the person who had imposed sexual prohibitions in the patient's childhood. By means of the therapeutic ego-dissociation a standpoint of intellectual contemplation, a 'measure of ascendancy', had formed itself in her mind, in opposition to her defensive behaviour: in that dissociation the 'reality' elements in the ego were separated not only from those elements which bore the stamp of that unhappy experience and signalled their warning, but also from those other elements which acted as the executive of the super-ego.

In the case we are considering, the next result of the analysis was that the positive transference began to reveal itself, taking more openly possession of the ego and manifesting itself in the claims which the patient made on the analyst's love. Once more, dissociation had to be induced in the ego, so as to separate out of the processes of dramatic enactment an island of intellectual contemplation, from which the patient could perceive that her behaviour was determined by her infantile experiences in relation to her father. This, naturally, only proved possible after prolonged therapeutic work.

I hope that this short account may have sufficed to make clear what I believe to be one of the most important processes in analytic therapy, namely, the effecting of a dissociation within the ego by interpretation of the patient's instinctually conditioned conduct and his defensive reaction to it. Perhaps I may say in conclusion that the therapeutic dissociation of the ego in analysis is merely an extension, into new fields, of that self-contemplation which from all time has been regarded as the most essential trait of man in distinction to other living beings. For example, Herder expressed the view that *speech* originated in this objectifying process which works by the dissociation of the mind in self-contemplation. This is what he says about it: 'Man shews reflection when the power of his mind works so freely that, out of the whole ocean of sensations which comes flooding in through the channel of every sense, he can separate out, if I may so put it, a single wave and hold it, directing his attention upon it and being conscious of this attention. . . . He shews reflection when he not only has a vivid and distinct perception of every sort of attribute, but can acknowledge in himself one or more of them as distinguishing attributes: the first such act of acknowledgment yields a clear conception; it is the mind's first judgement. And how did this acknowledgment take place? Through a characteristic which he had had to separate out and which, as a characteristic due to conscious reflection, presented itself clearly to his mind. Good! Let us greet him with a cry of "eureka"! This first characteristic due to conscious reflection was a word of the mind! With it human speech was invented!' (*Über den Ursprung der Sprache.*)

In the therapeutic dissociation which is the fate of the ego in analysis, the analysand is called on 'to answer for himself'[3] and the unconscious, ceasing to be expressed in behaviour, becomes articulate in *words*. We may say, then, that in this ego-dissociation we have an extension of reflection beyond what has hitherto been accessible. Thus, from the standpoint also of the human faculty of speech, we may justly claim that analytic therapy makes its contribution to the humanizing of man.

---

3. [German: '*zur Rede gestellt*'; literally, 'is put to speech'.]

27

CURRENT CONCEPTS OF TRANSFERENCE

Elizabeth R. Zetzel

EDITOR'S NOTE

This paper, a contribution to a symposium on transference, is often credited as the first effort to carefully distinguish the transference neurosis from the therapeutic alliance—a clarification foreshadowed both by Sterba's 1934 paper (chapter 26) and by Bibring (1937). The paper is also well known for its comparison of the Kleinian and classical Freudian views of transference, and is one of several such critiques to have appeared in the literature. It may be contrasted with the paper by Segal (1967; see chapter 35) in which the Kleinians' position is presented from their own vantage point. This contribution also initiated a series of investigations of the analytic relationship, its genetic underpinnings, and the therapeutic alliance by this author (see Zetzel 1970).

Zetzel's criticism of the Kleinians for overvaluing primitive fantasies and neglecting the resistance aspects of regression is counterbalanced by her own emphasis on regression as a manifestation of resistance—a position that may lead to premature efforts on the part of classical analysts to circumvent the necessary therapeutic regression essential for complete analytic work. A brief discussion of modifications in basic psychoanalytic technique typifies the position of classical analysts who advocate the use of these variations in the presence of ego disturbances in the patient (see Eissler 1953 [chapter 35]). The paper deserves a special place in the history of psychoanalysis for having provided a stimulus for the consideration of the transference and alliance sectors of the patient's relationship with the analyst, and for having sparked the first debates regarding the attributes, merits, and deficiencies of the classical Freudian and the Kleinian views of transference, the analytic relationship and interaction, and related techniques.

There are few current problems concerning the problem of transference that Freud did not recognize either implicitly or explicitly in the development of his theoretical and clinical framework. For all essential purposes, moreover, his formulations, in spite of certain shifts in emphasis, remain integral to contemporary psycho-analytic theory and practice. Recent developments mainly concern the impact of an ego-psychological approach; the significance of object relations, both current and infantile, external and internal; the role of aggression in mental life,

Reprinted from *International Journal of Psycho-Analysis* 37:369–376, 1956.

and the part played by regression and the repetition compulsion in the transference. Nevertheless, analysis of the infantile oedipal situation in the setting of a genuine transference neurosis is still considered a primary goal of psycho-analytic procedure.

Originally, transference was ascribed to displacement on to the analyst of repressed wishes and fantasies derived from early childhood. The transference neurosis was viewed as a compromise formation similar to dreams and other neurotic symptoms. Resistance, defined as the clinical manifestation of repression, could be diminished or abolished by interpretation mainly directed towards the content of the repressed. Transference resistance, both positive and negative, was ascribed to the threatened emergence of repressed unconscious material in the analytic situation. Soon, with the development of a structural approach, the superego described as the heir to the genital oedipal situation was also recognized as playing a leading part in the transference situation. The analyst was subsequently viewed not only as the object of displacement of infantile incestuous fantasies, but also as the substitute by projection for the prohibiting parental figures which had been internalized as the definitive superego. The effect of transference interpretation in mitigating undue severity of the superego has, therefore, been emphasized in many discussions of the concept of transference.

Certain expansions in the structural approach related to increased recognition of the role of early object relations in the development of both ego and superego have affected current concepts of transference. In this connection, the significance of the analytic situation as a repetition of the early mother-child relationship has been stressed from different points of view. An equally important development relates to Freud's revised concept of anxiety which not only led to theoretical developments in the field of ego psychology, but also brought about related clinical changes in the work of many analysts. As a result, attention was no longer mainly focused on the content of the unconscious. In addition, increasing importance was attributed to the defensive processes by means of which the anxiety which would be engendered if repression and other related mechanisms were broken down, was avoided in the analytic situation. Differences in the interpretation of the role of the analyst and the nature of transference developed from emphasis, on the one hand, on the importance of early object relations, and on the other, from primary attention to the role of the ego and its defences. These defences first emerged clearly in discussion of the technique of child analysis, in which Melanie Klein (1) and Anna Freud (2), the pioneers in this field, played leading roles.

From a theoretical point of view, discussion foreshadowing the problems which face us today was presented in 1934 in well-known papers by Richard Sterba (3) and James Strachey (4), and further elaborated at the Marienbad Symposium at which Edward Bibring (5) made an important contribution. The importance of identification with, or introjection of, the analyst in the transference situation was clearly indicated. Therapeutic results were attributed to the effect of this process in mitigating the need for pathological defences. Strachey, however, considerably influenced by the work of Melanie Klein, regarded transference as essentially a projection on to the analyst of the patient's own superego. The therapeutic process was attributed to subsequent introjection of a modified superego as a result of 'mutative' transference interpretation. Sterba and Bibring, on the other hand, intimately involved with development of the ego-psychological approach, emphasized the central role of the ego, postulating a therapeutic split and identification with the analyst as an essential feature of transference. To some extent, this difference of opinion may be regarded as semantic. If the superego is explicitly defined as the heir of the genital Oedipus conflict, then earlier intra-systemic conflicts within the ego, although they may be related retrospectively to the definitive superego, must, nevertheless, be defined as contained within the ego. Later divisions within the ego of the type indicated by Sterba and very much expanded by Edward Bibring in his concept of therapeutic alliance between the analyst and the healthy part of the patient's ego, must also be excluded from superego significance. In contrast, those who attribute pregenital intra-systemic conflicts within the ego primarily to the introjection of objects, consider that the resultant state of internal conflict resembles in all dynamic respects the situation seen in later conflicts between ego and superego. They, therefore, believe that these structures develop simultaneously and suggest that no sharp distinction should be made between pre-oedipal, oedipal, and post-oedipal superego.

The differences, however, are not entirely verbal, since those who attribute superego formation to the early months of life tend to attribute a significance to early object relations which differs from the conception of those who stress control and neutralization of instinctual energy as primary functions of the ego. This theoretical difference necessarily implies some disagreement as to the dynamic situation both in childhood and in adult life, inevitably reflected in the concept of transference and in hypotheses as to the nature of the therapeutic process. From one point of view, the role of the ego is central and crucial at every phase of analysis. A differentiation is made between transference as therapeutic alliance and the transference neurosis, which, on the whole, is considered a manifestation of resistance. Effective analysis depends on a sound therapeutic alliance, a prerequisite for which is the existence, before analysis, of a degree of mature ego functions, the absence of which in certain severely disturbed patients and in young children may preclude traditional psycho-analytic procedure. Whenever indicated, interpretation must deal with transference manifestations, which means, in effect, that the transference must be analysed. The process of analysis, however, is not exclusively ascribed to transference interpretation. Other interpretaitions of unconscious material, whether related to defence or to early fantasy, will be equally effective provided they are accurately timed and provided a satisfactory therapeutic alliance has been made. Those, in contrast, who stress the importance of early object relations emphasize the crucial role of transference as an object relationship, distorted though this may be, by a variety of defences against primitive unresolved conflicts. The central role of the ego, both in the early stages of development and in the analytic process, is definitely accepted. The nature of the ego is, however, considered at all times to be determined by its external and internal objects. Therapeutic progress indicated by changes in ego function results, therefore, primarily from a change in object relations through interpretation of the transference situation. Less differentiation is made between transference as therapeutic alliance and the transference neurosis as a manifestation of resistance. Therapeutic progress depends almost exclusively on transference interpretation. Other interpretations, although indicated at times, are not, in general, considered an essential feature of the analytic process. From this point of view, the preanalytic maturity of the patient's ego is not stressed as a prerequisite for analysis; children and relatively disturbed patients are considered potentially suitable for traditional psycho-analytic procedure.

These differences in theoretical orientation are not only reflected in the approach to children and disturbed patients. They may also be recognized in significant variations of technique in respect to all clinical groups, which inevitably affect the opening phases, understanding of the inevitable regressive features of the transference neurosis, and handling of the terminal phases of analysis. I shall try to underline the main problems by emphasizing contrast, rather than similarity. I shall also try to avoid too detailed discussion of controversial theory regarding the nature of early ego development by a somewhat arbitrary differentiation between those who relate ego analysis to the analysis of defences and those who stress the primary significance of object relations both in the transference, and in the development and definitive structures of the ego. Needless to say, this involves some oversimplification. I hope, however, that it may, at the same time, clarify certain important issues. To take up first the analysis of patients generally agreed to be suitable for classical analytic procedure, the transference neuroses. Those who emphasize the role of the ego and the analysis of defences, not only maintain Freud's conviction that analysis should proceed from surface to depth, but also consider that early material in the analytic situation derives, in general, from defensive processes rather than from displacement on to the analyst of early instinctual fantasies. Deep transference interpretation in the early phases of analysis will, therefore, either be meaningless to the patient since its unconscious significance is so inaccessible, or, if the defences are precarious, will lead to premature and possibly intolerable anxiety. Premature interpretation of the equally unconscious automatic defensive processes by means of which instinctual fantasy has been kept unconscious is also ineffective and undesirable. There are, however, differences of opinion within this group, as to how far analysis of defence can be separated from analysis of content. Waelder (6), for example, has stressed the impossibility of such separation. Fenichel (7), however, considered that at least theoretical separation should be made and indicated that, as far as possible, analysis of defence should precede analysis of unconscious fantasy. It is, nevertheless, generally agreed that the transference neurosis develops, as a rule, after ego defences have been sufficiently undermined to mobilize previously hidden instinctual conflict. During both the early stages of analysis, and at frequent points after the development of the transference neurosis, defence against the transference will become a main feature of the analytic situation.

This approach, as already indicated, is based on certain definite premises regarding the nature and function of the ego in respect to the control and neutralization of instinctual energy and unconscious fantasy. While the importance of early object relations is not neglected, the conviction that early transference interpretation is ineffective and potentially dangerous is related to the hypothesis that the instinctual energy available to the mature ego has been neutralized and is, for all effective purposes, relatively or absolutely divorced from its unconscious fantasy meaning at the beginning of analysis. In contrast, there are a number of analysts of differing theoretical orientation who do not view the development of the mature ego as a relative separation of ego functions from unconscious sources, but consider that unconscious fantasy continues to operate in all conscious mental activity. These analysts also tend on the whole to emphasize the crucial significance of primitive fantasy in respect to the development of the transference situation. The individual entering analysis will inevitably have unconscious fantasies concerning the analyst derived from primitive sources. This material, although deep in one sense, is, nevertheless, strongly current and accessible to interpretation. Mrs. Klein (8, 9), in addition, relates the development and definitive structure of both ego and superego to unconscious fantasy determined by the earliest phases of object relationship. She emphasizes the role of early introjective and projective processes in relation to primitive anxiety ascribed to the death instinct and related aggressive fantasies. The unresolved difficulties and conflicts of the earliest period continue to colour object relations throughout life. Failure to achieve an essentially satisfactory object relationship in this early period, and failure to master relative loss of that object without retaining its good internal representative, will not only affect all object relations and definitive ego function, but more specifically determine the nature of anxiety-provoking fantasies on entering the analytic situation. According to this point of view, therefore, early transference interpretation, even though it may relate to fantasies derived from an early period of life, should result not in an increase, but a decrease of anxiety.

In considering next problems of transference in relation to analysis of the transference neurosis, two main points must be kept in mind. First, as already indicated, those who emphasize the analysis of defence tend to make a definite differentiation between transference as therapeutic alliance and the transference neurosis as a compromise formation which serves the purposes of resistance. In contrast, those who emphasize the importance of early object relations view the transference primarily as a revival or repetition, sometimes attributed to symbolic processes of early struggles in respect to objects. Here, no sharp differentiation is made between the early manifestations of transference and the transference neurosis. In view, moreover, of the weight given to the role of unconscious fantasy and internal objects in every phase of mental life, healthy and pathological functions, though differing in essential respects, do not differ with regard to their direct dependence on unconscious sources.

In the second place, the role of regression in the transference situation is subject to wide differences of opinion. It was, of course, one of Freud's earliest discoveries that regression to earlier points of fixation is a cardinal feature, not only in the development of neurosis and psychosis, but also in the revival of earlier conflicts in the transference situation. With the development of psycho-analysis and its application to an ever increasing range of disturbed personalities, the role of regression in the analytic situation has received increased attention. The significance of the analytic situation as a means of fostering regression as a prerequisite for the therapeutic work has been emphasized by Ida Macalpine (10) in a recent paper. Differing opinions as to the significance, value, and technical handling of regressive manifestations form the basis of important modifications of analytic technique which will be considered presently. In respect, however, to the transference neurosis, the view recently expressed by Phyllis Greenacre (11) that regression, an indispensable feature of the transference situation, is to be resolved by traditional technique would be generally accepted. It is also a matter of general agreement that a prerequisite for successful analysis is revival and repetition in the analytic situation of the struggles of primitive stages of development. Those who emphasize defence analysis, however, tend to view regression as a manifestation of resistance; as a primitive mechanism of defence employed by the ego in the setting of the transference neurosis. Analysis of these regressive manifestations with their potential dangers depends on the existing and continued functioning of adequate ego strength to maintain therapeutic alliance at an adult level. Those, in contrast, who stress the significance of transference as a revival of the early mother-child relationship do not emphasize regression as an indication of resistance or defence. The revival of these primitive experiences in the transference situation is, in fact, regarded as an essential prerequisite for satisfactory psychological maturation and true genitality. The Kleinian school, as already indicated, stress the continued activity of primitive conflicts in determining essential features of the transference at every stage of analysis. Their increasingly overt revival in the analytic situation, therefore, signifies a deepening of the analysis, and in general, is regarded as an indication of diminution rather than increase of resistance. The dangers involved according to this point of view are determined more by failure to mitigate primitive anxiety by suitable transference interpretation, than by failure to achieve, in the early phases of analysis, a sound therapeutic alliance based on the maturity of the patient's essential ego characteristics.

In considering, briefly, the terminal phases of analysis, many unresolved problems concerning the goal of therapy and definition of a completed psycho-analysis must be kept in mind. Distinction must also be made between the technical problems of the terminal phase and evaluation of transference resolution after the analysis has been terminated. There is widespread agreement as to the frequent revival in the terminal phases of primitive transference manifestations apparently resolved during the early phase of analysis. Balint (12), and those who accept Ferenczi's concept of primary passive love, suggest that some gratification of primitive passive needs may be essential for successful termination. To Mrs. Klein (13) the terminal phases of analysis also represent a repetition of important features of the early mother-child relationship. According to her point of view, this period represents, in essence, a revival of the early weaning situation. Completion depends on a mastery of early depressive struggles culminating in successful introjection of the analyst as a good object. Although, in this connection, emphasis differs considerably, it should be noted that those who stress the importance of identification with the analyst as a basis for therapeutic alliance, also accept the inevitability of some permanent modifications of a similar nature. Those, however, who make a definite differentiation between transference and the transference neurosis stress the importance of analysis and resolution of the transference neurosis as a main prerequisite for successful termination. The identification based on therapeutic alliance must be interpreted and understood, particularly with reference to the reality aspects of the analyst's personality. In spite, therefore, of significant important differences, there are, as already indicated in connection with the earliest papers of Sterba and Strachey, important points of agreement in respect to the goal of psycho-analysis.

The differences already considered indicate some basic current problems of transference. So far, however, discussion has been limited to variations within the framework of a traditional technique. We must now consider problems related to overt modifications. Here it is essential to distinguish between variations introduced in respect to certain clinical conditions, often as a preliminary to classical psycho-analysis, and modifications based on changes in basic approach which lead to significant alterations with regard both to the method and to the aim of therapy. It is generally agreed that some variations of technique are indicated in the treatment of certain character neuroses, borderline patients, and the psychoses. The nature and meaning of such changes is, however, viewed differently according to the relative emphasis placed on the ego and its defences, on underlying unconscious conflicts, and on the significance and handling of regression in the therapeutic situation. In 'Analysis Terminable and Interminable' (14), Freud suggested that certain ego attributes may be inborn or constitutional and, therefore, probably inaccessible to psycho-analytic procedure. Hartmann (15, 16, 17) has suggested that in addition to these primary attributes, other ego characteristics, originally developed for defensive purposes, and the related neutralized instinctual energy at the disposal of the ego, may be relatively or absolutely divorced from unconscious fantasy. This not only explains the relative inefficacy of early transference interpretation, but also hints at possible limitations in the potentialities of analysis attributable to secondary autonomy of the ego which is considered to be relatively irreversible. In certain cases, moreover, it is suggested that analysis of precarious or seriously pathological defences — particularly those concerned with the control of aggressive impulses — may be not only ineffective, but dangerous. The relative failure of ego development in such cases not only precludes the development of a genuine therapeutic alliance, but also raises the risk of a serious regressive, often predominantly hostile transference situation. In certain cases, therefore, a preliminary period of psychotherapy is recommended in order to explore the capacities of the patient to tolerate traditional psycho-analysis. In others, as Robert Knight (18) in his paper on Borderline States, and as many analysts working with psychotic patients have suggested, psycho-analytic procedure is not considered applicable. Instead, a therapeutic approach based on analytic understanding which, in essence, utilizes an essentially implicit positive transference as a means of reinforcing, rather than analysing the precarious defenses of the individual, is advocated. In contrast, Herbert Rosenfeld (19) has approached even severely disturbed psychotic patients with minimal modifications of psycho-analytic technique. Only changes which the severity of the patient's condition enforces are introduced. Here, the dangers of regression in therapy are not emphasized since primitive fantasy is considered to be active under all circumstances.

This most primitive period is viewed in terms of early object relations with special stress on persecutory anxiety related to the death instinct. Interpretation of this primitive fantasy in the transference situation, as already indicated, is considered to diminish rather than to increase psychotic anxiety and to offer the best opportunity of strengthening the severely threatened psychotic ego. Other analysts, Dr. Winnicott (20), for example, attribute psychosis mainly to severe traumatic experiences, particularly of deprivation in early infancy. According to this point of view, profound regression offers an opportunity to fulfil, in the transference situation, primitive needs which had not been met at the appropriate level of development. Similar suggestions have been proposed by Margolin (21) and others, in the concept of anaclitic treatment of serious psychosomatic disease. This approach is also based on the premise that the inevitable regression shown by certain patients, should be utilized in therapy, as a means of gratifying, in an extremely permissive transference situation, demands which had not been met in infancy. It must, in this connection, be noted that the gratifications recommended in the treatment of severely disturbed patients are determined by the conviction that these patients are incapable of developing transference as we understand it in connection with neuroses and must therefore be handled by a modified technique.

The opinions so far considered, however much they may differ in certain respects, are nonetheless all based on the fundamental premise that an essential difference between analysis and other methods of therapy depends on whether or not interpretation of transference is an integral feature of technical procedure. Results based on the effects of suggestion are to be avoided, as far as possible, whenever traditional technique is employed. This goal has, however, proved more difficult to achieve than Freud expected when he first discerned the significance of symptomatic recovery based on positive transference. The importance of suggestion, even in the most strict analytic methods, has been repeatedly stressed by Edward Glover and others (22, 23). Widespread and increasing emphasis as to the part played by the analyst's personality in determining the nature of the individual transference also implies recognition of unavoidable suggestive tendencies in the therapeutic process. Many analysts to-day believe that the classical conception of analytic objectivity and anonymity cannot be maintained. Instead, thorough analysis of reality aspects of the therapist's personality and point of view is advocated as an essential feature of transference analysis and

an indispensable prerequisite for the dynamic changes already discussed in relation to the termination of analysis. It thus remains the ultimate goal of psycho-analysts, whatever their theoretical orientation, to avoid, as far as is humanly possible, results based on the unrecognized or unanalysed action of suggestion, and to maintain, as a primary goal, the resolution of such results through consistent and careful interpretation.

There are, however, a number of therapists, both within and outside the field of psycho-analysis, who consider that the transference situation should not be handled only or mainly as a setting for interpretation even in the treatment or analysis of neurotic patients. Instead, they advocate utilization of the transference relationship for the manipulation of corrective emotional experience. The theoretical orientation of those utilizing this concept of transference may be closer to, or more distant from, a Freudian point of view according to the degree to which current relationships are seen as determined by past events. At one extreme, current aspects and cultural factors are considered of predominant importance; at the other, mental development is viewed in essentially Freudian terms and modifications of technique are ascribed to inherent limitations of the analytic method rather than to essentially changed conceptions of the early phases of mental development. Of this group, Alexander (24) is perhaps the best example. It is thirty years since, in his Salzburg paper, he indicated the tendency for patients to regress, even after apparently successful transference analysis of the oedipal situation to narcissistic dependent pregenital levels which prove stubborn and refractory to transference interpretation. In his more recent work, the role of regression in the transference situation has been increasingly stressed. The emergence and persistence of dependent, pregenital demands in a very wide range of clinical conditions, it is argued, indicates that the encouragement of a regressive transference situation is undesirable and therapeutically ineffective. The analyst, therefore should when this threatens, adopt a definite role explicitly differing from the behaviour of the parents in early childhood in order to bring about therapeutic results through a corrective emotional experience in the transference situation. This, it is suggested, will obviate the tendency to regression, thus curtailing the length of treatment and improving therapeutic results. Limitation of regressive manifestations by active steps modifying traditional analytic procedure in a variety of ways is also frequently indicated, according to this point of view.

It will be clear that to those who maintain the

conviction that interpretation of all transference manifestations remains an essential feature of psycho-analysis, the type of modification here described, even though based on a Freudian reconstruction of the early phases of mental development, represents a major modification. It is determined by a conviction that psycho-analysis, as a therapeutic method, has limitations related to the tendency to regression, which cannot be resolved by traditional technique. Moreover, the fundamental premise on which the conception of corrective emotional experience is based minimizes the significance of insight and recall. It is, essentially, suggested that corrective emotional experience alone may bring about qualitative dynamic alterations in mental structure, which can lead to a satisfactory therapeutic goal. This implies a definite modification of the analytic hypothesis that current problems are determined by the defences against instinctual impulses and/or internalized objects which had been set up during the decisive periods of early development. An analytic result therefore depends on the revival, repetition and mastery of earlier conflicts in the current experience of the transference situation with insight an indispensable feature of an analytic goal.

Since certain important modifications are related to the concept of regression in the transference situation, I should like briefly to consider this concept in relation to the repetition compulsion. That transference, essentially a revival of earlier emotional experience, must be regarded as a manifestation of the repetition compulsion is generally accepted. It is, however, necessary to distinguish between repetition compulsion as an attempt to master traumatic experience and repetition compulsion as an attempt to return to a real or fantasied earlier state of rest or gratification. Lagache (25), in a recent paper, has related the repetition compulsion to an inherent need to return to any problem previously left unsolved. From this point of view, the regressive aspects of the transference situation are to be regarded as a necessary preliminary to the mastery of unresolved conflict. From the second point of view, however, the regressive aspects of transference are mainly attributed to a wish to return to an earlier state of rest or narcissistic gratification, to the maintenance of the *status quo* in preference to any progressive action, and finally, to Freud's original conception of the death instinct. There is a good deal to suggest that both aspects of the repetition compulsion may be seen in the regressive aspects of every analysis. To those who feel that regressive self-destructive forces tend to be stronger than progressive libidinal impulses, the potentialities of the analytic approach will inevitably appear to be limited. Those, in contrast, who regard the reappearance in the transference situation of earlier conflicts as an indication of tendencies to master and progress will continue to feel that the classical analytic method remains the optimal approach to psychological illness wherever it is applicable.

To conclude: I have tried in this paper to outline some current problems of transference both in relation to the history of psycho-analytic thought and in relation to the theoretical premises on which they are based. With regard to contemporary views which advocate serious modification of analytic technique, I cannot improve on the remarks made by Ernest Jones (26) in his Introduction to the Salzburg Symposium thirty years ago. 'Depreciation of the Freudian (infantile) factors at the expense of the pre-Freudian (pre-infantile and post-infantile) is a highly characteristic manifestation of the general human resistance against the former, being usually a flight from the Oedipus conflict which is the centre of infantile factors. We also note that the practice of psycho-analysis does not always insure immunity from this reaction.' With regard, finally, to the important problems which arise from genuine scientific differences within the framework of traditional technique, I have tried to focus the issues for discussion by emphasizing as objectively as possible divergence rather than agreement. I should like, however, to close on a more personal note. I have had the unusual opportunity over the past ten years to observe at close quarters impressive achievements by analysts of widely divergent theoretical orientation. All of them are in complete agreement as to the primary importance of transference analysis. None have accepted any significant modifications of traditional technique as a means of either shortening analysis or accepting a modified analytic goal. All finally agree as to the basic importance of understanding the significance and possible dangers of counter-transference manifestations. Unfortunately, however, this vitally important unconscious reaction is not limited to the individual analytic situation. It may also be aroused in respect to scientific theories both within and outside our special field of knowledge. Just as, therefore, resolution of the individual transference situation depends on the analyst's understanding of his own counter-transference, so too, similar insight and objectivity on a wider scale may determine resolution of the problems I have outlined to-day.

BIBLIOGRAPHY

(1) Klein, M. 'Symposium on Child Analysis' (1927). Published in *Contributions to Psychoanalysis, 1941–45*. (London: Hogarth, 1948.)

(2) Freud, A. (1926). 'Introduction to the Technique in the Analysis of Children' (Vienna): *The Psychoanalytic Treatment of Children*. (Imago Publishing Co., 1945.)

(3) Sterba, R. 'The Fate of the Ego in Analytic Therapy', *Int. J. Psycho-Anal.*, 1934, 15, 117–126.

(4) Strachey, J. 'The Nature of the Therapeutic Action of Psycho-Analysis', *Int. J. Psycho-Anal.*, 1934, 15, 130–137.

(5) Bibring, E. 'Therapeutic Results of Psycho-Analysis', *Int. J. Psycho-Anal.*, 1937, 18, 170–189.

(6) Waelder, R. Contribution to Panel on Defence Mechanisms and Psychoanalytic Technique. Mid-Winter meeting of the American Psychoanalytic Association 1953. (Report published in the *Journal of the American Psychoanalytic Association*, April 1954.)

(7) Fenichel, O. 'Problems of Psychoanalytic Technique', *Psychoanal. Quart.*, 1941.

(8) Klein, M. *Contribution to Psychoanalysis, 1941–45*. (London: Hogarth, 1948.)

(9) Klein, M., *et al.* (1952). *Developments in Psychoanalysis*. (London: Hogarth.)

(10) Macalpine, I. 'The Development of the Transference', *Psychoanal. Quart.*, 1950, 19, 501–519.

(11) Greenacre, P. 'The Role of Transference. Practical Considerations in Relation to Psychoanalytic Therapy', *J. Amer. Psychoanal. Assoc.*, 1954, 2, 671–684.

(12) Balint, M. *Primary Love and Psycho-Analytic Technique*. (London: Hogarth, 1952.)

(13) Klein, M. 'On the Criteria for the Termination of an Analysis', *Int. J. Psycho-Anal.*, 1950, 31, Part 3.

(14) Freud, S. (1937). 'Analysis Terminable and Interminable', *Collected Papers*, V. (London: Hogarth, 1950.)

(15) Hartmann, H. (1950). 'Psychoanalysis and Development Psychology', *Psychoanal. Study of the Child*, V. (New York: International Universities Press.)

(16) ———(1952). 'The Mutual Influences in the Development of Ego and Id', *Psychoanal. Study of the Child*, VII. (New York: International Universities Press.)

(17) ——— Kris, E., and Loewenstein, R. (1946). 'Comments on the Formation of Psychic Structure', *Psychoanal. Study of the Child*, II. (New York: International Universities Press.

(18) Knight, R. 'Borderline States', *Psychoanalytic Psychiatry and Psychology*, 1954, 1, 97–109.

(19) Rosenfeld, H. 'Transference-phenomena and Transference-analysis in an Acute Catatonic Schizophrenic Patient', *Int. J. Psycho-Anal.*, 1952, 33, 457–464.

(20) Winnicott, D. W. 'Metapsychological and Clinical Aspects of Regression within the Psychoanalytical Set-up', *Int. J. Psycho-Anal.*, 1955, 36, 16–26.

(21) Margolin, S. 'Genetic and Dynamic Psychophysiological Determinants of Pathophysiological Processes'. *The Psychosomatic Concept in Psychoanalysis*, ed. Felix Deutsch. (New York: International Universities Press, 1953, pp. 8–36.)

(22) Glover, E. *The Technique of Psychoanalysis*. (New York: International Universities Press, 1955.)

(23) Glover, E. 'Therapeutic Criteria of Psychoanalysis', *Int. J. Psycho-Anal.*, 1954.

(24) Alexander, F. Contribution to the Symposium held at the Eighth International Psycho-Analytic Congress, Salzburg, April 21, 1924. Published in *Int. J. Psycho-Anal.*, 1925, 6, 13–34.

(25) Lagache, D. 'Quelques Aspects du Transfert' (Some Aspects of Transference)', *Revue Française de Psychanalyse*, 15, 407–424.

(26) Jones, E. 'Introduction to the Symposium on Theories of Therapeutic Results.' Published in *Int. J. Psycho-Anal.*, 1925, 6, 1–4.

28

THE WORKING ALLIANCE AND THE TRANSFERENCE NEUROSIS

RALPH R. GREENSON

EDITOR'S NOTE

While Zetzel is generally credited with having mapped out the alliance sector and having distinguished it from the realm of the transference neurosis, the present paper by Greenson is the first (and to this day perhaps the most complete) attempt to explore this aspect of the analytic relationship in careful clinical and theoretical detail. While a number of analysts have recently attempted to distinguish the therapeutic and working alliances (see Dickes 1975, Kanzer 1975 [chapter 30], Langs 1976b), the main thrust of these studies of alliance is to establish two distinctive though overlapping areas: one in which the patient's psychopathology is expressed primarily through transference, and another, relatively free of disturbance, in which patient and analyst reasonably and rationally work together toward the goals of analysis.

Greenson studies the contributions of patient, analyst, and analytic setting to the alliance sector, and considers too the means of identifying and analyzing disturbances in this area. There is some tendency here, as is characteristic of writings on this topic, to shift toward conscious communication and noninterpretive interventions in this regard, an approach that may lead one to overlook the unconscious qualities and implications of the alliance sector (see Langs 1975a). The present paper, part of Greenson's efforts to explore and define aspects of the analytic relationship that fall largely outside the sphere of transference, is an outstanding result of his capacity for fresh thinking.

The clinical material on which this presentation is based is derived from patients who developed unexpected difficulties in the course of psychoanalytic therapy. Some of these patients had undergone one or more analyses with other analysts; others were patients of mine who returned for further analysis. In this group there were patients who were unable to get beyond the preliminary phases of analysis. Even after several years of analysis they were not really 'in analysis'. Others seemed interminable; there was a marked discrepancy between the copiousness of insight and the paucity of change. The clinical syndromes these cases manifested were heterogeneous in diagnostic category, ego functions, or dynamics of personality. The key to understanding the essential pathology as well as the therapeutic stalemate was in the failure of the patient to develop a reliable working relation with the analyst. In each case the patient was either unable to establish or maintain a durable working

Reprinted from *Psychoanalytic Quarterly* 34:155–181, 1965.

alliance with the analyst and the analyst neglected this fact, pursuing instead the analysis of other transference phenomena. This error in technique was observable in psychoanalysts with a wide range of clinical experience and I recognized the same shortcoming in myself when I resumed analysis with patients previously treated.

In working with these seemingly unanalyzable or interminable patients I became impressed by the importance of separating the patient's reactions to the analyst into two distinct categories: the transference neurosis and the working alliance. Actually this classification is neither complete nor precise. However, this differentiation helps make it possible to give equal attention to two essentially different transference reactions.

My clinical experiences in regard to the working alliance were enhanced and clarified by Elizabeth Zetzel in Current Concepts of Transference (32). In that essay she introduced the term 'therapeutic alliance' and indicated how important she considered it by demonstrating that one could differentiate between the classical psychoanalysts and the British school by whether they handled or ignored this aspect of the transference. Leo Stone (31) gave further insight and fresh impetus in my attempts to clarify and formulate the problem of the working alliance and its relation to other transference phenomena.

The concept of a working alliance is an old one in both psychiatric and psychoanalytic literature. It has been described under a variety of labels but, except for Zetzel and Stone, it either has been considered of secondary importance or has not been clearly separated from other transference reactions. It is the contention of this paper that the working alliance is as essential for psychoanalytic therapy as the transference neurosis. For successful psychoanalytic treatment a patient must be able to develop a full-blown transference neurosis and also to establish and maintain a reliable working alliance. The working alliance deserves to be recognized as a full and equal partner in the patient-therapist relationship.

DEFINITION OF TERMS

Transference is the experiencing of feelings, drives, attitudes, fantasies, and defenses toward a person in the present which are inappropriate to that person and are a repetition, a displacement of reactions originating in regard to significant persons of early childhood (4, 6, 11). I emphasize that for a reaction to be considered transference it must have two characteristics: it must be a repetition of the past and it must be inappropriate to the present.

During analysis several transference phenomena can be distinguished. In the early phases we see usually sporadic, transient reactions, aptly called 'floating' transference reactions by Glover (17). Freud described more enduring transference phenomena which develop when the transference situation is properly handled. Then all the patient's neurotic symptoms are replaced by a neurosis in the transference relation of which he can be cured by therapeutic work. 'It is a new edition of the old disease' (9, 11). I would modify this concept and say that the transference neurosis is in effect when the analyst and the analysis become the central concern in the patient's life. The transference neurosis includes more than the infantile neurosis; the patient also relives the later editions and variations of his original neurosis. The 'floating' transference phenomena ordinarily do not belong to the transference neurosis. However, for simplification, the phrase, transference neurosis, here refers to the more regressive and inappropriate transference reactions.

The term, working alliance, is used in preference to diverse terms others have employed for designating the relatively nonneurotic, rational rapport which the patient has with his analyst. It is this reasonable and purposeful part of the feelings the patient has for the analyst that makes for the working alliance. The label, working alliance, was selected because it emphasizes its outstanding function: it centers on the patient's ability to work in the analytic situation. Terms like the 'therapeutic alliance' (32), the 'rational transference' (2), and the 'mature transference' (31) refer to similar concepts. The designation, working alliance, however, has the advantage of stressing the vital elements: the patient's capacity to work purposefully in the treatment situation. It can be seen at its clearest when a patient, in the throes of an intense transference neurosis, can yet maintain an effective working relationship with the analyst.

The reliable core of the working alliance is formed by the patient's motivation to overcome his illness, his conscious and rational willingness to cooperate, and his ability to follow the instructions and insights of his analyst. The actual alliance is formed essentially between the patient's reasonable ego and the analyst's analyzing ego (29). The medium that makes this possible is the patient's partial identification with the analyst's approach as he attempts to understand the patient's behavior.

The working alliance comes to the fore in the analytic situation in the same way as the patient's reasonable ego: the observing, analyzing ego is split off from his experiencing ego (30). The analyst's interventions separate the working attitudes from the neurotic transference phenomena just as his interventions split off the reasonable ego from the irrational one. These two sets of phenomena are parallel and express analogous psychic events from different points of reference. Patients who cannot split off a reasonable, observing ego will not be able to maintain a working relation and vice versa.

This differentiation between transference neurosis and working alliance, however, is not absolute since the working alliance may contain elements of the infantile neurosis which eventually will require analysis. For example, the patient may work well temporarily in order to gain the analyst's love, and this ultimately will lead to strong resistances; or the overvaluation of the analyst's character and ability may also serve the working alliance well in the beginning of the analysis, only to become a source of strong resistance later. Not only can the transference neurosis invade the working alliance but the working alliance itself can be misused defensively to ward off the more regressive transference phenomena. Despite these intermixtures, the separation of the patient's reactions to the analyst into these two groupings, transference neurosis and working alliance, seems to have clinical and technical value.

SURVEY OF THE LITERATURE

Freud spoke of the friendly and affectionate aspects of the transference which are admissible to consciousness and which are 'the vehicle of success in psychoanalysis . . .' (6, p. 105). Of rapport he wrote: 'It remains the first aim of the treatment to attach him [the patient] to it and to the person of the doctor. To ensure this, nothing need be done but to give him time. If one exhibits a serious interest in him, carefully clears away the resistances that crop up at the beginning and avoids making certain mistakes, he will of himself form such at attachment. . . . It is certainly possible to forfeit this first success if from the start one takes up any standpoint other than one of sympathetic understanding' (8, pp. 139-140).

Sterba (30) wrote about the patient's identification with the analyst which leads to the patient's concern with the work they have to accomplish in common — but he gave this aspect of the transference no special

designation. Fenichel (2, p. 27) described the 'rational transference' as an aim-inhibited positive transference which is necessary for analysis. Elizabeth Zetzel's emphasis on the importance of the 'therapeutic alliance' was discussed above. Loewald's paper on the therapeutic action of psychoanalysis is a penetrating and sensitive study of the different kinds of relations the patient develops toward the analyst during psychoanalysis (23). Some of his ideas are directly concerned with what I call the working alliance. Leo Stone devotes himself to the complexities in the relation between analyst and patient. He refers to the 'mature transference' which he believed to be: (a) in opposition to the 'primordial transference' reactions and (b) essential for a successful analysis (31, p. 106).

The Symposium on Curative Factors in Psychoanalysis presented before the Twenty-second Congress of the International Psychoanalytical Association (1962) contained many references to the special transference reactions that make for a therapeutic alliance and also some discussion of the analyst's contribution to the 'good' analytic situation. Gitelson (16) spoke of the rapport on which we depend in the beginning of analysis and which eventuates in transference. He stressed the necessity for the analyst to present himself as a good object and as an auxiliary ego. Myerson (25), Nacht (26), Segal (27), Kuiper (22), Garma (13), King (21), and Heimann (20) took issue with him on one or another aspect of his approach. In some measure the disagreement seems to be due to failure to distinguish clearly between the working alliance and the more regressive transference phenomena.

This brief and incomplete survey reveals that many analysts, including Freud, recognized that in psychoanalytic treatment another kind of relation to the analyst is necessary besides the more regressive transference reactions.

DEVELOPMENT OF THE WORKING ALLIANCE

Aberrations

The first clinical examples show how the course of development of the working alliance deviated markedly from that of the usual psychoanalytic patient. The reason for proceeding this way stems from the fact that in the classical analytic patient the working alliance develops almost imperceptibly, relatively silently, and seemingly independently of any special activity on the part of the analyst. The irregular cases highlight different processes and procedures which take place almost invisibly in the usual analytic patient.

Some years ago an analyst from another city referred an intelligent middle-aged man who had had more than six years of previous analysis. Certain general conditions had improved but his original analyst believed the patient needed additional analysis because he was still unable to marry and was very lonely. From the beginning of the therapy I was struck by the fact that he was absolutely passive about recognizing and working with his resistances. It turned out that he expected them to be pointed out continuously as his previous analyst had done. It also impressed me that the moment I made some intervention he had an immediate response, although often incomprehensible. I discovered that he thought it his duty to reply immediately to every intervention since he believed it would be a sign of resistance, and therefore bad, to keep silent for a moment or so to mull over what had been said. Apparently his previous analyst had never recognized his fear of being silent as a resistance. In free association the patient searched actively for things to talk about and, if more than one idea occurred to him, he chose what seemed to be the item he thought I was looking for without mentioning the multiple choices. When I requested information, he often answered by free association so that the result was bizarre. For example, when I asked him what his middle name was he answered: 'Raskolnikov', the first name that occurred to him. When I recovered my composure and questioned this he defended himself by saying that he thought he was supposed to free associate. I soon gained the impression that this man had never really established a working relation with his first analyst. He did not know what he was supposed to do in the analytic situation. He had been lying down in front of an analyst for many years, meekly submitting to what he imagined the previous analyst had demanded, constant and instant free association. Patient and analyst had been indulging in a caricature of psychoanalysis. True, the patient had developed some regressive transference reactions, some of which had been interpreted, but the lack of a consistent working alliance left the whole procedure amorphous, confused, and ineffectual.

Although I realized that the magnitude of the patient's problems could not be due solely or even mainly to the first analyst's technical shortcomings, I thought the patient ought to be given a fair opportunity to see whether he could work in an analytic situation. Besides, this clarification would also expose the patient's pathology more vividly. Therefore, in the first months of our work together, I carefully explained, whenever it seemed appropriate, the different tasks that psychoanalytic therapy requires of the patient. He reacted to this information as though it were all new to him and seemed eager to try to work in the way I described. However, it soon became clear that he could not just say what came to his mind, he felt compelled to find out what I was looking for. He could not keep silent and mull over what I said; he was afraid of the blank spaces, they signified some awful danger. If he were silent he might think; if he thought he might disagree with me, and to disagree was tantamount to killing me. His striking passivity and compliance were revealed as a form of ingratiation, covering up an inner emptiness, an insatiable infantile hunger, and a terrible rage. In a period of six months it became clear that this man was a schizoid 'as if' character who could not bear the deprivations of classical psychoanalysis (1). I therefore helped him obtain supportive psychotherapy with a woman therapist.

A woman I had previously analyzed for some four years resumed analysis after an interval of six years. We both knew when she had interrupted treatment that there was a great deal of unfinished analysis, but we agreed that an interval without analysis might clarify the unusual obscurities and difficulties we encountered in trying to achieve a better resolution of her highly ambivalent, complaining, clinging, sadomasochistic transference. I had suggested her going to another analyst, since, in general, I have found a change in analysts is more productive than a return to the old one. It usually offers new insights into the old transference reactions and adds new transference possibilities. However, for external reasons this was not feasible and I undertook the resumption of her analysis, although with some reservations.

In her first hours on the couch I was struck by the strange way the patient worked in the analysis. Then I quickly recalled that this had often happened in the past; it appeared more striking now since I was no longer accustomed to it; it seemed almost bizarre. After a certain moment in the hour the patient would speak almost incessantly; there would be disconnected sentences, part of a recital of a recent event, an occasional obscene phrase with no mention of its strangeness or that it was an obsessive thought, and then back to the recital of a past event. The patient seemed to be completely oblivious to her odd way of speaking and never spontaneously mentioned it. When I confronted her with this she at first seemed unknowing and then felt attacked.

I realized that in the previous analysis there had been many such hours or parts of hours whenever the patient was very anxious and tried to ward off her awareness of anxiety as well as analysis of it. I recalled that we had uncovered some of the meanings and historical determinants of such behavior. For example, her mother had been a great chatterer, had talked to the child as a grownup before she could understand. Her incomprehensible talking to me was an identification with her mother and an acting out in the analytic situation. Furthermore, the mother had used a stream of talk to express both anxiety and hostility to her husband, an essentially quiet man. The patient took over this pattern from her mother and re-enacted it in the analytic hour whenever she was anxious and hostile and when she was torn between hurting me and holding onto me.

We came to understand that this mode of behavior also denoted a regression in ego functions from secondary process toward primary process, a kind of 'sleep-talking' with me, a reenactment of sleeping with the parents. This peculiar way of talking had recurred many times during the first analysis and although various determinants had been analyzed it still persisted to some degree up to the interruption of that analysis. Whenever I tried to confront the patient with a misuse of one of the analytic procedures, we would be sidetracked by her reactions to my confrontation or by new material that came up. She might recall some past event which seemed relevant or, in the next hours, dreams or new memories would appear and we never really returned to the subject of why she was unable to do some part of the psychoanalytic work. In her second analysis, I would not be put off. Whenever the merest trace of the same disconnected manner of talking appeared, or whenever it seemed relevant, I confronted her with the problem and kept her to this subject until she at least acknowledged what was under discussion. The patient attempted to use all her old methods of defense against confrontations of her resistances. I listened only for a short time to her protestations and evasions and repeatedly pointed out their resistive function. I did not work with any new material until convinced the patient was in a good working alliance with me.

Slowly the patient began to face her misuse of the basic rule. She herself became aware of how she at times consciously, at others preconsciously, and, at still other times, unconsciously, blurred the real purpose of free association. It became clear that when the patient felt anxious in her relation to me she would let herself slip into this regressive 'sleep-talking' manner of speech. It was a kind of 'spiteful

obedience'—spiteful in so far as she knew it was an evasion of true free association. It was obedience inasmuch as she submitted to this regressive or, one might say, incontinent way of talking. This arose whenever she felt a certain kind of hostility toward me. She felt this as an urge to pour out a stream of poison upon me that led her to feel I would be destroyed and lost to her and she would feel alone and frightened. Then she would quickly dive into sleep-talking as though saying: 'I am a little child who is partly asleep and is not responsible for what is coming out of me. Don't leave me; let me sleep on with you; it is just harmless urine that is coming out of me.' Other determinants will not be discussed since they would lead too far afield.

It was fascinating to see how differently this analysis proceeded from the previous one. I do not mean to imply that this patient's tendency to misuse her ability to regress in ego functioning completely disappeared. However, my vigorous pursuit of the analysis of the defective working alliance, my constant attention to the maintenance of a good working relation, my refusal to be misled into analyzing other aspects of her transference neurosis had their effects. The second analysis had a completely different flavor and atmosphere. In the first analysis I had an interesting and whimsical patient who was frustrating because I was so often lost by her capricious wanderings. In the second, though still a whimsical patient she also was an ally who not only helped me when I was lost but pointed out that I was being led astray even before I realized it.

The third patient, a young man, entered analysis with me after he had spent two and one half years with an analyst in another city, which had left him almost completely untouched. He had obtained certain insights but had the distinct impression that his former analyst really disapproved of infantile sexuality even though the young man realized that analysts were not supposed to be contemptuous of it. In the preliminary interviews the patient told me that he had the greatest difficulty in talking about masturbation and previously often consciously withheld this information. He had informed the former analyst about the existence of many conscious secrets but nevertheless stubbornly refused to divulge them. He had never wholeheartedly given himself up to free association and reported many hours of long silence. However, the patient's manner of relating his history to me and my general clinical impression led me to believe that he was analyzable despite the fact that he had not been able to form a working alliance with his first analyst.

I undertook the analysis and learned a great deal about this patient's negative reactions to his previous analyst, some of which stemmed from his way of conducting that analysis. For example, in one of the first hours on the couch the patient took out a cigarette and lit it. I asked him what he was feeling when he decided to light the cigarette. He answered petulantly that he knew he was not supposed to smoke in his previous analysis and now he supposed that I too would forbid it. I told him that I wanted to know what feelings, ideas, and sensations were going on in him at the moment that he decided to light the cigarette. He then revealed that he had become somewhat frightened in the hour and to hide this anxiety from me he decided to light the cigarette. I replied that it was preferable for such feelings and ideas to be expressed in words instead of actions because then I would understand more precisely what was going on in him. He realized then that I was not forbidding him to smoke but only pointing out that it was more helpful to the process of being analyzed if he expressed himself in words and feelings. He contrasted this with his first analyst who told him before he went to the couch that it was customary not to smoke during sessions. There was no explanation for this and the patient felt that his first analyst was being arbitrary.

In a later hour the patient asked me whether I was married. I countered by asking him what he imagined about that. He hesitantly revealed that he was torn between two sets of fantasies, one that I was a bachelor who loved his work and lived only for his patients; the other that I was a happily married man with many children. He went on spontaneously to tell me that he hoped I was happily married because then I would be in a better position to help him with his sexual problems. Then he corrected himself and said it was painful to think of me as having sexual relations with my wife because that was embarrassing and none of his business. I then pointed out to him how, by not answering his question and by asking him instead to tell his fantasies about the answer, he revealed the cause of his curiosity. I told him I would not answer questions when I felt that more was to be gained by keeping silent and letting him associate to his own question. At this point the patient became somewhat tearful and, after a short pause, told me that in the beginning of his previous analysis he had asked many questions. His former analyst never answered nor did he explain why he was silent. He felt his analyst's silence as a degradation and humiliation and now realized that his own later silences were a retaliation for this imagined injustice. Somewhat later he saw that he had

identified himself with his first analyst's supposed contempt. He, the patient, felt disdain for his analyst's prudishness and at the same time was full of severe self-reproach for his own sexual practices which he then projected onto the analyst.

It was instructive to me to see how an identification with the previous analyst based on fear and hostility led to a distortion of the working relationship instead of an effective working alliance. The whole atmosphere of the first analysis was contaminated by hostile, mistrustful, retaliative feelings and attitudes. This turned out to be a repetition of the patient's behavior toward his father, a point the first analyst had recognized and interpreted. The analysis of this transference resistance, however, was ineffectual, partly because the first analyst worked in such a way as to justify constantly the patient's infantile neurotic behavior and so furthered the invasion of the working alliance by the transference neurosis.

I worked with this patient for approximately four years and almost from the beginning a relatively effective working alliance was established. However, my manner of conducting analysis, which seemed to him to indicate some genuine human concern for his welfare and respect for his position as a patient also mobilized important transference resistances in a later phase of the analysis. In the third year I began to realize that, despite what appeared to be a good working alliance and a strong transference neurosis, there were many areas of the patient's outside life that did not seem to change commensurately with the analytic work. Eventually I discovered that the patient had developed a subtle but specific inhibition in doing analytic work outside the analytic hour. If he became upset outside he would ask himself what upset him. Usually he succeeded in recalling the situation in question. Sometimes he even recalled the meaning of that event that he had learned from me at some previous time, but this insight would be relatively meaningless to him; it felt foreign, artificial, and remembered by rote. It was not his insight; it was mine, and therefore had no living significance for him. Hence, he was relatively blank about the meaning of the upsetting events.

Apparently, although he seemed to have established a working alliance with me in the analytic situation, this did not continue outside. Analysis revealed that the patient did not allow himself to assume any attitude, approach, or point of view that was like mine outside the analytic hour. He felt that to permit himself to do so would be tantamount to admitting that I had entered into him. This was intolerable because he felt this to be a homosexual assault, a repetition of several childhood and adolescent traumas. Slowly we uncovered how the patient had sexualized and aggressivized the process of introjection.

This new insight was the starting point for the patient to learn to discriminate among the different varieties of 'taking in'. Gradually he was able to re-establish a nonhomosexual identification with me in adapting an analytic point of view. Thus a working relation that had been invaded by the transference neurosis was once again relatively free of infantile neurotic features. The previous insights that had remained ineffectual eventually led to significant and lasting changes.[1]

Those patients who cling tenaciously to the working alliance because they are terrified of the regressive features of the transference neurosis should be briefly mentioned. They develop a reasonable relation to the analyst and do not allow themselves to feel anything irrational, be it sexual, aggressive, or both. Prolonged reasonableness in an analysis is a pseudo-reasonableness for a variety of unconscious neurotic motives.

For about two years a young social scientist who had an intellectual knowledge of psychoanalysis maintained a positive and reasonable attitude toward me, his analyst. If his dreams indicated hostility or homosexuality he acknowledged this but claimed that he knew he was supposed to feel such things toward his analyst but he 'really' did not. If he came late or forgot to pay his bill he again admitted that it might seem that he did not want to come or pay his bill but 'actually' it was not so. He had violent anger reactions to other psychiatrists he knew, but insisted they deserved it and I was different. He became infatuated with another male analyst for a period of time and 'guessed' he must remind him of me, but this was said playfully. All of my attempts to get the patient to recognize his persistent reasonableness as a means of avoiding or belittling his deeper feelings and impulses failed. Even my attempts to trace the historical origins of this mode of behavior were unproductive. He had adopted the role of 'odd ball', clown, harmless nonconformist in his high school years and was repeating this in the analysis. Since I could not get the patient to work further or consistently on this problem, I finally told him that we had to face the fact that we were getting nowhere and we

ought to consider some alternative besides continuing psychoanalysis with me. The patient was silent for a few moments and said 'frankly' he was disappointed. He sighed and then went on to make a free association-like remark. I stopped him and asked him what in the world he was doing. He replied that he 'guessed' I sounded somewhat annoyed. I assured him it was no guess. Then slowly he looked at me and asked if he might sit up. I nodded and he did. He was quite shaken, sober, pale, and in obvious distress. After some moments of silence he said that maybe he would be able to work better if he could look at me. He had to be sure I was not laughing at him, or angry, or getting sexually excited. I asked him about the last point. He told me that he often fantasied that perhaps I was being sexually excited by what he said but hid it from him. This he had never brought up before, it was just a 'fleeting idea'. But this fleeting idea led quickly to many memories of his father repeatedly and unnecessarily taking his temperature rectally. He proceeded to a host of homosexual and sadomasochistic fantasies. The persistent reasonableness was a defense against these as well as a playful attempt to tease me into acting out with him. My behavior, in the hour described above, was not well controlled, but it led to awareness that the patient's working alliance was being used to ward off the transference neurosis.

The working alliance had become the façade for the transference neurosis. It was his neurotic character structure hiding as well as expressing his underlying neurosis. Only when the patient's acting out was interrupted and he realized he was about to lose the transference object did his rigidly reasonable behavior become ego-alien and accessible to therapy. He needed several weeks of being able to look at me, to test out whether my reactions could be trusted. Then he became able to distinguish between genuine reasonableness and the teasing, spiteful reasonableness of his character neurosis and the analysis began to move.

The classical analytic patient

The term classical in this connection refers to a heterogeneous group of patients who are analyzable by the classical psychoanalytic technique without major modifications. They suffer from some form of transference neurosis, a symptom or character neurosis, without any appreciable defect in ego functions. In such patients the working transference develops almost imperceptibly, relatively silently, and seemingly independently of any special activity or intervention on the part of the analyst. Usually

---

1. This case is described in greater detail in a paper entitled The Problem of Working Through. In: *Tribute to Marie Bonaparte.* Edited by Max Schur. (In process of publication.)

signs of the working alliance appear in about the third to sixth month of analysis. Most frequently the first indications of this development are: the patient becomes silent and then, instead of waiting for the analyst to intervene, he himself ventures the opinion that he seems to be avoiding something. Or he interrupts a rather desultory report of some event and comments that he must be running away from something. If the analyst remains silent the patient spontaneously asks himself what it can be that is making him so evasive and he will let his thoughts drift into free associations.

It is obvious that the patient has made a partial and temporary identification with me and now is working with himself in the same manner as I have been working on his resistances. If I review the situation I usually find that prior to this development the patient has experienced some sporadic sexual or hostile transference reaction which has temporarily caused a strong resistance. I patiently and tactfully demonstrate this resistance, then clarify how it operated, what its purpose was, and eventually interpret and reconstruct its probable historical source. Only after effective transference-resistance analysis is the patient able to develop a partial working alliance. However, it is necessary to go back to the beginning of the analysis to get a detailed view of its development.

There is great variety in the manner in which a patient enters into the preliminary interviews. In part this is determined by his past history in regard to psychoanalysts, physicians, and authority figures and strangers, as well as his reactions to such conditions as being sick or needing and asking for help (15). Furthermore, his knowledge or lack of it about procedures of psychoanalysis and the reputation of the psychoanalyst also influence his initial responses. Thus the patient comes to the initial interview with a preformed relationship to me, partly transference and partly based on reality, depending on how much he fills in the unknowns inappropriately out of his own past.

The preliminary interviews heavily color the patient's reactions to the analyst. This is determined mainly by the patient's feelings about exposing himself as well as his responses to my method of approach and my personality. Here too I believe we see a mixture of transference and realistic reactions. Exposure of one's self is apt to stir up reverberations of past denudings in front of parents, doctors, or others, and is therefore likely to produce transference reactions. My technique of conducting the interviews will do the same the more it seems strange, painful,

or incomprehensible to the patient. Only those methods of approach that seem understandable to him may lead to realistic reactions. My 'analyst' personality as it is manifested in the first interviews may also stir up both transference and realistic reactions. It is my impression that those qualities that seem strange, threatening, or nonprofessional evoke strong transference reactions along with anxiety. Traits the patient believes indicate a therapeutic intent, compassion, and expertness may produce realistic responses as well as positive transference reactions. The clinical material from the third case indicates how the manner, attitude, and technique of the analyst in the beginning of both analyses decisively colored the analytic situation.

By the time I have decided that psychoanalysis is the treatment of choice, I shall have gained the impression that the patient in question seems to have the potential for forming a working alliance with me along with his transference neurosis. My discussion with the patient of why I believe psychoanalysis is the best method of therapy for him, the explanations of the frequency of visits, duration, fee, and similar matters, and the patient's own appraisal of his capacity to meet these requirements will be of additional value in revealing the patient's ability to form a working alliance.

The first few months of analysis with the patient lying on the couch attempting to free associate can best be epitomized as a combination of testing and confessing. The patient tests his ability to free associate and to expose his guilt and anxiety-producing experiences. Simultaneously he is probing his analyst's reactions to these productions (10, 18). There is a good deal of history telling and reporting of everyday events. My interventions are aimed at pointing out and exploring fairly obvious resistances and inappropriate affects. When the material is quite clear I try to make connections between past and present behavior patterns. As a consequence, the patient usually begins to feel that perhaps I understand him. Then he dares to regress, to let himself experience some transient aspect of his neurosis in the transference in regard to my person. When I succeed in analyzing this effectively then I have at least temporarily succeeded in establishing a reasonable ego and a working alliance alongside of the experiencing ego and the transference neurosis. Once the patient has experienced this oscillation between transference neurosis and working alliance in regard to one area, he becomes more willing to risk future regressions in that same area of the transference neurosis. However every new aspect of the transference neurosis may bring about an impairment of the working alliance and temporary loss of it.

Origins of the Working Alliance

Contributions of the patient

For a working alliance to take place, the patient must have the capacity to form object relations since all transference reactions are a special variety of them. People who are essentially narcissistic will not be able to achieve consistent transferences. Furthermore, the working alliance is a relatively rational, desexualized, and deaggressivized transference phenomenon. Patients must have been able to form such sublimated, aim-inhibited relations in their outside life. In the course of analysis the patient is expected to be able to regress to the more primitive and irrational transference reactions that are under the influence of the primary process. To achieve a working alliance, however, the patient must be able to re-establish the secondary process, to split off a relatively reasonable object relationship to the analyst from the more regressive transference reactions. Individuals who suffer from a severe lack of or impairment in ego functions may well be able to experience regressive transference reactions but will have difficulty in maintaining a working alliance. On the other hand, those who dare not give up their reality testing even temporarily and partially, and those who must cling to a fixed form of object relationship are also poor subjects for psychoanalysis. This is confirmed by the clinical findings that psychotics, borderline cases, impulse ridden characters, and young children usually require modifications in the classical psychoanalytic technique (13, 14, 17). Freud had this in mind when he distinguished transference neuroses which are readily analyzable from narcissistic neuroses which are not.

The patient's susceptibility to transference reactions stems from his state of instinctual dissatisfaction and his resultant need for opportunities for discharge. This creates a hunger for objects and a proneness for transference reactions in general (3). Satisfied or apathetic people have fewer transference reactions. The awareness of neurotic suffering also compels the patient to establish a relationship to the analyst. On a conscious and rational level the therapist offers realistic hope of alleviating the neurotic misery. However, the patient's helplessness in regard to his suffering mobilizes early longings for an omnipotent parent. The working alliance has both a rational and irrational component. The above indicates that the analyzable patient must have the need for transference reactions, the capacity to regress and permit neurotic transference reactions, and have the ego strength or that particular form of ego resilience that enables him to interrupt his regression in order to reinstate the reasonable and purposeful working alliance (Cf. 23). The patient's ego functions play an important part in the implementation of the working alliance in addition to a role in object relations. In order to do the analytic work the patient must be able to communicate in a variety of ways; in words, with feelings, and yet restrain his actions. He must be able to express himself in words, intelligibly with order and logic, give information when indicated and also be able to regress partially and do some amount of free association. He must be able to listen to the analyst, comprehend, reflect, mull over, and introspect. To some degree he also must remember, observe himself, fantasy, and report. This is only a partial list of ego functions that play a role in the patient's capacity to establish and maintain a working alliance; we also expect the patient simultaneously to develop a transference neurosis. Thus his contribution to the working alliance depends on two antithetical properties: his capacity to maintain contact with the reality of the analytic situation and also his willingness to risk regressing into his fantasy world. It is the oscillation between these two positions that is essential for analytic work.

Contributions of the analytic situation

Greenacre (18), Macalpine (24), and Spitz (28) all have pointed out how different elements of the analytic setting and procedures promote regression and the transference neurosis. Some of these same elements also aid in forming the working alliance. The high frequency of visits and long duration of the treatment not only encourage regression but also indicate the long-range objectives and the importance of detailed, intimate communication. The couch and the silence give opportunity for introspection and reflection as well as production of fantasy. The fact that the patient is troubled, unknowing, and being looked after by someone relatively untroubled and expert stirs up the wish to learn and to emulate. Above all the analyst's constant emphasis on attempting to gain understanding of all that goes on in the patient, the fact that nothing is too small, obscure, ugly, or beautiful to escape the analyst's search for comprehension—all this tends to evoke in the patient the wish to know, to find answers, to find causes. This does not deny that the analyst's probings stir up resistances: it merely asserts that it also stirs up the patient's curiosity and his search for causality.

Freud stated that in order to establish rapport one needs time and an attitude of sympathetic understanding (8). Sterba (29) stressed the identificatory processes. The fact that the analyst continuously observes and interprets reality to the patient leads the patient to identify partially with this aspect of the analyst. The invitation to this identification comes from the analyst. From the beginning of treatment, the analyst comments about the work they have to accomplish together. The use of such terms as 'let us look at this', or 'we can see', promotes this. Loewald stresses how the analyst's concern for the patient's potentials stimulates growth and new developments (23).

Fenichel (2) believed it is the analytic atmosphere that is the most important factor in persuading the patient to accept on trial something formerly rejected. Stone (31) emphasized the analyst's willingness to offer the patient certain legitimate, controlled gratifications. I would add that the constant scrutiny of how the patient and the analyst seem to be working together, the mutual concern with the working alliance, in itself serves to enhance it.

Contributions of the analyst

It is interesting to observe how some analysts take theoretical positions apparently in accord with their manifest personality and others subscribe to theories that seem to contradict their character traits. Some use technique to project, others to protect, their personality. This finding is not meant as a criticism of either group, since happy and unhappy unions can be observed in both. Some rigid analysts advocate strictest adherence to the 'rule of abstinence' and I have seen the same type of analyst attempt to practice the most crass manipulative, gratifying 'corrective emotional experience' psychotherapy. Many apparently care-free and easy-going analysts practice a strict 'rule of abstinence' type of therapy while some of this same character provoke their patients to act out or indulge them in some kind of mutual gratification therapy. Some analysts practice analysis that suits their personality; some use their patients to discharge repressed desires. Be that as it may, these considerations are relevant to the problems inherent in the establishment of the working alliance. Here, however, only a brief outline of the problems can be attempted. The basic issue is: what characteristics of personality and what theoretical orientation in the analyst will insure the development of a working alliance as well as the development of a full-blown transference neurosis?

I have already briefly indicated how certain aspects of the analytic situation facilitate production of a transference neurosis. This can be condensed to the following: we induce the patient to regress and to develop a transference neurosis by providing a situation that consists of a mixture of deprivation, a sleep-like condition, and constancy. Patients develop a transference neurosis from a variety of different analysts as long as the analytic situation provides a goodly amount of deprivation administered in a predictable manner over a suitable length of time. For a good therapeutic result, however, one must also achieve a good working relationship.

What attitudes of the analyst are most likely to produce a good working alliance? My third case indicates how the patient identified himself with his previous analyst on the basis of identification with the aggressor, on a hostile basis. This identification did not produce a therapeutic alliance; it produced a combination of spite and defiance, and interfered with the psychoanalytic work. The reason for this was that the personality of the first analyst seemed cold and aloof; traits which resembled the patient's father and he was not able to differentiate his first analyst from his regressive transference feelings. How differently he reacted to me in the beginning. He was clearly able to differentiate me from his parent and therefore he was able to make a temporary and partial identification with me, and thus to do the analytic work.

The most important contribution of the psychoanalyst to a good working relationship comes from his daily work with the patient. His consistent and unwavering pursuit of insight in dealing with any and all of the patient's material and behavior is the crucial factor. Other inconsistencies may cause the patient pain, but they do not interfere significantly with the establishment of a working alliance. Yet there are analysts who work consistently and analytically and still seem to have difficulty in inducing their patients to develop a working alliance. I believe this may be due to the kind of atmosphere they create. In part, the disturbance may be the result of too literal acceptance of two suggestions made by Freud: the concept of the analyst as a mirror and the rule of abstinence (7, 10, 12). These two rules have led many analysts to adopt an austere, aloof, and even authoritarian attitude toward their patients. I believe this to be a misunderstanding of Freud's intention; at best, an attitiude incompatible with the formulation of an effective working alliance.

The reference to the mirror and the rule of abstinence were suggested to help the analyst safeguard the transference from contamination, a point Greenacre *(18)* has amplified. The mirror refers to the notion that the analyst should be 'opaque' to the patient, nonintrusive in terms of imposing his values and standards upon the patient. It does not mean that the analyst shall be inanimate, cold, and unresponsive. The rule of abstinence refers to the importance of not gratifying the patient's infantile and neurotic wishes. It does not mean that all the patient's wishes are to be frustrated. Sometimes one may have to gratify a neurotic wish temporarily. Even the frustration of the neurotic wishes has to be carried on in such a way as not to demean or traumatize the patient.

While it is true that Freud stressed the deprivational aspects of the analytic situation, I believe he did so because at that time (1912–1919) the danger was that analysts would permit themselves to overreact and to act out with their patients. Incidentally, if one reads Freud's case histories, one does not get the impression that the analytic atmosphere of his analyses was one of coldness or austerity. For example, in the original record of the case of the Rat man, Freud appended a note, dated December 28, to the published paper *(5)*, 'He was hungry and was fed'. Then on January 2, 'Besides this he apparently only had trivialities to report and I was able to say a great deal to him today'.

It is obvious that if we want the patient to develop a relatively realistic and reasonable working alliance, we have to work in a manner that is both realistic and reasonable despite the fact that the procedures and processes of psychoanalysis are strange, unique, and even artificial. Smugness, ritualism, timidity, authoritarianism, aloofness, and indulgence have no place in the analytic situation.

The patient will not only be influenced by the content of our work but by how we work, the attitude, the manner, the mood, and the atmosphere in which we work. He will react to and identify himself particularly with those aspects that need not necessarily be conscious to us. Glover *(17)* stressed the need of the analyst to be natural and straightforward, decrying the pretense, for example, that all arrangements about time and fee are made exclusively for the patient's benefit. Fenichel *(2)* emphasized that above all the analyst should be human and was appalled that so many of his patients were surprised by his naturalness and freedom. Sterba *(30)*, stressing the 'let us look, we shall see' approach, hints at his way of working. Stone *(31)* goes even further in emphasizing legitimate gratifications and the therapeutic attitude and intention of the psychoanalyst that are necessary for the patient.

All analysts recognize the need for deprivations in psychoanalysis; they would also agree in principle on the analyst's need to be human. The problem arises, however, in determining what is meant by humanness in the analytic situation and how does one reconcile this with the principle of deprivation. Essentially the humanness of the analyst is expressed in his compassion, concern, and therapeutic intent toward his patient. It matters to him how the patient fares, he is not just an observer or a research worker. He is a physician or a therapist, and his aim is to help the patient get well. He keeps his eye on the long-range goal, sacrificing temporary and quick results for later and lasting changes. Humanness is also expressed in the attitude that the patient is to be respected as an individual. We cannot repeatedly demean a patient by imposing rules and regulations upon him without explanation and then expect him to work with us as an adult. For a working alliance it is imperative that the analyst show consistent concern for the rights of the patient throughout the analysis. Though I let my patient see that I am involved with him and concerned, my reactions have to be nonintrusive. I try not to take sides in any of his conflicts except that I am working against his resistances, his damaging neurotic behavior, and his self-destructiveness. Basically, however, humanness consists of understanding and insight conveyed in an atmosphere of serious work, straightforwardness, compassion, and restraint *(19)*.

The above outline is my personal point of view on how to resolve the conflict between the maintenance of distance and the closeness necessary for analytic work and is not offered as a prescription for all analysts. However, despite great variation in analysts' personalities, these two antithetical elements must be taken into account and handled if good analytic results are to be obtained. The transference neurosis and the working alliance are parallel antithetical forces in transference phenomena; each is of equal importance.

SUMMARY

Some analyses are impeded or totally thwarted by failure of patient and analyst to form a working alliance. Clinical examples of such failures are examined, showing how they were corrected. Formation of the working alliance, its characteristics, and its relation to transference are discussed. It is contended that the working alliance is equally as important as the transference neurosis.

REFERENCES

1. Deutsch, Helene: *Some Forms of Emotional Disturbance and Their Relationship to Schizophrenia.* This Quarterly, XI, 1942, pp. 301–321.
2. Fenichel, Otto: *Problems of Psychoanalytic Technique.* New York: The Psychoanalytic Quarterly, Inc., 1941.
3. Ferenczi, Sandor: Introjection and Transference (1909). In: *Sex in Psychoanalysis.* New York: Basic Books, Inc., 1950.
4. Freud: *Fragment of an Analysis of a Case of Hysteria (1905* [1901]). Standard Edition, VII, pp. 116–117.
5. ———: *Notes upon a Case of Obsessional Neurosis* (1909). Standard Edition, X, p. 303.
6. ———: *The Dynamics of Transference* (1912). Standard Edition, XII.
7. ———: *Recommendations to Physicians Practicing Psychoanalysis.* (1912). *Ibid.*
8. ———: *On Beginning the Treatment* (1913). *Ibid.*
9. ———: *Remembering, Repeating and Working Through* (1914). *Ibid.*
10. ———: *Observations on Transference Love* (1915 [1914]). *Ibid.*
11. ———: *Introductory Lectures on Psychoanalysis* (1916–1917 [1915–1917]). Standard Edition, XV, XVI.
12. ———: *Lines of Advance in Psychoanalytic Therapy* (1919 [1918]). Standard Edition, XVII.
13. Garma, Angel: Contribution to Discussion on *The Curative Factors in Psychoanalysis.* Int. J. Psa., XLIII, 1962, pp. 221–224.
14. Gill, Merton M.: *Psychoanalysis and Exploratory Psychotherapy.* J. Amer. Psa. Assn., II, 1954, pp. 771–797.
15. ———; Newman, Richard; and Redlich, Frederick, C.: *The Initial Interview in Psychiatric Practice.* New York: International Universities Press, Inc., 1954.
16. Gitelson, Maxwell: *The Curative Factors in Psychoanalysis. The First Phase of Psychoanalysis.* Int. J. Psa., XLIII, 1962, pp. 194–205.
17. Glover, Edward: *The Technique of Psychoanalysis.* (Chapters I–III, VII–VIII.) New York: International Universities Press, Inc., 1955.
18. Greenacre, Phyllis: *The Role of Transference. Practical Considerations in Relation to Psychoanalytic Therapy.* J. Amer. Psa. Assn., II, 1954, pp. 671–684.
19. Greenson, Ralph R.: *Variations in Classical Psychoanalytic Technique: An Introduction.* Int. J. Psa., XXXIX, 1958, pp. 200–201.
20. Heimann, Paula: Contribution to Discussion on *The Curative Factors in Psychoanalysis.* Int. J. Psa., XLIII, 1962, pp. 228–231.
21. King, Pearl: Contributions to Discussion on *The Curative Factors in Psychoanalysis. Op. cit.,* pp. 225–227.
22. Kuiper, Pieter: Contribution to Discussion on *The Curative Factors in Psychoanalysis. Op. cit.,* pp. 218–220.
23. Loewald, Hans: *On the Therapeutic Action of Psychoanalysis.* Int. J. Psa., XLI, 1960, pp. 16–33.
24. Macalpine, Ida: *The Development of Transference.* This Quarterly, XIX, 1950, pp. 501–539.
25. Myerson, Paul G.: Footnote in Gitelson, Maxwell: *The Curative Factors in Psychoanalysis. Op cit.,* p. 202.
26. Nacht, Sacha: *The Curative Factors in Psychoanalysis. Op. cit.,* pp. 206–211.
27. Segal, Hanna: *The Curative Factors in Psychoanalysis. Op. cit.,* pp. 212–217.
28. Spitz, René A.: *Transference: The Analytical Setting and Its Prototype.* Int. J. Psa., XXXVII, 1956, pp. 380–385.
29. Sterba, Richard: *The Fate of the Ego in Analytic Therapy.* Int. J. Psa., XV, 1934, pp. 117–126.
30. ———: *The Dynamics of the Dissolution of the Transference Resistance.* This Quarterly, IX, 1940, pp. 363–379.
31. Stone, Leo: *The Psychoanalytic Situation.* New York: International Universities Press, Inc., 1961.
32. Zetzel, Elizabeth R.: *Current Concept of Transference.* Int. J. Psa., XXXVII, 1956, pp. 369–376.

29

THERAPEUTIC MISALLIANCES

Robert Langs

EDITOR'S NOTE

This paper offers the most extensive and detailed consideration of disturbances in the therapeutic alliance available. It adopts a distinctly interactional approach to the subject and carefully explores the contributions of both patient and analyst to these very subtle and therefore often unrecognized problems. There is a similarly detailed consideration of the conscious and unconscious efforts by both participants to identify and resolve their collusion in these disturbances. The maladaptive symptom relief often achieved by such collusion is termed *misalliance cure,* a concept that provides considerable insight into the general subject of noninsightful "cure."

In addition to detailing the basis and manifestations of this particular type of disturbance in the therapeutic alliance, the misalliance concept leads to a further clarification of the analytic interaction itself. It provides considerable impetus for the definition of interactional mechanisms, and of the actualities of the analyst and the unconscious implications of his interventions. As such, it serves as an important basis for my subsequent studies of the unconscious communicative interaction (Langs 1976a,b, 1978a,b).

This paper will study aspects of the psychopathology of the patient-analyst and patient-therapist relationships[1] and the therapeutic alliance, and in particular the efforts by either the patient or the analyst—or both—to effect a *therapeutic misalliance.* If we briefly define the therapeutic alliance as the conscious and unconscious agreement—and subsequent actual work—on the part of both patient and analyst to join forces in effecting symptom alleviation and characterological changes through insight and inner structural change within the patient, then therapeutic misalliances constitute interactions that are designed either to undermine such goals or to achieve symptom modification, however temporary, on some other basis. I believe that there are inherent needs in both patient and analyst to both create and resolve therapeutic misalliances in every analytic and psychotherapeutic situation, and that the recognition, analysis, and modification of these propensities and actualities is a first-order therapeutic task. In this paper I want to define therapeutic misalliances, to discuss their development, recognition, and resolution in analysis and psychotherapy, and to explore the main technical considerations which evolve from these observations.

While there had been occasional passing references to deviant alliances in the literature (see Corwin 1972 and Greenacre 1959 for examples), I believe that the first extensive and explicit use of the term *therapeutic misalliance* (alternately, *antitherapeutic alliance* to delineate its dimensions as a deviant search for "cure" that is opposed to insight) appeared in my two-volume work, *The Technique of Psychoanalytic*

Reprinted from *International Journal of Psychoanalytic Psychotherapy* 4:77–105, 1975.

Psychotherapy (Langs 1973b, 1974). In general, this area has been studied under the rubrics of transference and countertransference gratification, resistance, mutual acting out, and acting in—topics which still merit further study in themselves. As I shall demonstrate, the concept of therapeutic misalliances overlaps with each of these but goes beyond them as well, enabling us to develop aspects of these and other problems in technique that have otherwise been relatively neglected. In particular, this concept is especially relevant to the adaptive and interactional aspects of the patient-analyst dyad, including the mutual influence of patient and analyst upon each other, and the realistic and intrapsychic consequences of the relationship for both participants. While not all disturbances in the therapeutic alliance take the form of misalliances (there may be primarily uniliteral impairments in the alliance, so that the mutuality inherent in the concept of misalliance is missing), it seems advisable to make a special study of these particular interactions, since they are basic to many disturbances in the analytic situation and are probably the single most common dimension to stalemated or failed analyses. The concept also highlights the analyst's contributions, however large or small, to such impasses or temporary difficulties in the treatment situation.

Actually, the concept of therapeutic misalliance has been implicit in many of the more extensive studies of the patient-analyst relationship, including those which focused on the therapeutic (or working) alliance dimension of it. (Freud 1915, Fenichel 1941, Greenacre 1959, 1971, Tarachow, 1962, Greenson 1965, 1957, 1971, 1972, Greenson and Wexler 1969, Friedman 1969, Myerson 1973, and Langs 1973a,b, 1974, 1975a), and it is reflected in Freud's case histories as well (1905, 1909, 1918; see Langs, in press, for a discussion of this topic). As background for the present study, I shall confine myself to succinctly defining the concept of the therapeutic alliance and to describing some of the main indirect allusions to therapeutic misalliances in the literature (for a fuller résumé of the subject of the therapeutic alliance see Zetzel 1956, 1958, 1966–1969, Stone 1961, 1967, Greenson 1965, 1967, Dickes 1967, Friedman 1969, Binstock 1973, and Langs 1973b, 1974).

To be brief, we may view the patient-analyst (and patient-therapist) relationship as an interaction based on the respective intrapsychic needs and sets, evocations and reactions—and adaptive responses—of each party. It has primarily realistic (nontransference—see Greenson and Wexler 1969, Greenson 1971, 1972, and Langs 1973a,b, 1974, 1975a) and primarily unrealistic or fantasied (transference) dimen-

sions that readily intermix—intrapsychically and interactionally—for both participants. These two polarities are weighted differently for each, however; the latter are disproportionately greater in the patient (Racker 1968). It is out of this matrix that we isolate for study those facets, conscious and unconscious, that constitute the therapeutic alliance—the pact between that part of the patient that is motivated to cooperate with the analyst and is seeking adaptive and appropriate symptom relief, and that part of the analyst which is competent to offer it to him through his professional empathy with the patient and his relatively neutral interventions that are geared toward interpretations. Founded on both a basic mother-child relatedness (Zetzel 1958, Greenacre 1959, Stone 1961, 1967) and more mature relationships (Stone 1961, Greenson 1965), the therapeutic alliance is an agreement between the mature ego sectors of both parties (Sterba 1943) to work in consort toward the goals of treatment. However, there are also more primitive ego and id contributions to this pact (Friedman 1969) which must be well neutralized and sublimated to contribute positively to the alliance.

The therapeutic alliance has conscious and unconscious, explicit and implicit components (Myerson 1973, Langs 1973b, 1974), and is shaped by the needs and ego functions of both patient and analyst, especially by the latter's ground rules, personality, stance, work style, and interventions. It is these that guide the unfolding of this alliance in the direction of work toward inner structural change for the patient, based on a variety of communications from the analyst that are soon understood on some level by the patient.

Efforts toward therapeutic misalliances arise primarily out of unresolved intrapsychic conflicts—inappropriate instinctual drive needs, and superego and ego disturbances—and prior disturbed object relations and interactions experienced by either patient or analyst, which prompt either to seek gratifications and defensive reinforcements in their relationship that are not in keeping with the search for insight and inner change. The factors which lead to such efforts are on a continuum with those that contribute to a viable therapeutic alliance, and they intermingle; we are therefore faced with a delicate and sensitive issue. It is one that may be described in still another way: transference and countertransference inevitably contribute to and may interfere with alliance; when they do so, they must be detected, analyzed, and resolved (Zetzel 1958, Greenson 1965, Friedman 1969, Myerson 1973, Langs 1973b, 1974). It is in this realm that transference and countertransference fantasies influence reality and contribute to the ongoing adaptive efforts of each party to the therapeutic relationship. It is here that fantasy and memory are translated into actualities, gross or subtle—e.g., maladaptive conflict "resolutions" and pathological unconscious identifications—that are experienced as resistances and the search for alternative solutions to the patient's neuorsis. If the resolution of such efforts is not given precedence in the analysis, little else will be accomplished; failure to detect and modify actual misalliances undermines the work toward more lasting adaptive solutions to the patient's conflicts—structural and characterological change based on insight and constructive identifications (Fenichel 1941, Langs 1974).

Elsewhere (Langs 1973b, 1974, 1975a), I have discussed in detail the manner in which misalliances arise, especially from efforts by the patient to act out primarily transference-based fantasies and from unneeded deviations in analytic or therapeutic technique and technical errors on the part of the analyst that serve as expressions of his countertransference problems (Langs 1975b). Far more subtle means of generating and maintaining misalliances also exist, though not all misalliances stem from transference and countertransference problems. They may arise primarily through extraneous sources, such as third parties to treatment (insurance companies, supervisors, etc.), manipulative nontransference motives for therapy (e.g., court remands), and personal noncountertransference needs in the analyst (e.g., a candidate's needs with a patient whom he is analyzing to fulfil his requirements at an analytic institute). Such situations may impose limiting realities on the analytic outcome and may effect unmodifiable sectors of misalliance—aspects I will discuss in a later paper (Langs 1975b).

Sectors of misalliance offer, in the realities of the therapist's involvement, an image of him that interferes critically with the three basic and interrelated avenues of sound symptom resolution: positive identifications with the therapist based on his behavior within his therapeutic role; curative interactions in which the therapist's interpretations and maintenance of the boundaries replace living out and misalliance (Racker 1968); and the development of cognitive insights based on the interpretations of the therapist. This latter is itself based on a maximal opportunity for the patient to project his intrapsychic fantasies onto the therapist and on the patient's experience of the therapist as a sound figure whose interpretations have a constructive impact on him.

These introductory considerations were first developed empirically from clinical observations of analytic psychotherapy (Langs 1973, 1974a) and psychoanalysis. It was reassuring to find in studying the literature that many others had made similar observations, though they were conceptualized in somewhat different terms. Freud, for instance, was well aware of such occurrences and the dangers they entail. This is most apparent in his paper on transference love (1915), where he warns analysts against accepting transference love as a conquest of the patient; he developed the rule of abstinence in this context. Should there be compliance by the analyst, "the Patient would achieve *her* aim, but he would never achieve *his*" p. 165). Nor, Freud goes on, must the analyst actively repulse this transference love; he should "treat it as something unreal" (p. 166; see also Tarachow 1962) and analyze it. Then Freud refers to those women with whom attempts to analyze the erotic transference will not succeed. "These are women of elemental passionateness who tolerate no surrogates. They are the children of nature who refuse to accept the psychical in place of the material, who, in the poet's words, are accessible only to the logic of soup with dumplings for arguments" (pp. 166–167). In the terms being presented here, their sole wish is for misalliance with their analyst. Throughout his writings, Freud emphasized that gratifications of this kind preclude successful analytic work.

Nunberg (1926, 1955) observed that patients have narcissistic and magical concepts of "cure" through fulfillment of their infantile wishes and through a different kind of work than that expected by their analysts. His presentations provide considerable clinical material related to inevitable efforts by patients to create misalliances. Fenichel (1941) put this concept succinctly: "In what is called 'handling of the transference,' 'not joining the game' is the principal task. Only thus is it possible subsequently to make interpretations" (p. 73)—in essence, avoiding a misalliance is fundamental for interpretive work. Throughout her writings on technique, Greenacre (1971) shows a sensitivity to the problem. In one notable allusion, she refers to the importance of the preservation of the patient's autonomy by the analyst. She therefore counsels against the use of active support or manipulation which impair the analytic result and weaken the patient's ego. "The therapeutic alliance is thus insidiously diluted with ingredients of a narcissistic alliance" (Greenacre 1959, p. 487). Corwin (1972) also studied narcissistic alliances.

Tarachow (1962) writes: "*The task of setting aside the other as a real object I regard as the central problem* in the theory of the treatment process" (p. 377). This problem arises out of the mutual object need of the patient and the analyst; rather than gratify these needs, the latter imposes a therapeutic barrier by interpreting and not participating in reality. This promotes expressions of unconscious fantasies in the patient's free associations and the development of the transference neurosis. The analyst must be capable of renunciation, especially of his wishes for fusion with the patient. The slightest alteration in the analyst's behavior calls for self-scrutiny; collusion (i.e., misalliance) with the patient has usually been involved.

Greenson's discussion of the working alliance (1965, 1967) alludes to aberrations in this alliance which clearly reflect therapeutic misalliances; he emphasizes that analytic efforts in this area must take precedence over all other aspects, including work related to the transference neurosis. Inherent in the modifications of the misalliances described by Greenson was the recogntition of the analyst's participation in the aberrant interaction with the patient, and the need for the analyst to modify his contributing behavior as well as to analyze the sources for the difficulty with the patient. In describing one such misalliance, Greenson noted: "The analysis of this transference resistance, however, was ineffectual, partly because the first analyst worked in such a way as to justify the patient's infantile neurotic behavior and so furthered the invasion of the working alliance by the transference neurosis" (1965, pp. 166–167).

Friedman (1969) studied a paradox within the patient-analyst relationship: transference is the major motivating factor in analysis and yet the prime weapon—resistance—that the patient uses to combat these efforts, and to try to gain actual fulfillment of his neurotic needs. Similarly, the emphasis on the therapeutic alliance as a compact between the mature and relatively autonomous parts of the egos of both patient and analyst presents the paradox that such an alliance, to be effective, must also rely on contributions from instinctual needs and entail some degree of gratification of these needs. In traversing the fine line between offering the patient too little and too much gratification, the danger of participating in misalliance is ever present.

In another vein, Myerson's studies of the analytic modus vivendi (1969, 1973) describe ways in which certain patients attempt to work in analysis with either too little or too much involvement with the analyst, thereby limiting analytic progress. He states that the prime task with such patients is the disruption of these deviant modi vivendi (i.e., efforts

toward misalliance) through various types of interventions, some of which are noninterpretive.

Kanzer (1975) calls into question the common tendency in analysts who deal technically with aberrations in the therapeutic alliance to suggest noninterpretive interventions. His contention that such measures are antitherapeutic suggests that these techniques actually foster new sectors of misalliance, rather than constructively modifying the original problem in the alliance. My own observations support those of Kanzer (see Langs 1973b, 1974, 1975b; and see below).

There are, of course, many descriptions of misalliances in the literature on countertransference problems (for a partial bibliography, see Langs 1974). Space will not permit a survey of this aspect here except to note that Searles (1965) and Racker (1968) have been especially sensitive to this kind of problem; the latter's profound studies most clearly foreshadowed the findings to be presented here. In particular, Racker's paper (1968 [1957]) on the meanings and uses of countertransference (for him, defined as all of the analyst's reactions to his analysand) documented the occurrence of "vicious circles" in which the analyst enters the patient's neurosis and thereby cannot interpret it. Racker emphasized the role of the analyst's self-observations in preventing misalliances and demonstrated repeatedly how reactions in the analyst that complement the patient's neurotic needs preclude a proper understanding of the patient. In one pertinent statement among many, he wrote (1968, p. 152):

The transference, insofar as it is determined by the infantile situations and archaic objects of the patient, provokes in the unconscious of the analyst infantile situations and an intensified vibration of archaic objects of his own. . . . the analyst, if not conscious of such countertransference responses, may make the patient feel exposed once again to an archaic object (the vicious circle), and . . . in spite of his having some understanding of what is happening in the patient, the analyst is prevented from giving an adequate interpretation.

Lastly, in quite a different vein, Glover's early paper (1931) on the therapeutic effects of inexact interpretations may be viewed as one of the first psychoanalytic studies of therapeutic misalliances. Briefly, Glover defined an inexact interpretation as one in which the specific fantasy system on which a symptom is based is not uncovered; a related fantasy system is instead interpreted to the patient. He described the manner in which the patient may seize upon the inexact interpretation and convert it into a displacement-substitute that is sufficiently remote from the real sources of the patient's anxiety as to afford him considerable symptom relief. He also noted that such improvement occurs at the cost of refractoriness to deeper analysis. In addition, Glover described a variety of defenses, suggestions, offers of sanction, and other efforts toward providing the patient the kind of displacement systems commonly offered by nonanalysts. In the terms defined within this paper, Glover was, indeed, exploring a variety of therapeutic misalliances and their effects.

Overall, the literature reflects the inevitability of efforts toward misalliance, major or minor, the infinitely varied forms that such endeavors may take, and the prime importance of their detection, analysis, and modification. It is, however, relatively lacking in specific discussions of the means of detecting misalliances, the techniques related to their resolution, the special efforts of the patient toward modifying them, and the mutual influence of patient and analyst upon each other in creating, maintaining, and altering misalliances. Some clinical data will enable us to clarify these and other aspects of this problem.

CLINICAL MATERIAL

Every patient who seeks psychoanalysis or psychotherapy will attempt on some level to effect a therapeutic misalliance with his analyst or therapist. The direction of these efforts is the product of his past history, character makeup, unresolved intrapsychic conflicts and symptoms, current life situation, and responses to the analyst and the analytic situation.

It is characteristic of such efforts that they tend to re-create pathogenic and unresolved infantile relationships and traumas, and unmastered conflicts—along with efforts at adaptive and maladaptive mastery. They represent attempts to gratify infantile and unfulfilled pathological fantasies directly with the analyst. Simultaneously, they defend the patient against anxiety and guilt, intrapsychic conflicts, unresolved unconscious fantasies, and the threats posed by the relationship with the analyst. Patients try to involve the analyst in living out complex, pathological, unconscious fantasies and relationships, usually as an alternative to their verbal communication in derivative form.

It is one of the analyst's tasks in the opening phase of psychoanalysis to detect expressions of the patient's—and his own—wishes for a misalliance

with him (Nunberg 1926). Throughout the subsequent therapy or analysis, the therapist remains alert for such a development at any juncture, especially at times of difficulty and at termination—the latter being a very common period for needs of this kind to occur in both participants. In general, the patient's efforts may appear in derivative or direct form in his associations, or may be attempted through some behavior and actual effort to engage the analyst in this type of involvement. These efforts need not be grossly acted out, but are often reflected in the manner and content of the patient's free associations and in his general analytic modus vivendi (Myerson 1969, 1973). While these intentions and fantasies, which are initially strongly related to the patient's unconscious motives for seeking analysis and to what has been termed *the pre-formed transference* (Langs 1974), contain the potential for misalliance, they also prove to be a rich source of analyzable material if the analyst does not consciously or unconsciously join in the misalliance. The analyst or therapist may have unresolved needs for a misalliance with his patients in general, or with a specific patient, that are mobilized upon his beginning a new therapeutic venture. The underlying motives are similar to those already described for the patient, with some specific additional aspects related to his role as analyst, and they reflect a variety of countertransferences and counterresistances to his patient.

The intermingling of the sources of misalliances is such that an unconscious circular interaction is characteristic. Both patient and analyst are attempting to adapt to their own inner needs and to the stimuli emanating from the other person. One of them may initiate a move toward misalliance or may respond to some cue from, or reaction by, the other; in turn, the second one will unconsciously participate or resist, or may communicate his own need for a different type of neurotic relationship, to which the first will then react. Unconscious evocation of, reaction to, acceptance of, resistance against, attempts to intensify, and attempts to rectify the area of misalliance occur in quick succession on both sides.

As previously noted (Langs 1974), misalliances may be classified as mutually narcissistic, sadomasochistic, exhibitionistic-voyeuristic, seductive, and infantilizing. However, such terms tend to offer a classification that fails to reflect the specific nuances and richness of these interactions; a deep, dynamic clinical description and formulation promises to offer a more precise picture.

In this spirit, then, let us move directly to a vignette drawn from the opening phase of a psychotherapy; as we will see, the principles and concepts to be derived from it are fully applicable to the psychoanalytic situation as well.[2]

Dr. Z. presented a patient, Mr. A., to me in supervision. Mr. A. was a man in his fifties who sought therapy for recurrent moderate depressions and failures to advance in his work despite apparent strong abilities. He served as a consultant to an electronics firm and was concerned that his contract would not be renewed. His wife was depressed and currently in therapy. Of note regarding his past history is the fact that his parents had both died in an automobile accident when the patient was in his late teens; he had dissipated his inheritance in the years that followed and was currently worried about finances. Diagnostically, he was assessed as an obsessive character disorder with depression.

In his first sessions, Mr. A. spoke repeatedly of his financial worries and of his failure to provide his wife with security, closeness or an adequate sexual relationship. He envied the younger men who always appeared to replace him in his work. He tended to withdraw whenever he was under stress. When others failed, he always felt better.

Mr. A. detailed his current realistic problems in this manner over several hours, and the therapist asked occasional questions about them. When the patient then revealed that he was currently having joint sessions with his wife's therapist, Dr. Z. asked him how he felt about it, but otherwise did not explore or deal with it. In his associations, Mr. A. spoke of not wanting to hear about his wife's problems and of how he lacked family ties. His brother hated Mr. A.'s wife and never spoke to either of them; Mr. A. allowed his guilt to plague and inhibit him. He alluded to a previous psychotherapy in which the therapist unnecessarily reduced his fee and which got nowhere. That therapist had also seen his wife and had been overtly seductive; Mrs. A. had stopped seeing him when she caught him in an error—a contradiction—and he asked her to leave. When the therapist asked further about this past therapy, Mr. A. spoke of his anger over his wife's seductiveness with other men; he did not trust her. He would end up having to fix things himself.

In the next few hours, allusions to the sessions with his wife's therapist, which are soon discontinued at that therapist's request, were intermingled with recollections of his parents' deaths, in which his own hostility toward them was hinted at. He then recalled primal observations from his childhood, his attachment to male friends, and vaguely wondered if he was homosexually attracted to a cousin who had

understood and helped him as a teenager. Later, he spoke of a cousin who had had a nervous breakdown and of how two therapists were too much to handle. His guilt immobilized him and he preferred to be left alone; maybe hypnosis would help him. He never committed himself.

I shall pause here to describe the relevant supervisory discussions and formulations. In brief, Mr. A. consciously sought help for his depression, guilt, and need to fail. Unconsciously, he initially indicated that a misalliance in which the therapist would fail would temporarily reassure ("cure") him. His associations suggested that he would also accept a situation of mutual withdrawal in which his hostile and sexual impulses were covered over (and somewhat gratified) as another sector of misalliance. This became especially clear when his associations revealed that the other therapist was protecting Mr. A. from experiencing, and therefore facing, his unconscious homosexual fantasies toward his present therapist.

Despite supervisory discussions, the therapist chose to ignore the emerging derivatives of Mr. A.'s unconscious fantasies and did not deal with the evident resistances embedded in the deviation in technique—the sessions with the second therapist (Langs 1975b). Unconsciously, he communicated to the patient his own wishes to avoid both closeness with Mr. A. and meaningful material and interaction, and his preference for focusing on realistic problems in which intrapsychic conflicts and disturbing affects and fantasies were relatively ignored.

Mr. A. and Dr. Z., each prompting and responding to the other, rather quickly and unconsciously had arranged a ruminative intellectualizing, reality-focused, fantasy-avoiding misalliance of major proportions. Despite supervisory comments, the therapist did virtually nothing to modify his position. Soon Mr. A., who had unconsciously perpetuated the misalliance, also initiated unconscious efforts to modify it. Such curative endeavors by patients toward their analysts and therapists have been described previously by Little (1951), Searles (1965), and myself (1973a, 1975a). More recently, Searles (1975) in an extensive study of the curative work of his schizophrenic and neurotic patients toward himself as their analyst, has suggested that they reflect a basic human need that arises in the infant in his earliest relationship and symbiotic experiences with his mother.

Empirically I have found that patients are exquisitely sensitive to and unconsciously perceptive of their therapist's errors, and that they respond by efforts to correct and assist the therapist at such moments. Their unconscious communications at such junctures bear the hallmark of sound confrontations and interpretations; they express ideas and formulations remarkably parallel to my own thinking and direct interventions with their therapists in supervision. Upon reflection, the underlying principle is a sound one: if the therapist is blocked or unhelpful in his therapeutic work, his cure must take precedence so that he can ultimately help the patient.

In a well-run treatment, such efforts are relatively infrequent and generally minor, though nonetheless quite important (Searles 1975). The patient's reactions at such moments are, as always, based on a mixture of valid unconscious perceptions and bona fide therapeutic efforts on the one hand, and their own intrapsychic fantasies, conflicts, and needs— including transference distortions—on the other. In emphasizing the need to recognize and implicitly make use of the patient's helpful endeavors, we must not overlook the ultimate shift of the focus of treatment to the therapy of the patient. However, the therapist who treats these efforts entirely as distortions and ignores their realistic aspects (Searles 1975) will make hurtful and insensitive interventions. Here, I shall merely attempt a preliminary sketch of patients' efforts at cure, pending more conclusive investigations.

As we have seen, Mr. A., quite early in the therapy, and well after the first sectors of misalliance had been established, spoke of withdrawing under stress and of his own failures to provide his family with a growth-promoting relationship. In part this material reflects his unconscious perception of the therapist's failings—indeed, of his need to fail—and of the misalliance; it reflects too his subsequent incorporative identification with these aspects of the therapist. While this may well appear somewhat speculative, in part because I have condensed the initial material to an extreme degree, let us follow the subsequent developments.

Mr. A. had soon revealed that he had a second therapist. In addition to reflecting his own fears of closeness and his homosexual anxieties, this is an indication of the patient's unconscious awareness of Dr. Z.'s supervisor (such communications are common among clinic patients). Perhaps Mr. A. was also suggesting that supervision might be a factor in Dr. Z.'s fears of the therapeutic relationship; this indeed was an impression that I had in the supervision. More important, however, it represented an effort to alert the therapist to the presence of a third

(and fourth—his wife) party to the treatment, and its implicit defensive and neurotically gratifying dimensions. When Dr. Z. failed to explore the situation, thereby accepting and participating in it, we can observe a variety of unconscious reactions in Mr. A.—incorporative identification, what I term *unconscious interpretations,* and further extensive efforts to "cure" the therapist.

Thus, Mr. A. alluded to the way he allows guilt to plague and inhibit him, a view—again confirmed by my supervisory observations—of an aspect of the therapist's countertransference problems. He also suggested through displaced derivatives that the therapist had an underlying hatred for him (and therefore permitted a detrimental situation to continue, while protecting himself from his anger by having an observer present); he also spoke of his own refusal to listen to his wife (the therapist who will not hear). He referred to the therapist who inappropriately reduced his fee, failed to help, was seductive, made a blunder, and sent his wife away. When these indirect allusions to the present therapist went unheeded, we hear of the patient's growing mistrust and his despairing conclusion that he will have to cure himself.

Further derivatives connect the two-therapist situation to Mr. A.'s rage at his deserting parents (the therapist) and to primal scene experiences (threesomes). There is then a strikingly condensed association that contains another unconscious interpretation, one that was exquisitely intended to bring to the therapist's awareness the underlying, interfering homosexual conflicts that prompted him to accept a third party to his relationship with Mr. A. As his supervisor, I could not have expressed such insights into Dr. Z.'s countertransference difficulties and motives for misalliance more clearly. It is evident, of course, that these associations also reflect Mr. A.'s own latent homosexual conflicts. Such condensations and multiple functions of communications from the patient are the rule.

Finally, Mr. A. went on to express his fears for his own mental integrity if the blind spot and misalliance prevailed. Simultaneously he offered a confrontation and interpretation of the therapist's anxieties: that they were based on guilt, primal scene and homosexual conflicts, and fears of being overwhelmed. Lastly, there was another reference to the therapist's striking failure to intervene—commit himself—and to another search for self-cure through hypnosis. In actuality, many of these derivatives convey unconsciously from Mr. A. direct comments that had been made in supervision to Dr. Z.

To continue more briefly with this vignette, the

patient was soon told that his business contract would not be renewed. He spent many sessions ruminating about this problem and how to deal with it, and from time to time the therapist questioned him about it or pointed out an obvious aspect of Mr. A.'s concern. Soon the patient conveyed feelings that he was getting nowhere in his therapy and the therapist reported to me that he felt bored and was annoyed with his patient. In supervision, I too experienced the sessions as uninteresting and hollow. Since the therapist made no effort to deal with the resistances and misalliance that he and the patient had effected, I more strongly recommended confrontations with the patient's failure to communicate expressions of his inner conflicts (derivatives of his unconscious fantasies) and a modification of the therapist's stance: he should no longer participate in the reality focus and should confine himself to confronting and analyzing the patient's defenses and to exploring any expressions of intrapsychic conflicts that emerged. I also used Mr. A.'s unconscious interpretations to Dr. Z. to alert the latter to the underlying basis for his block.

As the therapist very tentatively began to modify his stance, Mr. A.'s associations—which had been undecipherable in connection with any type of unconscious fantasy other than those related to the misalliance—came alive again. He spoke of how he should give his son more responsibilities, and of the lack of dialogue between himself and his wife. When confronted with the lack of reference to his inner stirrings he, for the first time, told the story of the man who gets a flat and needs to borrow a jack to fix it. On walking to a house to ask for help, he is so convinced that he will be refused, and builds the scene so much in his mind, that he rings the bell and attacks the man who answers it. Mr. A. also anticipates a royal shafting wherever he goes; he becomes the good guy, and then no one feels bad.

In other sessions, he spoke of his anger when his wife stirred him up, adding, however, that he wanted to take on responsibilities with her. His friend had been in therapy and had not changed; he just accepted it. His son did nothing—it was Mr. A.'s own fault for being permissive and not meddling in his problems; he was afraid he might crush his son. His own father never intervened with him, though his mother did.

As the therapist continued to explore Mr. A.'s fears of revealing himself, the patient spoke of how he pressured his inactive son to do things and to communicate. He played psychiatrist with his son but not with himself. He disliked having the same conversation with his wife over and over; his first

therapist never got behind the same old reality issues. If he exposed himself to the therapist, the latter would be just like his wife and give him advice.

We see, then, that the therapist's constructive efforts to modify the misalliance were unconsciously perceived by the patient, who also appears to have positively identified with the correctly and unconsciously perceived newfound strengths of the therapist. Derivatives of Mr. A.'s own intrapsychic conflicts become available for cognitive-emotional insight through interpretation by the therapist. Thus were opened up crucial routes for the modification of misalliances and for new, constructive avenues of conflict resolution and change for the patient.

I have presented this vignette in some detail because it demonstrates in its two misalliances— the accepted third party to the therapy and the shared obsessive-avoidance defenses—many typical characteristics of these misalliances: their mutuality, and the clues whereby they can be recognized and resolved.

Subjectively, therapeutic misalliances should be considered when the therapist senses a lack of progress or depth in the therapy, or in the unfolding of the material from the patient. Beyond such cognitive awareness, the therapist may experience a range of thoughts, feelings, and fantasies: things are not right; he dislikes the patient, or has other unusual attitudes or feelings toward him; he feels used or manipulated, or that he is ineffectual as a therapist; he is aware of notably seductive or aggressive felings toward the patient that he is unable to resolve; he cannot understand a stalemate or a regression in the patient. Subjectively experienced disturbances in his therapeutic attitudes, or any unusual manner of intervening or behaving, are clues to the presence of countertransference problems, and direct the therapist to search for their expression in the actual interaction with the patient.

Subjective clues lead the therapist to listening especially carefully to the patient's associations with the suspected misalliance in mind. A correct and sensitive subjective appraisal that leads to the identification of a misalliance should be confirmed in the patient's associations. At times, when the therapist is especially blocked, these will stimulate him to focus on his own inner feelings and fantasies. Themes of noncommunication, of manipulation, of poor parental functioning, of poor therapy of any kind, of collusion, and other misalliance-related content should alert him. The valid understanding of these associations as they relate to a misalliance or any aspect of the patient-therapist relationship should always, in turn, be confirmed by the therapist's subjective experiences and realizations (see Langs 1975a).

In this vignette, the therapist's sense of boredom and anger could have alerted him to the obsessive misalliance (not simply Mr. A.'s resistances). A review of his interventions (e.g., repeated realistic inquiries and avoidance of instinctual-drive derivatives) would have been helpful, as would other, inevitable feelings that he did not report to me. In my supervision, I detected many clues to the misalliance. Mr. A.'s multiple communications were also available.

Therapeutic misalliances foster symptom relief through pathological, shared defenses and inappropriate gratifications. They repeat and confirm the patient's neurotic fantasies, needs, and past pathogenic interactions, and the participating therapist cannot interpret and modify such pathology; he is, for the moment, an integral part of it.

Modification of misalliances entails the following steps:

1. Recognition by the therapist.
2. Modification of the therapist's participation through self-analysis, without burdening the patient, though full use should be made of the patient's unconscious perceptions and interpretations. The therapist's failure to resolve his inner conflicts will promote new versions of the misalliance.
3. Full analysis, without blame, of the patient's own needs for the misalliance, and his role in effecting it.

When a major technical error, deviation in technique, or erroneous stance by the therapist has contributed to the misalliance, the therapist in proper context may *implicitly* acknowledge his contribution— a practice that is largely misused by patient and therapist, and therefore best confined to indirect means. Basically, even if the therapist's participation was inadvertent, he should never deny his role, should tacitly accept the actuality of his contribution, and not treat the patient's perceptions of it as fantasy-based. However, this does not preclude a full exploration of the patient's involvement in the misalliance, his extensions of reality into conscious and unconscious fantasies, and his frequent attempts to misuse the misalliance to sanction his own pathology. A full analysis of the unconscious motives for seeking and maintaining a misalliance not only clears the way to a viable therapeutic alliance, but is the vehicle for vital therapeutic work.

In fact, the analytic resolution of misalliances is a moving experience for both patient and therapist, providing both an intense kind of experience that is appropriately gratifying in a way that is unique even in the therapeutic relationship. The final mutual triumph over pathological inner needs and defenses is especially satisfying.

The interaction between the patient and the therapist has alternating thrusts toward misalliance and rectification of the misalliance—restoring the therapeutic alliance. In focusing on the efforts of one or the other toward maladaptive equilibrium, we must not overlook their respective efforts toward healthier adaptations. While we tend to focus on the therapist's conscious efforts toward resolution of the misalliance, this vignette clearly indicates consistent efforts by the patient to alert the therapist to the misalliance and to help him modify it.

Having established some basic concepts and technical principles, let us now attempt to apply and expand upon them with a second vignette.

Mrs. B. was a young teacher who had sought therapy for marital difficulties. She had been in psychotherapy for several months with a woman therapist who was, at the time of the sessions to be described, in her sixth month of a pregnancy. The patient appeared to have some phobic systems, primarily a fear of driving and an anxiety that she would be physically damaged in an accident caused by another car; these symptoms had been reported in recent sessions.

The patient had missed a session because of a legal holiday and for her following hour knocked on the therapist's door fifteen minutes early; in the session itself, she spoke of feeling isolated and lonely in her marriage, and complained about her husband's incessant nagging. She recalled having had some facial moles removed when she was thirteen years of age, a procedure that included cosmetic plastic surgery as well. While her appearance had improved, the changes had intensified her anxieties and especially exacerbated a choking sensation in her throat and difficulty in swallowing. The therapist responded with a lengthy intervention, in which she related the patient's feelings of loneliness to the missed session and connected this to her coming early; in addition, she suggested that this also related to the anticipated separation that would occur at the time of her delivery. The patient responded with some general agreement.

Mrs. B. was late to her next session; she stated that she no longer felt lonely and that she was not attached to her therapist, who she felt was somehow implying that she had had feelings during her mother's pregnancy in her childhood (a sister had been born when she was five and a brother when she was eight); she rather elaborately denied any such reaction. She also complained that the sessions were exhausting her and that the therapist was too silent.

In the next hour, the patient was five minutes late but eager to talk. She had quarreled with her husband and had been angry over his attachment to his mother, stating that he did not seem to understand that she and he were a couple and that they should function as a couple. They had argued and the patient had slept alone, but then became frightened. That night she slept at her sister's house and when the therapist asked why the patient was behaving in this way now, Mrs. B. related it to being in treatment, feeling stronger, and not seeing any change in her husband. The therapist asked her to relate it more clearly to treatment and the patient reiterated what she had said. She then spoke of her difficulties in opening up in treatment and suggested that she had to work on that. The therapist made another lengthy intervention in which she attempted to link the patient's becoming more freely verbal in her sessions to her wish to leave her husband, adding that it also seemed to reflect feelings of hurt in response to the therapist's recent comments and to the missed session. The patient said that she was thinking of reducing her sessions from two to one weekly, and the therapist commented that this represented an effort to deny any need for her.

Mrs. B. said that she had felt hurt and criticized by the therapist and had thought of not coming for her session, adding that she overreacts in an unproductive way. Doing things when she was hurt would not change the problem and her husband simply would not change. The therapist seemed not to realize how frightened she was of leaving him; she added that she had her faults too, and had to accept the marriage since she could not expect anything better. The therapist made another long intervention about the manner in which the patient was feeling criticized and therefore angry with her, relating it to her conflict with her husband. The patient responded by ruminating about her exaggerated sensitivity to hurts, relating it to her father's hitting her as a child, and contrasting it to her parents' efforts to be supportive at other times.

I shall pause here to formulate the interaction between this patient and her therapist. The material begins essentially with a missed hour and with derivatives related to what is quite evidently the primary adaptive task intrapsychically for Mrs. B., her therapist's pregnancy. The associations indicate that this patient is experiencing the pregnancy as a development through which she will suffer a great loss and a rupture of the close twosome that she had been experiencing with the therapist. In addition,

there is evidence of an unconscious incorporative identification with the pregnant therapist, with related bodily anxieties—the fear of being smashed by a car and being damaged bodily, and the reparative references to the plastic surgery. On the basis of the therapist's subsequent interventions, we might speculate that the allusions to the nagging husband relate to an unconscious perception of the manner in which this therapist intervenes.

In the following hour, Mrs. B.'s denial of any reaction to the therapist's pregnancy offers a genetic clue to its unconscious meaning and is apparently designed, however defensively, to alert the therapist to the fact that it is a crucial source of anxiety and conflict—the main adaptive and therapeutic context for the moment. When the therapist failed to recognize these implications, the patient complained about treatment.

In the next hour, the patient, through displaced derivatives, expressed her anger regarding the anticipated rupture of the therapeutic couple, acting out the denial of her need for her therapist in her relationship with her husband. When the therapist failed to recognize the central source of this behavior and of the underlying conflicts (her own pregnancy), the patient soon undertook unconscious efforts to alert her to this blind spot—talking about her own problems in opening up in the sessions and in being in touch, and her thoughts of canceling her hours. When the therapist responded with lengthy, apparently anxious and inaccurate interventions, the patient spoke of the manner in which she herself overreacted unproductively—a formulation that was anticipated in supervision.

Mrs. B. goes on to again express her conflicts over leaving treatment, once more displacing these reactions onto her husband. Her own devalued self-image and an incorporative identification with the impaired (pregnant and insensitive) therapist lead her to allusions to her own faults. Another generally incorrect intervention follows, and Mrs. B. speculates on her own sensitivity to hurts, an unconscious interpretation to the therapist, perhaps an unconscious perception of the therapist's excessive sensitivity, with a related genetic intervention—that the therapist's sensitivity is related to a disturbed interaction with her parents.

The sectors of misalliance between Mrs. B. and her therapist primarily involved the establishment of a somewhat sadomasochistic and intellectualized defensive interaction designed to avoid and deny the main areas of intrapsychic conflict evoked—probably for both of them—by the pregnancy.

I would view the patient's momentary feeling that

she was stronger as a *misalliance cure* (for the earlier roots of this concept see Langs 1974 and Barchilon 1958) in which the patient found support and reassurance through the therapist's difficulties and mobilized her own resources because of the latter's failure. The mutual avoidance of the patient's central anxieties and conflicts afforded her momentary relief through the shared defenses. In general, then, it is important to accurately identify the underlying basis of symptom relief and to recognize the indicators of a momentarily successful "cure" through therapeutic misalliance.

The patient began the next hour by reporting that she felt better and had worked things out with her husband; it was not completely satisfactory, but she had made an effort. She went on to describe a movie that she had seen in which several people were crippled and paralyzed; she had fled the theater. She now remembered a dream from that night, one in which she was working with crippled children. On the night prior to the present session, she had dreamt of sitting in a luncheonette and hearing some children criticize her singing.

In the session, she stated that if she were crippled or handicapped like the men in the movie, she would kill herself, even though they seemed to make the adjustment. She felt that the dream meant that she could not imagine herself being damaged and that the second dream alluded to her difficulty in taking criticism as a child, something that she could handle better now. She related this to treatment and stated that it bothered her that she ruminated in her sessions; she felt guilty with her husband because she did not do the things that she should do for him — she did not give enough to him.

These communications condensed a variety of unconscious perceptions and fantasies. The dream and associations to them reflect the patient's unconscious identification with the pregnant therapist in a manner that indicates that pregnancy is seen by Mrs. B. as a potentially crippling experience that is evoking considerable anxiety in her. This material also reflects unconscious perceptions of the therapist, who did not intervene or understand these communications — that is, failed to do the things that she should have done in the sessions. Further, the associations represent another effort on the part of Mrs. B. to direct the therapist to the source of their respective conflicts and anxieties. Mrs. B. sensed, apparently correctly, that her therapist was anxious about her pregnancy and avoiding it in the treatment situation. On this basis, she offered a series of unconscious interpretations which are amalgams of her fantasies with efforts to direct the therapist to the possible sources of her anxieties. These efforts are best illustrated in the reference to the handicapped and crippled men. In this context, the flight from the theater dramatizes the therapist's own massive avoidance.

Mrs. B. began her next hour by describing minor surgery that her husband would be having; she would have to drive him home because he would be groggy (another allusion to the necessity for this patient to take responsibility for her therapy). She had had a pleasant visit with her in-laws but had been demeaned by her husband when she had reacted to his tormenting of a waitress. There was a period of silence; when the therapist inquired into it, Mrs. B. said she had been thinking of menstruation. Her periods had been irregular for the past couple of months and her gynecologist had said it was her nerves. It made her feel that there was something wrong with her and that she would not be able to have babies; she somehow connected this to her fears of accidents and damage. When she was thirteen, she had had similar anxieties.

The therapist intervened, reiterating the various themes to which the patient had alluded, and pointed out that the patient's increased anxiety undoubtedly reflected concerns about her pregnancy and delivery, and worries that she — the therapist — would be damaged. Mrs. B. responded with a broad smile; she said that she envied her therapist's Ph.D. — she actually had an M.D. — and added that she was worried that she herself would be unable to have children when she wanted them. She suddenly recalled that she had had a dream where she had delivered a baby who was fine but was taken away. She guessed that she was, after all, concerned about her therapist's pregnancy and delivery.

In this session, relatively undisguised derivatives of Mrs. B.'s unconscious fantasies, conflicts, and anxieties as they are related to the therapist's pregnancy unfold. The onset of the patient's irregular periods coincided with the recognition of the therapist's pregnancy and affords further evidence of the patient's identification with her therapist. In addition, it hints at unconscious wishes to destroy the fetus and at rage in the rivalry with the therapist, a thesis that is supported by her own fear that she would not be able to have a child, the allusion to accidents and damage, and the element of the final dream in which the baby disappears. The therapist failed to recognize these derivatives as related to specific aggressive fantasies — a failure that could form the nucleus of another misalliance, and demonstrates how a therapist's failure to resolve his contributing intrapsychic conflicts can lead to new versions of the search for unconscious collusion.

Perhaps because the patient's unconscious interventions were of some help to this therapist, she was finally able to identify some of the important meanings of these less and less disguised associations and to interpret aspects of them. Her relatively correct intervention evoked a strongly confirmatory response in the patient in the form of the recall of a previously repressed dream (Langs 1974a). The dream also suggests an unconscious incorporative identification with a more positive image of the therapist, in that it portrays the patient as being capable of delivering a baby, although this is marred by the disappearance of the child—an element which undoubtedly refers to the patient's own hostile wishes, but may also be a further unconscious attempt to suggest to the therapist that the latter's need to avoid the subject of her pregnancy was related to her own unresolved hostility toward her fetus. A further acknowledgment of the therapist's capacities is contained in the reference to her degree, although the patient again showed her hostility by mentioning a Ph.D., which, her later associations revealed, she considered lower than the M.D. the therapist had actually attained.

As with the first vignette, the material presented here strongly indicates that this patient's apparent resistances against dealing with the conflicts, fantasies, and anxieties evoked by her therapist's pregnancy were not solely evoked by intrapsychic defenses. It is clear that the therapist's own unconscious defensive avoidance of the pregnancy significantly contributed to and reinforced the patient's defensiveness. It follows, then, that the first step toward resolving this resistance was a modification of the therapist's defenses so that she could consciously acknowledge and deal with the derivatives from the patient related to her pregnancy, and would no longer unconsciously communicate to the patient her own wishes to avoid the subject.

This material also demonstrates the manner in which a patient who is faced with a seriously defensive therapist, and who also has mounting inner anxieties and distrusting fantasies, will actively attempt to cure the therapist of her difficulty in order to obtain much-needed help in return. The therapist's correct though limited intervention was subsequently confirmed by associations that included both the further modification of repressive barriers and indications of a momentary positive incorporative identification.

In retrospect, it appears that if the therapist had properly understood the communications regarding the patient's marital problems as a means of expressing Mrs. B.'s unconscious perception of her misalliance with the therapist, and if she had more sensitively monitored the patient's associations for unconscious perceptions of her own role in the stalemate that she herself had sensed, she would have been directed much sooner to her own difficulties. Discussions with the therapist suggested that her anxieties regarding her pending delivery, and her own conscious and unconscious fantasies of bodily damage, were so intense that she did indeed unconsciously share many of these disturbing fantasies with the patient and therefore utilized comparable defenses.

We see also that the therapist's difficulties in dealing with this area created pressures within the patient toward greater self-confidence and more effective communications, and therefore afforded her a momentary misalliance cure. The symptom relief obtained by the patient through these shared defenses, and through the gratification of being more in tune with her anxieties than the therapist was with hers, was short-lived, and the patient's anxieties soon returned. The subsequent material clearly reflects the fact that the patient had in no way understood her intrapsychic conflicts and anxieties as related to the pregnancy, but that she had found temporary relief through bypassing them. As her anxiety intensified, it became necessary for her to return to the specific unconscious fantasies that were disturbing her and to seek the assistance of the therapist in resolving them. In a small way, these observations provide clues regarding the vicissitudes of the identificatory processes in the therapeutic relationship as they fluctuate with the therapist's actual capacities and thereby strengthen or weaken the patient's self-image and general ego capacities. The interpretation of derivatives of unconscious transference fantasies, by contrast, offers specific cognitive insights that enable the patient to master areas of conflict.

In concluding my discussion of this vignette, I would note that the material supports the thesis that the development of a firm therapeutic alliance depends on both the nonparticipation of the therapist in a misalliance and correctly timed, pertinent interpretations. Attempts to be reassuring, to offer so-called reparative deviations in technique, and any other kind of noninterpretive intervention could only foster additional sectors of misalliance and further convey the therapist's difficulties in understanding the patient's intrapsychic conflicts. In addition, any effort to reassure the patient regarding the therapist's good intentions (Zetzel 1966–1969) or to discuss the patient's realistic concerns (Greenson and

Wexler 1969) would not only reflect an insensitivity to the main source of the patient's conflicts and difficulties, but would also entail at times the conscious denial of the patient's valid, unconscious perceptions of the therapist. Such a noninterpretive stance reflects the therapist's failure to appreciate both the transference and realistic elements in the patient's communications, and their unconscious elaborations.

I am well aware of the danger of reading too much into the patient's associations. I want to emphasize that it was the striking correspondence between my own conscious assessment as a supervisor, and the unconscious perceptions and communications of the patient that led me to recognize the remarkable extent to which patients are in touch with their therapist's failings, and the extent of their endeavors to assist the therapist with them. Similarly, when in this case I formulated that the therapist had made a sound and helpful intervention, the patient's unconscious communications reflected a perception and incorporation of these positive attributes. Once this exquisite sensitivity on the part of the patient is fully appreciated, it enables the therapist to understand and predict the unfolding of many previously confusing sessions—a powerful means of understanding the patient-therapist and patient-analyst interactions.

DISCUSSION AND CONCLUSIONS

Therapeutic misalliances, as sectors of the patient-analyst relationship, are related to the intermixtures of transference and countertransference, as well as to other aspects of the patient's and the analyst's mutual attempts to adapt. They may be present in patients or analysts who appear to be working well and seem overtly to be cooperating and not acting out or acting in. They offer, however, momentary maladaptive resolutions to the patient's and/or analyst's conflicts, and foster maladaptive identifications of each with the other, undermining the therapist's effectiveness. They must, therefore, be analyzed and resolved to permit other aspects of the analytic work to unfold effectively. Yet, as inevitable expressions of the patient's pathology and of the residuals of the pathology in the analyst, these efforts at misalliance are, paradoxically, a major opportunity for effective and necessary analytic work and for growth within both participants.

Although misalliances are always embedded in the specific conflicts, character structure, and genetic history of the patient and the analyst, we may identify certain general motives for the creation of misalliances. On the patient's part, the search for misalliance stems from the hope for maladaptive relief from the anxiety and guilt related to his intrapsychic conflicts. A misalliance can serve as a major defense against closeness with the analyst and all that such intimacy represents to the patient. It may also provide him inappropriate gratification of his neurotic needs and be a means by which he repeats past interactions that fostered his neurosis and justifies its continuation. Through a misalliance, the patient also bypasses the painful process of renunciation and inner change. A misalliance can reinforce inappropriate superego sanctions and punishments, and offer a wide range of pathological defenses to the patient—as well as to the analyst. For any given moment, it may provide the patient temporary and usually unstable symptomatic relief so that he does not attempt to seek out other, more adaptive but arduous solutions to his conflicts. To the extent that misalliances gratify wishes to circumvent reasonable boundaries and to deny separateness, they also provide the patient illusions of symbiotic ties, and a false sense of omnipotence and of a right to special gratification, which can momentarily reassure him to the extent that he is not plagued by his intrapsychic conflicts. The inherent depreciation and destruction of the analyst who becomes involved in a misalliance provides the patient neurotic feelings of power and pathologically gained self-esteem.

Through a misalliance, the analyst no longer represents insight, delay, optimal adaptation, renunciation, and the process of analytic scrutiny; the patient thereby is able to unconsciously justify his abandonment of meaningful analytic work toward inner change. More broadly, the analyst is for the moment no longer a "good object" with which the patient can constructively identify, but has become instead a "bad object" who is incorporated to the detriment of the patient's self-representation and functioning. In all, the inevitable wish to maladaptively and momentarily lessen conflict, anxiety, and guilt at any cost, the universal human search for unlimited closeness and immediate discharge, and the need to repeat and master past traumatic relationships prompt these efforts toward misalliances in patients.

Despite these gains, the inherently maladaptive, destructive and inappropriately gratifying aspects of an effected misalliance will prompt the patient to make efforts to modify and renounce the collusion with the help of the analyst. Unconsciously aware of the ultimately self-defeating dimensions of a misalliance, the patient communicates his perceptions to the analyst in his efforts to find a new and healthier adaptation. In addition, he unconsciously attempts to resolve the misalliance through curing the therapist as well as himself.

In general, despite the momentary symptomatic relief that misalliances afford, they are often followed by serious regressive and acting out episodes if they are not detected and modified. Further, if the patient's efforts to modify the misalliance go unheeded and if the analyst has unresolved unconscious needs to maintain it, the patient will either abruptly terminate the therapy or will continue in the stalemated therapeutic situation in which he can maintain the inappropriate relationship and gratifications so obtained.

The analyst's inevitable residuals of unmastered anxiety and guilt, neurotic and maladaptive defensive needs, his longings for personal or magical closeness and for inappropriate gratifications, his struggles against the severe limits imposed by the analytic relationship, and his own search to repeat and master past pathological interactions prompt him to search for misalliances with his patients. Specific unresolved intrapsychic conflicts stirred up by a particular patient may prompt him to seek out a misalliance rather than to assist the patient in resolving his difficulties analytically. It should be noted, however, that the analyst's or therapist's responsibilities in this area differ from those of the patient. He must recognize and master a developing misalliance as quickly as possible, to prevent it from permanently impairing the therapeutic relationship and derailing the analytic work. While the patient, for his analysis to be successful, must be willing at some point to explore, analyze, and resolve his quest for misalliance with the analyst, the analyst, the analyst carries the responsibility to resolve his inner difficulties along these lines largely on his own, tacitly accepting whatever assistance the patient consciously or unconsciously offers. He should not feel unduly guilty over a misalliance that he has evoked, but should utilize his disturbed interaction as a means of understanding the patient and his own neurotic needs.

I will conclude by briefly listing the main heuristic and technical implications of the concept of the therapeutic misalliance.

1. The misalliance concept leads directly to a study of the patient-analyst interaction and its intrapsychic consequences when impairments arise in the therapeutic alliance and in the treatment situation. This is a viable alternative to the more common focus at such moments on the patient's damaged capacities, such as an inability for mature object relationships and trust (Zetzel 1958, 1966–1969).

While recognizing the importance of such factors, the misalliance concept points to the frequency with which difficulties arise from shared unconscious interactions and communications.

2. The concept of therapeutic misalliance fosters use of the adaptational-interactional viewpoint, in which the intrapsychic repercussions of the actualities of the therapeutic relationship and the behaviors of the analyst are considered, along with manifestations of the effects of transference and countertransference fantasies.

The therapist's ongoing relationship with the patient, his therapeutic stance and "hold," and his projections and communications to the patient as an actual person ("object"—Loewald 1960) contribute to important incorporative identifications into the patient's self-representations and psychic structures, and create the basic background for effective interpretive work. They are as important as the capacity of the therapist to offer meaningful insights through interpretation.

3. The misalliance concept leads to a full appreciation of the importance of the patient's unconscious perceptions of the therapist, and the kernels of reality in his relationship with the therapist. It establishes them as a constituent to be added to unconscious fantasies and memories (transference) as the main determinants of the patient's reactions to the therapist or analyst, and the main basis for neurotic symptom formation.

4. The concept also leads us to recognize the vital importance of who the analyst is, and how he behaves and structures the relationship with the patient—in addition to how and what he interprets. The therapist's need and identity are conveyed in the way he uses the ground rules of therapy, in his maintenance of the boundaries of the relationship, and in his capacity to interpret rather than participate in a pathogenic interaction. These now become important focuses of therapy, rather than peripheral factors.

5. This concept leads to a recognition that the patient's intrapsychic resistances and pathogenic needs often find unconscious reinforcement in the responses of the therapist, and to a more careful study of the manner in which intrapsychic conflicts and defenses are, in general, supported by interactions with others.

6. This concept focuses on a facet of the treatment situation that must be analyzed first before other effective work can be done, and on an aspect of the therapist's interaction with the patient that must be modified, along with the intrapsychic basis on which it has developed; for true resolution to occur, words are not enough.

7. The concept helps to create a better perspective on the therapeutic relationship and the contributions of transference and countertransference (distortions) on the one hand, and nontransference and non-countertransference (reality) on the other. It leads, also, to a fuller appreciation of the pathological needs of both participants, and especially to the curative needs and capacities of both. It shows us, too, that in pathological interactions lie the seeds of growth and constructive change.

My emphasis on the patient's curative efforts toward his therapist is not intended to suggest that this dimension of their relationship should be prominent or central to therapy. The therapeutic situation is designed for the patient's needs and should center upon them; however, we should not neglect the potential for adaptive change available to the therapist at those moments (hopefully relatively infrequent) of need. I am aware that I have dealt briefly with many pertinent issues, but hope primarily that I have stimulated fresh considerations of the patient-analyst interaction and its role in impediments and progress in therapy. The spirit of this report is reflected in a quote from Freud (1937, p. 221):

"Instead of an enquiry into how a cure by analysis comes about (a matter which I think has been sufficiently elucidated) the question should be asked, what are the obstacles that stand in the way of such a cure."

NOTES

1. I shall use the terms *therapist* and *analyst* interchangeably here because the segment of the therapeutic relationship that I am investigating is largely (though not entirely) comparable. The clinical data that I can specifically report in this paper are drawn from analytic psychotherapy, though I have made countless comparable observations in the psychoanalytic situation as well.

2. For a variety of reasons, I have made the decision to not use material from my own clinical practice, past and present, in any of my writings. In part, this decision has derived from the observation that such use of one's therapeutic or analytic work entails serious risk of misalliance with the patient (see also Langs 1975b).

REFERENCES

Binstock, W. (1973). The therapeutic relationship. *Journal of the American Psychoanalytic Association* 21:543–557.

Barchilon, J. (1958). On countertransference "cures." *Journal of the American Psychoanalytic Association* 6:222–236.

Corwin, H. (1972). The scope of therapeutic confrontation. *International Journal of Psychoanalytic Psychotherapy* 1(3):68–89.

Dickes, R. (1967). Severe regressive disruptions of the therapeutic alliance. *Journal of the American Psychoanalytic Association* 15:508–533.

Fenichel, O. (1941). *Problems of Psychoanalytic Technique.* New York: Psychoanalytic Quarterly.

Freud, S. (1905). Fragment of an analysis of a case of hysteria. *Standard Edition* 7:3–124.

———(1909). Notes upon a case of obsessional neurosis. *Standard Edition* 10:153–320.

———(1915). Observations on transference-love (further recommendations on the technique of psycho-analysis III). *Standard Edition* 12:157–171.

———(1918). From the history of an infantile neurosis. *Standard Edition* 17:3–122.

———(1937). Analysis terminable and interminable. *Standard Edition* 23:209–253.

Friedman, L. (1969). The therapeutic alliance. *International Journal of Psycho-Analysis* 50:139–154.

Glover, E. (1931). The therapeutic effect of inexact interpretation: a contribution to the theory of suggestion. *International Journal of Psycho-Analysis* 12:397–411.

Greenacre, P. (1959). Certain technical problems in the transference relationship. *Journal of the American Psychoanalytic Association* 7:484–502.

———(1971). *Emotional Growth,* Vol. 2. New York: International Universities Press.

Greenson, R. (1965). The working alliance and the transference neurosis. *Psychoanalytic Quarterly* 34:155–181.

———(1967). *The Technique and Practice of Psychoanalysis,* Vol. 1. New York: International Universities Press.

———(1971). The "real" relationship between the patient and the psychoanalyst. In *The Unconscious Today,* ed. M. Kanzer. New York: International Universities Press.

———(1972). Beyond transference and interpretation. *International Journal of Psycho-Analysis* 53:213–217.

———, and Wexler, M. (1969). The non-transference relationship in the psychoanalytic situation. *International Journal of Psycho-Analysis* 50:27–39.

Kanzer, M. (1975). The therapeutic and working alliances. *International Journal of Psychotherapy* 4:48–68.

Langs, R. (1973a). The patient's view of the therapist: reality or fantasy? *International Journal of Psychoanalytic Psychotherapy* 2:411–431.

————(1973b). *The Technique of Psychoanalytic Psychotherapy,* Vol. 1. New York: Jason Aronson.

————(1974). *The Technique of Psychoanalytic Psychotherapy,* Vol. II. New York: Jason Aronson.

————(1975a). The patient's unconscious perception of the therapist's errors. In *Tactics and Techniques in Psychoanalytic Therapy, Vol. II: Countertransference,* ed. P. Giovacchini. New York: Jason Aronson.

————(1975b). The therapeutic relationship and deviations in technique. *International Journal of Psychoanalytic Psychotherapy* 4:106–141.

————(in press). The misalliance dimension in Freud's case histories. In *Freud and His Patients,* ed. M. Kanzer and J. Glenn. New York: Jason Aronson.

Little, M. (1951). Counter-transference and the patient's response to it. *International Journal of Psycho-Analysis* 32:32–40.

Loewald, H. (1960). On the therapeutic action of psychoanalysis. *International Journal of Psycho-Analysis* 41:16–33.

Myerson, P. (1969). The hysteric's experience in psychoanalysis. *International Journal of Psycho-Analysis* 50:373–384.

————(1973). The establishment and disruption of the psychoanalytic *modus vivendi. International Journal of Psycho-Analysis* 54:133–142.

Nunberg, H. (1926). The will to recovery. *International Journal of Psycho-Analysis* 7:64–78.

————(1955). *Principles of Psychoanalysis.* New York: International Universities Press.

Racker, H. (1968). *Transference and Counter-Transference.* London: Hogarth Press.

Searles, H. (1965). *Collected Papers on Schizophrenia and Related Subjects.* New York: International Universities Press.

————(1975). The patient as therapist to his analyst. In *Tactics and Techniques in Psychoanalytic Therapy, Vol. II: Countertransference,* ed. P. Giovacchini. New York: Jason Aronson.

Sterba, R. (1934). The fate of the ego in analytic therapy. *International Journal of Psycho-Analysis* 15:117–126.

Stone, L. (1961). *The Psychoanalytic Situation.* New York: International Universities Press.

————(1967). The psychoanalytic situation and transference: postscript to an earlier communication. *Journal of the American Psychoanalytic Association* 15:3–58.

Tarachow, S. (1962). Interpretation and reality in psychotherapy. *International Journal of Psycho-Analysis* 43:377–387.

Zetzel, E. (1956). Current concepts of transference. *International Journal of Psycho-Analysis* 37:369–376.

————(1958). Therapeutic alliance in the psychoanalysis of hysteria. In *The Capacity for Emotional Growth,* pp. 197–215. New York: International Universities Press, 1970.

30

THE THERAPEUTIC AND WORKING ALLIANCES

MARK KANZER

EDITOR'S NOTE

This paper by Mark Kanzer includes both a cogent review of the relevant psychoanalytic writings and an important and extended criticism of the fundamental writings of Zetzel and Greenson on this topic. Kanzer clearly indicates the many problems inherent in the definitions of the therapeutic and working alliances offered by these authors, and discusses the dangers these pose to sound analytic technique. Kanzer was among the first analysts to take issue with a number of widespread and uncritically accepted ideas in these areas. While retaining the valuable contributions developed through the alliance concept, he points to the need for caution and for careful psychoanalytic consideration.

This contribution can be supplemented by an early critique of Zetzel's work by Arlow and Brenner (1966) and by a number of discussants who participated with them in the first Pan-American Congress for Psychoanalysis. In addition, a recent contribution by Brenner (1979) covers much of this same territory from another vantage point.

The concepts of the "therapeutic alliance" (Zetzel, 1956) and "working alliance" (Greenson, 1965) are traced in their antecedents to Freud and other analysts and compared especially with Freud's "analytic pact." Differences both in theory and practice are elucidated with the aid of case material. While the therapeutic and working alliances are often used interchangeably, they are found to take up their positions at diametrically opposite points along a continuum defined by the analytic pact and show a marked tendency to depart from the guidance offered the traditional analysis by the fundamental rule. They should be regarded more as exercises in analytically oriented psychotherapy than parameters of the traditional technique. Nevertheless, as a basis for comparisons, it should be recognized that the

Reprinted from *International Journal of Psychoanalytic Psychotherapy* 4:48–73, 1975.

latter technique: (1) does not formulate in theory many of the measures left for pragmatic fulfillment; (2) does not include genetic, structural and adaptive viewpoints that later developments require. Current tendencies to include the analyst's self-observations in relation to the total analytic process point up the growing influence of these more recent considerations.

* * *

The terms "therapeutic alliance" (Zetzel, 1956) and "working alliance" (Greenson, 1965) stress the collaborative, healthy and realistic aspects of the patient-physician relationship during psychoanalysis. In general, these are contrasted with the unrealistic, neurotic, and irrational aspects—more specifically the manifestations of the transference neurosis. Nevertheless, there can be no precise distinction between the two, any more than is possible between health and neurosis. Psychoanalysis above all does justice to the irrational, often looking to it for support of therapeutic goals where these are opposed by the rational side of the patient's personality. Even the patient's antagonism toward therapy, therefore, may play a constructive part in the treatment.

EARLY ALLIANCE CONCEPTS

While the delineation of the alliances is of relatively recent origin and reflects the influence of modern structural and genetic considerations, precursors may be noted from the very beginnings of psychoanalysis. Thus, Freud was already remarking in the *Studies on Hysteria* (Breuer and Freud, 1893–95) that "we make of the patient a collaborator" (p. 282) whose receptivity to insights overcomes resistances. Nevertheless, it was the conflicts and resistances which shaped more of analytic theory, while collaboration was much taken for granted and relegated to pragmatic descriptions. However, it drew recognition in such concepts as "the effective positive transference" (Freud, 1912a, 1913), the "ego alliance" (Sterba, 1934), the "auxiliary superego" (Strachey, 1934), and "analytic atmosphere" (Bibring 1937) and the "analytic pact" (Freud, 1937, 1940).

In tracing the development of the concepts of the alliance, which are considerably at variance with each other as they stress one or another aspect of collaboration, we find it useful to begin with the first specific classification of transference types which Freud undertook in his paper on "The Dynamics of Transference" (1912a). Here he stated:

We must make up our minds to distinguish a "positive" transference from a "negative" one, the transference of affectionate feelings from that of hostile ones, and to treat the two sorts of transference to the doctor separately. Positive transference is then further divisible into transference of friendly or affectionate feelings which are admissible to consciousness and transference of prolongations of those feelings into the unconscious. As regards the latter, analysis shows that they invariably go back to erotic sources. And we are thus led to the discovery that all the emotional relations of sympathy, friendship, trust, and the like, which can be turned to good account in our lives, are genetically linked with sexuality and have developed from purely sexual desires through a softening of their sexual aim, however pure and unsensual they may appear to our conscious self-perception. Originally we knew only sexual objects, and psychoanalysis shows us the people who in our real life are merely admired or respected may still be sexual objects for our unconscious (p. 105).

It is the last form which, in more contemporary descriptions, would be called the sublimated or neutralized aspect of the transference, in contrast to the "untamed" affective or instinctual aspects. Freud defined the "aim-softened" transference as "the vehicle of success in psychoanalysis exactly as it is in other methods of treatment" (p. 105). This is a most significant statement inasmuch as (1) it is repeated in virtually all of his subsequent discussions of the therapeutic process; (2) it specifically links the efficacy of psychoanalysis with the substratum of suggestion which operates in a variety of ways in other forms of therapy:

To this extent we readily admit that the results of psychoanalysis rests upon suggestion; by suggestion, however, we must understand, as Ferenczi (1909) does, the influencing of a person by means of transference phenomena which are possible in his case. We take care of the patient's final independence by employing suggestion in order to get him to accomplish a piece of psychical work which has as its necessary result a permanent improvement in his psychical situation (pp. 105–6).

This latter was to be achieved by the integrative results of making the unconscious conscious. Today, the task would be placed in relation to the structural growth of the personality, so that the "permanent improvement" brought about by the analyst's influence could be compared to maturation brought about under wise parental guidance.

While Freud at the time was primarily concerned with unconscious and libidinal aspects of the personality, he was making advances in his consideration of the parts played by the ego and outer reality in both normal and abnormal states. Ultimately, the various forms of transference would have to be described in structural and phase-specific terms, so that "trust" and "admiration" for the analyst require a fuller description than the semi-metaphorical "softening" of sex drives, while the guidance of the analyst has to be extended beyond suggestion and interpretation of the unconscious to include more specific reality-testing functions for the ego and models for the superego.

Trends in this direction may already be noted in Freud's technical paper, "On Beginning the Treatment" (1913), inasmuch as it sketches not only the patient's transferences from the past, but also the analyst's influence as a professional practitioner and humane individual during the first stage of treatment—an influence which, preceding interpretations, permits the patient to sense the "sympathetic understanding" and the "serious interest" that the physician is prepared to place at his disposal. These attitudes encourage the patient to put the analyst in the category of "people by whom he was accustomed to be treated with affection" (pp. 139–40).

Though this is certainly true, they also help place the analyst in a wider category of useful and more contemporary relationships with other persons and permit preliminary realistic impressions to be formed of his professional methodology, skill, tact and human qualities (see especially Gitelson, 1962, on the testing of the analyst during the first phase of treatment). Moreover, they imply that transferences are not merely spontaneous and endogenous endowments of some blank screen with meaning, but include responses to demonstrations of friendliness and helpfulness from a real person. All interpretations and other interventions by the analyst provide opportunities to convey such attitudes and thereby strengthen the helpful positive transferences.

Almost simultaneously, however, Freud has been recommending neutrality and the famous "mirror technique" on the part of the analyst (1912b), and if he saw contradictions in these precepts, he never indicated as much. Presumably he had in mind neither an automaton in the analyst's chair, nor a concerned mother, nor even a personal friend. He seems rather to have envisioned a professionally realistic and humane basis of operations for the development of a flexible relationship which enables the patient to explore the many images stored in his unconscious that seek projection on to the analyst. The latter in turn acquires freedom for a variety of responses which keep him in close touch with the patient's mental processes on different levels. A "real" friend or relative makes a poor analyst; so does a coldly detached investigator.

The analyst's theoretical orientation as well as his personality enter into the choice of levels he maintains with the patient. Entire eras of analytic history have been marked by predilections for unconscious communication between the therapeutic collaborators or for intellectual alliances that will propagate insight. Although ego psychology has been considered prone to further the latter, we find that its most eminent exponents have never overlooked the unconscious core of the patient-physician relationship and have underlined the need to keep this in mind in formulating both the theoretical and pragmatic course of the analytic process. Thus Heinz Hartmann was careful to point out that

Freud was admittedly and intentionally rather restrained in formulating technical rules; and we are still far from dispensing a collection of technical prescriptions that would cover every given situation. . . . In teaching one must avoid giving the student the impression that actually a complete set of rules exists [1951, pp. 32–33].

Ernst Kris (1951) suggested that it was the "personal equation" of the analyst which determined the degree to which he permitted scope for his unconscious in relating to the patient and cited instances in which his own intuition had guided him more surely to a correct interpretation than had his conscious reasoning. At the same time, however, he warned of the desirability of coupling intuition with self-analysis. Robert Waelder's approach to the neutrality-humanitarian controversy was to remark that "Freud took it for granted, if not explicitly stated, that the analyst has a human helpful attitude—that this is ego-syntonic for the analyst" (1958, p. 563).

Precepts about neutrality are thus to be reconciled with warm interest, humanness and the close affective bonds of empathy and intuition. However, the functions of a therapeutic alliance are not limited to positive feelings or to reason on either side. The analytic rituals and particularly the maintenance of the fundamental rule call for discipline and abstinence for both partners, for re-education of the patient and for the assumption of responsibilities by the physician that are definitely of a parental nature. This extends to control over behavior in the external world and cautioning against major decisions, though

one willingly leaves untouched as much of the patient's personal freedom as is compatible with these restrictions, nor does one hinder him from carrying out unimportant intentions, even if they are foolish; one does not forget that it is in fact only through his own experience and mishaps that a person learns sense [Freud, 1914, p. 153].

The model evoked here suggests a permissive but responsible parent contemplating an adolescent whose conduct is not likely to create serious problems. Regression to still earlier levels of the parent-child relationship are then fostered within the analytic situation itself:

The main instrument, however, for curbing the patient's compulsion to repeat and for turning it into a motive for remembering lies in the handling of the transference.

We render the compulsion harmless, and indeed useful, by giving it the right to assert itself in a definite field. We admit it into the transference as a playground in which it is allowed to expand in almost complete freedom and in which it is expected to display to us everything in the way of pathogenic instincts that is hidden in the patient's mind. Provided only that the patient shows *compliance enough to respect the necessary conditions of the analysis,* we regularly succeed in giving all the symptoms of the illness a new transference meaning and in replacing his ordinary neurosis by a "transference-neurosis" of which he can be cured by the therapeutic work [Freud, 1914; p. 154. Italics mine].

The eventful introduction of the concept of the transference neurosis is coupled with and dependent upon the transference alliance. Now the stage is set for childhood memories to be acted out in the presence of the analyst. To be sure, by such "acting out," Freud had in mind especially the formation of fantasies on the couch which could be granted verbal and to a limited degree, affective expression. It is in confronting these fantasies with his own "real self" (humane and understanding but not involved like the original prototype of the transference) that the "neutrality" of the analyst and his mirror technique prove of such great value. In this sense, his self-restraint should also be seen as a contribution to the therapeutic alliance. Thus the transference neurosis and the behavior of the analyst are also inextricably intertwined and dependent on each other.

The 1914 formulation is carried over virtually intact, but with structural elaborations, into Freud's account of the "analytic pact" a generation later (1937, 1940). Here the "normal ego" of the patient is defined by his ability to adhere to the fundamental rule, i.e., to verbalize without reservation all the contents of his mind (free association). The neurotic portion of the personality demands, however, different forms of alliance with the analyst as parent, lover, financial adviser, etc. These demands the analyst utilizes for his own therapeutic purposes. "If the patient puts the analyst in the place of his father (or mother), he is also giving him the powers which his superego exercises over his ego," Freud observed, "since his parents were, as we know, the origin of his superego. The new superego now has an opportunity for a sort of *after-education* of the neurotic; it can correct mistakes for which his parents were responsible in educating him" (1940, p. 175; italics Freud's). Thus the analyst undertakes not only to revive the memories of the past but to promote a new growth of the personality in which he functions as an enlightened parent.

Such re-education was to take place in the course of teaching the patient to overcome the resistances

and encounter with understanding and tolerance the natural impulses that parents had originally condemned. Typically, however, Freud warned the analyst (in an apparent extension of the neutrality concept) not to be carried away by a proprietary attitude and zeal for the patient's welfare:

However much the analyst may be tempted to become a teacher, model and ideal for other people and to create men in his own image, he should not forget that it is not his task in the analytic relationship, and indeed that he will be disloyal to his task, if he allows himself to be led on by his inclinations. If he does, he will only be repeating a mistake of the parents who crushed their child's independence by their influence and he will only be replacing the patient's earlier dependence by a new one. In all his attempts at improving and educating the patient the analyst should respect his individuality. The amount of influence which he may legitimately allow himself will be determined by the amount of developmental inhibition present in the patient.

Apparently this may be considerable, for he adds a cryptic comment: "Some neurotics have remained so infantile that in analysis too they can only be treated as children" (p. 175).

The permissiveness and respect for the individuality of the patient that Freud demanded were deeply ingrained in his own code of human rights and may well be seen, in a larger context, as part of the liberal and middle-class outlook of his youth. He was unusually self-reliant, of course, in following his own destiny and even revolutionary in re-educating patients so that their perspectives included his feelings on the unconscious and sex. The expectation that the very removal of restraints would promote normal growth, a view resembling Rousseau's ideas about natural man, underlies such cornerstones of psychoanalytic practice as free association, permissiveness toward milder forms of acting out, and neutrality. If it is correct, however, that the patient has regressed to oedipal and pre-oedipal phases of development, is it to be expected that the process of maturation, to be undertaken anew, now calls for permissiveness such as Freud envisions or more active functioning as "a teacher, model and ideal?" Are the mistakes of the parents limited to crushing the child's independence or their failure to fulfill these positive needs?

Relevant here is the conception Freud outlines in the *Introductory Lectures on Psychoanalysis* (1916–17) of the actual progress of re-education as seen in the analytic setting: "If the patient is to fight his way through the normal conflict which we have uncovered for him in the analysis [i.e., *after* the unconscious has been made conscious] he is in need of a powerful stimulus which will influence the decision *in the sense which we desire, leading to recovery"* (p. 445; italics mine). I have underlined here the analyst's sense of commitment to therapeutic aims, as Freud distinguished it from therapeutic zeal. "At this point, what turns the scale in his struggle is not his intellectual insight—which is neither strong enough nor free enough for such achievement—but simply and solely his relation to the doctor" (p. 445).

This relationship, through the freeing of libido from the original parents, has become all the stronger. The analyst becomes a "new object" (p. 455) who mediates the libido centered in himself into new channels of direct satisfaction and sublimation. While Freud did not actually make this point, it seems likely that the "harmless acting out" toward which the analyst assumes a benign stand must also include, in the form of working through, belated efforts to acquire experiences that would normally have gone with earlier stages of maturation. To be able to place these in the developmental scale through appropriate constructions would offer a more dynamic approach than merely to contemplate them with indulgence (Kanzer, 1966).

There is, for example, the not uncommon situation in which a patient neurotically relives the past in relation to his own wife and child. From unconscious incestuous motives toward the former and counteroedipal rivalry with the latter, he advances toward a belated superego formation under the aegis of the "new object" relationship to the analyst. His own father's "mistake" had been a failure, as a passive person, to provide companionship and leadership. Now the patient began to act out constructive fantasies in relation to the father, as mobilized in the analytic relationship, by giving his son companionship and leadership that had been denied him at a comparable period in his own life. Such indirect "re-education" for himself required no special "fathering" attitudes on the part of the analyst beyond his interpretation of the significant new behavior toward the son.

We learn more of the "new object" aspect of the analyst, as might be expected, from the experiences of child analysts. Anna Freud finds that the latter must serve in a double capacity, not only representing the urge to repeat the past that is so prominent in the transference of adults, but also a "hunger for new experiences" that is equally strong and demanding on the therapist (1965, p. 32). (In the case just described, the patient was, of course, in a better position than a child to seek out means for acquiring new experiences.) The "mistakes of the parents"

must often be rectified by their own treatment before a genuine re-education can take place. For the child analyst, however, it is a typical experience that "a therapeutic method is assigned a task which, by rights, should be carried out on the one hand by the ego and on the other by the parents of the child" (A. Freud, 1965, p. 218).

Anna Freud, proceeding to review from this standpoint traditional analytic goals and methods with adults, places them in a broader framework than is often customary.

All authors writing on the subject (of adult analysis) agree that more elements are contained in the analytic method than the *interpretation* of transference and resistance, the *widening of consciousness* at the expense of the unconscious parts of id, ego and superego, and the consequent increase in *ego dominance"* (p. 227; italics Freud's).

Anna Freud lists verbalization, clarification, suggestion, education, corrective emotional experiences and reassurance, with the analyst able to function through these instruments as the "new object" that will foster maturation (see also Bibring, 1954, on the curative forces in psychoanalysis). Then, following lines of thought we have already encountered, she points out that while the classical analyst is taught to rely as little as possible on noninterpretative mechanisms, the choice in the end may lie not so much with the physician as with the patient. She quotes Sigmund Freud as saying: "We may treat a neurotic in any way we like, he always treats himself with transferences" (p. 228). The delineation of transference as a potentially creative force abetted by relationships to parents and analysts may be found in a study by Loewald, 1960.

In summary, then, we find that early formulations of the therapeutic alliance, such as the "effective positive transference," recognized a broad scheme of interactions by means of which patient and analyst influenced each other in arriving at common therapeutic goals, reproducing in this way forces between parent and child generated through maturation, and providing opportunities for a beneficial outcome of previous failures in the maturational processes. Nor should we overlook "effective negative transferences," which in treatment as in real life find solution in constructive individual and social patternings of aggressive drives. We certainly cannot agree with the formula that the patient "must retain maximal basic trust" in the analyst (Zetzel, 1966, p. 100). This would in fact retain suggestibility. The patient should become better able to find the reasons for and tolerate distrust while gradually replacing trust in the analyst by trust in himself.

THE THERAPEUTIC ALLIANCE

It is not surprising that analysts with backgrounds in child observation and child analysis have made important contributions to elucidation of the after-education which takes place in the course of adult analysis. Thus in 1956, Spitz put forward new conceptions of countertransference that supplemented Zetzel's ideas about the therapeutic alliance, published the same year. Whereas notions of countertransference had usually assumed a pejorative note, suggesting distortions of the analytic attitude as the result of intrusion of personal feelings, Spitz pointed out that empathy and intuition also required the ability to counteridentify on an affective level with the patient. He therefore distinguished between primitive and uncontrolled countertransferences and more sublimated forms that played a constructive part in the treatment (much as Freud had done with the transferences). He further compared the patient to a "helpless infant" with anaclitic needs to which the analyst responded with "diatrophic" (maternally supporting) attitudes. This "dyad" permitted the analyst to regress with the patient but to maintain controls for himself that would ultimately assist his collaborator in establishing similar controls. To act out the diatrophic attitude was to court countertransference reactions in the adverse sense. While the "helplessness" of a patient does not necessarily bear comparison with an infant's, the continuum which Spitz postulated between human sympathy and neutrality seems quite useful in bringing together the connections between the two attitudes.

Elizabeth Zetzel accepted the anaclitic diatropic dyad as did Gitelson (1962), who did not limit it to the infant-mother model but felt that the analyst could and indeed should express adequate supportive feelings in the treatment. While she, like most analysts, found the focus of the therapeutic alliance in the mature ego of the patient, she constructed a theorem that such maturity was to be found only where a good object relationship had been formed in infancy. Where the latter condition was lacking (which seemed usually to be the case), the first phases of treatment elicited genuine anxiety, rather than transferences, in the patient, and intuitive supportive reactions on the part of the analyst were required for a therapeutic alliance to be formed. In further amplification of her views, Zetzel came to see the entire course of analysis as closely paralleling stages of maturation, with different phase-specific types of support necessary to maintain the alliance. Thus the latter had to be dealt with separately from the transference neurosis (1966).

Criticisms were inevitably forthcoming from exponents of traditional views about adult analysis. Their objections included: (1) rejection of the notion that there were any simple analogies to be drawn between stages of treatment and of normal maturation—indeed, there is much to suggest the opposite trend, with the slow relinquishment of established defenses; (2) criticisms of the disposition to invoke genetic explanations that are difficult to validate and to overlook later factors in the complex determination of behavior; (3) the argument that confusion is bound to arise through alternations between neutrality directed to the unraveling of the transference neurosis and a series of interventions to support the therapeutic alliance (Arlow and Brenner, 1966; Rangell, 1969; Modell, 1972). (Actually, the analytic pact which Freud developed related the neurosis to deflections from the analytic rule which was supported by the normal ego [1940, p. 173]; this provides for an organic unity that is prone to be overlooked in more recent formulations about the "alliances." It is quite true, however, that traditional analysis, emphasizing the resistances and defenses, left the collaborative aspects and especially the intrusion of external determinants in relative obscurity.)

It was a foremost contention of Elizabeth Zetzel that only on the level of nonverbal contacts could early formations of the personality be reached, but Anna Freud felt that such aspirations were not to be fulfilled by analytic methods:

The therapeutic alliance between analyst and patient is not carried by any of these earlier stages of object-relationship, although all these earlier stages are "material." The therapeutic alliance is based, I believe, on ego-attitudes that go with later stages, namely, on self-observation, insight, give-and-take in object-relationships, the willingness to make sacrifices. It is the oedipal relationship which offers those advantages; thus, it serves as material for interpretations, as well as for cementing the alliance between analyst and patient [1962, p. 192].

(I believe that the normal adult ego best fits the qualifications mentioned, while "cement" could presumably be provided by preoedipal as well as oedipal strivings. However, it would be very difficult to demonstrate either in pure culture among the multidetermined factors in adult behavior.)

Zetzel's constructs are bolstered by ample and fascinating clinical material which permits the reader to apply his own experience and draw independent conclusions — a rarity in a science that acknowledgedly finds difficulty in presenting its complicated case histories. In several areas one may take issue with Zetzel. One case (selected because it illustrates with particular clarity cardinal assumptions of Zetzel) describes a young woman who began treatment with an inexperienced candidate. Unfavorable developments are compared with the reactions of a newborn child maladroitly handled by an inexperienced mother (1966).

During the first session on the couch, the patient recalled as an initial communication a recent experience in which she had been part of an audience attending a conference of distinguished psychologists. It had occurred to her that to these sophisticated speakers, the audience must seem pathetic and full of "crackpots." Associations went on to her own passive nature and a rejecting mother who "hoarded" things from her. I agree with Zetzel that the patient gives an impression of anxiety when confronted with the analytic situation and that we do receive preliminary glimpses of the mother-child relationship which do not yet permit interpretation. Where an area of difference and some mystification now opens is in the vague alternative Zetzel advocates: "What I am suggesting rather, is that some activity on the part of the analyst which would convey to the patient that he was not a 'hoarder' would have fostered the development of a secure working relationship" (p. 96).

From the word "hoarder" as verbal bridge the patient now went off in an entirely different direction and brought up the subject of the fee, which she regarded as too high. With only moderate displacement she mentioned a printer whom she told off angrily when he sent an outrageously high bill. Then there was a long pause; I would agree with Zetzel's conclusion that it indicated "anger at the analyst, combined with fears of rejection" and transference "anxieties relevant to situations in which she had not felt free to protest" (p. 96).

Apparently the candidate did not respond, and it is difficult to know whether the allusion to the desirability of showing he was not a hoarder had reference to decreasing the fee. Certainly the gap between this and the implication of appropriate interventions by a breast-mother is great. In any event, an impasse seems to have developed, with the patient reverting to the same type of material and the candidate (perhaps with an eye on the supervisor) remaining silent. Finally (probably under supervisory prodding) he adopted "a slightly more active and human attitude,

indicating to the patient his recognition of her anxiety. As a result, the patient reported that until yesterday she had thought of the analyst as a distant, Olympian, somewhat magical figure. If, for example, he were taking notes, these must be written on a special pad, with a special pen which would make no noise. Now she realized that this picture had been fantastic. He was, after all, an ordinary man. If he were taking notes, it would be on an ordinary pad with ordinary pen" (pp. 96–97).

Zetzel draws conclusions very fundamental for her theorems: (1) there is a comparison between the ineptitude of the candidate and that of an inexperienced mother; (2) the patient thereupon regressed and endowed the therapist with primitive magic such as might have been exercised by an omnipotent mother; (3) the candidate's warmer participation encouraged a return to reality (he was an "ordinary man"). She makes the point that warm intuitive responses are needed prior to interpretations in order to launch a therapeutic alliance, just as they are needed to promote good object relationships between mother and child.

Such conclusions do not seem to be in accord with the actual material. An analytic pact is not in operation merely because an individual sits behind a couch. To be meaningful, it requires a competent analyst or, in the case of an inexperienced candidate, the ability to transmit auxiliary competence. The mother-child model seems to have been introduced one-sidedly and with little evidence; the patient herself had stressed in her first associations her professional inadequacy to judge the proceedings as compared to the supposed equipment of the therapist. Trust, under such circumstances, is not limited to the basic trust of an infant. The analytic situation in particular makes reality-testing on the part of the patient difficult; presumably the analyst has realistic reasons which he is not prepared to communicate.

The patient did indeed fix on a realistic problem, the fee, which called for some definite response rather than warm and intuitive signs of maternal understanding. The kindly "acknowledgment" of the patient's "infantile" anxiety, after long delay, seems condescending and gratuitously assumes that a display of motherliness will be an adequate substitute for correct procedures. Moreover, the patient's own verbalized associations point in other directions. The analyst is endowed in her fantasies not with breast-equivalents but with a "magic pen" whose phallic implications are sufficiently familiar to warrant consideration. Feminine masochism was suggested by the opening communication concerning well-equipped psychologists looking down upon a "crackpot" (vaginal symbol?) like herself. The displacement of his demands to the economic issue should also be taken into account. We feel justified in suggesting that the period of the impasse was sustained for the patient by masturbatory fantasies and that the reaction to the "kindliness" of the analyst—i.e., that he was merely an "ordinary man"—combined disappointment and a growing capacity to confront him with her misgivings about his therapeutic capacities.

In more than one respect, this case and its management lead ideally into a consideration of Greenson's "working alliance," which is very different, in a remarkably complementary way, from Zetzel's "therapeutic alliance," though many (including the principals) have used the terms interchangeably.

THE WORKING ALLIANCE

Greenson's stress is on the realistic and nontransference aspects of the patient-physician relationship, which are all too often submerged in one-sided considerations of the transferences. Thus presumably Greenson would have taken up the fee situation quite realistically in the last case. (While justified, it would have been oversimple, however, to ignore transference elements which were becoming enmeshed with it.) Greenson would be on safe enough ground in suggesting that some analysts lean too exclusively toward transference interpretations (Zetzel's candidate does not appear to give weight to the implied justification for believing that the fee was indeed rather high). He might also argue that analytic methodology itself weighs the scales toward the side of inner rather than outer reality. However, commentators have raised the question whether Greenson himself does not lean in the other direction (Zetzel, 1969; Rangell, 1969; Heimann, 1970).

Thus Greenson, writing in collaboration with Wexler, seems to take as a target some ultrapurist image of an analyst oriented exclusively to transference and limiting his pronouncements to interpretations:

The technique of "only analysing" or "only interpreting" transference phenomena may stifle the development and clarification of the transference neurosis and act as an obstacle to the maturation of the transference-free or "real" reactions of the patient. . . . It is also important to deal with the non-transference interactions between patient and analyst" [1969, p. 28].

I have seen an analysis almost founder because the analyst demanded his fee for sessions missed quite early in treatment because of the death of a close relative. His own guilt emerged in very unsatisfactory explanations he gave the patient and the assurance that associations would reveal her "fantasies."

Actually, transference must always arise in the context of reality. Interpretations separate fantasy from reality and automatically enhance reality-testing. The analyst cannot make a valid interpretation unless he is well acquainted with the patient's current as well as past realities. The comment: "You treat your wife as though she were your mother" must rest upon observable facts of everyday life and should result in a more realistic treatment of the wife as well as clearer insight into past relationships to the mother. A similar differentiation should be promoted by the observation: "You expect me to behave like your mother"—a step toward reality-testing which will probably be more difficult to make if the analyst does in fact behave like a mother.

Greenson's demand that the analyst "recognize, acknowledge, clarify, differentiate, and even nurture the non-transference or relatively transference-free reactions between patient and analyst" (p. 27) seems to go beyond this bipolar aspect of interpretations to deal with actual reality, so that, as Heimann puts it, the working alliance embodies a demand for "not analyzing certain sectors of the patient-analyst relationship" (1970, p. 145). Greenson himself acknowledges difficulties in this definition of "reality" (Greenson and Wexler, 1970, p. 149). As a clinical example, he offers the case of Kevin who, in an angry outburst, criticized him as overtalkative, given to exaggeration, and likely to be hurt if told such personal truths (Greenson and Wexler, 1969, p. 28). Greenson felt that this called for the direct acknowledgment that the patient was correct, a measure which he regarded as strengthening the latter's reality-testing as well as the working alliance between them. "Acknowledging that the patient was right in his criticism was certainly unanalytical," he avers, but will further the development of the analysis.

What is controversial here is not so much the acknowledgment that a patient may be correct in realistic criticisms of the analyst or the acknowledgment on the analyst's part that he is at fault—to do otherwise may well be "unanalytical"—but rather the oversimplified way in which the problem is presented. The traditional analytic response might well have been: "You are aware that you should voice all thoughts that come to mind. Direct criticisms of the analyst are among the most difficult to express but you will find it rewarding to do so." The principle of unsuppressed communication and the tolerance of the analyst for such criticisms of himself seem valuable modes of reality-testing and cementing the working alliance; they do not necessarily preclude, if there is a special indication to do so, the more specific acknowledgment that Greenson undertook in this case.

Moreover, we are given no adequate reason that Kevin chose this time, after more than four years, to find his analyst's traits intolerable. We do learn that his outburst followed an interpretation, but learn nothing of the interpretation or of the ultimate working through after the discussion of the analyst's shortcomings. It is a familiar enough tendency, even outside the analytic situation, to respond to a criticism with an attack, and to seek to promote "flights into reality" by diverting attention from the self. The clinical wisdom of selecting the attack on the analyst for attention under such circumstances cannot be judged without data on the transference and the interpretation. Any suggestion that only the former is worthy of consideration, or should necessarily receive priority, would indeed be unanalytical. The analyst traditionally considers and balances both possibilities, not one alone.

There is no question, however, that both the notions of the therapeutic alliance and the working alliance have stirred analysts to reappraisal of themselves and their methods, and to this extent have been beneficial. There is, for example, the recent study by Olinick et al. (1973), which portrays "the analyst at work" (p. 142). The authors draw on Fliess (1942) in describing the "temporarily built-up person who (functions) under the circumstances and for the period of his work—defined in terms of therapeutic function" (p. 225). The work ego is further defined as a relatively stable and autonomous group of functions which operates in a matrix of empathy, uses trial identifications, is motivated by curiosity and diatrophic interests and finds expression in interpretations and other therapeutic interventions.

Olinick and his co-workers further search out the functions of the analyst which serve these purposes (observing, experiencing, etc.) as they are influenced by the analytic process. They postulate that his own regressive pulls in the direction of cognitive and affective feedback pose threats to the maintenance of the therapeutic alliance which disturb the work ego and the superego–ego-ideal monitoring system that has been prepared for its task by personal analysis and training. The "primary data"

of the work ego includes the analyst's self-observations. These emit signals that influence him in a continuum ranging from empathy to intellectual insight. Interpretations resolve the tensions not only of the patient but also of the analyst, and thus restore the therapeutic alliance (cf. Spitz, 1956; Loewald, 1960).

The laudable tendency to present detailed material not only from the patient's case history but from the therapist's responses, as part of the dyadic concept of the alliances, also leads to self-scrutiny in this instance. One vignette describes a twenty-six-year-old male patient who alternately wept and berated the analyst as he relived a period during which his father deserted the family. The analyst became aware of

a strange physical sensation in his arms, related to tenderness, but not quite a tender feeling. He said to the patient, "You are wanting me to take you in my arms." The patient relaxed on the couch and said, "Yes." After a moment of silence, he began to talk about his affection for his father, and his yearning for an affectionate relationship with an older man" (p. 147).

The analyst's response seems here closer to Zetzel, who called for intuitive demonstrations of warmth, than to that of Spitz, who warned against overt introduction of countertransference material into the sessions. The analyst had his misgivings, as he recounts, which he sought to overcome by discussions with students and colleagues, and later in the more daring form of a publication. I am not in a position to form a definite opinion, but certainly the procedure described above departed from the well-founded rule that interpretations shall be made only when the patient is on the threshold of discovering them for himself. Instead, it is the analyst's self-discovery that is invoked for this purpose with the tacit assumption that his trial identification (Fliess, 1942) with the patient is actually valid. We do not find convincing evidence that this is the case and the subsequent calming of the patient may represent not so much a restoration of the therapeutic alliance as a seduction and a stifling of the inherent trends of his thoughts and feelings. To be sure, the trial identifications of an experienced analyst may be closer to the inner events of the patient's mind than can be translated into words. The dangers we have mentioned, however, cannot be readily discounted. To apply Spitz's admonitions, could not the "intuition" of the analyst have been kept in mind as an orienting device until the course of the patient's associations had more distinctly verified his surmise?

Such validation is more precisely offered by Robert Langs in a study of the mirroring through the patient's reactions of the therapist's errors (in press). He leaves the strict boundaries of the analytic situation and in fact describes the supervision of inexperienced therapists from this standpoint (without limiting himself to the early mother-child framework!). Thus, a young man who had lost his wife and children through divorce repeatedly bemoaned his fate. The therapist just as repeatedly took note of the disposition to blame others, with severe damage to the therapeutic and working alliances as well as to the course of treatment. The recognition that the patient was actually seeking his sympathy proved a more effective lever in treating him.

Here too a self-observing signal might have assisted the therapist in correcting negative counter-transference reactions — a function which the supervisor had to take over (and indeed a regular task of supervisors). In analysis, the inexperienced therapist is likely to use such experiences to promote his own self-understanding. Langs makes the point that awareness of certain typical reactions on the part of the patient will assist the therapist in detecting his own errors. Signs that he mentions include affective disturbances, symptoms, and associations immediately after the error, such as references to blind and insensitive persons. Later there may be acting out, recourse to drugs between sessions, coming late, and discouragement with the treatment process. There are also predictive potentials in the ability to compare alternative therapeutic constructions with the reactions to their use.

"Mirroring" by the patient need not be limited, of course, to the errors of the analyst and may offer unexpected vistas into the process of therapy, especially where the classical method, with its potentials for revealing the finer nuances of transferences, is not in use. In one such instance a business executive treated by the reviewer, fifty years old, rejecting analysis, came for a modified form of treatment (twice a week, sitting up) that evolved essentially into an abreactive and counseling relationship. He was motivated most by a fear of airplanes, and worries and hypochondriacal symptoms that in effect kept him chained to his desk. Here he surrounded himself with "yes-men" whose work he supervised so closely that he preferred to do it himself, sending his assistants on the travels and holidays that he had to renounce for himself. Nevertheless, he felt imposed upon and smoldered with anger in the midst of the vicious cycle his neurosis had created.

Progress followed the reconstruction of a situation in his youth when his father had assumed a similar position in the office while he and his brother had been kept from developing their abilities and sent off instead for travels and vacations. On one such holiday, which the patient shared with a girlfriend, he suddenly received word that his father had been stricken with a heart attack which ultimately proved fatal. On his way home, when he flew for the first time, the patient experienced his initial dread of airplane travel. It had also emerged that the treatment began as the patient was approaching the age at which the father died and quite consciously, if superstitiously, anticipated a similar end for himself. Little was said of transference reactions, but the material, even on a superficial level, was enlightening.

When the patient had outlived his father, he ventured one day to inform the therapist that he planned a vacation to begin the following week. As he said nothing of his feelings about the interruption of the treatment, it was considered essential to bring them up before his departure. "I am sure *you* will not like it," he remarked in this connection. Since the therapist had often counseled such holidays, he expressed surprise (actually, no arrangements had ever been made for fees to be paid under such circumstances). "You will be remaining hard at work here," the patient continued, quite seriously. "How can you want me to be off enjoying myself?" This comment unexpectedly opened vistas into an underlying transference which illuminated feelings of guilt toward the father, unrealistic aspects of the patient-therapist relationship, and the significance of the patient's attitude toward his own assistants. Such a flash of transference, properly understood, illuminated the therapeutic and working alliances that had been established, and proved them to be facades covering the more powerful fantasies that actually guided the course of treatment. "In the last resort, the choice of therapeutic process does not seem to lie with [the therapists' intentions] but with their patients" (Anna Freud, 1965, p. 228).

COMMENTARY

Historically and functionally, the therapeutic and working alliances continue traditional tendencies in psychoanalysis, but highlight areas that have often been left for pragmatic solution or have not been sufficiently brought into line with the implications of child development, structural psychology and the adaptive framework.

Analytic therapy, evolving from hypnosis and from the doctrines of cathartic therapy (each invoking its own therapeutic and working alliances), placed emphasis on the recovery of traumatic memories, most especially in the sphere of infantile sexuality. Attention was directed accordingly to the inner boundaries between the patient's unconscious and consciousness (the topographic framework). The analyst functioned as a "censor" directing the search inwardly for the elusive memory, interpreting its manifestations and persuading the patient with his superego authority to permit its passage into consciousness. In line with these efforts, he was an educator with respect to mental processes and an instructor as to the psychology of sexual life.

The discovery of transference diminished the distance between the patient and the analyst, drawing attention to the latter's current and multiple implications in representing the very memories that were the objects of search. A key instrument in differentiating the past from the present, and fantasy from reality, was provided by the analyst's demonstrable neutrality (Freud, 1915). Nevertheless, other roles assigned the analyst were not compatible with neutrality—an inconsistency inherent not so much in the limitations of technique as in the complexities of life. Transference itself was no merely endogenous reflection of the past but was influenced by displays of interest and sympathy, the analyst's capacity for empathy and insight, and constant interactions between the analytic partners on a hierarchy of levels and in a complex and ever-changing context of past and present determinants.

The ultimate model of the transference relationship has to be the experience of realistic interactions with parents and with other individuals and situations in the past during the course of maturation, as extended into behavior in the present and anticipatory reactions to the future. Transference from the past is not limited to the re-enactment of the preoedipal or oedipal phases but extends to the "hunger for new experiences" that entered into the constitution of "new objects" and also of new self-representations. Freud's concept of Eros (1920) seeking unprecedented combinations, as compared to a death drive demanding a return to the past, requires this more dynamic concept of transference and the analyst's role in mediating transitions to the future.

The indispensable organizer of these various interactions for purposes of analytic therapy remained, throughout the history of psychoanalysis, the use of the fundamental rule. Whereas, in earlier days, the resistances received foremost consideration and the areas of collaboration were much taken for granted, the therapeutic and working alliances have come to focus on the latter. Concomitantly, however, they often seem to seek autonomy in their own right rather than recognize their inherent connections with the substratum of past analytic experience. Moreover, applications of an analytic orientation beyond the traditional boundaries of the classical situation foster such tendencies and call for greater integration between the treatment of adults, adolescents, and children as guided by a variety of experiences within a wide framework of therapeutic conditions. Conversely, the curative forces mobilized within the classical situation are by no means exhausted or understood merely by detailing the analytic process in relation to resistances and their interpretations.

While research in the future seems likely to extend the continuity between the classical analytic and other analytically oriented forms of treatment, the maintenance of the fundamental rule in the former appears to be a necessary control if confusion is not to become synonymous with a self-conscious "humane" viewpoint, with injudicious experiments that give free rein to "intuition" and with loosely conceived exercises in "reality-testing."

REFERENCES

Arlow, J. and Brenner, C. (1966): Discussion: The psychoanalytic situation. In *Psychoanalysis in the Americas*, ed. R. E. Litman, pp. 133–138. New York: International Universities Press.

Bibring, E. (1937): Therapeutic results of psychoanalysis. *International Journal of Psycho-Analysis*, 18:170–189.

———(1954): Psychoanalysis and the dynamic psychotherapies. *Journal of the American Psychoanalytic Association*, 2:745–770.

Breuer, J. and Freud, S. (1893–95): *Studies on Hysteria*. Standard Ed., 2.

Ferenczi, S. (1909): Introjection and transference. In *Sex in Psychoanalysis*, pp. 35–93. New York: Basic Books, 1950.

Fliess, R. (1942): The metapsychology of the analyst. *Psychoanalytic Quarterly*, 11:211–227.

Freud, A. (1962): The theory of the parent-child relationship. In *The Writings of Anna Freud*, 5:187–193. New York: International Universities Press, 1969.

———(1965): *Normality and Pathology in Childhood*. New York: International Universities Press.

Freud, S. (1912a): The dynamics of transference. *Standard Ed.*, 12:97–108.

————(1912b): Recommendations to physicians practising psychoanalysis. *Ibid.*, pp. 109–120.

————(1913): On beginning the treatment. *Ibid.*, pp. 121–144.

————(1914): *Remembering, repeating and working through. Ibid.*, pp. 145–156.

————(1915): Observations on transference love. *Ibid.*, pp. 157–171.

————(1916–17): *Introductory Lectures on Psychoanalysis. Standard Ed.*, 16:431–447.

————(1920): *Beyond the Pleasure Principle. Standard Ed.*, 18:7–64.

————(1937): Analysis terminable and interminable. *Standard Ed.*, 23:216–253.

————(1940): *An Outline of Psychoanalysis. Ibid.*, pp. 147–207.

Gitelson, M. (1962): The curative factors in psychoanalysis. *International Journal of Psychoanalysis*, 43:194–205.

Greenson, R. (1965): The working alliance and the transference neurosis. *Psychoanalytic Quarterly*, 34:155–181.

———— and Wexler, M. (1969): The non-transference relationship in the psychoanalytic situation. *International Journal of Psychoanalysis*, 50:27–39.

————(1970): Discussion: The non-transference relationship in the psychoanalytic situation. *International Journal of Psychoanalysis*, 51:143–150.

Hartmann, H. (1951): Technical implications of ego psychology. *Psychoanalytic Quarterly*, 20:31–43.

Heimann, P. (1970): Discussion: The non-transference relationship in the psychoanalytic situation. *International Journal of Psycho-Analysis*, 51:143–150.

Kanzer, M. (1966): The motor sphere of the transference. *Psychoanalytic Quarterly*, 35:522–539.

Kris, E. (1951): Ego psychology and interpretation in psychoanalytic therapy. *Psychoanalytic Quarterly*, 20:15–30.

Langs, R. (1973): The patient's unconscious perception of the therapist's errors. In: *Tactics and Techniques in Psychoanalytic Therapy*, ed. P. Giovacchini. New York: Jason Aronson.

Loewald, H. (1960): On the therapeutic action of psychoanalysis. *International Journal of Psycho-Analysis*, 41:16–33.

Modell, A. (1972): Book Review: E. R. Zetzel, *The Capacity for Emotional Growth. Psychoanalytic Quarterly*, 41:261–265.

Olinick, S., Poland, W., Grigg, K., and Granatir, W. (1973): The psychoanalytic work ego: Process and interpretation. *International Journal of Psycho-Analysis*, 54:143–152.

Rangell, L. (1969): The intrapsychic process and its interpretation. *International Journal of Psycho-Analysis*, 50:65–78.

Spitz, R. (1956): Countertransference. *Journal of the American Psychoanalytic Association*, 4:256–265.

Sterba, R. (1934): The fate of the ego in analytic therapy. *International Journal of Psycho-Analysis*, 15:117–125.

Strachey, J. (1934): The nature of the therapeutic action of psychoanalysis. *International Journal of Psycho-Analysis*, 15:127–159.

Waelder, R. (1958): Panel: Technical aspects of transference. Reporter: D. Leach. *Journal of the American Psychoanalytic Association*, 6:563.

Zetzel, E. (1956): Current concepts of transference. *International Journal of Psycho-Analysis*, 37:369–376.

————(1966): The analytic situation. In *Psychoanalysis in the Americas*, ed. R. Litman, pp. 86–106. New York: International Universities Press.

————(1969): Book review: R. Greenson. *The Technique and Practice of Psychoanalysis. International Journal of Psycho-Analysis*, 50:411–412.

PART VI

THE THERAPEUTIC INTERACTION

There is a clear and significant trend among psychoanalysts of all backgrounds toward a growing appreciation of the implications of the analytic and therapeutic interactions. In its broadest form, this adaptational-interactional approach takes into account transference and nontransference, as well as countertransference and non-countertransference, and in addition considers the sphere of the therapeutic alliance and the framework of the therapeutic situation. It is therefore a conceptualization that encompasses every dimension of the analytic situation and experience.

While Freud, in his papers on technique (1912a,b [chapters 1 and 38], 1913, 1914, 1915), wrote implicitly of the analytic interaction, his emphasis fell for the most part on the transference dimension and only occasionally—and even then in a way that viewed it as isolated—on countertransference. It was Ferenczi (1909) who first specifically investigated the identificatory and introjective aspects of transference, and who thereby introduced a more definitive approach to the analytic interaction. Some years later, Strachey (1934) made a bold and ingenious effort to examine this dimension, and to explore and define its introjective and projective qualities. In a paper that was to spawn an extensive literature—first Kleinian but later to become more general—on this subject, Strachey examined in detail the implications for theory and technique of an essentially interactional approach.

The task of developing Strachey's remarkable insight fell, as I have noted, mainly to the Kleinians, and their response is represented by the papers by Baranger and Baranger, Malin and Grotstein, and Segal reprinted here. In these and other contributions, the mechanism of projective identification has been identified as a central dynamism of the analytic interaction, a finding that has increased immeasurably our understanding of the therapeutic experience. In addition, the Barangers (1966; see chapter 33) put forward the bipersonal field as a metaphor for the analytic situation and interaction, a concept that furthered clinical understanding and technique (see also Viderman 1974, for the comparable metaphor of the psychoanalytic space). My own discussion of the communicative properties of the bipersonal field (Langs 1978e) owes much to both Strachey and the advances in Kleinian thinking. I have not included it here only because it has already appeared in the *International Journal of Psychoanalytic Psychotherapy* (Vol. 7), in my collected papers (1978b), and as an appendix to my *The Listening Process* (1978a).

Virtually independent of these trends, a few classical analysts have made their own significant contributions to our understanding of the interactional dimension. Loewald (1960) presented the most important of these studies, and, while his paper is often referred to, little has been done to extend his basic thesis that growth within analysis depends on identificatory processes on the part of the patient in his relationship with an analyst capable of more mature, higher-order functioning. Later authors have, however, implicitly expanded upon this line of thought, and have relied more and more on an essentially interactional approach. Most notable among these are Sandler's study (1976; see chapter 24) of role evocations and Beres and Arlow's considerations of empathy and intuition within the analyst (1974; see chapter 23). Nonetheless, classical analysts continue to stress transference and relatively isolated intra-psychic stirrings within the patient, and have a long way to go in developing a thoroughgoing interactional approach to the analytic experience.

Many analysts outside the mainstream of classical Freudian or Kleinian lines of thought have contributed important studies of the analytic interaction. Of these, the investigations of counter-transference and noncountertransference by Margaret Little (1951 [chapter 12], 1957), the extensive writings of Winnicott (1959, 1965), the elaborate papers by Khan (1974), the creative presentations by Searles (1965, 1970, 1971, 1972, 1973 [chapter 36], 1975 [chapter 10]) and my own work (Langs 1976a,b, 1978a,b) are among the most outstanding. There seems little doubt that the interactional approach to the therapeutic experience is the most comprehensive available, and that the most innovative work currently being done in this area is achieved within this perspective.

31

THE NATURE OF THE THERAPEUTIC ACTION OF PSYCHOANALYSIS

JAMES STRACHEY

EDITOR'S NOTE

This brilliant paper by the chief translator into English of Freud's collected works is a truly remarkable contribution in many ways, not the least of which is the surprising fact that it constitutes virtually the sole original contribution by this gifted writer to the psychoanalytic literature. In tribute to its rich originality, the paper was reprinted in the *International Journal of Psycho-Analysis* in 1969 and was in 1972 the subject of a critical appreciation by Herbert Rosenfeld.

Published in 1934, this study was the beneficiary of the increasing attention that the structural hypotheses and object relations had received in the eleven years following Freud's *The Ego and the Id* (1923). Written under the noticeable influence of Melanie Klein, the paper became the fountainhead for virtually all of the later Kleinian investigations of the analytic interaction, and indeed for almost all specific discussions, from any quarter, of the interaction between patient and analyst. It contains within it, in germinal form, a host of ideas being investigated and clarified even to this day.

Strachey's study of transference rests on a consideration of the immediate object relationship and interaction between patient and analyst, as these reflect both earlier significant genetic experiences of the patient and the realities of the here and now. The latter are seen not only in terms of surface actualities, but also in light of their extensive unconscious implications. In addition to displacement, both projection and introjection are accorded great importance in the analytic experience. Strachey coined the term *mutative interpretation* for an intervention in which some aspect of transference is interpreted in terms of a current cathectic investment by the patient in his relationship with the analyst, as this illuminates present interactional experiences and mechanisms as well as the genetic past. Strachey thereby laid the basis for our understanding of how the cognitive insight derived from transference interpretations can combine with actual interactional experiences to effect adaptive structural change.

While Strachey focused, as Rosenfeld (1972) has noted, on adaptive alterations in the superego, his formulations have relevance as well for modifications in the ego and the self. Appearing at a time when the psychoanalytic understanding of the therapeutic experience was in its infancy, this contribution presented some of the most remarkable insights ever achieved in this area.

INTRODUCTORY

It was as a therapeutic procedure that psycho-analysis originated.[1] It is in the main as a therapeutic agency that it exists to-day. We may well be surprised, therefore, at the relatively small proportion of psychoanalytic literature which has been concerned with the mechanisms by which its therapeutic effects are achieved. A very considerable quantity of data have been accumulated in the course of the last thirty or forty years which throw light upon the nature and workings of the human mind; perceptible progress has been made in the task of classifying and subsuming such data into a body of generalized hypotheses or scientific laws. But there has been a remarkable hesitation in applying these findings in any great detail to the therapeutic process itself. I cannot help feeling that this hesitation has been responsible for the fact that so many discussions upon the practical details of analytic technique seem to leave us at cross-purposes and at an inconclusive end. How, for instance, can we expect to agree upon the vexed question of whether and when we should give a 'deep interpretation', while we have no clear idea of what we *mean* by a 'deep interpretation', while, indeed, we have no exactly formulated view of the concept of 'interpretation' itself, no precise knowledge of what 'interpretation' is and what effect it has upon our patients? We should gain much, I think, from a clearer grasp of problems such as this. If we could arrive at a more detailed understanding of the workings of the therapeutic process we should be less prone to those occasional feelings of utter disorientation which few analysts are fortunate enough to escape; and the analytic movement itself might be less at the mercy of proposals for abrupt alterations in the ordinary technical procedure—proposals which derive much of their strength from the prevailing uncertainty as to the exact nature of the analytic therapy. My present paper is a tentative attack upon this problem; and even though it should turn out that its very doubtful conclusions cannot be maintained, I shall be satisfied if I have drawn attention to the urgency of the problem itself. I am most anxious, however, to make it clear that what follows is not a practical discussion upon psychoanalytic technique. Its immediate bearings are merely theoretical. I have taken as my raw material the various

sorts of procedures which (in spite of very considerable individual deviations) would be generally regarded as within the limits of 'orthodox' psychoanalysis and the various sorts of effects which observation shows that the application of such procedures tends to bring about; I have set up a hypothesis which endeavours to explain more or less coherently why these particular procedures bring about these particular effects; and I have tried to show that, if my hypothesis about the nature of the therapeutic action of psychoanalysis is valid, certain implications follow from it which might perhaps serve as criteria in forming a judgment of the probable effectiveness of any particular type of procedure.

RETROSPECT

It will be objected, no doubt, that I have exaggerated the novelty of my topic.[2] 'After all', it will be said, 'we *do* understand and have long understood the main principles that govern the therapeutic action of analysis'. And to this, of course, I entirely agree; indeed I propose to begin what I have to say by summarizing as shortly as possible the accepted views upon the subject. For this purpose I must go back to the period between the years 1912 and 1917 during which Freud gave us the greater part of what he has written directly on the therapeutic side of psychoanalysis, namely the series of papers on technique (1912–15) and the twenty-seventh and twenty-eighth chapters of the *Introductory Lectures* (1916–17).

'RESISTANCE ANALYSIS'

This period was characterized by the systematic application of the method known as 'resistance analysis'. The method in question was by no means a new one even at that time, and it was based upon ideas which had long been implicit in analytical theory, and in particular upon one of the earliest of Freud's views of the function of neurotic symptoms. According to that view (which was derived essentially from the study of hysteria) the function of the neurotic symptom was to defend the patient's personality against an unconscious trend of thought

---

1. Portions of this paper were read at a meeting of the British Psycho-Analytical Society on 13 June 1933. [Reprinted from *Int. J. Psycho-Anal.* (1934), 15, 127–159.]

Reprinted from *International Journal of Psycho-Analysis* 15:117–126, 1934.

2. I have not attempted to compile a full bibliography of the subject, though a number of the more important contributions to it are referred to in the following pages.

that was unacceptable to it, while at the same time gratifying the trend up to a certain point. It seemed to follow, therefore, that if the analyst were to investigate and discover the unconscious trend and make the patient aware of it—if he were to make what was unconscious conscious—the whole *raison d'être* of the symptom would cease and it must automatically disappear. Two difficulties arose, however. In the first place some part of the patient's mind was found to raise obstacles to the process, to offer resistance to the analyst when he tried to discover the unconscious trend; and it was easy to conclude that this was the same part of the patient's mind as had originally repudiated the unconscious trend and had thus necessitated the creation of the symptom. But, in the second place, even when this obstacle seemed to be surmounted, even when the analyst had succeeded in guessing or deducing the nature of the unconscious trend, had drawn the patient's attention to it and had apparently made him fully aware of it—even then it would often happen that the symptom persisted unshaken. The realization of these difficulties led to important results both theoretically and practically. *Theoretically,* it became evident that there were two senses in which a patient could become conscious of an unconscious trend; he could be made aware of it by the analyst in some intellectual sense without becoming 'really' conscious of it. To make this state of things more intelligible, Freud devised a kind of pictorial allegory. He imagined the mind as a kind of map. The original objectionable trend was pictured as being located in one region of this map and the newly discovered information about it, communicated to the patient by the analyst, in another. It was only if these two impressions could be 'brought together' (whatever exactly that might mean) that the unconscious trend would be 'really' made conscious. What prevented this from happening was a force within the patient, a barrier—once again, evidently, the same 'resistance' which had opposed the analyst's attempts at investigating the unconscious trend and which had contributed to the original production of the symptom. The removal of this resistance was the essential preliminary to the patient's becoming 'really' conscious of the unconscious trend. And it was at this point that the *practical* lesson emerged: as analysts our main task is not so much to investigate the objectionable unconscious trend as to get rid of the patient's resistance to it.

But how are we to set about this task of demolishing the resistance? Once again by the same process of investigation and explanation which we have already applied to the unconscious trend. But this time we are not faced by such difficulties as before, for the forces that are keeping up the repression, although they are to some extent unconscious, do not belong to the unconscious in the systematic sense; they are a part of the patient's ego, which is co-operating with us, and are thus more accessible. Nevertheless the existing state of equilibrium will not be upset, the ego will not be induced to do the work of re-adjustment that is required of it, unless we are able by our analytic procedure to mobilize some fresh force upon our side.

What forces can we count upon? The patient's will to recovery, in the first place, which led him to embark upon the analysis. And, again, a number of intellectual considerations which we can bring to his notice. We can make him understand the structure of his symptom and the motives for his repudiation of the objectionable trend. We can point out the fact that these motives are out-of-date and no longer valid; that they may have been reasonable when he was a baby, but are no longer so now that he is grown up. And finally we can insist that his original solution of the difficulty has only led to illness, while the new one that we propose holds out a prospect of health. Such motives as these may play a part in inducing the patient to abandon his resistances; nevertheless it is from an entirely different quarter that the decisive factor emerges. This factor, I need hardly say, is the transference. And I must now recall, very briefly, the main ideas held by Freud on that subject during the period with which I am dealing.

TRANSFERENCE

I should like to remark first that, although from very early times Freud had called attention to the fact that transference manifested itself in two ways—negatively as well as positively, a good deal less was said or known about the negative transference than about the positive. This of course corresponds to the circumstance that interest in the destructive and aggressive impulses in general is only a comparatively recent development. Transference was regarded predominantly as a *libidinal* phenomenon. It was suggested that in everyone there existed a certain number of unsatisfied libidinal impulses, and that whenever some new person came upon the scene these impulses were ready to attach themselves to him. This was the account of transference as a universal phenomenon. In neurotics, owing to the abnormally large quantities of unattached libido present in them, the tendency to transference would be correspondingly greater; and the peculiar circumstances of the analytic situation would further increase it. It was evidently the existence of these feelings of love, thrown by the patient upon the analyst, that provided the necessary extra force to induce his ego to give up its resistances, undo the repressions and adopt a fresh solution of its ancient problems. This instrument, without which no therapeutic result could be obtained, was at once seen to be no stranger; it was in fact the familiar power of suggestion, which had ostensibly been abandoned long before. Now however it was being employed in a very different way, in fact in a contrary direction. In pre-analytic days it had aimed at bringing about an increase in the degree of repression; now it was used to overcome the resistance of the ego, that is to say, to allow the repression to be removed.

But the situation became more and more complicated as more facts about transference came to light. In the first place, the feelings transferred turned out to be of various sorts; besides the loving ones there were the hostile ones, which were naturally far from assisting the analyst's efforts. But, even apart from the hostile transference, the libidinal feelings themselves fell into two groups: friendly and affectionate feelings which were capable of being conscious, and purely erotic ones which had usually to remain unconscious. And these latter feelings, when they became too powerful, stirred up the repressive forces of the ego and thus increased its resistances instead of diminishing them, and in fact produced a state of things that was not easily distinguishable from a negative transference. And beyond all this there arose the whole question of the lack of permanence of all suggestive treatments. Did not the existence of the transference threaten to leave the analytic patient in the same unending dependence upon the analyst?

All of these difficulties were got over by the discovery that the transference itself could be analysed. Its analysis, indeed, was soon found to be the most important part of the whole treatment. It was possible to make conscious its roots in the repressed unconscious just as it was possible to make conscious any other repressed material—that is, by inducing the ego to abandon its resistances—and there was nothing self-contradictory in the fact that the force used for resolving the transference was the transference itself. And once it had been made conscious, its unmanageable, infantile, permanent characteristics disappeared; what was left was like any other 'real' human relationship. But the necessity for constantly analysing the transference became still more apparent from another discovery. It was found

that as work proceeded the transference tended, as it were, to eat up the entire analysis. More and more of the patient's libido became concentrated upon his relation to the analyst, the patient's original symptoms were drained of their cathexis, and there appeared instead an artificial neurosis to which Freud gave the name of the 'transference neurosis'. The original conflicts, which had led to the onset of neurosis, began to be re-enacted in the relation to the analyst. Now this unexpected event is far from being the misfortune that at first sight it might seem to be. In fact it gives us our great opportunity. Instead of having to deal as best we may with conflicts of the remote past, which are concerned with dead circumstances and mummified personalities, and whose outcome is already determined, we find ourselves involved in an actual and immediate situation, in which we and the patient are the principal characters and the development of which is to some extent at least under our control. But if we bring it about that in this revivified transference conflict the patient chooses a new solution instead of the old one, a solution in which the primitive and unadaptable method of repression is replaced by behaviour more in contact with reality, then, even after this detachment from the analysis, he will never be able to fall back into his former neurosis. The solution of the transference conflict implies the simultaneous solution of the infantile conflict of which it is a new edition. 'The change', says Freud in his *Introductory Lectures* (p. 381), 'is made possible by alterations in the ego occurring as a consequence of the analyst's suggestions. At the expense of the unconscious the ego becomes wider by the work of interpretation which brings the unconscious material into consciousness; through education it becomes reconciled to the libido and is made willing to grant it a certain degree of satisfaction; and its horror of the claims of its libido is lessened by the new capacity it acquires to expend a certain amount of the libido in sublimation. The more nearly the course of the treatment corresponds with this ideal description the greater will be the success of the psychoanalytic therapy'. I quote these words of Freud's to make it quite clear that at the time he wrote them he held that the ultimate factor in the therapeutic action of psychoanalysis was suggestion on the part of the analyst acting upon the patient's ego in such a way as to make it more tolerant of the libidinal trends.

THE SUPEREGO

In the years that have passed since he wrote this

passage Freud has produced extremely little that bears directly on the subject; and that little goes to shew that he has not altered his views of the main principles involved. Indeed, in the additional lectures which were published last year, he explicitly states that he has nothing to add to the theoretical discussion upon therapy given in the original lectures fifteen years earlier (1933, p. 194). At the same time there has in the interval been a considerable further development of his theoretical opinions, and especially in the region of ego-psychology. He has, in particular, formulated the concept of the super-ego. The re-statement in superego terms of the principles of therapeutics which he laid down in the period of resistance analysis may not involve many changes. But it is reasonable to expect that information about the superego will be of special interest from our point of view; and in two ways. In the first place, it would at first sight seem highly probable that the superego should play an important part, direct or indirect, in the setting-up and maintaining of the repressions and resistances the demolition of which has been the chief aim of analysis. And this is confirmed by an examination of the classification of the various kinds of resistances made by Freud in *Inhibitions, Symptoms and Anxiety* (1926, pp. 149–50). Of the five sorts of resistance there mentioned it is true that only one is attributed to the direct intervention of the superego, but two of the ego-resistances— the repression-resistance and the transference-resistance—although actually originating from the ego, are as a rule set up by it out of fear of the super-ego. It seems likely enough therefore that when Freud wrote the words which I have just quoted, to the effect that the favourable change in the patient 'is made possible by alterations in the ego' he was thinking, in part at all events, of that portion of the ego which he subsequently separated off into the super-ego. Quite apart from this, moreover, in another of Freud's more recent works, the *Group Psychology* (1921), there are passages which suggest a different point—namely, that it may be largely through the patient's superego that the analyst is able to influence him. These passages occur in the course of his discussion on the nature of hypnosis and suggestion (p. 77). He definitely rejects Bernheim's view that all hypnotic phenomena are traceable to the factor of suggestion, and adopts the alternative theory that suggestion is a partial manifestation of the state of hypnosis. The state of hypnosis, again, is found in certain respects to resemble the state of being in love. There is 'the same humble subjection, the same compliance, the same absence of criticism towards

the hypnotist as towards the loved object'; in particular, there can be no doubt that the hypnotist, like the loved object, 'has stepped into the place of the subject's ego-ideal'. Now since suggestion is a partial form of hypnosis and since the analyst brings about his changes in the patient's attitude by means of suggestion, it seems to follow that the analyst owes his effectiveness, at all events in some respects, to his having stepped into the place of the patient's superego. Thus there are two convergent lines of argument which point to the patient's superego as occupying a key position in analytic therapy: it is a part of the patient's mind in which a favourable alteration would be likely to lead to general improvement, and it is a part of the patient's mind which is especially subject to the analyst's influence.

Such plausible notions as these were followed up almost immediately after the superego made its first *début*.[3] They were developed by Ernest Jones, for instance, in his paper on 'The Nature of Auto-Suggestion' (1923). Soon afterwards[4] Alexander launched his theory that the principal aim of all psychoanalytic therapy must be the complete demolition of the superego and the assumption of its functions by the ego (Alexander, 1925). According to his account, the treatment falls into two phases. In the first phase the functions of the patient's superego are handed over to the analyst, and in the second phase they are passed back again to the patient, but this time to his ego. The superego, according to this view of Alexander's (though he explicitly limits his use of the word to the *unconscious* parts of the ego-ideal), is a portion of the mental apparatus which is essentially primitive, out of date and out of touch with reality, which is incapable of adapting itself, and which operates automatically, with the monotonous uniformity of a reflex. Any useful functions that it performs can be carried out by the ego, and there is therefore nothing to be done with it but to scrap it. This wholesale attack upon the superego seems to be of questionable validity. It seems probable that its abolition, even if that were practical politics, would involve the abolition of a large number of highly desirable mental activities. But the idea that the analyst temporarily takes over the functions of the patient's superego during the treatment and by so doing in some way alters it agrees with the tentative remarks which I have already made.

So, too, do some passages in a paper by Radó

---

3. In Freud's paper at the Berlin Congress in 1922, subsequently expanded into *The Ego and the Id* (1923).

4. At the Salzburg Congress in 1924.

upon 'The Economic Principle in Psycho-Analytic Technique'.[5] The second part of this paper, which was to have dealt with psychoanalysis, has unfortunately never been published; but the first one, on hypnotism and catharsis (1925),[6] contains much that is of interest. It includes a theory that the hypnotic subject introjects the hypnotist in the form of what Radó calls a 'parasitic superego', which draws off the energy and takes over the functions of the subject's original superego. One feature of the situation brought out by Radó is the unstable and temporary nature of this whole arrangement. If, for instance, the hypnotist gives a command which is too much in opposition to the subject's original superego, the parasite is promptly extruded. And, in any case, when the state of hypnosis comes to an end, the sway of the parasitic superego also terminates and the original superego resumes its functions.

However debatable may be the details of Radó's description, it not only emphasizes once again the notion of the superego as the fulcrum of psychotherapy, but it draws attention to the important distinction between the effects of hypnosis and analysis in the matter of permanence. Hypnosis acts essentially in a temporary way, and Radó's theory of the parasitic superego, which does not really replace the original one but merely throws it out of action, gives a very good picture of its apparent workings. Analysis, on the other hand, in so far as it seeks to affect the patient's superego, aims at something much more far-reaching and permanent — namely, at an integral change in the nature of the patient's superego itself.[7] Some even more recent developments in psychoanalytic theory give a hint, so it seems to me, of the kind of lines along which a clearer understanding of the question may perhaps be reached.

INTROJECTION AND PROJECTION

This latest growth of theory has been very much occupied with the destructive impulses and has brought them for the first time into the centre of interest; and attention has at the same time been concentrated on the correlated problems of guilt and anxiety. What I have in mind especially are the ideas upon the formation of the superego recently developed by Melanie Klein and the importance which she attributes to the processes of introjection and projection in the development of personality. I will re-state what I believe to be her views in an exceedingly schematic outline.[8] The individual, she holds, is perpetually introjecting and projecting the objects of its id-impulses, and the character of the introjected objects depends on the character of the id-impulses directed towards the external objects. Thus, for instance, during the stage of a child's libidinal development in which it is dominated by feelings of oral aggression, its feelings towards its external object will be orally aggressive; it will then introject the object, and the introjected object will now act (in the manner of a superego) in an orally aggressive way towards the child's ego. The next event will be the projection of this orally aggressive introjected object back on to the external object, which will now in its turn appear to be orally aggressive. The fact of the external object being thus felt as dangerous and destructive once more causes the id-impulses to adopt an even more aggressive and destructive attitude towards the object in self-defence. A vicious circle is thus established. This process seeks to account for the extreme severity of the superego in small children, as well as for their unreasonable fear of outside objects. In the course of the development of the normal individual, his libido eventually reaches the genital stage, at which the positive impulses predominate. His attitude towards his external objects will thus become more friendly, and accordingly his introjected object (or superego) will become less severe and his ego's contact with reality will be less distorted. In the case of the neurotic, however, for various reasons — whether on account of frustration or of an incapacity of the ego to tolerate id-impulses, or of an inherent excess of the destructive components — development to the genital

5. Also first read at Salzburg in 1924.

6. Also in a revised form in German (1926).

7. This hypothesis seems to imply a contradiction of some authoritative pronouncements, according to which the structure of the superego is finally laid down and fixed at a very early age. Thus Freud appears in several passages to hold that the superego (or at all events its central core) is formed once and for all at the period at which the child emerges from its Oedipus complex. (See, for instance, Freud, 1923, pp. 68–9.) So, too, Melanie Klein speaks of the development of the superego 'ceasing' and of its formation 'having reached completion' at the onset of the latency period (Klein, 1932, pp. 250 and 252), though in many other passages (e.g., p. 369) she implies that the superego can be altered at a later age under analysis. I do not know how far the contradiction is a real one. My theory does not in the least dispute the fact that in the normal course of events the superego becomes fixed at an early age and subsequently remains essentially unaltered. Indeed, it is a part of my view that in practice nothing except the process of psychoanalysis *can* alter it. It is of course a familiar fact that in many respects the analytic situation re-constitutes an infantile condition in the patient, so that the fact of being analysed may, as it were, throw the patient's superego once more into the melting-pot. Or, again, perhaps it is another mark of the non-adult nature of the neurotic that his superego remains in a malleable state.

8. See Klein (1932), passim, especially Chapters VIII and IX.

stage does not occur, but the individual remains fixated at a pre-genital level. His ego is thus left
exposed to the pressure of a savage id on the one
hand and a correspondingly savage superego on the
other, and the vicious circle I have just described is
perpetuated.

The Neurotic Vicious Circle

I should like to suggest that the hypothesis which I
have stated in this bald fashion may be useful in
helping us to form a picture not only of the mechanism of a *neurosis* but also of the mechanism of its
cure. There is, after all, nothing new in regarding a
neurosis as essentially an obstacle or deflecting force
in the path of normal development; nor is there anything new in the belief that psychoanalysis (owing to
the peculiarities of the analytic situation) is able to
remove the obstacle and so allow the normal
development to proceed. I am only trying to make
our conceptions a little more precise by supposing
that the pathological obstacle to the neurotic individual's further growth is in the nature of a vicious circle
of the kind I have described. If a breach could somehow or other be made in the vicious circle, the processes of development would proceed upon their nor-
normal course. If, for instance, the patient could be
made less frightened of his superego or introjected
object, he would project less terrifying imagos on to
the outer object and would therefore have less need
to feel hostility towards it; the object which he then
introjected would in turn be less savage in its pressure upon the id-impulses, which would be able to
lose something of their primitive ferocity. In short, a
benign circle would be set up instead of the vicious
one, and ultimately the patient's libidinal development would proceed to the genital level, when, as in
the case of a normal adult, his superego will be
comparatively mild and his ego will have a relatively
undistorted contact with reality.[9]

But at what point in the vicious circle is the breach
to be made and how is it actually to be effected? It is
obvious that to alter the character of a person's
superego is easier said than done. Nevertheless, the
quotations that I have already made from earlier discussions of the subject strongly suggest that the
superego will be found to play an important part in

the solution of our problem. Before we go further,
however, it will be necessary to consider a little more
closely the nature of what is described as the analytic
situation. The relation between the two persons concerned in it is a highly complex one, and for our
present purposes I am going to isolate two elements
in it. In the first place, the patient in analysis tends
to centre the whole of his id-impulses upon the analyst. I shall not comment further upon this fact or its
implications, since they are so immensely familiar. I
will only emphasize their vital importance to all that
follows and proceed at once to the second element of
the analytic situation which I wish to isolate. The
patient in analysis tends to accept the analyst in
some way or other as a substitute for his own superego. I propose at this point to imitate with a slight
difference the convenient phrase which was used by
Radó in his account of hypnosis and to say that in
analysis the patient tends to make the analyst into an
'auxiliary superego'. This phrase and the relation
described by it evidently require some explanation.

The Analyst as 'Auxiliary Superego'

When a neurotic patient meets a new object in
ordinary life, according to our underlying hypothesis
he will tend to project on to it his introjected archaic
objects and the new object will become to that extent
a phantasy object. It is to be presumed that his introjected objects are more or less separated out into two
groups, which function as a 'good' introjected object
(or mild superego) and a 'bad' introjected object (or
harsh superego). According to the degree to which
his ego maintains contacts with reality, the 'good'
introjected object will be projected on to benevolent
real outside objects and the 'bad' one on to malignant
real outside objects. Since, however, he is by
hypothesis neurotic, the 'bad' introjected object will
predominate, and will tend to be projected more
than the 'good' one; and there will further be a tendency, even where to begin with the 'good' object
was projected, for the 'bad' one after a time to take its
place. Consequently, it will be true to say that in
general the neurotic's phantasy objects in the outer
world will be predominantly dangerous and hostile.
Moreover, since even his 'good' introjected objects
will be 'good' according to an archaic and infantile
standard, and will be to some extent maintained
simply for the purpose of counteracting the 'bad'
objects, even his 'good' phantasy objects in the outer
world will be very much out of touch with reality.

---

9. A similar view has often been suggested by Melanie Klein.
See, for instance, Klein (1932, p. 369). It has been developed
more explicitly and at greater length by Melitta Schmideberg
(1932).

Going back now to the moment when our neurotic patient meets a new object in real life and supposing (as will be the more usual case) that he projects his 'bad' introjected object on to it—the phantasy external object will then seem to him to be dangerous; he will be frightened of it and, to defend himself against it, will become more angry. Thus when he introjects this new object in turn, it will merely be adding one more terrifying imago to those he has already introjected. The new introjected imago will in fact simply be a duplicate of the original archaic ones, and his superego will remain almost exactly as it was. The same will be also true *mutatis mutandis* where he begins by projecting his 'good' introjected object on to the new external object he has met with. No doubt, as a result, there will be a slight strengthening of his kind superego at the expense of his harsh one, and to that extent his condition will be improved. But there will be no *qualitative* change in his superego, for the new 'good' object introjected will only be a duplicate of an archaic original and will only re-inforce the archaic 'good' superego already present.

The effect when this neurotic patient comes in contact with a new object *in analysis* is from the first moment to create a different situation. His superego is in any case neither homogeneous nor well-organized; the account we have given of it hitherto has been over-simplified and schematic. Actually the introjected imagos which go to make it up are derived from a variety of different stages of his history and function to some extent independently. Now, owing to the peculiarities of the analytic circumstances and of the analyst's behaviour, the introjected imago of the analyst tends in part to be rather definitely separated off from the rest of the patient's superego. (This, of course, presupposes a certain degree of contact with reality on his part. Here we have one of the fundamental criteria of accessibility to analytic treatment; another, which we have already implicitly noticed, is the patient's ability to attach his id-impulses to the analyst.) This separation between the imago of the introjected analyst and the rest of the patient's superego becomes evident at quite an early stage of the treatment; for instance in connection with the fundamental rule of free association. The new bit of superego tells the patient that he is allowed to say anything that may come into his head. This works satisfactorily for a little; but soon there comes a conflict between the new bit and the rest, for the original superego says: 'You must *not* say this, for, if you do, you will be using an obscene word or betraying so-and-so's confidences'. The separation off of the new bit—what

I have called the 'auxiliary' superego—tends to persist for the very reason that it usually operates in a different direction from the rest of the superego. And this is true not only of the 'harsh' superego but also of the 'mild' one. For, though the auxiliary superego is in fact kindly, it is not kindly in the same archaic way as the patient's introjected 'good' imagos. The most important characteristic of the auxiliary superego is that its advice to the ego is consistently based upon *real* and *contemporary* considerations and this in itself serves to differentiate it from the greater part of the original superego.

In spite of this, however, the situation is extremely insecure. There is a constant tendency for the whole distinction to break down. The patient is liable at any moment to project his terrifying imago on to the analyst just as though he were anyone else he might have met in the course of his life. If this happens, the introjected imago of the analyst will be wholly incorporated into the rest of the patient's harsh superego, and the auxiliary superego will disappear. And even when the *context* of the auxiliary superego's advice is realized as being different from or contrary to that of the original superego, very often its *quality* will be felt as being the same. For instance, the patient may feel that the analyst has said to him: 'If you don't say whatever comes into your head, I shall give you a good hiding', or, 'If you don't become conscious of this piece of the unconscious I shall turn you out of the room'. Nevertheless, labile though it is, and limited as is its authority, this peculiar relation between the analyst and the patient's ego seems to put into the analyst's grasp his main instrument in assisting the development of the therapeutic process. What is this main weapon in the analyst's armoury? Its name springs at once to our lips. The weapon is, of course, interpretation. And here we reach the core of the problem that I want to discuss in the present paper.

INTERPRETATION

What, then, *is* interpretation? and how does it work? Extremely little seems to be known about it, but this does not prevent an almost universal belief in its remarkable efficacy as a weapon: interpretation has, it must be confessed, many of the qualities of a *magic* weapon. It is, of course, felt as such by many patients. Some of them spend hours at a time in providing interpretations of their own—often ingenious, illuminating, correct. Others, again, derive a direct libidinal gratification from being given interpretations and may even develop something parallel to a drug-addiction to them. In non-analytical circles interpretation is usually either scoffed at as something ludicrous, or dreaded as a frightful danger. This last attitude is shared, I think, more than is often realized, by a certain number of analysts. This was particularly revealed by the reactions shewn in many quarters when the idea of giving interpretations to small children was first mooted by Melanie Klein. But I believe it would be true in general to say that analysts are inclined to feel interpretation as something extremely powerful whether for good or ill. I am speaking now of our *feelings* about interpretation as distinguished from our reasoned beliefs. And there might seem to be a good many grounds for thinking that our feelings on the subject tend to distort our beliefs. At all events, many of these beliefs seem superficially to be contradictory; and the contradictions do not always spring from different schools of thought, but are apparently sometimes held simultaneously by one individual. Thus, we are told that if we interpret too soon or too rashly, we run the risk of losing a patient; that unless we interpret promptly and deeply we run the risk of losing a patient; that interpretation may give rise to intolerable and unmanageable outbreaks of anxiety by 'liberating' it; that interpretation is the only way of enabling a patient to cope with an unmanageable outbreak of anxiety by 'resolving' it; that interpretations must always refer to material on the very point of emerging into consciousness; that the most useful interpretations are really deep ones; 'Be cautious with your interpretations!' says one voice; 'When in doubt, interpret!' says another. Nevertheless, although there is evidently a good deal of confusion in all of this, I do not think these views are necessarily incompatible; the various pieces of advice may turn out to refer to different circumstances and different cases and to imply different uses of the word 'interpretation'.

For the word is evidently used in more than one sense. It is, after all, perhaps only a synonym for the old phrase we have already come across — 'making what is unconscious conscious', and it shares all of that phrase's ambiguities. For in one sense, if you give a German-English dictionary to someone who knows no German, you will be giving him a collection of interpretations, and this, I think, is the kind of sense in which the nature of interpretation has

been discussed in a recent paper by Bernfeld (1932).[10] Such descriptive interpretations have evidently no relevance to our present topic, and I shall proceed without more ado to define as clearly as I can one particular sort of interpretation, which seems to me to be actually the ultimate instrument of psychoanalytic therapy and to which for convenience I shall give the name of 'mutative' interpretation.

I shall first of all give a schematized outline of what I understand by a mutative interpretation, leaving the details to be filled in afterwards; and, with a view to clarity of exposition, I shall take as an instance the interpretation of a hostile impulse. By virtue of his power (his strictly limited power) as auxiliary superego, the analyst gives permission for a certain small quantity of the patient's id-energy (in our instance, in the form of an aggressive impulse) to become conscious.[11] Since the analyst is also, from the nature of things, the *object* of the patient's id-impulses, the quantity of these impulses which is now released into consciousness will become consciously directed towards the analyst. This is the critical point. If all goes well, the patient's ego will become aware of the contrast between the aggressive character of his feelings and the real nature of the analyst, who does not behave like the patient's 'good' or 'bad' archaic objects. The patient, that is to say, will become aware of a distinction between his archaic phantasy object and the real external object. The interpretation has now become a mutative one, since it has produced a breach in the neurotic vicious circle. For the patient, having become aware of the lack of aggressiveness in the real external object, will be able to diminish his own aggressiveness; the new object which he introjects will be less aggressive, and consequently the aggressiveness of his superego will also be diminished. As a further corollary to these events, and simultaneously with them, the patient will obtain access to the infantile material which is being re-experienced by him in his relation to the analyst.

Such is the general scheme of the mutative interpretation. You will notice that in my account the process appears to fall into two phases. I am anxious not to pre-judge the question of whether these two phases are in temporal sequence or whether they may not really be two simultaneous aspects of a single event. But for descriptive purposes it is easier

10. A critical summary of this by Gerö will be found in *Imago* (1933), 19.

11. I am making no attempt at describing the process in correct metapsychological terms. For instance, in Freud's view, the antithesis between conscious and unconscious is not, strictly speaking, applicable to instinctual impulses themselves, but only to the ideas which represent them in the mind (1915, p. 109). Nevertheless, for the sake of simplicity, I speak throughout this paper of 'making id-impulses conscious'.

to deal with them as though they were successive. First, then, there is the phase in which the patient becomes conscious of a particular quantity of id-energy as being directed towards the analyst; and secondly there is the phase in which the patient becomes aware that this id-energy is directed towards an archaic phantasy object and not towards a real one.

THE FIRST PHASE OF INTERPRETATION

The first phase of mutative interpretation — that in which a portion of the patient's id-relation to the analyst is made conscious in virtue of the latter's position as auxiliary superego — is in itself complex. In the classical model of an interpretation, the patient will first be made aware of a state of tension in his ego, will next be made aware that there is a repressive factor at work (that his superego is threatening him with punishment), and will only then be made aware of the id-impulse which has stirred up the protests of his superego and so given rise to the anxiety in his ego. This is the classical scheme. In actual practice, the analyst finds himself working from all three sides at once, or in irregular succession. At one moment a small portion of the patient's superego may be revealed to him in all its savagery, at another the shrinking defencelessness of his ego, at yet another his attention may be directed to the attempts which he is making at restitution — at compensating for his hostility; on some occasions a fraction of id-energy may even be directly encouraged to break its way through the last remains of an already weakened resistance. There is, however, one characteristic which all of these various operations have in common; they are essentially upon a small scale. For the mutative interpretation is inevitably governed by the principle of minimal doses. It is, I think, a commonly agreed clinical fact that alterations in a patient under analysis appear almost always to be extremely gradual: we are inclined to suspect sudden and large changes as an indication that suggestive rather than psychoanalytic processes are at work. The gradual nature of the changes brought about in psychoanalysis will be explained if, as I am suggesting, those changes are the result of the summation of an immense number of minute steps, each of which corresponds to a mutative interpretation. And the smallness of each step is in turn imposed by the very nature of the analytic situation. For each interpretation involves the release of a certain quantity of id-energy, and, as we shall see in a moment, if the quantity released is too large, the highly unstable state of equilibrium which enables the analyst to function as the patient's auxiliary superego is bound to be upset. The whole analytic situation will thus be imperilled, since it is only in virtue of the analyst's acting as auxiliary superego that these releases of id-energy can occur at all.

Let us examine in greater detail the effects which follow from the analyst attempting to bring too great a quantity of id-energy into the patient's consciousness all at once.[12] On the one hand, nothing whatever may happen, or on the other hand there may be an unmanageable result; but in neither event will a mutative interpretation have been effected. In the former case (in which there is apparently no effect) the analyst's power as auxiliary superego will not have been strong enough for the job he has set himself. But this again may be for two very different reasons. It may be that the id-impulses he was trying to bring out were not in fact sufficiently urgent at the moment: for, after all, the emergence of an id-impulse depends on two factors — not only on the permission of the superego, but also on the urgency (the degree of cathexis) of the id-impulse itself. This, then, may be one cause of an apparently negative response to an interpretation, and evidently a fairly harmless one. But the same apparent result may also be due to something else; in spite of the id-impulse being really urgent, the strength of the patient's own repressive forces (the degree of repression) may have been too great to allow his ego to listen to the persuasive voice of the auxiliary superego. Now here we have a situation dynamically identical with the next one we have to consider, though economically different. This next situation is one in which the patient accepts the interpretation, that is, allows the id-impulse into his consciousness, but is immediately overwhelmed with anxiety. This may shew itself in a number of ways: for instance, the patient may produce a manifest anxiety-attack, or he may exhibit signs of 'real' anger with the analyst with complete lack of insight, or he may break off the analysis. I any of these cases the analytic situation will, for the moment at least, have broken down. The patient will be behaving just as the hypnotic subject behaves when, having been ordered by the hypnotist to perform an action too much at variance with his own conscience, he breaks off the hypnotic relation and

---

12. Incidentally, it seems as though a *qualitative* factor may be concerned as well: that is, some *kinds* of id-impulses may be more repugnant to the ego than others.

wakes up from his trance. This state of things, which is *manifest* where the patient responds to an interpretation with an actual outbreak of anxiety or one of its equivalents, may be *latent* where the patient shews no response. And this latter case may be the more awkward of the two, since it is masked, and it may sometimes, I think, be the effect of a greater overdose of interpretation than where manifest anxiety arises (though obviously other factors will be of determining importance here and in particular the nature of the patient's neurosis). I have ascribed this threatened collapse of the analytic situation to an overdose of interpretation: but it might be more accurate in some ways to ascribe it to an *insufficient* dose. For what has happened is that the second phase of the interpretative process has not occurred: the phase in which the patient becomes aware that his impulse is directed towards an archaic phantasy object and not towards a real one.

THE SECOND PHASE OF INTERPRETATION

In the second phase of a complete interpretation, therefore, a crucial part is played by the patient's sense of reality: for the successful outcome of that phase depends upon his ability, at the critical moment of the emergence into consciousness of the released quantity of id-energy, to distinguish between his phantasy object and the real analyst. The problem here is closely related to one that I have already discussed, namely that of the extreme lability of the analyst's position as auxiliary superego. The analytic situation is all the time threatening to degenerate into a 'real' situation. But this actually means the opposite of what it appears to. It means that the patient is all the time on the brink of turning the real external object (the analyst) into the archaic one; that is to say, he is on the brink of projecting his primitive introjected imagos on to him. In so far as the patient actually does this, the analyst becomes like anyone else that he meets in real life — a phantasy object. The analyst then ceases to possess the peculiar advantages derived from the analytic situation; he will be introjected like all other phantasy objects into the patient's superego, and will no longer be able to function in the peculiar ways which are essential to the effecting of a mutative interpretation. In this difficulty the patient's sense of reality is an essential but a very feeble ally; indeed, an improvement in it is one of the things that we hope the analysis will bring about. It is important, therefore, not to submit it to any unnecessary strain; and

that is the fundamental reason why the analyst must avoid any real behaviour that is likely to confirm the patient's view of him as a 'bad' or a 'good' phantasy object. This is perhaps more obvious as regards the 'bad' object. If, for instance, the analyst were to show that he was really shocked or frightened by one of the patient's id-impulses, the patient would immediately treat him in that respect as a dangerous object and introject him into his archaic severe superego. Thereafter, on the one hand, there would be a diminution in the analyst's power to function as an auxiliary superego and to allow the patient's ego to become conscious of his id-impulses — that is to say, in his power to bring about the *first* phase of a mutative interpretation; and, on the other hand, he would, as a real object, become sensibly less distinguishable from the patient's 'bad' phantasy object and to that extent the carrying through of the *second* phase of a mutative interpretation would also be made more difficult. Or again, there is another case. Supposing the analyst behaves in an opposite way and actively urges the patient to give free rein to his id-impulses. There is then a possibility of the patient confusing the analyst with the imago of a treacherous parent who first encourages him to seek gratification, and then suddenly turns and punishes him. In such a case, the patient's ego may look for defence by itself suddenly turning upon the analyst as though he were his own id, and treating him with all the severity of which his superego is capable. Here again, the analyst is running a risk of losing his privileged position. But it may be equally unwise for the analyst to act really in such a way as to encourage the patient to project his 'good' introjected object on to him. For the patient will then tend to regard him as a good object in an archaic sense and will incorporate him with his archaic 'good' imagos and will use him as a protection against his 'bad' ones. In that way, his infantile positive impulses as well as his negative ones may escape analysis, for there may no longer be a possibility for his ego to make a comparison between the phantasy external object and the real one. It will perhaps be argued that, with the best will in the world, the analyst, however careful he may be, will be unable to prevent the patient from projecting these various imagos on to him. This is of course indisputable, and indeed, the whole effectiveness of analysis depends upon its being so. The lesson of these difficulties is merely to remind us that the patient's sense of reality has the narrowest limits. It is a paradoxical fact that the best way of ensuring that his ego shall be able to distinguish between phantasy and reality is to withhold reality from him as much as possible. But it is true. His ego is so weak — so much at the mercy of his id and superego — that he can only cope with reality if it is administered in minimal doses. And these doses are in fact what the analyst gives him, in the form of interpretations.

INTERPRETATION AND REASSURANCE

It seems to me possible that an approach to the twin practical problems of interpretation and reassurance may be facilitated by this distinction between the two phases of interpretation. Both procedures may, it would appear, be useful or even essential in certain circumstances and inadvisable or even dangerous in others. In the case of interpretation,[13] the first of our hypothetical phases may be said to 'liberate' anxiety, and the second to 'resolve' it. Where a quantity of anxiety is already present or on the point of breaking out, an interpretation, owing to the efficacy of its second phase, may enable the patient to recognize the unreality of his terrifying phantasy object and so to reduce his own hostility and consequently his anxiety. On the other hand, to induce the ego to allow a quantity of id-energy into consciousness is obviously to court an outbreak of anxiety in a personality with a harsh superego. And this is precisely what the analyst does in the first phase of an interpretation. As regards 'reassurance', I can only allude briefly here to some of the problems it raises.[14] I believe, incidentally, that the term needs to be defined almost as urgently as 'interpretation', and that it covers a number of different mechanisms. But in the present connection reassurance may be regarded as behaviour on the part of the analyst calculated to make the patient regard him as a 'good' phantasy object rather than as a real one. I have already given some reasons for doubting the expediency of this, though it seems to be generally felt that the procedure may sometimes be of great value, especially in psychotic cases. It might, moreover, be supposed at first sight that the adoption of such an attitude by the analyst might actually directly favour the prospect of making a mutative interpretation. But I believe that it will be seen on

reflection that this is not in fact the case: for precisely in so far as the patient regards the analyst as his phantasy object, the second phase of the interpretation does not occur — since it is of the essence of that phase that in it the patient should make a distinction between his phantasy object and the real one. It is true that his anxiety may be reduced; but this result will not have been achieved by a method that involves a permanent qualitative change in his superego. Thus, whatever tactical importance reassurance may possess, it cannot, I think, claim to be regarded as an ultimate operative factor in psychoanalytic therapy.

It must here be noticed that certain other sorts of behaviour on the part of the analyst may be dynamically equivalent to the giving of a mutative interpretation, or to one or other of the two phases of that process. For instance, an 'active' injunction of the kind contemplated by Ferenczi may amount to an example of the first phase of an interpretation; the analyst is make use of his peculiar position in order to induce the patient to become conscious in a particularly vigorous fashion of certain of his id-impulses. One of the objections to this form of procedure may be expressed by saying that the analyst has very little control over the dosage of the id-energy that is thus released, and very little guarantee that the second phase of the interpretation will follow. He may therefore be unwittingly precipitating one of those critical situations which are always liable to arise in the case of an incomplete interpretation. Incidentally, the same dynamic pattern may arise when the analyst requires the patient to produce a 'forced' phantasy or even (especially at an early stage in an analysis) when the analyst asks the patient a question; here again, the analyst is in effect giving a blindfold interpretation, which it may prove impossible to carry beyond its first phase. On the other hand, situations are fairly constantly arising in the course of an analysis in which the patient becomes conscious of small quantities of id-energy without any direct provocation on the part of the analyst. An anxiety situation might then develop, if it were not that the analyst, by his behaviour or, one might say, absence of behaviour, enables the patient to mobilize his sense of reality and make the necessary distinction between an archaic object and a real one. What the analyst is doing here is equivalent to bringing about the second phase of an interpretation, and the whole episode may amount to the making of a mutative interpretation. It is difficult to estimate what proportion of the therapeutic changes which occur during analysis may not be due to *implicit*

---

13. For the necessity for 'continuous and deep-going interpretations' in order to diminish or prevent anxiety-attacks, see Melanie Klein (1932, pp. 58-9). On the other hand: 'The anxiety belonging to the deep levels is far greater, both in amount and intensity, and it is therefore imperative that its liberation should be duly regulated' (*ibid.*, p. 139).

14. Its uses were discussed by Melitta Schmideberg in a paper read to the British Psycho-Analytical Society on 7 February 1934.

mutative interpretations of this kind. Incidentally, this type of situation seems sometimes to be regarded, incorrectly as I think, as an example of reassurance.

'IMMEDIACY' OF MUTATIVE INTERPRETATIONS

But it is now time to turn to two other characteristics which appear to be essential properties of every mutative interpretation. There is in the first place one already touched upon in considering the apparent or real absence of effect which sometimes follows upon the giving of an interpretation. A mutative interpretation can only be applied to an id-impulse which is actually in a state of cathexis. This seems self-evident; for the dynamic changes in the patient's mind implied by a mutative interpretation can only be brought about by the operation of a charge of energy originating in the patient himself: the function of the analyst is merely to ensure that the energy shall flow along one channel rather than along another. It follows from this that the purely informative 'dictionary' type of interpretation will be non-mutative, however useful it may be as a prelude to mutative interpretations. And this leads to a number of practical inferences. Every mutative interpretation must be emotionally 'immediate'; the patient must experience it as something actual. This requirement, that the interpretation must be 'immediate', may be expressed in another way by saying that interpretations must always be directed to the 'point of urgency'. At any given moment some particular id-impulse will be in activity; *this* is the impulse that is suceptible of mutative interpretation at that time, and no other one. It is, no doubt, neither possible nor desirable to be giving mutative interpretations all the time; but, as Melanie Klein has pointed out (1932, pp. 58–9) it is a most precious quality in an analyst to be able at any moment to pick out the point of urgency.

'DEEP' INTERPRETATION

But the fact that every mutative interpretation must deal with an 'urgent' impulse takes us back once more to the commonly felt fear of the explosive possibilities of interpretation, and particularly of what is vaguely referred to as 'deep' interpretation. The ambiguity of the term, however, need not bother us. It describes, no doubt, the interpretation of material which is either genetically early and historically distant from the patient's actual experience or which is under an especially heavy weight of repression — material, in any case, which is in the normal course of things exceedingly inaccessible to his ego and remote from it. There seems reason to believe, moreover, that the anxiety which is liable to be aroused by the approach of such material to consciousness may be of peculiar severity (*ibid.,* p. 139). The question whether it is 'safe' to interpret such material will, as usual, mainly depend upon whether the second phase of the interpretation can be carried through. In the ordinary run of case the material which is urgent during the earlier stages of the analysis is not deep. We have to deal at first only with more or less far-going displacements of the deep impulses, and the deep material itself is only reached later and by degrees, so that no sudden appearance of unmanageable quantities of anxiety is to be anticipated. In exceptional cases, however, owing to some peculiarity in the structure of the neurosis, deep impulses may be urgent at a very early stage of the analysis. We are then faced by a dilemma. If we give an interpretation of this deep material, the amount of anxiety produced in the patient may be so great that his sense of reality may not be sufficient to permit of the second phase being accomplished, and the whole analysis may be jeopardized. But it must not be thought that, in such critical cases as we are now considering, the difficulty can necessarily be avoided simply by not giving any interpretation or by giving more superficial interpretations of non-urgent material or by attempting reassurances. It seems probable, in fact, that these alternative procedures may do little or nothing to obviate the trouble; on the contrary, they may even exacerbate the tension created by the urgency of the deep impulses which are the actual cause of the threatening anxiety. Thus the anxiety may break out in spite of these palliative efforts and, if so, it will be doing so under the most unfavourable conditions, that is to say, outside the mitigating influences afforded by the mechanism of interpretation. It is possible, therefore, that, of the two alternative procedures which are open to the analyst faced by such a difficulty, the interpretation of the urgent id-impulses, deep though they may be, will actually be the safer.

'SPECIFICITY' OF MUTATIVE INTERPRETATIONS

I shall have occasion to return to this point for a moment later on, but I must now proceed to the mention of one further quality which it seems necessary for an interpretation to possess before it can be mutative, a quality which is perhaps only another aspect of the one we have been describing. A mutative interpretation must be *'specific'*: that is to say, detailed and concrete. This is, in practice, a matter of degree. When the analyst embarks upon a given theme, his interpretations cannot always avoid being vague and general to begin with; but it will be necessary eventually to work out and interpret all the details of the patient's phantasy system. In proportion as this is done the interpretations will be mutative, and much of the necessity for apparent repetitions of interpretations already made is really to be explained by the need for filling in the details. I think it possible that some of the delays which despairing analysts attribute to the patient's id-resistance could be traced to this source. It seems as though vagueness in interpretation gives the defensive forces of the patient's ego the opportunity, for which they are always on the lookout, of baffling the analyst's attempt at coaxing an urgent id-impulse into consciousness. A similarly blunting effect can be produced by certain forms of reassurance, such as the tacking on to an interpretation of an ethnological parallel or of a theoretical explanation: a procedure which may at the last moment turn a mutative interpretation into a non-mutative one. The apparent effect may be highly gratifying to the analyst; but later experience may show that nothing of permanent use has been achieved or even that the patient has been given an opportunity for increasing the strength of his defences. Here we have evidently reached a topic discussed not long ago by Edward Glover in one of the very few papers in the whole literature which seriously attacks the problem of interpretation (1931). Glover argues that, whereas a *blatantly* inexact interpretation is likely to have no effect at all, a *slightly* inexact one may have a therapeutic effect of a non-analytic, or rather anti-analytic, kind by enabling the patient to make a deeper and more efficient repression. He uses this as a possible explanation of a fact that has always seemed mysterious, namely, that in the earlier days of analysis, when much that we now know of the characteristics of the unconscious was still undiscovered, and when interpretation must therefore often have been inexact, therapeutic results were nevertheless obtained.

ABREACTION

The possibility which Glover here discusses serves to remind us more generally of the difficulty of being certain that the effects that follow any given interpretation are genuinely the effects of interpretation and not transference phenomena of one kind of another. I have already remarked that many patients derive direct libidinal gratification from interpretation as such; and I think that some of the striking signs of abreaction which occasionally follow an interpretation ought not necessarily to be accepted by the analyst as evidence of anything more than that the interpretation has gone home in a libidinal sense.

The whole problem, however, of the relation of abreaction to psychoanalysis is a disputed one. Its therapeutic results seem, up to a point, undeniable. It was from them, indeed, that analysis was born; and even to-day there are psychotherapists who rely on it almost exclusively. During the War, in particular, its effectiveness was widely confirmed in cases of 'shell-shock'. It has also been argued often enough that it plays a leading part in bringing about the results of psychoanalysis. Ferenczi and Rank, for instance, declared that in spite of all advances in our knowledge abreaction remained an essential agent in analytic therapy (1924, p. 27). More recently, Reik (1933) has supported a somewhat similar view in maintaining that 'the element of surprise is the most important part of analytic technique'. A much less extreme attitude is taken by Nunberg in the chapter upon therapeutics in his text-book of psychoanalysis (1932, pp. 303–4).[15] But he, too, regards abreaction as one of the component factors in analysis, and in two ways. In the first place, he mentions the improvement brought about by abreaction in the usual sense of the word, which he plausibly attributes to a relief of endo-psychic tension due to a discharge of accumulated affect. And in the second place, he points to a similar relief of tension upon a small scale arising from the actual process of becoming conscious of something hitherto unconscious, basing himself upon a statement of Freud's (1920, p. 28) that the act of becoming conscious involves a discharge of energy. On the other hand, Radó (1925) appears to regard abreaction as opposed in its function to analysis. He asserts that the therapeutic effect of catharsis is to be attributed to the fact

15. This chapter appears in English in an abbreviated version as a contribution to Lorand (1933). There is very little, I think, in Nunberg's comprehensive catalogue of the factors at work in analytic therapy that conflicts with the views expressed in the present paper, though I have given a different account of the interrelation between those factors.

that (together with other forms of non-analytic psychotherapy) it offers the patient an artificial neurosis in exchange for his original one, and that the phenomena observable when abreaction occurs as akin to those of an hysterical attack. A consideration of the views of these various authorities suggests that what we describe as 'abreaction' may cover two different processes: one a discharge of affect and the other a libidinal gratification. If so, the first of these might be regarded (like various other procedures) as an occasional adjunct to analysis, sometimes, no doubt, a useful one, and possibly even as an inevitable accompaniment of mutative interpretations; whereas the second process might be viewed with more suspicion, as an event likely to impede analysis—especially if its true nature were unrecognized. But with either form there would seem good reason to believe that the effects of abreaction are permanent only in cases in which the predominant etiological factor is an external event: that is to say, that it does not in itself bring about any radical qualitative alteration in the patient's mind. Whatever part it may play in analysis is thus unlikely to be of anything more than an ancillary nature.

Extra-transference Interpretations

If we now turn back and consider for a little the picture I have given of a mutative interpretation with its various characteristics, we shall notice that my description appears to exclude every kind of interpretation except those of a single class—the class, namely, of *transference* interpretations. Is it to be understood that no extra-transference interpretation can set in motion the chain of events which I have suggested as being the essence of psycho-analytical therapy? That is indeed my opinion, and it is one of my main objects in writing this paper to throw into relief—what has, of course, already been observed, but never, I believe, with enough explicitness—the dynamic distinctions between transference and extra-transference interpretations. These distinctions may be grouped under two heads. In the first place, extra-transference interpretations are far less likely to be given at the point of urgency. This must necessarily be so, since in the case of an extra-transference interpretation the object of the id-impulse which is brought into consciousness is not the analyst and is not immediately present, whereas, apart from the earliest stages of an analysis and other exceptional circumstances, the point of urgency

is nearly always to be found in the transference. It follows that extra-transference interpretations tend to be concerned with impulses which are distant both in time and space and are thus likely to be devoid of immediate energy. In extreme instances, indeed, they may approach very closely to what I have already described as the handing-over to the patient of a German-English dictionary. But in the second place, once more owing to the fact that the object of the id-impulse is not actually present, it is less easy for the patient, in the case of an extra-transference interpretation, to become directly aware of the distinction between the real object and the phantasy object. Thus it would appear that, with extra-transference interpretations, on the one hand what I have described as the first phase of a mutative interpretation is less likely to occur, and on the other hand, if the first phase *does* occur, the second phase is less likely to follow. In other words, an extra-transference interpretation is liable to be both less effective and more risky than a transference one.[16] Each of these points deserves a few words of separate examination.

It is, of course, a matter of common experience among analysts that it is possible with certain patients to continue indefinitely giving interpretations without producing any apparent effect whatever. There is an amusing criticism of this kind of 'interpretation-fanaticism' in the excellent historical chapter of Ferenczi and Rank (1924, p. 31). But it is clear from their words that what they have in mind are essentially extra-transference interpretations, for the burden of their criticism is that such a procedure implies neglect of the analytic situation. This is the simplest case, where a waste of time and energy is the main result. But there are other occasions, on which a policy of giving strings of extra-transference interpretations is apt to lead the analyst into more positive difficulties. Attention was drawn by Reich (1927)[17] a few years ago in the course of some technical discussions in Vienna to a tendency among inexperienced analysts to get into trouble by eliciting from the patient great quantities of material in a disordered and unrelated fashion: this may, he maintained, be carried to such lengths that the analysis is brought to an irremediable state of chaos. He pointed

---

16. This corresponds to the fact that the pseudo-analysts and 'wild' analysts limit themselves as a rule to extra-transference interpretations. It will be remembered that this was true of Freud's original 'wild' analyst (1910).

17. This has recently been re-published as a chapter in Reich (1933), which contains a quantity of other material with an interesting bearing on the subject of the present paper.

out very truly that the material we have to deal with is stratified and that it is highly important in digging it out not to interfere more than we can help with the arrangement of the strata. He had in mind, of course, the analogy of an incompetent archaeologist, whose clumsiness may obliterate for all time the possibility of reconstructing the history of an important site. I do not myself feel so pessimistic about the results in the case of a clumsy analysis, since there is the essential difference that our material is alive and will, as it were, restratify itself of its own accord if it is given the opportunity: that is to say, in the analytic situation. At the same time, I agree as to the presence of the risk, and it seems to me to be particularly likely to occur where extra-transference interpretation is excessively or exclusively resorted to. The means of preventing it, and the remedy if it has occurred, lie in returning to transference interpretation at the point of urgency. For if we can discover which of the material is 'immediate' in the sense I have described, the problem of stratification is automatically solved; and it is a characteristic of most extra-transference material that it has no immediacy and that consequently its stratification is far more difficult to decipher. The measures suggested by Reich himself for preventing the occurrence of this state of chaos are not inconsistent with mine; for he stresses the importance of interpreting *resistances* as opposed to the primary id-impulses themselves— and this, indeed, was a policy that was laid down at an early stage in the history of analysis. But it is, of course, one of the characteristics of a resistance that it arises in relation to the analyst; and thus the interpretation of a resistance will almost inevitably be a transference interpretation.

But the most serious risks that arise from the making of extra-transference interpretations are due to the inherent difficulty in completing their second phase or in knowing whether their second phase has been completed or not. They are from their nature unpredictable in their effects. There seems, indeed, to be a special risk of the patient not carrying through the second phase of the interpretation but of projecting the id-impulse that has been made conscious on to the analyst. This risk, no doubt, applies to some extent also to transference interpretations. But the situation is less likely to arise when the object of the id-impulse is actually present and is moreover the same person as the maker of the interpretation.[18] (We may here once more recall the problem of 'deep' interpretation, and point out that its dangers, even in the most unfavourable circumstances, seem to be greatly diminished if the interpretation in question is a transference interpretation.) Moreover, there appears to be more chance of this whole process occurring silently and so being overlooked in the case of an extra-transference interpretation, particularly in the earlier stages of an analysis. For this reason, it would seem to be important after giving an extra-transference interpretation to be specially on the *qui vive* for transference complications. This last peculiarity of extra-transference interpretations is actually one of their most important from a practical point of view. For on account of it they can be made to act as 'feeders' for the transference situation, and so to pave the way for mutative interpretations. In other words, by giving an extra-transference interpretation, the analyst can often provoke a situation in the transference of which he can then give a mutative interpretation.

It must not be supposed that because I am attributing these special qualities to transference interpretations, I am therefore maintaining that no others should be made. On the contrary, it is probable that

---

18. It even seems likely that the whole possibility of effecting mutative interpretations may depend upon this fact that in the analytic situation the giver of the interpretation and the object of the id-impulse interpreted are one and the same person. I am not thinking here of the argument mentioned above—that it is easier under that condition for the patient to distinguish between his phantasy object and the real object—but of a deeper consideration. The patient's original superego is, as I have argued, a product of the introjection of his archaic objects distorted by the projection of his infantile id-impulses. I have also suggested that our only means of altering the character of this harsh original superego is through the mediation of an auxiliary superego which is the product of the patient's introjection of the analyst as an object. The process of analysis may from this point of view be regarded as an infiltration of the rigid and unadaptable original superego by the auxiliary superego with its greater contact with the ego and with reality. This infiltration is the work of the mutative interpretations; and it consists in a repeated process of introjection of imagos of the analyst—imagos, that is to say, of a real figure and not of an archaic and distorted projection— so that the quality of the original superego becomes gradually changed. And since the aim of the mutative interpretations is thus to cause the introjection of the analyst, it follows that the id-impulses which they interpret must have the analyst as their object. If this is so, the views expressed in the present paper will require some emendation. For in that case, the first criterion of a mutative interpretation would be that it must be a transference interpretation. Nevertheless, the quality of urgency would still remain important; for, of all the possible transference interpretations which could be made at any particular moment, only the one which dealt with an urgent id-impulse would be mutative. On the other hand, an extra-transference interpretation even of an extremely urgent id-impulse could never be mutative— though it might, of course, produce temporary relief along the lines of abreaction or reassurance.

a large majority of our interpretations are outside the transference—though it should be added that it often happens that when one is ostensibly giving an extra-transference interpretation one is implicitly giving a transference one. A cake cannot be made of nothing but currants; and, though it is true that extra-transference interpretations are not for the most part mutative, and do not themselves bring about the crucial results that involve a permanent change in the patient's mind, they are none the less essential. If I may take an analogy from trench warfare, the acceptance of a transference interpretation corresponds to the capture of a key position, while the extra-transference interpretations correspond to the general advance and to the consolidation of a fresh line which are made possible by the capture of the key position. But when this general advance goes beyond a certain point, there will be another check, and the capture of a further key position will be necessary before progress can be resumed. An oscillation of this kind between transference and extra-transference interpretations will represent the normal course of events in an analysis.

Mutative Interpretations and the Analyst

Although the giving of mutative interpretations may thus only occupy a small portion of psychoanalytic treatment, it will, upon my hypothesis, be the most important part from the point of view of deeply influencing the patient's mind. It may be of interest to consider in conclusion how a moment which is of such importance to the patient affects the analyst himself. Mrs. Klein has suggested to me that there must be some quite special internal difficulty to be overcome by the analyst in giving interpretations. And this, I am sure, applies particularly to the giving of mutative interpretations. This is shown in their avoidance by psychotherapists of non-analytic schools; but many psychoanalysts will be aware of traces of the same tendency in themselves. It may be rationalized into the difficulty of deciding whether or not the particular moment has come for making an interpretation. But behind this there is sometimes a lurking difficulty in the actual *giving* of the interpretation, for there seems to be a

constant temptation for the analyst to do something else instead. He may ask questions, or he may give reassurances or advice or discourses upon theory, or he may give interpretations—but interpretations that are not mutative, extra-transference interpretations, interpretations that are non-immediate, or ambiguous, or inexact—or he may give two or more alternative interpretations simultaneously, or he may give interpretations and at the same time show his own scepticism about them. All of this strongly suggests that the giving of a mutative interpretation is a crucial act for the analyst as well as for the patient, and that he is exposing himself to some great danger in doing so. And this in turn will become intelligible when we reflect that at the moment of interpretation the analyst is in fact deliberately evoking a quantity of the patient's id-energy while it is alive and actual and unambiguous and aimed directly at himself. Such a moment must above all others put to the test his relations with his own unconscious impulses.

Summary

I will end by summarizing the four main points of the hypothesis I have put forward:

(1) The final result of psychoanalytic therapy is to enable the neurotic patient's whole mental organization, which is held in check at an infantile stage of development, to continue its progress towards a normal adult state.

(2) The principal effective alteration consists in a profound qualitative modification of the patient's superego, from which the other alterations follow in the main automatically.

(3) This modification of the patient's superego is brought about in a series of innumerable small steps by the agency of mutative interpretations, which are effected by the analyst in virtue of his position as object of the patient's id-impulses and as auxiliary superego.

(4) The fact that the mutative interpretation is the ultimate operative factor in the therapeutic action of psychoanalysis does not imply the exclusion of many other procedures (such as suggestion, reassurance, abreaction, etc.) as elements in the treatment of any particular patient.

References

Alexander, F. (1925). A metapsychological description of the process of cure. *Int. J. Psycho-Anal.* 6, 13–34.

Bernfeld, S. (1932). Der Begriff der 'Deutung' in der Psychoanalyse. *Z. angew. Psychol.* 42, 448–497.

Ferenczi, S. & Rank, O. (1924). *Entwicklungsziele der Psychoanalyse.* [Transl. 1925: *The Development of Psychoanalysis.* New York: Nervous and Mental Disease Publishing Co.]

Freud, S. (1910). Observations on 'wild' psychoanalysis. *Collected Papers,* vol. 2. [*S.E.* 11.]

Freud, S. (1912–15). Papers on technique. *Collected Papers,* vol. 2. [*S.E.* 12–13.]

Freud, S. (1915). The unconscious. *Collected Papers,* vol. 4. [*S.E.* 14.]

Freud, S. (1916–17). *Introductory Lectures on Psycho-Analysis.* London: Allen & Unwin. [*S.E.* 15–16.]

Freud, S. (1920). *Beyond the Pleasure Principle.* London: Hogarth Press. [*S.E.* 18.]

Freud, S. (1921). *Group Psychology and the Analysis of the Ego.* London: Hogarth Press. [*S.E.* 18.]

Freud, S. (1923). *The Ego and the Id.* London: Hogarth Press. [*S.E.* 19.]

Freud, S. (1926). *Inhibitions, Symptoms and Anxiety.* London: Hogarth Press. [*S.E.* 20.]

Freud, S. (1933). *New Introductory Lectures on Psycho-Analysis.* London: Hogarth Press. [*S.E.* 22.]

Glover, E. (1931). The therapeutic effect of inexact interpretation: a contribution to the theory of suggestion. *Int. J. Psycho-Anal.* 12, 397–411.

Jones, E. (1923). The nature of auto-suggestion. *Int. J. Psycho-Anal.* 4, 293–312.

Klein, M. (1932). *The Psycho-Analysis of Children.* London: Hogarth Press.

Lorand, S. (1933). *Psycho-Analysis Today.* New York: Covici, Friede.

Nunberg, H. (1932). *Allgemeine Neurosenlehre auf psychoanalytischer Grudlage.* [Transl. *Principles of Psychoanalysis.* New York: Int. Univ. Press.]

Radó, S. (1925). The economic principle in psychoanalytic technique. *Int. J. Psycho-Anal.* 6, 35–44.

Radó, S. (1926). Das ökonomische Prinzip der Technik. *Int. Z. Psychoanal.* 12, 15–24.

Reich, W. (1927). Bericht über das 'Seminar für psychoanalytische Therapie' in Wien. *Int. Z. Psychoanal.* 13, 241–244.

Reich, W. (1933). *Charakteranalyse.* [Transl. *Character Analysis.* New York: Noonday Press.]

Reik, T. (1933). New ways in psycho-analytic technique. *Int. J. Psycho-Anal.* 14, 321–334.

Schmideberg, M. (1932). Zur Psychoanalyse asozialer Kinder und Jugendlicher. *Int. Z. Psychoanal.* 18, 474–527.

32

THE THERAPEUTIC ACTION
OF PSYCHO-ANALYSIS
(Abstract by Robert Langs)

HANS W. LOEWALD

EDITOR'S NOTE

This paper is one of a series of publications by this classical analyst (see also Loewald 1970, 1971, 1975) in which he reexamined the concept of transference and, in particular, explored the role of the actual interaction between patient and analyst in the process of cure. Despite the remarkable similarity in titles, Loewald does not refer to the earlier paper by Strachey (1934; see chapter 31) on this subject, an illustration of the extensive lack of communication between the British and Europeans on the one hand and the Americans on the other, as well as between Kleinians and classical Freudians.

The significance of Loewald's paper lies in its being the first major discussion by a classical psychoanalyst of the influence of the actual analytic interaction on the patient. Loewald's basic thesis — that the resumption of ego development in analysis is based on the new object relationship with the analyst, and largely on the patient's identification with the analyst's higher level of functioning — allowed classical analysts to consider the interplay between the intrapsychic realm and the environment. He stresses the importance of analytic interpretation in this process and also reconsiders forms of transference, both normal and pathological, and the distorted and realistic aspects of the patient's relationship to the analyst.

It should be noted, however, that Loewald does not consider the specifics of the analytic interaction in any detail, and that he tends to assume an ideal and well-functioning analyst and to stress identificatory processes while underplaying those related to projection and projective identification. But the paper nevertheless represents a major breakthrough and can still be read and elaborated with profit by analysts of every persuasion.

Because permission to publish the paper in its entirety could not be obtained, I have included here the abstract of this paper written for *The Therapeutic Interaction* (Langs 1976b). The reader is well advised to seek out and study the original.

The framework of this discussion is the role that interaction with the environment plays in the formation, development, and continued integrity of the psychic apparatus. The discussion focuses on the relation between the development of psychic structures and interaction with other structures and the connection between ego formation and object

Reprinted from *The Therapeutic Interaction, Vol. 1*, by Robert Langs, pp. 218–220. New York: Jason Aronson, 1976.

relations. Its basic thesis is that there is a resumption of ego development in psychoanalysis which is contingent on the relationship with the new object, the analyst. The interaction processes that transpire between patient and analyst lead to periods of ego integration and disintegration, with the ultimate development of a higher integration and differentiation of the psychic apparatus for the patient. This contradicts the view of the psychic apparatus as a closed system and modifies the general thinking regarding the neutrality of the analyst. This latter is properly considered in terms of his need for scientific objectivity and his role as an individual onto whom the patient may project his transferences. It is also related to the need of the analyst to avoid falling into the role of an environmental figure or its opposite, in terms of the relationship the patient is transferring to the analyst.

On the other hand, the analyst must set ego development in motion and make himself available to the patient and for the development of a new object relationship, if the patient is to modify his pathology. To do so, he must possess certain qualifications, including objectivity in reference to the patient's transference distortions. Interpretations of these distortions eliminate the impediments represented by transferences as they interfere with the development of new object relationships.

However, the analyst does not only reflect transference distortions; through his interpretations "he implies aspects of undistorted reality which the patient begins to grasp step by step as transferences are interpreted. This undistorted reality is mediated to the patient by the analyst, mostly by the process of chiselling away the transference distortions" (p. 18). The heart of this process is that of identification, and in a progressive analysis, the patient and analyst identify to an increasing degree; identification forms the foundation for the new object relationship developed by the patient.

The development of an ego function is dependent upon interaction and takes place in a favorable environment that becomes increasingly internalized by the observing ego of the patient. The analyst's realistic neutrality and objectivity, love and respect, interact with the organization and reorganization of the patient's ego, and this interaction is based on the model of the parent and child. The child's internalization of aspects of the parent, including the parent's image of the child, is based on his early handling, bodily and emotionally, and is crucial to ego development, which takes place partly through introjection. The development of mature object relations is characterized by an optimal range of related-

ness and by the ability to relate to different objects according to their particular level of maturity.

In another section, Loewald demonstrates how the id, as well as the ego, develops in interaction with the external environment, although on a different level of organization. He traces out Freud's thinking regarding instinctual drives and shows that Freud eventually emphasized the manner in which these drives are related to objects and are integrated in object relationships. They become organized in the context of such relationships much as does the ego. Thus, there are adaptive aspects to both the ego and the id organization.

The author next returns to the mother-child model to further clarify the patient-analyst relationship, emphasizing that the mother's unconscious responsiveness is a prerequisite for introjection and identification; this is conveyed through her caring activities, which mediate the development of structure. Projection also plays a role in the organization of the psychic apparatus and of the environment. There is, however, a crucial "differential" between the organism and the environment that forces the development of the former; in analysis, this is based on the analyst's greater maturity and understanding. His interpretive work organizes experience for the patient and enables the latter to reach a higher level of organization. These integrative experiences in analysis show that the classical mirror model is not tenable.

In general, interactions in analysis take place through language and allow for sublimated gratifications. There must be experiences of satisfaction for integrative experiences to occur, and "Analytic interpretations represent, on higher levels of interaction, the mutual recognition involved in the creation of identity of experience in two individuals of different levels of ego-organization. Insight gained in such interaction is an integrative experience" (p. 25). Thus, an interpretation comprises two elements: first, it takes the patient a step toward true regression, which enables clarification of the defensive operations and structures; and second, by this very step it mediates to the patient the higher integrative level to be reached, allowing for a freer interplay between the unconscious and preconscious. Internalization is dependent on interaction and is made possible through the analytic process, thereby leading to a reorganization of the ego and to structural change.

The analytic patient is tempted to seek improvement in terms of unsublimated satisfaction through interaction with the analyst on levels closer to the primary process, and the analyst mediates a higher organization to the patient as long as the patient has a sufficiently strong positive transference and the analyst is in tune with the patient's productions. In a sense, the patient in speaking to the analyst is attempting to reach the analyst as a representative of the higher stages of ego-reality organization, and he thereby creates insight for himself through language communication. This is only feasible if the analyst in his own communications reveals himself as indeed a more mature person than the patient. This process is much like regression in the service of the ego, and, to varying degrees, patients are constantly striving for these integrative experiences through and despite their resistances.

In his concluding section, Loewald notes that Freud used the term "transference neurosis," first, to distinguish it from narcissistic neuroses, and second, to delineate the transfer of relations with infantile objects onto later objects, especially the analyst. In developing this theme, Loewald notes that there is an important development in the Interpretation of Dreams in Freud's (1900) discussion of day residues for dreams. Basic to the relevant process is the compulsion to associate an unconscious complex with one that is conscious, and transference gives present contemporary objects their "blood" without which they remain "ghosts."

Transference is pathological only as far as the unconscious is imprisoned by defenses, and analysis leads to a modification of these conditions. The analyst offers himself to the patient as a contemporary object to revive the "ghosts" of the past; Loewald sees this as related to the mutual attraction of unconscious and day-residue elements in dreams. Thus, transference is not a mark of man's immaturity, as Silverberg (1948) noted, but is the dynamism by which the instinctual life of man becomes ego and by which reality becomes integrated and maturity is achieved. Without such transferences or when they miscarry, human life becomes sterile and empty. Here transference takes on the meaning of an evolving relationship with objects.

Loewald notes that transference has a double aspect in that it refers to the interaction between the psychic apparatus and the object-world, as well as to the interplay between the preconscious and the unconscious within the psychic apparatus. This can be best understood through the concept of internalization of an interaction process, rather than through the simpler notion of the internalization of objects. Thus, the need of the unconscious for transference is one of the ways in which primary process is transformed into secondary process; this leads to the idea that psychic health has to do with an optimal communication between unconscious and preconscious. Through the relationship with the analyst, these transformations from primary into secondary processes are reopened.

In concluding, Loewald considers the transference and so-called "real" relationship between the patient and analyst. While these two must be differentiated, it cannot be stated that realistic relationships are devoid of transference, since there is no such thing as a reality or a real relationship without transference.

33

INSIGHT IN THE ANALYTIC SITUATION

Madeleine Baranger and Willy Baranger

EDITOR'S NOTE

The concept of the bipersonal field found its first expression in this paper by Madeleine and Willy Baranger. As a means of conceptualizing the analytic relationship and situation, it stresses projective identification by the patient and projective counteridentification by the analyst as the central mechanisms of the field. Its greatest virtue, however, is the room it provides for expanded understanding of the analytic interaction. Symptoms, resistances, and insights are all viewed as products of the field and therefore as interactional outcomes to which both patient and analyst contribute. In this way, every occurrence within either member of the analytic dyad is investigated for contributions from both participants. On the whole, the paper offers an extensive consideration of the implications of its basic concept and reflects the imaginative thinking regarding the analytic interaction that characterizes the best of the Kleinian contributions.

> What do they do? They dialogue.
> — Freud

Insight is the seed for rules which determine the distinctive characteristics of the analytic situation; the purpose for the study of its dynamics; the aim of the instrument of action in psychoanalysis—namely interpretation—and the core of its specific process of cure.

In view of the central importance of this phenomenon, insight, one cannot help but wonder at the lack of more numerous and more systematic specific studies on the subject, and at the fact that the concept has not been clarified in a more precise manner.

The present paper has as its purpose, the study of insight in terms of its functions within the analytic situation, starting from the concept that has generally (though not universally) been accepted among the analysts since Freud—that insight is the essential aim in all analytic processes.

This implies, naturally, that the analyst works through his interpretation and not through his *"being,"* in opposition to what some believe, erroneously, from our point of view. The analytic experience is bsaed on natural communication, artificially modified and codified by the preestablished framework of the analytic situation, between two human beings, with functions determined by the very structure of the situation. The communication evolves into material for psychoanalytic knowledge and work to the extent that it has been interpreted, and this interpretation produces, in turn, a new communication between both protagonists, on a different level, elaborated in the order of the "logos." When this dialectic inversion does not take place, the psychoanalytic process fails, no matter what "therapeutic" result is obtained.

We shall begin our study of insight by basing it on certain conclusions or, to state it differently, by

Reprinted from *Psychoanalysis in the Americas,* ed. Robert E. Litman. New York: International Universities Press, 1966.

working from a frame of reference expressed in a previous work by Baranger and Baranger (1961–1962). We shall make a brief summary of these points.

I. CHARACTERISTICS OF THE ANALYTIC SITUATION

a. The analytic situation is, essentially, bipersonal. All that occurs within this situation, all that can be stated about it, rests on this basic fact.

This artifical situation has a definite structure in space, in time, and in the basic asymmetric functional relationship (an analyst and an analysand).

Although this situation is materially bipersonal, the absent-present third is introduced immediately, thus reproducing the Oedipus triangle, "central in the neurosis" and also in normal evolution. Special states lead this triangular relationship to give way, regressively, to a truly bipersonal situation, or to modify itself into a multipersonal relationship. In any case, the triangle is the central situation on which all others are based.

b. The analytic situation is essentially ambiguous. It functions according to the "as if" principle (*as if* my analyst were my father, mother, etc.). If it loses its quality of ambiguity (if my analyst *is* my persecutor, or if he *is* only my analyst), the process stops functioning. The analytic situation is also ambiguous in time (living past or future situations in a present situation); in space (being there and here at the same time); in the corporeal aspects (the corporeal experiences of the analyst and of the analysand erase the real physical limits—e.g., the patient can experience the analyst as a foetus within his own body).

c. The bipersonal field of the analytic situation is structured according to three basic configurations: the structure defined by the analytic contract (fundamental rule, the undertaking of understanding, and not of judging, etc.); the structure of the overt material (the analysand tells his analyst, who is presumably gratifying, of the frustrations caused, for example, by his wife); the unconscious fantasy which determines the emergence of this overt content—the latent, or unconscious material (e.g., fantasy of homosexual union with the analyst father).

The moment which calls for interpretation, "the urgency point," is given by the meaningful intercrossing of these three configurations. It is the point where they converge.

d. This urgency point does not depend on the patient alone. Although the analyst may make

efforts to neither suggest nor impose anything, through his interpretation and selection of material, he assumes direction of the process (Lacan, 1961). The urgency point is the same as unconscious fantasy, but it is the fantasy of a pair (which is created within a pair as such). In spite of the "passivity" of the analyst, he is involved in the patient's fantasy. His unconscious responds to it and *contributes to its emergence and formation*. This fantasy can be defined as "the dynamic structure (of a pair) which, at every moment, confers meaning to the bipersonal field."

e. The analytic situation can be defined as "a pair situation where all imaginable pair situations (as well as others) can be experienced, without acting any of them." Its mobility and indefiniteness are thus essential.

The analytic pair is defined by the reciprocal projective identification (Klein, 1955) of its members, that is, by an interplay of projective identification on the part of the analysand and of projective identification and projective counteridentification on the part of the analyst. This process has its special characteristics in the patient and in the analyst.

f. The dynamics of the analytic situation—or of the primary structure, which we later define as transference-countertransference—depend on two things: (1) the primary field, which is structured as the "gestalt" of the unconscious experience of the analyst and analysand, and is shared between them, and (2) the interpretation of the analyst. The interpretation, in turn, because of its orientation and because of the selection of the material, partly conditions the dynamics of the field. A common language between analyst and analysand is established, and for each analytic situation is experienced differently by the same analyst. The dynamics of the analytic situation depend as much on the analyst's personality, technical manner, tools, and frame of reference, as on the patient's personality, conflicts, and resistances.

g. What has, from Freud's time, been called "neurosis in transference" and also later, "psychosis in transference" is in reality a microneurosis or micropsychosis of transference-countertransference. It is not a pathological process of the patient, but is rather, a function of the bipersonal field. Each analyst knows how involved he is in these processes.

It is part of the essence of the analytic process that the patient tends to repeat, in the analytic situation, the vicious cycles of his own life, and that the analyst does the same. The function of the analyst is to let himself become involved—in part—in a specific pathological process of the field in which he is already partly involved through his relationship with the patient. Consequently, he must try to rescue the patient, and himself as well, since both are participating in the same drama.

h. This double rescue can be made effectively only through interpretation. Interpretation, if adequate, permits the transition from the primary couple link of the bipersonal field to another type of link in which a part of the field neurosis or psychosis has already been overcome or worked through. One of the essential purposes of the analyst's training is to permit him to become involved in the pathology of the field and to furnish him with the tools which will make it possible for him to work through it. In this, the previous and remaining aspects of his personal neurosis are of major importance. Herein lies the suitability for certain patients to be analyzed by a given analyst.

i. The concept of the patient's neurosis or psychosis has no operative value of its own. By this we do not mean that we discard the fact that the diagnosis or structure of a patient may have importance, but rather, that it has value only in relation to his eventual analyst and to the foreseeable phenomena of the bipersonal field.

Insight can be defined as a characteristic of an individual who has easy access to his intrapsychic processes, a certain number of which may be differentiated. Here, we shall consider it as a bipersonal process, correlated to the interpretation, and specific to the analytic situation.

j. The working through of the field is a process involving interpretation by the analyst and "understanding" by the patient. Upon closer examination, it becomes apparent that these are not two separate processes, but a single one. An interpretation that does not reach the patient is an ineffective interpretation, and one that can be omitted. A patient's comprehension (if it is only his) has little importance in the analytic process. The insight that is specifically analytic, is that process of joint comprehension by analyst and patient of an unconscious aspect of the field, which consequently leads to a reduction in the pathology of the field, and the rescue of the respective parts involved.

II. Underlying Processes of the Analytic Situation

What makes up the field of the analytic situation? What is it that establishes it as such? At first sight, it is a field of communication, where things are said and heard and where other things are transmitted and received in nonverbal ways. It is logical to think, as Liberman (1962) does, that the intrapersonal communication in the patient, with its hindrances, is reproduced in the intrapersonal communication of the field. The same can be said of the analyst, except for the obvious differences.

The field is structured by the interaction of the communication toward and from both centers: analyst and patient. But the communications are established on very different stratified levels, intermingling and separating in accordance with the vicissitudes of the dynamic processes which are taking place. Underneath the verbalized "material," a fantasied interchange takes place, the transmission of numerous experiences, sometimes even in the corporeal field (transference and countertransference somatic reactions to the nonverbalized aspects of the communication).

What structures the field is an unconscious fantasy which we can conceive, by analogy, as being similar to what we know of the unconscious fantasy of the individual psyche. In reality, the definition should operate in the opposite direction from the object immediate to our knowledge (the fantasy of the analytic situation) toward the fantasy of the individual, one of the components of the situation considered as separate. The bipersonal unconscious fantasy of the field gives it its significance at any given moment of its functioning, and is that which conditions the appearance of the overt verbal content. It includes a distribution of roles between the analyst and analysand, the putting in to play of different impulses, the awareness of danger for the patient (and, eventually, for the analyst), the action of defense mechanisms, the reciprocal projections of subject, and parts of both selves present.

The fantasy of the field tends essentially to erase the individual limits between analyst and analysand, including the spatial limits between their respective bodies, which is one of the reasons why the patient is in a position where he cannot look at the analyst; direct visual contact, as a means of establishing and controlling the distance, would ultimately inhibit the communicative process. In this sense, the analytic situation tends to facilitate the projective identification. The field is constituted and functions with projective identifications as starting points, together with their natural corollaries, the introjective identifications (Klein, 1952, 1955).

Nevertheless, the nature of the processes of projective and introjective identification, in the analyst and in the patient, should be differentiated. It is this differentiation, which is not merely quantitative, that gives the field its asymmetric character.

At a given level, the phenomena of projective and introjective identification coincide, in essence, both in analyst and patient. In this way, the analyst can experience the patient in accordance with different aspects of his own self, or in terms of his internalized objects, or react with "projective counteridentification" (Grinberg, 1956) to the projective identification unconsciously accepted by him from within the patient. But, at a different level, the analyst normally keeps these phenomena under control and avoids the invasion on the part of the patient. It is this difference which led to the original belief that countertransference was to be regarded as a perturbing phenomenon of the analytic process and not as an integrating part of it, and which contributed to maintaining the myth of the analyst as a mirror. At this second level, the analyst makes use of the introjective identification to permit his patient's projection to penetrate him, up to a certain limit, as well as his own projective identification which he recognizes in that which has been introjected by the patient. These two phenomena can take place in the analyst in either a correlated and communicated way, or in an isolated manner. In the first event, the spontaneous, introjective-projective situation serves as material for the interpretation. In the second, the understanding and interpretation of the analyst barely touch the analytic situation, without going into it, and a stumbling block begins to form. Expressed differently, we see an aspect of the neurosis of the field. We do not consider the second situation as one which can be totally avoided. It would be an illusion to try to avoid the analysand's neurosis from becoming a neurosis in the transference or the bipersonal field reflecting the neurotic circles.

Translated into metapsychological terms, this means that the observing ego of the analyst can or cannot be in communication with its own spontaneous processes in relation to the patient. Thus understood, the observing ego is not merely pure observation, but is also an interpreting ego within the analyst's theoretic frame of reference. This includes his fantasy and his concept of the analytic work, his fantasy and his concept of what is happening in the field and in the patient, as well as what he has acquired in terms of self-knowledge and as technical aptitude in the course of his training and his personal analysis.

In the patient, on the contrary, and because of the regression induced by the analytic situation itself, the observing ego generally stops functioning and submerges itself in less differentiated functioning of the psychic structures. Two exceptions to this phenomenon can be observed. One of these exceptions involves states of "resistance" (which correspond to feelings of noncommunication on the part of the analyst) when the subject, threatened by an unconscious danger, refuses to regress and maintains for his defense, a schizoid splitting, isolating part of his ego in order to keep an eye on the imminent danger, and to defend the frontiers of his internal world while protecting himself from encroachment by the analyst. In this case, the analysand may use false insight as a means of defending himself against an interpretation, thus reducing it to its abstract terms and emptying it of its living content. Such a situation gives the analyst an excellent sign of the temporary failure of his efforts.

The other exception to the undifferentiated functioning of the patient, is the process of true insight. We shall return to this, shortly.

These considerations merely develop that which Freud (1916, 1921) implied in his descriptions of the analytic situation, fundamental rule, and floating attention.

III. STEREOTYPING OF THE FIELD AND PARALYSIS OF INSIGHT

The interaction of regressive and repetitive phenomena characterizing the analytic situation, necessarily renders it pathological. This is the basic condition by which the analytic situation is able to achieve its therapeutic aims and results. A truly "finished" analysis, if it were conceivable, would manifest itself in a field functioning freely, where no pathological crystallization were produced. The analytic process can be conceived as the consecutive resolution of all the difficulties which, time after time, prevent communication and mobility in the field.

If, as Freud expressed in one of his unfinished works (1940), all mechanisms of defense imply a certain "spaltung," or a certain splitting within the ego, every pathological formation of the field will imply the splitting of one of its sections, this section escaping from the general dynamics of the field and creating a more or less pronounced paralysis. Even if a certain remobilization of the field is produced, its function now leaves aside the split section in such a way as to leave it out of the dynamics of the situation. This splitting does not correspond to a repression; certain parts of the split-off section are conscious or can be made conscious with little difficulty. Other parts, on the contrary, are repressed and very much correspond to the archaic splittings underlying the present splitting (M. Baranger, 1960, and W. Baranger, 1961–1962a, 1961–1962b).

In the bipersonal situation, this process becomes really harmful when the patient's essay of splitting finds an unconscious complicity or a blind spot in the analyst. One sees, then, a partialization of the analytic process. Events continue taking place; part of the material continues being worked through, but something that is very important escapes the process and remains crystallized. This, naturally, limits the result of the analysis more than is necessary.

In this way, a "bastion" which is opposed to progress, is formed. Of course, certain bastions exist within the patient himself, which he is implicitly determined not to put into play in the contract. It can be an object relation or a pleasing activity which the patient feels is perverse, or an aspect of his economic situation, an ideology, etc. When it does not produce any complicity on the part of the analyst, the patient's bastion constitutes a difficulty in the analytic work or a "resistance," but not a bastion within the field. The patient tries, in one way or another, to evade the fundamental rule and the analyst struggles to reintegrate into the general movement, the content avoided by the patient. On the other hand, when there is complicity, the communication is divided: a section of the field is crystallized, enclosing the patient's resistance and the analyst's counterresistance, unconsciously communicated between them and operating together, at the same time that an apparently normal communication continues to take place on a separate level.

But the inconvenience of such situations is soon felt and, if the field bastion is important, the general dynamics also tend toward stasis. This is what happens in analyses that "don't work." Freud (1916) described the processes in somewhat different terms, but in this same sense when he compared analysis to the reconquest of a territory invaded by neurosis, and noted that the invading army could enter into battle at any point considered convenient and not necessarily at the same places where battles had been fought at the time of the conquest. We would add, that if the analyst has allies within the invaded territory, the invader also has informers in the liberating army which lead to the paralysis of some of its forces and, eventually, to the failure of the reconquest.

In any case, this complicity in the resistance-counterresistance transforms the dynamics of the field, which E. Pichon Riviere (1956) has compared to a "process in spiral," to a monotonous and uniformly circular movement that patients, metaphorically, frequently refer to as a treadmill. Analyst and patient continue revolving around the treadmill or the bastion which they have unintentionally built together.

The most extreme process in the pathology of the field could be expressed in terms of parasitism of the analyst by the patient. If a part of the work of the analyst is to be penetrated by the projective identifications of the patient, or to serve as a deposit for the patient's experiences, the session generally finishes by a restitution of what has been deposited. But sometimes the restitution cannot be made (perhaps because the penetration was too violent or invading) and the analyst remains "inhabited" by a part of the patient after the session is over. If the process becomes chronic, the situation resembles a type of parasitism exercised by the patient.

Subjectively, the analyst feels impotent, flooded by the patient. The analytic situation loses its temporal frame and overflows outside the sessions, and the preoccupation about the patient fills the non-analytic hours. This type of situation is not uncommon when there is a threat of self-destructive acting-out on the part of the patient (possibility of suicide, self-inflicted accidents, psychotic crisis of unforeseeable consequences, etc.). The parasitism of the analyst can, at times, be appreciated in a material way through the active intervention of persons related to the patient (relatives, friends, doctors) who forcefully introduce themselves into the life of the analyst in their attempts to manipulate his behavior as they see fit (e.g., demanding that he take action with regard to internment, psychiatric treatment, etc.). In these cases, the analytic situation has burst out of the field. The analyst and the environment now act as bearers of fragments of the patient's own self, as actors in a drama whose director would be the very patient.

Sometimes, a clear sequence between the phenomenon of paralysis of the field by a bastion and the explosion of the analytic situation can be observed. The bastion, in these cases, covers and defends a "psychotic nucleus" of the patient, the mobilization of which provokes something analogous to a sudden explosion, and as a consequence, the analyst becomes parasitized. The analyst's impotence within the field gives way to an impotence resulting from the parasitic invasion by a part of the patient, and the dispersion of other parts of the patient in many other persons.

The cases in which the analyst becomes parasitic to the patient are also frequent, and here too, it is the result of projective and introjective identifications. Up to a certain point, this is a general situation, which prompted Rado (1959) to describe the analyst as the "parasite superego" of the patient, but in certain cases the phenomenon becomes massive. The analysand feels as if he were a puppet being manipulated by the analyst. He lives as a function of the analysis and acts as if the analyst were commanding him at every moment. These cases coincide with a transitory impoverishment of the patient's ego, which empties itself in favor of the analyst through idealization, and which experiences itself as empty or as the receptacle of all his dead or useless objects.

Every phenomenon of parasitism, to the degree that it presupposes a stereotyped functioning of both real participants in the bipersonal field existing outside the reciprocal basic functions defined in the analytic contract, belongs to the pathology of the field. This does not occur necessarily in a symbiotic situation. We could even say that the analytic situation is essentially symbiotic; first, because it reproduces regressive repetitions of the symbiotic dependence on the parents, and secondly, because it is directed toward the production of projective identifications. We understand as symbiotic, a situation where, in certain moments and to a certain degree, the individual's boundary limits are erased; the processes of projective identification are in control; and where, as a consequence, a distribution of function between the symbiotic persons takes place. We believe that a certain degree of symbiosis necessarily exists in any couple (even more so, in a lasting couple) and in any human group which functions as one. "Strictly speaking," says Jose Bleger (1961), "we must talk of symbiosis when a crossed projective identification has taken place and when each one of the receivers acts according to the function of the complementary roles of the others and vice versa." To a certain degree, the analytic situation corresponds to the definition that the analyst is the "adult," the "healthy ego," etc., of the analysand, and the analysand is the "child," the "neurotic," etc. which remains within the analyst. We must not forget that there are moments during which the roles are interchanged—the analyst being the sick child, and the analysand the healthy adult.

Strictly speaking, the analytic situation is also a partial and artificial symbiosis which is always being corrected and "desymbiotisized" by the analyst. That is, the analytic situation is designed to both produce and reduce the symbiosis. When, due to the characteristics of both members, the symbiotic situation goes beyond the limits of reducibility, a true symbiotic situation is produced and a bastion is created. When attempts to reduce this situation fail, the limited symbiosis is transformed into an overflowing symbiosis which rapidly becomes parasitism.

IV. FUNCTION OF INSIGHT

In view of the previous considerations, we may regard insight as a phenomenon of the bipersonal field. One has to differentiate radically between insight as a personal quality, or as a moment of self-discovery, and insight as given in the analytic situation. Although the word is the same, the phenomena are only comparable in their result, while being totally dissimilar in their essence. Analytic insight is the work of two persons.

In general, insight is the result of the interpretation made by the analyst. In some cases, the stage has been set for the moment of insight, by virtue of the previous material, and the analyst has given partial interpretations. A dialogue has been established, reaching a particular point where the analyst formulates the "mutative interpretation" (Strachey, 1934) which produces the insight.

In other cases, it is the patient, himself, who gives the final touch to the dialogue and reaches the expression that throws light on the situation of the bipersonal field and the internal situation which has structured it. In this latter case, it is the analyst who learns something, taught by the patient.

It was probably Freud's "opus magnum" that he permitted his patients (Dora, the "Wolf man," "Little Hans") to teach him, and that he transmitted this knowledge to us; i.e., to be receptive to the teachings of another. Even at this moment, the theoretic progress of analysis is the result of the cooperation of an analyst and his patients.

Discovery—and insight is always that, even though the analyst does nothing but face situations already known and experienced—is always tinged with surprise. That is why Freud considered the patient's "this would never have occurred to me," as a confirmation of the interpretation.

Insight does not occur after each of the analyst's interpretations, nor at any moment in the evolution of the field. It requires a previous mobilization of the field. Paralysis, which we saw as one of the basic phenomena of the pathology of the field is, par excellence, the anti-insight condition. Insight implies the reintegration of situations which have been paralyzed in a "bastion," into the general dynamics of the analytic situation, recovering what has been alienated and recognizing it as part of the self. In that sense, it is an overcoming of a splitting, and coincides with what Melanie Klein has called the "depressive position." It is the reparation of a situation of the field which was threatened or destroyed by the splitting processes. It is a reassociation. In this reparation, the analyst never acts alone. He can repair the situation if the patient is momentarily in accord with him to repair it, or better said, if both feel the urge to do it.

This means that insight appears as something that occurs within a symbiotic situation. It is a double vision of the field, permitting a double interior vision. Technically, it is between these two phases that insight occurs as a symbiotic situation which is one no longer. Insight is the moment in which the joint efforts of analyst and patient are able to make conscious and to formulate the symbiotic situation as such. This runs parallel to a process of discrimination, both of the temporal and spatial order: "I'm repeating such a childhood situation in a context that does not justify it; this does not belong to me; it belongs to the other—that which the other has does not belong to him, but to me." Insight thus permits a redistribution of the analyst's as well as the patient's parts, which had been placed in the field as a consequence of the establishment of the symbiotic situation. One or the other becomes aware of what the previous situation of the field had been, of the specific ways in which it had been blocked; they reindividualize and replace themselves in their reciprocal situation, determined by basic contract. But meanwhile, something has happened: an obstacle has been overcome; something which had been split off has been reintegrated; the internal object situation of the patient has been modified and, to a lesser degree, so has that of the analyst.

The touchstone of insight and of the value of the interpretive formulation, which constitutes one of its essential moments, is the felt change in the type of communication taking place during transference and countertransference. Analyst and analysand are no longer defined by their complementarity but rather, by their sharing of common experience. Although this experience is one of discovery and enrichment, of free communication, and noneroticized affection, it does not deny the aggressive tensions which are produced and which will be produced again. It opens the future for the field, and for life, in the measure in which life depends on the field. It is experiencing the shared analytic work as something positive, something which was worth the effort. This experience has nothing to do, qualitatively, with the "beatific" moments which can be produced in any analysis, and which reproduce the happy moments of union with the breast, with the mother, with the idealized object. It is not contemplation; it is life with the perspective of future evolution. The moment of insight, thus described, is the essential, specific, and authentic gratification which

the analyst can find in his work, in addition to the other less fundamental ones.

Being in communication in the field and with each other at the moment of insight, analyst and analysand find that they are also in communication within themselves; they enjoy a wide accessibility to the different regions of their psychic lives. It is, however, a controlled internal communication which takes into account the differences between regions and functions. It is not an invasion or a confusion, but a discriminating unity. The observing ego, or the ego in its function as observer—which, in the patient, had gone into regression and had lost its autonomy in the conflict of the field, and which, in the analyst, had been reduced to the impotent contemplation of the bastion—reappears in both, in complete functional control.

One perceives with clarity, two extreme types of functioning of the observing ego in the analytic situation. At certain moments of stumbling against the bastion, the observing ego of the patient functions with the defensive aim of watching the field. In these cases, it may even take recourse in false insight and intellectualizations (Richfield, 1954), which give no real meaning to or lead to any progress in the communication. The same phenomenon can exist on the part of the analyst. When this occurs, the observing egos in the analyst and in the patient cannot coincide since each of them is in a defensive position against the other. They intellectualize in order to separate themselves. In the moment of insight, on the contrary, the observing ego in the patient and that in the analyst discriminate themselves from the rest of the intrapersonal field to coincide in the interpersonal field. They do not unite but, coexisting and collaborating, work, even intellectually, to *reunite* themselves. In such moments, analyst and analysand share the analytic work. That is to say, the fantasies of illness and cure are able to coincide in the patient and in the analyst. At the beginning and underlying all of his rational concepts about treatment, the patient expects magical conduct from his analyst. The patient comes to the analysis with a fantasy of what is occurring to him, of his "sickness," and also with a fantasy of the work of his analyst towards his cure. The analyst, as well, has a general fantasy of his work, and a particular one of the structure of the patient, of his disturbances, of what his treatment is going to be. In one, as in the other, these original fantasies are structured as the bipersonal field is established, and evolve with its dynamics. Thus, a fantasy of the bipersonal field, of its evolution, of the role played in it by each of the participants, of its pathology, and of its possible cure is created. In general, these fantasies do not coincide in the patient and in the analyst (the analysand may be looking, for example, for something that the analyst can never give: e.g., a penis to a woman). The evolution of the field produces a gradual approximation of the fantasy pertaining to the illness and the cure, on the one hand, and the fantasy of the analysand and of that of the analyst, on the other.

This fantasy of the pathology of the field and of the type of work to be done, largely determines the conduct of the patient and his way of cooperating or not cooperating with the work. Similarly, this fantasy determines the attitude of the analyst, his selection of interpretations, and the directions he imprints on the process (Lacan, 1961).

The moment of insight occurs when both fantasies coincide: analyst and analysand coincide in their comprehension and statement of the present state of the field, and both realize, at the same time, the exact nature of their common work at that moment. After this moment has passed, the field will be restructured once again, and in a pathologic form, but differently. The fantasies of analyst and analysand will once again separate, reintegrating another part of history, another conflict, until the analytic work permits another stumbling-block to be overcome and a new instance of insight is produced.

CONCLUSION

Analytic insight is the process by which a situation of paralyzed, parasitic, or symbiotic communication changes into a situation of object communication through a discriminative process.

Insight is characterized by:

1. A previous mobilization of the bipersonal field, with the crumbling of a pathological bastion.

2. A redistribution, within the field, of the parts which had been symbiotically mixed in both the patient and in the analyst.

3. A discriminating reindividuation, with the appearance in both of their separate egos, each performing its discriminatory and observing function.

4. An intra- and interpersonal union in the common task.

5. An integration of the fantasy of illness of the field and of the fantasy of its cure, both in the analysand and in the analyst.

34

PROJECTIVE IDENTIFICATION IN THE THERAPEUTIC PROCESS

ARTHUR MALIN AND JAMES S. GROTSTEIN

EDITOR'S NOTE

Later Kleinian studies of the analytic interaction tended toward an overriding stress on the role of projective identification, primarily as a means of pathological communication and expression stemming from the patient. Until recently, this meant ignoring pathological projective identifications arising largely from the analyst (see Part III). But these otherwise valuable investigations have received considerable attention of late from non-Kleinians, and promise eventually to take their place as fundamental investigations of one important component of the analytic interaction.

First used by Melanie Klein (1946), the term *projective identification* refers to actual interactional efforts to place into an object some aspect of the intrapsychic world and functioning of the subject— an aspect with which he remains identified. The term also implies efforts by the subject to evoke an identification by the object, and might better be termed *interactional projection*.

The present paper is included in this volume for its clarity of exposition and relevance to the Kleinian concept of transference, as well as to the interactional mechanisms that prevail in the analytic experience. It considers both the patient's efforts at interactional projection and variations in how these communications are received and processed by the analyst—considerations that have received more specific attention in recent years.

Recent articles by Loewald (1960) and Searles (1963) having to do with certain aspects of the therapeutic process have stimulated us to investigate what we believe may be the basis of the therapeutic effect in psycho-analysis. In our view the concept of projective identification can be fruitfully applied to an understanding of the therapeutic process. We shall attempt to describe the concept of projective identification and then discuss the relevance of this idea to normal and pathological development with a view toward clarifying the therapeutic process in light of it.

The term projective identification was first used by Melanie Klein (1946) and was meant to indicate a process in which parts of the self are split off and projected into an external object or part object. Hanna Segal (1964) states,

Projective identification is the result of the projection of parts of the self into an object. It may result in the object's being perceived as having acquired the characteristics of the projected part of the self, but it can also result in the self becoming identified with the object of its projection.

This idea was developed from Klein's (1932, 1934) earlier concept of object relations existing from the start of extrauterine life. Klein had indicated that the

Reprinted from *International Journal of Psycho-Analysis* 47:26–31, 1966.

relation to the first object, the breast, is through introjection. She also demonstrated that object relations from the beginning depend for their development on projective and introjective mechanisms. Klein (1946) suggested that these mechanisms are seen in the earliest period of normal development, which she described as the paranoid-schizoid position. She stated further that these mechanisms are also a type of defence found particularly in schizophrenic patients.

We wish to emphasize at this point that projective identification to us has come to mean many different things and embraces many concepts. Our paper is an attempt, both to clarify and to expand on it, and to place it in its proper perspective in psychoanalytic theory and practice.

First, we should like to say why we use the term projective identification and not projection. Projection alone is a mechanism for dealing with instinctual drives, akin to incorporation. It is an instinctual mode. We feel, as does Fairbairn (1954), that all intra-psychic and inter-personal relations are transacted on the basis of object relationships, rather than on the basis of instinctual drives alone. The object is the irreducible vehicle in human interaction.

Once we make this assumption, we then conceive of the psychic apparatus as a dynamic structure composed of internalized objects (and part-objects) with drive charges inseparably attached to them. We feel that these charged parts of self (or identifications) are projected outward and that the status of the identification changes by virtue of the projection, thus enabling the ego to discharge, for instance, unwanted or disclaimed parts of the self (purified pleasure ego of Freud, 1915). The external object now receives the projected parts, and then this alloy—external object plus newly arrived projected part—is re-introjected to complete the cycle.

In the preceding paragraph, we have dealt with the defensive nature of projective identification. We wish to emphasize that it is also, at the same time, a way of relating to objects. As Freud (1921) has stated, the infant relates by identification prior to making anaclitic object choices. We agree with this and go two steps further; first, we believe that all identification includes projection, as we hope to show; and second, that projective identification is also a normal as well as abnormal, way of relating which persists into mature adulthood.

We hope to develop the reasons why these burdensome emendations of theory are necessary, especially since the advent of object-relations theory has imposed this task upon us.

An article by Knight (1940) appears to anticipate the concept of projective identification although it is not described directly by that name. In this short article Knight attempts to describe the different ways in which identification may be used and defined. Knight states,

. . . Identification is never an irreducible process or state of affairs, but is always based on a subtle interaction of both introjective and projective mechanisms.

Knight makes a point that Bibring's term, 'altruistic surrender', involves a projection of one's own desires for pleasure and gratification into another person with whom one then identifies. Knight goes further and states,

The awareness of how we would feel under similar circumstances enables us to project our own needs and wishes on to the object and then to experience his feelings as if they were ours through the resultant temporary identification with him. Even though this vicarious experience would appear to be an instantaneous process, it seems to me valuable to reduce it to its constituent mechanisms of projection and possibly also introjection.

It is obvious that Knight is referring to identification with whole objects rather than part objects as emphasized by Klein, but Knight's ideas are certainly compatible with the concept of projective identification.

In line with Knight's thinking, we want to emphasize what seems obvious in the concept of identification, namely, that all identification includes projection, and all projection includes identification.[1] Before we are ready to internalize (take in psychically, incorporate), we must be in some state of readiness for this process. That is, we must tentatively project out a part of our inner psychic contents in order to be receptive to the object for introjection and subsequently to form an identification with it. When we start with the projection it is necessary that there be some process of identification or internalization in general, or else we can never be aware of the projection. That is, what is projected would be lost like a satellite rocketed out of the gravitational pull of the earth. Eventually all contact with the satellite will be lost. Although the satellite has left Earth, it must remain under the influence of Earth's

---

1. We define introjection as a psychic phenomenon in which the object is taken into the psychic apparatus but is kept separate from the self; in other words, it is within the ego but unassimilated, much like a foreign body. Following introjection, identification may take place by the object's becoming assimilated into the ego or self. See Greenson (1954).

gravitational pull to remain in orbit in order for it to maintain some contact with Earth. A projection, of itself, seems meaningless unless the individual can retain some contact with what is projected. That contact is a type of internalization, or loosely, an identification. We want to show that Klein's concept of projective identification can be broadened greatly in order to understand many phenomena in psychic life both normal and pathological, and to enhance our knowledge of identification itself.

Rosenfeld (1952a, 1952b, 1954) and Bion (1955, 1956) have applied the concept of projective identification to the understanding and treatment of the psychotic patient. They state that when a patient splits off a part of himself and projects it into the object, such as the analyst, he has a feeling of relatedness to the analyst but with some corresponding feelings of inner impoverishment. Very often the patient feels that the split-off part, now in the external object, is a persecutor. They emphasize the importance of projective identification in understanding delusional transference material.

Searles (1963) describes very similar phenomena. He relates much of his material to the Kleinian concept of projective identification, but he does emphasize some important differences between his ideas and Klein's. In a more broadly defined manner, however, we would view Searles's ideas on transference psychosis as being another aspect of projective identification. Searles makes an important point, for instance, of the schizophrenic patient's need to project a part of himself into the therapist. The therapist must provide, according to Searles, a suitable and receptive object in himself to receive this projection from the patient. Searles suggests,

Moreover, it is my experience that he [the chronic schizophrenic patient] actively needs a degree of symbiotic relatedness in the transference, which would be interfered with were the analyst to try, recurrently, to establish with him the validity of verbalized transference interpretations.

Searles suggests here that the projective identification from the patient to the analyst must first be accepted by the analyst before verbal interpretations will be of any help.

Loewald (1960) writes of therapeutic change as involving structural change in the ego. In speaking of the patient's reaction to the analyst, Loewald states,

A higher stage of organization, of both himself and his environment, is thus reached, by way of the organizing understanding which the analyst provides.

Loewald emphasizes throughout his article the importance of higher levels of ego integration which the patient can achieve through the analytic treatment. We suggest that projective identification helps explain the development of these higher levels of ego integration.

Transference phenomena are obviously very closely related to projective identification. Transference implies the projection of inner attitudes which came from earlier object relationships into the figure of the analyst during the analysis. A much broader concept of transference would state that all subsequent relationships are modified on the basis of the earliest object relationship of the individual which is now established in the inner psychic life. This view very closely approximates the concept of primary objects which was advanced by Balint (1937). If we accept a broad view of transference to include all object relations, internal and external, after the primary relationship with the breast-mother which is now internalized, then we are stating that all object relations and all transference phenomena are examples, at least in part, of projective identification. This implies that there must be a projection from within the psychic apparatus into the external object. We emphasize that this includes parts of self as well as internal object representations. To go back to Klein's ideas for a moment, some of her lack of emphasis on the environment in human development can be understood in terms of projective identification. It can be understood in the sense that the early instinctual representations, including the death instinct, are projected into the breast-mother, and then the bad breast-mother is introjected on the basis of the earlier projection and not so much on the basis of the actual environmental situation of that breast-mother. We should like to modify this idea, however, with the suggestion that it is just the fact that the inner psychic contents related to earliest object relations are projected into the external objects that makes for the tremendous influence of the environment. *It seems to us that it is only upon perceiving how the external object receives our projection and deals with our projection that we now introject back into the psychic apparatus the original projection, but now modified and on a newer level.* Hopefully, the mother has helped the infant by allowing this projection to be met with a response of understanding, care, and love. It is the mother who cannot do this, and who sees the child's projections as destructive and frightening, who will confirm the infant's fears of his own bad destructive self.[2] We suggest,

---

2. Erikson (1959) has shown that the mother also projects her

moreover, that this method of projecting one's inner psychic contents into external objects and then perceiving the response of these external objects and introjecting this response on a new level of integration is the way in which the human organism grows psychically, nurtured by his environment. The environment must meet the needs of these projections and be able to reinterpret for the developing individual the inner workings of their psychic apparatus and to demonstrate that these are not destructive, 'bad' parts. The external object must confirm those constructive and 'good' aspects of the developing individual and thus facilitate higher ego integration which will mitigate the effect of the destructive components of the self.

We propose that these concepts are of crucial importance in understanding the earliest experiences of the infant, the further growth and development of children and adults, and to a great extent the therapeutic effect of psycho-analysis. We have all observed how patients must project into the analyst their inner psychic contents. These consist of objects and part objects with associated feelings and attitudes. It is mainly through his perception of the manner in which the analyst handles these projections that the patient can find a new level of integration. As Searles (1963) emphasizes, what is important is a receptiveness without an encouragement of these projections, and an attempt at understanding their meaning without the fear that these projections will destroy the analyst.

The essence of the therapeutic process is through modification of internal object relationships within the ego, and this is largely brought about by projective identification. Correct interpretations can be seen as an important way in which the patient can observe how his projections have been received and acknowledged by the analyst. If this does not take place the patient is left with futility, despair, and doubt in regard to his inner self worth.

One of the most common defences of the schizophrenic borderline patient, as well as of many neurotics, is the need to preserve the analyst as a good object by maintaining a distance which paradoxically is not very helpful to developing understanding. Much of this is related to what seems to be a negative therapeutic reaction. It would appear that these patients are trying to preserve the analyst by avoiding closeness to him, i.e. not projecting any of their bad parts into the analyst which they feel will destroy the analyst and therefore their only hope for

---

needs and feelings into the infant and responds to the child's perception of these needs.

survival. For example, a borderline patient could rarely speak of any positive feelings toward the analyst, but would occasionally, with great disappointment, point out what he felt was an error on the part of the analyst. It was learned in the analysis that in this way the patient would demonstrate his great reliance and positive attitude toward the analyst, but only through this method of expressing disappointment. To speak directly of his concern and closeness to the analyst would be forbidden because the patient felt that any closeness and trust would mean that the analyst would have to handle the patient's destructiveness and would therefore be destroyed. Therefore, to keep some distance from the analyst was to preserve him. Conversely, a patient may often keep his distance because he has already projected bad objects into the analyst and therefore sees the analyst as a persecutor.

The following case history will illustrate some of the above ideas:

A 23-year-old civil engineer came into analysis because of increasing anxiety over his loneliness. He found himself very aloof from his fellow office workers toward whom he felt a mixture of fear and contempt and did not dare, as a consequence, to get close to them. His sexual life, other than masturbation, consisted of a few contacts with prostitutes and one contact with a girl toward whom he had begun to develop feelings. Subsequent sexual attempts with her resulted in humiliating impotent failures, however, so he abruptly terminated the relationship with her. His life otherwise was characterized by a lonely, stark impoverishment in which he spent most of his spare time in his apartment, drinking, playing the guitar, or reading.

He is the second eldest of four children, having an older sister and a younger brother and sister respectively. His father was described as an angry, loud, drunk, martinet of a man who once was a prizefighter. His mother was a willowy, soft-spoken, subtly patronizing martyr of a woman who was frequently beaten by the father while the children watched in paralyzed horror. When the patient was 12, the mother 'escaped' from the father and encouraged her children to come with her. Only the oldest child obliged, however; the others remained with the father. Immediately thereafter the father moved them away from New York to a small town in California where he forced them to use assumed names so that the mother could not trace them and have them brought back to New York.

Life with father consisted of hearing his insults and temper fits, subjecting oneself to Spartan discipline (the father enforced regular calisthenics upon them as if they were in training), and consistently being reminded of what a better parent he was than their mother who, he claimed, wanted them sent to an orphan's home. After graduating from high school the patient left home against his father's will and used his savings to enter college to become an engineer.

His initial behaviour in analysis was cold, formal, and detached. He would describe a very lonely, impoverished life with an eerie detachment. He did not seem to be involved with his own life. Provocative gestures at work, such as frequently arriving late, allowing himself to be seen idle, and arguments with the supervisor, changed into transference phenomena of professing mild to enormous contempt and ridicule toward the analyst, whose weaknesses and deficiencies almost invariably bore a striking resemblance to the patient's own shortcomings, in addition to shortcomings of both parents. Examples of some of the projections are as follows: frequently he would accuse the analyst of being weak and poorly integrated and possibly suffering from a huge inner impoverishment. Along with this he would state that he felt the analyst also had a hidden homosexual problem. These all were projections of his weak self-concept. On other occasions he would berate the analyst as being too rigid and demanding, and he would freely express how he hated pleasing him—that would be like giving in. This perception of the analyst as rigid, autocratic, and hard to please, represented a projection of the father identification. On still other occasions he would perceive the analyst as supercilious, polite, ingratiating, insincere, and martyr-like. All these qualities belonged to his mother identification.

The projections were accepted by the analyst for their psychic validity, and then interpreted as his need to put bad parts of himself, including bad objects and part objects, into the analyst in order to rid his ego of these bad contents. In addition he was symbolically entering the analyst through these projections, to take control of him by weakening his self-esteem through consistent criticism and denigration. Not only was he repeating with the analyst what he had experienced with his father and mother, but he was also taking possession, in fantasy, of the analyst from within to guarantee total possession of the object. In his life history there was no precedent for him to assume he could have any relationship with anyone without total control or total subjugation. Without this guarantee, as it were, there existed no relationship for him.

The projection of bad parts of himself (and bad objects and part objects) had still another purpose which closely dovetailed with the mechanisms described. This patient was so trapped in his schizoid world that he could not trust his good, positive love feelings to be truly good. He had the conviction that his very love was bad and would be rejected; thus he related with his overtly bad self in order to establish a relationship and, paradoxically, protect the external object and himself from destruction. Moreover, he got a particular delight if he felt the analyst was hurt by his tirades of abuse. As long as the analyst was hurt (i.e. affected), then he as an individual was having some effect on another person and was therefore asserting his identity and was at the same time dealing with his deep envy of the analyst's immutability.

Consistent interpretations of all of these mechanisms wherever they occurred considerably lessened the negative transference, and the patient was subsequently able to recognize that he was warding off his deep feelings of dependency on the analyst. Changes occurred by virtue of analysing the projections rather than by the analyst's unconsciously or consciously responding as if they were objectively valid. In other words, this was a new experience for the patient which allowed him to integrate the previously projected parts, now reintegrated into the ego, so that a higher level of functioning could occur. This is an example of transference, but it is also something more than is ordinarily conveyed by that term. The patient was not merely displacing from the past; he was projecting from within himself bad contents into the analyst. By permitting the patient to project into the analyst, that is, to accept the psychic validity of the projection, a way of establishing a relationship with the patient was developed which allowed successful interpretation and resolution of this archaic way of relating. It also anticipated and precluded a negative therapeutic reaction and aided the patient to heal his ego fragments.

In the light of all the above material we should like to offer some speculative ideas in regard to the general concept of identification. We suggest the possibility that there is an early primary identification with the breast-mother and that in a sense no further real identification takes place. Instead, there is a constant modifying and integrating of this earliest identification. This might explain the contradiction that appears in the literature in regard to identification at one point appearing as a normal process of development and at another point as a pathological defence mechanism. It would seem that normal identification refers to the primary identification and that any further identification later on in life would be of a more pathological defensive nature more likely on the level of introjection, that is, an unassimilated foreign-body reaction in the psychic apparatus. However, normal development does include identification, but of a far more transient nature than originally assumed, which really has to do with further structuring, integrating, and synthesizing of the earliest primary identification. What is commonly thought of as good identifications can be seen to be growth of the self through these mechanisms. It may be stated that we can never change the facts of what has happened to the patient in his life. What we hope to do, however, is to help the patient integrate his experiences in a new way so that he may have a choice in the way he relates to the world.[3]

Fairbairn (1952) has made an interesting contribution to the concept of identification. He feels that primary identification takes place with the pre-ambivalent object, which is then split into good and bad objects. All future identifications are made solely with the bad objects. The good objects, he states, do not need to be identified with. There is a different kind of internalizing of the good objects, but this is transitory and is given up as one matures. In other words, the good objects are loosely held as a scaffold-ing, as it were, for ego growth and differentiation. As this takes place, the scaffolding is removed.

To summarize, we are suggesting that projective identification is a normal process existing from birth. It is one of the most important mechanisms by which growth and development take place through object relations. This mechanism can be described as one in which objects and associated affects are re-experienced on a new integrative level so that fur-ther synthesis and development will take place within the ego.

We have taken Klein's concept of projective identification and have attempted to show how this idea can be greatly broadened to increase our understanding of normal and pathological development and the therapeutic process. In our view projective identification seems to be the way in which human beings are able to test their own inner psychic life by projecting psychic contents out into the environment and perceiving the environment's reaction to these projected parts of oneself. This process gives rise to newer psychic integrations leading to normal growth and development, and is, moreover, of crucial importance in the therapeutic process.

REFERENCES

Balint, M. (1937). 'Early developmental states of the ego: primary object love.' In: *Primary Love and Psycho-Analytic Technique.* (London: Hogarth, 1952; New York: Liveright, 1953.)

Bion, W. R. (1955). 'Language and the schizophrenic.' In: *New Directions in Psycho-Analysis* ed. Klein, Heimann and Money-Kyrle. (London: Tavistock, New York: Basic Books.) (1956). 'Development of schizophrenic thought.' *Int. J. Psycho-Anal.,* 37.

Erikson, E. H. (1959). *Identity and the Life Cycle: Selected Papers. Psychological Issues,* Monogr. 1. (New York: Int. Univ. Press.)

Fairbairn, W. R. D. (1952). *Psychoanalytic Studies of the Personality.* (London: Tavistock.) (Amer. title: *An Object-Relations Theory of the Personality.* (New York: Basic Books, 1954.))

Freud, S. (1951). 'Instincts and their vicissitudes.' *S.E.,* 14.

——(1921). *Group Psychology and the Analysis of the Ego. S.E.,* 18.

Greenson, R. R. (1954). 'The struggle against identification.' *J. Amer. Psychoanal. Assoc.,* 2.

Klein, M. (1932). *The Psycho-Analysis of Children.* (London: Hogarth, 1950.)

——(1934). 'A contribution to the psychogenesis of manic-depressive states.' In: *Contributions to Psycho-Analysis 1921–1945.* (London: Hogarth 1950.)

——(1946). 'Notes on some schizoid mechanisms.' In: *Developments in Psycho-Analysis* ed. Riviere. (London: Hogarth, 1952.)

Knight, R. P. (1940). 'Introjection, projection and identification.' *Psychoanal. Quart.,* 9.

Lichtenstein, H. (1961). 'Identity and sexuality: a study of their interrelationship in man.' *J. Amer. Psychoanal. Assoc.,* 9.

Loewald, H. W. (1960). 'On the therapeutic action of psycho-analysis.' *Int. J. Psycho-Anal.,* 41.

Rosenfeld, H. (1952a). 'Notes on the psychoanalysis of the super-ego conflict of an acute schizophrenic patient.' *Int. J. Psycho-Anal.,* 33.

——(1952b). 'Transference-phenomena and transference-analysis in an acute catatonic schizophrenic patient.' *Int. J. Psycho-Anal.,* 33.

——(1954). 'Considerations regarding the psycho-analytic approach to acute and chronic schizophrenia.' *Int. J. Psycho-Anal.,* 35.

Searles, H. F. (1963). 'Transference psychosis in the psychotherapy of chronic schizophrenia.' *Int. J. Psycho-Anal.,* 44.

Segal, H. (1964). *Introduction to the Work of Melanie Klein.* (London: Heinemann; New York: Basic Books.)

---

3. See Lichtenstein's (1961) concept of 'identity theme'.

35

MELANIE KLEIN'S TECHNIQUE

HANNA SEGAL

EDITOR'S NOTE

In this paper Hanna Segal outlines the basic components of the Kleinian therapeutic technique and the fundamentals of Kleinian theory on which they are based. Written with exceptional clarity, the contribution delineates the basic principles under which Kleinian analysts operate in the analytic situation. It offers the reader an excellent opportunity to understand the Kleinian position and to take issue where necessary. For some readers it may occasion the abandonment of unfounded and unflattering ideas they may have held regarding Kleinian practice.

THE RATIONALE

The Kleinian technique is psychoanalytical and strictly based on Freudian psychoanalytic concepts. The formal setting is the same as in classical Freudian analysis; the patient is offered five or six fifty-minute sessions a week; a couch is provided for him to recline on, with the analyst sitting behind him; he is invited to free-associate, and the analyst interprets his associations. Not only is this formal setting the same as that in classical technique, but in all essentials the psychoanalytical principles as laid down by Freud are adhered to. The role of the analyst is confined to interpreting the patient's material, and all criticism, advice, encouragement, reassurance, and the like, is rigorously avoided. The interpretations are centered on the transference situation, impartially taking up manifestations of positive and negative transference as they appear. By transference I mean here not only the "here-and-now" relation to the analyst, but the relation to the analyst including reference to past relationships as transferred onto the analyst, and current problems and relationships in their interrelationship to the transference. Special attention is paid to the transference onto the analyst

of internal figures from the patient's inner world. The level at which the interpretations are given, again as indicated by Freud, is determined by the level of the patient's maximum unconscious anxiety. In these respects, the Kleinian analyst may be considered to be following the classical Freudian technique with the greatest exactitude, more so indeed than most other Freudian analysts, who find that they have to alter their analytical technique in some of its essential aspects when dealing with prepsychotic, psychotic, or psychopathic patients. Analysts using the Kleinian approach (Rosenfeld, 1965; Segal, 1950, 1956; Bion, 1956, 1957, 1958, 1959) find it both possible and useful to retain the strictly psychoanalytical technique even with these patients.

Could it be said, therefore, that there is no room for the term "Kleinian technique"? It seems to me that it is legitimate to speak of a technique as developed by Melanie Klein in that the nature of the interpretations given to the patient and the changes of emphasis in the analytical process show, in fact, a departure, or, as Melanie Klein saw it, an evolution from the classical technique. She saw aspects of material not seen before, and interpreting those aspects, she revealed further material that might not have been reached otherwise and that, in turn, dictated new interpretations, seldom, if ever, used in the classical technique.

To understand the rationale of the Kleinian

Reprinted from *Psychoanalytic Forum* 2:212-225; 226-227, 1967, ed. J. Lindon. Permission granted by the Psychiatric Research Foundation.

approach and to appreciate the way in which the technique grew, it is best to place it in its historical setting. When Melanie Klein, in the 1920's, started her work with children, she assumed that Freud's method could be applied to children with only such modifications as would not alter the essence of the psychoanalytical relationship and the interpretative process. Since children do not verbalize easily, and since play is one of their major means of expression, she provided each child patient with a drawer of small, simple toys and play material, and she interpreted their play, behavior, and verbal communications in the way in which she would have interpreted an adult's free associations. She observed that children develop a transference, both positive and negative, very rapidly and very intensely. She found that the children's communications, through various activities in the session, revealed their unconscious conflicts with the same, and often indeed greater, clarity as the adults' free associations. The analysis of children fully confirmed Freud's deductions about childhood derived from work with adults, but, as might be expected, certain new facts emerged. The Oedipus complex and the superego seemed both to be in evidence at an earlier age than one would have expected and to have pregenital, as well as genital, forms. Indeed, the roots of the Oedipal situation seemed to lie as far back as the second oral phase. The superego of the small child was equally well in evidence, possessed of savage and primitive oral, anal, and urethral characteristics. She was impressed by the prevalence and power of the mechanisms of projection and introjection; the introjections leading to the building of a complex inner world and the projections coloring most of the child's perceptions of reality. Splitting was very active as an early mechanism preceding repression, and the child's development appeared to be a constant struggle toward integration and the ovecoming of powerful splitting mechanisms. Once seen in the child, those more primitive levels of experience could be understood and detected in the material of adult patients.

THE CONCEPT OF PHANTASY

Working at the primitive level of the child's world led Melanie Klein to broaden the concept of unconscious phantasy.

As the work of psychoanalysis, in particular the analysis of young children, has gone on and our knowledge of early mental life has developed, the relationships which we have come to discern between the earliest mental processes and the later more specialized types of mental functioning commonly called "phantasies" have led many of us to extend the connotation of the term "phantasy" in the sense which is now to be developed. (A tendency to widen the significance of the term is already apparent in many of Freud's own writings, including a discussion of unconscious phantasy.) (Susan Isaacs, 1952.)

Unconscious phantasy springs directly from the instincts and their polarity and from the conflicts between them. Susan Isaacs defined it as "the mental correlate of the instincts" or "the psychic equivalent of the instincts." In the infant's omnipotent world instincts express themselves as the phantasy of their fulfillment. "To the desire to love and eat corresponds the phantasy of an ideal love-, life- and food-giving breast; to the desire to destroy, equally vivid phantasies of an object shattered, destroyed and attacking" (Segal, 1964). Phantasy in the Kleinian view is primitive, dynamic, and constantly active, coloring external reality and constantly interplaying with it. "Reality experience interacting with unconscious phantasy gradually alters the character of phantasies, and memory traces of reality experiences are incorporated into phantasy life. I have stressed earlier that the original phantasies are of a crude and primitive nature, directly concerned with the satisfaction of instincts, experienced in a somatic as well as a mental way, and, since our instincts are always active, so a primitive layer of primary phantasies are active in all of us. From the core, later phantasies evolve. They become altered by contact with reality, by conflict, by maturational growth. As instincts develop instinct derivatives, so the early primitive phantasies develop later derivatives and they can be displaced, symbolized and elaborated and can even penetrate into consciousness as daydreams, imagination, etc." (Segal, 1964). This broader concept of phantasy provides a link between the concept of instinct and that of ego mechanisms.

What Freud picturesquely calls here "the language of the oral impulse," he elsewhere calls "the mental expression" of an instinct, i.e. the phantasies which are the psychic representatives of a bodily aim. In this actual example,[1] Freud is showing us the phantasy that is the mental equivalent of an *instinct*. But he is at one and the same time formulating the subjective aspect of the *mechanism* of introjection (or projection). Thus *phantasy is the link between the id impulse and the ego mechanism,* the means by which the one is transmuted into the other. "I want to eat that and therefore I have eaten it" is a phantasy which represents

---

1. The example of introjection is from Freud's paper on "Negation."

the id impulse in the psychic life; it is at the same time the subjective experiencing of the mechanism or function of the introjection (Isaacs, 1952).

This applies to all mental mechanisms, even when they are specifically used as defenses.

We are all familiar with phantasying as a defensive function. It is a flight from reality and a defence against frustration. This seems contradictory to the concept of phantasy as an expression of instinct. The contradiction, however, is more apparent than real; since phantasy aims at fulfilling instinctual striving in the absence of reality satisfaction, that function in itself is a defence against reality. But, as mental life becomes more complicated, phantasy is called upon as a defence in various situations of stress. For instance, manic phantasies act as a defence against the underlying depression. The question arises of the relation between the defensive function of phantasy and mechanisms of defence. It is Isaacs' contention that what we call mechanisms of defence is an abstract description from an observer's point of view of what is in fact the functioning of unconscious phantasy. That is, for instance, when we speak of repression, the patient may be having a detailed phantasy, say, of dams built inside his body holding back floods, floods being the way he may represent in phantasy his instincts. When we speak of denial, we may find a phantasy in which the denied objects are actually annihilated, and so on. The mechanisms of introjection and projection, which long precede repression and exist from the beginning of mental life, are related to phantasies of incorporation and ejection; phantasies which are, to begin with, of a very concrete somatic nature. Clinically, if the analysis is to be an alive experience to the patient, we do not interpret to him mechanisms, we interpret and help him to relive the phantasies contained in the mechanisms (Segal, 1964).

The understanding of Melanie Klein's use of the concept of phantasy is necessary for the understanding of her technical approach to resistance, if we take resistance to be synonymous with defenses against insight. The criticism has been advanced that the Kleinian analyst interprets the content of unconscious phantasies and neglects the analysis of defenses. This criticism is, I think, based on a misunderstanding of our way of handling defenses. We attach great importance to analyzing the unconscious anxiety that is defended against in conjunction with the analysis of the defenses against it, so that the emergence of the defended material into consciousness is facilitated not only by the analysis of the defenses but also by the lessening of the unconscious anxiety. This is particularly important when one reaches into the deep psychotic layers of the personality, as otherwise the ego may be flooded by psychotic anxieties. In the early days of psycho-

analysis it was considered dangerous to analyze prepsychotics because it was believed that analysis of defenses could expose the weak ego to a psychotic breakdown. This anxiety was fully justified. It is far safer to analyze prepsychotics now, when we do not analyze predominantly resistance or defenses, leaving the ego defenseless but have some understanding of the psychotic phantasies and anxieties that necessitate these defenses and can modify these anxieties by interpretations, which are directed at the content as well as at the defenses against it. The concept of mental mechanisms as one facet of phantasy life implies also that there is less division between interpretations of defense and those of content, and interpretation can deal more readily with the patient's total experience.

The same applies to the interpretation of structure. Susan Isaacs established the connection between the concepts of instinct, mental mechanism, and phantasy. I have extended it further, connecting phantasy with ego and superego structure, a connection that is implied in Susan Isaacs' paper, but not explicitly stated.

If one views the mechanisms of projection and introjection as being based on primitive phantasies of incorporation and ejection, the connection between phantasy and mental structure becomes immediately apparent. The phantasies of objects which are being introjected into the ego, as well as the loss of the ego by phantasies of projective identification, affect the structure of personality. When Freud described the super ego as an internal object in active relationship with the id and the ego, he was accused by academic psychologists of being "anthropomorphic," but what was he in fact describing? This structure within the ego is the end result of complex phantasies. The child in phantasy projects some of his own aggression into a parental figure; he then in phantasy incorporates this figure and, again in phantasy, attributes to this figure various attitudes and functions. Melanie Klein has shown that other objects, earlier than the superego described by Freud, are similarly introjected, and a complex internal world is built in phantasy and structuralized. The fact that structure is partly determined by unconscious phantasy is of paramount importance from the therapeutic point of view, since we have access to these phantasies in the analytic situation and, through mobilizing them and helping the patient to relive and remodel them in the process of analytic treatment, we can affect the structure of the patient's personality (Segal, 1963).

THE FIRST SESSION

This view of phantasy affects the technique, in that the patient's material is looked at differently than in the classical technique. All the patient's communications in the session are viewed as containing an element of unconscious phantasy, though they may seem concerned with incontrovertible external facts. For instance, a patient may open a session by complaining that it is cold and raining. The analyst will keep an open mind about a possible phantasy content. Is the patient complaining of the analyst's unfriendliness? Is he complaining about the interval between sessions, and if so, did he feel like a baby left crying in the cold or like a baby left with a wet nappy? Did he feel that his omnipotent urination has led to a flood? No interpretation will be given, of course, until further material provides the meaning, but the analyst is alerted to the fact of coldness and wetness as a communication about something in the patient's inner world as well as in the weather.

In the phantasy world of the analysand, the most important figure is the person of the analyst. To say that all communications are seen as communications about the patient's phantasy as well as current external life is equivalent to saying that all communications contain something relevant to the transference situation. In Kleinian technique the interpretation of the transference is often more central than in the classical technique.

Our understanding of the central role played by unconscious phantasy and transference affects the course of the analysis from the very first session. The question is often asked by students, should transference be interpreted in the first session? If we follow the principle that the interpretation should be given at the level of the greatest unconscious anxiety and that what we want to establish contact with is the patient's unconscious phantasy, then it is obvious that, in the vast majority of cases, a transference interpretation will impose itself. In my own experience I have not had a case in which I did not have to interpret the transference from the start. A patient undertaking a psychoanalysis is bound to come to his first session full of hopes and fears and is sure to have formed phantasies about the analyst as soon as he came in contact with him, or even before—as soon as he knew he was going to meet him. These hopes and fears, and the resistance against them, are often more clearly presented in the first session than in later ones. Interpreting them has the effect of both lessening the unconscious anxiety and, from the start, focusing the patient's attention on the central role of the analyst in his unconscious. These interpretations have, of course, to be formulated in a way that is acceptable and understandable to a patient as yet unfamiliar with the analytic technique. To give a not uncommon example, an obviously frigid and

"shut-in" woman patient, in her first session, is first silent, then expresses some anxiety about how to behave, what to say, and so forth. The analyst may interpret her fear of his getting in touch with her mind. Then the patient proceeds to describe her father as a violent man, often drunk, who used to terrify her. The analyst can interpret that she hopes he will get in touch with her and understand her, but is also frightened that his interpretations will be violent and terrifying and that he will penetrate her mind and damage it. In this situation the fear of being physically raped, which may already be clear to the analyst, need not be interpreted, but its mental equivalent is near enough to the patient's anxieties to be brought into consciousness. A correct interpretation of this anxiety is necessary to enable the patient to "open out."

Another question, often asked in relation to the first session, concerns the level of interpretation. Should interpretations be deep or superficial? This again is dictated by the principle of interpreting at the level at which anxiety is active. It is by no means true that the patient presents first genital, then anal, and finally oral material. He presents material at the level at which, at that moment, anxiety is centered. For instance, to establish contact with a schizophrenic, it is usually necessary from the start to interpret the most primitive forms of projective identification if one is to get in touch with him at all. Thus, I interpreted, in the first session, to a schizophrenic adolescent, that she felt she had put all her "sickness" (the word she used) into me the moment she entered the room, and, as a result, felt me to be a sick and frightening person. A little later in the session I interpreted that she was afraid that my talking would put the "sickness" back into her. These interpretations, in my view, lessened her immediate paranoid reactions and enabled her to stay in the room and communicate with me.

Even in the relatively healthy individual, however, oral or anal anxieties may be clearly presented in the transference situation in the first session. Thus, a candidate started the session by declaring his determination to be qualified in the minimum time and to get in all the analysis he could in the shortest possible time. Later in the session he spoke of his digestive troubles and, in another context, of cows, presenting a picture of his phantasy about the relation to the analyst so clearly as to enable me to make the interpretation that I was the cow, like the mother who breast-fed him, and that he felt that he was going to empty me greedily, as fast as possible, of all my analysis—milk; this interpretation which immediately brought out material about his guilt in relation to exhausting and exploiting his mother.

I have described the approach to the first session in order to emphasize that, from the start, we try to get in touch with the patient's unconscious phantasy, as manifested in the transference. This does not mean, however, that analysis is concerned with the description of phantasies in the void. A full interpretation of an unconscious phantasy involves all its aspects. It has to be traced to its original instinctual source, so that the impulses underlying the phantasy are laid bare. At the same time, the defensive aspects of the phantasy have to be taken into account, and the relation has to be traced between phantasy and external reality in the past and the present.

It is the contention of Melanie Klein and her co-workers that the application of these principles in the analysis of children, adults and, in more recent years, psychotic patients as well, has enabled us to reach deeper layers of the unconscious. These deeper layers must be taken into consideration if we are to understand the analysand's anxieties and the structure of his internal world, the basis of which is laid in early infancy. This accounts for the fact that interpretations at an oral or anal level and of introjective or projective mechanisms play a much larger part than in the classical technique.

The Paranoid-Schizoid Position

In the development of psychoanalysis, as in most sciences, there is an interrelation between technical innovations and theoretical concepts, changes in technique revealing new material, leading to new theoretical formulations, and the theoretical concepts in turn leading to new techniques. It is impossible to speak of Melanie Klein's technique without bringing in some aspects of theory. As is probably well known by now, Melanie Klein describes two stages in the oral phase, corresponding roughly to Abraham's preambivalent and ambivalent stages. She calls them the paranoid-schizoid and the depressive positions and describes two different types of ego and object-relation organization belonging to these two stages. In the paranoid-schizoid position, the infant has no concept of a whole person. He is related to part objects, primarily the breast. He also experiences no ambivalence. His object is split into an ideal and a persecutory one, and the prevalent anxiety at that stage is of a persecutory nature, the fear that the persecutors may invade and destroy the self and the ideal object. The aim of the infant is to

acquire, possess, and identity with the ideal object and to project and keep at bay both the bad objects and his own destructive impulses. Splitting, introjection, and projection are very active as mechanisms of defense. The analysis of these persecutory anxieties and of the defenses against them plays an important part in Kleinian technique. For instance, if the analyst if very idealized, he will be particularly watchful for the appearance of bad figures in the patient's extra-analytical life and take every opportunity of interpreting them as split-off bad aspects of himself. He will also be watchful for the projection of the patient's own destructive impulses into these bad figures.

An important mechanism evolved in the paranoid-schizoid position is that of projective identification. In projective identification, a part of the patient's ego is in phantasy projected into the object controlling it, using it and projecting into it his own characteristics. Projective identification illustrates perhaps most clearly the connection between instincts, phantasy, and mechanisms of defense. It is a phantasy that is usually very elaborate and detailed; it is an expression of instincts that both libidinal and aggressive desires are felt to be omnipotently satisfied by the phantasy; it is, however, also a mechanism of defense in the same way in which projection is; it rids the self of unwanted parts. It may also be used as a defense, for instance, against separation anxiety. Here is an example of the difference between interpreting only projection and interpreting projective identification. A student reported a case in which his woman patient, preceding a holiday break, was describing how her children bickered and were jealous of one another in relation to her. The student interpreted that the children represented herself, jealous about him in relation to the holiday break, an interpretation that she accepted without being much moved. He did not interpret that she felt that she had put a jealous and angry part of herself into the children and that that part of her was changing and controlling them. The second interpretation, for which there was plenty of material in preceding and subsequent sessions, was of very great importance, in that it could be shown to the patient how, by subtle manipulations, she was in fact forcing the children to carry those parts of herself. Often a transference situation can only be understood in terms of projective identification, a situation, for instance, in which the patient is silent and withdrawn, inducing in the analyst a feeling of helplessness, rejection, and lack of understanding, because the patient has projected into the analyst the child part of himself with all its feelings.

A schizophrenic patient, whose analysis I super-vised, at the beginning of his analysis used to stand with his back to the analyst, a huge table separating them. This patient had been separated from his mother and sent overseas when he was a small child. The analyst interpreted mainly that the table repre-sented the ocean that separated him from his mother and how he used it to "turn the tables on her." In turning his back to her, he was the rejecting mother, and he was putting into the analyst the desperate child part of himself. Following certain indications, such as the patient's change of posture, and using her countertransference feelings, she could interpret in great detail the kind of feeling he felt he was pro-jecting into her. The patient reacted to this interpre-tation sometimes as a persecution, which would then be interpreted as his feeling that she was forcibly and perhaps vengefully pushing these feelings back into him. Gradually the feelings of persecution lessened, the patient gave up his posture behind the table and felt able to communicate with the analyst by speech. Such a situation can also be seen as reversal, a well-known mechanism described by Freud. It is not, however, sufficient to interpret to the patient that he is reversing the situation of separation. One has to interpret in detail his introjective identification with the rejecting mother and the projective identification of the rejected child part of himself, identifying and describing its feelings and interpreting the detail of the phantasy how this part is projected. For instance, the feces and flatus may contain the parts that the patient wishes to project. Hence, turning his back to the analyst could have not only a symbolic meaning but could also relate to phantasies con-nected with his wish to defecate into the analyst.

States of mind in which projective identification predominates may leave the patient feeling depleted, since part of himself is missing, persecuted by the analyst filled with his projections, and confused with the analyst. This is particularly noticeable in the case of the schizophrenic, who immediately forms a violent psychotic transference, whose anxiety and confusion can only be relieved by interpretations of identification (Rosenfeld, 1965; Segal, 1964).

It is to be emphasized, however, that the analysis of the paranoid-schizoid object relationships and defenses is not confined to the analysis of the psy-chotic and the prepsychotic only; in that the schizoid defenses, though originating in the earliest stages of development, are repeatedly regressed to and re-vived as a defense against feelings aroused in the depressive position.

THE DEPRESSIVE POSITION

The depressive position starts when the infant begins to recognize his mother. Throughout the paranoid-schizoid position, normal processes of maturation are helped by, and help in turn, the psychological drive to integration, and eventually, sufficient integration is achieved for the infant to recognize his mother as a whole object. The concept of the whole object contrasts both with that of the part object and that of the object split into good and bad. The infant begins to recognize his mother not as a collection of anatomical parts, breasts that feed him, hands that tend him, eyes that smile or frighten, but as a whole person with an independent existence of her own, who is the source of both his good and his bad experiences. This integration in his perception of his object goes *pari passu* with the inte-gration in his own self. He gradually realizes that it is the same infant, himself, who both loves and hates the same person, his mother. He experiences ambiv-alence. This change in his object relations brings with it a change in the content of his anxieties. While he was previously afraid that he would be destroyed by his persecutors, now he dreads that his own aggression will destroy his ambivalently loved object. His anxiety has changed from a paranoid to a depressive one. Since at that stage the infant's phan-tasies are felt as omnipotent, he is exposed to the experience that his aggression has destroyed his mother, leaving in its wake feelings of guilt, irre-trievable loss, and mourning. His mother's absence is often experienced as a death. As the depressive position starts in the oral stage of development, where the infant's love and hatred are linked with phantasies of incorporation, this ambivalence is felt also in relation to the mother as an internal object, and in states of depressive anxiety and mourning, the infant feels that he has lost not only his mother in the external world, but that his internal object is destroyed as well. Melanie Klein viewed these depressive anxieties as part of normal development and an unavoidable corollary to the process of inte-gration. They become reawakened up to a point in any subsequent situation of loss. There is a differ-ence here between the Kleinian view and the clas-sical view. In the classical view, melancholic illness involves ambivalence in relation to an internal object and regression to an oral fixation (Freud, 1917; Abraham, 1912), but normal mourning involves only the loss of the external object. In the

Kleinian view, ambivalence toward an internal object and the depressive anxieties associated with it are a normal stage of development and are reawakened in the normal mourning. It is often contended by classical Freudian analysts that when a patient is actually mourning it is usually an unproductive period in his analysis. Kleinian analysts, in contrast, find that analysis of mourning situations and tracing them to their early roots often helps the patient greatly in working through the mourning and coming out of it enriched by the experience.

I should like to describe here the dream of a patient soon after his mother's death. He dreamed that he was crawling on all fours around marshy ground, a kind of bog. He woke up with a sinking feeling, a mixture of depression and nausea. He described the nausea as a feeling as though the marshy ground were bubbling up inside his stomach. He associated first to crawling on all fours and connected it with an incident too long to report in detail, referring to his mother's pregnancy when he was a toddler, and the acute feelings of rage and loss he experienced in relation to his mother about the time of his sister's birth. Then he tried to describe the marshy ground, but found it very difficult, until he suddenly realized that it looked exactly like a microscope slide of a cancerous breast. His mother did not die of cancer of the breast, but he always thought this was the disease she would die of. He remembered hitting her in the breast and being terrified she would develop cancer. A further analysis of his dream led to a great deal of material about his early phantasies of attacking his mother's breast orally and anally and incorporating a destroyed breast as a focal point of his depression and the psychosomatic ailments in his childhood, reproduced in his nausea on the morning following his dream. The death of his mother reawakened all his earlier experiences of losing her, as at the birth of his sister and at weaning, and made him experience the loss as one of his internal mother as well, now experienced as the marshy bog in his internal world. This bog also represented the analytical breast identified with the original breast of his mother, and he expressed anxiety that his analysis might be "bogged down." Thus, his mourning situation could be analyzed both in relation to its early genetic roots and in the transference.

THE MANIC DEFENSES

The intensity of pain and anxiety in the depressive position mobilizes new and powerful defenses, namely the system of manic defenses. The manic defenses involve a regression to splitting, denial, idealization, and projection, basically schizoid mechanisms, but organized into a system to protect the ego from the experience of depressive anxiety. Since the depressive anxiety arises out of the infant's recognition of the mother as a whole object on whom he depends and in relation to whom he can experience ambivalence and the subsequent guilt and fear of loss, this whole relation has to be denied. Denial of the importance of his object and triumph over it, control, contempt, and devaluation take the place of depressive feelings.

A patient, following recognition of his oral attachment to the analyst, his greed for analysis, and his angry urinary attacks against her, had the following two dreams. In the first dream, he saw a house on fire and collapsing, but he drove past it, thinking it had little importance. In the second dream, he stole two buns from a bread shop, but he thought it did not matter very much, as they were such little buns. He defended himself against his depressive feelings about phantasies of stealing the analyst's breasts and destroying her body with his urine by denial and contempt. The anxiety and guilt about the fire is dealt with by denial—"it had little importance"—and the guilt about stealing by contempt, the analysis being represented by "such little buns." The fire associated among other things with the burning in his stomach (he had a gastric ulcer), and the collapsing house reminded him of his recurrent anxieties about a depressive collapse, so that it could be clearly shown to him how those attacks were directed at the analyst and analysis in his internal world. He frequently dealt with his anxieties about his mental and physical health in typically manic ways illustrated in this dream.

The manic defenses lead to a vicious circle. The depression results from the original attack on the object; the manic defenses preclude the ego from the experience of depression, but they also preclude a working through of the depressive position and necessitate a further attack on the object by denial, triumph, and contempt, thereby increasing the underlying depression. It is well known that where manic phenomena are encountered one has to look for the underlying depression. It is less well known that where there is a presenting depressive illness, one has to look for unconscious manic defense systems, precluding the working through of the depressive feelings. In the Kleinian view, the triumph over the internal object, which Freud describes as a feature of melancholic illness, is part of manic defenses perpetuating a situation of depression.

The working through of the depressive position in normal development depends on the capacity to make reparation. When the infant feels that in his hatred he has destroyed his good external and internal object, he experiences not only an intense feeling of guilt and loss but also pining and a longing to restore the lost loved object externally and internally, and to re-create the lost harmony and well-being. He mobilizes all his love and creativity to that end. It is this reparative drive that, in the Kleinian view, is the most important source of mental growth and creativity. The dream of a patient illustrates this. She dreamed that she was putting together a jigsaw puzzle representing a house in a landscape. The associations led to many past situations, particularly in her parental home. The putting together of the jigsaw puzzle was the analytical process, felt by her as a restoration and re-creation inside her of what was felt by her as a very shattered internal world, but it also represented a book she was currently writing, her wish to write being stimulated by this need to produce a whole picture out of shattered fragments.

With the repeated experiences of loss and recovery of his object, a recovery that is felt by him to be also a re-creation, the infant acquires an increasing confidence in the strength of his good object and in his own love and creativity. It is in the depressive position also that reality sense gradually develops. The depressive anxiety about the object leads the infant to withdraw his projections and to allow his object a more independent and separate existence. In recognizing his own ambivalence and his phantasies, he becomes aware of his inner reality and begins to differentiate it from the external reality of his object. A successful working through of the depressive position is fundamental to mental health. In the process of working through, the ego becomes integrated, capable of reality-testing and sublimation, and it is enriched from the introjection and assimilation of good objects. This in turn lessens his omnipotence and therefore his guilt and fear of loss.

It will be clear from the foregoing that technically we attach the greatest importance to the analysis of the manic and schizoid defenses to enable the patient to experience depressive anxiety and to work it through by way of restoration of the internal objects and the self. The paranoid-schizoid and depressive positions are not only stages of development. They are two types of ego integration and organization, and the ego has a constant struggle to maintain a state of integration.

Throughout his lifetime an individual oscillates between a paranoid-schizoid and a depressive internal organization. These oscillations vary in force with each individual psychopathology. At one end of the spectrum there is the schizophrenic or autistic patient who may rarely reach a depressive integration. At the other end is the fully mature individual with the well-integrated inner world, a person who has largely overcome depressive anxiety, who has a trust in a well-established good internal object and his own creative potential, and who has the capacity to deal with such depressive anxiety as is unavoidably stirred in realistic and creative ways. The analysis of the Oedipus complex in the Kleinian, as in the Freudian, technique remains a central task, but the technique is affected by the considerations stated above, and the paranoid-schizoid and depressive components in the Oedipal situation are carefully taken up.

OEDIPUS COMPLEX

A patient presented the following dream. He dreamed that he was in a strange place where the wash place was out in the open, so that he had to undress and wash naked. There were other naked people present. He suddenly noticed on a kind of platform a couple facing one another, each pointing at the other an identical lethal weapon. It was like a camera, but more bottle-shaped, and it was covered by something like a camera hood made out of tinfoil. If the tinfoil were lifted, a lethal ray or radiation would be released. He was absolutely sick with anxiety, knowing beforehand what would happen. One of them, probably the woman, lifted the hood, and he hoped for a moment that the other one would not retaliate, since it was so senseless, but of course he retaliated immediately, and the dreamer felt a sense of hopelessness, doom, and despair at the senselessness of the destruction. He also felt some anxiety about himself because he thought that he might have been in the field of the rays and that they might have got into him. His associations started with the fear of nuclear warfare, but then turned to memories of his sexual curiosity in childhood. The camera with the lethal ray associated in his mind with his fear of his mother's eyes, who, he felt, could control and attack his father and himself by looking. Sometimes he felt that her looks could kill. The association he found most upsetting was to the tinfoil. He knew precisely what it reminded him of. He had purchased two bottles of brandy as Christmas presents, one for his analyst (a woman) and one for his wife's analyst (a man). He was shocked at the thought that his gifts to this couple of analysts appeared in his dream as lethal weapons, with which they were supposed to annihilate one another. This dream is clearly concerned with the patient's Oedipal feelings, his sexual curiosity about his parents, and his hostility, which changed their intercourse into a lethal combat.

In the analysis of this dream, in addition to analyzing the patient's curiosity about the parents' sexual intercourse and his jealous feelings about it, both in the transference and in terms of his memories emerging from the repression, the following elements have been taken up: (1) The projective elements in his voyeurism. (2) Its effect on his perception of his parents in relation to himself (his fear of his mother's controlling eyes) and to one another (their intercourse becoming a mutual lethal attack). (3) The introjection of the situation, expressed in the dream by the patient's feeling that he is "in the field of the rays," that they "may have got into him" and the effect of this introjection on the patient's internal world, particularly his hypochondriacal anxiety, always fairly active in this patient and referred to by him in connection with anxiety about himself in the dream. (4) The depressive element, which is evidenced by his tremendous feeling of pity and loss; though the hostility is projected into the parents and they become dangerous to one another and to him, they are felt in the dream to be victims as much as persecutors, and obviously love and concern for them are retained in a large measure.[2]

I have stated before that Melanie Klein found in the analysis of very small children that the Oedipus complex has very early roots in the oral phase. When she developed later the concept of the depressive position, it became clear that the Oedipus complex begins at the same time. This indeed is implicit in the definition of the depressive position. If the infant becomes aware of his mother as a whole person, a whole separate person leading a life of her own, having other relationships of her own, he is immediately exposed to the experience of sexual jealousy. The fact that his world is still colored by his omnipotent projections increases his jealousy, for when he senses the emotional tie between his parents, he fantasies them as giving one another precisely those satisfactions he desires for himself. Thus he will experience his jealousy first of all in oral terms, but the triangular situation will have the configuration and the intensity of the Oedipus complex described by Freud.

The child's experience of the Oedipal situation will be dictated by the stage of his own libidinal development and expresses itself to begin with in oral terms. Also, the earlier the stage of the Oedipus complex, the more it will be dominated by the infant's omnipotent projections. This is very important technically because, in analyzing the early roots of the Oedipal conflict, one liberates it from the dominance of omnipotent mechanisms and phantasies. Tracing the Oedipus complex to its early roots enables one also to analyze the complex interplay between the early relationship to the breast and the Oedipus complex; for instance, how anxieties experienced in relation to the breast make the infant turn to the penis or, conversely, how the Oedipal jealousy may affect the feeding relationship to the breast.

Here is an example of how Oedipal jealousy interferes with the introjection of a good breast. The patient had been for months, off and on, preoccupied with a situation in his office. There was a young couple, Mr. and Mrs. L., of whom he was constantly complaining. They were interfering with his work and his relationships and were in a collusive relationship with their boss, Mr. R., who was thoroughly hated by the patient. In the session preceding the one I am going to describe in more detail he told me that he had heard that Mrs. L. was on the point of a breakdown and might be leaving the office. He felt suddenly terribly sorry for the L.'s. He realized that for months he had been complaining what a nuisance they were to him and had never given a thought to their predicament and the pressure they were under from Mr. R., whose paranoia, intrigues, and incessant demands were preying upon them and poisoning them. He was near tears speaking about them. He said that Mr. R. was behaving mentally just the way he was physically. The patient had often referred in the past to Mr. R.'s tendency to diarrhea—"just shitting all over the place." Mr. R. often, in the analysis, played the role of the bad sexual father, who dirtied the mother, but also that of the patient's split-off "dirtying" self projected into the father. The next day the patient started the session by complaining of headache and diarrhea. He then said that he had had three short dreams. In the first dream he had spent twenty-four hours speaking to Mrs. M. (the wife of a psychoanalyst). In the second, he saw some beautiful mountains, round and white, like a woman's breast, with a most beautiful lake, but he knew that the lake was full of some infection or poison, so that he could neither drink nor bathe in it, and he had to go away. In the third dream, he was in a holiday resort. The mistress of

---

2. The appearance of the phallic woman (she has the same weapon as the man) as related to the patient's projection into her of his own dangerous penis—the brandy bottle.

the hotel was a kind of courtesan and he wanted to kiss her, but had some anxiety about her as a dirty prostitute. The first associations were to Mrs. M. A few days previously he had seen Dr. M. giving me a lift in a Rolls-Royce and felt very jealous. The mountain landscape made him think of the forthcoming analytic holiday. The poison in the water associated in his mind with a typhoid epidemic in Switzerland, which in turn reminded him of his own diarrhea. He had also the previous day read in a newspaper about an infection in tinned food, so that a couple of tins could poison a whole family. He was particularly impressed by the thought of secret poison or infection because the lake looked so beautiful and unspoilt.

The interpretation dealt in essence with the situation in which the patient's Oedipal jealousy, stirred by the holiday and by the sight of the rich Dr. M. driving his analyst off in a car, interrupts the idealized feeding situation represented in the first dream and leads to a secret anal attack by diarrhea against the analyst as the feeding mother, so that the lake connected with the beautiful white mountains (the breast) becomes poisonous to him, like a couple of tins of poisoned food. The interpretation also emphasized how secret these attacks were, since on the face of it his relation to the analyst was so good. The interpretation mobilized an admission of many hostile thoughts about the analysis and the analyst personally and suspicions that the analytical treatment would make him worse. His thoughts then returned to the couple at the office, expressing tremendous concern and anxiety about them, particularly Mrs. L., repeating, "This poor woman, will she ever recover?" He knew that his concern was for the analyst and the analysis, would it ever recover from his secret dirtying? As he went on speaking of the couple, it gradually sounded more and more as if he were speaking about himself, because the expressions he applied to them were increasingly reminiscent of things he said about himself when he was depressed—"How will they ever get out of this mess? They will never recover from it, they won't be able to cope," and one got an increasingly clear picture of his introjection of, and his identification with, a parental couple irrecoverably ruined and destroyed by the Mr. R. part of himself. In this patient's experience, one can also see a move from a paranoid to a more depressive experience of his Oedipus complex. He starts by being completely persecuted by the L.'s as a parental couple. In his dreams and the associations to it there is also a paranoid suspicion of the feeding breast, represented by the infected lake, and, in the transference, his suspicions of the

analyst. Toward the end of the session, his feeling in relation to mother—"this poor woman"—and the parental couple is full of guilt and concern. He is particularly concerned with this destroyed couple in his internal world and with his identification with them.

WORKING THROUGH

These oscillations between the paranoid-schizoid and the depressive feelings underlie, in my opinion, the process of working through. In the analytic situation, the patient relives his relation to his original objects. His attachment to them has to be lived through again and given up again. In Freud's view, no object can be given up without being introjected into the ego. In the Kleinian view, this introjection is part of the depressive process. No object can be given up successfully without a complete process of mourning, as in the depressive position, ending in the introjection of a good internal object, strengthening the ego. Any new insight of any importance necessitates this process. The pain of the mourning situation mobilizes new manic and schizoid defenses, but with each repeated experience the ego is strengthened, the good object is more securely established, and the need to have recourse to new defenses is lessened. The process of working through is completed when some aspect of the object has been given up in this way.

It is impossible to speak of the Kleinian technique of today without mentioning the special attention paid to the factor of envy. Since the publication of *Envy and Gratitude* (Klein, 1957), the analysis of envy has played an increasingly important role. The analysis of early oral anxieties led Melanie Klein to believe that envy has very early roots and plays a large part in the infant's relation to the breast. She distinguishes between it and greed and jealousy and considers it more primitive than jealousy. "Jealousy is based on love and aims at the possession of the loved object and the removal of the rival. It pertains to a triangular relationship and therefore to a time of life when objects are clearly recognized and differentiated from one another. Envy, on the other hand, is a two-part relation in which the subject envies the object for some possession or quality; no other live object need enter into it. Jealousy is necessarily a whole-object relationship, while envy is essentially experienced in terms of part-objects, though it persists into whole-object relationships.

Greed aims at the possession of all the goodness that

can be extracted from the object, regardless of consequences; this may result in the destruction of the object and the spoiling of its goodness, but the destruction is incidental to the ruthless acquirement. Envy aims at being as good as the object, but, when this is felt as impossible, it aims at spoiling the goodness of the object, to remove the source of envious feelings. It is this spoiling aspect of envy that is so destructive to development, since the very source of goodness that the infant depends on is turned bad, and good introjections, therefore, cannot be achieved. Envy, though arising from primitive love and admiration, has a less strong libidinal component than greed and is suffused with the death instinct. As it attacks the source of life, it may be considered to be the earliest direct externalization of the death instinct. Envy stirs as soon as the infant becomes aware of the breast as a source of life and good experience; the real gratification which he experiences at the breast, reinforced by idealization, so powerful in early infancy, makes him feel that the breast is the source of all comforts, physical and mental, an inexhaustible reservoir of food and warmth, love, understanding and wisdom. The blissful experience of satisfaction which this wonderful object can give will increase his love and his desire to possess, preserve and protect it, but the same experience stirs in him also the wish to be himself the source of such perfection. He experiences painful feelings of envy which carry with them the desire to spoil the qualities of the object which can give him such painful feelings (Segal, 1964).

The importance of envy lies in the fact that it interferes with the normal operation of the schizoid mechanisms. Splitting into an ideal and a bad object cannot be established, since it is the ideal object that is the object of envy, and therefore hostility. Thus, the introjection of an ideal object, which could become the core of ego, is disturbed at its very roots. Defenses against envy may be equally detrimental to growth. The devaluation of the object and the projection of envy into it give rise to persecutory anxiety and lead to the formation of an envious superego, which interferes with the development of the ego. The analysis of patients suffering from an excessively severe superego often reveals that it is the envious aspect of the superego that is felt as most damaging, since it is directed not only against the aggressive wishes of the ego, but also, and often predominantly, against any positive or creative strivings of the ego. In the analytical situation, envy manifests itself often by negative therapeutic reactions. As soon as the analysis is felt as good, and the analyst is felt as the source of the good analysis, it has to be attacked and destroyed. Envy brings in its wake feelings of hopelessness. Bad experiences are bad, but good experiences also become bad, since they stir envy; therefore there seems to be no hope

for a good experience. Since a good object cannot be introjected, the ego does not feel that it can grow and eventually bridge the gap between the self and the original object by introspection and assimilation, and this in turn increases envy, leading again to hopelessness. The analysis of envy, which has been split off, denied, and projected, is extremely painful and disturbing, but it reintroduces hope through the establishment of a good and enviable object. Latent appreciation can be mobilized and the battle can be fought again between love and gratitude and envy.

It is difficult to give a brief example here, since envy is usually heavily defended against and has to be tracked in painful detail, but I would like to describe the dream of one patient, showing some emergence of hope, when, for the first time, he could admit some envy in relation to the analyst. This patient, a borderline case, came to the first session carrying two bags of food, a Thermos bottle of coffee and one of tea, and throughout the session fed himself a number of drugs, such as dexidrine. He made it clear from the start who had possession and control of the feeding breast. In the early stages of his analysis, he developed the following pattern. He would frequently miss or come very late, but after the session he would spend hours in the lavatory, doing his "post analysis," that is, writing notes on his session, categorizing them, drawing conclusions, and so forth. He often said that this "post analysis" was of far more value to him than the analysis. Since the patient had a large number of anal perversions, it was not difficult to show him, with the help of his dreams, that in his phantasy he was feeding himself on his own feces, considered as far superior to the mother's food. His feeling of superiority was so absolute that an interpretation of envy would have been quite laughable to him, though the enormity of his envy of both men and women, particularly women, was blatantly obvious. One could, however, get at it by interpreting his projective identification. There was no doubt in his mind about the analyst's inferiority and her feelings of dependence on him, rejection by him, envy of his riches, and so forth. The analyst, in his mind, had the same characteristics as his extremely envious superego, by which he was controlled to such a degree that he was not allowed, for instance, to read a book or listen to the radio, because it wasted time. He felt equally controlled and nagged by his analyst. Accompanying this was a state of despair of such absoluteness that it had become painless. When finally he began to be aware of his own envy in relation to the analyst, primarily as a feeding breast, he had the following dream. He dreamed that under an enormous pile of dead leaves he found a single snowdrop, white as a drop of milk. His waking association was that at last, under a pile of feces, he had found a single drop of milk as a sign of hope.

The discovery of early envy and the way in which it operates has given great impetus to new work, particularly with psychotics (Bion, 1959) and other intractable cases, for instance, severe acting out and drug addiction (Rosenfeld, 1965). It is, however, impossible in this chapter to treat of it at length.

TERMINATION OF ANALYSIS

Has the Kleinian outlook on analysis altered the criteria for the termination of an analysis and the therapeutic aim? In certain basic ways the criteria remain the same—the lifting of repression, insight, freeing the patient from early fixations and inhibitions, and enabling him to form full and satisfactory personal relationships.

The Kleinian analyst will be guided in his evaluation of the therapeutic progress mainly by his assessment of the patient's internal world; he will try to evaluate the state of integration in the patient's ego and his internal objects and his capacity to maintain the state of integration in situations of stress.

Melanie Klein (1950) wrote:

My criterion for the termination of an analysis is, therefore, as follows: have persecutory and depressive anxieties been sufficiently reduced in the course of the analysis, and has the patient's relation to the external world been sufficiently strengthened to enable him to deal satisfactorily with the situation of mourning arising at this point? By analysing as fully as possible both the negative and the positive transference, persecutory and depressive anxieties are diminished and the patient becomes increasingly able to synthesize the contrasting aspects of the primary objects, and the feelings towards them, thus establishing a more realistic and secure attitude to the internal and external world. If these processes have been sufficiently experienced in the transference situation both the idealisation of the analyst and the feelings of being persecuted by him are diminished; the patient can then cope more successfully with the feelings of loss caused by the termination of the analysis and with that part of the work of mourning which he has to carry out by himself after the end of the analysis.

REFERENCES

Bion, W. R. Development of schizophrenic thought. *International Journal of Psychoanalysis*. 1956, 37, 344-346.

Bion, W. R. The differentiation of the psychotic from the non-psychotic personalities. *International Journal of Psychoanalysis*, 1957, 38, 266-275.

Bion, W. R. On hallucination. *International Journal of Psychoanalysis*, 1958, 39, 341-349.

Bion, W. R. Attacks on linking. *International Journal of Psychoanalysis*, 1959, 40, 308-315.

Isaacs, Susan. The nature and function of phantasy. (*Developments in psychoanalysis*, 1952.) *International Journal of Psychoanalysis*, 1948, 29, 73-97.

Klein, Melanie. Psychoanalysis of children. (*Contributions to Psychoanalysis*) (Trans. by Alix Strachey). New York: Norton, 1932.

Klein, Melanie. On the criteria for the termination of an analysis. *International Journal of Psychoanalysis*, 1950, 31, 78-80, 204.

Klein, Melanie. *Envy and gratitude*. New York: Basic Books, 1957.

Rosenfeld, Herbert A. *Psychotic states: a psychoanalytical approach*. London: Hogarth Press, 1965.

Segal, Hanna. Some aspects of the analysis of a schizophrenic. *International Journal of Psychoanalysis*, 1950, 31, 268-278.

Segal, Hanna. Depression in the schizophrenic. *International Journal of Psychoanalysis*, 1956, 37, 339-343.

Segal, Hanna. Curative factors in psychoanalysis. *International Journal of Psychoanalysis*, 1962, 43, 212-217.

Segal, Hanna. *Introduction to the work of Melanie Klein*. New York: Basic Books, 1964.

36

VICISSITUDES OF BEING, KNOWING AND EXPERIENCING IN THE THERAPEUTIC SITUATION

M. Masud R. Khan

EDITOR'S NOTE

One of an extensive series of penetrating contributions by this British psychoanalyst and follower of Winnicott (see Khan 1974), this paper seems to defy classification. While it has a distinctly interactional quality, it has a bearing also on the nature of the analytic setting (Part VII) and on both transference (Part I) and nontransference (Part II). But it deals as well with aspects of the patient's analytic experience that cannot really be considered under any of these rubrics. The distinctions he draws between the patient's experiences of being, knowing, and experiencing suggest qualities of the analytic process and the nature of cure that have seldom been investigated, and the implications he sees these as having for technique have a cast quite unusual for this literature. Khan's use of the concept of not interpreting, which follows upon earlier remarks by Winnicott (1956), offers a perspective on the ego building aspects of analysis that have to this day been quite neglected. The paper itself is an artistic product capable of generating in the reader that experience of discovery so rarely encountered in the psychoanalytic literature.

All psychotherapeutic experiences that we hear discussed in various types and styles of psychotherapies today derive in one way or another from Freud's invention of the psychoanalytic situation. Stone (1961) has given a very detailed and authentic account of the nature and character of the analytic situation (cf. Khan, 1962). Here I shall only briefly state the essential features of the psychoanalytic situation. I am approaching the whole area and issue of psychotherapeutic experiences from the classical Freudian point of view. It is my belief, however, that what is true in this frame of reference is also valid for all other types of psychotherapeutic ventures.

The total analytic situation, as arranged and established by the analyst for his patient, functions in terms of: (1) the analytic setting; (2) the transference; (3) interpretations.

Analytic setting is, of course, the physical ambience that the analyst provides: the room, the light, the furniture, the couch and his own presence. Transference is something very specialized, which the analyst also provides. The concept of transference, as defined by Freud (1912), has become too generalized today. The important thing about transference is that the potentiality in the patient for transference experience is mobilized and harnessed only by the analytic setting and by the analyst's behaviour, in which verbal interpretation plays a very mutative role. Furthermore, it is necessary to distinguish what the transference provides towards the total clinical process from that which the analytic setting provides (Winnicott, 1955; Balint, 1968).

The analytic setting provides space, time, and the presence of the analyst towards the clinical process,

Reprinted from *British Journal of Medical Psychology* 42:383–393, 1969.

and the experiential yield from this for the patient is 'holding'. I am borrowing the concept of 'holding' from Winnicott's theory of parent-infant relationship. Winnicott (1960*a*) uses this concept

to denote not only the actual holding of the infant, but also the total environmental provision prior to the concept of *living with*. In other words, it refers to a three-dimensional or space relationship with time gradually added.

The inference here is that the clinical analytic situation is essentially modelled on the infant-mother relationship. It is here that the researches into infant care on the one hand and the theories of modern ego psychologists on the other have substantially enlarged the more restricted concept of Freud of both the role of the analyst and that of the analytic situation. What Winnicott designates as 'the actual physical holding of the infant' in the clinical situation, metaphorically as well as sentiently, is represented by the role of the couch. The result of this 'holding' in terms of time and space for the patient is the experience of *being*.

In parallel and yet in contrast, the transference in the total analytic situation provides the means for an object-relationship, and thus the scope for the processing of inner psychic reality with its attendant defence mechanisms. If this comes through correctly, then it leads to *experiencing* in the patient of himself. A concomitant of the act of *experiencing* is that of *knowing*—that is, insight. Here I am trying to relate the function of the analytic setting in terms of 'holding' to *being*, and transference through object relationships to *experiencing* in the patient.

Knowing in the psychotherapeutic experience results largely from the act of interpretation on the part of the analyst. Verbal interpretation is a very specialized and limited function of the *total* behaviour of the analyst *vis-à-vis* his patient in the *total* analytic situation. Interpretation is that act of verbal and affective intervention, contribution, and evaluation by the analyst which crystallizes two new experiences for the patient: (*a*) recognition of his *being*, and (*b*) the *knowing* of his *experiencing*.

The whole of the psychoanalytic theory of analytic technique is more or less centred on explicating the different modalities of *knowing* through interpretation and transference. What is less often discussed is the fluctuating interplay in the patient's total experience of himself in the analytic setting in terms of *being*, through the object-relationships provided via transference towards *experiencing*, and the *knowing* of his intrapsychic reality and interpersonal conflicts through interpretation.

Interpretation in this context has highly specialized characteristics in terms of the given climate of psychodynamics and psychic reality operating in the clinical situation at a given moment (Heimann, 1956). The act of interpreting, however, should include also the analyst's reticence—that is, his *not-interpreting*. As Winnicott (1954) and Balint (1968), among others, have stressed in recent years, in the area of analytic work where the setting is facilitating holding and being, it is essentially *not-interpreting* that is the analyst's contribution. To the question of *what* is not being interpreted, the answer is ambiguous. What one can identify is that the act of not-interpreting is not a simple passive act. It is the result of intensive analytic work that precedes it, in which a patient's resistances, deriving from his ego pathology interfering with his own authentic experiencing of his *being* in the analytic setting, have been mitigated. Balint (1968) has defined this role of the analyst as 'the unobtrusive analyst', and Winnicott (1954) calls it 'the holding of the regressed patient in the clinical setting'. Both these, of course, are highly sophisticated artifacts of clinical experience, arrived at through diligent interpretative work.

To put it paradoxically, un-interpretation is the climax only of interpretation. It is not possible to arrive at un-interpretation without interpretation. It is this that is implied by the statement often made that the basic ego strength and complexity of psychic functioning has to establish itself in the patient before he can arrive at the point where the non-interpretation of the analyst crystallizes the experience of being in the patient (Khan, 1964).

The second function of interpretation is that of inhibiting and organizing the inessential and discursive exploitation of transference by the patient towards discharge through mentation. There is a very great deal of compulsive material-producing which runs counter to the need of *experiencing* himself by the patient in the analytic situation.

It is only when the vectors of *being* and *experiencing* are reliably established in a patient's capacity and functioning in the analytic situation that one can begin to discuss the mutative role of interpretation towards facilitating *knowing* of all the conflictual areas of intrapsychic and interpersonal realities in the patient. Only thus can interpretation facilitate insight.

In the above re-statement of the psychodynamics of the total psychoanalytic situation, the emphasis is very much on what the analyst does, contributes, and abstains from intrusively inflicting on his patient. Our contemporary gains from the study of infant-mother relationships, as well as ego psychology, have brought us to a point where it is largely the understanding of the countertransference discipline and functioning that will yield the true definition of the nature of interpretation in the analytic process.

Countertransference is here being defined as a non-pathological capacity of the analyst's affectivity, intelligence, and imagination to comprehend the total reality of the patient. The word 'counter' in the concept countertransference is most significant, because it establishes the fact of the separateness of the analyst from that which he is identifying and empathizing with in the patient's experience. This differentiation of the analyst's self from the patient's experience in the area of countertransference is essential to keep in focus, because any blurring of boundaries in this context leads merely to a clinical confusion of psychic realities. It is imperative that, in the clinical equation, the psychic boundaries and processes of at least one party, namely the analyst, should always be distinctly structured and defined in terms of their functions and aims.

I shall now give clinical material from three patients to define the nature and character of specific psychotherapeutic experiences in their analyses.

INTERPRETATION, SYMBOLIZATION AND KNOWING

I shall report now from the clinical material of a young, highly educated, sensitive, and intelligent female patient, who had sought analysis because, in her own statement: 'There is something in myself that I find lacking and which I would like to know more about.' Emphasis on *knowing* in this case from the very beginning was the patient's, not mine. She suffered from a poverty of fantasy life. She was too rational, she felt. Analysis has now been in progress for some four years, and I report from a recent session.

The patient came in a rather robust mood of well-being, lay down, and in her usual style started to talk quietly. She had gone to the theatre over the weekend with a female friend who had suddenly got very upset and depressed by something in the play and they had to leave the theatre. The next day, this friend had rung up the patient and talked at length about her inner problems, to which the patient was very sympathetic, and the friend had been almost crying on the phone from depression and distress. The patient, who has as a person an explicit capacity to understand others and empathize with their

moods, was left wondering afterwards how can someone become so depressed; someone who is in her own life otherwise very creative. This made her talk about how in her own life she has never felt bored, and there has always been a sort of solid sense of well-being in her, and then she commented that the sense of well-being in her somewhere always makes her think it is because an area of her own inner life is shut away from her and which she needs to know in order to be a deeper sort of person. She described her state of affairs as being well from a lack. Then she was silent for a little while, and I could feel that she was absorbed with herself. She suddenly remembered that she had had a dream which had upset her very much. She prefaced telling the dream by the statement that 'it was a new sort of dream for her'. The dream was as follows:

Dream about my mother carrying my father's coffin downstairs. I was standing to one side at the bottom of the stairs and was upset to see that his head had to be in a separate coffin and that both coffins were so thin, I wondered how they'd managed to get his body in and thought his feet must have been hurt in getting them to lie flat. My mother opened the coffin with his head in — it looked like a cold joint of meat — skull shaped — and my mother got a knife and made an incision where the nose would have been and then scrubbed at a place on his cheek till some of the flesh came up. Then she put two apples in one eye socket and one apple in the other socket. While this ritual was going on, I felt very miserable and watched my tears sinking into the carpet.

In her associations to the dream, the patient had singled out four features as being important:

1. That though the dream's narrative may strike one as sadistic, in fact the affects experienced by her while dreaming had not that quality. Her mother in the dream, she felt, was doing something almost autistically and had no comprehension at all of its meaning. She was, as it were, involved in a ritual act without affect.

2. Her own helplessness *vis-à-vis* the mother particularly, and all the events of the dream during the act of dreaming. She was merely a passive onlooker, who registered the events without understanding anything of their meaning.

3. Though she had been able to cry for the first time in a dream, she felt distressed at the fact that her tears had aridly fallen on to the carpet and made no real impression either on her mother or in her own experience.

4. She had the distinct feeling that the dream's narrative was saying more than the imagery of the dream, but she could not quite grasp what. This was

in marked contrast to her other dreams, where the imagery had always been very explicitly representative of instinctual needs and conflicts.

In terms of the dream specifically and what I knew from the patient's history and material in the past, I decided to give a long interpretation. I pointed out that the most important element in the dream was that she was witnessing something profoundly disturbing in her mother, of which her mother herself had no understanding. Furthermore, she, that is the patient, could also contribute nothing towards ameliorating either the mother's predicament or incapacity. I here offer a construction to her that what the dream was symbolically trying to process was what the patient had grown up with and registered throughout her childhood in her mother, but had not the psychic capacity to print and make conscious at the time.

It was this particular inability to make reparation to the mother, and the phase-inadequacy of her maturational capacities that had led to the arrest of her fantasy life and pushed her to a precocious alignment with reality and extroverted rationality (see Winnicott, 1948). Mourning and sadness became unfeasible in her developmental process as a child, because neither she nor her mother had the means to cope with it at that time. I also reminded her how, during her early childhood, she had been thrown very much on her mother's resources because of long absences of her father on war service, when she was between two and six years of age.

It was most striking how this patient, who so far had been able to recall very little from her childhood and had given almost no material about her mother, now seemed to open up and describe most succinctly and meaningfully some basic aspects of her early development and relationship to her mother. I am here abstracting from material of some three weeks that followed the dream session. The features that turned out to be most important were:

(a) How clearly she had registered but not allowed it to become elaborated by fantasy, her mother's state of chronic and static dismay vis-à-vis life and her own marriage, which she had compensated for by fetishistic over-involvement with her daughter's body hygiene.

(b) The total absence of ambivalence and conflict vis-à-vis her mother because of the mother's incapacity to tolerate any form of distress, anger, and fractiousness in the child.

(c) How she had not at all experienced the absence of her father through all those years.

(d) A premature opting out for the exploitation of ego-functions in actual living, both in games and in studies, leading to the curtailment of the fantasy elaboration of inner psychic reality. Along with this was combined a very severe restriction of aggressive behaviour, largely due to the mother's intolerance of it, and the mother's highly obsessional defences in herself against hostility and aggression (cf. James, 1960; Greenson, 1958).

For me and the patient, the important thing about the dream had been her use of the capacity for symbolization, without which there is no knowing possible. For this patient, life had never been a problem—intellectually, socially, or sexually—but yet she herself had always been aware of a certain element of lack of depth in her experience of life. She had felt that my interpretation, which enabled her to see in the dream-imagery a metaphorical and symbolic way of knowing her past, had opened up for her a completely new way of looking at herself. From now on, she began to take a much deeper interest in literature and the arts, and her relationship to people, also, changed significantly. She felt she could now begin to know others instead of merely coping with them.

Similarly, she felt for the first time insight related her to herself rather than being experienced merely as an attack on her very private and unshareable self.

I am using the concept of 'knowing' in a rather complex way. Knowing is more than just mental reportage of self-awareness or verbalization of memories of life experiences. There is a distinct quality of ego-cathexis plus imagination added to the remembered facts or the mental representations of past experiences for the experience of knowing to crystallize, and it is one of the basic functions of interpretation to sponsor this particular imaginative, affective ego-cathexis in the patient of her own self-awareness. Self-awareness by itself is an insufficient source of experience. It is the augmentation of self-awareness by ego-cathexis that alone leads to reflectiveness, and reflectiveness is the true matrix for insight to crystallize as a creative psychotherapeutic experience for the patient. I can perhaps best establish my point here by using an argument from W. H. Auden (1956), who in his paper 'Making, Knowing, and Judging', following Coleridge's distinction between primary imagination and secondary imagination, argued:

The concern of the Primary Imagination, its only concern, is with sacred beings and sacred events. . . A sacred being cannot be anticipated; it must be encountered. . . The impression made by a sacred event is of an overwhelming but undefinable significance. The Secondary

Imagination is of another character and at another mental level. It is active not passive, and its categories are not the sacred and the profane, but the beautiful and the ugly. . . the Secondary Imagination is social and craves agreement with other minds. . . Both kinds of imagination are essential to the health of the mind. Without the inspiration of sacred awe, its beautiful forms would soon become banal, its rhythms mechanical; without the activity of the Secondary Imagination the passivity of the Primary would be the mind's undoing; sooner or later its sacred beings would possess it, it would come to think of itself as sacred, exclude the outer world as profane and so go mad. . . The value of a profane thing lies in what it usefully does, the value of a sacred thing lies in what it *is*.

I want to elaborate on Auden's definitions to establish my point *vis-à-vis* the reported dream. It is easily demonstrable how the patient draws upon her social experience of her friend's distress and works it symbolically towards a knowing of her internalization of her mother's predicament and its impact upon her development. Her experiences of well-being derived from the idolization of very archaic body-experiences from infant-care with corresponding idealized attachment to primary mother. This I would attribute to primary imagination, and postulate that here, though there can be experience of *being*, little complexity of psychic elaboration through symbolization, secondary imagination and its fruition into *knowing*, can actualize (Khan, 1968). It was the provision of the interpretative work that had gradually mobilized the patient's capacity for symbolic work and knowing of her inner reality. Only through the secondary imagination can a person relate external reality (persons) to inner reality (internal objects), and arrive at that symbolic work which is the basis of all *knowing*. The fundamental role of interpretation with such patients is to facilitate their true use of their secondary imagination and symbolic process towards their own *knowing* (cf. Rycroft, 1956).

The final detail of the dream deserves further mention—namely, the patient's incapacity to *experience* her own crying, as well as her mother's unresponsiveness to it. At this stage of her analysis this patient is still unable to surrender to grief and sadness in a meaningful way. Crying in the sessions is a collapse of her ego capacities, and she feels reduced to nothing by it. It has no value as yet. It is important to bear in mind how there is no rigid chronological sequence of mutative therapeutic stages from *being* to *experiencing* to *knowing* or the other way round. In each case, one has gradually to discover with and through the patient what is the true psychic reality of a given phase of work. This patient

who is solidly anchored in her *being* and has now the means of *knowing*, has yet to establish her potentiality for *experiencing* deeply and truly, which would entail also true object-relating. I abstained deliberately from interpreting the sadistic elements in the dream and did not interpret to the patient at any point that her mother's behaviour in the dream was also a projection of the patient's own rage and sadistic fantasies about the absent father on to her mother.

Today, when we have a vast conceptual vocabulary available to us to translate a patient's dream-imagery with, it is important to restrict our range to the patient's symbolic capacity in our interpretative work. Also, this reticence is part of what I have earlier on defined as the analyst's *un-interpretative* function (Khan, 1963).

EXPERIENCING VERSUS MENTATION

I shall now report briefly from the analysis of a male patient with brilliant academic achievements, who had had some five years of analysis in another country which had been most helpful to him in getting him through his academic career. Laing (1961) and Guntrip (1968) have given succinct phenomenological descriptions of this type of schizoid person.

He had come seeking further analysis because of his incapacity to rest from what he described as his 'interminable mental constructs', which were his only way of attaching to others, apart from absurdly passive and perverse sexual experiences with women, that left him always depleted and enraged. He politely and passively blamed his previous analysis for having exaggerated his tendency to read meanings into everything rather than experiencing, and it was from this that he felt he needed to be cured.

One of the basic difficulties this patient lived with was what he called the 'insatiable chatter in his head', which he could never stop. He arrived for every session with his customary load of already interpreted material and left every session with a sense of acute futility at having experienced nothing. There was a total absence of reverie in him. His dreams were very much like pictorializations of psychological abstractions of his daily contacts. Any interpretative work that one did at this stage merely added to the 'chatter in his head' and exacerbated his cancerous mentation.

Not to interpret was equally futile, because it gave him the feeling of having destroyed the analyst in the clinical setting and filled him with both panic and dismay. To find the sort of interpretation that would 'shut up the chatter in his head' was the first task, if he was to experience anything. I shall now report on the session in which this happened, but I shall have to give a little bit of background material to it.

Alongside his interminable 'chatter in his head' this patient also suffered from inexhaustible hypochondriacal symptoms which his first analyst had diligently interpreted in terms of their psychodynamic meanings. I had taken exactly the opposite course with him. I had found him a very able physician and handed over that side of the equation of his total behaviour to the physician, and adamantly refused to interpret it. He had arrived on a Monday session and reported that he had had various minor surgical operations done on his body over the weekend. He emphasized how physical pain was one thing that gave him momentary rest from the 'chatter in his head'. He did something very simple in this session which was unusual for him. He took the blanket from the chair and wrapped himself in it and lay down. After a little while, he complained that I had given no interpretation at all, to which I responded that any interpretation on my part would undo his gain from having experienced respite from his mentation during the pain incurred by him over the weekend from his surgeons. He lay down quietly and gradually his breathing sank to a low rhythm, and he fell asleep.

He woke himself up automatically just about five minutes before the end of the session. He said he had been asleep and had not dreamt. 'What a relief!' he added.

The next session is the one that I want to report on. The patient arrived, requested that one of the lights be switched off, which darkened the room considerably, lay down, and after a little while I could hear him crying. He cried the whole length of the session; then he gradually collected himself, sat up, thanked me for not having disrupted his experience, and said that so far as he could recall, this was the first time he had experienced himself as a person living through a private emotional state to which he had absolutely no clue, and yet he had tolerated not tinkering with it mentally. The real gain to the patient from this experience of himself was that he felt now he had available to him in himself a real experience of quietude and affective sentience, which he could contrast to his 'chatter in the head'. Up till now, one of the most aggravating features of his endless mentation was that though he knew it to be a morbid and wasteful state of self-dissipation, he had no other type of self-experience to correct it with. This helped him to move from obsessive introspection to a reflective evaluation of himself.

After this experience, which happened some six months before writing of this account, this patient has, by his own volition, changed his whole way of life. From living a compulsively collusive and cluttered existence with others where his main form of self-dissipation was conversation, he is living for the first time in his life a sort of private existence. In his work, also, he has shifted from being compulsively productive to long stretches of reading and studying. In analysis he speaks thoughtfully, and it is possible for him to relate meaningfully to his past and present. What I wish to emphasize here is a very distinctive use of interpretation towards delimiting and curtailing the mentation. Unfortunately, even this description is hardly adequate to the complexity of the affective interchange between the patient and myself in the analytic situation through our very presences in the setting. It is my contention here that excessive interpretative work with such a patient turns us into the accomplice of their psychopathology and dissociates the patient for ever from experiencing himself as a person.

For this particular patient, *experiencing* had to be first a very private and unshareable state before it could become possible for him to relate from this capacity to others both symbolically and sentiently. Here, the basic function of the interpretation was to *neutralize* the transference object-relationship towards enabling the patient to use the setting as the vehicle of his self-sustenance in the analytic situation.

That session emphasized the importance for him of my recognition of his need to be in the crying state without needing help or intervention. It is this avoidance of the intrusion of even *knowing*, that is insight, on the one hand, and facilitation of his presence as a person, who was to all practical purposes unrelated to me in the transference, that enabled him to arrive at *experiencing something* in himself to which he could neither put a mental construct nor infest with erotic tensions. This is what, temporarily at least, shut up the 'chatter in his head' and shifted him from mentation to *experiencing* in the analytic situation.

This is in marked contrast to the female patient I have reported, where interpretation through transference relationship had provided the symbolic instruments with which to psychically know herself, and learn to be reflective insightfully towards her own experiences and others.

THE DREAD OF BEING (THE TRUE SELF)

Winnicott (1960a) has introduced the concepts of true and false self in the psychoanalytic literature. Briefly stated, his argument is that dissociation of a person into a true and false self is the result of the deficiency of primary environmental (maternal) provisions in infant-care. The chief characteristics of the false self organization are:

1. Its defensive function is to hide and protect the true self, whatever that might be.
2. The false self has as its main concern a search for conditions which will make it possible for the true self to come into its own.
3. When a false self becomes organized in an individual who has a high intellectual potential, there is a strong tendency for the mind to become the location of the false self.
4. The point of origin of the false self is in a defence against that which is unthinkable, namely the 'exploitation of the true self, which would result in its annihilation'.

Using Winnicott's hypotheses, I would now recount clinical experiences from the analysis of a young female patient of 24, who could tolerate living only through a hectic exploitation of her false self organization, and who had a terrible dread of ever being found and met in her true self—that is, her authentic being as a person.

This girl, with an inordinately high IQ, has had a long and chequered 'career' as a patient since she was 16. She had been referred to me by a female colleague who had patiently and heroically managed her illness for some three years, and had eventually got so worn down by this patient's violent physical attacks on her person and clinical setting that she could take no more of it. The patient had been physically unmanageable throughout her treatment and even hospitalization had not helped, because she had charmed the hospital staff with her compliant helpfulness. Her violence was exclusively directed at the person of her analyst and her familial environment. The patient is a hefty, wilful girl, with a diabolical will and cunning. My chief reason for believing that perhaps I could help her better than her female analyst was that physically I felt stronger than her, and knew I could meet her compulsion to test me in that area. I had also staff available to me, should I need them. I mention these details because ordinarily we do not take such factors into consideration with our patients, but they become of fateful importance in the management and treatment of a patient like this.

This girl, who has an extraordinary capacity to talk and think in her relation to others, cannot use language to express herself in the analytic situation. Instead of speech and verbalization, *action* was her sole mechanism of defence. Hence, she could not use the couch either. She simply stood and stared at one with a violent and explosive intensity.

She had no tolerance of interpretations. They created a mad, berserk panic in her and compelled her to thrash about. She had no use for insight either. She wanted only *the truth*: and it had to be the given and not the found truth. If she helped one to understand her predicament, then she felt she had betrayed herself. From this frenzied muddle which was her presence in the room, one had to decide to aim towards some one experience that could be focalized as a point of reference. I decided, quite arbitrarily I confess, to make it her refusal to use the couch and lie down. I knew perfectly well she would react violently against it.

For months we battled over this issue of not using the couch. I tried out every interpretation, and she mocked and rejected them all. Eventually, one day I said to her that I can see that so long as she is *in action*, she is not existing in her own being and person. But if she were to lie down she would then be vulnerable, because she would be present in her being and thus could be damaged and annihilated. 'By what?' she asked menacingly. To which I replied that I did not know by what, but I knew what I said was true of her behaviour. We bickered and battled over this for a few more weeks. Eventually, to prove me wrong, she agreed to try lying down and did. It was a bizarre sight indeed. I can only describe it by the absurd statement that what I could see was a person standing up in a horizontal position. Of course, she did not stay on the couch for more than a minute, and was up on her feet and lunging about all over the room.

In the next session, however, she arrived tearful and chastened in mood. After asking her usual silly and provocative questions, for the first time she volunteered to tell me a dream. Her exact words were: 'I had the same ghastly dream again. You know it.' She would not accept that I did not know the dream for the simple reason that she had not told it to me yet. She said that was irrelevant. If I really cared and tried I would be able to know the dream. A few more weeks passed battling around this. Then one day she told me the dream while she was lying down on the couch, which she had been doing fitfully now and then. The dream was: 'All my teeth were rotting and falling away. In fact if I had not awakened myself, all of me would have rotted.' She has had this dream recurrently since childhood and never told it before to any one of her three previous therapists. She asked me what it meant, and hastened to add: 'Oh, don't tell me!' Then she asked again what it meant. I said that so far as I could tell, *she had an anxiety dream about the dream she cannot dream.* She was thoughtfully silent, and remarked: 'I know — you mean I cannot dream about me in the other world, where I am perfect and everything is perfect.' This was the first time she had mentioned 'the other world' where she is a perfect being. She added further: 'I see what you mean about not being able to use the couch and that annihilation lark. It is the same as my not being able to sleep properly in my bed. If I dreamt the real dream, then it would not be all in my own possession; some of it will always be the dream's, even if it is my own dream. Me in the other world has to be all in my keeping. Only thus it can be kept perfect.'

Suddenly she was up and laughing 'n her maniacal way where one cannot tell whether she is shrieking or laughing. And she said: 'You think it is all mad, don't you.' I agreed with her that to me it all sounded very mad, but I also knew it was very real and meaningful to her. She accepted that gracefully.

In the following months she talked a little more about her two 'me's'— the 'me in this world' and the 'me in the other world'. How she is always trying to arrange her 'me in this world' to become something where her 'perfect me in the other world' could live from, but it never works. Something always goes wrong. So it never starts. Living for this girl is a terrible anguish and ordeal. Her only respite from herself is when she is acting for others. One thing, however, is now quite clear — that to bring her 'perfect me in the other world' into the clinical situation is to take the risk of annihilation. Hence all she can communicate is the terror and dread of that eventuality. And yet she insists it must happen one day if 'I am to really live. It cannot go on for ever like this.' Maybe she will have to kill her 'me in this world' in the end, she says; which in her case is not an idle hysterical threat. It could go that way (cf. Winnicott, 1960*b*).

CONCLUSIONS

I have given three clinical examples of how patients *use* the analyst as an object in the clinical situation. These examples are perhaps extreme cases. Of course, there are endless variations of such *use* of the analyst that mix these modalities in different proportions. I would like now to discuss briefly each *use* of the analyst described in the case material.

In the case of the girl whose dream was about her mother's unconscious and its impact on her developmental process and maturation, it is clear that the child had been able to internalize the experience and the corresponding object-relationship. Only she could not bring all her later developmental and socio-sexual experiences to bear upon this experience and modify, correct and enlarge it. It stayed dissociated and hidden in a very special way, and the essential task she had set herself and the analyst was the rediscovery and resolution of this internalized and dissociated relation to her mother. Here, the emphasis in the transference neurosis was on *knowing* and that freeing of both imagination and intellectual capacities which alone enables a person to cognize themselves meaningfully. The crucial task for the analyst was to provide through interpretations those links which facilitated the process of symbolization, as in the dream, and thus enabling the repressed material to become both sentient and remembered personal experiential data. Here, insight is the aim as well as the vehicle of integration in a person.

In the second example of the male patient, the emphasis was quite different. He needed a respite from the continuous defensive exploitation of his mind in order to *experience* his affects. One can here talk of automatic defence. The anxiety affects were not allowed to develop in the service of the ego. The ego prematurely anticipated potential anxiety-situations and defended itself with stereotyped and archaic defences. Such patients dread any sort of experience of helplessness, and all their clinging is a way of rejecting both the object and their own instinctual needs. Hence the role of the analyst in the clinical setting was to curtail interpretative work because it merely reinforced the patient's own style of self-defence. Only by this dosage of refusal to supplement the patient's intellectual defensive organization was it possible to sponsor that basic trust in the clinical situation where he could take the risk of being undefended and sentiently be a person in his affectivity. No true object-relation is involved in this *use* of the analyst by the patient. The analyst is a living and responsive part of the total environment that the patient has put himself in the care of. To introduce the bias of object-relationship in the transference interpretation in this climate of the *use* of the analyst is to distort the true dynamics of the analytic situation in terms of the bias of our theories, and regardless of the need of the patient and his psychic reality.

The third case cited is more difficult to discuss in terms of the accredited analytic theory of technique because she has been unable to use the analytic situation in any meaningful way. Here, the crux of the clinical situation lies in finding ways of enabling a patient to tolerate their violent rejection of the analytic process, and helping them to discover how they defend the exposure of their inner reality, which they both hide and cling to with a fetishistic and fanatical fervour. Though they demand cure almost with an intensity of a craving, they regard participation in the therapeutic process as a betrayal of their true self (to use Winnicott's phrase). Freud had always emphasized that in the clinical situation what is most important and relevant is not *what* a patient hides but *how* he hides it. No human being can or ever does reveal the whole of their inner reality and truth.

The question is whether their *privacy* constitutes a relatedness to their true self or a paranoid and aggressive exclusion of others from any link with it. If it is the latter, then the patient brings his or her needfulness as a *challenge* to the analytic task. The need and compulsion to be found out is here tantamount to what Winnicott (1956) has described as the element of hope in the antisocial tendency, and it has to be met as such (Milner, 1969). I have given material from the third case merely to indicate the limiting point of analytic process and situation.

REFERENCES

Auden, W. H. (1956). Making, knowing and judging. In *The Dyer's Hand*. London: Faber & Faber, 1962.

Balint, M. (1968). *The Basic Fault*. London: Tavistock Publications.

Freud, S. (1912). The dynamics of transference. *S.E.* 12.

Greenson, R. (1958). On screen defences, screen hunger and screen identity. *J. Am. psychoanal. Ass.* 6, 242–262.

Guntrip, H. (1968). *Schizoid Phenomena, Object Relations and the Self*. London: Hogarth Press.

Heimann, P. (1956). Dynamics of transference interpretation. *Int. J. Psycho-Anal.* 37, 288–294.

James, M. (1960). Premature ego development. *Int. J. Psycho-Anal.* 41, 288–294.

Khan, M. M. R. (1962). Dream psychology and the evolution of the psycho-analytic situation. *Int. J. Psycho-Anal.* 43, 21–31.

Khan, M. M. R. (1963). Silence as communication. *Bull. Menninger Clin.* 27, 300–313.

Khan, M. M. R. (1964). Ego distortion, cumulative trauma, and the role of reconstruction in the analytic situation. *Int. J. Psycho-Anal.* 45, 272–279.

Khan, M. M. R. (1968). Reparation to the self as an idolised internal object. *Dynamische Psychiatrie* 1, 92–97.

Laing, R. D. (1961). *The Self and Others*. London: Tavistock Publications.

Milner, M. (1969). *Hands of the Living God*. London: Hogarth Press.

Rycroft, C. (1956). The nature and function of the analyst's communication to the patient. *Int. J. Psycho-Anal.* 37, 469–472.

Stone, L. (1961). *The Psychoanalytic Situation*. New York: International Universities Press.

Winnicott, D. W. (1948). Reparation in respect of mother's organized defence against depression. In *Collected Papers*. London: Tavistock Publications, 1958.

Winnicott, D. W. (1954). Metapsychological and clinical aspects of regression within the psychoanalytical set-up. In *Collected Papers*. London: Tavistock Publications, 1958.

Winnicott, D. W. (1955). Clinical varieties of transference. In *Collected Papers*. London: Tavistock Publications, 1958.

Winnicott, D. W. (1956). The antisocial tendency. In *Collected Papers*. London: Tavistock Publications, 1958.

Winnicott, D. W. (1960a). The theory of the parent-infant relationship. *Int. J. Psycho-Anal.* 41, 585–595.

Winnicott, D. W. (1960b). Ego distortion in terms of true and false self. In *The Maturational Processes and the Facilitating Environment*. London: Hogarth Press, 1965.

37

CONCERNING THERAPEUTIC SYMBIOSIS

HAROLD F. SEARLES

EDITOR'S NOTE

This paper is another in a series of remarkably original investigations of the analytic interaction by this extremely perceptive analyst (see Searles 1965, 1979). Here Searles explores the autistic and symbiotic phases of the analytic experience, offering essentially interactional conceptions with full consideration of contributions from both patient and analyst. The author's capacity to maintain a consistent perspective on the contributions and experiences of both analyst and patient, and to resist prevailing prejudices in regard to the nature of the analytic exchange, enables him to generate rewarding new insights into the analytic interaction — including the patient's function as what Searles terms a *symbiotic therapist* (see also Part II and Searles 1975 [chapter 10]). Finally, note should be taken of his comments on the role of jealousy in analysis; here his use of interactional concepts brings him quite close to the Kleinian discussions of envy.

In 1958 I postulated that symbiotic relatedness constitutes a necessary phase in psychoanalysis or psychotherapy with either neurotic or psychotic patients, and introduced the term "therapeutic symbiosis" for this mode of patient-analyst relatedness (Searles, 1959a). In 1959 I stated that what the analyst offers the patient which is new and therapeutic, in this regard, is not an avoidance of the development of symbiotic, reciprocal dependency with the patient, but rather an acceptance of this (1959b). My several subsequent discussions of this subject have included mention of the role of symbiotic relatedness in healthy, adult living (1965, 1967).

The present paper is the third in a series of reports on what I have learned in recent years concerning autism, symbiosis, and individuation. In these papers I am concerned not only with patients suffering from schizophrenia of varying degrees of severity but also with, for example, the subtle autism that

Reprinted from the *Annual of Psychoanalysis* 1:247–262, 1973.

emerges in the course of the neurotic patient's analysis. The first two papers included these passages:

The categories . . . of pathologic symbiosis, autism, therapeutic symbiosis, and individuation depict what I regard as successive phases of ego development in therapy. Whether any one patient needs to run that whole course will depend upon the level of ego development he has already attained at the beginning. He may already have achieved, for example, a strong capacity for a therapeutically symbiotic relatedness, in which case the first two phases of ego development would be relatively little in evidence in one's work with him [Searles, 1971, p. 70].

I have described it as characteristic of this phase of transition between autism and therapeutic symbiosis that the analyst now begins to find it feasible effectively to make transference-interpretations. This is in contrast to the earlier, autistic phase, during which he has had to adapt to long stretches of time during which he has been given to feel useless, neglectful, irrelevant, uncaring, incompetent and, more than anything else, essentially non-human, precisely for the reason that the patient has needed to regress, in his experience of the analyst, to the level of the young child's experience of the mother as being something far more than merely human as a person is seen through adult eyes. The patient has needed to come to experience the analyst as being equivalent to the early mother who comprises the whole world of which the infant is inextricably a part, and before he has achieved sufficient of an own self to be able to tolerate the feeling-experience of sensing her as separate from his own body, and the two of them as separate from the rest of the actual world. The transition phase likewise stands in contrast, as regards the timeliness of transference-interpretations, to the subsequent phase of therapeutic symbiosis, in which such interpretations are almost limitlessly in order [Searles, 1970, pp. 12–13].

I shall use the term "therapeutic symbiosis" in this paper to include both ambivalent and pre-ambivalent types of symbiosis in the patient-analyst relationship, although earlier I had reserved that term for pre-ambivalent symbiosis—that is, a symbiosis which is felt as a thoroughly adoring, contented oneness, and which is traceable genetically to experiences in the very early infant-mother relationship, before significant increments of hate had come to intrude into this oneness and transform the emotional matrix of it into one of pervasive ambivalence. Both types of symbiosis are clearly full of potential for therapeutic effect, as, indeed, is each of the other phases of ego development that are mentioned in the first quotation above. Moreover, I have come to regard it as impossible to find any clearly defined, long-sustained instance of pre-ambivalent symbiosis and am more than ever mindful of a reservation I expressed in 1961:

> There is no sure criterion by which we can know . . . whether we are involved in a genuinely preambivalent symbiosis with the patient, or rather in the predominantly paranoid symbiosis which is a defense against hatred . . . and we must remain open-minded to the ever-present possibility that . . . a basically constructive, subjectively preambivalent symbiosis will be misused unconsciously from time to time, by both participants, to keep increments of particularly intense hostility out of awareness [1961, p. 181].

THE PATIENT AS SYMBIOTIC THERAPIST

An understanding of the nature of therapeutic symbiosis requires that one grasp something of the extent to which the patient is himself devoted to functioning as a therapist in relationship to his officially designated analyst, as well as in his relationships with other persons in his life. Not only is the striving for an essentially psychotherapeutic effect upon the other person a concern of those relatively few persons who select the practice of psychoanalysis or psychotherapy as their life work, but it is also a basic and pervasive concern of human beings generally. But probably it is those persons whose childhoods to a large extent were devoted to functioning as therapist to other family members, and whose therapist-functioning proved both complex and absorbing and fundamental to their sense of personal identity, as well as frustrated in clear and lasting and acknowledgedly successful results, for whom such activity becomes a naturally absorbing adult-life work.

Although one can usefully explore the ways in which a genuine individual—that is a person who possesses a whole self, a person who has a relatively whole ego—thus unofficially functions as therapist to other persons who likewise have experienced psychological individuation and are thus whole individuals, I am concerned here with the "symbiotic therapist," the person who himself has not firmly achieved individuation, and whose most deeply meaningful human relationships consist in his complementing the aras of ego-incompleteness in other persons. This mode of relatedness is founded upon a relationship with his mother in which his ego-functioning was fixated similarly at a level of relatively infantile fragmentation and nondifferentiation, partially because the precarious family-intactness required that he not become a whole person but remain instead available for complementing the ego-incompleteness of the others in the family, individually and collectively.

The patient seen in this light is not merely a victim exploited by mother and family; to leave the conceptualization at that is to take into account only the potentially hostile components of what is transpiring. In these symbiotic processes, just as self and object are not clearly demarcated, neither are hate and love clearly differentiated. It is as much as anything the patient's nascent capacity for love, and for the development of mature human responsibility, which impels him to perpetuate this mode of relatedness. From the not-yet-well-differentiated, "selfish" point of view, he strives, for his psychological and physical survival, to maintain the only mode of relatedness he knows, and hopefully so to enhance, so strengthen the mother as to enable her to mature further, to provide himself with a model for identification, for the sake of his own maturation. From the "altruistic" point of view, which is also not well differentiated, he goes on literally sacrificing his own potential self, for the sake of complementing the mother and thus ensuring her survival.

Just as the seeds of the most intense paranoid hate can be found in all this, so, too, can be found here the sources of the most genuinely selfless human love. The more ill a patient is, the more deeply indispensable does he need to become, at this pre-individuation level of ego-functioning, to his transference-mother, the analyst. This necessary transference evolution is made all but impossible by the traditional view of the analyst as the healthy one, the one with the intact ego, who is endeavoring to give help to the ill one, the patient, seen as afflicted with an "ego defect" or "ego deficit." The latter is thus "afflicted," indeed, but to some real degree, so (like everyone else) is the analyst. Without this "affliction," in fact, he could not hope to function effectively as the analyst in the therapeutically symbiotic phase of the patient's treatment.

No one becomes so fully an individual, so fully "mature," as to have lost his previously achieved capacity for symbiotic relatedness. The so-called "ego defect" of the schizophrenic patient, seen in its dynamic function rather than as static crippledness, is really the area of his most intense, though fixedly symbiotic aliveness, and is of the same nature as the symbiotic basis of healthy adult ego-functioning—that basis which enables a healthy adult to come to feel, creatively and restoratively, at one with (or, one might say, part of) another individual, a group of his fellow human beings, mankind generally, the whole external world, a creative idea, or whatever.

In psychoanalytic treatment what is needed, more than anything else, to resolve the fixation in the patient's ego development—his having achieved, that is, only a fragment, or fragments, of an ego—is his discovery that a fellow human being, the analyst, can come to know, and to work with him in implicit acknowledgment of his indispensably important role in the analyst's own ego-functioning. Only through such a process can the patient become a more whole individual. Further, the individuation which he undergoes more successfully this time, in the context of the transference relationship, is in a real sense mutual, in that the analyst too, having participated with the patient in the therapeutic symbiosis, emerges with a renewed individuality which has been enriched and deepened by this experience. Just as we need to realize that, in healthy human living, symbiotic relatedness is not confined to infancy and early childhood but forms, at largely though not entirely unconscious levels, the dynamic substrate of adult living, so, too, individuation is not a once-and-for-all, irreversible process. It is not only a deeply ill patient who can achieve, in psychoanalytic treatment, a fuller individuation than the relatively fragmentary and superficial individuation he had achieved in childhood. A healthy adult, too, by definition, lives a daily and yearly life which involves, in its most essential ingredients, experiences—whether measured in moments or phases of his life—of symbiotic relatedness and re-individuation.

It is currently one of our great human tragedies that hundreds of thousands of persons are living out their lives in gigantic mental hospitals, existing largely in chemical cocoons, because behind our scornful shunning of them is our unformulated sensing that any one of them, if we were to permit him or her to do so, would become personally more a part of us than we dare to allow.

In recent years I have learned that one of the most heavily defended emotions in the schizophrenic patient is his sense of guilt at having failed to enable his fragmented mother to become a whole and successful mother to him. This sense of guilt is based partially upon subjective omnipotence and is therefore to a degree irrational; in this regard it is analogous to the guilt we would have the supposedly omnipotent "schizophrenigenic mother" bear, single-handedly, for the fact of the patient's schizophrenic illness. But it is essential for us to perceive that the patient's sense of guilt at having thus failed his mother has also a realistic aspect, for it is this realistic component which provides the key to his capacity for developing a sense of more mature responsibility in his interpersonal relationships in general. It is only as he comes to enable his analyst to function as analyst—analogous to mother—in relation to him (despite whatever intense hatred and other "negative" feelings) that the crippling effect of this heretofore unconscious guilt can be undone. We can now see, in retrospect, that the pathogenic introjects which have comprised the core of his schizophrenia have reprsented not only his unconscious means of coping with an otherwise intolerable outer reality, but also his unconscious, primitive way of trying to heal that "outer reality"—that is, those most deeply ill components of mother and subsequent mother-transference figures—by taking those components into himself and trying thus to free her (and her successors) from the burden of them.

THE PHASE OF AMBIVALENT SYMBIOSIS

As regression deepens in the analytic relationship—regression not only on the part of the heretofore autistic patient but also on the part of the analyst, who, as I described in an earlier paper (1970), has become considerably caught up, himself, in autistic processes—there are now encountered sudden and increasingly frequent bits of the ego-splitting, intense ambivalence against which, in the history of each participant, autistic processes had developed as a defense. In this stage of ambivalent symbiosis, in which ego boundaries are by definition unrealiable in either participant, there is much of both projecting and introjecting, with each person feeling threatened by the other by reason of the other's personifying one's own as-yet-unintegratable inner contents. For example, each projects upon the other his own murderous feelings, and feels correspondingly in fear for his life. The loss, for each, of what he has felt to be entirely his own (autistic) world—its disruption by, for example, one's patient who now feels to be chaotically permeating one's whole life—is accompanied by intense rage, fear, and the most primitive kinds of loss reactions. One's subjective experience is that one no longer has either a world, or a self, of one's own.

It is to be noted that ambivalence which is largely unconscious, rather than conscious and therefore integratable by the ego, requires symbiotic relatedness with the other person, relatedness in which the other personifies those components of the ambivalent feelings which one is having to repress at the moment. Contrariwise, when one can face and accept his own ambivalent feelings, one can be a separate person and can react to the other as being, also, a separate person. I shall never forget the sense of achieved inner freedom which enabled me to tell a hebephrenic woman, in relation to whom I had been enmeshed in anguished symbiotic relatedness for years, that I would never allow her to visit my home—as she long had yearned to do—even if my refusal meant that she would stay in a mental hospital all her life. Where one draws the line, in such matters, is an expression of the analyst's individual self; this is where *I* draw the line. Theoretically, it is not essential, and it may be unwise, although in my experience rarely if ever disastrous, to say these things to the patient; the important thing is that one become able to feel them—to feel, in this instance, a degree of intense rejectingness which I had projected for years, heretofore, upon this, in truth, remarkably rejecting woman. The degree of ambivalence of which I am writing is so intense that it can be met, as I hope to show further in this paper, only if the two participants function to a high degree as one in the experiencing and acknowledging of it.

Some years ago, at a time when I had not experienced enough *pre*ambivalently symbiotic relatedness

with my patients to be able to conceptualize it, and when I assumed all symbiotic relatedness to be highly ambivalent, I wrote in my notes, following a session with this same woman:

I have referred to symbiotic relationships in two recent papers and have been wanting lately to try to describe in detail what are the characteristics of such a relationship. I have just come from an hour with Carol Fleming[1] which has been like hundreds of similar hours with her and which is, I think, a typical one to represent the [ambivalently] symbiotic relationship.

When I went up to see her she was lying in bed, silently, in her bare-walled room—lying in her steel bed—and the only other items of furniture were the two chairs. I felt a sense of deep discouragement when I went in there, and aversion to going ahead with the work. As the hour progressed, an hour in which she said little and this only in a fragmentary fashion, while looking antagonistically toward me most of the time, I noticed that what I felt was perhaps most of all a sense of helplessness in the face of my own feelings, and a non-acceptance of them, whether these were feelings of antagonism, or sympathy, or tenderness, or what-not. I felt strong urges to simply abandon the work with her and abandon her, but felt again a sense of conflict and helplessness at doing this.

I felt a sense of what one might call being at the mercy of her own playing upon my feelings, whether by making me antagonistic through hateful behavior, or by evoking tenderness and sympathy from me when she would suddenly have a friendly look on her face and make a kind of beseeching gesture. Another thing to be stressed is that my feelings were in quite a welter and were rapidly changing. At one period in the hour I got to feeling as though we were two rattlesnakes with our fangs in one another's necks, each refusing to let go because by staying in the relationship we were best expressing the boundless hatefulness we felt toward one another. Throughout the hour there was an element of dissatisfaction on my part with my own feelings.

A few months earlier I had written:

The entire time of the small group [one of several groups into which the overall therapist-staff were divided, which met regularly to discuss, informally and as candidly as we could, whatever were the most pressing problem situations at the moment] today was taken up with my presenting my work with Carol Fleming. I brought it up because I was feeling under a good deal of pressure about the forthcoming visit of the mother and father. As I was telling the others about the way it was going with Carol, I began to see more and more indications in myself of a massive submerged rage at her because of my feelings of failure in the work. I felt as though there were a large, heavy stone in me . . . it felt unmistakably like depression

---

1. A pseudonym.

with a good deal of rage associated with it. The thing that came to me in the course of presenting this was that even my "positive," tender feelings toward her were a burden to me, as well as my formerly strong feelings of cruelty and sadism. These "positive" feelings were a burden, I felt, because I did not feel free to express them to her—as by, for instance, touching her head when I felt like it. I have felt all along that such expressions of tenderness were a kind of misuse of my therapist position, something which would frighten her and would simply be a kind of gratifying of my own dependency feelings, using her as a mother-figure. In the course of the rest of the day it came to me that the *most important thing in my life at Chestnut Lodge*[2] at present is my anger at Carol Fleming. It was a quite startling thing, indeed, to come to this realization; it occurred to me later that this may be some measure, too, of the importance of the relationship to the patient herself.

No one or two vignettes can be fully typical of the varied clinical phenomena which I am conceptualizing. This patient, for instance, was still more invested in her years'-long autism, still relatively little invested in explicitly discernible, ambivalently symbiotic relatedness, than have been most of the patients I have in mind as I write.

With these latter patients, most of whom in my experience have been borderline schizophrenic or ambulatorily schizophrenic—considerably more readily accessible, that is, than the woman I have just mentioned—there is the additional circumstance that both participants almost constantly react to one another, whether in a verbal, or in a tangibly nonverbal, fashion and with feelings that shift rapidly about over the whole spectrum, from fury to tenderness to scorn, and so on, often in extraordinary mixtures of emotions.

Much of my own experience with ambivalently symbiotic relatedness has occurred during the final several months of my eleven years of work with a hebephrenic man who had achieved by now this way of functioning, at a time when both of us knew that before long I would be leaving the hospital where he dwelt; and during my work with some hundreds of borderline or ambulatorily schizophrenic patients with whom I have had one-time interviews for consultative and/or teaching purposes. I have wondered about the role of mutual separation anxiety in this so-active responding, under these special

---

2. I am chagrined to see that I had to write, and to feel, this qualification: "at Chestnut Lodge"; I could not experience this simply as the most important thing in my life. This I regard as evidence of my then-unconscious resistance to acknowledging the patient's full importance to me—my own resistance, that is, to the development of a fully felt, pre-ambivalently symbiotic relatedness with her.

circumstances of approaching termination or one-time interviews. But my experiences with various other long-range treatment cases have confirmed my belief that the separation anxiety involved has less to do with the imminence of physical separation than with the imminent threat to both participants lest their lively symbiotic relatedness give way at any moment, unpredictably and uncontrollably, to autism or individuation (outcomes which do not seem differentiated in the patient's grasp of the situation, nor at all well differentiated in my own understanding in that context). Thus the imminence of either outcome poses the same subjective threat of one's being torn asunder at any moment.

The symbiotic instability of ego boundaries makes it impossible to know whether the anger or depression, for instance, which one suddenly experiences is one's "own," or whether one is empathically sensing a feeling of the patient's "own" against which *he* is successfully defended unconsciously (as by projection). Also, as regards the patient's verbal communications, it is often impossible to know, and it feels urgently important to ascertain, whence and to whom these communications are coming.

For example, one such patient who at a nonverbal level was well established in ambivalently symbiotic relatedness with me, but who had not yet achieved a comparable level of verbal articulateness, confined his verbal communications over many months to certain stereotyped comments. In one session, he expressed each of the following stereotyped comments at least once: "Take your time." "Abide with what ya have." "Remain happy." "Time and place f'r everything." "No need to say." For me it was something like listening to one side of a telephone conversation. I told him that I had no way of knowing whether each of these comments was—and here I utilize numbers, which I did not use in communicating to him—(1) his response to thoughts he was having, (2) his response to voices he was hearing, (3) his conjecture as to what I was thinking, (4) his accurate report to me of what he was hearing the voices say, or (5) some mixture of all these. Not surprisingly, in response to so complex a comment from me, he offered no illuminating reply. I assume that he was quite unable to differentiate among these various possibilities, to which I now added another: (6) were his stereotyped comments giving behavioral expression, by processes of introjection, to what he tended unconsciously to perceive as being my own silently hallucinated state? I was not in fact subject to hallucinations, stressful though these sessions often were; but one of his most discernible transference reactions was in terms of my being his "shell-shocked" father (who had died long ago), a man so ego-fragmented as to have been incapacitated from useful career activity throughout the patient's childhood, and a man who may well have suffered, therefore, from hallucinations.

Considerably earlier in the work I had become aware, more simply, that things he said could be expressive of *my* presumed feelings or attitudes, from his point of view, as well as of his own feelings and attitudes. When, for example, in the middle of a prolonged silence he would say reproachfully, "You don't ever intend to say," this seemingly could refer variously to how he viewed me, or how he viewed himself, or how he assumed I viewed him. On another occasion, when I went into the building where he lived to have the hour with him, I found him standing outside the nearby nurses' office, and he made no move to follow me down the corridor to his room. After a few minutes of my sitting in his room with the door open, waiting for him, I went out and got a newspaper near that office and brought it back to the room, ignoring him as I went by. After a relatively brief time he came into the room, saying, "Who the hell needs *you,* you slimy son-of-a-bitch?," which could express equally well his attitude or the one I had manifested in getting the newspaper. What makes it feel so important to the analyst, at this stage of things, to try to locate the ego boundaries is that there is so much unintegrated, and therefore uncontrollable, hostility in the relationship. For example, the memory was still fresh in my mind of a time when he evidently had suddenly heard a hallucinatory voice, coming from me, saying deeply insulting things to him, and had reacted with such barely-contained, explosive fury that I felt physically frightened of him and thoroughly helpless to affect what was going on in him.

THE ROLE OF JEALOUSY IN THE FRAGMENTED EGO[3]

In my work with the above-mentioned man, as well as with another patient earlier and many subsequently, I have seen that ambivalently symbiotic relatedness often comes to have, at first weirdly, a quality of *group* relatedness, with jealousy a most important and difficult complicating factor. It is

commonly assumed that jealousy is an emotion that occurs in a context of three actual persons (Farber, 1961). But in these patients—and, again, I refer not merely to grossly ego-fragmented hebephrenic patients, but to any patients in whom schizoid components come to light in the course of analysis, which in my opinion then includes patients generally—the pathogenic introjects have the subjective personal identity value, and interpersonal impact, of persons. It is when the analyst comes to be invested, by the patient, with a personal significance approximately equivalent to that with which the introject in question is invested—when, in simpler words, the analyst comes to be as important to the patient as the latter's own "self" is to him—that the analyst now feels, and the remainder of the patient's identity (i.e. the area not comprised of the introject) now feels, pitted in an intense three- (or more) way jealous competition.

For example, the hebephrenic man I have been mentioning used to relate during the sessions to hallucinatory voices which made me feel, by contrast, totally insignificant to him. When I would try to interrupt his dialogue with a hallucinatory figure, he would snap in vitriolic fury, "Shut up! I got company!" But it was only as my feeling-significance to him increased that I began to feel jealous when he would turn from relating to me, to relating to an hallucinatory voice. At such times I had a distinct sense that a group relationship was going on in the room, and I have often had this feeling with a similarly ego-fragmented woman with whom I have worked for many years. Still later, in my treatment of the hebephrenic man, I became so sure of my importance to him that I could know that the hallucinatory phenomena he manifested were secondary to the events transpiring between us, and I no longer felt vulnerable to such jealousy.

The patient's own jealousy of himself, springing from a part of him which feels left out from another part to "whom" the analyst is responding, constitutes an enormous resistance in the treatment. That is, when one island among those comprising the patient's collective "self" is able to work with the analyst in making a step forward in the work, another such island "who" feels left behind and intensely jealous, reacts with savage vindictiveness against what the two coworkers have accomplished together, and against the collaborative relationship between them. Such a patient's "self" is largely comprised of a collection of poorly integrated introjects. I surmise that the jealousy is traceable in part to early life experiences of unmasterable jealousy at the closeness between two other actual persons—the parents, for

---

3. An excellent paper by Pao (1969), "Pathological Jealousy," while not containing the concepts I am putting forward here, provides a useful psychodynamic background for them, as well as a valuable survey of the literature concerning jealousy.

example, or the mother and a sibling adored by her—jealousy which was not resolved in the patient but was unconsciously defended against by his introjection of the two, emotionally close, other persons. But I surmise that, more importantly, the jealousy had a counterpart *within the mother* (or other mothering ones) *herself,* such that the child had to cope with, and to try introjectively—by taking into himself, that is—to make whole a mother whose ego was fragmented and ridden with just such "intrapsychic" jealousy.

In the course of treatment, this jealousy can best be dealt with as an unconscious defense against the therapeutically necessary, but at first frightening to both patient and analyst, fusion involved in pre-ambivalent symbiosis. It seems to me that the instances of the acting out of such jealousy that are most disruptive of the treatment occur before there has developed any strong pre-ambivalent relatedness in the transference. Any jealousy phenomena which occur later, after individuation has occurred, while perhaps not inconsiderable, can be dealt with by the now whole patient and the now whole analyst, as they explore the meaning to their relationship of some third whole person outside the office.

Finally, I shall give an example from my work with a schizoid patient—a patient whose degree of illness is common in an office practice. For several years I found this man infuriatingly smug. But the time came when, to my astonishment, I realized that what I was feeling now was jealousy; *he* so clearly favored his *self* over *me* that I felt deeply jealous, bitterly left out of this mutually cherishing and cozy relationship between the two "persons" who comprised him. I emphasize that this did not happen until after several years of my work with him. In retrospect, I saw that I previously had not developed sufficient personal significance to him (in classically psychoanalytic terms, had not been sufficiently cathected as a separate object in his experience of me), to sense these two now relatively well-differentiated "persons" in him and to feel myself capable of and desirous of participating in the "three"-way, intensely jealousy-laden competition. It is my impression that such schizoid patients usually prove so discouragingly inaccessible to psychoanalysis that the analyst and the patient give up the attempt at psychoanalysis before they have reached this lively but disturbing (to analyst as well as patient) stratum, this stratum in which the patient's ego fragmentation becomes revealed and the nature of the transference becomes one of a murderously jealous "three"-way competitiveness.

Technique During the Phase of Transition from Autism to Therapeutic Symbiosis

The oftentimes long, seemingly static phase of autism proves in retrospect not to have been a mere marking of time before the onset of the discernibly active therapeutic processes of the symbiotic phase, but rather to have comprised the necessary establishing of the reliably strong context within which these latter changes can be allowed to occur. For me, this finding substantiates the positive emphasis which Milner (1969) places upon what I am calling autism. She writes of "the theme of premature ego-development and the necessity, for healthy mental growth, for recurrent times when retreat into absent-mindedness [i.e., autism] is possible," and suggests that "behind the states that are talked about by analysts as auto-erotic and narcissistic [i.e., autistic] there can be an attempt to reach a beneficent kind of narcissism, a primary self-enjoyment . . . which, if properly understood, is not a rejection of the outer world but a step towards a renewed and revitalized investment in it" (Milner, 1969). She also cites Heimann's (1962) paper which concerns narcissistic withdrawal for creative work and the need for research into the changes that narcissism undergoes from its primitive manifestations, so that it becomes compatible with ego creativity and object relations.

The autistic phase involves the formation, in my view, of what Hartmann (1939) has termed "the average expectable environment," what Winnicott (1941) has called "the good-enough holding environment," and what Khan (1963, 1964) describes in terms of the mother's role as protective shield.

A high degree of reliability develops during the autistic phase. This reliability, whether expressed in terms of punctuality, regularity of seating arrangements, or whatever constellation of outward trappings in the treatment situation, must have to do with both participants' developing sureness as to what the situation will, and will not, permit. Sometimes extraordinary patience and what might seem to be inexcusable leniency are necessary on the analyst's part; other times demand murderously impatient firmness—whatever gives truest expression to the analyst's individual self in meeting the needs of the immediate treatment situation.

In my work with one chronically schizophrenic woman, I developed a technique which I described with some embarrassment to my Chestnut Lodge colleagues as the Chinese water-torture method, for reason that it appeared on the surface to be so highly sadistic. In fact, this technique developed out of absolute necessity and proved to be immensely useful. It consisted simply in a maddeningly rigorous application of a technique emphasized many years ago by Rogers (1942): repeating what the patient said and simultaneously indicating a readiness to hear more, but without going a single step beyond her. The woman had an extremely tenuous sense of identity and was terribly afraid, therefore, of venturing forward on her own; individuality was equivalent, for her, to hopeless insanity. On the hundreds of occasions in the past when I had ventured encouragingly a bit beyond her, she had immediately reacted to me in totally alienated horror and condemnation, typically cutting me off from her with a shocked, awed, "You're crazy, Dr. Searles!" I had learned the hard way that I must be *with* her at each of her most tentative steps, repeating each of her tentative comments — often only the first part of an intendedly full sentence, which unaided she could not complete — but that I must not get at all *ahead* of her.

I was amused when, in a staff presentation, one of my colleagues, who had found my presentation of one of my typical interviews with her quite disturbing, said in angry protest:

. . . in that interview, every word practically that she said, you seized on it, you repeated it back to her and then you asked her some further data on it, as if you had to control each and every thing that she did. I wonder, God, this would be an awful rigidly structured business, and I wonder what she might think of the meaning of that in terms of her own aggressive feelings — why this has to be done. Surely when she said something was driving her crazy, I think I would have had the same feeling, that if somebody was doing this to me, I'd really feel that I was going nuts and would feel like tearing out my hair or something.

I was amused at his reaction both because of what I felt to be the accuracy of his description of what I was doing with her, and because the nature of his emotional reaction to it was so akin to the emotional reaction which was developing within the patient herself — a therapeutically most welcome development. My relationship with her progressed through a subsequent phase of ambivalently symbiotic relatedness, during which there were a great many stormy sessions in which we both participated most actively; and a later, clearly identifiable and prolonged, phase of pre-ambivalently therapeutic symbiosis which was of enormous growth-value for both of us, and which enabled her to achieve a stronger degree of subsequent individuation than any others among my chronically schizophrenic patients have, so far, ever achieved. These later developments could not have occurred, I am convinced, without my having functioned during that autistic phase as a kind of exoskeleton for her.

In my paper concerning neutral therapist responses (1963), I detailed something of the clinical events which indicated that, in my work with one chronically schizophrenic patient who lay mute and motionless throughout the analytic sessions for months — months during which he evidently was hovering on the brink of death — it was my functioning meanwhile as a progressively mute and motionless inanimate object which served eventually, where more "active" measures had all failed, to help him to become genuinely alive and increasingly functional.

One way of construing all this is to see that the analyst must come to personify the patient's own autistic rigidity, in order for that rigidity to become translated into increasingly well-differentiated and consciously utilizable ego strength. This is achieved partially through the patient's identification with the analyst's timely and skillful "becoming alive" and his readiness to venture forth in various constructive ways from so rigid and "inanimate," but for all patients at times so necessary, a transference position. In everyday office analytic practice, the patients — and these include not only ambulatorily schizophrenic and borderline patients, but also neurotic ones — who complain most of the analyst's remoteness and changelessness are the very persons who need most, for the sake of the resolution and integration of erstwhile autistic components within themselves, to have him function thus in relation to them.

In my experience, for the resolution of the patient's autism to occur, the analyst must do more than function as a more reliable maternally protective shield for the patient than the latter's biological mother had been during his infancy and early childhood, in the manner that Khan has described. First the analyst must have become increasingly free in his acceptance of the *patient's* functioning as *his* — the analyst's — maternally protective shield. In my own way of conceptualizing it: to the extent that the analyst can become able comfortably and freely to immerse himself in the autistic patient as comprising his (the analyst's) world, the patient can then utilize him as a model for identification as regards the acceptance of such very primitive dependency needs, and can come increasingly to exchange his erstwhile autistic world for the world comprised of, and personified by, the analyst. This progression of events is in actuality comprised not of discrete, once-and-for-all shifts forward, but rather of blended and ever-oscillating processes, so that at one moment the exoskeleton is being provided by the analyst, at the next moment by the patient, and, increasingly, by both at once and at one.

What I am describing here requires, again, an appreciation of the patient's therapist-orientation. Through the evolution of the transference the analyst, in finding the patient's autistic functioning to be serving as an increasingly important maternal-shield in his own ego-functioning, is reacting like the ego-fragmented mother whose own functioning has required that the patient remain fixated at the level of autism, as the foundation stone of her own precarious existence. What the analyst brings into the patient's life that is new is that he, unlike the mother earlier, has a sufficiently well-integrated ego to dare to *know* how indispensably important to him is this patient, this autistic patient who is able meaningfully to relate to him, at first, only as the maternal shield for those least well-integrated components of the analyst upon which the patient's transference to him as an ego-fragmented mother is based.

In other words, the analyst must dare to know that, at this very primitive level, the patient is functioning, and has been functioning, as his mother-therapist. To the extent that he is conscious of this, he need not acknowledge it explicitly to the patient. It becomes mutually and implicitly understood that the patient has been helping him to confront areas of himself with which he had been previously largely unacquainted. As these areas become integrated into the analyst's conscious ego-functioning, he becomes more and more the strong mother the patient has been needing. Since the patient has been mothering him successfully, as the patient's infant or fetus, there is now no humiliation for the patient in becoming increasingly aware of his own infant-need, now, for the analyst as mother.

In a recent paper (1972) concerning my work, extending over many years and still continuing, with a deeply ego-fragmented and delusional woman, I described my gradual discovery of the awesome extent to which her highly delusional world was in actuality flowing from, and thus was based upon, her responding to various real but predominantly unconscious components of my personality—that is,

heretofore largely unconscious ways of my functioning with her during the sessions. Notable for me in this increasingly clear realization of the extent to which I have been personifying a God-the-creator, early mother to the patient, is the extent to which I previously had shied away from experiencing myself as possessing this degree of importance to her. For me personally, it has been easier to adore the patient as God-like, than to feel so adored by her.

In my recent papers (1970, 1971) concerning autism I have described how the analyst is thrown, in response to the autistic patient, back upon his own autistic processes. A development which comes eventually to contribute to the resolution of this autistic mode of relatedness is the analyst's surprised, recurrent, and deepening realization and acceptance of the fact that these two seemingly so separate worlds, his world and that of the patient, are but separate outcroppings of the unconscious ground joining the two of them. This principle is commonly manifested in the analyst's finding, during, for example, one of the frequent periods of silence with a boringly schizoid patient, that his self-examination of his preoccupying and supposedly quite free associations, as he is managing to get through this workaday time by dint of such inner "freedom," yields, as he begins to examine these associations, new and highly informative cues to what is going on between himself and the patient, and within the patient. The analyst's own "private" or "autistic" inner world is not nearly so far apart from the patient as he, the analyst, assumed it to be.

Summary

In this paper I have discussed various processes which are relevant to therapeutic symbiosis, including the patient's functioning as symbiotic therapist to the analyst, the phase of ambivalent symbiosis and various matters of analytic technique during that phase, and the realm of "intrapsychic" jealousy—jealousy, that is, based upon the fragmented state of the ego. Throughout the paper, I have attempted to highlight the therapeutic role of reciprocal identification processes between patient and analyst.

Bibliography

Farber, L. H. (1961), Faces of Envy, *Rev. Existential Psychol. and Psychiat.*, I (Spring 1961), No. 2. Reprinted on pp. 118–130 of his book, *The Ways of the Will—Essays toward a Psychology and Psychopathology of Will.* New York and London: Basic Books, 1966.

Hartmann, H. (1939), *Ego Psychology and the Problem of*

Adaptation. London & New York: Imago; New York: International Universities Press, 1958.

Heimann, P. (1962), Notes on the Anal Stage, *Internat. J. Psycho-Anal.,* 43:406–414.

Khan, M. M. R. (1963), The Concept of Cumulative Trauma. *The Psychoanalytic Study of the Child,* 18:286–306.

——(1964), Ego Distortion, Cumulative Trauma, and the Role of Reconstruction in the Analytic Situation. *Internat. J. Psycho-Anal.,* 45:272–278.

Milner, M. (1969), *The Hands of the Living God: An Account of a Psychoanalytic Treatment.* New York: International Universities Press, pp. 155, 383.

Pao, P-N. (1969), Pathological Jealousy. *Psychoanal. Quart.,* 38:616–638.

Rogers, C. (1942), *Counseling and Psychotherapy.* Cambridge: The Riverside Press.

Searles, H. F. (1959a), Integration and Differentiation in Schizophrenia. *J. Nerv. and Ment. Dis.,* 129:542–550.

——(1959b), The Effort to Drive the Other Person Crazy: An Element in the Aetiology and Psychotherapy of Schizophrenia. *Brit. J. Med. Psychol.,* 32:1–18.

——(1961), Phases of Patient-Therapist Interaction in the Psychotherapy of Chronic Schizophrenia. *Brit. J.*

Med. Psychol., 34:169–193.

——(1963), The Place of Neutral Therapist Responses in Psychotherapy with the Schizophrenic Patient. *Internat. J. Psycho-Anal.,* 44:42–56.

——(1965), *Collected Papers on Schizophrenia and Related Subjects.* London & New York: Hogarth; New York: International Universities Press.

——(1967), Concerning the Development of an Identity. *Psychoanal. Rev.,* 53:507–530.

——(1970), Autism and the Phase of Transition to Therapeutic Symbiosis. *Contemporary Psychoanalysis,* 7:1–20.

—— (1971), Pathologic Symbiosis and Autism. In: *In the Name of Life—Essays in Honor of Erich Fromm,* ed. B. Landis and E. S. Tauber. New York: Holt, Rinehart and Winston, pp. 69–83. (This paper is actually the first in my current series, but appeared second because of a one-year delay in publication.)

——(1972), The Function of the Patient's Realistic Perceptions of the Analyst in Delusional Transference. *Brit. J. Med. Psychol.,* 45:1–18.

Winnicott, D. W. (1941), The Observation of Infants in a Set Situation. In: *Collected Papers.* London & New York: Tavistock; New York: Basic Books, 1958.

Part VII

THE THERAPEUTIC SETTING AND HOLD

Despite the deceptive simplicity of the concept of a set of ground rules for the analytic and therapeutic situations, no aspect of the therapeutic experience has proven more controversial or more difficult to conceptualize. Basing itself on Freud's papers on technique (1912b [chapter 38], 1913, 1915), the classical psychoanalytic literature that followed was for the most part satisfied to view the ground rules simply as a means of establishing a workable therapeutic situation and of safeguarding the transference. In the years that followed, sporadic articles appeared on one or another ground rule, almost all of them advocating flexibility for the sake of supposed humanness. To these was added Eissler's important delineation (1953; see chapter 39) of *parameters* of technique—specific deviations or alterations of the ground rules necessitated by ego dysfunctions within the patient.

Milner (1952) provided a means of extending the conceptualization of these ground rules by likening them to the frame of a painting: the frame provides the medium within its confines properties that are distinctive and unique as compared to the world around it. This metaphor allowed thinking about the ground rules to assume a more graphic quality, and their nature and functions were thereby clarified. This line of thought was then extended through studies by Bleger (1967; see chapter 41) and myself (1975b; see chapter 42). The framework model proved especially suitable as an element of the bipersonal field concept (Baranger and Baranger 1966 [chapter 33], Langs 1976a), in that it fostered the realization of the importance of a secure frame as a means of establishing clear-cut boundaries between patient and therapist and, more broadly, as a means of creating not only a distinctive set of conditions within the field, but also a specific set of communicative properties essential for analytic work.

Winnicott (1956 [chapter 40], 1959, 1965) developed still another dimension of the analytic setting—its holding qualities and function as a background of safety. Here, as noted by both Modell (1976; see chapter 43) and myself (1975b; see chapter 42), the object relational aspects of the management of the setting could be appreciated, especially those properties that relate to an ego-building, growth-promoting hold as offered by the therapist or analyst to the patient.

More recently (Langs 1978d,f; see chapters 18 and 25), I was able to extend this conception into a view of the establishment and management of the ground rules and setting as part of the conscious and unconscious communicative interaction between patient and therapist. This led to a further reconsideration of the therapist's functioning in this sphere as a reality filled with unconscious implications. Along different but related lines, it proved possible also to identify the holding functions of both patient and setting for the therapist or analyst, and to establish certain containing functions for the ground rules — an extension of Bion's studies of the container and the contained (1977) as they refer to projective identifications and their recipients. The therapist's maintenance of the ground rules and setting, then, creates the background of safety, a hold and a container — a defined therapeutic space and communicative medium — within which the patient may grow and develop, and resolve his intrapsychic and interpersonal conflicts.

38

RECOMMENDATIONS TO PHYSICIANS PRACTISING PSYCHO-ANALYSIS

SIGMUND FREUD

EDITOR'S NOTE

In this, the second of Freud's five fundamental studies of transference and technique (see Freud 1912a [chapter 1], 1913, 1914, 1915), Freud develops a series of technical rules for psychoanalysis. These are related mainly to the analyst's noncountertransference functioning (see Part IV), in that Freud delineates the use of evenly suspended attention, the surgeon and mirror models as inherent to the analyst's basic stance, the need for anonymity, and the disturbing influence of noninterpretive interventions. In his 1913 companion paper Freud discussed such matters as fees, length of sessions, the use of the sofa, and the fundamental rule of free association, while in 1915, in discussing transference love, he developed the rule of abstinence.

It is remarkable, then, that despite his own very loose interpretations of the basic ground rules he developed, Freud was able to supplement his investigations of transference with a surprisingly detailed delineation of the structure and function of the analytic setting and the basic stance of the analyst. On the whole, Freud advocated adherence by the analyst to these ground rules, except for special circumstances and certain types of stalemated analyses (see also Freud 1918, 1937) though his own case studies (Freud 1905, 1908, 1918) reveal many additional deviations. Nonetheless, it is a tribute to Freud's genius that he saw and defined transference and the structure of the analytic setting as two of the most crucial components of the analytic experience.

The technical rules which I am putting forward here have been arrived at from my own experience in the course of many years, after unfortunate results had led me to abandon other methods. It will easily be seen that they (or at least many of them) may be summed up in a single precept. [Cf. p. 115.]

Reprinted from *The Standard Edition of the Complete Psychological Works of Sigmund Freud*, volume 12, pp. 111–120, trans. and ed. James Strachey, by permission of Sigmund Freud Copyrights Ltd., The Institute of Psycho-Analysis, The Hogarth Press Ltd., and (for U.S. rights) Basic Books Inc.

My hope is that observance of them will spare physicians practising analysis much unnecessary effort and guard them against some oversights. I must however make it clear that what I am asserting is that this technique is the only one suited to my individuality; I do not venture to deny that a physician quite differently constituted might find himself driven to adopt a different attitude to his patients and to the task before him.

(*a*) The first problem confronting an analyst who is treating more than one patient in the day will seem to him the hardest. It is the task of keeping in mind all the innumerable names, dates, detailed memories and pathological products which each patient communicates in the course of months and years of treatment, and of not confusing them with similar material produced by other patients under treatment simultaneously or previously. If one is required to analyse six, eight, or even more patients daily, the feat of memory involved in achieving this will provoke incredulity, astonishment or even commiseration in uninformed observers. Curiosity will in any case be felt about the technique which makes it possible to master such an abundance of material, and the expectation will be that some special expedients are required for the purpose.

The technique, however, is a very simple one. As we shall see, it rejects the use of any special expedient (even that of taking notes). It consists simply in not directing one's notice to anything in particular and in maintaining the same 'evenly-suspended attention' (as I have called it)[1] in the face of all that one hears. In this way we spare ourselves a strain on our attention which could not in any case be kept up for several hours daily, and we avoid a danger which is inseparable from the exercise of deliberate attention. For as soon as anyone deliberately concentrates his attention to a certain degree, he begins to select from the material before him; one point will be fixed in his mind with particular clearness and some other will be correspondingly disregarded, and in making this selection he will be following his expectations or inclinations. This, however, is precisely what must not be done. In making the selection; if he follows his expectations he is in danger of never finding anything but what he already knows; and if he follows his inclinations he will certainly falsify what he may perceive. It must not be forgotten that the things one hears are for the most part things whose meaning is only recognized later on.

It will be seen that the rule of giving equal notice to everything is the necessary counterpart to the demand made on the patient that he should communicate everything that occurs to him without criticism or selection. If the doctor behaves otherwise, he is throwing away most of the advantage which

results from the patient's obeying the 'fundamental rule of psycho-analysis'.[2] The rule for the doctor may be expressed: 'He should withhold all conscious influences from his capacity to attend, and give himself over completely to his "unconscious memory".' Or, to put it purely in terms of technique: 'He should simply listen, and not bother about whether he is keeping anything in mind.'

What is achieved in this manner will be sufficient for all requirements during the treatment. Those elements of the material which already form a connected context will be at the doctor's conscious disposal; the rest, as yet unconnected and in chaotic disorder, seems at first to be submerged, but rises readily into recollection as soon as the patient brings up something new to which it can be related and by which it can be continued. The undeserved compliment of having 'a remarkably good memory' which the patient pays one when one reproduces some detail after a year and a day can then be accepted with a smile, whereas a conscious determination to recollect the point would probably have resulted in failure.

Mistakes in this process of remembering occur only at times and places at which one is disturbed by some personal consideration (see below [p. 450])— that is, when one has fallen seriously below the standard of an ideal analyst. Confusion with material brought up by other patients occurs very rarely. Where there is a dispute with the patient as to whether or how he has said some particular thing, the doctor is usually in the right.[3]

(b) I cannot advise the taking of full notes, the keeping of a shorthand record, etc., during analytic sessions. Apart from the unfavourable impression which this makes on some patients, the same considerations as have been advanced with regard to attention apply here too.[4] A detrimental selection from the material will necessarily be made as one writes the notes or shorthand, and part of one's own mental activity is tied up in this way, which would be better employed in interpreting what one has heard. No objection can be raised to making exceptions to this rule in the case of dates, the text of dreams, or

---

1. [The reference seems to be to a sentence in the case history of 'Little Hans' (1909b), Standard Ed., 10, 23, though the wording there is slightly different. The present phrase occurs again later, in 'Two Encyclopaedia Articles' (1923a), Standard Ed., 18, 239.]

2. [See footnote 2, above, p. 107.]

3. A patient will often assert that he has already told the doctor something on a previous occasion, while the doctor can assure him with a quiet feeling of superiority that it has come up now for the first time. It then turns out that the patient had

previously had the intention of saying it, but had been prevented from performing his intention by a resistance which was still present. His recollection of his intention is indistinguishable to him from a recollection of its performance. [Freud enlarged on this point not long afterwards in a short paper on 'Fausse Reconnaissance' occurring during analysis (1914a), Standard Ed., 13, 201.]

4. [A footnote to the same effect had been inserted by Freud in his 'Rat Man' case history (1909d), Standard Ed., 10, 159.]

particular noteworthy events which can easily be detached from their context and are suitable for independent use as instances.[5] But I am not in the habit of doing this either. As regards instances, I write them down from memory in the evening after work is over; as regards texts of dreams to which I attach importance, I get the patient to repeat them to me after he has related them so that I can fix them in my mind.

(*c*) Taking notes during the session with the patient might be justified by an intention of publishing a scientific study of the case. On general grounds this can scarcely be denied. Nevertheless it must be borne in mind that exact reports of analytic case histories are of less value than might be expected. Strictly speaking, they only possess the *ostensible* exactness of which 'modern' psychiatry affords us some striking examples. They are, as a rule, fatiguing to the reader and yet do not succeed in being a substitute for his actual presence at an analysis. Experience invariably shows that if readers are willing to believe an analyst they will have confidence in any slight revision to which he has submitted his material; if, on the other hand, they are unwilling to take analysis and the analyst seriously, they will pay no attention to accurate verbatim records of the treatment either. This is not the way, it seems, to remedy the lack of convincing evidence to be found in psychoanalytic reports.

(*d*) One of the claims of psycho-analysis to distinction is, no doubt, that in its execution research and treatment coincide; nevertheless, after a certain point, the technique required for the one opposes that required for the other. It is not a good thing to work on a case scientifically while treatment is still proceeding—to piece together its structure, to try to foretell its further progress, and to get a picture from time to time of the current state of affairs, as scientific interest would demand. Cases which are devoted from the first to scientific purposes and are treated accordingly suffer in their outcome; while the most successful cases are those in which one proceeds, as it were, without any purpose in view, allows oneself to be taken by surprise by any new turn in them, and always meets them with an open mind, free from any presuppositions. The correct behaviour for an analyst lies in swinging over according to need from the one mental attitude to the other, in avoiding speculation or brooding over

cases while they are in analysis, and in submitting the material obtained to a synthetic process of thought only after the analysis is concluded. The distinction between the two attitudes would be meaningless if we already possessed all the knowledge (or at least the essential knowledge) about the psychology of the unconscious and about the structure of the neuroses that we can obtain from psychoanalytic work. At present we are still far from that goal and we ought not to cut ourselves off from the possibility of testing what we have already learnt and of extending our knowledge further.

(*e*) I cannot advise my colleagues too urgently to model themselves during psycho-analytic treatment on the surgeon, who puts aside all his feelings, even his human sympathy, and concentrates his mental forces on the single aim of performing the operation as skilfully as possible. Under present-day conditions the feeling that is most dangerous to a psychoanalyst is the therapeutic ambition to achieve by this novel and much disputed method something that will produce a convincing effect upon other people. This will not only put him into a state of mind which is unfavourable for his work, but will make him helpless against certain resistances of the patient, whose recovery, as we know, primarily depends on the interplay of forces in him. The justification for requiring this emotional coldness in the analyst is that it creates the most advantageous conditions for both parties: for the doctor a desirable protection for his own emotional life and for the patient the largest amount of help that we can give him to-day. A surgeon of earlier times took as his motto the words: 'Je le pansai, Dieu le guérit.'[6] The analyst should be content with something similar.

(*f*) It is easy to see upon what aim the different rules I have brought forward converge. [See p. 111.] They are all intended to create for the doctor a counterpart to the 'fundamental rule of psychoanalysis' which is laid down for the patient. Just as the patient must relate everything that his self-observation can detect, and keep back all the logical and affective objections that seek to induce him to make a selection from among them, so the doctor must put himself in a position to make use of everything he is told for the purposes of interpretation and of recognizing the concealed unconscious material without substituting a censorship of his own for the selection that the patient has forgone. To put it in a

---

5. [Presumably for scientific purposes.]
6. ['I dressed his wounds, God cured him.' The saying is attributed to the French surgeon, Ambroise Paré (*c.* 1517-1590).]

formula, he must turn his own unconscious like a receptive organ towards the transmitting unconscious of the patient. He must adjust himself to the patient as a telephone receiver is adjusted to the transmitting microphone. Just as the receiver converts back into sound waves the electric oscillations in the telephone line which were set up by sound waves, so the doctor's unconscious is able, from the derivatives of the unconscious which are communicated to him, to reconstruct that unconscious, which has determined the patient's free associations.

But if the doctor is to be in a position to use his unconscious in this way as an instrument in the analysis, he must himself fulfil one psychological condition to a high degree. He may not tolerate any resistances in himself which hold back from his consciousness what has been perceived by his unconscious; otherwise he would introduce into the analysis a new species of selection and distortion which would be far more detrimental than that resulting from concentration of conscious attention. It is not enough for this that he himself should be an approximately normal person. It may be insisted, rather, that he should have undergone a psycho-analytic purification and have become aware of those complexes of his own which would be apt to interfere with his grasp of what the patient tells him. There can be no reasonable doubt about the disqualifying effect of such defects in the doctor; every unresolved repression in him constitutes what has been aptly described by Stekel[7] as a 'blind spot' in his analytic perception.

Some years ago I gave as an answer to the question of how one can become an analyst: 'By analysing one's own dreams.'[8] This preparation is no doubt enough for many people, but not for everyone who wishes to learn analysis. Nor can everyone succeed in interpreting his own dreams without outside help. I count it as one of the many merits of the Zurich school of analysis that they have laid increased emphasis on this requirement, and have embodied it in the demand that everyone who wishes to carry out analyses on other people shall first himself undergo an analysis by someone with expert knowledge. Anyone who takes up the work seriously should choose this course, which offers more than one advantage; the sacrifice involved in laying oneself open to another person without being driven to it by illness is amply rewarded. Not only is one's aim of learning to know what is hidden in one's own mind far more rapidly attained and with less expense of affect, but impressions and convictions will be gained in relation to oneself which will be sought in vain from studying books and attending lectures. And lastly, we must not under-estimate the advantage to be derived from the lasting mental contact that is as a rule established between the student and his guide.[9]

An analysis such as this of someone who is practically healthy will, as may be imagined, remain incomplete. Anyone who can appreciate the high value of the self-knowledge and increase in self-control thus acquired will, when it is over, continue the analytic examination of his personality in the form of a self-analysis, and be content to realize that, within himself as well as in the external world, he must always expect to find something new. But anyone who has scorned to take the precaution of being analysed himself will not merely be punished by being incapable of learning more than a certain amount from his patients, he will risk a more serious danger and one which may become a danger to others. He will easily fall into the temptation of projecting outwards some of the peculiarities of his own personality, which he has dimly perceived, into the field of science, as a theory having universal validity; he will bring the psycho-analytic method into discredit, and lead the inexperienced astray.

(g) I shall now add a few other rules, that will serve as a transition from the attitude of the doctor to the treatment of the patient.

Young and eager psycho-analysts will not doubt be tempted to bring their own individuality freely into the discussion, in order to carry the patient along with them and lift him over the barriers of his own narrow personality. It might be expected that it would be quite allowable and indeed useful, with a view to overcoming the patient's existing resistances, for the doctor to afford him a glimpse of his own mental defects and conflicts and, by giving him intimate information about his own life, enable him to put himself on an equal footing. One confidence deserves another, and anyone who demands intimacy

---

7. [Stekel, 1911a, 532.]

8. [The reference is to the third of Freud's Clark University lectures (1910a [1909]), *Standard Ed.*, 11, 33. Some account of his varying views on the subject will be found in an Editor's footnote to the 'History of the Psycho-Analytic Movement' (1914d), ibid., 14, 20–1.]

9. [See, however, a less optimistic view expressed in Section II of 'Analysis Terminable and Interminable' (1937c). That paper, one of the very last of Freud's writings, touches at many points (especially in Section VII) on the subject discussed in this and the next paragraph.]

from someone else must be prepared to give it in return.

But in psycho-analytic relations things often happen differently from what the psychology of consciousness might lead us to expect. Experience does not speak in favour of an affective technique of this kind. Nor is it hard to see that it involves a departure from psycho-analytic principles and verges upon treatment by suggestion. It may induce the patient to bring forward sooner and with less difficulty things he already knows but would otherwise have kept back for a time through conventional resistances. But this technique achieves nothing towards the uncovering of what is unconscious to the patient. It makes him even more incapable of overcoming his deeper resistances, and in severer cases it invariably fails, by encouraging the patient to be insatiable: he would like to reverse the situation, and finds the analysis of the doctor more interesting than his own. The resolution of the transference, too—one of the main tasks of the treatment—is made more difficult by an intimate attitude on the doctor's part, so that any gain there may be at the beginning is more than outweighed at the end. I have no hesitation, therefore, in condemning this kind of technique as incorrect. The doctor should be opaque to his patients and, like a mirror, should show them nothing but what is shown to him. In practice, it is true, there is nothing to be said against a psychotherapist combining a certain amount of analysis with some suggestive influence in order to achieve a perceptible result in a shorter time—as is necessary, for instance, in institutions. But one has a right to insist that he himself should be in no doubt about what he is doing and should know that his method is not that of true psycho-analysis.

(*h*) Another temptation arises out of the educative activity which, in psycho-analytic treatment, devolves on the doctor without any deliberate intention on his part. When the developmental inhibitions are resolved, it happens of itself that the doctor finds himself in a position to indicate new aims for the trends that have been liberated. It is then no more than a natural ambition if he endeavours to make something specially excellent of a person whom he has been at such pains to free from his neurosis and if he prescribes high aims for his wishes. But here again the doctor should hold himself in check, and take the patient's capacities rather than his own desires as guide. Not every neurotic has a high talent for sublimation; one can assume of many of them that they would not have fallen ill at all if they had possessed the art of sublimating their instincts. If we press them unduly towards sublimation and cut them off from the most accessible and convenient instinctual satisfactions, we shall usually make life even harder for them than they feel it in any case. As a doctor, one must above all be tolerant to the weakness of a patient, and must be content if one has won back some degree of capacity for work and enjoyment for a person even of only moderate worth. Educative ambition is of as little use as therapeutic ambition. It must further be borne in mind that many people fall ill precisely from an attempt to sublimate their instincts beyond the degree permitted by their organization and that in those who have a capacity for sublimation the process usually takes place of itself as soon as their inhibitions have been overcome by analysis. In my opinion, therefore, efforts invariably to make use of the analytic treatment to bring about sublimation of instinct are, though no doubt always laudable, far from being in every case advisable.

(*i*) To what extent should the patient's intellectual co-operation be sought for in the treatment? It is difficult to say anything of general applicability on this point: the patient's personality is the determining factor. But in any case caution and self-restraint must be observed in this connection. It is wrong to set a patient tasks, such as collecting his memories or thinking over some particular period of his life. On the contrary, he has to learn above all—what never comes easily to anyone—that mental activities such as thinking something over or concentrating the attention solve none of the riddles of a neurosis; that can only be done by patiently obeying the psycho-analytic rule, which enjoins the exclusion of all criticism of the unconscious or of its derivatives. One must be especially unyielding about obedience to that rule with patients who practise the art of sheering off into intellectual discussion during their treatment, who speculate a great deal and often very wisely about their condition and in that way avoid doing anything to overcome it. For this reason I dislike making use of analytic writings as an assistance to my patients; I require them to learn by personal experience, and I assure them that they will acquire wider and more valuable knowledge than the whole literature of psycho-analysis could teach them. I recognize, however, that under institutional conditions it may be of great advantage to employ reading as a preparation for patients in analysis and as a means of creating an atmosphere of influence.

I must give a most earnest warning against any attempt to gain the confidence or support of parents or relatives by giving them psycho-analytic books to read, whether of an introductory or an advanced kind. This well-meant step usually has the effect of bringing on prematurely the natural opposition of the relatives to the treatment — an opposition which is bound to appear sooner or later — so that the treatment is never even begun.

Let me express a hope that the increasing experience of psycho-analysts will soon lead to agreement on questions of technique and on the most effective method of treating neurotic patients. As regards the treatment of their relatives I must confess myself utterly at a loss, and I have in general little faith in any individual treatment of them.

39

THE EFFECT OF THE STRUCTURE OF THE EGO ON PSYCHOANALYTIC TECHNIQUE

K. R. EISSLER

EDITOR'S NOTE

After Freud's basic contributions classical analysts wrote only occasional papers on one or another ground rule. In these two main themes emerged: first, that the ground rules were a means of safeguarding the transference and enabling its analytic resolution (Freud 1912a, 1913, Greenacre 1954, Greenson 1967), and second, that flexibility should be the overriding principle in the application of these tenets lest the analyst appear insensitive and inhuman. The most striking exception to this trend is seen in the present paper by Eissler, in which he specifically defines a particular form of deviation in technique—an alteration in the basic ground rules—necessitated by ego dysfunctions within the patient. This type of deviation he termed the *parameter*. In this carefully reasoned essay, Eissler details its constructive and possibly detrimental effects, as well as the particulars of its technical application.

The paper is often referred to in discussions of modifications and deviations in technique. While the constructive aspects of parameters have never been psychoanalytically validated, these measures tend to be recommended and used rather freely. Later writers have seldom addressed the detrimental potential of parameters, nor have they tended to distinguish parameters from other types of deviations.

The subject matter of this paper is closely related to a problem which has occupied the minds of analysts for decades. It is within the scope of the question which Freud raised at the Berlin Psychoanalytic Convention (1922) when he asked: "What is the relationship between psychoanalytic technique and psychoanalytic theory?" Freud's question encompassed a vast area, only one portion of which pertains to the subject matter of this paper.

Freud's question of 1922 will interest us today particularly in conjunction with the structure of the ego. During the last two decades a certain sentiment has spread which might be formulated as follows:

If our knowledge of the structure of the ego were complete, then a variety of techniques—ideally adapted to the requirements of the individual disturbance—could be perfected; thus we could assure definite mastery of the ego over those areas in which it had suffered defeat, that is to say, assure complete recovery. Like all sentiments, this one does not adequately reflect objective reality, but it is probably correct to say that greatly deepened, almost complete, insight into the structure of the ego would multiply the clinical effectiveness of psychoanalytic techniques. The pessimist's claim, however, must be conceded: Full knowledge of the structure of the ego would, no doubt, make the task of changing that structure appear in its true and gigantic proportion, inducing us as a consequence to withdraw modestly from such heroic attempts.

Reprinted from *Journal of the American Psychoanalytic Association* 1: 104–143 by permission of International Universities Press, Inc. Copyright © 1953 by American Psychoanalytic Association.

Before delving into the subject matter, I want to exclude two variables which have great bearing on psychoanalytic techniques. Such delimitation will facilitate a more precise formulation of basic issues and avoid the bewilderment which might arise in view of the great variety of problems involved. Psychoanalytic techniques depend chiefly on three variables: the patient's disorder and personality, the patient's present life circumstances, and the psychoanalyst's personality. In the following discussion the last two variables will be excluded. It is assumed that the living conditions of the patient and the personality of the analyst are both ideal; that is, entirely favorable to the analytic process. Thus in our assumption no disturbance of the psychoanalytic process originates either from the patient's actual life circumstances or the analyst's personality.

Failure to distinguish these variables has considerably lowered the standards of discussion of psychoanalytic technique.[1] Clinical reality, of course, is so highly varied and provides so many unforeseen situations that it is impossible to set up a standard technique which would meet all exigencies of practice. This is also true of other specialties. All accepted rules of asepsis are thrown aside in some emergency situations; nevertheless, when operating under optimal conditions, the surgeon follows these rules faithfully, and they are still taught in approved medical schools although the teacher knows well the many situations in which there will be no occasion for their application.

While the patient's particular life circumstances may necessitate a certain technical measure, it is a grave mistake to conclude that this measure has general validity because it has proved its usefulness under special conditions. To overlook the specificity of variables to which a technical measure is correlated means to discard sound scientific standards.

For the purpose of demonstrating the errors we may fall into when we do not distinguish between the variables of the technique, I wish to cite only one example. In discussing the principle of flexibility, Alexander and French (3) quote Freud's technical advice that at certain points of the treatment phobic patients should be urged to expose themselves to the fear-arousing situation. Alexander uses this technical device as an additional argument in favor of his technique of giving his patients ample advice and encouragement. However, Freud's technical measure, as will be seen presently, does not lend itself at all to generalization if it is seen in its true proportion and context; that is to say, if it is correlated with that variable which forced its introduction.

Another general remark comes to mind. I mentioned earlier as one variable of psychoanalytic technique the psychoanalyst's personality. Freud reported some of the subjective factors which influenced the evolving of his technique. For example, in explaining his request that the patient take the supine position during analysis, Freud (17) mentions his dislike of being stared at for several hours. And he goes on to add other reasons which make the supine position preferable.

When she discussed her deviation from classical psychoanalysis, analyzing in a face-to-face situation, Frieda Fromm-Reichmann (30, p. 11) supported her argument by quoting Freud's idiosyncrasy. Her argument is out of place. An analyst may be an exhibitionist and may therefore prefer a face-to-face technique. Whatever technique a therapist may devise can be used in the service of his pleasure principle. The value of a technical measure must rest on objective factors. If it coincides with the therapist's pleasure, all the better, but this coincidence is not a decisive factor in judging and evaluating the given technique.

Fromm-Reichmann calls the reader's attention to another factor which deserves consideration when we speak of Freud's aversion to being gazed at for eight hours. She claims that the therapist of the time was "liable to share the embarrassment of his patient while listening to difficult communications" (30, p. 11) and this made him prefer the patient's supine position.[2] Fromm-Reichmann's reasoning, whether it is correct or not, brings into the picture a cluster of factors which I have deliberately deleted from my earlier enumeration of variables, namely, the historical situation. There have been attempts to correlate all kinds of historical factors with classical psychoanalysis: Victorianism and anti-Victorianism,

---

1. Following Freud's concept of wild analysis (16) one may really talk of wild discussions on psychoanalytic technique in this context.

2. Fromm-Reichmann's reasoning in favor of face-to-face interviews cannot be thoroughly discussed here; therefore I will limit myself to one statement. If the author means to identify Freud with the above-quoted statement, as the content suggests, she was mistaken. Freud reported that he had used the supine position before he had discovered the sexual etiology of the neuroses, and further that he had gained the full conviction regarding the correctness of the theory from his interviews with neurasthenics whose sexual life he investigated in a face-to-face position. (see Freud, 25, p. 42.)

feudalism, Puritanism, etc. No individual can divorce himself from the historical period in which he is living any more than he can put himself beyond time or space. Valuable as the sociology of science is, it does not decide which scientific finding is correct and which is not. The historical viewpoint can be applied to any of the so-called modern psychoanalytic innovations. Let us consider, for example, the technique of the staggering of interviews which is now so often advised.

As is well known, Freud attributed to the constancy and continuity of the technique—that is to say, to the technique of daily interviews—great importance, whereas some contemporary psychoanalysts believe the frequency of interviews should be adapted to the therapeutic needs of the patient; that is to say, he should be seen less often when it is desirable to increase his emotional participation and more often to assuage anxiety. The resulting technique accustoms the patient to see his analyst some times rarely and other times frequently. A historical evaluation of this technique will show that the living pattern of many analysts, certainly of those who are nationally prominent, is quite different from that of Freud. They are prominent figures on the national scene, being called to Washington as government advisers, serving on numerous committees, at all times of the year, lecturing at places hundreds or thousands of miles apart, participating in conventions—in short, they are kept busy in many extracurricular activities, so to speak. Can such analysts indulge in the luxury of daily interviews for ten months of the year without sinking into national oblivion? I have mentioned only the crudest historical reasons for the technique of staggered interviews; there are other, more subtle, ones. A historical factor may well be a valid aspect of research. But we must remember that although historical factors may be easily correlated with the techniques of a given period, the correctness or incorrectness of any technique is not decided by such correlation. Everything that is created by man must be deeply imbued by the historical climate at the time of its creation. In considering the creations of scientists we observe that at certain times and under certain circumstances the historical climate has led to a correct interpretation of reality; at other times it has led to an incorrect interpretation. Since it is idle to raise the historical argument in weighing the pros and cons of a scientific proposition, I have omitted the historical factor as one of the variables of psychoanalytic technique to be discussed here.

To return to the discussion of the effect of ego structure on technique: I will begin with a clinical example in which the psychoanalytic technique can be applied with the fewest complications. The basic model of the psychoanalytic technique can be discussed with relative ease in a case of hysteria. In such a case, we assume—and in this abstract context it is unimportant whether this assumption is clinically correct or not—that the hysteric patient has reached the phallic level and that his ego has all the potentialities for developing into an organization which can maintain an adequate relationship to reality. The task of therapy, at this point, is to give the patient that support which is necessary for the attainment of the genital level and to make possible the realization of those potentialities of the ego which have been held in abeyance chiefly because of traumatic experiences. Such a patient is informed of the basic rule and of his obligation to follow it. He adheres to it to the best of his ability, which is quite sufficient for the task of achieving recovery. The tool with which the analyst can accomplish this task is interpretation, and the goal of interpretation is to provide the patient with insight. Insight will remove the obstacles which have so far delayed the ego in attaining its full development. The problem here is only when and what to interpret; for in the ideal case the analyst's activity is limited to interpretation; no other tool becomes necessary.

In order to avoid misunderstandings, I want to stress that I do not discuss here the problem of what is therapeutically effective in the analysis of a neurosis. The therapeutically effective factors are, of course, of a far greater diversity than interpretation; among many others there is, for example, transference. It would, however, be a mistake to consider transference a tool of therapy, particularly in a case of hysteria. Transference in this instance is a source of energy which if properly used leads to recovery through the application of interpretation.

Another point should be clarified. There are other therapeutically effective factors which may look like tools, such as the denial of wish fulfillment, to which the patient must submit throughout the treatment or, more generally, the psychoanalytic therapeutic attitude. I believe that these factors are secondary; that is to say, they are the necessary consequences when interpretation is the only tool of the analyst. Similarly, working through is a specific technique for using interpretation.

I have left out one tool which is indispensable for the basic model technique. It is doubtful if any person was ever analyzed without being asked questions by the analyst in the course of the psychoanalytic treatment. Indeed, I think that the question as a type of communication is a basic and therefore indispensable tool of analysis, and one essentially different from interpretation. Unfortunately this tool has been taken for granted. The principal investigations at the present time pertain to the proper use of questions in interviews and not in the psychoanalytic process itself (F. Deutsch, 8, 9). The psychology of "question" in terms of structural psychology has not yet been written. But though it offers a most challenging task, I shall not consider it further in this paper but shall proceed to another neurosis, investigating the minimum tools necessary in the case of a phobia.

The technique required in a classical case of phobia is likely to be surprising at one point. The treatment begins and proceeds for a long time like that of a hysteria; that is to say, the analyst uses interpretation as the exclusive tool of therapy. However, in the treatment of some cases a point is reached when it becomes evident that interpretation does not suffice as a therapeutic tool and that pathogenic material is warded off despite the analysis of all those resistances which become clinically visible. In other words, despite maximum interpretation, the pathogenic area cannot be tapped. Even if all resistances are interpreted and every reconstruction obtainable from the material is conveyed to the patient, and even if the patient ideally adheres to the basic rule, the area constituting the core of the psychopathology will not become accessible to the analyst. At that moment a new technical tool becomes necessary. As is well known, this new tool is advice or command.

The analyst must impose on the patient a command: to expose himself to the dreaded situation despite his fear of it and regardless of any anxiety which might develop during that exposure. In extreme cases it may become necessary to threaten the discontinuance of treatment unless the patient takes on the burden of voluntarily suffering anxiety. Advising the patient to perform a certain action or even forcing him indirectly to do it is beyond the scope of interpretation and introduces a therapeutic tool which is of an entirely different type. In order to facilitate communication I introduce here the term *parameter of a technique*. I define the parameter of a technique as the deviation, both quantitative and qualitative, from the basic model of technique, that

is to say, from a technique which requires interpretation as the exclusive tool. In the basic model technique the parameter is, of course, zero throughout the whole treatment. We therefore would say that the parameter of the technique necessary for the treatment of a phobia is zero in the initial phases as well as in the concluding phases; but to the extent that interpretation is replaced by advice or command in the middle phase, there is a parameter which may, as in the instance cited here, be considerable, though temporary.

The justification of introducing a parameter into the treatment of phobia is based exclusively on clinical observation. Early experience demonstrated that the basic model technique had led to a stalemate. It became clear to Freud that if phobias were to be treated at all by psychoanalysis, he had to deviate from the basic technical position; namely, not to impose advice or command on a patient after treatment had started. The parameter which he introduced was the minimum, without which no progress could be made. The great advantage of this parameter was that it needed to be used for only a short time, that once it had proved its usefulness it could be dispensed with, and the treatment could proceed with the basic model technique. The parameter introduced into the psychoanalysis of phobia may serve as a model from which the ideal conditions which a parameter ought to fulfill can be deduced. We formulate tentatively the following general criteria of a parameter if it is to fulfill the conditions which are fundamental to psychoanalysis: (1) A parameter must be introduced only when it is proved that the basic model technique does not suffice; (2) the parameter must never transgress the unavoidable minimum; (3) a parameter is to be used only when it finally leads to its self-elimination; that is to say, the final phase of the treatment must always proceed with a parameter of zero. These three conditions are ideally fulfilled by the parameter which has become part and parcel of the analytic treatment of phobic patients.

If we now turn to the next group of neuroses, the compulsive-obsessive ones, we encounter a still different situation. Here we can take the history of the "Wolfman" as paradigmatic (20).[3] As far as can be

---

3. This patient has been diagnosed in various ways. Before his analysis some authorities claimed manic-depressive insanity (20, p. 474). Freud's diagnosis was "a condition following upon an obsessional neurosis which has come to an end spontaneously, but has left a defect behind it after recovery" (20, p. 474), but another passage suggests that Freud may have considered the patient an obsessional neurotic: "It [the patient's intestinal trouble] represented the small trait of hysteria which is regularly

found at the root of an obsessional neurosis" (20, p. 552). Freud later (28, p. 318) referred to the paranoic character of some of the patient's symptoms. Yet the problems of technique which Freud discussed in the original paper pertained to those which are generally encountered in analyses of compulsive neuroses. I do not agree with Binswanger (5) who considers the early history of the "Wolfman" as typical of childhood schizophrenia.

seen, for the greater part of the treatment Freud used the basic model technique. Toward the end— "not until trustworthy signs had led me to judge that the right moment had come" (20, p. 478)—Freud introduced two parameters. One of them is well known: He appointed a fixed time for the conclusion of the treatment. The second, rarely mentioned, impresses me as even more consequential: "I promised the patient a complete recovery of his intestinal activity" (20, p. 552). The patient must have experienced this as a definite surrender of the analytic reserve and as the analyst's admission and promise of omnipotence; hence the resurgence of the disease when the analyst became sick and proved himself to be not omnipotent (Brunswick, 7, p. 442).

These two parameters are of a different order than that encountered in the treatment of phobias. They fulfill the first demand we put upon a parameter; they were introduced when it was proved that the basic model technique would not bring about the patient's recovery. It is questionable whether they fulfill the second demand, of presenting the indispensable minimum deviation. Undoubtedly they do not fulfill the third requirement; they are not self-eliminating for two reasons: (1) Since the patient is to be dismissed at an appointed time, there is no time left for a concluding phase in which the basic model technique will be the exclusive one. (2) The other parameter, the promise of omnipotence, extends vastly over the termination of the treatment and seems to have been, in the case of the "Wolfman," a precondition necessary for the patient's maintenance of mental health during the years following his analysis. This deviation is of interest for other reasons: It is possible that the introduction per se of some parameters has a lasting effect on the patient's transference, an effect which cannot be undone by interpretation. Deviations from the basic model technique are occasionally lightheartedly suggested by some analysts under the assumption that the effect of any therapeutic measure can be "analyzed" later. As a general statement this is definitely

wrong. Unfortunately, the boundaries have not yet been ascertained beyond which therapeutic measures create an irreparable damage to the transference relationship. One must expect individual variations from one patient to another in this respect.[4]

Freud made a definitive statement with regard to this problem when he discussed the treatment of negative therapeutic reactions. After describing the parameter of the technique which he would have to introduce if he were to effect clinical recovery in patients showing negative therapeutic reactions, he went on to state clearly and emphatically that this particular parameter is irreconcilable with psychoanalytic technique because it would convert transference into a relationship per se inaccessible to psychoanalytic interpretations.[5] Thus a fourth proposition must be introduced in order to delineate the conditions which a parameter must fulfill if the technique is to remain within the scope of psychoanalysis: The effect of the parameter on the transference relationship must never be such that it cannot be abolished by interpretation.

Returning to Freud's technique in the treatment of the "Wolfman," I want to re-emphasize what is generally known: that neither of the technical innovations in this case has become an integral part of analysis. We do not have a technique for this type of compulsive neurosis which is comparable in either adequacy or precision to the parameter of technique used in the treatment of phobias.

If we now approach the other two groups of disorders, the schizophrenias and delinquencies, the situation becomes infinitely more complicated. The technique of free association cannot be applied in either group. In the schizophrenias the patient would be incapable of co-operating; moreover, the technique might precipitate regressions. In the delinquencies the basic rule is inapplicable because of the patient's intentional and adamant refusal to follow it. In these two groups, not only is the basic rule inapplicable, but simultaneously the main tool of interpretation is thrown out of gear, and insight

---

4. Of the many examples which could be cited I arbitrarily select one. There are patients in whom the slightest deviation of the rule of conducting the treatment in the situation of frustration can have an extremely detrimental effect and the fulfillment of a wish, trivial as the request for a cigarette, may endanger the further course of the treatment by establishing a fixed fantasy inaccessible to further analysis. Other patients, and I believe they are the majority, are less rigid. Whatever may, in them, be evoked in terms of transference formation by trivial wish fulfillments can easily be analyzed and does not become a stumbling block to further treatment.

5. See (22, footnote on p. 72). The content of this footnote is

of formidable importance. Perusal of most books on psychoanalytic technique of recent date will show that Freud's spirit of intellectual honesty has largely been lost. Technical innovations are introduced in large number and are supported by the simple-minded justification that the innovator has noticed subsequent disappearance of symptoms. The question of "at what cost to and limitation of the ego" is no longer asked; instead pride in the alleged superiority of the contemporary analysts' knowledge makes many authors believe that Freud's safeguards against the effect of the therapist's personality—in situations where a structural change, induced by the analytical process, ought to take place—have become superfluous.

cannot be conveyed to these patients by verbal interpretation—at least not in the initial phase of treatment. Therefore the parameters of the necessary techniques cannot be used to alter the basic model technique at certain spots nor can they be introduced as new devices in certain phases, as in the neuroses just mentioned: In the schizophrenias and the delinquences the whole technique must be changed in all essential aspects.

Nevertheless the four criteria just formulated, which a parameter must fulfill if a technique is to be accepted as psychoanalytic, are valid also for these two groups.[6]

It is impossible to demonstrate here the consequences which must follow when the basic model technique is adapted to the necessities of such grave disorders as the schizophrenias always are and the delinquencies in almost all instances prove to be, but I do want to stress that, despite the claim to the contrary by a few analysts, I am convinced that it has not yet been proved that schizophrenic patients ever reach a state in which they can be treated in accordance with the basic model technique. That is, to a certain extent, coincidental with a doubt that schizophrenic patients can be "cured" by psychoanalysis in that sense in which we commonly say neuroses can be cured. This statement is not to be construed as a denial of the effectiveness of psychoanalysis in the treatment of schizophrenic patients.

To return to the neuroses: We have taken the minimum requirements of a case of hysteria as our basic model and have compared them with the minimum requirements of other disorders. For historical reasons hysteria can be taken as the base line of the psychoanalytic therapy, since Freud demonstrated the basic technique and the basic concepts of psychoanalysis in conjunction with his clinical experiences with hysterias. However, there is also an intrinsic reason why psychoanalysis was evolved in the course of the treatment of hysterias. Tentatively I would say that the discovery of psychoanalysis would have been greatly impeded, delayed, or even made impossible if in the second half of the nineteenth century the prevailing neurosis had not been hysteria. Notwithstanding some inaccuracy, it can be said that the earliest psychoanalytic model of hysteria pertains to an ego which has suffered that minimum

of injury without which no neurosis would develop at all. It is of interest to peruse the earliest publication by Breuer and Freud (6) from this point of view.

In the paper of 1892, two different functions were assigned to the ego in the course of the development of hysteria: (a) Most hysterical symptoms were recognized as being consequences of traumata. Any experience which could elicit intensive painful affects could become a trauma, depending upon the sensitivity of the ego. This sensitivity was the only factor through which the ego contributed to the development of the disease, but nothing further was said about it. The psychic trauma had penetrated the patient like a foreign body and accomplished— well protected in its hideout—the whole variety of hysterical symptomatology. This early theory comes close to picturing the disease process as an event in which a part of reality has intruded into the psychic organism and pushed aside for a while the normal personality. Because of this interpretation of clinical observations, the structure of the ego did not need consideration. (b) That part of reality which remains isolated in the patient obtains its privileged function from the lack of affective abreaction, which would have been necessary in order to assimilate it. Two groups of factors were held responsible for the want of abreaction. First, the patient did not abreact because the nature of the trauma made it impossible or because the patient did not want to take notice of the trauma; that is to say, he did not want to abreact. The second group of factors concerned the state of the ego at the time when the trauma occurred. The ego was either paralyzed by an inordinately strong affect or by a hypnoid state and therefore was incapable of contributing that amount of work which would have been necessary for rendering innocuous the poisonous effect of reality— if this kind of imagery is permitted.[7]

All these explanations had one point in common: They conjured away the bearing of the ego upon the disease process; the ego does not want to, or cannot, function and thus an area is established in which the ego-alien puts forth roots and flourishes.[8] This disregard of the ego shows up also in the therapy, which was based on a maximum paralysis of the ego, induced by means of hypnosis.

We are not, in this paper, concerned with

---

6. The fourth condition, that the parameter must not give the transference a lasting direction, will be difficult to fulfill during the acute phases of the disease. If it has happened that a parameter has influenced the transference in a way which cannot be undone by interpretation, a change of analyst may become necessary.

7. One receives the impression that these earlier theories might have been influenced by contemporary concepts of internal medicine regarding the origin of infectious disorders.

8. To be sure, one of the authors must have seen beyond these conceptions, since at one point he speaks of "a hysterical individuality."

investigating the extent to which these conceptions correctly reflected clinical reality, but only with noting that in hysteria it was apparently possible to study the disease process quite apart from the rest of the personality. Consequently a technique was evolved which permitted concentration on the clinically most conspicuous part of the disease process and which succeeded in eliminating it, at least temporarily.[9]

A late statement of Freud's may now be brought into genetic connection with early theories. In "Analysis Terminable and Interminable," Freud reported that complete recovery could be achieved with relative ease in patients whose pathology was caused mainly by traumata (28, p. 321). Despite their symptomatology, the ego had not been noticeably modified in such patients. In view of this statement the following conclusion can be drawn: The basic model technique, without emendations, can be applied to those patients whose neurotic symptomatology is borne by an ego not modified to any noteworthy degree. In other words, if the ego has preserved its integrity, it will make maximum use of the support it receives from the analyst in the form of interpretation. The exclusive technical problem in such instances is simply to find that interpretation which will provide the ego, in the respective phases of the treatment, with maximum support.[10]

For the type of phobia which I presented initially, this diagram must be slightly changed. Despite maximum assistance by means of interpretations, the ego cannot recover from the damage caused by the past. I believe that this fact has not made us marvel enough. It is still a riddle why a human being should refuse to make maximal use of the insight which is conveyed to him. It must be remembered that the insight offered him comprehends not only the history of his sickness but also all those resistances checking his recovery which manifest themselves during this treatment phase. Nonetheless, though recovery does not follow the offer of maximum insight, the process of recovery can be initiated after the patient has been forced to expose himself to the very danger he is so much afraid of.

---

9. Cf. for the foregoing A. Freud (11, pp. 11f.).

10. I will pursue this problem further in connection with Freud's concept of the hypothetically normal ego. The question of whether such a technique, based principally on interpretations, leads to intellectualization and lack of emotional participation on the patient's side will not be discussed here. Freud's papers on metapsychology and on the technique of psychoanalysis refute this argument. See also Alexander's (1) incisive criticism of Ferenczi's and Rank's book *The Development of Psychoanalysis*.

The patient behaves like someone who has in his grasp all the riches of the world but who refuses to take them and must be forced by threat to do so.

Of course we know some of the reasons which make it necessary in such cases to deviate from the model technique and to demand of the patient that he expose himself to the feared situation. The prospect of anxiety is such a deterrent that it cannot be overcome unless the patient is threatened with the even greater pain of losing a beloved object. But this does not explain why such an ego can give up a resistance and turn toward pathogenic, repressed material only when it is re-exposed to the pain of a dreaded anxiety. It is necessary to conclude that this ego had lost its capacity of adjustment to a larger extent than the ego of a hysteric patient. The ego organization in phobia must be significantly different from that of hysteria.

At this point it is wise to remember that the state of affairs alluded to above is not encountered in all patients suffering from phobias. Some of them recover without having recovery imposed upon them. Therefore it may be appropriate to say that it is not so much the particular combination of symptoms and defenses — that is to say, the structure of the symptom — which necessitates the specific technique but the ego organization in which the particular symptom is embedded. We must also remember that the pattern of the basic model technique does not always suffice in the treatment of hysterias; sometimes a technique resembling that for phobias becomes necessary. A hysterical patient who consistently consults internists for the treatment of conversion symptoms or who uses physical means of therapy may have to be told that he must either abstain from such escapes or face a discontinuance of his psychoanalysis. In such instances we must assume that the ego has become modified to a larger extent than was to be expected from the classical description of the dynamics of hysteria. On the other hand, as Freud (14) has shown in the history of the "Ratman," it is possible to have a compulsive-obsessive neurosis which will subside on the mere application of the basic model technique, and a comparison of the "Ratman's" history with that of the "Wolfman" will show that fairly similar symptoms may be combined with two entirely different ego organizations — one barely, the other severely, modified.

It may be worth while to demonstrate how little or how much a mechanism or a symptom as such may count, depending on the all-inclusive ego organization in which it occurs. In his essay on Leonardo da Vinci Freud (15) investigated the circumstances which may have been responsible for the relative lack of artistic productivity which became increasingly noticeable in Leonardo's life. Science and scientific research gradually gained ground over artistic achievements. Freud thought that Leonardo's hesitation was caused by a lack of power to isolate the work of art by pulling it out of a broader context. Leonardo's want of capacity to isolate was correlated with a craving to express all of the associations linked with the artistic intention.

In contrast to this example of the lack of capacity to isolate, I want to cite a passage from a letter (21 November 1782) which Goethe wrote to a friend during a time when he was overburdened with administrative work as a Privy Councilor at the Court of Weimar: "I have totally separated (externally of course) my political and social life from my moral and poetic one and in this way I feel at my very best . . . . I leave separated the Privy Councilor and my other self without which the Privy Councilor can exist very well. Only in my innermost plans and purposes and endeavors do I remain mysteriously self-loyal and thus tie my social, political, moral, and poetic life again together into a hidden knot." Here isolation—and quantitatively a rather extensive isolation, cutting across Goethe's existence—functions as a truly life-saving device. I cannot go into the details of this period in the life of Goethe; suffice it to say that it was an extremely critical one, and that without some very felicitous circumstances he might have suffered injuries which could have endangered his future as an artist. Isolation was one of the mechanisms which enabled him to survive this period in a way which was of greater benefit to him. I want to point out that the isolation of which Goethe speaks here is dangerous, and one which can be found in cases suffering from severe psychopathology; nevertheless, the mechanism which Goethe described cannot be classified clinically as part of a disease. Fortunately, Goethe made another remark which enlightens us as to the reason why isolation did not lead to psychopathology. He mentioned briefly his loyalty to himself and the hidden knot by dint of which the isolated activities were tied again into a unit; that is to say, the powerful isolation was counterpoised by an unusually strong capacity for synthesis. This mysterious knot of which Goethe speaks is really the subject matter of my exposition.

My third example is a patient whose whole personality organization was interwoven with the effects of isolation, the mechanism which dominated her life. For her time had separated into isolated moments and her childhood recollections were remembered as disconnected flashes of an ego-alien past. Likewise her various contemporary activities were isolated from each other, and probably body space, too, had fallen apart into disconnected space units as evidenced by her difficulty in distinguishing right from left. Time and space had become an aggregate. Isolation had achieved its maximum effect. As can be easily foreseen, a most severe psychopathology must flourish on such fertile ground. Interestingly enough, the patient had no feeling of suffering about this part of her psychopathology.

These three clinical examples show us three totally different effects of the mechanism of isolation:[11] first, a deficit in the capacity for isolation, leading to a deficit in artistic creativity; second, a profusion preserving the continuity of manifold functions; and third, an excessive growth decomposing the ego into innumerable fragments.

In view of the relative independence of ego structure and mechanism the following conclusion can be drawn: The behavior of the ego in the situation of the basic model technique is specific. Here is the critical point where it can be determined whether or not the ego has suffered a modification. The symptoms or behavior deviations do not necessarily betray the true structure of the ego organization. This was brought conspicuously to my attention during the analysis of a patient who had spent one and a half years in voluntary commitment. At times this patient was believed to be schizophrenic because of the bewildering variety of bizarre behavior patterns. She made an astounding improvement under a technique which, with rather rare exceptions, followed the rules of classical analysis. Very much to my surprise, the many bizarre features melted away under the impact of a purely interpretative technique and a relatively unharmed ego strongly interested in and strongly attached to the world appeared from behind the maze of symptoms.

The rule that symptoms can only remotely be correlated with ego organization is true also for the allegedly symptom-free ego. I once had an opportunity to analyze a person who gave the impression, in the two initial interviews, of being relatively symptom-free and well adjusted, in accordance with his own claim of wanting treatment only for professional reasons. After several months the treatment was discontinued at the patient's request. It was my impression that the patient was not analyzable. His acting out, under the guise of conforming with

---

11. Of course, such variety of effects could be shown for any defense mechanism; it is not true of isolation only.

the necessities of reality, firmly rooted mechanisms which compensated for an excessive castration fear and his tenuous object relationships, not unlike those often found in schizophrenics, both made me decide for a time that I would never again try the analysis of a "normal" person.

The problem which deserves keenest attention concerns the concept of ego modifications.[12] It must first be differentiated from an ego change. The ego, as are all parts of the personality, is constantly changing. Through new perceptions and by the acquisition of new knowledge and the formation of new memories it enriches itself; by the interplay of defense mechanisms it tries to discard part of these new acquisitions: The ever-changing constellations of reality and the unceasing rhythm of biological processes make it face an infinite variation of tasks. It is correct to say that while two cross-sections of the ego are never identical, nevertheless it is always the same. It shares this property with most organisms which can maintain their identity and constancy by means of constant and rapidly occurring changes. All of these changes — primarily changes of content — do not add up to modifications of the ego. However, some of these changes may in certain frames of reference be looked upon as modifications. In the state of sleep, for example, a profound — perhaps the greatest possible — reorganization of the ego occurs. If the state of sleep is considered as a preparation for the return to a temporarily relinquished state characterized by a series of constant indices, then it will be called an ego change. If, however, we are investigating thought processes — which appear greatly modified during sleep as compared with the thought processes of the state of wakefulness — or the laws of dream work or the shifts of cathexis which take place during sleep, then the sleeping ego will be classified as a highly modified one. Disregarding the rather special question of whether the biologically enforced fluctuations of ego states ought to be called changes or modifications, it can be said that if an ego is not normal it has been modified. But what is a normal ego? Freud answered this question in the course of devising a conceptual scale which permits the ranging of all possible ego modifications from a zero point (the hypothetically normal ego) to an absolute maximum (the psychotic ego). According to Freud's definition, a normal ego is one which "would guarantee unswerving loyalty to the analytic compact"

(28, p. 342), and since such an ego is a theoretical construction, he called it a hypothetically normal ego (*fiktives Normal-Ich*).

In my estimation, such an ego would be one which would react properly to the basic model technique as outlined above. It would be an ego — and this I think is a crucial point — not characterized by specific defenses, attitudes, functions or by any other structural property, but characterized exclusively by a certain mode of behavior in the comprehensive situation of the analytic treatment situation.[13]

According to Freud's definition, the hypothetically normal ego is an ego which uncompromisingly assists in the psychoanalytic therapy. It surrenders, so to speak, to the voice of reason and unflinchingly makes maximum use of the help proffered during the treatment. This description of the hypothetically normal ego (though never encountered in clinical reality) introduces a new concept into psychoanalysis. The whole troublesome question of normal behavior is thus taken out of the contexts in which it has been discussed up to now. It is no longer question of whether or not a person has adjusted to reality, whether or not he has integrated current value systems or has achieved mastery over his biological needs. The whole question of symptomatology has been brushed aside with one stroke, and all current static definitions of normality superseded by a new dynamic definition. Freud's separation of the concepts of "normality" and "health" and their redefinition were great steps forward and ought to facilitate communication. Here Freud laid the foundation of a metapsychology of the psychoanalytic technique in structural terms.[14] Thus a normal ego is one which, notwithstanding its symptoms, reacts to rational therapy with a dissolution of its symptoms.

It is necessary to follow up the implications of this concept. It implies that the normal ego also may suffer disease. The ego of the child, because of its weakness, cannot help building up defenses and in most instances cannot escape the formation of symptoms. Indeed, Freud's definition implies that under certain circumstances neurosis is a "normal" phenomenon. Once the seed of a psychopathological disorder has been planted in the child's personality, the later, adult ego has no other choice under certain stresses but to fall back on the earlier adjustive process (Hartmann, 33). The discovery that, in some of its most important aspects, the ego also is unconscious

---

12. Dr. Hartmann suggests in a personal communication "ego deformation" instead of "ego modification." The latter term follows Joan Riviere's translation of Freud's "Analysis Terminable and Interminable."

13. This definition presupposes optimal conditions in regard to the analyst's conduct of treatment as well as to the external conditions under which the treatment takes place.

14. For a discussion of the concept of mental health from the point of view of ego psychology see Hartmann (33).

adds to the plausibility of this description. However, an ego which has thus been coerced into falling back on inappropriate solutions may have preserved its "normality" if it is still endowed with the capacity for capitalizing on proper help. If we may assume that psychoanalytic treatment is the most comprehensive psychological therapy because its goal is to provide the ego with all the knowledge and all the support it needs to regain its full competency, then psychoanalysis becomes the only procedure by which "normality" can be gauged.

In more general terms, the concept of the hypothetically normal ego presupposes that a childhood neurosis has developed as a result of the ego's infantile incapability of mastering the tasks put upon it by external as well as by internal reality. Yet, despite those neurotic solutions which were imposed upon the childhood ego, the development and the maturation of the ego organization were not essentially delayed or injured. Owing to the inheritance of childhood, the adult ego has not acquired its full freedom, but when it is brought into a situation in which it can obtain the assistance needed, it fights against this inheritance, and the ego's potentialities, which have been unharmed by past traumata, achieve full realization; in other words, one of the significant features of an ego essentially unharmed by traumata or constitutional factors or archaic fixations of libido is its responsiveness to rational, verbal communications which do not contain more than interpretations. [15]

I think this conception of the normal ego is in substantial agreement with a profound thought which Goethe (31) expressed (probably in conjunction with an experience of impotence): "The disease only avers the healthy" (Die Krankheit erst bewähret den Gesunden). Illness thus becomes the unavoidable accident of life; that is to say, it is a manifestation of life itself, and the ego's reaction to the sickness is the exclusive frame of reference of health.

At the other end of the scale is the ego of the psychotic, with whom the analytic compact is impossible (Freud, 28, p. 337). There is scarcely anything to say about this end of the scale aside from a historical remark: When Freud was sketching the maximal ego modification, he probably had in mind the acute hallucinatory confusion which so often had served him as the prototype of psychosis. [16] Indeed,

during the acute phase of a psychosis, psychoanalysis in its usual form is of no therapeutic avail. At that stage the ego is at least temporarily "modified" in such a way as to make direct psychoanalytic interference impossible. [17] In the case of an acute hallucinatory confusion, the ego derives all its wish fulfillments out of itself even in its state of wakefulness. Tension is removed by the hallucination of instinctual gratification. The ego falsifies reality in accordance with its own wishes and can thus dispense with reality. The analyst has lost every avenue of approach because the ego has become inaccessible. It is exclusively engaged in its subservience to the id. Since the normal ego is fictitious, it is evident that in clinical reality elements of the other extreme are always intermixed. [18]

As Freud said, ". . . . every normal person is only approximately normal; his ego resembles that of the psychotic in one point or another, in a greater or lesser degree, and its distance from one end of the scale and proximity to the other may provisionally serve as a measure of what we have indefinitely spoken of as 'modification of the ego'" (28, p. 337).

This view of normality as cursorily outlined by Freud seems to coincide remarkably well with views advanced by modern biologists and physiologists. In describing the variety of meanings which the concept of normality has in biology, Ivy (35) mentions the nonarbitrary statistical view which maintains "that a sharp distinction between 'normal' and 'abnormal' does not exist for a group or even an individual. . . . It recognizes that degrees of normality and abnormality exist. . . . It permits an absolute diagnosis of abnormality only when death occurs." Freud set up a series from the acute hallucinatory psychosis to the hypothetically normal ego and thereby established a point at one end of the scale of "absolute diagnosis of abnormality" from which various degrees of normality and abnormality lead to the hypothetically normal ego at the other end of the scale.

In an attempt to clarify the meanings which the concept of normality should have in physiology, Ivy makes a significant remark about physiological processes in disease. Defensive processes, he says, such as fever or leucocytosis are normal although their effects may be abnormal. The defensive processes "are the usual physiological responses to insult. The process concerned is a statistically and

---

15. See A. Freud (12) for a brilliant clinical application of this theoretical problem.

16. See Freud (13, 19). See also Freud (23) where he calls Meynert's amentia, the acute hallucinatory confusion, the most extreme and striking form of psychosis.

17. This remark does not militate against psychotherapeutic

measures of a different kind.

18. I think that the clincial varieties of ego modification cannot be completely dissolved into varying mixtures of these two extremes but require a third component whose extreme is the criminal. The analyst cannot establish with him any kind of alliance for which the hypothetically normal ego is ideally adapted.

physiologically normal response. The response, however, may produce abnormal effects in certain instances and hence is physiologically abnormal." Here, the problem of the "normal disease" is solved by differentiating process from response, the latter leading sometimes to abnormal effects. For example, the abnormal effect of a rise in body temperature is seen in its eventual disturbance of "other functions and margins of safety," when the fever reaches a certain height.

Likewise, according to Freud's conceptual frame of reference, psychogenic symptoms must be viewed as the logical and unavoidable consequences of the impact of external and internal reality on the childhood ego, still weak because still immature; thus symptoms may be the signs of the ego's basic health. The "physiologically normal response" would, then, become abnormal as soon as it led to an ego modification. Freud's concepts—(1) the hypothetically normal ego as defined by the response in the situation of the basic model technique; (2) a scale leading by degrees to a state of absolute unresponsiveness to the analytic compact; and (3) the intervening variety of ego modifications to which a variety of techniques must be correlated—provide, in my estimation, a system which is ideally flexible and superbly adaptable to actual clinical work. Their heuristic value impresses me as enormous and—finally, but of greatest importance—these concepts ought to bring some rationale and order into psychoanalytical discussions of technique and thus end the contemporary arguments, most of which are based exclusively on utilitarian viewpoints. Points of expediency will always deflect the strict course which practice should take according to theory, but psychoanalysis will lose its standing as a science if problems of technique are discussed exclusively from the viewpoint of expediency.

I am aware that I follow a thought of Freud's, possibly too rigorously, by insisting that the baseline of psychoanalytic technique is one which uses a single technical tool, to wit, interpretation. In support of my contention, repeated clinical experience shows that there is a group of patients whose treatment does need scarcely more than interpretation to usher in the process of recovery and to lead the ego to the therapeutic goal. Clinical experience shows also that this group has an important structural factor in common—a relatively unmodified ego. Furthermore, it can be demonstrated that the introduction of an additional tool, one which will play a prominent part in the analytic technique, is necessitated by a structural defect in the ego. Therefore, we are warranted in classifying personality structures in accordance with the techniques required to deal adequately with their defects. This aspect justifies our assigning a special place to a purely interpretative technique.[19]

It is well known that the proper use of interpretation is difficult and complicated. But so central is this tool that any proposed variation or addition should be scrutinized with the greatest care. The introduction of parameters, even of such simple ones as are necessary in some cases of phobia, contains dangers which must not be overlooked. Each parameter increases the possibility that the therapeutic process may be falsified, inasmuch as it may offer the patient's ego the possibility of substituting obedience for a structural change.

The term obedience, not entirely an accurate one, is used here to designate all those improvements which a patient may show under the pressure of the therapy but which are not based on a dissolution of the corresponding conflicts. A patient often prefers to produce adjusted behavior instead of a structural change.[20]

Every introduction of a parameter incurs the danger that a resistance has been temporarily eliminated without having been properly analyzed. Therefore, after an obstacle has been removed by the use of a parameter, the meaning which this parameter has had for the patient and the reasons which necessitated the choice of the parameter must retrospectively be discussed; that is to say, interpretation must become again the exclusive tool to straighten out the ruffle which was caused by the use of a parameter.

At this point I must strongly emphasize that in my use of the term interpretation I always presuppose the proper use of this technique. It would, of course, be foolish to suggest that just any kind of interpretation, or the mere act of interpreting, will do. Again, this paper is not the place for a discussion of what a proper interpretative technique is; it is mandatory, however, that a warning be raised against the quick introduction of parameters under the justification that interpretations have been of no avail. There is a great temptation to cover up, by the introduction of parameters, one's own inability to use properly the interpretative technique.

---

19. This is not the place to discuss the epistemology of interpretation. For a comprehensive treatise on interpretation, see a paper by Bernfeld (4) which regrettably is not available in English. See also Waelder (44).

20. This is one of the many reasons why in psychotherapy one so frequently has an opportunity of enjoying bristling clinical successes and why the proper psychoanalytic technique always works against a much heavier resistance than any other technique.

In view of the paramount importance which one must attribute to ego modification as an obstacle to psychoanalytic therapy and therefore to recovery, the question of the cause of ego modification must be raised. It is again Freud who gives us the answer by delineating the twofold effect which defense mechanisms may have on the ego. They may protect the ego or they may destroy the ego. "The purpose of the defense mechanisms is to avert dangers. It cannot be disputed that they are successful; it is doubtful whether the ego can altogether do without them during its development, but it is also certain that they themselves may become dangerous. Not infrequently it turns out that the ego has paid too high a price for the services which these mechanisms render" (Freud, 28, p. 340; see also A. Freud, 11, p. 54). And Freud suggests that we consider these deleterious effects of the defenses upon the ego as ego modification.

I want to illustrate such an effect briefly with a clinical example. A three-year-old girl was awakened one morning by her mother, who carried a newborn baby, the girl's sister, in her arms, saying: "Look here, Mary, this is Marguerit. Isn't she sweet?" Showing all the signs of enjoyment, the little girl agreed that Marguerit was sweet. Twenty-eight years later, in her analysis, the girl described the incident, reporting that her mother had descended with incredible swiftness upon her and complaining that her mother had no reason to assume that Mary knew Marguerit was the name of a girl. She claimed she was given no choice but to show the same emotion as her mother and that to meet the situation "requested" by her mother, she had to rally an incredible amount of energy. At the time of the analysis the patient reported that after a day of responsible work, which she performed to the satisfaction of her superiors, she would return home in a state of complete exhaustion. However, she was not exhausted by the exigencies of her work, but because she must rally an incredible amount of energy to show the emotion requested by her environment. To say good morning to her co-workers, to "pitch in with the elevator man" when he made a trivial remark about the weather, absorbed her energy. She found it necessary to brace herself constantly when in the company of others in order to respond appropriately to the respective social realities. She really would have liked to sit in a rocking chair alone in her room and hold her head in her arms.

Here we see that the defense accomplished its goal ideally in the little child in terms of facilitating social behavior, and this patient's history may serve as an example that the relatively symptom-free child is often the most endangered one. The whole jealousy, the whole terrific anger about her mother's unfaithfulness and rejection were excluded from consciousness and were replaced by the socially required admiration of and love for the baby.[21] The little sister soon became the patient's favorite, and she cheerfully spent all her free time with the new companion, developing with surprising quickness strong maternal attitudes. None of her recollections indicated a disturbance of behavior or outward signs of ambivalence toward the baby. The ideal result of the defense, however, must be viewed simultaneously with the catastrophic effect it had on the ego organization. It seems that the defense devoured the ego like a cancerous growth devours the organisms harboring it.

A high degree of modification has occurred in the schizophrenic ego. The single defense mechanism and the individual patterns of defense mechanisms do not assist the ego but are destructive; they burden the ego to such an extent that it is constantly on the verge of breaking off its relationship with reality. This appears to be a complete contradiction to what is usually described as the fundamental process in schizophrenia, that is to say, the ego's being made subservient to the id. No doubt, in most phases of the schizophrenic psychosis, wish fulfillments of the id play a great role, but the function of defense was not deleted from Freud's metapsychological diagram of psychosis. ". . . . the falsifications of memory, the delusional systems and hallucinations," writes Freud (24, p. 280), "in so many cases and forms of psychosis are of a most distressing character and are bound up with a development of dread, which is surely a sign that the whole process of remodelling reality is conducted in the face of most strenuous opposition. We may, for our own purposes, reconstruct the process on the model of a neurosis, which is more familiar to us. Here we see that a reaction of anxiety takes place every time the repressed instinct makes a move forward, and that the result of the conflict is after all but a compromise and as a satisfaction is incomplete. Probably in a psychosis the rejected part of reality reasserts its claim, just as in neurosis the repressed instinct does; hence the consequences in both are the same." Here one of the defensive purposes is clearly described. The ego of the psychotic must defend itself constantly against the perception, recognition, and acknowledgment of objective reality. As the ego can postpone awakening by responding to the arousal stimulus by an arousal dream, so can the psychotic prevent the intrusion of objective reality by the maintenance of his own self-created

---

21. I delete from this description the severe anxiety this patient suffered as a child and delineate only the effect which the defense had on the child's external behavior.

reality. The arousal dream requires a minimum of cathexis, and the unmodified ego suffers the pain of having overruled reality when, upon awakening, it pays the price for having unduly indulged in the desire to sleep. The psychotic ego must garner a very large amount of energy in order to feed constantly its own reality, and the unceasing struggle against the pain which would be aroused by the perception of objective reality in turn results in pain.

In a thoughtful study, Katan (36) clearly describes the defensive function of one of Schreber's hallucinations of little men descending upon his head and then perishing after a short period of existence. Schreber reached a stage in his psychosis where he could masturbate without erection and emission. ". . . . The hallucination occurs instead of the excitement. . . . In the hallucination, sexual excitement does not occur at all, and instead of the idea of Schreber perishing, we find the idea of the other men losing their lives" (36, p. 34). By hallucination, the ego anticipated danger and warded it off. The remarkable feature, however, is that a fantasy or daydream or a passing thought of the same (though usually less bizarre) content may occur in the neurotic for the same purpose and with the same effect of sparing himself anxiety or excitement. Indeed, one may even venture to say that an ego relatively free of symptoms may maintain its functional organization by a passing thought of such a kind. Yet in Schreber the defensive process, leading to a hallucination, imposed itself upon the total ego, absorbed all its functions, and took full possession of the visual apparatus. It is permissible to say that at that moment the ego could not do anything else but hallucinate or, in other words, that the defensive process had spread itself out at the cost of the rest of the ego.

In the case of Schreber's hallucination, the content against which the defense was directed (passive homosexual wishes) was not different from those which one finds quite often in neurotics, if Katan's reconstruction is correct. Yet sometimes the contents which the schizophrenic tries to ward off are quite surprising. The schizophrenic patient I have mentioned before assured me for years that there was only hatred in her, that she would like to see the people killed with whom she had to deal and that she was incapable of feeling any interest in or longing for any human being. However, when she started to tell me the daydreams which filled her mind during the hour it took her to fall asleep—until then she had chiefly reported the feelings and fantasies which she had in the company of others—I was amazed to hear of a fantasy in which she took care of a crippled and mentally disturbed girl whom she knew. With great skill and tact she got me acquainted in her fantasy with the child and arranged for the child's treatment and cure. Aside from the narcissistic-erotic elements which undoubtedly are to be found in that daydream, there was expressed a core of real warmth and affection. There was no doubt that this patient had kept repressed her social inclinations and that her elaborate fantasies of killing also served the purpose of denying her sociability.[22] This paradoxical constellation is not essentially different from that which Freud described when he wrote: "I recollect a case of chronic paranoia in which after each attack of jealousy a dream conveyed to the analyst a correct picture of the cause, free from any trace of delusion. An interesting contrast was thus brought to light: For, while we are accustomed to discover from the dreams of neurotic patients jealousies which are alien to their waking lives, in the present psychotic case the delusion which dominated the patient's daytime existence was corrected by a dream" (29, p. 78).

A few factors may be mentioned which are involved in the ego's being victimized by its defensive apparatus. I believe that all defense mechanisms are initially fed by energy which has not been neutralized, just as the child's early thought processes are closer to the primary process than to the secondary. In the course of development the defense mechanisms are subjected to a process which is comparable to the change from the primary to the secondary thought processes. The energy which they consume is delibidinized and freed of primary aggression. The schizophrenic ego does not achieve this.[23] Its defenses are driven by passion and destruction. The use of destructive energy seems to explain why the schizophrenic ego is primarily a masochistic or self-destructive one; the use of libidinal energies would explain why some schizophrenics in certain phases of their disorder can substitute defensive processes for the whole sexual gratification.[24]

In the unmodified ego the whole apparatus of defense mechanisms functions vis-à-vis internal stimulation in the same way that the stimulus barrier functions to prevent overstimulation by external

22. It is questionable whether my description of the patient's repressing her social tendencies is correct. One of her problems was to be different from her mother. Since her mother was social, the patient had to add to any expression of friendliness the feeling that this was pretense only. The feeling of hatred was the last anchor left to her for the purpose of making sure that she was not identical with her mother.

23. I am continuing here Hartmann's (34, p. 88) suggestions regarding the energetics of defense mechanisms.

24. Cf Katan (36).

stimuli. In the schizophrenic the defensive apparatus does not possess the firmness necessary for this function. Therefore the ego is forced to respond in its totality without being able to channel adequately the internal or external demands, which threaten to engulf the whole ego. The world—the external as well as the internal one—always descends with incredible swiftness upon the schizophrenic.

The defense mechanisms, however, become particularly visible after the acute schizophrenic symptomatology has vanished and there emerges the organization of the ego which lies behind the picturesque schizophrenic symptomatology per se. Then one can observe the excessive demand which the schizophrenic puts upon the synthetic function (Nunberg, 38). One can also see his inability to bear up under the impact of internal contradictions and his desperate fight for an ego purified of contradictory feelings; that is to say, for a purified pleasure ego—the only ego state known when we were completely one with ourselves, a state accessible to and desired by the adult chiefly in sleep. The fact that the defense mechanisms of the schizophrenic are still set in motion by, and use up, instinctual energy greatly reduces the seeming contradiction which I initially mentioned, the contradiction between the two metapsychological formulations: (1) That in schizophrenia the ego loses territory to the id, (2) that the ego is devoured by its defenses. The vast majority of schizophrenic patients who are clinically observed are in a stage in which the defenses are still working, but independently of and unchecked by a comprehensive, over-all ego organization; yet, since these defense mechanisms work in close co-operation with the id owing to energic conditions, it is also correct to speak of the id's encroachment on the ego.

The hypothesis that in schizophrenia the defensive apparatus is kept in motion by energy which has not been desexualized or neutralized must not be confused with another psychoanalytic proposition; namely, that many defense mechanisms may lead to instinctual gratifications, despite their defensive function. The degree of gratification, of course, varies. We are accustomed to find this coincidence of gratification and defense in the neurotic symptom, but it is also true of some defense mechanisms.[25] This does not, however, mean that a defense mechanism—which, apart from its effect as a tool of warding off instincts, leads to a partial discharge of id energy—is itself cathected by id energy. I think that at this point one must distinguish with particular exactness between the accomplishment of a defensive mechanism within the personality and the cathexis of the defense mechanism per se. Projection leads always to the transfer of a content from within the personality to without, but a comparison of the sporadic, neurotic projections in a hysteria and the stable, rigid projections in a paranoid psychosis shows that the energic factors are quite different. The hypothesis that such differences are also based on the difference of the energies used by the mechanisms per se, facilitates, I think, the understanding of the ego modification encountered in schizophrenia.

Be this as it may, it is important to keep in mind Freud's statement that the defense mechanisms themselves present only one of the difficulties to be overcome in analysis. If the effect of these defense mechanisms has resulted in a modification of the ego, the analysis will face even greater difficulties, necessitating deviations from the basic model technique.

Unfortunately we do not yet have an adequate conceptual frame of reference to describe these ego modifications although we are constantly struggling with them in most patients who now come for analysis. Freud compared ego modifications with "dislocation or crippling,"[26] but the metapsychology of such ego modifications has scarcely been established.[27] Observing a patient, we watch the defense mechanisms and their interplay. We see single functions like judgment and perception and note their bearing upon each other. We observe some of the results such as the identifications and projections, but we are not able to perceive the ego organization which underlies them, the mysterious knot of which Goethe spoke and which makes a human being more than the aggregate of his defense mechanisms and functions. Indeed, it is most tantalizing to know of a problem, to observe its manifestation in clinical reality, but to be unable to evolve an adequate conceptual framework necessary for its solution.

Since the ego modification presents itself most conspicuously in the schizophrenias, one is forced to

---

25. See Waelder (42), Nunberg (37, p. 94), and others. The quantitative relationship between gratification and defense is probably quite different in symptom and defense mechanism.

26. See (27, p. 321). The German words are *Verrenkung* and *Einschränkung*. See also A. Freud (11, p. 54): "Thus repression becomes the basis of compromise-formation and neurosis. The consequences of the other defensive methods are not less serious but, even when they assume an acute form, they remain more within the limits of the normal. They manifest themselves in innumerable transformations, distortions and deformities of the ego, which are in part the accompaniment of and in part substitutes for neurosis."

27. See A. Freud (11, pp. 100–113, particularly p. 111) for an attempt in that direction.

to return to this group of disorders when discussing the chances and limitations of psychoanalysis in grappling with this sector of psychopathology.[28]

Despite our great ignorance one statement can be made with certainty. The parameters necessary in the psychoanalysis of schizophrenia will be most extensive and numerous. The most remarkable difference, of course, concerns the essentially different technique of handling the transference.[29] In most neuroses the transference develops spontaneously, and the technical problem consists of converting transference into a helper of the analytic process by means of interpretation, while in some phases of the treatment of the schizophrenic transference must be produced by action, gesture, or words, and for long stretches the chief technical problem consists of manipulating the therapeutic situation in such a way as to effect, quantitatively and qualitatively, the proper accretion of transference.

In discussing parameters enforced by the ego modification which is prevalent in schizophrenia, a therapeutic task must be mentioned which holds no place, or only a very subordinate one, in the treatment of neurotic ego modifications. The schizophrenic must acquire a capacity which the neurotic possesses fully unless he is temporarily deprived of it under the onslaught of an acute, emotional upsurge. I refer to the capacity for putting a mental distance between oneself and the phenomena of the mind, whether these are correlated to external or internal stimulation. It is the privilege of man to possess the antithetical capabilities of feeling at one with his experiences and also of elevating himself above them. What may be now an experience which fills out completely the borders of his consciousness, may become at any moment a content of observation, judgment, or evaluation. The schizophrenic, however, has lost this capacity in respect to certain contents, although the function per se is not destroyed. But to one sector of his life at least he is bound so firmly that he is incapable of elevating himself beyond its sphere. This lack is one of the most significant indices of the profound modification which the ego of the schizophrenic has suffered.[30]

A schizophrenic once impressively said: "I could rather believe that you or the world around me do not exist than assume that the voices I hear are not real." The schizophrenic has lost the ability to differentiate between the possible and the real in certain sectors of reality.[31] This incapacity to lift himself out of the context of phenomena at one point at least must make the technique of treating schizophrenics essentially different from that of neurotics if one extends the treatment to the treatment of the ego modification. It is strange to notice that this technical problem which is most typical of the treatment of schizophrenics is barely mentioned in the contemporary literature on the psychotherapy of schizophrenia.[32] The analyst meets in this instance a task of formidable extent which cannot be sufficiently discussed here. It can only be said that sometimes when one succeeds in demonstrating to the schizophrenic that the symptom is a derivative of bodily sensations, one may reach a point where the schizophrenic can extend his faculty of objectivation also to this sector of his psychopathology.

In the following brief description, I have arbitrarily chosen two parameters which fairly regularly play a role in the treatment of schizophrenics: (1) goal construction, and (2) reduction of symptomatology.

(1) The goal toward which psychoanalytic treatment strives is implicitly, though vaguely, represented in the neurotic's mind. The schizophrenic is deprived of such an integrated and elaborated goal. He must be provided with a diagram of the unmodified ego. Since the patient often does not know how such an ego does function, it is up to the analyst to provide the frame of reference, which often may be an entirely new one to the patient.[33]

Certainly the argument will be raised that such measures do not fall within the scope of psychoanalysis but belong to education or instruction or correction. Yet I wonder whether this parameter necessarily leads us outside psychoanalysis. Education is essentially a technique which tries to force the ego to assimilate the ego alien or, in other words, to convert the ego alien into the ego syntonic.[34] The parameter which I am briefly mentioning here

---

28. See (18, pp. 357–373) and (27, pp. 82–112) for Freud's remarks about psychoses in general and schizophrenia in particular as sources of insight into the structure of the ego.

29. See Waelder (41) for a comparison of the techniques in the treatment of neurosis and psychosis.

30. For a description and discussion of this problem see the consequential thoughts about a typology of psychopathology as presented by Waelder (43). See also Freud (27, p. 84) and Sterba (40).

31. I take this formulation from Waelder (43, p. 477).

32. Fromm-Reichmann (30) seems to claim that there is essentially no difference between the technique of treatment of schizophrenics and neurotics, a point of view which in my opinion is tenable only if the field of therapeutic action is limited to the patient's interpersonal relationships with disregard of the patient's ego modification.

33. Personal communication of Dr. Edith Jacobson.

34. I am aware of the insufficiency of such a broad and vague statement, but to clarify it would necessitate the enumeration of its many exceptions.

concerns the reconstruction of a viable ego. It concerns a goal which the patient once upon a time had aspired to though probably he had never reached it. Education always tries to implant values; this parameter is essentially divorced from any value system, although admittedly if it is not used wisely, it may become tainted by the tacit application of value systems.

Education always restricts the ego in some way despite the accretion of content which it provides. This parameter, however, must never lead to a restrictive process within the ego. In other words, the reconstructive processes initiated by this parameter must lay the foundation for the later education of the ego. Therefore I would rather say that this parameter is essentially outside of education.

(2) One of the most difficult tasks is to find and to demonstrate to the patient which function or which functions of the ego have been impaired and in what way. The dysfunctions which can be clinically seen on the surface are, of course, not the primary ones. The production of a delusion may occur owing to the injury of quite different functions of the ego. If the modification of the ego is to be undone, the specific function which is disturbed must be drawn into the treatment and brought to the patient's attention.[35]

This parameter partly overlaps one which may occur in the analysis of a neurotic. In the neurotic, however, the parameter will usually not transgress interpretation whereas in the treatment of the schizophrenic it concerns a tool which is essentially beyond the scope of interpretation. The disturbed function must be isolated from interplay with others, and the patient must learn to study the way in which this particular function becomes altered under the impact of specific conditions. If a disturbed function is discussed while it is still riveted to others, interpretation will be far less successful than when the disturbed function has been presented to the patient in isolation. In one instance, distortions of reality which appeared like true delusions based on projection turned out to be supplements and confirmations of certain delusions which the patient had formed about herself. The complicated symptomatology could be reduced finally to a certain annoying bodily feeling on which the delusion of self was based. The distortions of reality were only a secondary formation produced by the patient's need (and her fear) of finding supported by external evidence that which

she had assumed beforehand to be true regarding a process belonging to internal reality.

I want to try to narrow down as much as possible the problem on which, in my opinion, the chief question of psychoanalytic theory as well as practice hinges today. It goes back to a point which Freud (21) advanced for the first time in 1920 and which was taken up and continued by Alexander (2, p. 5) seven years later before being discussed once more by Freud (28) in "Analysis Terminable and Interminable" when he spoke of the resistance against the uncovering of resistances. These secondary resistances become noticeable in the course of psychoanalytic treatment when the analyst tries to make the patient's consciousness focus on those resistances which ward off id impulses.[36] Then it becomes surprisingly evident that the modified ego is highly disinclined not only to become aware of id contents but also to become aware of some of those processes and contents which occur within its own boundaries.[37] Yet these secondary resistances are also active outside of the analytic situation, just as the primary resistances (directed against the id) are constantly active although they become palpable mainly in the psychoanalytic situation. What is the function of these secondary resistances? The primary ones protect the ego against the spread of the id, and one of the functions of the secondary resistances is to prevent the spread of the primary defenses.[38] They also would like to arrogate to themselves the maximum territory as would the eternally insatiable id drives. Under normal conditions—that is to say, in an unmodified ego—they utilize neutralized energy and are fully occupied with their work against the id. In the modified ego, however, they turn also against the ego. In extreme instances the secondary defenses are swept away, and there is no barrier against that cancerous growth of which I have spoken figuratively before.

A clinical example may illustrate how the secondary resistances can make themselves noticeable in the treatment. A patient of superior intelligence, with unusually strong pregenital fixations but well-preserved psychosexual genital activity, filled long stretches of his analysis with repetitive complaints about trivial matters regarding his wife. He did not show any understanding of the obvious fact that the discrepancy between the intensity of his complaints and the triviality of their content required a discussion and explanation. One day he reported,

---

35. See also Waelder (41).

36. For the stratification of defenses, see Gero (31).

37. See Freud (26, pp. 25-27). Helene Deutsch (9, p. 11) describes the narcissistic gratification which some patients derive

from their defenses. This of course reduces the motivation to give up these defenses.

38. See Rapaport (39, p. 692) for the effect of delay in the formation of psychic structure.

somewhat abruptly, that he enjoyed his wife's doing the very things he had always complained of and that he knew how secretly to manipulate situations in such a way as to make his wife act the way he had considered so obnoxious and which gave him occasion to be cold and unfriendly to her.

When the sadistic, aggressive nature of this impulse was explained, he acknowledged it and even volunteered that he had known this for a long time. He showed some understanding of the uncanny sadistic technique with which he maneuvered his wife into the situation of a helpless victim without giving her an opportunity of defending herself.

The sadistic impulse had been warded off by means of denial and substitution of the opposite, since the patient tried to prove to himself and to the analyst that he was not cruel, but that he deserved pity owing to his wife's deficiencies. I tried to show the patient that his incessant complaining had also served the purpose of assuaging his feelings of guilt. The more successful he was in gratifying his sadism in the camouflaged way he used so expertly, the more he had to present himself the next day as injured and unjustly treated by fate in being married to an allegedly unsatisfactory partner. This interpretation was not accepted by the patient. He could not understand it; he could not follow me; and he insisted upon the validity of his complaints, although he had just agreed that he himself secretly induced his wife to behave in the manner about which he habitually complained to me the following day.

Here we encounter the paradoxical situation in which a patient accepts the interpretation of an id impulse and admits its existence but shows an excessive resistance against the interpretation of the corresponding defense mechanism. There are several reasons for the latter type of resistance. The patient's complaining was done with much emotion. The defense had become partly cathected with instinctual energy. Furthermore, in some instances it is questionable which is easier for the ego to give up, the gratification of an id impulse or the defense. I believe that this patient had come to a point when he would more readily forego the sadistic gratification and acquire mastery over this force than he would sacrifice the feeling of being unjustly treated by fate. Indeed, there is some wisdom in the paradox. As long as he holds to the defense which consists of his playing the role of the victim, there is hope that possibly in the future he can permit himself sadistic gratifications. Only after he has discarded this defense would his conscience no longer tolerate the camouflaged enjoyment of sadistic pleasures. In this instance the defense provided masochistic gratifications which rooted the mechanism with particular firmness in the ego. I have the impression that it is usually the masochism of the ego which makes the interpretation of defense mechanisms excessively

difficult. The ego seems to feel particularly safe when the masochistic gratification is achieved in a process which genuinely wards off another drive.

In accordance with well-known features of the pathology of repression one can safely assume that the pathology of the secondary resistances will take one of two forms: It will be too strongly or too weakly cathected. Tentatively I would like to suggest that possibly the neurotic ego modification belongs to the former and the psychotic to the latter group. However, it is not probable that clinical reality would follow such neatly drawn lines. Be this as it may, in the patient just mentioned, the excessive growth of a defense mechanism can be observed although the ego modification was not of the schizophrenic type. A less modified ego would have received the interpretation with some relief and the resistance against the interpretation of the id impulse would have been much sharper.

The secondary defenses which do their main work subterraneously and which can be gauged predominantly by the study of their effect on the primary defenses probably form a part of a special organization within the ego and—depending on these secondary defenses—ego modification can, or cannot, be altered by psychoanalysis. There can be no doubt that the neurotic ego modification, such as that found in phobia, can be altered by psychoanalysis. In certain compulsive-obsessive neuroses of long standing, the possibility is questionable.

Although techniques have been devised to undo, at least temporarily, acute schizophrenic symptoms, it is highly debatable whether the modification which the schizophrenic ego so impressively shows can be altered by psychoanalysis. The psychotherapeutic techniques which are applied most commonly in the treatment of schizophrenics do not add substantially to our knowledge and understanding of schizophrenia, since most of them disregard the clinical fact that the problem of the therapy of schizophrenia is essentially the problem of undoing an ego modification. Many a psychotherapist takes on the schizophrenic to demonstrate his psychotherapeutic courage. He will not hesitate to apply any psychotherapeutic tool so long as it gives hope of forcing the schizophrenic out of his acute condition. In so far as such endeavors are heavily sprinkled with pseudoanalytic interpretations, one must call these techniques "wild" psychoanalysis. I think that the concept of a parameter and adherence to the four rules I mentioned may prevent us from falling into wild analysis, which is particularly tempting in the case of schizophrenia. In general, I think, one can say that the most promising source of knowledge of the structure of the ego will be found in an exact description and a justification—both in terms of metapsychology—of any deviation from the basic

model technique whenever such deviation becomes necessary.

BIBLIOGRAPHY

1. Alexander, F. Review of Ferenczi, S. and Rank, O., "The Development of Psychoanalysis." *Internat. Ztschr. f. Psychoanal., 11*:113-122, 1925.

2. Alexander, F. *The Psychoanalysis of the Total Personality.* New York and Washington: Nerv. and Ment. Dis. Publ. Co., 1927.

3. Alexander, F. and French, T. M. *Psychoanalytic Therapy.* New York: Ronald Press, 1946.

4. Bernfeld, S. Der Begriff der "Deutung" in der Psychoanalyse. *Ztschr. f. angewandte Psychol., 42*:448-497, 1932.

5. Binswanger, L. Zur Frage der Häufigkeit der Schizophrenie im Kindersalter. *Ztschr. f. Kinderpsychiat., 12*: 33-50, 1945.

6. Breuer, J. and Freud, S. (1892) The psychic mechanism of hysterical phenomena. *Studies in Hysteria.* New York and Washington: Nerv. and Ment. Dis. Publ. Co., 1936.

7. Brunswick, R. M. Supplement to Freud's "History of an Infantile Neurosis." *Internat. J. Psycho-Anal., 9*: 439-476, 1928.

8. Deutsch, F. The associative anamnesis. *Psychoanal. Quart., 8*:354-381, 1939.

9. Deutsch, F. *Applied Psychoanalysis.* New York: Grune & Stratton, 1949.

10. Deutsch, H. Ueber bestimmte Widerstandsformen. *Internat. Ztschr. f. Psychoanal. u. Imago, 24*:10-20, 1939.

11. Freud, A. *The Ego and the Mechanisms of Defense.* New York: Internat. Univ. Press, 1946.

12. Freud, A. Indications for child analysis. *The Psychoanalytic Study of the Child, 1*:127-149. New York: Internat. Univ. Press, 1945.

13. Freud, S. (1894) The defence neuro-psychoses. *Coll. Papers, 1*:59-75. London: Hogarth Press, 1924.

14. Freud, S. (1909) Notes upon a case of obsessional neurosis. *Ibid., 3*:293-383.

15. Freud, S. (1910) *Leonardo da Vinci.* New York: Dodd, Mead, 1932.

16. Freud, S. (1910) Observations on "wild" psychoanalysis. *Coll. Papers, 2*:297-304. London: Hogarth Press, 1924.

17. Freud, S. (1913) Further recommendations in the technique of psycho-analysis. On beginning the treatment. *Ibid., 2*:342-365.

18. Freud, S. (1917) *A General Introduction to Psychoanalysis.* New York: Garden City Publ. Co., 1935.

19. Freud, S. (1917) Metapsychological supplement to the theory of dreams. *Coll. Papers, 4*:137-151. London: Hogarth Press, 1925.

20. Freud, S. (1918) From the history of an infantile neurosis. *Ibid., 3*:473-605.

21. Freud, S. (1920) *Beyond the Pleasure Principle.* London: Hogarth Press, 1922.

22. Freud, S. (1923) *The Ego and the Id.* London: Hogarth Press, 1949.

23. Freud, S. (1924) Neurosis and psychosis. *Coll. Papers, 2*:250-254. London: Hogarth Press, 1924.

24. Freud, S. (1924) The loss of reality in neurosis and psychosis. *Ibid., 2*:277-282.

25. Freud, S. (1925) *An Autobiographical Study.* London: Hogarth Press, 1950.

26. Freud, S. (1926) *The Problem of Anxiety.* New York: W. W. Norton & Co., 1936.

27. Freud, S. (1933) *New Introductory Lectures on Psychoanalysis.* New York: W. W. Norton & Co., 1933.

28. Freud, S. (1937) Analysis terminable and interminable. *Coll. Papers, 5*:316-357. London: Hogarth Press, 1950.

29. Freud, S. (1938) *An Outline of Psychoanalysis.* New York: W. W. Norton and Co., 1950.

30. Fromm-Reichmann, F. *Principles of Intensive Psychotherapy.* Chicago: Univ. of Chicago Press, 1950.

31. Gero. G. The concept of defense. *Psychoanal. Quart., 20*:565-578, 1951.

32. Goethe, J. W. *Das Tagebuch.* Sopienausgabe, Vol. 5/2, p. 345.

33. Hartmann, H. Psycho-analysis and the concept of health. *Internat. J. Psycho-Anal., 20*:308-321, 1939.

34. Hartmann, H. Comments on the psychoanalytic theory of the ego. *The Psychoanalytic Study of the Child, 5*:74-96. New York: Internat. Univ. Press, 1950.

35. Ivy, A. C. What is normal or normality? *Quart. Bull. Northwest. Univ. Med. School, 18*:22-32, 1944.

36. Katan, M. Schreber's hallucinations about the "little men." *Internat. J. Psycho-Anal., 31*:32-35, 1950.

37. Nunberg, H. *Allgemeine Neurosenlehre.* Bern: Huber, 1932.

38. Nunberg, H. The synthetic function of the ego. *Internat. J. Psycho-Anal., 12*:123-140, 1931.

39. Rapaport, D. *Organization and Pathology of Thought.* New York: Columbia Univ. Press, 1951.

40. Sterba, R. The fate of the ego in analytic therapy. *Internat. J. Psycho-anal., 15*:117-126, 1934.

41. Waelder, R. The psychoses: their mechanisms and accessibility to influence. *Ibid., 6*:259-281, 1925.

42. Waelder, R. On the principle of multiple function and overdetermination. *Psychoanal. Quart., 5*:43-62, 1936.

43. Waelder, R. Das Freiheitsproblem in der Psychoanalyse. *Imago, 20*:467-484, 1934.

44. Waelder, R., Kritieron der Deutung. *Internat. Ztschr. f. Psychoanal. u. Imago, 24*:136-145, 1939.

40

ON TRANSFERENCE

D. W. WINNICOTT

EDITOR'S NOTE

This brief gem offers fresh insights on transference (see Part I) and interaction (see Part VI), while providing a strikingly unique conception of the role and functions of the analytic setting. In respect to transference, Winnicott's studies of its manifestations with non-neurotic patients is a pioneering effort. His sensitivity to the environment and the good-enough adaptation of the analyst provide fresh perspectives on the analytic interaction, to the point where Winnicott is able to recognize that often what appears as resistance within the patient is actually an indication that the analyst has made a mistake.

The paper is included in this section because of the great importance Winnicott's view of the analytic setting as a critical means of holding the patient and providing him an opportunity for ego maturation, through which he might subsequently become involved in the arduous task of the more usual analytic work. In this way Winnicott was able to recognize that the analytic setting and the basic stance of the analyst—a mixture of human and nonhuman factors—constitute the fundamental matrix that offers the patient both ego support and an opportunity for growth-promoting identifications. The basic ground rules of analysis are no longer simply a set of tenets designed to safeguard the transference (Freud 1912b [chapter 38], 1913, Greenacre 1954 [chapter 3]) but also embody important efforts at stabilization and cure.

My contribution to this Symposium on Transference[1] deals with one special aspect of the subject. It concerns the influence on analytical practice of the new understanding of infant care which has, in turn, derived from analytical theory.

There has often, in the history of psychoanalysis, been a delay in the direct application of analytical metapsychology in analytical practice. Freud was able to formulate a theory of the very early stages of the emotional development of the individual at a time when theory was being applied only in the treatment of the well-chosen neurotic case. (I refer to the period of Freud's work between 1905, the *Three Contributions,* and 1914, *Narcissism.*)

For instance, the part of theory that concerns the primary process, primary identification, and primary repression appeared in analytical practice only in the form of a greater respect that analysts had, as compared with others, for the dream and for psychic reality.

As we look back now we may say that cases were

1. Contribution to the *Discussion of Problems of Transference.* 19th International Psycho-Analytical Congress, Geneva, 24–28 July, 1955.

Reprinted from *International Journal of Psycho-Analysis* 37:386–388, 1956.

well chosen as suitable for analysis if in the very early personal history of the patient there had been enough infant-care. This good enough adaptation to need at the beginning had enabled the individual's ego to come into being, with the result that the earlier stages of the establishment of the ego could be taken for granted by the analyst. In this way it was possible for analysts to talk and write as if the human infant's first experience was the first feed, and as if the object-relationship between mother and infant that this implied was the first significant relationship. This was satisfactory for the practising analyst, but it could not satisfy the direct observer of infants in the care of their mothers.

At that time theory was groping towards a deeper insight into this matter of the mother with her infant, and indeed the term 'primary identification' implies an environment that is not yet differentiated from that which will be the individual. When we see a mother holding an infant soon after birth, or an infant not yet born, at this same time we know that there is another point of view, that of the infant if the infant were already there; and from this point of view the infant is either not yet differentiated out, or else the process of differentiation has started and there is absolute dependence on the immediate environment and its behaviour. It has now become possible to study and use this vital part of old theory in a new and practical way in analytical work, work either with borderline cases or else with the psychotic phases or moments that occur in the course of the analyses of neurotic patients or normal people. This work widens the concept of transference since at the time of the analysis of these phases the ego of the patient cannot be assumed as an established entity, and there can be no transference neurosis for which, surely, there must be an ego, and indeed an intact ego, an ego that is able to maintain defences against anxiety that arises out of instinct the responsibility for which is accepted.

I have referred to the state of affairs that exists when a move is made in the direction of emergence from primary identification. Here at first is absolute dependence. There are two possible kinds of outcome: by the one environmental adaptation to need is good enough, so that there comes into being an ego which, in time, can experience id-impulses; by the other environmental adaptation is not good enough, and so there is no true ego establishment, but instead there develops a pseudo-self which is a collection of innumerable reactions to a succession of failures of adaptation. I would like here to refer to Anna Freud's paper: 'The Widening Scope of Indications for Psycho-Analysis'.[2] The environment, when it successfully adapts at this early stage, is not recognized, or even recorded, so that in the original stage there is no feeling of dependence; whenever the environment fails in its task of making active adaptation, however, it automatically becomes recorded as an impingement, something that interrupts the continuity of being, that very thing which, if not broken up, would have formed itself into the ego of the differentiating human being.

There may be extreme cases in which there is no more than this collection of reactions to environmental failures of adaptation at the critical stage of emergence from primary identification. I am sure this condition is compatible with life, and with physical health. In the cases on which my work is based there has been what I call a true self hidden, protected by a false self. This false self is no doubt an aspect of the true self. It hides and protects it, and it reacts to the adaptation failures and develops a pattern corresponding to the pattern of environmental failure. In this way the true self is not involved in the reacting, and so preserves a continuity of being. This hidden true self suffers an impoverishment, however, that results from lack of experience.

The false self may achieve a deceptive false integrity, that is to say a false ego-strength, gathered from an environmental pattern, and from a good and reliable environment; for it by no means follows that early maternal failure must lead to a general failure of child-care. The false self cannot, however, experience life, and feel real.

In the favourable case the false self develops a fixed maternal attitude towards the true self, and is permanently in a state of holding the true self as a mother holds a baby at the very beginning of differentiation and of emergence from primary identification.

In the work that I am reporting the analyst follows the basic principle of psycho-analysis, that the patient's unconscious leads, and is alone to be pursued. In dealing with a regressive tendency the analyst must be prepared to follow the patient's unconscious process if he is not to issue a directive and so step outside the analyst's role. I have found that it is not necessary to step outside the analyst's role and that it is possible to follow the patient's unconscious lead in this type of case as in the analysis of neurosis. There are differences, however, in the two types of work.

Where there is an intact ego and the analyst can take for granted these earliest details of infant-care,

---

2. *J. Amer. Psychoanal. Assoc.*, 2, 1954.

then the setting of the analysis is unimportant relative to the interpretative work. (By setting, I mean the summation of all the details of management.) Even so there is a basic ration of management in ordinary analysis which is more or less accepted by all analysts.

In the work I am describing the setting becomes more important than the interpretation. The emphasis is changed from the one to the other.

The behaviour of the analyst, represented by what I have called the setting, by being good enough in the matter of adaptation to need, is gradually perceived by the patient as something that raises a hope that the true self may at last be able to take the risks involved in starting to experience living.

Eventually the false self hands over to the analyst. This is a time of great dependence, and true risk, and the patient is naturally in a deeply regressed state. (By regression here I mean regression to dependence and to the early developmental processes.) This is also a highly painful state because the patient is aware, as the infant in the original situation is not aware, of the risks entailed. In some cases so much of the personality is involved that the patient must be in care at this stage. The processes are better studied, however, in those cases in which these matters are confined, more or less, to the time of the analytic sessions.

One characteristic of the transference at this stage is the way in which we must allow the patient's past to *be* the present. This idea is contained in Mme. Sechehaye's book and in her title *Symbolic Realization*. Whereas in the transference neurosis the past comes into the consulting room, in this work it is more true to say that the present goes back into the past, and *is* the past. Thus the analyst finds himself confronted with the patient's primary process in the setting in which it had its original validity.

Good enough adaptation by the analyst produces a result which is exactly that which is sought, namely, a shift in the patient of the main site of operation from a false to a true self. There is now for the first time in the patient's life an opportunity for the development of an ego, for its integration from ego nuclei, for its establishment as a body ego, and also for its repudiation of an external environment with the initiation of a relatedness to objects. For the first time the ego can experience id-impulses, and can feel real in so doing, and also in resting from experiencing. And from here there can at last follow an ordinary analysis of the ego's defences against anxiety.

There builds up an ability of the patient to use the analyst's limited successes in adaptation, so that the ego of the patient becomes able to begin to recall the original failures, all of which were recorded, kept ready. These failures had a disruptive effect at the time, and a treatment of the kind I am describing has gone a long way when the patient is able to take an example of original failure and to be angry about it. Only when the patient reaches this point, however, can there be the beginning of reality-testing. It seems that something like primary repression overtakes these recorded traumata once they have been used.

The way that this change from the experience of being disrupted to the experience of anger comes about is a matter that interests me in a special way, as it is at this point in my work that I found myself surprised. The patient makes use of the analyst's failures. Failures there must be, and indeed there is no attempt to give perfect adaptation; I would say that it is less harmful to make mistakes with these patients than with neurotic patients. The analyst may be surprised as I was to find that while a gross mistake may do but little harm, a very small error of judgement may produce a big effect. The clue is that the analyst's failure is being used and must be treated as a *past* failure, one that the patient can perceive and encompass, and be angry about. The analyst needs to be able to make use of his failures in terms of their meaning for the patient, and he must if possible account for each failure even if this means a study of his unconscious counter-transference.

In these phases of analytic work resistance or that which would be called resistance in work with neurotic patients always indicates that *the analyst has made a mistake,* or in some detail has behaved badly; in fact, the resistance remains until the analyst has found out the mistake and has tried to account for it, and has used it. If he defends himself just here the patient misses the opportunity for being angry about a past failure just where anger was becoming possible for the first time. Here is a great contrast between this work and the analysis of neurotic patients with intact ego. It is here that we can see the sense in the dictum that every failed analysis is a failure not of the patient but of the analyst.

This work is exacting partly because the analyst has to have a sensitivity to the patient's needs and a wish to provide a setting that caters for these needs. The analyst is not, after all, the patient's natural mother.

It is exacting, also, because of the necessity for the analyst to look for his own mistakes whenever resistances appear. Yet it is only by using his own mistakes that he can do the most important part of the treatment in these phases, the part that enables the patient to become angry for the first time about the details of failure of adaptation that (at the time when they happened) produced disruption. It is this part of the work that frees the patient from dependence on the analyst.

In this way the negative transference of 'neurotic' analysis is replaced by objective anger about the analyst's failures, so here again is an important difference between the transference phenomena in the two types of work.

We must not look for an awareness at a deep level of our adaptation successes, since these are not felt as such. Although we cannot work without the theory that we build up in our discussions, undoubtedly this work finds us out if our understanding of the patient's need is a matter of the mind rather than of the psyche-soma.

I have discovered in my clinical work that one kind of analysis does not preclude the other. I find myself slipping over from one to the other and back again, according to the trend of the patient's unconscious process. When work of the special kind I have referred to is completed it leads naturally on to ordinary analytic work, the analysis of the depressive position and of the neurotic defences of a patient with an ego, an intact ego, an ego that is able to experience id-impulses and to take the consequences.

What I have described is only the beginning. For me it is the application of the statements I made in my paper 'Primitive Emotional Development' (1945). What needs to be done now is the study in detail of the criteria by which the analyst may know when to work with the change of emphasis, how to see that a need is arising which is of the kind that I have said must be met (at least in a token way) by active adaptation, the analyst keeping the concept of Primary Identification all the time in mind.

41

PSYCHO-ANALYSIS OF THE PSYCHO-ANALYTIC FRAME

JOSÉ BLEGER

EDITOR'S NOTE

José Bleger, a Kleinian psychoanalyst strongly influenced by Winnicott (1956 [chapter 40], 1959, 1965), sets out in this paper to investigate the nature and function of the ground rules of psychoanalysis—here termed the *psychoanalytic frame*. The result is a paper rich in insight, though one that has unfortunately attracted little notice by other writers. Bleger views the setting or frame as an institution and nonprocess, and as the essential representation of the early mother-child symbiosis in the analytic relationship. Out of these fundamental constants and their correct management by the analyst basic ego development is seen to unfold in the analytic experience. From this recognition—and here is the paper's major virtue—Bleger draws an invaluable technical conclusion: the analysis of impingements upon the frame must precede all other therapeutic work.

Winnicott (1956) defines "setting" as "the summation of all the details of management."[1] I suggest, for reasons that will become clearer further on, that we should apply the term "psycho-analytic situation" to the totality of phenomena included in the therapeutic relationship between the analyst and the patient. This situation comprises phenomena which constitute a *process* that is studied, analysed, and interpreted; but it also includes a *frame*, that is to say, a "non-process", in the sense that it is made up of constants within whose bounds the process takes place.[2]

The analytic situation may be thus studied from the point of view of the methodology it stands for, its frame corresponding to the *constants* of a phenomenon, a method or technique, and the process to the

set of *variables*. Methodological considerations will, however, be left out and they have only been mentioned here to make it clear that a process can only be examined when the same constants (frame) are being kept up. Thus, we include within the psychoanalytic frame the role of the analyst, the set of space (atmosphere) and time factors, and part of the technique (including problems concerning the fixing and keeping of times, fees, interruptions, etc.). The frame refers to a strategy rather than to a technique. One part of the frame includes "the psycho-analytic contract" which "is an agreement between two people into which enter two formal elements of mutual exchange: time and money" (Liberman, 1961).

I am here concerned with the psycho-analysis of the psycho-analytic frame, and there is a great deal in the literature about the need for keeping it up and about the breaks and distortions caused by the patient in the course of any psycho-analysis (varying in intensity and features from exaggerated obsessive fulfilment to repression, acting out, or psychotic disintegration). My work in the psycho-analysis of psychotic cases has clearly revealed to me the importance of maintaining and protecting the fragments or

---

1. Paper read at the Second Argentine Psychoanalytic Congress, Buenos Aires, June 1966.

2. Here we might compare this terminology with that used by Liberman (1962) and Rodrigué (1966) respectively.

Reprinted from *International Journal of Psycho-Analysis* 48:511–519, 1967.

elements which might have remained and which can sometimes only be achieved by hospitalization. Yet I do not want to consider now the problem of "disruption of" or "attack on" the frame. I want to study what is involved in the maintenance of an *ideally normal frame*. The problem is similar to what physicists call an ideal experiment, that is to say a problem which does not occur fully and precisely in the way it is being described or stated, but which is of great theoretical and practical use. This is perhaps what Rodrigué had in mind when he once referred to the patient whose history nobody has written and nobody will ever be able to write.

The way I have stated the problem seems to imply that such study is impossible, since ideal analysis does not exist, and I agree with this opinion. The fact is that at times permanently, and at other times sporadically, the frame changes from the mere background of a Gestalt into a figure, that is to say, a process. But even in these cases, it is not the same thing as the process of the analytic situation itself because, whenever "flaws" occur in the frame, we still tend to maintain it or restore it with our interpretation; this is quite different from our attitude in the analysis of the process itself. In this sense, I am interested in examining the psycho-analytic meaning of the frame *when it is not a problem,* in the "ideal" analysis (or at the moments or stages when it is ideal). Thus, I am interested in the psycho-analysis of the frame when it is maintained and not when it is broken, when it remains a set of constants and not when it has turned into variables. The problem I want to look into concerns those analyses in which the frame is not a problem—precisely to show that it is a problem—a problem, however, which has not been defined or hitherto recognized.

A relationship which lasts for years, in which a set of norms and attitudes is kept up, is nothing less than a true definition of *institution*. The frame is then an institution within whose bounds certain phenomena take place which we call behaviour. I was led to this study partly by a series of seminars on Institutional Psychology and as a result of my experience in this field (though at present limited). What became evident to me was that each institution is a portion of the individual's personality; and it is of such importance that identity is always, wholly or partially, institutional, in the sense that at least one part of the identity always shapes itself by belonging to a group, institution, ideology, party, etc. Fenichel (1945) wrote: "Unquestionably the individual structures created by institutions help conserve these institutions." But besides this interaction between individuals and institutions, institutions always work in varying degrees as the limits of the body image and as the basic centre of identity.

The frame is maintained and tends to be maintained (actively, by the psycho-analyst) as invariable; and while it exists as such it seems to be non-existent or it does not count, just as we become aware of institutions or relationships only when they are missing, are blocked, or have ceased to exist. (I do not know who it was who said about love and children that we only know they exist when they cry.) But, what is the meaning of the frame when it is maintained, when "it does not cry"? It is, in all instances, the problem of symbiosis, which is "dumb" and only reveals itself when it breaks or is on the verge of rupture. This is what happens, too, with the body image whose study started with pathology which first proved its existence. In the same way as we speak of the "ghost member", we must accept that institutions and the frame *always* make up a "ghost world", that of the most primitive and undifferentiated organization. What is always there is never noticed unless it is missing; we might apply to the frame the term used by Wallon for what he called "ultra-things", that is to say, all that which in experience appears as vague, undefined, without conception or knowledge of itself. What makes up the ego are not only the steady relationships with objects and institutions but the ulterior frustrations and gratifications with them. There is no awareness of what is always present. Awareness of the missing or gratifying object comes later; the first step is the perception of a certain "incompleteness". What exists in the individual's perception is that which experience has taught him might be missing. On the other hand, steady or motionless relationships (the non-absences) are those which organize and preserve the non-ego, and serve as a basis for the building up of the ego according to frustrating and gratifying experiences. The fact that the non-ego is not perceived does not mean it does not exist psychologically for the organization of personality. The knowledge of something is only apparent in the absence of that something, until it is incorporated as an internal object. But what we do not perceive is also present. And precisely because of this, that "ghost world" is also present in the frame even when this has not been broken.

I want to digress again, hoping to provide more elements for the present study. Until recently, we were comfortably working in the field of science, language, logic, etc., without realizing that all of these phenomena or behaviours (I am interested in all of them in so far as they are behaviours, that is to say, human phenomena) take place within a context of assumptions which we ignored or thought nonexistent or invariable; but we know now that communication contains a meta-communication, science is a meta-science, theory a meta-theory, language a meta-language, logics a meta-logics, etc., etc. If the "meta-" varies the contents vary radically.[3] Thus, the frame is constant, and is therefore decisive in the phenomena of the process of behaviour. In other words, the frame is a *meta-behaviour*, and the phenomena we are going to distinguish as behaviour depend on it. It is what remains implicit, but on which the explicit depends.

The meta-behaviour works as a "bulwark", as M. and W. Baranger have called it, a phase in which the analysand tries not to risk avoiding the basic rule. In the meta-behaviour, I am interested in analysing the cases in which the basic rule is fulfilled, and I am concerned precisely with examining that fulfilment. I agree with these authors in regarding the analytic relationship as a symbiotic relationship; but in the cases in which the frame is being respected, the problem lies in the fact that the frame itself is the receiver of the symbiosis and that the latter is not present in the analytic process itself. Symbiosis with the mother (immobility of the non-ego), enables the child to develop his ego. The frame has a similar function: it acts as support, as mainstay, but, so far, we have been able to perceive it only when it changes or breaks. The most powerful, endurable, and at the same time least apparent, "bulwark" is, then, the one that lies on the frame.

I want to illustrate the description I have offered of the frame with the example of a patient Mr A., with a phobic character and an intense dependence disguised under the form of reactive independence. For a long time he wavered between hesitation, desire and fear of buying a flat in a purchase that was never accomplished. At a certain point, he came to know by mere chance that I had, some time before, bought a flat that was still being built, and this was the starting point of a period of anxiety and acting out.

One day he told me about what he had learnt and I interpreted his reaction: the way he said it contained reproach at my not informing him of my purchase, knowing it was a fundamental problem of his. He tried to ignore or forget the incident by presenting strong resistance every time I insistently related this fact to his acting out, till strong feelings of hatred, envy, frustration, coupled with verbal attacks, began to appear, and were followed by a feeling of detachment and hopelessness. As we advanced further in the analysis of these situations, the "background" of his childhood experience gradually began to emerge from the narration of different recollections. At home, his parents had done nothing without informing or consulting him about it; he knew all the details of the development of the family life. After the emergence of these memories and my interpretation of them against great resistance, he began accusing me of having broken our connexion, and he said that he would not be able to trust me. Fantasies of suicide appeared as well as derangement, frequent confusion and hypochondriacal symptoms.[4]

For the patient, something had broken, something which *was so* and *had to be* as it had always been; and he could not conceive of its being otherwise. He was demanding a repetition of what had been lived, of what for him had "always been so", a demand or feature he had managed to keep through his life by restricting or limiting his ego in social relationships and by constantly controlling relationships himself, demanding a strong dependence from his objects.

I want to stress in this example how the "non-repetition", because the frame was respected, brought to light the steadiest and most permanent element of his personality, his "ghost world". The delusional transference (Little) or the psychotic part of his personality was a non-ego that constituted the groundwork of his ego and his identity. It was only with the "unfulfilment" of his "ghost world" that he was able to see that my frame was different from his, that even before the unfulfilment, his "ghost world" already existed. I must emphasize, however, that the maintenance of the frame was what led to the analysis of the psychotic part of his personality. The important question is not how many of these phenomena are due to frustration or the clash with reality (the frame), but how much of this area does not appear and is therefore never likely to be analysed. I am able not to give an answer to this question, but only to delineate the problem. It is similar to what

---

3. This variation in the "meta-" or variation of the fixed or constant assumptions is the origin of non-Euclidean geometry and Boolean algebra (Lieber, 1960). In psychotherapy, each technique has its assumptions (its frame) and therefore, its own "contents" or processes.

4. As Little (1958) describes it in patients whose transference is delusional, body associations of very early experiences began to appear in my patient. When he felt immobilized he associated to having been wrapped up as a baby in a band that kept him motionless. The non-ego of the frame includes the body and if the frame breaks, the limits of the ego made up by the non-ego have to be recovered through hypochondriacal symptoms.

happens with the character feature that must be turned into a symptom in order to be analysed, that is to say, it must stop being ego-syntonic. Should not whatever is done in the analysis of character be done with the frame? The problem is different and more difficult since the frame is not ego-syntonic on the one hand, and on the other hand is the groundwork on which the ego and the identity of the individual are built up; and it is strongly separated off from the analytic process, from the ego that shapes the neurotic transference.

Even if we assume that, in the case mentioned above, this material would have emerged in one way or another because it was there, the problem persists in reference to the psycho-analytic meaning of the frame.

Summing up, one might say that the frame (thus defined as a problem) is the most perfect repetition compulsion[5] and that actually there are two frames, one which is suggested and kept up by the analyst, and consciously accepted by the patient, and the other, that of the "ghost world", on which the patient projects.[6] The latter is the most perfect repetition compulsion since it is the most complete, the least known, and the least noticeable one. Rodrigué (1966) talks about a "pending transference" and the "difficulty arises because we are speaking about a phenomenon which, if it existed in its pure form, would have to be dumb by definition."

It has always seemed surprising and exciting to me, in the analysis of psychotic cases, to note the coexistence of a total denial of the analyst with exaggerated sensitivity to the infringement of any detail of the "habitual", the frame, and how the patient might become confused or violent, for example, because of a few minutes' difference in starting or finishing the session. Now I understand it better in that what becomes disorganized is his "meta-ego", which to a great extent, is all he has got. I think it is jumping to conclusions to talk all the time about a patient's "attack" on the frame when he does not adhere to it. He brings what he has got and it is not always an "attack" but his own organization, even though disordered.

In psychotic transference, affection is not transferred but "a total situation, the whole of a development" (Lagache); it would be better to say, the whole of a "non-development". For Melanie Klein, transference repeats the primitive object

relationships, but I think that what is still most primitive (the non-differentiation) repeats itself in the frame. The ambiguity of the "as if" of the analytic situation studied by W. and M. Baranger (1961–62) does not cover "all the aspects of the analytic field" as they express it, but only the process. The frame does not accept ambiguity, either on the part of the patient or on the part of the analyst's technique. Each frame *is*, and does not admit ambiguity. Similarly, I believe that the phenomenon of participation (Lévy-Bruhl) or of syncretism admitted by these authors for the analytic situation, only applies to the frame.

Jaques (1955) says that social institutions are unconsciously used as a defence against psychotic anxiety. I believe them to be the depository of the psychotic part of the personality, i.e. the undifferentiated and non-dissolved portion of the primitive symbiotic links. Psychotic anxieties take place within the institution, and, in the case of the psychoanalytic situation, within what we have described as the process—what "is in motion" against what is not: the frame. Reider (1953) describes different types of transference to the institution instead of the therapist and psycho-analysis as an institution seems to be a means of recovering the lost omnipotence of sharing in the prestige of a great institution. I believe that what is important here is to consider the psychoanalytic situation as an institution in itself, especially the frame.

The development of the ego, in analysis, in the family, or in any institution, depends on the immobility of the non-ego. This denomination of non-ego makes us think about it as something non-existent, but which actually exists to the extent that it is the "meta-ego" on which the very possibility of formation and maintenance of the ego depends. Hence we might say that identity depends upon the manner in which the non-ego is kept up or handled. If the meta-behaviour varies, the whole ego undergoes changes in proably equivalent degrees as regards its quantity and its quality. García Reinoso (1956) has said that just as it is true—as Freud had pointed out—that the ego is corporal, so is the non-ego. We might add something else: that the non-ego is a different ego, having different features, and I suggest (Bleger, 1967) calling it a *syncretic ego*. This also implies that there is not only *one* sense of reality and a lack of it: there are different structures of the ego and sense of reality.

The non-ego is the background or the frame of the organized ego; the "background" and "figure" of a unique Gestalt. Between the ego and the non-ego, or between the neurotic and psychotic part of the

---

5. This repetition compulsion is not only a way of remembering but a way of life on the requirement to live.

6. Wender (1966) has said that there are two patients and two analysts, to which I now add: two frames.

personality, there is no dissociation but a cleavage, as I have described it in a previous paper.

Miss N was a very rigid and limited patient who always lived with her parents in hotels in different countries; the only thing she always carried with her was a small picture. The unsatisfactory relationship with her parents and the constant moving had turned this picture into her "frame", what gave her the "non-change" for her identity.

The frame is the most primitive part of the personality, it is the fusion ego-body-world, on whose immobility depend the formation, existence, and differentiation (of the ego, the object, the body image, the body, the mind, etc., etc.). Patients with "acting-in" tendencies or psychotic patients also bring "their own frame", and *the institution of their primitive symbiotic relationship*; yet not only they, but all patients bring it too. Hence we can better recognize the catastrophic situation which to a variable degree is always created by the analyst's breaking the frame, e.g. holiday, changes of time, etc., because in these breakings a "crevice" is opened into which enters a reality that appears catastrophic to the patient; "his" frame, his "ghost world" remains without depository and it becomes evident that his frame is not the psycho-analytic frame, as happened with Mr A.

I now want to give an example of a "crevice" that the patient maintained till he felt the need to recover his omnipotence, "his" frame.

Mr Z, the only son of a family who in his childhood was wealthy and socially influential and united, lived in a huge, luxurious mansion with his parents and grandparents, for whom he was the centre of attention. For political reasons, a lot of their possessions were expropriated, and this brought about a great economic decline. The whole family tried hard for a while to live like rich people, concealing their disaster and poverty, but his parents finally moved into a small apartment and accepted a job. (In the meantime his grandparents had died.) When the family faced and accepted the change, he continued living up to appearances. He withdrew from his parents to live on his profession as an architect and he covered up his great insecurity and economic instability so well that everybody thought him rich. He lived and encouraged his fantasy that "nothing had happened", preserving in this way the safe and idealized world of his childhood, his "ghost world". The impression he gave me in the course of treatment was that of a "well-to-do" person, belonging to the social and economic upper class, who, without the showing-off of a "parvenu", maintained an air of security, dignity, and superiority, of being over and beyond the "miseries" and "pettiness" of life, including money.

The frame was well kept, the patient paying regularly and punctually. As the cleavage in his personality was being more deeply analysed, as well as his acting in two worlds, he began to owe me money, to be unpunctual, and to speak—with great difficulty—about his lack of money, a fact which made him feel very "humiliated". The breaking of the frame meant here a certain disruption of his omnipotent organization, the appearance of a "breach" which became the way to get in "against" his omnipotence (the steady and safe world of his childhood). The fulfilment of the frame was the depository of his omnipotent magic world, his childish dependence, his psychotic transference. His most profound fantasy was that analysis would strengthen that omnipotence and would give him back his "ghost world". "To live" in the past was the basic organization of his existence.

The following material comes from a session just after his parents were seriously injured in an accident. During the previous session he paid me part of his debt, and he began the present session by telling me that he had brought me so much money and still owed me so much. He felt the debt "as a breach, as something missing". After a pause, he went on: "Yesterday I had sexual intercourse with my wife and at the beginning I was impotent and that frightened me". (He had been impotent at the beginning of his marriage.) I interpreted that as he was now living a difficult situation because of his parents' accident, he wanted to go back to the security he enjoyed in his childhood, to his parents and grandparents within him, and the relationship with his wife, with me, and with the present reality made him impotent to accomplish that. He had a need to close the breach by paying me the whole of the debt, so that the money might disappear between us, so that I, and everything that made him suffer now, might also disappear. He answered that the day before he had thought that he in fact only needed his wife not to be alone, she was a mere addition in his life. I interpreted that he also wished me to satisfy his reality-needs so that they might disappear and he might thus go back to the security of his childhood, and to his fantasy of reunion with his grandparents, father and mother, just as had happened in his early years.

After a silence, he said that when he heard the word fantasy he found it strange that I should talk of fantasies, and was afraid of going mad. I told him that he wanted me to give him back all the security of his childhood which he tried to preserve within himself so as to cope with the difficult situation and that, on the other hand, he felt that I, and reality with its needs and sufferings, got in through the breach which his debt had created between us. He finished the session by talking about a transvestist; and I interpreted that he felt like a transvestist: at times like a rich and only son, at times like his father, at times like his mother, at times like his grandfather, and in each one of them both *poor and rich*.

Any variation in the frame brings the non-ego to a crisis, "contradicts" the fusion, "challenges" the ego, and compels reintrojection, re-elaboration of the ego, or stirs the defences to immobilize or reproject the psychotic part of the personality. Mr Z could accept the analysis of "his" frame till he had defensively to get it back; and what is important is that his "ghost world" appears and is questioned with "flaws" to the frame (his debt) and that the recovery of his "ghost world" was linked to the fulfilment of *my* frame precisely to ignore me or destroy me.

The phenomenon of reactivation of symptoms at the end of a psycho-analytic treatment, which has often been described, is due, too, to a mobilization and regression of the ego because of a mobilization of the "meta-ego". The background of the Gestalt becomes a figure.[7] The frame, in this way, may be considered as an "addiction" which, if not systematically analysed, may become a stabilized organization, the foundation of the organization of the personality, and the individual gets an ego "adjusted" and modelled upon the institutions of which he is part. It is the basis, I believe, of what Alvarez de Toledo, Grinberg, and Langer (1966) have called the "analytic character", which the existentialists call a "factic" existence, and which we might recognize as a "factic ego".[8]

This "factic ego" is an "ego of belonging"; it is made up and sustained by the admission of the subject to an institution (which may be the therapeutic relationship, the psycho-analytical society, a study group, or any other institution); there is no "internalized ego" to give internal stability to the subject.

Let us say, in other words, that his whole personality is made up of "characters", that is to say, of roles, or — to put it another way — that his whole personality is a façade. I am now describing the "extreme case" but quantitative variation must be

taken into account because there is no way to abolish completely this "factic ego"; neither do I think this necessary.

The "pact" or the negative therapeutic reaction represents a perfect fixation of the patient's non-ego in the frame and even its non-recognition and acceptance by the psycho-analyst; moreover, we might say that the negative therapeutic reaction is a real perversion of the transference-countertransference relationship. The "therapeutic alliance" is, on the contrary, an alliance with the healthiest part of the patient (Greenacre, 1959); and this is true of the process but not of the frame. In the latter, the alliance is established with the psychotic (or symbiotic) part of the patient's personality (whether with the corresponding part of the psycho-analyst's personality I do not know yet).[9]

Winnicott (1947) says:

For the neurotic, the couch and warmth and comfort can be *symbolical* of the mother's love; for the psychotic it would be more true to say that these things *are* the analyst's physical expression of love. The couch *is* the analyst's lap or womb, and the warmth *is* the live warmth of the analyst's body. And so on.

As to the frame, this is always the most regressive, psychotic part of the patient (for every type of patient). The frame is a permanent presence, like the parents for the child. Without them, there is no development of the ego, but to keep the frame beyond necessity, or to avoid any change in the relationship with the frame or with the parents, there may be even a paralysis of development. Rodrigué, in a book on transference (1966), compares the psycho-analytic process with the process of evolution.

It has been emphasized that the child's ego organizes itself according to the mobility of the medium that creates and provides his needs. The rest of the medium which does not generate needs, is not distinguished and remains as a background in the structure of personality, and as yet this has not been given proper considerations.

In every analysis, even one with an ideally kept frame, the frame must become an object of analysis. I do not mean that this is not occurring in practice, but I want to stress the meaning or significance of what is being done or remains undone, and its

---

7. It must be this fact which has led some authors (Christoffel, 1952) to the breaking of the frame as a technique (giving up the couch and having the interview face to face) a point of view I do not share.

8. I have dealt more intensively with the "factic ego" and

the "syncretic ego", the "corporal ego" and the "internalized ego" elsewhere (Bleger, 1967).

9. I do not believe that this psychotic split transference which is placed on the frame is the consequence of repression of infantile amnesia.

importance. The de-symbiotization of the analyst-patient relationship is only reached with the systematic analysis of the frame at the right moment. And here we are likely to find the strongest resistance because it is not a repressed thing but something split and never differentiated; its analysis disturbs the ego and the most mature identity reached by the patient. In these cases we don't interpret what is repressed; we give rise to the secondary process. It is not interpreted on amnesic gaps but on what never was part of the memory. It is not projective identification either; it is the expression of syncretism or the patient's "participation."

The frame is part of the patient's body image; it *is* the body image in the part that has not been structured and differentiated. It is thus something different from the body image itself; it is the body-space and body setting non-differentiation. That is why the interpretation of gestures and body attitudes frequently becomes persecutory, because we do not "move" the patient's ego, but rather his "meta-ego".

I want to present now another example which also has the peculiarity that I cannot describe the "dumbness" of the frame but only the moment when it reveals itself, when it has stopped being dumb. I have already compared it with the body image, the study of which was started precisely by the consideration of its disturbances. In this case, however, the psycho-analyst's frame was vitiated.

A colleague brought to a supervision session the analysis of a patient whose transference neurosis he had been interpreting for several years; but the intractability of the case induced him to bring it to supervision. The patient "respected" the frame and in this sense "there were no problems"; he associated well; there was no "acting-out"; and the analyst interpreted well in the area on which he was working. But the patient and the therapist used the familiar form of address to each other because the patient had suggested this at the beginning of his analysis, and the therapist had accepted it. The analysis of the therapist's countertransference took many months till he finally "dared" to correct this familiar form of address, interpreting to the patient what was happening and what was hidden behind it. To stop using the familiar "tu" to each other as a result of its systematic analysis revealed the narcissistic relationship and the omnipotent control, and how the person and role of the analyst had been suppressed because of this familiarity.

By using this familiar form of address, the patient imposed his own frame, overlapping the analyst's, but really destroying the latter. The analyst was compelled to cope with a task that represented too great an effort in the session with his patient (and in his countertransference), and this led to an intensive change in the analytic process and rupture in the patient's ego, which was surviving under unsafe conditions and with a very limited "spectrum" of interest, with intensive and extensive inhibitions. The change of the form of address through analysis led to the conclusion that this was not an obsessive phobic character but a simple schizophrenia with a phobic-obsessive characterological "façade".

I do not think it would have been efficient enough to modify the familiar form of address from the very beginning since the candidate did not have the technical experience to handle a patient with a strong narcissistic organization. The analyst must not agree to use the familiar form of address himself, though he may accept it on the part of his patient and analyse it at a suitable time (which I cannot place retrospectively). The analyst should accept the frame the patient brings (which is his "meta-ego") because there the non-solved primitive symbiosis is found summed up. But we must state, at the same time, that to accept the patient's "meta-ego" (the frame) does not mean to abandon one's own, by means of which one is able to analyse the process and to transform the frame itself into a process. Any interpretation of the frame (not altered) stirs the psychotic part of the personality. It makes up what I have called a split interpretation. But the analyst-patient relationship outside the strict frame (as in this example), as well as the "extra-analytic" relationships, enable the psychotic transference to be concealed and favour the "development" of the "psycho-analytic character."

Another patient, Mrs C, maintained her frame until she progressed in her pregnancy. She had never shaken hands since treatment started, but she now stopped greeting me when arriving or leaving. I strongly resisted including in the interpretation that she had stopped greeting me, but I could see in this the mobilization of her symbiotic relationship with her mother, of highly persecutory features, which became active because of her pregnancy. Not to shake hands when arriving or leaving has been maintained but there still lies an important part of "her frame", which is different from "mine". I believe that the situation is even more complex, because not to shake hands is not a mere detail which is missing to round up the frame. It is evidence that she has another frame, another Gestalt which is not mine (that of the psycho-analytic treatment) and in which her idealized relationship with her mother remained split. The more we deal with the psychotic part of the personality, the more we must take into account that a detail is not just a detail, but an expression of a Gestalt, that is to say, of a special organization or structure.

Summing up, we may say that a patient's frame is his most primitive fusion with the mother's body and that the psycho-analyst's frame must help to re-establish the original symbiosis in order to be able to change it. The disruption of the frame, as well as its ideal or normal maintenance, are technical and theoretical problems, but what basically blocks off any possibility of a profound treatment is the disruption the analyst himself introduces or admits in the frame. *The frame can only be analysed within the frame,* or, in other words, the patient's most primitive dependence and psychological organization can only be analysed within the analyst's frame, which should be neither ambiguous, nor changeable, nor altered.

SUMMARY

I propose to call the *psycho-analytic situation* the sum total of phenomena involved in the therapeutic relationship between the analyst and the patient. This situation includes phenomena which make up a *process* and which is studied, analysed and interpreted; but it also includes a *frame,* that is to say "a non-process" in the sense that it represents the constants, within whose limits the process occurs. The relationship between them is studied and the frame is explained as the set of constants within whose limits the process takes place (variables). The basic aim is to study, not the breaking of the frame, but its psycho-analytic meaning when "ideally normal" conditions are maintained.

Thus, the frame is studied as an *institution* within whose limits phenomena occur which are called "behaviours". In this sense, the frame is "dumb" but not non-existent. It makes up the non-ego of the patient, according to which the ego shapes itself. This non-ego is the "ghost world" of the patient, that lies in the frame and represents a "meta-behaviour".

The role of the frame is illustrated with some clinical examples which reveal the placement in the frame of the patient's most primitive "family institution". It is thus the perfect repetition compulsion, which brings up the primitive undifferentiation of the first stages of the organization of personality. The frame as an institution is the receiver of the psychotic part of the personality, i.e. of the undifferentiated and non-solved part of the primitive symbiotic links. The psycho-analytic meaning of the frame defined in this way is then examined, as well as the relevance of these considerations for clinical work and technique.

REFERENCES

Abraham, K. (1919). "A particular form of neurotic resistance against the psycho-analytic method." *Selected Papers.* (London: Hogarth, 1927.)

Alvarez de Toledo, L. C., Grinberg, L. and Langer, M. (1964). "Termination of training analysis." In: *Psycho-analysis in the Americas.* ed. Litman. (New York: Int. Univ. Press, 1966.)

Baranger, W. and Baranger, M. (1961–2). 'La situatión analítica como campo dinámico." *Rev. Urug. Psicoanal., 4.*

———(1964). "El insight en la situación analítica." *Rev. Urug. Psicoanal., 6.*

Bleger, J. (1964). "Simbiosis: estudio de la parte psicótica de la personalidad." *Rev. Urug. Psicoanal., 6.*

———(1966). *Psicohigiene y Psicologia institucional.* (Buenos Aires: Paidos.)

———(1967). *Simbiosis y Ambiguedad.* (Buenos Aires: Paidos.)

Christoffel, H. (1952). "Le problème du transfert." *Rev. franc. psychoanal., 16.*

Fenichel, O. (1945). *The Psychoanalytic Theory of Neurosis.* (New York: Norton.)

Freud, S. (1914). "Remembering, repeating and working-through." S.E., 12.

García Reinoso, D. (1956). "Cuerpo y mente." *Rev. Psicoanal., 13.*

Greenacre, P. (1959). "Certain technical problems in the transference relationship." *J. Amer. Psychoanal. Assoc., 7.*

Jaques, E. (1951). *The Changing Culture of a Factory.* (London: Tavistock.)

———(1955). "Social systems as a defence against persecutory and depressive anxiety." In: *New Directions in Psycho-Analysis.* ed. Klein *et al.* (London: Tavistock.)

Klein, M. (1955). "The psycho-analytic play technique: its history and significance." *ibid.*

Lagache, D. (1952). "Le problème du transfert." *Rev. franc. psychoanal., 16.* (Spanish: *Rev. Urug. Psicoanal.,* 1956, 1.)

Liberman, D. (1962). *La communicación en terapeutica psicoanalítica.* (Buenos Aires: Eudeba).

Liberman, D., Ferschtut, G., Sor, D. (1961). "El contrato analítico." *Rev. Psicoanal., 18.*

Lieber, L. R. (1960). "The great discovery of modern mathematics." *General Semantics Bull., 26–27.*

Little, M. (1958). "On delusional transference." *Int. J. Psycho-Anal.*, 39.

Nunberg, H. (1951). "Transference and reality." *Int. J. Psycho-Anal.*, 32.

Reider, N. (1953). "A type of transference at institutions." *Bull. Menning Clin.*, 17.

Rodrigué, E. and Rodrigué, G. T. de (1966). *El Contexto del Proceso Analítico*. (Buenos Aires: Paidos.)

Wender, L. (1966). "Reparación patalógica y perversión." Paper read to the Argentine Psychoanaltic Assoc.

Winnicott, D. W. (1945). "Primitive emotional development." *Collected Papers*. (London: Tavistock, 1958.)

———(1947). "Hate in the countertransference." *ibid.*

———(1956). "Clinical varieties of transference." *ibid.*

42

THE THERAPEUTIC RELATIONSHIP AND DEVIATIONS IN TECHNIQUE

Robert Langs

EDITOR'S NOTE

This paper offers, in addition to a condensed review of the literature on the ground rules or framework, an extensive set of postulates regarding (1) the therapist's management of the ground rules and boundaries of the therapeutic relationship, and (2) the unconscious meanings and functions of deviations.

It is suggested that the humanistic maintenance of the therapeutic hold, setting, and framework is an essential component of a sound therapeutic experience, and that most if not all deviations contain important countertransference-based inputs. This is a position that has evoked extensive controversy despite what I consider successful efforts at extensive clinical documentation. Clearly I feel it is a position to be carefully considered and evaluated.

The framework and boundaries of the patient-analyst and patient-therapist relationships are a relatively neglected but important area. It is my main thesis that the manner in which the analyst or therapist[1] establishes and maintains the ground rules and boundaries of the therapeutic setting and interaction is among the most important means through which he conveys to the patient the essence of his identity and the dynamic state of his own intrapsychic structures, conflicts, and balances. The therapist's management of the therapeutic relationship therefore influences the ongoing identificatory and incorporative processes in the patient vis-à-vis the therapist, and contributes to the nature of the analytic "field" or "screen"—the person with whom the patient interacts and onto whom he projects his intrapsychic fantasies. It therefore influences the transference dimension as well. As a result, modifications or deviations in the established ground rules and boundaries of the therapeutic setting and relationship have a wide range of deeply significant consequences, of which only a certain portion is

modifiable through subsequent analytic-interpretive work in the cognitive-verbal sphere. Actual changes in the therapist's stance are essential to correct the detrimental consequences of such deviations and, further, it may prove virtually impossible to alter certain effects on the patient through any means.

Specifically defined, the ground rules and boundaries of the therapeutic relationship include the following: set fee, hours, and length of sessions; the fundamental rule of free association with communication occurring while the patient is in his chair or on the couch; the absence of physical contact and other extratherapeutic gratifications; the therapist's relative anonymity, physicianly concern, and use of neutral interventions geared primarily toward interpretations; and the exclusive one-to-one relationship with total confidentiality. While the psychoanalytic and psychotherapeutic situations may differ in the placement of the patient and the analyst or therapist, and in frequency of sessions, they nonetheless are both created with a definable set of ground rules that offer as good as possible a therapeutic situation and relationship. I shall focus in this paper on the management of these ground rules and boundaries; I shall be less concerned here with the consequences arising from the different framework of the two

Reprinted from *International Journal of Psychoanalytic Psychotherapy* 4:106–141, 1975.

therapeutic modalities. For both settings, it is these ground rules and boundaries that delimit the therapeutic "hold" (Winnicott 1958) and the boundaries of the therapeutic interaction; they are experiences that, per se, offer important opportunities for identification, structure building, and the projection of intrapsychic fantasies by the patient. Further, they influence the manner in which the patient perceives and assimilates the therapist's verbal interventions.

With this as our basic definition, let us now consider the relevant literature. With the single exception of Bleger (1967), explorations of the ground rules and boundaries of the analytic relationship derive initially from the technical issue of whether ego defects or dysfunctions in the patient call for modification of the usual limits of psychoanalytic technique, i.e., for *parameters* of technique, a term suggested by Eissler (1953). From there, such exploration extends into considerations of the therapist's flexibility (A. Freud 1954a,b) and, more recently, into the degree of deprivation necessary and optimal in the psychoanalytic situation (e.g., Stone 1961) and into those deviations in technique supposedly designed to foster the therapeutic alliance (e.g., Zetzel 1966–69 and Greenson and Wexler 1969). While, as we shall see, a wide range of deviations and parameters in technique have been advocated by various writers, the specific consequences of these deviations for the therapeutic relationship and the intrapsychic conflicts and structures of the patient are virtually neglected. Most writers limit themselves to general impressions of the productivity of such maneuvers—a factor I shall discuss later in this paper.

The papers on parameters and deviations in technique raise a host of issues, only some of which are pertinent here. The most unavoidable of these important secondary problems is that of delineation of classical psychoanalytic technique (Eissler 1953, Greenson 1958). Here I shall simply offer a brief definition of the classical psychoanalytic situation as one in which a relationship between a patient and analyst is established in order to assist the patient in resolving his neurotic difficulties through constructive unconscious identifications and the greatest possible development of insight and adaptive, inner-structural change; the latter is reflected in symptom alleviation and in constructive characterological alterations. The treatment milieu is designed to foster the fullest possible expression of the patient's intrapsychic conflicts, fantasies, and memories, especially as revealed in the relationship between the patient and the analyst. Thus, it is a setting in which all efforts are made to minimize the contribution of the analyst's unresolved intrapsychic conflicts and fantasies to the unfolding interaction between himself and the patient, and, further, to offer the patient an opportunity for inevitable identifications with the analyst based on the latter's constructive manner of functioning and relating. Without digressing, I would suggest that the psychotherapeutic situation is of comparable design, though less intensely so (for details, see Langs 1973b, 1974; since the literature on deviations is founded on the psychoanalytic situation, I will base my own discussion here on that modality).

In creating a climate in which these goals can be achieved, the analyst directly and indirectly indicates to the patient the nature of their respective roles and responsibilities; he delineates a set of explicit ground rules and implicit boundaries in the relationship. In this context, the analyst develops and maintains an atmosphere of warm and growth-promoting concern (Loewald 1960, Greenson 1967), while his primary goal is to understand the patient's communications and to intervene in a relatively neutral manner, ultimately through interpretations that lead to the patient's achievement of insight into his unconscious fantasies, memories, and conflicts. Other types of interventions, such as directives, manipulations, and counterreactions to the patient's associations, fall beyond the scope of such standard technique.

Within this classical framework, *variations* in technique are inevitable (Greenson 1958); they reflect each analyst's personality, style of work, and his appropriate, limited, flexible responses to momentary clinical situations. Beyond these variations, which fall clearly within the classical psychoanalytic framework, lie minor and major *deviations* in technique. Greenson (1958), for example, refers to minor deviations as modifications in technique—necessary and temporary interruptions of the basic procedures and aims of psychoanalysis—and speaks of major deviations as measures that entail "permanent changes in the psychoanalytic method with a consequent renunciation of its results" (p. 200). *Minor deviations* in technique may therefore be defined as consciously intended or inadvertent extensions of the basic psychoanalytic stance that are within such limits for any given patient and analyst that the essential therapeutic relationship and analytic work are not significantly modified, providing that they are recognized, corrected, and the patient's reactions to them analyzed. The ultimate determination of this group of relatively benign deviations, which fall into the gray area between standard technique and extensions which modify it significantly, depends on a careful assessment of the patient's—and analyst's—total reaction to the deviation in question. As I shall show later, patients in analysis and therapy are exquisitely sensitive to these deviations and universally react to them. The issue is whether, by exploring the consequences, such a deviation can be clearly distinguished from a technical error evoked by faulty knowledge and especially by the analyst's countertransference needs, and whether it—in any case—can be worked through so that there is no lasting impairment in the analytic relationship and situation. If this is impossible, then the intervention is best designated a major deviation which has altered to some degree the analysis and its outcome. If the measure was used because of the patient's unmodifiable psychopathology, the intervention may be termed a *parameter* of technique.

Major deviations and parameters clearly transcend the boundaries of the standard psychoanalytic situation. They will usually result in a permanent modification of the patient-analyst relationship and the outcome of the psychoanalytic work. Even when indicated, these deviations always provide considerable inappropriate gratification for the patient and they may affect constructive structural change. It is here that the distinction between necessary parameters and unneeded deviations—technical errors—becomes critical. Since major deviations also generally provide the analyst with momentary gratifications which extend beyond those usually available to him in the analytic situation, the deviation itself may have countertransference-based motives which must be separated from the realistic, patient-oriented indications for the measure.

Turning now to the literature, I shall bypass here a study of Freud's deviations in technique since I have made a separate exploration of them (Langs, in press). The findings, it may be noted, are in keeping with data to be presented here: these deviations have major consequences; the distinction between deviations and technical errors or countertransference-evoked measures is often difficult; the deviations may permanently modify the patient-analyst relationship and compromise the analytic outcome; and they generally evoke strong, regressive responses in the analysand in addition to any positive consequences.

The definitive paper on the subject of parameters was that of Eissler (1953), who, following leads developed by Freud (1937), proposed that our theoretical understanding of the structure of the ego leads us to develop varieties of (deviant) psychoanalytic technique to enhance the ego's achievement of mastery. While he defined standard psychoanalytic technique as one in which interpretations alone are made, he acknowledged the idealization of this model and attempted to modify it in a later paper (Eissler 1958). In his original presentation, he coined the term *parameter* for a technique which he defined as a deviation that is both quantitatively and qualitatively different from the basic model of psychoanalysis, which requires interpretation as an exclusive tool. He stated that such parameters are introduced only when: (1) the basic model of analysis does not suffice in the analytic situation; (2) the alteration never transgresses the unavoidable minimum; (3) its use can finally lead to its self-elimination; and (4) its effects on the patient's transference can be undone by interpretation.

However, Eissler (1953) himself acknowledged possible dangers in the use of parameters. He described three: (1) that the therapeutic process might be falsified so that obedience is substituted for structural change and for the resolution of the corresponding conflicts; (2) that resistances might be temporarily eliminated without having been properly analyzed; and (3) that the concept of parameters might be used to cover an inability to use interpretations properly. In addition, he commented that parameters might have a lasting effect on the patient's transference—one that could not be undone by interpretation. In a later panel discussion (1958) Eissler also raised the point that an analyst might utilize a parameter when an interpretation was feasible and it was not necessary for him to be directive. He introduced the concept of "pseudo-parameters" so that he could include relatively neutral interventions other than interpretations within the framework of classical technique, and indicated that at times these might have interfering qualities, such as, for instance, a gift to the patient.

In the same panel, Loewenstein (1958) pointed out the dangers of modifying psychoanalytic technique in noting these possible consequences: that it may curtail the spontaneous productions of the patient and therefore lead the analyst to misunderstand his unconscious; that interpretation may be minimized and manipulation maximized; and that it may hamper analyzability and jeopardize the transference neurosis. His own discussion centered upon variations in analytic technique rather than clear-cut deviations, although he included several of these as well. He also noted that deviations in technique may occur in many forms, on many levels, and entail a variety of meanings.

Bouvet's (1958) presentation at this panel was based on his particular concepts of object relationships and of the distance between patient and analyst. While recognizing that deviations may be rationalized and actually stem from countertransference problems, he advocated modifications that help to modulate the distance between patient and analyst, thereby fostering the analytic work, and he noted that they must subsequently be eliminated and analyzed.

Reich (1958), in her contribution to this panel, described a special variation of technique in which she utilized strong confrontations regarding an analysand's mother in a manner which was unusual for her, and which she felt conveyed value judgments which went beyond her usual neutrality. This proved necessary with a sadomasochistic, guilt-ridden, acting-out patient who had idealized her mother and had developed an analytic impasse of acting out and acting in, which alternated with unbearable guilt. The devaluation of the patient's mother proved vital to the resolution of this stalemate.

Nacht (1958), in discussing the panel presentation, pointed out that parting from the analyst's neutrality can provide unconscious neurotic satisfactions for the patient; these may become an end in themselves and, as a result, make the transference neurosis unresolvable. On the other hand, rigid neutrality can create the same type of situation by creating a sadomasochistic couple. He suggested that with certain types of patients, after a full countertransference exploration, an abandonment of neutrality is necessary in order to establish the analyst's "presence" and at times in order to provide some type of reality to his relationship with the patient in the form of a reparative gift. He emphasized that he did not mean by this concrete gratification, but primarily a gratifying attitude. Rosenfeld (1958) stated his preference for interpretations rather than parameters.

Frank (1956) stated that every analysis includes moments of advice and injunctions, and he spoke out against ritualism in analytic technique. He described two patients, who appeared to be schizophrenic or severely disturbed, and with whom he used grossly modified analytic techniques. (I shall not examine the use of deviations with such patients here.)

Allen (1956) pointed out that the analyst's wish to "break" or change the basic rules of analysis always creates considerable conflict within him; she emphasized that such decisions should always be based on the needs of the patient's personality. In considering such changes, the analyst inevitably struggles against the introjects of his own analyst, teachers, and parents—his superego figures—and he must

therefore fully analyze within himself both any inappropriate need to comply rigidly with these figures or to rebel against them. She then presented patients with whom she felt that the classical model was creating either stasis or undue emergencies; she found it useful for the progress of the analytic work to modify the use of the couch and to have the patient sit facing her at times.

Lorand (1963) pointed out that complete neutrality is a myth; advice and manipulation are part of every analytic situation. He noted that these can be excessive, reflecting countertransference problems, but presented one patient with whom such advice, in the form of a confrontation with alternatives in reality, appeared to be beneficial. He also offered two vignettes from his supervisory experiences in which deviations in technique were clearly a reflection of countertransference problems and constituted technical errors. Balint (1968) wrote of the difficulties in treating certain types of severe character disorder on borderline patients, and described in a general way the use of certain variations and deviations in analytic technique which, he felt, fostered analytic work with these patients.

Hoedemaker (1960) discussed variations in technique used primarily with delinquent and schizophrenic patients. His emphasis on setting limits as part of the standard analytic technique led him to describe situations in which he ejected patients from analysis and from his office. Stating that such limit-setting fosters healthy identifications, he yet leaves a number of unanswered questions in his discussion of the issue of deviations in technique. Similarly, Rodgers (1965) advocated the parameter of concurrent psychotherapy of the spouse of an analysand by the same analyst in order to overcome a stalemate supported by the spouse, and Calogeras (1967) sanctioned silence and nonadherence to the fundamental rule of free association with a patient who was apparently unable to adhere to this ground rule. They describe pragmatic success with these measures, but the presentations do not permit a thorough study of the reasons the parameter worked as it did—a comment that is pertinent to almost all of the presentations reviewed here.

Greenacre (1959, 1971) generally recommended adherence to basic analytic technique, emphasizing that deviations tend to undermine the patient's autonomy and to create narcissistic alliances (misalliances; see Langs 1975b). Anna Freud (1954a,b) attempted to define the dangers of both inflexibility and excessive flexibility in regard to the technical rules of analysis, and suggested that deviations in these rules are usually "necessary whenever the aspects of a case leads us to expect manifestations of transference or resistance which exceed in force or in malignancy the amounts with which we are able to cope" (1954a, p. 50).

Lastly, Stone (1954, 1961, 1967) has spoken out against rigid adherence to technical rules, including those related to anonymity and the absence of transference gratifications. In a series of complex presentations that are too detailed for full discussion here, he advocates the use of parameters and deviations in technique as long as they bring about the ultimate analytic outcome. Under these conditions they can, he states, usually be deprived of their negative effects on the transference.

While Stone (1961) was reacting primarily to inappropriate rigidities in the clinical stance of many psychoanalysts, the present paper has arisen out of repeated observations that therapists and analysts currently tend all too readily to discard or modify the ground rules and boundaries in their relationship with their parents. The concept of parameters is often used to justify countertransference-based interventions and technical errors. In the literature, these issues are discussed without the specific study of clinical data (a striking feature of the literature). Often there is a failure to recognize the far-reaching and universal effects of all variations in technique—correct or erroneous—on their patients (Langs 1973b).

In general, there have been many additional reasons offered to justify temporary deviations in technique. The purported or expected effects are too often taken at face value, while the latent and implicit content and meanings of the deviation and its consequences are ignored. Deviations have been advocated to enhance the therapeutic alliance, to express the "real" relationship between patient and therapist, to lessen the deprivation inherent in analysis and therapy, to promote the therapeutic relationship, to avoid unnecessary frustration of the patient, to avoid a trauma that the patient will not be able to tolerate, to make the therapist seem more human, and to demonstrate his flexibility. The far-reaching effects of deviations per se are relatively neglected, as is the basic psychoanalytic methodology of probing the meanings of the analyst's interventions and the patient's responses to them rather than confining one's considerations to preconceived theories or to naive, surface-oriented assessments of manifest meanings and reactions (see Kanzer 1975).

As noted, Bleger's contribution (1967) is along different lines. Taking as his starting point Winnicott's definition (1958) of the analytic setting as the summation of all of the details of management,

Bleger considers the total psychoanalytic relationship and defines the frame of this relationship as non-process, made up of constants within whose bounds the process of analysis takes place. He then focuses on the silently maintained protective elements in the frame and the necessity of their ultimate analysis, relating that frame to the concept of institutions that are viewed as contributing to the individual's identity. It is invariable and nonpalpable, and Bleger therefore postulates that it is related to the most primitive and undifferentiated psychic organization out of which the ego is built, and that it has a strong basis in the bodily ego and in the early symbiosis between mother and child. The frame therefore contains the symbiotic elements of the patient-analyst relationship and acts as a support and mainstay, interfering only when it changes or breaks.

Modifications in the frame may occur at the patient's behest and compliance by the analyst repeats the neurotic interaction of the patient's childhood. However, when the frame is respected, the repetition does not occur, and this brings out and makes available for analysis the most permanent elements in the patient's personality, viewed by Bleger as his psychotic core.

Bleger also suggests that the patient brings his own frame—in the institution of his primitive, symbiotic relatedness—to the analytic situation. On the one hand, the patient may attempt to have the analyst modify the frame in order to create a sense of magical union with him and to evoke a magical cure; on the other, any break or variation in the frame, necessary or unnecessary, induced by the analyst, is disruptive and creates a catastrophic situation for the patient, bringing the "non-ego" to a crisis, contradicting the fusion, challenging the ego, and compelling ego changes and defenses. Moreover, the frame may become a kind of addiction if it is not systematically analyzed, leading to a false ego development without internal stability. While the analyst must initially accept the frame that the patient brings to the analysis and the primitive symbiosis that it contains, Bleger suggests that he should not bend his own frame, since it is through that vehicle that he is able to analyze the disturbance within the patient and to transform the frame itself into useful processes for the patient. Any patient-analyst relationship outside this strict frame enables the psychotic transference to be concealed; instead, there develops a facade which he terms *the psychoanalytic character*. Since the frame is viewed as the most primitive fusion with the mother's body, Bleger feels that the psychoanalyst's frame helps reestablish the original symbiosis as a step toward modifying it. In all, then, for Bleger the psychoanalytic setting or frame—the ground rules and boundaries—contributes to the deepest levels of the patient-therapist interaction and may have profound effects on the patient.

SOME POSTULATES

This brings me now to the results of a re-examination of my own earlier observations in this area (Langs 1973a,b, 1974). It is evident to me that every patient has an identifiable, predictable, and intense response to the slightest deviation in the framework of the therapeutic relationship. A careful investigation of responses to such interventions reveals that these measures have extensive meanings and consequences for the patient, and makes clear the inherent and silent meanings of the therapeutic framework itself, as well as the implications of altering it. Before presenting additional clinical material, I shall therefore briefly list the main meanings of this framework, the basic consequences of deviations from it, and techniques for modifying detrimental consequences and fostering positive effects in such deviations.

1. The manner in which the therapist delineates and explicates the ground rules and boundaries of the therapeutic relationship significantly reflects his identity as a therapist, and his resolution and management of his own intrapsychic conflicts and inner needs.

(a) Modifications that are not specifically and clearly indicated by the therapeutic needs and pathology of the patient will reflect intrapsychic disturbances—countertransference problems—within the therapist. In so doing, they convey important unconscious meanings.

(b) This framework is the basic vehicle for the therapeutic "hold" which provides the stability, security, and boundaries necessary for the patient properly to relate and communicate in the therapeutic situation.

(c) It is also the backdrop onto which the patient projects his intrapsychic fantasies—the transference dimension—and is one factor that influences the specific timing and nature of these projections and their extensions in interactions with the therapist.

2. Proper maintenance of the framework of the therapeutic relationship provides the patient constructive interactional experiences which lead to positive, ego-enhancing, inner-structural changes through incorporative identification with the positive qualities of the therapist. Such changes are to be distinguished from the structural effects of interpretations, though they contribute to and interact with them.

3. The maintenance of proper therapeutic boundaries in response to inappropriate efforts by the patient to evoke deviations—an important type of behavioral transference expression—or in the face of the therapist's own inappropriate needs to modify them, is one means through which the therapist avoids pathogenic interactions with the patient that repeat his—and the therapist's—past pathogenic object relationships within the therapeutic situation. This fosters experiential modification of such relatedness, the development of analyzable expression of the related unconscious fantasies and memories, and avoids therapeutic misalliances (Langs 1975b).

4. The proper maintenance of the boundaries of the therapeutic relationship is essential not only for maximal projection of the patient's intrapsychic pathological fantasies (transference), but is also vital for the greatest effectiveness of the therapist's interpretations, which will be undermined or modified if the therapist's management behavior has evoked a negative image of himself, one that fosters negative and traumatic incorporative identifications, and unconscious needs in the patient to defend himself against the therapist's communications.

5. Because they fall into the realm of behavior, the management of the boundaries of the relationship must be secure for verbal interventions to convey their intended meanings and to have their greatest insight-producing effects.

6. Deviations in technique evoke intense reactions because of their actual unconscious meanings, which are elaborated in the patient's own needs and fantasies. Such reactions may include interference with the most basic hold and necessary symbiotic ties offered by the therapist to the patient, and shifts in the more mature sectors of relatedness between the two. Deviations alter the boundaries between patient and therapist, arousing issues of failure to maintain separate identities, incest barriers, and the like. Deviations by the therapist may also reflect impairment in both sexual and aggressive, instinctual-drive–discharge management.

7. All deviations in technique, regardless of the indications for them, entail inappropriate gratifications for both therapist and patient. The extent and specific unconscious meanings of such gratification must be recognized and ultimately analyzed. Whenever a deviation in technique is undertaken without clearcut indication, the first step must be to modify

the deviation in reality. Those deviations that are clearly indicated must also eventually be retracted as far as possible. Only thus can verbal analysis of the consequences of a deviation for the patient be carried out to the fullest.

8. Deviations in technique may reflect and evoke modifications in the psychoanalytic relationship and process that are lasting and unmodifiable through verbal interventions. Especially if they are not recognized, they create sectors of therapeutic misalliance and compromise the therapeutic outcome. Even when recognized, those deviations that have been undertaken out of the therapist's countertransference needs may leave a lasting—and often incorporated— image of the therapist, derived from the patient's conscious and unconscious realistic perceptions, and from its subsequent intrapsychic extensions within himself, in terms of his own psychopathology, unconscious fantasies, intrapsychic conflicts, past and present object relationships, and other inner factors.

9. Deviations in technique of all kinds, therefore, lead to intense adaptive responses, often rather pervasive and productive on the part of the patient. The specific meaning of this material, however, can be properly understood and analyzed only if the deviation itself is recognized as the major adaptive context and organizing factor in the patient's reactions and communications, and constructive inner change will follow only if the meaning of the deviation is fully analyzed, and the boundaries to the relationship properly restored.

10. Many deviations in technique are not undertaken primarily because of the patient's needs, but are rationalizations of the extensive countertransference gratifications they offer the therapist. In so doing, therapists neglect the ego-strengthening factors and structural reinforcements that are inherent in the firm maintenance of proper and clear-cut boundaries and ground rules. Also missed are the anxiety-provoking and disruptive aspects inherent in the therapist's failure to maintain these much-needed boundaries.

11. My cumulative observations suggest— although I shall not pursue this in detail here—that deviations and parameters in techniques should be limited to clear-cut emergencies and to those relatively rare clinical situations in which the genetic basis and unconscious fantasies maintaining the patient's ego dysfunctions have been thoroughly analyzed, the therapist's countertransference has been carefully subjected to self-analysis and controlled as a disturbing factor, and a stalemate based on the patient's ego dysfunctions appears to be present. Before deviating, a full consideration of all other disturbing factors should be made, since problems within the therapist and with his technique are often more important to the stalemate than is the psychopathology of the patient.

12. Therapists who tend to deviate in technique once will tend to do so again. In addition, patients who are successful in evoking deviations in technique from their therapists will endeavor to evoke further deviations. There is a strong tendency for patients to accept the therapeutic misalliances inherent in such deviations as a means of temporarily affording themselves symptom relief without structural change (Langs 1975b), and for therapists to maintain such misalliances for their own inappropriate reasons as well.

13. Once evoked, any deviation in technique must be a primary adaptive and therapeutic context (Langs 1973b) for subsequent listening and analytic work. Their residual manifestations must be modified so that the boundaries and ground rules are restored to the relationship, and the patient's reaction to the deviation itself and to its subsequent elimination is fully explored and resolved.

14. Unconsciously, patients will often initially accept the therapeutic misalliance evoked by a deviation in technique because of the momentary relief and the neurotic gratification which it offers, but they will also subsequently attempt to modify the misalliance and help the therapist restore the proper boundaries in seeking lasting symptom relief (Langs 1975b). In their search for ultimate conflict resolution through inner structural change, they make unconscious efforts to alert the therapist to the presence of the deviation and to their unconscious understanding of the inner basis within the therapist for the deviation he has evoked. Patients also make efforts that I have described elsewhere (Langs 1975b) as "unconscious interpretations" designed to help the therapist resolve the countertransference problems which led to his deviation. However, recognition of the detrimental consequences of an unneeded deviation in technique is primarily the responsibility of the therapist, who should assess his use of a deviation through a close study of the patient's reactions and of his own subjective state.

15. In general, then, in those circumstances where the therapist formulates the need for a deviation in technique because of some emergency with the patient, an otherwise unresolvable stalemate, or the need to respond in a human and unusual manner under extraordinary conditions, he should counterbalance his assessment of the indications for the deviation with a full anticipation of the possible

negative consequences. Only such an assessment can lead to a final conclusion that will restrict deviations to those that are truly constructive to the therapeutic relationship and outcome.

This is a rather lengthy list of basic principles, and their many ramifications cannot be fully discussed in this paper. In order to illustrate their validity and to briefly discuss some of their main implications, let us turn now to a few representative vignettes.

CLINICAL MATERIAL

Mr. A. was a young man with a severe character disorder, in twice-weekly psychotherapy for a severe depression that followed the suicide of an older sister who had terminated her psychotherapy just weeks before her death. In addition, he was confused about his goals in life, seriously concerned about again becoming a homosexual, and disturbed over his inability to find a suitable marriage partner. His parents had had a stormy marriage and were divorced, and another sibling, a brother, was divorced and having emotional problems.

From the outset, the treatment, which I occasionally supervised, did not go well. The therapist had considerable difficulty in understanding his patient, especially his underlying conflicts and fantasies, and his interventions tended to be naive and inaccurate. The patient had responded with a great deal of open resentment, with questions about the efficacy of therapy, and with occasional absences. There was considerable evidence that he had quickly joined the therapist in a misalliance with bilateral obsessional, sadomasochistic, and latent homosexual qualities, one that he alternately accepted and attempted to modify (Langs 1975b).

In the sessions prior to those that we will study here, Mr. A. had been questioning the frequency of his hours and was worried that he would not get any help in his treatment. He had had an argument with a male cousin who had referred him for therapy and described a variety of fantasies about leaving treatment; he had been depressed. Without available derivatives, the therapist had attempted to relate this depression to the death of Mr. A.'s sister. The material actually pointed strongly both to feelings of hopelessness regarding the therapeutic situation and to rage at the therapist as the underlying factors in this symptom—an assessment that was made in supervision. In response to the therapist's intervention, the patient spoke in considerable detail of the manner in which his mother never accepted

responsibility for failures in their family—a comment that reflected a rather sensitive, indirect unconscious perception of the therapist's difficulties.

In the next session, the patient described feeling exceptionally well, although the previous day had been his sister's birthday and he had been quite depressed; he had thought of calling the therapist. He ruminated about fears of becoming dependent on the therapist and about the guilt that the therapist had suggested he had experienced in regard to the death of his sister. When the therapist commented that Mr. A. seemed to have difficulties in discussing certain feelings with him, the patient complained about the therapist's coldness and likened him to a fellow with whom he had lived and with whom he had frequently quarreled. He thought of changing therapists; he felt that they were getting nowhere, and yet he feared offending the therapist. He recalled that when he got mad at his father, he was beaten, and when he was angry with his mother, she would cry; as a result, he always controlled his anger with other people.

Mr. A. arrived for his next session, which was early on a Saturday morning, in the midst of a snowstorm. The therapist began the hour by asking Mr. A. how the driving had been, and the patient responded that it had been pretty bad; in turn, he asked the therapist if he had had difficulties driving to his office. The therapist said that he lived nearby, within walking distance of his office, and the patient fell silent. Next, he said that he felt quite shy. He had seen his father and had discussed his sister's suicide; he had decided not to visit his father again. He did not hate him, but rather felt sorry for him; he then thought of the snow falling on his sister's grave.

The therapist commented that he seemed preoccupied with his sister, and the patient said that he felt guilty and that he also did not want to see his mother again. With her, he gave the peace sign but inside he was full of hate. His mother had gone to the West Coast because his brother had been ill, but the situation was not serious and it was an unnecessary trip. It would have been better if she had stayed with her sister, who was quite ill, and if she had given better care to the daughter she had lost. His parents had a way of tearing their children to pieces; he then thought of the manner in which his sister had died. He was afraid that if he told his mother he didn't want to see her, she would go crazy, but felt if he didn't say something, he would go crazy.

At this point, the therapist chose to convey to the patient some information regarding his mother that he had taken from the assessment interview carried out by another therapist in the clinic in which the patient was being seen; this related to an apparent psychotic depression and hospitalization which the patient's mother had gone through after Mr. A.'s birth. The patient said that he really ought to find out more about what happened and that he had not heard from his mother for several days; she would disappear on purpose so that everybody would fear that she had killed herself. Sometimes things that he himself said led people to be afraid that he would kill himself, but he had no recollection of making such remarks. He had some fear that his mother might commit suicide and that somehow he would be blamed.

To discuss briefly the material to this point, we may identify the first deviation in technique as the therapist's revelation to the patient that he lived near the clinic—a modification in his relative anonymity. Despite this deviation's human qualities, it was predicted in supervision that it would be experienced by the patient as a homosexual gift and seduction offered as compensation for the therapist's failure adequately to intervene and as an attempt to undo his unresolved hostilities toward Mr. A. It appeared to reflect a homosexual countertransference problem in the therapist, one that existed beyond any technical confusion on his part. As supervisor, I anticipated that it would evoke homosexual longings and anxious suicidal fantasies, and that the patient would seek out further deviations in order both to gratify his own neurotic unconscious fantasies and needs, and to reinforce the defensive misalliance. Along other lines, however, he would also attempt to assist the therapist in reestablishing the boundaries of their relationship and in modifying the therapist's unresolved countertransference difficulties.

In view of these predictions, we may note that the patient had responded to the therapist's self-revelation with a period of silence and a feeling of shyness—an initial withdrawal reaction, and an effort to reestablish distance and appropriate boundaries (this may also be an unconscious suggestion to the therapist that he be less open). There followed allusions to his sister's suicide and thoughts of not wanting to see his father again. Implied here are feelings of rage toward his father who, he felt, had contributed to his sister's suicide, and a sense of compassion for him—feelings, in the present adaptive context, that are displaced from the therapist. Next comes the thought of not seeing his mother—another effort to create distance—and then the comment that the patient gives the sign of peace but is full of hate inside. This reflects in part an incorporative identification with the angry and somewhat destructive therapist. It also conveys a sensitive,

unconscious recognition that the deviation in technique was meant in part as a peace offering (the therapist spoke of it to me as an attempt to further the failing therapeutic alliance), that it was an attempt by the therapist to deny his countertransference anger.

The next associations reflect the patient's unconscious recognition of the deviation as a misguided effort on the part of the therapist—as was that of his mother—to offer an expression of concern; the patient also comments that such efforts should find more appropriate expression. I consider these associations a valuable commentary, one that is generally applicable to therapists' misguided efforts to reinforce the therapeutic alliance through deviations in technique, rather than through the more appropriate channels of correct interventions leading to valid interpretations and a proper maintenance of the therapeutic boundaries. The latter avoid mutual acting out of transference-countertransference fantasies—misalliances—and their consequences. In his own way, the patient went on to describe the manner in which such unfortunate efforts only tear their patients to pieces, and how they will, in patients so predisposed, evoke suicidal fantasies and reactions, rather than constructive inner change.

It is in this latter material that we begin to see some of the specific intrapsychic elaborations and unconscious meaning that the deviation in technique has evoked in Mr. A. Despite the emphasis in this paper on the actual detrimental unconscious meanings and implications of unneeded deviations in technique—the kernel of truth—we should not overlook the manner in which these veridical perceptions and experiences are then processed through the patient's own intrapsychic pathology and adaptive resources. Each patient will respond to deviations in technique in a manner that reflects both the broader general meanings of the deviation and their highly specific implications for him.

The next associations reflect the dilemma in which the patient is placed when faced with an unnecessary deviation in technique: on the one hand, if he attempts to reestablish the boundaries, he will create anxiety in the therapist, who has been unable to tolerate the necessary deprivation required by the therapeutic situation, and who has failed to maintain his own intrapsychic integration and to renounce his inappropriate instinctual drives. On the other hand, however, if he fails to assist the therapist in reestablishing the proper framework to their relationship, the patient himself will be under pressure. Through the perception of this disturbance in the therapist and through incorporative identification with him, this aspect of the deviation threatens the structural balances and mental integrity of the patient as well.

In keeping with my previous observation that the therapist who deviates once will be prone to repeat, we find that the therapist at this point in the session introduced information that he had obtained from an extratherapeutic source—the assessment notes. This brings to the fore a third party to the therapy, bypasses the associations, and is introduced solely in terms of the therapist's need to present it. On the basis of my discussion with this therapist, I speculated that this was an attempt to deflect the focus away from the patient-therapist interaction and an unconscious effort to create a situation in which the patient, rather than himself, would be disturbed. Mr. A. responded with a reference to his mother's disappearance and her intention that others be concerned with her suicide. This may be viewed as an unconscious perception of the therapist's insensitivities; it also conveys the patient's own suicidal feelings and hostility toward the therapist. Mr. A.'s subsequent allusion to his not remembering something that he was purported to have said may be viewed as a response to the therapist's use of material that was drawn from outside sources. As the session ended, we sense the patient's mounting rage at the therapist and the possibility of its being turned inward.

Briefly, in the following hour, the patient began by saying that his mother had turned up and seemed to be well. The cousin who had referred Mr. A. to therapy had exposed himself to the patient, and this had led Mr. A. to feel dominant; the cousin had confessed a whole series of personal troubles that he was having with his wife and daughter. The therapist suggested that this reflected Mr. A.'s concern over the fact that he—the therapist—had revealed something about himself in the previous hour. The patient heartily agreed, adding that he felt that the therapist was in love with him in the previous hour, as if they were two women; he had felt that he was about to become the dominant one because the therapist was losing his objectivity. Mr. A.'s associations then went on to his concerns about becoming a homosexual and a fantasy of being dominated homosexually by a huge black man who had become his lover. He had thought of calling the therapist soon after the previous hour because he was in a panic over his mother's absence, but he was afraid he would evoke a panic in the therapist.

We see from this material that the patient's view of the deviations in technique contains some validity and some intrapsychic elaboration. In response to the therapist's correct intervention, Mr. A. revealed his impression that the therapist was involved homosexually with him, that he had lost his objectivity, and that he had reacted out of anxiety. These conscious and unconscious interpretations are clearly shaped by the patient's own homosexual anxieties and conflicts; they cannot, however, simply be dismissed as reflecting them since there is considerable evidence that the deviation in technique had indeed reflected the therapist's own unresolved homosexual countertransference.

In the next hour, Mr. A. reported that he had clarified the facts of his mother's early illness. He recalled being teased by a delivery man as a child and spoke of a childhood injury that had been misdiagnosed by a doctor who had believed that there had been some brain damage, although this was subsequently ruled out. He recalled a few sessions with a psychiatrist during his college years in which the therapist directed him to avoid his father and told the patient that he was retarded. He then spoke of his mother's concerns; she had arranged for the patient to have a nevus removed although it turned out there was nothing wrong with it.

In this session, we may recognize unconscious attempts by the patient to alert the therapist to his technical errors and erroneous deviations in technique, and to call to his attention his need to manipulate and to underestimate the patient's capacities. In addition to the themes of doctor's mistakes and of unnecessary therapeutic measures, the material reflects an incorporative identification with the therapist, who is behaving in a somewhat incompetent manner.

The hour had been concluded with an allusion to how the patient himself had been a likable and bright little child. This reflects, in part, Mr. A.'s continued mixed image of the therapist. It is based largely on the fact that the latter had made a correct intervention, but had not been able to follow it up with additional interpretations and with a specific reestablishment of the proper boundaries of the therapeutic relationship.

The patient began the next hour by telling the therapist that he had confessed some of his homosexual fantasies to his cousin, who seemed more favorably inclined toward him after that revelation. The patient had dreamt that his mouth was stuffed with sand and that someone's head was cut off. The therapist immediately asked for thoughts about the dream and whether there was any additional content to it, and Mr. A. said that it reminded him of fellatio and of a teenage homosexual experience. The stuffed head reminded him of his need to keep his feelings back; he then spoke of some suicidal feelings that he had had some months ago. The therapist said that he was trying to express his feelings and the patient agreed, adding that he did not want to kill himself. He remembered getting attention when he was injured in his childhood.

In the following hour, the patient spoke of how strange the early Saturday morning session seemed, and he reviewed the events that led to his sister's suicide. The therapist intervened and suggested that the patient was afraid of going crazy and was trying to disrupt his relationships by revealing his homosexual conflicts to his cousin. The patient disagreed, stating that it was all right to be crazy and that one should accept his imperfections. He then told the therapist that he had joined a choir and had been singing a great deal, asking the therapist if he had a good voice and inquiring into the therapist's religion. He also wondered if treatment could be extended beyond the one-year deadline established by clinic policy and said that he had thought of calling the therapist, but had been afraid that the therapist would be angry.

In these two sessions, the relationship between the material and the deviation in technique is less clear. The associations reflect the patient's unconscious awareness of the homosexual misalliance, and suggests both a wish to participate in it, and rage at himself and the therapist because of it. There appears to be a fear of losing control and a dread of excessive guilt that might evoke a suicidal reaction. Finally there are a number of additional efforts by the patient to extend the boundaries of the relationship and further to modify the therapist's anonymity; the therapist neither complied nor attempted to confront or interpret these efforts.

The patient began the next hour by asking the therapist if he was a psychiatrist, since he was so young. The therapist explained his status as a trainee in the clinic, and the patient said that he had really wanted someone older, who could be the ideal mother he had never had. The therapist intervened, stating that the patient seemed to feel that he was not an ideal therapist; Mr. A. agreed that this was so. He was wondering if he could seduce the therapist and saw the therapist as being very much like his mother, who would get upset when others revealed themselves. He could remember wanting to sleep with his mother and using girlfriends to cover over these wishes. He was afraid there would be a crisis in treatment and he would have to leave it even though he shouldn't do so.

In this hour, we discover that the therapist had not resolved the countertransference problems that had prompted him to reveal information regarding himself and that quite without rational purpose he

had revealed his status in the clinic. The patient responded with disappointment; he saw the therapist as a poor mother and as someone who could be seduced. He then offered an unconscious interpretation to the effect that the therapist was upset when his patients revealed thoughts about themselves, thereby suggesting that the therapist's self-revelations were unconsciously designed to deflect focus from these disturbing revelations from his patient. This latest deviation in technique, one that the patient sought out, is also unconsciously viewed and interpreted to the therapist by the patient as an incestuous seduction, based on unresolved incestuous conflicts in the therapist. These interventions to the therapist are, of course, once again intermixed with the patient's own intrapsychic fantasies and conflicts. These seductive deviations evoked thoughts of flight from therapy, accompanied by wishes to remain.

In the next hour, the patient began by saying that he was furious that the therapist told him when to end their sessions. He was also furious with his cousin, who had revealed additional personal facts about his life. Mr. A. had had a dream in which he was in a small town and being hassled by the police. There was a black man in a fancy foreign car and the people wanted him to go on the radio. There also was a black boxer who had been on television as an entertainer, and the patient asked him for a ride out of town to West Virginia. The man agreed but said that he was going to Alaska. They were on the road and there was a huge oil truck behind them that honked to pass them. The patient felt that the people from town were after them. The truck passed and the car broke down; the man said that it was all right to go fishing. They pulled off the road and did so.

In his associations, the patient recalled a time that he and a homosexual friend had been briefly put into jail for petty thievery. He spoke of some foreign students who were extremely incompetent and knew nothing about anything; they thought he was a snob because he looked down upon them, but he felt that it was realistic since he had more experience.

The therapist pointed out that the patient seemed to be angry at him, since had had told him that he was a trainee at the clinic, and that the patient viewed him as incompetent. The patient said that he had been wondering how competent the therapist actually was and that he felt that in therapy he had to do most of the work. Nonetheless, he felt that the two of them could grow together and he wanted to stay with the therapist beyond the one-year limit. He had the impression that the therapist did not read enough, and recalled a fantasy of screaming at the therapist and calling him names. He somehow saw the therapist as overintellectual, unfeeling, of a different religion than himself, and as a momma's boy; he felt guilty telling the therapist these things and was afraid of hurting his feelings.

It is of interest that the patient begins this hour by expressing anger over the way in which the therapist established one of the boundaries of treatment—the length of the session. From this, we see that the boundaries of the therapeutic relationship and setting are very much on his mind, and next we learn again of his anger toward those who reveal too much about themselves. Lacking extensive associations to the dream, we may speculate that it reflects the patient's unconscious perception of the therapist's need to exhibit himself, perceptions and acceptance of the homosexual misalliance offered by the therapist through the deviation, and a sense of absurdity regarding the therapeutic situation in which the therapist was having difficulty in maintaining the boundaries. In addition, we see that the therapist's deviations offered a momentary "misalliance cure" (Langs 1975b) in that the patient felt, appropriately to some extent, that he was more competent than his therapist and that he was in a position to teach a great deal to the therapist so that they could grow together. It is in this context that he wanted to yell at the therapist and then confronted him with some of his difficulties, indirectly suggesting that they were based in part on the therapist's conflicts with his mother.

Mr. A. was late to the next hour and said that his brother was feeling better but was on tranquilizers. The patient had planned a business trip for the following week, one that would interrupt the therapy; he had not told the therapist because he felt that he would be annoyed and ask him to stay. He asked the therapist his diagnosis and speculated that he was manic-depressive. He liked the idea of that diagnosis because he could do anything he wanted. He asked the therapist if he liked traveling and the therapist, in turn, asked the patient for his thoughts. Mr. A. spoke of leaving the area and treatment; he thought of going to Australia, where people were closer, and of finding a girlfriend. The therapist spoke of Mr. A.'s wish to be close to people, including himself, and of the difficulty that Mr. A. seemed to be having in taking a trip that would entail two missed sessions. The patient said that he would like to be closer to the therapist and would like to get to know him because the therapist's failure to answer his questions made him feel that it wasn't a human relationship and that he was being put in a box without any concern. He told the therapist to enjoy sleeping late while he was away and then missed the next two hours.

To discuss this hour, we may suggest that the patient attempted to establish boundaries on his own, by missing two sessions, in part to fend off his seductive therapist and in part out of his fears of his own reactions to the therapist. Mr. A.'s speculation as to his underlying illness is an unconscious reflection of his concerns about the therapist, and the subsequent association to using the diagnosis as an excuse for doing anything that he wants to do tentatively touches upon the therapist's status as a trainee who can justify behaving carelessly. His further associations indicate that the missed hours are an acting out of fantasies of termination, and the hour concludes with a mixture of the patient's longings to join the therapist in a latent homosexual misalliance and his continued wishes to establish reasonable boundaries—the box—as well. It is of interest that the patient complained that the therapist did not answer his questions, while the latent material indicates that he had been deeply disturbed by the fact that the therapist had, indeed, done so.

Very briefly, upon his return the patient began his hour by expressing a fear that the therapist would not be there. He spoke of a movie that he had seen while he was away, in which an extremely self-centered man promiscuously made love to many different women. The therapist commented that the patient seemed conflicted about returning and was afraid of getting to close to him, and Mr. A. agreed, saying that he had had an image during his absence of begging the therapist not to seduce him. He directly asked if the therapist intended to seduce him and stated that he did not want another lover, but that he just wanted someone who understood him and knew what conflicts about homosexuality are like. The therapist intervened, telling the patient that his sexual feelings toward him had apparently intensified because of the self-revelations he had made, adding that this seemed to be interfering with his talking in the sessions and with others. Mr. A. responded that his homosexual feelings did seriously interfere with his relations with men, and he illustrated this with a man he had met on his trip.

In the next hour, the patient felt considerably better and expressed gratitude toward the therapist, stating that for the first time he could see the therapist as a real person who understood him. He had told his cousin of his homosexual fantasies toward the therapist and this had terrified the cousin, who was afraid of such things. He then went on to describe how he had once tried to seduce a very close friend, who had refused him, and he then spoke further about the death of his sister.

This material begins with a further unconscious perception of the therapist's difficulties and emphasizes the seductive aspects of his deviations in technique. The patient's actual fear of being seduced strongly reflects his own psychopathology, including some degree of difficulty in reality testing and his extensive homosexual conflicts. On the other hand, his statement about not wanting another lover—the therapist—but just someone who understands him, is a poignant expression of the specific need of every patient in psychotherapy: inappropriate love repeats past neurotic interactions and reinforces the neurosis; reasonable "love" in the form of concern offers a positive identification; but only insightful understanding leading to interpretations can promote lasting, adaptive, inner change based on conflict resolution.

In this session, the therapist made a sensitive and correct intervention which the patient confirmed to some extent in his recollection of his meeting with another man during his trip. In the following hour we then see the indications of a positive incorporative identification with the therapist, who was now viewed as attempting to establish appropriate boundaries—a close friend who refused to be seduced. The patient remained concerned that the therapist is frightened of his own and the patient's homosexuality. We see, too, that he continues to struggle with his own anxieties regarding the therapist's self-revelations, and the unconscious homosexual perceptions and fantasies they had stirred up within him.

Before drawing together some general inferences from this material about both psychotherapeutic and psychoanalytic technique, I shall supplement this vignette in two ways: by offering a brief summary of reactions to deviations in technique in patients presented elsewhere and by offering a brief vignette from the psychoanalytic literature to establish the fact that comparable responses occur in patients in psychoanalysis when their analysts deviate from the basic ground rules. The following vignettes typify the material already presented in my book, *The Technique of Psychoanalytic Psychotherapy* (Langs 1973b, 1974):

Mr. S.W. (1973b, pp. 539–551) was advised by his therapist that his homosexual fantasies and anxieties were being stirred up by sharing a bedroom with his mother, and it was suggested to him that he sleep elsewhere. The following themes were most striking in this patient's reaction, one that occupied him over a period of many weeks: fears of excessive dependency; the therapist as a god who must be refuted; a dream in which his father is dead and that, in context, reflected murderous wishes toward the therapist, who was attempting to control the patient; references to lying; an allusion to how people intruded into his bathroom and permitted him no privacy in his house; his father looking at his pubic hair; mutual exhibitionism with his sister; references to the fact that the therapist could be missing something; a homosexual attraction to a coworker which led to direct homosexual fantasies about the therapist; anger at his father who told him what to do; a dream of someone who killed everybody, which was directly associated to the therapist's telling this patient what to do. Further themes included a homosexual advance made by the patient to someone else and additional intense homosexual fantasies toward the therapist; a fantasy of the therapist attempting homosexual penetration but being impotent; fantasies of mutual fellatio; having intercourse with a woman since he could not have relations with the therapist; and a revelation that the patient had fantasied that the therapist was telling him not to be interested in women, but to be interested in him.

We begin to see common themes in the patient's unconscious perceptions of unneeded deviations in technique, their unconscious meanings, and the manner in which they are then elaborated upon in the patient's own psychopathology. With Mr. S.W. this included extensive latent homosexual conflicts and their vicissitudes.

Mrs. H.Y. (Langs 1973b, pp. 202–204) reacted to her therapist's holding her up as she fell while leaving a session with unanalyzed associations to the manner in which her mother had frightened her regarding heights and bodily injury, references to a psychotic uncle, threats of leaving treatment, missed sessions, direct and indirect allusions to the therapist's being unaware of things, a repetition of the falling behavior, to which the therapist did not respond with assistance, allusions to her own problems with anger and the ways in which she avoids problems, and references to her husband as a reckless driver.

In contrast, Miss B. (Langs 1973b, p. 417), whose therapist did not accept a gift, reacted to the establishment of these boundaries by developing a new relationship that was far less destructive than her previous relationships had been. In brief, this last response reflects the kinds of positive incorporative identifications that follow from the appropriate maintenance of the ground rules and boundaries of the therapeutic relationship, a subject I will not pursue in any detail in this paper.

A paper by Gudeman (1974) describes a clinical vignette pertinent to this presentation. In brief, the material relates to a married woman, the mother of two children, who came to analysis because of frigidity and a poor marriage. In her analysis, there was an initial flood of instinctualized material and a description of her kleptomania after her grandfather died, her masturbatory practices, and the recall of a seduction by an older man in her early adolescence; though no sexual intimacy had occurred, the patient had felt guilty, since she had contributed to what had happened.

While in the opening months of the treatment, following the description of the death of her grandfather, the patient came early to a session carrying a bouquet of flowers. While the analyst saw that she was living out the wish for a wedding, he accepted the flowers with some discomfort and said nothing immediately. He knew that the acceptance of the gift could enhance the erotic components of the "transference," but he felt that rejection of it would mobilize separation, anxiety and anger beyond the patient's ability to understand and analyze. He also viewed the gift as a possible harbinger of fragile ego boundaries and a reflection of significant regressive potential. His goal in accepting the gift was to foster the therapeutic alliance and to prevent undue regression.

In the session, after giving her gift, the patient spoke of wanting to be loved by her analyst and wanting him to be her father. She wanted to know his first name and the analyst responded that it would be of most use to talk about these feelings and not always useful to give him a present, although she might want to do so. The patient was angry when the analyst did not give her a pat on the head.

Later on, when her husband was away, the patient brought her children to the waiting room. At another time, she gave her analyst tobacco as a present, having had a gynecological examination on the previous day. Other material demonstrated that the patient had set up a triangular situation in which the analyst was the loving, good person who could provide her gratification, while the husband was seen as withholding and hostile.

After nine months of treatment, the patient took a one-week vacation (we are not informed as to whether she was held responsible for these sessions). Then, a month after the analyst's summer vacation, the patient brought in a request from her husband that the analyst write a letter justifying a vasectomy for him because of his wife's emotional illness. In associating to this request, the patient said that she preferred that it be done, since it would eliminate the problem of her being a woman or having her own tubes tied. The analyst eventually indicated that there was no psychiatric basis for such a letter and that he would not write it. The patient responded by saying that she could then have another child and cut it into little pieces. She felt pleased and disappointed, as if the analyst had taken something away from her. She probably thought that she could get him to write the letter and felt that her husband would be cross with her but would survive.

Soon after, the patient dreamt that she was in a bathroom where there were toilets for deaf and blind people. She felt exposed and there was a younger man being seduced by an older woman. She came to the analyst's office and the analyst told her, "That's it," and the patient sat up and they ended up talking. An intervention that the dream indicated that the analyst was not hearing or seeing something led to associations about her not getting away with the vasectomy request, but little else.

There followed fears that the analyst would abandon her and then a phone call from her husband because the patient was disturbed. In the next session, she appeared psychotic and, in a disorganized way, she spoke of taking a knife to herself, of her father beating her, of her grandfather teaching her to masturbate, of lies, of being seduced by the analyst, of masturbating, of blaming the analyst, and of secrets. The analyst became more active and in subsequent sessions, the patient brought in a long biographical sketch, and she spoke of dead babies and being raped by her father and everyone. When the patient did not respond well one particular session, the analyst called her by telephone and had her return that day, seeing her in the sitting position. He decribed to the patient his sense of confusion and medicated her, and over the following several days the patient became calmer.

In confining my discussion of this vignette to the question of deviations in technique, we can see that central to this patient's psychotic episode was a series of deviations in technique, rationalized by the analyst on the basis of promoting the therapeutic alliance and the wish to avoid so-called undue regression, that apparently remained relatively unanalyzed with the patient. They evoked in her intense wishes for erotic gratification from the analyst, desires to modify a number of other boundaries in the relationship, and the offer of further gifts to him. The sequence culminated in the request that the analyst justify the vasectomy for the husband, and when the analyst now modified his stance and attempted to establish that particular boundary, a psychotic episode followed.

In dealing with the dream that was reported at this time, the analyst chose to allude to the possible representations of his deafness and blindness, but apparently missed the other communications (both perceptions and fantasies), thereby confirming the very unconscious perception that he was attempting to clarify. As we have already seen, the dream contains elements characteristic in communications from patients when they are adapting to deviations in technique. It was undoubtedly prompted by the change in the therapist's stance, which the patient perceived as a reflection of his own unconscious guilt and anxieties regarding the extent to which he had permitted the patient to seduce him. In a manner that is typical of reactions to technical errors of this kind (Langs 1975a), the patient dreamt of deaf and blind people, alluding to the analyst who had missed the implications of his erroneous interventions— here the deviations in technique. The patient feels exposed, in part because of an incorporative identification with the analyst who exposed himself, and the manifest dream (we have few associations) reflects her unconscious perception of her having seduced the analyst, who then suddenly tells her the analysis is at an end. A subsequent association alludes to seduction and to her great confusion over the boundaries between herself and the analyst.

We may speculate that the dream is an effort to communicate the patient's unconscious interpretations of the basis of the analyst's behavior in his bodily anxieties and erotic countertransference. Most striking in this situation is the analyst's abrupt shift in his management of the boundaries of the analytic relationship, and this is reflected in the manifest dream in the shift from exposure and seduction to the words "that's it" and the patient's sitting up in the session. The analyst's confusion—which he later directly acknowledged to the patient—is reflected in the patient's psychotic confusion. Here, both incorporative identification and the patient's own pathology played a role.

It seems clear that rather than enhancing this patient's therapeutic alliance, reality testing, and self-boundaries, and rather than assisting this patient to avoid disruptive regression, the deviations in technique significantly contributed to the patient's potential for disturbance in each of these areas. Once again, we see that this patient's regressive reaction, her sense of fusion with the analyst, and her guilt over seducing him and being seduced by him, were all intensified by the analyst's failure to provide appropriate boundaries and to indicate his own ability to maintain appropriate limits to their relationship. While this reaction certainly reflects the patient's own psychopathology, it seems likely that it would have emerged in a more gradual and manageable fashion, and in the context of a viable therapeutic alliance, if the analyst had not permitted the patient to seduce him into modifying the boundaries of their relationship and had, instead, adhered to the ground rules and extensively analyzed the patient's wishes to modify them.

Discussion and Conclusions

In concluding, I will briefly highlight the main implications of these observations and suggest some important areas of further study.

1. The manner in which the therapist or analyst establishes and maintains the ground rules and boundaries of the therapeutic relationship is an important manifestation of his identity, the state of his controls, and his capacity for renunciation, for managing his own intrapsychic conflicts, for handling the stirrings within himself evoked by the patient, and for avoiding pathogenic interactions. Modifications of these boundaries and ground rules often stem from unresolved countertransference problems and reflect difficulties that are unconsciously detected by the patient. Even when deviations are invoked in emergency situations, or when a ground rule is altered for some other real reason, they generally provide the therapist—and the patient—with inappropriate gratifications and repetitions of pathogenic object relationships of which the therapist must be aware since this too will be unconsciously perceived by the patient.

2. The therapist's maintenance of the ground rules and boundaries of the therapeutic relationship is an area of activity that is constantly monitored by the patient and is utilized as a basis for unconscious, incorporative identification. Constructively handled, it provides a basis for positive and adaptive inner change that supplements the patient's endeavors to achieve conflict resolution and symptom relief through cognitive insight based on the therapist's interpretations. In addition, the proper maintenance of these boundaries is essential to give the patient the best opportunity to project his intrapsychic fantasies and to attempt to enact his past pathogenic object relationships in his interaction with the analyst in a manner that can be recognized and analyzed. Modifications in these boundaries lead to significant contaminations of the patient's intrapsychic projections, and to a situation in which the pathological introjects, unconscious fantasies,

and past object relationships are repeated and justified in the therapeutic relationship, rather than frustrated and not confirmed in reality so that they can be analyzed primarily in terms of the patient's unconscious conflicts, fantasies, and memories.

3. The idea that deviations in technique are necessary to foster the therapeutic alliance appears to be based on a naive treatment of the subject, one that fails to recognize the extensive unconscious meanings and implications of these deviations. Such an attitude overlooks the manner in which firm, analytically justified maintenance of the ground rules offers to the patient a structured framework and secure image of the therapist through which a strong and viable therapeutic relationship can be established. In this context, it is to be noted that, empirically, deviations in technique of all kinds often stem from uncontrolled anxieties in the therapist and from doubts regarding his capacity to analyze the patient; further, the patient unconsciously recognizes such sources of deviations and reacts strongly to these unconscious meanings.

4. Clinically, the ramifications of unneeded deviations in technique are unconsciously perceived by the patient, who attempts to alert the therapist to the unconscious meanings of the deviation, to offer— interpret—to the therapist his ideas as to the neurotic difficulties that have prompted the therapist to undertake these deviations, and to assist the therapist in restoring the proper boundaries of the therapeutic relationship. On the other hand, the hope of sharing inappropriate defenses and of finding momentary gratifications and symptom relief through the misalliance engendered by the acceptance of the therapist's deviations in technique will lead the patient to accept these deviations and seek out others. However, as the guilt and anxiety mount, in response to the unconscious awareness of the mutual corruption in the lack of boundaries and in reaction to its hidden, forbidden meanings, the patient will react by ultimately terminating the treatment or interrupting it temporarily, withdrawing from the therapist in some other way, and acting out in keeping with the model offered by the therapist. Other, contrasting efforts are made to reestablish the necessary boundaries in the hope of some ultimate benefit from the treatment.

With considerable unconscious perceptiveness, patients recognize that deviations in technique tend to promote undue surrender and loss of autonomy; reflect inappropriate and destructive mothering; have exhibitionistic and seductive implications; reflect a lack of barriers, including those that range from separateness of self and object to the incest barrier; are unconscious attempts at seduction; are inherently destructive toward the patient; reflect some degree of loss of control in the therapist; and often serve to conceal underlying sexual and aggressive conflicts in the therapist—to name but a few of the kinds of communications latently inherent in these measures. The appearance of such themes in the material from patients should prompt the therapist to examine his management of the ground rules and boundaries of the therapeutic relationship for any gross or subtle modification in his stance.

5. Technically, a deviation in technique, however minor, that has been evoked by a patient or offered by the therapist, calls for the following measures:

(a) Identification of the deviation and modification of the therapeutic stance so that the deviation is not continued unnecessarily, and it is made clear to the patient, implicitly or explicitly, that the boundaries will be restored and maintained. Without the modification of the deviant situation in reality, all other therapeutic endeavors will be of no avail.

(b) A full exploration and analysis of the patient's reaction to the deviation and to the reestablishment of the boundaries. During such an analysis, it is generally not advisable for the therapist to directly acknowledge that his deviation was in error, but his attitude should *implicitly* reflect his awareness that the deviation was inappropriate and that the patient's perceptions of this aspect of the deviation are not fantasy but have significant kernels of realistic perceptiveness in them. The advice that the therapist acknowledge his errors to the patient has generally been based on a wish to appear human and fallible to the patient when it seems appropriate. This stance overlooks the deviation in boundaries that such an explicit acknowledgment entails, and the consequences thereof. This is a complex issue that deserves fuller study; my present observations suggest that implicit acceptance of appropriate responsibility is the most helpful therapeutic attitude for the patient.

The therapist must carefully and sensitively separate the patient's valid perceptions of the implications of the deviation and the therapist's unconscious need for it from the extension of these perceptions into the patient's fantasies. In addition, he should try to understand how the deviation in technique was perceived by the patient as a loss of control, an acting out, and a failure to maintain inner and outer boundaries on the part of the therapist. Failure to analyze the implications of these nonverbal aspects will prompt a negative incorporative identification and acting out on the part of the patient, who will often attempt to misuse the therapist's countertransference problems as an inappropriate sanction for his own acting out. In addition, the specific working through of these aspects of the deviation in technique fosters the reestablishment of the patient's own inner and outer boundaries and controls.

(c) The therapist should be prepared for derivatives related to deviations in technique to appear in the patient's associations and his adaptive responses for some time following such an incident; he should also be prepared for their reemergence throughout the subsequent treatment and especially at the time of termination. Continued analytic work with the repercussions of such deviations will reveal their genetic and current dynamic unconscious meanings for the patient. It will enable an assessment of the extent to which the deviation did in reality repeat the pathogenic behavior of, and interaction with, early significant figures, and the extent to which the patient used the stimulus of the deviation as a source of more distorted transference fantasies. Clearly, reactions to deviations in technique cannot be viewed simply as transference responses, but must be understood in terms of the mixture of reality and fantasy involved.

6. The marked productivity of patients following deviations in technique can now be understood to reflect the traumatic impact that such deviations have on them and the intense adaptive efforts that they make in response. Such efforts include attempts to cure the therapist of his own intrapsychic conflicts as reflected in the unneeded deviation (Searles 1975, Langs 1975), attempts to rectify the actual therapeutic situation, and efforts to readapt to the intrapsychic conflicts and memories stirred up by the deviation in technique.

7. The present findings suggest that deviations in technique should be restricted to emergency situations and to the use of parameters that are truly necessitated by ego dysfunctions in the patient. They point to a need to reevaluate the indications for deviations in technique and parameters, and should promote extensive self-scrutiny by the therapist when he is considering or has made a modification in technique. In addition, these observations suggest that even in those emergency situations where deviations prove necessary for the patient, their unconscious ramifications are extensive and require considerable subsequent analysis and modification.

Tentatively it would appear that many of the therapeutic crises that prompt therapists to deviate in their technique are evoked by the interaction between the patient's psychopathology and that of the therapist. These data suggest that the therapist's initial stance at such times should center on an effort to understand the specific precipitants of the crisis and on self-analytic work toward modifying his own contribution, as well as the basic use of correct interpretations to the patient. This not only provides the patient cognitive insight, but affords him an actual experience in which the therapist does not repeat the past pathogenic interaction, but instead detaches himself from it and is capable of interpreting it (Racker 1968). The danger of mutual acting out and misalliance through deviations should, if at all possible, be considered before they are invoked. The therapist should engage in considerable self-scrutiny and in a reassessment of his interaction with the patient and of his understanding of the material; he should preferably restrict the use of deviations to those situations where he is unable to detect any countertransference difficulties and there is an emergency need, such as a suicidal or homicidal patient. In doing so, the deviation should be kept to the absolute minimum and modified in reality as quickly as possible, with a full analysis of all the dimensions of the experience (Eissler 1953).

8. Technically, the therapeutic stance used when the deviation is entirely necessary and justified is different from those situations in which the deviation proves to have been unneeded and in large measure a product of the therapist's countertransference. In the former situation, the inappropriate gratifications afforded to both patient and therapist can be analyzed as inevitable side effects of an essential technical measure, while in the latter situation the neurotic gratifications and the repetition of past neurotic object relationships is the central contributing factor and must be recognized as such.

9. The counterpart of these findings regarding deviations in technique is the postulate that the present ground rules and boundaries of the therapeutic relationship in adult psychoanalysis and psychotherapy offer an optimal therapeutic hold and setting for the patient. The finding that patients are exquisitely sensitive to the seemingly most trivial alterations in the boundaries and ground rules—e.g., a necessary change of hour—also attests the importance of this dimension of the therapeutic relationship.

10. The present findings should, however, not be construed as a brief for therapeutic rigidity or misconstrued as a basis upon which to advocate a lack of humanity and concern in the psychotherapist or analyst. To the contrary, it is intended to help the therapist become aware of the major ramifications of any deviation in technique so that these factors can be considered along with other dimensions when such a measure is contemplated. These observations prepare the therapist who has expressed human

concern or other controlled, noninterpretive reactions to the patient for those consequences that he might not otherwise have anticipated. They can serve to remind us that the most meaningful expression of the therapist's or analyst's humanity in the treatment setting lies in his usual attitude of concern and in his capacity to offer the patient a correct interpretation, especially at a moment when he has not participated in a neurotic interaction with the patient. Without deviating, the therapist who wishes to be appropriately supportive can respond to emergency situations with implicit concern, an increased rate of intervening, and by affording the patient a model of someone who is reasonably involved, interpretively helpful, and also has the capacity to maintain necessary limits. Many who have written on the subject of deviations in technique have failed to appreciate the powerful supportive dimensions inherent in nondeviant analytic technique and seem to underestimate the power of a correct interpretation that emanates from an analyst who is not involved in a misalliance or embroiled in a countertransference conflict.

11. These findings also remind us of the powerful inner forces that move the therapist or analyst toward deviations in technique and misalliances, ranging from deep personal needs to deny one's own limitations and mortality to the search for specific countertransference-based neurotic interactions, gratifications, and defenses (Langs 1975b).

12. Finally, this study also emphasizes the importance of the distinction between reality and fantasy in the therapeutic relationship (Langs 1973a). It is insufficient to explore and analyze the content of the patient's reactions to deviations in technique in terms of his intrapsychic fantasies, without recognition of their basis and stimulus in reality and the actual, nonverbal meanings and effects of these deviations on the patient. Here, the distinctions between interpretation and management, free association and interaction, fantasy and actuality, and verbal interaction and nonverbal communication became pertinent.

Who and what the therapist is becomes as important as what he says. The culmination of analytic work in insight gained from the analyst's interpretations does not thereby lose status, but is supplemented by another important dimension of technique: the management of the analytic relationship.

NOTES

1. The area under study in this presentation is largely comparable for psychotherapy and psychoanalysis, and I shall therefore use the term *therapist* generically to allude to both the psychotherapist and the psychoanalyst, and reserve the latter two terms when referring specifically to a psychotherapeutic or psychoanalytic situation. I have not included material from my own psychotherapeutic and psychoanalytic practice because of a decision to not use these sources in my writings. Among the many reasons for this decision is the empirical discovery that such use of one's clinical experience, past and present, significantly modifies the framework and boundaries of the therapeutic situation. It is, in effect, a deviation in technique that has all the consequences, more or less, of the deviations described in the body of this paper. Since some degree of deviation is already inherent in the supervisory situation and in material published by others, I shall use vignettes drawn from these sources to develop the theses offered here.

2. Upon completion of this paper, I came across Milner's (1952) intriguing comments, made in the context of a study of symbolism and child analysis, regarding the frame that demarks the reality that prevails within the psychoanalytic situation from that which exists outside of it. She views the frame as essential to the creation of the transference illusions — a suggestion that clearly relates to the ground rules and boundaries discussed in this paper.

REFERENCES

Allen, S. (1956). Reflections on the wish of the analyst to "break" or change the basic rule. *Bulletin of the Menninger Clinic* 20:192–200.

Arlow, J., and Brenner, C. (1966). Discussion of papers on the psychoanalytic situation. In *Psychoanalysis in the Americas,* ed. R. Litman. New York: International Universities Press.

Balint, M. (1968). *The Basic Fault: Therapeutic Aspects of Regression.* London: Tavistock Publications.

Bleger, J. (1967). Psycho-analysis of the psycho-analytic frame. *International Journal of Psycho-Analysis* 48:511–519.

Bouvet, M. (1958). Technical variations and the concept of distance. *International Journal of Psycho-Analysis* 39:211–221.

Calogeras, R. (1967). Silence as a technical parameter in psychoanalysis. *International Journal of Psycho-Analysis* 48:536–558

Eissler, R. (1953). The effect of the structure of the ego on psychoanalytic technique. *Journal of the American Psychoanalytic Association* 1:104–143.

———(1958). Remarks on some variations in psychoanalytic technique. *International Journal of Psycho-Analysis* 39:222–229.

Frank, J. (1956). Indications and contraindications for the application of the "standard technique." *Journal of the American Psychoanalytic Association* 4:266–284.

Freud, A. (1954a). Problems of technique in adult analysis (with discussion by several others). *Bulletin of the Philadelphia Association of Psychoanalysis* 4:44–69.

———(1954b). The widening scope of indications for psychoanalysis, discussion. *Journal of the American Psychoanalytic Association* 2:607–620.

Freud, S. (1937). Analysis terminable and interminable. *Standard Edition* 23:209–254.

Greenacre, P. (1959). Certain technical problems in the transference relationship. *Journal of the American Psychoanalytic Association* 7:484–502.

———(1971). *Emotional Growth*, Vol. II. New York: International Universities Press.

Greenson, R. (1958). Variations in classical psychoanalytic technique: an introduction. *International Journal of Psycho-Analysis* 39:200–201.

———(1967). *The Technique and Practice of Psychoanalysis*, Vol. 1. New York: International Universities Press.

———(1972). Beyond transference and interpretation. *International Journal of Psycho-Analysis* 53:213–217.

———, and Wexler, M. (1969). The non-transference relationship in the psychoanalytic situation. *International Journal of Psycho-Analysis* 50:27–39.

Gudeman, J. (1974). Uncontrolled regression in therapy and analysis. *International Journal of Psychoanalytic Psychotherapy* 3:325–338.

Hoedemaker, E. (1960). Psycho-analytic technique and ego modification. *International Journal of Psycho-Analysis* 41:34–45.

Kanzer, M. (1975). The therapeutic and working alliances. *International Journal of Psychoanalytic Psychotherapy* 4:48–68.

Langs, R. (1972). A psychoanalytic study of material from patients in psychotherapy. *International Journal of Psychoanalytic Psychotherapy* 1:4–45.

———(1973a). The patient's view of the therapist: reality or fantasy? *International Journal of Psychoanalytic Psychotherapy* 2:411–431.

———(1973b). *The Technique of Psychoanalytic Psychotherapy*, Vol. I. New York: Jason Aronson.

———(1974). *The Technique of Psychoanalytic Psycho-*

therapy, Vol. II. New York: Jason Aronson.

———(1975a). The patient's unconscious perception of the therapist's errors. In *Tactics and Techniques in Psychoanalytic Therapy, Vol. II: Countertransference*, ed. P. Giovacchini. New York: Jason Aronson.

———(1975b). Therapeutic misalliances. *International Journal of Psychoanalytic Psychotherapy* 4:77–105.

———(in press). The misalliance dimension in Freud's case histories. In *Freud and His Patients*, ed. M. Kanzer and J. Glenn. New York: Jason Aronson.

Loewald, H. (1960). On the therapeutic action of psychoanalysis. *International Journal of Psycho-Analysis* 41:16–33.

Loewenstein, R. (1958). Remarks on some variations in psychoanalytic technique. *International Journal of Psycho-Analysis* 39:202–210.

Lorand, S. (1963). Modifications in classical psychoanalysis. *Psychoanalytic Quarterly* 32:192–204.

Milner, M. (1952). Aspects of symbolism in comprehension of the not-self. *International Journal of Psycho-Analysis* 33:181–195.

Nacht, S. (1958). Variations in technique. *International Journal of Psycho-Analysis* 39:235–237.

Racker, H. (1968). *Transference and Countertransference*. London: Hogarth Press.

Reich, A. (1958). A special variation of technique. *International Journal of Psycho-Analysis* 39:230–234.

Rodgers, T. (1965). A specific parameter: concurrent psychotherapy of the spouse of an analysand by the same analyst. *International Journal of Psycho-Analysis* 46:237–243.

Rosenfeld, H. (1958). Contribution to the discussion on variations in classical technique. *International Journal of Psycho-Analysis* 39:238–239.

Searles, H. (1975). The patient as therapist to his analyst. In *Tactics and Techniques in Psychoanalytic Therapy, Vol. II: Countertransference*, ed. P. Giovacchini. New York: Jason Aronson.

Stone, L. (1954). The widening scope of indications for psychoanalysis. *Journal of the American Psychoanalytic Association* 2:567–594.

———(1961). *The Psychoanalytic Situation*. New York: International Universities Press.

———(1967). The psychoanalytic situation and transference: postscript to an earlier communication. *Journal of the American Psychoanalytic Association* 15:3–58.

Tarachow, S. (1962). Interpretation and reality in psychotherapy. *International Journal of Psycho-Analysis* 43:377–387.

Winnicott, D. W. (1958). *Collected Papers*. London: Tavistock Publications.

Zetzel, E. (1966). The analytic situation. In *Psychoanalysis in the Americas*, ed. R. Litman. New York: International Universities Press.

43

"THE HOLDING ENVIRONMENT" AND THE THERAPEUTIC ACTION OF PSYCHOANALYSIS

Arnold H. Modell

EDITOR'S NOTE

Modell's paper extends and elaborates Winnicott's ideas regarding the holding environment and its functions. He stresses the object relationship aspects of the therapist's hold and its basis in the actual aspects of the analyst's technique, which are then penetrated by fantasy. There is emphasis too on the background of safety provided for the patient in this way, and the importance of interpretive interventions in securing the hold. Much is made of the analogy between the mother's hold of the infant and that of the analyst toward his patient. However, as with almost all other writings on the subject, Modell fails to note the important differences between these two holds. The maternal hold strives to be almost entirely protective, while the analytic hold is both protective and a means of facilitating a growth-promoting, therapeutic regression; the latter is therefore both anxiety alleviating and anxiety provoking.

Modell's work, which specifically considers the functions of the holding environment in the treatment of narcissistic character disorders, also reflects a trend among classical analysts to integrate the contributions of Kernberg (1975) Kohut (1971, 1977), and certain Kleinians into their thinking.

At the Congress in Marienbad in 1936, Glover (1937) observed that "it is essential that our theory of therapeutic results should keep pace with the complexity of ego development and with the complexity of our etiological formulae" (p. 127). This paper is an attempt to respond to Glover's succinct advice, for, as we enlarge the scope of psychoanalysis to include an ever-increasing range of people who are said to suffer from disorders of ego development, we are forced to consider for these people a theory of the therapeutic action of psychoanalysis different from that we use with the so-called "classical case."

The isolation of those factors which underlie therapeutic change in psychoanalysis is not a secure area of knowledge; it is easier to identify the forces that interfere with the progress of an analysis than to understand what contributes to its therapeutic success. Our theory of therapeutic change in psychoanalysis may itself be constantly changing due to the changing nature of the neuroses. This theory is obviously linked to the subject of transference where a final understanding also seems continually to elude us. A thorough examination of the theory of therapeutic action of psychoanalysis is beyond the scope of this paper: it should be understood that the following account is necessarily cursory and simplified.

I believe that most analysts would accept James Strachey's description (1934) that structural growth is effected by means of sparingly employed mutative interpretations. Interpretations are only effective when certain conditions are met: in Strachey's words, "every mutative interpretation must be emotionally 'immediate'; the patient must experience it

Reprinted from *Journal of the American Psychoanalytic Association* 24: 285–308 by permission of International Universities Press, Inc. Copyright © 1976 by American Psychoanalytic Association.

as something actual" (p. 286). He says further that the interpretation must be directed to the "point of urgency." This means that very precise conditions must be present regarding the state of the patient's affects. It must be assumed that the patient is in a state of affective relatedness so that the "point of urgency" can be perceived by means of the psychoanalyst's empathy—that is to say, there must be an affective bond. It must further be assumed that the patient's affective experience is of a certain intensity— that is, intense enough to experience the immediacy of feeling but not so intense as to overwhelm him. We know that Strachey believed that the transference interpretations are likely to have the greatest "urgency" and that mutative changes are most likely to occur through the interpretation of a transference. Differences of opinion exist regarding this point: there are those who would place transference interpretation at the very center of the therapeutic process, while others, such as Anna Freud (1969), would give equal weight to interpretive reconstruction utilizing memory, free association, and dreams. Further controversy exists over the effectiveness of interpretation in the presence or absence of a therapeutic alliance: a majority opinion would believe that transference interpretations are mutative, that is, that they produce structural change only when self/object differentiation has been achieved so that the patient can accept the analyst as a separate person and can collaborate actively (Zetzel, 1956). Kleinian analysts would take a minority view, believing that transference interpretations can be effective even in the absence of a therapeutic alliance. (For a discussion of this controversy see Greenson, 1974; Rosenfeld, 1974.)

But if we leave these controversies aside, all analysts are united in the view that interpretations can be effective only when there is, in Strachey's terms, a "point of urgency," that is to say, affect that is genuine and communicated.

It is further believed that mutative interpretations lead to structural change by means of a series of innumerable small steps. This results in a growing identification of the patient with the analyst's "analytic attitude" (Bibring, 1937). Strachey emphasized the modification of the patient's superego, but we would now include the modification of the ego and the sense of self.

The theory that the therapeutic action of psychoanalysis requires a certain state of affective relatedness would have to be modified as it applies to the psychoanalysis of narcissistic character disorders. For in the opening phase of the psychoanalytic treatment (a phase which may last for a year or more) there is a persistent state of affective nonrelatedness.

We can confirm Kohut's (1971) description of a syndrome defined operationally by the development of a transference consisting of externalizations of part of the self or the undifferentiated self-object, which he called the mirror transference, and the idealizing transference. The uniformity of this particular transference manifestation, in contrast to the transference neurosis, whose content is unique, is of special interest and will be discussed later in this paper. We agree with Kohut that this group is essentially neurotic and not psychotic and can be distinguished from borderline patients (see also Kernberg, 1974; Modell, 1975b). The diagnosis of this syndrome is also aided by a particular form of the countertransference response (Modell, 1973), which is the result of the patient's state of nonrelatedness. The analyst reacts with a sense of boredom and sleepiness to this massive affect block and to the realization that he is continuously in the presence of another person who does not seem to be interested in him. Although the analyst's withdrawal may be defensive, I do not believe it is necessarily neurotic— it is a human reaction to the patient's state of nonrelatedness. The patient's speech usually has a monotonous, dry, or empty quality, traumatic events are related with such absence of feeling that the analyst must struggle against becoming indifferent. Dreams are also shorn of affect and can only rarely be interpreted. Strachey's criterion for interpretation—the state of affective relatedness— "the point of urgency" is lacking, and, further, there is an absence of a therapeutic alliance. In the absence of both transference neurosis and a therapeutic alliance, and without a point of affective urgency that permits mutative interpretations, what then provides the motive force for the therapeutic action of psychoanalysis in these patients (Kohut, 1971)?

Kohut attributes the structural growth that occurs in these cases to a process that he calls "transmuting internalization." He describes it as follows (1971): "Preceding the withdrawal of the cathexis from the object there is a breaking up of those aspects of the object imago that are being internalized" (p. 49). And further, "there takes place . . . a depersonalizing of the introjected aspects of the image of the object" (p. 50). I find Kohut's concept of the "transmuting internalization" an unsatisfactory explanation of the therapeutic action of psychoanalysis in narcissistic personality disorders. It is not that I question that "transmuting internalizations" occur, for this has long been recognized: my principal objection is his theoretical frame of reference—one that focuses nearly exclusively on changes in the self, and describes these changes in terms of a distribution of narcissistic object libido. Kohut does not make use of the psychoanalytic theory of object relations; to describe qualitative differences in libido is reminiscent of Freud's 1914 paper, "On Narcissism," a paper that preceded structural theory. Although Kohut does employ structural concepts, narcissism is separated from the development of object relations, a view antithetical to object-relations theory. (For a similar criticism see Loewald, 1973; Kernberg, 1974.)

Theory has a selective influence upon what we choose to observe. Kohut's theoretical position that narcissism and object relations proceed along separate developmental lines would minimize the interplay of the human environment upon the vicissitudes of development and the sense of self. This is not a minor theoretical disagreement, but a radically different model of the mind (see my discussion in Panel, 1971). Object-relations theory describes intrapsychic processes in the context of a human environment. Such a view is consistent with contemporary biological theory in that it views the world around the organism with the organism in it. This is what, in psychoanalytic jargon, has come to be called a "two-body" theory.

It is our contention, therefore, that the syndrome of the narcissistic character disorder that Kohut has so accurately described requires a theory of object relations for its fuller understanding. There is a theory of the therapeutic action of psychoanalysis that derives from the object-relations point of view. We are referring to those analysts who view the analytic setting itself as containing some elements of the mother-child relation. This point of view includes the contributions of Winnicott (1965), Balint (1968), Spitz (1956), Loewald (1960) and Gitelson (1962), among others. It is a view that would see the analytic setting as an open system, a view in which the ego must be considered in relation to its human environment.

We have adopted Winnicott's term, "the holding environment," as an evocative description of this human environment, but it should be understood that in applying Winnicott's term we are emphasizing a theory that is not exclusively Winnicott's. Winnicott introduced the term "holding environment" as a metaphor for certain aspects of the analytic situation and the analytic process. The term derives from the maternal function of holding the infant, but, taken as a metaphor, it has a much broader application and extends beyond the infantile period—where the holding is literal and not metaphorical—to the broader caretaking functions of the parent in relation to the older child (Khan, 1963). We suggest that the mother, or more

accurately, the caretaking adults, stand between the child and the actual environment and that the child and its caretaker are an open system joined by means of the communication of affects. As Winnicott (1963) put it, ". . . the analyst is *holding* the patient, and this often takes the form of conveying in words at the appropriate moment something that shows that the analyst knows and understands the deepest anxiety that is being experienced, or that is waiting to be experienced" (p. 240). The holding environment provides an illusion of safety and protection, an illusion that depends upon the bond of affective communication between the caretaker and the child. We are reminded of the war-time experience of children who remained with their mothers, contrasted with those who were separated. The study made by Freud and Burlingham (1943), demonstrated that the mothers' affective signals took precedence over the actual, the external, reality: the children remained calm when the mothers were unafraid, despite the real danger. The holding environment suggests not only protection from the dangers from without, but also protection from the dangers from within. For the holding implies a restraint, a capacity to hold the child having a temper tantrum so that his aggressive impulses do not prove destructive to either himself or the caretaker. In this regard it is not uncommon to observe at the beginning of an analysis that patients will test the analyst's capacity to survive aggressive onslaughts. The holding environment provides, in Sandler's (1960) terms, a background of safety. When there is a loss of this holding environment, which may occur for a variety of reasons, such as the illness of the parents or their emotional unavailability, the child is forced into a premature maturation and, in a sense, for a period at least, ceases to be a child, for to have a childhood requires the presence of a holding environment. A child who is forced into a premature self-sufficiency does so by means of an illusion (Modell, 1975b), an illusion for which the ego pays a price.

THE HOLDING ENVIRONMENT AND THE ANALYTIC SETTING AS AN OBJECT RELATIONSHIP

Others, however, have questioned whether the analytic situation does in fact recapitulate an early mother-child relation. Anna Freud (1969) states: "There is, further, the question whether the transference really has the power to transport the patient back as far as the beginning of life. Many are convinced that this is the case. Others, myself among them, raise the point that it is one thing for the preformed object-related fantasies to return from repression and be redirected from the inner to the outer world (i.e., to the person of the analyst); but that it is an entirely different, almost magical expectation, to have the patient in analysis change back into the prepsychological, undifferentiated, unstructured state, in which no division exists between body and mind or self and object" (p. 40). Leo Stone (1961) is also skeptical about whether the analytic setting can reproduce aspects of an early object relationship.

As Anna Freud indicates, it would be foolish to insist that regression in analysis goes back to structurally undifferentiated states of the first or second year of life. Nevertheless, there are actual elements in the analyst's technique that are reminiscent of an idealized maternal holding environment, and these can be enumerated: the analyst is constant and reliable; he responds to the patient's affects; he accepts the patient, and his judgment is less critical and more benign; he is there primarily for the patient's needs and not for his own; he does not retaliate; and he does at times have a better grasp of the patient's inner psychic reality than does the patient himself and therefore may clarify what is bewildering and confusing.

Strachey (1934) underlined an important paradox that is implicit in psychoanalytic technique. He stated: "It is a paradoxical fact that the best way of ensuring that his [the patient's] ego shall be able to distinguish between phantasy and reality is to withhold reality from him as much as possible" (p. 285). This paradox is also relevant to our consideration of the "holding environment." For although there are "real" caretaking elements in the analyst's customary activity, if he does in fact assume an actual protective role (such as might be necessary in certain emergencies), this will interfere with the analytic process. We wish to reiterate, therefore, that the caretaking elements we have described are implicit in the classic analytic technique itself (in Eissler's terms, without parameters). If active measures are introduced into the analytic situation, there is the paradoxical effect of weakening the analytic holding environment. (The same point has been made by Rosenfeld, 1972, and Gitelson, 1962.)

It should also be made clear that when we speak of "real" elements in the object relation between patient and analyst as part of the caretaking function, we are not referring to the very different issue of the patient's perception of the analyst and a "real" person (Greenson and Wexler, 1969). The word "real" is used here in a different context. Again, to refer back to

Strachey's paradox, the introduction of special measures to reveal to the patient the "reality" of the analyst's personality may, in the treatment of the neuroses at least, have the opposite effect. The use of this technique in borderline and other psychotic illnesses is a separate issue.

We have discussed the so-called "actual" elements in the object tie between the patient and the analyst. We know that the situation is further complicated by the fact that this actual object tie is penetrated by the products of fantasy. That these fantasies may be primitive and may occur in young children does not mean that the patient has in fact regressed in a structural sense to the age of one or two, as Anna Freud has questioned. The fantastic elements include the magical wish to be protected from the dangers of the world and the illusion that the person of the analyst in some way stands between these dangers and shields the patient. It is the illusion that the patient is not "really in the world." There is the wish that the analyst can make the world better for the patient, without the patient's being required to do any work — that mere contiguity to this powerful analyst will transfer the analyst's magical powers to himself.

A patient in the termination phase dreamed that she was lying on the floor holding a life-sized doll while I was seated watching her. The patient identified the doll as the analytic process that she was in danger of losing. What is of interest here is that the analytic process itself was invested with the qualities of a transitional object, apart from the person of the analyst. Although the qualities of the holding environment are generated by the analyst's technique, they may become separated from the analyst and take on a life of their own. The analytic process is not infrequently observed in dreams as a more or less protective container, such as a house or an automobile.

The gratifications that result from the analyst's functioning as a "holding environment," we must again emphasize, are not the consequence of the analyst's special activity, that is, actively giving reassurance, love, or support, but are an intrinsic part of "classical" technique. Here, gratification appears to contradict the rule of abstinence, but the nature of the gratification is quite different from that associated with libidinal or aggressive discharge. It moves silently, it is not orgastic. I have suggested elsewhere (Modell, 1975a) that the instinctual backing of object relations is of a different order from what Freud described as the instincts of the id. While this assertion remains controversial, it is not controversial to assume that the healing forces of the "holding environment" have biological roots.

The Psychoanalytic Process
in Narcissistic
Character Disorders

**The first phase—the cocoon: transference
and the "holding environment"**

Kohut's description of the idealizing and mirror transference in the narcissistic character disorder is now widely known, and we have accepted his description as an operational method of defining the syndrome itself. What we are to describe now are other facets of transference that can be observed if we shift the focus from the self to the broader context of object relations—that is to say, the self in an environment. The complexity of the analytic process is such that what we can offer here are only partial approximations. We have the impression that the early part of the first phase of analysis, as we shall describe it, corresponds to Kohut's description of the idealizing transference. Kohut's mirror transference in its less archaic forms occurs toward the end of the first phase and the beginning of the second or middle phase of analysis. It is also to be understood that the separation of these phases is a fluid, dynamic process; the boundaries between phases are not sharp and, due to progressive and regressive movements, their sequence may be interrupted. The situation is not unlike the changing of seasons.

The initial period usually extends for a year or a year and a half, or may persist longer. It is a period of great frustration for the psychoanalyst: the patient behaves in the main as if there are not two people in the consulting room—the patient remains essentially in a state of nonrelatedness. This state of affective nonrelatedness induces a particular countertransference response that has been widely observed (Kohut, 1971; Modell, 1973; Kernberg, 1974). It is one of boredom, sleepiness, and indifference. In contrast to borderline patients who make intense demands upon the analyst and consequently induce intense countertransference affects, these patients attempt to maintain an illusion of self-sufficiency. They report an intrapsychic perception of this state of self-sufficiency and feel encased in a "plastic bubble" (Modell, 1968; Volkan, 1973) or behind a

sheet of glass (Guntrip, 1968) or feel that they are a mummy in a case or, as I have described earlier (Modell, 1968), they feel encased in a cocoon.[1] I have chosen the cocoon metaphor because it implies a potential for life. A cocoon, unlike a mummy or a plastic bubble, contains something alive and must be attached to something else that is essential for its nourishment.[2] The illusion of self-sufficiency and disdainful aloofness that these people display defends against the very opposite—that is, yearnings that are intense and insatiable. Patients' descriptions of feeling as if they were inside a plastic bubble attest to their endopsychic perceptions of deadness. It should also be obvious that these analogies may be variations of a womb fantasy—a state where one is cut off from interaction from the environment, where one is not "really in the world"; where there is an illusion of self-sufficiency and yet a total dependence upon the caretaking functions of the maternal environment.[3]

During this phase of the analytic process, although the analyst may experience boredom and indifference, the patient may be enjoying the analytic experience. With some patients we have the impression of a child playing happily by himself content to know that his mother is in the next room. The patient is talking to himself, but he does experience a sense that he is safe in the analytic setting.

Although the analyst in the initial period may have a feeling that nothing is happening, we believe that the analytic process is set in motion by the holding environment and the tie to the analyst himself. During this period there cannot be said to be a therapeutic alliance, for this requires a sense of separateness that has not yet been established. Instead of a therapeutic alliance, we see a magic belief reminiscent of what has been described in borderline patients as a transitional-object relationship—the object stands between them and the dangers of the real world. It is as if the patient really believes that he is not "in the world" and that there is no need for him to obtain anything for himself—there is a denial of the need to work. Implicit here is the belief that the analyst can rescue the patient in spite of himself and that the analyst has sufficient power to preserve the analysis in spite of the patient's efforts to sabotage it. In this idealizing phase, the analyst implicitly

---

1. Slap (1974) has also described this phenomenon, but has mistakenly associated it with Lewin's dream screen.

2. Some patients, if they are able to, will come very early to their appointments to obtain the feeling of safety and pleasure of remaining alone in the waiting room with the knowledge that I am next door.

3. Freud used the analogy of an egg in another context (1911):

"A neat example of a psychical system shut off from the stimuli of the external world, and able to satisfy even its nutritional requirements autistically (to use Bleuler's term), is afforded by a bird's egg with its food supply enclosed in its shell; for it, the care provided by its mother is limited to the provision of warmth" (p. 220n).

possesses some powerful qualities so that change may be effected merely by being in his presence. It is a sense of magic based on contiguity: merely to be in the presence of the powerful object is to share his power. What I am describing corresponds, of course, to some aspects of Kohut's idealizing transference. This positively toned transference gradually gives way, for reasons to be described, to negative transference. For a cocoon is also similar to a fortress, where nothing leaves and nothing enters. The analyst begins to observe that his comments tend to be forgotten or not even heard—nothing seems to get through. The analyst's emotional position is one of acceptance, patience, and empathy—he must be able to wait. Winnicott has observed (1969): "For instance, it is only in recent years that I have been able to sit and wait for the natural evolution of the transference arising out of the patient's growing trust in the psychoanalytic technique and setting, and to avoid breaking up the natural process by making interpretations" (p. 86). Interpretations at this stage tend to be either dismissed, not heard, or resented as an intrusion. (We will return in a later section to discuss the function of interpretation.)

The middle period: the emergence of rage and the development of the therapeutic alliance

In this portion of the analysis the positively toned transference gradually changes into its opposite. We begin to enter the period that can be described as one of narcissistic rage. The time of onset of this phase may be due in part to the emotional capacities of the analyst, that is, how long he can tolerate the patient's prolonged state of nonrelatedness. But we suspect that even with the most tolerant and accepting analyst the process would shift of its own accord, for, as the regression deepens, the insatiable demands that have been warded off by denial will become more manifest. The analyst becomes more aware of the patient's insatiable needs for admiration and total attention and, in turn, becomes more confronting. This is not simply the empathic acceptance of the patient's grandiose self that Kohut has described. Here I share the observation of Loewald (1973) who states: "To my mind a not inconsiderable share of the analytic work consists of more or less actively and consistently confronting these freed narcissistic needs of the narcissistic transferences" (p. 447) (see also Kernberg [1974] on confronfrontation). The confrontation of the patient's grandiosity gradually gives way to a systematic interpretation of the cocoon fantasy itself. With this activity on the part of the analyst, the affect block and state of nonrelatedness is gradually and imperceptibly

altered and gives way to genuine affects, albeit that of intense rage. We have arrived at the "point of urgency" that Strachey described as the necessary precondition for giving mutative interpretations. This rage in some patients takes on murderous proportions or may lead to a defensive indifference, a regressive movement back to the earlier cocoon fantasy. I believe, with Winnicott (1969), that the rage itself supports the process of individuation. In contrast to the rage that accompanies the Oedipus complex, the wish to destroy the parent of the opposite sex, this rage is not aimed at the analyst as a parental imago. It is less definite and more diffuse. For example, as the analyst is equated with the environment itself, he becomes the target of rage directed against external reality. This rage may also be fueled by envy—the envy itself is again diffuse and nonspecific: the patient may envy the analyst for what he is and for what he has, that is, his knowledge. As one moves through this stormy period in the analysis, a period that may occupy months or perhaps a year or longer, one observes that the cocoon transference has been gradually dissolving—the patient no longer believes in his self-sufficiency, he is able to acknowledge his demands more directly, his extreme dependency is no longer denied. With this, comes the beginning of individuation, a sense of separateness, and the development of the therapeutic alliance. Although this may be a difficult and painful period, there is a sense that two people are present. The patient gradually, although reluctantly, begins to accept the fact that he has a responsibility for the work in the analysis.

We believe that the holding environment of the first phase has led to sufficient ego consolidation to permit a shift in the focus of therapeutic action of psychoanalysis in the second phase. And we believe that the motive force for the therapeutic action of psychoanalysis in the second phase is interpretation. Interpretation effects the dissolution of the cocoon transference in a manner analogous to the use of interpretation to effect the dissolution of a transference neurosis. It should be understood that, in contrast to the classical case, the dissolution of the cocoon transference permits the establishment of a therapeutic alliance. We can say that at the end of this middle phase the patient is emerging from the cocoon—he is beginning to hatch. With this there is a greater sense of aliveness. As patients report it—they feel as if they are beginning to live their own lives.

Third phase—the end phase

In this phase the analysis approximates that of a classical case. This is not to say that it is identical to that of a classical case, in that the potentiality for regressive movement is ever-present. During weekend separations for example, there may be a renewal of the cocoon transference. Elements, however, of the historically idiosyncratic transference neurosis begin to emerge—that is, there is a repetition of imagos of whole persons and not the externalization of parts of the self.

We have now entered the realm of the Oedipus complex. In the male, indications of castration anxiety appear in the transference, which has shifted from the conflict with the environment to recapitulate historically determined facets of the transference neurosis. Correspondingly, there is a shift of focus, both within the transference and outside of it, from dyadic to triangular relationships. While the vicissitudes of the Oedipus complex may not emerge as completely as in a "classical" case, they are unmistakably present.

Affects are now experienced with great intensity—now it is only rarely that the analyst experiences the sense of boredom and sleepiness that so characterized the opening phase. In short, during this period the analysis is not unlike that of a classical neurosis, with the exception that there is the readiness to establish a narcissistic affect block that characterizes the cocoon transference.

Because of extreme dependency, it can be understood that the phase of termination may be prolonged. It should be clear that a true termination can be achieved only if the cocoon transference has been resolved through interpretation. In some patients with narcissistic character disorders, this middle and stormy phase in which the cocoon transference is resolved is never traversed. Consequently, the patient remains unanalyzed and persists in a state where the analytic situation itself is used as a transitional object. It can be said with some truth that such patients become addicted to the analytic process.

EMPATHY AND MUTATIVE INTERPRETATION

We have suggested that interpretations only become mutative during the second phase of the treatment of narcissistic character disorders, that is, when there is a state of affective relatedness. Interpretations are, of course, not confined to the second phase of analysis, and we suspect that their therapeutic action in the first phase may be of a different order. Interpretations may function principally as a sign of the analyst's empathy and understanding—that is, they may function as part of the analytic holding environment.

I believe Rycroft (1956) had something of the same idea in mind when he stated: "In addition therefore to their symbolic function of communicating ideas, interpretations also have the sign-function of conveying to the patient the analyst's emotional attitude towards him. They combine with the material setting provided by the analyst to form the analyst's affective contribution to the formation of a trial relationship, within which the patient can recapture the ability to make contact and communication with external objects" (p. 472).

It is unlikely therefore that interpretations can be mutative until there is sufficient maturation of the ego for the acceptance of self/object differentiation. In the opening phase, the analyst's interpretations, although accurate, may not be distinguished by the patient from the analyst's general empathic response (see also Gedo and Goldberg [1973] for a discussion of the hierarchy of treatment modalities).

THE NARCISSISTIC TRANSFERENCE AND THE TRANSFERENCE NEUROSIS

It is the underlying assumption in this paper that, as our psychoanalytic nosology is broadened to include syndromes of varying disturbances of ego structure, we will correspondingly have broadened our understanding of the analytic process and the process of transference. This is the point of view developed by Gedo and Goldberg (1973). We believe it is important to resist a tendency to blur the nosological distinction between the transference neurosis and the narcissistic character disorders. We suspect that the increased attention to the narcissistic disorders may reflect an actual increase in their frequency—a shift in the ecology of neuroses—and that a shifting nosology of neurosis may be the manifestation of yet unidentified psychosocial processes. Fenichel (1938) observed that "neurotics who demand analytic treatment today differ from those that went to Freud thirty or forty years ago." And we now say that the neurotic who seeks treatment today differs from those who consulted Fenichel in 1938. For we have now come to view the capacity to form a transference neurosis as a sign of health. Elements of the transference neurosis appear only after a certain degree of ego growth and consolidation has been achieved. The development of the transference neurosis requires a capacity for illusion (Khan, 1973). (For a more general discussion of the transference neurosis, see Blum, 1971.) As Greenson has noted (see Workshop, 1974), it is fluid, changeable, and different in every patient. This is in marked contrast to the narcissistic transferences, which are uniform to the extent that they can be said to form an operational basis for defining the syndrome. This is not to say that the delineation of the narcissistic transferences occurs regardless of the analyst's technique or skill. Nevertheless, their uniformity suggests that they are based upon the externalization of psychic structures, that is, various portions of the self, or self-object, and that they do not require a condition of basic trust for their emergence. This suggests that the more familiar externalization of the superego is also a noncreative structural transference element, to be distinguished from the transference neurosis.

EGO DISTORTION AND THE EGO'S CONFLICT WITH THE ENVIRONMENT

In his paper, "Neurosis and Psychosis," Freud (1924) suggested that the ego's conflict with the environment was characteristic of psychosis: ". . . *neurosis is the result of a conflict between the ego and its id, whereas psychosis is the analogous outcome of a similar disturbance in the relations between the ego and the external world*" (p. 149). Our psychoanalytic experience with narcissistic character disorders has shown us that Freud's formula no longer applies, for this syndrome, where the ego is in conflict with the environment, must be categorized as a neurosis. Yet in the same paper Freud suggests a solution to this apparent contradiction, for he states that it is possible for the ego to avoid a psychic rupture by ". . . deforming itself, by submitting to encroachments on its own unity and even perhaps by effecting a cleavage or division of itself" (pp. 152–153). Freud had a specific form of ego distortion in mind, which he elaborated in later papers (1927, 1940). This is the ego's capacity, such as in cases of fetishism, to maintain two opposite views simultaneously, with a resultant loss in its synthetic functions. An example given was that of the fetishist's accurate perception of the female genitals held in the mind side-by-side with the belief in the existence of a female penis. Splitting of this sort, with a loss of synthetic functions, exists in narcissistic character disorders which Kohut described as a "vertical" split.

In our description of the cocoon transference we have suggested that the underlying fantasy of self-sufficiency is defensive and is the consequence of the ego's conflict with the environment. The belief in a state of omnipotent self-sufficiency exists side-by-side with an intense and overwhelming dependency expressed as a craving hunger for admiration and approval. This deformation of the ego is also a split,

as Freud described, whose content follows directly from the ego's conflict with the environment. As we have depicted earlier, the specific deformation provides the basis for a specific transference response in which the ego's conflict with the environment is relived in the analytic setting.

We are led to a closer consideration of the nature of the trauma and the resultant ego disturbance or distortion. It would be naïve to suggest that there is a simple or direct relationship between developmental trauma and a specific characterological syndrome. We know of many instances where the developmental trauma is similar and the resultant characterological response quite variable. In questions of this sort Freud (1937) has emphasized the factor of the quantitative strength of the instincts at the time of the environmental trauma, so that it is ultimately a question of inner rather than outer reality.

Further, we know that the reconstruction of childhood trauma from the analytic material of an adult patient is on a less firm footing than our direct observations of the psychoanalytic process itself. Nevertheless, we are not able to minimize the importance of trauma in the etiology of the narcissistic character disorder, which in a very general way may be described as a developmental failure of the "holding environment."

In our patients we can infer through historical reconstruction that there has been a relative failure in the parental holding environment which takes several forms. The child's sense of safety and ultimately his sense of basic trust depends on his reliance on the parents' judgments in their dealings with him and the external world. Intelligent children can easily perceive that their parents' judgment is "off." We were able to determine that several of our patients who suffered from narcissistic character disorders had mothers who were at times childishly fatuous and silly or extremely unpredictable in their judgments of reality. Kohut has described that the mothers of these patients are lacking in empathy and are overly intrusive, an observation we were able to confirm. This failure of empathy can also take the form of a relative failure of the parents' protective function, that is, to protect the child from excessive stimulation. This may mean the failure to protect the child from sadistic or bullying attacks from other members of the household, as well as a failure to protect the child from excessive sexual stimulation. For there to be a failure of the holding environment, we believe that it is necessary that both parents in some way be involved. We have the impression that in the older child the father's role is significant either in opposing or augmenting the maternal element.

Although the specific form of the failure of the

parental shield may vary, we believe there is a common denominator in that it induces the formation of a precocious and premature sense of self, a sense of self that retains its fragility and must be supported by omnipotent, grandiose fantasies (Modell, 1975b). It is this defensive structure that we see re-emerging in the psychoanalytic process—the cocoon transference. The conflict with the environment that emerges in the middle period of the analytic process reaches a climax when there is a breaking up of the cocoon transference so that the hatred transferred to the analyst is the patient's hatred of reality.

To return to our question—that of the failure of the holding environment in the "classical" case. Trauma and conflict with the environment are of course not absent in the histories of our so-called classical case, but do not lead to a structural deformation of the ego. We have the impression that such traumas may be reflected in periods of "acting in" during the early phase of psychoanalysis and in the relative abandonment of the therapeutic alliance, as if the patient needs to experience regressively the illusion of the magical protection of the analytic setting. In contrast to the patients with narcissistic character disorders, such episodes do not require any lengthy period of ego consolidation before yielding to interpretation.

It should be clear that we approached the problem of the "holding environment" from several points of view. We believe that there are elements of caretaking functions implicit in the object tie of the patient to the analyst, functions that are part of ordinary psychoanalytic technique. Loewald (1960) has said that the analytic setting represents a *new* object tie. In addition to these "real" elements, there is the fantasy that the analytic setting functions in some magical way to protect the patient from the dangers of the environment, a fantasy similar to that of perceiving the analyst as a transitional object (Modell, 1968).

These fantasies commonly appear in the termination phase and are no different from other transference fantasies that can be dealt with by interpretation. In so-called classical cases, the analytic setting functions as a "holding environment" silently; it is something that is taken for granted and can be described as part of the "confident" transference. Where there is ego distortion, the analytic setting as a holding environment is central to the therapeutic action.

Conclusion

The therapeutic action of the holding environment in the transference neuroses can easily be contrasted to that in the narcissistic character disorders. In the former, the holding environmental functions in the manner of a vessel or container that permits the unfolding of the transference neurosis—it provides the necessary background of safety to support illusion. With the narcissistic character disorders, in contrast, the analytic setting facilitates necessary ego consolidation so that mutative interpretations may be eventually effective and a therapeutic alliance may be established. It is only then that elements of the transference neurosis emerge in a form that can be analyzed.

Interpretation leads to the dissolution of magical fantasies associated with the holding environment in a manner analogous to the dissolution of the transference neurosis. If these fantasies associated with the holding environment are not sufficiently analyzed, there is a danger, in the narcissistic character disorder, that the analytic process itself may become a transitional object and the patient would then be addicted to an interminable analysis.

References

Balint, M. (1968), *The Basic Fault*. London: Tavistock Publications.

Bibring, E. (1937), Symposium on the theory of the therapeutic results of psychoanalysis. *Internat. J. Psycho-Anal.*, 18:170-189.

Blum, H. (1971), On the conception and development of the transference neurosis. *This Journal*, 19:41-53.

Fenichel, O. (1938), Ego disturbances and their treatment. In: *Collected Papers*, second series. New York: Norton, 1954, pp. 109-128.

Freud, A. (1969), *Difficulties in the Path of Psychoanalysis*. New York: International Universities Press.

———— & Burlingham, D. (1943), *War and Children*. New York: International Universities Press, 1944.

Freud, S. (1911), Formulations on the two principles of mental functioning. *Standard Edition*, 12:218-226. London: Hogarth Press, 1957.

————(1914), On narcissism: An introduction. *Standard Edition*, 14:67-102. London: Hogarth Press, 1957.

————(1924), Neurosis and psychosis. *Standard Edition*, 19:149–153. London: Hogarth Press, 1961.

————(1927), Fetishism. *Standard Edition*, 21:149–157. London: Hogarth Press, 1964.

————(1937), Analysis terminable and interminable. *Standard Edition*, 23:216–253. London: Hogarth Press, 1964.

————(1940), Splitting of the ego in the process of defence. *Standard Edition*, 23:271–278. London: Hogarth Press, 1964.

Gedo, J. & Goldberg, A. (1973), *Models of the Mind*. Chicago: University of Chicago Press.

Gitelson, M. (1962), On the curative factors in the first phase of analysis. In: *Psychoanalysis: Science and Profession*. New York: International Universities Press, 1973, pp. 311–341.

Glover, E. (1937), Symposium on the theory of the therapeutic results of psychoanalysis. *Internat. J. Psycho-Anal.*, 18:125–132.

Greenson, R. (1974), Transference: Freud or Klein. *Internat. J. Psycho-Anal.*, 55:37–48.

———— & Wexler, M. (1969). The non-transference relationship in the psychoanalytic situation. *Internat. J. Psycho-Anal.*, 50:27–39.

Guntrip, H. (1968), *Schizoid Phenomena, Object Relations, and the Self*. New York: International Universities Press.

Kernberg, O. (1974), Further contributions to the treatment of narcissistic personalities. *Internat. J. Psycho-Anal.*, 55:215–240.

Khan, M. (1963), The concept of cumulative trauma. In: *The Privacy of the Self*. New York: International Universities Press, 1974, pp. 42–58.

————(1973), The role of illusion in the analytic space and process. In: *The Annual of Psychoanalysis*, 1. New York: Quadrangle, pp. 231–246.

Kohut, H. (1971), *The Analysis of the Self*. New York: International Universities Press.

Loewald, H. (1960). On the therapeutic action of psychoanalysis. *Internat. J. Psycho-Anal.*, 41:16–33.

————(1973), Review of Kohut's *The Analysis of the Self*. *Psychoanal. Quart.*, 42:441–451.

Modell, A. H. (1968), *Object Love and Reality*. New York: International Universities Press.

————(1973), Affects and psychoanalytic knowledge. In: *The Annual of Psychoanalysis*, 1. New York: Quadrangle, pp. 117–124.

————(1975a), The ego and the id—fifty years later. *Internat. J. Psycho-Anal.*, 56:57–68.

————(1975b), A narcissistic defense against affects and the illusion of self-sufficiency. *Internat. J. Psycho-Anal.*, 56:275–282.

Panel (1971). Models of the Psychic Apparatus, S. Abrams, reporter. *This Journal*, 19:131–142.

Rosenfeld, H. (1972), A critical appreciation of James Strachey's paper on the nature of the therapeutic action of psychoanalysis. *Internat. J. Psycho-Anal.*, 53:454–461.

————(1974), Discussion of R. R. Greenson's "Transference: Freud or Klein." *Internat. J. Psycho-Anal.*, 55:49–51.

Rycroft, C. (1956), The nature and function of the analysts' communication to the patient. *Internat. J. Psycho-Anal.*, 37:469–472.

Sandler, J. (1960), The background of safety. *Internat J. Psycho-Anal.*, 41:352–356.

Slap, J. (1974), On waking screens. *This Journal*, 22:844–853.

Spitz, R. (1956), Countertransference. *This Journal*, 4:256–265.

Stone, L. (1961), *The Psychoanalytic Situation*. New York: International Universities Press.

Strachey, J. (1934), The nature of the therapeutic action of psychoanalysis. *Internat. J. Psycho-Anal.*, 50:277–292.

Volkan, V. (1973), Transitional fantasies in the analysis of a narcissistic personality. *This Journal*, 21:351–376.

Winnicott, D. (1963), Psychiatric disorders in terms of infantile maturational processes. In: *The Maturational Process and the Facilitating Environment*. New York: International Universities Press, 1965, pp. 230–241.

————(1965), *The Maturational Process and the Facilitating Environment*. New York: International Universities Press.

————(1969), The use of an object and relating through identifications. In: *Playing and Reality*. New York: Basic Books, 1971, pp. 86–94.

Workshop (1974), The Fate of the Transference Neurosis after Analysis, A. Balkoura, reporter. *This Journal*, 22:895–903.

Zetzel, E. (1956), The concept of transference. In: *The Capacity for Emotional Growth*. New York: International Universities Press, 1970, pp. 168–181.

Epilogue

TRUTH THERAPY/LIE THERAPY

ROBERT LANGS

EDITOR'S NOTE

This paper has been chosen to conclude this volume in the belief that it presents a view of the therapeutic experience quite unfamiliar to most therapists. The vantage point adopted in this paper leads to a series of realizations pertinent to the literature sampled in the preceding pages, and brings into question its very foundation. It befits a volume of this kind that it first present the best the field has to offer, and then conclude by taking issue with some of its basic precepts. To the extent that the questions raised are valid and pertinent—and of course it is my belief that they are—this final paper will allow the reader to question those aspects of the psychoanalytic understanding of the therapeutic interaction which rest on questionable premises and means of observation, and which therefore require revision. It is my hope that this volume, representing the best in our psychoanalytic heritage, will prepare the way for what is best in its future.

There have been many efforts of late to characterize and distinguish what has become an enormous variety of therapeutic modalities—psychoanalysis, analytic psychotherapy, supportive therapy, gestalt and existential therapies, behavior modification, and so on. These have been classified along various lines: exploratory versus supportive, breaking down defenses versus reinforcing them, interpersonal versus intrapsychic, individual versus group, individual versus family, etc. There remains, however, a sense of dissatisfaction regarding these distinctions and considerable question in respect to their empirical validity and specific implications for patient-therapist interactions.

The inconclusive status of these distinctions is reflected, too, in a multiplicity of related topics. Issues stand unresolved in respect to the conscious and unconscious motivations within patients as they

Reprinted from *Interactions: The Realm of Transference and Counter-transference*, pp. 401–434. New York: Jason Aronson, 1980.

approach a treatment situation; there is also the question of the conscious and unconscious motives of the therapist who offers such help, as well as of the underlying factors that determine the choice and explication of the therapeutic modality he will use. This touches upon the problem of fundamental resistances within patients in response to a given treatment format, as well as on the issue of counter-resistances within therapists. It also suggests the complicated issue of the process "cure" or symptom alleviation (a term used in its broadest sense to include all types of characterological, behavioral, and symptomatic change) as well as the broader question of the essential nature of the therapeutic interaction itself.

This chapter is an effort to elaborate a *selected fact* (Bion 1962)—a realization that provides a new meaning and synthesis to previously unclarified and disparate clinical observations. This fact crystallized for me, in my clinical and supervisory work, in the opposition (or continuum) that lends this chapter its title: truth therapy/lie therapy. With this as our framework, let us turn to a reconsideration of certain selected concepts pertinent to the therapeutic situation.

SOME BASIC DEFINITIONS

Patient

Let us begin by considering the term *patient*, a term whose meaning is too often taken for granted. Almost without thinking, we could readily state that a patient is an individual who seeks out (or is directed to) and engages a professional—a therapist—in an effort designed for relief of mental suffering and its consequences (neurosis, as I will later term it).

It seems evident, however, that this generally accepted characterization is not only naive but lacks substantial and functional meaning. For example, it would provide no basis for distinguishing a stated wish for help from actual participation in a manner conducive to symptom alleviation. It would allow no room for the differentiation between the conscious wish for cure and unconscious wishes that may contradict this manifest intention.

Similarly, this definition would provide little reason to explore the patient's conscious and unconscious motives for seeking therapy, his expectations as to how it will be carried out, or the implications of his efforts to actually shape the therapy along particular lines. Finally, it would preclude an important distinction that has been largely overlooked: that between the *designated patient* (the person seeking or pushed toward help) and the *functional patient* (the person within the therapeutic dyad who, at a given juncture, is consciously or unconsciously expressing a need for help, that is, for a curative response from the other member of the dyad).

We need a definition of the term, then, that will take into account both stated and unstated— unconsciously expressed—needs and functions. The latter involve factors beyond the former delineation of the patient's role and requisites (e.g., his position vis-à-vis the therapist, his responsibility for the fees and hours, the fundamental rule of free association, etc.). It becomes a matter of defining the characteristics of the functional patient, the range of behaviors and attitudes that characterize a meaningful and workable quest for psychological and emotional help. Beyond the simplistic definition of the designated patient, we must consider whether the designated patient is at any particular point also a functional patient. Similarly, we need criteria to

determine when a designated therapist is, for long or short periods, operating as a functional patient. The final delineation depends on our definition of a number of related terms.

Therapist

The prevailing definition of the term *therapist* is based on his manifest roles and functions: it is actually a definition of what I would term more specifically the *designated therapist*. So defined, the therapist is an individual who, it is supposed, has the expertise to provide symptom relief to the neurotic patient. This definition encompasses the entire range of therapeutic approaches, analytic or not. But if we choose to go deeper, we are faced with the need to define the *functional therapist*. Here we must identify a set of conscious and unconscious behaviors and functions that characterize therapeutic endeavors. On this basis, we could then empirically decide, in examining a particular therapeutic interlude, whether the designated therapist or the designated patient is at that moment serving as the functional therapist, and whether he is doing so consciously or unconsciously.

Therapy

The term *therapy* encompasses, in common parlance, any endeavor to provide symptom relief to the neurotic patient. As such, it embraces many divergent modalities. Here the specific nature of the curative process comes into question. Such issues as effectiveness, durability of outcome, detrimental consequences, and the actual basis for change come under scrutiny. Here it would be particularly helpful if we could identify the actual healing transactions in a given treatment situation. Their surface and underlying aspects must be delineated, including the nature of the spiraling communicative unconscious interaction between patient and therapist, as well as all that it touches upon, both past and present.

In this way, we can shift from the superficially descriptive definition of therapy to one more in keeping with the actuality of unconscious processes. We can then delineate the standards or practices, stated with full sensitivity to both direct and indirect expression, conscious and unconscious meaning and function, that define the various treatment forms.

Neurosis

I propose that we use the term *neurosis* to refer to any symptomatic or characterological disturbance—

somatic, psychic, or behavioral—that derives to some significant degree from inner mental conflict and dysfunction. A neurosis, then, is a maladaptive response, one that is inappropriate to consensually validated reality. It is a reaction based largely on pathological unconscious fantasies, memories, and introjects, as well as on dysfunctions and disturbances in each of the macrostructures: id, ego, and superego. At the core of every neurosis lies the most primitive and psychotic part of the personality: major separation and bodily anxieties, internal structural conflicts, pathological identifications, and fears of highly disruptive mental configurations and elements (see Grotstein 1977a,b). This constellation is built up through the years and therefore involves important genetic factors.

Neurotic responses are maladaptations evoked by current realities and their manifest and latent implications. For patients in therapy or analysis, these *adaptive contexts* occur primarily in the realm of the therapeutic interaction; they derive from the behaviors and verbalizations of the therapist or analyst. Traumatic contexts stemming from relationships outside of treatment are secondary. The discovery, analysis, working through, and resolution-modification of the unconscious factors in a neurosis is one important means of providing a patient the opportunity for an insightful, lasting revision of his maladaptive responses and their replacement with relatively nonsymptomatic, adaptive resources and reactions founded on genuine structural change.

Truth

We require for our purposes a definition of truth relevant to the patient and his neurosis, and to the therapist and his interventions—relevant, in short, to the nature of therapy. It must therefore be a definition that encompasses the immediate unconscious therapeutic communicative interaction as this pertains to the patient's illness. This implies that there can be but one truth system in this context, though patient or therapist can deal with it in a variety of ways. Truths must be formulated as hypotheses through an in-depth evaluation of an activated context and derivative response, and must then be confirmed through an unanticipated Type Two derivative expression.

The search for truth begins with the surface relationship and transactions between patient and therapist, however the two participants are defined. It then extends into the conscious and unconscious implications—meanings and functions—of these transactions, specifically as they pertain to factors underlying the development and maintenance of the patient's neurosis and activated in the patient-therapist interaction.

This definition has many implications. First, it indicates that the most basic truths in psychotherapy pertain to the designated patient's illness. It therefore implies that the neurosis of the designated therapist is secondary and has meaning only as it relates to the emotional difficulties of the patient. However, it does leave room for the recognition that under certain conditions the neurosis of the therapist may take center stage—at which point he becomes, by the definitions developed here, the functional patient.

Second, this conception places the spiraling unconscious communicative interactions between patient and therapist at the very heart of the treatment situation. It encompasses the surface and depths of this interaction, its manifest and latent dimensions, and suggests that the truth about the patient's neurosis can be known only by taking this interaction as the starting point and tracing out its constituents from there—intrapsychically, interactionally, dynamically, and genetically.

Third, this definition permits the understanding of truth in terms of both reality and fantasy. It allows consideration of both accurate and erroneous perceptions of actuality, of both realistic and unrealistic forms of imagination. It accommodates both the introjective and the projective aspects of the patient's experiences within the therapeutic interaction, and fosters the understanding of the patient's illness in terms of sources in both the present and the past, within the therapeutic situation as well as outside it. Empirically, however, it stresses the overriding primacy of the former.

Truth, as defined here, can be stated in terms related to the psychoanalytic validation within the clinical situation. The formulation of such truths requires a maximal degree of self-knowledge within the therapist, who must be capable of generating validatable assessments of his own mental state, his conscious and unconscious communications to the patient, the nature of the conscious and unconscious therapeutic interaction, and the full scope of the communications from the patient. The ultimate test for the truth of an interpretation is whether, when imparted to the patient, it meets with interactional and cognitive validation. Interactional validation occurs through *derivative* representations of positive introjective identifications with a therapist considered capable of understanding the truth. Cognitive validation is afforded the therapist by the revelation of indirect, surprising, and unique Type Two derivatives (i.e., disguised material which organizes meaningfully around an immediate adaptive context related to therapy), often in the form of the emergence of a *selected fact*.

In the actual development of this definition, it was the search for postulates for which Type Two derivative validation could be consistently obtained that led to the selection of truth as it pertains to the patient's neurosis as a key dimension of the therapeutic experience. It is therefore possible to propose that therapeutic modalities can be defined in terms of their approach to and handling of this particular form of truth in the treatment situation. Before doing so, it will be necessary for us to define the opposite of truth, the lie.

Lie

We may define the term *lie* free of any pejorative implications (see Bion 1970). In our context, it may be defined as any communication or behavior, conscious or unconscious, designed on some level to avoid, falsify, break the link to, or create the barrier against the dynamically cogent meanings and functions of the patient's neurosis within the therapeutic interaction. In short, a lie is any effort to seal off or destroy awareness of the truth—the actual factors and expressions of the patient's neurosis. As we shall see, most lies in therapy are expressed unconsciously. Our definition does not refer to conscious and deliberate lies, since these may either express or obliterate the truth of the patient's illness.

While the term *lie* has a penumbra of meanings that might adversely affect its scientific usage, it serves remarkably well as a selected fact. Attempts to develop a different term, such as barrier, fiction, or falsification, proved unsuccessful. None of these were able to convey the essential implications of the term *lie*.

Empirically, a lie is revealed when the material from the patient fails to permit a meaningful interpretation—an assessment that must be subjected carefully to validation. In addition, whenever an interpretation or management of the framework is met with a nonvalidating response, we may suspect the presence of lie communication in patient or therapist.

The implications of the term *lie* may be made somewhat clearer by recognizing that defenses and resistances may be expressed as potential truths or functional lies. If their manifestations can be organized around a specific adaptive context to yield Type Two derivative meaning, they have truthful qualities. I have previously described their presence in the Type A communicative field, in which the use of symbols and illusion prevails (Langs 1978). In this instance, the communicative expressions of defense and resistance contain within them derivative (unconscious) elements of truth and meaning. Therefore, even though they function for purposes of defense, they also serve to search for and express the truth of the patient's neurosis.

On the other hand, there is another constellation of defenses and resistances which have rather different communicative qualities in respect to truth and lie. They serve to destroy meaning, rather than to reveal it in disguised form. They deal with truth by creating lies and barriers to its expression. They are functional falsifications quite divorced from any derivative expression of the prevailing truth about the therapeutic interaction and the patient's neurosis. The lie-defense is a barrier to the truth, rather than a disguised expression of it. This is a form of communication that I attempted to delineate in describing the static Type C communicative field, characterized by barrier formations and falsifications and in which relatedness and meaning are destroyed (Bion 1977, Langs 1978e).

This is a specific definition of the lie, one based on the unconscious functions of a communication. A conscious lie in these terms may serve to either express or obliterate underlying truths; it may be a derivative of the truth or a barrier to it. If the former, it is not a lie as defined here. If the latter, it is the most flagrant and pervasive form of the lie-barrier that we know of.

To my knowledge, these distinctions have not been specified in the prior literature. They are, however, foreshadowed by Bion's discussion (1977) of the Column Two function of the grid. This column represents statements known by the speaker to be false on one level of discourse (however truthful on another), statements that serve as barriers to underlying chaotic truths. Bion has also given unique consideration to the conscious liar and the lie system (1970), and his comments on − K, efforts to destroy knowledge and understanding (1962), are also relevant. The key concept is that of two distinctive types of defensive formation: (1) those based on derivatives which upon analysis reveal both their own unconscious meanings and functions and that which is defended against (the usual psychoanalytic conception); and (2) those based on impervious barriers which do not reflect or reveal upon analysis either their underlying meanings and functions or that which is thereby sealed off.

In the clinical situation this distinction can be made by identifying the prevailing adaptive context within the therapeutic interaction. If the material organizes meaningfully as Type Two derivatives in response to that context, in terms of unconscious fantasies and perceptions, we have an expression of some underlying truth. If, on the other hand, there is either a distinct absence of any representation of the adaptive context, or if there is an evident context without a meaningful derivative constellation, we have evidence for the presence of lies and barriers.

While there is only one constellation of truth, there are many lies and barriers. Some serve as intrapsychic walls and as a means of rupturing interpersonal ties (links) between patient and therapist. Others function primarily as projective identifications and as a means of action-discharge through which disturbing falsifications are placed into the object either in the service of riddance or as evocation-of-proxy responses (Wangh 1962).

Some projective identifications express and impart truths, while others entail lies. This suggests a distinction regarding Type B communicators, who make extensive use of action-discharge mechanisms and projective identification, that had never previously been delineated: some patients use these mechanisms in the service of a search for the truth, while others use them in order to destroy the truth and maintain the lie. Interpretations of the underlying meanings and functions of the projective identification prove feasible with the first group, though not with the second, with whom interventions must center on the nature and functions of the prevailing lie and barrier.

The Polarization of Two Basic Therapeutic Modalities

With these definitions in mind, let us now take our concepts of patient, therapist, and therapy and superimpose each on the axis connecting (and separating) our concepts of truth and lie. Such a process will in all likelihood allow us to provide a more specific content for each of the concepts involved. Several avenues of approach suggest themselves here, of which I shall choose but one: a discussion of psychoanalysis and psychoanalytically oriented psychotherapy. I choose these modalities because of their avowed intention to seek out, identify, and analyze the truth of the patient's neurosis. Many noninterpretive therapeutic approaches would accept readily the characterization if not the appellation of lie-barrier therapy outlined here. They do not profess to approach psychoanalytic truth, sometimes

not acknowledging it at all. Their self-understanding is that they effect their therapeutic results in some other manner. I will return to this subject in my final discussion, since I hope to offer a point of view that will foster a sympathetic understanding of the nature of these therapeutic modalities and of the patients and therapists who turn to them.

Truth therapy

We can distinguish two extreme types of patients, therapists, and therapies. With respect to truth or lie communication, a number of combinations of patients and therapists are possible. However, truth therapy can exist and be perpetuated only in the presence of a patient and a therapist who are both of them truth-receiving (listening) and truth-telling (associating and intervening). While this is the ideal model for insight-oriented therapy and is taken for granted in most analytic writings, once we define the relevant attributes we will be in a position to discover just how rare this type of treatment actually is.

In brief, truth therapy is a treatment situation in which the conditions are created that permit the patient to express analyzable derivatives, the therapist to impart sound interpretations, and the patient to receive and meaningfully utilize the proffered understanding. If we focus first on the patient, it can be readily seen that our considerations go well beyond his surface announcement that he wishes to understand himself or, more vaguely, to be relieved of his symptoms. It is also insufficient to state that the truth-seeking patient is capable of free associating and of tolerating the deprivations and limited gratifications of a sound analytic setting and interpretive approach. Similarly, it is inadequate to suggest that such a patient is capable of forming a manifest therapeutic alliance with the therapist based on apparent cooperative efforts directed toward insight and understanding.

The criteria for a truth-seeking patient involve the manner in which he expresses himself and receives and processes the interventions from the therapist. In regard to the former, the truth patient utilizes the Type A communicative mode. Over brief sequences of sessions, these patients represent directly or through relatively undisguised derivatives the prevailing adaptive context within the therapeutic interaction. They provide as well a coalescing derivative network in which meaningful unconscious perceptions, fantasies, memories, and introjects are available. Their material leads to a validated interpretative intervention related to a pertinent therapeutic context or indicator that touches ultimately upon the patient's symptomatology and its genetic and current underpinnings.

Quite unconsciously, then, truth patients express their genuine wish to understand by becoming engaged in meaningful *derivative communication*, viable indirect communications organizable around an adaptive context derived from the therapist's interventions. This is the hallmark of a truth-telling patient. And while ultimately his search is directed toward the truth about his own inner mental world and neurosis, he is also prepared to touch upon the true meanings of the therapist's communications as they reflect both the latter's neurosis and his sound functioning. The patient seeks ultimately to know and understand both his unconscious fantasies and his unconscious perceptions of the therapist. These are consistently developed in response to their spiraling communicative interaction, an ongoing reality filled with unconscious implications. All other adaptive contexts and communications, however meaningful, will accrue specific pertinence through linkages to this communicative interaction. In fact, the absence of any such link implies a departure from the search for the ultimate truth about the patient and a shift toward lie-barrier therapy. Thus, while the truths which must be dealt with in the therapeutic situation are layered hierarchically, a sine qua non is the link to the central adaptive context within the therapeutic interaction. Only interpretations that take into account the main adaptive contexts within the interaction, and the patient's unconscious responses to them, receive Type Two derivative validation.

Next, we can consider the therapist, who has been attending to the patient's associations. Let's assume a truth-seeking patient who has represented the main adaptive context and his derivative responses. For the therapist to be in a position to comprehend and interpret such material, and to have his intervention experienced by the patient as a statement of truth, there must exist a secure and stable therapeutic environment. While a patient may express truth-seeking derivatives in a modified frame (almost always, these are references to the deviation itself), he will have major difficulties in experiencing the therapist's interventions as similarly truth-seeking unless the framework is secured or in the process of being rectified. This is the case largely because deviations in the basic ground rules and therapeutic contract serve as barriers to the truth; they convey a valid image of the therapist as lying and lie-seeking. For a patient to experience the therapist's interventions as an entirely symbolic effort directed toward

understanding the truth, there must be no contradictory communications. Alterations in the framework, for example, usually belie such efforts.

The truth therapist, then, is capable of securing and maintaining a stable and consistent therapeutic environment, of adhering to the frame in the face of nonemergency efforts by the patient to evoke deviations, and of responding interpretively to such pressures as well. In the presence of an inadvertent or patient-evoked alteration of the framework, such a therapist is capable of both rectifying the frame and interpreting the patient's responsive unconscious fantasies and perceptions. When the frame is stable, he is able to offer sound interpretations based on an integrated approach that involves the prevailing indicators and adaptive context, as well as the most meaningful aspects of the derivative complex.

The capacity of a therapist to effect truth therapy is by no means a simply cognitive accomplishment. In order to generate an interpretation or reconstruction that will receive Type Two derivative validation, he must first be capable of appreciating the unconscious implications of his interventions — silences, interpretations, reconstructions, and managements of the framework. This requires a capacity for self-analysis and an ability to organize the material from the patient as a Type Two derivative commentary on the adaptive context of each of his interventions, including their manifest and latent implications. This requires a great deal of the therapist: a capacity for frustration and tolerance and for delay; an ability to renounce the gratification of pathological instinctual drives and the use of pathological defenses; a healthy and secure superego and ego-ideal system; the capacity to tolerate and contain projective identifications and role and image evocations; and a relative mastery of his own pathological tendencies. It seems likely, then, that an unanalyzed therapist can only hope to approximate truth therapy and that only a truth analysis can enable a therapist to develop fully the use of this treatment modality.

While there are many additional requisites the therapist must meet in order to do truth therapy, I would add but one, a factor that applies equally to patient and therapist. Stating it in terms of the therapist, I am referring to a set of interrelated capacities to tolerate and analyze the emergence of a therapeutic regression in the patient (the expression of primitive and sometimes terrifying derivatives of his inner mental world), to experience disruptive and pathological pressures and projective identifications, and to tolerate some degree of parallel regression and primitive expression within himself. The search for truth always entails such regression, as well as significant pain. On the positive side, to the extent that the therapist experiences a limited and appropriate regression, he can grow in personal insight. It is, however, essential to delineate the positive and negative attributes of truth therapy, or of any truth system, and to recognize both its pain and its adaptive rewards. We will return to this issue once we have further clarified the patient's contribution to truth therapy.

We now turn to the truth-seeking patient once he has received a correct interpretation (i.e., an understanding of a segment of the truth in respect to the most active and pertinent neurotic manifestations within the therapeutic bipersonal field at a given moment, be it in the patient or therapist). In my earlier investigations (Langs 1978a,b, 1979), I had assumed that truth-seeking patients (and actually, virtually all patients) respond to a correct interpretation with two forms of validation: (1) derivatives reflecting an inevitable positive introjective identification with the understanding therapist (the interactional and relationship spheres); and (2) Type Two derivative validation with the report of surprising new material that not only confirms the interpretation in an unexpected manner but that also functions quite often as a *selected fact,* giving new meaning to previously disparate material. The latter is a cognitive validation.

My more recent studies, however, have indicated that this dual validation does not in itself suffice as a means of identifying the truth seeker. There are actually three attributes to the truth patient: (1) the expression of analyzable derivatives stemming from an adaptive context within therapy; (2) a response with Type Two derivative validation to correct interpretation or management of the frame by the therapist; and (3) his actual utilization of the insights derived in this way to achieve conscious understanding, the development and use of new adaptive resources, conflict resolution, and the modification of ego dysfunctions and maladaptive responses. Thus the patient's validating response takes place primarily on an unconscious level. He may then react in one of several ways to his experience of a correct interpretation and his responsive associations. Continued truth seeking is only one of several possibilities.

The patient who is fully accepting of truth therapy is both a *truth seeker* and *truth receiver.* He will therefore process his cognitive insights and introjective experiences in a way that leads him to consciously recognize at least some fragment of the truth as it had not previously been known to him. He is able to broaden his self-understanding and to link other realizations to this new truth. He makes use of his direct insight into himself—and the therapist—in effecting new and more constructive adaptive responses. When such responses, founded upon conscious insight and unconscious conflict resolution, become durable, we speak of insightful structural change.

Truth-seeking patients make use of these insights in a manner that constructively influences their behavior. They soon embark upon new adaptive behaviors and offer fresh communications unconsciously designed to reach out toward additional repressed, denied, or split-off truths. This thrust toward growth, however gratifying, is studded with periods of defense-resistance, anxiety, regression, and suffering. Eventually, however, come new resolution and relative peace.

There is another kind of patient, who communicates truth-containing derivatives, who then obtains a truthful interpretive response from the therapist, who next provides almost immediate cognitive and interactional validation, and who yet proves incapable of processing this understanding toward adaptive structural change. At the very last moment, so to speak, they turn away from the truth and prove refractory. They do not work through the insights they have indirectly validated and acknowledged. Their maladaptive behavior and symptoms remain unchanged. They may be characterized as *truth seekers* and as *lie receivers (obliterators).*

Implicit to this conception of truth therapy is the understanding that the neuroses develop through two interrelated factors: (1) pathological and distorting intrapsychic fantasies, introjects, and memories; and (2) pathological behaviors and attitudes in external objects (in particular, the maternal figure and the therapist), which form the basis for disruptive introjects and distortions in id, ego, and superego functioning. Because of this, truth therapy requires an understanding of the unconscious implications of the therapist's actual behaviors and interactions, as well as of the patient's inner mental world. While all truths related to the therapeutic interaction must ultimately be traced out to those within the patient, it remains critical to understand that important truths within the bipersonal field may stem from the therapist as well.

Truth therapy may be considered a commensal relationship (Bion 1970) or healthy symbiosis (Searles 1975) in which the patient is able to individuate himself. While it entails a frightening disequilibrium, it is optimally nondestructive and devoid of any degree of pathological symbiosis or parasitism (Bion 1970). In general, available surface insights and understanding are in keeping with the under-lying unconscious truths, so that there is a sense of consistency and integrity that is relatively lacking in lie therapy. A major motivation for truth therapy lies in the wish within both patient and therapist to cope through understanding, active mastery, knowledge, and integrity—whatever their temporary cost. By no means do all patients and therapists prefer this par-ticular adaptive mode.

There are many motives within both patient and therapist that prompt them to depart from truth therapy. In structural terms, these motives involve defensiveness, superego corruption, and the wish for pathological instinctual drive gratifications. On an object relationship level, they entail wishes for inappropriate fusion and merger. In terms of affects, they involve active wishes to immediately and mal-adaptively obliterate anxiety, depression, guilt, and the like. Intrapsychically, the hope is to submerge and bypass inner conflict and to create rigid barriers against the influence of pathological unconscious fantasies, memories, and introjects. In terms of the therapeutic process and the role of necessary but temporary therapeutic regression, the wish is to avoid such experiences and the more primitive parts of the personality that would find expression in its course. There are needs as well to deny the neces-sary degree of separateness between patient and therapist. More broadly, the wish is to deny dreaded anticipations of nonexistence and death.

When the search for truth exists in only one of the two participants to the therapeutic dyad, destructive envy is mobilized in the other participant. A truth-seeking therapist is experienced at times by all patients, and in particular by lie patients, as perse-cutory and attacking, since he threatens to unleash the painful affects and contents related to their most disturbing inner constellations. In this light, we can begin to appreciate the extent to which psycho-analysts and others have failed, despite the intensity of their quest, to develop a validated, truth-seeking treatment modality, and the pervasive struggle among individual therapists against work of this kind.

Lie therapy

While there is but one form of truth therapy, there are many types of lie therapy, and of lie patients and lie therapists. In this context, it is well to be reminded that the term *lie* as used here implies ultimately an unconsciously determined falsification and the development of impenetrable barriers to underlying truths, accompanied as a rule by significant breaks

in interpersonal relatedness. The lie is a form of nonrepresentation, of *nonderivative communication.* Functionally, it serves to obliterate and seal off expressions of the patient's neurosis and his valid unconscious perceptions of disturbances in the ther-apist. The hallmark of the lie patient can be found in the clinical validation of the impossibility of meaningfully organizing his material around an adaptive context known to the therapist and derived from the therapeutic interaction.

Lie patients range from those who tell deliberate, obliterating untruths to those who use surface truths as barriers to unconscious truths. A lie patient may consciously believe in the veracity of a particular communication, despite its essential function as an untruth vis-à-vis the actively mobilized neurotic constellation within the bipersonal field, primarily within the patient, though secondarily within the therapist as well. Unconsciously, then, lie patients often use apparent truths as barriers to more cata-strophic truths connected to the most pressing mani-festations of neurosis within the therapeutic inter-action (Bion 1977).

Lies, then, are designed to substitute either falsifi-cations or superficial truths for more disturbing and compelling underlying truths, and to create impene-trable barriers to these inner and outer actualities. It is here that the difference in the defenses of the truth seeker and the lie patient can be identified: the truth-ful patient will defend himself with communications designed to cover underlying fantasies, conflict, and disturbance; nonetheless, he ultimately reveals in some derivative form the hidden unconscious mean-ings and functions of both the defense and the underlying neurotic disturbance. On the other hand, the lie patient does not communicate such derivative meaning; his expressions are designed essentially for the destruction and concealment of meaning.

On another level, the truth seeker maintains a sig-nificant degree of relatedness with the therapist even as he defends himself, while the lie patient attempts to destroy meaningful interpersonal links. His goal is the destruction of meaning and the creation of nonmeaning and defensive chaos; he is a negative rather than a positive communicator. The truth seeker intends to create understanding, however dis-guised, and to seek it out, while the lie patient has no such purpose; he wishes instead to obliterate the possibility of any emergence of meaning and truth. (These considerations are comparable to, but extend, my recent discussion of the Type A and Type C patient; see Langs 1978e.)

It has been remarkably difficult for psychoanalysts

to recognize the existence of lie patients. This blind spot appears based in part on a lack of insight into the attitude and propensities of many analysts in regard to the search for meaning or its destruction. A lie therapist is inconceivable to most analysts. Nonetheless, in the specific clinical situation, both patient and therapist may operate under the influence of lie systems. These may be based on shared premises, which will tend to make the two participants quite compatible, or they may be founded on distinctly different assumptions (falsifications or barriers), creating distinct clashes. The latter situation can be thought of as an unrecognized version of what Bion (1963) has termed *reversing perspective*: therapist and patient experience the same sensory cues—verbal and nonverbal—though each makes use of the material for a different lie system.

With a lie patient, a truth therapist will focus his therapeutic efforts on the unconscious meanings and functions of the patient's lie-barrier needs and propensities. Any other effort is bound to be hollow, and is tantamount to joining in the patient's lie system and maintaining a pretense of therapy, a false illusion that will function on some level as a neurotic (open to reality testing) or psychotic (closed to reality testing) delusion.

If we define the lie therapist as communicating in a way that avoids the critical unconscious communicative interaction, that is, the prevailing adaptive context and the patient's unconscious responses, then the literature suggests that lie therapists and lie patients are extremely common in both the psychotherapeutic and the psychoanalytic situations. It appears, in fact, that lie patients are the rule. It is therefore essential to understand the nature of the symptom alleviation that may occur in a lie therapy setting.

The essence of lie therapy is the creation of falsifications and barriers to the truth of the patient's neurosis, and secondarily that of the therapist, as activated within the therapeutic interaction. There is considerable evidence that some degree of symptom relief can take place on this basis, entirely without true understanding. This entails the commonly referred to reinforcement of the patient's defenses, many of which are pathological, and the gratification as well of pathological conscious and unconscious needs and fantasies. It also involves the offer of new lie systems to the patient. Unconsciously, the lie therapist proposes new types of impenetrable barriers to the underlying truths within the bipersonal field and new means of rupturing meaningful interpersonal links to the point where these formations may seal off an active pathological core within the patient, providing him temporary symptom relief. Pathological symbiosis is also offered.

The situation is, as a rule, even more complex than this initial description would imply. The lie therapist generates a series of unconscious perceptions, projections, and projective identifications which are by and large introjected by the patient. These may have very complicated effects, including a reinforcement of the patient's own lie system, his defensively obliterating functions and his Type C barriers. This also exacerbates the patient's unconscious need to protect himself from the therapist's neurosis.

While lie-based introjects may prove to be symptom alleviating, they also entail distinctly detrimental elements. As Bion (1970) has noted, the relationship between the overt liar and his audience is essentially parasitic and unconsciously designed to destroy both participants; the same holds true for the unwitting liar, whether patient or therapist. Whatever other mechanisms of symptom alleviation are available in lie therapy, there is little development of unencumbered adaptive resources, little possibility for true growth and individuation, and the creation instead of a need for relatively rigid and fixed barriers and systems of falsification. In addition, the interactions in the lie therapy are at bottom destructive, weak, uninsightful, and envious. Nonetheless, the lie is for many an attractive barrier against underlying catastrophic truths and is frequently put to such use by both members of the therapeutic dyad.

Thus, lie systems and therapy involve the development of usually brittle and rigid Type C barriers and falsifications that require endless reinforcement and repetition, though they may very well succeed in temporarily sealing off the most primitive and disturbing parts of the patient's or therapist's personality, as well as of their interaction. The lie offers an immediate sense of relief at the expense of a full definition of inner and outer reality, and leads to the formation of illusory and delusional phenomena. In this light, many symptomatic acts and slips of the tongue can be understood as what I would call neurotic hallucinations and delusions, in that such false impressions and beliefs occur in otherwise nonpsychotic persons and yield readily to reality testing while nonetheless being unconsciously maintained. Yet despite these liabilities, the lie system offers immediate protection, a quick means of modifying anxiety and frustration, and a potential barrier to underlying disturbance. It is a system and form of therapy, then, with its own assets and liabilities: it may sometimes lead to rather stable and nondisruptive symptom alleviation, though quite often this proves to be a fragile equilibrium vulnerable to deterioration.

CLASSIFYING PATIENTS AND THERAPISTS

Lie patients

It is possible tentatively to clinically identify some relatively common types of lie patients.

The overt liar. This type of patient is, as a rule, diagnosed as either schizophrenic or psychopathic, and has proven refractory to most treatment modalities. While the psychopath is almost always a lie patient, the schizophrenic is less frequently so, even if he does use lies. Much depends here on the extent to which these lies function unconsciously as derivative and therefore revealing communications. In general, these patients are extremely vulnerable to frustration or hurt. They respond with lies and barriers, and often with action, flight, or a rupture of personal relatedness.

The deliberate, nonderivative liar epitomizes certain characteristics of all individuals inclined toward the use of unconscious lie systems: an inability to tolerate frustrating realities, a need to evade such actualities through direct falsifications rather than deal with them, and a strong sense of underlying destructiveness and pathological symbiotic need.

Interventions built upon the contents of a falsification are absurdities; they demean and ridicule the therapist. This quality demonstrates the parasitic effects of the liar in his relationship with his audience—here, the therapist. It must be stressed that even though seemingly meaningful derivatives may be contained in surface lie communications, the very presence of the deliberate lie tends to undermine their deeper truthful implications.

In intervening, the therapist must keep in mind that this communicative style involving the blatant lie must first be modified interpretively before any other type of therapeutic work can be undertaken. The therapist must be quite certain he has not unconsciously contributed to the liar's propensity. He must recognize that the therapeutic modification of this style, as well as of any unconscious lie system, must be founded upon development of a secure therapeutic framework and on an essentially truth-seeking interpretive approach. Both insight and inevitable introjective identifications serve as vehicles for the shift from deliberate lying to a more truthful communicative style.

This touches upon the basic issue of whether it is possible to modify a patient's use of lie systems to the extent that he becomes, in the main, a truth-seeker. While a definitive answer to this question would require extensive empirical investigation, my general impression is that such a change would be, at the very least, extremely difficult to accomplish. In general, the more blatant and pervasive the need to consciously lie, the more difficult it is to develop such a transformation. Unconscious lie systems and patients are more amenable to analytic change. Much depends on the extent to which the patient's use of deliberate and covert lies alternates with truth-seeking communication, since it is the latter that will reveal the unconscious meanings, functions, and genetics of the patient's need to lie.

The mindless patient. This type of lie patient is usually diagnosed as schizophrenic or borderline. He tends to be under intense pressure from the psychotic part of his personality, which is both quite active and quite primitive. By obliterating the presence of thoughts, this type of lie patient attempts to create impervious barriers to the catastrophic qualities of his most immediate fantasies and perceptions.

There are degrees of mindlessness, the most extensive of which is the obliteration of any awareness of thought, feeling, and the like. Next are patients who permit isolated, fragmented contents to register, though they obliterate all intrapsychic connections and interpersonal links. As some of these fragments begin to coalesce, this type of patient may disown them and experience them as arising either through the influence of someone else or involuntarily from within. They tend to respond with other distancing devices, endeavoring to destroy or obliterate any thoughts or affects that manage to emerge. In verbalizing, they are hollow and repetitious. They place themselves outside of their conscious fantasies and talk about such neutral issues as how they should indeed get around to exploring and dealing with what is on their mind. There is a failure in containing function and a need for either autism or for a pathological symbiotic mode of relatedness with the therapist.

These patients may be silent in therapy for long periods. At best they offer fragmented and terse associations using a single image or lacking imagery entirely. Even the single-image associations are generally stated in an empty and barren way, without specificity and with little nuance. Only rarely is an adaptive context represented and linked to a derivative complex, and even then it tends to be greatly disguised. The links between other actual and potential thoughts are severed, and in addition the basic interrelatedness with the therapist is restricted or seemingly absent. Should thoughts appear, they are usually so disturbing and evidently psychotic—often intensely paranoid and depressive—that the patient makes strong secondary efforts to obliterate their existence or to take physical flight from the situation in which the thoughts occurred.

Despite these restrictions, some of these patients are in part truth-seeking. From time to time they communicate a represented adaptive context and a fragmented derivative network, thereby producing unconscious meanings which can then be interpreted to them. Often, however, the therapist is restricted technically to the playback of representations of this type of lie-barrier defensiveness, since the underlying anxieties, fantasies, memories, and introjects are nowhere in evidence. A great deal of patient holding and containing is called for, though care must be taken to not miss opportunities for interpretive comments and to mistakenly remain fixated with unhelpful confronting and noninterpretive interventions.

The lie narrator. This type of patient, whom I have described elsewhere (Langs 1978e) as the Type C narrator, is often richly imaginative and superficially appealing. He engages in long and sometimes dramatic narrative tales filled with deceptively attractive imagery. However, the failure of this material to organize meaningfully around an adaptive context betrays its primary function as an unconscious lie-barrier to underlying chaotic truths. On other occasions, these patients will go on in endless detail about a particular adaptive context, reporting flat direct thoughts and fantasies about the therapist or analyst, but without offering meaningful indirect derivatives. When they display imagination in elaborating their conscious fantasies about the analyst, it is always in the absence of any representation of a significant adaptive context.

The unwary therapist will tend to treat such material in terms of its surface meanings, or as Type One derivatives without an adaptive context, and so will offer functionally meaningless lie-interventions involving purported unconscious meanings and genetic sources. Such interventions do not receive Type Two derivative validation but instead evoke continued rumination and surface elaborations. Under such conditions the therapist has joined the patient in his lie system. The therapeutic work takes place entirely in terms of content that is either manifest or hollowly latent; the underlying chaos within patient, therapist, and their interaction is entirely avoided. It seems likely that many false analyses have taken place with patients of this kind

in treatment with analysts who have understood the basic function neither of these communications nor of their own interventions.

The frame changer. Largely on an unconscious level, patients sense that the very existence of truth therapy can be undermined by modifications in the ideal or standard framework of the therapeutic and analytic situations (Langs 1979). As a result these patients will attempt in both gross and subtle ways, sometimes repeatedly, to engage the therapist in alterations of the therapeutic environment. These are attempts not only to create a lie-dominated bipersonal field but also to provide intrapsychic and interpersonal barriers to underlying truths. In addition, they involve pathological projective identification and relatedness.

Two distinct types of frame changes can be identified: (1) those who attempt to modify the frame in order to express their own propensities toward lie communication and to destroy any possibility of truth therapy; and (2) those who generate thrusts toward lie therapy in the hope of establishing a truth therapy situation. With the first group, efforts to secure the frame and to interpret the implications of the patient's efforts at deviation will prove difficult, since the patient seldom provides a meaningful communicative network—a represented adaptive context and a coalescing derivative complex. These are patients in whom lying and pathological symbiosis are deeply ingrained. They wish only for a lie therapy and will obliterate virtually every meaningful interpretation from the therapist, as also every genuine effort on his part to create a secure and truthful bipersonal field. Such patients are reminiscent of those described by Balint (1968) in terms of regression in search of gratification rather than in search of adaptive change. The second type of patient is more inclined toward truth seeking, and attempts to provide, for himself and the therapist, an opportunity to analyze and modify their propensities for lying. His efforts at modifying the framework will be accompanied by meaningful derivative communication, and he will respond favorably to the therapist's interpretations and managements of the framework, and to a healthier mode of relatedness.

It is in this context that we may stress the extent to which a secure framework is necessary for truth therapy. Lie patients attempt to modify the basic conditions of treatment by altering the framework and hope to achieve *framework deviation cures, therapeutic misalliances,* and pathological symbioses through the establishment of falsifications and Type C barriers designed to seal off all access to the psychotic and other disturbing parts of their personalities.

The somatizer. There is some indication that the somatization of unconscious fantasies, memories, and introjects is a form of lie communication. Somatizers tend to make frequent use of unconscious lies and barriers; there is reason to postulate that this type of somatization tends to occur in a Type C field. More rarely, there may be a meaningful derivative network associated with such symptoms.

This list is by no means exhaustive. It emphasizes the expressive side of this communicative style and leaves the receptive side untouched. Those who obliterate, falsify, or destroy the meaning and implications of what they see, hear, and momentarily understand must receive attention as well. These patients are *lie receivers* or *obliterators of truth,* and their responses to the analyst's interventions are greatly influenced by this factor.

Lie therapists and analysts

The lie therapist can be identified through the nature of his interventions, which reflect his receptive and expressive communicative propensities. All noninterpretive therapists may be classified as lie therapists, while interpretive therapists and analysts may be categorized along several lines. I will offer two such classifications.

The first is based on the identification of what appear to be the basic false premises of clinical psychoanalysis. These are passed on from analyst to analyst through their own personal analyses and the formal teaching they receive. They contribute to their functioning as lie therapists and analysts. Space permits the listing of only two of these false premises—one regarding the analyst, the other the patient—and a true premise regarding each of these.

False premise. The analyst is a participant-observer whose main function is to create a flexible, relatively safe background and relationship for the patient's pathological projections and transferences. These transferences are distortions based on displacements from past relationships. In general, the analyst functions well and is effective. His interventions are to be understood primarily in terms of their intended, conscious meanings and functions. They should be largely interpretive, though noninterpretive interventions have their place, often as preliminary to interpretation and reconstruction. Management of the ground rules relies on common sense and requires flexibility.

The analyst's countertransferences—his pathological responses—are relatively rare and isolated. Though based on unconscious fantasies they are usually gross, self-evident, and limited. Only rarely do they significantly influence the course of an analysis.

True premise. The analyst is in a continuous unconscious communicative interaction with the patient. His behaviors, silences, interventions, and managements of the ground rules or framework convey not only their consciously intended implications but also crucial unconscious communications. The patient consistently adapts to these stimuli, which prove to be the primary source of his associations and behaviors, whether conscious or unconscious; outside stimuli are secondary and exert their effects through their influence on the continuing communicative interaction. The analyst has two major functions—interpreting-reconstructing and managing the framework—and all departures from an interpretive stance and the maintenance of a steady and secure frame are filled with pathological unconscious communications to which the patient is exquisitely sensitive.

As a dimension of the ever-present communicative interaction, the influence of unconscious countertransference fantasies, memories, introjects, and the like is always present to some degree. In addition to these inevitable countertransferences, which exert a low-level continuous influence, there may be interludes in which preponderant countertransference is the central feature of the therapeutic interaction. As a rule the therapist or analyst becomes the functional patient at such times, and the designated patient may respond by becoming the functional therapist.

In sum, the false premise tends to isolate the therapist from the patient, and to imply that the two are involved in a static relationship in which the therapist's communications are given only surface consideration, while those from the patient are sometimes viewed in depth. The true premise sees the patient and therapist in an extensive and continuous unconscious communicative interaction; every nuance of the therapist's work has a strong unconscious influence on the patient and vice versa.

False premise. The patient is emotionally ill. Because of this, he largely distorts his relationship with the therapist or analyst so that his associations and behaviors are based primarily on pathological fantasies and on displacements from the past and projections—transferences. In the main, the patient's free associations are derived from intrapsychic conflicts and derivatives, which tend to be viewed as isolated mental products. In the face of occasional empathic failures or inevitable separations, the therapist's behaviors are evocative of material from the patient, which nonetheless can best be understood intrapsychically and in terms of displacements from past significant relationships.

In the main, transference expressions are conveyed through direct allusions to the therapist, or through evident displacement figures. While healthy functioning is acknowledged in the patient, much of it is confined to his rational capability to maintain a cooperative relationship with the therapist—the therapeutic alliance. Little attention is paid to other valid (nontransference) capacities, and the patient's sound unconscious perceptiveness, especially as it pertains to the analyst's conscious and unconscious communications, is virtually ignored. Resistances are intrapsychically based and are to be interpreted as such.

True premise. The patient is indeed ill, likely to project and distort, and bound to express his pathological mental world through projections and transferences. Nonetheless, these reactions are consistently stimulated by aspects of the immediate relationship with the therapist, and by the latter's conscious and unconscious communications. The patient's reactions to the therapist are always a mixture of transference and nontransference, unconscious distortion and valid perceptiveness. The transference component, which is represented in every communication from the patient, can be identified only after the valid elements. Every interpretation from the therapist should, in principle, account for both the distorted and the veridical aspects of the patient's associations and behaviors.

The patient, then, is capable of extensive areas of valid functioning and communication, much of it unconscious. When faced with expressions of illness—countertransference—in the therapist, he has the ability to unconsciously perceive many latent aspects of this disturbance and to respond with usually unconscious therapeutic efforts, thereby serving as the functional therapist. Such unconscious valid functioning will eventually be extended into distorted and inappropriate responses and communications, the contributions of the patient's unconscious transferences.

In sum, the patient's behaviors and communications are always a mixture of transference and nontransference, that is, transversal communications (Langs 1978a). He is engaged in an unconscious communicative interaction with the therapist, and everything he imparts has some bearing on that interaction. His associations and behaviors do not reflect isolated contents, but derive their most immediate meaning and their genetic implications from the ongoing therapeutic interaction.

Many techniques and therapeutic practices have arisen on the basis of these false premises, creating the conditions for lie therapy. Perhaps the primary motive for these erroneous assumptions resides in the needs of therapists and analysts to deny the presence and influence of their own unconscious countertransferences and to defend themselves ultimately against the most primitive and disturbed parts of their own personalities. Many additional motives contribute, including the fear of the patient's most regressed communications and fears of separateness and loss. The dread and anxiety are such that these false premises are almost rigidly maintained, thereby revealing their brittle but self-protective qualities.

In principle, every therapist is a mixture of lie therapist and truth therapist. It seems that at this point in psychoanalytic history the former predominates in most individual practitioners. This observation, which is unfortunately both realistic and harsh, will be better understood if we turn now to some common types of lie therapists and lie analysts. These will be identified in terms of their behaviors in the therapeutic interaction, that is, the nature of their interventions. In general, the therapist in whom the lie modality predominates will make use of a mixture of these techniques, often without significant awareness of the unconscious implications of his interventions. Following are the common techniques of lie therapists.

The framework changer. Analysts and therapists in this group—and the literature bears witness to few exceptions—tend to take a very lax attitude toward the ground rules of psychotherapy and psychoanalysis. Most believe that psychotherapy is a distinctly different treatment modality from psychoanalysis, implying in part that in the former situation alterations in the basic ground rules and the use of noninterpretive interventions are more than justified. More broadly, these therapists tend to modify the standard framework quite readily, cancelling sessions, changing hours, intervening noninterpretively, modifying total confidentiality through such measures as signing insurance forms, and so on. Some will attempt to explore the patient's material after such a deviation, though few will do so in advance. Even fewer will take the material from the patient in advance of such a deviation as a commentary on the proposal and as reflecting in part the patient's unconscious, valid awareness of the actual consequences of the proposed deviation. Without exception, these alterations in the standard frame create the conditions for lie therapy. They are themselves unconscious lie communications—

falsifications and barriers—even in those rare emergencies in which such steps are justified.

In general, there is a tendency among frame-changing therapists to deploy the naive rationalization of the need for flexibility and humanity as justification for deviations. This is an attitude that is itself a lie and a falsification, since it cannot be validated in Type Two derivative form by the material from a patient subsequent to the invocation of such a technical measure. Instead, such material unfailingly indicates the patient's need for a therapeutic environment, based on a secure frame, that provides a full openness to the communicative relationship in the form of a growth-promoting (healthy) symbiosis, and the opportunity for unconscious and analyzable expressions from the patient.

A therapist who deviates gratifies some aspects of his unconscious countertransferences, conveys some type of pathological projective identification, and offers the patient Type C barriers against prevailing and disturbing adaptive contexts that impinge upon the necessary separateness and disturbed parts of the personality of both participants. Because deviations create pathological symbiosis, patients consciously accept them, while universally indicating in derivative form an unconscious awareness of their destructiveness. Deviations reflect a need for Type C barriers and lies within the therapist and invite the patient to move away from or seal off the truth about his own neurosis and that of the therapist. Because truth therapy can take place only within a secure therapeutic environment, we must realize the frequency with which therapists turn from truth to lie therapy in current practice.

The genetic reconstructionist. This type of lie therapist epitomizes the therapist or analyst who utilizes Type One derivatives isolated from adaptive contexts related to the immediate therapeutic interaction. The patient's associations are treated as isolated contents without immediate interactional pertinence and are interpreted in terms of isolated unconscious fantasies and memories within the patient himself. Their derivative roots are consistently traced to past genetic figures; in particular, unconscious perceptions of the analyst are thereby denied.

Such an attitude is, of course, based on the premise that the patient is expressing himself primarily through transferences—distortions derived from past relationships. His associations are therefore interpreted in terms of their roots in earlier relationships (or as having isolated unconscious meanings and fantasied contents). Often the manifest content is addressed and simply translated in terms involving genetic antecedents. Implicit to this approach is the assumption that the analyst has in no way actually behaved like the earlier figure (Little 1951) or otherwise stimulated the patient's communications.

Another aspect of such work is the extent to which it lacks any effort at Type Two derivative, psychoanalytic validation. Instead, direct and conscious elaboration, and the repetition of familiar memories, are often viewed as confirming the analyst's interpretation or reconstruction; such work is characteristically linear and flat. It lacks both the convoluted, coalescing, and truly unique qualities of sound interpretive efforts and the originality of unanticipated validation.

Under these conditions the patient's material is consistently formulated as inappropriately defensive and resistant, as well as distorted and pathological, based primarily on early pathogenic experiences. The patient is viewed as caught up in his own intrapsychic fantasies to which the analyst has essentially made no contribution and which refer only rarely to the ongoing analytic interaction. When conscious fantasies and impressions about the analyst emerge, they are treated as transferences per se, rather than as derivatives which may well contain not only disguised unconscious fantasies and memories but unconscious perceptions as well. The latter type of functioning in response to the analyst's conscious and unconscious communications is virtually never considered.

The total effect is the development of a lie therapy in which the analyst's own unconscious communications, both valid and distorted, are not consistently taken into account. As a result, the treatment situation serves in large measure as a barrier and falsification in respect to the analyst's own inner disturbances. In addition, the patient's pathology is often misconstrued, in that many of his nonpathological and nontransference-based communications, which are in fact validly related to unconscious perceptions of the therapist, are treated as distortions.

The patient is therefore offered a lie system that stems largely from the therapist's pathological (mainly defensive) needs. At the heart of this lie system is the substitute of a genetic explanation for an understanding of the immediate unconscious communicative interaction, with its pathological and nonpathological elements to which ultimately the patient makes genetic links. Functionally it is irrelevant whether these genetic interpretations are true or false; they serve in either case as barriers to the unconscious truths within the bipersonal field. Sometimes these truths involve aspects of the patient's pathology other than those interpreted, and, very often, contributions from the analyst's unconscious countertransferences. As a result, this type of lie system (with its strong sadistic component) may or may not interdigitate with the patient's own falsifications and barriers (if these are present), which make up his own particular lie system. This often takes the form of strong masochistic trends. If concordant, there may be symptom relief based on a shared lie system. If discordant, the patient may incorporate the analyst's lie system and thereby gain temporary symptom alleviation, or he may, consciously or unconsciously, violently oppose the lie system, leading to therapeutic chaos, stalemate, and sudden, unexplained termination. These are major resistances whose unconscious sources are not understood by the therapist. Much of the outcome depends on the extent to which the patient is able to incorporate the therapist's lie system as a means of sealing off underlying and disturbing truths related to expressions of his own and the therapist's most disruptive psychopathology.

Genetic reconstructionists intervene in a manner entirely divorced from the prevailing adaptive context within the therapeutic interaction. Often this entails erroneous interpretations and mismanagements of the framework. Since attention is directed to the past, however, conscious awareness of these present errors is split off and denied by both patient and analyst— sealed off and falsified. The concept of genetic and projected transferences serves here as a lie system. This is reflected in the finding that many responses from the patient that the analyst identifies as transference-based are in actuality nontransference-based. Genetic interpretations are used as barriers to the truths of the immediate analytic situation and interaction, and to the central neurotic expressions of both participants. Freud's dedicated quest for the truth, which brought mankind far closer to the inner and outer actuality of neuroses than ever before, nevertheless provided a model of lie therapy that prevails to this day. In this context, it is well to recall my own discussion (1976a,b) and, earlier, those of Szasz (1963) and Chertok (1968). Using different approaches, we have suggested that despite the undeniable brilliance of his insights, Freud's discovery of transference served in part as a defensive means of denying his countertransference-based contributions to the therapeutic interactions in which he participated. This remarkable fact shows how treacherous the search for the truth within the therapeutic interaction may be, and how conscious integrity cannot protect the therapist from his unconscious need for lies and barriers.

The interpreter of outside relationships. This is another common type of lie therapist. Here,

purported dynamic interpretations and genetic derivations are developed in terms of the patient's relationships with figures outside the treatment situation, without any correlation being drawn to the patient-therapist interaction. Such interventions virtually never receive Type Two derivative validation. Functionally, they serve to create lies and barriers to the compelling and relatively chaotic truths within the therapeutic interaction. They serve mainly to generate a lie system which is often shared by patient and therapist, and which is elaborated in a flat and linear fashion.

The user of the psychoanalytic cliché. This type of lie therapist uses a technique which overlaps with those discussed earlier. Because of its prevalence, however, it deserves separate mention. As in other forms of lie therapy, the material from the patient is treated in isolated fashion, considered on a manifest or readily inferential level, and viewed largely in terms of intrapsychic dynamics and distortions. A large number of psychoanalytic clichés are thereby introduced through the therapist's interventions. At times these are highly intellectualized and abstract: allusions to the patient's dependency, hostility, symbiotic needs, and the like. At other times they draw upon well-worn psychoanalytic hypotheses such as those related to the oedipus complex, preoedipal disturbances, and such. It is the absence of dynamic specificity, of unconscious links to the therapeutic interaction, and of derivative meaning that transforms these overt truths into functional lies.

As with other forms of lie interventions, there is total disregard for the crucial adaptive contexts within the therapeutic interaction. The psychoanalytic cliché offers powerful Type C barriers to psychic truths, and patients willingly accept them on the surface. They then weave elaborate though essentially falsified responsive tales as a means of avoiding their own inner disturbance and their disturbed unconscious perceptions of the therapist.

Who then among us does not recognize some aspect of his psychoanalytic and psychotherapeutic techniques among these characterizations of lie therapy? It seems quite evident that lie therapy and lie therapists are the rule rather than the exception. From this we may infer that there is a powerful attraction in falsifications and barriers and among us all an enormous dread of the chaotic and terrible truths of our neuroses and those of our patients. Immediate safety is sought at the expense of both growth and the development of adaptive resources. It seems evident that the consistent utilization of truth therapy techniques requires of the therapist a considerable degree of self-understanding, self-scrutiny, tolerance of anxiety and psychic pain, and acceptance of relative separateness.

DISCUSSION

This delineation of truth and lie therapy raises a number of unique clinical issues, while offering substantially new perspectives on time-worn clinical debates. Perhaps the most important suggestion in this discussion is that psychoanalysis and psychoanalytically oriented psychotherapy, as usually practiced, are forms of lie therapy. While these treatment modalities differ from other types of lie therapies in a number of ways, they share in common with virtually every form of therapeutic endeavor practiced today the existence of significant lie systems inherent in its clinical methodology and practice. This understanding reflects the universal need in all human beings, patients and therapists alike, for lie therapy and lie systems. Corollary to this is the recognition that the adoption of truth systems by truth patients and truth therapists is an accomplishment not easily won.

This realization could provide dynamically oriented therapists new perspectives on the noninterpretive treatment modalities and on therapeutic approaches that propose to seek out the truth but that include in their basic assumptions such evident flaws as the implicit acceptance of lie fictions and lie barriers. Perhaps the most important judgment we can make of a therapeutic modality is whether it is committed to the full search for the truth. Modalities so inclined would allow the revision in clinical observation, theory, and practice that ultimately characterizes the truth therapy modality.

It is in this context that we can recognize that classical psychoanalysis is distinguished by its total commitment to the truth, despite its failing to have as yet attained this goal clinically. Other dynamic therapies have built into their theoretical edifices significant lie-barrier systems that pose major obstacles to their own avowed search for the truth. It is in fact precisely the classical psychoanalytic viewpoint that permits the discovery of lie systems, whether in its own practice or within other treatment modalities. This implies that this particular approach is most open to the modifications in understanding and technique called for by this presentation.

Paradoxically, though no longer unexpectedly, the discovery and application of truth therapy lead to the realization that, until now, the perpetuation of a given therapeutic approach has relied heavily on its

lie propensities, the lie systems it offers its patients. The growth and development of truth therapy will be arduous, and initially one can expect only a small number of truth patients and truth therapists. Yet despite the emphasis here on the universal need for lies there is also part of every human being that wishes to know and deal with the truth, however painful. As truth systems are accorded greater value by both individuals and groups (professional and lay), truth therapy should establish itself as a significant form of therapeutic practice.

A number of pressing clinical issues arise. One important question is how a truth therapist can best develop the treatment setting and approach for the lie patient. We are now aware of the nature of certain resistances that prompt patients initially to be refractory to truth therapy. Perhaps the best approach is one in which the therapist establishes truth conditions and quite naturally concentrates his interpretations on the patient's responses (efforts to modify the framework, to obtain noninterpretative interventions, etc.), in the expectation that the insights developed in this way will provide the patient a first important step toward becoming a truth patient. But how then should we approach the lie patient who envies the truth therapist, and who self-protectively, unconsciously feels that he must destroy any possibility of truthful unconscious communication? Is it possible to knowingly deviate and offer relatively well-understood and well-modulated sectors of lie communication to such patients, as an initial effort to permit their involvement in the therapeutic situation, in the hope that subsequently there can be a gradual shift toward definitive truth therapy? It may well be that such compromises leave lasting and relatively unmodifiable unconscious images of the therapist as a lie communicator, and the therapeutic outcome would thereby be significantly affected. And yet this may nonetheless be the most optimal treatment setting and outcome possible for these patients, given their own pathological needs and propensities.

Similar questions arise regarding therapists and analysts. It seems inconceivable that any therapist would compromise his commitment to knowing the truth about both his patient and himself within a therapeutic interaction, whatever its structure and nature might be. A therapist with unconscious needs for lie communication is an inherently destructive and parasitic figure; even his utilization of the lie therapy modality is bound to suffer. But what then of the lie therapist who knowingly utilizes a lie-barrier system *as the basis* for his therapeutic work? Is it possible for a therapist, once he knows the truth, to effectively function as a lie therapist? And is today's patient population such that we need knowledgeable lie therapists who, while practicing a given form of lie therapy, are at least aware of its presence and some of the prevailing unconscious dynamics? Such may be the overriding practical necessity, though a serious danger lies in accepting such pragmatic needs as a basis for turning away from the truth. These considerations should in no way lessen the pursuit of establishing truth therapy as a basic and important treatment modality for emotional ills. Nor should we abandon the hope that this approach, with its great pain and yet its enormous promise, could someday become the prevailing form of psychotherapy.

Along somewhat different lines, the recognition of truth and lie systems provides a means of viewing the conscious and unconscious therapeutic communicative interaction in a new light. There is much to be learned in defining the truth or lie system being offered by a therapist to a particular patient, while simultaneously identifying the prevailing truth or lie system in the latter's communications. Lie systems function as barriers, fictions, unconscious communications, and projective identifications, much of this infused with massive defensiveness, parasitism, and destructiveness, however self-protective. However, a lie system relies in substance upon a particular constellation of elements which must exclude all other possibilities lest it be damaged or collapse. Because of this, rival lie systems or any truth system poses a threat to its maintenance. All psychopathology entails the use of some type of lie system, permeable or not. Truth systems serve to modify pathological defenses, and function essentially as constructive unconscious communications and projective identifications, however much they may threaten a particular lie patient (or lie therapist) and his system.

Finally, having made repeated use of the extremes of this continuum—truth tellers and lie communicators—for the purposes of exposition, I must remind the reader that neither type exists in pure form, whether patient or therapist. Sectors of lie within the truth patient inevitably reflect significant aspects of his psychopathology and its genetics, and therefore provide meaningful opportunities for interpretive work. On the other hand, it is the nucleus of truth expression and seeking in the lie patient that offers a viable potential for the analytic modification of his lie system (and his need for it) to the point where his truthful tendencies can predominate. Much analytic work, however, must be done to develop a capacity within patients to tolerate the truth, to work with it and grow by it.

For the therapist, matters are somewhat different. The lie therapist will generally express his truthful propensities quite unconsciously, and while they may generate isolated positive introjects within the patient, they will not provide him the cognitive insights and adaptive resources necessary for sound structural change. The kernels of truth conveyed by such a therapist will provide the truth-seeking patient with islands of hope which tend, in the long run, not to be fulfilled, since the therapist's lie tendencies inevitably predominate.

The truth therapist will also express himself from time to time through lies, and these involve his inevitable countertransferences. While the patient may respond to these communications in a manner that proves analyzable and even growth-promoting, sound interpretive work requires that the therapist must become aware of his lie and resolve these propensities. While such interludes usually replicate aspects of the patient's earlier pathological interactions, their rectification and interpretation prove constructive for the patient—and for the therapist.

In conclusion, it is my hope that this chapter will be seen as an effort to break down our current, fixed, somewhat stale, and apparently lie-infused conceptualizations of the therapeutic interaction. Such ideas have taken us as far as they can; it is time now to discover their flaws and untruths. On this basis a new and clinically validated system of truth can be developed. And of course this must be done with the recognition that, as was true of our predecessors, we can generate only the best truths available to us for the moment. Eventually flaws must be discovered even in our new system, and psychoanalysis will prepare for yet another step in its progress as a science.

REFERENCES

For Epilogue references, see Editor's References, pp. 516–518.

EDITOR'S REFERENCES

Arlow, J., and Brenner, C. (1966). Discussion of the analytic situation, by E. Zetzel. In *Psychoanalysis In The Americas,* ed. R. Litman, New York: International Universities Press.

Balint, M. (1968). *The Basic Fault: Therapeutic Aspects of Regression.* London: Tavistock.

Balint, A., and Balint, M. (1939). On transference and countertransference. *International Journal of Psycho-Analysis* 20:223-230.

Baranger, M., and Baranger, W. (1966). Insight in the analytic situation. In *Psychoanalysis in the Americas,* ed. R. Litman, New York: International Universities Press. [Chapter 33, this volume]

Beres, D., and Arlow, J. A. (1974). Fantasy and identification in empathy. *Psychoanalytic Quarterly* 43:26-50. [Chapter 23, this volume]

Bibring, E. (1937). Contributions to the symposium on the theory of therapeutic results of psycho-analysis. *International Journal of Psycho-Analysis* 18:170-189.

———(1954). Psychoanalysis and the dynamic psychotherapies. *Journal of the American Psychoanalytic Association* 2:745-770.

Bion, W. (1962). *Learning from Experience.* In W. Bion, *Seven Servants.* New York: Jason Aronson, 1977.

———(1963). *Elements of Psycho-Analysis.* In W. Bion, *Seven Servants.* New York: Jason Aronson, 1977.

———(1967). *Second Thoughts.* New York: Jason Aronson.

———(1970). *Attention and Interpretation.* In W. Bion, *Seven Servants.* New York: Jason Aronson, 1977.

———(1977). *Seven Servants.* New York: Jason Aronson.

Bird, B. (1972). Notes on transference: universal phenomenon and hardest part of analysis. *Journal of the American Psychoanalytic Association* 20:267-301. [Chapter 6, this volume]

Bleger, J. (1967). Psycho-analysis of the psycho-analytic frame. *International Journal of Psycho-Analysis* 48:511-510. [Chapter 41, this volume]

Brenner, C. (1979). Working alliance, therapeutic alliance, and transference. *Journal of the American Psychoanalytic Association.* 27 (Supplement): 137-158.

Chertok, L. (1968). The discovery of the transference: toward an epistemological interpretation. *International Journal of Psycho-Analysis* 49:560-576.

Dickes, R. L. (1975). Technical considerations of the therapeutic and working alliances. *International Journal of Psychoanalytic Psychotherapy* 4:1-24.

Edelson, M. (1975). *Language and Interpretation in Psychoanalysis.* New Haven: Yale University Press.

Ferenczi, S. (1909). Introjection and transference. In S. Ferenczi, *Sex in Psychoanalysis.* New York: Robert Bruner, 1950.

———(1910). On the technique of psycho-analysis. In S. Ferenczi, *Further Considerations of the Technique of Psycho-Analysis.* London: Hogarth Press, 1950.

Fliess, R. (1953). Countertransference and counteridentification. *Journal of the American Psychoanalytic Association* 1:268-284.

Freud, S. (1905). Fragment of an analysis of a case of hysteria. *Standard Edition* 7:3-122.

———(1909). Notes upon a case of obsessional neurosis. *Standard Edition* 17:3-122.

———(1910). The future prospects of psycho-analytic therapy. *Standard Edition* 11:141-151.

———(1912a). The dynamics of transference. *Standard Edition* 12:97-108. [Chapter 1, this volume]

———(1912b). Recommendations to physicians practising psycho-analysis. *Standard Edition* 12:111-120. [Chapter 38, this volume]

———(1913). On beginning the treatment (further recommendations on the technique of psycho-analysis, I) *Standard Edition* 12:121-144.

———(1914). Remembering, repeating, and working-through (further recommendations on the technique of psycho-analysis, II). *Standard Edition* 12:145-156.

———(1915). Observations on transference-love (further recommendations on the technique of psycho-analysis, III). *Standard Edition* 12:157-171.

———(1918). From the history of an infantile neurosis. *Standard Edition* 17:3-122.

———(1920). Beyond the pleasure principle. *Standard Edition* 18:3-64.

———(1923). The ego and the id. *Standard Edition* 19: 3-66.

———(1937). Analysis terminable and interminable. *Standard Edition* 23:209-253.

Gill, M. (1979). The analysis of the transference. *Journal of the American Psychoanalytic Association* 27:263-288. [Chapter 7, this volume]

Greenacre, P. (1954). The role of transference. *Journal of the American Psychoanalytic Association* 2:671-684. [Chapter 3, this volume]

———(1971). *Emotional Growth.* 2 Vols. New York: International Universities Press.

Greenson, R. (1965). The working alliance and the transference neurosis. *Psychoanalytic Quarterly* 34:155-181. [Chapter 28, this volume]

———(1967). *The Technique and Practice of Psychoanalysis* Vol. 1. New York: International Universities Press.

———(1969). The non-transference relationship in the psychoanalytic situation. *International Journal of Psycho-Analysis* 50:27-39.

———(1972). Beyond transference and interpretation. *International Journal of Psycho-Analysis* 53:213-217. [Chapter 9, this volume]

———(1974). Loving, hating, and indifference towards the patient. *International Review of Psycho-Analysis* 1: 259-266.

———(1978). *Explorations in Psychoanalysis*. New York: International Universities Press.

Grotstein, J. (1977a). The psychoanalytic concept of schizophrenia: I. The dilemma. *International Journal of Psycho-Analysis* 58:403-426.

———(1977b). The psychoanalytic concept of schizophrenia: II. Reconciliation. *International Journal of Psycho-Analysis* 58:427-452.

Hann-Kende, F. (1933). On the role of transference and countertransference in psychoanalysis. In *Psychoanalysis and the Occult*, ed. G. Devereux. New York: International Universities Press, 1953, 1970. Originally published in 1933, tr. G. Devereux.

Kanzer, M. (1975). The therapeutic and working alliances: an assessment. *International Journal of Psychoanalytic Psychotherapy* 4:48-68. [Chapter 30, this volume]

Kernberg, O. (1975). *Borderline Conditions and Pathological Narcissism*. New York: Jason Aronson.

Khan, M. (1974). *The Privacy of the Self*. New York: International Universities Press.

Klein, M. (1946). Notes on some schizoid mechanisms. *International Journal of Psycho-Analysis* 33:433-438.

Kohut, H. (1971). *The Analysis of the Self*. New York: International Universities Press.

———(1977). *The Restoration of the Self*. New York: International Universities Press.

Langs, R. (1975a). Therapeutic misalliances. *International Journal of Psychoanalytic Psychotherapy* 4:77-105. [Chapter 29, this volume]

———(1975b). The therapeutic relationship and deviations in technique. *International Journal of Psychoanalytic Psychotherapy* 4:106-141.

———(1975c). The patient's unconscious perception of the therapist's errors.

———(1976a). *The Bipersonal Field*. New York: Jason Aronson.

———(1976b). *The Therapeutic Interaction*. New York: Jason Aronson.

———(1978a). *The Listening Process*. New York: Jason Aronson.

———(1978b) *Technique in Transition*. New York: Jason Aronson.

———(1978c). Responses to creativity in psychoanalysts. In *Technique in Transition* by R. Langs, New York: Jason Aronson.

———(1978d). Interventions in the bipersonal field. In *Technique in Transition* by R. Langs, New York: Jason Aronson. [Chapter 25, this volume]

———(1978e). Some communicative properties of the bipersonal field. In *Technique in Transition* by R. Langs, New York: Jason Aronson.

———(1978f). The adaptational-interactional dimension of countertransference. In *Technique in Transition* by R. Langs, New York: Jason Aronson. [Chapter 18, this volume]

———(1979). *The Therapeutic Environment*. New York: Jason Aronson.

Little, M. (1951). Countertransference and the patient's response to it. *International Journal of Psycho-Analysis* 32:32-40. [Chapter 12, this volume]

———(1957). "R"—the analyst's total response to his patient's needs. *International Journal of Psycho-Analysis* 38: 240-254.

Loewald, H. (1970). Psychoanalytic theory and the psychoanalytic process. *Psychoanalytic Study of the Child* 25:45-68.

———(1971). The transference neurosis: comments on the concept and the phenomenon. *Journal of the American Psychoanalytic Association* 19:54-56.

———(1975). Psychoanalysis as an art and the fantasy character of the psychoanalytic situation. *Journal of the American Psychoanalytic Association* 23:277-300.

Milner, M. (1952). Aspects of symbolism in comprehension of the not-self. *International Journal of Psycho-Analysis* 33:181-195.

Racker, H. (1957). The meanings and uses of countertransference. *Psychoanalytic Quarterly* 26:303-357. [Chapter 15, this volume]

———(1968). *Transference and Countertransference*. London: Hogarth Press.

Reich, A. (1960). Further remarks on countertransference. *International Journal of Psycho-Analysis* 41: 380-395.

Rosen, V. (1974). The nature of verbal interventions in psychoanalysis. *Psychoanalysis and Contemporary Science* 3: 189-209.

Rosenfeld, H. (1972). A critical appreciation of James Strachey's paper on the nature of the therapeutic action of psycho-analysis. *International Journal of Psycho-Analysis* 53:455-461.

Sandler, J. (1976). Countertransference and role-responsiveness. *International Review of Psycho-Analysis* 3:43-47.

Sandler, J. et al. (1969). Notes on some theoretical and clinical aspects of transference. *International Journal of Psycho-Analysis*. 50:633-645. [Chapter 5, this volume]

———(1973). *The Patient and the Analyst: The Basis of the Psychoanalytic Process*. International Universities Press, chapters 1-6.

Schafer, R. (1959). Generative empathy in the treatment situation. *Psychoanalytic Quarterly* 28:342-373.

Searles, H. (1965). *Collected Papers on Schizophrenia and Related Subjects*. New York: International Universities Press.

———(1970). Autism and the phase of transition to therapeutic symbiosis. *Contemporary Psychoanalysis* 7 1-20.

————(1971). Pathological symbiosis and autism. In *The Name of the Life,* ed. B. Landis and E. Tauber. New York: Holt, Rinehart and Winston, 1971.

————(1972). The functions of the patient's realistic perception of the analyst's delusional transference. *British Journal of Medical Psychology* 45:1-18.

————(1973). Concerning therapeutic symbiosis. *The Annual of Psycho-Analysis* 1:247-262. [Chapter 37, this volume]

————(1975). The patient as therapist to his analyst. In *Tactics and Techniques of Psychoanalytic Therapy, Vol. II: Countertransference,* ed. P. Giovacchini, New York: Jason Aronson. [Chapter 10, this volume]

————(1979). Concerning transference and counter-transference. *International Journal of Psychoanalytic Psychotherapy* 7:165-188.

Segal, H. (1967). Melanie Klein's technique. *Psychoanalytic Forum* 2:197-211. [Chapter 35, this volume]

Shapiro, T. (1970). Interpretation and naming. *Journal of the American Psychoanalytic Association* 18:399-421.

Sterba, R. (1934). The fate of the ego in analytic therapy. *International Journal of Psycho-Analysis* 15:117-126. [Chapter 26, this volume]

Strachey, J. (1934). The nature of the therapeutic action of psychoanalysis. *International Journal of Psycho-Analysis* 15: 127-159. Reprinted in *International Journal of Psycho-Analysis* 50 (1969):275-292. [Chapter 31, this volume]

Szasz, T. (1963). The concept of transference. *International Journal of Psycho-Analysis* 44:432-443. [Chapter 4, this volume]

Ticho, E. (1972). The effects of the analyst's personality on psychoanalytic treatment. *Psychoanalytic Forum* 4: 137-151.

Viderman, S. (1974). Interpretation in the analytic space. *International Review of Psycho-Analysis* 1:467-480.

Wangh, M. (1962). The "evocation of a proxy": a psychological maneuver, its use as a defense, its purposes and genesis. *Psychoanalytic Study of the Child* 17:461-469.

Winnicott, D. (1956). On transference. In Winnicott 1958.

————(1958). *Collected Papers.* London: Tavistock Publications.

————(1965). *The Maturational Process and the Facilitating Environment.* New York: International Universities Press.

Zac, J. (1972). An investigation of how interpretations arise in the analyst. *International Journal of Psycho-Analysis* 53:315-320.

Zetzel, E. (1956). Current concepts of transference. *International Journal of Psycho-Analysis* 37:369-376. [Chapter 27, this volume]

————(1970). *The Capacity for Emotional Growth.* New York: International Universities Press.

INDEX